CW00369997

ARCHBOLD

2016

SECOND SUPPLEMENT TO THE 2016 EDITION

EDITOR

P.J. RICHARDSON, Q.C. (Hon.), LL.M. (LOND.), Dip. Crim. (CANTAB.)
of Gray's Inn and the Inner Temple, Barrister

SUPPLEMENT EDITORS

WILLIAM CARTER, M.A. (OXON.)
of Gray's Inn, Barrister

STEPHEN SHAY, B.A. (OXON.)
of the Middle Temple, Barrister

SWEET & MAXWELL

Published in 2016 by Sweet & Maxwell, Friars House, 160 Blackfriars Road, London, SE1 8EZ, part of Thomson Reuters (Professional) UK Limited (Company No. 1679046). Registered in England and Wales. Registered office: 2nd Floor, 1 Mark Square, Leonard Street, London EC2A 4EG.

Printed and bound by CPI Group (UK) Ltd, Croydon, CR0 4YY.

Typeset by Sweet & Maxwell, Friars House, 160 Blackfriars Road, London, SE1 8EZ.

For further information on our products and services, visit:

http://www.sweetandmaxwell.co.uk

No natural forests were destroyed to make this product; only farmed timber was used and replanted.

A CIP catalogue record for this book is available from the British Library

ISBN MAINWORK 9780414050235
ISBN SECOND SUPPLEMENT 9780414054318

SERVICE INFORMATION

The Archbold service

Archbold: Criminal Pleading, Evidence and Practice consists of one main text volume (including the tables and index). This volume is re-issued annually, and is updated by cumulative supplements, the e-update service (see below) and *Archbold Review*.

The supplement

Three cumulative supplements, containing updating material for the main volume, are published in each year as part of the service.

This is the second supplement of 2016.

New material is incorporated into this supplement using the same paragraph numbers as appear in the mainwork. All material new to this supplement is marked in the text by a **bold star in the margin.** ★

After consulting the main work on any given subject, reference should always be made to the same paragraph number in the current supplement to check that there have been no new developments since the main text volume was published. The supplement will also track material which has been removed or relocated as part of the re-issue process.

The back cover contains a list of all important developments included in this supplement for the first time and where they can be found.

All references in the text to cases, statutes and statutory instruments are contained in the tables printed at the beginning of this supplement.

Please email smg.archbold@thomson.com with comments/suggestions for any of the Archbold services.

Archbold eBook upgrade

Archbold 2016 is available as an eBook on the iPad, PC and Mac. As a purchaser of *Archbold: Criminal Pleading, Evidence and Practice* 2016, 64th edition you are also entitled to purchase one copy of the Archbold eBook at a special upgrade price. To find more information about the Archbold eBook please visit the Archbold website www.sweetandmaxwell.co.uk/archbold or contact our customer services team on 0845 600 9355.

Archbold e-update activation code

As a subscriber to Archbold 2016 you have free and unlimited access to the accompanying weekly e-update service and online archive. If you are a new user accessing the service for the first time then please visit www.sweetandmaxwell.co.uk/archbold where you will be asked to complete a simple short registration process, and to enter the following activation code to start receiving updates:

| AB2016 |

If you are an existing user of the e-update then your access will automatically be updated for the new edition and there is no need to re-register.

TABLE OF CONTENTS

TABLE OF CONTENTS

ABBREVIATIONS OF LEGISLATION

The following abbreviations have been adopted throughout.

AFA	Armed Forces Act
CAA	Criminal Appeal Act
CDA	Crime and Disorder Act
CDDA	Company Directors Disqualification Act
CEMA	Customs and Excise Management Act
CJA	Criminal Justice Act
CJCA	Criminal Justice and Courts Act
CJCSA	Criminal Justice and Court Services Act
CJIA	Criminal Justice and Immigration Act
CJPA	Criminal Justice and Police Act
CJPOA	Criminal Justice and Public Order Act
CLA	Criminal Law Act
CPIA	Criminal Procedure and Investigations Act
C(S)A	Crime (Sentences) Act
CYPA	Children and Young Persons Act
DTA	Drug Trafficking Act
DTOA	Drug Trafficking Offences Act
ECHR	European Convention on Human Rights
FSMA	Financial Services and Markets Act
LASPOA	Legal Aid, Sentencing and Punishment of Offenders Act
MCA	Magistrates' Courts Act
MHA	Mental Health Act
PACE	Police and Criminal Evidence
PCA	Proceeds of Crime Act
PCCA	Powers of Criminal Courts Act
PCC(S)A	Powers of Criminal Courts (Sentencing) Act
PJA	Police and Justice Act
RIPA	Regulation of Investigatory Powers Act
RSA	Road Safety Act
RSC	Rules of the Supreme Court (Revision)
RTA	Road Traffic Act
RTOA	Road Traffic Offenders Act
SCA	Serious Crime Act
SOA	Sexual Offences Act
SOCPA	Serious Organised Crime and Police Act
VCRA	Violent Crime Reduction Act
YJCEA	Youth Justice and Criminal Evidence Act

TABLE OF STATUTES

References in bold indicate where legislation is reproduced in full

ix

TABLE OF NON-UK LEGISLATION

TABLE OF INTERNATIONAL TREATIES AND CONVENTIONS

References in bold indicate where legislation is reproduced in full

TABLE OF EC REGULATIONS AND DIRECTIVES

TABLE OF STATUTORY INSTRUMENTS

References in bold indicate where legislation is reproduced in full

TABLE OF CASES

1

TABLE OF NON-UK CASES

TABLE OF PRACTICE DIRECTIONS

CHAPTER 1

THE INDICTMENT

III. SENDINGS FOR TRIAL

B. PRINCIPAL PROVISIONS

(2) Sending of cases to the Crown Court

Crime and Disorder Act 1998, ss.50A, 51-51E

A magistrates' court has no power to conduct sending proceedings under section 51 of the ★**1-31** 1998 Act (§ 1-25 in the main work) in the absence of the accused: *R. (Lord Janner) v. Westminster Magistrates' Court,* 179 J.P. 465, DC (refusing to interfere with an order of a district judge that the claimant, an elderly man suffering from advanced dementia, should attend sending proceedings, having regard to the procedural importance of the proceedings and the principle of open justice). For criticism of the decision, see CLW/15/41/1.

D. MODE OF TRIAL FOR OFFENCES TRIABLE EITHER WAY AND CERTAIN SUMMARY OFFENCES

(2) Procedure

(a) *Statutory provisions*

Magistrates' Courts Act 1980, ss.24-24D

Mode of trial of children and young persons

The Sentencing Council has issued a revised definitive guideline on allocation relating to deci- ★**1-115** sions as to mode of trial (i) for adults charged with offences triable either way (as to whom, see *post*, § 1-118), and (ii) for youths charged jointly with an adult who is being or has been sent for trial. It is to apply with effect from March 1, 2016. As to youths jointly charged with adults, whereas section 51(7) of the CDA 1998 (§ 1-25 in the main work) provides for a child or young person who is jointly charged with an adult who is being, or has been, sent to the Crown Court for trial, also to be sent for trial in the Crown Court if this is considered "necessary in the interests of justice", the guideline lists considerations relevant to this test as including: (a) whether separate trials will cause injustice to witnesses or to the case as a whole (consideration should be given to the YJCEA 1999, ss.27 (video-recorded evidence in chief) and 28 (video-recorded cross-examination or re-examination) (*ibid.*, §§ 8-99, 8-93)), (b) the youth's age, (c) the age gap between the youth and the adult, (d) the youth's level of maturity, (e) the alleged role of the youth and the alleged relative culpability, and (f) the youth's history. The guideline adds that a court should bear in mind that a youth court now has a general power to commit for sentence following conviction pursuant to the PCC(S)A 2000, s.3B (*ibid.*, § 5-27), which power, in appropriate cases, would permit the Crown Court to sentence both an adult and a youth who have been tried separately.

(c) *Allocation guideline*

The Sentencing Council has issued a revised definitive guideline on allocation relating to deci- ★**1-118** sions as to mode of trial (i) for adults charged with offences triable either way, and (ii) for youths charged jointly with an adult who is being or has been sent for trial (as to whom, see *ante*, § 1-115). It is to apply with effect from March 1, 2016. As to mode of trial for adults, the guideline now states that either-way offences should be tried summarily, unless (a) after taking into account personal mitigation and any potential reduction for plea, the sentence would clearly be in excess of a magistrates' court's powers or would be likely to be a very substantial fine, or (b) for reasons of "unusual legal, procedural or factual complexity", the case should be tried in the Crown Court.

V. THE FORM OF AN INDICTMENT

A. RULES AS TO INDICTMENTS

★**1-177**   As to the intended replacement of the Indictments (Procedure) Rules 1971 (S.I. 1971 No. 2084) (see the main work), see *post*, § 1-302.

C. CONTENTS

(2) Statement and particulars of offence(s) and signature

Particulars of offence

★**1-190**   For a case considering whether an indictment alleging several money laundering offences in a single count was bad for duplicity or uncertainty, see *R. v. William*, *post*, § 26-52.

E. DUPLICITY

(4) Rule 10.2(2) of the Criminal Procedure Rules 2015 (S.I. 2015 No. 1490)

Application of the rule and potential problems with it

★**1-222**   For a case considering whether an indictment alleging several money laundering offences in a single count was bad for duplicity or uncertainty, see *R. v. William*, *post*, § 26-52.

★**1-224**   For a case considering *R. v. Tomlin* (see the main work), see *R. v. T.J.C.*, *post*, § 21-341.

VII. PREFERRING THE BILL OF INDICTMENT

A. WHEN A BILL OF INDICTMENT MAY BE PREFERRED

Administration of Justice (Miscellaneous Provisions) Act 1933, s.2(1), (2)

★**1-277**   As to the procedure for making and determining an application to a High Court judge for consent to prefer a bill of indictment in accordance with section 2(2)(b) of the 1933 Act, see *post*, § 1-302.

Indictment based on voluntary bill

★**1-288**   As to the intended replacement of the Indictments (Procedure) Rules 1971 (S.I. 1971 No. 2084) (as to which, see the main work), see *post*, § 1-302.

Administration of Justice (Miscellaneous Provisions) Act 1933, s.2(3)-(8) and Sched. 2

★**1-296**   As to new rules made under section 2(6) of the 1933 Act regulating the procedure for making an application to a High Court judge for consent to prefer a bill of indictment ("a voluntary bill"), see *post*, § 1-302.

B. RULES AS TO PROCEDURE

★**1-298**   As to the intended replacement of the Indictments (Procedure) Rules 1971 (S.I. 1971 No. 2084) (as to which, see the main work), see *post*, § 1-302.

Voluntary bill procedure

Indictments (Procedure) Rules 1971 (S.I. 1971 No. 2084), r.2

★**1-302**   With effect from April 4, 2016, rules 4.3 and 4.4 (§§ 2-164, 2-165 in the main work, and *post*) of the Criminal Procedure Rules 2015 (S.I. 2015 No. 1490) are amended, and a new rule 10.3 (application to a High Court judge for consent to prefer a voluntary bill (*post*)) is inserted in the 2015 rules, by rules 5 and 6 of the Criminal Procedure (Amendment) Rules 2016 (S.I. 2016 No. 120). New rule 10.3 makes provision in relation to an application to a High Court judge for consent to prefer a voluntary bill and for the procedure for making and determining such an application (in accordance with the Administration of Justice (Miscellaneous Provisions) Act 1933, s.2(2)(b) (§ 1-277 in the main work)). It should also be noted that, whilst new rule 10.3 is plainly intended to replace the extant provisions of the Indictments (Procedure) Rules 1971 (S.I. 1971 No. 2084) (see the main work *et seq.*), the 1971 rules have not been revoked.

Criminal Procedure Rules 2015 (S.I. 2015 No. 1490), r.10.3

Application to a High Court judge for permission to serve a draft indictment

10.3.—(1) This rule applies where a prosecutor wants a High Court judge's permission to serve a draft indictment.

(2) Such a prosecutor must—
(a) apply in writing;
(b) serve the application on—
   (i) the court officer, and
   (ii) the proposed defendant, unless the judge otherwise directs; and
(c) ask for a hearing, if the prosecutor wants one, and explain why it is needed.

(3) The application must—
(a) attach—
   (i) the proposed indictment,
   (ii) copies of the documents containing the evidence on which the prosecutor relies, including any written witness statement or statements complying with rule 16.2 (content of written witness statement) and any documentary exhibit to any such statement,
   (iii) a copy of any indictment on which the defendant already has been arraigned, and
   (iv) if not contained in such an indictment, a list of any offence or offences for which the defendant already has been sent for trial;
(b) include—
   (i) a concise statement of the circumstances in which, and the reasons why, the application is made, and
   (ii) a concise summary of the evidence contained in the documents accompanying the application, identifying each passage in those documents said to evidence each offence alleged by the prosecutor and relating that evidence to each count in the proposed indictment; and
(c) contain a statement that, to the best of the prosecutor's knowledge, information and belief—
   (i) the evidence on which the prosecutor relies will be available at the trial, and
   (ii) the allegations contained in the application are substantially true
   unless the application is made by or on behalf of the Director of Public Prosecutions or the Director of the Serious Fraud Office.

(4) A proposed defendant served with an application who wants to make representations to the judge must—
(a) serve the representations on the court officer and on the prosecutor;
(b) do so as soon as practicable, and in any event within such period as the judge directs; and
(c) ask for a hearing, if the proposed defendant wants one, and explain why it is needed.

(5) The judge may determine the application—
(a) without a hearing, or at a hearing in public or in private;
(b) with or without receiving the oral evidence of any proposed witness.

(6) At any hearing, if the judge so directs a statement required by paragraph (3)(c) must be repeated on oath or affirmation.

(7) If the judge gives permission to serve a draft indictment, the decision must be recorded in writing and endorsed on, or annexed to, the proposed indictment.

[Rule 10.3 is inserted, with effect from April 4, 2016, by the Criminal Procedure (Amendment) Rules 2016 (S.I. 2016 No. 120), r.5.]

Indictments (Procedure) Rules 1971 (S.I. 1971 No. 2084), r.6

As to the intended replacement of S.I. 1971 No. 2084 (see the main work), see *ante*, § 1-302.   **★1-303**

Indictments (Procedure) Rules 1971 (S.I. 1971 No. 2084), rr.7, 8

As to the intended replacement of S.I. 1971 No. 2084 (see the main work), see *ante*, § 1-302.   **★1-305**

Indictments (Procedure) Rules 1971 (S.I. 1971 No. 2084), rr.9, 10

As to the intended replacement of S.I. 1971 No. 2084 (see the main work), see *ante*, § 1-302.   **★1-306**

★**1-307**   As to the intended replacement of S.I. 1971 No. 2084 (see the main work), see *ante*, § 1-302.

XI. POWERS AND DUTIES OF PARTICULAR PROSECUTION AGENCIES

A. Crown Prosecution Service

(8) Guidelines for crown prosecutors

Prosecution of Offences Act 1985, s.10

★**1-337**   The Guidance on a Victim's Right to Review issued by the DPP (with effect from June 5, 2013), which provides that a suspect is not to be made aware of a victim's request for a review during the review process (the suspect thus having no opportunity to make representations to the independent reviewing prosecutor), is lawful: *S. v. CPS and Oxford Magistrates' Court* [2016] 1 Cr.App.R. 14 (considering *L. v. DPP and Commr of Police for the Metropolis*; *Pratt v. CPS* (see the main work) and *R. v. Killick* (*ibid.*, § 4-93)).

(15) Consents to prosecutions

Prosecution of Offences Act 1985, s.25

★**1-365**   Whereas section 4 of the CLA 1977 (§ 33-34 in the main work) prohibits the institution of proceedings for certain offences of conspiracy "except by or with the consent of" the Attorney-General, (i) the modern process of entering a charge on the register of a magistrates' court is a formal and administrative step and, accordingly, does not in itself involve the institution of proceedings; thus, consent need not be obtained before that step is undertaken; it is within the scope of section 25(2) (see the main work) of the 1985 Act in that it is purely part of the administrative process that follows arrest, charging and remand in custody or on bail; (ii) consent is, however, required to be obtained prior to the sending of a case to the Crown Court pursuant to section 51 (§ 1-25 in the main work) of the CDA 1998; a sending under section 51 is not within the protection afforded by section 25(2) of the 1985 Act: *R. v. Welsh (Christopher Mark) (Senior)* [2016] 1 Cr.App.R. 9 (considering, *inter alia*, *R. v. Lambert* (as to which, see the main work), and *R. v. W. (C.) and M. (M.)* (as to which, see the main work, and now reported at [2016] 1 Cr.App.R. 8, *sub nom. R. v. Welsh (Christopher) (Junior)*).

B. Serious Fraud Office

(2) Investigation powers

Criminal Justice Act 1987, s.2

Director's investigation powers

★**1-373**   For new rules relating to applications for warrants under section 2 of the 1987 Act (see § 1-372 in the main work), see *post*, § 15-272.

Chapter 2

THE CRIMINAL JURISDICTION OF THE CROWN COURT

I. THE CROWN COURT

C. Constitution

(1) Judges of the Crown Court

Criminal Procedure Rules 2015 (S.I. 2015 No. 1490), r.34.11

Constitution of the Crown Court

★**2-8**   With effect from April 4, 2016, a new rule 34.11 of S.I. 2015 No. 1490 is substituted by rule 11(c) of the Criminal Procedure (Amendment) Rules 2016 (S.I. 2016 No. 120), as follows-

"Constitution of the Crown Court
34.11.— (1) On the hearing of an appeal the general rule is that—
  (a) the Crown Court must comprise—
    (i) a judge of the High Court, a Circuit judge, a Recorder or a qualifying judge advocate, and
    (ii) no less than two and no more than four justices of the peace, none of whom took part in the decision under appeal; and
  (b) if the appeal is from a youth court—
    (i) each justice of the peace must be qualified to sit as a member of a youth court, and
    (ii) the Crown Court must include a man and a woman.
(2) Despite the general rule—
  (a) the Crown Court may include only one justice of the peace and need not include both a man and a woman if—
    (i) the presiding judge decides that otherwise the start of the appeal hearing will be delayed unreasonably, or
    (ii) one or more of the justices of the peace who started hearing the appeal is absent; and
  (b) the Crown Court may comprise only a judge of the High Court, a Circuit judge, a Recorder or a qualifying judge advocate if—
    (i) the appeal is against conviction, under section 108 of the Magistrates' Courts Act 1980, and
    (ii) the respondent agrees that the court should allow the appeal, under section 48(2) of the Senior Courts Act 1981.
(3) Before the hearing of an appeal begins—
  (a) the Crown Court may comprise only a judge of the High Court, a Circuit judge, a Recorder or a qualifying judge advocate; and
  (b) so constituted, the court may, among other things, exercise the powers to which the rules in this Part and in Part 3 (case management) apply.".

(2) Additional powers

Courts Act 2003, s.66

Judges having powers of District Judges (Magistrates' Courts)

Section 66 of the 2003 Act does not give the Crown Court the ability to reconstitute itself as a magistrates' court; where it does operate, the judge continues to sit as a judge of the Crown Court, but merely exercises powers available to a district judge in criminal causes and matters: *R. v. Frimpong*, unreported, December 16, 2015, CA ([2015] EWCA Crim. 1933) (considering *R. (W. (a minor)) v. Leeds Crown Court* (as to which, see § 2-12 in the main work)).   ★2-10

V. APPELLATE JURISDICTION OF CROWN COURT IN CRIMINAL CASES

B. RIGHTS OF APPEAL TO CROWN COURT

(10) Appeals relating to investigation anonymity orders

Part 47 of the Criminal Procedure Rules 2015 (S.I. 2015 No. 1490) (as to which, see the main work) is replaced by a new Part 47 by the Criminal Procedure (Amendment) Rules 2016 (S.I. 2016 No. 120) with effect from April 4, 2016. New rules 47.45 to 47.49 make corresponding provision to that previously made by rules 47.23 to 47.26, with rule 47.49 corresponding to the former rule 47.26 (appeals to the Crown Court).   ★2-106

F. PROCEDURE

(1) Rules of court

Criminal Procedure Rules 2015 (S.I. 2015 No. 1490), Pt 34

Application to introduce further evidence

With effect from April 4, 2016, rule 34.7 (including the heading) of S.I. 2015 No. 1490 (see the main work) is amended by rule 11(a) of the Criminal Procedure (Amendment) Rules 2016 (S.I. 2016 No. 120), so as to (i) to substitute *"Application to introduce further evidence or for ruling on procedure, evidence or other question of law"* as the new heading, (ii) to substitute the words   ★2-123

"Paragraph (2) of this rules applies where", for the words "This rule applies where" in paragraph (1), and (iii) to insert new paragraphs (3) and (4), as follows—

"(3) Paragraph (4) of this rule applies to an application—
    (a) about—
        (i) case management, or any other question of procedure, or
        (ii) the introduction or admissibility of evidence, or any other question of law;
    (b) that has not been determined before the hearing of the appeal begins.
(4) The application is subject to any other rule that applies to it (for example, as to the time and form in which the application must be made).".

VI. CRIMINAL PROCEDURE RULES

Criminal Procedure Rules 2015 (S.I. 2015 No. 1490), Pt 2

Definitions

★2-160   With effect from April 4, 2016, the definition of "live link" in rule 2.2 of S.I. 2015 No. 1490 is amended by rule 3 of the Criminal Procedure (Amendment) Rules 2016 (S.I. 2016 No. 120), so as to substitute the words "in the courtroom" for the words "in court".

Criminal Procedure Rules 2015 (S.I. 2015 No. 1490), Pt 4

Service by handing over a new document

★2-164   There is an error in rule 4.3 of S.I. 2015 No. 1490 as set out in the main work. A new paragraph (3) was included in S.I. 2015 No. 1490, as follows—

"(3) Unless the court otherwise directs, for the purposes of paragraph (1)(c) or (d) (service by handing a document to a party's representative) "representative" includes an advocate appearing for that party at a hearing.".

What is shown as paragraph (3) in the main work became paragraph (4). Paragraph (4) has now been amended by rule 5(a) of the Criminal Procedure (Amendment) Rules 2016 (S.I. 2016 No. 120), with effect from April 4, 2016. The effect of the amendment is to re-number paragraph (4)(b) as paragraph (4)(c), and to insert a new paragraph (b) as follows-
    "(b) in relation to an application to a High Court judge for permission to serve a draft indictment—
        (i) in London, the Queen's Bench Listing Office, Royal Courts of Justice, Strand, London WC2A 2LL, and
        (ii) elsewhere, the office at which court staff administer the business of any court then constituted of a High Court judge;".

Service by leaving or posting a document

★2-165   With effect from April 4, 2016, rule 4.4 of S.I. 2015 No. 1490 is amended by rule 5(b) of the Criminal Procedure (Amendment) Rules 2016 (S.I. 2016 No. 120), so as to re-number paragraph (3)(b) as paragraph (3)(c), and to insert a new paragraph (b), as follows—
    "(b) in relation to an application to a High Court judge for permission to serve a draft indictment—
        (i) in London, the Listing Office of the Queen's Bench Division of the High Court, and
        (ii) elsewhere, the office at which court staff administer the business of any court then constituted of a High Court judge;".

CHAPTER 3

BAIL, APPEARANCE OF ACCUSED FOR TRIAL, PRESENCE DURING TRIAL

I. BAIL

A. GENERAL

(7) Place of remand

(b) *Persons under 21 years*

Secure accommodation for children remanded to local authority accommodation

The Children (Secure Accommodation) Regulations 1991 (S.I. 1991 No. 1505) (see the main work), have been further amended by the Children (Secure Accommodation) (Amendment) (England) Regulations 2015 (S.I. 2015 No. 1883) (with effect from December 7, 2015).   ★3-107

B. SPECIFIC PROVISIONS

(1) The police

(a) *The Police and Criminal Evidence Act 1984*

Police and Criminal Evidence Act 1984, s.37

Duties of custody officer before charge

With effect from October 26, 2015 (Criminal Justice and Courts Act 2015 (Commencement No. 3 and Transitional Provisions) Order 2015 (S.I. 2015 No. 1778)), section 42 of the 2015 Act (see the main work) was brought into force.   3-141

Police and Criminal Evidence Act 1984, s.46A

Power of arrest for failure to answer police bail

As to the application of section 46A of the 1984 Act (§ 3-167 in the main work) to investigations conducted, and persons detained, by Revenue and Customs officers, see S.I. 2015 No. 1783, *post*, § 15-27.   ★3-168

III. PRESENCE OF ACCUSED IN COURT DURING THE TRIAL

A. GENERAL RULE

Trial

Where the appellant had been prosecuted for breaching an anti-social behaviour order (which prohibited him from appearing in public naked), contrary to the CDA 1998, s.1(10) (§ 5-1199 in the 2015 edition of this work), and where he had wished to represent himself, but had refused to wear any clothes in court, the judge had been right to exclude him from the courtroom and try him *in absentia*; were he to have appeared naked in court, it would have been a further breach of the order; that a court should contemplate concurrence with the commission of a criminal offence during proceedings before it was a bizarre notion and, without more, fatal to the appeal; the judge's failure to consider any *ad hoc* alternative arrangement, such as use of a screen, did not render her decision irrational; it had always been open to the appellant to appear in court; had he clothed himself he could have taken a part in proceedings; that he opted by his response to the court's inevitable ruling to stay out of court was his decision; he had known the consequences: *R. v. Gough (Stephen)*, 179 J.P. 416, CA.   ★3-223

CHAPTER 4

TRIAL

I. PRELIMINARIES

A. COMMENCEMENT DATE

Senior Courts Act 1981, s.77

Sending for trial: date of trial

★**4-1**   As to the prescription of time periods for the purposes of section 77 of the 1981 Act (see the main work), see the amendment to rule 3.24 of the Criminal Procedure Rules 2015 (S.I. 2015 No. 1490), *post*, § 4-121.

B. HEARING IN OPEN COURT

(2) Statutory exceptions

(c) *Rules of court*

★**4-13**   As to the intended replacement of the Indictments (Procedure) Rules 1971 (S.I. 1971 No. 2084) (as to which, see the main work), see *ante*, § 1-302.

C. PUBLICITY

(2) Restrictions

(b) *Child or young person as victim, witness or defendant*

Youth Justice and Criminal Evidence Act 1999, ss.44, 45, 45A

Power to restrict reporting of criminal proceedings involving persons under 18

★**4-27**   Given the similarity of their terms, the case law relating to section 39 of the CYPA 1933 (as to which, see §§ 4-28, 4-29 in the main work) may still provide guidance as to the principles and practice to be followed when dealing with applications under section 45 of the YJCEA 1999 (as to which, see the main work): *R. v. H.* [2016] 1 Cr.App.R.(S.) 13, CA.

Power to restrict reporting of criminal proceedings for lifetime of witnesses and victims under 18

★**4-28**   With effect from November 15, 2015, the Youth Justice and Criminal Evidence Act 1999 (Application to Service Courts) Order 2009 (S.I. 2009 No. 2083) (see the main work) was further amended by the Youth Justice and Criminal Evidence Act 1999 (Application to Service Courts) (Amendment) (No. 2) Order 2015 (S.I. 2015 No. 1805) so as to extend its provisions to proceedings before the Summary Appeal Court. The amended articles include article 13.

(c) *Certain adult witnesses and victims*

Youth Justice and Criminal Evidence Act 1999, s.46

Power to restrict reports about certain adult witnesses in criminal proceedings

★**4-33**   As to the further amendment of S.I. 2009 No. 2083 (see the main work), see S.I. 2015 No. 1805, *ante*, § 4-28.

Youth Justice and Criminal Evidence Act 1999, s.47

Restrictions on reporting directions under Chapter 1, 1A or 2

★**4-34**   As to the further amendment of S.I. 2009 No. 2083 (see the main work), see S.I. 2015 No. 1805, *ante*, § 4-28.

Youth Justice and Criminal Evidence Act 1999, s.52

Decisions as to public interest for purposes of Chapter IV

As to the further amendment of S.I. 2009 No. 2083 (see the main work), see S.I. 2015 No. ★**4-36**
1805, *ante*, § 4-28.

D. Identity and Impartiality of Judge

Impartiality

The fact that a judge was only one of ten judges on an appellate bench was irrelevant where ★**4-53**
the applicant had objective grounds to fear the impartiality of that particular judge: *Morice v.*
France (2016) 62 E.H.R.R. 1.

G. Representation of the Defendant

(1) Legal representation

For a case considering *R. v. Ulcay* (see the main work), see *R. (Sanjari) v. Crown Court at* ★**4-67**
Birmingham, *post*, § 6-286.

J. Retrial

R. v. Burton is now reported at [2016] 1 Cr.App.R. 7. ★**4-72**

K. Limited Discretionary Power to Prevent Prosecution Proceeding

(2) Abuse of process

(b) *Where it will be impossible to give the defendant a fair trial*

General

Prosecutorial failings (here, in relation to their disclosure duties) are not relevant to whether ★**4-77**
the defendant can have a fair trial; and unjustified delay on its own cannot justify a stay; serious
prejudice to the defendant consequent on the delay must be shown (*R. v. S. (S.P.)*, and *R. v. F.*
(S.) (as to both of which, see § 4-79 in the main work)), and "prejudice" here refers to prejudice
to a fair trial, not personal prejudice: *R. v. R.* (2016) 160(1) S.J. 43, CA ([2015] EWCA Crim.
1941). As to this case, see also *post*, §§ 4-87, 12-59.

Delay and the right to trial "within a reasonable time"

Common law principles

For a case considering *R. v. S. (S.P.)* and *R. v. F. (S.)* (see the main work), see *R. v. R.*, *ante*, § ★**4-79**
4-77.

(c) *Where a stay is necessary to protect the integrity of the criminal justice system*

General

It is important that conduct or results that may merely be the consequence of state ★**4-87**
incompetence or negligence should not necessarily justify the abandonment of a trial of serious
allegations; to grant a stay where neither prosecutorial misconduct of the type identified in the
authorities (e.g. *R. v. Horseferry Road Magistrates' Court, ex p. Bennett* and *R. v. Mullen* (as to both of
which, see § 4-99 in the main work)), nor delay such as would prejudice a fair trial, can be
established would provide a perverse incentive for defendants to procrastinate and seek to
undermine the prosecution by creating hurdles to overcome, in the hope that a particular hurdle
will cause it to fail: *R. v. R.* (2016) 160(1) S.J. 43, CA ([2015] EWCA Crim. 1941). As to this case,
see also *ante*, § 4-77; and *post*, § 12-59.

N. Pre-Trial Hearings

(2) Plea and trial preparation hearings

Arraigning the defendant on the indictment

With effect from April 4, 2016, rule 3.24 of S.I. 2015 No. 1490 (see the main work) is amended ★**4-121** by rule 4 of the Criminal Procedure (Amendment) Rules 2016 (S.I. 2016 No. 120) to prescribe periods for the purposes of section 77 of the Senior Courts Act 1981 (§ 4-1 in the main work). This is effected by the insertion of a new paragraph (5), as follows—

> "(5) In a case in which a magistrates' court sends the defendant for trial, the Crown Court must take the defendant's plea—
>> (a) not less than 2 weeks after the date on which that sending takes place, unless the parties otherwise agree; and
>> (b) not more than 16 weeks after that date, unless the court otherwise directs (either before or after that period expires).".

Criminal Procedure Rules 2015 (S.I. 2015 No. 1490), rr.3.13-3.25

★**4-124**   The Lord Chief Justice has authorised the use in the Crown Court of two new forms of certificate of readiness for trial, one to be completed by the defendant and one by the prosecutor. Both forms can be found in the Criminal Procedure Rules section of the Ministry of Justice website, under Part 3 - Case management (http://www.justice.gov.uk/courts/procedure-rules/crimi nal/formspage).

VI. CRIMINAL PROCEDURE RULES: TRIAL AND SENTENCE

Criminal Procedure Rules 2015 (S.I. 2015 No. 1490), Pt 25

Procedure on plea of not guilty

★**4-265f**   With effect from April 4, 2016, rule 10(a) of the Criminal Procedure (Amendment) Rules 2016 (S.I. 2016 No. 120) amends rule 25.9 of S.I. 2015 No. 1490 (see the main work), so as: (i) to substitute a new paragraph (2)(b), as follows—
> "(b) the prosecutor may summarise the prosecution case, concisely outlining the facts and the matters likely to be in dispute;",

(ii) to insert a new paragraph (2)(c), as follows—
> "(c) where there is a jury, to help the jurors to understand the case and resolve any issue in it the court may—
>> (i) invite the defendant concisely to identify what is in issue, if necessary in terms approved by the court,
>> (ii) if the defendant declines to do so, direct that the jurors be given a copy of any defence statement served under rule 15.4 (defence disclosure), edited if necessary to exclude any reference to inappropriate matters or to matters evidence of which would not be admissible;";

(iii) to re-number paragraphs (2)(c) to (2)(j) accordingly; (iv) in paragraph (3), for "Paragraph (2)(d)" to substitute "Paragraph (2)(e)"; and (v) in paragraph (4), for "Paragraph (2)(e)" to substitute "Paragraph (2)(f)".

Directions to the jury and taking the verdict

★**4-265g**   With effect from April 4, 2016, rule 25.14(6) of S.I. 2015 No. 1490 (see the main work) is amended by rule 10(c) of the Criminal Procedure (Amendment) Rules 2016 (S.I. 2016 No. 120) to correct the drafting mistake referred to in the main work.

VII. THE JURY

F. THE JUDGE'S DISCRETION TO STAND JURORS DOWN

★**4-293**   For a further appeal in the case of *R. v. Khan* (see the main work), see *R. v. Hanif (No. 2)*, *post*, § 7-89.

XIV. THE DEFENCE CASE

B. WARNING AS TO GIVING OF EVIDENCE BY DEFENDANT

Criminal Justice and Public Order Act 1994, s.35

Effect of accused's silence at trial

★**4-379**   Whether the drawing of an adverse inference from an accused's silence at trial infringes his right to a fair trial under Article 6 of the ECHR (§ 16-72 in the main work) is to be determined in light of the circumstances of the particular case; in practice, adequate safeguards must be in place to ensure that any adverse inferences do not go beyond what is permitted under Article 6 (*i.e.* silence may be taken into account in situations that clearly call for an explanation (*Murray v. U.K.* (as to which, see §§ 15-172, 16-94 in the main work)); the critical question will be whether the proceedings as a whole were fair; and the trial judge's direction to the jury will be of particular relevance to the inquiry: *O'Donnell v. U.K.* (2015) 61 E.H.R.R. 37. Where, therefore, the defendant in a murder case (the applicant) had an I.Q. of 62 and an understanding of spoken English equivalent to a six-year-old, where there had been competing medical evidence as to whether it was "undesirable" for him to give evidence (see s.35(2)(b) of the 1994 Act), and where the trial judge concluded on a *voire dire* that his mental condition did not make it undesirable for him to do so and that, accordingly, the jury should be permitted to draw an adverse inference from his failure to give evidence, taking all the circumstances into account, including the weight of the circumstantial evidence that called for an explanation, the competing medical evidence and the judge's clear and detailed direction to the jury (setting out the expert evidence, explaining that the prosecution retained the burden of proof, regardless of whether or not the defendant chose to testify, and instructing them that they could only draw an adverse inference from his silence if they were satisfied beyond a reasonable doubt that the evidence relied upon by him to justify his silence did not adequately explain his absence from the witness box), there was no violation of Article 6(1); the circumstantial evidence meant that the resulting conviction could not have been based solely or mainly on the defendant's failure to testify; and there had been nothing unreasonable about the manner in which the judge preferred the prosecution's medical expert, particularly since he allowed the defence expert to give evidence to the jury as to the defendant's intellectual capacity and the effect that this might have on his ability to give evidence on his own behalf: *ibid.* (also considering *Beckles v. U.K.* (§§ 15-370, 16-94 in the main work)).

CHAPTER 5

SENTENCES AND ORDERS ON CONVICTION

II. PRELIMINARIES

(1) Procedure following plea of guilty or conviction by court or jury

Criminal Procedure Rules 2015 (S.I. 2015 No. 1490), r.25.16

Procedure if the court convicts
    R. v. Thames Water Utilities Ltd is now reported at [2015] 2 Cr.App.R.(S.) 63.   **5-11b**

III. GENERAL PRINCIPLES

B. DETERMINING THE SERIOUSNESS OF AN OFFENCE

(2) Factual basis for sentence

(a) *On conviction following a plea of not guilty*

Relevance of other offences apparently committed by the offender disclosed by the evidence against him
    R. v. O'Prey (see the main work) was considered in *R. v. O'Leary, post,* § 5-122.   **5-80**

(b) *Following plea of guilty*

Agreed basis of plea
    R. v. Thames Water Utilities Ltd is now reported at [2015] 2 Cr.App.R.(S.) 63.   **5-96**

(3) Information about the effect of the offence on the victim

★**5-104**   As to whether the guideline on domestic violence (Appendix K-82) allows for the imposition of a more lenient sentence because of representations on the victim's behalf, see *R. v. Moore, post,* Appendix K-412.

C. REDUCTION IN SENTENCE FOR GUILTY PLEA

Advance indication of sentence (before plea)

5-111   Where, following a *Goodyear* indication (*R. v. Goodyear (Practice note)* (see the main work)), the defendant pleaded guilty but then absconded before sentence, and where he subsequently surrendered to custody and pleaded guilty to failing to surrender to bail for which he received a consecutive sentence, the judge had been bound by the indication he had given in relation to the primary offence; an indication, once given, is, save in exceptional circumstances (see *R. v. Newman* (§ 5-111 in the main work)), binding on the judge who gave it and any other judge, subject to overriding statutory obligations such as those following a finding of dangerousness: *R. v. Davies* [2015] 2 Cr.App.R.(S.) 57, CA.

D. INREASE IN SENTENCES FOR RACIAL OR RELIGIOUS AGGRAVATION OR AGGRAVATION RELATED TO DISABILITY OR SEXUAL ORIENTATION

Procedure

5-122   In *R. v. O'Leary* [2016] 1 Cr.App.R.(S.) 11, CA, it was held that section 145 of the CJA 2003 (increase in sentences for racial or religious aggravation (§ 5-120 in the main work)) obliges a court to consider whether an offence was racially or religiously aggravated even if the offence in question could have been charged under one of sections 29 to 32 of the CDA 1998. Thus, in the particular circumstances, it had been open to the judge to sentence for an offence of wounding, contrary to the Offences against the Person Act 1861, s.20 (§ 19-252 in the main work), on the basis that it was racially aggravated, even though section 29 of the 1998 Act (*ibid.,* § 19-266) makes specific provision for an offence of racially aggravated wounding. However, the court said that this was not to be taken as supporting the view that the prosecution are thereby relieved of the duty to consider the indictment with care; in the majority of cases where the evidence supports an aggravated form of assault, it should be pleaded as such in the indictment. The court considered, *inter alia, R. v. O'Prey* (*ibid.,* § 5-80).

E. MITIGATION

(3) Selected mitigating factors

Age/ill health

5-131   Where the appellant was blind and had impaired hearing, where he had been involved in the high-level distribution of cocaine and heroin and fell to be sentenced for three conspiracies to supply Class A drugs, the judge had been entitled not to reduce the appropriate sentence on account of his disabilities; they had not prevented him from playing a leading role in a sophisticated, large-scale operation from which he obtained a lavish lifestyle; the prison authorities had taken steps to ensure he had appropriate accommodation and support: *R. v. Arshad* [2015] 2 Cr.App.R.(S.) 54, CA (considering *R. v Hall* (as to which, see the main work)).

Assistance to law enforcement agencies

Serious Organised Crime and Police Act 2005, ss.73-75A

Assistance by defendant: review of sentence

★**5-133**   As to whether the common law principle allowing a discount in sentencing for assistance given to prosecuting authorities could be extended to an offender who, having given no assistance prior to sentence, thereafter provided material assistance, but could not bring his case within section 74 of the 2005 Act (as to which, see the main work), see *R. v. Z., post,* § 5-140.

Assistance given otherwise than in accordance with the 2005 Act

The common law principle that a discount in sentencing would be provided where help had ★**5-140**
been given, or was expected to be given, to law enforcement authorities (see *R. v. A. and B.* and
R. v. A. in the main work), should not be extended to allow an offender who had given no assistance prior to sentence thereafter to provide material assistance, and then to obtain a reduction
in sentence by way of a belated appeal against sentence: *R. v. Z.* [2016] 1 Cr.App.R.(S.) 15, CA.

F. SENTENCING GUIDELINES

Sentencing Council for England and Wales

R. v. Thames Water Utilities Ltd is now reported at [2015] 2 Cr.App.R.(S.) 63.   ★**5-147**

The Sentencing Council for England and Wales has issued a definitive guideline covering the
offences of theft, contrary to the Theft Act 1968, s.1 (§ 21-15 in the main work), abstracting
electricity, contrary to section 13 of the 1968 Act (*ibid.*, § 21-169), handling stolen goods, contrary
to section 22 of the 1968 Act (*ibid.*, § 21-221), going equipped, contrary to section 25 of the 1968
Act (*ibid.*, § 21-288), and making off without payment, contrary to section 3 of the Theft Act 1978
(*ibid.*, § 21-303), applying to all offenders aged 18 or over who are sentenced on or after February
1, 2016. For the details thereof, see *post*, Appendix K-315 *et seq.*

The Sentencing Council has issued a definitive guideline on corporate manslaughter and   ★
certain offences under legislation relating to health and safety and food safety and hygiene. It applies to all organisations and individuals aged 18 or over, sentenced on or after February 1, 2016,
regardless of the date of the offence. So far as corporate manslaughter is concerned, the new
guideline is clearly intended to replace the former guideline (Appendix K-252 *et seq.* in the first
supplement to this edition). So far as health and safety offences are concerned, this was presumably the intention, but there is no express statement to this effect and it may be noted that the
former guideline was not confined to any particular offences, but was confined to offences that
caused death, whereas the new guideline is not confined to offences causing death or any other
harm but is expressed as applying to only certain offences under the Health and Safety at Work
etc. Act 1974. For the detail of the guideline relating to corporate manslaughter, see *post*, Appendix K-252 *et seq.*

The Sentencing Council has also issued a definitive guideline on robbery offences, which are   ★
divided into "street and less sophisticated commercial" robberies, "professionally planned commercial" robberies, and robberies in a dwelling. It applies to all offenders aged 18 and over who
are sentenced on or after April 1, 2016, regardless of the date of the offence. For the detail of the
guideline, see *post*, Appendix K-80a *et seq.*

The Sentencing Council has also conducted a consultation on a draft guideline relating to the   ★
imposition of community and custodial sentences. This closed on February 25, 2016.

Most recently, the Sentencing Council launched a consultation on a draft revised guideline
relating to reduction in sentence for a guilty plea. The consultation closes on May 5, 2016.

H. TAKING OFFENCES INTO CONSIDERATION

Significance

Where an offender was given the maximum sentence available for an offence, which was   ★**5-163**
discounted to give credit for a guilty plea, the judge had been entitled slightly to inflate the
discounted sentence in order to reflect offences (which would have resulted in substantial sentences
in their own right) being taken into consideration: *R. v. Kennedy* [2015] 2 Cr.App.R.(S.) 61, CA.

V. COMMUNITY SENTENCES

C. COMMUNITY ORDERS

(1) General
Criminal Justice Act 2003, s.177

Community orders

With effect from January 30, 2016, the Legal Aid, Sentencing and Punishment of Offenders Act   ★**5-253**

2012 (Alcohol Abstinence and Monitoring Requirements) Piloting Order 2014 (S.I. 2014 No. 1777) (see the main work) was further amended by the Legal Aid, Sentencing and Punishment of Offenders Act 2012 (Alcohol Abstinence and Monitoring Requirements) Piloting (Amendment) Order 2016 (S.I. 2016 No. 1) so as to extend the period that section 76 of the 2012 Act (alcohol abstinence and monitoring requirement (as to which, see *ibid.*)) is in force in relation to the South London local justice area to March 31, 2016. In consequence, any alcohol abstinence and monitoring order imposed on or before that date will continue to have effect after that date: art. 4(2) of S.I. 2014 No. 1777.

(3) Requirements available in the case of all offenders
Criminal Justice Act 2003, ss.199-213

Alcohol abstinence and monitoring requirement

★**5-279**   With effect from January 30, 2016, the Criminal Justice Act 2003 (Alcohol Abstinence and Monitoring Requirement) (Prescription of Arrangement for Monitoring) Order 2014 (S.I. 2014 No. 1787) (see the main work) was amended by the Criminal Justice Act 2003 (Alcohol Abstinence and Monitoring Requirement) (Prescription of Arrangement for Monitoring) (Amendment) Order 2016 (S.I. 2016 No. 10) so as to keep in place, until March 31, 2016, the specification for monitoring compliance with an alcohol abstinence and monitoring requirement (*ibid.*), to take account of the extended period of the pilot scheme (as to which, see S.I. 2016 No. 1, *ante*, § 5-253).

D. Youth Community Orders

Introduction

5-291   Attendance centre orders under section 60 of the PCC(S)A 2000 were just one of several "youth community orders" that could be made under that Act. As explained in the main work, however, the sections of the Act that provided for the making of a curfew order (s.37), an exclusion order (s.40A), a supervision order (ss.63, 64 and 67, and Sched. 6) and an action plan order (ss.69–71) were repealed by the CJIA 2008, and these repeals came fully into force on November 30, 2009, except that they continue to apply to offences committed before that date. With the passage of time, it was unlikely that, by the time of publication of the 2013 edition of this work, further reference would need to be made to these provisions. Should it be necessary, however, they can be found in the supplements to the 2012 edition. The position with regard to section 60 is rather different (see the annotations thereto (*post*, § 5-292)).

Powers of Criminal Courts (Sentencing) Act 2000, s.60

Attendance centre orders

5-292   **60.**—(1) Where—

    (a) (subject to 148, 150 and 156 of the Criminal Justice Act 2003) a person aged under *21* [16] is convicted by or before a court of an offence punishable with imprisonment, or

    (b) a court [has power or] would have power, but for section 89 below (restrictions on imprisonment of young offenders and defaulters), to commit a person aged under *21* [16] to prison in default of payment of any sum of money or for failing to do or abstain from doing anything required to be done or left undone, *or*

    (c) *a court has power to commit a person aged at least 21 but under 25 to prison in default of payment of any sum of money,*

the court may, if it has been notified by the Secretary of State that an attendance centre is available for the reception of persons of his description, order him to attend at such a centre, to be specified in the order, for such number of hours as may be so specified.

(2) An order under subsection (1) above is in this Act referred to as an "attendance centre order".

(3) The aggregate number of hours for which an attendance centre order may require a person to attend at an attendance centre shall not be less than 12 except where—

    (a) he is aged under 14; and

    (b) the court is of the opinion that 12 hours would be excessive, having regard to his age or any other circumstances.

(4) The aggregate number of hours shall not exceed 12 except where the court is of the opinion, having regard to all the circumstances, that 12 hours would be inadequate, and in that case [shall not exceed 24]—

    (a) *shall not exceed 24 where the person is aged under 16; and*

    (b) *shall not exceed 36 where the person is aged 16 or over but under 21 or (where subsection (1)(c) above applies) under 25.*

(5) A court may make an attendance centre order in respect of a person before a previous attendance centre order made in respect of him has ceased to have effect, and may determine the number of hours to be specified in the order without regard—

    (a) to the number specified in the previous order; or

    (b) to the fact that order is still in effect.

(6) An attendance centre order shall not be made unless the court is satisfied that the attendance centre to be specified in it is reasonably accessible to the person concerned, having regard to his age, the means of access available to him and any other circumstances.

(7) The times at which a person is required to attend at an attendance centre shall, as for as practicable, be such as to avoid—

    (a) any conflict with his religious beliefs or with the requirements of any other [youth] community order to which he may be subject; and

    (b) any interference with the times, if any, at which he normally works or attends school or any other educational establishment.

(8) The first time at which the person is required to attend at an attendance centre shall be a time at which the centre is available for his attendance in accordance with the notification of the Secretary of State, and shall be specified in the order.

(9) The subsequent times shall be fixed by the officer in charge of the centre, having regard to the person's circumstances.

(10) A person shall not be required under this section to attend at an attendance centre on more than one occasion on any day, or for more than three hours on any occasion.

(11) Where a court makes an attendance centre order, the clerk of the court shall—

    (a) deliver or send a copy of the order to the officer in charge of the attendance centre specified in it; and

    (b) deliver a copy of the order to the person in respect of whom it is made or send a copy by registered post or the recorded delivery service addressed to his last or usual place of abode.

(12) Where a person ("the defaulter") has been ordered to attend at an attendance centre in default of the payment of any sum of money—

    (a) on payment of the whole sum to any person authorised to receive it, the attendance centre order shall cease to have effect;

    (b) on payment of a part of the sum to any such person, the total number of hours for which the defaulter is required to attend at the centre shall be reduced proportionately, that is to say by such number of complete hours as bears to the total number the proportion most nearly approximating to, without exceeding, the proportion which the part bears to the whole sum.

[This section is printed as amended by the CJA 2003, s.304, and Sched. 32, para. 102(1), (2)(a) (substitution of references to sections 148, 150 and 156 of the 2003 Act for references to corresponding provisions of the 2000 Act, and substitution of "16" for "21" in subs. (1)(a)), and (4) (substitution of "youth community order" for "community order" in subs. (7)); and as amended, as from a day to be appointed, by the CJCSA 2000, s.74 and Sched. 7, para. 173 (insertion of words in first set of square brackets in subs. (1)(b)); and the CJA 2003, s.304, and Sched. 32, paras 90 and 102(1), and (2)(b) and (c), and (3) (substitution of "16" for "21" in subs. (1)(b), omission of subs. (1)(c) and the word "or" immediately preceding it, substitution of words in square brackets for italicised words in subs. (4)). The amendments to subss. (1)(a) and (7) came into force on April 4, 2005: Criminal Justice Act 2003 (Commencement No. 8 and Transitional and Saving Provisions) Order 2005 (S.I. 2005 No. 950), save that, in the case of persons aged 16 or 17 upon conviction, the substitution of "16" for "21" in subs. (1)(a) and the insertion of the word "youth" before "community order" in subs. (7) have no application in relation to offences committed before November 30, 2009, or in relation to any failure to comply with an order made in respect of an offence committed before that date: *ibid.*, Sched. 2, paras 12 and 13. The whole of this section is repealed as from a day to be appointed (as to which, see §§ 5-1, 5-185, 5-186 in the main work) by the CJIA 2008, ss.6(1) and 149, and Sched. 28, Pt 1. To the extent that this repeal relates to subs. (1)(a), it was brought into force on November 30, 2009: Criminal Justice and Immigration Act 2008 (Commencement No. 13 and Transitory Provision) Order 2009 (S.I. 2009 No. 3074).]

As to the requirements to be complied with before imposing an attendance centre order, see **5-293** (for offences committed before April 4, 2005) sections 35 and 36 of the PCC(S)A 2000 (§§ 5-189, 5-190 in the supplements to the 2012 edition) (it being a "community order" within that Act), and (for offences committed after that date) section 148 of the CJA 2003 (§ 5-248 in the main work) (it being a "community sentence" within that Act).

It is not entirely clear whether a court may make attendance centre orders on the same occasion in respect of a number of offences with an aggregate in excess of the limits in subsection (4). It is submitted that the better view is that it cannot; section 60(1) appears to be concerned with defining an *occasion* when an attendance centre order may be made. On any such occasion *one* order may be made. Subsection (5) appears to confirm the correctness of this approach: if it were incorrect, subsection (5) would not be needed.

Section 61 gives effect to Schedule 5 (*post*, §§ 5-365 *et seq.*).

F. Enforcement, etc.

(2) Of youth community orders

Curfew, exclusion and supervision orders

5-364   As to curfew and exclusion orders, see Schedule 3 to the PCC(S)A 2000 (§§ 5-228 *et seq.* in the supplements to the 2012 edition); and as to supervision orders, see Schedule 7 to that Act (§§ 5-371 *et seq.* in the supplements to the 2012 edition).

Powers of Criminal Courts (Sentencing) Act 2000, Sched. 5

Section 61   SCHEDULE 5

Breach, Revocation and Amendment of Attendance Centre Orders

Breach of order or attendance centre rules

5-365   1.—(1) Where an attendance centre order is in force and it appears on information to a justice that the offender—
    (a) has failed to attend in accordance with the order, or
    (b) while attending has committed a breach of rules made under section 222(1)(d) or (e) of the Criminal Justice Act 2003 which cannot be adequately dealt with under those rules,
the justice may issue a summons requiring the offender to appear at the place and time specified in the summons or, if the information is in writing and on oath, may issue a warrant for the offender's arrest.

(2) Any summons or warrant issued under this paragraph shall direct the offender to appear or be brought—
    (a) before a magistrates' court acting for the petty sessions area in which the offender resides; or
    (b) if it is not known where the offender resides, before a magistrates' court acting for the petty sessions area in which is situated the attendance centre which the offender is required to attend by the order or by virtue of an order under paragraph 5(1)(b) below.

2.—(1) If it is proved to the satisfaction of the magistrates' court before which an offender appears or is brought under paragraph 1 above that he has failed without reasonable excuse to attend as mentioned in sub-paragraph (1)(a) of that paragraph or has committed such a breach of rules as is mentioned in sub-paragraph (1)(b) of that paragraph, that court may deal with him in any one of the following ways—
    (a) it may impose on him a fine not exceeding £1,000;
    (b) where the attendance centre order was made by a magistrates' court, it may deal with him, for the offence in respect of which the order was made, in any way in which he could have been dealt with for that offence by the court which made the order if the order had not been made; or
    (c) where the order was made by the Crown Court, it may commit him to custody or release him on bail until he can be brought or appear before the Crown Court.

(2) Any exercise by the court of its power under sub-paragraph (1)(a) above shall be without prejudice to the continuation of the order.

(3) A fine imposed under sub-paragraph (1)(a) above shall be deemed, for the purposes of any enactment, to be a sum adjudged to be paid by a conviction.

(4) Where a magistrates' court deals with an offender under sub-paragraph (1)(b) above, it shall revoke the attendance centre order if it is still in force.

(5) In dealing with an offender under sub-paragraph (1)(b) above, a magistrates' court—

  (a) shall take into account the extent to which the offender has complied with the requirements of the attendance centre order; and

  (b) in the case of an offender who has wilfully and persistently failed to comply with those requirements, may impose a custodial sentence notwithstanding anything in section 152(2) of the Criminal Justice Act 2003.

(5A) Where a magistrates' court dealing with an offender under sub-paragraph (1)(a) above would not otherwise have the power to amend the order under paragraph 5(1)(b) below (substitution of different attendance centre), that paragraph has effect as if references to an appropriate magistrates' court were references to the court dealing with an offender.

(6) A person sentenced under sub-paragraph (1)(b) above for an offence may appeal to the Crown Court against the sentence.

(7) A magistrates' court which deals with an offender's case under sub-paragraph (1)(c) above shall send to the Crown Court—

  (a) a certificate signed by a justice of the peace giving particulars of the offender's failure to attend or, as the case may be, the breach of the rules which he has committed; and

  (b) such other particulars of the case as may be desirable;

and a certificate purporting to be so signed shall be admissible as evidence of the failure or the breach before the Crown Court.

3.—(1) Where by virtue of paragraph 2(1)(c) above the offender is brought or appears before the Crown Court and it is proved to the satisfaction of the court—

  (a) that he has failed without reasonable excuse to attend as mentioned in paragraph 1(1)(a) above, or

  (b) that he has committed such a breach of rules as is mentioned in paragraph 1(1)(b) above,

that court may deal with him, for the offence in respect of which the order was made, in any way in which it could have dealt with him for that offence if it had not made the order.

(2) Where the Crown Court deals with an offender under sub-paragraph (1) above, it shall revoke the attendance centre order if it is still in force.

(3) In in dealing with an offender under sub-paragraph (1) above, the Crown Court—

  (a) shall take into account the extent to which the offender has complied with the requirements of the attendance centre order; and

  (b) in the case of an offender who has willfully and persistently failed to comply with those requirements, may impose a custodial sentence notwithstanding anything in section 152(2) of the Criminal Justice Act 2003.

(4) In proceedings before the Crown Court under this paragraph any question whether there has been a failure to attend or a breach of the rules shall be determined by the court and not by the verdict of a jury.

Revocation of order with or without re-sentencing

4.—(1) Where an attendance centre order is in force in respect of an offender, an appropriate **5-366** court may, on an application made by the offender or by the officer in charge of the relevant attendance centre, revoke the order.

(2) In sub-paragraph (1) above "an appropriate court" means—

  (a) where the court which made the order was the Crown Court and there is included in the order a direction that the power to revoke the order is reserved to that court, the Crown Court;

  (b) in any other case, either of the following—

    (i) a magistrates' court acting for the petty sessions area in which the relevant attendance centre is situated;

    (ii) the court which made the order.

(3) Any power conferred by this paragraph—

  (a) on a magistrates' court to revoke an attendance centre order made by such a court, or

  (b) on the Crown Court to revoke an attendance centre order made by the Crown Court,

includes power to deal with the offender, for the offence in respect of which the order was made, in any way in which he could have been dealt with for that offence by the court which made the order if the order had not been made.

(4) A person sentenced by a magistrates' court under sub-paragraph (3) above for an offence may appeal to the Crown Court against the sentence.

(5) The proper officer of a court which makes an order under this paragraph revoking an attendance centre order shall—

   (a) deliver a copy of the revoking order to the offender or send a copy by registered post or the recorded delivery service addressed to the offender's last or usual place of abode; and

   (b) deliver or send a copy to the officer in charge of the relevant attendance centre.

(6) In this paragraph "the relevant attendance centre", in relation to an attendance centre order, means the attendance centre specified in the order or substituted for the attendance centre so specified by an order made by virtue of paragraph 5(1)(b) below.

(7) In this paragraph "proper officer" means—

   (a) in relation to a magistrates' court, the justices' chief executive for the court; and

   (b) in relation to the Crown Court, the appropriate officer.

Amendment of order

5-367   5.—(1) Where an attendance centre order is in force in respect of an offender, an appropriate magistrates' court may, on application made by the offender or by the officer in charge of the relevant attendance centre, by order—

   (a) vary the day or hour specified in the order for the offender's first attendance at the relevant attendance centre; or

   (b) substitute for the relevant attendance centre an attendance centre which the court is satisfied is reasonably accessible to the offender, having regard to his age, the means of access available to him and any other circumstances.

(2) In sub-paragraph (1) above "an appropriate magistrates' court" means—

   (a) a magistrates' court acting for the petty sessions area in which the relevant attendance centre is situated; or

   (b) (except where the attendance centre order was made by the Crown Court) the magistrates' court which made the order.

(3) The justices' chief executive for a court which makes an order under this paragraph shall—

   (a) deliver a copy to the offender or send a copy by registered post or the recorded delivery service addressed to the offender's last or usual place of abode; and

   (b) deliver or send a copy—

     (i) if the order is made by virtue of sub-paragraph (1)(a) above, to the officer in charge of the relevant attendance centre; and

     (ii) if it is made by virtue of sub-paragraph (1)(b) above, to the officer in charge of the attendance centre which the order as amended will require the offender to attend.

(4) In this paragraph "the relevant attendance centre" has the meaning given by paragraph 4(6) above.

Orders made on appeal

5-368   6.—(1) Where an attendance centre order has been made on appeal, for the purposes of this Schedule it shall be deemed—

   (a) if it was made on an appeal brought from a magistrates' court, to have been made by that magistrates' court;

   (b) if it was made on an appeal brought from the Crown Court or from the criminal division of the Court of Appeal, to have been made by the Crown Court.

(2) In relation to an attendance centre order made on appeal, paragraphs 2(1)(b) and 4(3) above shall each have effect as if the words "if the order had not been made" were omitted and paragraph 3(1) above shall have effect as if the words "if it had not made the order" were omitted.

Orders for defaulters

5-369   7.—(1) References in this Schedule to an "offender" include a person who has been ordered to attend at an attendance centre for such a default or failure as is mentioned in section 60(1)(b) or (c) of this Act.

(2) Where a person has been ordered to attend at an attendance centre for such a default or failure—

   (a) paragraphs 2(1)(b), 3(1) and 4(3) above shall each have effect in relation to the order as if the words ", for the offence in respect of which the order was made," and "for that offence" were omitted; and

   (b) paragraphs 2(5)(b) and 3(3)(b) above (which relate to custodial sentences for offences) do not apply.

[This schedule is printed as amended by the CJA 2003, s.304, and Sched. 32, paras 90 and 126; and the Domestic Violence, Crime and Victims Act 2004, s.29, and Sched. 5, para. 6. The whole schedule is repealed as from a day to be appointed (as to which, see §§ 5-1, 5-185, 5-186 in the main work) by the CJIA 2008, ss.6(1) and 149, and Sched. 28, Pt 1.]

When dealing with an offender under paragraph 3(1), the court must observe any limitations **5-370** related to his age which applied at the time when he was sentenced: he must be sentenced on the basis of his age when he was originally convicted of the offence for which the attendance centre order was made.

In a case coming within paragraph 4, the failure to attend the attendance centre, or breach of the rules, must be proved to the satisfaction of the Crown Court: the certificate of the magistrates' court is merely evidence.

VI. CUSTODIAL SENTENCES

A. Mandatory Life Sentence

(2) Legislation

Criminal Justice Act 2003, Sched. 22, paras 1, 2, 9 and 10

Section 276　　　　　　　　　　　SCHEDULE 22

Mandatory Life Sentences: Transitional Cases

Interpretation

1. In this Schedule—　　　　　　　　　　　　　　　　　　　　　　　　　　**5-428**
　　"the commencement date" means the day on which section 269 comes into force;
　　"the early release provisions" means the provisions of section 28(5) to (8) of the Crime (Sentences) Act 1997;
　　"existing prisoner" means a person serving one or more mandatory life sentences passed before the commencement date (whether or not he is also serving any other sentence);
　　"life sentence" means a sentence of imprisonment for life or custody for life passed in England and Wales or by a court-martial outside England and Wales;
　　"mandatory life sentence" means a life sentence passed in circumstances where the sentence was fixed by law.

Existing prisoners notified by Secretary of State

2. Paragraph 3 applies in relation to any existing prisoner who, in respect of any mandatory life **5-429** sentence, has before the commencement date been notified in writing by the Secretary of State (otherwise than in a notice that is expressed to be provisional) either—
　　(a)　of a minimum period which in the view of the Secretary of State should be served before the prisoner's release on licence, or
　　(b)　that the Secretary of State does not intend that the prisoner should ever be released on licence.

Sentences passed on or after commencement date in respect of offences committed before that date

9. Paragraph 10 applies where—　　　　　　　　　　　　　　　　　　　　　　**5-430**
　　(a)　on or after the commencement date a court passes a life sentence in circumstances where the sentence is fixed by law, and
　　(b)　the offence to which the sentence relates was committed before the commencement date.
10. The court—
　　(a)　may not make an order under subsection (2) of section 269 specifying a part of the sentence which in the opinion of the court is greater than that which, under the practice followed by the Secretary of State before December 2002, the Secretary of State would have been likely to notify as mentioned in paragraph 2(a), and
　　(b)　may not make an order under subsection (4) of section 269 unless the court is of the opinion that, under the practice followed by the Secretary of State before December 2002, the Secretary of State would have been likely to give the prisoner a notification falling within paragraph 2(b).

B. Automatic Life Sentences

Powers of Criminal Courts (Sentencing) Act 2000, s.109

Life sentence for second serious offence

5-440   **109.**—(1) This section applies where—

(a) a person is convicted of a serious offence committed after 30th September 1997; and

(b) at the time when that offence was committed, he was 18 or over and had been convicted in any part of the United Kingdom of another serious offence.

(2) The court shall impose a life sentence, that is to say—

(a) *where the offender is 21 or over when convicted of the offence mentioned in subsection (1)(a) above, a sentence of imprisonment for life,*

(b) where he is under 21 at that time, a sentence of custody for life under section 94 above,

[a sentence of imprisonment for life] unless the court is of the opinion that there are exceptional circumstances relating to either of the offences or to the offender which justify its not doing so.

(3) Where the court does not impose a life sentence, it shall state in open court that it is of that opinion and what the exceptional circumstances are.

(4) An offence the sentence for which is imposed under *subsection (2)* above shall not be regarded as an offence the sentence for which is fixed by law.

(5) An offence committed in England and Wales is a serious offence for the purposes of this section if it is any of the following, namely—

(a) an attempt to commit murder, a conspiracy to commit murder or an incitement to murder;

(b) an offence under section 4 of the Offences Against the Person Act 1861 (soliciting murder);

(c) manslaughter;

(d) an offence under section 18 of the Offences Against the Person Act 1861 (wounding, or causing grievous bodily harm, with intent);

(e) rape or an attempt to commit rape;

(f) an offence under section 5 of the Sexual Offences Act 1956 (intercourse with a girl under 13);

(g) an offence under section 16 (possession of a firearm with intent to injure), section 17 (use of a firearm to resist arrest) or section 18 (carrying a firearm with criminal intent) of the Firearms Act 1968; and

(h) robbery where, at some time during the commission of the offence, the offender had in his possession a firearm or imitation firearm within the meaning of that Act.

(6) An offence committed in Scotland is a serious offence for the purposes of this section if the conviction for it was obtained on indictment in the High Court of Justiciary and it is any of the following, namely—

(a) culpable homicide;

(b) attempted murder, incitement to commit murder or conspiracy to commit murder;

(c) rape or attempted rape;

(d) clandestine injury to women or an attempt to cause such injury;

(e) sodomy, or an attempt to commit sodomy, where the complainer, that is to say, the person against whom the offence was committed, did not consent;

(f) assault where the assault—

(i) is aggravated because it was carried out to the victim's severe injury or the danger of the victim's life; or

(ii) was carried out with an intention to rape or to ravish the victim;

(g) robbery where, at some time during the commission of the offence, the offender had in his possession a firearm or imitation firearm within the meaning of the Firearms Act 1968;

(h) an offence under section 16 (possession of a firearm with intent to injure), section 17 (use of a firearm to resist arrest) or section 18 (carrying a firearm with criminal intent) of that Act;

(i) lewd, libidinous or indecent behaviour or practices; and

(j) an offence under section 5(1) of the Criminal Law (Consolidation) (Scotland) Act 1995 (unlawful intercourse with a girl under 13).

(7) An offence committed in Northern Ireland is a serious offence for the purposes of this section if it is any of the following, namely—

(a) an offence falling within any of paragraphs (a) to (e) of subsection (5) above;

(b) an offence under section 4 of the Criminal Law Amendment Act 1885 (intercourse with a girl under 14);

(c) an offence under Article 17 (possession of a firearm with intent to injure), Article 18(1) (use of a firearm to resist arrest) or Article 19 (carrying a firearm with criminal intent) of the Firearms (Northern Ireland) Order 1981; and

(d) robbery where, at some time during the commission of the offence, the offender had in his possession a firearm or imitation firearm within the meaning of that Order.

[This section is printed as amended, as from a day to be appointed, by the CJCSA 2000, s.74, and Sched. 7, para. 189 (substitution of words in square brackets for paras (a) and (b) in subs. (2)). It is repealed, as from April 4, 2005 (Criminal Justice Act 2003 (Commencement No. 8 and Transitional and Saving Provisions) Order 2005 (S.I. 2005 No. 950), by the CJA 2003, s.332, and Sched. 37 Pt 7. For the saving provisions in relation to an offence committed before April 4, 2005, see § 5-2 in the main work.]

Serious offences

The only attempts which are serious offences are those specifically mentioned: *R. v. Buckland*; **5-441** *R. v. Newman* [2000] 1 Cr.App.R. 471, CA. Offences under the Firearms Act 1968, s.17(2) are serious offences: *ibid.*; as are offences under sections 16, 17 and 18 of that Act where the firearm was an imitation only: *ibid.*

An offence of robbery is a "serious offence" within section 109(2)(h) if the offence was committed as a joint enterprise where a firearm or imitation was used, even though the offender himself had never had possession of it, provided that there was joint possession of it; where, in relation to the alleged index offence, there is an issue as to whether this was established against the offender, the court must be satisfied that at the earlier hearing the offender admitted, or it was admitted on his behalf, that he was in joint possession of the firearm: *R. v. Flamson* [2002] 2 Cr.App.R.(S.) 48, CA. The court considered that *R. v. Eubank* [2002] 1 Cr.App.R.(S.) 4, CA (§ 24-49 in the main work) had no application to the facts of the case. In *R. v. Murphy* [2003] 1 Cr.App.R.(S.) 39, CA, however, it was held, without reference to *Flamson*, that where there was an issue as to whether the defendant had been in possession of a firearm, the proper way to resolve the issue was, in accordance with *Eubank*, for an appropriate count under the Firearms Act 1968 to be included in the indictment. Where this course had not been adopted, it was not open to the judge to conclude in relation to either the index offence or the fresh offence that it fell within section 109(1)(h); absent an unequivocal admission on the part of the defendant (see *R. v. Benfield*; *R. v. Sobers* [2004] 1 Cr.App.R.(S.) 52, CA).

R. v. Benfield; *R. v. Sobers* was followed in *R. v. Hylands* [2005] 2 Cr.App.R.(S.) 25, CA, where it was said that for an offence of robbery to fall within section 109(5)(h) of the 2000 Act, the qualifying condition relating to a firearm or imitation firearm had to be established either by means of an appropriate count under the Firearms Act 1968 being included in the indictment, or there had to be an unequivocal admission in relation thereto; and this applies where the only issue in relation to the robbery is identity (there being unchallenged evidence before the jury that the robber was in possession of a firearm at the time of the robbery); if there was any doubt about the matter, it was to be resolved in favour of the defendant.

As to whether a conviction at a court-martial in Germany for an offence of wounding with intent to cause grievous bodily harm committed whilst a serving member of the armed forces in Germany may qualify as a "serious offence" within the meaning of section 109(1)(a) of the PC-C(S)A 2000, see *R. v. Sanders, post*, § 5-447.

"exceptional circumstances"

The meaning of "exceptional circumstances" (s.109(2)) was reconsidered in *R. v. Offen* [2001] 1 **5-442** W.L.R. 253, CA. Lord Woolf C.J. said that quite apart from the impact of the Human Rights Act 1998, the rationale of the section should be highly relevant in deciding whether or not exceptional circumstances existed. The question whether circumstances were appropriately regarded as "exceptional" must be influenced by the context in which the question was being asked. The policy and intention of Parliament were to protect the public against a person who had committed two serious offences. It therefore could be assumed that the section was not intended to apply to someone in relation to whom it was established that there would be no need for protection in the future. In other words, if the facts showed the statutory assumption was misplaced, then this, in the statutory context, was not the normal situation and in consequence, for the purposes of the section, the position was exceptional. The time that elapsed between the two offences could, but would not necessarily, reflect on whether, after the second serious offence was committed, there was any danger against which the public would need protection. The same was true of two differing offences, and the age of the offender. These were all circumstances which could give rise to the conclusion that what could be normal and not exceptional in a different context was exceptional in this context. If this approach was not adopted, then in the case of the serious offences listed in the section, the gravity of which could vary greatly, the approach to "exceptional circumstances" could be unduly restrictive. The aim of section 2 was not to increase the time offenders spent in prison as a punishment for the offence they had committed, but to provide for an assessment to be made to see whether the offender posed a real risk to the public, in which event his release was deferred. Section 109 established a norm. The norm was that those who commit two serious offences were a danger or risk to the public. If in fact, taking into account all the circumstances relating to a particular offender, he did not create an unacceptable risk to the public, he was an exception to this norm.

Construing section 109 in accordance with the duty imposed on the court by section 3 of the 1998 Act, and taking into account the rationale of the section, gave content to "exceptional circumstances". In the court's judgment, section 109 would not contravene Convention rights if courts applied the section so that it did not result in offenders being sentenced to life imprisonment when they did not constitute a significant risk to the public. Whether there was a significant risk would depend on the evidence which was before the court. If the offender was a significant risk, the court could impose a life sentence under section 109 without contravening the Convention. It would be part of the responsibility of judges to assess the risk to the public that offenders constituted. In many cases the degree of risk that an offender constituted would be established by his record, with or without the assistance of assessments made in reports which were available to the court. If courts needed further assistance, they could call for it when deciding whether a discretionary life sentence should be imposed. There should be no undue difficulty in making a similar assessment when considering whether the court was required to impose an automatic life sentence, although the task would not be straightforward, because of the lack of information as to the first serious offence which will sometimes exist because of the passage of time. This did not mean that the court was approaching the passing of an automatic life sentence as if it was no different from the imposition of a discretionary life sentence. Notwithstanding the interpretation resulting from the application of section 3(1) of the 1998 Act suggested, section 109 would give effect to the intention of Parliament. It would do so, however, in a more just, less arbitrary and more proportionate manner. Section 109 would still mean that a judge was obliged to pass a life sentence in accordance with its terms unless, in all the circumstances, the offender posed no significant risk to the public. There was no such obligation in cases where section 109 did not apply. In addition, if the judge decided not to impose a life sentence under section 109, he would have to give reasons as required by section 109(3). Furthermore, the issue of dangerousness would have to be addressed in every case and a decision made as to whether or not to impose a life sentence.

Offen has since been applied in *R. v. McDonald* [2001] 2 Cr.App.R.(S.) 127, CA (having regard, in particular, to the length of time since the appellant's conviction for his previous "serious" offences (14 years) and to the fact that it was not the appellant but a co-defendant who had produced an imitation firearm in the course of the robbery, although it belonged to the appellant, it would be wrong to conclude that the appellant presented a serious risk of harm to the public so as to justify the imposition of an automatic life sentence); and in *R. v. Kelly (No. 2)* [2002] 1 Cr.App.R.(S.) 85, CA, it was held that the statutory presumption that arises under section 109(2), and which flows from the existence of two qualifying offences remains in place, and has to be displaced by the defendant in any given case; and such displacement may be achieved in a number of ways, including scrutiny of the offending and behaviour pattern, or by positive psychiatric or similar evidence, such evidence being likely to be required if the court is to be persuaded that the presumption cannot apply since the criterion to be established is that there is "no need to protect the public in the future" or "no significant risk to the public".

In *R. v. Baff* [2003] 2 Cr.App.R.(S.) 37, CA, it was said that the use of imitation firearms for the purpose of robbery caused as much fear and alarm to vulnerable members of the public as robbery with a real firearm; and that, if the court were to rule that section 109 did not as a matter of principle apply where the offender limited his offending to robberies with an imitation firearm, it would be creating an exception to an express provision flatly contradicting an aspect of sentencing policy laid down by Parliament.

In *R. v. Richards* [2002] 2 Cr.App.R.(S.) 26, CA, it was held that in considering whether a defendant who qualifies for an automatic life sentence under section 109 presents a significant risk to the public, the judge may take account of a significant risk of the commission of serious offences other than those listed as "serious" in the section itself, for example, burglaries of dwellings or a conspiracy to import hard drugs. For a criticism of this decision, see the commentary in the *Criminal Law Review*. It is inconsistent with the view of the court in *R. v. Fletcher*; *R. v. Smith* [2002] 1 Cr.App.R.(S.) 82, CA, to the effect that the "danger in point is that of violent or sexual offending."

Richards was not cited in *R. v. Stark* [2002] 2 Cr.App.R.(S.) 104, CA, where there was a high risk of further offences being committed by the appellant, but no significant risk of danger to the public by way of either violent or sexual offences; accordingly, it was held that the case was to be regarded as an exception to the norm, which was that those who committed two serious offences were a danger or risk to the public.

The approach in *R. v. Stark* and *R. v. Fletcher*; *R. v. Smith* was followed, and that in *Richards* expressly disapproved in *R. v. Magalhaes* [2005] 2 Cr.App.R.(S.) 13, CA.

In *R. v. Frost* [2001] 2 Cr.App.R.(S.) 26, CA, the appellant had been found guilty by a youth court in 1991 of wounding with intent to resist arrest. He was later convicted of wounding with intent to cause grievous bodily harm. The court held that the finding of guilt by the youth court amounted to a "conviction" for the purposes of PCC(S)A 2000, s.109(1), by virtue of the CYPA 1933, s.59. If the appellant had been older and had been subject to a probation order, the "conviction" would have been deemed not to be a conviction by virtue of the PCCA 1973, s.13(1) (*rep.*), but this provision did not apply to a supervision order. The anomaly which resulted from this amounted to an "exceptional circumstance" for the purposes of section 109, and the sentence of life imprisonment was quashed, even though it could not be said that the offender presented no significant risk to the public.

The fact that the offender is mentally ill and eligible for a hospital order does not in itself amount to an "exceptional circumstance" for this purpose: see *R. v. Newman* [2000] 2 Cr.App.R.(S.) 227, CA; *R. v. Drew* [2003] 2 Cr.App.R. 24, HL (where a submission that an automatic life sentence on conviction of wounding with intent constituted inhuman or degrading treatment was rejected; having been transferred administratively to hospital within a few days of the passing of sentence, the appellant was receiving the same treatment as he would have received had he been made subject to a hospital order, and he could not complain of the stigma attaching to the sentence as he had been convicted by a jury, who must therefore have been satisfied as to his intent).

On appeal, the issue is whether the offender created an unacceptable risk to the public at the time when he was sentenced, not at the time when the Court of Appeal is considering the matter: see *R. v. Watkins* [2003] 1 Cr.App.R.(S.) 16, CA; *R. v. Noorkoiv* [2002] 2 Cr.App.R.(S.) 91, CA.

C. Minimum Fixed Term Sentences

(1) Legislation

Powers of Criminal Courts (Sentencing) Act 2000, ss.112–115

Offences under service law

In *R. v. Sanders* [2007] 1 Cr.App.R.(S.) 74, CA, it was held that the effect of section 114 of the **5-447** PCC(S)A 2000 was limited to deeming the conviction to have been in England and Wales; it did not deem the offence to have been committed in England and Wales; where, therefore, the appellant had previously been convicted of an offence under section 70 of the Army Act 1955 and the corresponding civil offence had been one of those listed in section 109(5), but the offence had been committed abroad, he was not to be regarded as having previously been convicted of a serious offence, since, under section 109(5), an offence would only be "serious" if committed in England and Wales; section 114 would bite only in relation to convictions under section 70 where the offence occurred in England and Wales. It should be noted that the repeal of the words "a serious offence" in section 114(1)(b) is of no effect where an offender is being dealt with for an offence committed prior to April 4, 2005.

(2) Practice

"unjust"

★**5-452** As a matter of principle, a sentencing court should not water down the effect of the minimum sentence provisions in the PCC(S)A 2000, by reference to considerations of totality, when passing sentence for one or more other offences at the same time as imposing a required minimum sentence, or when sentencing an offender already serving such a sentence (but this is not to say that no allowance should be made for totality in such cases): *R. v. Chaplin* [2016] 1 Cr.App.R.(S.) 10, CA. *Cf. R. v. Sparkes* (in the main work).

Totality principle

★**5-456** For a further case considering the operation of the totality principle in the context of statutory provisions relating to minimum sentences, see *R. v. Chaplin, ante*, § 5-452.

D. Discretionary Custodial Sentences

(1) General restrictions

(c) *Legislation (offences committed before April 4, 2005)*

Powers of Criminal Courts (Sentencing) Act 2000, ss.79, 80

General restrictions on imposing discretionary custodial sentences

5-469   **79.**—(1) This section applies where a person is convicted of an offence punishable with a custodial sentence other than one—

    (a) fixed by law; or

    (b) falling to be imposed under section 109(2), 110(2) or 111(2) below.

(2) Subject to subsection (3) below, the court shall not pass a custodial sentence on the offender unless it is of the opinion—

    (a) that the offence, or the combination of the offence and one or more offences associated with it, was so serious that only such a sentence can be justified for the offence; or

    (b) where the offence is a violent or sexual offence, that only such a sentence would be adequate to protect the public from serious harm from him.

(3) Nothing in subsection (2) above shall prevent the court from passing a custodial sentence on the offender if he fails to express his willingness to comply with—

    (a) a requirement which is proposed by the court to be included in a community rehabilitation order or supervision order and which requires an expression of such willingness; or

    (b) a requirement which is proposed by the court to be included in a drug treatment and testing order or an order under section 52(4) above (order to provide samples). In relation to an offence committed before 1st October 1997:

(4) Where a court passes a custodial sentence, it shall—

    (a) in a case not falling within subsection (3) above, state in open court that it is of the opinion that either or both of paragraphs (a) and (b) of subsection (2) above apply and why it is of that opinion; and

    (b) in any case, explain to the offender in open court and in ordinary language why it is passing a custodial sentence on him.

(5) A magistrates' court shall cause a reason stated by it under subsection (4) above to be specified in the warrant of commitment and to be entered in the register.

[This section is printed as amended by the CJCSA 2000, s.74 and Sched. 7, para. 1. It is repealed, as from April 4, 2005 (Criminal Justice Act 2003 (Commencement No. 8 and Transitional and Saving Provisions) Order 2005 (S.I. 2005 No. 950)), by the CJA 2003, s.332, and Sched. 37, Pt 7. As to the saving provision in relation to offences committed before April 4, 2005, see § 5-2 in the main work.]

In relation to an offence committed before October 1, 1997, see the transitional provision in Sched. 11, para. 4(d).

Length of discretionary custodial sentences: general provision

5-470   **80.**—(1) This section applies where a court passes a custodial sentence other than one fixed by law or falling to be imposed under section 109(2) below.

(2) Subject to sections 110(2) and 111(2) below, the custodial sentence shall be—

    (a)   for such term (not exceeding the permitted maximum) as in the opinion of the court is commensurate with the seriousness of the offence, or the combination of the offence and one or more offences associated with it; or

    (b)   where the offence is a violent or sexual offence, for such longer term (not exceeding that maximum) as in the opinion of the court is necessary to protect the public from serious harm from the offender.

(3) Where the court passes a custodial sentence for a term longer than is commensurate with the seriousness of the offence, or the combination of the offence and one or more offences associated with it, the court shall—

    (a)   state in open court that it is of the opinion that subsection (2)(b) above applies and why it is of that opinion; and

    (b)   explain to the offender in open court and in ordinary language why the sentence is for such a term.

(4) A custodial sentence for an indeterminate period shall be regarded for the purposes of subsections (2) and (3) above as a custodial sentence for a term longer than any actual term.

(5) Subsection (3) above shall not apply in any case where the court passes a custodial sentence falling to be imposed under subsection (2) of section 110 or 111 below which is for the minimum term specified in that subsection.

[This section is repealed, as from April 4, 2005 (Criminal Justice Act 2003 (Commencement No. 8 and Transitional and Saving Provisions) Order 2005 (S.I. 2005 No. 950)), by the CJA 2003, s.332, and Sched. 37, Pt 7. As to the saving provision in relation to offences committed before April 4, 2005, see § 5-2 in the main work.]

Powers of Criminal Courts (Sentencing) Act 2000, s.161

Meaning of "associated offence", "sexual offence", "violent offence" and "protecting the public from serious harm"

161.—(1) [*See § 5-2 in the main work.*]   **5-471**

(2) In this Act, "sexual offence" means any of the following—

    (f)   an offence under the Protection of Children Act 1978;

    (fa) an offence under section 3 of the Sexual Offences (Amendment) Act 2000;

    (fa) an offence under any provision of Part 1 of the Sexual Offences Act 2003; except section 52, 53 or 71

    (g)   an offence under section 1 of the Criminal Law Act 1977; of conspiracy to commit any of the offences in paragraphs (a) to (f) above;

    (h)   an offence under section 1 of the Criminal Attempts Act 1981; of attempting to commit any of those offences;

    (i)   an offence of inciting another to commit any of those offences.

(3) In this Act, "violent offence" means an offence which leads, or is intended or likely to lead, to a person's death or to physical injury to a person, and includes an offence which is required to be charged as arson (whether or not it would otherwise fall within this definition).

(4) In this Act any reference, in relation to an offender convicted of a violent or sexual offence, to protecting the public from serious harm from him shall be construed as a reference to protecting members of the public from death or serious personal injury, whether physical or psychological, occasioned by further such offences committed by him.

[Subss. (2) to (4) are printed as amended and repealed in part, by the Sexual Offences (Amendment) Act 2000, s.6(1); and the SOA 2003, ss.139 and 140, and Sched. 6, para. 4 (insertion of second para. (fa) in subs. (2)), and Sched. 7 (repeal of subs. (2)(a)–(e), the failure to repeal the first para. (fa) being accounted for by the draftsman having overlooked the amendment made by the 2000 Act). The amendments effected by the 2003 Act took effect on May 1, 2004 (Sexual Offences Act 2003 (Commencement) Order 2004 (S.I. 2004 No. 874)). For the former provisions, which will continue to apply in relation to offences committed before that date (Interpretation Act 1978, s.16 (*post*, Appendix F-16)), see the 2004 edition of this work. Subss. (2) to (4) are repealed, as from April 4, 2005 (Criminal Justice Act 2003 (Commencement No. 8 and Transitional and Saving Provisions) Order 2005 (S.I. 2005 No. 950)), by the CJA 2003, s.332, and Sched. 7. As to the saving provision in relation to offences committed before April 4, 2005, see § 5-2 in the main work.]

"Violent" and "sexual" offences

    Whether any particular offence is a violent offence depends on the facts of the individual   **5-472** offence. An offence which leads to or is intended to lead only to psychological injury is not a "violent offence" but it is not necessary that serious harm should have been caused (see *R. v. Robinson* [1994] 1 W.L.R. 168, CA). Nor does it have to be established that physical injury was a probability: *R. v. Szczerba* [2002] 2 Cr.App.R.(S.) 86, CA.

In *R. v. Cochrane*, 15 Cr.App.R.(S.) 708, CA, it was held that a robbery in which the victim was threatened with a knife was a "violent offence" as the incident could have resulted in injury, either accidentally or if the victim had resisted. See also *R. v. Bibby*, 16 Cr.App.R.(S.) 127, CA. For cases of robbery by persons armed with a firearm, see *R. v. Touriq Khan*, 16 Cr.App.R.(S.) 180, CA, *R. v. Palin*, 16 Cr.App.R.(S.) 888, CA, and *R. v. Baker* [2001] 1 Cr.App.R.(S.) 55, CA. An offence of threatening to kill which does not involve the infliction of physical injury will not normally be a "violent offence": see *R. v. Richart*, 16 Cr.App.R.(S.) 977, CA, *R. v. Ragg* [1996] 1 Cr.App.R.(S.) 176, CA and *R. v. Birch* [2002] 1 Cr.App.R.(S.) 129, CA; but see *R. v. Wilson* [1998] 1 Cr.App.R.(S.) 341, CA.

Attempted arson is "an offence which is required to be charged as arson" and is accordingly a "violent offence" within section 161(3): *R. v. Guirke* [1997] 1 Cr.App.R.(S.) 170, CA.

"Serious harm" (s.161(4) of the Act of 2000)

5-473   See § 5-495 in the main work.

The criterion of seriousness

5-474   For discussion of the relevant authorities in relation to section 79(1), see § 5-465 in the main work.

Sentences commensurate with the seriousness of the offence

5-475   For relevant considerations where a court is deciding what term of custody is commensurate with an offence or group of offences, see § 5-466 in the main work.

Longer than normal sentences

5-476   For the definitions of "sexual offence" and "violent offence", see section 161(2) and (3) of the PCC(S)A 2000 (*ante*, § 5-471); and for the authorities in relation thereto, see *ante*, § 5-472. For the construction of references to "protecting the public from serious harm", see section 161(4) of the 2000 Act (*ante*, § 5-471); and the authorities referred to at §§ 5-495 *et seq.* in the main work.

An isolated offence, however serious, will rarely be sufficient to justify a longer than normal sentence under section 80(2)(b), whether the offence is violent or sexual, or both: *R. v. Walsh*, 16 Cr.App.R.(S.) 204, CA; *R. v. Mumtaz Ali*, 16 Cr.App.R.(S.) 692, CA. A longer than commensurate sentence may be passed on an offender with no previous convictions: *R. v. Thomas*, 16 Cr.App.R.(S.) 616, CA.

A court deciding whether to draw the inference that the offender is likely to commit further violent or sexual offences may need to examine the circumstances of the current offence in some detail, going beyond what would be necessary if only a commensurate sentence were in issue: *R. v. Oudkerk*, 16 Cr.App.R.(S.) 172, CA. Equally, if the inference is to be based on a previous conviction, the court may need to examine the circumstances of that offence in detail: *R. v. Samuels*, 16 Cr.App.R.(S.) 856, CA.

An offender may satisfy the requirements of section 80(2)(b) even though the members of the public who are at risk from him are a small group, or possibly an individual: *R. v. Hashi*, 16 Cr.App.R.(S.) 121, CA. Where the offender's behaviour is directed at a small group of people, who can be protected from him by other means, a longer than commensurate sentence may not be justified: *R. v. Nicholas*, 15 Cr.App.R.(S.) 381, CA; *R. v. Swain*, 15 Cr.App.R.(S.) 765, CA; *R. v. L.*, 15 Cr.App.R.(S.) 501, CA.

In many cases the inference of dangerousness will be based in part on psychiatric evidence: *R. v. Lyons*, 15 Cr.App.R.(S.) 460, CA; *R. v. Fawcett*, 16 Cr.App.R.(S.) 55, CA; *R. v. Etchells* [1996] 1 Cr.App.R.(S.) 163, CA.

The principles which should be applied in deciding the length of a longer than commensurate sentence were considered in *R. v. Mansell*, 15 Cr.App.R.(S.) 771, CA; and *R. v. Crow*; *R. v. Pennington*, 16 Cr.App.R.(S.) 409, CA. Lord Taylor C.J. said that some allowance should usually be made, even in the worst cases, for a plea of guilty. A sentence imposed under section 80(2)(b), whilst long enough to give necessary protection for the public, should still bear a reasonable relationship to the offence for which it was imposed.

This principle was not applied in *R. v. Chapman* [2000] 1 Cr.App.R. 77, CA, where it was said that there was no necessary ratio between the part of the sentence intended to punish and the part intended to protect. There was no objection in principle if the court regarded a sentence of two years as necessary to punish, but an additional term of six or eight years as necessary to protect, making a total term of eight or 10 years. *Chapman* was followed in *R. v. Wilson* [2000] 2 Cr.App.R.(S.) 323, CA, but not apparently in *R. v. De Silva* [2000] 2 Cr.App.R.(S.) 408, CA.

The question whether a longer than commensurate sentence may properly be imposed to run **5-477** consecutively to a sentence of imprisonment was considered by the Court of Appeal in *R. v. Everleigh* [2002] 1 Cr.App.R.(S.) 32. The court considered *R. v. King*, 16 Cr.App.R.(S.) 987; *R. v. Walters* [1997] 2 Cr.App.R.(S.) 87; *R. v. Johnson* [1998] 1 Cr.App.R.(S.) 126; *R. v. Cuthbertson and Jenks* [2000] 1 Cr.App.R.(S.) 359; *R. v. Parsons* [2000] 1 Cr.App.R.(S.) 428; *R. v. Blades* [2000] 1 Cr.App.R.(S.) 463; *R. v. Sullivan* [2000] 2 Cr.App.R.(S.) 318; *R. v. Sowden* [2000] 2 Cr.App.R.(S.) 360; *R. v. Wilson* [2000] 2 Cr.App.R.(S.) 323; and *R. v. Ellis* [2001] 1 Cr.App.R.(S.) 43. Accepting that not all of these of authorities could be reconciled, the court held that they showed that it was inappropriate to pass a longer than the normal sentence to run consecutively to another sentence imposed on the same occasion, because a longer than normal sentence is intended in itself to protect the public from serious harm, without the need for any additional penalty in relation to other conduct punishable at the same time. Secondly, there was nothing inappropriate, but on the contrary it might be desirable, for a longer than normal sentence to be passed consecutively either to a sentence passed on an earlier occasion (*Wilson*) or to a period of return to custody ordered under the PCC(S)A 2000, s.116, which was a consequence of a sentence passed on an earlier occasion (*Blades*). As was pointed out in *Blades*, it was important that both the public and the defendant should know that a sentence once passed would have to be served (subject to any reduction which might be appropriate in accordance with *R. v. Taylor* [1998] 1 Cr.App.R.(S.) 312). It was desirable that the sentencing judge, if imposing a consecutive sentence, should make it plain what were the factors which he had taken into consideration in so passing the sentence under section 80(2)(b).

In *R. v. Christie*, 16 Cr.App.R.(S.) 469, CA, it was said to be wrong to add an additional period to the sentence under section 80(2)(b) if the commensurate sentence already incorporated an element for the protection of the public. In *R. v. Campbell* [1997] 1 Cr.App.R.(S.) 119, CA, it was held that if the sentencing guidelines for a particular offence included an element for the protection of the public, the sentencer should decide what was the appropriate sentence, leaving out of account any element for the protection of the public, and should then add the greater element needed for the protection of the public from serious harm under section 80(2)(b). This would avoid the risk of imposing an element of the sentence twice over. In *R. v. Gabbidon and Bramble* [1997] 2 Cr.App.R.(S.) 19, CA, this approach was described as too difficult an exercise in forensic archaeology; it was better that the sentencer simply applied the principle of balance stated by Lord Taylor C.J. in *R. v. Mansell*, 15 Cr.App.R.(S.) 771.

In a case where a longer than normal sentence is passed on one offender and a commensurate sentence on the other, it does not necessarily follow that there is any disparity of sentence, provided that there is evidence of continuing dangerousness on the part of one offender and not in the case of the other: *R. v. Bestwick and Huddlestone*, 16 Cr.App.R.(S.) 168, CA.

A longer than commensurate sentence may be imposed on an offender under section 80(2)(b) even though he does not qualify for a sentence of life imprisonment under the criteria established for that form of sentence: *R. v. Helm*, 16 Cr.App.R.(S.) 834, CA. The enactment of section 80(2)(b) has not reduced the requirements for a life sentence: *R. v. Roche*, 16 Cr.App.R.(S.) 849, CA.

Where a sentencer has in mind the possibility of passing a longer than commensurate sentence, he should warn counsel for the defendant of his intentions and invite submissions on the question: *R. v. Baverstock*, 96 Cr.App.R. 435, CA. This point has been repeated in many cases; it is particularly important when any question arises as to whether the offence is a "violent offence" for the purposes of the Act. Where a court passes a longer than commensurate sentence it is required by the PCC(S)A 2000, s.80(3) to state in open court that it is of the opinion that subsection (2)(b) applies and why it is of that opinion, and explain to the offender in open court and in ordinary language why the sentence is for such a term. Failure to comply with this obligation does not invalidate the sentence: *Baverstock, ante*; *R. v. Thomas*, 16 Cr.App.R.(S.) 616, CA. Even where the nature of the expected future harm is obvious, the sentencer should ensure that he has properly identified what the harm was before he proceeded to sentence, and should point out clearly and in straightforward terms what it was that he considered to be the serious harm in question: *R. v. Bacon*, 16 Cr.App.R.(S.) 1031, CA.

Where a court fails to pass a longer than commensurate sentence where such a sentence should be passed, the resulting sentence may be "unduly lenient" and may be the subject of a reference by the Attorney-General under the CJA 1988, s.36: *Att-Gen.'s Reference (No. 9 of 1994) (R. v. Groves)*, 16 Cr.App.R.(S.) 366, CA. Where a person sentenced to a longer than commensurate sentence persuades the Court of Appeal that the case is not one in which a longer than commensurate sentence should have been passed, the court is not bound to substitute a shorter sentence; its powers are at large, and it may approve the sentence passed as a commensurate sentence if it considers it appropriate to do so: *R. v. Palmer* [1996] 2 Cr.App.R.(S.) 68, CA; and see also *R. v. Henshaw* [1996] 2 Cr.App.R.(S.) 310, CA; and *R. v. Rai and Robinson* [2000] 2 Cr.App.R.(S.) 120, CA.

(2) Imprisonment

(c) *Dangerous offenders*

Discretionary life sentences and extended sentences

(iv) *Assessment of significant risk*

★5-512   Resort to sentences under the dangerousness provisions of the CJA 2003 (§§ 5-495 *et seq.* in the main work) is not limited to cases where the public in general (as opposed to a single individual or a small group of identifiable individuals) are at risk: *R. v. Laverick* [2015] 2 Cr.App.R.(S.) 62, CA.

Fixing the minimum term (life sentences not fixed by law)

Powers of Criminal Courts (Sentencing) Act 2000, s.82A

Determination of tariffs

5-531   It is not a requirement, when fixing, pursuant to section 82A of the 2000 Act (see the main work), the minimum term that should attach to a discretionary life sentence, to fix it by reference to the practice of the courts that prevailed at the date at which the offence was committed: *R. v. Bell* [2016] 1 Cr.App.R.(S.) 16, CA (considering *R. v Sullivan*; *R. v. Gibbs*; *R. v. Elener (Barry) and R. v. Elener (Derek)* (*post*, Appendix B-178), and *R. (Uttley) v. Secretary of State for the Home Department* (§ 16-135 in the main work), but following the approach adopted in *R. v H.* and *R. v. Masefield* (as to both of which, see § 19-136 in the main work)).

(e) *Suspended sentences*

Criminal Justice Act 2003, ss.189-192

Imposition of requirements by suspended sentence order

★5-550   As to the further amendment of the Legal Aid, Sentencing and Punishment of Offenders Act 2012 (Alcohol Abstinence and Monitoring Requirements) Piloting Order 2014 (S.I. 2014 No. 1777), see S.I. 2016 No. 1, *ante*, § 5-253.

E. Release on Licence

Criminal Justice Act 2003, s.240A

Calculation of credit period

★5-649   While it used to be the case that a judge had a general discretion to direct that time spent on a qualifying curfew should not count against sentence, that is no longer so; the primary rule now is that half the number of days spent on qualifying curfew are to be deducted, although this number is to be reduced in certain circumstances set out in section 240A(3) (as to which, see § 5-645 in the main work): *R. v. Love*, unreported, August 14, 2015, CA ([2015] EWCA Crim. 1545).

Criminal Justice Act 2003, s.265

Restriction on consecutive sentences for released prisoners

Where a prisoner, having committed an offence whilst on temporary release, is arrested and **5-669** remanded in custody, the court may not make any sentence for the fresh offence consecutive to the sentence being served at the time the offence was committed if, by the time of sentence, he has passed the date on which he would have been released on licence from the earlier sentence: *R. v. Hookway* [2015] 2 Cr.App.R.(S.) 43, CA. The court relied in large part on section 265 of the 2003 Act (§ 5-668 in the main work); but, for a submission that the provisions of that section were not engaged (unless critical details have been omitted from the judgment), and that the point must remain open to argument, see the commentary at CLW/15/34/22.

Modifications of Chapter 6 in certain transitional cases

As explained in the main work (see § 5-619), the effect of LASPOA 2012 is to apply Chapter 6 **5-670a** of Part 12 of the CJA 2003 to all prisoners regardless of the date of their offence or the date of sentence. However, two new Schedules (20A and 20B) are inserted into the 2003 Act (by the 2012 Act, s.121(5) and (6), and Scheds 16, paras 1 and 3, and 17, paras 1 and 10) for the purpose of preserving the transitional provisions that existed prior to their commencement. These have the effect of modifying Chapter 6 where they apply. It is submitted that they now only have potential relevance to the release date of an offender sentenced after their commencement in one situation, *viz.* where an offender serving a "1991 Act sentence" who has never been released from that sentence (and theoretically also an offender serving a "1967 Act sentence" who has never been released) is sentenced to a consecutive term for a fresh offence (see paras 22 and 33, *post*).

As to the commencement of these provisions of the 2012 Act, see § 5-2a in the main work.

Criminal Justice Act 2003, Sched. 20B, paras 1–3, 7, 8, 18–20, 22, 23, 30, 33

Part 1

Introductory

Interpretation

1.—(1) The following provisions apply for the purposes of this Schedule.   **5-670b**

(2) "The commencement date" means the date on which section 121 of the Legal Aid, Sentencing and Punishment of Offenders Act 2012 comes into force.

(3) "The 1967 Act" means the Criminal Justice Act 1967.

(4) "The 1991 Act" means the Criminal Justice Act 1991.

(5) A "section 85 extended sentence" means an extended sentence under section 85 of the Sentencing Act and includes (in accordance with paragraph 1(3) of Schedule 11 to that Act) a sentence under section 58 of the Crime and Disorder Act 1998.

(6) In relation to a section 85 extended sentence, "the custodial term" and "the extension period" have the meaning given by that section.

(7) References to section 86 of the Sentencing Act include (in accordance with paragraph 1(3) of Schedule 11 to that Act) section 44 of the 1991 Act as originally enacted.

(8) A "1967 Act sentence" is a sentence imposed before 1 October 1992.

(9) A "1991 Act sentence" is a sentence which is—

(a) imposed on or after 1 October 1992 but before 4 April 2005, or

(b) imposed on or after 4 April 2005 but before the commencement date and is either—

(i) imposed in respect of an offence committed before 4 April 2005, or

(ii) for a term of less than 12 months.

(10) A "2003 Act sentence" is a sentence which is—

(a) imposed on or after the commencement date, or

(b) imposed on or after 4 April 2005 but before the commencement date and is both—

(i) imposed in respect of an offence committed on or after 4 April 2005, and

(ii) for a term of 12 months or more.

(11) Where an offence is found to have been committed over a period of two or more days, or at some time during a period of two or more days, it is to be taken for the purposes of this Schedule to have been committed on the last of those days.

Explanation of dates

2. The following dates (which are mentioned in this Schedule) are dateson which changes to the **5-670c** law relating to the release and recall of prisoners came into force—

1 October 1992 is the date on which Part 2 of the 1991 Act came into force;

30 September 1998 is the date on which certain provisions of the Crime and Disorder Act 1998 came into force;

4 April 2005 is the date on which this Chapter came into force;

9 June 2008 is the date on which section 26 of the Criminal Justice and Immigration Act 2008 came into force;

14 July 2008 is the date on which certain other provisions of that Act came into force;

2 August 2010 is the date on which section 145 of the Coroners and Justice Act 2009 came into force.

PART 2

Prisoners Serving 1991 Act Sentences, etc.

5-670d 3.—(1) This Part applies to certain persons serving a 1991 Act sentence.

(2) This Part also applies to a person serving a 2003 Act sentence which is—

(b) an extended sentence imposed under section 227 or 228 before 14 July 2008.

(3) But this Part does not apply to a person who—

(a) has been released on licence under Part 2 of the 1991 Act,

(b) has been recalled to prison, and

(c) (whether or not having returned to custody in consequence of that recall) is unlawfully at large on the commencement date.

[Para. 3(2)(a) was repealed by the Criminal Justice and Courts Act 2015, s.15(8).]

Release on licence at one-half of sentence: section 85 extended sentence prisoners

5-670e 7. This paragraph applies to a person if—

(a) the person has been convicted of an offence committed on or after 30 September 1998 but before 4 April 2005,

(b) the person is serving a section 85 extended sentence in respect of that offence,

(c) the person has not previously been released from prison on licence in respect of that sentence, and

(d) paragraph 4 does not apply to the person.

5-670f 8.—(1) As soon as a person to whom paragraph 7 applies has served one-half of the custodial term, it is the duty of the Secretary of State to release the person on licence under this paragraph.

(2) Sub-paragraph (1) applies in place of section 243A or 244, as the case may be (release of prisoners serving less than 12 months, or serving 12 months or more).

It should be noted that paragraph 4 (see para. 7(d)) has no application to a person sentenced after "the commencement date".

Period for which licence to remain in force: section 85 extended sentence prisoners

5-670g 18. This paragraph applies to a person who—

(a) has been convicted of an offence committed on or after 30 September 1998 but before 4 April 2005,

(b) is serving a section 85 extended sentence imposed in respect of that offence, and

(c) has not previously been released from prison on licence in respect of that sentence.

5-670h 19.—(1) Where a person to whom paragraph 18 applies is released on licence and the custodial term is less than 12 months, the licence shall remain in force until the end of the period found by adding—

(a) one-half of the custodial term, and

(b) the extension period.

(2) Where a person to whom paragraph 18 applies is released on licence and the custodial term is 12 months or more, the licence shall remain in force until the end of the period found by adding—

(a) three-quarters of the custodial term, and

(b) the extension period.

(3) Sub-paragraphs (1) and (2) are subject to any revocation under section 254.

(4) Sub-paragraphs (1) to (3) apply in place of section 249 (duration of licence).

Concurrent or consecutive terms

5-670i 20. Paragraphs 21 and 22 apply where a person ("P") is serving two or more sentences of imprisonment imposed on or after 1 October 1992 and—

(a) the sentences were passed on the same occasion, or

(b) where they were passed on different occasions, the person has not been released under

30

Part 2 of the 1991 Act or under this Chapter at any time during the period beginning with the first and ending with the last of those occasions.

22.—(1) This paragraph applies where two or more sentences are to be served consecutively on each other and— **5-670j**

   (a) one or more of those sentences is a 1991 Act sentence, and

   (b) one or more of them is a 2003 Act sentence.

(2) Section 264 does not affect the length of the period which P must serve in prison in respect of the 1991 Act sentence or sentences.

(3) Nothing in this Chapter requires the Secretary of State to release P until P has served a period equal in length to the aggregate of the length of the periods which P must serve in relation to each of the sentences mentioned in sub-paragraph (1).

(3A) If P is subject to supervision requirements under section 256AA (by virtue of section 264(3C)(b)), section 256AA(4)(b) (end of supervision period) applies in relation to P as if the reference to the requisite custodial period were to the period described in sub-paragraph (3) of this paragraph.

(4) If P is also serving one or more 1967 Act sentences, paragraphs 32 and 33 apply instead of this paragraph.

[Sub-para. (3A) was inserted, as from February 1, 2015 (Offender Rehabilitation Act 2014 (Commencement No. 2) Order 2015 (S.I. 2015 No. 40)) by the Offender Rehabilitation Act 2014, s.5(1), (6) and (7). This amendment applies only in relation to any person who falls to be released under Chapter 6 of Part 12 of the 2003 Act on or after the day on which it came into force: 2014 Act, s.21, and Sched. 7, paras 1 and 2.]

PART 3

Prisoners Serving 1967 Act Sentences

23.—(1) This Part applies to certain persons serving a 1967 Act sentence. **5-670k**

(2) But this Part does not apply to a person who—

   (a) has been released on licence,

   (b) has been recalled to prison, and

   (c) (whether or not having returned to custody in consequence of that recall) is unlawfully at large on the commencement date.

(3) In this Part, references to release under Part 2 of the 1991 Act include release under section 60 of the 1967 Act.

Concurrent or consecutive terms

30. Paragraphs 31 to 33 apply where a person ("P") is serving two or more sentences of imprisonment and— **5-670l**

   (a) the sentences were passed on the same occasion, or

   (b) where they were passed on different occasions, the person has not been released under Part 2 of the 1991 Act or under this Chapter at any time during the period beginning with the first and ending with the last of those occasions.

33.—(1) This paragraph applies where two or more sentences are to be served consecutively on each other and— **5-670m**

   (a) one or more of those sentences is a 1967 Act sentence, and

   (b) one or more of them is a 2003 Act sentence.

(2) Section 264 does not affect the length of the period which P must serve in prison in respect of the 1967 Act sentence or sentences.

(3) Nothing in this Chapter requires the Secretary of State to release P until P has served a period equal in length to the aggregate of the length of the periods which P must serve in relation to each of the sentences mentioned in sub-paragraph (1).

(4) If P is subject to supervision requirements under section 256AA (by virtue of section 264(3C)(b)), section 256AA(4)(b) (end of supervision period) applies in relation to P as if the reference to the requisite custodial period were to the period described in sub-paragraph (3) of this paragraph.

[Sub-para. (4) was inserted, as from February 1, 2015 (Offender Rehabilitation Act 2014 (Commencement No. 2) Order 2015 (S.I. 2015 No. 40)) by the Offender Rehabilitation Act 2014, s.5(1), (6) and (8). This amendment applies only in relation to any person who falls to be released under Chapter 6 of Part 12 of the 2003 Act on or after the day on which it came into force: 2014 Act, s.21, and Sched. 7, paras 1 and 2.]

VII. FINES

Powers of Criminal Courts (Sentencing) Act 2000, ss.139, 140, 142

Enforcement of fines imposed and recognizances forfeited by Crown Court

★5-677   As to the proper interpretation of section 79(2) of the MCA 1980 (see s.140(3) of the 2000 Act in the main work), see *R. (Gibson) v. Secretary of State for Justice* [2016] Lloyd's Rep F.C. 11, CA (Civ. Div.).

Determining the amount of the fine

5-685a   *R. v. Thames Water Utilities Ltd* is now reported at [2015] 2 Cr.App.R.(S.) 63.

VIII. COMPENSATION, RESTITUTION AND REPARATION

A. Compensation Orders

Sale of assets to raise funds

5-708   While there are decisions to the effect that it is generally inappropriate to make a compensation order that is likely to result in the sale of the family home (see, *inter alia*, *R. v. Hackett* and *R. v. Holah* (as to both of which, see the main work)), those authorities pre-dated the PCA 2002, which undoubtedly allows for a defendant's interest in the family home to be included in his realisable assets (for the purposes of confiscation proceedings); one consequence of that is the possibility that its sale would be necessitated if he had no other assets to meet a confiscation order; there could be no general principle, therefore, to the effect that a compensation order should not be made if the offender could only discharge the order if the family home were to be sold so that he could realise his interest therein; *R. v. Beaumont* (§ 5-813a in the main work) was decided by two judges and is not decisive authority for any contrary proposition; a potential forced sale of the family home would be a matter to take into account, but it is not in principle some kind of trump card; each case must be decided by reference to its own facts: *R. v. Parkinson* [2016] 1 Cr.App.R.(S.) 6.

IX. DEPRIVATION AND CONFISCATION

B. Confiscation under the Drug Trafficking Act 1994

Assessment of benefit

5-737   When determining for the purposes of section 2 of the DTA 1994 (confiscation orders) whether an offender has benefited from an offence of drug trafficking in respect of which he has not been convicted at trial, the statutory assumptions provided for in section 4(3) are not the only way in which the Act permits the court to determine the fact (or extent) of such benefit; where those assumptions are not applicable, the court is entitled to rely on other evidence led at trial to show that one or more offences of drug trafficking (other than those charged) have been committed (and then to estimate the benefit that must have been obtained from those offences): *R. v. Briggs-Price* [2009] 1 A.C. 1026, HL. A majority of their Lordships held, however, that a judge should only rely on evidence of other offences not charged if he was satisfied to the criminal standard that they had been proved (the minority taking the view that the civil standard was the applicable standard).

Valuation of property

5-738   Where a judge assessed the value of the defendant's proceeds of drug trafficking at £3.2 million, he was correct in taking the view that he was required by the DTA 1994 to make a confiscation order in that amount, unless the defendant satisfied him (to the civil standard) that his realisable assets were less than that amount; and where the defendant had failed to do so, there was no obligation on the judge to assume that the defendant would have incurred some expenses to be set against that figure, and to make some discount in respect thereof; such approach was misconceived; his task under the statute was to assess the value of the proceeds in accord with the provisions of the statute (which was not the same as profit), and to make an order in that amount unless the value of the realisable assets was less than that amount, and the burden of proof in that regard was on the defendant: *R. v. Versluis* [2005] 2 Cr.App.R.(S.) 26, CA.

"drug trafficking offence"

Where the defendant was convicted of a conspiracy to convert the proceeds of drug trafficking **5-739** "or" the proceeds of criminal conduct (the substantive offences being created by the DTA 1994, s.49, and the CJA 1988, s.93C, respectively), this was to be construed as a finding that the agreement was not restricted to the laundering of the proceeds of drug trafficking or to the proceeds of criminal conduct other than drug trafficking, but was an agreement to launder money, whatever its provenance; it was, in effect, an agreement to launder both the proceeds of drug trafficking and the proceeds of other criminal conduct; accordingly, the defendant was properly to be regarded as having been convicted of a "drug trafficking offence" for the purposes of the confiscation provisions of the 1994 Act as the definition of that expression extended to a conspiracy to commit an offence contrary to section 49; and the judge had, therefore, erred in declining to conduct confiscation proceedings under the 1994 Act: *R. v. Suchedina (Att.-Gen.'s Reference (No. 4 of 2003))* [2005] 1 Cr.App.R. 2, CA.

Increase in realisable property

In *Re Peacock (Secretary of State for the Home Department intervening)* [2012] 2 Cr.App.R.(S.) 81, **5-740** SC, it was held that the High Court has power, under section 16(2) of the 1994 Act, to certify that the amount that might be realised is greater than the amount taken into account at the time a confiscation order under that Act was made, and to do so by reference to assets honestly acquired since the date of the making of the order. As to the argument that increasing a confiscation order by reference to after-acquired assets would militate against a defendant's reform and rehabilitation, and be likely to discourage him from engaging in lawful and openly profitable employment, the court pointed out that section 16(4) confers a discretion on the Crown Court, rather than obliging it to order an increase in the amount of the confiscation order in parallel with the assessment of the amount of increase in the defendant's realisable property under section 16(2).

Certificate of inadequacy

It is unambiguously clear from the wording of sections 6 and 8(1) of the 1994 Act that the **5-741** value of a gift made by a defendant will be included in the amount of a confiscation order and will constitute "realisable property", even though it may not itself be realisable by the defendant because it is no longer in his power or control; and it is implicit in the statutory scheme that, where the value of a gift has been included in the amount of a confiscation order pursuant to section 6(1), it will not then be open to the defendant to seek a certificate of inadequacy under section 17(1) on the basis that he cannot realise or recover that gift; section 17 cannot be used as a device for upsetting an original finding that an item is "realisable property" within section 6(2), and thus to be included in the "amount that might be realised" under section 6(1), and thus within the amount of the confiscation order: *Re L.*, unreported, June 23, 2010, QBD (Hickinbottom J.) ([2010] EWHC 1531 (Admin.)).

Variation of realisable amount

Where, following the grant of a certificate of inadequacy by the High Court under section 17 of **5-742** the 1994 Act, the Crown Court had, pursuant to subsection (4) of that section, substituted a nil amount as the amount to be recovered, it was possible, if the defendant thereafter came into funds, for the amount to be varied upwards again if the High Court issued a certificate under section 16(2) that the amount that might be realised was now more than the amount that had been substituted for the original amount; but the Crown Court had a discretion as to whether to accede to an application for the amount to be increased following such certification, and one factor to be taken into account by it in deciding how to exercise its discretion would be whether the state had sat on its hands after significant and clear evidence about the defendant's change in financial circumstances had come to its attention or had unreasonably delayed in re-opening the issue: *R. v. Griffin* [2009] 2 Cr.App.R.(S.) 89, CA.

Restraint orders; payment of legal expenses out of restrained assets

5-743   See *Revenue and Customs Prosecution Office v. Briggs-Price and O'Reilly, post,* § 5-761.

C. Confiscation under the Criminal Justice Act 1988

Postponement of determinations

5-756   In *R. v. Haisman* [2004] 1 Cr.App.R.(S.) 63, CA, it was held that where prosecuting counsel had invited the judge to postpone confiscation proceedings and to proceed to sentence, and the judge responded by saying, "If everyone agrees to that, I will do that" and there was no dissent from any counsel to that course, the judge had "manifestly reached a decision" (*R. v. Ross* [2001] 2 Cr.App.R.(S.) 109, CA) to postpone the confiscation proceedings under section 72A of the CJA 1988, with the consequence that the confiscation orders made subsequent to the imposition of sentence were lawful.

In *R. v. Paivarinta-Taylor* [2010] 2 Cr.App.R.(S.) 64, CA, the court said that whereas section 72A(1) of the CJA 1988 enables a court to postpone making a determination as to a defendant's benefit for the purpose of a confiscation order, or as to the amount to be recovered from him under such an order, for such period as it may specify in certain circumstances, and whereas section 72A(9) provides that, in sentencing the defendant at any time during the specified postponement period, the court shall not impose any fine on him, the decision in *R. v. Soneji* [2006] 1 A.C. 340, HL (that where there is a breach of a procedural requirement in a statute, a court should ask itself what Parliament intended should be the consequences and whether it fairly could be taken to have intended total invalidity), remains binding authority, as do *R. v. Ruddick* [2004] 1 Cr.App.R.(S.) 7, CA, *R. v. Simpson* [2003] 2 Cr.App.R. 36, CA, and *R. v. Donohoe* [2007] 1 Cr.App.R.(S.) 88, CA, in so far as they add to the principles identified in *Soneji* as to the correct approach to the consequences of a breach of the procedural provisions relating to confiscation orders under the 1988 Act. Cases such as *R. v. Threapleton* [2002] 2 Cr.App.R.(S.) 46, CA, were decided without reference to *Soneji*, and the Court of Appeal said that they should in future be disregarded when considering the consequences of such a breach. It was held that Parliament could not be taken to have intended that a breach of section 72A(9) would lead to total invalidity, that the imposition of a fine before making a confiscation order would render the fine itself invalid, that, having imposed such a fine, the court could then no longer proceed to consider the making of a confiscation order, or that any confiscation order so made would itself be rendered invalid.

Assessment of benefit/making of assumptions

5-757   The assumption provided for in section 72AA(4)(a) of the 1988 Act (*viz.* that any property transferred to the defendant since the beginning of the relevant period was received by him "in connection with the commission of offences to which this Part of this Act applies") includes within its scope offences committed by persons other than the defendant; thus it is not sufficient to rebut the presumption to show that the property was obtained by the defendant as a result of somebody else's criminal conduct; but the defendant's knowledge or lack of knowledge would be highly material in deciding whether to apply the safety valve in subsection (5) (assumption not to be made if court is satisfied that there would be a serious risk of injustice): *R. v. Ilyas* [2009] 1 Cr.App.R.(S.) 59, CA. See the commentary by David Thomas Q.C. in the *Criminal Law Review* ([2008] Crim.L.R. 908) for the suggestion that this decision will not carry across to the PCA 2002 regime; and see the commentary in CLW/08/39/9 as to the limitations of the actual decision, and, in particular, for the suggestion that it is out of kilter with the decision of the House of Lords in *R. v. May* (§ 5-1044 in the main work).

Whereas section 72AA of the 1988 Act provided that in certain cases it was to be assumed against the defendant that he had committed offences other than those of which he had been convicted or which he had asked to be taken into consideration, and that this assumed criminal conduct should be included within his "relevant criminal conduct" (the assessed benefit from which would form the basis of any confiscation order, subject only to his realisable assets being insufficient), there was nothing objectionable in imposing on the defendant the burden of showing in the particular case that the assumptions should not be made; the assumptions were founded on his holding of property or expenditure of money, and there was nothing unfair in requiring him to show that the source of his property was legitimate: *R. v. Bagnall and Sharma* [2013] 1 W.L.R. 204, CA.

As to the assessment of benefit under the 1988 Act, see also *R. v. Ahmad (Shakeel) and Ahmad (Syed Mubarak)* (§ 5-1051 in the main work).

Factual basis for making order

Where an agreement is reached as to the amount of a confiscation order, that agreement will **5-758** be binding on the defendant unless there are the sort of exceptional circumstances referred to in *R. v. Hirani*, unreported, June 11, 2008, CA ([2008] EWCA Crim. 1463) (save in most exceptional circumstances, a confiscation order based on an agreed amount will not be set aside where the essence of complaint is that, in seeking to secure the best deal available, erroneous advice was given to a party to the agreement; without exhaustively identifying such circumstances, there would need to be a well-founded submission that the whole process was unfair): *R. v. Ayankoya*, unreported, May 24, 2011, CA ([2011] EWCA Crim. 1488). The circumstances had, however, been wholly exceptional where: (i) the defendant had agreed to the amount after being incorrectly informed by his counsel that the judge had ruled that an adjournment to await bank statements supporting his claims would be impossible and that he therefore had a choice of either agreeing the amount or giving evidence without the statements with the inherent risk that a higher amount would result, and (ii) where the bank statements had in fact shown that there was force in the defendant's claims; in these circumstances, the erroneous advice had been of a potentially fundamental nature: *ibid.*

Amount that might be realised

In *R. v. Blee* [2004] 1 Cr.App.R.(S.) 33, CA, it was held that whereas section 74(3) of the CJA **5-759** 1988 provides that "the amount that might be realised at the time a confiscation order is made" includes "the total of the values at that time of all gifts caught by this Part of this Act" and whereas section 74(10) provides that a gift is caught by that part of the Act if "(a) it was made by the defendant at any time after the commission of the offence ...; and (b) the court considers it appropriate in all the circumstances to take the gift into account" it follows that the fact that the property held by the donee at the time of the confiscation order is less than the value of the gift does not *per se* preclude the court from taking the full value of the gift into account; the court is given a discretion by section 74(10) and the question for it to decide is whether it is "appropriate" to take the gift into account; if it considers it appropriate to take it into account (in whole or in part), then to the extent that it does so, the value of the gift is to be included in the computation of the amount that might be realised; in exercising the discretion, the court may have regard to the timing of the gift (here, made when the defendant, having been on the run, had decided to surrender), to the fact that it was made to a person from whom the defendant would be likely to be able to receive an equivalent benefit in return, if he wished, and to the fact that whilst the donee currently had assets worth considerably less than the value of the gift, he was in highly paid employment and would be likely again to hold substantial assets; and, where it is said that the gift has been dissipated prior to the confiscation order, this is a matter to be considered under section 74(10), rather than on a subsequent application for a certificate of inadequacy.

As to the approach to be taken where the prosecution allege that the defendant is the beneficial owner of property registered in the name of a third party, see *Revenue and Customs Prosecutions Office v. May* [2010] 3 All E.R. 1173, CA (Civ. Div.) (§ 5-1059 in the main work).

Valuation of property

In *R. v. Hedges* (2004) 148 S.J. 974, CA, it was held that in making a confiscation order against **5-760** a defendant whose only realisable asset was the house which he owned jointly with his wife, the correct approach to valuation of his interest in the property had been to determine the market value of the property, then deduct the outstanding mortgage and the reasonable costs of sale before making a confiscation order in respect of half the remaining amount; such an approach properly reflected the intention of section 74(4) of the CJA 1988 and was to be preferred to that of dividing the value of the house and then deducting the remaining mortgage and costs of sale from the defendant's half share, on the basis that he was responsible for payment of the mortgage;

whilst it was true that the defendant was in theory liable to repay the whole mortgage, being jointly and severally liable, the reality was that the mortgage and the costs of sale would be discharged out of the proceeds of sale, the net effect of which would be to reduce his share in the value of the house by half the amount of the mortgage and costs of sale.

In *R. v. Ahmed* [2005] 1 All E.R. 128, CA, it was held that where a court concludes that an offender has benefited from relevant criminal conduct (CJA 1988, s.71(1A)), the court has no discretion, in valuing the realisable assets for the purposes of determining the amount of the confiscation order, to exclude from the computation, the value of the defendant's share in the matrimonial home, notwithstanding the probability that the home would have to be sold to meet the confiscation order; the words "the amount appearing to the court" in subsection (6)(b) ("... the sum which an order made by a court under this section requires an offender to pay shall be equal to (a) ...; or (b) the amount appearing to the court to be the amount that might be realised at the time the order is made, whichever is the less") did not give the court a discretion; it merely referred to the valuation process to be carried out under section 74, and section 3 of the Human Rights Act 1998 (§ 16-16 in the main work) did not require it to be read as construing such a discretion on the court on account of the possible interference with innocent third parties' rights under Article 8 of the ECHR (*ibid.*, § 16-137); the court is merely concerned with the arithmetic exercise of computing what is, in effect, a statutory debt; such process does not involve any assessment of the way in which the debt may ultimately be paid; different considerations would apply if the debt is not met and the prosecution determine to take enforcement action; if a court is asked to make an order for the sale of the matrimonial home then the third party's rights under Article 8 would clearly be engaged; and it would be at that stage that the court would have to consider whether or not it would be proportionate to make an order for the sale of the home. In connection with this case, see *Webber v. Webber (CPS intervening)*, § 5-1062 in the main work.

In the earlier case of *R. v. Goodenough* [2005] 1 Cr.App.R.(S.) 88, CA, it was held that where a defendant's only realisable asset was his equity in the matrimonial home, the making of a confiscation order in accordance with the requirements of the 1988 Act for the amount by which he had benefited from his offending (being an amount less than the value of his equity) did not infringe or interfere with his rights under Article 8 or under Article 1 of the First Protocol (right to peaceful enjoyment of possessions); the rights of the defendant's wife might be infringed if the house were to be sold in order to raise the money to pay the amount of the confiscation order, and it would be open to the wife to oppose any application to appoint a receiver to enforce the order.

Restraint orders; payment of legal expenses out of restrained assets

5-761 In *Revenue and Customs Prosecution Office v. Briggs-Price and O'Reilly* [2007] L.S. Gazette, June 28, 32, CA (Civ. Div.) ([2007] EWCA Civ. 568) it was held, in relation to the confiscation regimes under the CJA 1988 and the DTA 1994, that the principle in *Customs and Excise Commrs v. Norris* [1991] 2 Q.B. 293, CA (Civ. Div.) (defendant's legal expenses may be met from restrained assets), applies both to legal expenses incurred prior to conviction (and any appeal against conviction) and to legal expenses incurred in connection with the making of a confiscation order and an appeal against such order; there is a discretion in such cases, which will be exercised for a proper and legitimate purpose within the scope of the statutory regime where the released assets are to meet expenses for a prospective appeal which are neither excessive nor improperly incurred (such amount as is released being capable of control by assessment).

Restraint orders; appointment of receiver

5-762 See *Revenue and Customs Prosecutions Office v. Pigott (Lamb, interested party)* [2010] S.T.C. 1190, CA (Civ. Div.) (§ 5-874 in the main work).

Certificate of inadequacy

5-763 There is no rule of law that says that, on an application under section 83 of the 1988 Act for a certificate of inadequacy, the High Court could not be persuaded that a defendant was unable to pay the outstanding amount by reason of a worsening of his financial circumstances unless he gave full disclosure of what had happened in the meantime to all his assets, including previously unidentified assets (that the Crown Court had found to exist when making the confiscation order); any such rule would trammel the width of section 83 by imposing a restriction which was not in the statute; and it would also be capable of causing not merely hardship, but hardship amounting to injustice; in the case of previously unidentified assets, it is possible that a defendant may genuinely have no idea or only a dim recollection of what originally happened to them; he should be allowed to try to persuade the court, if this be the case, that his identified assets have shrunk in value and that as a result he is not able to pay the amount outstanding: *Glaves v. CPS* [2011] Costs L.R. 556, CA (Civ. Div.) (considering *Telli v. Revenue and Customs Prosecutions Office* (see § 5-1057 in the main work)).

It was held in *Escobar v. DPP* [2009] 1 W.L.R. 64, DC, that when making an order under section 83(4) of the CJA 1988 for the reduction of a sum payable under a confiscation order (following the issue of a certificate of inadequacy), the Crown Court has jurisdiction to fix a time for payment (by way of extension of the original date). The court said that although there is no express power to extend time in section 83, section 75(1) ("(1) Where the Crown Court orders the defendant to pay an amount under this Part ..., sections 139(1) to (4) ... of the Powers of Criminal Courts (Sentencing) Act 2000 (powers of Crown Court in relation to fines and enforcement of Crown Court fines) shall have effect as if that amount were a fine imposed on him by the Crown Court.") operates so as to incorporate section 139(1) of the 2000 Act (§ 5-676 in the main work), which in turn gives the court power to extend the time for payment when it substitutes a lesser sum under section 83. When read as a whole, section 75 is generally concerned to make provision for orders made under section 83 as well as those under other provisions in Part VI, and this is consistent with the natural and grammatical meaning of the relevant provisions, in that the Crown Court is making an order under section 83(4) and the effect of that order is that the defendant has to pay an amount due under Part VI. For the suggestion that the court's conclusion is out of kilter with the legislative structure, see CLW/09/02/5. For the relevant provisions of the PCA 2002, see sections 23 and 39 (§§ 5-824, 5-840 in the main work), neither of which contain any provision for an extension of the time allowed to pay.

Enforcement

See *Revenue and Customs Prosecutions Office v. May* [2010] 3 All E.R. 1173, CA (Civ. Div.) (§ 5-1059 in the main work). **5-764**

Presence of the accused

See *R. v. Spearing* (§ 3-225 in the main work). **5-765**

D. CONFISCATION UNDER THE PROCEEDS OF CRIME ACT 2002

(2) Legislation

(a) *Statute*

Proceeds of Crime Act 2002, ss.6–91

Making of order

In *R. v. Davenport* [2016] Lloyd's Rep. F.C. 21, CA, it was said that, where the prosecution seek a confiscation order, under section 6 of the 2002 Act (§ 5-805 in the main work), and a compensation order, under section 130 of the PCC(S)A 2000 (*ibid.*, § 5-691), in circumstances where section 13(5) (*ibid.*, § 5-813) of the 2002 Act is not engaged (*i.e.* the court believes the person has sufficient means to satisfy both orders in full), the court should bear in mind: (i) it is empowered to make both orders; (ii) it should be alert to any risk of double-counting, and to the risk of making a disproportionate confiscation order; (iii) ordinarily, it should not make a compensation and confiscation order representing the full amount of benefit where there has been actual restitution to the victim(s) prior to the confiscation hearing (*R. v. Waya* (§ 5-1042 in the main work), and *R. v. Jawad* (*ibid.*, § 5-813a)); (iv) where a defendant asserts that restitution will be made after the hearing, the court should scrutinise carefully and critically the supporting evidence and arguments; (v) if it remains uncertain whether the victims will be repaid under the compensation order, then a confiscation order including that amount will not ordinarily be disproportionate (*Jawad*); (vi) mathematical certainty of restitution is not, however, required; the court should decide practically and realistically whether restitution is assured; (vii) future restitution is capable **★5-806** of being properly assessed as assured, depending on the circumstances, notwithstanding that it will not be immediate, or almost immediate, at the time of the hearing; and (viii) while a defendant who is truly intent on making full restitution ordinarily should have arranged this prior to the hearing, there may be cases where that is impossible; if the court then has firm, evidence-based grounds for believing that restitution may still be forthcoming, albeit it cannot be taken as "assured" at the time of the hearing, it has a discretion to adjourn for further inquiry.

Effect of order on court's other powers

5-813a *R. v. Beaumont* (see the main work) was doubted in *R. v. Parkinson, ante,* § 5-708.

★ For a case considering what a court may wish to bear in mind where the prosecution seek a confiscation order and a compensation order in circumstances where the defendant has sufficient assets to meet both orders in full and where section 13(5) of the 2002 Act (as to which, see § 5-813 in the main work) is therefore not engaged, see *R. v. Davenport, ante,* § 5-806.

Postponement

★5-815 An application by the prosecution for leave to appeal from the decision of the criminal division of the Court of Appeal in *R. v. Guraj* (see the main work) has been allowed: see [2016] 1 W.L.R. 389, SC.

Conditions for exercise of powers

★5-856 With effect from March 1, 2016 (Serious Crime Act 2015 (Commencement No. 5 and Transitional Provisions and Savings) Regulations 2016 (S.I. 2016 No. 148)), section 13 of the 2015 Act (see the main work) was brought into force.

"Appropriate approval"

★5-861 As to the coming into force of section 13 of the SCA 2015 (see the main work), see *ante,* § 5-856.

Tainted gifts

★5-908 *R. v. Lehair* is now reported at [2016] 1 Cr.App.R.(S.) 2.

Proceeds of Crime Act 2002, Sched. 2

Lifestyle offences

★5-924 As from a day to be appointed, a new paragraph 1A is inserted in Schedule 2 to the PCA 2002 by the Psychoactive Substances Act 2016, s.60, and Sched. 5, para. 2(1) and (2), as follows—

"1A. An offence under any of the following provisions of the Psychoactive Substances Act 2016—
(a) section 4 (producing a psychoactive substance);
(b) section 5 (supplying, or offering to supply, a psychoactive substance);
(c) section 7 (possession of psychoactive substance with intent to supply);
(d) section 8 (importing or exporting a psychoactive substance).".

(b) *Subordinate legislation*

Commencement

Proceeds of Crime Act 2002 (Commencement No. 5, Transitional Provisions, Savings and Amendment) Order 2003 (S.I. 2003 No. 333)

Citation and interpretation

5-937 **1.**—(1) [*Citation.*]

(2) In this Order, "the Act" means the Proceeds of Crime Act 2002.

(3) Where an offence is found to have been committed over a period of two or more days, or at some time during a period of two or more days, it shall be taken for the purposes of this order to have been committed on the earliest of those days.

Commencement of provisions

5-938 **2.**—(1) The provisions of the Act listed in column 1 of the Schedule to this Order shall come into force on 24th March 2003, subject to the transitional provisions and savings contained in this order.

(2) But where a particular purpose is specified in relation to any such provision in column 2 of that Schedule, the provision concerned shall come into force only for that purpose.

Transitional provisions relating to confiscation orders—England and Wales

3.—(1) Section 6 of the Act (making of confiscation order) shall not have effect where the offence, **5-939** or any of the offences, mentioned in section 6(2) was committed before 24th March 2003.

(2) Section 27 of the Act (defendant convicted or committed absconds) shall not have effect where the offence, or any of the offences, mentioned in section 27(2) was committed before 24th March 2003.

(3) Section 28 of the Act (defendant neither convicted nor acquitted absconds) shall not have effect where the offence, or any of the offences, in respect of which proceedings have been started but not concluded was committed before 24th March 2003.

4. [*Transitional provisions relating to confiscation orders—Northern Ireland.*]

It was held in *R. v. Moulden* [2009] 1 Cr.App.R. 27, CA, that where the respondent appeared before the Crown Court to be dealt with in respect of two indictments, one alleging offences committed before March 24, 2003, and the other alleging offences committed after that date, each indictment represented a separate set of "proceedings" for the purposes of section 6(2)(a) of the 2002 Act (see § 5-805 in the main work) and accordingly, by virtue of article 3(1), the 2002 Act had no application to the pre-March 24, 2003, indictment, but did apply to the post-March 24, 2003, indictment. The judge had, therefore, been correct to apply the confiscation provisions of the CJA 1988 to the one indictment and the confiscation provisions of the 2002 Act to the other indictment, and to reject the prosecution submission that the effect of these provisions was to disapply the 2002 Act in relation to both indictments, thereby triggering the assumptions provided for by section 72AA of the 1988 Act.

Where the defendant pleaded guilty to a count of conspiracy to make false instruments, the particulars of offence alleging that the offence took place "between the 1st day of January 2003 and the 16th day of May 2007", and where his written basis of plea was to the effect that his first admitted act in pursuance of the criminal agreement took place only on October 29, 2003, his offence had begun before March 24, 2003, for the purposes of article 3(1) (having regard to article 1(3)), such that the applicable confiscation provisions were those under Part VI of the CJA 1988, not Part 2 of the PCA 2002, see *R. v. Evwierhowa* [2011] 2 Cr.App.R.(S.) 77, CA.

As to whether, in principle, rental income from criminally-obtained properties could properly be regarded as benefit even though it was derived from properties obtained subject to offences, in respect of which there were convictions, that were committed before the commencement of Part 2 of the 2002 Act, see *R. v. Oyebola*, (§ 5-1049a in the main work).

By virtue of articles 3(1) and 10(1)(e) (*post*, § 5-942), section 16 of the DTA 1994 (increase in realisable property) continues to have effect where an offence mentioned in section 6(2) of the PCA Act 2002 (making of confiscation order (§ 5-805 in the main work)) was committed before March 24, 2003: *Re Peacock (Secretary of State for the Home Department intervening)* [2012] 2 Cr.App.R.(S.) 81, SC. For the suggestion that the court misconstrued the order (albeit reaching the correct result), see CLW/12/08/5.

Transitional provisions relating to restraint orders and enforcement abroad—England and Wales

5. Sections 41 (restraint orders) and 74 (enforcement abroad) of the Act shall not have effect **5-940** where—

    (a) the powers in those sections would otherwise be exercisable by virtue of a condition in section 40(2) or (3) of the Act being satisfied; and

    (b) the offence mentioned in section 40(2)(a) or 40(3)(a), as the case may be, was committed before 24th March 2003.

6. [*Transitional provisions relating to restraint orders and enforcement abroad—Northern Ireland.*]

Transitional provisions relating to criminal lifestyle—England and Wales

7.—(1) This article applies where the court is determining under section 6(4)(a) of the Act whether **5-941** the defendant has a criminal lifestyle.

(2) Conduct shall not form part of a course of criminal activity under section 75(3)(a) of the Act where any of the three or more offences mentioned in section 75(3)(a) was committed before 24th March 2003.

(3) Where the court is applying the rule in section 75(5) of the Act on the calculation of relevant

benefit for the purposes of determining whether or not the test in section 75(2)(b) of the Act is satisfied by virtue of conduct forming part of a course of criminal activity under section 75(3)(a) of the Act, the court must not take into account benefit from conduct constituting an offence mentioned in section 75(5)(c) of the Act which was committed before 24th March 2003.

(4) Conduct shall form part of a course of criminal activity under section 75(3)(b) of the Act, notwithstanding that any of the offences of which the defendant was convicted on at least two separate occasions in the period mentioned in section 75(3)(b) were committed before 24th March 2003.

(5) Where the court is applying the rule in section 75(5) of the Act on the calculation of relevant benefit for the purposes of determining whether or not the test in section 75(2)(b) of the Act is satisfied by virtue of conduct forming part of a course of criminal activity under section 75(3)(b) of the Act, the court may take into account benefit from conduct constituting an offence committed before 24th March 2003.

(6) Where the court is applying the rule in section 75(6) of the Act on the calculation of relevant benefit for the purposes of determining whether or not the test in section 75(2)(c) of the Act is satisfied, the court must not take into account benefit from conduct constituting an offence mentioned in section 75(6)(b) of the Act which was committed before 24th March 2003.

[This article is printed as substituted by the Proceeds of Crime Act 2002 (Commencement No. 5) (Amendment of Transitional Provisions) Order 2003 (S.I. 2003 No. 531).]

8. [*Transitional provisions relating to criminal lifestyle—Northern Ireland.*]

Transitional provisions relating to particular criminal conduct
9. Conduct which constitutes an offence which was committed before 24th March 2003 is not particular criminal conduct under section 76(3) or 224(3) of the Act.

Savings for England and Wales

5-942   **10.**—(1) Where, under article 3 or 5, a provision of the Act does not have effect, the following provisions shall continue to have effect—

    (a) sections 71 to 89 (including Schedule 4) and 102 of the Criminal Justice Act 1988;

    (b) paragraphs 83 and 84 of Schedule 17 to the Housing Act 1988;

    (c) sections 21(3)(e) to (g), 27, 28 and 34 of the Criminal Justice Act 1993;

    (d) paragraph 36 of Schedule 9 to the Criminal Justice and Public Order Act 1994;

    (e) sections 1 to 36 and 41 of the Drug Trafficking Act 1994;

    (f) sections 1 to 10, 15(1) and (3) (including Schedule 1), 16(2), (5) and (6) of the Proceeds of Crime Act 1995;

    (g) section 4(3) of the Private International Law (Miscellaneous Provisions) Act 1995;

    (h) sections 35 to 38 of the Proceeds of Crime (Scotland) Act 1995;

    (i) the Proceeds of Crime (Enforcement of Confiscation Orders made in England and Wales or Scotland) Order (Northern Ireland) 1997 and the Proceeds of Crime (Northern Ireland) Order 1996, so far as necessary for the continued operation of the Proceeds of Crime (Enforcement of Confiscation Orders made in England and Wales or Scotland) Order (Northern Ireland) 1997;

    (j) paragraphs 23 and 36 of Schedule 5 to the Justices of the Peace Act 1997;

    (k) section 83 of, paragraph 114 of Schedule 8 to and paragraph 8 of Schedule 9 to the Crime and Disorder Act 1998;

    (l) paragraphs 139 and 172 of Schedule 13 to the Access to Justice Act 1999;

    (m) paragraphs 105 to 113 and 163 to 173 of Schedule 9 to the Powers of Criminal Courts (Sentencing) Act 2000;

    (n) paragraphs 6(1) to (3) and 10 of Schedule 15 to the Terrorism Act 2000.

(2) Where under article 3 or 5, a provision of the Act does not have effect, the following provisions shall continue to have effect as if they had not been amended by Schedule 11 to the Act—

    (a) section 13(6) of the Criminal Justice (International Co-operation) Act 1990;

    (b) paragraph 17(3) of Schedule 8 to the Terrorism Act 2000.

11. [*Savings for Northern Ireland.*]

12. [*Savings for enforcement of Scottish orders in England, Wales and Northern Ireland.*]

13. [*Savings in relation to external orders.*]

14. [*Amendment of arts 3 and 5 of S.I. 2003 No. 120, §§ 26-4, 26-5 in the main work.*]

Article 2   THE SCHEDULE

Column 1	*Column 2*
Part 2 (sections 6 to 91, including Schedule 2) (Confiscation: England and Wales).	So far as not already in force.
Part 4 (sections 156 to 239, including Schedule 5) (Confiscation: Northern Ireland).	
Part 9 (sections 417 to 434) (Insolvency *etc.*).	
Part 10 (sections 435 to 442) (Information).	So far as not already in force.
Section 444 (External requests and orders).	
Section 445 (External investigations).	
Section 447 (Interpretation).	
Section 456 (Amendments).	Commenced for the purposes of the provisions of Schedule 11 to the Act commenced by this Order.
Section 457 (Repeals).	Commenced for the purposes of the provisions of Schedule 12 to the Act commenced by this Order.
In Schedule 11, paragraphs 1, 4, 5, 7, 8, 9, 11, 14(2) and (3), 15, 16, 17(2), (4) and (6), 19(2) and (3), 20, 21, 25(2)(a) and (h) to (j), 26, 27, 28(1) and (2)(e) and (g), 31(2) and (3)(a) to (c), 32, 37 and 39.	Paragraphs 7, 11, 15, 16, 20, 21 and 39 are commenced except to the extent that they relate to Part 3 of the Act. Paragraph 17(2) is commenced so far as it repeals sections 71 to 89, 94 and 99 to 102 of the Criminal Justice Act 1988. Paragraph 25(2)(a) is commenced so far as it repeals sections 1 to 38 and 41 of the Drug Trafficking Act 1994. Paragraph 27 is commenced so far as not already in force. Paragraph 31(2) is commenced so far as it repeals articles 4 to 41 of the Proceeds of Crime (Northern Ireland) Order 1996.
In Schedule 12, the following entries; the entry relating to the Criminal Appeal (Northern Ireland) Act 1980; the entry relating to the Police and Criminal Evidence Act 1984; the entry relating to the Criminal Justice Act 1988; the entry relating to the Housing Act 1988; the entry relating to the Police and Criminal Evidence (Northern Ireland) Order 1989; in the entry relating to the Criminal Justice (International Co-operation) Act 1990, the entry in the second column concerning section 13 of that Act; the entry relating to the Criminal Justice (Confiscation) (Northern Ireland) Order 1990; the entry relating to the Criminal Justice Act 1993; the entry relating to the Drug Trafficking Act 1994; the entry relating to the Proceeds of Crime Act 1995; in the entry relating to the Criminal Procedure (Consequential Provisions) (Scotland) Act 1995, the entry in the second column concerning Schedule 4 of that Act; the entry relating to the Private International Law (Miscellaneous Provisions) Act 1995; in the entry relating to the Proceeds of Crime (Scotland) Act 1995, the entry in the second column concerning sections 35 to 39 of that Act, the entry in the second column concerning section 40 of that Act and the entry in the second column concerning section 42 of that Act; the entry relating to	The entry relating to sections 71 to 102 of the Criminal Justice Act 1988 is commenced so far as it repeals sections 71 to 89, 94 and 99 to 102 of that Act. The entries relating to the Criminal Justice Act 1993, the Proceeds of Crime Act 1995 and the Access to Justice Act 1999 are commenced so far as not already in force. The entry relating to sections 1 to 54 of the Drug Trafficking Act 1994 is commenced so far as it repeals sections 1 to 38 and 41 of that Act. The entry relating to Parts II and III of the Proceeds of Crime (Northern Ireland) Order 1996 is commenced so far as it repeals articles 4 to 41 of that Order. The entry relating to the Terrorism Act 2000 is commenced so far as it repeals paragraphs 6 and 10 of Schedule 15 to that Act.

Column 1

Column 2

the Proceeds of Crime (Northern Ireland) Order 1996; the entry relating to the Justices of the Peace Act 1997; in the entry relating to the Crime and Disorder Act 1998, the entry in the second column concerning section 83 of that Act, the entry in the second column concerning Schedule 8 of that Act and the entry in the second column concerning Schedule 9 of that Act; the entry relating to the Access to Justice Act 1999; the entry relating to the Powers of Criminal Courts (Sentencing) Act 2000; the entry relating to the Terrorism Act 2000; and the entry relating to the Criminal Justice and Police Act 2001.

Appeals

Proceeds of Crime Act 2002 (Appeals under Part 2) Order 2003 (S.I. 2003 No. 82)

Leave to appeal to Supreme Court

★**5-1014**   With effect from November 30, 2015, article 11 of S.I. 2003 No. 82 was amended by the Proceeds of Crime Act 2002 (Appeals under Part 2) (Amendment) Order 2015 (S.I. 2015 No. 1855) so as to insert "13B(4)," before "33".

Application for leave to appeal

★**5-1015**   With effect from November 30, 2015, article 12(1) of S.I. 2003 No. 82 was amended by the Proceeds of Crime Act 2002 (Appeals under Part 2) (Amendment) Order 2015 (S.I. 2015 No. 1855) so as to insert a reference to an appeal to the Supreme Court under section 13B(4) of the 2002 Act (as to which, see § 5-813c in the main work).

Presence at hearing

★**5-1016**   With effect from November 30, 2015, article 14 of S.I. 2003 No. 82 was amended by the Proceeds of Crime Act 2002 (Appeals under Part 2) (Amendment) Order 2015 (S.I. 2015 No. 1855) so as to insert "13B(4)," before "33".

(3) Authorities

Lack of discretion/abuse of process/proportionality

★**5-1042**   *Paulet v. U.K.* is now reported at (2015) 61 E.H.R.R. 39.

Benefit

Property

★**5-1047**   **Miscellaneous offences**. As to the benefit obtained from an offence of insider dealing, see *DPP (Cth) v. Gay, post*, § 30-43.

★**5-1050b**   **Offences committed in connection with the running of a business through a company or otherwise.** The Supreme Court has reversed the judgment of the Court of Appeal in *R. v. Harvey*: see *R. v. Harvey (Jack)* [2016] 2 W.L.R. 37. The appellant was convicted of handling stolen goods after it was discovered that a significant proportion (the trial judge assessed this at 38 per cent) of the machinery that was hired out by his company was stolen. It being a case to which the "criminal lifestyle" provisions applied, the judge calculated his benefit by taking 38 per cent of the total turnover (including value added tax) during the relevant period and this approach had been upheld by the Court of Appeal. The Supreme Court held: (i) value added tax for which a defendant has accounted to Her Majesty's Revenue and Customs is in a different category to income or corporation tax (or expenses connected to acquiring money or an asset); such taxes are computed on net income, and cannot be allocated to a particular transaction, whereas a value added tax liability can be precisely related to the obtaining of the property in question; where money is paid to a person as a result of a transaction liable to value added tax, he is regarded under European

Union law as collecting the tax element on behalf of the Revenue; where the tax has been accounted for to the Revenue, the judge's approach would lead to the government enjoying double recovery; (ii) there was a powerful argument for saying that these considerations should lead to the conclusion that, when value added tax has been accounted for to the Revenue, it has not been "obtained" by the defendant as a matter of statutory construction of the 2002 Act; however, the 2002 Act is complex and it is important to hold fast to the principle in *R. v. Waya* (§ 5-1042 in the main work), that, once property has been obtained as a result of or in connection with crime, it remains the defendant's benefit whether or not he retains it; accordingly, that argument of the appellant fell to be rejected; (iii) those considerations were, however, relevant to proportionality and Article 1 of the First Protocol to the ECHR (right to peaceful enjoyment of possessions); any provision entitling the executive to effect double recovery from an individual, although not absolutely forbidden by that article, is clearly at risk of being found disproportionate; although, therefore, it would be appropriate under the 2002 Act, as traditionally interpreted, to make a confiscation order calculated on the basis that the value added tax had been "obtained" by the defendant, it would be disproportionate to do so, at least when that tax had been accounted for (either by remittance or being set off against input tax); and (iv) there is nothing disproportionate about a judge taking a "broad-brush" approach to questions of what sums were received or paid in value added tax in the context of criminal activity where the evidence is confusing, unreliable, and/or incomplete; the risk of disproportionality may lie more in spending time and money pursuing a precise answer that is at best elusive and, more frequently, unattainable.

Offences involving the fraudulent evasion of duty or VAT.

R. v. Chahal and Singh is now reported at [2015] Lloyd's Rep. F.C. 601, *sub nom. R. v. Chahal.*   ★**5-1051**

Pecuniary advantage
Paulet v. U.K. is now reported at (2015) 61 E.H.R.R. 39.   ★**5-1053**

X. DISQUALIFICATION, RESTRICTION, EXCLUSION, ETC., ORDERS

A. BANNING ORDERS UNDER THE FOOTBALL SPECTATORS ACT 1989

(2) Legislation
Football Spectators Act 1989, ss.14A-14H

The Football Spectators (2016 European Championship Control Period) Order 2016 (S.I. 2016   ★**5-1069**
No. 141) provides that, in relation to the UEFA 2016 European Championship tournament in France, section 14(6) of the 1989 Act (definition of "control period" in relation to an external tournament (see the main work)) shall have effect as if, for the reference to five days, there were substituted a reference to 10 days, and that the period beginning on May 31, 2016 (which is 10 days before the first match), and ending when the last match included in the tournament is finished or cancelled (which, subject to postponement, is due to be July 10, 2016), is a control period for the purposes of Part II of the Act.

There is no power to make a football banning order prohibiting the defendant from attending   ★**5-1072**
only regulated football matches involving specified teams, and Article 8 of the ECHR (right to respect for private and family life (§ 16-137 in the main work)) is not engaged when a person is prevented from attending as a spectator an event to which the public are invited in return for payment, and subject to contractual terms; in any event, the right under Article 8(1) is not unqualified (see Art. 8(2)); by stipulating that, if the conditions for making an order are met, an order in the terms of section 14(4) must be made, Parliament has struck the necessary balance for the purposes of Article 8(2): *Commr of Police of the Metropolis v. Thorpe*, 180 J.P. 16, QBD (Edis J.) (conceding, however, that the power under s.14G of the 1989 Act (*ibid.*, § 5-1079) to impose requirements, that are additional to the mandatory terms of an order, might engage Art. 8).

H. SERIOUS CRIME PREVENTION ORDERS

(2) Legislation
Serious Crime Act 2007, ss.1, 2, 4, 5

Serious crime prevention orders
With effect from March 1, 2016 (Serious Crime Act 2015 (Commencement No. 5 and   ★**5-1151**

Transitional Provisions and Savings) Regulations 2016 (S.I. 2016 No. 148)), section 46 of, and Schedule 1 to, the 2015 Act (see the main work) were brought into force.

Involvement in serious crime: Scotland and Northern Ireland orders

★**5-1152a**   As to the commencement of section 46 of, and Schedule 1 to, the SCA 2015, see *ante*, § 5-1151.

Involvement in serious crime: supplementary

★**5-1153**   As to the commencement of section 46 of, and Schedule 1 to, the SCA 2015, see *ante*, § 5-1151.

Type of provision that may be made by orders

★**5-1154**   As to the commencement of section 46 of, and Schedule 1 to, the SCA 2015, see *ante*, § 5-1151.

Serious Crime Act 2007, ss.6-10

Other exceptions

★**5-1156**   As to the commencement of section 46 of, and Schedule 1 to, the SCA 2015, see *ante*, § 5-1151..

Limited class of applicants for making of orders

★**5-1157**   As to the commencement of section 46 of, and Schedule 1 to, the SCA 2015, see *ante*, § 5-1151.

Right of third parties to make representations

★**5-1158**   As to the commencement of section 46 of, and Schedule 1 to, the SCA 2015, see *ante*, § 5-1151.

Notice requirements in relation to orders

★**5-1159**   As to the commencement of section 46 of, and Schedule 1 to, the SCA 2015, see *ante*, § 5-1151.

Serious Crime Act 2007, ss.11-15

Restrictions for legal professional privilege

★**5-1161**   As to the commencement of section 46 of, and Schedule 1 to, the SCA 2015, see *ante*, § 5-1151.

Restrictions on excluded material and banking information

★**5-1162**   As to the commencement of section 46 of, and Schedule 1 to, the SCA 2015, see *ante*, § 5-1151.

Serious Crime Act 2007, ss.16-18

★**5-1166**   As to the commencement of section 46 of, and Schedule 1 to, the SCA 2015, see *ante*, § 5-1151.
★**5-1167**   As to the commencement of section 46 of, and Schedule 1 to, the SCA 2015, see *ante*, § 5-1151.

Serious Crime Act 2007, ss.19-22

Inter-relationship between different types of orders in England and Wales and Northern Ireland

★**5-1172**   As to the commencement of section 46 of, and Schedule 1 to, the SCA 2015, see *ante*, § 5-1151.

Scotland

★**5-1172a**   As to the commencement of section 46 of, and Schedule 1 to, the SCA 2015, see *ante*, § 5-1151.

Serious Crime Act 2007, ss.30-34

Other partnerships

★**5-1179**   As to the commencement of section 46 of, and Schedule 1 to, the SCA 2015, see *ante*, § 5-1151.

Providers of information society services

★**5-1182**   As to the commencement of section 46 of, and Schedule 1 to, the SCA 2015, see *ante*, § 5-1151.

Serious Crime Act 2007, ss.35-41

Compliance with orders: authorised monitors

★**5-1187**   As to the commencement of section 46 of, and Schedule 1 to, the SCA 2015, see *ante*, § 5-1151.

Costs in relation to authorised matters

★**5-1188**   As to the commencement of section 46 of, and Schedule 1 to, the SCA 2015, see *ante*, § 5-1151.

Serious offences

★**5-1192**   As from a day to be appointed, a new paragraph 1A is inserted in Schedule 1 to the SCA 2007 by the Psychoactive Substances Act 2016, s.60, and Sched. 5, para. 8(1) and (2). This new paragraph (the draftsman has overlooked the fact that a new para. 1A has already been inserted by the Modern Slavery Act 2015) refers to the offences under sections 4, 5, 7 and 8 of the 2016 Act (producing, supplying or offering to supply, possessing with intent to supply, importing or exporting, a psychoactive substance (*post*, §§ 27-135 *et seq.*)).

I. CRIMINAL BEHAVIOUR ORDERS

(3) Authorities

(b) *Criminal behaviour orders*

DPP v. Bulmer is now reported at [2016] 1 Cr.App.R.(S.) 12.   ★5-1218a

J. FINANCIAL REPORTING ORDERS

With effect from March 1, 2016 (Serious Crime Act 2015 (Commencement No. 5 and   ★5-1219
Transitional Provisions and Savings) Regulations 2016 (S.I. 2016 No. 148)), section 85(1) of, and paragraph 71 of Schedule 4 to, the 2015 Act (see the main work) were brought into force, so far as they were not already in force (along with s.50(1)(b), which repealed s.77 (financial reporting orders in Scotland) of the 2005 Act).

K. PROCEDURE

Criminal Procedure Rules 2015 (S.I. 2015 No. 1490), Pt 31

Application for behaviour order and notice of terms of proposed order: special rules

In *R. v. Uddin*, unreported, December 11, 2015, CA ([2015] EWCA Crim. 1918), it was held: (i)   ★5-1222
rule 31.3 of the Criminal Procedure Rules 2015 (S.I. 2015 No. 1490) should be interpreted as requiring a prosecutor's intention to apply for an anti-social behaviour order (or criminal behaviour order) to be in writing, (ii) if the prosecution significantly alter the nature of their case in support of the application, the defendant must have clear and specific notice of the change, and (iii) where the defendant would have been left unsure about the case he had to meet, an order is liable to be quashed on appeal on this ground alone.

XV. MISCELLANEOUS MATTERS

D. SURCHARGES

Criminal Justice Act 2003, ss.161A, 161B

A court may not impose a second surcharge on an offender who is brought back to court and   5-1300
re-sentenced following his failure to comply with the requirements of a community sentence (an appropriate surcharge having been ordered when that sentence was imposed): *R. v. George* [2015] 2 Cr.App.R.(S.) 58, CA. No counsel for the Crown appeared on the appeal and the court did not therefore consider an argument that might have been advanced to the effect that revocation of the original sentence would have the effect that the surcharge that was parasitic on it would also fall away, allowing for a surcharge appropriate to the substituted penalty to be imposed. As to this, see CLW/15/34/26.

It is not open to a court (magistrates' court or Crown Court), when sentencing a defendant to a   ★
term of imprisonment, to order the defendant to pay a surcharge under section 161A of the CJA 2003 (§ 5-1298 in the main work) and, on the same occasion, to impose a period of imprisonment for non-payment of the surcharge: *R. v. Frimpong*, unreported, December 16, 2015, CA ([2015] EWCA Crim. 1933) (the court was actually concerned with the criminal courts charge under s.21A of the Prosecution of Offences Act 1985 (§ 6-53a in the main work), but made it plain that it took the same view in relation to the surcharge required by s.161A).

CHAPTER 6

COSTS AND LEGAL AID

I. COSTS

B. PROSECUTION OF OFFENCES ACT 1985

(7) Court costs in criminal cases

Prosecution of Offences Act 1985, ss.21A-21F

Criminal courts charge

★6-53a   For a case considering whether it was lawful for a magistrates' court to impose an immediate sentence of imprisonment together with the criminal courts charge (see the main work) and, on the same occasion, a period of imprisonment in respect of non-payment of the charge just imposed, see *R. v. Frimpong, ante,* § 5-1300.

Prosecution of Offences Act 1985 (Criminal Courts Charge) Regulations 2015 (S.I. 2015 No. 796), regs 1-4

Amount of the criminal courts charge

★6-53i   With effect from December 24, 2015, regulation 3 of, and the schedule (§ 6-53j in the main work) to, S.I. 2015 No. 796 were revoked by the Prosecution of Offences Act 1985 (Criminal Courts Charge) (Amendment) Regulations 2015 (S.I. 2015 No. 1970).

★6-53j   As to the revocation of the schedule to S.I. 2015 No. 796, see S.I. 2015 No. 1970, *ante,* § 6-53i.

D. MISCELLANEOUS ENACTMENTS

(12) Criminal Procedure Rules 2015 (S.I. 2015 No. 1490)

Criminal Procedure Rules 2015 (S.I. 2015 No. 1490), Pt 45

When this Part applies

★6-109   It should be noted that in the Queen's Printer copy of the 2015 rules, rule 45.1(1)(c) concluded with a reference to "rule 76.6 or rule 76.7". As this was an obvious error that should have been corrected as part of the rearrangement of the rules in 2015 (when Pt 76 of the 2014 rules became Pt 45 of the 2015 rules), it was corrected in the main work. For the sake of completeness, it should be noted that the error has now been formally corrected by rule 14(a) of the Criminal Procedure (Amendment) Rules 2016 (S.I. 2016 No. 120).

Court's power to vary requirements under Sections 2, 3 and 4

★6-111   With effect from April 4, 2016, rule 45.3(1) of S.I. 2015 No. 1490 (see the main work) is amended by rule 14(b) of the Criminal Procedure (Amendment) Rules 2016 (S.I. 2016 No. 120), so as to substitute the words "Unless other legislation otherwise provides, the court may" for the words "The court may".

Costs resulting from unnecessary or improper act, etc.

★6-116   With effect from April 4, 2016, rule 45.8 of S.I. 2015 No. 1490 is amended by rule 14(c) of the Criminal Procedure (Amendment) Rules 2016 (S.I. 2016 No. 120), so as (i) to insert, at the end of paragraph (4)(a) ", and in any event no later than the end of the case", and (ii) to insert new paragraphs (8) to (10), as follows—

> "(8) To help assess the amount, the court may direct an enquiry by—
>> (a) the Lord Chancellor, where the assessment is by a magistrates' court or by the Crown Court; or
>> (b) the Registrar, where the assessment is by the Court of Appeal.
> (9) In deciding whether to direct such an enquiry, the court must have regard to all the circumstances including—

46

(a) any agreement between the parties about the amount to be paid;

(b) the amount likely to be allowed;

(c) the delay and expense that may be incurred in the conduct of the enquiry; and

(d) the particular complexity of the assessment, or the difficulty or novelty of any aspect of the assessment.

(10) If the court directs such an enquiry—

(a) paragraphs (3) to (8) inclusive of rule 45.11 (assessment and re-assessment) apply as if that enquiry were an assessment under that rule (but rules 45.12 (appeal to a costs judge) and 45.13 (appeal to a High Court judge) do not apply);

(b) the authority that carries out the enquiry must serve its conclusions on the court officer as soon as reasonably practicable after following that procedure; and

(c) the court must then assess the amount to be paid.".

Costs against a legal representative

With effect from April 4, 2016, rule 45.9 of S.I. 2015 No. 1490 is amended by rule 14(d) of the ★6-117 Criminal Procedure (Amendment) Rules 2016 (S.I. 2016 No. 120), so as (i) to insert, at the end of paragraph (4)(a) ", and in any event no later than the end of the case", (ii) to insert new paragraphs (8) to (10) (in identical terms to the new paras (8) to (10) in r.45.8, *ante*), and (iii) to re-number the current paragraph (8) as "(9)" (this is a drafting error, in that it should plainly be re-numbered "(11)").

Costs against a third party

With effect from April 4, 2016, rule 45.10 of S.I. 2015 No. 1490 is amended by rule 14(e) of the ★6-118 Criminal Procedure (Amendment) Rules 2016 (S.I. 2016 No. 120), so as to insert new paragraphs (8) to (10) (in identical terms to the new paras (8) to (10) in r.45.8, *ante*).

II. LEGAL AID

C. SECONDARY LEGISLATION

Criminal legal aid

Criminal Legal Aid (General) Regulations 2013 (S.I. 2013 No. 9), Pt 1

Interpretation

The amendments of regulation 2 of S.I. 2013 No. 9 that were due to come into force on Janu- ★6-233 ary 11, 2016 are now due to come into force on April 1, 2016: Criminal Legal Aid (Remuneration etc.) (Amendment) (No. 2) Regulations 2015 (S.I. 2015 No. 2049). However, in light of the Justice Secretary's ministerial statement on January 28, 2016, that what had become known as the "dual contracting" model, and which was to be implemented by the January 11/April 1 amendments, it now appears inevitable that, prior to April 1, further legislation will be brought forward that will cancel the April 1 amendments. How this is to be achieved remains to be seen (nothing having been published as at February 26, 2016).

In the inserted definition of "relevant contract", there are now inserted the words "2010 ★ Standard Crime Contract" after the words "whichever of the": S.I. 2015 No. 2049.

If the April 1, 2016, amendments come into force, the definition of "Unit of Work" will read ★ "'Unit of Work' has the meaning given in the relevant contract": S.I. 2015 No. 2049.

If the April 1, 2016, amendments come into force, the definition of "2010 Standard Crime ★ Contract" will be replaced by the following "'2010 Standard Crime Contract', '2015 Duty Provider Contract' and '2015 Own Client Contract' mean the contracts so named between the Lord Chancellor and a provider of advice and assistance or representation made available under sections 13, 15 or 16 of the Act": S.I. 2015 No. 2049.

Criminal Legal Aid (General) Regulations 2013 (S.I. 2013 No. 9), Pt 2

Application

The amendment of regulation 8 of S.I. 2013 No. 9 that was due to come into force on January ★6-239 11, 2016 is now due to come into force on April 1, 2016 (but see *ante*, § 6-233): Criminal Legal Aid (Remuneration etc.) (Amendment) (No. 2) Regulations 2015 (S.I. 2015 No. 2049).

Criminal Legal Aid (General) Regulations 2013 (S.I. 2013 No. 9), Pt 4

General

★**6-242**   The amendment of regulation 11 of S.I. 2013 No. 9 that was due to come into force on January 11, 2016 is now due to come into force on April 1, 2016 (but see *ante*, § 6-233): Criminal Legal Aid (Remuneration etc.) (Amendment) (No. 2) Regulations 2015 (S.I. 2015 No. 2049).

Applications

★**6-245**   The amendment of regulation 14 of S.I. 2013 No. 9 that was due to come into force on January 11, 2016 is now due to come into force on April 1, 2016 (but see *ante*, § 6-233): Criminal Legal Aid (Remuneration etc.) (Amendment) (No. 2) Regulations 2015 (S.I. 2015 No. 2049).

Determinations

★**6-246**   The amendment of regulation 15 of S.I. 2013 No. 9 that was due to come into force on January 11, 2016 is now due to come into force on April 1, 2016 (but see *ante*, § 6-233): Criminal Legal Aid (Remuneration etc.) (Amendment) (No. 2) Regulations 2015 (S.I. 2015 No. 2049).

Withdrawal

★**6-247**   The amendment of regulation 16 of S.I. 2013 No. 9 that was due to come into force on January 11, 2016 is now due to come into force on April 1, 2016 (but see *ante*, § 6-233): Criminal Legal Aid (Remuneration etc.) (Amendment) (No. 2) Regulations 2015 (S.I. 2015 No. 2049).

Appeal

★**6-248**   The amendment of regulation 17 of S.I. 2013 No. 9 that was due to come into force on January 11, 2016 is now due to come into force on April 1, 2016 (but see *ante*, § 6-233): Criminal Legal Aid (Remuneration etc.) (Amendment) (No. 2) Regulations 2015 (S.I. 2015 No. 2049).

Determinations by a court and choice of representative

S.I. 2013 No. 614, regs 10-14

Change of provider

★**6-286**   Whereas regulation 9 of the Criminal Legal Aid (Determinations by a Court and Choice of Representative) Regulations 2013 (S.I. 2013 No. 614) (§ 6-280 in the main work) provides for the circumstances in which a court may withdraw a determination that the defendant qualifies for legal aid (including that "the provider named in the representation order ... declines to continue to represent the individual"), and whereas regulation 14 (*ibid.*, § 6-285) provides for the circumstances in which the court "may" determine that the individual can select a new provider in lieu of the original provider ("there has been a breakdown in the relationship between the individual and the original provider such that effective representation can no longer be provided by the original provider"/ "there is some other compelling reason why effective representation can no longer be provided by the original provider"/ "the original provider considers there to be a duty to withdraw from the case in accordance with the provider's professional rules of conduct" and has provided the court with details in relation thereto), (i) defendants cannot be permitted unnecessarily to delay and complicate proceedings by the device of changing their representatives; a judge must be astute to guard against this risk; it is particularly important that lawyers should give realistic advice to defendants; a defendant's unhappiness or disagreement with such advice is not a ground that ordinarily will justify the transfer of a representation order; and legal aid resources being limited, judges must, in the current state of the market for legal services, be sensitive to the risk that some lawyers will try to induce a defendant to change his solicitor for commercial reasons and therefore be astute to the conflicts of interest that might arise; (ii) only in extremely rare cases, and where full particulars are given, will a general ground of loss of confidence or incompetence be entertained; and it will not suffice simply to say that there has been a breakdown in the relationship (*R. v. Ulcay* (§ 4-67 in the main work)); (iii) where the judge is satisfied that the defendant is responsible for the situation in which the original provider declines to continue, then the proper course is to withdraw the representation order and leave the defendant to represent himself (or instruct solicitors privately): *R. (Sanjari) v. Crown Court at Birmingham* [2015] 2 Cr.App.R. 30, DC. As to this case, see also *post*, § 7-11.

Financial eligibility (magistrates' courts)

The amendment of regulation 5(2) of the Criminal Legal Aid (Financial Resources) Regulations 2013 (S.I. 2013 No. 471) that was due to come into force on January 11, 2016 (as to which, see the main work), is now due to come into force on April 1, 2016 (but see *ante*, § 6-233): Criminal Legal Aid (Remuneration etc.) (Amendment) (No. 2) Regulations 2015 (S.I. 2015 No. 2049). As well as altering the date of commencement of the amendment, S.I. 2015 No. 2049 also alters the text of the amendments (substituting a new reg. 7 in S.I. 2015 No. 1369), but this does not affect the text of the main work. ★6-321

Chapter 7

CRIMINAL APPEAL

II. HIGH COURT JURISDICTION IN CROWN COURT PROCEEDINGS

A. Jurisdiction

(2) Judicial review

(c) *Matters relating to trial on indictment*

Matters not relating to trial on indictment

The decision of the Divisional Court in *R. (Wang Yam) v. Central Criminal Court* was upheld by the Supreme Court (see *R. (Yam) v. Central Criminal Court* [2016] 2. W.L.R. 19), but the jurisdictional issue referred to in the main work was not before the Supreme Court. ★7-11

Matters relating to trial on indictment

For *obiter* observations to the effect that a refusal by a judge to authorise the transfer of a legal aid order to a new provider was a matter "relating to trial on indictment" within section 29(3) of the Senior Courts Act 1981 (§ 7-4 in the main work), see *R. (Sanjari) v. Crown Court at Birmingham* [2015] 2 Cr.App.R. 30, DC. As to this case, see also *ante*, § 6-286. ★7-13

IV. APPEAL TO COURT OF APPEAL BY THE DEFENDANT

A. Appeal Against Conviction on Indictment

(3) Determination of appeals

Conviction "unsafe"

Grounds of appeal unrelated to the issue of guilt

For a case considering whether, where a jury are found not to have constituted an "independent and impartial" tribunal, as required by Article 6 of the ECHR (§ 16-72 in the main work), a conviction can ever be upheld, see *R. v. Hanif (No. 2)*, *post*, § 7-89. ★7-45

Appeals following pleas of guilty

In *R. v. McCarthy* [2016] Crim.L.R. 145, CA, the appellant had pleaded guilty to wounding with intent (Offences Against the Person Act 1861, s.18 (§ 19-251 in the main work)). He appealed against conviction, arguing that it was unsafe on account of his plea having resulted from undue pressure and/or incompetent legal representation. The court held: (i) as to undue pressure, this was said to result from his being advised that his chances of acquittal were no better than 30 per cent and from the fact that the prosecution had indicated that they would accept a plea to affray (to be added to the indictment) from his co-accused (his mother), if he were to plead guilty (rais- ★7-46 ing the possibility that his mother might escape a custodial sentence), but these were the sort of pressures that defendants frequently faced in this sort of situation; and (ii) as to incompetent legal representation, (a) whilst various aspects of counsel's conduct of the case were open to criticism (holding conferences with his lay client at the latter's home without a solicitor present/ not informing his solicitor what he was doing or advising/ failing to keep notes of conferences/ failing to explain strengths of prosecution case until late in the day/ failing to consider whether a joint family conference was appropriate/ failing to ensure his brief was endorsed/ failing to explore a basis of plea and record the same/ failing to record his advice and the client's agreement with it leading to a change in plea/ adopting far too informal an approach throughout), it did not follow that the appellant should be allowed to vacate his plea for those reasons alone; what mattered was the nature and extent of the legal advice he was given; however, the case was a paradigm example of why some formality and distance between advocates and their lay clients were required; however (b) whether or not the appellant appreciated he was pleading guilty to an offence under section 18, rather than the lesser offence of unlawful wounding under section 20 of the 1861 Act (*ibid.*, § 19-252), it was apparent that the distinction between the two (and what had to be proved on a s.18 count) had never been properly explained to him; this had improperly narrowed his freedom of choice and rendered the conviction unsafe.

(4) Grounds of appeal

Miscellaneous

(viii) *Bias*

★**7-89**   In *R. v. Hanif (No. 2)*, unreported, July 31, 2014, CA, the court heard a second appeal in the case of *R. v. Khan* (as to which, see the main work) following the successful application of the appellants to the European Court of Human Rights (see *Hanif and Khan v. U.K.* (in the main work)). It was held: (i) if a jury are found not to have constituted an "independent and impartial" tribunal, as required by Article 6 of the ECHR (*ibid.*, § 16-72), then, even if in every other respect a conviction is safe, there can be no question of upholding it (*Millar v. Dickson*; *Payne v. Heywood*; *Stewart v. Same*; *Tracey v. Same* (*ibid.*, § 7-45); *R. v. Abdroikov*; *R. v. Green*; *R. v. Williamson* (*ibid.*, §§ 4-266, 4-293)); (ii) it is clear from the decision in *R. v. Abdroikov*; *R. v. Green*; *R. v. Williamson*, that the presence of a police officer on a jury where there is no challenge to the evidence of the police will not affect the impartiality and independence of the jury; however, if the evidence of the police is in dispute, then it is a matter of judgment in each case, applying the test in *Porter v. Magill*; *Weeks v. Magill* (see the main work), as to whether the relationship between the police officers giving evidence and the police officer on the jury is such that a fair-minded and informed observer would consider there was a real possibility that the tribunal was biased; in making that judgment, it is necessary to have regard to matters such as whether the officers knew each other, whether they had worked together, whether they shared the same local service background, and other matters of that kind. The court did not expressly reject the distinction drawn in *R. v. Khan* between partiality to a witness and partiality to a party (see the main work), but such, it is submitted, is the effect of the court's approach. On the facts, it was held that Article 6 had been violated in the case of the first appellant, where a police officer juror had known a police officer witness (whose evidence was disputed by the first appellant) for 10 years and, although not from the same police station, had on three occasions worked with him on an investigation; but not in the case of the second appellant. In the latter's case, the Strasbourg court had held that, as the appellants were co-defendants and convicted by the same jury, given its ruling in relation to the first appellant, it would be artificial to reach a different conclusion regarding the independence of the "tribunal" that tried the second appellant. The Court of Appeal said that the Strasbourg court would not have so decided if it had properly understood English criminal procedure (in particular, that a jury are always directed (as here) to consider the case of each defendant, and the evidence against each, separately).

G. Procedure from Notice of Appeal to Hearing

(7) Extension of time

7-171   An extension of time to appeal against conviction would not be granted, especially when there has been a plea of guilty, unless refusal would give rise to a substantial injustice, and where the only ground of appeal is a subsequent change in the law, the court would look with even greater circumspection upon the issue whether a substantial injustice could be established: *R. v. McGuffog* [2015] R.T.R. 34, CA (granting, however, an appropriate extension where, following advice from counsel (that it was no defence to say that there was an absence of contributory fault on the part of the driver), the applicant had pleaded guilty to causing death by driving when unlicensed, contrary to section 3ZB (§ 32-71 in the main work) of the RTA 1988, where, following the Supreme Court decision in *R. v. Hughes* [2014] 1 Cr.App.R. 6 (there must be something open to proper criticism in the driving of the defendant, beyond the mere presence of the vehicle on the road), the applicant sought an extension of time (three plus years) in which to apply for leave to appeal against conviction, and where it was not merely the change in the law that was creating an injustice (the prosecution conceded that, were a trial to take place now, there would have been no conviction), but also the remoter consequences of the conviction (the applicant was unable to obtain insurance for less than £2,700, and he was prohibited (for five years) from driving his 11-year-old disabled daughter); the circumstances were exceptional, and the delay was not the fault of the applicant).

I. Notification of Result of Appeal and Matters Depending Thereon

(2) Alteration of decision, relisting of cases

Whilst the jurisdiction and powers of the criminal division of the Court of Appeal, like those of **7-222** the civil division, are entirely statutory, there is an implicit power to revise any order pronounced before it is recorded as an order of the court in the record of the relevant court; where, however, the order has been recorded, the power of revision is strictly limited; this is subject to two exceptions on the authorities in the criminal jurisdiction, *viz.* the court does have power to re-open an appeal if (a) on a proper analysis, the previous order was a nullity (*R. v. Majewski* (as to which, see the main work)), or (b) a defect in the procedure may have led to some real injustice (*R. v. Daniel* (*ibid.*)); however, in *Taylor v. Lawrence* (*ibid.*, § 7-223), it was held that the civil division had an implicit power to reopen an appeal if the circumstances were exceptional, it was necessary to do so to avoid real injustice and there was no alternative remedy; the same principle should apply in the criminal division, although the manner of its application might vary; in the criminal division, the jurisdiction is probably confined to procedural errors, particularly as there are alternative remedies for fresh evidence cases through the Criminal Cases Review Commission: *R. v. Yasain* [2015] 2 Cr.App.R. 28, CA.

V. APPEAL TO COURT OF APPEAL BY THE PROSECUTION

E. Rules of Procedure

Criminal Procedure Rules 2015 (S.I. 2015 No. 1490), Pt 38

Crown Court judge's permission to appeal
With effect from April 4, 2016, rule 38.5 of S.I. 2015 No. 1490 is amended by rule 12 of the ★**7-269** Criminal Procedure (Amendment) Rules 2016 (S.I. 2016 No. 120), so as to correct the reference in paragraph (1)(b) to "rule 67.2" as noted in the main work.

X. APPEAL TO THE SUPREME COURT FROM THE COURT OF APPEAL

A. The Appeal

(2) Application for leave to appeal

Criminal Procedure Rules 2015 (S.I. 2015 No. 1490), Pt 43

Application for permission or reference
With effect from April 4, 2016, rule 43.2(1)(b)(i) of S.I. 2015 No. 1490 is amended by rule 13 of ★**7-401** the Criminal Procedure (Amendment) Rules 2016 (S.I. 2016 No. 120), so as to correct the reference to "Part 70" as noted in the main work.

CHAPTER 8

ORAL TESTIMONY OF WITNESSES

I. PRELIMINARIES

A. SECURING ATTENDANCE OF WITNESSES, PRODUCTION OF DOCUMENTS, ETC.

(1) Summons to witness to attend Crown Court

Criminal Procedure Rules 2015 (S.I. 2015 No. 1490), Pt 17

Application for summons, warrant or order: general rules

★8-17   With effect from April 4, 2016, rule 17.3 of S.I. 2015 No. 1490 is amended by rule 7(a) of the Criminal Procedure (Amendment) Rules 2016 (S.I. 2016 No. 120) so as: (i) in paragraph (2), to substitute the words "A party applying for a witness summons or order must" for the words "The party applying must"; (ii) to insert a new paragraph (3), as follows—

> "(3) A party applying for an order to be allowed to inspect and copy an entry in bank records must—
>> (a) identify the entry;
>> (b) explain the purpose for which the entry is required; and
>> (c) propose—
>>> (i) the terms of the order, and
>>> (ii) the period within which the order should take effect, if 3 days from the date of service of the order would not be appropriate.";

(iii) to re-number paragraph (3) as paragraph (4), and (iv) to insert, after paragraph (4), as so re-numbered, a new paragraph (5), as follows—

> "(5) The applicant must serve any order made on the witness to whom, or the bank to which, it is directed.".

Application for summons to produce a document, etc.: special rules

★8-19   With effect from April 4, 2016, rule 17.5(5) of S.I. 2015 No. 1490 is amended by rule 7(b) of the Criminal Procedure (Amendment) Rules 2016 (S.I. 2016 No. 120) so as to substitute the words "bank records" for "a banker's book".

II. SWEARING OF WITNESSES

B. GIVING OF SWORN OR UNSWORN EVIDENCE

Youth Justice and Criminal Evidence Act 1999, s.55

Determining whether witness to be sworn

★8-43   With effect from November 15, 2015, the Youth Justice and Criminal Evidence Act 1999 (Application to Service Courts) Order 2009 (S.I. 2009 No. 2083) was amended by the Youth Justice and Criminal Evidence Act 1999 (Application to Service Courts) (Amendment) (No. 2) Order 2015 (S.I. 2015 No. 1805) so as to extend its provisions to proceedings before the Summary Appeal Court.

III. COMPETENCE AND COMPELLABILITY

(8) The spouse or civil partner of the defendant

Police and Criminal Evidence Act 1984, s.80

★8-65   The correct citation for *R. v. A. (B.)* is [2012] 2 Cr.App.R. 34, not [2012] 1 Cr.App.R. 34.

IV. RULES OF EVIDENCE AND PRACTICE RELATING TO THE QUESTIONING OF WITNESSES

C. Cross-Examination

(6) As to credit

(c) *Finality of answers*

Exceptions

(iv) *Medical evidence relating to reliability of witness's evidence*

A judge should not direct a jury to regard a witness's evidence with caution, because he has ★8-288 some history of mental illness, without properly considering whether there is a medical foundation for regarding the particular evidence as unreliable; that would be an invitation to a form of irrationality and stereotypical prejudice that should have no part in the criminal justice system: *Milton v. The Queen* [2015] 1 W.L.R. 5356, PC.

Chapter 10

MISCELLANEOUS SOURCES OF EVIDENCE

III. DEPOSITIONS AND WRITTEN STATEMENTS

C. Witness Statements

Criminal Procedure Rules 2015 (S.I. 2015 No. 1490), Pt 16

Written statement in evidence

With effect from April 4, 2016, rule 25.12 of S.I. 2015 No. 1490 is amended by rule 10(b) of ★10-19 the Criminal Procedure (Amendment) Rules 2016 (S.I. 2016 No. 120). It now provides that, if a court admits the written statement of a witness to which Part 16 (written witness statements), 19 (expert evidence) or 20 (hearsay) of the 2015 rules applies, each relevant part of the statement must be read or summarised aloud, unless the court otherwise directs.

VII. EXPERT EVIDENCE

A. Legislation

Criminal Procedure Rules 2015 (S.I. 2015 No. 1490), Pt 19

As to the amendment of rule 25.12 of S.I. 2015 No. 1490 (as to which, see the main work), see ★10-46b *ante*, § 10-19.

B. Opinion Evidence

Scope

Pora v. The Queen is now reported at [2016] 1 Cr.App.R. 3. ★10-51

In *Myers v. The Queen*; *Cox v. Same*; *Brangman v. Same* [2016] 1 Cr.App.R. 11, PC it was held: (i) ★ evidence from a police officer expert in local gang culture that the defendants in three murder cases were members of a gang that was violently feuding (often to the death) with another gang to which the victims belonged, was admissible because it was relevant to identity and the defendants' motives (even though it was evidence of shared motive between all gang members rather than a motive harboured uniquely by the defendants), and supported the other evidence; but evidence of the gangs' other unlawful activities, or the cause of their animosity, was not relevant and should not have been admitted; the ambit of admissible gang evidence will depend, in any particular case, on what legitimate role it may have in helping the jury to resolve one or more issues in the case; (ii) a police officer giving expert evidence must meet the ordinary threshold requirements for expertise and observe the ordinary rules as to the giving of expert evidence; these exacting standards can be difficult for an officer who is effectively combining the duties of an investigator with those of an independent expert, but he must fully understand his duty to the court to give independent evidence, whichever side it may favour; his duty as an expert witness would involve at least the following; (a) he must set out his qualification to give expert evidence, by reference to his training and experience; (b) he must state not only his conclusions but also how he has arrived at them; if they are based on his own observations or contacts with particular persons, he must say so; if they are based on information provided by other officers, he must show how it is collected and exchanged and, if recorded, how (and in respect of such third party evidence, careful consideration should be given to the rule against hearsay, and the dividing line between opinion evidence and specific evidence of observable fact); if they are based on informers, he must at least acknowledge that such is his source, although of course he need not name them; and (c) in relation to primary conclusions concerning the defendant or other key persons, he must go beyond a mere general statement that he has sources of kinds A, B and C, and say whence the particular information he is advancing has come. As to this case, see also *post*, § 13-30.

Proper approach

★**10-52**   As to what is required of a police officer giving evidence as an expert witness in a case where he is also an active investigator, particularly where the case relates to gang culture, see *Myers v. The Queen*; *Cox v. Same*; *Brangman v. Same*, *ante*, § 10-51.

Duty of disclosure

★**10-53**   As to the disclosure duties of a police officer giving evidence as an expert witness in a case where he is also an active investigator, particularly where the case relates to gang culture, see *Myers v. The Queen*; *Cox v. Same*; *Brangman v. Same*, *ante*, § 10-51.

CHAPTER 11

HEARSAY EVIDENCE

II. STATUTE

A. CRIMINAL JUSTICE ACT 2003

(4) Rules of court

Criminal Procedure Rules 2015 (S.I. 2015 No. 1490), Pt 20

★**11-56a**   As to the amendment of rule 25.12 of S.I. 2015 No. 1490 (as to which, see the main work), see *ante*, § 10-19.

C. BANKERS' BOOKS EVIDENCE ACT 1879

(4) Case in which banker, etc. not compellable to produce book, etc.; court order for inspection

Bankers' Books Evidence Act 1879, ss.6, 7

★**11-63**   As to the amendment of the Criminal Procedure Rules 2015 (S.I. 2015 No. 1490) to clarify the procedure where an application is made for an order under section 7 of the 1879 Act (see the main work), see *ante*, § 8-17.

CHAPTER 12

PRIVILEGE, PUBLIC INTEREST IMMUNITY AND DISCLOSURE

I. PRIVILEGE

B. ANSWERS WHICH MAY INCRIMINATE A WITNESS

Privilege against self-incrimination

In *R. (DPP) v. Leicester Magistrates' Court* [2016] 1 Cr.App.R. 5, DC, it was held that where a wit-   ★**12-2** ness had refused to sign a statement based upon answers previously given in interviews under caution, despite assurances given by the police that she would not herself be prosecuted, where she was then summoned to appear before a magistrates' court for a deposition to be taken from her, where the prosecutor had repeated the assurances that, in the event that she gave evidence in accordance with her unsigned statement, she would not be prosecuted, the district judge had been wrong to rule that she could decline to be sworn by invoking the privilege against self-incrimination; evidence obtained from a witness under compulsion, where the witness had claimed the privilege against self-incrimination and had been entitled to do so but the privilege had been wrongly denied to him, could not subsequently be used in evidence against him; moreover, it was doubtful whether asking a witness to sign, or verify on oath, the contents of a witness statement, reflecting answers given in interview, would materially increase such risk as there was of the witness being prosecuted; and the witness in the instant case had the additional protection of the doctrine of abuse of process, since any attempt to prosecute her would be in breach of the assurance given to the magistrates' court, which had been repeated in the Divisional Court. For criticism of the court's conclusions, see CLW/15/45/4.

C. LEGAL PROFESSIONAL PRIVILEGE

(1) The nature of legal professional privilege

Legal advice privilege

The Court of Appeal of Hong Kong (in *Citic Pacific Ltd v. Secretary of State for Justice,* unreported,   ★**12-11** June 29, 2015 (CACV 7/2012)), after lengthy consideration of the authorities, took the view that the civil division of the Court of Appeal (in *Three Rivers D.C. v. Governor and Company of the Bank of England (No. 5)* (as to which, see the main work)) had adopted an approach to who was a lawyer's client, in a corporate context, that was too restrictive. The Hong Kong court was of the opinion that whether or not an internal communication should attract privilege should not depend on the position within the organisation occupied by its author, but on whether or not it was produced or brought into existence with the dominant purpose that its contents should be used to obtain legal advice.

(2) Communications in furtherance of crime

R. v. Brown is now reported at [2015] 2 Cr.App.R. 31, *sub nom. R. v. Brown (Edward).*   ★**12-13**

(3) Duration and waiver of privilege

Waiver

Where the appellant company received a report indicating that there may have been fraud   ★**12-15** involving some of its overseas operations and had instructed the respondent solicitors to conduct an investigation, where, as a result of a leak of the report, the Serious Fraud Office had begun their own criminal investigation, and where the appellant applied for an order for taxation of the respondent's bills, it was held that the hearing of the application and any subsequent assessment of the bills should be conducted in private; although there had been an implied waiver of privilege to enable the respondent to contest the challenge to its charges, there was no ground for finding that privilege had thereby been waived generally; in appropriate circumstances, an implied waiver could be limited in the same way as an express waiver, and there was no reason in principle or practice why the circumstances giving rise to a limited waiver should not extend to a party who was already in possession of the privileged documents at the time of the waiver; where it was clear that, if the application were heard in public, the Serious Fraud Office would attend in order to glean information of assistance to its criminal inquiry, and where at least some of the material relied on by the respondent could potentially and significantly prejudice the appellant's interests in that inquiry, and where some of the privileged documents were created for the very purpose of enabling the respondent to assist the appellant in the fraud investigation and its dealings with the Serious Fraud Office, there was potential for very real prejudice to the appellant if the application were to be held in public; whilst the respondent had a legitimate interest in clearing its name in relation to allegations of gross and deliberate overcharging that had appeared in the press, this concern could be met by the issuing of a public judgment at the end of the proceedings: *Eurasian Natural Resources Ltd v. Dechert LLP* [2015] 1 W.L.R. 4621, Ch D (Roth J.).

(7) "Without prejudice" negotiations in civil proceedings

★**12-20**   The public policy on which the "without prejudice" rule was based was capable of applying to communications involving genuine settlement discussions between a regulated body and its statutory regulator (here the Financial Conduct Authority): *Property Alliance Group Ltd v. Royal Bank of Scotland plc* [2016] 1 W.L.R. 361, Ch D (Birss J.).

III. DISCLOSURE

B. LEGISLATION

(1) Criminal Procedure and Investigations Act 1996

Criminal Procedure and Investigations Act 1996, ss.3, 4

Initial duty of prosecutor to disclose

★**12-59**   In *R. v. R.* (2016) 160(1) S.J. 43, CA ([2015] EWCA Crim. 1941), the Court of Appeal gave detailed guidance on the duties of the prosecution, defence and the court in relation to disclosure, and, in particular, at the stage of initial disclosure, in the context of a prosecution for a substantial fraud, in which the computers seized contained seven terabytes of data: (i) the prosecution are in the driving seat at this stage and must get a grip on the case and its disclosure requirements from the outset, adopting a considered and appropriately resourced approach, which must include the overall disclosure strategy, selection of software tools, identifying and isolating material which is subject to legal professional privilege, and proposing search terms to be applied; they must explain what they are doing and what they will not be doing at this stage, ideally in the form of a "Disclosure Management Document"; (ii) they must encourage dialogue with, and prompt engagement of, the defence, whose duty it is to engage with them and thus assist the court; (iii) they are not required to do the impossible, nor should the duty of giving initial disclosure be rendered incapable of fulfilment through the physical impossibility of reading and scheduling each and every item of material seized; common sense must be applied and the prosecution are entitled to use appropriate sampling and search terms, and their record-keeping and scheduling obligations are modified accordingly; the right course, at this stage, is to formulate a strategy, to canvass that strategy with the court and the defence, and to utilise technology to make an appropriate search or conduct an appropriate sampling exercise of the material seized; (iv) the process must be subject to robust case management by the judge, with regard, critically, to the structure of the scheme under the 1996 Act, keeping well in mind that, at the stage of initial disclosure, the true issues in the case may yet be unclear; and (v) flexibility is critical and disclosure is not to be conducted as a "box-ticking" exercise; in a document-heavy case, there can be no objection to the judge, after discussion with the parties, devising a tailored or bespoke approach to disclosure, but, whatever the approach adopted, the scheme of the 1996 Act must be kept firmly in mind and not subverted. As to this case, see also *ante*, § 4-77.

(4) Sexual offences

Sexual Offences (Protected Material) Act 1997

Introductory

[Meaning of "protected material"

1.—(1) In this Act "protected material", in relation to proceedings for a sexual offence, means a **12-129** copy (in whatever form) of any of the following material, namely—

   (a) a statement relating to that or any other sexual offence made by any victim of the offence (whether the statement is recorded in writing or in any other form),

   (b) a photograph or pseudo-photograph of any such victim, or

   (c) a report of a medical examination of the physical condition of any such victim,

which is a copy given by the prosecutor to any person under this Act.

(2) For the purposes of subsection (1) a person is, in relation to any proceedings for a sexual offence, a victim of that offence if—

   (a) the charge, summons or indictment by which the proceedings are instituted names that person as a person in relation to whom that offence was committed; or

   (b) that offence can, in the prosecutor's opinion, be reasonably regarded as having been committed in relation to that person;

and a person is, in relation to any such proceedings, a victim of any other sexual offence if that offence can, in the prosecutor's opinion, be reasonably regarded as having been committed in relation to that person.

(3) In this Act, where the context so permits (and subject to subsection (4))—

   (a) references to any protected material include references to any part of any such material; and

   (b) references to a copy of any such material include references to any part of any such copy.

(4) Nothing in this Act—

   (a) so far as it refers to a defendant making any copy of—

      (i) any protected material, or

      (ii) a copy of any such material,

      applies to a manuscript copy which is not a verbatim copy of the whole of that material or copy; or

   (b) so far as it refers to a defendant having in his possession any copy of any protected material, applies to a manuscript copy made by him which is not a verbatim copy of the whole of that material.]

[Meaning of other expressions

2.—(1) In this Act— **12-130**

    "contracted out prison" means a contracted out prison within the meaning of Part IV of the Criminal Justice Act 1991;

    "defendant", in relation to any proceedings for a sexual offence, means any person charged with that offence (whether or not he has been convicted);

    "governor", in relation to a contracted out prison, means the director of the prison;

    "inform" means inform in writing;

    "legal representative", in relation to a defendant, means a person who, for the purposes of the Legal Services Act 2007, is an authorised person in relation to an activity which constitutes the exercise of a right of audience or the conduct of litigation (within the meaning of that Act) and who is acting for the defendant in connection with any proceedings for the sexual offence in question;

    "photograph" and "pseudo-photograph" shall be construed in accordance with section 7(4) and (7) of the Protection of Children Act 1978;

    "prison" means any prison, young offender institution or remand centre which is under the general superintendence of, or is provided by, the Secretary of State under the Prison Act 1952, including a contracted out prison;

    "proceedings" means (subject to subsection (2)) criminal proceedings;

    "the prosecutor", in relation to any proceedings for a sexual offence, means any person acting as prosecutor (whether an individual or a body);

    "relevant proceedings", in relation to any material which has been disclosed by the prosecutor under this Act, means any proceedings for the purposes of which it has been so disclosed or any further proceedings for the sexual offence in question;

"sexual offence" means one of the offences listed in the Schedule to this Act.

(2) For the purposes of this Act references to proceedings for a sexual offence include references to—

 (a) any appeal or application for leave to appeal brought or made by or in relation to a defendant in such proceedings;

 (b) any application made to the Criminal Cases Review Commission for the reference under section 9 or 11 of the Criminal Appeal Act 1995 of any conviction, verdict, finding or sentence recorded or imposed in relation to any such defendant; and

 (c) any petition to the Secretary of State requesting him to recommend the exercise of Her Majesty's prerogative of mercy in relation to any such defendant.

(3) In this Act, in the context of the prosecutor giving a copy of any material to any person—

 (a) references to the prosecutor include references to a person acting on behalf of the prosecutor; and

 (b) where any such copy falls to be given to the defendant's legal representative, references to the defendant's legal representative include references to a person acting on behalf of the defendant's legal representative.]

[The definition of "legal representative" is printed as amended by the Legal Services Act 2007, s.208(1), and Sched 21, para. 123.]

Regulation of disclosures to defendant

[Regulation of disclosures by prosecutor

12-131 **3.**—(1) Where, in connection with any proceedings for a sexual offence, any statement or other material falling within any of paragraphs (a) to (c) of section 1(1) would (apart from this section) fall to be disclosed by the prosecutor to the defendant—

 (a) the prosecutor shall not disclose that material to the defendant; and

 (b) it shall instead be disclosed under this Act in accordance with whichever of subsections (2) and (3) below is applicable.

(2) If—

 (a) the defendant has a legal representative, and

 (b) the defendant's legal representative gives the prosecutor the undertaking required by section 4 (disclosure to defendant's legal representative),

the prosecutor shall disclose the material in question by giving a copy of it to the defendant's legal representative.

(3) If subsection (2) is not applicable, the prosecutor shall disclose the material in question by giving a copy of it to the appropriate person for the purposes of section 5 (disclosure to unrepresented defendant) in order for that person to show that copy to the defendant under that section.

(4) Where under this Act a copy of any material falls to be given to any person by the prosecutor, any such copy—

 (a) may be in such form as the prosecutor thinks fit, and

 (b) where the material consists of information which has been recorded in any form, need not be in the same form as that in which the information has already been recorded.

(5) Once a copy of any material is given to any person under this Act by the prosecutor, the copy shall (in accordance with section 1(1)) be protected material for the purposes of this Act.]

[Disclosure to defendant's legal representative

12-132 **4.**—(1) For the purposes of this Act the undertaking which a defendant's legal representative is required to give in relation to any protected material given to him under this Act is an undertaking by him to discharge the obligations set out in subsections (2) to (7).

(2) He must take reasonable steps to ensure—

 (a) that the protected material, or any copy of it, is only shown to the defendant in circumstances where it is possible to exercise adequate supervision to prevent the defendant retaining possession of the material or copy or making a copy of it, and

 (b) that the protected material is not shown and no copy of it is given, and its contents are not otherwise revealed, to any person other than the defendant, except so far as it appears to him necessary to show the material or give a copy of it to any such person—

  (i) in connection with any relevant proceedings, or

  (ii) for the purposes of any assessment or treatment of the defendant (whether before or after conviction).

(3) He must inform the defendant—

(a) that the protected material is such material for the purposes of this Act,

(b) that the defendant can only inspect that material, or any copy of it, in circumstances such as are described in subsection (2)(a), and

(c) that it would be an offence for the defendant—

(i) to have that material, or any copy of it, in his possession otherwise than while inspecting it or the copy in such circumstances, or

(ii) to give that material or any copy of it, or otherwise reveal its contents, to any other person.

(4) He must, where the protected material or a copy of it has been shown or given in accordance with subsection (2)(b)(i) or (ii) to a person other than the defendant, inform that person—

(a) that that person must not give any copy of that material, or otherwise reveal its contents—

(i) to any other person other than the defendant, or

(ii) to the defendant otherwise than in circumstances such as are described in subsection (2)(a); and

(b) that it would be an offence for that person to do so.

(5) He must, where he ceases to act as the defendant's legal representative at a time when any relevant proceedings are current or in contemplation—

(a) inform the prosecutor of that fact, and

(b) if he is informed by the prosecutor that the defendant has a new legal representative who has given the prosecutor the undertaking required by this section, give the protected material, and any copies of it in his possession, to the defendant's new legal representative.

(6) He must, at the time of giving the protected material to the new legal representative under subsection (5), inform that person—

(a) that that material is protected material for the purposes of this Act, and

(b) of the extent to which—

(i) that material has been shown by him, and

(ii) any copies of it have been given by him,

to any other person (including the defendant).

(7) He must keep a record of every occasion on which the protected material was shown, or a copy of it was given, as mentioned in subsection (6)(b).]

[Disclosure to unrepresented defendant

5.—(1) This section applies where, in accordance with section 3(3), a copy of any material falls to **12-133** be given by the prosecutor to the appropriate person for the purposes of this section in order for that person to show that copy to the defendant under this section.

(2) Subject to subsection (3), the appropriate person in such a case is—

(a) if the defendant is detained in a prison, the governor of the prison or any person nominated by the governor for the purposes of this section; and

(b) otherwise the officer in charge of such police station as appears to the prosecutor to be suitable for enabling the defendant to have access to the material in accordance with this section or any person nominated by that officer for the purposes of this section.

(3) The Secretary of State may by regulations provide that, in such circumstances as are specified in the regulations, the appropriate person for the purposes of this section shall be a person of any description so specified.

(4) The appropriate person shall take reasonable steps to ensure—

(a) that the protected material, or any copy of it, is only shown to the defendant in circumstances where it is possible to exercise adequate supervision to prevent the defendant retaining possession of the material or copy or making a copy of it,

(b) that, subject to paragraph (a), the defendant is given such access to that material, or a copy of it, as he reasonably requires in connection with any relevant proceedings, and

(c) that that material is not shown and no copy of it is given, and its contents are not otherwise revealed, to any person other than the defendant.

(5) The prosecutor shall, at the time of giving the protected material to the appropriate person, inform him—

(a) that that material is protected material for the purposes of this Act, and

(b) that he is required to discharge the obligations set out in subsection (4) in relation to that material.

(6) The prosecutor shall at that time also inform the defendant—

(a) that that material is protected material for the purposes of this Act,

(b) that the defendant can only inspect that material, or any copy of it, in circumstances such as are described in subsection (4)(a), and

    (c) that it would be an offence for the defendant—

        (i) to have that material, or any copy of it, in his possession otherwise than while inspecting it or the copy in such circumstances, or

        (ii) to give that material or any copy of it, or otherwise reveal its contents, to any other person,

as well as informing him of the effect of subsection (7).

    (7) If—

    (a) the defendant requests the prosecutor in writing to give a further copy of the material mentioned in subsection (1) to some other person, and

    (b) it appears to the prosecutor to be necessary to do so—

        (i) in connection with any relevant proceedings, or

        (ii) for the purposes of any assessment or treatment of the defendant (whether before or after conviction),

the prosecutor shall give such a copy to that other person.

    (8) The prosecutor may give such a copy to some other person where no request has been made under subsection (7) but it appears to him that in the interests of the defendant it is necessary to do so as mentioned in paragraph (b) of that subsection.

    (9) The prosecutor shall, at the time of giving such a copy to a person under subsection (7) or (8), inform that person—

    (a) that the copy is protected material for the purposes of this Act,

    (b) that he must not give any copy of the protected material or otherwise reveal its contents—

        (i) to any person other than the defendant, or

        (ii) to the defendant otherwise than in circumstances such as are described in subsection (4)(a); and

    (c) that it would be an offence for him to do so.

    (10) If the prosecutor—

    (a) receives a request from the defendant under subsection (7) to give a further copy of the material in question to another person, but

    (b) does not consider it to be necessary to do so as mentioned in paragraph (b) of that subsection and accordingly refuses the request,

he shall inform the defendant of his refusal.

    (11) [*Making of regulations under subs. (3).*]]

[Further disclosures by prosecutor

12-134   **6.**—(1) Where—

    (a) any material has been disclosed in accordance with section 3(2) to the defendant's legal representative, and

    (b) at a time when any relevant proceedings are current or in contemplation the legal representative either—

        (i) ceases to act as the defendant's legal representative in circumstances where section 4(5)(b) does not apply, or

        (ii) dies or becomes incapacitated,

that material shall be further disclosed under this Act in accordance with whichever of section 3(2) or (3) is for the time being applicable.

    (2) Where—

    (a) any material has been disclosed in accordance with section 3(3), and

    (b) at a time when any relevant proceedings are current or in contemplation the defendant acquires a legal representative who gives the prosecutor the undertaking required by section 4,

that material shall be further disclosed under this Act, in accordance with section 3(2), to the defendant's legal representative.]

12-135   **7.** [*Regulation of disclosures by Criminal Cases Review Commission.*]]

Supplementary

[Offences

12-136   **8.**—(1) Where any material has been disclosed under this Act in connection with any proceedings for a sexual offence, it is an offence for the defendant—

    (a) to have the protected material, or any copy of it, in his possession otherwise than while inspecting it or the copy in circumstances such as are described in section 4(2)(a) or 5(4)(a), or

(b) to give that material or any copy of it, or otherwise reveal its contents, to any other person.

(2) Where any protected material, or any copy of any such material, has been shown or given to any person in accordance with section 4(2)(b)(i) or (ii) or section 5(7) or (8), it is an offence for that person to give any copy of that material or otherwise reveal its contents—

(a) to any person other than the defendant, or

(b) to the defendant otherwise than in circumstances such as are described in section 4(2)(a) or 5(4)(a).

(3) Subsections (1) and (2) apply whether or not any relevant proceedings are current or in contemplation (and references to the defendant shall be construed accordingly).

(4) A person guilty of an offence under this section is liable—

(a) on summary conviction, to imprisonment for a term not exceeding *six* [12] months or a fine not exceeding the statutory maximum or both;

(b) on conviction on indictment, to imprisonment for a term not exceeding two years or a fine or both.

(5) Where a person is charged with an offence under this section relating to any protected material or copy of any such material, it is a defence to prove that, at the time of the alleged offence, he was not aware, and neither suspected nor had reason to suspect, that the material or copy in question was protected material or (as the case may be) a copy of any such material.

(6) The court before which a person is tried for an offence under this section may (whether or not he is convicted of that offence) make an order requiring him to return any protected material, or any copy of any such material, in his possession to the prosecutor.

(7) Nothing in subsection (1) or (2) shall be taken to apply to—

(a) any disclosure made in the course of any proceedings before a court or in any report of any such proceedings, or

(b) any disclosure made or copy given by a person when returning any protected material, or a copy of any such material, to the prosecutor or the defendant's legal representative;

and accordingly nothing in section 4, or 5 shall be read as precluding the making of any disclosure or the giving of any copy in circumstances falling within paragraph (a) or (as the case may be) paragraph (b) above.]

[In subs. (4)(a), "12" is substituted for "six", as from a day to be appointed, by the CJA 2003, s.282(2) and (3). The increase has no application to offences committed before the substitution takes effect: s.282(4).]

[Modification and amendment of other enactments
9.—(1) [*Repealed by CJA 2003, s.332, and Sched. 37, Pt 4.*] **12-137**

(2) Despite section 20(1) of the Criminal Procedure and Investigations Act 1996 (disclosure provisions of the Act not affected by other statutory duties), section 3(3) to (5) of that Act (manner of disclosure) shall not apply in relation to any disclosure required by section 3, 7 or 9 of that Act if section 3(1) above applies in relation to that disclosure.

(3) [*See ss.17 and 18 of the Criminal Procedure and Investigations Act 1996, §§ 12-88et seq. in the main work*]

(4) [*Inserts subs. 1(6) into the Criminal Procedure and Investigations Act 1996, § 12-56 in the main work.*]]

10. [*Financial provision.*]] **12-138**

[Short title, commencement and extent
11.—(1) [*Short title.*] **12-139**

(2) This Act shall come into force on such day as the Secretary of State may appoint by order made by statutory instrument.

(3) Nothing in this Act applies to any proceedings for a sexual offence where the defendant was charged with the offence before the commencement of this Act.

(4) This Act extends to England and Wales only.]

[Section 2   SCHEDULE

SEXUAL OFFENCES FOR PURPOSES OF THIS ACT

5. Any offence under section 1 of the Protection of Children Act 1978 or section 160 of the **12-140** Criminal Justice Act 1988 (indecent photographs of children).

5A. Any offence under any provision of Part 1 of the Sexual Offences Act 2003 except section 64, 65, 69 or 71.

6. Any offence under section 1 of the Criminal Law Act 1977 of conspiracy to commit any of the offences mentioned in paragraphs 5 and 5A.

7. Any offence under section 1 of the Criminal Attempts Act 1981 of attempting to commit any of those offences.

8. Any offence of inciting another to commit any of those offences.]

[This schedule is printed as amended by the SOA 2003, ss.139 and 140, and Scheds 6, para. 36, and 7. The reference in para. 8 to inciting another to commit an offence has effect as a reference to the offences under Part 2 of the SCA 2007: 2007 Act, s.63(1), and Sched. 6, para. 34.]

CHAPTER 13

EVIDENCE OF BAD CHARACTER

I. INTRODUCTION

C. INTERPRETATION

Criminal Justice Act 2003, s.98

Evidence having to do with alleged facts of offence charged

★**13-6**   While there may be exceptions, evidence of the "criminal educational opportunity" provided by prior offending of a like nature did not afford a sufficient nexus to the offence with which the defendant was charged to mean that it was "to do with" the instant charge: *R. v. Sullivan*, 179 J.P. 552, CA (considering, *inter alia*, *R. v. Mullings* (as to which, see the main work)). As to this case, see also § 13-63a.

III. DEFENDANTS

B. THE SEVEN GATEWAYS

(3) Important explanatory evidence (ss.101(1)(c), 102)

Criminal Justice Act 2003, s.102

"Important explanatory evidence"

★**13-30**   In *Myers v. The Queen*; *Cox v. Same*; *Brangman v. Same* [2015] 3 W.L.R. 1145, PC (as to which, see *ante*, § 10-51), it was said that the principle in *R. v. Pettman* (as to which, see the main work) requires cautious handling.

(4) Important matter in issue between defendant and prosecution (ss.101(1)(d), 103)

(b) *Evidence that would have been admissible at common law*

Particular topics

Directing the jury

★**13-63a**   In *R. v. Sullivan*, *ante*, § 13-6, the court stressed the importance, with non-conviction bad character evidence, of directing the jury, first, as to the need to be satisfied that the evidence does indeed establish the defendant's "bad character" as alleged, and, secondly, if it does, as to the significance of the evidence to the issues in the case they are trying.

IV. PROCEDURE

(5) Rules of court

Criminal Procedure Rules 2015 (S.I. 2015 No. 1490), Pt 21

Notice to introduce evidence of a defendant's bad character

★**13-114**   With effect from April 4, 2016, rule 21.4 of S.I. 2015 No. 1490 is amended by rule 8 of the

Criminal Procedure (Amendment) Rules 2016 (S.I. 2016 No. 120), so as: (i) to substitute the words "A prosecutor or co-defendant who wants to introduce such evidence" for the words "That party" in paragraph (2); (ii) to substitute the words "A prosecutor must serve any such notice" for the words "A prosecutor who wants to introduce such evidence must serve the notice" in paragraph (3); (iii) to substitute the words "A co-defendant must serve any such notice" for the words "A co-defendant who wants to introduce such evidence must serve the notice" in paragraph (4); (iv) to insert the words "identified by such a notice" after the words "A party who objects to the introduction of the evidence" in paragraph (5); (v) to insert the word "such" after the word "determine" in paragraph (6)(a); (vi) to insert the word "such" after the word "receive" in paragraph (7); and (vii) to insert a new paragraph (8), as follows—

"(8) A defendant who wants to introduce evidence of his or her own bad character must—
(a) give notice, in writing or orally—
  (i) as soon as reasonably practicable, and in any event
  (ii) before the evidence is introduced, either by the defendant or in reply to a question asked by the defendant of another party's witness in order to obtain that evidence; and
(b) in the Crown Court, at the same time give notice (in writing, or orally) of any direction about the defendant's character that the defendant wants the court to give the jury under rule 25.14 (directions to the jury and taking the verdict).".

V. REHABILITATION OF OFFENDERS

(1) Introduction

A challenge to the lawfulness of the approach taken in the Rehabilitation of Offenders Act 1974 (Exceptions) Order 1975 (Amendment) (England and Wales) Order 2013 (S.I. 2013 No. 1198) (as to which, see the main work) (that it was too crude and led to arbitrary results in that it excluded convictions for certain offences from protection from disclosure whatever their age and whatever disposal had been adopted by the court) was rejected in *R. (W.) v. Secretary of State for Justice* [2015] A.C.D. 139, QBD (Simon J.) ([2015] EWHC 1952 (Admin.)) (his Lordship commenting that almost any system that could be devised might lead to harsh results at the margins). **13-120**

CHAPTER 14

EVIDENCE OF IDENTIFICATION

II. IDENTIFICATION BY OTHER PERSONAL CHARACTERISTICS
C. BLOOD, BODY SAMPLES, SECRETIONS, SCENT AND ODONTOLOGY

DNA

In *R. v. F.N.C.* [2016] 1 Cr.App.R. 12, CA ([2015] EWCA Crim. 1732), it was held (considering, *inter alia*, *R. v. Ogden* and *R. v. Bryon* (as to both of which, see the main work), *R. v. Adams (No. 2)* (*ibid.*, § 14-81) and *R. v. Hookway* (*ibid.*, § 14-66)) that where DNA is directly deposited in the course of the commission of a crime by the offender, a very high DNA match with the defendant is sufficient to raise a case for the defendant to answer; there is a clear distinction between such a case and cases where the DNA was deposited on an article left at the scene. The court further observed, *obiter*, that the analysis and techniques of analysis of DNA have improved markedly in the past decade and, thus, the fact that the DNA was on an article left at the scene (as distinct from being directly deposited in the course of the commission of the offence by the offender) may, without more, be sufficient to raise a case to answer where the match probability is in the order of one in a billion. **★14-81a**

III. IDENTIFICATION BY OTHER EVIDENCE

Identification and judicial notice of the legal process

In *Bates v. CPS* [2016] Crim.L.R. 55, DC, it was held (considering, *inter alia*, *Creed v. Scott* (as to **★14-94** which, see the main work)) that where the name, address and date of birth of the defendant matched those given to a police officer by the driver of a vehicle stopped for speeding on the occasion giving rise to the prosecution, that was sufficient to raise a case to answer; there had been no requirement to hold an identification parade because the officer was not an eye-witness who had identified a suspect or purported to do so, but was merely reporting that the details given by the driver were those of the person who subsequently appeared at court in answer to the summons.

CHAPTER 15

INVESTIGATORY POWERS; CONFESSIONS; DISCRETION TO EXCLUDE EVIDENCE, ETC.

I. INVESTIGATORY POWERS

A. POLICE AND CRIMINAL EVIDENCE ACT 1984

(2) Codes of practice

(b) *Commencement*

★**15-6**   With effect from February 2, 2016, the Police and Criminal Evidence Act 1984 (Codes of Practice) (Revision of Code E) Order 2016 (S.I. 2016 No. 35) brings into force a revised Code E (*post*, Appendix A-162 *et seq.*) on the audio recording of interviews with suspects. The revisions exempt four offences from the requirement that the interviews of individuals regarding indictable offences must be audio recorded. The conditions that must be met before the exemption can apply are set out in a new annex to the code.

(3) "Reasonable grounds for suspicion"

★**15-15**   *R. (Chatwani) v. National Crime Agency and Birmingham Magistrates' Court* is now reported at [2015] A.C.D. 110, *sub nom. R. (Chatwani) v. National Crime Agency.*

(9) Application of Act to Revenue and Customs and immigration officers
Police and Criminal Evidence Act 1984, s.114

Application of Act to Revenue and Customs

★**15-26**   With effect from November 4, 2015, the Police and Criminal Evidence Act 1984 (Application to Revenue and Customs) Order 2015 (S.I. 2015 No. 1783) consolidates the Police and Criminal Evidence Act 1984 (Application to Revenue and Customs) Order 2007 (S.I. 2007 No. 3175), and its amending orders, all of which are revoked.

S.I. 2007 No. 3175

Interpretation

★**15-27**   As to the revocation and replacement of the Police and Criminal Evidence Act 1984 (Application to Revenue and Customs) Order 2007 (S.I. 2007 No. 3175) (see the main work) by S.I. 2015 No. 1783, see *ante*, § 15-26. The new articles 2 to 4 are set out below.

Interpretation

2. (1) In this Order—
"the Act" means the Police and Criminal Evidence Act 1984;
"the Commissioners" means the Commissioners for Her Majesty's Revenue and Customs;
"the customs and excise Acts" has the meaning given to it by section 1 of the Customs and Excise Management Act 1979;
"designated customs official" has the meaning given to it by section 14(6) of the Borders, Citizenship and Immigration Act 2009;

"Home Office custody suite" means premises wholly or partly used for the detention of persons by designated customs officials;

"office of Revenue and Customs" means premises wholly or partly occupied by Her Majesty's Revenue and Customs;

"relevant indictable offence" means an indictable offence which relates to a matter in relation to which Her Majesty's Revenue and Customs have functions;

"relevant investigation" means a criminal investigation conducted by officers of Revenue and Customs which relates to a matter in relation to which Her Majesty's Revenue and Customs have functions.

(2) A person is in Revenue and Customs detention for the purpose of this Order if—

    (a) he has been taken to an office of Revenue and Customs after being arrested for an offence; or

    (b) he is arrested at an office of Revenue and Customs after attending voluntarily at the office or accompanying an officer of Revenue and Customs to it,

and is detained there or detained elsewhere in the charge of an officer of Revenue and Customs.

(3) A person is in Home Office detention for the purpose of this Order if—

    (a) he has been taken to a Home Office custody suite after being arrested for an offence; or

    (b) he is arrested at a Home Office custody suite after attending voluntarily at that suite or accompanying a designated customs official to it,

and is detained there or detained elsewhere in the charge of a designated customs official.

Application

3. (1) The provisions of the Act contained in Schedule 1 to this Order, which relate to investigations of offences conducted by police officers or to persons detained by the police, shall apply to relevant investigations conducted by officers of Revenue and Customs and to persons detained by such officers.

This is subject to the modifications in paragraphs (2) and (3) and articles 4 to 19 and Schedule 2.

(2) The Act shall have effect as if the words and phrases in Column 1 of Part 1 of Schedule 2 to this Order were replaced by the substitute words and phrases in Column 2 of that Part.

(3) Where in the Act any act or thing is to be done by a constable of a specific rank, that act or thing shall be done by an officer of Revenue and Customs of at least the grade specified in Column 2 of Part 2 of Schedule 2 to this Order, and the Act shall be construed accordingly.

Exceptions

4. Nothing in the application of the Act to Revenue and Customs confers on an officer of Revenue and Customs any power—

    (a) to charge a person with any offence;

    (b) to release a person on bail; or

    (c) to detain a person for an offence after he has been charged with that offence.

Seizure and retention of things found

As to the revocation and replacement of the Police and Criminal Evidence Act 1984 (Application to Revenue and Customs) Order 2007 (S.I. 2007 No. 3175) by S.I. 2015 No. 1783, see *ante*, § 15-26. The new articles 5 to 8 are set out below.   ★**15-28**

Seizure and retention of things found upon search

5.—(1) Where in the Act a constable is given power to seize and retain any thing found upon a lawful search of person or premises, an officer of Revenue and Customs shall have the same power, notwithstanding that the thing found is not evidence of an offence which relates to a matter in relation to which Her Majesty's Revenue and Customs have functions.

(2) Nothing in the application of the Act to Revenue and Customs prevents any thing lawfully seized by a person under any enactment from being accepted and retained by an officer of Revenue and Customs.

(3) Section 21 of the Act (access and copying) shall not apply to any thing seized as liable to forfeiture under the customs and excise Acts.

Excluded and special procedure material

6. In its application by virtue of article 3 above the Act shall have effect as if the following section were inserted after section 14—

[*See s.114(2)(b)(i) of the 1984 Act, § 15-25 in the main work, for text of section 14A, but note that the section is now headed "Exception for Revenue and Customs" and "section 9(2)" in the last line now reads as "subsection 9(2)".*]

7. In its application by virtue of article 3 above the Act shall have effect as if the following section were inserted after section 14A—

[*See s.114(2)(b)(i) of the 1984 Act, § 15-25 in the main work, for text of section 14B.*]

Modification of section 18 of the Act (entry and search after arrest)

8.—(1) Section 18 of the Act (entry and search after arrest) is modified as follows.

(2) For subsection 18(1) substitute—

"(1) Subject to the following provisions of this section, an officer of Revenue and Customs may enter and search any premises occupied or controlled by a person who is under arrest for any relevant indictable offence if he has reasonable grounds for suspecting that there is on the premises evidence, other than items subject to legal privilege, that relates—

(a) to that offence; or

(b) to some other indictable offence which is connected with or similar to that offence.

(3) In sub-sections (5) and (5A), after "police station", insert ", office of Revenue and Customs or Home Office custody suite".

(4) In sub-section (8), after "police detention", insert ", Revenue and Customs detention or Home Office detention".

Modification of section 35 of the Act (designated police stations)

★**15-29** As to the revocation and replacement of the Police and Criminal Evidence Act 1984 (Application to Revenue and Customs) Order 2007 (S.I. 2007 No. 3175) by S.I. 2015 No. 1783, see *ante*, § 15-26. New article 9 has no equivalent in previous legislation. Old articles 9 to 13 are renumbered as 10 to 14. The new articles 9 to 13 are set out below.

Modification of section 30 of the Act (arrest elsewhere than at police station)

9.—(1) Section 30 of the Act (arrest elsewhere than at police station) is modified as follows.

(2) In subsections (1A), (2), (3), subsection (4)(a), and subsections (5), (6), (7), (7A), (10), (10A) and (11), after "police station", wherever that expression occurs, insert ", office of Revenue and Customs or Home Office custody suite."

(3) In subsection (2), subsections (4)(a) and (5)(b), and subsection (6), after "designated police station", wherever that expression occurs, insert ", designated office of Revenue and Customs or designated Home Office custody suite".

(4) In subsection (3), before "detention", delete "police".

(5) In its application by virtue of article 3 above the Act shall have effect as if the following subsection were inserted after subsection 30(6)—

"(6A) An arrested person may be transferred between Revenue and Customs detention and Home Office detention, and between Revenue and Customs detention and police detention.".

Modification of section 35 of the Act (designated police stations)

10.—(1) Section 35 of the Act (designated police stations) is modified as follows.

(2) For subsection 35(1) substitute—

"(1) The Commissioners shall designate offices of Revenue and Customs which, subject to subsections 30(3) and (5), are to be the offices to be used for the purposes of detaining arrested persons.".

(3) For subsection 35(2) substitute—

"(2) The Commissioners' duty under subsection (1) above is to designate offices of Revenue and Customs appearing to them to provide enough accommodation for that purpose.".

(4) For subsection 35(3) substitute—

"(3) Without prejudice to section 12 of the Interpretation Act 1978 (continuity of duties) the Commissioners—

(a) may designate an office which was not previously designated; and

(b) may direct that a designation of an office previously made shall cease to operate.".

Modification of section 36 of the Act (custody officers at police stations)

11.—(1) Section 36 of the Act (custody officers at police stations) is modified as follows.

(2) For subsection (2) substitute—

"(2) A custody officer for an office of Revenue and Customs designated under subsection 35(1) above shall be appointed—

    (a) by the Commissioners; or

    (b) by such officer of Revenue and Customs as the Commissioners may direct.".

Modification of section 41 of the Act (limits on period of detention without charge)

12.—(1) Section 41 of the Act (limits on period of detention without charge) is modified as follows.

(2) For paragraph (2)(b) substitute—

    "(b) in the case of a person arrested outside England and Wales, shall be—

        (i) the time at which that person arrives at the office of Revenue and Customs in England and Wales in which the offence for which he was arrested is being investigated; or

        (ii) the time 24 hours after the time of that person's entry into England and Wales".

13. [*Modification of section 50 of the Act (keeping of records of detention).*]

Modification of section 55 of the Act (intimate searches)

As to the revocation and replacement of the Police and Criminal Evidence Act 1984 (Application to Revenue and Customs) Order 2007 (S.I. 2007 No. 3175) by S.I. 2015 No. 1783, see *ante*, § 15-26. Old article 13 has been renumbered as article 14. The new articles 14 to 16 are set out below.   ★**15-30**

Modification of section 55 of the Act (intimate searches)

14.—(1) Section 55 of the Act (intimate searches) shall have effect as if it related only to things such as are mentioned in paragraph (1)(a) of that section.

(2) [*Information to be included in Commissioners' annual report (s.55(15)).*]

Modification of section 77 of the Act (definition of independent person)

15. Subsection 77(3) of the Act (definition of independent person) shall be modified to the extent that the definition of "independent person" shall, in addition to the persons mentioned therein, also include an officer of Revenue and Customs or any other person acting under the authority of the Commissioners.

Use of reasonable force

16. Where any provision of the Act as applied to Revenue and Customs—

    (a) confers a power on an officer of Revenue and Customs, and

    (b) does not provide that the power may only be exercised with the consent of some person other than that officer,

the officer may use reasonable force, if necessary, in the exercise of the power.

Arrest without warrant

As to the revocation and replacement of the Police and Criminal Evidence Act 1984 (Application to Revenue and Customs) Order 2007 (S.I. 2007 No. 3175) by S.I. 2015 No. 1783, see *ante*, § 15-26. The new articles 17 to 20 are set out below.   ★**15-31**

Arrest without warrant

17. Subsection 24(2) of the Act (arrest without warrant) does not limit—

    (a) subsection 138(1) of the Customs and Excise Management Act 1979;

    (b) section 20 and paragraph 4 of Schedule 3 to the Criminal Justice (International Co-operation) Act 1990;

    (c) any other enactment, including any enactment contained in subordinate legislation, for the time being in force which confers upon officers of Revenue and Customs the power to arrest or detain persons.

Search of persons

18. Where an officer of Revenue and Customs searches premises in reliance on a warrant under section 8 of, or paragraph 12 of Schedule 1 to, the Act (power of justice of the peace to authorise entry and search of premises), he may search any person found on the premises—

    (a) where he has reasonable cause to believe that person to be in possession of material which is likely to be of substantial value (whether by itself or together with other material) to the investigation of the offence;

    (b) but no person should be searched except by a person of the same sex.

Authorisation
    19. Powers and functions in the provisions of the Act contained in Schedule 1 to this Order may be exercised only by officers of Revenue and Customs acting with the authority (which may be general or specific) of the Commissioners.

Revocation
    20. [*Revocation of statutory instruments referred to at § 15-26, ante.*]

Provisions of the Act applied to Revenue and Customs

★**15-32**   As to the revocation and replacement of the Police and Criminal Evidence Act 1984 (Application to Revenue and Customs) Order 2007 (S.I. 2007 No. 3175) by S.I. 2015 No. 1783, see *ante*, § 15-26. The provisions listed in the main work appear in Schedule 1 to S.I. 2015 No. 1783, with the addition of a reference to section 46A(1) and (1A) (power of arrest for failure to answer to police bail (§ 3-167 in the main work)) of the Act.

Equivalent words and phrases

★**15-33**   As to the revocation and replacement of the Police and Criminal Evidence Act 1984 (Application to Revenue and Customs) Order 2007 (S.I. 2007 No. 3175) by S.I. 2015 No. 1783, see *ante*, § 15-26. Part 1 of Schedule 2 to S.I. 2015 No. 1783 replicates Part 1 of Schedule 2 to S.I. 2007 No. 3175 (see the main work).

Equivalent grades

★**15-34**   As to the revocation and replacement of the Police and Criminal Evidence Act 1984 (Application to Revenue and Customs) Order 2007 (S.I. 2007 No. 3175) by S.I. 2015 No. 1783, see *ante*, § 15-26. Part 2 of Schedule 2 to S.I. 2015 No. 1783 replicates Part 2 of Schedule 2 to S.I. 2007 No. 3175 (see the main work).

Borders, Citizenship and Immigration Act 2009

★**15-35**   As to the revocation and replacement of the Police and Criminal Evidence Act 1984 (Application to Revenue and Customs) Order 2007 (S.I. 2007 No. 3175) (see the main work), see *ante*, § 15-26. As explained in the main work, it had in any event ceased to apply to criminal investigations conducted by designated customs officials with effect from mid-2013.

B. Stop and Search

(2) Criminal Justice and Public Order Act 1994
Criminal Justice and Public Order Act 1994, s.60

Powers to stop and search in anticipation of, or after, violence
★**15-48**   The decision of the Court of Appeal in *R. (Roberts) v. Commr of Police of the Metropolis (Liberty intervening)* has been upheld by the Supreme Court (see *R. (Roberts) v. Commr of Police of the Metropolis* [2016] 1 W.L.R. 210), insofar as it related to Article 8 of the ECHR. The Court of Appeal's decision in relation to Article 5 was not the subject of appeal.

C. Entry, Search and Seizure

(2) Statute
Police and Criminal Evidence Act 1984, s.8

Power of justice of the peace to authorise entry and search of premises
★**15-55**   For new rules relating to applications for warrants under section 8 of the 1984 Act (see § 15-54 in the main work), see *post*, § 15-272.

Police and Criminal Evidence Act 1984, Sched. 1

Special procedure

For rules about applications for production orders under paragraph 4 of Schedule 1 to the 1984 Act (see the main work), see *post*, § 15-272.   ★**15-58**

For rules about applications for search warrants under paragraph 12 of Schedule 1 to the 1984 Act (see the main work), see *post*, § 15-272.   ★**15-60**

Data protection

R. v. Bhatti is now reported at [2016] 1 Cr.App.R. 1.   ★**15-71a**

Police and Criminal Evidence Act 1984, ss.15, 16

Search warrants: procedure

As to the substitution of Part 47 of the Criminal Procedure Rules 2015 (S.I. 2015 No. 1490) (see the main work), see *post*, § 15-272.   ★**15-85**

Execution of warrants

R. (Chatwani) v. National Crime Agency and Birmingham Magistrates' Court is now reported at [2015] A.C.D. 110, *sub nom. R. (Chatwani) v. National Crime Agency.*   ★**15-87**

Criminal Justice and Police Act 2001, ss. 59-62

Application to the appropriate judicial authority

In *R. (H.S) v. South Cheshire Magistrates' Court*; *R. (M.U.) v. North Cheshire Magistrates' Court*; *R. (A.M.) v. South Cheshire Magistrates' Court*; *R. (H.S.) v. Crown Court at Manchester*, unreported, November 30, 2015, DC ([2015] EWHC 3415 (Admin.)), it was said that the decision in *R. (Cheema) v. Nottingham and Newark Magistrates' Court* (see the main work) is not to be taken to have laid down a general rule that there can be no application by the police to the Crown Court, under section 59 of the 2001 Act, for an order authorising the retention of property that has been seized, until every issue raised in a related judicial review claim (challenging the lawfulness of a warrant under which the property was seized and/ or the lawfulness of the entry and seizure, and seeking a remedy in the form of an order for the return of the property, and/or a declaration, and/or damages) has been resolved by the High Court.   ★**15-112**

R. (Chatwani) v. National Crime Agency and Birmingham Magistrates' Court (see the main work) is now reported at [2015] A.C.D. 110, *sub nom. R. (Chatwani) v. National Crime Agency.*   ★

For rules about orders for the retention or return of property under section 59 of the 2001 Act (see the main work), see *post*, §§ 15-125, 15-272 *et seq.*   ★

Applications under section 59

A new Part 47 of the Criminal Procedure Rules 2015 (S.I. 2015 No. 1490) (as substituted by the Criminal Procedure (Amendment) Rules 2016 (S.I. 2016 No. 120), and as to which, see *post*, § 15-272 *et seq.*) now makes specific provision in relation to applications under section 59 of the CJPA 2001 (see, in particular, new rr.47.35-47.40 (*post*, §§ 15-292 *et seq.*)). Whilst rule 39 of the Crown Court Rules 1982 (see the main work) has not been revoked, it was always doubtful whether it survived the amendment (by the Courts Act 2003 (Consequential Amendments) Order 2004 (S.I. 2004 No. 2035) to the rule-making power in section 84(1) of the Senior Courts Act 1981 of the Crown Court Rule Committee (now the Lord Chief Justice), and it may now safely be ignored.   ★**15-125**

D. Arrest

(2) The Police and Criminal Evidence Act 1984

Police and Criminal Evidence Act 1984, s.24

Arrest without warrant: constables

The cases of *Shields v. Chief Constable of Merseyside Police*, *Richardson v. Chief Constable of West Midlands Police* and *Hayes v. Chief Constable of Merseyside Police* (all cited in the main work) were considered in *R. (B. and others (former soldiers)) v. Chief Constable of the Police Service of Northern*   ★**15-131**

Ireland, unreported, December 17, 2015, DC ([2015] EWHC 3691 (Admin.)), where it was held that the proposed arrests of former soldiers in relation to alleged offences committed during "Bloody Sunday" in 1972 would be unlawful; the suspects were prepared to attend voluntarily at a police station in England and Wales for interview under caution; their arrests were not necessary to allow "prompt and effective" investigation (within the meaning of Northern Irish legislation in identical terms to s.24(5)(e) of the 1984 Act); "prompt and effective" is to be read conjunctively; "effective" means tending to achieve its purpose, not "efficient" or "cost-effective"; and whether an investigation is "prompt" must be considered in context; an arrest could not lead to a "prompt" investigation where the alleged offences occurred 43 years ago.

E. QUESTIONING AND TREATMENT OF PERSONS

(6) Tape recording of interviews

Police and Criminal Evidence Act 1984, s.60

★**15-174**   As to the coming into force of a revised Code of Practice on Audio Recording Interviews with Suspects ("Code E"), see *ante*, § 15-6.

(8) Fingerprints, photographs, intimate and other samples

National DNA database

15-189a   The Protection of Freedoms Act 2012 (Destruction, Retention and Use of Biometric Data) (Transitional, Transitory and Saving Provisions) (Amendment) Order 2015 (S.I. 2015 No. 1739) has amended the Protection of Freedoms Act 2012 (Destruction, Retention and Use of Biometric Data) (Transitional, Transitory and Saving Provisions) Order 2013 (S.I. 2013 No. 1813) (as to which, see the main work) so as to extend the transitional periods in articles 6 (see the main work) and 7 (*ibid.*, § 15-198) by one year.

Destruction, retention and use of fingerprints, etc.

★**15-197**   As to the substitution of Part 47 of S.I. 2015 No. 1490 (see the main work), see *post*, § 15-272.

Material not subject to existing statutory restrictions

15-198   As to the extension of the transitional period in article 7 of the Protection of Freedoms Act 2012 (Destruction, Retention and Use of Biometric Data) (Transitional, Transitory and Saving Provisions) Order 2013 (S.I. 2013 No. 1813) (as to which, see the main work, and § 25-145j in the main work), see *ante*, § 15-189a.

F. POLICE ACT 1997 AND REGULATION OF INVESTIGATORY POWERS ACT 2000

★**15-205**   In *R.E. v. U.K.*, *The Times*, January 8, 2016, ECtHR, it was held: (i) the regime put in place by S.I. 2010 No. 461 (see the main work) is compatible with Article 8 of the ECHR, to the extent that it allows for the covert surveillance of legal consultations; and (ii) consultations between a detainee and an appropriate adult are not subject to legal professional privilege and therefore do not involve the same expectation of privacy; accordingly, it was permissible for the covert surveillance of such conversations to be classified as "directed" rather than "intrusive" surveillance.

★**15-206**   With effect from January 15, 2016, the Equipment Interference (Code of Practice) Order 2016 (S.I. 2016 No. 38), *inter alia*, brought into force a code of practice prepared under section 71 of the 2000 Act, relating to the authorisation of interference with property under section 5 of the Intelligence Services Act 1994. It also contains information on the exercise of powers under section 7 of the 1994 Act (interference with equipment outside the British islands). So far as section 5 is concerned, paragraph 1.2 of the code declares that, to the extent that the guidance provided by the code with respect to equipment interference under section 5 overlaps with the guidance provided by the code of practice brought into force by the Regulation of Investigatory Powers (Covert Surveillance and Property Interference: Code of Practice) Order 2014 (S.I. 2014 No. 3103) (as to which, see the main work), this code takes precedence.

H. Proceeds of Crime Act 2002

(1) Summary

Introduction

With effect from November 30, 2015, (i) the Proceeds of Crime Act 2002 (External Investigations) (Amendment) Order 2015 (S.I. 2015 No. 1751) amended the Proceeds of Crime Act 2002 (External Investigations) Order 2013 (S.I. 2013 No. 2605); and (ii) the Proceeds of Crime Act 2002 (External Investigations) (Amendment) (No. 2) Order 2015 (S.I. 2015 No. 1752) amended the Proceeds of Crime Act 2002 (External Investigations) Order 2014 (S.I. 2014 No. 1893). ★**15-220**

As to the substitution of Part 47 of the Criminal Procedure Rules 2015 (S.I. 2015 No. 1490), see *post*, § 15-272. The new Part 47 continues to make procedural provision in relation to both the 2002 Act and S.I. 2014 No. 1893 (*ante*). ★

(2) Statute

Proceeds of Crime Act 2002, ss.341-345

Investigations

With effect from March 1, 2016 (Serious Crime Act 2015 (Commencement No. 5 and Transitional Provisions and Savings) Regulations 2016 (S.I. 2016 No. 148)), sections 38(1) and 85(1) of, and paragraph 55 of Schedule 4 to, the 2015 Act (see the main work) were brought into force. ★**15-228**

Proceeds of Crime Act 2002, ss.346-369

Supplementary

As to the substitution of Part 47 of S.I. 2015 No. 1490 (see the main work), see *ante*, § 15-272. ★**15-238**

Search and seizure warrants

For procedural provision in relation to proceedings under section 352 of the 2002 Act (see the main work), see *post*, § 15-272. ★**15-239**

Requirements where production order not available

With effect from March 1, 2016 (Serious Crime Act 2015 (Commencement No. 5 and Transitional Provisions and Savings) Regulations 2016 (S.I. 2016 No. 148)), section 38(2) of the 2015 Act (see the main work) was brought into force. ★**15-240**

(3) Procedural rules

Criminal Procedure Rules 2015 (S.I. 2015 No. 1490), Pt 47

When this Part applies

With effect from April 4, 2016, a whole new Part 47 of S.I. 2015 No. 1490 (investigation orders and warrants (see the main work for Sections 1 to 4, 7 and 8, § 2-106 in the main work for Section 5, and §§ 25-401c and 25-401d in the main work for Section 6)) is substituted by rule 15 of the Criminal Procedure (Amendment) Rules 2016 (S.I. 2016 No. 120)). The new part now includes rules about production orders under paragraph 4 of Schedule 1 (*ibid.*, §§ 15-58 *et seq.*) to the PACE Act 1984 and section 157 of the Extradition Act 2003, orders to grant entry under paragraph 5(5) (*ibid.*, § 25-106) of Schedule 5 to the Terrorism Act 2000, search warrants under paragraph 12 of Schedule 1 (*ibid.*, § 15-58) to the 1984 Act, paragraph 11 (*ibid.*, § 25-111) of Schedule 5 to the 2000 Act, section 352 (*ibid.*, § 15-239) of the PCA 2002, article 13 of the Proceeds of Crime Act 2002 (External Investigations) Order 2014 (S.I. 2014 No. 1893), and section 160 of the 2003 Act, and orders for the retention or return of property under section 1 of the Police (Property) Act 1897 and section 59 (*ibid.*, § 15-112) of the CJPA 2001. In addition to the new material, existing material in the part is rearranged and, in some instances, amended or consolidated in consequence. In particular, new Section 3 (rr.47.24-47.34) relates to investigation warrants, with rules 47.24 to 47.27 containing general provisions, and rules 47.28 to 47.34 relating to applications for warrants under section 8 of the 1984 Act (*ibid.*, § 15-54), section 2 of the CJA 1987 (*ibid.*, § 1-372), paragraph 12 of Schedule 1 to the 1984 Act (*ante*), paragraph 11 of ★**15-272**

Schedule 5 to the 2000 Act (*ante*), section 352 of the 2002 Act (*ante*) (and article 13 of the 2014 order), section 160 of the 2003 Act, and "any other power" respectively. The current rules about investigation anonymity orders (Section 5 (rr.47.23-47.26)), investigation approval orders under the RIPA 2000 (Section 6 (rr.47.27, 47.28)) and orders for the retention of fingerprints, *etc.* (Section 8 (rr.47.34-47.36)) are rearranged and renumbered but are unchanged in substance: what was Section 5 becomes Section 6 (rr.47.45-47.49), what was Section 6 becomes Section 7 (rr.47.50-47.52), and what was Section 8 becomes Section 5 (rr.47.41-47.44).

Criminal Procedure Rules 2015 (S.I. 2015 No. 1490), Pt 47 (as substituted by the Criminal Procedure (Amendment) Rules 2016 (S.I. 2016 No. 120), r.15)

Section 1: General rules

When this Part applies

★**15-272a**   **47.1.** This Part applies to the exercise of the powers listed in each of rules 47.4, 47.24, 47.35, 47.41, 47.45 and 47.50.

Meaning of "court", "applicant" and "respondent"

★**15-272b**   **47.2.** In this Part—

    (a) a reference to the "court" includes a reference to any justice of the peace or judge who can exercise a power to which this Part applies;

    (b) "applicant" means a person who, or an authority which, can apply for an order or warrant to which this Part applies; and

    (c) "respondent" means any person—

        (i) against whom such an order is sought or made, or

        (ii) on whom an application for such an order is served.

Documents served on the court officer

★**15-272c**   **47.3.**—(1) Unless the court otherwise directs, the court officer may—

    (a) keep a written application; or

    (b) arrange for the whole or any part to be kept by some other appropriate person, subject to any conditions that the court may impose.

(2) Where the court makes an order when the court office is closed, the applicant must, not more than 72 hours later, serve on the court officer—

    (a) a copy of the order; and

    (b) any written material that was submitted to the court.

(3) Where the court issues a warrant—

    (a) the applicant must return it to the court officer as soon as practicable after it has been executed, and in any event not more than 3 months after it was issued (unless other legislation otherwise provides); and

    (b) the court officer must—

        (i) keep the warrant for 12 months after its return, and

        (ii) during that period, make it available for inspection by the occupier of the premises to which it relates, if that occupier asks to inspect it.

Section 2: Investigation orders

When this Section applies

★**15-273**   **47.4.** This Section applies where—

    (a) a Circuit judge can make, vary or discharge an order for the production of, or for giving access to, material under paragraph 4 of Schedule 1 to the Police and Criminal Evidence Act 1984, other than material that consists of or includes journalistic material;

    (b) for the purposes of a terrorist investigation, a Circuit judge can make, vary or discharge—

        (i) an order for the production of, or for giving access to, material, or for a statement of its location, under paragraphs 5 and 10 of Schedule 5 to the Terrorism Act 2000,

        (ii) an explanation order, under paragraphs 10 and 13 of Schedule 5 to the 2000 Act,

        (iii) a customer information order, under paragraphs 1 and 4 of Schedule 6 to the 2000 Act;

    (c) for the purposes of a terrorist investigation, a Circuit judge can make, and the Crown

Court can vary or discharge, an account monitoring order, under paragraphs 2 and 4 of Schedule 6A to the 2000 Act;

(d) for the purposes of an investigation to which Part 8 of the Proceeds of Crime Act 2002 or the Proceeds of Crime Act 2002 (External Investigations) Order 2014 applies, a Crown Court judge can make, and the Crown Court can vary or discharge—

    (i) a production order, under sections 345 and 351 of the 2002 Act or under articles 6 and 12 of the 2014 Order,

    (ii) an order to grant entry, under sections 347 and 351 of the 2002 Act or under articles 8 and 12 of the 2014 Order,

    (iii) a disclosure order, under sections 357 and 362 of the 2002 Act or under articles 16 and 21 of the 2014 Order,

    (iv) a customer information order, under sections 363 and 369 of the 2002 Act or under articles 22 and 28 of the 2014 Order,

    (v) an account monitoring order, under sections 370, 373 and 375 of the 2002 Act or under articles 29, 32 and 34 of the 2014 Order;

(e) in connection with an extradition request, a Circuit judge can make an order for the production of, or for giving access to, material under section 157 of the Extradition Act 2003.

Exercise of court's powers

47.5.—(1) Subject to paragraphs (2), (3) and (4), the court may determine an application for an ★**15-274** order, or to vary or discharge an order—

(a) at a hearing (which must be in private unless the court otherwise directs), or without a hearing; and

(b) in the absence of—

    (i) the applicant,

    (ii) the respondent (if any),

    (iii) any other person affected by the order.

(2) The court must not determine such an application in the applicant's absence if—

(a) the applicant asks for a hearing; or

(b) it appears to the court that—

    (i) the proposed order may infringe legal privilege, within the meaning of section 10 of the Police and Criminal Evidence Act 1984, section 348 or 361 of the Proceeds of Crime Act 2002 or article 9 of the Proceeds of Crime Act 2002 (External Investigations) Order 2014,

    (ii) the proposed order may require the production of excluded material, within the meaning of section 11 of the 1984 Act, or

    (iii) for any other reason the application is so complex or serious as to require the court to hear the applicant.

(3) The court must not determine such an application in the absence of any respondent or other person affected, unless—

(a) the absentee has had at least 2 business days in which to make representations; or

(b) the court is satisfied that—

    (i) the applicant cannot identify or contact the absentee,

    (ii) it would prejudice the investigation if the absentee were present,

    (iii) it would prejudice the investigation to adjourn or postpone the application so as to allow the absentee to attend, or

    (iv) the absentee has waived the opportunity to attend.

(4) The court must not determine such an application in the absence of any respondent who, if the order sought by the applicant were made, would be required to produce or give access to journalistic material, unless that respondent has waived the opportunity to attend.

(5) The court officer must arrange for the court to hear such an application no sooner than 2 business days after it was served, unless—

(a) the court directs that no hearing need be arranged; or

(b) the court gives other directions for the hearing.

(6) The court must not determine an application unless satisfied that sufficient time has been allowed for it.

(7) If the court so directs, the parties to an application may attend a hearing by live link or telephone.

(8) The court must not make, vary or discharge an order unless the applicant states, in writing or orally, that to the best of the applicant's knowledge and belief—

    (a) the application discloses all the information that is material to what the court must decide; and

    (b) the content of the application is true.

(9) Where the statement required by paragraph (8) is made orally—

    (a) the statement must be on oath or affirmation, unless the court otherwise directs; and

    (b) the court must arrange for a record of the making of the statement.

(10) The court may—

    (a) shorten or extend (even after it has expired) a time limit under this Section;

    (b) dispense with a requirement for service under this Section (even after service was required); and

    (c) consider an application made orally instead of in writing.

(10) A person who wants an extension of time must—

    (a) apply when serving the application for which it is needed; and

    (b) explain the delay.

Application for order: general rules

★**15-275**   **47.6.**—(1) This rule applies to each application for an order to which this Section applies.

(2) The applicant must—

    (a) apply in writing and serve the application on the court officer;

    (b) demonstrate that the applicant is entitled to apply, for example as a constable or under legislation that applies to other officers;

    (c) give the court an estimate of how long the court should allow—

        (i) to read the application and prepare for any hearing, and

        (ii) for any hearing of the application;

    (d) attach a draft order in the terms proposed by the applicant;

    (e) serve notice of the application on the respondent, unless the court otherwise directs;

    (f) serve the application on the respondent to such extent, if any, as the court directs.

(3) A notice served on the respondent must—

    (a) specify the material or information in respect of which the application is made; and

    (b) identify—

        (i) the power that the applicant invites the court to exercise, and

        (ii) the conditions for the exercise of that power which the applicant asks the court to find are met.

(4) The applicant must serve any order made on the respondent.

Application containing information withheld from a respondent or other person

★**15-276**   **47.7.**—(1) This rule applies where an application includes information that the applicant thinks ought to be revealed only to the court.

(2) The application must—

    (a) identify that information; and

    (b) explain why that information ought not to be served on the respondent or another person.

(3) At a hearing of an application to which this rule applies—

    (a) the general rule is that the court must consider, in the following sequence—

        (i) representations first by the applicant and then by the respondent and any other person, in the presence of them all, and then

        (ii) further representations by the applicant, in the others' absence; but

    (b) the court may direct other arrangements for the hearing.

Application to vary or discharge an order

★**15-277**   **47.8.**—(1) This rule applies where one of the following wants the court to vary or discharge an order to which a rule in this Section refers—

    (a) an applicant;

    (b) the respondent; or

    (c) a person affected by the order.

(2) That applicant, respondent or person affected must—

    (a) apply in writing as soon as practicable after becoming aware of the grounds for doing so;

(b) serve the application on—
(i) the court officer, and
(ii) the respondent, applicant, or any person known to be affected, as applicable;
(c) explain why it is appropriate for the order to be varied or discharged;
(d) propose the terms of any variation; and
(e) ask for a hearing, if one is wanted, and explain why it is needed.

Application to punish for contempt of court
47.9.—(1) This rule applies where a person is accused of disobeying— ★**15-278**
(a) a production order made under paragraph 4 of Schedule 1 to the Police and Criminal Evidence Act 1984;
(b) a production etc. order made under paragraph 5 of Schedule 5 to the Terrorism Act 2000;
(c) an explanation order made under paragraph 13 of that Schedule;
(d) an account monitoring order made under paragraph 2 of Schedule 6A to that Act;
(e) a production order made under section 345 of the Proceeds of Crime Act 2002 or article 6 of the Proceeds of Crime Act 2002 (External Investigations) Order 2014;
(f) an account monitoring order made under section 370 of the 2002 Act or article 29 of the 2014 Order; or
(g) a production order made under section 157 of the Extradition Act 2003.
(2) An applicant who wants the court to exercise its power to punish that person for contempt of court must comply with the rules in Part 48 (contempt of court).

Orders under the Police and Criminal Evidence Act 1984

Application for a production order under the Police and Criminal Evidence Act 1984
47.10.—(1) This rule applies where an applicant wants the court to make an order to which rule ★**15-279**
47.4(a) refers.
(2) As well as complying with rule 47.6 (application for order: general rules), the application must, in every case—
(a) specify the offence under investigation (and see paragraph (3)(a));
(b) describe the material sought;
(c) identify the respondent;
(d) specify the premises on which the material is believed to be, or explain why it is not reasonably practicable to do so;
(e) explain the grounds for believing that the material is on the premises specified, or (if applicable) on unspecified premises of the respondent;
(f) specify the set of access conditions on which the applicant relies (and see paragraphs (3) and (4)); and
(g) propose—
(i) the terms of the order, and
(ii) the period within which it should take effect.
(3) Where the applicant relies on paragraph 2 of Schedule 1 to the Police and Criminal Evidence Act 1984 ("the first set of access conditions": general power to gain access to special procedure material), the application must—
(a) specify the indictable offence under investigation;
(b) explain the grounds for believing that the offence has been committed;
(c) explain the grounds for believing that the material sought—
(i) is likely to be of substantial value to the investigation (whether by itself, or together with other material),
(ii) is likely to be admissible evidence at trial for the offence under investigation, and
(iii) does not consist of or include items subject to legal privilege or excluded material;
(d) explain what other methods of obtaining the material—
(i) have been tried without success, or
(ii) have not been tried because they appeared bound to fail; and
(e) explain why it is in the public interest for the respondent to produce the material, having regard to—
(i) the benefit likely to accrue to the investigation if the material is obtained, and
(ii) the circumstances under which the respondent holds the material.
(4) Where the applicant relies on paragraph 3 of Schedule 1 to the Police and Criminal Evidence

Act 1984 ("the second set of access conditions": use of search warrant power to gain access to excluded or special procedure material), the application must—

    (a) state the legislation under which a search warrant could have been issued, had the material sought not been excluded or special procedure material (in this paragraph, described as "the main search power");

    (b) include or attach the terms of the main search power;

    (c) explain how the circumstances would have satisfied any criteria prescribed by the main search power for the issue of a search warrant; and

    (d) explain why the issue of such a search warrant would have been appropriate.

Orders under the Terrorism Act 2000

Application for an order under the Terrorism Act 2000

★**15-280**   **47.11.**—(1) This rule applies where an applicant wants the court to make one of the orders to which rule 47.4(b) and (c) refers.

(2) As well as complying with rule 47.6 (application for order: general rules), the application must—

    (a) specify the offence under investigation;

    (b) explain how the investigation constitutes a terrorist investigation within the meaning of the Terrorism Act 2000;

    (c) identify the respondent; and

    (d) give the information required by whichever of rules 47.12 to 47.16 applies.

Content of application for a production etc. order under the Terrorism Act 2000

★**15-280a**   **47.12.** As well as complying with rules 47.6 and 47.11, an applicant who wants the court to make an order for the production of, or for giving access to, material, or for a statement of its location, must—

    (a) describe that material;

    (b) explain why the applicant thinks the material is—

        (i) in the respondent's possession, custody or power, or

        (ii) expected to come into existence and then to be in the respondent's possession, custody or power within 28 days of the order;

    (c) explain how the material constitutes or contains excluded material or special procedure material;

    (d) confirm that none of the material is expected to be subject to legal privilege;

    (e) explain why the material is likely to be of substantial value to the investigation;

    (f) explain why it is in the public interest for the material to be produced, or for the applicant to be given access to it, having regard to—

        (i) the benefit likely to accrue to the investigation if it is obtained, and

        (ii) the circumstances in which the respondent has the material, or is expected to have it; and

    (g) propose—

        (i) the terms of the order, and

        (ii) the period within which it should take effect.

Content of application for an order to grant entry under the Terrorism Act 2000

★**15-280b**   **47.13.** An applicant who wants the court to make an order to grant entry in aid of a production order must—

    (a) specify the premises to which entry is sought;

    (b) explain why the order is needed; and

    (c) propose the terms of the order.

Content of application for an explanation order under the Terrorism Act 2000

★**15-280c**   **47.14.** As well as complying with rules 47.6 and 47.11, an applicant who wants the court to make an explanation order must—

    (a) identify the material that the applicant wants the respondent to explain;

    (b) confirm that the explanation is not expected to infringe legal privilege; and

    (c) propose the terms of the order.

Content of application for a customer information order under the Terrorism Act 2000

★**15-280d**   **47.15.** As well as complying with rules 47.6 and 47.11, an applicant who wants the court to make a customer information order must—

(a) explain why it is desirable for the purposes of the investigation to trace property said to be terrorist property within the meaning of the Terrorism Act 2000;

(b) explain why the order will enhance the effectiveness of the investigation; and

(c) propose the terms of the order.

Content of application for an account monitoring order under the Terrorism Act 2000

47.16. As well as complying with rules 47.6 and 47.11, an applicant who wants the court to make ★**15-280e** an account monitoring order must—

(a) specify—

    (i) the information sought,

    (ii) the period during which the applicant wants the respondent to provide that information (to a maximum of 90 days), and

    (iii) where, when and in what manner the applicant wants the respondent to provide that information;

(b) explain why it is desirable for the purposes of the investigation to trace property said to be terrorist property within the meaning of the Terrorism Act 2000;

(c) explain why the order will enhance the effectiveness of the investigation; and

(d) propose the terms of the order.

Orders under the Proceeds of Crime Act 2002

Application for an order under the Proceeds of Crime Act 2002

47.17.—(1) This rule applies where an applicant wants the court to make one of the orders to ★**15-281** which rule 47.4(d) refers.

(2) As well as complying with rule 47.6 (application for order: general rules), the application must—

(a) identify—

    (i) the respondent, and

    (ii) the person or property the subject of the investigation;

(b) in the case of an investigation in the United Kingdom, explain why the applicant thinks that—

    (i) the person under investigation has benefited from criminal conduct, in the case of a confiscation investigation, or committed a money laundering offence, in the case of a money laundering investigation, or

    (ii) the cash involved is property obtained through unlawful conduct, or is intended to be used in unlawful conduct, in the case of a detained cash investigation;

(c) in the case of an investigation outside the United Kingdom, explain why the applicant thinks that—

    (i) there is an investigation by an overseas authority which relates to a criminal investigation or to criminal proceedings (including proceedings to remove the benefit of a person's criminal conduct following that person's conviction), and

    (ii) the investigation is into whether property has been obtained as a result of or in connection with criminal conduct, or into the extent or whereabouts of such property;

(d) give the additional information required by whichever of rules 47.18 to 47.22 applies.

Content of application for a production order under the Proceeds of Crime Act 2002

47.18. As well as complying with rules 47.6 and 47.17, an applicant who wants the court to make ★**15-282** an order for the production of, or for giving access to, material, must—

(a) describe that material;

(b) explain why the applicant thinks the material is in the respondent's possession or control;

(c) confirm that none of the material is—

    (i) expected to be subject to legal privilege, or

    (ii) excluded material;

(d) explain why the material is likely to be of substantial value to the investigation;

(e) explain why it is in the public interest for the material to be produced, or for the applicant to be given access to it, having regard to—

    (i) the benefit likely to accrue to the investigation if it is obtained, and

    (ii) the circumstances in which the respondent has the material; and

(f) propose—

(i)   the terms of the order, and

(ii)   the period within which it should take effect, if 7 days from the date of the order would not be appropriate.

Content of application for an order to grant entry under the Proceeds of Crime Act 2002

★**15-283**   **47.19.** An applicant who wants the court to make an order to grant entry in aid of a production order must—

(a)   specify the premises to which entry is sought;

(b)   explain why the order is needed; and

(c)   propose the terms of the order.

Content of application for a disclosure order under the Proceeds of Crime Act 2002

★**15-284**   **47.20.** As well as complying with rules 47.6 and 47.17, an applicant who wants the court to make a disclosure order must—

(a)   describe in general terms the information that the applicant wants the respondent to provide;

(b)   confirm that none of the information is—

(i)   expected to be subject to legal privilege, or

(ii)   excluded material;

(c)   explain why the information is likely to be of substantial value to the investigation;

(d)   explain why it is in the public interest for the information to be provided, having regard to the benefit likely to accrue to the investigation if it is obtained; and

(e)   propose the terms of the order.

Content of application for a customer information order under the Proceeds of Crime Act 2002

★**15-285**   **47.21.** As well as complying with rules 47.6 and 47.17, an applicant who wants the court to make a customer information order must—

(a)   explain why customer information about the person under investigation is likely to be of substantial value to that investigation;

(b)   explain why it is in the public interest for the information to be provided, having regard to the benefit likely to accrue to the investigation if it is obtained; and

(c)   propose the terms of the order.

Content of application for an account monitoring order under the Proceeds of Crime Act 2002

★**15-286**   **47.22.** As well as complying with rules 47.6 and 47.17, an applicant who wants the court to make an account monitoring order for the provision of account information must—

(a)   specify—

(i)   the information sought,

(ii)   the period during which the applicant wants the respondent to provide that information (to a maximum of 90 days), and

(iii)   when and in what manner the applicant wants the respondent to provide that information;

(b)   explain why the information is likely to be of substantial value to the investigation;

(c)   explain why it is in the public interest for the information to be provided, having regard to the benefit likely to accrue to the investigation if it is obtained; and

(d)   propose the terms of the order.

Orders under the Extradition Act 2003

★**15-286a**   **47.23.** [*Application for a production order under the Extradition Act 2003.*]

Section 3: Investigation warrants

When this Section applies

★**15-287**   **47.24.** This Section applies where—

(a)   a justice of the peace can issue a warrant under—

(i)   section 8 of the Police and Criminal Evidence Act 1984,

(ii)   section 2 of the Criminal Justice Act 1987;

(b)   a Circuit judge can issue a warrant under—

(i)   paragraph 12 of Schedule 1 to the Police and Criminal Evidence Act 1984,

(ii)   paragraph 11 of Schedule 5 to the Terrorism Act 2000,

(iii)   section 160 of the Extradition Act 2003;

(c)   a Crown Court judge can issue a warrant under—

(i)   section 352 of the Proceeds of Crime Act 2002, or

(ii)   article 13 of the Proceeds of Crime Act 2002 (External Investigations) Order 2014;

(d)   a court to which these rules apply can issue a warrant to search for and seize articles or persons under a power not listed in paragraphs (a), (b) or (c).

Exercise of court's powers

47.25.—(1) The court must determine an application for a warrant—   ★**15-288**

(a)   at a hearing, which must be in private unless the court otherwise directs;

(b)   in the presence of the applicant; and

(c)   in the absence of any person affected by the warrant, including any person in occupation or control of premises which the applicant wants to search.

(2) If the court so directs, the applicant may attend the hearing by live link or telephone.

(3) The court must not determine an application unless satisfied that sufficient time has been allowed for it.

(4) The court must not determine an application unless the applicant confirms, on oath or affirmation, that to the best of the applicant's knowledge and belief—

(a)   the application discloses all the information that is material to what the court must decide, including any circumstances that might reasonably be considered capable of undermining any of the grounds of the application; and

(b)   the content of the application is true.

(5) If the court requires the applicant to answer a question about an application—

(a)   the applicant's answer must be on oath or affirmation;

(b)   the court must arrange for a record of the gist of the question and reply; and

(c)   if the applicant cannot answer to the court's satisfaction, the court may—

(i)   specify the information the court requires, and

(ii)   give directions for the presentation of any renewed application.

(6) Unless to do so would be inconsistent with other legislation, on an application the court may issue—

(a)   a warrant in respect of specified premises;

(b)   a warrant in respect of all premises occupied or controlled by a specified person;

(c)   a warrant in respect of all premises occupied or controlled by a specified person which specifies some of those premises; or

(d)   more than one warrant—

(i)   each one in respect of premises specified in the warrant,

(ii)   each one in respect of all premises occupied or controlled by a person specified in the warrant (whether or not such a warrant also specifies any of those premises), or

(iii)   at least one in respect of specified premises and at least one in respect of all premises occupied or controlled by a specified person (whether or not such a warrant also specifies any of those premises).

Application for warrant: general rules

47.26.—(1) This rule applies to each application to which this Section applies.   ★**15-289**

(2) The applicant must—

(a)   apply in writing;

(b)   serve the application on—

(i)   the court officer, or

(ii)   if the court office is closed, the court;

(c)   demonstrate that the applicant is entitled to apply, for example as a constable or under legislation that applies to other officers;

(d)   give the court an estimate of how long the court should allow—

(i)   to read and prepare for the application, and

(ii)   for the hearing of the application; and

(e)   tell the court when the applicant expects any warrant issued to be executed.

(3) The application must disclose anything known or reported to the applicant that might reasonably be considered capable of undermining any of the grounds of the application.

(4) Where the application includes information that the applicant thinks should not be supplied

under rule 5.7 (supply to a party of information or documents from records or case materials) to a person affected by a warrant, the applicant may—

    (a) set out that information in a separate document, marked accordingly; and

    (b) in that document, explain why the applicant thinks that that information ought not to be supplied to anyone other than the court.

  (5) The application must include—

    (a) a declaration by the applicant that to the best of the applicant's knowledge and belief—

        (i) the application discloses all the information that is material to what the court must decide, including anything that might reasonably be considered capable of undermining any of the grounds of the application, and

       (ii) the content of the application is true; and

    (b) a declaration by an officer senior to the applicant that the senior officer has reviewed and authorised the application.

  (6) The application must attach a draft warrant or warrants in the terms proposed by the applicant.

Information to be included in a warrant

★**15-290**   **47.27.**—(1) A warrant must identify—

    (a) the person or description of persons by whom it may be executed;

    (b) any person who may accompany a person executing the warrant;

    (c) so far as practicable, the material, documents, articles or persons to be sought;

    (d) the legislation under which it was issued;

    (e) the name of the applicant;

    (f) the court that issued it, unless that is otherwise recorded by the court officer;

    (g) the court office for the court that issued it; and

    (h) the date on which it was issued.

  (2) A warrant must specify—

    (a) either—

        (i) the premises to be searched, where the application was for authority to search specified premises, or

       (ii) the person in occupation or control of premises to be searched, where the application was for authority to search any premises occupied or controlled by that person; and

    (b) the number of occasions on which specified premises may be searched, if more than one.

  (3) A warrant must include, by signature, initial, or otherwise, an indication that it has been approved by the court that issued it.

  (4) Where a warrant comprises more than a single page, each page must include such an indication.

  (5) A copy of a warrant must include a prominent certificate that it is such a copy.

Application for warrant under section 8 of the Police and Criminal Evidence Act 1984

★**15-290a**   **47.28.**—(1) This rule applies where an applicant wants a magistrates' court to issue a warrant or warrants under section 8 of the Police and Criminal Evidence Act 1984.

  (2) As well as complying with rule 47.26, the application must—

    (a) specify the offence under investigation (and see paragraph (3));

    (b) so far as practicable, identify the material sought (and see paragraph (4));

    (c) specify the premises to be searched (and see paragraphs (5) and (6));

    (d) state whether the applicant wants the premises to be searched on more than one occasion (and see paragraph (7)); and

    (e) state whether the applicant wants other persons to accompany the officers executing the warrant or warrants (and see paragraph (8)).

  (3) In relation to the offence under investigation, the application must—

    (a) state whether that offence is—

        (i) an indictable offence, or

       (ii) a relevant offence as defined in section 28D of the Immigration Act 1971; and

    (b) explain the grounds for believing that the offence has been committed.

  (4) In relation to the material sought, the application must explain the grounds for believing that that material—

    (a) is likely to be of substantial value to the investigation (whether by itself, or together with other material);

    (b) is likely to be admissible evidence at trial for the offence under investigation; and

    (c) does not consist of or include items subject to legal privilege, excluded material or special procedure material.

(5) In relation to premises which the applicant wants to be searched and can specify, the application must—

    (a) specify each set of premises;

    (b) in respect of each set of premises, explain the grounds for believing that material sought is on those premises; and

    (c) in respect of each set of premises, explain the grounds for believing that—

        (i) it is not practicable to communicate with any person entitled to grant entry to the premises,

        (ii) it is practicable to communicate with such a person but it is not practicable to communicate with any person entitled to grant access to the material sought,

        (iii) entry to the premises will not be granted unless a warrant is produced, or

        (iv) the purpose of a search may be frustrated or seriously prejudiced unless a constable arriving at the premises can secure immediate entry to them.

(6) In relation to premises which the applicant wants to be searched but at least some of which the applicant cannot specify, the application must—

    (a) explain the grounds for believing that—

        (i) because of the particulars of the offence under investigation it is necessary to search any premises occupied or controlled by a specified person, and

        (ii) it is not reasonably practicable to specify all the premises which that person occupies or controls which might need to be searched;

    (b) specify as many sets of premises as is reasonably practicable;

    (c) in respect of each set of premises, whether specified or not, explain the grounds for believing that material sought is on those premises; and

    (d) in respect of each specified set of premises, explain the grounds for believing that—

        (i) it is not practicable to communicate with any person entitled to grant entry to the premises,

        (ii) it is practicable to communicate with such a person but it is not practicable to communicate with any person entitled to grant access to the material sought,

        (iii) entry to the premises will not be granted unless a warrant is produced, or

        (iv) the purpose of a search may be frustrated or seriously prejudiced unless a constable arriving at the premises can secure immediate entry to them.

(7) In relation to any set of premises which the applicant wants to be searched on more than one occasion, the application must—

    (a) explain why it is necessary to search on more than one occasion in order to achieve the purpose for which the applicant wants the court to issue the warrant; and

    (b) specify any proposed maximum number of occasions.

(8) In relation to any set of premises which the applicant wants to be searched by the officers executing the warrant with other persons authorised by the court, the application must—

    (a) identify those other persons, by function or description; and

    (b) explain why those persons are required.

Application for warrant under section 2 of the Criminal Justice Act 1987

47.29.—(1) This rule applies where an applicant wants a magistrates' court to issue a warrant or warrants under section 2 of the Criminal Justice Act 1987.   ★**15-290b**

(2) As well as complying with rule 47.26, the application must—

    (a) describe the investigation being conducted by the Director of the Serious Fraud Office and include—

        (i) an explanation of what is alleged and why, and

        (ii) a chronology of relevant events;

    (b) specify the document, documents or description of documents sought by the applicant (and see paragraphs (3) and (4)); and

    (c) specify the premises which the applicant wants to be searched (and see paragraph (5)).

(3) In relation to each document or description of documents sought, the application must—

    (a) explain the grounds for believing that each such document—

        (i) relates to a matter relevant to the investigation, and

        (ii) could not be withheld from disclosure or production on grounds of legal professional privilege; and

    (b) explain the grounds for believing that—

        (i) a person has failed to comply with a notice by the Director to produce the document or documents,

(ii) it is not practicable to serve such a notice, or

(iii) the service of such a notice might seriously impede the investigation.

(4) In relation to any document or description of documents which the applicant wants to be preserved but not seized under a warrant, the application must—

(a) specify the steps for which the applicant wants the court's authority in order to preserve and prevent interference with the document or documents; and

(b) explain why such steps are necessary.

(5) In respect of each set of premises which the applicant wants to be searched, the application must explain the grounds for believing that a document or description of documents sought by the applicant is on those premises.

(6) If the court so directs, the applicant must make available to the court material on which is based the information given under paragraph (2).

Application for warrant under paragraph 12 of Schedule 1 to the Police and Criminal Evidence Act 1984

★ **15-290c**   **47.30.**—(1) This rule applies where an applicant wants a Circuit judge to issue a warrant or warrants under paragraph 12 of Schedule 1 to the Police and Criminal Evidence Act 1984.

(2) As well as complying with rule 47.26, the application must—

(a) specify the offence under investigation (and see paragraph (3)(a));

(b) specify the set of access conditions on which the applicant relies (and see paragraphs (3) and (4));

(c) so far as practicable, identify the material sought;

(d) specify the premises to be searched (and see paragraphs (6) and (7)); and

(e) state whether the applicant wants other persons to accompany the officers executing the warrant or warrants (and see paragraph (8)).

(3) Where the applicant relies on paragraph 2 of Schedule 1 to the Police and Criminal Evidence Act 1984 ("the first set of access conditions": general power to gain access to special procedure material), the application must—

(a) specify the indictable offence under investigation;

(b) explain the grounds for believing that the offence has been committed;

(c) explain the grounds for believing that the material sought—

(i) is likely to be of substantial value to the investigation (whether by itself, or together with other material),

(ii) is likely to be admissible evidence at trial for the offence under investigation, and

(iii) does not consist of or include items subject to legal privilege or excluded material;

(d) explain what other methods of obtaining the material—

(i) have been tried without success, or

(ii) have not been tried because they appeared bound to fail; and

(e) explain why it is in the public interest to obtain the material, having regard to—

(i) the benefit likely to accrue to the investigation if the material is obtained, and

(ii) the circumstances under which the material is held.

(4) Where the applicant relies on paragraph 3 of Schedule 1 to the Police and Criminal Evidence Act 1984 ("the second set of access conditions": use of search warrant power to gain access to excluded or special procedure material), the application must—

(a) state the legislation under which a search warrant could have been issued, had the material sought not been excluded or special procedure material (in this paragraph, described as "the main search power");

(b) include or attach the terms of the main search power;

(c) explain how the circumstances would have satisfied any criteria prescribed by the main search power for the issue of a search warrant; and

(d) explain why the issue of such a search warrant would have been appropriate.

(5) Where the applicant relies on the second set of access conditions and on an assertion that a production order made under paragraph 4 of Schedule 1 to the 1984 Act in respect of the material sought has not been complied with—

(a) the application must—

(i) identify that order and describe its terms, and

(ii) specify the date on which it was served; but

(b) the application need not comply with paragraphs (6) or (7).

(6) In relation to premises which the applicant wants to be searched and can specify, the application must (unless paragraph (5) applies)—

(a) specify each set of premises;

(b) in respect of each set of premises, explain the grounds for believing that material sought is on those premises; and

(c) in respect of each set of premises, explain the grounds for believing that—

  (i) it is not practicable to communicate with any person entitled to grant entry to the premises,

  (ii) it is practicable to communicate with such a person but it is not practicable to communicate with any person entitled to grant access to the material sought,

  (iii) the material sought contains information which is subject to a restriction on disclosure or an obligation of secrecy contained in an enactment and is likely to be disclosed in breach of the restriction or obligation if a warrant is not issued, or

  (iv) service of notice of an application for a production order under paragraph 4 of Schedule 1 to the 1984 Act may seriously prejudice the investigation.

(7) In relation to premises which the applicant wants to be searched but at least some of which the applicant cannot specify, the application must (unless paragraph (5) applies)—

(a) explain the grounds for believing that—

  (i) because of the particulars of the offence under investigation it is necessary to search any premises occupied or controlled by a specified person, and

  (ii) it is not reasonably practicable to specify all the premises which that person occupies or controls which might need to be searched;

(b) specify as many sets of premises as is reasonably practicable;

(c) in respect of each set of premises, whether specified or not, explain the grounds for believing that material sought is on those premises; and

(d) in respect of each specified set of premises, explain the grounds for believing that—

  (i) it is not practicable to communicate with any person entitled to grant entry to the premises,

  (ii) it is practicable to communicate with such a person but it is not practicable to communicate with any person entitled to grant access to the material sought,

  (iii) the material sought contains information which is subject to a restriction on disclosure or an obligation of secrecy contained in an enactment and is likely to be disclosed in breach of the restriction or obligation if a warrant is not issued, or

  (iv) service of notice of an application for a production order under paragraph 4 of Schedule 1 to the 1984 Act may seriously prejudice the investigation.

(8) In relation to any set of premises which the applicant wants to be searched by the officers executing the warrant with other persons authorised by the court, the application must—

(a) identify those other persons, by function or description; and

(b) explain why those persons are required.

Application for warrant under paragraph 11 of Schedule 5 to the Terrorism Act 2000

47.31.—(1) This rule applies where an applicant wants a Circuit judge to issue a warrant or war- **★15-290d** rants under paragraph 11 of Schedule 5 to the Terrorism Act 2000.

(2) As well as complying with rule 47.26, the application must—

(a) specify the offence under investigation;

(b) explain how the investigation constitutes a terrorist investigation within the meaning of the Terrorism Act 2000;

(c) so far as practicable, identify the material sought (and see paragraph (4));

(d) specify the premises to be searched (and see paragraph (5)); and

(e) state whether the applicant wants other persons to accompany the officers executing the warrant or warrants (and see paragraph (6)).

(3) Where the applicant relies on an assertion that a production order made under paragraph 5 of Schedule 5 to the 2000 Act in respect of material on the premises has not been complied with—

(a) the application must—

  (i) identify that order and describe its terms, and

  (ii) specify the date on which it was served; but

(b) the application need not comply with paragraphs (4) or (5)(b).

(4) In relation to the material sought, unless paragraph (3) applies the application must explain the grounds for believing that—

(a) the material consists of or includes excluded material or special procedure material but does not include items subject to legal privilege;

(b) the material is likely to be of substantial value to a terrorist investigation (whether by itself, or together with other material); and

(c) it is not appropriate to make an order under paragraph 5 of Schedule 11 to the 2000 Act in relation to the material because—

(i) it is not practicable to communicate with any person entitled to produce the material,

(ii) it is not practicable to communicate with any person entitled to grant access to the material or entitled to grant entry to premises to which the application for the warrant relates, or

(iii) a terrorist investigation may be seriously prejudiced unless a constable can secure immediate access to the material.

(5) In relation to the premises which the applicant wants to be searched, the application must—

(a) specify—

(i) where paragraph (3) applies, the respondent and any premises to which the production order referred, or

(ii) in any other case, one or more sets of premises, or any premises occupied or controlled by a specified person (which may include one or more specified sets of premises); and

(b) unless paragraph (3) applies, in relation to premises which the applicant wants to be searched but cannot specify, explain why—

(i) it is necessary to search any premises occupied or controlled by the specified person, and

(ii) it is not reasonably practicable to specify all the premises which that person occupies or controls which might need to be searched;

(c) explain the grounds for believing that material sought is on those premises.

(6) In relation to any set of premises which the applicant wants to be searched by the officers executing the warrant with other persons authorised by the court, the application must—

(a) identify those other persons, by function or description; and

(b) explain why those persons are required.

Application for warrant under section 352 of the Proceeds of Crime Act 2002

★**15-290e**   **47.32.**—(1) This rule applies where an applicant wants a Crown Court judge to issue a warrant or warrants under—

(a) section 352 of the Proceeds of Crime Act 2002; or

(b) article 13 of the Proceeds of Crime Act 2002 (External Investigations) Order 2014.

(2) As well as complying with rule 47.26, the application must—

(a) explain whether the investigation is a confiscation investigation, a money laundering investigation, a detained cash investigation or an external investigation;

(b) in the case of an investigation in the United Kingdom, explain why the applicant suspects that—

(i) the person under investigation has benefited from criminal conduct, in the case of a confiscation investigation, or committed a money laundering offence, in the case of a money laundering investigation, or

(ii) the cash involved is property obtained through unlawful conduct, or is intended to be used in unlawful conduct, in the case of a detained cash investigation;

(c) in the case of an investigation outside the United Kingdom, explain why the applicant believes that—

(i) there is an investigation by an overseas authority which relates to a criminal investigation or to criminal proceedings (including proceedings to remove the benefit of a person's criminal conduct following that person's conviction), and

(ii) the investigation is into whether property has been obtained as a result of or in connection with criminal conduct, or into the extent or whereabouts of such property;

(d) indicate what material is sought (and see paragraphs (4) and (5));

(e) specify the premises to be searched (and see paragraph (6)); and

(f) state whether the applicant wants other persons to accompany the officers executing the warrant or warrants (and see paragraph (7)).

(3) Where the applicant relies on an assertion that a production order made under sections 345 and 351 of the 2002 Act or under articles 6 and 12 of the 2014 Order has not been complied with—

(a) the application must—

(i) identify that order and describe its terms,

(ii) specify the date on which it was served, and

(iii) explain the grounds for believing that the material in respect of which the order was made is on the premises specified in the application for the warrant; but

(b) the application need not comply with paragraphs (4) or (5).

(4) Unless paragraph (3) applies, in relation to the material sought the application must—

(a) specify the material; or

(b) give a general description of the material and explain the grounds for believing that it relates to the person under investigation and—

(i) in the case of a confiscation investigation, relates to the question whether that person has benefited from criminal conduct, or to any question about the extent or whereabouts of that benefit,

(ii) in the case of a money laundering investigation, relates to the question whether that person has committed a money laundering offence,

(iii) in the case of a detained cash investigation into the derivation of cash, relates to the question whether that cash is recoverable property,

(iv) in the case of a detained cash investigation into the intended use of the cash, relates to the question whether that cash is intended by any person to be used in unlawful conduct,

(v) in the case of an investigation outside the United Kingdom, relates to that investigation.

(5) Unless paragraph (3) applies, in relation to the material sought the application must explain also the grounds for believing that—

(a) the material consists of or includes special procedure material but does not include excluded material or privileged material;

(b) the material is likely to be of substantial value to the investigation (whether by itself, or together with other material); and

(c) it is in the public interest for the material to be obtained, having regard to—

(i) other potential sources of information,

(ii) the benefit likely to accrue to the investigation if the material is obtained.

(6) In relation to the premises which the applicant wants to be searched, unless paragraph (3) applies the application must—

(a) explain the grounds for believing that material sought is on those premises;

(b) if the application specifies the material sought, explain the grounds for believing that it is not appropriate to make a production order under sections 345 and 351 of the 2002 Act or under articles 6 and 12 of the 2014 Order because—

(i) it is not practicable to communicate with any person against whom the production order could be made,

(ii) it is not practicable to communicate with any person who would be required to comply with an order to grant entry to the premises, or

(iii) the investigation might be seriously prejudiced unless an appropriate person is able to secure immediate access to the material;

(c) if the application gives a general description of the material sought, explain the grounds for believing that—

(i) it is not practicable to communicate with any person entitled to grant entry to the premises,

(ii) entry to the premises will not be granted unless a warrant is produced, or

(iii) the investigation might be seriously prejudiced unless an appropriate person arriving at the premises is able to secure immediate access to them;

(7) In relation to any set of premises which the applicant wants to be searched by those executing the warrant with other persons authorised by the court, the application must—

(a) identify those other persons, by function or description; and

(b) explain why those persons are required.

47.33. [*Application for warrant under section 160 of the Extradition Act 2003.*]   ★**15-290f**

Application for warrant under any other power

47.34.—(1) This rule applies—   ★**15-291**

(a) where an applicant wants a court to issue a warrant or warrants under a power (in this rule, "the relevant search power") to which rule 47.24(d) (other powers) refers; but

(b) subject to any inconsistent provision in legislation that applies to the relevant search power.

(2) As well as complying with rule 47.26, the application must—

   (a) demonstrate the applicant's entitlement to apply;

   (b) identify the relevant search power (and see paragraph (3));

   (c) so far as practicable, identify the articles or persons sought (and see paragraph (4));

   (d) specify the premises to be searched (and see paragraphs (5) and (6));

   (e) state whether the applicant wants the premises to be searched on more than one occasion, if the relevant search power allows (and see paragraph (7)); and

   (f) state whether the applicant wants other persons to accompany the officers executing the warrant or warrants, if the relevant search power allows (and see paragraph (8)).

  (3) The application must—

   (a) include or attach the terms of the relevant search power; and

   (b) explain how the circumstances satisfy the criteria prescribed by that power for making the application.

  (4) In relation to the articles or persons sought, the application must explain how they satisfy the criteria prescribed by the relevant search power about such articles or persons.

  (5) In relation to premises which the applicant wants to be searched and can specify, the application must—

   (a) specify each set of premises; and

   (b) in respect of each, explain how the circumstances satisfy any criteria prescribed by the relevant search power—

     (i) for asserting that the articles or persons sought are on those premises, and

     (ii) for asserting that the court can exercise its power to authorise the search of those particular premises.

  (6) In relation to premises which the applicant wants to be searched but at least some of which the applicant cannot specify, the application must—

   (a) explain how the relevant search power allows the court to authorise such searching;

   (b) specify the person who occupies or controls such premises;

   (c) specify as many sets of such premises as is reasonably practicable;

   (d) explain why—

     (i) it is necessary to search more premises than those specified, and

     (ii) it is not reasonably practicable to specify all the premises which the applicant wants to be searched;

   (e) in respect of each set of premises, whether specified or not, explain how the circumstances satisfy any criteria prescribed by the relevant search power for asserting that the articles or persons sought are on those premises; and

   (f) in respect of each specified set of premises, explain how the circumstances satisfy any criteria prescribed by the relevant search power for asserting that the court can exercise its power to authorise the search of those premises.

  (7) In relation to any set of premises which the applicant wants to be searched on more than one occasion, the application must—

   (a) explain how the relevant search power allows the court to authorise such searching;

   (b) explain why the applicant wants the premises to be searched more than once; and

   (c) specify any proposed maximum number of occasions.

  (8) In relation to any set of premises which the applicant wants to be searched by the officers executing the warrant with other persons authorised by the court, the application must—

   (a) identify those other persons, by function or description; and

   (b) explain why those persons are required.

Section 4: Orders for the retention or return of property

When this Section applies

★15-292   47.35.—(1) This Section applies where—

   (a) under section 1 of the Police (Property) Act 1897, a magistrates' court can—

     (i) order the return to the owner of property which has come into the possession of the police or the National Crime Agency in connection with an investigation of a suspected offence, or

     (ii) make such order with respect to such property as the court thinks just, where the owner cannot be ascertained;

   (b) a Crown Court judge can—

     (i) order the return of seized property under section 59(4) of the Criminal Justice and Police Act 2001, or

(ii) order the examination, retention, separation or return of seized property under section 59(5) of the Act.

(2) In this Section, a reference to a person with "a relevant interest" in seized property means someone from whom the property was seized, or someone with a proprietary interest in the property, or someone who had custody or control of it immediately before it was seized.

Exercise of court's powers

47.36.—(1) The court may determine an application for an order— ★**15-292a**

    (a) at a hearing (which must be in private unless the court otherwise directs), or without a hearing;

    (b) in a party's absence, if that party—

        (i) applied for the order, or

        (ii) has had at least 14 days in which to make representations.

(2) The court officer must arrange for the court to hear such an application no sooner than 14 days after it was served, unless—

    (a) the court directs that no hearing need be arranged; or

    (b) the court gives other directions for the hearing.

(3) If the court so directs, the parties to an application may attend a hearing by live link or telephone.

(4) The court may—

    (a) shorten or extend (even after it has expired) a time limit under this Section;

    (b) dispense with a requirement for service under this Section (even after service was required); and

    (c) consider an application made orally instead of in writing.

(5) A person who wants an extension of time must—

    (a) apply when serving the application or representations for which it is needed; and

    (b) explain the delay.

47.37. [*Application for an order under section 1 of the Police (Property) Act 1897.*] ★**15-292b**

Application for an order under section 59 of the Criminal Justice and Police Act 2001

47.38.—(1) This rule applies where an applicant wants the court to make an order to which rule 47.35(1)(b) refers. ★**15-292c**

(2) The applicant must apply in writing and serve the application on—

    (a) the court officer; and

    (b) as appropriate—

        (i) the person who for the time being has the seized property,

        (ii) each person whom the applicant knows or believes to have a relevant interest in the property.

(3) In each case, the application must—

    (a) explain the applicant's interest in the property (either as a person with a relevant interest, or as possessor of the property in consequence of its seizure, as appropriate);

    (b) explain the circumstances of the seizure of the property and identify the power that was exercised to seize it (or which the person seizing it purported to exercise, as appropriate); and

    (c) include or attach a list of those on whom the applicant has served the application.

(4) On an application for an order for the return of property under section 59(4) of the Criminal Justice and Police Act 2001, the application must explain why any one or more of these applies—

    (a) there was no power to make the seizure;

    (b) the property seized is, or contains, an item subject to legal privilege which is not an item that can be retained lawfully in the circumstances listed in section 54(2) of the Act;

    (c) the property seized is, or contains, excluded or special procedure material which is not material that can be retained lawfully in the circumstances listed in sections 55 and 56 of the Act;

    (d) the property seized is, or contains, something taken from premises under section 50 of the Act, or from a person under section 51 of the Act, in the circumstances listed in those sections and which cannot lawfully be retained on the conditions listed in the Act.

(5) On an application for an order for the examination, retention, separation or return of property under section 59(5) of the 2001 Act, the application must—

    (a) specify the direction that the applicant wants the court to make, and explain why;

   (b) if applicable, specify each requirement of section 53(2) of the Act (examination and return of property) which is not being complied with;

   (c) if applicable, explain why the retention of the property by the person who now has it would be justified on the grounds that, even if it were returned, it would immediately become appropriate for that person to get it back under—

      (i) a warrant for its seizure, or

      (ii) a production order made under paragraph 4 of Schedule 1 to the Police and Criminal Evidence Act 1984, section 20BA of the Taxes Management Act 1970 or paragraph 5 of Schedule 5 to the Terrorism Act 2000.

Representations in response

★**15-292d**   **47.39.**—(1) This rule applies where a person wants to make representations about an application under rule 47.37 or rule 47.38.

   (2) Such a person must—

   (a) serve the representations on—

      (i) the court officer, and

      (ii) the applicant and any other party to the application;

   (b) do so not more than 14 days after service of the application; and

   (c) ask for a hearing, if that person wants one.

   (3) Representations in opposition to an application must explain why the grounds on which the applicant relies are not met.

Application to punish for contempt of court

★**15-292e**   **47.40.**—(1) This rule applies where a person is accused of disobeying an order under section 59 of the Criminal Justice and Police Act 2001.

   (2) A person who wants the court to exercise its power to punish that person for contempt of court must comply with the rules in Part 48 (contempt of court).

Section 5: Orders for the retention of fingerprints, etc.

When this Section applies

★**15-293**   **47.41.** This Section applies where—

   (a) a District Judge (Magistrates' Court) can make an order under—

      (i) section 63F(7) or 63R(6) of the Police and Criminal Evidence Act 1984, or

      (ii) paragraph 20B(5) or 20G(6) of Schedule 8 to the Terrorism Act 2000;

   (b) the Crown Court can determine an appeal under—

      (i) section 63F(10) of the Police and Criminal Evidence Act 1984, or

      (ii) paragraph 20B(8) of Schedule 8 to the Terrorism Act 2000.

Exercise of court's powers

★**15-293a**   **47.42.**—(1) The court must determine an application under rule 47.43, and an appeal under rule 47.44—

   (a) at a hearing, which must be in private unless the court otherwise directs; and

   (b) in the presence of the applicant or appellant.

   (2) The court must not determine such an application or appeal unless any person served under those rules—

   (a) is present; or

   (b) has had an opportunity—

      (i) to attend, or

      (ii) to make representations.

Application to extend retention period

★**15-293b**   **47.43.**—(1) This rule applies where a magistrates' court can make an order extending the period for which there may be retained material consisting of—

   (a) fingerprints taken from a person—

      (i) under a power conferred by Part V of the Police and Criminal Evidence Act 1984,

      (ii) with that person's consent, in connection with the investigation of an offence by the police, or

      (iii) under a power conferred by Schedule 8 to the Terrorism Act 2000 in relation to a person detained under section 41 of that Act;

(b) a DNA profile derived from a DNA sample so taken; or

(c) a sample so taken.

(2) A chief officer of police who wants the court to make such an order must—

(a) apply in writing—

    (i) within the period of 3 months ending on the last day of the retention period, where the application relates to fingerprints or a DNA profile, or

    (ii) before the expiry of the retention period, where the application relates to a sample;

(b) in the application—

    (i) identify the material,

    (ii) state when the retention period expires,

    (iii) give details of any previous such application relating to the material, and

    (iv) outline the circumstances in which the material was acquired;

(c) serve the application on the court officer, in every case; and

(d) serve the application on the person from whom the material was taken, where—

    (i) the application relates to fingerprints or a DNA profile, or

    (ii) the application is for the renewal of an order extending the retention period for a sample.

(3) An application to extend the retention period for fingerprints or a DNA profile must explain why that period should be extended.

(4) An application to extend the retention period for a sample must explain why, having regard to the nature and complexity of other material that is evidence in relation to the offence, the sample is likely to be needed in any proceedings for the offence for the purposes of—

(a) disclosure to, or use by, a defendant; or

(b) responding to any challenge by a defendant in respect of the admissibility of material that is evidence on which the prosecution proposes to rely.

(5) On an application to extend the retention period for fingerprints or a DNA profile, the applicant must serve notice of the court's decision on any respondent where—

(a) the court makes the order sought; and

(b) the respondent was absent when it was made.

Appeal

47.44.—(1) This rule applies where, under rule 47.43, a magistrates' court determines an application relating to fingerprints or a DNA profile and— ★**15-293c**

(a) the person from whom the material was taken wants to appeal to the Crown Court against an order extending the retention period; or

(b) a chief officer of police wants to appeal to the Crown Court against a refusal to make such an order.

(2) The appellant must—

(a) serve an appeal notice—

    (i) on the Crown Court officer and on the other party, and

    (ii) not more than 21 days after the magistrates' court's decision, or, if applicable, service of notice under rule 47.43(5); and

(b) in the appeal notice, explain, as appropriate, why the retention period should, or should not, be extended.

(3) Rule 34.11 (constitution of the Crown Court) applies on such an appeal.

For Section 6 of Part 47 (rr.47.45–47.49) relating to investigation anonymity orders, see *ante*, § ★**15-294**
2-106.

For Section 7 of Part 47 (rr.47.50-47.52) relating to investigation approval orders under RIPA ★
2000, see *post*, §§ 25-401c *et seq.*

II. CONFESSIONS AND RELATED TOPICS

B. ACCUSATIONS MADE IN THE PRESENCE OF THE DEFENDANT

(3) Criminal Justice and Public Order Act 1994

Silence when questioned or charged

R. v. Brizzalari (see the main work) was applied in *R. v. Harris (Henricko)* [2016] 1 Cr.App.R. 4, ★**15-364**

CA, where it was held that the judge was right not to give a section 34 direction where the prosecution made it clear that they were not seeking to draw an adverse inference from matters mentioned at trial but omitted from the defendant's interview, but merely wished to rely on the inconsistencies as going to the defendant's credit.

III. DISCRETION TO EXCLUDE EVIDENCE

A. UNDER STATUTE

(6) Confessions

★**15-423**   For a decision of the Supreme Court where it was held that a judge had been correct not to exclude evidence (under the exact equivalent of the PACE Act 1984, s.78 (§ 15-401 in the main work) in Northern Ireland) of admissions contained in the appellant's unsuccessful application for asylum in Sweden, on the basis of which he had been convicted of membership of an illegal organisation, see *R. v. McGeough* [2016] 1 Cr. App.R. 10, SC (disclosure to the United Kingdom authorities was lawful under Swedish law and European Union law, there was no legitimate expectation of confidentiality (Swedish law, about which he had had legal advice at the time, was explicit about asylum applications being public documents), and no element of compulsion to the making of the admissions).

CHAPTER 16

HUMAN RIGHTS

II. THE HUMAN RIGHTS ACT

D. APPLICATION TO PUBLIC AUTHORITIES

Human Rights Act 1998, s.9

Judicial acts

★**16-30**   *Webster v. Lord Chancellor* is now reported at [2015] 3 W.L.R. 1909, *sub nom. W. v. Ministry of Justice*.

III. GENERAL PRINCIPLES OF INTERPRETATION

B. THE EUROPEAN CONVENTION ON HUMAN RIGHTS

Limitations on rights

★**16-39**   *Beghal v. DPP (Secretary of State for the Home Department intervening)* is now reported at [2016] A.C. 88.

★   The decision of the Divisional Court (as to which, see the main work) in *R. (Miranda) v. Secretary of State for the Home Department (Liberty intervening)* has been upheld on appeal: see *R. (Miranda) v. Secretary of State for the Home Department (Liberty intervening)* unreported, January 19, 2016, CA (Civ. Div.) ([2016] EWCA Civ. 6). As to this case, see also *post*, §§ 25-13, 25-124a.

IV. THE RIGHTS GUARANTEED

D. RIGHT TO LIBERTY AND SECURITY

Article 5

General

★**16-56**   *Beghal v. DPP (Secretary of State for the Home Department intervening)* is now reported at [2016] A.C. 88.

Detention following conviction

M. v. Germany (see the main work) was followed and applied in *Jendrowiak v. Germany* (2015) 61 ★**16-58**
E.H.R.R. 32. As to this case, see also *post*, § 16-60a.

Detention when reasonably considered necessary to prevent commission of offence

Preventive detention of a dangerous offender cannot be justified under Article 5(1)(c) of the ★**16-60a**
ECHR (§ 16-53 in the main work): *Jendrowiak v. Germany* (2015) 61 E.H.R.R. 32 (the potential
further offences were not sufficiently concrete and specific). As to this case, see also *ante*, § 16-58.

Bail

Zenati v. Commr of Police of the Metropolis is now reported at [2015] Q.B. 758. ★**16-63**

E. RIGHT TO A FAIR TRIAL

Article 6

Jury trial

Abdulla Ali v. U.K. is now reported at (2016) 62 E.H.R.R. 7, *sub nom. Ali v. U.K.* ★**16-82**

The protection against self-incrimination

Beghal v. DPP (Secretary of State for the Home Department intervening) is now reported at [2016] ★**16-90**
A.C. 88.

The protection against self-incrimination

For a case considering *Murray v. U.K.* and *Beckles v. U.K.* (as to both of which, see the main ★**16-94**
work), see *O'Donnell v. U.K.*, *ante*, § 4-379.

Trial within a reasonable time

The European Court of Human Rights' ruling in *Minshall v. U.K.* (see the main work) that a ★**16-100**
delay between the appellant's conviction and the determination of his appeal against a confiscation order was in breach of the reasonable time requirement in Article 6 of the ECHR (§ 16-72 in
the main work) did not affect the validity of the confiscation order and enforcement proceedings
relating to it (as to which, see *R. (Minshall) v. Marylebone Magistrates' Court* in the main work):
Minshall v. Commrs for H.M. Revenue and Customs [2015] Lloyd's Rep. F.C. 515, CA (Civ. Div.).

Impartiality

For a further appeal following the application to the European Court of Human Rights in ★**16-102**
Hanif and Khan v. U.K. (see the main work), see *R. v. Hanif (No. 2)*, *ante*, § 7-89.

The fact that a judge was only one of ten judges on an appellate bench was irrelevant where ★
the applicant had objective grounds to fear the impartiality of that particular judge, see *Morice v.
France* (2016) 62 E.H.R.R. 1.

F. NO PUNISHMENT WITHOUT LAW

Retroactive penalties

It should be noted that the citation given for *Gough v. Chief Constable of Derbyshire Constabulary* is ★**16-134**
for the decision of the Divisional Court (the decision being reported as *Gough v. Chief Constable of
Derbyshire Constabulary*; *R. (Miller) v. Leeds Magistrates' Court*; *Lilley v. DPP*). The Court of Appeal
decision (reported as *Gough v. Chief Constable of Derbyshire Constabulary* at [2002] Q.B. 1213) was
concerned only with banning orders under section 14B. Thus, it is the Divisional Court decision
that constitutes the authority in relation to section 14A and the Court of Appeal decision that
constitutes the authority in relation to section 14B.

G. Right to Respect for Private and Family Life

Article 8

Interference

★**16-141**   For a case considering the extent to which (if at all) football banning orders under the Football Spectators Act 1989 (§§ 5-1071 *et seq.* in the main work) engage Article 8 of the ECHR (§ 16-137 in the main work), see *Commr of Police of the Metropolis v. Thorpe, ante,* § 5-1072.

Justification

★**16-142**   *Beghal v. DPP (Secretary of State for the Home Department intervening)* is now reported at [2016] A.C. 88.

Intrusive surveillance, interception of communications, etc.

★**16-148**   For a case considering *Bykov v. Russia* and *Kennedy v. U.K.* (as to both of which, see the main work), see *R.E. v. U.K., ante,* § 15-205.

I. Freedom of Expression

Article 10

Public order

★**16-166**   It is not for a trial court to rule on the question whether a decision to prosecute was proportionate for the purposes of Article 10 (§ 16-157 in the main work) or 11 (freedom of assembly and association (*ibid.,* § 16-171)) of the ECHR: *James v. DPP,* 180 J.P. 1, DC. As to this case, see also post, § 29-44.

J. Freedom of Assembly and Association

Article 11

Justification

★**16-174**   See *James v. DPP, ante,* § 16-166.

Chapter 17

THE MENTAL ELEMENT IN CRIME

III. MENTAL ELEMENT IN ACCESSORIES

A. Intention

★**17-67**   The Supreme Court (sitting also as the Privy Council) in *R. v. Jogee; Ruddock v. R.,* unreported, February 18, 2016 ([2016] UKSC 8 & [2016] UKPC 7), held that the Privy Council in *Chan Wing-Siu v. R.,* and the House of Lords in *R. v. Powell; R. v. English* (as to both of which, see the main work), had taken a wrong turn in relation to the mental element that has to be established in respect of a person accused of crime on the basis of accessorial liability. Whilst the court declared that the principles were the same whatever the offence charged, the two cases being considered both involved convictions for murder (as did so many of the earlier cases on the subject), which makes it more convenient to set out the detail in Chapter 19 (*post,* § 19-24).

D. Alternative Intents

(1) Principle

★**17-71**   In light of the abandonment of *R. v. Powell; R. v. English* (as to which, see the main work), by the Supreme Court and Privy Council in *R. v. Jogee; Ruddock v. R.* (as to which, see *ante,* § 17-67, and *post*, § 19-24), it is submitted that the second sentence of this paragraph in the main work should now begin: "If he *intends* that one of a number of crimes should be committed, and one of those crimes is committed ...".

CHAPTER 18

PRINCIPALS AND SECONDARY PARTIES

III. SECONDARY PARTIES

A. ACCESSORIES

(2) Aiders and abettors

(f) *Joint enterprise/common design*

As to *R. v. Anderson and Morris* and *R. v. Powell*; *R. v. English* (as to both of which, see the main work), see *R. v. Jogee*; *Ruddock v. The Queen*, *post*, § 19-24. ★**18-15**

CHAPTER 19

OFFENCES AGAINST THE PERSON

I. HOMICIDE

A. MURDER

(1) Definition

"Under the Queen's peace"

Whereas the definition of murder based on that contained in *Coke's Institutes* (Co. Inst. Pt III (1797 ed.), ch. 7, p.47) (§ 19-1 in the main work) states that the killing must be of a person who is "under the Queen's peace", whilst "the Queen's peace" may still play some part in the elements that have to be proved for murder as regards the status of the victim, it has nothing whatsoever to do with the status of the killer; therefore, any belief of the defendant, however genuine, as to the existence of a state of war between him and the Queen was entirely irrelevant: *R. v. Adebolajo* [2015] 4 All E.R. 194, CA. **19-16**

(2) Liability of secondary parties

As to a decision of the Supreme Court (sitting also as the Privy Council) overruling *R. v. Powell*; *R. v. English* (as to which, see the main work), see *R. v. Jogee*; *Ruddock v. The Queen*, *post*, § 19-24. As with so many previous cases, the case concerned convictions for murder, but the decision reinforced the message (set out in the main work) that there are no special principles governing the liability of secondary parties to murder. ★**19-23**

Principle

In *R. v. Jogee*; *Ruddock v. R.*, unreported, February 18, 2016, SC & PC ([2016] UKSC 8 & [2016] UKPC 7), it was held: ★**19-24**
  (i) the principle that, if two people set out to commit an offence (crime A), and, in the course of it, one of them commits another offence (crime B), the second person is guilty as an accessory to crime B if he foresaw its commission by the principal as a possibility but neither intended it, nor agreed to it, expressly or tacitly, even on a conditional basis, as laid down

in *Chan Wing-Siu v. R.*, and then developed in *R. v. Powell*; *R. v. English* (as to both of which, see the main work), could not be supported; the Privy Council in *Chan Wing-Siu v. R.* and the House of Lords in *R. v. Powell*; *R. v. English*, had taken a wrong turn;

(ii) there is no reason why ordinary principles of secondary liability should not be of general application (the mental element required being that the accessory intended to encourage or assist the principal to commit the crime, acting with whatever mental element the offence requires of the principal); the correct approach is to treat foresight as evidence (albeit sometimes strong evidence) of intent to assist or encourage, but not as an inevitable yardstick of common purpose;

(iii) (a)   where the prosecution cannot prove whether a defendant was a principal or accessory, it will be sufficient to prove that he participated in the crime in one way or another;

(b)   when the question is whether D2, who joined with others in a venture to commit crime A, shared a common purpose or common intent (the two are the same) which included, if things came to it, the commission of crime B, the offence with which D2 is charged, and which was physically committed by D1, a time honoured way of inviting a jury to consider such a question is to ask whether they are sure that D1's act was within the scope of the joint venture, that is, whether D2 expressly or tacitly agreed to a plan that included D1 going as far as he did, and committing crime B, if the occasion arose; if the jury are satisfied that there was an agreed common purpose to commit crime A, and if they are satisfied also that D2 must have foreseen that, in the course of committing crime A, D1 might well commit crime B, they may in appropriate cases be justified in drawing the conclusion that D2 had the necessary conditional intent that crime B should be committed, if the occasion arose; or, in other words, that it was within the scope of the plan to which D2 gave his assent and intentional support; but that will be a question of fact for the jury in all the circumstances;

(c)   where there is a more or less spontaneous outbreak of multi-handed violence, the evidence may be too nebulous for the jury to find that there was some form of agreement, express or tacit; but secondary liability does not necessarily depend on there being some form of agreement between the defendants; it depends on proof of intentional assistance or encouragement, conditional or otherwise; if the accessory joins with a group which he realises is out to cause serious injury, the jury may well infer that he intended to encourage or assist the deliberate infliction of serious bodily injury and or intended that that should happen if necessary; in that case, if the principal acts with intent to cause serious bodily injury and death results, the principal and accessory will each be guilty of murder; if a person is a party to a violent attack on another, without an intent to assist in the causing of death or really serious harm, but the violence escalates and results in death, he will be not guilty of murder but guilty of manslaughter; so also if he participates by encouragement or assistance in any other unlawful act which all sober and reasonable people would realise carried the risk of some harm (not necessarily serious) to another, and death in fact results; the test is objective;

(d)   a qualification to this (recognised *R. v. Anderson and Morris* (as to which, see the main work, and § 18-15 in the main work)) is that it is possible for death to be caused by some overwhelming supervening act by the perpetrator, which nobody in the defendant's shoes could have contemplated might happen, and is of such a character as to relegate his acts to history; in that case the defendant will bear no criminal responsibility for the death;

(e)   this type of case apart, there will normally be no occasion to consider the concept of "fundamental departure" as derived from *Powell*; in particular, an intention to assist in a crime of violence is not determined only by whether the accessory knows what kind of weapon the principal has in his possession; knowledge or ignorance that weapons generally, or a particular weapon, is or are carried by the principal will be evidence going to what the intention of the accessory was, and may be irresistible evidence one way or the other, but it is evidence and no more; and

(iv) this restatement of the law does not render invalid all convictions arrived at by faithfully applying the law as laid down in *Chan Wing-Siu* and *Powell*; it may not have been important on the facts to the outcome of a trial or the safety of a conviction; the Court of Appeal can grant exceptional leave to appeal out of time, and may do so if substantial injustice is demonstrated, but it will not do so simply because the law applied has now been declared to have been mistaken (*R. v. Cottrell*; *R. v. Fletcher* (§ 7-171 in the main work)).

As to *R. v. Powell*; *R. v. English* (as to which, see the main work), see *R. v. Jogee*; *Ruddock v. R.*, *ante*, § 19-24.   ★**19-25**

As to *Chan Wing-Siu v. R.* (as to which, see the main work),see *R. v. Jogee*; *Ruddock v. R.*, *ante*, § 19-24.   ★**19-27**

As to *R. v. Powell*; *R. v. English* (as to which, see the main work), see *R. v. Jogee*; *Ruddock v. R.*, *ante*, § 19-24.   ★**19-29**

Guidance

As to *R. v. Powell*; *R. v. English* (as to which, see the main work), see *R. v. Jogee*; *Ruddock v. R.*, *ante*, § 19-24.   ★**19-30**

Application of principle

As to *R. v. Powell*; *R. v. English* (as to which, see the main work), see *R. v. Jogee*; *Ruddock v. R.*, *ante*, § 19-24.   ★**19-31**

(3) Lawful homicide

"Householder" cases

In *R. (Collins) v. Secretary of State for Justice*, unreported, January 15, 2016, DC ([2016] EWHC 33 (Admin.)), it was held: (i) section 76(5A) of the CJIA 2008 (§ 19-40 in the main work) does no more than stipulate that, in a householder case, grossly disproportionate force cannot be reasonable (and therefore the defence must fail); the negative drafting of the subsection would allow a jury to find either that the force used was not reasonable, though it was not grossly disproportionate, or that it was reasonable though it was not proportionate (provided that it was not grossly disproportionate); similarly, the negative drafting of subsection (6) would permit a finding (in a non-householder case) that the force used was not reasonable though it was proportionate; whilst, in almost all cases, if the degree of force is proportionate, it will also be reasonable, the two cannot be equated (considering *R. v. Keane*; *R. v. McGrath* (as to which, see § 19-41 in the main work)); and (ii) subsection (5A) is compatible with the state's obligation under Article 2 of the ECHR (*ibid.*, § 16-41) to protect the right to life. For a suggestion as to how a jury might be directed in light of the court's separation of reasonableness and proportionality, see CLW/16/03/3.   ★**19-48a**

(4) Defences

(b) *Provocation*

Common law

At common law, provocation reduced murder to manslaughter; and was available as a potential defence both for a principal and an accessory: *R. v. Marks* [1998] Crim.L.R. 676, CA. It was irrelevant on the issue of guilt in all other crimes.   **19-65**

The jury should be directed that before they have to consider the issue of provocation the Crown must have proved beyond reasonable doubt that all the other elements of murder were present, including the necessary intent: see *Lee Chun-Chuen v. R.* [1963] A.C. 220, PC; and *R. v. Martindale*, 50 Cr.App.R. 273, Ct-MAC.

The law as to provocation immediately prior to October 4, 2010 (as to which, see § 19-54 in the main work) was governed by a blend of common law and statute, *viz.* the Homicide Act 1957, s.3 (*post*, § 19-66).

Homicide Act 1957, s.3

Provocation

3. Where on a charge of murder there is evidence on which the jury can find that the person   **19-66**

charged was provoked (whether by things done or by things said or by both together) to lose his self-control, the question whether the provocation was enough to make a reasonable man do as he did shall be left to be determined by the jury; and in determining that question the jury shall take into account everything both done and said according to the effect which, in their opinion, it would have on a reasonable man.

This section altered as well as clarified the common law on this subject.

Duty of judge

19-67   Section 3 involves two questions: (a) is there any evidence of specific provoking conduct of the accused, and (b) is there any evidence that the provocation caused him to lose his self-control? If both questions are answered in the affirmative, the issue of provocation should be left to the jury notwithstanding the fact that in the opinion of the judge no reasonable jury could conclude on the evidence that a reasonable person would have been provoked to lose his self-control: *R. v. Gilbert*, 66 Cr.App.R. 237, CA; *Franco v. R., The Times*, October 11, 2001, PC; notwithstanding that there may be circumstances suggesting that the accused acted in revenge, rather than as a result of a sudden and temporary loss of self-control: *R. v. Baillie* [1995] 2 Cr.App.R. 31, CA; and notwithstanding that the issue has not been raised by the defence: *Bullard v. R.* [1957] A.C. 635, PC; *DPP v. Camplin* [1978] A.C. 705, HL; *R. v. Rossiter*, 95 Cr.App.R. 326, CA; and would prefer it not to be left to the jury: *R. v. Dhillon* [1997] 2 Cr.App.R. 104, CA.

Where, however, there is only a speculative possibility of the accused having acted as a result of provoking conduct, the issue should not be left to the jury: *R. v. Acott* [1997] 2 Cr.App.R. 94, HL (there must be some evidence of specific provoking conduct resulting in a loss of control by the accused; the source of such evidence is immaterial as is reliance thereon by the accused); and *R. v. Evans (John Derek)* [2010] Crim.L.R. 491, CA (§ 19-62 in the main work). Evidence of a loss of self-control is insufficient, for a loss of self-control might be brought on by fear, panic or sheer bad temper, as well as by provoking conduct: *ibid*. Questions put in cross-examination are not evidence: *ibid*. The observations in *Acott* are equally apt when considering whether there is sufficient evidence that a defendant was provoked, as they are when considering whether there was evidence of provoking conduct: *R. v. Miao, The Times*, November 26, 2003, CA. For the issue to be left to the jury, there has to be evidence from which a reasonable jury might conclude that the defendant was or may have been provoked: *R. v. Cambridge*, 99 Cr.App.R. 142, CA. See also *R. v. Jones (Robert James)* [2000] 3 *Archbold News* 2, CA (where the defence is self-defence, with no reliance by the defence on provocation, the judge should not leave provocation to the jury where the evidence of provoking conduct by the deceased, or the evidence that such conduct caused a loss of self-control by the defendant is minimal or fanciful).

In *Daniel v. State of Trinidad and Tobago* [2014] A.C. 1290, PC, it was held that while, in the event of dispute, it is for the judge to rule whether the issue of provocation arises on the evidence in relation to the first, subjective, limb of the test (namely, whether there was provocative behaviour and whether the defendant was in fact provoked by it to lose his self-control and kill in consequence), it is of great importance that judges respect the clear principle that the question as to whether the second, objective, limb of the test for provocation (namely, whether the provocation was such as might cause a reasonable man to act as the accused had) has been met, is a matter for the jury. Provocation has to be left to the jury, it was held, even if it is not the accused's primary case if, taking the evidence at its most favourable to the accused and remembering that the onus of proof is on the prosecution to rebut it, manslaughter by reason of provocation is a conclusion to which a jury might reasonably come. The board added that a judge could not withdraw the issue simply because he would decide the issue against the accused, nor even if he regarded the answer as obvious; but in a case where no jury, properly directed, could possibly find the test met, it is in the interests of a fair trial and of coherent law that an issue that does not arise ought not to be inserted into the jury's deliberations. As to this case, see also *ante*, § 19-56a; and *post*, § 19-75.

Where a judge is obliged to leave provocation to the jury, he should indicate to them, unless it is obvious, what evidence might support the conclusion that the defendant had lost his self-control; this is particularly important where the defence have not raised the issue: *R. v. Stewart* [1996] 1 Cr.App.R. 229, CA. See also *R. v. Humphreys* [1995] 4 All E.R. 1008, CA (similar duty where there is a complex history with several distinct strands of potentially provocative conduct, building up over time until the final encounter).

Where provocation is not left to the jury when it should have been, a conviction for manslaughter will be substituted unless the court is sure that the jury would inevitably have convicted: *R. v. Dhillon, ante*, but an appellate court should be cautious in drawing inferences or making findings about how the jury would have resolved issues which were never before them; and that is particularly so in the context of section 3, since Parliament had gone out of its way, unusually, to stipulate that resolution of the objective issue should be exclusively reserved to the jury; to the extent that an appellate court took it upon itself to decide that issue, it was doing what Parliament had said that the jury should do, and section 3 could not be read as applying only to the trial court: *Franco v. R., ante*.

In *R. v. Van Dongen and Van Dongen* [2005] 2 Cr.App.R. 38, CA, it was held that: (i) section 3 is concerned with provocative conduct, as opposed to merely causative conduct; yet a judgment that particular conduct was no more than causative risks straying into an evaluation of the objective element of the defence, which statute has left to the jury; accordingly, the prudent course for judges to take, in borderline cases, especially if the defence ask for a provocation direction to be given, is to leave the issue to the jury; (ii) where, therefore, in a case in which the defence had been self-defence and/or lack of intent and/or accident, but not provocation, there was evidence of conduct that was capable of being provoking conduct and there was evidence of a loss of self-control, the matter should have been left to the jury, more particularly as defence counsel had sought such a direction; but (iii) the failure to leave it did not mean that the conviction could not be upheld, notwithstanding that the Act specifically provides for the jury to determine the objective issue; *Franco v. R., ante*, was not authority for the proposition that a conviction could not be upheld in such circumstances; whilst it was necessary to be cautious in drawing inferences or making findings about how the jury would have resolved issues which were never before them, the court must not overlook the matter of justice for those concerned with the victim, nor the requirements of a proportionate appellate system, which included that those who were surely and fairly shown to be guilty of murder, and were so found by a jury, should not escape the consequences on gossamer grounds; where, therefore, the unavoidable facts of the case and the necessary logic of the jury's verdict ruled out any possibility of a miscarriage of justice, the conviction should be upheld.

Duty of counsel

See *R. v. Cox (A.M.)* [1995] 2 Cr.App.R. 513, CA (§ 19-61 in the main work).   **19-68**

Onus of proof

Once there is evidence from any source, sufficient to be left to the jury on the issue of provoca- **19-69** tion, the onus remains throughout upon the Crown to prove absence of provocation beyond reasonable doubt: *R. v. McPherson*, 41 Cr.App.R. 213, CCA. As to the necessity for a careful direction on onus of proof, see *R. v. Wheeler*, 52 Cr.App.R. 28, CA (§ 19-48 in the main work).

"Provoked … to lose his self control"

(i) *Meaning of "provocation"*

In *R. v. Whitfield*, 63 Cr.App.R. 39 at 42, the Court of Appeal said that the meaning of provoca- **19-70** tion was still that given to it by Devlin J. in *R. v. Duffy* [1949] 1 All E.R. 932, as cited by Lord Goddard C.J. when giving the judgment of the Court of Criminal Appeal:

> "Provocation is some act, or series of acts, done [or words spoken] [by the dead man to the accused] which would cause in any reasonable person, and actually causes in the accused, a sudden and temporary loss of self-control, rendering the accused so subject to passion as to make him or her for the moment not master of his mind" (at p.932).

The words in the first pair of square brackets were not actually said by Devlin J. but appear in the quotation of him by Lord Lane C.J. as if spoken by him (presumably to take account of the express reference to "things said" in section 3 of the 1957 Act, *ante*, § 19-66); the words in the second pair of square brackets must be ignored in view of the wording of section 3. See also *post*, § 19-73.

(ii) *Loss of self-control must be associated with the act which causes death*

The point was considered in *R. v. Ibrams and Gregory*, 74 Cr.App.R. 154, CA. Provocation is **19-71** available only in the case of a sudden and temporary loss of self-control of such a kind as to make the accused for the moment not master of his mind: see *R. v. Duffy* and *R. v. Whitfield, ante*. Circumstances which induce a desire for revenge are inconsistent with provocation, since the conscious formulation of a desire for revenge means that a person has had time to think, to reflect and that would negative a sudden temporary loss of self-control, which is the essence of provocation. But the mere existence of such circumstances does not mean that the judge should not leave the issue to the jury if there is evidence that the accused was in fact provoked; it is for the jury to decide: see *R. v. Baillie* [1995] 2 Cr.App.R. 31, CA.

(iii) *Cumulative provocation*

19-72   Although it is established that a temporary and sudden loss of self-control arising from an act of provocation is essential, it is less clear to what extent previous acts of provocation are admissible. Each case must be considered against the background of its own particular facts: *R. v. Thornton*, 96 Cr.App.R. 112, CA. In *R. v. Brown* [1972] 2 Q.B. 229, 56 Cr.App.R. 564, CA, a direction that the jury had to find provocation in something done on the morning of the killing was approved. In *R. v. Davies (P.)* [1975] Q.B. 691, 60 Cr.App.R. 253, the Court of Appeal described as "too generous" a direction that the jury could review the whole of the deceased's conduct throughout the years preceding death: and see *R. v. Ibrams and Gregory, ante*. In *R. v. Pearson* [1992] Crim.L.R. 193, the Court of Appeal substituted manslaughter for a conviction for murder on the grounds, *inter alia*, that the jury may have been left with the impression that an eight-year history of violent conduct by the deceased towards his younger son was not to be taken into account when considering the case of the elder son, who had spent much of that time away from home.

A general approach can, however, be discerned from the authorities, namely that evidence of previous provocative acts or past conduct, particularly in cases of domestic violence, is admissible in order to place in its appropriate context the reaction of the accused to the alleged provocation on the occasion of the killing: see *R. v. Thornton, ante*, at p. 118. For the proper approach in relation to a history of provocation leading to a post-traumatic stress syndrome or "battered woman syndrome", see *R. v. Ahluwalia*, 96 Cr.App.R. 133, CA, and *R. v. Thornton (No. 2)* [1996] 2 Cr.App.R. 108, CA (a jury might more easily find that there was a sudden loss of self-control triggered even by a minor incident if the defendant had endured abuse over a period, on a last-straw basis).

"Things done or said"

19-73   The things done or said may be done or said by the deceased or anyone else: *R. v. Davies (P.), ante*; *R. v. Doughty (S.)*, 83 Cr.App.R. 319, CA.

"Reasonable man"

19-74   The "reasonable man" means "an ordinary person of either sex, not exceptionally excitable or pugnacious, but possessed of such powers of self-control as everyone is entitled to expect that his fellow citizens will exercise in society as it is today": *per* Lord Diplock in *DPP v. Camplin* [1978] A.C. 705 at 771, HL; means "a man of ordinary self-control": *ibid., per* Lord Simon at p.726. Both formulations were approved by the majority in *Att.-Gen. for Jersey v. Holley* [2005] 2 A.C. 580, PC, in which an enlarged board of nine was assembled for the purpose of considering the conflict between *Camplin* and *Luc Thiet Thuan v. R.* [1997] A.C. 131, PC, on the one hand, and *R. v. Smith (Morgan)* [2001] 1 A.C. 146, HL, on the other, and to "clarify definitively the present state of English law". That it had done so was accepted by the Court of Appeal in *R. v. James; R. v. Karimi* [2006] 1 Cr.App.R. 29.

The majority opinion in *Holley* was that the jury, in deciding whether the defendant lost his self-control and, if he did, whether he did so as a result of provocation, should take the defendant exactly as they find him ("warts and all" (including that he had a violent temperament: see *R. v. Mohammed (Faqir)* [2005] 9 *Archbold News* 3, CA)); but, having assessed the gravity of the provocation to the defendant (for which purpose they must, for example, take account of the fact that he is a homosexual if taunted for his homosexuality, that he is disabled if taunted for being a "cripple", *etc.*), the standard of self-control by which his conduct is to be evaluated is the external standard of a person having and exercising the ordinary powers of self-control to be expected of a person of the defendant's age and sex. The majority ruling in *Smith* was held to be wrong in that section 3 of the 1957 Act adopted a uniform, objective standard; whether the provocative act or words and the defendant's response met the "ordinary person" standard prescribed by the statute is the question the jury must consider, not the altogether looser question (suggested by *Smith*) of whether, having regard to all the circumstances, the jury consider the loss of self-control was sufficiently excusable; the statute, it was said, does not leave each jury free to set whatever standard they consider appropriate. Accordingly, it was held to follow that if the defendant had been taunted by reference to his being an alcoholic or a drug addict, his alcoholism or addiction might be relevant to the jury's consideration of the gravity of the taunt to the defendant, but it would not be relevant to the question whether he exercised ordinary self-control.

Self-induced provocation

The mere fact that the defendant caused a reaction in others which in turn led him to lose his   **19-75**
self-control does not preclude a successful defence of provocation: *R. v. Johnson (C.)*, 89 Cr.App.R. 148, CA.

In *Edwards v. R.* [1973] A.C. 648, PC, the appellant's case was that the man whom he was blackmailing attacked him with a knife and he thereupon lost his temper and killed him. The relevant ordinance in Hong Kong was in the same terms as section 3 of the Homicide Act 1957, *ante*. The Board said (at p. 658):

> "No authority has been cited with regard to what may be called 'self-induced provocation'. On principle it seems reasonable to say that: (1) a blackmailer cannot rely on the predictable results of his own blackmailing conduct as constituting provocation sufficient to reduce his killing of the victim from murder to manslaughter, and the predictable results may include a considerable degree of hostile reaction by the person sought to be blackmailed, for instance vituperous words and even some hostile action such as blows with a fist; (2) but, if the hostile reaction by the person sought to be blackmailed goes to extreme lengths, it might constitute sufficient provocation even for a blackmailer; (3) there would in many cases be a question of degree to be decided by the jury."

In *Daniel v. State of Trinidad and Tobago* [2014] A.C. 1290, PC, it was held that there is no room for any general rule of law that provocation cannot arise because the accused himself generated the provocative conduct in issue. Subject to the proper role of the judge, the issue is for the jury, and the jury should ordinarily be directed that, if they find conduct by the accused which generates the provocative behaviour in question, that conduct will be directly relevant to both the subjective and the objective limbs of provocation. As to the subjective limb, it will go to both (a) the question whether the accused killed as a result of the provocative behaviour relied upon and (b) whether he lost self-control as a result of that behaviour. Generally, the more he generates the reaction of the deceased, the less likely it will be that he lost control and killed as a result of it; he might have been out of control from the outset, but that is not loss of control as a result of the provocative behaviour of the deceased. As to the objective limb, it will go to whether the provocative behaviour was enough to make a reasonable man in the defendant's position do as he did. Generally, the more he has himself generated the provocative behaviour, the less likely it will be that a reasonable man would have killed in consequence of it, but there may be cases where the jury may judge that the provocative behaviour may have induced a similar reaction in a reasonable man, notwithstanding the origins of the dispute between the accused and the deceased. On both limbs of the test of provocation, the extent to which the provocative behaviour relied upon was or was not a predictable result of what the accused did, *i.e.* how far it was to be expected, is itself a jury question and clearly a relevant factor, which the jury should take into account along with all the other circumstances of the killing. As to this case, see also *ante*, §§ 19-56a, 19-67.

Provocation and lies

Lies and attempts to cover up a killing are not necessarily inconsistent with provocation. In   **19-76**
directions about lies, when the issue was murder or manslaughter, the jury should be alerted to the fact that, before they could treat lies as proof of guilt of the offence charged, they had to be sure that there was not some possible explanation which destroyed their potentially probative effect. A failure to give such a direction, coupled with an indication that the jury might regard lies as probative of murder rather than manslaughter, amounted to a material misdirection: *R. v. Richens*, 98 Cr.App.R. 43, CA; *R. v. Taylor* [1998] 7 *Archbold News* 3, CA.

Provocation and good character

19-77   Where there is evidence of the defendant's good character, the judge should direct the jury as to the relevance of that both to credibility and propensity; and, in particular, should remind them that, as a man of good character, the defendant might have been unlikely to indulge in serious violence without first being provoked: *Paria v. R.* [2004] Crim.L.R. 228, PC.

Sentence

19-78   See the guideline issued by the Sentencing Guidelines Council (*post*, K-71 *et seq.*). Of the pre-guideline authorities, see, in particular, *Att.-Gen.'s References (Nos 74, 95 and 118 of 2002) (R. v. Suratan; R. v. Humes; R. v. Wilkinson)* [2003] 2 Cr.App.R.(S.) 42, CA, which is summarised at paragraph 2.1 of the guideline (Appendix K-74).

See also *R. v. Brook (Neil)*, § 5-520 in the main work.

B. Manslaughter

(8) Sentence

Involuntary manslaughter

★19-134   Authorities predating *Att.-Gen.'s Reference (No. 60 of 2009) (R. v. Appleby)* (as to which, see the main work) are now of no real value in considering the appropriate level of sentence in unlawful act manslaughter cases (in particular, *R. v. Carter* [2003] 2 Cr.App.R.(S.) 88, CA, is not to be regarded as representing good current sentencing guidance): *Att.-Gen.'s Reference (No. 36 of 2015) (R. v. Nicholles)* [2015] Crim.L.R. 918, CA.

★   The bracket for "one-punch" manslaughter cases, after trial, is now of the order of four to six years' imprisonment; *R. v. Furby* (as to which, see the main work) was an extreme case, and *Att.-Gen.'s Reference (No. 60 of 2009) (R. v. Appleby)*, *ante*, had signalled an upward movement for all manslaughter cases: *R. v. Lynch* [2015] 2 Cr.App.R.(S.) 73, CA.

19-136   *R. v. H.* and *R. v. Masefield* (as to both of which, see the main work) were followed in *R. v. Bell*, *ante*, § 5-531.

C. Corporate Manslaughter

(1) The offence

Corporate Manslaughter and Corporate Homicide Act 2007, s.1

The offence

★19-140   The Sentencing Council for England and Wales has now issued a definitive guideline on, *inter alia*, corporate manslaughter. It will replace the guideline issued by the Sentencing Guidelines Council in 2010. It applies to all organisations sentenced on or after February 1, 2016, regardless of the date of the offence. For the details, see *post*, Appendix K-252 *et seq.*

IV. COMMON ASSAULT AND BATTERY

C. Defences

Defence of property

★19-239   Where three people share a flat, each having their own bedroom, any one of them would be entitled to use reasonable force to remove either of the other two from their bedroom if they refused to leave upon being requested to do so; and the same would apply to a guest of any one of them who was sharing a bedroom; where, therefore, two females and a male shared a flat, each with their own bedroom, a female friend (the appellant) of one of the females would have been entitled to use reasonable force to eject the male flatmate from the bedroom that she was sharing with her friend, and the judge had been wrong not to leave the issue of reasonable force used for this purpose to the jury on the ground that, as a guest in the premises, she had no entitlement to use force: *R. v. Day*, unreported, April 17, 2015, CA ([2015] EWCA Crim. 1646).

VI. WOUNDING, CAUSING GRIEVOUS BODILY HARM

(5) Sentence

Racial or religious aggravation

For a case considering whether sentence could be passed for an offence under section 20 of the **19-257a** Offences against the Person Act 1861 (§ 19-252 in the main work) on the basis that the offence was racially aggravated where there was no count under section 29 of the CDA 1998 (*ibid.*, § 19-266), see *R. v. O'Leary, ante*, § 5-122.

VII. RACIALLY OR RELIGIOUSLY AGGRAVATED OFFENCES

(4) Sentence

For a case considering whether sentence could be passed for an offence under section 20 of the **19-269** Offences against the Person Act 1861 (§ 19-252 in the main work) on the basis that the offence was racially aggravated where there was no count under section 29 of the CDA 1998 (§ 19-266 in the main work), see *R. v. O'Leary, ante*, § 5-122.

IX. OFFENCES IN RELATION TO POLICE OFFICERS

A. ASSAULTS

In the execution of duty

Common law

In *McCann v. CPS* [2016] 1 Cr.App.R. 6, it was held: (i) whereas it had been said in *Rice v. Con-* **19-329** *nolly* (as to which, see the main work), that it is "part of the obligations and duties of a police constable to take all steps which appear to him to be necessary for keeping the peace, for preventing crime or for protecting property from criminal injury", this should today be read with the word "reasonably" inserted before the word "appear"; (ii) it followed that, where a police officer reasonably believed that the appellant was committing an offence of obstruction of the highway (Highways Act 1980, s.137), she was acting in the execution of her duty in directing the appellant to move where it reasonably appeared necessary to her that the appellant should move in order to prevent continuation of the offence; and this was so even though she was mistaken as to the appellant committing an offence under section 137 as the road in question was a private road; and it made no difference that, in giving the direction to move, she referred to the incorrect offence; and (iii) it further followed that, in refusing to move, the appellant was obstructing the officer in the execution of her duty, and that the officer had grounds for arresting the appellant on suspicion of committing an offence under section 137 (albeit she was not in fact committing such offence), and for an offence of obstructing a constable in the execution of her duty (Police Act 1996, s.89(2)), of which she had been properly convicted. The court also considered *O'Hara v. Chief Constable of the Royal Ulster Constabulary* and *R. (Rawlinson & Hunter Trustees) v. Central Criminal Court; R. (Tchenguiz) v. Director of the Serious Fraud Office* (as to both of which, see § 15-15 in the main work), and *B. v. DPP* (*ibid.*, § 15-41)).

X. OFFENCES INVOLVING THE CAUSING OF ALARM OR DISTRESS TO ANOTHER OR AN INTENT TO DO SO

A. HARASSMENT (INCLUDING BY STALKING)

(1) Introduction

Crawford v. Jenkins is now reported at [2015] 3 W.L.R. 843. **19-337**

C. CONTROLLING OR COERCIVE BEHAVIOUR

Serious Crime Act 2015, s.76

Controlling or coercive behaviour in an intimate or family relationship

With effect from December 29, 2015 (Serious Crime Act 2015 (Commencement No. 4) Regula- **★19-358** tions 2015 (S.I. 2015 No. 1976)), section 76 of the 2015 Act was brought into force.

XII. FEMALE GENITAL MUTILATION

Duty to notify police of female genital mutilation

★**19-368o**   With effect from October 31, 2015 (Serious Crime Act 2015 (Commencement No. 3) Regulations 2015 (S.I 2015 No. 1809)), section 74 of the 2015 Act (see the main work) was brought into force.

Guidance

★**19-368p**   With effect from October 31, 2015 (Serious Crime Act 2015 (Commencement No. 3) Regulations 2015 (S.I 2015 No. 1809)), section 75 of the 2015 Act (see the main work) was brought into force.

XV. TORTURE, SLAVERY AND HUMAN TRAFFICKING

B. SLAVERY AND HUMAN TRAFFICKING

(1) Offences

Modern Slavery Act 2015, ss.1-5

Human trafficking

★**19-440**   *R. v. Ali and Ashraf* is now reported at [2015] 2 Cr.App.R. 33, *sub nom. R. v. Ali (Yasir).*

CHAPTER 20

SEXUAL OFFENCES

II. OFFENCES

A. GENERAL INTERPRETATION

(1) Consent

Sexual Offences Act 2003, s.74

"Consent"

★**20-10a**   *R. v. Ali and Ashraf* is now reported at [2015] 2 Cr.App.R. 33, *sub nom. R. v. Ali (Yasir).*

N. TRAFFICKING

Modern Slavery Act 2015

★**20-182**   *R. v. Ali and Ashraf* is now reported at [2015] 2 Cr.App.R. 33, *sub nom. R. v. Ali (Yasir).*

IV. NOTIFICATION AND ORDERS

D. SEXUAL HARM PREVENTION ORDERS

(2) Legislation

Sexual Offences Act 2003, ss.103A-103K

Sexual harm prevention orders: applications and grounds

★**20-324**   The appellant police chief should not have had costs awarded against him (under the Courts Act 1971, s.52(3)) where he had made an application for a sexual offences prevention order and had subsequently withdrawn it because the respondent had moved out of the appellant's police area: *Chief Constable of Warwickshire Police v. M.T.*, 179 J.P. 454, QBD (Hickinbottom J.). The application had been made under section 104(5) of the 2003 Act. Whilst that section has now been repealed, the provisions of subsections (4) and (5) of section 103A of the 2003 Act (taken together (see the main work)) are in materially the same terms.

The making of a sexual harm prevention order (2003 Act, s.103A (§ 20-324 in the main work)) ★**20-328** was held to have been appropriate for an offence of distributing an indecent photograph of a child (Protection of Children Act 1978, s.1(1)(b) (*ibid.*, § 31-107)) in *R. v. Bingham* [2016] 1 Cr.App.R.(S.) 3, CA. The appellant contacted the complainant (17, but autistic, and functioned as if 12) online and showed him a video of a man in non-penetrative sexual activity with a child of primary school age, claiming this was live footage, and asked the complainant to show the child his penis. The court said that it was understandable that the appellant should have relied on *R. v. Smith* (as to which, see the main work), but distinguished the factual situations. The court reasoned that not every case of distribution will warrant such an order, and distribution to a 17-year-old will not necessarily demonstrate a risk to younger children; it all depends on the facts; and whilst the requirement of necessity must not be diluted, this was not simple distribution; it was distribution to a young person for a particular purpose, *viz.* to entice him to expose himself to the offender. As to *Smith*, it should also be noted that the threshold for making a sexual harm prevention order is lower than that for a sexual offences prevention order (with which the court in *Smith* was concerned). The court did not refer to this lowering of the bar (as to which, see § 20-325 in the main work).

CHAPTER 21

OFFENCES UNDER THE THEFT AND FRAUD ACTS

II. THEFT

(4) Sentence

The Sentencing Council for England and Wales has issued a definitive guideline on "theft of- **21-24** fences", *viz.* "general theft" (Theft Act 1968, s.1 (§ 21-15 in the main work)), theft from a shop or stall (*ibid.*), abstracting electricity (s.13 of the 1968 Act (*ibid.*, § 21-169)) handling stolen goods (s.22 of the 1968 Act (*ibid.*, § 21-221)), going equipped for theft or burglary (s.25 of the 1968 Act (*ibid.*, § 21-288)), and making off without payment (Theft Act 1978, s.3 (*ibid.*, § 21-303)). It applies to all offenders aged 18 or over who are sentenced on or after February 1, 2016. For the details, see *post*, Appendix K-315 *et seq.*

(5) Elements of the offence of theft

(d) *"Property"*

Intangible property

The decision of the New Zealand Court of Appeal in *Dixon v. The Queen* (as to which, see the ★**21-51** main work) has been reversed: *Dixon v. The Queen*, unreported, October 20, 2015, Supreme Court of New Zealand ([2015] NZSC 147). It was held that digital files did come within the definition of "property". As it was outside the scope of the appeal, the court did not consider what the Court of Appeal had described as the "orthodox view" that "pure information" is not "property".

III. ROBBERY AND ASSAULT WITH INTENT TO ROB

A. ROBBERY

(4) Sentence

Guideline cases

The Sentencing Council for England and Wales has issued a definitive guideline on robbery of- ★**21-90** fences (Theft Act 1968, s.8(1) (§ 21-84 in the main work)), which are divided into "street and less sophisticated commercial" robberies, "professionally planned commercial" robberies, and robberies in a dwelling. It applies to all offenders aged 18 and over who are sentenced on or after April 1, 2016, regardless of the date of the offence. For the detail, see *post*, Appendix K-80a *et seq.*

Street robberies, robberies of small businesses, and "less sophisticated commercial robberies"

★**21-93**   As to a new guideline applying to all robberies, but applying only to those aged 18 and over, see *ante*, § 21-90. The preamble to that guideline makes clear that the guideline of the Sentencing Guidelines Council (*post*, Appendix K-80) will continue to apply to the sentencing of youths pending a replacement guideline being issued.

VI. TAKING CONVEYANCES WITHOUT AUTHORITY

B. THE AGGRAVATED OFFENCE

(6) Elements of the offence

"Owing to the driving of the vehicle"

★**21-166**   Whereas section 12A(2)(b) of the Theft Act 1968 (§ 21-158 in the main work) makes a person guilty of an offence if he commits the basic offence of taking a vehicle without authority, contrary to section 12(1) of the 1968 Act (*ibid.*, § 21-141) and, "owing to the driving of the vehicle, an accident occurred by which injury was caused to any person", the test set out in *R. v. Hughes* (see the main work), in relation to the offence contrary to section 3ZB of the RTA 1988 (§ 32-72 in the main work), is to be applied to the offence under section 12A(2)(b), *viz.* there must be "at least some act or omission in the control of the car, which involves some element of fault, whether amounting to careless or inconsiderate driving or not, and which contributes in some more than minimal way" to the injury; the driving could not be said to have caused the accident if it merely explained how the vehicle came to be in the place where the accident occurred: *R. v. Taylor (Jack)* [2016] 1 W.L.R. 500, SC (effectively overruling *R. v. Marsh* (as to which, see the main work)).

VII. ABSTRACTION OF ELECTRICITY

(4) Sentence

21-172   As to the new sentencing guideline on "theft offences", including the offence of abstraction of electricity (s.13 of the Theft Act 1968 (§ 21-169 in the main work)), see *ante*, § 21-24.

XIII. HANDLING STOLEN PROPERTY

(4) Sentence

Guidelines

21-232   As to the new sentencing guideline on "theft offences", including the offence of handling stolen goods (s.22 of the Theft Act 1968 (§ 21-221 in the main work)), see *ante*, § 21-24.

XV. GOING EQUIPPED TO STEAL

(4) Sentence

21-291   As to the new sentencing guideline on "theft offences", including the offence of going equipped for theft or burglary (s.25 of the Theft Act 1968 (§ 21-288 in the main work)), see *ante*, § 21-24.

XVII. THEFT ACT 1978

C. MODE OF TRIAL AND PENALTIES

Theft Act 1978, s.4

Punishments

21-308   As to the new sentencing guideline on "theft offences", including the offence of making off without payment (s.3 of the Theft Act 1978 (§ 21-303 in the main work)), see *ante*, § 21-24.

XVIII. FRAUD ACT

A. Fraud

(5) The elements of the offence

(d) *Fraud by abuse of position*

Position

R. v. Valujevs is now reported at [2015] Q.B. 745.   ★21-340

Abuse of the position

In *R. v. T.J.C.* [2015] Crim.L.R. 1018, CA, the defendant held a lasting power of attorney in   ★21-341
relation to her father. His bills were paid from his bank account, but, *inter alia*, "significant sums"
were drawn from his accounts and transferred to hers. The defendant had admitted spending
some money on herself and others in a manner not in her father's best interests, and the indictment charged her with fraud by abuse of position (Fraud Act 2006, ss.1 and 4 (§§ 21-310, 21-313
in the main work)) between dates that were 28 months apart, but without identifying payments
said to be fraudulent or dishonest. Where the prosecution declined to produce further particulars
and accepted that they could not identify particular transactions as being unlawful, it was held
that the judge had been wrong to stay the count on the ground that it would be unfair and an
abuse of process to try the defendant in the absence of further particulars; this was a case where
the prosecution alleged a "general deficiency" of funds that they contended had been misap-
propriated, not that specific transactions were unlawful; and the indictment was sufficient for such
a purpose. The court said that the case was similar to *R. v. Tomlin* (§ 1-224 in the main work),
with the difference that it was not possible to arrive at the exact amount of the general deficiency.
It added that the judge should merely have required the prosecution to set out the case being
made in relation to general deficiency, which could easily have been done by a written opening
note. For critical consideration of this case, see CLW/15/42/4.

Chapter 24

FIREARMS AND OFFENSIVE WEAPONS

I. FIREARMS

A. Firearms Act 1968

(2) Offences relating to firearms certificates

"Air weapon"

The purpose of the words "which does not fall within section 5(1) and which is" (in section   ★24-11
1(3)(b) of the 1968 Act (§ 24-4 in the main work), and which were inserted by the Anti-social
Behaviour Act 2003, s.39(1) and (2)) was to impose a requirement of certification in relation to air
weapons falling within section 5(1)(af) (inserted by the 2003 Act, s.39(1) and (3)): *R. v. Law
(Nathan)* [2016] 1 Cr.App.R. 13, CA. As to this case, see also *post*, § 24-32.

(4) Prohibited weapons and ammunition

Firearms Act 1968, s.5

R. v. Goldsborough is now reported at [2015] 2 Cr.App.R. 29.   ★24-25

Special exemptions from prohibition of small firearms

In *R. v. Law (Nathan)* [2016] 1 Cr.App.R. 13, CA (as to which, see also *ante*, § 24-11), it was held   ★24-32
that the effect of the words "other than an air weapon" in section 5(1)(aba) (which was inserted by

the Firearms (Amendment) Act 1997, s.1(2)) was, when taken with section 1(3)(b) (§ 24-4 in the main work), to exclude only those air weapons that were not specially dangerous. For a submission that this conclusion was wrong, and that section 5(1)(aba) excludes all air weapons, see the commentary at CLW/16/02/6.

CHAPTER 25

OFFENCES AGAINST THE CROWN AND GOVERNMENT

III. TERRORISM

A. TERRORISM ACT 2000

Terrorism Act 2000, s.1

Terrorism: interpretation

★**25-13**   In *R. (Miranda) v. Secretary of State for the Home Department (Liberty intervening)*, unreported, January 19, 2016, CA (Civ. Div.) ([2016] EWCA Civ. 6), the court considered the definition of "terrorism" in section 1 of the 2000 Act, and held that "action" falling within subsection (2) has to be considered as importing a mental element; if Parliament had intended to provide that a person could commit an act of terrorism (and thus be a "terrorist") unwittingly or accidentally, it would have spelt this out clearly; publication of material can therefore amount to an act of terrorism under section 1(2)(c) or (d), but only if the person publishing it intends it to have (or is reckless as to whether it has) the effect set out in paragraph (c) or (d). As to this case, see also *ante*, § 16-39; and *post*, § 25-124a.

Terrorism Act 2000, Sched. 5

Terrorist investigations: searches

★**25-101**   As to *Sher v. Chief Constable of Greater Manchester* (as to which, see the main work), an application by the claimant to the European Court of Human Rights was unsuccessful: see *Sher v. U.K., The Times*, January 15, 2016. It was held that the specificity of the list of items susceptible to seizure in a search conducted by law enforcement officers will vary according to the nature of the allegations; allegations of a planned large-scale terrorist attack pose particular challenges, since, while there may be sufficient evidence to give rise to a reasonable suspicion that an attack is under preparation, an absence of specific information about the intended nature of the attack or its targets will make precise identification of the items to be sought during a search impossible; and the complexity of such cases may justify a search based on terms that are wider than would otherwise be permissible; multiple suspects and use of coded language compound the difficulties faced by the police in seeking to identify in advance of a search the specific nature of the items and documents to be sought; and the urgency of the situation cannot be ignored; to impose a requirement that a search warrant identify in detail the precise nature of the items sought could seriously jeopardise the effectiveness of an investigation where numerous lives might be at stake; in cases of this nature, the police must be permitted some flexibility to assess, on the basis of what is encountered during the search, which items might be linked to terrorist activities, and to seize them for further examination. As to this case, see also *post*, § 25-158.

Excluded and special procedure material: production & access

★**25-107**   For rules about production orders and orders to grant entry under paragraph 5 of Schedule 5 to the 2000 Act (§ 25-106 in the main work), see *ante*, §§ 15-272 *et seq.*

★**25-110**   As to the substitution of Part 47 of S.I. 2015 No. 1490 (see the main work), see *ante*, §§ 15-272 *et seq.*

Excluded or special procedure material: search

★**25-111**   For rules about applications for search warrants under paragraph 11 of Schedule 5 to the 2000 Act (see the main work), see *ante*, §§ 15-272 *et seq.*

Explanations

As to the substitution of Part 47 of S.I. 2015 No. 1490 (see the main work), see *ante*, §§ 15-272 **★25-113** *et seq.*

Terrorism Act 2000, Sched. 6A

Rules of court

As to the substitution of Part 47 of S.I. 2015 No. 1490 (see the main work), see *ante*, §§ 15-272 **★25-120** *et seq.*

Terrorism Act 2000, Sched. 7

Beghal v. DPP (Secretary of State for the Home Department intervening) is now reported at [2016] **★25-124a** A.C. 88.

In *R. (Miranda) v. Secretary of State for the Home Department (Liberty intervening)*, unreported, **★** January 19, 2016, CA (Civ. Div.) ([2016] EWCA Civ. 6), it was held (upholding, in part, the decision of the Divisional Court (as to which, see the main work), but for different reasons): (i) the "true and dominant purpose" (*R. v. Southwark Crown Court, ex p. Bowles* (as to which, see § 15-252 in the main work)) for stopping the claimant (which can be judged by reference to the state of mind of the examining officers' superior officers: *R. (Pearce) v. Metropolitan Police Commr* (as to which, see § 15-87 in the main work)) was, on the evidence, to determine whether the claimant (the partner of a journalist who was believed to be carrying "stolen encrypted material, the release or compromise of which would be likely to cause very great damage to security interests and possible loss of life") appeared to be a "terrorist" (having regard to the definition of "terrorism" in s.1 of the 2000 Act (as to which, see *ante*, § 25-13)), as permitted by Schedule 7; the fact that the stop also promoted the Security Service's different but overlapping purpose (to ascertain the nature of the material which the claimant was carrying and, if on examination it proved to be as was feared, to neutralise the effect of its release (or further release) or dissemination) did not mean that the power was not exercised for the Schedule 7 purpose; in determining whether the true and dominant purpose fell within Schedule 7, it was permissible to take account of intelligence supplied by the Security Service to the superior officers of the examining officers where that was a factor in the superior officers' instruction to the examining officers to carry out the stop; (ii) on the facts, the stop involved no violation of Article 10 of the ECHR (freedom of expression (§ 16-157, in the main work)); it was prescribed by law, pursued a legitimate aim and was proportionate, even though those directing the minds of the examining officers were aware that the material carried by the claimant might be journalistic material; when determining the proportionality of a decision taken by the police in the interests of national security, the court should accord a substantial degree of deference to their expertise in assessing the risk to national security and in weighing it against countervailing interests; further, the greater the potential harm, the greater the weight that should be accorded to community interests; however (iii) in general, the power under Schedule 7 is incompatible with Article 10 in relation to journalistic material, in that it is not subject to adequate safeguards against its arbitrary exercise; in particular, the availability of judicial review, after the event, cannot cure a breach of Article 10 resulting from the disclosure of a confidential source or other confidential material. As to this case, see also *ante*, §§ 16-39, 25-13.

Terrorism Act 2000, Sched. 8

Destruction and retention of fingerprints and samples etc: United Kingdom

As to the substitution of Part 47 of S.I. 2015 No. 1490 (see the main work), see *ante*, § 15-272. **★25-145b**

As to the substitution of Part 47 of S.I. 2015 No. 1490 (see the main work), see *ante*, § 15-272 **★25-145g**

Article 7 of the Protection of Freedoms Act 2012 (Destruction, Retention and Use of Biometric **25-145j** Data) (Transitional, Transitory and Saving Provisions) Order 2013 (S.I. 2013 No. 1813) (as to which, see the main work) has been amended by Protection of Freedoms Act 2012 (Destruction, Retention and Use of Biometric Data) (Transitional, Transitory and Saving Provisions) (Amendment) Order 2015 (S.I. 2015 No. 1739) so as to substitute "October 31, 2016" for "October 31, 2015".

Warrants of further detention

As to *Sher v. Chief Constable of Greater Manchester* (as to which, see the main work), an application **★25-158** by the claimant to the European Court of Human Rights was unsuccessful: see *Sher v. U.K., The Times*, January 15, 2016. The court held (in agreement with the Divisional Court) that the procedure for applying for a warrant of further detention, in relation to a person arrested as a suspected terrorist under section 41 of the 2000 Act (§ 25-52 in the main work), is not incompatible with Article 5(4) of the ECHR (right to review of lawfulness of detention under Art. 5(1)(c) (*ibid.*, § 16-53)) by reason of (a) the fact that it allows evidence to be given in closed session (see Sched. 8, para. 33 (*ibid.*, § 25-157)), or (b) the fact that it makes no provision for the appointment of a special advocate. As to (a), the court said that, terrorism falling into a special category, Article 5(4) cannot require disclosure of confidential sources of supporting information or even facts that would be susceptible of indicating such sources or their identity or preclude the holding of a closed hearing to allow a court to consider confidential material; but the authorities must disclose adequate information to enable the applicant to know the nature of the allegations against him and have the opportunity to lead evidence to refute them; they must also ensure that the applicant or his legal advisers are able effectively to participate in court proceedings concerning continued detention. As to (b), the court pointed out that the Divisional Court had held that a district judge hearing an application for a warrant of further detention did have power to appoint a special advocate if he considered such appointment necessary to secure the fairness of the proceeding. As to this case, see also *ante*, § 25-101.

★ In *Magee v. U.K.* (2016) 62 E.H.R.R. 10, it was held that the detention of the applicants, who had been arrested under section 41 of the 2000 Act (§ 25-52 in the main work), for 12 days under Schedule 8 to the 2000 Act, prior to their release without charge, involved no violation of Article 5 of the ECHR. That the judicial authority considering applications for warrants of further detention was not empowered to order conditional release was of no relevance.

IV. IMMIGRATION

Immigration Act 1971, ss.25-25C

★**25-292**   In *Att.-Gen.'s References (Nos 49 and 50 of 2015) (R. v. Bakht)* [2016] 1 Cr.App.R.(S.) 4, CA, the court had regard to *R. v. Oliveira*; *R. v. Cina* (as to which, see the main work), in listing the following factors as being relevant to sentencing in a case of conspiracy to contravene section 25 of the 1971 Act: (a) whether the offence was isolated or repeated, (b) the duration of the offending, (c) whether the offenders had previous similar convictions, (d) whether the motivation was commercial or humanitarian, (e) the number of individuals involved in the breach, (f) whether they were strangers or family, (g) the degree of organisation involved, (h) whether the offenders recruited others, (i) the offender's role, and (j) whether the conduct involved exploitation of, or pressure put upon, others.

XI. OFFENCES RELATING TO POSTS AND TELECOMMUNICATIONS

C. REGULATION OF INVESTIGATORY POWERS ACT 2000

Compatibility with ECHR

★**25-385a**   For a case considering, *inter alia*, *Kennedy v. U.K.*, see *R.E. v. U.K.*, *ante*, § 15-205.

Regulation of Investigatory Powers Act 2000, ss.21-23B

Obtaining and disclosing communications data

★**25-400**   The decision of the Divisional Court in *R. (Davis) v. Secretary of State for the Home Department (Open Rights Group intervening)* is now reported at [2016] Crim.L.R. 48, *sub nom. R. (Davis) v. Secretary of State for the Home Department*.

★ On an appeal against the decision of the Divisional Court (see the main work and *ante*), two questions were referred to the Court of Justice of the European Union (*viz.* (i) "Did the court in *Digital Rights Ireland Ltd* [see the main work] intend to lay down mandatory requirements of European Union law with which the national legislation of member states must comply?" and (2) "Did the court in *Digital Rights Ireland Ltd* intend to expand the effect of Articles 7 (right to privacy and family life) and/or 8 (right to the protection of personal data) of the Charter of

Fundamental Rights of the European Union beyond the effect of Article 8 [(§ 16-137) in the main work)] of the ECHR as established in the jurisprudence of the European Court of Human Rights?"): see *R. (Davis) v. Secretary of State for the Home Department (Open Rights Group intervening)*, unreported, November 20, 2015, CA (Civ. Div.) ([2015] EWCA Civ. 1185) (expressing the provisional view that the decision in *Digital Rights* did not go so far as to lay down specific mandatory requirements of European Union law with which national legislation had to comply).

Criminal Procedure Rules 2015 (S.I. 2015 No. 1490), rr.47.50–47.52

Investigation approval orders

As to the substitution, with effect from April 4, 2016, of Part 47 of S.I. 2015 No. 1490 (see the main work), see *ante*, § 15-272. The provision made by the former rules 47.27 and 47.28 is now made by rules 47.50 to 47.52.

★25-401c

Criminal Procedure Rules 2015 (S.I. 2015 No. 1490), rr.47.50–47.52 (as substituted by the Criminal Procedure (Amendment) Rules 2016 (S.I. 2016 No. 120), r.15)

Section 7: Investigation approval orders under the Regulation of Investigatory Powers Act 2000

When this Section applies

47.50. This Section applies where a justice of the peace can make an order approving—

★25-401d

   (a) the grant or renewal of an authorisation, or the giving or renewal of a notice, under section 23A of the Regulation of Investigatory Powers Act 2000;

   (b) the grant or renewal of an authorisation under section 32A of the 2000 Act.

Exercise of court's powers

47.51.—(1) This rule applies where a magistrates' court refuses to approve the grant, giving or renewal of an authorisation or notice.

★25-401e

(2) The court must not exercise its power to quash that authorisation or notice unless the applicant has had at least 2 business days from the date of the refusal in which to make representations.

Application for approval for authorisation or notice

47.52.—(1) This rule applies where an applicant wants a magistrates' court to make an order approving—

★25-401f

   (a) under sections 23A and 23B of the Regulation of Investigatory Powers Act 2000—

      (i) an authorisation to obtain or disclose communications data, under section 22(3) of the 2000 Act, or

      (ii) a notice that requires a postal or telecommunications operator if need be to obtain, and in any case to disclose, communications data, under section 22(4) of the 2000 Act;

   (b) under sections 32A and 32B of the Regulation of Investigatory Powers Act 2000, an authorisation for—

      (i) the carrying out of directed surveillance, under section 28 of the 2000 Act, or

      (ii) the conduct or use of a covert human intelligence source, under section 29 of the 2000 Act.

(2) The applicant must—

   (a) apply in writing and serve the application on the court officer;

   (b) attach the authorisation or notice which the applicant wants the court to approve;

   (c) attach such other material (if any) on which the applicant relies to satisfy the court—

      (i) as required by section 23A(3) and (4) of the 2000 Act, in relation to communications data,

      (ii) as required by section 32A(3) and (4) of the 2000 Act, in relation to directed surveillance, or

      (iii) as required by section 32A(5) and (6), and, if relevant, section 43(6A), of the 2000 Act, in relation to a covert human intelligence source; and

   (d) propose the terms of the order.

XIII. REVENUE AND CUSTOMS OFFENCES

B. Customs and Excise Management Act 1979

(2) Definitions and application

Customs and Excise Management Act 1979, s.5

Time of importation, exportation, etc.

★**25-428**   As to the application of section 5 of the 1979 Act (see the main work), from a day to be appointed, in relation to the importation or exportation of psychoactive substances, see section 55(2) and (4) of the Psychoactive Substances Act 2016 (*post*, § 27-186).

(11) General powers of examination and search

Customs and Excise Management Act 1979, s.164

Power of search

★**25-468**   As to the application of section 164 of the 1979 Act (see § 25-467 in the main work), from a day to be appointed, to psychoactive substances, see section 55 of the Psychoactive Substances Act 2016 (*post*, § 27-186).

(13) Fraudulent evasion offences

Taking steps to evade excise duty

Customs and Excise Management Act 1979, s.170B

Offence of taking preparatory steps for evasion of excise duty

★**25-505**   A conviction under section 170B(1) of the 1979 Act is not required before goods can be liable to forfeiture under subsection (2): *Amber Services Europe Ltd v. Director of Border Revenue* (2016) 160(5) S.J. 43, DC ([2015] EWHC 3665 (Admin.)).

CHAPTER 26

MONEY LAUNDERING OFFENCES

I. PROCEEDS OF CRIME ACT 2002

B. Offences

(4) Legislation

Proceeds of Crime Act 2002, s.327

Concealing, etc., criminal property

26-12   Where a defendant is charged with converting criminal property, contrary to section 327(1)(c) of the PCA 2002 (§ 26-11 in the main work), the prosecution can rely upon alternative or several allegations of different criminal conduct, provided that they can prove at least one to the criminal standard to the satisfaction of the jury; the decisions in *Prosecution Appeal (No. 11 of 2007)*; *R. v. W.* and *R. v. Anwoir* (as to both of which, see the main work), as to the necessity to identify the criminal conduct, are reconciled by "the clear adjudication in each" that criminal conduct, specific or generic, has to be evidenced and proved to the criminal standard; however, a specific crime or criminal conduct does not have be specified and proved by the prosecution; the statute does not support that narrow construction, and neither *R. v. W. (N.)* nor *R. v. Anwoir* supports such a proposition: *R. v. Kuchhadia* [2015] 2 Cr.App.R. 32, CA.

★   In *R. v. Ogden*, unreported, January 26, 2016, CA ([2016] EWCA Crim. 6), it was held (considering *R. v. Loizou* (as to which, see the main work)) that, if A, being in possession of a controlled drug (within the Misuse of Drugs Act 1971 (§§ 27-5 *et seq.* in the main work)), agrees with B to supply it to B (who is aware that the substance in question is a controlled drug), A and B will be guilty of a conspiracy to convert criminal property, contrary to section 1 of the CLA 1977 (*ibid.*, § 33-2), and section 327(1)(c) of the 2002 Act; "illegal [*sic*] drugs always represent criminal property". The court commented that, whilst this would entail every person who buys "illicit" drugs even for their own personal use also being guilty of an offence under section 327, the spectre of the authorities charging offences under that Act in such circumstance is unreal, as "good sense" would prevail. For criticism of the decision, see CLW/16/05/3.

For a case considering whether an indictment alleging several money laundering offences (contrary to s.327) in a single count was bad for duplicity or uncertainty, see *R. v. William, post*, § 26-52. ★**26-13**

D. Interpretation

Proceeds of Crime Act 2002, ss.339A, 340

In *R. v. William* [2015] Lloyds Rep. F.C. 704, CA, it was held: (i) whereas an offence under section 327 of the PCA 2002 (§ 26-11 in the main work) is committed where, *inter alia*, a person converts or transfers criminal property, and whereas section 340(3) (*ibid.*, § 26-51) provides that "(3) Property is criminal property if - (a) it constitutes a person's benefit from criminal conduct or it represents such a benefit (in whole or part and whether directly or indirectly), and (b) the alleged offender knows or suspects that it constitutes or represents such a benefit.", the reference to "in whole or part" shows that the whole property is treated as criminal property, even where only part of it represents benefit from criminal conduct; (ii) the effect of section 340(6) is that someone who cheats the revenue by failing to pay the tax he should pay (such as W, who had pleaded guilty to 10 counts of cheating the public revenue (the three appellants, W's wife (X) and daughters (Y and Z) were convicted of offences under s.327 in relation to the funnelling of large sums of money, coming from W, into and out of accounts in their names)) has obtained a pecuniary advantage and is to be taken to have obtained a benefit equal to the value of the tax unpaid (considering *R. v. K. (I.)* (as to which, see § 26-53 in the main work)); in cases where turnover is falsely represented, the benefit is the tax due on the undeclared turnover; however, the criminal property (as defined by s.340) is the entirety of the undeclared turnover, and not merely the tax due because the benefit is represented in part by that sum; (iii) where the appellants submitted that the indictment (which alleged that they "on multiple occasions between [two dates five years apart] converted and transferred criminal property, namely ...") was bad for duplicity (and/ or uncertainty), while there was no doubt that the count alleged multiple offending (because on each occasion money was taken out of the account, an offence would have been completed), and while in general this was not permitted, what is now rule 10.2(2) of the Criminal Procedure Rules 2015 (S.I. 2015 No. 1490) (*ibid.*, § 1-188) does permit an indictment to be framed in this way in certain circumstances, for example, where there is no identifiable victim, as in money laundering cases. ★**26-52**

As to whether "illegal" drugs always represent "criminal property" for the purposes of Part 7 of the 2002 Act, see *R. v. Ogden, ante*, § 26-12.

E. Sentence

Proceeds of Crime Act 2002, s.334

As to sentencing considerations where a person is convicted of a money laundering offence under Part 7 of the PCA 2002, but the prosecution allege, and the court accepts, that the underlying criminal activity in which the defendant was himself involved was dealing in controlled drugs, see *R. v. Ogden, post*, Appendix K-626a. ★**26-55**

CHAPTER 27

HARMFUL OR DANGEROUS DRUGS

A. INTRODUCTION

(3) Definition of a "controlled drug"

Misuse of Drugs Act 1971, s.2

Temporary class drug orders

★**27-5a**   With effect from November 27, 2015, the Misuse of Drugs Act 1971 (Temporary Class Drug) (No. 3) Order 2015 (S.I. 2015 No. 1929), specifies the following substances and products as drugs subject to temporary control—

> "(a) N-methyl-1-(thiophen-2-yl)propan-2-amine (methiopropamine or MPA);
> (b) any stereoisomeric form of N-methyl-1-(thiophen-2-yl)propan-2-amine;
> (c) any salt of a substance specified in paragraph (a) or (b); and
> (d) any preparation or other product containing a substance specified in any of paragraphs (a) to (c)."

The order stipulates that the provisions of the Misuse of Drugs (Safe Custody) Regulations 1973 (S.I. 1973 No. 798) (see § 27-91 in the main work) apply to these substances and products (art. 3(1)), and that the Misuse of Drugs Regulations 2001 (S.I. 2001 No. 3998) (see § 27-83 in the main work) are to apply to them as if they were specified as controlled drugs to which Schedule 1 to those regulations applied (art. 3(2)). The specified substances and products will cease to be subject to temporary control after one year, or, if earlier, upon the coming into force of an order under section 2(2) listing them in Schedule 2 to the 1971 Act (s.2A(6) of the 1971 Act).

(5) Interpretation

Intoxicating substances

★**27-19**   As from a day to be appointed, the Intoxicating Substances (Supply) Act 1985 (see the main work) is repealed by the Psychoactive Substances Act 2016, s.60, and Sched. 5, para. 1(1).

F. AUTHORISATION OF ACTIVITIES OTHERWISE UNLAWFUL UNDER SECTIONS 3 TO 6

Misuse of Drugs Act 1971, ss.7, 7A

★**27-83**   As to the application of the Misuse of Drugs Regulations 2001 (S.I. 2001 No. 3998) (as to which, see the main work) to the substances and products subject to the Misuse of Drugs Act 1971 (Temporary Class Drug) (No. 3) Order 2015 (S.I. 2015 No. 1929), see *ante*, § 27-5a.

J. POWERS OF SECRETARY OF STATE FOR PREVENTING MISUSE OF CONTROLLED DRUGS

Misuse of Drugs Act 1971, s.10

★**27-91**   As to the application of the Misuse of Drugs (Safe Custody) Regulations 1973 (S.I. 1973 No. 798) (as to which, see the main work) to the substances and products subject to the Misuse of Drugs Act 1971 (Temporary Class Drug) (No. 3) Order 2015 (S.I. 2015 No. 1929), see *ante*, § 27-5a.

V. PSYCHOACTIVE SUBSTANCES

(1) Background

★**27-131**   The Psychoactive Substances Act 2016 creates a blanket ban on the production, distribution, sale and supply of psychoactive substances in the United Kingdom. The Act is intended to counter the increasing emergence of new substances or products that are designed to mimic the effects of traditional drugs. These substances are known collectively as "new psychoactive substances" and, together with other substances which have been used as intoxicants for many years, are often referred to as "legal highs". Many such substances are only legal because they have not yet been assessed for their harm and considered for control under the 1971 Act, not because they are inherently safe to use. Such is the speed and scale at which new substances are now emerging and such their diversity, that regulation on a substance by substance, or even group by group, basis has resulted in a significant time lag between a new psychoactive substance coming onto the market and a response under the 1971 Act. The 2016 Act aims to address that difficulty by a blanket prohibition.

Section 1 (not set out *post*) merely provides an "overview" of the Act. Sections 2 and 3 define "psychoactive substance" and "exempted substance". Sections 4 to 11 provide for offences of production, supply or offering to supply, possession with intent to supply, importing or exporting, and possession in a custodial institution of a psychoactive substance, and for penalties on conviction. The offences are triable either way and the maximum sentence on conviction on indictment is seven years' imprisonment (two years in the case of a s.9 offence). Sections 12 to 35 provide for prohibition notices, premises notices, prohibition orders and premises orders and offences of failing to comply with such orders. Sections 36 to 48 provide for powers of entry, search and seizure. Sections 49 to 54 provide for the retention and disposal of seized items. Sections 55 to 63 contain supplementary and final matters. Schedule 1 lists exempt substances. Schedule 2 lists exempted activities. Schedule 3 applies to applications for search warrants and their execution.

(2) Commencement

Sections 59 and 61 to 63 of the 2016 Act, and any power to make regulations under the Act,　★**27-132** came into force on Royal Assent (January 28, 2016): s.63(1). The remainder of the Act comes into force on a day to be appointed: s.63(2).

(3) Psychoactive substances and exempted substances

Psychoactive Substances Act 2016, ss.2, 3

Meaning of "psychoactive substance" etc.
　2.—(1) In this Act "psychoactive substance" means any substance which—　★**27-133**
　　(a)　is capable of producing a psychoactive effect in a person who consumes it, and
　　(b)　is not an exempted substance (see section 3).
　(2) For the purposes of this Act a substance produces a psychoactive effect in a person if, by stimulating or depressing the person's central nervous system, it affects the person's mental functioning or emotional state; and references to a substance's psychoactive effects are to be read accordingly.
　(3) For the purposes of this Act a person consumes a substance if the person causes or allows the substance, or fumes given off by the substance, to enter the person's body in any way.

Exempted substances
　3.—(1) In this Act "exempted substance" means a substance listed in Schedule 1.　★**27-134**
　(2) The Secretary of State may by regulations amend Schedule 1 in order to—
　　(a)　add or vary any description of substance;
　　(b)　remove any description of substance added under paragraph (a).
　(3) Before making any regulations under this section the Secretary of State must consult—
　　(a)　the Advisory Council on the Misuse of Drugs, and
　　(b)　such other persons as the Secretary of State considers appropriate.
　(4) The power to make regulations under this section is exercisable by statutory instrument.
　(5) A statutory instrument containing regulations under this section may not be made unless a draft of the instrument has been laid before, and approved by a resolution of, each House of Parliament.

(3) Offences

Psychoactive Substances Act 2016, ss.4-11

Producing a psychoactive substance
　4.—(1) A person commits an offence if—　★**27-135**

    (a)   the person intentionally produces a psychoactive substance,

    (b)   the person knows or suspects that the substance is a psychoactive substance, and

    (c)   the person—

        (i)   intends to consume the psychoactive substance for its psychoactive effects, or

        (ii) knows, or is reckless as to whether, the psychoactive substance is likely to be consumed by some other person for its psychoactive effects.

    (2) This section is subject to section 11 (exceptions to offences).

Supplying, or offering to supply, a psychoactive substance

★**27-136**   **5.**—(1) A person commits an offence if—

    (a)   the person intentionally supplies a substance to another person,

    (b)   the substance is a psychoactive substance,

    (c)   the person knows or suspects, or ought to know or suspect, that the substance is a psychoactive substance, and

    (d)   the person knows, or is reckless as to whether, the psychoactive substance is likely to be consumed by the person to whom it is supplied, or by some other person, for its psychoactive effects.

    (2) A person ("P") commits an offence if—

    (a)   P offers to supply a psychoactive substance to another person ("R"), and

    (b)   P knows or is reckless as to whether R, or some other person, would, if P supplied a substance to R in accordance with the offer, be likely to consume the substance for its psychoactive effects.

    (3) For the purposes of subsection (2)(b), the reference to a substance's psychoactive effects includes a reference to the psychoactive effects which the substance would have if it were the substance which P had offered to supply to R.

    (4) This section is subject to section 11 (exceptions to offences).

Aggravation of offence under section 5

★**27-137**   **6.**—(1) This section applies if—

    (a)   a court is considering the seriousness of an offence under section 5, and

    (b)   at the time the offence was committed the offender was aged 18 or over.

    (2) If condition A, B or C is met the court—

    (a)   must treat the fact that the condition is met as an aggravating factor (that is to say, a factor that increases the seriousness of the offence), and

    (b)   must state in open court that the offence is so aggravated.

    (3) Condition A is that the offence was committed on or in the vicinity of school premises at a relevant time.

    (4) For the purposes of subsection (3) a "relevant time" is—

    (a)   any time when the school premises are in use by persons under the age of 18;

    (b)   one hour before the start and one hour after the end of any such time.

    (5) In this section—

    "school premises" means land used for the purposes of a school, other than any land occupied solely as a dwelling by a person employed at the school;

    "school" has the same meaning—

        (a) in England and Wales, as in section 4 of the Education Act 1996;

        (b), (c) *[Scotland and Northern Ireland]*.

    (6) Condition B is that in connection with the commission of the offence the offender used a courier who, at the time the offence was committed, was under the age of 18.

    (7) For the purposes of subsection (6) a person ("P") uses a courier in connection with an offence under section 5 if P causes or permits another person (the courier)—

    (a)   to deliver a substance to a third person, or

    (b)   to deliver a drug-related consideration to P or a third person.

    (8) A drug-related consideration is a consideration of any description which—

    (a) is obtained in connection with the supply of a psychoactive substance, or

    (b) is intended to be used in connection with obtaining a psychoactive substance.

    (9) Condition C is that the offence was committed in a custodial institution.

    (10) In this section—

    "custodial institution" means any of the following—

        (a) a prison;

        (b) a young offender institution, secure training centre, secure college, young offenders institution, young offenders centre, juvenile justice centre or remand centre;

(c) a removal centre, a short-term holding facility or pre-departure accommodation;

(d) service custody premises;

"removal centre", "short-term holding facility" and "pre-departure accommodation" have the meaning given by section 147 of the Immigration and Asylum Act 1999;

"service custody premises" has the meaning given by section 300(7) of the Armed Forces Act 2006.

Possession of psychoactive substance with intent to supply

7.—(1) A person commits an offence if—　　　　　　　　　　　　　　　　　　★**27-138**

(a) the person is in possession of a psychoactive substance,

(b) the person knows or suspects that the substance is a psychoactive substance, and

(c) the person intends to supply the psychoactive substance to another person for its consumption, whether by any person to whom it is supplied or by some other person, for its psychoactive effects.

(2) This section is subject to section 11 (exceptions to offences).

Importing or exporting a psychoactive substance

8.—(1) A person commits an offence if—　　　　　　　　　　　　　　　　　　★**27-139**

(a) the person intentionally imports a substance,

(b) the substance is a psychoactive substance,

(c) the person knows or suspects, or ought to know or suspect, that the substance is a psychoactive substance, and

(d) the person—

(i) intends to consume the psychoactive substance for its psychoactive effects, or

(ii) knows, or is reckless as to whether, the psychoactive substance is likely to be consumed by some other person for its psychoactive effects.

(2) A person commits an offence if—

(a) the person intentionally exports a substance,

(b) the substance is a psychoactive substance,

(c) the person knows or suspects, or ought to know or suspect, that the substance is a psychoactive substance, and

(d) the person—

(i) intends to consume the psychoactive substance for its psychoactive effects, or

(ii) knows, or is reckless as to whether, the psychoactive substance is likely to be consumed by some other person for its psychoactive effects.

(3) In a case where a person imports or exports a controlled drug suspecting it to be a psychoactive substance, the person is to be treated for the purposes of this section as if the person had imported or exported a psychoactive substance suspecting it to be such a substance.

In this subsection "controlled drug" has the same meaning as in the Misuse of Drugs Act 1971 .

(4) Section 5 of the Customs and Excise Management Act 1979 (time of importation, exportation, etc) applies for the purposes of this section as it applies for the purposes of that Act.

(5) This section is subject to section 11 (exceptions to offences).

For section 5 of the 1979 Act, see § 25-428 in the main work.

Possession of a psychoactive substance in a custodial institution

9.—(1) A person commits an offence if—　　　　　　　　　　　　　　　　　　★**27-140**

(a) the person is in possession of a psychoactive substance in a custodial institution,

(b) the person knows or suspects that the substance is a psychoactive substance, and

(c) the person intends to consume the psychoactive substance for its psychoactive effects.

(2) In this section "custodial institution" has the same meaning as in section 6.

(3) This section is subject to section 11 (exceptions to offences).

Penalties

10.—(1) A person guilty of an offence under any of sections 4 to 8 is liable—　　★**27-141**

(a) on summary conviction in England and Wales—

(i) to imprisonment for a term not exceeding 12 months (or 6 months, if the offence was committed before the commencement of section 154(1) of the Criminal Justice Act 2003), or

(ii) to a fine,

or both;

(b), (c) [*Scotland and Northern Ireland*];

    (d) on conviction on indictment, to imprisonment for a term not exceeding 7 years or a fine, or both.

  (2) A person guilty of an offence under section 9 is liable—

    (a) on summary conviction in England and Wales—

       (i) to imprisonment for a term not exceeding 12 months (or 6 months, if the offence was committed before the commencement of section 154(1) of the Criminal Justice Act 2003), or

      (ii) to a fine,

    or both;

    (b), (c) [*Scotland and Northern Ireland*];

    (d) on conviction on indictment, to imprisonment for a term not exceeding 2 years or a fine, or both.

Exceptions to offences

★27-142   **11.**—(1) It is not an offence under this Act for a person to carry on any activity listed in subsection (3) if, in the circumstances in which it is carried on by that person, the activity is an exempted activity.

  (2) In this section "exempted activity" means an activity listed in Schedule 2.

  (3) The activities referred to in subsection (1) are—

    (a) producing a psychoactive substance;

    (b) supplying such a substance;

    (c) offering to supply such a substance;

    (d) possessing such a substance with intent to supply it;

    (e) importing or exporting such a substance;

    (f) possessing such a substance in a custodial institution (within the meaning of section 9).

  (4) The Secretary of State may by regulations amend Schedule 2 in order to—

    (a) add or vary any description of activity;

    (b) remove any description of activity added under paragraph (a).

  (5)-(7) [*Identical to s.3(3)-(5), ante, § 27-134.*]

(5) Powers for dealing with prohibited activities

Psychoactive Substances Act 2016, ss.12-35

Meaning of "prohibited activity"

★27-143   **12.**—(1) In this Act "prohibited activity" means any of the following activities—

    (a) producing a psychoactive substance that is likely to be consumed by individuals for its psychoactive effects;

    (b) supplying such a substance;

    (c) offering to supply such a substance;

    (d) importing such a substance;

    (e) exporting such a substance;

    (f) assisting or encouraging the carrying on of a prohibited activity listed in any of paragraphs (a) to (e).

  (2) The carrying on by a person of an activity listed in any of paragraphs (a) to (e) of subsection (1) is not the carrying on of a prohibited activity if the carrying on of the activity by that person would not be an offence under this Act by virtue of section 11.

★27-144   **13.** [*Prohibition notices prohibitions.*]

★27-145   **14.** [*Premises notices.*]

★27-146   **15.** [*Prohibition notices and premises notices: supplementary.*]

★27-147   **16.** [*Further provision about giving notices under sections 13 to 15.*]

Meaning of "prohibition order"

★27-148   **17.**—(1) In this Act a "prohibition order" means an order prohibiting the person against whom it is made from carrying on any prohibited activity or a prohibited activity of a description specified in the order.

  (2) A prohibition order may be made—

    (a) on application (see section 18), or

    (b) following conviction of an offence under any of sections 4 to 8 or a related offence (see section 19).

(3) For the meaning of "prohibited activity", see section 12.

18. [*Prohibition orders on application.*] ★**27-149**

Prohibition orders following conviction

19.—(1) Where a court is dealing with a person who has been convicted of a relevant offence, the ★**27-150** court may make a prohibition order under this section if the court considers it necessary and proportionate for the purpose of preventing the person from carrying on any prohibited activity.

(2) A prohibition order may not be made under this section except—

(a) in addition to a sentence imposed in respect of the offence concerned, or

(b) in addition to an order discharging the person conditionally or, in Scotland, discharging the person absolutely.

(3) If a court makes a prohibition order under this section, any prohibition notice that has previously been given to the person against whom the order is made is to be treated as having been withdrawn.

(4) A prohibition order under this section made against an individual who is under the age of 18 at the time the order is made—

(a) must specify the period for which it has effect, and

(b) may not have effect for more than 3 years.

(5) In this section "relevant offence" means—

(a) an offence under any of sections 4 to 8;

(b) an offence of attempting or conspiring to commit an offence under any of sections 4 to 8;

(c) an offence under Part 2 of the Serious Crime Act 2007 in relation to an offence under any of sections 4 to 8;

(d) an offence of inciting a person to commit an offence under any of sections 4 to 8;

(e) an offence of aiding, abetting, counselling or procuring the commission of an offence under any of sections 4 to 8.

20. [*Premises orders.*] ★**27-151**

21. [*Applications for prohibition orders and premises orders.*] ★**27-152**

Provision that may be made by prohibition orders and premises orders

22.—(1) A court making a prohibition order or a premises order, or a court varying such an order ★**27-153** under or by virtue of any of sections 28 to 31, may by the order impose any prohibitions, restrictions or requirements that the court considers appropriate (in addition to the prohibition referred to in section 17(1) or the requirement referred to in section 20(2) (as the case may be)).

(2) Subsections (3) to (6) contain examples of the type of provision that may be made under subsection (1), but they do not limit the type of provision that may be so made.

(3) The prohibitions, restrictions or requirements that may be imposed on a person by a prohibition order or a premises order include prohibitions or restrictions on, or requirements in relation to, the person's business dealings (including the conduct of the person's business over the internet).

(4) The requirements that may be imposed on a person by a prohibition order include a requirement to hand over for disposal an item belonging to the person that the court is satisfied—

(a) is a psychoactive substance, or

(b) has been, or is likely to be, used in the carrying on of a prohibited activity.

(5) An item that is handed over in compliance with a requirement imposed by virtue of subsection (4) may not be disposed of—

(a) before the end of the period within which an appeal may be made against the imposition of the requirement (ignoring any power to appeal out of time), or

(b) if such an appeal is made, before it is determined or otherwise dealt with.

(6) The prohibitions that may be imposed on a person by a prohibition order or a premises order include a prohibition prohibiting access to premises owned, occupied, leased, controlled or operated by the person for a specified period (an "access prohibition").

(7) The period specified under subsection (6) may not exceed 3 months (but see subsections (3) to (5) of section 28).

(8) An access prohibition may prohibit access—

(a) by all persons, or by all persons except those specified, or by all persons except those of a specified description;

(b) at all times, or at all times except those specified;

(c) in all circumstances, or in all circumstances except those specified.

(9) An access prohibition may—

(a) be made in respect of the whole or any part of the premises;

(b)   include provision about access to a part of the building or structure of which the premises form part.

(10) In this section "specified" means specified in the prohibition order or the premises order (as the case may be).

(11) Subsection (6) of section 14 (when a person "owns" premises) applies for the purposes of subsection (6) of this section as it applies for the purposes of that section.

★**27-154**   **23.** [*Enforcement of access prohibitions.*]

★**27-155**   **24.** [*Access prohibitions: reimbursement of costs.*]

★**27-156**   **25.** [*Access prohibitions: exemption from liability.*]

Offence of failing to comply with a prohibition order or premises order

★**27-157**   **26.**—(1) A person against whom a prohibition order or a premises order is made commits an offence by failing to comply with the order.

(2) A person guilty of an offence under this section is liable—

(a)   on summary conviction in England and Wales—

(i)   to imprisonment for a term not exceeding 12 months (or 6 months, if the offence was committed before the commencement of section 154(1) of the Criminal Justice Act 2003), or

(ii)   to a fine,

or both;

(b), (c)   [*Scotland and Northern Ireland*];

(d)   on conviction on indictment, to imprisonment for a term not exceeding 2 years or a fine, or both.

(3) A person does not commit an offence under this section if—

(a)   the person took all reasonable steps to comply with the order, or

(b)   there is some other reasonable excuse for the failure to comply.

★**27-158**   **27.** [*Summary offences of failing to comply with access prohibition in prohibition order or premises order, and of obstructing, without reasonable excuse, a person acting under s.23(1).*]

Variation and discharge on application

★**27-159**   **28.**—(1) The court may vary or discharge a prohibition order or a premises order on the application of—

(a)   the person who applied for the order (if any),

(b)   the person against whom the order was made, or

(c)   any other person who is significantly adversely affected by the order.

(2) Where a prohibition order is made under section 19, the court may also vary or discharge the order on the application of—

(a)   in the case of an order made in England and Wales, the chief officer of police for a police area or the chief constable of the British Transport Police Force;

(b)   in the case of an order made in Scotland, the Lord Advocate or a procurator fiscal;

(c)   in the case of an order made in Northern Ireland, the chief constable of the Police Service of Northern Ireland;

(d)   in the case of an order made in England and Wales or Northern Ireland, the Director General of the National Crime Agency;

(e)   in the case of an order made in England and Wales or Northern Ireland, the Secretary of State by whom general customs functions are exercisable.

(3) Subsection (4) applies where—

(a)   a prohibition order or a premises order imposes an access prohibition (see section 22(6)), and

(b)   an application for the variation of the order is made by the person who applied for the order, or by a person mentioned in subsection (2), before the expiry of the period for which the access prohibition has effect.

(4) Where this subsection applies, the court may vary the order by extending (or further extending) the period for which the access prohibition has effect.

(5) The period for which an access prohibition has effect may not be extended so that it has effect for more than 6 months.

(6) In this section "the court" means—

(a)   the court that made the order, except where paragraph (b) or (c) applies;

(b)   where—

> (i) the order was made under section 19 on an appeal in relation to a person's conviction or sentence for an offence, or
>
> (ii) the order was made by a court under that section against a person committed or remitted to that court for sentencing for an offence,
>
> the court by or before which the person was convicted (but see subsection (7));

(c) where the court that made the order was a youth court but the person against whom the order was made is aged 18 or over at the time of the application, a magistrates' court or, in Northern Ireland, a court of summary jurisdiction.

(7) Where the person mentioned in subsection (6)(b)—

(a) was convicted by a youth court, but

(b) is aged 18 or over at the time of the application,

the reference in subsection (6)(b) to the court by or before which the person was convicted is to be read as a reference to a magistrates' court or, in Northern Ireland, a court of summary jurisdiction.

(8) An order that has been varied under this section remains an order of the court that first made it for the purposes of—

(a) section 24;

(b) any further application under this section.

Variation following conviction

29.—(1) This section applies where—   ★**27-160**

(a) a court is dealing with a person who has been convicted of a relevant offence and against whom a prohibition order or a premises order has previously been made, or

(b) a court is dealing with a person who has been convicted of an offence under section 26 of failing to comply with a prohibition order or a premises order.

(2) The court may vary the prohibition order or (as the case may be) the premises order.

(3) An order that has been varied under subsection (2) remains an order of the court that first made it for the purposes of sections 24 and 28.

(4) An order may not be varied under this section except—

(a) in addition to a sentence imposed in respect of the offence concerned, or

(b) in addition to an order discharging the person conditionally or, in Scotland, discharging the person absolutely.

(5) In this section "relevant offence" has the same meaning as in section 19.

Appeals against making of prohibition orders and premises orders

30.—(1)-(4) [*Orders made under section 18 or 20.*]   ★**27-161**

(5) A person against whom a prohibition order is made under section 19 may appeal against the making of the order as if it were a sentence passed on the person for the offence referred to in section 19(1) (to the extent it would not otherwise be so appealable).

Appeals about variation and discharge

Decisions under section 28

31.—(1) [*Appeal against a decision under s.28 of a magistrates' court shall be to the Crown Court.*]   ★**27-162**

(2) The right of appeal under subsection (1) is exercisable by—

(a) the person against whom the relevant order was made, and

(b) any other person who is significantly adversely affected by that order.

(3) In subsections (1) and (2) the "relevant order" means the order that was the subject of the application under section 28.

(4) An appeal under subsection (1) against the making of a decision must be made before the end of the period of 28 days starting with the date of the decision.

(5) On an appeal under subsection (1) the court hearing the appeal may (to the extent it would not otherwise have power to do so) make such orders as may be necessary to give effect to its determination of the appeal, and may also make such incidental or consequential orders as appear to it to be just.

(6) A prohibition order or a premises order that has been varied by virtue of subsection (5) remains an order of the court that first made it for the purposes of sections 24 and 28.

Decisions under section 29

(7) A person against whom a prohibition order or a premises order has been made may appeal against a variation of the order under section 29 as if the varied order were a sentence passed on the person for the offence referred to in section 29(1) (to the extent it would not otherwise be so appealable).

Nature of proceedings under sections 19 and 29, etc.

32.—(1) Proceedings before a court arising by virtue of section 19 or 29 are civil proceedings (like   ★**27-163**
court proceedings under section 18, 20 or 28).

(2) The standard of proof to be applied by the court in the proceedings is the balance of probabilities.

(3) The court is not restricted in the proceedings to considering evidence that would have been admissible in the criminal proceedings in which the person concerned was convicted.

(4) The court may adjourn any proceedings arising by virtue of section 19 or 29 even after sentencing the person concerned.

(5) [*Scotland.*]

(6) A prohibition order may be made or varied as mentioned in section 19(2)(b) or 29(4)(b) (as the case may be) in spite of anything in the following provisions (which relate to orders discharging a person conditionally or absolutely and their effect)—

    (a) sections 12 and 14 of the Powers of Criminal Courts (Sentencing) Act 2000;

    (b), (c) [*Scotland and Northern Ireland*].

Special measures for witnesses: England and Wales

★**27-164**
    33.—(1) Chapter 1 of Part 2 of the Youth Justice and Criminal Evidence Act 1999 (special measures directions in the case of vulnerable and intimidated witnesses) applies to relevant proceedings under this Act as it applies to criminal proceedings, but with—

    (a) the omission of the provisions of that Act mentioned in subsection (2) (which make provision only in the context of criminal proceedings), and

    (b) any other necessary modifications.

(2) The provisions are—

    (a) section 17(4) to (7);

    (b) section 21(4C)(e);

    (c) section 22A;

    (d) section 32.

(3) Rules of court made under or for the purposes of Chapter 1 of Part 2 of that Act apply to relevant proceedings under this Act—

    (a) to the extent provided by rules of court, and

    (b) subject to any modifications provided by rules of court.

(4) Section 47 of that Act (restrictions on reporting special measures directions etc.) applies with any necessary modifications—

    (a) to a direction under section 19 of that Act as applied by this section;

    (b) to a direction discharging or varying such a direction.

Sections 49 and 51 of that Act (offences) apply accordingly.

(5) In this section "relevant proceedings under this Act" means—

    (a) proceedings in England and Wales under section 18, 20, 28, 30 or 31, and

    (b) proceedings in England and Wales arising by virtue of section 19 or 29.

★**27-165**
    34. [*Special measures for witnesses: Northern Ireland.*]

★**27-166**
    35. [*Transfer of proceedings from youth court.*]

(6) Powers of entry search and seizure

Psychoactive Substances Act 2016, ss.36-48

Power to stop and search persons

★**27-167**
    36.—(1) This section applies where a police or customs officer has reasonable grounds to suspect that a person has committed, or is likely to commit, an offence under any of sections 4 to 9 or section 26.

(2) The officer may—

    (a) search the person for relevant evidence, and

    (b) stop and detain the person for the purposes of the search.

(3) The powers conferred by this section may be exercised in any place to which the officer lawfully has access (whether or not it is a place to which the public has access).

(4) In this Act—

"police or customs officer" means—

    (a) a constable,

    (b) a general customs official, or

    (c) a designated NCA officer authorised by the Director General of the National Crime Agency (whether generally or specifically) to exercise the powers of a police or customs officer under this Act;

"relevant evidence" means evidence that an offence has been committed under any of sections 4 to 9 or section 26 .

Power to enter and search vehicles

37.—(1) This section applies where—   ★**27-168**
  (a) a police or customs officer has reasonable grounds to suspect that there is relevant evidence in a vehicle, and
  (b) the vehicle is not a dwelling.
(2) The officer may at any time—
  (a) enter the vehicle and search it for relevant evidence;
  (b) stop and detain the vehicle for the purposes of entering and searching it.
(3) Where—
  (a) a police or customs officer has stopped a vehicle under this section, and
  (b) the officer considers that it would be impracticable to search the vehicle in the place where it has stopped,
the officer may require the vehicle to be taken to such place as the officer directs to enable the vehicle to be searched.
(4) A police or customs officer may require—
  (a) any person travelling in a vehicle, or
  (b) the registered keeper of a vehicle,
to afford such facilities and assistance with respect to matters under that person's control as the officer considers would facilitate the exercise of any power conferred by this section.
(5) The powers conferred by this section may be exercised in any place to which the officer lawfully has access (whether or not it is a place to which the public has access).
(6) In this section "vehicle" does not include any vessel or aircraft.
(7) For provision conferring additional powers to enter and search vehicles, see section 39.

Power to board and search vessels or aircraft

38.—(1) This section applies where—   ★**27-169**
  (a) a police or customs officer has reasonable grounds to believe that there is relevant evidence in or on any vessel or aircraft, and
  (b) the vessel or aircraft is not a dwelling.
(2) The officer may at any time—
  (a) board the vessel or aircraft, and
  (b) search it for relevant evidence.
(3) For the purposes of exercising the power conferred by subsection (2), the officer may require a vessel or aircraft—
  (a) to stop, or
  (b) to do anything else that will facilitate the boarding of that or any other vessel or aircraft.
(4) A police or customs officer who has boarded a vessel or aircraft may, for the purposes of disembarking from the vessel or aircraft, require that or any other vessel or aircraft—
  (a) to stop, or
  (b) to do anything else that will enable the officer to disembark from the vessel or aircraft.
(5) A police or customs officer may require any person on board a vessel or aircraft to afford such facilities and assistance with respect to matters under that person's control as the officer considers would facilitate the exercise of any power conferred by this section.
(6) For provision conferring additional powers to enter and search vessels and aircraft, see section 39.

Power to enter and search premises

39.—(1) Where a justice is satisfied that the requirements in subsection (4) are met in relation to   ★**27-170**
any premises, the justice may issue a warrant (a "search warrant") authorising a relevant enforcement officer—
  (a) to enter the premises, and
  (b) to search them for relevant evidence.
(2) A search warrant may be issued only on the application of—
  (a) a relevant enforcement officer, in England and Wales or Northern Ireland;
  (b) a relevant enforcement officer or a procurator fiscal, in Scotland.
(3) A search warrant may be either—
  (a) a warrant that relates only to premises specified in the warrant (a "specific-premises warrant"), or

(b) in the case of a warrant issued in England and Wales or Northern Ireland, a warrant that relates to any premises occupied or controlled by a person specified in the warrant (an "all-premises warrant").

(4) The requirements of this subsection are met in relation to premises if there are reasonable grounds to suspect that—

    (a) there are items on the premises that are relevant evidence, and

    (b) in a case where the premises are specified in the application, any of the conditions in subsection (5) is met.

(5) The conditions referred to in subsection (4)(b) are—

    (a) that it is not practicable to communicate with any person entitled to grant entry to the premises;

    (b) that it is not practicable to communicate with any person entitled to grant access to the items;

    (c) that entry to the premises is unlikely to be granted unless a warrant is produced;

    (d) that the purpose of entry may be frustrated or seriously prejudiced unless a relevant enforcement officer arriving at the premises can secure immediate entry to them.

(6) In this Act "relevant enforcement officer" means—

    (a) a police or customs officer (see section 36(4)), or

    (b) an officer of a local authority.

Further provision about search warrants

★**27-171**   **40.**—(1) An application for a search warrant may be made without notice being given to persons who might be affected by the warrant.

(2) The application must be supported—

    (a) in England and Wales, by an information in writing;

    (b), (c) [*Scotland and Northern Ireland*].

(3) A person applying for a search warrant must answer on oath any question that the justice hearing the application asks the person.

In the case of an application made by a procurator fiscal, that requirement may be met by a relevant enforcement officer.

(4) A search warrant may be executed by any relevant enforcement officer.

(5) A search warrant may authorise persons to accompany any relevant enforcement officer who is executing it.

(6) A person authorised under subsection (5) to accompany a relevant enforcement officer may exercise any power conferred by sections 39 to 45 which the officer may exercise as a result of the warrant.

But the person may exercise such a power only in the company of, and under the supervision of, a relevant enforcement officer.

(7) Schedule 3 contains further provision about—

    (a) applications for search warrants made in England and Wales or Northern Ireland, and

    (b) search warrants issued in England and Wales or Northern Ireland.

(8) An entry on or search of premises under a search warrant issued in England and Wales or Northern Ireland is unlawful unless it complies with the provisions of Part 3 of that Schedule (execution of search warrants).

Powers of examination, etc.

★**27-172**   **41.**—(1) This section applies where a relevant enforcement officer is exercising a power of search conferred by section 37, 38 or 39 in relation to any premises.

(2) The officer may examine anything that is in or on the premises.

(3) The officer may carry out any measurement or test of anything which the officer has power under this section to examine.

(4) The power conferred by subsection (3) includes power to take a sample from any live plant.

(5) For the purpose of exercising—

    (a) a power of search conferred by section 37, 38 or 39, or

    (b) any power conferred by this section,

the officer may, so far as is reasonably necessary for that purpose, break open any container or other locked thing.

(6) The officer may require any person in or on the premises to afford such facilities and assistance with respect to matters under that person's control as the officer considers would facilitate the exercise of—

(a) a power of search conferred by section 37, 38 or 39, or

(b) any power conferred by this section.

(7) Nothing in this section confers any power to search a person.

Power to require production of documents, etc

42.—(1) This section applies where a relevant enforcement officer is exercising a power of search ★**27-173** conferred by section 37, 38 or 39 in relation to any premises.

(2) The officer may require any person in or on the premises to produce any document or record that is in the person's possession or control.

(3) A reference in this section to the production of a document includes a reference to the production of—

(a) a hard copy of information recorded otherwise than in hard copy form, or

(b) information in a form from which a hard copy can be readily obtained.

(4) For the purposes of this section—

(a) information is recorded in hard copy form if it is recorded in a paper copy or similar form capable of being read (and references to hard copy have a corresponding meaning);

(b) information can be read only if—

(i) it can be read with the naked eye, or

(ii) to the extent that it consists of images (for example photographs, pictures, maps, plans or drawings), it can be seen with the naked eye.

Powers of seizure, etc

43.—(1) A police or customs officer who is exercising the power of search conferred by section 36 ★**27-174** may seize and detain anything found in the course of the search.

(2) This subsection applies where a relevant enforcement officer—

(a) is exercising a power of search conferred by section 37, 38 or 39 in relation to any premises, or

(b) is otherwise lawfully on premises.

(3) Where subsection (2) applies, the officer may—

(a) seize and detain or remove any item found on the premises;

(b) take copies of or extracts from any document or record found on the premises.

(4) A relevant enforcement officer to whom any document or record has been produced in accordance with a requirement imposed under section 42 may—

(a) seize and detain or remove that document or record;

(b) take copies of or extracts from that document or record.

In this subsection "document" includes anything falling within paragraph (a) or (b) of section 42(3).

(5) The powers under this section may only be exercised—

(a) for the purposes of determining whether an offence under any of sections 4 to 9 or section 26 has been committed, or

(b) in relation to an item which a relevant enforcement officer reasonably believes to be—

(i) relevant evidence, or

(ii) a psychoactive substance (whether or not it is relevant evidence).

(6) Nothing in this section confers power on a relevant enforcement officer to seize an item which is an excluded item (see section 44).

Excluded items

44.—(1) This section defines what is meant by "excluded items" for the purposes of section 43. ★**27-175**

(2) In England and Wales "excluded items" means—

(a) items subject to legal privilege, within the meaning of the Police and Criminal Evidence Act 1984 (see section 10 of that Act);

(b) excluded material, within the meaning of that Act (see section 11 of that Act);

(c) special procedure material, within the meaning of that Act (see section 14 of that Act).

(3), (4)

[*Scotland and Northern Ireland.*]

Further provision about seizure under section 43

45.—(1) Where— ★**27-176**

(a) any items which a relevant enforcement officer wishes to seize and remove are in a container, and

(b)   the officer reasonably considers that it would facilitate the seizure and removal of the items if they remained in the container for that purpose,

any power to seize and remove the items conferred by section 43 includes power to seize and remove the container.

(2) If a container is seized under this section, reasonable efforts must be made to return it to—

(a)   the person from whom it was seized, or

(b)   (if different) a person to whom it belongs.

(3) Subsection (2) does not apply—

(a)   if the container appears to be of negligible value,

(b)   if it is not practicable for the container to be returned, or

(c)   while the container is or may be needed for use as evidence at a trial for an offence.

(4) If, in the opinion of a relevant enforcement officer, it is not for the time being practicable for the officer to seize and remove any item, the officer may require—

(a)   the person from whom the item is being seized, or

(b)   where the officer is exercising a power of search conferred by section 37, 38 or 39 in relation to any premises, any person in or on the premises,

to secure that the item is not removed or otherwise interfered with until such time as the officer may seize and remove it.

Notices and records in relation to seized items

★**27-177**   **46.**—(1) This section applies where a relevant enforcement officer, or a person accompanying a relevant enforcement officer, seizes any item under section 43.

(2) When the item is seized, the officer must make reasonable efforts to give written notice to each of the following persons—

(a)   in the case of an item seized from a person, the person from whom the item was seized;

(b)   in the case of an item seized from premises, any person who appears to the officer to be the occupier of the premises or otherwise to be in charge of the premises;

(c)   if the officer thinks that the item may belong to any person not falling within paragraph (a) or (b), that other person.

A person falling within any of paragraphs (a) to (c) is referred to in this section as an "affected person".

(3) If—

(a)   the item is seized from premises, and

(b)   at the time of the seizure it is not reasonably practicable to give a notice to any affected person,

the officer must leave a copy of the notice in a prominent place on the premises.

(4) The notice must—

(a)   state what has been seized and the reason for its seizure;

(b)   specify any offence which the officer believes has been committed;

(c)   explain the effect of sections 49 to 51 and 53.

(5) The officer must make a record of what has been seized.

(6) If a person who appears to a relevant enforcement officer to be an affected person asks for a copy of that record, the officer must, within a reasonable time, provide a copy of that record to that person.

Powers of entry, search and seizure: supplementary provision

★**27-178**   **47.**—(1) A relevant enforcement officer may use reasonable force, if necessary, for the purpose of exercising any power conferred by sections 36 to 45.

(2) A person authorised under section 40(5) to accompany a relevant enforcement officer may use reasonable force, if necessary, for the purpose of exercising any power conferred by sections 39 to 45.

(3) The powers conferred on a relevant enforcement officer by any of sections 36 to 45 do not affect any powers exercisable by the officer apart from that section.

Offences in relation to enforcement officers

★**27-179**   **48.**—(1) A person commits an offence if, without reasonable excuse, the person intentionally obstructs a relevant enforcement officer in the performance of any of the officer's functions under sections 36 to 45.

(2) A person commits an offence if—

(a)   the person fails without reasonable excuse to comply with a requirement reasonably made,

or a direction reasonably given, by a relevant enforcement officer in the exercise of any
power conferred by sections 37 to 45, or

(b) the person prevents any other person from complying with any such requirement or
direction.

(3) In this section any reference to a relevant enforcement officer includes a reference to a person
authorised under section 40(5) to accompany a relevant enforcement officer.

(4) A person who is guilty of an offence under this section is liable—

(a) on summary conviction in England and Wales, to either or both of the following—

(i) imprisonment for a term not exceeding 51 weeks (or 6 months, if the offence was
committed before the commencement of section 281(5) of the Criminal Justice Act
2003);

(ii) a fine;

(b), (c)[*Scotland and Northern Ireland*].

(7) Retention and disposal of items

Psychoactive Substances Act 2016, ss.49-54

Retention of seized items

49.—(1) This section applies to any item seized under section 43.   ★**27-180**

(2) The item may be retained so long as is necessary in all the circumstances and in particular—

(a) for use as evidence at a trial for an offence under this Act, or

(b) for forensic examination or for investigation in connection with an offence under this Act.

(3) No item may be retained for either of the purposes mentioned in subsection (2) if a photograph
or a copy would be sufficient for that purpose.

50. [*Power of police, etc., to dispose of seized psychoactive substances.*]   ★**27-181**

51. [*Forfeiture of seized items by court on application.*]   ★**27-182**

52. [*Appeal against decision under s.51.*]   ★**27-183**

53. [*Return of item to person entitled to it, or disposal if return impracticable.*]   ★**27-184**

Forfeiture by court following conviction

54.—(1) This section applies where a person is convicted of—   ★**27-185**

(a) an offence under any of sections 4 to 9 and 26, or

(b) an ancillary offence (see subsection (11)).

(2) In this section "the court" means—

(a) the court by or before which the person is convicted of the offence, except where paragraph
(b) or (c) applies;

(b) if the person is committed to the Crown Court to be dealt with for that offence, the Crown
Court;

(c) [*Scotland.*]

(3) The court must make an order for the forfeiture of any psychoactive substance in respect of
which the offence was committed.

(4) The court may also make an order for the forfeiture of any other item that was used in the
commission of the offence.

(5) An order under subsection (3) or (4) is referred to in this section as a "forfeiture order".

(6) Before making a forfeiture order under subsection (4) in relation to any item, the court must
give an opportunity to make representations to any person (in addition to the convicted person) who
claims to be the owner of the item or otherwise to have an interest in it.

(7) A forfeiture order may not be made so as to come into force at any time before there is no
further possibility (ignoring any power to appeal out of time) of the order being varied or set aside
on appeal.

(8) Where the court makes a forfeiture order, it may also make such other provision as it considers
to be necessary for giving effect to the forfeiture.

(9) That provision may, in particular, include provision relating to the retention, handling,
destruction or other disposal of the item.

(10) Provision made by virtue of this section may be varied at any time by the court that made it.

(11) In this section "ancillary offence" means—

(a) an offence of attempting or conspiring to commit an offence under any of sections 4 to 9
and 26;

(b) an offence under Part 2 of the Serious Crime Act 2007 in relation to an offence under any of sections 4 to 9 and 26;

(c) an offence of inciting a person to commit an offence under any of sections 4 to 9 and 26;

(d) an offence of aiding, abetting, counselling or procuring the commission of an offence under any of sections 4 to 9 and 26.

(8) Supplementary and final provisions

Psychoactive Substances Act 2016, ss.55-63

Application of Customs and Excise Management Act 1979

★**27-186**   **55.**—(1) Section 164 of the Customs and Excise Management Act 1979 (power to search persons) applies in relation to a psychoactive substance as it applies in relation to an article with respect to the importation or exportation of which any prohibition or restriction is for the time being in force under or by virtue of any enactment.

(2) A psychoactive substance is liable to forfeiture under the Customs and Excise Management Act 1979 if—

(a) the psychoactive substance—

(i)   is imported or exported, or

(ii) is entered for exportation or brought to any place in the United Kingdom for exportation,

(b) the psychoactive substance is likely to be consumed by any individual for its psychoactive effects, and

(c) the importation or (as the case may be) exportation of the psychoactive substance is not an exempted activity.

(3) For the purposes of subsection (2) the importation or exportation of a psychoactive substance is an "exempted activity" if it would not be an offence under this Act by virtue of section 11.

(4) Section 5 of the Customs and Excise Management Act 1979 (time of importation, exportation, etc) applies for the purposes of subsection (2) as it applies for the purposes of that Act.

For section 5 of the 1979 Act, see § 25-428 in the main work; for section 164 of the 1979 Act, see § 25-467 in the main work.

Offences by directors, partners, etc

27-187   **56.**—(1) Where an offence under this Act has been committed by a body corporate and it is proved that the offence—

(a) has been committed with the consent or connivance of a person falling within subsection (2), or

(b) is attributable to any neglect on the part of such a person,

that person (as well as the body corporate) is guilty of that offence and liable to be proceeded against and punished accordingly.

(2) The persons are—

(a) a director, manager, secretary or similar officer of the body corporate;

(b) any person who was purporting to act in such a capacity.

(3) Where the affairs of a body corporate are managed by its members, subsection (1) applies in relation to the acts and defaults of a member, in connection with that management, as if the member were a director of the body corporate.

(4) [*Scotland.*]

Providers of information society services

27-188   **57.** Schedule 4 contains provision about the application of certain provisions of this Act in relation to persons providing information society services within the meaning of that Schedule.

27-189   **58.** [*Review.*]

Interpretation

27-190   **59.**—(1) In this Act—

"access prohibition" has the meaning given by section 22(6);

"designated NCA officer" means a National Crime Agency officer designated under section 10 of the Crime and Courts Act 2013 as a person having either or both of the following—

(a) the powers and privileges of a constable;

(b) the powers of an officer of Revenue and Customs;

"exempted substance" has the meaning given by section 3 ;

"general customs function" has the meaning given by section 1(8) of the Borders, Citizenship and Immigration Act 2009;

"general customs official" means a person designated as a general customs official under section 3(1) of the Borders, Citizenship and Immigration Act 2009;

"item" includes any substance;

"justice" means—

> (a) in England and Wales, a justice of the peace,
>
> (b), (c) [*Scotland and Northern Ireland*];

"local authority" means—

> (a) in England, a county council, a district council, a London borough council, the Common Council of the City of London or the Council of the Isles of Scilly,
>
> (b) in Wales, a county council or county borough council,
>
> (c), (d) [*Scotland and Northern Ireland*];

"police or customs officer" has the meaning given by section 36(4);

"premises" includes any place and, in particular, includes—

> (a) any vehicle, vessel or aircraft;
>
> (b) any offshore installation within the meaning given by section 1 of the Mineral Workings (Offshore Installations) Act 1971;
>
> (c) any renewable energy installation within the meaning given by section 104 of the Energy Act 2004;
>
> (d) any tent or movable structure;

"premises notice" is to be read in accordance with section 14;

"premises order" is to be read in accordance with section 20;

"prohibited activity" has the meaning given by section 12;

"prohibition notice" is to be read in accordance with section 13;

"prohibition order" is to be read in accordance with section 17;

"psychoactive effects", in relation to a substance, is to be read in accordance with section 2(2);

"psychoactive substance" has the meaning given by section 2(1);

"relevant enforcement officer" has the meaning given by section 39(6);

"relevant evidence" has the meaning given by section 36(4);

"search warrant" means a warrant under section 39;

"senior officer" has the meaning given by section 13(7);

"vessel" is to be read in accordance with subsection (4).

(2) In this Act—

> (a) any reference to producing a substance is a reference to producing it by manufacture, cultivation or any other method;
>
> (b) any reference to supplying a substance includes a reference to distributing it;
>
> (c) any reference to consuming a substance is to be read in accordance with section 2(3).

(3) For the purposes of this Act the items which are in a person's possession include any items which are—

> (a) subject to that person's control, but
>
> (b) in the custody of another person.

(4) In this Act any reference to a vessel includes a reference to—

> (a) any ship or boat or any other description of vessel used in navigation, and
>
> (b) any hovercraft, submersible craft or other floating craft,

but does not include a reference to anything that permanently rests on, or is permanently attached to, the sea bed.

(5) [*Scotland.*]

★**27-191**   60. [*Gives effect to Sched. 5 (consequential amendments).*]

★**27-192**   61. [*Power to make further consequential amendments.*]

★**27-193**   62. [*Extent.*]

★**27-194**   63. [*Commencement and short title.*]

(9) Exempted activities and substances, search warrants, information society service providers

Exempted substances (Sched. 1)

★**27-195**   Schedule 1 (given effect by s.3 (*ante*, § 27-134)) lists the following exempt substances: controlled drugs within the Misuse of Drugs Act 1971; medicinal products (within the meaning of the Human Medicines Regulations 2012 (S.I. 2012 No. 1916), reg. 2); alcohol and alcoholic products; nicotine; tobacco products (*i.e.* anything that is such a product within the Tobacco Products Duty Act 1979, s.1, and any other product that contains nicotine and does not contain any psychoactive substance); caffeine and caffeine products (*i.e.* any product that contains caffeine and does not contain any psychoactive substance); and any substance that is ordinarily consumed as food and does not contain a prohibited ingredient ("food" including drink, and "prohibited ingredient", in relation to a substance, meaning any psychoactive substance, which is not naturally occurring in the substance, and the use of which in or on food is not authorised by an EU instrument).

Exempted activities

★**27-196**   Schedule 2 (given effect by s.11 (*ante*, § 27-142)) exempts healthcare-related activities (paras 1-3), and research (para. 4).

Psychoactive Substances Act 2016, Sched. 3

SCHEDULE 3

SEARCH WARRANTS: ENGLAND AND WALES AND NORTHERN IRELAND

PART 1

Application of this Schedule

★**27-197**   1. This Schedule applies to—
    (a)   applications for search warrants made in England and Wales or Northern Ireland, and
    (b)   search warrants issued in England and Wales or Northern Ireland.

PART 2

Search Warrants: Applications and Safeguards

Applications for warrants

★**27-198**   2.—(1) A person applying for a search warrant must—
    (a)   state that the application is made under section 39 of this Act;
    (b)   specify the matters set out in sub-paragraph (2) or (3) (as the case may be);
    (c)   state what are the grounds for suspecting that relevant evidence is on the premises;
    (d)   identify, so far as is possible, the offence to which the relevant evidence relates.
    (2) If the person is applying for a specific-premises warrant, the person must specify each set of premises that it is desired to enter and search.
    (3) If the person is applying for an all-premises warrant, the person must specify—
    (a)   as many of the sets of premises that it is desired to enter and search as it is reasonably practicable to specify;
    (b)   the person who is in occupation or control of those premises and any others that it is desired to enter and search;
    (c)   why it is necessary to search more premises than those specified under paragraph (a);
    (d)   why it is not reasonably practicable to specify all the premises that it is desired to enter and search.

(4) If the person is applying for a search warrant authorising entry and search on more than one occasion, the person must also state—

(a) the ground on which the person applies for such a warrant, and

(b) whether the person seeks a warrant authorising an unlimited number of entries, or (if not) the maximum number of entries desired.

(5) In this paragraph "specific-premises warrant" and "all-premises warrant" have the meaning given by section 39(3).

Safeguards in connection with power of entry conferred by warrant

3. A search warrant authorises entry on one occasion only, unless it specifies that it authorises   ★**27-199**
multiple entries.

4.—(1) A search warrant must—   ★**27-200**

(a) specify the name of the person who applies for it;

(b) specify the date on which it is issued;

(c) state that the warrant is issued under section 39 of this Act;

(d) specify each set of premises to be searched, or (in the case of an all-premises warrant) the person who is in occupation or control of premises to be searched, together with any premises to be searched that are under the person's occupation or control and can be specified;

(e) identify, so far as is possible, the offence to which the relevant evidence suspected to be on the premises relates.

(2) In sub-paragraph (1)(d) "all-premises warrant" has the meaning given by section 39(3).

5.—(1) Two copies must be made of a search warrant that specifies only one set of premises and   ★**27-201**
does not authorise multiple entries.

(2) As many copies as are reasonably required may be made of any other kind of search warrant.

(3) The copies must be clearly certified as copies.

PART 3

Execution of Search Warrants

Warrant to be executed within one month

6. Entry and search under a search warrant must be within one month from the date of its issue.   ★**27-202**

All-premises warrants

7.—(1) In the case of an all-premises warrant, premises that are not specified in the warrant may   ★**27-203**
be entered and searched only if a relevant enforcement officer of the appropriate grade has authorised them to be entered.

(2) An authorisation under sub-paragraph (1) must be in writing.

(3) In this paragraph—

"all-premises warrant" has the meaning given by section 39(3) ;

"relevant enforcement officer of the appropriate grade" means—

(a) a senior officer (see section 13(7)), or

(b) in the case of a search warrant issued on the application of an officer of a local authority, a person designated by the local authority for the purposes of this paragraph.

Search of premises more than once

8.—(1) Premises may be entered or searched for the second or any subsequent time under a   ★**27-204**
search warrant authorising multiple entries only if a relevant enforcement officer of the appropriate grade has authorised that entry to the premises.

(2) An authorisation under sub-paragraph (1) must be in writing.

(3) In this paragraph "relevant enforcement officer of the appropriate grade" has the same meaning as in paragraph 7 .

Time of search

9. Entry and search under a search warrant must be at a reasonable hour unless it appears to the   ★**27-205**
relevant enforcement officer executing it that the purpose of a search may be frustrated on an entry at a reasonable hour.

Evidence of authority etc

10.—(1) Where the occupier of premises to be entered and searched under a search warrant is   ★**27-206** present at the time when a relevant enforcement officer seeks to execute the warrant, the following requirements must be satisfied—

    (a) the occupier must be told the officer's name;

    (b) if not a constable in uniform, the officer must produce to the occupier documentary evidence that the officer is a relevant enforcement officer;

    (c) the officer must produce the warrant to the occupier;

    (d) the officer must supply the occupier with a copy of it.

(2) Where the occupier of premises to be entered and searched under a search warrant is not present at the time when a relevant enforcement officer seeks to execute the warrant—

    (a) if some other person who appears to the officer to be in charge of the premises is present, sub-paragraph (1) has effect as if a reference to the occupier were a reference to that other person;

    (b) if not, the officer must leave a copy of the warrant in a prominent place on the premises.

Extent of search

★**27-207**   11. A search under a search warrant may only be a search to the extent required for the purpose for which the warrant was issued.

Securing premises after entry

★**27-208**   12. A relevant enforcement officer who enters premises under a search warrant must take reasonable steps to ensure that when the officer leaves the premises they are as secure as they were before the officer entered.

Return and retention of warrant

★**27-209**   13.—(1) A search warrant must be returned to the appropriate person (see sub-paragraph (2))—

    (a) when the warrant has been executed, or

    (b) on or before the expiry of the period of one month from the date of its issue, if the warrant is—

        (i) a specific-premises warrant that has not been executed,

        (ii) an all-premises warrant, or

        (iii) a warrant authorising multiple entries.

(2) The appropriate person is—

    (a) in the case of a warrant issued in England and Wales, the designated officer for the local justice area in which the justice of the peace was acting when issuing the warrant;

    (b) [*Northern Ireland*].

(3) The appropriate person must retain a search warrant returned under sub-paragraph (1) for 12 months from the date of its return.

(4) If during that period the occupier of premises to which the search warrant relates asks to inspect it, the occupier must be allowed to do so.

(5) In this paragraph "specific-premises warrant" and "all-premises warrant" have the meaning given by section 39(3) .

Providers of information society services

★**27-210**   Schedule 4 (given effect by s.57) relates to the providers of information society services. Part 1 (paras 1-5) makes provision for the liability of information society service providers for offences under section 5(2) of the Act (offering to supply a psychoactive substanc (*ante*, § 27-136)), extending the liability of domestic service providers in respect of things done abroad, restricting the institution of proceedings against non-U.K. service providers and providing exceptions for mere conduits, caching and hosting. Part 2 (paras 6-9) makes provision in relation to prohibition notices and prohibition orders, extending the liability of domestic service providers for offences under section 26 (*ante*, § 27-157), placing restrictions on the terms of a prohibition notice or order in the case of a non-U.K. service provider and creating protections for service providers of intermediary services. Part 3 (paras 10 and 11) contains interpretation provisions.

CHAPTER 28

OFFENCES AGAINST PUBLIC JUSTICE

III. CONTEMPT OF COURT

B. COMMON LAW

(13) Publication of matter relating to proceedings in private

In *R. (Yam) v. Central Criminal Court* [2016] 2 W.L.R. 19, SC, the Supreme Court upheld the ★**28-51**
decision of the Divisional Court in *R. (Wang Yam) v. Central Criminal Court* (see the main work).
However, the court found that the relevant power to make an order restraining disclosure to the
European Court of Human Rights existed at common law, and it therefore gave no consideration
to section 12 of the Administration of Justice Act 1960, or section 11 of the Contempt of Court
Act 1981 (*ibid.*, 28-79). It was held that non-disclosure to the Strasbourg court of sensitive material heard *in camera* during the appellant's criminal trial would not involve any breach of any
obligation under Article 34 of the ECHR, that, if such a breach were to be found, it would have to
be by the Strasbourg court, and that that court could request further material under Article 38 of
the convention to enable it to consider the appellant's case both at the admissibility stage and, if
the matter were to go further, on the merits.

C. CONTEMPT OF COURT ACT 1981

(2) The strict liability rule
Contempt of Court Act 1981, ss.1, 2

Limitation of scope of strict liability

The decision of the Divisional Court in *R. (Wang Yam) v. Central Criminal Court* (see the main ★**28-56**
work) was upheld by the Supreme Court (as to which, see *ante*, § 28-51), but that court did not
consider whether or not the staff and judges of the Strasbourg court could be described as a "section of the public" (see the main work).

Publication of material prejudicial to a defendant

For an example of a publication of material prejudicial to a defendant during the recent ★**28-63**
"phone-hacking" trial being held to have been in contempt of court, see *Att.-Gen. v. Condé Nast
Publications Ltd,* unreported, November 18, 2015, DC ([2015] EWHC 3322 (Admin.)) (magazine
article going beyond mere comment or observation in relation to Rupert Murdoch and two of the
defendants). It was said that while there would have been a general expectation that the jury
would have followed the judge's directions to ignore any comment about the case, there was
nothing on the cover of the magazine to alert a juror that the inside article was not conventional,
fair and balanced reporting; in the circumstances, it was unrealistic to expect a juror who had
turned to the article and read it to be uninfluenced by, or to put out of his mind, its contents,
published as it was during the trial; there would therefore have been a "seriously arguable
ground of appeal" that the jury should have been discharged (*Att.-Gen. v. Birmingham Post and
Mail Ltd* and *Att.-Gen. v. M.G.N. Ltd and News Group International Ltd* (as to both of which, see §
28-61 in the main work)); it was immaterial that no application had been made to discharge the
jury.

(5) Restriction of publication of matters exempted from disclosure
Contempt of Court Act 1981, s.11

Publication of matters exempted from disclosure in court

The decision of the Divisional Court in *R. (Wang Yam) v. Central Criminal Court* (see the main ★**28-80**
work) was upheld by the Supreme Court (as to which, see *ante*, § 28-51), but section 11 of the
1981 Act (§ 28-79 in the main work) was not considered.

VII. PRISON SECURITY

E. Smuggling and Unauthorised Photography, etc

Prison Act 1952, ss. 40A-40E

Throwing articles into prison

★**28-195b**   With effect from November 10, 2015 (Serious Crime Act 2015 (Commencement No. 3) Regulations 2015 (S.I. 2015 No. 1809)), section 79 of the 2015 Act (see the main work) was brought into force. The statement in the main work that section 79 came into force on June 1, 2015, is a mistake. Section 78 (inserting s.40CA of the 1952 Act (§ 28-195a in the main work)) came into force on that date, but not section 79.

Chapter 29

PUBLIC ORDER OFFENCES

I. PUBLIC ORDER ACT 1986

B. Offences (Pt I (ss.1–10))

(5) Harassment, alarm or distress

Public Order Act 1986, s.4A

Intentional harassment, alarm or distress

★**29-44**   In *James v. DPP*, 180 J.P. 1, DC, it was held that whether a decision to prosecute for an offence under the 1986 Act was proportionate for the purposes of Article 10 (freedom of expression (§ 16-157 in the main work)) or 11 (freedom of assembly and association (*ibid.*, § 16-171)) of the ECHR was not an issue for trial courts to deal with; that was a decision for the prosecutor; the decision in *Dehal v. CPS* (where Art. 10 was engaged, a prosecution for an offence under s.4 of the 1986 Act (*ibid.*, § 29-30) would be unlawful unless it could be established that it was necessary to prevent public disorder (see the main work)), had been "uprooted" by *Bauer v. DPP (Liberty intervening)* [2013] 1 W.L.R. 3617, DC, and was wrongly decided; a contention that a decision to prosecute was disproportionate was not one that the criminal courts could rule on unless it amounted to an abuse of process, which was itself an exceptional and limited remedy.

Chapter 30

COMMERCE, FINANCIAL MARKETS AND INSOLVENCY

I. FRAUDULENT TRADING, ETC

A. Fraudulent Trading

(5) The nature of the offence

★**30-6**   · *Bilta (U.K.) Ltd (in liquidation) v. Nazir (No. 2)* is now reported at [2016] A.C. 1.

III. INSIDER DEALING

(2) Legislation

(d) Miscellaneous

Criminal Justice Act 2003, ss.61-64

Penalties and prosecution

★**30-43**   For a decision of the Supreme Court of Tasmania (Estcourt J.) considering the offender's "benefit" for the purposes of Australian federal legislation relating to confiscation of the proceeds of crime (broadly corresponding to the PCA 2002 (§§ 5-785 *et seq.* in the main work)), see *DPP (Cth) v. Gay*, 295 F.L.R. 91 ([2015] TASSC 15). The offender was convicted of insider trading (under the Corporations Act 2001 (Cth), ss.1043A(1) and 1311(1)), having sold shares in a company of which he was a director and chairman while he had price-sensitive information, but he had not kept the sale secret from the company, had planned to sell the shares for some time prior to having the information, had discussed the sale with the board, and was selling the shares because of a serious, possibly life-threatening illness he had at the time. It was held that his benefit for the purposes of a pecuniary penalty under the legislation (the "penalty" to be assessed in the amount of the benefit, less certain specified deductions) was not the gross proceeds of the sale of the shares, but should take account of the cost price of the shares; to decide otherwise would be manifestly unjust; although there are authorities relating to illegal drugs in which no account had been taken of the acquisition costs, there was no parallel with this case, where the shares were acquired legally, and where their sale was not absolutely prohibited but only prohibited at certain times; not all acquisition costs will be expenses or outgoings "incurred in relation to the illegal activity"; here, the acquisition of the shares bore no relevant relationship to the offender's later unlawful conduct. The judge said that the question whether the benefit should be valued as the amount of profit made by the person, or the difference between the price achieved on the sale of the shares and that which would have been achieved had the market been fully informed by reason of the inside information being generally available, was a question for further argument and evidence.

CHAPTER 32

MOTOR VEHICLE OFFENCES

II. DRIVING OFFENCES

G. CAUSING DEATH BY DRIVING: UNLICENSED OR UNINSURED DRIVERS

(6) Ingredients of the offence

For a case considering whether an extension of time to appeal against conviction should have been granted where the applicant had pleaded guilty to an offence contrary to section 3ZB of the 1988 Act (§ 32-71 in the main work), before the Supreme Court decision in *R. v. Hughes* (see the main work), but in circumstances where the Crown conceded that there could have been no conviction had the prosecution been brought after that decision was handed down, see *R. v. McGuffog, ante*, § 7-171. **32-76**

P. DRIVING WITHOUT A LICENCE

(5) Grant and form of licences

Road Traffic Act 1988, s.97

Grant of licences

The Motor Vehicles (Driving Licences) Regulations 1999 (S.I. 1999 No. 2864) have been further amended by the Motor Vehicles (Driving Licences) (Amendment) (No. 4) Regulations 2015 (S.I. 2015 No. 1797) (with effect from December 31, 2015), and the Road Traffic Offenders Act 1988 and Motor Vehicles (Driving Licences) (Amendment) Regulations 2015 (S.I. 2015 No. 2004) (with effect from January 4, 2016). **★32-160**

R. NO INSURANCE

(5) Burden of proof

DPP v. Whittaker is now reported at [2015] R.T.R. 30. **★32-179**

T. Failing to Give Information as to Identity of Driver

(1) Statute

Road Traffic Act 1988, s.172

Duty to give information as to identity of driver etc in certain circumstances

★**32-187**   *Atkinson v. DPP* (see the main work) was considered in *Marshall v. CPS*, 180 J.P. 33, DC, where it was said that a defendant will find it extremely difficult to bring himself within the defence in subsection (4) if, in fact, he did not exercise reasonable diligence with a view to ascertaining the driver's identity at the time of the alleged offence.

W. Disqualification and Endorsement

(11) Effect of disqualification

Road Traffic Offenders Act 1988, s.37

Effect of order of disqualification

★**32-275**   With effect from January 4, 2016, section 37 of the RTOA 1988 is amended by the Road Traffic Offenders Act 1988 and Motor Vehicles (Driving Licences) (Amendment) Regulations 2015 (S.I. 2015 No. 2004), so as to add a new subsection at the end, as follows:-

> "(4) Notwithstanding anything in Part III of the Road Traffic Act 1988, a person who holds a Community licence which authorises that person to drive motor vehicles of a particular class, but who is disqualified by an order of a court under section 36 of this Act, is (unless the person is also disqualified otherwise than by virtue of such an order) entitled to drive a motor vehicle of that class in accordance with the same conditions as if the person were authorised to drive a motor vehicle of that class by a provisional licence.".

Chapter 33

CONSPIRACY, ENCOURAGEMENT AND ATTEMPT TO COMMIT CRIME

I. CONSPIRACY

B. Statutory Offence of Conspiracy

(6) Restrictions on institution of proceedings

Criminal Law Act 1977, s.4

Restrictions on the institution of proceedings for conspiracy

★**33-34**   *R. v. W. (C.) and M. (M.)* (see the main work) is now reported at [2016] 1 Cr.App.R. 8, *sub nom. R. v. Welsh (Christopher) (Junior)*. For a case considering that decision, and further considering the relationship between section 4 of the 1977 Act (see the main work) and section 25 of the Prosecution of Offences Act 1985 (*ibid.*, § 1-365), see *R. v. Welsh (Christopher Mark) (Senior)*, *ante*, § 1-365.

APPENDIX A
Codes of Practice and Attorney-General's Guidelines

I. CODES OF PRACTICE

A. UNDER THE POLICE AND CRIMINAL EVIDENCE ACT 1984

(1) Introduction

The Police and Criminal Evidence Act 1984 makes provision for the issuing by the Secretary of ★**A-1**
State of codes of practice in connection with the tape-recording of interviews (s.60, § 15-173 in
the main work), the visual recording of interviews (s.60A, § 15-177 in the main work), the
exercise by police officers of statutory powers of "stop and search" (s.66(1)(a)(i) and (ii), § 15-2 in
the main work), the exercise by police officers of statutory powers to arrest a person (s.66(1)(a)(iii),
§ 15-2 in the main work) the detention, treatment, questioning and identification of persons by
police officers (s.66(1)(b), § 15-2 in the main work), and searches of premises and seizure of
property (s.66(1)(c) and (d), § 15-2 in the main work).

There are eight extant codes: Code A (stop and search); Code B (search and seizure); Code C
(detention, treatment and questioning of persons), Code D (identification), Code E (audio-
recording of interviews), Code F (visual recording of interviews), Code G (arrest) and Code H
(detention, treatment and questioning of persons under section 41 of, and Schedule 8 to, the Terrorism Act 2000).

Code D came into force on March 7, 2011: Police and Criminal Evidence Act 1984 (Codes of
Practice) (Revision of Codes A, B and D) Order 2011 (S.I. 2011 No. 412). Code G came into force
on November 12, 2012: Police and Criminal Evidence Act 1984 (Codes of Practice) (Revision of
Codes C, G and H) Order 2012 (S.I. 2012 No. 1798).

The Police and Criminal Evidence Act 1984 (Codes of Practice) (Revisions to Codes A, B, C, E,
F and H) Order 2013 (S.I. 2013 No. 2685) brought revised Codes A, B, C, E, F and H into force
on October 27, 2013. The revisions were required in order to give effect to (i) the United
Kingdom's obligations under European Parliament and Council Directive 2010/64/EU on the
right to interpretation and translation in criminal proceedings, and (ii) the decision of the
Divisional Court in *R. (C.) v. Secretary of State for the Home Department* (as to which, see §§ 15-6, 15-
165, 16-141 in the main work).

The Police and Criminal Evidence Act 1984 (Codes of Practice) (Revisions to Codes C and H)
Order 2014 (S.I. 2014 No. 1237) brought revised Codes C and H into force on June 2, 2014. The
revisions implemented obligations under European Parliament and Council Directive 2012/13/
EU, in relation to the right to information in criminal proceedings. In particular, every detainee
must be given a revised written notice setting out his rights and entitlements whilst in custody,
which has been updated to reflect the new substantive rights conferred by the 2012 directive.

The Police and Criminal Evidence Act 1984 (Revision of Code A) Order 2015 (S.I. 2015 No.
418) brought a revised Code A into force on March 19, 2015. The main changes were intended to
make clear what constitutes "reasonable grounds for suspicion". The revised code also emphasises
that where officers are not using their powers properly they will be subject to formal performance
or disciplinary proceedings.

The Police and Criminal Evidence Act 1984 (Codes of Practice) (Revision of Code E) Order ★

2016 (S.I. 2016 No. 35) brought a revised Code E on the audio recording of interviews with suspects into force on February 2, 2016. The revisions exempt four offences from the requirement that the interviews of individuals regarding indictable offences must be audio-recorded. The conditions that must be met before the exemption can apply are set out in a new annex to the code.

For further details of the various versions of the codes and their revisions, see §§ 15-5, 15-6 in the main work. For further details in relation to the codes generally, see the main work at §§ 15-2 *et seq.* (primary legislation), § 15-5 (commencement), § 15-7 (status of codes), § 15-8 (who is bound by the codes), § 15-10 (admissibility), and § 15-11 (breaches).

It should be noted that the original text of the codes has a series of errors. Only in the most obvious cases has any change been made to the wording, but the punctuation, use of case, use of number and paragraphing have been amended with a view to injecting consistency and intelligibility.

(2) Stop and search

A. CODE OF PRACTICE FOR THE EXERCISE BY: POLICE OFFICERS OF STATUTORY POWERS OF STOP AND SEARCH; POLICE OFFICERS AND POLICE STAFF OF REQUIREMENTS TO RECORD PUBLIC ENCOUNTERS

Commencement—transitional arrangements

This code applies to any search by a police officer and the recording of public encounters taking place after 00.00 on 19 March 2015.

A:1.0 General

A-2   A:1.01 This code of practice must be readily available at all police stations for consultation by police officers, police staff, detained persons and members of the public.

A:1.02 The notes for guidance included are not provisions of this code, but are guidance to police officers and others about its application and interpretation. Provisions in the annexes to the code are provisions of this code.

A:1.03 This code governs the exercise by police officers of statutory powers to search a person or a vehicle without first making an arrest. The main stop and search powers to which this code applies are set out in Annex A, but that list should not be regarded as definitive [see *Note 1*]. In addition, it covers requirements on police officers and police staff to record encounters not governed by statutory powers (see paras 2.11 and 4.12). This code does not apply to:

(a) the powers of stop and search under:

    (i) the Aviation Security Act 1982, s.27(2), and

    (ii) the Police and Criminal Evidence Act 1984, s.6(1) (which relates specifically to powers of constables employed by statutory undertakers on the premises of the statutory undertakers);

(b) searches carried out for the purposes of examination under Schedule 7 to the Terrorism Act 2000 and to which the code of practice issued under paragraph 6 of Schedule 14 to the Terrorism Act 2000 applies;

(c) the powers to search persons and vehicles and to stop and search in specified locations to which the code of practice issued under section 47AB of the Terrorism Act 2000 applies.

A:1 Principles governing stop and search

A-3   A:1.1 Powers to stop and search must be used fairly, responsibly, with respect for people being searched and without unlawful discrimination. Under the Equality Act 2010, s.149, when police officers are carrying out their functions, they also have a duty to have due regard to the need to eliminate unlawful discrimination, harassment and victimisation, to advance equality of opportunity between people who share a relevant protected characteristic and people who do not share it, and to take steps to foster good relations between those persons. [See *Notes 1* and *1A*.] The Children Act 2004, s.11, also requires chief police officers and other specified persons and bodies to ensure that in the discharge of their functions they have regard to the need to safeguard and promote the welfare of all persons under the age of 18.

A:1.2 The intrusion on the liberty of the person stopped or searched must be brief and detention for the purposes of a search must take place at or near the location of the stop.

A:1.3 If these fundamental principles are not observed the use of powers to stop and search may be drawn into question. Failure to use the powers in the proper manner reduces their effectiveness. Stop and search can play an important role in the detection and prevention of crime, and using the powers fairly makes them more effective.

A:1.4 The primary purpose of stop and search powers is to enable officers to allay or confirm suspicions about individuals without exercising their power of arrest. Officers may be required to justify the use or authorisation of such powers, in relation both to individual searches and the overall pattern of their activity in this regard, to their supervisory officers or in court. Any misuse of the powers is likely to be harmful to policing and lead to mistrust of the police. Officers must also be able to explain their actions to the member of the public searched. The misuse of these powers can lead to disciplinary action (see paras 5.5 and 5.6).

A:1.5 An officer must not search a person, even with his or her consent, where no power to search is applicable. Even where a person is prepared to submit to a search voluntarily, the person must not be searched unless the necessary legal power exists, and the search must be in accordance with the relevant power and the provisions of this code. The only exception, where an officer does not require a specific power, applies to searches of persons entering sports grounds or other premises carried out with their consent given as a condition of entry.

A:1.6 Evidence obtained from a search to which this code applies may be open to challenge if the provisions of this code are not observed.

A:2 Types of stop and search powers

A:2.1 This code applies, subject to paragraph 1.03, to powers of stop and search as follows: **A-4**

(a) powers which require reasonable grounds for suspicion, before they may be exercised; that articles unlawfully obtained or possessed are being carried such as section 1 of PACE for stolen and prohibited articles and section 23 of the Misuse of Drugs Act 1971 for controlled drugs;

(b) authorised under section 60 of the Criminal Justice and Public Order Act 1994, based upon a reasonable belief that incidents involving serious violence may take place or that people are carrying dangerous instruments or offensive weapons within any locality in the police area, or that it is expedient to use the powers to find such instruments or weapons that have been used in incidents of serious violence;

(c) [*not used*];

(d) the powers in Schedule 5 to the Terrorism Prevention and Investigation Measures (TPIM) Act 2011 to search an individual who has not been arrested, conferred by:

    (i) paragraph 6(2)(a) at the time of serving a TPIM notice;

    (ii) paragraph 8(2)(a) under a search warrant for compliance purposes; and

    (iii) paragraph 10 for public safety purposes;

    see paragraph 2.18A;

(e) powers to search a person who has not been arrested in the exercise of a power to search premises (see Code B, para. 2.4).

(a) Stop and search powers requiring reasonable grounds for suspicion – explanation

General

A:2.2 Reasonable grounds for suspicion is the legal test which a police officer must satisfy before **A-5** they can stop and detain individuals or vehicles to search them under powers such as section 1 of PACE (to find stolen or prohibited articles) and section 23 of the Misuse of Drugs Act 1971 (to find controlled drugs). This test must be applied to the particular circumstances in each case and is in two parts:

    (i) firstly, the officer must have formed a genuine suspicion in their own mind that they will find the object for which the search power being exercised allows them to search (see Annex A, second column, for examples); and

    (ii) secondly, the suspicion that the object will be found must be reasonable. This means that there must be an objective basis for that suspicion based on facts, information and/or intelligence which are relevant to the likelihood that the object in question will be found, so that a reasonable person would be entitled to reach the same conclusion based on the same facts and information and/or intelligence.

    Officers must therefore be able to explain the basis for their suspicion by reference to intelligence or information about, or some specific behaviour by, the person concerned (see paras 3.8(d), 4.6 and 5.5).

A:2.2A The exercise of these stop and search powers depends on the likelihood that the person searched is in possession of an item for which they may be searched; it does not depend on the person concerned being suspected of committing an offence in relation to the object of the search. A police officer who has reasonable grounds to suspect that a person is in innocent possession of a stolen or prohibited article, controlled drug or other item for which the officer is empowered to search, may stop and search the person even though there would be no power of arrest. This would apply when a child under the age of criminal responsibility (10 years) is suspected of carrying any such item, even if they knew they had it. (See *Notes 1B* and *1BA*.)

Personal factors can never support reasonable grounds for suspicion

A-5a

A:2.2B Reasonable suspicion can never be supported on the basis of personal factors. This means that unless the police have information or intelligence which provides a description of a person suspected of carrying an article for which there is a power to stop and search, the following cannot be used, alone or in combination with each other, or in combination with any other factor, as the reason for stopping and searching any individual, including any vehicle which they are driving or are being carried in:

    (a) a person's physical appearance with regard, for example, to any of the "relevant protected characteristics" set out in the Equality Act 2010, s.149, which are age, disability, gender reassignment, pregnancy and maternity, race, religion or belief, sex and sexual orientation (see para. 1.1 and *Note 1A*), or the fact that the person is known to have a previous conviction; and

    (b) generalisations or stereotypical images that certain groups or categories of people are more likely to be involved in criminal activity.

A:2.3 [*Not used.*]

Reasonable grounds for suspicion based on information and/or intelligence

A-5b

A:2.4 Reasonable grounds for suspicion should normally be linked to accurate and current intelligence or information, relating to articles for which there is a power to stop and search, being carried by individuals or being in vehicles in any locality. This would include reports from members of the public or other officers describing:

- a person who has been seen carrying such an article or a vehicle in which such an article has been seen;
- crimes committed in relation to which such an article would constitute relevant evidence, for example, property stolen in a theft or burglary, an offensive weapon or bladed or sharply pointed article used to assault or threaten someone or an article used to cause criminal damage to property.

A:2.4A Searches based on accurate and current intelligence or information are more likely to be effective. Targeting searches in a particular area at specified crime problems not only increases their effectiveness but also minimises inconvenience to law-abiding members of the public. It also helps in justifying the use of searches both to those who are searched and to the public. This does not, however, prevent stop and search powers being exercised in other locations where such powers may be exercised and reasonable suspicion exists.

A:2.5 [*Not used.*]

Reasonable grounds for suspicion and searching groups

A-5c

A:2.6 Where there is reliable information or intelligence that members of a group or gang habitually carry knives unlawfully or weapons or controlled drugs, and wear a distinctive item of clothing or other means of identification in order to identify themselves as members of that group or gang, that distinctive item of clothing or other means of identification may provide reasonable grounds to stop and search any person believed to be a member of that group or gang. [See *Note 9*.]

A:2.6A A similar approach would apply to particular organised protest groups where there is reliable information or intelligence:

    (a) that the group in question arranges meetings and marches to which one or more members bring articles intended to be used to cause criminal damage and/or injury to others in support of the group's aims;

    (b) that at one or more previous meetings or marches arranged by that group, such articles have been used and resulted in damage and/or injury; and

    (c) that on the subsequent occasion in question, one or more members of the group have brought with them such articles with similar intentions.

These circumstances may provide reasonable grounds to stop and search any members of the group to find such articles (see *Note 9A*). See also paragraphs 2.12 to 2.18, "Searches authorised under section 60 of the Criminal Justice and Public Order Act 1994", when serious violence is anticipated at meetings and marches.

Reasonable grounds for suspicion based on behaviour, time and location

A:2.6B Reasonable suspicion may also exist without specific information or intelligence and on the basis of the behaviour of a person. For example, if an officer encounters someone on the street at night who is obviously trying to hide something, the officer may (depending on the other surrounding circumstances) base such suspicion on the fact that this kind of behaviour is often linked to stolen or prohibited articles being carried. An officer who forms the opinion that a person is acting suspiciously or that they appear to be nervous must be able to explain, with reference to specific aspects of the person's behaviour or conduct which they have observed, why they formed that opinion (see paras 3.8(d) and 5.5). A hunch or instinct which cannot be explained or justified to an objective observer can never amount to reasonable grounds. **A-5d**

A:2.7 [*Not used.*]

A:2.8 [*Not used.*]

Securing public confidence and promoting community relations

A:2.8A All police officers must recognise that searches are more likely to be effective, legitimate and secure public confidence when their reasonable grounds for suspicion are based on a range of objective factors. The overall use of these powers is more likely to be effective when up-to-date and accurate intelligence or information is communicated to officers and they are well-informed about local crime patterns. Local senior officers have a duty to ensure that those under their command who exercise stop and search powers have access to such information, and the officers exercising the powers have a duty to acquaint themselves with that information (see paras 5.1 to 5.6). **A-5e**

Questioning to decide whether to carry out a search

A:2.9 An officer who has reasonable grounds for suspicion may detain the person concerned in order to carry out a search. Before carrying out the search the officer may ask questions about the person's behaviour or presence in circumstances which gave rise to the suspicion. As a result of questioning the detained person, the reasonable grounds for suspicion necessary to detain that person may be confirmed or, because of a satisfactory explanation, be dispelled. [*See Notes 2 and 3.*] Questioning may also reveal reasonable grounds to suspect the possession of a different kind of unlawful article from that originally suspected. Reasonable grounds for suspicion however cannot be provided retrospectively by such questioning during a person's detention or by refusal to answer any questions asked. **A-5f**

A:2.10 If, as a result of questioning before a search, or other circumstances which come to the attention of the officer, there cease to be reasonable grounds for suspecting that an article of a kind for which there is a power to stop and search is being carried, no search may take place. [*See Note 3.*] In the absence of any other lawful power to detain, the person is free to leave at will and must be so informed.

A:2.11 There is no power to stop or detain a person in order to find grounds for a search. Police officers have many encounters with members of the public which do not involve detaining people against their will and do not require any statutory power for an officer to speak to a person (see para. 4.12 and *Note 1*). However, if reasonable grounds for suspicion emerge during such an encounter, the officer may detain the person to search them, even though no grounds existed when the encounter began. As soon as detention begins, and before searching, the officer must inform the person that they are being detained for the purpose of a search and take action in accordance with paragraphs 3.8 to 3.11 under *"Steps to be taken prior to a search".*

(b) Searches authorised under section 60 of the Criminal Justice and Public Order Act 1994

A:2.12 Authority for a constable in uniform to stop and search under section 60 of the Criminal Justice and Public Order Act 1994 may be given if the authorising officer reasonably believes: **A-5g**

(a) that incidents involving serious violence may take place in any locality in the officer's police area, and it is expedient to use these powers to prevent their occurrence;

(b) that persons are carrying dangerous instruments or offensive weapons without good reason in any locality in the officer's police area; or

(c) that an incident involving serious violence has taken place in the officer's police area, a dangerous instrument or offensive weapon used in the incident is being carried by a person in any locality in that police area, and it is expedient to use these powers to find that instrument or weapon.

A:2.13 An authorisation under section 60 may only be given by an officer of the rank of inspector or above and in writing, or orally if paragraph 2.12(c) applies and it is not practicable to give the authorisation in writing. The authorisation (whether written or oral) must specify the grounds on which it was given, the locality in which the powers may be exercised and the period of time for which they are in force. The period authorised shall be no longer than appears reasonably necessary to prevent, or seek to prevent incidents of serious violence, or to deal with the problem of carrying dangerous instruments or offensive weapons or to find a dangerous instrument or offensive weapon that has been used. It may not exceed 24 hours. An oral authorisation given where paragraph 2.12(c) applies must be recorded in writing as soon as practicable. [See *Notes 10–13.*]

A:2.14 An inspector who gives an authorisation must, as soon as practicable, inform an officer of or above the rank of superintendent. This officer may direct that the authorisation shall be extended for a further 24 hours, if violence or the carrying of dangerous instruments or offensive weapons has occurred, or is suspected to have occurred, and the continued use of the powers is considered necessary to prevent or deal with further such activity or to find a dangerous instrument or offensive weapon that has been used. That direction must be given in writing unless it is not practicable to do so, in which case it must be recorded in writing as soon as practicable afterwards. [See *Note 12.*]

A:2.14A The selection of persons and vehicles under section 60 to be stopped and, if appropriate, searched should reflect an objective assessment of the nature of the incident or weapon in question and the individuals and vehicles thought likely to be associated with that incident or those weapons [see *Notes 10* and *11*]. The powers must not be used to stop and search persons and vehicles for reasons unconnected with the purpose of the authorisation. When selecting persons and vehicles to be stopped in response to a specific threat or incident, officers must take care not to discriminate unlawfully against anyone on the grounds of any of the protected characteristics set out in the Equality Act 2010 (see paragraph 1.1).

A:2.14B The driver of a vehicle which is stopped under section 60 and any person who is searched under section 60 are entitled to a written statement to that effect if they apply within twelve months from the day the vehicle was stopped or the person was searched. This statement is a record which states that the vehicle was stopped or (as the case may be) that the person was searched under section 60 and it may form part of the search record or be supplied as a separate record.

Powers to require removal of face coverings

A-6   A:2.15 Section 60AA of the Criminal Justice and Public Order Act 1994 also provides a power to demand the removal of disguises. The officer exercising the power must reasonably believe that someone is wearing an item wholly or mainly for the purpose of concealing identity. There is also a power to seize such items where the officer believes that a person intends to wear them for this purpose. There is no power to stop and search for disguises. An officer may seize any such item which is discovered when exercising a power of search for something else, or which is being carried, and which the officer reasonably believes is intended to be used for concealing anyone's identity. This power can only be used if an authorisation given under section 60, or under section 60AA, is in force. [See *Note 4.*]

A:2.16 Authority under section 60AA for a constable in uniform to require the removal of disguises and to seize them may be given if the authorising officer reasonably believes that activities may take place in any locality in the officer's police area that are likely to involve the commission of offences and it is expedient to use these powers to prevent or control these activities.

A:2.17 An authorisation under section 60AA may only be given by an officer of the rank of inspector or above, in writing, specifying the grounds on which it was given, the locality in which the powers may be exercised and the period of time for which they are in force. The period authorised shall be no longer than appears reasonably necessary to prevent, or seek to prevent the commission of offences. It may not exceed 24 hours. [See *Notes 10–13.*]

A:2.18 An inspector who gives an authorisation must, as soon as practicable, inform an officer of or above the rank of superintendent. This officer may direct that the authorisation shall be extended for a further 24 hours, if crimes have been committed, or are suspected to have been committed, and the continued use of the powers is considered necessary to prevent or deal with further such activity. This direction must also be given in writing at the time or as soon as practicable afterwards. [See *Note 12.*]

(c) [Not used]

(d) Searches under Schedule 5 to the Terrorism Prevention and Investigation Measures Act 2011

A-7   A:2.18A Paragraph 3 of Schedule 5 to the TPIM Act 2011 allows a constable to detain an individual to be searched under the following powers:

- (i) paragraph 6(2)(a) when a TPIM notice is being, or has just been, served on the individual for the purpose of ascertaining whether there is anything on the individual that contravenes measures specified in the notice;
- (ii) paragraph 8(2)(a) in accordance with a warrant to search the individual issued by a justice of the peace in England and Wales, a sheriff in Scotland or a lay magistrate in Northern Ireland who is satisfied that a search is necessary for the purpose of determining whether an individual in respect of whom a TPIM notice is in force is complying with measures specified in the notice (see para. 2.20); and
- (iii) paragraph 10 to ascertain whether an individual in respect of whom a TPIM notice is in force is in possession of anything that could be used to threaten or harm any person.

See paragraph 2.1(e).

A:2.19 The exercise of the powers mentioned in paragraph 2.18A does not require the constable to have reasonable grounds to suspect that the individual:

- (a) has been, or is, contravening any of the measures specified in the TPIM notice; or
- (b) has on them anything which:
  - in the case of the power in sub-paragraph (i), contravenes measures specified in the TPIM notice;
  - in the case of the power in sub-paragraph (ii) is not complying with measures specified in the TPIM notice; or
  - in the case of the power in sub-paragraph (iii), could be used to threaten or harm any person.

A:2.20 A search of an individual on warrant under the power mentioned in paragraph 2.18A(ii) must carried [*sic*] out within 28 days of the issue of the warrant and:

- the individual may be searched on one occasion only within that period;
- the search must take place at a reasonable hour unless it appears that this would frustrate the purposes of the search.

A:2.21–2.25 [*Not used.*]

A:2.26 The powers under Schedule 5 allow a constable to conduct a search of an individual only for specified purposes relating to a TPIM notice as set out above. However, anything found may be seized and retained if there are reasonable grounds for believing that it is or it contains evidence of any offence for use at a trial for that offence or to prevent it being concealed, lost, damaged, altered, or destroyed. However, this would not prevent a search being carried out under other search powers if, in the course of exercising these powers, the officer formed reasonable grounds for suspicion.

(e) Powers to search persons in the exercise of a power to search premises

A:2.27 The following powers to search premises also authorise the search of a person, not under arrest, who is found on the premises during the course of the search: **A-8**

- (a) section 139B of the Criminal Justice Act 1988 under which a constable may enter school premises and search the premises and any person on those premises for any bladed or pointed article or offensive weapon;
- (b) under a warrant issued under section 23(3) of the Misuse of Drugs Act 1971 to search premises for drugs or documents but only if the warrant specifically authorises the search of persons found on the premises; and
- (c) under a search warrant or order issued under paragraph 1, 3 or 11 of Schedule 5 to the Terrorism Act 2000 to search premises and any person found there for material likely to be of substantial value to a terrorist investigation.

A:2.28 Before the power under section 139B of the Criminal Justice Act 1988 may be exercised, the constable must have reasonable grounds to suspect that an offence under section 139A or 139AA of the Criminal Justice Act 1988 (having a bladed or pointed article or offensive weapon on school premises) has been or is being committed. A warrant to search premises and persons found therein may be issued under section 23(3) of the Misuse of Drugs Act 1971 if there are reasonable grounds to suspect that controlled drugs or certain documents are in the possession of a person on the premises.

A:2.29 The powers in paragraph 2.27 do not require prior specific grounds to suspect that the person to be searched is in possession of an item for which there is an existing power to search. However, it is still necessary to ensure that the selection and treatment of those searched under these powers is based upon objective factors connected with the search of the premises, and not upon personal prejudice.

A:3 Conduct of searches

A:3.1 All stops and searches must be carried out with courtesy, consideration and respect for the **A-9** person concerned. This has a significant impact on public confidence in the police. Every reasonable effort must be made to minimise the embarrassment that a person being searched may experience. [See *Note 4.*]

A:3.2 The co-operation of the person to be searched must be sought in every case, even if the person initially objects to the search. A forcible search may be made only if it has been established that the person is unwilling to co-operate or resists. Reasonable force may be used as a last resort if necessary to conduct a search or to detain a person or vehicle for the purposes of a search.

As to this paragraph, see *James v. DPP* (§ 15-41 in the main work).

A:3.3 The length of time for which a person or vehicle may be detained must be reasonable and kept to a minimum. Where the exercise of the power requires reasonable suspicion, the thoroughness and extent of a search must depend on what is suspected of being carried, and by whom. If the suspicion relates to a particular article which is seen to be slipped into a person's pocket, then, in the absence of other grounds for suspicion or an opportunity for the article to be moved elsewhere, the search must be confined to that pocket. In the case of a small article which can readily be concealed, such as a drug, and which might be concealed anywhere on the person, a more extensive search may be necessary. In the case of searches mentioned in paragraph 2.1(b) and (d), which do not require reasonable grounds for suspicion, officers may make any reasonable search to look for items for which they are empowered to search. [See *Note 5.*]

A:3.4 The search must be carried out at or near the place where the person or vehicle was first detained. [See *Note 6.*]

A:3.5 There is no power to require a person to remove any clothing in public other than an outer coat, jacket or gloves, except under section 60AA of the Criminal Justice and Public Order Act 1994 (which empowers a constable to require a person to remove any item worn to conceal identity). [See *Notes 4* and *6.*] A search in public of a person's clothing which has not been removed must be restricted to superficial examination of outer garments. This does not, however, prevent an officer from placing his or her hand inside the pockets of the outer clothing, or feeling round the inside of collars, socks and shoes if this is reasonably necessary in the circumstances to look for the object of the search or to remove and examine any item reasonably suspected to be the object of the search. For the same reasons, subject to the restrictions on the removal of headgear, a person's hair may also be searched in public (see paragraphs 3.1 and 3.3).

A:3.6 Where on reasonable grounds it is considered necessary to conduct a more thorough search (*e.g.* by requiring a person to take off a T-shirt), this must be done out of public view, for example, in a police van unless paragraph 3.7 applies, or police station if there is one nearby. [See *Note 6.*] Any search involving the removal of more than an outer coat, jacket, gloves, headgear or footwear, or any other item concealing identity, may only be made by an officer of the same sex as the person searched and may not be made in the presence of anyone of the opposite sex unless the person being searched specifically requests it. [See Code C, Annex L and *Notes 4* and *7.*]

A:3.7 Searches involving exposure of intimate parts of the body must not be conducted as a routine extension of a less thorough search, simply because nothing is found in the course of the initial search. Searches involving exposure of intimate parts of the body may be carried out only at a nearby police station or other nearby location which is out of public view (but not a police vehicle). These searches must be conducted in accordance with paragraph 11 of Annex A to Code C except that an intimate search mentioned in paragraph 11(f) of Annex A to Code C may not be authorised or carried out under any stop and search powers. The other provisions of Code C do not apply to the conduct and recording of searches of persons detained at police stations in the exercise of stop and search powers. [See *Note 7.*]

Steps to be taken prior to a search

A-10   A:3.8 Before any search of a detained person or attended vehicle takes place the officer must take reasonable steps, if not in uniform (see para. 3.9), to show their warrant card to the person to be searched or in charge of the vehicle to be searched and, whether or not in uniform, to give that person the following information:

  (a) that they are being detained for the purposes of a search;

  (b) the officer's name (except in the case of enquiries linked to the investigation of terrorism, or otherwise where the officer reasonably believes that giving their name might put them in danger, in which case a warrant or other identification number shall be given) and the name of the police station to which the officer is attached;

  (c) the legal search power which is being exercised; and

  (d) a clear explanation of:

      (i) the object of the search in terms of the article or articles for which there is a power to search; and

    (ii) in the case of:
- the power under section 60 of the Criminal Justice and Public Order Act 1994 (see para. 2.1(b)), the nature of the power, the authorisation and the fact that it has been given;
- the powers under Schedule 5 to the Terrorism Prevention and Investigation Measures Act 2011 (see paras 2.1(e) and 2.18A):
  - the fact that a TPIM notice is in force or (in the case of para. 6(2)(a)) that a TPIM notice is being served;
  - the nature of the power being exercised (for a search under para. 8 of Schedule 5, the warrant must be produced and the person provided with a copy of it);
- all other powers requiring reasonable suspicion (see para. 2.1(a)), the grounds for that suspicion (this means explaining the basis for the suspicion by reference to information and/or intelligence about, or some specific behaviour by, the person concerned (see para. 2.2));

(e) that they are entitled to a copy of the record of the search if one is made (see section 4 below) if they ask within 3 months from the date of the search and:

    (i) if they are not arrested and taken to a police station as a result of the search and it is practicable to make the record on the spot, that immediately after the search is completed they will be given, if they request, either:
- a copy of the record, or
- a receipt which explains how they can obtain a copy of the full record or access to an electronic copy of the record; or

    (ii) if they are arrested and taken to a police station as a result of the search, that the record will be made at the station as part of their custody record and they will be given, if they request, a copy of their custody record which includes a record of the search as soon as practicable whilst they are at the station. [See *Note 16*.]

A:3.9 Stops and searches under the power mentioned in paragraph 2.1(b) may be undertaken only by a constable in uniform.

A:3.10 The person should also be given information about police powers to stop and search and the individual's rights in these circumstances.

A:3.11 If the person to be searched, or in charge of a vehicle to be searched, does not appear to understand what is being said, or there is any doubt about the person's ability to understand English, the officer must take reasonable steps to bring information regarding the person's rights and any relevant provisions of this code to his or her attention. If the person is deaf or cannot understand English and is accompanied by someone, then the officer must try to establish whether that person can interpret or otherwise help the officer to give the required information.

A:4 Recording requirements

(a) Searches which do not result in an arrest

A:4.1 When an officer carries out a search in the exercise of any power to which this code applies **A-11** and the search does not result in the person searched or person in charge of the vehicle searched being arrested and taken to a police station, a record must be made of it, electronically or on paper, unless there are exceptional circumstances which make this wholly impracticable (*e.g.* in situations involving public disorder or when the recording officer's presence is urgently required elsewhere). If a record is to be made, the officer carrying out the search must make the record on the spot unless this is not practicable, in which case the officer must make the record as soon as practicable after the search is completed. [See *Note 16*.]

A:4.2 If the record is made at the time, the person who has been searched or who is in charge of the vehicle that has been searched must be asked if they want a copy and if they do, they must be given immediately, either:
- a copy of the record, or
- a receipt which explains how they can obtain a copy of the full record or access to an electronic copy of the record.

A:4.2A An officer is not required to provide a copy of the full record or a receipt at the time if they are called to an incident of higher priority. [See *Note 21*.]

(b) Searches which result in an arrest

A:4.2B If a search in the exercise of any power to which this code applies results in a person being **A-11a** arrested and taken to a police station, the officer carrying out the search is responsible for ensuring that a record of the search is made as part of their custody record. The custody officer must then ensure that the person is asked if they want a copy of the record and if they do, that they are given a copy as soon as practicable. [See *Note 16.*]

(c) Record of search

A:4.3 The record of a search must always include the following information:

(a) a note of the self-defined ethnicity, and if different, the ethnicity as perceived by the officer making the search, of the person searched or of the person in charge of the vehicle searched (as the case may be) [see *Note 18*];

(b) the date, time and place the person or vehicle was searched [see *Note 6*];

(c) the object of the search in terms of the article or articles for which there is a power to search;

(d) in the case of:

- the power under section 60 of the Criminal Justice and Public Order Act 1994 (see paragraph 2.1(b)), the nature of the power, the authorisation and the fact that it has been given [see *Note 17*];

- the powers under Schedule 5 to the Terrorism Prevention and Investigation Measures Act 2011 (see paras 2.1(e) and 2.18A):

  - the fact that a TPIM notice is in force or (in the case of para. 6(2)(a)) that a TPIM notice is being served;

  - the nature of the power, and

  - for a search under paragraph 8, the date the search warrant was issued, the fact that the warrant was produced and a copy of it provided and the warrant must also be endorsed by the constable executing it to state whether anything was found and whether anything was seized, and

- all other powers requiring reasonable suspicion (see para. 2.1(a)), the grounds for that suspicion;

(e) subject to paragraph 3.8(b), the identity of the officer carrying out the search. [See *Note 15.*]

A:4.3A For the purposes of completing the search record, there is no requirement to record the name, address and date of birth of the person searched or the person in charge of a vehicle which is searched. The person is under no obligation to provide this information and they should not be asked to provide it for the purpose of completing the record.

A:4.4 Nothing in paragraph 4.3 requires the names of police officers to be shown on the search record or any other record required to be made under this code in the case of enquiries linked to the investigation of terrorism or otherwise where an officer reasonably believes that recording names might endanger the officers. In such cases the record must show the officers' warrant or other identification number and duty station.

A:4.5 A record is required for each person and each vehicle searched. However, if a person is in a vehicle and both are searched, and the object and grounds of the search are the same, only one record need be completed. If more than one person in a vehicle is searched, separate records for each search of a person must be made. If only a vehicle is searched, the self-defined ethnic background of the person in charge of the vehicle must be recorded, unless the vehicle is unattended.

A:4.6 The record of the grounds for making a search must, briefly but informatively, explain the reason for suspecting the person concerned, by reference to information and/or intelligence about, or some specific behaviour by, the person concerned (see para. 2.2).

A:4.7 Where officers detain an individual with a view to performing a search, but the need to search is eliminated as a result of questioning the person detained, a search should not be carried out and a record is not required. [See paragraph 2.10, *Notes 3* and *22A.*]

A:4.8 After searching an unattended vehicle, or anything in or on it, an officer must leave a notice in it (or on it, if things on it have been searched without opening it) recording the fact that it has been searched.

A:4.9 The notice must include the name of the police station to which the officer concerned is attached and state where a copy of the record of the search may be obtained and how (if applicable) an electronic copy may be accessed and where any application for compensation should be directed.

A:4.10 The vehicle must if practicable be left secure.

Recording of encounters not governed by statutory powers

A:4.11 [*Not used.*]

A:4.12 There is no national requirement for an officer who requests a person in a public place to **A-11d** account for themselves, *i.e.* their actions, behaviour, presence in an area or possession of anything, to make any record of the encounter or to give the person a receipt. [See para. 2.11 and *Notes 22A* and *22B*.]

A:5 Monitoring and supervising the use of stop and search powers

General

A:5.1 Any misuse of stop and search powers is likely to be harmful to policing and lead to mistrust **A-12** of the police by the local community and by the public in general. Supervising officers must monitor the use of stop and search powers and should consider in particular whether there is any evidence that they are being exercised on the basis of stereotyped images or inappropriate generalisations. Supervising officers must satisfy themselves that the practice of officers under their supervision in stopping, searching and recording is fully in accordance with this code. Supervisors must also examine whether the records reveal any trends or patterns which give cause for concern, and if so take appropriate action to address this. (See para. 2.8A.)

A:5.2 Senior officers with area or force-wide responsibilities must also monitor the broader use of stop and search powers and, where necessary, take action at the relevant level.

A:5.3 Supervision and monitoring must be supported by the compilation of comprehensive statistical records of stops and searches at force, area and local level. Any apparently disproportionate use of the powers by particular officers or groups of officers or in relation to specific sections of the community should be identified and investigated.

A:5.4 In order to promote public confidence in the use of the powers, forces in consultation with police and crime commissioners must make arrangements for the records to be scrutinised by representatives of the community, and to explain the use of the powers at a local level. [See *Note 19*.]

Suspected misuse of powers by individual officers

A:5.5 Police supervisors must monitor the use of stop and search powers by individual officers to **A-12a** ensure that they are being applied appropriately and lawfully. Monitoring takes many forms, such as direct supervision of the exercise of the powers, examining stop and search records (particularly examining the officer's documented reasonable grounds for suspicion) and asking the officer to account for the way in which they conducted and recorded particular searches or through complaints about a stop and search that an officer has carried out.

A:5.6 Where a supervisor identifies issues with the way that an officer has used a stop and search power, the facts of the case will determine whether the standards of professional behaviour as set out in the Code of Ethics (see http://www.college.police.uk/en/20972.htm) have been breached and which formal action is pursued. Improper use might be a result of poor performance or a conduct matter, which will require the supervisor to take appropriate action such as performance or misconduct procedures. It is imperative that supervisors take both timely and appropriate action to deal with all such cases that come to their notice.

Notes for Guidance

Officers exercising stop and search powers

A:1 *This code does not affect the ability of an officer to speak to or question a person in the ordinary course of* **A-13** *the officer's duties without detaining the person or exercising any element of compulsion. It is not the purpose of the code to prohibit such encounters between the police and the community with the co-operation of the person concerned and neither does it affect the principle that all citizens have a duty to help police officers to prevent crime and discover offenders. This is a civic rather than a legal duty; but when a police officer is trying to discover whether, or by whom, an offence has been committed he or she may question any person from whom useful information might be obtained, subject to the restrictions imposed by Code C. A person's unwillingness to reply does not alter this entitlement, but in the absence of a power to arrest, or to detain in order to search, the person is free to leave at will and cannot be compelled to remain with the officer.*

A:1A *In paragraphs 1.1 and 2.2B(a), the "relevant protected characteristics" are: age, disability, gender reassignment, pregnancy and maternity, race, religion or belief, sex and sexual orientation.*

A:1B *Innocent possession means that the person does have* [sic] *the guilty knowledge that they are carrying an unlawful item which is required before an arrest on suspicion that the person has committed an offence in respect of the item sought (if arrest is necessary – see PACE Code G) and/or a criminal prosecution) can be considered. It is not uncommon for children under the age of criminal responsibility to be used by older children and adults to carry stolen property, drugs and weapons and, in some cases, firearms, for the criminal benefit of others, either:*

  • *in the hope that police may not suspect they are being used for carrying the items; or*

- *knowing that if they are suspected of being couriers and are stopped and searched, they cannot be arrested or prosecuted for any criminal offence.*

Stop and search powers therefore allow the police to intervene effectively to break up criminal gangs and groups that use young children to further their criminal activities.

A:1BA *Whenever a child under 10 is suspected of carrying unlawful items for someone else, or is found in circumstances which suggest that their welfare and safety may be at risk, the facts should be reported and actioned in accordance with established force safeguarding procedures. This will be in addition to treating them as a potentially vulnerable or intimidated witness in respect of their status as a witness to the serious criminal offence(s) committed by those using them as couriers. Safeguarding considerations will also apply to other persons aged under 18 who are stopped and searched under any of the powers to which this code applies. See paragraph 1.1 with regard to the requirement under the Children Act 2004, s.11, for chief police officers and other specified persons and bodies, to ensure that in the discharge of their functions, they have regard to the need to safeguard and promote the welfare of all persons under the age of 18.*

A:2 *In some circumstances preparatory questioning may be unnecessary, but in general a brief conversation or exchange will be desirable not only as a means of avoiding unsuccessful searches, but to explain the grounds for the stop/search, to gain cooperation and reduce any tension there might be surrounding the stop/ search.*

A:3 *Where a person is lawfully detained for the purpose of a search, but no search in the event takes place, the detention will not thereby have been rendered unlawful.*

A:4 *Many people customarily cover their heads or faces for religious reasons—for example, Muslim women, Sikh men, Sikh or Hindu women, or Rastafarian men or women. A police officer cannot order the removal of a head or face covering except where there is reason to believe that the item is being worn by the individual wholly or mainly for the purpose of disguising identity, not simply because it disguises identity. Where there may be religious sensitivities about ordering the removal of such an item, the officer should permit the item to be removed out of public view. Where practicable, the item should be removed in the presence of an officer of the same sex as the person and out of sight of anyone of the opposite sex (see Code C, Annex L).*

A:5 *A search of a person in public should be completed as soon as possible.*

A:6 *A person may be detained under a stop and search power at a place other than where the person was first detained, only if that place, be it a police station or elsewhere, is nearby. Such a place should be located within a reasonable travelling distance using whatever mode of travel (on foot or by car) is appropriate. This applies to all searches under stop and search powers, whether or not they involve the removal of clothing or exposure of intimate parts of the body (see paragraphs 3.6 and 3.7) or take place in or out of public view. It means, for example, that a search under the stop and search power in section 23 of the Misuse of Drugs Act 1971 which involves the compulsory removal of more than a person's outer coat, jacket or gloves cannot be carried out unless a place which is both nearby the place they were first detained and out of public view, is available. If a search involves exposure of intimate parts of the body and a police station is not nearby, particular care must be taken to ensure that the location is suitable in that it enables the search to be conducted in accordance with the requirements of paragraph 11 of Annex A to Code C.*

A:7 *A search in the street itself should be regarded as being in public for the purposes of paragraphs 3.6 and 3.7 above, even though it may be empty at the time a search begins. Although there is no power to require a person to do so, there is nothing to prevent an officer from asking a person voluntarily to remove more than an outer coat, jacket or gloves in public.*

A:8 [Not used.]

A:9 *Other means of identification might include jewellery, insignias, tattoos or other features which are known to identify members of the particular gang or group.*

A:9A *A decision to search individuals believed to be members of a particular group or gang must be judged on a case by case basis according to the circumstances applicable at the time of the proposed searches and in particular, having regard to:*

    (a) *the number of items suspected of being carried;*

    (b) *the nature of those items and the risk they pose; and*

    (c) *the number of individuals to be searched.*

      A group search will only be justified if it is a necessary and proportionate approach based on the facts and having regard to the nature of the suspicion in these cases. The extent and thoroughness of the searches must not be excessive.

      The size of the group and the number of individuals it is proposed to search will be a key factor and steps should be taken to identify those who are to be searched to avoid unnecessary inconvenience to unconnected members of the public who are also present.

      The onus is on the police to be satisfied and to demonstrate that their approach to the decision to search is in pursuit of a legitimate aim, necessary and proportionate.

Authorising officers

A-14   A:10 *The powers under section 60 are separate from and additional to the normal stop and search powers* which require reasonable grounds to suspect an individual of carrying an offensive weapon (or other article). Their overall purpose is to prevent serious violence and the widespread carrying of weapons which might lead to persons being seriously injured by disarming potential offenders or finding weapons that have been used in circumstances where other powers would not be sufficient. They should not therefore be used to replace or circumvent the normal powers for dealing with routine crime problems. A particular example might be an authorisation to prevent serious violence or the carrying of offensive weapons at a sports event by rival team supporters when the expected general appearance and age range of those likely to be responsible, alone, would not be sufficiently distinctive to support reasonable suspicion (see paragraph 2.6). The purpose of the powers under section 60AA is to prevent those involved in intimidatory or violent protests using face coverings to disguise identity.

A:11 *Authorisations under section 60 require a reasonable belief on the part of the authorising officer. This must have an objective basis, for example: intelligence or relevant information such as a history of antagonism and violence between particular groups; previous incidents of violence at, or connected with, particular events or locations; a significant increase in knife-point robberies in a limited area; reports that individuals are regularly carrying weapons in a particular locality; information following an incident in which weapons were used about where the weapons might be found or in the case of section 60AA previous incidents of crimes being committed while wearing face coverings to conceal identity.*

A:12 *It is for the authorising officer to determine the period of time during which the powers mentioned in paragraph 2.1(b) may be exercised. The officer should set the minimum period he or she considers necessary to deal with the risk of violence, the carrying of knives or offensive weapons, or to find dangerous instruments or weapons that have been used. A direction to extend the period authorised under the powers mentioned in paragraph 2.1(b) may be given only once. Thereafter further use of the powers requires a new authorisation.*

A:13 *It is for the authorising officer to determine the geographical area in which the use of the powers is to be authorised. In doing so the officer may wish to take into account factors such as the nature and venue of the anticipated incident or the incident which has taken place, the number of people who may be in the immediate area of that incident, their access to surrounding areas and the anticipated or actual level of violence. The officer should not set a geographical area which is wider than that he or she believes necessary for the purpose of preventing anticipated violence, the carrying of knives or offensive weapons, or for finding a dangerous instrument or weapon that has been used or, in the case of section 60AA, the prevention of commission of offences. It is particularly important to ensure that constables exercising such powers are fully aware of the locality within which they may be used. The officer giving the authorisation should therefore specify either the streets which form the boundary of the locality or a divisional boundary if appropriate within the force area. If the power is to be used in response to a threat or incident that straddles police force areas, an officer from each of the forces concerned will need to give an authorisation.*

A:14 [Not used.]

Recording

A:15 *Where a stop and search is conducted by more than one officer the identity of all the officers engaged in the search must be recorded on the record. Nothing prevents an officer who is present but not directly involved in searching from completing the record during the course of the encounter.* **A-15**

A:16 *When the search results in the person searched or in charge of a vehicle which is searched being arrested, the requirement to make the record of the search as part of the person's custody record does not apply if the person is granted "street bail" after arrest (see section 30A of PACE) to attend a police station and is not taken in custody to the police station. An arrested person's entitlement to a copy of the search record which is made as part of their custody record does not affect their entitlement to a copy of their custody record or any other provisions of PACE Code C section 2 (custody records).*

A:17 *It is important for monitoring purposes to specify when authority is given for exercising the stop and search power under section 60 of the Criminal Justice and Public Order Act 1994.*

A:18 *Officers should record the self-defined ethnicity of every person stopped according to the categories used in the 2001 census question listed in Annex B. The person should be asked to select one of the five main categories representing broad ethnic groups and then a more specific cultural background from within this group. The ethnic classification should be coded for recording purposes using the coding system in Annex B. An additional "Not stated" box is available but should not be offered to respondents explicitly. Officers should be aware and explain to members of the public, especially where concerns are raised, that this information is required to obtain a true picture of stop and search activity and to help improve ethnic monitoring, tackle discriminatory practice, and promote effective use of the powers. If the person gives what appears to the officer to be an "incorrect" answer (e.g. a person who appears to be white states that they are black), the officer should record the response that has been given and then record their own perception of the person's ethnic background by using the PNC classification system. If the "Not stated" category is used the reason for this must be recorded on the form.*

A:19 *Arrangements for public scrutiny of records should take account of the right to confidentiality of those stopped and searched. Anonymised forms and/or statistics generated from records should be the focus of the examinations by members of the public. The groups that are consulted should always include children and young persons.*

A:20 [Not used.]

A:21 *In situations where it is not practicable to provide a written copy of the record or immediate access to an electronic copy of the record or a receipt of the search at the time (see paragraph 4.2A above), the officer should consider giving the person details of the station which they may attend for a copy of the record. A receipt may take the form of a simple business card which includes sufficient information to locate the record should the person ask for copy [sic], for example, the date and place of the search, and a reference number or the name of the officer who carried out the search (unless paragraph 4.4 applies).*

A:22 [Not used.]

A:22A *Where there are concerns which make it necessary to monitor any local disproportionality, forces have discretion to direct officers to record the self-defined ethnicity of persons they request to account for themselves in a public place or who they detain with a view to searching but do not search. Guidance should be provided locally and efforts made to minimise the bureaucracy involved. Records should be closely monitored and supervised in line with paragraphs 5.1 to 5.6, and forces can suspend or re-instate recording of these encounters as appropriate.*

A:22B *A person who is asked to account for themselves should, if they request, be given information about how they can report their dissatisfaction about how they have been treated.*

Definition of offensive weapon

A:23 *"Offensive weapon" is defined as "any article made or adapted for use by him for causing injury to the person, or intended by the person having it with him for such use or by someone else". There are three categories of offensive weapons: those made for causing injury to the person; those adapted for such a purpose; and those not so made or adapted, but carried with the intention of causing injury to the person. A firearm, as defined by section 57 of the Firearms Act 1968, would fall within the definition of offensive weapon if any of the criteria above apply.*

ANNEX A

Summary of main stop and search powers to which Code A applies

A-16

This table relates to stop and search powers only. Individual statutes below may contain other police powers of entry, search and seizure.

Power	Object of search	Extent of Search	Where Exercisable
Unlawful articles general			
1. Public Stores Act 1875, s.6	HM Stores stolen or unlawfully obtained	Persons, vehicles and vessels	Anywhere where the constabulary powers are exercisable
2. Firearms Act 1968, s.47	Firearms	Persons and vehicles	A public place, or anywhere in the case of reasonable suspicion of offences of carrying rearms with criminal intent or trespassing with firearms
3. Misuse of Drugs Act 1971, s.23	Controlled drugs	Persons and vehicles	Anywhere
4. Customs and Excise Management Act 1979, s.163	Goods: (a) on which duty has not been paid; (b) being unlawfully removed, imported or exported; (c) otherwise liable to forfeiture to HM Revenue and Customs	Vehicles and vessels only	Anywhere
5. Aviation Security Act 1982, s.24B *Note: This power applies throughout the UK but the provisions of this code will apply only when the power is exercised at an aerodrome situated in England and Wales.*	Stolen articles or articles made, adapted or intended for use in the course of/in connection with conduct which constitutes an offence in the part of the UK where the aerodrome is situated or would do so, if it occurred there.	Persons, vehicles, aircraft Anything in or on a vehicle or aircraft	Any part of an aerodrome
6. Police and Criminal Evidence Act 1984, s.1	Stolen goods;	Persons and vehicles	Where there is public access
	Articles made, adapted or intended for use in the course of or in connection with, certain offences under the Theft Act 1968, Fraud Act and Criminal Damage Act 1971;	Persons and vehicles	Where there is public access
	Offensive weapons, bladed or sharply-pointed articles (except folding pocket knives with a blade cutting edge not exceeding 3 inches);	Persons and vehicles	Where there is public access
	Fireworks: category 4 (display grade) fireworks if possession prohibited, adult fireworks in possession of a person under 18 in a public place.	Persons and vehicles	Where there is public access

Power	Object of search	Extent of Search	Where Exercisable
7. Sporting Events (Control of Alcohol etc.) Act 1985, s.7	Intoxicating liquor	Persons, coaches and trains	Designated sports grounds or coaches and trains travelling to or from a designated sporting event.
8. Crossbows Act 1987, s.4	Crossbows or parts of crossbows (except crossbows with a draw weight of less than 1.4 kilograms)	Persons and vehicles	Anywhere except dwellings
9. Criminal Justice Act 1988 s.139B	Offensive weapons, bladed or sharply pointed article	Persons	School premises
Evidence of game and wildlife offences			
10. Poaching Prevention Act 1862, s.2	Game or poaching equipment	Persons and vehicles	A public place
11. Deer Act 1991, s.12	Evidence of offences under the Act	Persons and vehicles	Anywhere except dwellings
12. Conservation of Seals Act 1970, s.4	Seals or hunting equipment	Vehicles only	Anywhere
13. Protection of Badgers Act 1992, s.11	Evidence offences under the Act	Persons and vehicles	Anywhere
14. Wildlife and Countryside Act 1981, s.19	Evidence of wildlife offences	Persons and vehicles	Anywhere except dwellings
Other			
15. Paragraphs 6 & 8 of Schedule 5 to the Terrorism Prevention and Investigation Measures Act 2011	Anything that contravenes measures specied in a TPIM notice.	Persons in respect of whom a TPIM notice is being served or is in force	Anywhere
16. Paragraph 10 of Schedule 5 to the Terrorism Prevention and Investigation Measures Act 2011	Anything that could be used to threaten or harm any person.	Persons in respect of whom a TPIM notice is in force.	Anywhere
17. [*Not used.*]			
18. [*Not used.*]			
19. Section 60 Criminal Justice and Public Order Act 1994	Offensive weapons or dangerous instruments to prevent incidents of serious violence or to deal with the carrying of such items or nd such items which have been used in incidents of serious violence	Persons and vehicles	Anywhere within a locality authorised under subsection (1)

ANNEX B

Self-defined ethnic classification categories

White	W
A. White—British	W1
B. White—Irish	W2
C. Any other White background	W9
Mixed	**M**
D. White and Black Caribbean	M1
E. White and Black African	M2
F. White and Asian	M3
G. Any other Mixed background	M9
Asian/ Asian—British	**A**
H. Asian—Indian	A1
I. Asian—Pakistani	A2
J. Asian—Bangladeshi	A3
K. Any other Asian background	A9
Black / Black—British	**B**
L. Black—Caribbean	B1
M. Black African	B2
N. Any other Black background	B9
Other	**O**
O. Chinese	O1
P. Any other	O9
Not stated	**NS**

ANNEX C

Summary of powers of community support officers to search and seize

The following is a summary of the search and seizure powers that may be exercised by a com- **A-17a**
munity support officer (CSO) who has been designated with the relevant powers in accordance with
Part 4 of the Police Reform Act 2002.

When exercising any of these powers, a CSO must have regard to any relevant provisions of this
code, including section 3 governing the conduct of searches and the steps to be taken prior to a
search.

1. [*Not used.*]

2. Powers to search requiring the consent of the person and seizure

A CSO may detain a person using reasonable force where necessary as set out in Part 1 of Schedule 4 to the Police Reform Act 2002. If the person has been lawfully detained, the CSO may search the person provided that person gives consent to such a search in relation to the following:

Designation	Powers conferred	Object of Search	Extent of Search	Where Exercisable
Police Reform Act 2002, Schedule 4, paragraphs 7 and 7A	(a) Criminal Justice and Police Act 2001, s.12(2)	(a) Alcohol or a container for alcohol	(a) Persons	(a) Designated public place
	(b) Confiscation of Alcohol (Young Persons) Act 1997, s.1	(b) Alcohol	(b) Persons under 18 years old	(b) Public place
	(c) Children and Young Persons Act 1933, s.7(3)	(c) Tobacco or cigarette papers	(c) Persons under 16 years old found smoking	(c) Public place

3. Powers to search not requiring the consent of the person and seizure

A CSO may detain a person using reasonable force where necessary as set out in Part 1 of Schedule 4 to the Police Reform Act 2002. If the person has been lawfully detained, the CSO may search the person without the need for that person's consent in relation to the following:

Designation	Power conferred	Object of Search	Extent of Search	Where Exercisable
Police Reform Act 2002, Schedule 4, paragraph 2A	Police and Criminal Evidence Act 1984, s.32	(a) Objects that might be used to cause physical injury to the person or the CSO. (b) Items that might be used to assist escape.	Persons made subject to a requirement to wait.	Any place where the requirement to wait has been made.

4. Powers to seize without consent

This power applies when drugs are found in the course of any search mentioned above.

Designation	Power conferred	Object of Seizure	Where Exercisable
Police Reform Act 2002, Schedule 4, paragraph 7B	Police Reform Act 2002, Schedule 4, paragraph 7B	Controlled drugs in a person's possession.	Any place where the person is in possession of the drug.

Annex D—Deleted
Annex E—Deleted

ANNEX F

Establishing gender of persons for the purpose of searching

See Code C, Annex L. **A-17b**

(3) Search and seizure

The text that follows is of the version of the code that came into force on October 27, 2013: see **A-18** *ante*, Appendix A-1.

For authorities in relation to Code B, see, in particular, § 15-126 in the main work.

B. CODE OF PRACTICE FOR SEARCHES OF PREMISES BY POLICE OFFICERS AND THE SEIZURE OF PROPERTY FOUND BY POLICE OFFICERS ON PERSONS OR PREMISES

Commencement—transitional arrangements

This code applies to applications for warrants made after 00.00 on 27 October 2013 and to **A-19** searches and seizures taking place after 00.00 on 27 October 2013.

B:1 Introduction

B:1.1 This code of practice deals with police powers to: **A-20**
- search premises
- seize and retain property found on premises and persons.

B:1.1A These powers may be used to find:
- property and material relating to a crime
- wanted persons
- children who abscond from local authority accommodation where they have been remanded or committed by a court.

B:1.2 A justice of the peace may issue a search warrant granting powers of entry, search and seizure, *e.g.* warrants to search for stolen property, drugs, firearms and evidence of serious offences. Police also have powers without a search warrant. The main ones provided by the Police and Criminal Evidence Act 1984 (PACE) include powers to search premises:
- to make an arrest
- after an arrest.

B:1.3 The right to privacy and respect for personal property are key principles of the Human Rights Act 1998. Powers of entry, search and seizure should be fully and clearly justified before use because they may significantly interfere with the occupier's privacy. Officers should consider if the necessary objectives can be met by less intrusive means.

B:1.3A Powers to search and seize must be used fairly, responsibly, with respect for people who occupy premises being searched or are in charge of property being seized and without unlawful discrimination. Under the Equality Act 2010, s.149, when police officers are carrying out their functions, they also have a duty to have due regard to the need to eliminate unlawful discrimination, harassment and victimisation, to advance equality of opportunity between people who share a relevant protected characteristic and people who do not share it, and to take steps to foster good relations between those persons. [See *Note 1A*.]

B:1.4 In all cases, police should therefore:
- exercise their powers courteously and with respect for persons and property
- only use reasonable force when this is considered necessary and proportionate to the circumstances.

B:1.5 If the provisions of PACE and this code are not observed, evidence obtained from a search may be open to question.

Notes for guidance

B:1A *In paragraph 1.3A, "relevant protected characteristic" includes: age, disability, gender reassignment, pregnancy and maternity, race, religion/belief, sex and sexual orientation.*

B:2 General

A-21

B:2.1 This code must be readily available at all police stations for consultation by:
- police officers
- police staff
- detained persons
- members of the public.

B:2.2 The *Notes for Guidance* included are not provisions of this code.

B:2.3 This code applies to searches of premises:

(a) by police for the purposes of an investigation into an alleged offence, with the occupier's consent, other than:
- routine scene of crime searches;
- calls to a fire or burglary made by or on behalf of an occupier or searches following the activation of fire or burglar alarms or discovery of insecure premises;
- searches when paragraph 5.4 applies;
- bomb threat calls;

(b) under powers conferred on police officers by PACE, ss.17, 18 and 32;

(c) undertaken in pursuance of search warrants issued to and executed by constables in accordance with PACE, ss.15 and 16 [see *Note 2A*];

(d) subject to paragraph 2.6, under any other power given to police to enter premises with or without a search warrant for any purpose connected with the investigation into an alleged or suspected offence. [See *Note 2B*.]

For the purposes of this code, "premises" as defined in PACE, s.23, includes any place, vehicle, vessel, aircraft, hovercraft, tent or movable structure and any offshore installation as defined in the Mineral Workings (Offshore Installations) Act 1971, s.1. [See *Note 2D*.]

B:2.4 A person who has not been arrested but is searched during a search of premises should be searched in accordance with Code A. [See *Note 2C*.]

B:2.5 This code does not apply to the exercise of a statutory power to enter premises or to inspect goods, equipment or procedures if the exercise of that power is not dependent on the existence of grounds for suspecting that an offence may have been committed and the person exercising the power has no reasonable grounds for such suspicion.

B:2.6 This code does not affect any directions or requirements of a search warrant, order or other power to search and seize lawfully exercised in England or Wales that any item or evidence seized under that warrant, order or power be handed over to a police force, court, tribunal, or other authority outside England or Wales. For example, warrants and orders issued in Scotland or Northern Ireland [see *Note 2B(f)*] and search warrants and powers provided for in sections 14 to 17 of the Crime (International Co-operation) Act 2003.

B:2.7 When this code requires the prior authority or agreement of an officer of at least inspector or superintendent rank, that authority may be given by a sergeant or chief inspector authorised to perform the functions of the higher rank under PACE, s.107.

B:2.8 Written records required under this code not made in the search record shall, unless otherwise specified, be made:
- in the recording officer's pocket book ("pocket book" includes any official report book issued to police officers), or
- on forms provided for the purpose.

B:2.9 Nothing in this code requires the identity of officers, or anyone accompanying them during a search of premises, to be recorded or disclosed:

(a) in the case of enquiries linked to the investigation of terrorism; or

(b) if officers reasonably believe recording or disclosing their names might put them in danger.

In these cases officers should use warrant or other identification numbers and the name of their police station. Police staff should use any identification number provided to them by the police force. [See *Note 2E*.]

B:2.10 The "officer in charge of the search" means the officer assigned specific duties and responsibilities under this code. Whenever there is a search of premises to which this code applies one officer must act as the officer in charge of the search. [See *Note 2F*.]

B:2.11 In this code:

(a) "designated person" means a person other than a police officer, designated under the Police Reform Act 2002, Pt 4 who has specified powers and duties of police officers conferred or imposed on them [see Note 2G];

(b) any reference to a police officer includes a designated person acting in the exercise or performance of the powers and duties conferred or imposed on them by their designation;

(c) a person authorised to accompany police officers or designated persons in the execution of a warrant has the same powers as a constable in the execution of the warrant and the search and seizure of anything related to the warrant. These powers must be exercised in the company and under the supervision of a police officer. [See *Note 3C.*]

B:2.12 If a power conferred on a designated person:

(a) allows reasonable force to be used when exercised by a police officer, a designated person exercising that power has the same entitlement to use force;

(b) includes power to use force to enter any premises, that power is not exercisable by that designated person except:

(i) in the company and under the supervision of a police officer; or

(ii) for the purpose of:

• saving life or limb; or

• preventing serious damage to property.

B:2.13 Designated persons must have regard to any relevant provisions of the codes of practice.

Notes for guidance

B:2A *PACE ss.15 and 16 apply to all search warrants issued to and executed by constables under any enact-* **A-22** *ment, e.g. search warrants issued by a:*

(a) *justice of the peace under the:*

• *Theft Act 1968, s.26—stolen property;*

• *Misuse of Drugs Act 1971, s.23—controlled drugs;*

• *PACE, s.8—evidence of an indictable offence;*

• *Terrorism Act 2000, Sched. 5, para. 1;*

• *Terrorism Prevention and Investigation Measures Act 2011, Sched. 5, para. 8(2)(b)— search of premises for compliance purposes (see para. 10.1);*

(b) *circuit judge under:*

• *PACE, Sched. 1;*

• *Terrorism Act 2000, Sched. 5, para. 11.*

B:2B *Examples of the other powers in paragraph 2.3(d) include:*

(a) *Road Traffic Act 1988, s.6E(1) giving police power to enter premises under section 6E(1) to:*

• *require a person to provide a specimen of breath; or*

• *arrest a person following:*

– *a positive breath test;*

– *failure to provide a specimen of breath;*

(b) *Transport and Works Act 1992, s.30(4) giving police powers to enter premises mirroring the powers in (a) in relation to specified persons working on transport systems to which the Act applies;*

(c) *Criminal Justice Act 1988, s.139B giving police power to enter and search school premises for offensive weapons, bladed or pointed articles;*

(d) *Terrorism Act 2000, Sched. 5, paras 3 and 15 empowering a superintendent in urgent cases to give written authority for police to enter and search premises for the purposes of a terrorist investigation;*

(e) *Explosives Act 1875, s.73(b) empowering a superintendent to give written authority for police to enter premises, examine and search them for explosives;*

(f) *search warrants and production orders or the equivalent issued in Scotland or Northern Ireland endorsed under the Summary Jurisdiction (Process) Act 1881 or the Petty Sessions (Ireland) Act 1851 respectively for execution in England and Wales;*

(g) *Terrorism Prevention and Investigation Measures Act 2011, Sched. 5, paras 5(1), 6(2)(b) and 7(2), searches relating to TPIM notices (see para. 10.1).*

B:2C *The Criminal Justice Act 1988, s.139B provides that a constable who has reasonable grounds to suspect an offence under the Criminal Justice Act 1988, s.139A or 139AA has or is being committed may enter school premises and search the premises and any persons on the premises for any bladed or pointed article or offensive weapon. Persons may be searched under a warrant issued under the Misuse of Drugs Act 1971, s.23(3) to search premises for drugs or documents only if the warrant specifically authorises the search of persons on the premises. Powers to search premises under certain terrorism provisions also authorise the search of persons on the premises, for example, under paragraphs 1, 2, 11 and 15 of Schedule 5 to the Terrorism Act 2000 and section 52 of the Anti-terrorism, Crime and Security Act 2001.*

B:2D *The Immigration Act 1971, Pt III and Sched. 2 gives immigration officers powers to enter and search premises, seize and retain property, with and without a search warrant. These are similar to the powers available to police under search warrants issued by a justice of the peace and without a warrant under PACE, ss.17, 18, 19 and 32 except they only apply to specified offences under the Immigration Act 1971 and immigration control powers. For certain types of investigations and enquiries these powers avoid the need for the Immigration Service to rely on police officers becoming directly involved. When exercising these powers, immigration officers are required by the Immigration and Asylum Act 1999, s.145 to have regard to this code's corresponding provisions. When immigration officers are dealing with persons or property at police stations, police officers should give appropriate assistance to help them discharge their specific duties and responsibilities.*

B:2E *The purpose of paragraph 2.9(b) is to protect those involved in serious organised crime investigations or arrests of particularly violent suspects when there is reliable information that those arrested or their associates may threaten or cause harm to the officers or anyone accompanying them during a search of premises. In cases of doubt, an officer of inspector rank or above should be consulted.*

B:2F *For the purposes of paragraph 2.10, the officer in charge of the search should normally be the most senior officer present. Some exceptions are:*

    (a) *a supervising officer who attends or assists at the scene of a premises search may appoint an officer of lower rank as officer in charge of the search if that officer is:*

        • *more conversant with the facts;*

        • *a more appropriate officer to be in charge of the search;*

    (b) *when all officers in a premises search are the same rank. The supervising officer if available, must make sure one of them is appointed officer in charge of the search, otherwise the officers themselves must nominate one of their number as the officer in charge;*

    (c) *a senior officer assisting in a specialist role. This officer need not be regarded as having a general supervisory role over the conduct of the search or be appointed or expected to act as the officer in charge of the search.*

Except in (c), nothing in this note diminishes the role and responsibilities of a supervisory officer who is present at the search or knows of a search taking place.

B:2G *An officer of the rank of inspector or above may direct a designated investigating officer not to wear a uniform for the purposes of a specific operation.*

B:3 Search warrants and production orders

(a) *Before making an application*

B:3.1 When information appears to justify an application, the officer must take reasonable steps to check the information is accurate, recent and not provided maliciously or irresponsibly. An application may not be made on the basis of information from an anonymous source if corroboration has not been sought. See *Note 3A*.

B:3.2 The officer shall ascertain as specifically as possible the nature of the articles concerned and their location.

B:3.3 The officer shall make reasonable enquiries to:

    (i) establish if:

        • anything is known about the likely occupier of the premises and the nature of the premises themselves;

        • the premises have been searched previously and how recently;

    (ii) obtain any other relevant information.

B:3.4 An application:

    (a) to a justice of the peace for a search warrant or to a circuit judge for a search warrant or production order under PACE, Sched. 1 must be supported by a signed written authority from an officer of inspector rank or above; [Note: if the case is an urgent application to a justice of the peace and an inspector or above is not readily available, the next most senior officer on duty can give the written authority];

    (b) to a circuit judge under the Terrorism Act 2000, Sched. 5 for:

        • a production order;

        • search warrant; or

        • an order requiring an explanation of material seized or produced under such a warrant or production order,

    must be supported by a signed written authority from an officer of superintendent rank or above.

B:3.5 Except in a case of urgency, if there is reason to believe a search might have an adverse effect on relations between the police and the community, the officer in charge shall consult the local police/community liaison officer:

- before the search; or
- in urgent cases, as soon as practicable after the search.

(b) *Making an application*

B:3.6 A search warrant application must be supported in writing, specifying:

 (a) the enactment under which the application is made [see *Note 2A*];

 (b) (i) whether the warrant is to authorise entry and search of:
- one set of premises; or
- if the application is under PACE, s.8, or Sched. 1, para. 12, more than one set of specified premises or all premises occupied or controlled by a specified person, and

 (ii) the premises to be searched;

 (c) the object of the search [see *Note 3B*];

 (d) the grounds for the application, including, when the purpose of the proposed search is to find evidence of an alleged offence, an indication of how the evidence relates to the investigation;

 (da) where the application is under PACE, s.8, or Sched. 1, para. 12 for a single warrant to enter and search:

 (i) more than one set of specified premises, the officer must specify each set of premises which it is desired to enter and search;

 (ii) all premises occupied or controlled by a specified person, the officer must specify:
- as many sets of premises which it is desired to enter and search as it is reasonably practicable to specify;
- the person who is in occupation or control of those premises and any others which it is desired to search;
- why it is necessary to search more premises than those which can be specified;
- why it is not reasonably practicable to specify all the premises which it is desired to enter and search;

 (db) whether an application under PACE, s.8 is for a warrant authorising entry and search on more than one occasion, and if so, the officer must state the grounds for this and whether the desired number of entries authorised is unlimited or a specified maximum;

 (e) that there are no reasonable grounds to believe the material to be sought, when making application to a:

 (i) justice of the peace or a circuit judge consists of or includes items subject to legal privilege;

 (ii) justice of the peace, consists of or includes excluded material or special procedure material;

 [Note: this does not affect the additional powers of seizure in the Criminal Justice and Police Act 2001, Pt 2 covered in paragraph 7.7 [see *Note 3B*]];

 (f) if applicable, a request for the warrant to authorise a person or persons to accompany the officer who executes the warrant [see *Note 3C*].

B:3.7 A search warrant application under PACE, Sched. 1, para. 12(a), shall if appropriate indicate why it is believed service of notice of an application for a production order may seriously prejudice the investigation. Applications for search warrants under the Terrorism Act 2000, Schedule 5, paragraph 11 must indicate why a production order would not be appropriate.

B:3.8 If a search warrant application is refused, a further application may not be made for those premises unless supported by additional grounds.

Notes for guidance

B:3A *The identity of an informant need not be disclosed when making an application, but the officer should be* **A-24** *prepared to answer any questions the magistrate or judge may have about:*
- *the accuracy of previous information from that source, and*
- *any other related matters.*

B:3B *The information supporting a search warrant application should be as specific as possible, particularly in relation to the articles or persons being sought and where in the premises it is suspected they may be found. The meaning of "items subject to legal privilege", "excluded material" and "special procedure material" are defined by PACE, ss.10, 11 and 14 respectively.*

B:3C *Under PACE, s.16(2), a search warrant may authorise persons other than police officers to accompany the constable who executes the warrant. This includes, e.g. any suitably qualified or skilled person or an expert in a particular field whose presence is needed to help accurately identify the material sought or to advise where certain evidence is most likely to be found and how it should be dealt with. It does not give them any right to force entry, but it gives them the right to be on the premises during the search and to search for or seize property without the occupier's permission.*

B:4 Entry without warrant—particular powers

(a) *Making an arrest etc*

A-25   B:4.1 The conditions under which an officer may enter and search premises without a warrant are set out in PACE, s.17. It should be noted that this section does not create or confer any powers of arrest. See other powers in *Note 2B(a)*.

(b) *Search of premises where arrest takes place or the arrested person was immediately before arrest*

B:4.2 When a person has been arrested for an indictable offence, a police officer has power under PACE, s.32 to search the premises where the person was arrested or where the person was immediately before being arrested.

(c) *Search of premises occupied or controlled by the arrested person*

B:4.3 The specific powers to search premises which are occupied or controlled by a person arrested for an indictable offence are set out in PACE, s.18. They may not be exercised, except if section 18 (5) applies, unless an officer of inspector rank or above has given written authority. That authority should only be given when the authorising officer is satisfied that the premises are occupied or controlled by the arrested person and that the necessary grounds exist. If possible the authorising officer should record the authority on the Notice of Powers and Rights and, subject to paragraph 2.9, sign the notice. The record of the grounds for the search and the nature of the evidence sought as required by section 18(7) of the Act should be made in:

- the custody record if there is one, otherwise
- the officer's pocket book, or
- the search record.

B:5 Search with consent

A-26   B:5.1 Subject to paragraph 5.4, if it is proposed to search premises with the consent of a person entitled to grant entry the consent must, if practicable, be given in writing on the Notice of Powers and Rights before the search. The officer must make any necessary enquiries to be satisfied the person is in a position to give such consent. [See *Notes 5A* and *5B*.]

B:5.2 Before seeking consent the officer in charge of the search shall state the purpose of the proposed search and its extent. This information must be as specific as possible, particularly regarding the articles or persons being sought and the parts of the premises to be searched. The person concerned must be clearly informed they are not obliged to consent, that any consent given can be withdrawn at any time, including before the search starts or while it is under way and anything seized may be produced in evidence. If at the time the person is not suspected of an offence, the officer shall say this when stating the purpose of the search.

B:5.3 An officer cannot enter and search or continue to search premises under paragraph 5.1 if consent is given under duress or withdrawn before the search is completed.

B:5.4 It is unnecessary to seek consent under paragraphs 5.1 and 5.2 if this would cause disproportionate inconvenience to the person concerned. [See *Note 5C.*]

Notes for guidance

A-27   B:5A *In a lodging house, hostel or similar accommodation, every reasonable effort should be made to obtain the consent of the tenant, lodger or occupier. A search should not be made solely on the basis of the landlord's consent.*

B:5B *If the intention is to search premises under the authority of a warrant or a power of entry and search without warrant, and the occupier of the premises co-operates in accordance with paragraph 6.4, there is no need to obtain written consent.*

B:5C *Paragraph 5.4 is intended to apply when it is reasonable to assume innocent occupiers would agree to, and expect, police to take the proposed action, e.g. if:*

- *a suspect has fled the scene of a crime or to evade arrest and it is necessary quickly to check surrounding gardens and readily accessible places to see if the suspect is hiding, or*
- *police have arrested someone in the night after a pursuit and it is necessary to make a brief check of gardens along the pursuit route to see if stolen or incriminating articles have been discarded.*

B:6 Searching premises—general considerations

(a) *Time of searches*

B:6.1 Searches made under warrant must be made within three calendar months of the date the **A-28** warrant is issued or within the period specified in the enactment under which the warrant is issued if this is shorter.

B:6.2 Searches must be made at a reasonable hour unless this might frustrate the purpose of the search.

B:6.3 When the extent or complexity of a search mean it is likely to take a long time, the officer in charge of the search may consider using the seize and sift powers referred to in section 7.

B:6.3A A warrant under PACE, s.8 may authorise entry to and search of premises on more than one occasion if, on the application, the justice of the peace is satisfied that it is necessary to authorise multiple entries in order to achieve the purpose for which the warrant is issued. No premises may be entered or searched on any subsequent occasions without the prior written authority of an officer of the rank of inspector who is not involved in the investigation. All other warrants authorise entry on one occasion only.

B:6.3B Where a warrant under PACE, s.8, or Sched. 1, para. 12 authorises entry to and search of all premises occupied or controlled by a specified person, no premises which are not specified in the warrant may be entered and searched without the prior written authority of an officer of the rank of inspector who is not involved in the investigation.

(b) *Entry other than with consent*

B:6.4 The officer in charge of the search shall first try to communicate with the occupier, or any other person entitled to grant access to the premises, explain the authority under which entry is sought and ask the occupier to allow entry, unless:

(i) the search premises are unoccupied;

(ii) the occupier and any other person entitled to grant access are absent;

(iii) there are reasonable grounds for believing that alerting the occupier or any other person entitled to grant access would frustrate the object of the search or endanger officers or other people.

B:6.5 Unless sub-paragraph 6.4(iii) applies, if the premises are occupied the officer, subject to paragraph 2.9, shall, before the search begins:

(i) identify him or herself, show their warrant card (if not in uniform) and state the purpose of, and grounds for, the search; and

(ii) identify and introduce any person accompanying the officer on the search (such persons should carry identification for production on request) and briefly describe that person's role in the process.

B:6.6 Reasonable and proportionate force may be used if necessary to enter premises if the officer in charge of the search is satisfied the premises are those specified in any warrant, or in exercise of the powers described in paragraph 4.1 to 4.3, and if:

(i) the occupier or any other person entitled to grant access has refused entry;

(ii) it is impossible to communicate with the occupier or any other person entitled to grant access; or

(iii) any of the provisions of paragraph 6.4 apply.

(c) *Notice of powers and rights*

B:6.7 If an officer conducts a search to which this code applies the officer shall, unless it is **A-29** impracticable to do so, provide the occupier with a copy of a notice in a standard format:

(i) specifying if the search is made under warrant, with consent, or in the exercise of the powers described in paragraphs 4.1 to 4.3. Note: the notice format shall provide for authority or consent to be indicated (see paragraphs 4.3 and 5.1);

(ii) summarising the extent of the powers of search and seizure conferred by PACE and other relevant legislation as appropriate;

(iii) explaining the rights of the occupier and the owner of the property seized;

(iv) explaining compensation may be payable in appropriate cases for damages [*sic*] caused entering and searching premises, and giving the address to send a compensation application [see *Note 6A*]; and

(v) stating this code is available at any police station.

B:6.8 If the occupier is:

• present, copies of the notice and warrant shall, if practicable, be given to them before the

search begins, unless the officer in charge of the search reasonably believes this would frustrate the object of the search or endanger officers or other people;
- not present, copies of the notice and warrant shall be left in a prominent place on the premises or appropriate part of the premises and endorsed, subject to paragraph 2.9 with the name of the officer in charge of the search, the date and time of the search.

The warrant shall be endorsed to show this has been done.

(d) *Conduct of searches*

B:6.9 Premises may be searched only to the extent necessary to achieve the purpose of the search, having regard to the size and nature of whatever is sought.

B:6.9A A search may not continue under:
- a warrant's authority once all the things specified in that warrant have been found;
- any other power once the object of that search has been achieved.

B:6.9B No search may continue once the officer in charge of the search is satisfied whatever is being sought is not on the premises [see *Note 6B*]. This does not prevent a further search of the same premises if additional grounds come to light supporting a further application for a search warrant or exercise or further exercise of another power. For example, when, as a result of new information, it is believed articles previously not found or additional articles are on the premises.

B:6.10 Searches must be conducted with due consideration for the property and privacy of the occupier and with no more disturbance than necessary. Reasonable force may be used only when necessary and proportionate because the co-operation of the occupier cannot be obtained or is insufficient for the purpose. [See *Note 6C*.]

B:6.11 A friend, neighbour or other person must be allowed to witness the search if the occupier wishes unless the officer in charge of the search has reasonable grounds for believing the presence of the person asked for would seriously hinder the investigation or endanger officers or other people. A search need not be unreasonably delayed for this purpose. A record of the action taken should be made on the premises search record including the grounds for refusing the occupier's request.

B:6.12 A person is not required to be cautioned prior to being asked questions that are solely necessary for the purpose of furthering the proper and effective conduct of a search, see Code C, paragraph 10.1(c). For example, questions to discover the occupier of specified premises, to find a key to open a locked drawer or cupboard or to otherwise seek co-operation during the search or to determine if a particular item is liable to be seized.

B:6.12A If questioning goes beyond what is necessary for the purpose of the exemption in Code C, the exchange is likely to constitute an interview as defined by Code C, paragraph 11.1A and would require the associated safeguards included in Code C, section 10.

(e) *Leaving premises*

B:6.13 If premises have been entered by force, before leaving the officer in charge of the search must make sure they are secure by:
- arranging for the occupier or their agent to be present;
- any other appropriate means.

(f) *Searches under PACE, Schedule 1 or the Terrorism Act 2000, Schedule 5*

B:6.14 An officer shall be appointed as the officer in charge of the search (see paragraph 2.10), in respect of any search made under a warrant issued under PACE Act 1984, Sched. 1 or the Terrorism Act 2000, Sched. 5. They are responsible for making sure the search is conducted with discretion and in a manner that causes the least possible disruption to any business or other activities carried out on the premises.

B:6.15 Once the officer in charge of the search is satisfied material may not be taken from the premises without their knowledge, they shall ask for the documents or other records concerned. The officer in charge of the search may also ask to see the index to files held on the premises, and the officers conducting the search may inspect any files which, according to the index, appear to contain the material sought. A more extensive search of the premises may be made only if:
- the person responsible for them refuses to:
  - produce the material sought, or
  - allow access to the index;
- it appears the index is:
  - inaccurate, or
  - incomplete;

• for any other reason the officer in charge of the search has reasonable grounds for believing such a search is necessary in order to find the material sought.

Notes for guidance

B:6A *Whether compensation is appropriate depends on the circumstances in each case. Compensation for damage caused when effecting entry is unlikely to be appropriate if the search was lawful, and the force used can be shown to be reasonable, proportionate and necessary to effect entry. If the wrong premises are searched by mistake everything possible should be done at the earliest opportunity to allay any sense of grievance and there should normally be a strong presumption in favour of paying compensation.* **A-31**

B:6B *It is important that, when possible, all those involved in a search are fully briefed about any powers to be exercised and the extent and limits within which it should be conducted.*

B:6C *In all cases the number of officers and other persons involved in executing the warrant should be determined by what is reasonable and necessary according to the particular circumstances.*

B:7 Seizure and retention of property

(a) *Seizure*

B:7.1 Subject to paragraph 7.2, an officer who is searching any person or premises under any statutory power or with the consent of the occupier may seize anything: **A-32**
  (a) covered by a warrant;
  (b) the officer has reasonable grounds for believing is evidence of an offence or has been obtained in consequence of the commission of an offence but only if seizure is necessary to prevent the items being concealed, lost, disposed of, altered, damaged, destroyed or tampered with;
  (c) covered by the powers in the Criminal Justice and Police Act 2001, Pt 2 allowing an officer to seize property from persons or premises and retain it for sifting or examination elsewhere.
See *Note 7B*.

B:7.2 No item may be seized which an officer has reasonable grounds for believing to be subject to legal privilege, as defined in PACE, s.10, other than under the Criminal Justice and Police Act 2001, Pt 2.

B:7.3 Officers must be aware of the provisions in the Criminal Justice and Police Act 2001, s.59, allowing for applications to a judicial authority for the return of property seized and the subsequent duty to secure in section 60 (see paragraph 7.12(iii)).

B:7.4 An officer may decide it is not appropriate to seize property because of an explanation from the person holding it but may nevertheless have reasonable grounds for believing it was obtained in consequence of an offence by some person. In these circumstances, the officer should identify the property to the holder, inform the holder of their suspicions and explain the holder may be liable to civil or criminal proceedings if they dispose of, alter or destroy the property.

B:7.5 An officer may arrange to photograph, image or copy, any document or other article they have the power to seize in accordance with paragraph 7.1. This is subject to specific restrictions on the examination, imaging or copying of certain property seized under the Criminal Justice and Police Act 2001, Pt 2. An officer must have regard to their statutory obligation to retain an original document or other article only when a photograph or copy is not sufficient.

B:7.6 If an officer considers information stored in any electronic form and accessible from the premises could be used in evidence, they may require the information to be produced in a form:
  • which can be taken away and in which it is visible and legible; or
  • from which it can readily be produced in a visible and legible form.

(b) *Criminal Justice and Police Act 2001: specific procedures for seize and sift powers*

B:7.7 The Criminal Justice and Police Act 2001, Pt 2 gives officers limited powers to seize property from premises or persons so they can sift or examine it elsewhere. Officers must be careful they only exercise these powers when it is essential and they do not remove any more material than necessary. The removal of large volumes of material, much of which may not ultimately be retainable, may have serious implications for the owners, particularly when they are involved in business or activities such as journalism or the provision of medical services. Officers must carefully consider if removing copies or images of relevant material or data would be a satisfactory alternative to removing originals. When originals are taken, officers must be prepared to facilitate the provision of copies or images for the owners when reasonably practicable. [See *Note 7C*.] **A-33**

B:7.8 Property seized under the Criminal Justice and Police Act 2001, s.50 or 51 must be kept securely and separately from any material seized under other powers. An examination under section

53 to determine which elements may be retained must be carried out at the earliest practicable time, having due regard to the desirability of allowing the person from whom the property was seized, or a person with an interest in the property, an opportunity of being present or represented at the examination.

B:7.8A All reasonable steps should be taken to accommodate an interested person's request to be present, provided the request is reasonable and subject to the need to prevent harm to, interference with, or unreasonable delay to the investigatory process. If an examination proceeds in the absence of an interested person who asked to attend or their representative, the officer who exercised the relevant seizure power must give that person a written notice of why the examination was carried out in those circumstances. If it is necessary for security reasons or to maintain confidentiality officers may exclude interested persons from decryption or other processes which facilitate the examination but do not form part of it. [See *Note 7D.*]

B:7.9 It is the responsibility of the officer in charge of the investigation to make sure property is returned in accordance with sections 53 to 55. Material which there is no power to retain must be:

- separated from the rest of the seized property; and
- returned as soon as reasonably practicable after examination of all the seized property.

B:7.9A Delay is only warranted if very clear and compelling reasons exist, for example:

- the unavailability of the person to whom the material is to be returned; or
- the need to agree a convenient time to return a large volume of material.

B:7.9B Legally privileged, excluded or special procedure material which cannot be retained must be returned:

- as soon as reasonably practicable; and
- without waiting for the whole examination.

B:7.9C As set out in section 58, material must be returned to the person from whom it was seized, except when it is clear some other person has a better right to it. [See *Note 7E.*]

B:7.10 When an officer involved in the investigation has reasonable grounds to believe a person with a relevant interest in property seized under section 50 or 51 intends to make an application under section 59 for the return of any legally privileged, special procedure or excluded material, the officer in charge of the investigation should be informed as soon as practicable and the material seized should be kept secure in accordance with section 61. [See *Note 7C.*]

B:7.11 The officer in charge of the investigation is responsible for making sure property is properly secured. Securing involves making sure the property is not examined, copied, imaged or put to any other use except at the request, or with the consent, of the applicant or in accordance with the directions of the appropriate judicial authority. Any request, consent or directions must be recorded in writing and signed by both the initiator and the officer in charge of the investigation. [See *Notes 7F* and *7G.*]

B:7.12 When an officer exercises a power of seizure conferred by sections 50 or 51 they shall provide the occupier of the premises or the person from whom the property is being seized with a written notice:

(i) specifying what has been seized under the powers conferred by that section;

(ii) specifying the grounds for those powers;

(iii) setting out the effect of sections 59 to 61 covering the grounds for a person with a relevant interest in seized property to apply to a judicial authority for its return and the duty of officers to secure property in certain circumstances when an application is made; and

(iv) specifying the name and address of the person to whom:

- notice of an application to the appropriate judicial authority in respect of any of the seized property must be given;
- an application may be made to allow attendance at the initial examination of the property.

B:7.13 If the occupier is not present but there is someone in charge of the premises, the notice shall be given to them. If no suitable person is available, so the notice will easily be found it should either be:

- left in a prominent place on the premises; or
- attached to the exterior of the premises.

(c) *Retention*

B:7.14 Subject to paragraph 7.15, anything seized in accordance with the above provisions may be retained only for as long as is necessary. It may be retained, among other purposes: **A-34**
  (i) for use as evidence at a trial for an offence;
  (ii) to facilitate the use in any investigation or proceedings of anything to which it is inextricably linked [see *Note 7H*];
  (iii) for forensic examination or other investigation in connection with an offence;
  (iv) in order to establish its lawful owner when there are reasonable grounds for believing it has been stolen or obtained by the commission of an offence.

B:7.15 Property shall not be retained under paragraph 7.14(i), (ii) or (iii) if a copy or image would be sufficient.

(d) *Rights of owners etc*

B:7.16 If property is retained, the person who had custody or control of it immediately before seizure must, on request, be provided with a list or description of the property within a reasonable time.

B:7.17 That person or their representative must be allowed supervised access to the property to examine it or have it photographed or copied, or must be provided with a photograph or copy, in either case within a reasonable time of any request and at their own expense, unless the officer in charge of an investigation has reasonable grounds for believing this would:
  (i) prejudice the investigation of any offence or criminal proceedings; or
  (ii) lead to the commission of an offence by providing access to unlawful material such as pornography.
A record of the grounds shall be made when access is denied.

Notes for guidance

B:7A *Any person claiming property seized by the police may apply to a magistrates' court under the Police* **A-35** *(Property) Act 1897 for its possession and should, if appropriate, be advised of this procedure.*

B:7B *The powers of seizure conferred by PACE, ss.18(2) and 19(3) extend to the seizure of the whole premises when it is physically possible to seize and retain the premises in their totality and practical considerations make seizure desirable. For example, police may remove premises such as tents, vehicles or caravans to a police station for the purpose of preserving evidence.*

B:7C *Officers should consider reaching agreement with owners and/or other interested parties on the procedures for examining a specific set of property, rather than awaiting the judicial authority's determination. Agreement can sometimes give a quicker and more satisfactory route for all concerned and minimise costs and legal complexities.*

B:7D *What constitutes a relevant interest in specific material may depend on the nature of that material and the circumstances in which it is seized. Anyone with a reasonable claim to ownership of the material and anyone entrusted with its safe keeping by the owner should be considered.*

B:7E *Requirements to secure and return property apply equally to all copies, images or other material created because of seizure of the original property.*

B:7F *The mechanics of securing property vary according to the circumstances; "bagging up", i.e. placing material in sealed bags or containers and strict subsequent control of access is the appropriate procedure in many cases.*

B:7G *When material is seized under the powers of seizure conferred by PACE, the duty to retain it under the code of practice issued under the Criminal Procedure and Investigations Act 1996 is subject to the provisions on retention of seized material in PACE, s.22.*

B:7H *Paragraph 7.14(ii) applies if inextricably linked material is seized under the Criminal Justice and Police Act 2001, s.50 or 51. Inextricably linked material is material it is not reasonably practicable to separate from other linked material without prejudicing the use of that other material in any investigation or proceedings. For example, it may not be possible to separate items of data held on computer disk without damaging their evidential integrity. Inextricably linked material must not be examined, imaged, copied or used for any purpose other than for proving the source and/or integrity of the linked material.*

B:8 Action after searches

B:8.1 If premises are searched in circumstances where this code applies, unless the exceptions in paragraph 2.3(a) apply, on arrival at a police station the officer in charge of the search shall make or have made a record of the search, to include: **A-36**
  (i) the address of the searched premises;
  (ii) the date, time and duration of the search;

(iii) the authority used for the search:
   - if the search was made in exercise of a statutory power to search premises without warrant, the power which was used for the search:
   - if the search was made under a warrant or with written consent;
       - a copy of the warrant and the written authority to apply for it, see paragraph 3.4; or
       - the written consent;

shall be appended to the record or the record shall show the location of the copy warrant or consent;

(iv) subject to paragraph 2.9, the names of:
   - the officer(s) in charge of the search;
   - all other officers and any authorised persons who conducted the search;

(v) the names of any people on the premises if they are known;

(vi) any grounds for refusing the occupier's request to have someone present during the search, see paragraph 6.11;

(vii) a list of any articles seized or the location of a list and, if not covered by a warrant, the grounds for their seizure;

(viii) whether force was used, and the reason;

(ix) details of any damage caused during the search, and the circumstances;

(x) if applicable, the reason it was not practicable;
   (a) to give the occupier a copy of the notice of powers and rights, see paragraph 6.7;
   (b) before the search to give the occupier a copy of the notice, see paragraph 6.8;

(xi) when the occupier was not present, the place where copies of the notice of powers and rights and search warrant were left on the premises, see paragraph 6.8.

B:8.2 On each occasion when premises are searched under warrant, the warrant authorising the search on that occasion shall be endorsed to show:

(i) if any articles specified in the warrant were found and the address where found;

(ii) if any other articles were seized;

(iii) the date and time it was executed and if present, the name of the occupier or if the occupier is not present the name of the person in charge of the premises;

(iv) subject to paragraph 2.9, the names of the officers who executed it and any authorised persons who accompanied them; and

(v) if a copy, together with a copy of the notice of powers and rights was:
   - handed to the occupier; or
   - endorsed as required by paragraph 6.8; and left on the premises and where.

B:8.3 Any warrant shall be returned within three calendar months of its issue or sooner on completion of the search(es) authorised by that warrant, if it was issued by a:

   - justice of the peace, to the designated officer for the local justice area in which the justice was acting when issuing the warrant; or
   - judge, to the appropriate officer of the court concerned.

B:9 Search registers

A-37

B:9.1 A search register will be maintained at each sub-divisional or equivalent police station. All search records required under paragraph 8.1 shall be made, copied, or referred to in the register. [See *Note 9A*.]

Note for guidance

B:9A *Paragraph 9.1 also applies to search records made by immigration officers. In these cases, a search register must also be maintained at an immigration office.* [*See also Note 2D.*]

B:10 Searches under Schedule 5 to the Terrorism Prevention and Investigation Measures Act 2011

A-37a

B:10.1 This code applies to the powers of constables under Schedule 5 to the Terrorism Prevention and Investigation Measures Act 2011 relating to TPIM notices to enter and search premises subject to the modifications in the following paragraphs.

B:10.2 In paragraph 2.3(d), the reference to the investigation into an alleged or suspected offence include [*sic*] the enforcement of terrorism prevention and investigation measures which may be imposed on an individual by a TPIM notice in accordance with the Terrorism Prevention and Investigation Measures Act 2011.

B:10.3 References to the purpose and object of the entry and search of premises, the nature of articles sought and what may be seized and retained include (as appropriate):

    (a) in relation to the power to search without a search warrant in paragraph 5 (for purposes of serving TPIM notice), finding the individual on whom the notice is to be served;

    (b) in relation to the power to search without a search warrant in paragraph 6 (at time of serving TPIM notice), ascertaining whether there is anything in the premises, that contravenes measures specified in the notice [see *Note 10A*];

    (c) in relation to the power to search without a search warrant under paragraph 7 (suspected absconding), ascertaining whether a person has absconded or if there is anything on the premises which will assist in the pursuit or arrest of an individual in respect of whom a TPIM notice is force who is reasonably suspected of having absconded;

    (d) in relation to the power to search under a search warrant issued under paragraph 8 (for compliance purposes), determining whether an individual in respect of whom a notice is in force is complying with measures specified in the notice [see *Note 10A*].

Note for guidance

B:10A *Searches of individuals under Schedule 5, paras 6(2)(a) (at time of serving TPIM notice) and 8(2)(a) (for compliance purposes) must be conducted and recorded in accordance with Code A. See Code A, para. 2.18A for details.*

(4) Detention, treatment and questioning of persons

The text that follows is of the version of the code that came into force on June 2, 2014: see **A-38** *ante*, A-1.

For authorities in relation to Code C, see, in particular, §§ 15-167 *et seq.* (right of access to solicitor), § 15-204 (general), § 15-311 (confessions), § 15-372 (sufficient evidence for prosecution to succeed), §§ 15-401 *et seq.* (discretionary exclusion of evidence) in the main work.

C. CODE OF PRACTICE FOR THE DETENTION, TREATMENT AND QUESTIONING OF PERSONS BY POLICE OFFICERS

Commencement—transitional arrangements

This code applies to people in police detention after 00.00 on 2 June 2014, notwithstanding that **A-39** their period of detention may have commenced before that time.

C:1 General

C:1.0 The powers and procedures in this code must be used fairly, responsibly, with respect for **A-40** the people to whom they apply and without unlawful discrimination. Under the Equality Act 2010, s.149, when police officers are carrying out their functions, they also have a duty to have due regard to the need to eliminate unlawful discrimination, harassment and victimisation, to advance equality of opportunity between people who share a relevant protected characteristic and people who do not share it, and to take steps to foster good relations between those persons. See *Notes 1A* and *1AA*.

C:1.1 All persons in custody must be dealt with expeditiously, and released as soon as the need for detention no longer applies.

C:1.1A A custody officer must perform the functions in this code as soon as practicable. A custody officer will not be in breach of this code if delay is justifiable and reasonable steps are taken to prevent unnecessary delay. The custody record shall show when a delay has occurred and the reason. See *Note 1H*.

C:1.2 This code of practice must be readily available at all police stations for consultation by:

- police officers;
- police staff;
- detained persons;
- members of the public.

C:1.3 The provisions of this code:

- include the *Annexes*;
- do not include the *Notes for Guidance*.

C:1.4 If an officer has any suspicion, or is told in good faith, that a person of any age may be mentally disordered or otherwise mentally vulnerable, in the absence of clear evidence to dispel that suspicion, the person shall be treated as such for the purposes of this code. See *Note 1G*.

C:1.5 If anyone appears to be under 17, they shall in the absence of clear evidence that they are older, be treated as a juvenile for the purposes of this code and any other code.

C:1.5A If anyone appears to have attained the age of 17 and to be under the age of 18, they shall in the absence of clear evidence that they are older, be treated as a 17-year-old for the purposes of this and any other code. The provisions and *Notes for Guidance* which in accordance with paragraph 1.5 apply to a juvenile and the way they are to be treated shall also apply to them, except as described in sub-paragraphs (a) and (b) below:

> (a) the statutory provisions in section 38 of PACE (detention after charge) which apply only to an arrested juvenile as defined in section 37(15) of PACE and to which paragraphs 16.7 and 16.10 and *Note 16D* of this code relate, shall not apply to a person who appears to have attained the age of 17 for the purposes of:
>> (i) the grounds to keep them in police detention after charge; and
>> (ii) the requirement to transfer a person who has been kept in police detention after charge to local authority accommodation and the power of the local authority to detain them pending appearance at court;
> (b) the statutory provisions in section 65(1) of PACE (appropriate consent) which require appropriate consent for a person who has not attained the age of 17 to be given by them and their parent or guardian shall not apply to a person who appears to have attained the age of 17 and whose consent alone shall be sufficient. In this code, section 65(1) applies to Annex A, paras 2(b) and 2B (intimate searches), and Annex K, paras 1(b) and 3 (X-Ray and ultrasound scan), and in Code D (identification), to para. 2.12 and *Note 2A* with regards to taking fingerprints, samples, footwear impressions, photographs and evidential searches and examinations.

See *Notes 1L* and *1M*.

C:1.6 If a person appears to be blind, seriously visually impaired, deaf, unable to read or speak or has difficulty orally because of a speech impediment, they shall be treated as such for the purposes of this code in the absence of clear evidence to the contrary.

A-41 C:1.7 The "appropriate adult" means, in the case of a:

> (a) juvenile:
>> (i) the parent, guardian or, if the juvenile is in the care of a local authority or voluntary organisation, a person representing that authority or organisation (see *Note 1B*);
>> (ii) a social worker of a local authority (see *Note 1C*);
>> (iii) failing these, some other responsible adult aged 18 or over who is not a police officer or employed by the police;
>> note: paragraph 1.5A extends sub-paragraph (a) to the person called to fulfil the role of the appropriate adult for a 17-year-old detainee [*sic*];
> (b) person who is mentally disordered or mentally vulnerable (see *Note 1D*):
>> (i) a relative, guardian or other person responsible for their care or custody;
>> (ii) someone experienced in dealing with mentally disordered or mentally vulnerable people but who is not a police officer or employed by the police;
>> (iii) failing these, some other responsible adult aged 18 or over who is not a police officer or employed by the police.

C:1.8 If this code requires a person be given certain information, they do not have to be given it if at the time they are incapable of understanding what is said, are violent or may become violent or in urgent need of medical attention, but they must be given it as soon as practicable.

C:1.9 References to a custody officer include any police officer who for the time being, is performing the functions of a custody officer.

C:1.9A When this code requires the prior authority or agreement of an officer of at least inspector or superintendent rank, that authority may be given by a sergeant or chief inspector authorised to perform the functions of the higher rank under the Police and Criminal Evidence Act 1984 (PACE), s.107.

C:1.10 Subject to paragraph 1.12, this code applies to people in custody at police stations in England and Wales, whether or not they have been arrested, and to those removed to a police station as a place of safety under the Mental Health Act 1983, ss.135 and 136, as a last resort (see paragraph 3.16). Section 15 applies solely to people in police detention, *e.g.* those brought to a police station under arrest or arrested at a police station for an offence after going there voluntarily.

C:1.11 No part of this code applies to a detained person:

> (a) to whom PACE Code H applies because:
>> • they are detained following arrest under section 41 of the Terrorism Act 2000 (TACT) and not charged; or
>> • an authorisation has been given under section 22 of the Counter-Terrorism Act 2008 (CTACT) (post-charge questioning of terrorist suspects) to interview them;

(b) to whom the code of practice issued under paragraph 6 of Schedule 14 to TACT applies because they are detained for examination under Schedule 7 to TACT.

C:1.12 This code does not apply to people in custody:

(i) arrested by officers under the Criminal Justice and Public Order Act 1994, s.136(2), on warrants issued in Scotland, or arrested or detained without warrant under section 137(2) by officers from a police force in Scotland; in these cases, police powers and duties and the person's rights and entitlements whilst at a police station in England or Wales are the same as those in Scotland;

(ii) arrested under the Immigration and Asylum Act 1999, s.142(3), in order to have their fingerprints taken;

(iii) whose detention is authorised under Schedules 2 or 3 to the Immigration Act 1971 or section 62 of the Nationality, Immigration and Asylum Act 2002;

(iv) who are convicted or remanded prisoners held in police cells on behalf of the Prison Service under the Imprisonment (Temporary Provisions) Act 1980;

(v) [*not used*];

(vi) detained for searches under stop and search powers except as required by Code A.

The provisions on conditions of detention and treatment in sections 8 and 9 must be considered as the minimum standards of treatment for such detainees.

C:1.13 In this code:

(a) "designated person" means a person other than a police officer, designated under the Police Reform Act 2002, Pt 4, who has specified powers and duties of police officers conferred or imposed on them;

(b) reference to a police officer includes a designated person acting in the exercise or performance of the powers and duties conferred or imposed on them by their designation;

(c) where a search or other procedure to which this code applies may only be carried out or observed by a person of the same sex as the detainee, the gender of the detainee and other parties present should be established and recorded in line with Annex L of this code.

C:1.14 Designated persons are entitled to use reasonable force as follows:— **A-42**

(a) when exercising a power conferred on them which allows a police officer exercising that power to use reasonable force, a designated person has the same entitlement to use force; and

(b) at other times when carrying out duties conferred or imposed on them that also entitle them to use reasonable force, for example:

• when at a police station carrying out the duty to keep detainees for whom they are responsible under control and to assist any police officer or designated person to keep any detainee under control and to prevent their escape;

• when securing, or assisting any police officer or designated person in securing, the detention of a person at a police station;

• when escorting, or assisting any police officer or designated person in escorting, a detainee within a police station;

• for the purpose of saving life or limb; or

• preventing serious damage to property.

C:1.15 Nothing in this code prevents the custody officer, or other officer given custody of the detainee, from allowing police staff who are not designated persons to carry out individual procedures or tasks at the police station if the law allows. However, the officer remains responsible for making sure the procedures and tasks are carried out correctly in accordance with the codes of practice (see *Note 3F*). Any such person must be:

(a) a person employed by a police force and under the direction and control of the chief officer of that force; or

(b) employed by a person with whom a police force has a contract for the provision of services relating to persons arrested or otherwise in custody.

C:1.16 Designated persons and other police staff must have regard to any relevant provisions of the codes of practice.

C:1.17 References to pocket books include any official report book issued to police officers or other police staff.

Notes for guidance

C:1A *Although certain sections of this code apply specifically to people in custody at police stations, those there voluntarily to assist with an investigation should be treated with no less consideration, e.g. offered refreshments at appropriate times, and enjoy an absolute right to obtain legal advice or communicate with anyone outside the police station.*

C:1AA *In paragraph 1.0, "relevant protected characteristic" includes: age, disability, gender reassignment, pregnancy and maternity, race, religion/belief, sex and sexual orientation.*

C:1B *A person, including a parent or guardian, should not be an appropriate adult if they:*

- *are*
  - *– suspected of involvement in the offence;*
  - *– the victim;*
  - *– a witness;*
  - *– involved in the investigation;*
- *received admissions prior to attending to act as the appropriate adult.*

Note: if a juvenile's parent is estranged from the juvenile, they should not be asked to act as the appropriate adult if the juvenile expressly and specifically objects to their presence.

Note: Paragraph 1.5A applies this note to 17-year-old detainees.

C:1C *If a juvenile admits an offence to, or in the presence of, a social worker or member of a youth offending team other than during the time that person is acting as the juvenile's appropriate adult, another appropriate adult should be appointed in the interest of fairness.*

Note: Paragraph 1.5A applies this note to 17-year-old detainees.

C:1D *In the case of people who are mentally disordered or otherwise mentally vulnerable, it may be more satisfactory if the appropriate adult is someone experienced or trained in their care rather than a relative lacking such qualifications. But if the detainee prefers a relative to a better qualified stranger or objects to a particular person their wishes should, if practicable, be respected.*

C:1E *A detainee should always be given an opportunity, when an appropriate adult is called to the police station, to consult privately with a solicitor in the appropriate adult's absence if they want. An appropriate adult is not subject to legal privilege.*

C:1F *A solicitor or independent custody visitor present at the police station in that capacity may not be the appropriate adult.*

C:1G *"Mentally vulnerable" applies to any detainee who, because of their mental state or capacity, may not understand the significance of what is said, of questions or of their replies. "Mental disorder" is defined in the Mental Health Act 1983, s.1(2), as "any disorder or disability of mind". When the custody officer has any doubt about the mental state or capacity of a detainee, that detainee should be treated as mentally vulnerable and an appropriate adult called.*

C:1H *Paragraph 1.1A is intended to cover delays which may occur in processing detainees, e.g. if:*

- *a large number of suspects are brought into the station simultaneously to be placed in custody;*
- *interview rooms are all being used;*
- *there are difficulties contacting an appropriate adult, solicitor or interpreter.*

C:1I *The custody officer must remind the appropriate adult and detainee about the right to legal advice and record any reasons for waiving it in accordance with section 6.*

C:1J *[Not used.]*

C:1K *This code does not affect the principle that all citizens have a duty to help police officers to prevent crime and discover offenders. This is a civic rather than a legal duty; but when police officers are trying to discover whether, or by whom, offences have been committed they are entitled to question any person from whom they think useful information can be obtained, subject to the restrictions imposed by this code. A person's declaration that they are unwilling to reply does not alter this entitlement.*

C:1L *Paragraph 1.5A does not amend section 37(15) of PACE which defines the term "arrested juvenile" for the purposes of sections 34 to 51 of PACE, or provisions in any other enactment which expressly refer and apply to persons under the age of 17. Until amended by Parliament, these statutory provisions alone do not extend to persons who have attained the age of 17.*

C:1M *The purpose of paragraph 1.5A is to extend the safeguards for juveniles to 17-year-olds unless this is precluded by any statutory provisions. Sub-paragraphs 1.5A(a) and (b) identify the provisions of sections 38 and 65 of PACE concerning detention after charge and appropriate consent which for this reason do not extend to 17-year-olds. All other safeguards in this and other codes are extended and the requirements which are indicated in the relevant provisions and Notes for Guidance are as follows:*

(a) *under paragraph 3.13 of this code, to identify and inform someone responsible for the welfare of a 17-year-old which is in addition to their right in section 5 of this code not to be held incommunicado;*

(b) *under paragraph 3.14 of this code to notify a person who has statutory responsibility under a court order to supervise or monitor a 17-year-old;*

(c) *under paragraph 8.8 with regard to cell accommodation and keeping 17-year-old detainees separate from adults;*

(d) *to call a person described by paragraph 1.7(a) or Note 17G in relation to testing for the presence of Class A drugs, to fulfil the role of the appropriate adult for the purposes of this or any other code to support and assist a 17-year-old:*

   (i) *by being present when:*
- *they are informed of their rights and entitlements and the grounds for their detention (see paras 3.17 and 3.18);*
- *they are cautioned or given a special warning (see paras 10.12 and 10.11A);*
- *they are being interviewed in accordance with this code (see sections 11 and 12) or Codes E or F unless paragraph 11.15 of this code allows the interview to go ahead without the adult being present;*
- *their detention is being reviewed or an extension is being considered (see paras 15.3(c) and 15.3C(a)):*
- *they are charged and related action is taken (see paras 16.1, 16.3, 16.4A and 16.6);*
- *samples to test for Class A drugs are requested from a person who has not attained the age of 18 (see para. 17.7);*
- *an intimate search is carried out (see Annex A, paras 2A, 2B and 5);*
- *a strip search is carried out (see Annex A, para. 11(c));*
- *an x-ray or ultrasound scan is carried out (see Annex K, paras 2 and 3);*
- *procedures in Code D involving witness identification, taking fingerprints, samples, footwear impressions and photographs and when evidential searches and examinations are carried out (see paras 2.14 and 2.15).*

   (ii) *by allowing:*
- *the adult to inspect their custody record and to have a copy of their record (see paras 2.4, 2.4A and 2.5);*
- *a 17-year-old to consult the adult in private (see para. 3.18);*
- *the adult to request legal advice on their behalf to advise and assist them (see paras 3.19, 6.5A and 11.17).*

C:2 Custody records

C:2.1A When a person: **A-44**
- is brought to a police station under arrest
- is arrested at the police station having attended there voluntarily or
- attends a police station to answer bail

they must be brought before the custody officer as soon as practicable after their arrival at the station or if applicable, following their arrest after attending the police station voluntarily. This applies to both designated and non-designated police stations. A person is deemed to be "at a police station" for these purposes if they are within the boundary of any building or enclosed yard which forms part of that police station.

C:2.1 A separate custody record must be opened as soon as practicable for each person brought to a police station under arrest or arrested at the station having gone there voluntarily or attending a police station in answer to street bail. All information recorded under this code must be recorded as soon as practicable in the custody record unless otherwise specified. Any audio or video recording made in the custody area is not part of the custody record.

C:2.2 If any action requires the authority of an officer of a specified rank, subject to paragraph 2.6A, their name and rank must be noted in the custody record.

C:2.3 The custody officer is responsible for the custody record's accuracy and completeness and for making sure the record or copy of the record accompanies a detainee if they are transferred to another police station. The record shall show the:
- time and reason for transfer;
- time a person is released from detention.

C:2.3A If a person is arrested and taken to a police station as a result of a search in the exercise of any stop and search power to which PACE Code A (stop and search) or the "search powers code" issued under TACT applies, the officer carrying out the search is responsible for ensuring that the record of that stop and search, is made as part of the person's custody record. The custody officer must then ensure that the person is asked if they want a copy of the search record and if they do, that they are given a copy as soon as practicable. The person's entitlement to a copy of the search record which is made as part of their custody record is in addition to, and does not affect, their entitlement to a copy of their custody record or any other provisions of section 2 (custody records) of this code. (See Code A, para. 4.2B, and the TACT search powers code, para. 5.3.5.)

C:2.4 The detainee's solicitor and appropriate adult must be permitted to inspect the whole of the detainee's custody record as soon as practicable after their arrival at the station and at any other time on request, whilst the person is detained. This includes the following specific records relating to the reasons for the detainee's arrest and detention and the offence concerned, to which paragraph 3.1(b) refers:

> (a) the information about the circumstances and reasons for the detainee's arrest as recorded in the custody record in accordance with paragraph 4.3 of Code G; this applies to any further offences for which the detainee is arrested whilst in custody;
>
> (b) the record of the grounds for each authorisation to keep the person in custody; the authorisations to which this applies are the same as those described at items (i)(a) to (d) in the table in paragraph 2 of Annex M [*sic*] of this code.

Access to the records in sub-paragraphs (a) and (b) is in addition to the requirements in paragraphs 3.4(b), 11.1A, 15.0, 15.7A(c) and 16.7A to make certain documents and materials available and to provide information about the offence and the reasons for arrest and detention.

Access to the custody record for the purposes of this paragraph must be arranged and agreed with the custody officer and may not unreasonably interfere with the custody officer's duties. A record shall be made when access is allowed and whether it includes the records described in sub-paragraphs (a) and (b) above.

Note: paragraph 1.5A extends this paragraph to the person called to fulfil the role of the appropriate adult for a 17-year-old detainee.

C:2.4A When a detainee leaves police detention or is taken before a court they, their legal representative or appropriate adult shall be given, on request, a copy of the custody record as soon as practicable. This entitlement lasts for 12 months after release.

Note: paragraph 1.5A extends this paragraph to the person called to fulfil the role of the appropriate adult for a 17-year-old detainee.

C:2.5 The detainee, appropriate adult or legal representative shall be permitted to inspect the original custody record after the detainee has left police detention provided they give reasonable notice of their request. Any such inspection shall be noted in the custody record.

Note: paragraph 1.5A extends this paragraph to the person called to fulfil the role of the appropriate adult for a 17-year-old detainee.

C:2.6 Subject to paragraph 2.6A, all entries in custody records must be timed and signed by the maker. Records entered on computer shall be timed and contain the operator's identification.

C:2.6A Nothing in this code requires the identity of officers or other police staff to be recorded or disclosed:

> (a) [*not used*];
>
> (b) if the officer or police staff reasonably believe recording or disclosing their name might put them in danger.

In these cases, they shall use their warrant or other identification numbers and the name of their police station. See *Note 2A*.

C:2.7 The fact and time of any detainee's refusal to sign a custody record, when asked in accordance with this code, must be recorded.

Note for guidance

A-45

C:2A *The purpose of paragraph 2.6A(b) is to protect those involved in serious organised crime investigations or arrests of particularly violent suspects when there is reliable information that those arrested or their associates may threaten or cause harm to those involved. In cases of doubt, an officer of inspector rank or above should be consulted.*

C:3 Initial action

(a) *Detained persons—normal procedure*

A-46

C:3.1 When a person is brought to a police station under arrest or arrested at the station having gone there voluntarily, the custody officer must make sure the person is told clearly about:

> (a) the following continuing rights, which may be exercised at any stage during the period in custody:
>
> > (i) their right to consult privately with a solicitor and that free independent legal advice is available as in section 6;
> >
> > (ii) their right to have someone informed of their arrest as in section 5;
> >
> > (iii) their right to consult the codes of practice (see *Note 3D*); and
> >
> > (iv) if applicable, their right to interpretation and translation (see para. 3.12) and their

right to communicate with their high commission, embassy or consulate (see para. 3.12A).

(b) their right to be informed about the offence and (as the case may be) any further offences for which they are arrested whilst in custody and why they have been arrested and detained in accordance with paragraphs 2.4, 3.4(a) and 11.1A of this code and paragraph 3.3 of Code G.

C:3.2 The detainee must also be given a written notice, which contains information:

(a) setting out:

  (i) their rights under paragraph 3.1, paragraph 3.12 and 3.12A;

  (ii) the arrangements for obtaining legal advice, see section 6;

  (iii) their right to a copy of the custody record as in paragraph 2.4A;

  (iv) their right to remain silent as set out in the caution in the terms prescribed in section 10;

  (v) their right to have access to materials and documents which are essential to effectively challenging the lawfulness of their arrest and detention for any offence and (as the case may be) any further offences for which they are arrested whilst in custody, in accordance with paragraphs 3.4(b), 15.0, 15.7A(c) and 16.7A of this code;

  (vi) the maximum period for which they may be kept in police detention without being charged, when detention must be reviewed and when release is required;

  (vii) their right to medical assistance in accordance with section 9 of this code;

  (viii) their right, if they are prosecuted, to have access to the evidence in the case before their trial in accordance with the Criminal Procedure and Investigations Act 1996, the Attorney General's Guidelines on Disclosure, the common law and the Criminal Procedure Rules;

(b) briefly setting out their other entitlements while in custody, by:

  (i) mentioning:

    – the provisions relating to the conduct of interviews;

    – the circumstances in which an appropriate adult should be available to assist the detainee and their statutory rights to make representations whenever the need for their detention is reviewed;

  (ii) listing the entitlements in this code, concerning:

    – reasonable standards of physical comfort;

    – adequate food and drink;

    – access to toilets and washing facilities, clothing, medical attention, and exercise when practicable.

See *Note 3A.*

C:3.2A The detainee must be given an opportunity to read the notice and shall be asked to sign the custody record to acknowledge receipt of the notice. Any refusal to sign must be recorded on the custody record.

C:3.3 [*Not used.*]

C:3.3A An "easy read" illustrated version should also be provided if available (see *Note 3A*).

C:3.4 (a) The custody officer shall:

  • record the offence(s) that the detainee has been arrested for and the reason(s) for the arrest on the custody record (see para. 10.3 and Code G, paras 2.2 and 4.3);

  • note on the custody record any comment the detainee makes in relation to the arresting officer's account but shall not invite comment; if the arresting officer is not physically present when the detainee is brought to a police station, the arresting officer's account must be made available to the custody officer remotely or by a third party on the arresting officer's behalf; if the custody officer authorises a person's detention, subject to paragraph 1.8, that officer must record the grounds for detention in the detainee's presence and at the same time, inform them of the grounds; the detainee must be informed of the grounds for their detention before they are questioned about any offence;

  • note any comment the detainee makes in respect of the decision to detain them but shall not invite comment;

  • not put specific questions to the detainee regarding their involvement in any offence, nor in respect of any comments they may make in response to the arresting officer's account or the decision to place them in detention; such an exchange is likely to constitute an interview as in paragraph 11.1A and require the associated safeguards in section 11.

Note: this sub-paragraph also applies to any further offences and grounds for detention which come to light whilst the person is detained.

See paragraph 11.13 in respect of unsolicited comments.

(b) Documents and materials which are essential to effectively challenging the lawfulness of the detainee's arrest and detention must be made available to the detainee or their solicitor. Documents and materials will be "essential" for this purpose if they are capable of undermining the reasons and grounds which make the detainee's arrest and detention necessary. The decision about whether particular documents or materials must be made available for the purpose of this requirement therefore rests with the custody officer who determines whether detention is necessary, in consultation with the investigating officer who has the knowledge of the documents and materials in a particular case necessary to inform that decision. A note should be made in the detainee's custody record of the fact that documents or materials have been made available under this sub-paragraph and when. The investigating officer should make a separate note of what is made available and how it is made available in a particular case. This sub-paragraph also applies (with modifications) for the purposes of sections 15 (reviews and extensions of detention) and 16 (charging detained persons). See *Note 3ZA* and paragraphs 15.0 and 16.7A.

C:3.5 The custody officer or other custody staff as directed by the custody officer shall:

(a) ask the detainee, whether at this time, they:

(i) would like legal advice, see paragraph 6.5;

(ii) want someone informed of their detention, see section 5;

(b) ask the detainee to sign the custody record to confirm their decisions in respect of (a);

(c) determine whether the detainee:

(i) is, or might be, in need of medical treatment or attention, see section 9;

(ii) requires:

- an appropriate adult (see paras 1.4, 1.5, 1.5A and 3.15);
- help to check documentation (see para. 3.20);
- an interpreter (see para. 3.12 and *Note 13B*);

(d) record the decision in respect of (c).

Where any duties under this paragraph have been carried out by custody staff at the direction of the custody officer, the outcomes shall, as soon as practicable, be reported to the custody officer who retains overall responsibility for the detainee's care and treatment and ensuring that it complies with this code. See *Note 3F*.

C:3.6 When these needs are determined, the custody officer is responsible for initiating an assessment to consider whether the detainee is likely to present specific risks to custody staff or themselves. Such assessments should always include a check on the Police National Computer, to be carried out as soon as practicable, to identify any risks highlighted in relation to the detainee. Although such assessments are primarily the custody officer's responsibility, it may be necessary for them to consult and involve others, *e.g.* the arresting officer or an appropriate healthcare professional, see paragraph 9.13. Reasons for delaying the initiation or completion of the assessment must be recorded.

C:3.7 Chief officers should ensure that arrangements for proper and effective risk assessments required by paragraph 3.6 are implemented in respect of all detainees at police stations in their area.

C:3.8 Risk assessments must follow a structured process which clearly defines the categories of risk to be considered and the results must be incorporated in the detainee's custody record. The custody officer is responsible for making sure those responsible for the detainee's custody are appropriately briefed about the risks. If no specific risks are identified by the assessment, that should be noted in the custody record. See *Note 3E* and paragraph 9.14.

C:3.8A The content of any risk assessment and any analysis of the level of risk relating to the person's detention is not required to be shown or provided to the detainee or any person acting on behalf of the detainee. But information should not be withheld from any person acting on the detainee's behalf, for example, an appropriate adult, solicitor or interpreter, if to do so might put that person at risk.

C:3.9 The custody officer is responsible for implementing the response to any specific risk assessment, *e.g.*:

- reducing opportunities for self harm;
- calling an appropriate healthcare professional;
- increasing levels of monitoring or observation;
- reducing the risk to those who come into contact with the detainee.

See *Note 3E*.

C:3.10 Risk assessment is an ongoing process and assessments must always be subject to review if circumstances change.

C:3.11 If video cameras are installed in the custody area, notices shall be prominently displayed showing cameras are in use. Any request to have video cameras switched off shall be refused.

(b) *Detained persons—special groups*

C:3.12 If the detainee appears to be someone who does not speak or understand English or who **A-47** has a hearing or speech impediment, the custody officer must ensure:

    (a) that without delay, an interpreter is called for assistance in the action under paragraphs 3.1 to 3.5; if the person appears to have a hearing or speech impediment, the reference to "interpreter" includes appropriate assistance necessary to comply with paragraphs 3.1 to 3.5 (see para. 13.1C if the detainee is in Wales) (see section 13 and *Note 13B*);

    (b) that in addition to the continuing rights set out in paragraph 3.1(a)(i) to (iv), the detainee is told clearly about their right to interpretation and translation;

    (c) that the written notice given to the detainee in accordance with paragraph 3.2 is in a language the detainee understands and includes the right to interpretation and translation together with information about the provisions in section 13 and Annex M, which explain how the right applies (see *Note 3A*); and

    (d) that if the translation of the notice is not available, the information in the notice is given through an interpreter and a written translation provided without undue delay.

C:3.12A If the detainee is a citizen of an independent Commonwealth country or a national of a foreign country, including the Republic of Ireland, the custody officer must ensure that in addition to the continuing rights set out in paragraph 3.1(a)(i) to (iv), they are informed as soon as practicable about their rights of communication with their high commission, embassy or consulate set out in section 7. This right must be included in the written notice given to the detainee in accordance with paragraph 3.2.

C:3.13 If the detainee is a juvenile, the custody officer must, if it is practicable, ascertain the identity of a person responsible for their welfare. That person:

    • may be:
        – the parent or guardian;
        – if the juvenile is in local authority or voluntary organisation care, or is otherwise being looked after under the Children Act 1989, a person appointed by that authority or organisation to have responsibility for the juvenile's welfare;
        – any other person who has, for the time being, assumed responsibility for the juvenile's welfare;
    • must be informed as soon as practicable that the juvenile has been arrested, why they have been arrested and where they are detained. This right is in addition to the juvenile's right in section 5 not to be held incommunicado. See *Note 3C*.

Note: paragraph 1.5A extends the obligations in this paragraph to 17-year-old detainees.

C:3.14 If a juvenile is known to be subject to a court order under which a person or organisation is given any degree of statutory responsibility to supervise or otherwise monitor them, reasonable steps must also be taken to notify that person or organisation (the "responsible officer"). The responsible officer will normally be a member of a youth offending team, except for a curfew order which involves electronic monitoring when the contractor providing the monitoring will normally be the responsible officer.

Note: paragraph 1.5A extends the obligations in this paragraph to 17-year-old detainees.

C:3.15 If the detainee is a juvenile, mentally disordered or otherwise mentally vulnerable, the custody officer must, as soon as practicable:

    • inform the appropriate adult, who in the case of a juvenile may or may not be a person responsible for their welfare, as in paragraph 3.13, of:
        – the grounds for their detention;
        – their whereabouts;
    • ask the adult to come to the police station to see the detainee.

Note: paragraph 1.5A extends the obligation to call someone to fulfil the role of the appropriate adult to 17-year-old detainees.

C:3.16 It is imperative that a mentally disordered or otherwise mentally vulnerable person, detained under the Mental Health Act 1983, s.136, be assessed as soon as possible. A police station should only be used as a place of safety as a last resort but if that assessment is to take place at the police station, an approved mental health professional and a registered medical practitioner shall be called to the station as soon as possible to carry it out. See *Note 9D*. The appropriate adult has no role in the assessment process and their presence is not required. Once the detainee has been assessed and suitable arrangements made for their treatment or care, they can no longer be detained under section 136. A detainee must be immediately discharged from detention under section 136 if a registered medical practitioner, having examined them, concludes they are not mentally disordered within the meaning of the Act.

C:3.17 If the appropriate adult is:

- already at the police station, the provisions of paragraphs 3.1 to 3.5 must be complied with in the appropriate adult's presence;
- not at the station when these provisions are complied with, they must be complied with again in the presence of the appropriate adult when they arrive,

and a copy of the notice given to the detainee in accordance with paragraph 3.2, shall also be given to the appropriate adult.

Note: paragraph 1.5A extends the obligations in this paragraph to 17-year-old detainees.

C:3.18 The detainee shall be advised that:

- the duties of the appropriate adult include giving advice and assistance;
- they can consult privately with the appropriate adult at any time.

Note: paragraph 1.5A extends the obligations in this paragraph to 17-year-old detainees.

C:3.19 If the detainee, or appropriate adult on the detainee's behalf, asks for a solicitor to be called to give legal advice, the provisions of section 6 apply.

Note: paragraph 1.5A extends the obligations in this paragraph to 17-year-old detainees.

C:3.20 If the detainee is blind, seriously visually impaired or unable to read, the custody officer shall make sure their solicitor, relative, appropriate adult or some other person likely to take an interest in them and not involved in the investigation is available to help check any documentation. When this code requires written consent or signing the person assisting may be asked to sign instead, if the detainee prefers. This paragraph does not require an appropriate adult to be called solely to assist in checking and signing documentation for a person who is not a juvenile, or mentally disordered or otherwise mentally vulnerable (see para. 3.15 and *Note 13C*).

(c) *Persons attending a police station or elsewhere voluntarily*

A-48
C:3.21 Anybody attending a police station or other location (see para. 3.22) voluntarily to assist police with the investigation of an offence may leave at will unless arrested. See *Note 1K*. The person may only be prevented from leaving at will if their arrest on suspicion of committing the offence is necessary in accordance with Code G. See Code G, *Note 2G*.

(a) If during an interview it is decided that their arrest is necessary, they must:

- be informed at once that they are under arrest and of the grounds and reasons as required by Code G, and
- be brought before the custody officer at the police station where they are arrested or, as the case may be, at the police station to which they are taken after being arrested elsewhere. The custody officer is then responsible for making sure that a custody record is opened and that they are notified of their rights in the same way as other detainees as required by this code.

(b) If they are not arrested but are cautioned as in section 10, the person who gives the caution must, at the same time, inform them they are not under arrest, they are not obliged to remain at the station or other location but if they agree to remain, they may obtain free and independent legal advice if they want. They shall also be given a copy of the notice explaining the arrangements for obtaining legal advice and told that the right to legal advice includes the right to speak with a solicitor on the telephone and be asked if they want advice. If advice is requested, the interviewer is responsible for securing its provision without delay by contacting the defence solicitor call centre. The interviewer must ensure that other provisions of this code and Codes E and F concerning the conduct and recording of interviews of suspects and the rights and entitlements and safeguards for suspects who have been arrested and detained are followed insofar as they can be applied to suspects who are not under arrest. This includes:

- informing them of the offence and, as the case may be, any further offences, they are suspected of and the grounds and reasons for that suspicion and their right to be so informed (see para. 3.1(b));
- the caution as required in section 10;
- determining whether they require an appropriate adult and help to check documentation (see para. 3.5(c)(ii)); and
- determining whether they require an interpreter and the provision of interpretation and translation services and informing them of that right (see paras 3.1(a)(iv), 3.5(c)(ii) and 3.12, *Note 6B* and section 13),

but does not include any requirement to provide a written notice in addition to that above which concerns the arrangements for obtaining legal advice.

C:3.22 If the other location mentioned in paragraph 3.21 is any place or premises for which the interviewer requires the person's informed consent to remain, for example, the person's home, then the references that the person is "not obliged to remain" and that they "may leave at will" mean that the person may also withdraw their consent and require the officer to leave.

(d) *Documentation*

C:3.23 The grounds for a person's detention shall be recorded, in the person's presence if practicable. See paragraph 1.8.

C:3.24 Action taken under paragraphs 3.12 to 3.20 shall be recorded.

(e) *Persons answering street bail*

C:3.25 When a person is answering street bail, the custody officer should link any documentation held in relation to arrest with the custody record. Any further action shall be recorded on the custody record in accordance with paragraphs 3.23 and 3.24 above.

(f) *Requirements for suspects to be informed of certain rights*

C:3.26 The provisions of this section identify the information which must be given to suspects who have been cautioned in accordance with section 10 of this code according to whether or not they have been arrested and detained. It includes information required by EU Directive 2012/13 on the right to information in criminal proceedings. If a complaint is made by or on behalf of such a suspect that the information and (as the case may be) access to records and documents has not been provided as required, the matter shall be reported to an inspector to deal with as a complaint for the purposes of paragraph 9.2, or paragraph 12.9 if the challenge is made during an interview. This would include, for example:

    (a) in the case of a detained suspect:
- not informing them of their rights (see para. 3.1);
- not giving them a copy of the notice (see para. 3.2(a));
- not providing an opportunity to read the notice (see para. 3.2A);
- not providing the required information (see paras 3.2(a), 3.12(b) and, 3.12A);
- not allowing access to the custody record (see para. 2.4);
- not providing a translation of the notice (see para. 3.12(c) and (d)); and

    (b) in the case of a suspect who is not detained:
- not informing them of their rights or providing the required information (see para. 3.21(b)).

Notes for guidance

C:3ZA *For the purposes of paragraphs 3.4(b) and 15.0:*   **A-49**

    (a) *investigating officers are responsible for bringing to the attention of the officer who is responsible for authorising the suspect's detention or (as the case may be) continued detention (before or after charge), any documents and materials in their possession or control which appear to undermine the need to keep the suspect in custody; in accordance with Part IV of PACE, this officer will be either the custody officer, the officer reviewing the need for detention before or after charge (PACE, s.40), or the officer considering the need to extend detention without charge from 24 to 36 hours (PACE, s.42) who is then responsible for determining, which, if any, of those documents and materials are capable of undermining the need to detain the suspect and must therefore be made available to the suspect or their solicitor;*

    (b) *the way in which documents and materials are "made available", is a matter for the investigating officer to determine on a case by case basis and having regard to the nature and volume of the documents and materials involved: for example, they may be made available by supplying a copy or allowing supervised access to view; however, for view only access, it will be necessary to demonstrate that sufficient time is allowed for the suspect and solicitor to view and consider the documents and materials in question.*

C:3A *For access to currently available notices, including "easy-read" versions, see https://www.gov.uk/notice-of-rights-and-entitlements-a-persons-rights-in-police-detention.*

C:3B *[Not used.]*

C:3C *If the juvenile is in local authority or voluntary organisation care but living with their parents or other adults responsible for their welfare, although there is no legal obligation to inform them, they should normally be contacted, as well as the authority or organisation unless they are suspected of involvement in the offence concerned. Even if the juvenile is not living with their parents, consideration should be given to informing them.*

C:3D *The right to consult the codes of practice does not entitle the person concerned to delay unreasonably any necessary investigative or administrative action whilst they do so. Examples of action which need not be delayed unreasonably include:*

- *procedures requiring the provision of breath, blood or urine specimens under the Road Traffic Act 1988 or the Transport and Works Act 1992;*
- *searching detainees at the police station;*
- *taking fingerprints, footwear impressions or non-intimate samples without consent for evidential purposes.*

C:3E *The Detention and Custody Authorised Professional Practice (APP) produced by the College of Policing (see http://www.app.college.police.uk) provides more detailed guidance on risk assessments and identifies key risk areas which should always be considered.*

C:3F *A custody officer or other officer who, in accordance with this code, allows or directs the carrying out of any task or action relating to a detainee's care, treatment, rights and entitlements to another officer or any police staff must be satisfied that the officer or police staff concerned are suitable, trained and competent to carry out the task or action in question.*

C:4 Detainee's property

(a) *Action*

A-50   C:4.1 The custody officer is responsible for:
- (a) ascertaining what property a detainee:
  - (i) has with them when they come to the police station, whether on:
    - arrest or re-detention on answering to bail;
    - commitment to prison custody on the order or sentence of a court;
    - lodgement at the police station with a view to their production in court from prison custody;
    - transfer from detention at another station or hospital;
    - detention under the Mental Health Act 1983, s.135 or 136;
    - remand into police custody on the authority of a court;
  - (ii) might have acquired for an unlawful or harmful purpose while in custody;
- (b) the safekeeping of any property taken from a detainee which remains at the police station.

The custody officer may search the detainee or authorise their being searched to the extent they consider necessary, provided a search of intimate parts of the body or involving the removal of more than outer clothing is only made as in Annex A. A search may only be carried out by an officer of the same sex as the detainee. See *Note 4A* and Annex L.

C:4.2 Detainees may retain clothing and personal effects at their own risk unless the custody officer considers they may use them to cause harm to themselves or others, interfere with evidence, damage property, effect an escape or they are needed as evidence. In this event the custody officer may withhold such articles as they consider necessary and must tell the detainee why.

C:4.3 Personal effects are those items a detainee may lawfully need, use or refer to while in detention but do not include cash and other items of value.

(b) *Documentation*

C:4.4 It is a matter for the custody officer to determine whether a record should be made of the property a detained person has with him or had taken from him on arrest. Any record made is not required to be kept as part of the custody record but the custody record should be noted as to where such a record exists. Whenever a record is made the detainee shall be allowed to check and sign the record of property as correct. Any refusal to sign shall be recorded.

C:4.5 If a detainee is not allowed to keep any article of clothing or personal effects, the reason must be recorded.

Notes for guidance

A-51   C:4A *PACE, s.54(1), and paragraph 4.1 require a detainee to be searched when it is clear the custody officer will have continuing duties in relation to that detainee or when that detainee's behaviour or offence makes an inventory appropriate. They do not require every detainee to be searched, e.g. if it is clear a person will only be detained for a short period and is not to be placed in a cell, the custody officer may decide not to search them. In such a case the custody record will be endorsed "not searched", paragraph 4.4 will not apply, and the detainee will be invited to sign the entry. If the detainee refuses, the custody officer will be obliged to ascertain what property they have in accordance with paragraph 4.1.*

C:4B *Paragraph 4.4 does not require the custody officer to record on the custody record property in the detainee's possession on arrest if, by virtue of its nature, quantity or size, it is not practicable to remove it to the police station.*

C:4C *Paragraph 4.4 does not require items of clothing worn by the person to be recorded unless withheld by the custody officer as in paragraph 4.2.*

C:5 Right not to be held incommunicado

(a) *Action*

C:5.1 Subject to paragraph 5.7B, any person arrested and held in custody at a police station or **A-52** other premises may, on request, have one person known to them or likely to take an interest in their welfare informed at public expense of their whereabouts as soon as practicable. If the person cannot be contacted the detainee may choose up to two alternatives. If they cannot be contacted, the person in charge of detention or the investigation has discretion to allow further attempts until the information has been conveyed. See *Notes 5C* and *5D.*

C:5.2 The exercise of the above right in respect of each person nominated may be delayed only in accordance with Annex B.

C:5.3 The above right may be exercised each time a detainee is taken to another police station.

C:5.4 If the detainee agrees, they may at the custody officer's discretion, receive visits from friends, family or others likely to take an interest in their welfare, or in whose welfare the detainee has an interest. See *Note 5B.*

C:5.5 If a friend, relative or person with an interest in the detainee's welfare enquires about their whereabouts, this information shall be given if the suspect agrees and Annex B does not apply. See *Note 5D.*

C:5.6 The detainee shall be given writing materials, on request, and allowed to telephone one person for a reasonable time, see *Notes 5A* and *5E.* Either or both of these privileges may be denied or delayed if an officer of inspector rank or above considers sending a letter or making a telephone call may result in any of the consequences in:

> (a) Annex B, paragraphs 1 and 2 and the person is detained in connection with an indictable offence;
>
> (b) [*Not used.*]

Nothing in this paragraph permits the restriction or denial of the rights in paragraphs 5.1 and 6.1.

C:5.7 Before any letter or message is sent, or telephone call made, the detainee shall be informed that what they say in any letter, call or message (other than in a communication to a solicitor) may be read or listened to and may be given in evidence. A telephone call may be terminated if it is being abused. The costs can be at public expense at the custody officer's discretion.

C:5.7A Any delay or denial of the rights in this section should be proportionate and should last no longer than necessary.

C:5.7B In the case of a person in police custody for specific purposes and periods in accordance with a direction under the Crime (Sentences) Act 1997, Sched. 1 (productions from prison etc.), the exercise of the rights in this section shall be subject to any additional conditions specified in the direction for the purpose of regulating the detainee's contact and communication with others whilst in police custody. See *Note 5F.*

(b) *Documentation*

C:5.8 A record must be kept of any:

> (a) request made under this section and the action taken;
>
> (b) letters, messages or telephone calls made or received or visit received;
>
> (c) refusal by the detainee to have information about them given to an outside enquirer. The detainee must be asked to countersign the record accordingly and any refusal recorded.

Notes for guidance

C:5A *A person may request an interpreter to interpret a telephone call or translate a letter.* **A-53**

C:5B *At the custody officer's discretion and subject to the detainee's consent, visits should be allowed when possible, subject to having sufficient personnel to supervise a visit and any possible hindrance to the investigation.*

C:5C *If the detainee does not know anyone to contact for advice or support or cannot contact a friend or relative, the custody officer should bear in mind any local voluntary bodies or other organisations who might be able to help. Paragraph 6.1 applies if legal advice is required.*

C:5D *In some circumstances it may not be appropriate to use the telephone to disclose information under paragraphs 5.1 and 5.5.*

C:5E *The telephone call at paragraph 5.6 is in addition to any communication under paragraphs 5.1 and 6.1.*

C:5F *Prison Service Instruction 26/2012 (Production of Prisoners at the Request of Warranted Law Enforcement Agencies) provides detailed guidance and instructions for police officers and governors and directors of prisons regarding applications for prisoners to be transferred to police custody and their safe custody and treatments while in police custody.*

C:6 Right to legal advice

(a) Action

A-54   C:6.1 Unless Annex B applies, all detainees must be informed that they may at any time consult and communicate privately with a solicitor, whether in person, in writing or by telephone, and that free independent legal advice is available. See paragraph 3.1, *Notes 1I, 6B* and *6J.*

C:6.2 [*Not used.*]

C:6.3 A poster advertising the right to legal advice must be prominently displayed in the charging area of every police station. See *Note 6H.*

C:6.4 No police officer should, at any time, do or say anything with the intention of dissuading any person who is entitled to legal advice in accordance with this code, whether or not they have been arrested and are detained, from obtaining legal advice. See *Note 6ZA.*

C:6.5 The exercise of the right of access to legal advice may be delayed only as in Annex B. Whenever legal advice is requested, and unless Annex B applies, the custody officer must act without delay to secure the provision of such advice. If the detainee has the right to speak to a solicitor in person but declines to exercise the right the officer should point out that the right includes the right to speak with a solicitor on the telephone. If the detainee continues to waive this right, or a detainee whose right to free legal advice is limited to telephone advice from the Criminal Defence Service (CDS) Direct (see *Note 6B*) declines to exercise that right, the officer should ask them why and any reasons should be recorded on the custody record or the interview record as appropriate. Reminders of the right to legal advice must be given as in paragraphs 3.5, 11.2, 15.4, 16.4, 16.5, 2B of Annex A, 3 of Annex K and 5 of Annex M of this code and Code D, paragraphs 3.17(ii) and 6.3. Once it is clear a detainee does not want to speak to a solicitor in person or by telephone they should cease to be asked their reasons. See *Note 6K.*

C:6.5A In the case of a person who is a juvenile or is mentally disordered or otherwise mentally vulnerable, an appropriate adult should consider whether legal advice from a solicitor is required. If the person indicates that they do not want legal advice, the appropriate adult has the right to ask for a solicitor to attend if this would be in the best interests of the person. However, the person cannot be forced to see the solicitor if they are adamant that they do not wish to do so.

Note: paragraph 1.5A applies this paragraph to 17-year-old detainees.

C:6.6 A detainee who wants legal advice may not be interviewed or continue to be interviewed until they have received such advice unless:

    (a) Annex B applies, when the restriction on drawing adverse inferences from silence in Annex C will apply because the detainee is not allowed an opportunity to consult a solicitor; or

    (b) an officer of superintendent rank or above has reasonable grounds for believing that:

        (i) the consequent delay might:

- lead to interference with, or harm to, evidence connected with an offence;
- lead to interference with, or physical harm to, other people;
- lead to serious loss of, or damage to, property;
- lead to alerting other people suspected of having committed an offence but not yet arrested for it;
- hinder the recovery of property obtained in consequence of the commission of an offence; see *Note 6A*;

        (ii) when a solicitor, including a duty solicitor, has been contacted and has agreed to attend, awaiting their arrival would cause unreasonable delay to the process of investigation;

        note: in these cases the restriction on drawing adverse inferences from silence in Annex C will apply because the detainee is not allowed an opportunity to consult a solicitor;

    (c) the solicitor the detainee has nominated or selected from a list:

        (i) cannot be contacted;

        (ii) has previously indicated they do not wish to be contacted; or

        (iii) having been contacted, has declined to attend; and

- the detainee has been advised of the duty solicitor scheme but has declined to ask for the duty solicitor;
- in these circumstances the interview may be started or continued without further delay provided an officer of inspector rank or above has agreed to the interview proceeding;

note: the restriction on drawing adverse inferences from silence in Annex C will not apply because the detainee is allowed an opportunity to consult the duty solicitor;

(d) the detainee changes their mind about wanting legal advice or (as the case may be) about wanting a solicitor present at the interview and states that they no longer wish to speak to a solicitor; in these circumstances, the interview may be started or continued without delay provided that:

(i) an officer of inspector rank or above:

- speaks to the detainee to enquire about the reasons for their change of mind (see *Note 6K*), and
- makes, or directs the making of, reasonable efforts to ascertain the solicitor's expected time of arrival and to inform the solicitor that the suspect has stated that they wish to change their mind and the reason (if given);

(ii) the detainee's reason for their change of mind (if given) and the outcome of the action in (i) are recorded in the custody record;

(iii) the detainee, after being informed of the outcome of the action in (i) above, confirms in writing that they want the interview to proceed without speaking or further speaking to a solicitor or (as the case may be) without a solicitor being present and do not wish to wait for a solicitor by signing an entry to this effect in the custody record;

(iv) an officer of inspector rank or above is satisfied that it is proper for the interview to proceed in these circumstances and:

- gives authority in writing for the interview to proceed and, if the authority is not recorded in the custody record, the officer must ensure that the custody record shows the date and time of authority and where it is recorded, and
- takes, or directs the taking of, reasonable steps to inform the solicitor that the authority has been given and the time when the interview is expected to commence and records or causes to be recorded, the outcome of this action in the custody record;

(v) when the interview starts and the interviewer reminds the suspect of their right to legal advice (see paragraph 11.2, Code E, paragraph 4.5, and Code F, paragraph 4.5), the interviewer shall then ensure that the following is recorded in the written interview record or the interview record made in accordance with Code E or F:

- confirmation that the detainee has changed their mind about wanting legal advice or (as the case may be) about wanting a solicitor present and the reasons for it if given;
- the fact that authority for the interview to proceed has been given and, subject to paragraph 2.6A, the name of the authorising officer;
- that if the solicitor arrives at the station before the interview is completed, the detainee will be so informed without delay and a break will be taken to allow them to speak to the solicitor if they wish, unless paragraph 6.6(a) applies; and
- that at any time during the interview, the detainee may again ask for legal advice and that if they do, a break will be taken to allow them to speak to the solicitor, unless paragraph 6.6(a), (b), or (c) applies;

note: in these circumstances, the restriction on drawing adverse inferences from silence in Annex C will not apply because the detainee is allowed an opportunity to consult a solicitor if they wish.

C:6.7 If paragraph 6.6(a) applies, where the reason for authorising the delay ceases to apply, there **A-55** may be no further delay in permitting the exercise of the right in the absence of a further authorisation unless paragraph 6.6(b), (c) or (d) applies. If paragraph 6.6(b)(i) applies, once sufficient information has been obtained to avert the risk, questioning must cease until the detainee has received legal advice unless paragraph 6.6(a), (b)(ii), (c) or (d) applies.

C:6.8 A detainee who has been permitted to consult a solicitor shall be entitled on request to have the solicitor present when they are interviewed unless one of the exceptions in paragraph 6.6 applies.

C:6.9 The solicitor may only be required to leave the interview if their conduct is such that the interviewer is unable properly to put questions to the suspect. See *Notes 6D* and *6E*.

C:6.10 If the interviewer considers a solicitor is acting in such a way, they will stop the interview and consult an officer not below superintendent rank, if one is readily available, and otherwise an officer not below inspector rank not connected with the investigation. After speaking to the solicitor, the officer consulted will decide if the interview should continue in the presence of that solicitor. If they decide it should not, the suspect will be given the opportunity to consult another solicitor before the interview continues and that solicitor given an opportunity to be present at the interview. See *Note 6E*.

C:6.11 The removal of a solicitor from an interview is a serious step and, if it occurs, the officer of superintendent rank or above who took the decision will consider if the incident should be reported to the Solicitors Regulation Authority. If the decision to remove the solicitor has been taken by an officer below superintendent rank, the facts must be reported to an officer of superintendent rank or above who will similarly consider whether a report to the Solicitors Regulation Authority would be appropriate. When the solicitor concerned is a duty solicitor, the report should be both to the Solicitors Regulation Authority and to the Legal Aid Agency.

C:6.12 "Solicitor" in this code means:

- a solicitor who holds a current practising certificate;
- an accredited or probationary representative included on the register of representatives maintained by the Legal Aid Agency.

C:6.12A An accredited or probationary representative sent to provide advice by, and on behalf of, a solicitor shall be admitted to the police station for this purpose unless an officer of inspector rank or above considers such a visit will hinder the investigation and directs otherwise. Hindering the investigation does not include giving proper legal advice to a detainee as in *Note 6D*. Once admitted to the police station, paragraphs 6.6 to 6.10 apply.

C:6.13 In exercising their discretion under paragraph 6.12A, the officer should take into account in particular:

- whether:
  - the identity and status of an accredited or probationary representative have been satisfactorily established;
  - they are of suitable character to provide legal advice, *e.g.* a person with a criminal record is unlikely to be suitable unless the conviction was for a minor offence and not recent;
- any other matters in any written letter of authorisation provided by the solicitor on whose behalf the person is attending the police station. See *Note 6F*.

C:6.14 If the inspector refuses access to an accredited or probationary representative or a decision is taken that such a person should not be permitted to remain at an interview, the inspector must notify the solicitor on whose behalf the representative was acting and give them an opportunity to make alternative arrangements. The detainee must be informed and the custody record noted.

C:6.15 If a solicitor arrives at the station to see a particular person, that person must, unless Annex B applies, be so informed whether or not they are being interviewed and asked if they would like to see the solicitor. This applies even if the detainee has declined legal advice or, having requested it, subsequently agreed to be interviewed without receiving advice. The solicitor's attendance and the detainee's decision must be noted in the custody record.

(b) *Documentation*

C:6.16 Any request for legal advice and the action taken shall be recorded.

C:6.17 A record shall be made in the interview record if a detainee asks for legal advice and an interview is begun either in the absence of a solicitor or their representative, or they have been required to leave an interview.

Notes for guidance

C:6ZA *No police officer or police staff shall indicate to any suspect, except to answer a direct question, that period for which they are liable to be detained, or if not detained, the time taken to complete the interview, might be reduced:*

- *if they do not ask for legal advice or do not want a solicitor present when they are interviewed; or*
- *if they have asked for legal advice or (as the case may be) asked for a solicitor to be present when they are interviewed but change their mind and agree to be interviewed without waiting for a solicitor.*

C:6A *In considering if paragraph 6.6(b) applies, the officer should, if practicable, ask the solicitor for an estimate of how long it will take to come to the station and relate this to the time detention is permitted, the time of day (e.g. whether the rest period under paragraph 12.2 is imminent) and the requirements of other investigations. If the solicitor is on their way or is to set off immediately, it will not normally be appropriate to begin an interview before they arrive. If it appears necessary to begin an interview before the solicitor's arrival, they should be given* an indication of how long the police would be able to wait before 6.6(b) applies so there is an opportunity to make arrangements for someone else to provide legal advice.

C:6B *A detainee has a right to free legal advice and to be represented by a solicitor. This note for guidance explains the arrangements which enable detainees to obtain legal advice. An outline of these arrangements is also included in the Notice of Rights and Entitlements given to detainees in accordance with paragraph 3.2. The arrangements also apply, with appropriate modifications, to persons attending a police station or other location voluntarily who are cautioned prior to being interviewed. See paragraph 3.21.*

When a detainee asks for free legal advice, the Defence Solicitor Call Centre (DSCC) must be informed of the request.

Free legal advice will be limited to telephone advice provided by CDS Direct if a detainee is:

- *detained for a non-imprisonable offence;*
- *arrested on a bench warrant for failing to appear and being held for production at court (except where the solicitor has clear documentary evidence available that would result in the client being released from custody);*
- *arrested for drink driving (driving/in charge with excess alcohol, failing to provide a specimen, driving/in charge whilst unfit through drink); or*
- *detained in relation to breach of police or court bail conditions;*

unless one or more exceptions apply, in which case the DSCC should arrange for advice to be given by a solicitor at the police station, for example:

- *the police want to interview the detainee or carry out an eye-witness identification procedure;*
- *the detainee needs an appropriate adult;*
- *the detainee is unable to communicate over the telephone;*
- *the detainee alleges serious misconduct by the police;*
- *the investigation includes another offence not included in the list;*
- *the solicitor to be assigned is already at the police station.*

When free advice is not limited to telephone advice, a detainee can ask for free advice from a solicitor they know or if they do not know a solicitor or the solicitor they know cannot be contacted, from the duty solicitor.

To arrange free legal advice, the police should telephone the DSCC. The call centre will decide whether legal advice should be limited to telephone advice from CDS Direct, or whether a solicitor known to the detainee or the duty solicitor should speak to the detainee.

When a detainee wants to pay for legal advice themselves:

- *the DSCC will contact a solicitor of their choice on their behalf;*
- *they may, when free advice is only available by telephone from CDS Direct, still speak to a solicitor of their choice on the telephone for advice, but the solicitor would not be paid by legal aid and may ask the person to pay for the advice;*
- *they should be given an opportunity to consult a specific solicitor or another solicitor from that solicitor's firm; if this solicitor is not available, they may choose up to two alternatives; if these alternatives are not available, the custody officer has discretion to allow further attempts until a solicitor has been contacted and agreed to provide advice;*
- *they are entitled to a private consultation with their chosen solicitor on the telephone or the solicitor may decide to come to the police station;*
- *if their chosen solicitor cannot be contacted, the DSCC may still be called to arrange free legal advice.*

Apart from carrying out duties necessary to implement these arrangements, an officer must not advise the suspect about any particular firm of solicitors.

C:6C [*Not used.*]

C:6D *The solicitor's only role in the police station is to protect and advance the legal rights of their client. On occasions this may require the solicitor to give advice which has the effect of the client avoiding giving evidence which strengthens a prosecution case. The solicitor may intervene in order to seek clarification, challenge an improper question to their client or the manner in which it is put, advise their client not to reply to particular questions, or if they wish to give their client further legal advice. Paragraph 6.9 only applies if the solicitor's approach or conduct prevents or unreasonably obstructs proper questions being put to the suspect or the suspect's response being recorded. Examples of unacceptable conduct include answering questions on a suspect's behalf or providing written replies for the suspect to quote.*

C:6E *An officer who takes the decision to exclude a solicitor must be in a position to satisfy the court the decision was properly made. In order to do this they may need to witness what is happening.*

C:6F *If an officer of at least inspector rank considers a particular solicitor or firm of solicitors is persistently sending probationary representatives who are unsuited to provide legal advice, they should inform an officer of at least superintendent rank, who may wish to take the matter up with the Solicitors Regulation Authority.*

C:6G *Subject to the constraints of Annex B, a solicitor may advise more than one client in an investigation if*   **A-57** *they wish. Any question of a conflict of interest is for the solicitor under their professional code of conduct. If,* *however, waiting for a solicitor to give advice to one client may lead to unreasonable delay to the interview with another, the provisions of paragraph 6.6(b) may apply.*

C:6H *In addition to a poster in English, a poster or posters containing translations into Welsh, the main minority ethnic languages and the principal European languages should be displayed wherever they are likely to be helpful and it is practicable to do so.*

C:6I *[Not used.]*

C:6J *Whenever a detainee exercises their right to legal advice by consulting or communicating with a solicitor, they must be allowed to do so in private. This right to consult or communicate in private is fundamental. If the requirement for privacy is compromised because what is said or written by the detainee or solicitor for the purpose of giving and receiving legal advice is overheard, listened to, or read by others without the informed consent of the detainee, the right will effectively have been denied. When a detainee speaks to a solicitor on the telephone, they should be allowed to do so in private unless this is impractical because of the design and layout of the custody area or the location of telephones. However, the normal expectation should be that facilities will be available, unless they are being used, at all police stations to enable detainees to speak in private to a solicitor either face to face or over the telephone.*

C:6K *A detainee is not obliged to give reasons for declining legal advice and should not be pressed to do so.*

C:7 Citizens of independent Commonwealth countries or foreign nationals

(a) *Action*

A-58
C:7.1 A detainee who is a citizen of an independent Commonwealth country or a national of a foreign country, including the Republic of Ireland, has the right, upon request, to communicate at any time with the appropriate high commission, embassy or consulate. That detainee must be informed as soon as practicable of this right and asked if they want to have their high commission, embassy or consulate told of their whereabouts and the grounds for their detention. Such a request should be acted upon as soon as practicable. See *Note 7A.*

C:7.2 A detainee who is a citizen of a country with which a bilateral consular convention or agreement is in force requiring notification of arrest, must also be informed that subject to paragraph 7.4, notification of their arrest will be sent to the appropriate high commission, embassy or consulate as soon as practicable, whether or not they request it. A list of the countries to which this requirement currently applies and contact details for the relevant high commissions, embassies and consulates can be obtained from the Consular Directorate of the Foreign and Commonwealth Office (FCO) as follows:

- from the FCO web pages:
    - https://gov.uk/government/publications/table-of-consular-conventions-and-mandatory-notification-obligations, and
    - https://www.gov.uk/government/publications/foreign-embassies-in-the-uk
- by telephone to 020 7008 3100,
- by email to fcocorrespondence@fco.gov.uk.
- or by letter to the Foreign and Commonwealth Office, King Charles Street, London, SW1A 2AH.

C:7.3 Consular officers may, if the detainee agrees, visit one of their nationals in police detention to talk to them and, if required, to arrange for legal advice. Such visits shall take place out of the hearing of a police officer.

C:7.4 Notwithstanding the provisions of consular conventions, if the detainee claims that they are a refugee or have applied or intend to apply for asylum, the custody officer must ensure that the UK Visas and Immigration (UKVI) (formerly the UK Border Agency) is informed as soon as practicable of the claim. UKVI will then determine whether compliance with relevant international obligations requires notification of the arrest to be sent and will inform the custody officer as to what action police need to take.

(b) *Documentation*

A-59
C:7.5 A record shall be made:

- when a detainee is informed of their rights under this section and of any requirement in paragraph 7.2;
- of any communications with a high commission, embassy or consulate; and
- of any communications with UKVI about a detainee's claim to be a refugee or to be seeking asylum and the resulting action taken by police.

C:7A *The exercise of the rights in this section may not be interfered with even though Annex B applies.* **A-60**

C:8 Conditions of detention

(a) *Action*

C:8.1 So far as it is practicable, not more than one detainee should be detained in each cell. See **A-61** *Note 8C.*

C:8.2 Cells in use must be adequately heated, cleaned and ventilated. They must be adequately lit, subject to such dimming as is compatible with safety and security to allow people detained overnight to sleep. No additional restraints shall be used within a locked cell unless absolutely necessary and then only restraint equipment, approved for use in that force by the chief officer, which is reasonable and necessary in the circumstances having regard to the detainee's demeanour and with a view to ensuring their safety and the safety of others. If a detainee is deaf, mentally disordered or otherwise mentally vulnerable, particular care must be taken when deciding whether to use any form of approved restraints.

C:8.3 Blankets, mattresses, pillows and other bedding supplied shall be of a reasonable standard and in a clean and sanitary condition. See *Note 8A.*

C:8.4 Access to toilet and washing facilities must be provided.

C:8.5 If it is necessary to remove a detainee's clothes for the purposes of investigation, for hygiene, health reasons or cleaning, replacement clothing of a reasonable standard of comfort and cleanliness shall be provided. A detainee may not be interviewed unless adequate clothing has been offered.

C:8.6 At least two light meals and one main meal should be offered in any 24-hour period. See *Note 8B.* Drinks should be provided at meal times and upon reasonable request between meals. Whenever necessary, advice shall be sought from the appropriate healthcare professional, see *Note 9A,* on medical and dietary matters. As far as practicable, meals provided shall offer a varied diet and meet any specific dietary needs or religious beliefs the detainee may have. The detainee may, at the custody officer's discretion, have meals supplied by their family or friends at their expense. See *Note 8A.*

C:8.7 Brief outdoor exercise shall be offered daily if practicable.

C:8.8 A juvenile shall not be placed in a police cell unless no other secure accommodation is available and the custody officer considers it is not practicable to supervise them if they are not placed in a cell or that a cell provides more comfortable accommodation than other secure accommodation in the station. A juvenile may not be placed in a cell with a detained adult.

Note: paragraph 1.5A extends these requirements to 17-year-old detainees.

(b) *Documentation*

C:8.9 A record must be kept of replacement clothing and meals offered. **A-62**

C:8.10 If a juvenile is placed in a cell, the reason must be recorded.

Note: paragraph 1.5A extends this requirement to 17-year-old detainees.

C:8.11 The use of any restraints on a detainee whilst in a cell, the reasons for it and, if appropriate, the arrangements for enhanced supervision of the detainee whilst so restrained, shall be recorded. See paragraph 3.9.

Notes for guidance

C:8A *The provisions in paragraph 8.3 and 8.6 respectively are of particular importance in the case of a* **A-63** *person likely to be detained for an extended period. In deciding whether to allow meals to be supplied by family or friends, the custody officer is entitled to take account of the risk of items being concealed in any food or package and the officer's duties and responsibilities under food handling legislation.*

C:8B *Meals should, so far as practicable, be offered at recognised meal times, or at other times that take account of when the detainee last had a meal.*

C:8C *The Detention and Custody Authorised Professional Practice (APP) produced by the College of Policing (see http://www.app.college.police.uk) provides more detailed guidance on matters concerning detainee healthcare and treatment and associated forensic issues which should be read in conjunction with sections 8 and 9 of this code.*

C:9 Care and treatment of detained persons

(a) *General*

A-64   C:9.1 Nothing in this section prevents the police from calling an appropriate healthcare professional to examine a detainee for the purposes of obtaining evidence relating to any offence in which the detainee is suspected of being involved. See *Notes 9A* and *8C*.

C:9.2 If a complaint is made by, or on behalf of, a detainee about their treatment since their arrest, or it comes to notice that a detainee may have been treated improperly, a report must be made as soon as practicable to an officer of inspector rank or above not connected with the investigation. If the matter concerns a possible assault or the possibility of the unnecessary or unreasonable use of force, an appropriate healthcare professional must also be called as soon as practicable.

C:9.3 Detainees should be visited at least every hour. If no reasonably foreseeable risk was identified in a risk assessment, see paragraphs 3.6–3.10, there is no need to wake a sleeping detainee. Those suspected of being under the influence of drink or drugs or both or of having swallowed drugs, see *Note 9CA*, or whose level of consciousness causes concern must, subject to any clinical directions given by the appropriate healthcare professional, see paragraph 9.13:

- be visited and roused at least every half hour;
- have their condition assessed as in Annex H;
- and clinical treatment arranged if appropriate.

See *Notes 9B, 9C* and *9H.*

C:9.4 When arrangements are made to secure clinical attention for a detainee, the custody officer must make sure all relevant information which might assist in the treatment of the detainee's condition is made available to the responsible healthcare professional. This applies whether or not the healthcare professional asks for such information. Any officer or police staff with relevant information must inform the custody officer as soon as practicable.

(b) *Clinical treatment and attention*

A-65   C:9.5 The custody officer must make sure a detainee receives appropriate clinical attention as soon as reasonably practicable if the person:

(a) appears to be suffering from physical illness; or

(b) is injured; or

(c) appears to be suffering from a mental disorder; or

(d) appears to need clinical attention.

C:9.5A This applies even if the detainee makes no request for clinical attention and whether or not they have already received clinical attention elsewhere. If the need for attention appears urgent, *e.g.* when indicated as in Annex H, the nearest available healthcare professional or an ambulance must be called immediately.

C:9.5B The custody officer must also consider the need for clinical attention as set out in *Note for Guidance 9C* in relation to those suffering the effects of alcohol or drugs.

C:9.6 Paragraph 9.5 is not meant to prevent or delay the transfer to a hospital if necessary of a person detained under the Mental Health Act 1983, s.136. See *Note 9D*. When an assessment under that Act is to take place at a police station, see paragraph 3.16, the custody officer must consider whether an appropriate healthcare professional should be called to conduct an initial clinical check on the detainee. This applies particularly when there is likely to be any significant delay in the arrival of a suitably qualified medical practitioner.

C:9.7 If it appears to the custody officer, or they are told, that a person brought to a station under arrest may be suffering from an infectious disease or condition, the custody officer must take reasonable steps to safeguard the health of the detainee and others at the station. In deciding what action to take, advice must be sought from an appropriate healthcare professional. See *Note 9E*. The custody officer has discretion to isolate the person and their property until clinical directions have been obtained.

A-66   C:9.8 If a detainee requests a clinical examination, an appropriate healthcare professional must be called as soon as practicable to assess the detainee's clinical needs. If a safe and appropriate care plan cannot be provided, the appropriate healthcare professional's advice must be sought. The detainee may also be examined by a medical practitioner of their choice at their expense.

C:9.9 If a detainee is required to take or apply any medication in compliance with clinical directions prescribed before their detention, the custody officer must consult the appropriate healthcare professional before the use of the medication. Subject to the restrictions in paragraph 9.10, the custody officer is responsible for the safekeeping of any medication and for making sure the detainee is given the opportunity to take or apply prescribed or approved medication. Any such consultation and its outcome shall be noted in the custody record.

C:9.10 No police officer may administer or supervise the self-administration of medically prescribed controlled drugs of the types and forms listed in the Misuse of Drugs Regulations 2001, Sched. 2 or 3. A detainee may only self-administer such drugs under the personal supervision of the registered medical practitioner authorising their use or other appropriate healthcare professional. The custody officer may supervise the self-administration of, or authorise other custody staff to supervise the self-administration of, drugs listed in Schedule 4 or 5 if the officer has consulted the appropriate healthcare professional authorising their use and both are satisfied self-administration will not expose the detainee, police officers or anyone else to the risk of harm or injury.

C:9.11 When appropriate healthcare professionals administer drugs or authorise the use of other medications, supervise their self-administration or consult with the custody officer about allowing self-administration of drugs listed in Schedule 4 or 5, it must be within current medicines legislation and the scope of practice as determined by their relevant statutory regulatory body.

C:9.12 If a detainee has in their possession, or claims to need, medication relating to a heart condition, diabetes, epilepsy or a condition of comparable potential seriousness then, even though paragraph 9.5 may not apply, the advice of the appropriate healthcare professional must be obtained.

C:9.13 Whenever the appropriate healthcare professional is called in accordance with this section to examine or treat a detainee, the custody officer shall ask for their opinion about:
- any risks or problems which police need to take into account when making decisions about the detainee's continued detention;
- when to carry out an interview if applicable; and
- the need for safeguards.

C:9.14 When clinical directions are given by the appropriate healthcare professional, whether orally or in writing, and the custody officer has any doubts or is in any way uncertain about any aspect of the directions, the custody officer shall ask for clarification. It is particularly important that directions concerning the frequency of visits are clear, precise and capable of being implemented. See *Note 9F*.

(c) *Documentation*

C:9.15 A record must be made in the custody record of: **A-67**
- (a) the arrangements made for an examination by an appropriate healthcare professional under paragraph 9.2 and of any complaint reported under that paragraph together with any relevant remarks by the custody officer;
- (b) any arrangements made in accordance with paragraph 9.5;
- (c) any request for a clinical examination under paragraph 9.8 and any arrangements made in response;
- (d) the injury, ailment, condition or other reason which made it necessary to make the arrangements in (a) to (c); see *Note 9G*;
- (e) any clinical directions and advice, including any further clarifications, given to police by a healthcare professional concerning the care and treatment of the detainee in connection with any of the arrangements made in (a) to (c); see *Notes 9E* and *9F*;
- (f) if applicable, the responses received when attempting to rouse a person using the procedure in Annex H. See *Note 9H*.

C:9.16 If a healthcare professional does not record their clinical findings in the custody record, the record must show where they are recorded. See *Note 9G*. However, information which is necessary to custody staff to ensure the effective ongoing care and well-being of the detainee must be recorded openly in the custody record, see paragraph 3.8 and Annex G, paragraph 7.

C:9.17 Subject to the requirements of section 4, the custody record shall include:
- a record of all medication a detainee has in their possession on arrival at the police station;
- a note of any such medication they claim to need but do not have with them.

Notes for guidance

C:9A *A "healthcare professional" means a clinically qualified person working within the scope of practice as* **A-68** *determined by their relevant statutory regulatory body. Whether a healthcare professional is "appropriate" depends on the circumstances of the duties they carry out at the time.*

C:9B *Whenever possible juveniles and mentally vulnerable detainees should be visited more frequently. Note: paragraph 1.5A extends this note to 17-year-old detainees.*

C:9C *A detainee who appears drunk or behaves abnormally may be suffering from illness, the effects of drugs or may have sustained injury, particularly a head injury which is not apparent. A detainee needing or dependent on certain drugs, including alcohol, may experience harmful effects within a short time of being deprived of their supply. In these circumstances, when there is any doubt, police should always act urgently to call an appropriate healthcare professional or an ambulance. Paragraph 9.5 does not apply to minor ailments or injuries which do not need attention. However, all such ailments or injuries must be recorded in the custody record and any doubt must be resolved in favour of calling the appropriate healthcare professional.*

C:9CA *Paragraph 9.3 would apply to a person in police custody by order of a magistrates' court under the Criminal Justice Act 1988, s.152 (as amended by the Drugs Act 2005, s.8) to facilitate the recovery of evidence after being charged with drug possession or drug trafficking and suspected of having swallowed drugs. In the case of the healthcare needs of a person who has swallowed drugs, the custody officer subject to any clinical directions, should consider the necessity for rousing every half hour. This does not negate the need for regular visiting of the suspect in the cell.*

C:9D *Whenever practicable, arrangements should be made for persons detained for assessment under the Mental Health Act 1983, s.136 to be taken to a hospital. Chapter 10 of the Mental Health Act 1983 Code of Practice (as revised) provides more detailed guidance about arranging assessments under section 136 and transferring detainees from police stations to other places of safety.*

C:9E *It is important to respect a person's right to privacy and information about their health must be kept confidential and only disclosed with their consent or in accordance with clinical advice when it is necessary to protect the detainee's health or that of others who come into contact with them.*

C:9F *The custody officer should always seek to clarify directions that the detainee requires constant observation or supervision and should ask the appropriate healthcare professional to explain precisely what action needs to be taken to implement such directions.*

C:9G *Paragraphs 9.15 and 9.16 do not require any information about the cause of any injury, ailment or condition to be recorded on the custody record if it appears capable of providing evidence of an offence.*

C:9H *The purpose of recording a person's responses when attempting to rouse them using the procedure in Annex H is to enable any change in the individual's consciousness level to be noted and clinical treatment arranged if appropriate.*

C:10 Cautions

(a) *When a caution must be given*

C:10.1 A person whom there are grounds to suspect of an offence, see *Note 10A*, must be cautioned before any questions about an offence, or further questions if the answers provide the grounds for suspicion, are put to them if either the suspect's answers or silence (*i.e.* failure or refusal to answer or answer satisfactorily) may be given in evidence to a court in a prosecution. A person need not be cautioned if questions are for other necessary purposes, *e.g.*:

    (a) solely to establish their identity or ownership of any vehicle;

    (b) to obtain information in accordance with any relevant statutory requirement, see paragraph 10.9;

    (c) in furtherance of the proper and effective conduct of a search, *e.g.* to determine the need to search in the exercise of powers of stop and search or to seek co-operation while carrying out a search; or

    (d) to seek verification of a written record as in paragraph 11.13.

C:10.2 Whenever a person not under arrest is initially cautioned, or reminded they are under caution, that person must at the same time be told they are not under arrest and informed of the provisions of paragraph 3.21 which explain how they may obtain legal advice according to whether they are at a police station or elsewhere. See *Note 10C*.

C:10.3 A person who is arrested, or further arrested, must be informed at the time if practicable or, if not, as soon as it becomes practicable thereafter, that they are under arrest and of the grounds and reasons for their arrest, see paragraph 3.4, *Note 10B* and Code G, paragraphs 2.2 and 4.3.

C:10.4 As required by Code G, section 3, a person who is arrested, or further arrested, must also be cautioned unless:

    (a) it is impracticable to do so by reason of their condition or behaviour at the time;

    (b) they have already been cautioned immediately prior to arrest as in paragraph 10.1.

(b) *Terms of the cautions*

C:10.5 The caution which must be given on:

    (a) arrest; or

    (b) all other occasions before a person is charged or informed they may be prosecuted; see section 16,

should, unless the restriction on drawing adverse inferences from silence applies, see Annex C, be in the following terms:

"You do not have to say anything. But it may harm your defence if you do not mention when questioned something which you later rely on in court. Anything you do say may be given in evidence.".

Where the use of the Welsh language is appropriate, a constable may provide the caution directly in Welsh in the following terms:

"Does dim rhaid i chi ddweud dim byd. Ond gall niweidio eich amddiffyniad os na fyddwch chi'n sôn, wrth gael eich holi, am rywbeth y byddwch chi'n dibynnu arno nes ymlaen yn y Llys. Gall unrhyw beth yr ydych yn ei ddweud gael ei roi fel tystiolaeth.".

See *Note 10G.*

C:10.6 Annex C, paragraph 2, sets out the alternative terms of the caution to be used when the **A-70** restriction on drawing adverse inferences from silence applies.

C:10.7 Minor deviations from the words of any caution given in accordance with this code do not constitute a breach of this code, provided the sense of the relevant caution is preserved. See *Note 10D.*

C:10.8 After any break in questioning under caution, the person being questioned must be made aware they remain under caution. If there is any doubt the relevant caution should be given again in full when the interview resumes. See *Note 10E.*

C:10.9 When, despite being cautioned, a person fails to co-operate or to answer particular questions which may affect their immediate treatment, the person should be informed of any relevant consequences and that those consequences are not affected by the caution. Examples are when a person's refusal to provide:

- their name and address when charged may make them liable to detention;
- particulars and information in accordance with a statutory requirement, *e.g.* under the Road Traffic Act 1988, may amount to an offence or may make the person liable to a further arrest.

(c) *Special warnings under the Criminal Justice and Public Order Act 1994, ss.36 and 37*

C:10.10 When a suspect interviewed at a police station or authorised place of detention after ar- **A-71** rest fails or refuses to answer certain questions, or to answer satisfactorily, after due warning, see *Note 10F,* a court or jury may draw such inferences as appear proper under the Criminal Justice and Public Order Act 1994, ss.36 and 37. Such inferences may only be drawn when:

- (a) the restriction on drawing adverse inferences from silence, see Annex C, does not apply; and
- (b) the suspect is arrested by a constable and fails or refuses to account for any objects, marks or substances, or marks on such objects found:
  - on their person;
  - in or on their clothing or footwear;
  - otherwise in their possession; or
  - in the place they were arrested;
- (c) the arrested suspect was found by a constable at a place at or about the time the offence for which that officer has arrested them is alleged to have been committed, and the suspect fails or refuses to account for their presence there.

When the restriction on drawing adverse inferences from silence applies, the suspect may still be asked to account for any of the matters in (b) or (c) but the special warning described in paragraph 10.11 will not apply and must not be given.

C: 10.11 For an inference to be drawn when a suspect fails or refuses to answer a question about one of these matters or to answer it satisfactorily, the suspect must first be told in ordinary language:

- (a) what offence is being investigated;
- (b) what fact they are being asked to account for;
- (c) this fact may be due to them taking part in the commission of the offence;
- (d) a court may draw a proper inference if they fail or refuse to account for this fact; and
- (e) a record is being made of the interview and it may be given in evidence if they are brought to trial.

(d) *Juveniles and persons who are mentally disordered or otherwise mentally vulnerable*

C:10.11A The information required in paragraph 10.11 must not be given to a suspect who is a juvenile or who is mentally disordered or otherwise mentally vulnerable unless the appropriate adult is present.

C:10.12 If a juvenile or a person who is mentally disordered or otherwise mentally vulnerable is cautioned in the absence of the appropriate adult, the caution must be repeated in the adult's presence.

C:10.12A Paragraph 1.5A extends the requirements in paragraphs 10.11A and 10.12 to 17-year-old detainees.

(e) Documentation

C:10.13 A record shall be made when a caution is given under this section, either in the interviewer's pocket book or in the interview record.

Notes for guidance

A-72   C:10A *There must be some reasonable, objective grounds for the suspicion, based on known facts or informa-tion which are relevant to the likelihood the offence has been committed and the person to be questioned committed it.*

C:10B *An arrested person must be given sufficient information to enable them to understand that they have been deprived of their liberty and the reason they have been arrested, e.g. when a person is arrested on suspicion of committing an offence they must be informed of the suspected offence's nature, when and where it was committed. The suspect must also be informed of the reason or reasons why the arrest is considered necessary. Vague or technical language should be avoided.*

C:10C *The restriction on drawing inferences from silence, see Annex C, paragraph 1, does not apply to a person who has not been detained and who therefore cannot be prevented from seeking legal advice if they want, see paragraph 3.21.*

C:10D *If it appears a person does not understand the caution, the person giving it should explain it in their own words.*

C:10E *It may be necessary to show to the court that nothing occurred during an interview break or between interviews which influenced the suspect's recorded evidence. After a break in an interview or at the beginning of a subsequent interview, the interviewing officer should summarise the reason for the break and confirm this with the suspect.*

C:10F *The Criminal Justice and Public Order Act 1994, ss.36 and 37, apply only to suspects who have been arrested by a constable or an officer of Revenue and Customs and are given the relevant warning by the police or Revenue and Customs officer who made the arrest or who is investigating the offence. They do not apply to any interviews with suspects who have not been arrested.*

C:10G *Nothing in this code requires a caution to be given or repeated when informing a person not under ar-rest they may be prosecuted for an offence. However, a court will not be able to draw any inferences under the Criminal Justice and Public Order Act 1994, s.34, if the person was not cautioned.*

C:11 Interviews—general

(a) Action

A-73   C:11.1A An interview is the questioning of a person regarding their involvement or suspected involvement in a criminal offence or offences which, under paragraph 10.1, must be carried out under caution. Before a person is interviewed, they and, if they are represented, their solicitor must be given sufficient information to enable them to understand the nature of any such offence, and why they are suspected of committing it (see paras 3.4(a) and 10.3), in order to allow for the effective exercise of the rights of the defence. However, whilst the information must always be sufficient for the person to understand the nature of any offence (see *Note 11ZA*), this does not require the disclosure of details at a time which might prejudice the criminal investigation. The decision about what needs to be disclosed for the purpose of this requirement therefore rests with the investigating officer who has sufficient knowledge of the case to make that decision. The officer who discloses the information shall make a record of the information disclosed and when it was disclosed. This record may be made in the interview record, in the officer's pocket book or other form provided for this purpose. Procedures under the Road Traffic Act 1988, s.7, or the Transport and Works Act 1992, s.31, do not constitute interviewing for the purpose of this code.

C:11.1 Following a decision to arrest a suspect, they must not be interviewed about the relevant of-fence except at a police station or other authorised place of detention, unless the consequent delay would be likely to:

    (a) lead to:
- interference with, or harm to, evidence connected with an offence;
- interference with, or physical harm to, other people; or
- serious loss of, or damage to, property;

    (b) lead to alerting other people suspected of committing an offence but not yet arrested for it; or

(c) hinder the recovery of property obtained in consequence of the commission of an offence. Interviewing in any of these circumstances shall cease once the relevant risk has been averted or the necessary questions have been put in order to attempt to avert that risk.

C:11.2 Immediately prior to the commencement or re-commencement of any interview at a police station or other authorised place of detention, the interviewer should remind the suspect of their entitlement to free legal advice and that the interview can be delayed for legal advice to be obtained, unless one of the exceptions in paragraph 6.6 applies. It is the interviewer's responsibility to make sure all reminders are recorded in the interview record.

C:11.3 [*Not used.*]

C:11.4 At the beginning of an interview the interviewer, after cautioning the suspect, see section 10, shall put to them any significant statement or silence which occurred in the presence and hearing of a police officer or other police staff before the start of the interview and which have not been put to the suspect in the course of a previous interview. See *Note 11A*. The interviewer shall ask the suspect whether they confirm or deny that earlier statement or silence and if they want to add anything.

C:11.4A A significant statement is one which appears capable of being used in evidence against the suspect, in particular a direct admission of guilt. A significant silence is a failure or refusal to answer a question or answer satisfactorily when under caution, which might, allowing for the restriction on drawing adverse inferences from silence, see Annex C, give rise to an inference under the Criminal Justice and Public Order Act 1994, Pt III.

C:11.5 No interviewer may try to obtain answers or elicit a statement by the use of oppression. Except as in paragraph 10.9, no interviewer shall indicate, except to answer a direct question, what action will be taken by the police if the person being questioned answers questions, makes a statement or refuses to do either. If the person asks directly what action will be taken if they answer questions, make a statement or refuse to do either, the interviewer may inform them what action the police propose to take provided that action is itself proper and warranted.

C:11.6 The interview or further interview of a person about an offence with which that person has not been charged or for which they have not been informed they may be prosecuted, must cease when:

    (a) the officer in charge of the investigation is satisfied all the questions they consider relevant to obtaining accurate and reliable information about the offence have been put to the suspect, this includes allowing the suspect an opportunity to give an innocent explanation and asking questions to test if the explanation is accurate and reliable, *e.g.* to clear up ambiguities or clarify what the suspect said;

    (b) the officer in charge of the investigation has taken account of any other available evidence; and

    (c) the officer in charge of the investigation, or in the case of a detained suspect, the custody officer, see paragraph 16.1, reasonably believes there is sufficient evidence to provide a realistic prospect of conviction for that offence. See *Note 11B*.

This paragraph does not prevent officers in revenue cases or acting under the confiscation provisions of the Criminal Justice Act 1988 or the Drug Trafficking Act 1994 from inviting suspects to complete a formal question and answer record after the interview is concluded.

(b) *Interview records*

C:11.7 (a) An accurate record must be made of each interview, whether or not the interview takes **A-74** place at a police station.

    (b) The record must state the place of interview, the time it begins and ends, any interview breaks and, subject to paragraph 2.6A, the names of all those present; and must be made on the forms provided for this purpose or in the interviewer's pocket book or in accordance with Codes of Practice E or F.

    (c) Any written record must be made and completed during the interview, unless this would not be practicable or would interfere with the conduct of the interview, and must constitute either a verbatim record of what has been said or, failing this, an account of the interview which adequately and accurately summarises it.

C:11.8 If a written record is not made during the interview it must be made as soon as practicable after its completion.

C:11.9 Written interview records must be timed and signed by the maker.

C:11.10 If a written record is not completed during the interview the reason must be recorded in the interview record.

C:11.11 Unless it is impracticable, the person interviewed shall be given the opportunity to read the interview record and to sign it as correct or to indicate how they consider it inaccurate. If the person interviewed cannot read or refuses to read the record or sign it, the senior interviewer present shall read it to them and ask whether they would like to sign it as correct or make their mark or to indicate how they consider it inaccurate. The interviewer shall certify on the interview record itself what has occurred. See *Note 11E.*

C:11.12 If the appropriate adult or the person's solicitor is present during the interview, they should also be given an opportunity to read and sign the interview record or any written statement taken down during the interview.

Note: paragraph 1.5A extends the requirement in this paragraph to interviews of 17-year-old suspects.

C:11.13 A written record shall be made of any comments made by a suspect, including unsolicited comments, which are outside the context of an interview but which might be relevant to the offence. Any such record must be timed and signed by the maker. When practicable the suspect shall be given the opportunity to read that record and to sign it as correct or to indicate how they consider it inaccurate. See *Note 11E.*

C:11.14 Any refusal by a person to sign an interview record when asked in accordance with this code must itself be recorded.

(c) *Juveniles and mentally disordered or otherwise mentally vulnerable people*

A-75

C:11.15 A juvenile or person who is mentally disordered or otherwise mentally vulnerable must not be interviewed regarding their involvement or suspected involvement in a criminal offence or offences, or asked to provide or sign a written statement under caution or record of interview, in the absence of the appropriate adult unless paragraphs 11.1, 11.18 to 11.20 apply. See *Note 11C.*

Note: paragraph 1.5A extends the requirement in this paragraph to 17-year-old suspects.

C:11.16 Juveniles may only be interviewed at their place of education in exceptional circumstances and only when the principal or their nominee agrees. Every effort should be made to notify the parent(s) or other person responsible for the juvenile's welfare and the appropriate adult, if this is a different person, that the police want to interview the juvenile and reasonable time should be allowed to enable the appropriate adult to be present at the interview. If awaiting the appropriate adult would cause unreasonable delay, and unless the juvenile is suspected of an offence against the educational establishment, the principal or their nominee can act as the appropriate adult for the purposes of the interview.

Note: paragraph 1.5A extends the requirement in this paragraph to 17-year-old suspects.

C:11.17 If an appropriate adult is present at an interview, they shall be informed:

- that they are not expected to act simply as an observer; and
- that the purpose of their presence is to:
  - advise the person being interviewed;
  - observe whether the interview is being conducted properly and fairly; and
  - facilitate communication with the person being interviewed.

(d) *Vulnerable suspects—urgent interviews at police stations*

C:11.18 The following interviews may take place only if an officer of superintendent rank or above considers delaying the interview will lead to the consequences in paragraph 11.1(a) to (c), and is satisfied the interview would not significantly harm the person's physical or mental state (see Annex G):

(a) an interview of a juvenile or person who is mentally disordered or otherwise mentally vulnerable without the appropriate adult being present (note: paragraph 1.5A extends this requirement to 17-year-old detainees);

(b) an interview of anyone other than in (a) who appears unable to:
  - appreciate the significance of questions and their answers; or
  - understand what is happening because of the effects of drink, drugs or any illness, ailment or condition;

(c) an interview, without an interpreter being present, of a person whom the custody officer has determined requires an interpreter (see paras 3.5(c)(ii) and 3.12) which is carried out by an interviewer speaking the suspect's own language or (as the case may be) otherwise establishing effective communication which is sufficient to enable the necessary questions to be asked and answered in order to avert the consequences. See paragraphs 13.2 and 13.5.

C:11.19 These interviews may not continue once sufficient information has been obtained to avert the consequences in paragraph 11.1(a) to (c).

C:11.20 A record shall be made of the grounds for any decision to interview a person under paragraph 11.18.

Notes for guidance

C:11ZA *The requirement in paragraph 11.1A for a suspect to be given sufficient information about the offence* **A-76**
*applies prior to the interview and whether or not they are legally represented. What is sufficient will depend on the
circumstances of the case, but it should normally include, as a minimum, a description of the facts relating to the
suspected offence that are known to the officer, including the time and place in question. This aims to avoid
suspects being confused or unclear about what they are supposed to have done and to help an innocent suspect to
clear the matter up more quickly.*

C:11A *Paragraph 11.4 does not prevent the interviewer from putting significant statements and silences to a
suspect again at a later stage or a further interview.*

C:11B *The Criminal Procedure and Investigations Act 1996 code of practice, paragraph 3.5 states "In
conducting an investigation, the investigator should pursue all reasonable lines of enquiry, whether these point
towards or away from the suspect. What is reasonable will depend on the particular circumstances." Interviewers
should keep this in mind when deciding what questions to ask in an interview.*

C:11C *Although juveniles or people who are mentally disordered or otherwise mentally vulnerable are often
capable of providing reliable evidence, they may, without knowing or wishing to do so, be particularly prone in
certain circumstances to provide information that may be unreliable, misleading or self-incriminating. Special care
should always be taken when questioning such a person, and the appropriate adult should be involved if there is
any doubt about a person's age, mental state or capacity. Because of the risk of unreliable evidence it is also
important to obtain corroboration of any facts admitted whenever possible. Paragraph 1.5A extends this note to
17-year-old suspects.*

C:11D *Juveniles should not be arrested at their place of education unless this is unavoidable. When a juvenile
is arrested at their place of education, the principal or their nominee must be informed. Paragraph 1.5A extends
this note to 17-year-old suspects.*

C:11E *Significant statements described in paragraph 11.4 will always be relevant to the offence and must be
recorded. When a suspect agrees to read records of interviews and other comments and sign them as correct, they
should be asked to endorse the record with, e.g. "I agree that this is a correct record of what was said" and add
their signature. If the suspect does not agree with the record, the interviewer should record the details of any
disagreement and ask the suspect to read these details and sign them to the effect that they accurately reflect their
disagreement. Any refusal to sign should be recorded.*

C:12 Interviews in police stations

(a) *Action*

C:12.1 If a police officer wants to interview or conduct enquiries which require the presence of a **A-77**
detainee, the custody officer is responsible for deciding whether to deliver the detainee into the officer's custody. An investigating officer who is given custody of a detainee takes over responsibility for
the detainee's care and safe custody for the purposes of this code until they return the detainee to
the custody officer when they must report the manner in which they complied with the code whilst
having custody of the detainee.

C:12.2 Except as below, in any period of 24 hours a detainee must be allowed a continuous period
of at least 8 hours for rest, free from questioning, travel or any interruption in connection with the
investigation concerned. This period should normally be at night or other appropriate time which
takes account of when the detainee last slept or rested. If a detainee is arrested at a police station
after going there voluntarily, the period of 24 hours runs from the time of their arrest and not the
time of arrival at the police station. The period may not be interrupted or delayed, except:
  (a) when there are reasonable grounds for believing not delaying or interrupting the period
       would:
       (i) involve a risk of harm to people or serious loss of, or damage to, property;
       (ii) delay unnecessarily the person's release from custody; or
       (iii) otherwise prejudice the outcome of the investigation;
  (b) at the request of the detainee, their appropriate adult or legal representative;
  (c) when a delay or interruption is necessary in order to:
       (i) comply with the legal obligations and duties arising under section 15; or
       (ii) to take action required under section 9 or in accordance with medical advice.
   If the period is interrupted in accordance with (a), a fresh period must be allowed. Interruptions
under (b) and (c) do not require a fresh period to be allowed.

C:12.3 Before a detainee is interviewed the custody officer, in consultation with the officer in
charge of the investigation and appropriate healthcare professionals as necessary, shall assess whether
the detainee is fit enough to be interviewed. This means determining and considering the risks to the
detainee's physical and mental state if the interview took place and determining what safeguards are
needed to allow the interview to take place. See Annex G. The custody officer shall not allow a

detainee to be interviewed if the custody officer considers it would cause significant harm to the detainee's physical or mental state. Vulnerable suspects listed at paragraph 11.18 shall be treated as always being at some risk during an interview and these persons may not be interviewed except in accordance with paragraphs 11.18 to 11.20.

C:12.4 As far as practicable interviews shall take place in interview rooms which are adequately heated, lit and ventilated.

C:12.5 A suspect whose detention without charge has been authorised under PACE because the detention is necessary for an interview to obtain evidence of the offence for which they have been arrested may choose not to answer questions but police do not require the suspect's consent or agreement to interview them for this purpose. If a suspect takes steps to prevent themselves being questioned or further questioned, *e.g.* by refusing to leave their cell to go to a suitable interview room or by trying to leave the interview room, they shall be advised their consent or agreement to interview is not required. The suspect shall be cautioned as in section 10, and informed if they fail or refuse to co-operate, the interview may take place in the cell and that their failure or refusal to co-operate may be given in evidence. The suspect shall then be invited to co-operate and go into the interview room.

C:12.6 People being questioned or making statements shall not be required to stand.

A-78   C:12.7 Before the interview commences each interviewer shall, subject to paragraph 2.6A, identify themselves and any other persons present to the interviewee.

C:12.8 Breaks from interviewing should be made at recognised meal times or at other times that take account of when an interviewee last had a meal. Short refreshment breaks shall be provided at approximately two hour intervals, subject to the interviewer's discretion to delay a break if there are reasonable grounds for believing it would:

    (i) involve a:
- risk of harm to people;
- serious loss of, or damage to, property;

    (ii) unnecessarily delay the detainee's release; or

    (iii) otherwise prejudice the outcome of the investigation.

See *Note 12B*.

C:12.9 If during the interview a complaint is made by or on behalf of the interviewee concerning the provisions of any of the codes, or it comes to the interviewer's notice that the interviewee may have been treated improperly, the interviewer should:

    (i) record the matter in the interview record; and

    (ii) inform the custody officer, who is then responsible for dealing with it as in section 9.

(b) *Documentation*

A-79   C:12.10 A record must be made of the:
- time a detainee is not in the custody of the custody officer, and why;
- reason for any refusal to deliver the detainee out of that custody.

C:12.11 A record shall be made of:

    (a) the reasons it was not practicable to use an interview room; and

    (b) any action taken as in paragraph 12.5.

The record shall be made on the custody record or in the interview record for action taken whilst an interview record is being kept, with a brief reference to this effect in the custody record.

C:12.12 Any decision to delay a break in an interview must be recorded, with reasons, in the interview record.

C:12.13 All written statements made at police stations under caution shall be written on forms provided for the purpose.

C:12.14 All written statements made under caution shall be taken in accordance with Annex D. Before a person makes a written statement under caution at a police station, they shall be reminded about the right to legal advice. See *Note 12A*.

Notes for guidance

A-80   C:12A *It is not normally necessary to ask for a written statement if the interview was recorded in writing and the record signed in accordance with paragraph 11.11 or audibly or visually recorded in accordance with Code E or F. Statements under caution should normally be taken in these circumstances only at the person's express wish. A person may however be asked if they want to make such a statement.*

C:12B *Meal breaks should normally last at least 45 minutes and shorter breaks after two hours should last at least 15 minutes. If the interviewer delays a break in accordance with paragraph 12.8 and prolongs the interview, a longer break should be provided. If there is a short interview and another short interview is contemplated, the length of the break may be reduced if there are reasonable grounds to believe this is necessary to avoid any of the consequences in paragraph 12.8(i) to (iii).*

C:13 Interpreters

(a) *General*

C:13.1 Chief officers are responsible for making arrangements to provide appropriately qualified **A-81** independent persons to act as interpreters and to provide translations of essential documents for:

- detained suspects who, in accordance with paragraph 3.5(c)(ii), the custody officer has determined require an interpreter, and
- suspects who are not under arrest but are cautioned as in section 10 who, in accordance with paragraph 3.21, the interviewer has determined require an interpreter. In these cases, the responsibilities of the custody officer are, if appropriate, assigned to the interviewer. An interviewer who has any doubts about whether an interpreter is required or about how the provisions of this section should be applied to a suspect who is not under arrest should seek advice from an officer of the rank of sergeant or above.

If the suspect has a hearing or speech impediment, references to "interpreter" and "interpretation" in this code include appropriate assistance necessary to establish effective communication with that person. See paragraph 13.1C below if the person is in Wales.

C:13.1A The arrangements must comply with the minimum requirements set out in Directive 2010/64/EU of the European Parliament and of the Council of 20 October 2010 on the right to interpretation and translation in criminal proceedings (see *Note 13A*). The provisions of this code implement the requirements for those to whom this code applies. These requirements include the following:

- that the arrangements made and the quality of interpretation and translation provided shall be sufficient to "*safeguard the fairness of the proceedings, in particular by ensuring that suspected or accused persons have knowledge of the cases against them and are able to exercise their right of defence*"; this term which is used by the directive means that the suspect must be able to understand their position and be able to communicate effectively with police officers, interviewers, solicitors and appropriate adults as provided for by this and any other code in the same way as a suspect who can speak and understand English and who does not have a hearing or speech impediment and who would therefore not require an interpreter;
- the provision of a written translation of all documents considered essential for the person to exercise their right of defence and to "*safeguard the fairness of the proceedings*" as described above; for the purposes of this code, this includes any decision to authorise a person to be detained and details of any offence(s) with which the person has been charged or for which they have been told they may be prosecuted, see Annex M;
- procedures to help determine:
  - whether a suspect can speak and understand English and needs the assistance of an interpreter, see paragraph 13.1 and *Notes 13B* and *13C*; and
  - whether another interpreter should be called or another translation should be provided when a suspect complains about the quality of either or both, see paragraphs 13.10A and 13.10C.

C:13.1B All reasonable attempts should be made to make the suspect understand that interpretation and translation will be provided at public expense.

C:13.1C With regard to persons in Wales, nothing in this or any other code affects the application of the Welsh language schemes produced by police and crime commissioners in Wales in accordance with the Welsh Language Act 1993: see paragraphs 3.12 and 13.1.

(b) *Interviewing suspects—foreign languages*

C:13.2 Unless paragraphs 11.1 or 11.18(c) apply, a suspect who for the purposes of this code requires an interpreter because they do not appear to speak or understand English (see paras 3.5(c)(ii) and 3.12) must not be interviewed in the absence of a person capable of interpreting.

C:13.2A An interpreter should also be called if a juvenile is interviewed and their parent or guardian, present as the appropriate adult, does not appear to speak or understand English, unless the interview is urgent and paragraphs 11.1 or 11.18(c) apply.

Note: paragraph 1.5A extends the requirement in this paragraph to interviews of 17-year-old suspects.

C:13.3 When a written record of the interview is made (see para. 11.7), the interviewer shall make sure the interpreter makes a note of the interview at the time in the person's language for use in the event of the interpreter being called to give evidence, and certifies its accuracy. The interviewer should allow sufficient time for the interpreter to note each question and answer after each is put, given and interpreted. The person should be allowed to read the record or have it read to them and sign it as correct or indicate the respects in which they consider it inaccurate. If an audio or visual record of the interview is made, the arrangements in Code E or F shall apply.

C:13.4 In the case of a person making a statement under caution to a police officer or other police staff other than in English:

(a) the interpreter shall record the statement in the language it is made;

(b) the person shall be invited to sign it;

(c) an official English translation shall be made in due course.

(c) *Interviewing suspects who have a hearing or speech impediment*

C:13.5 Unless paragraphs 11.1 or 11.18(c) (urgent interviews) apply, a suspect who for the purposes of this code requires an interpreter or other appropriate assistance to enable effective communication with them because they appear to have a hearing or speech impediment (see paras 3.5(c)(ii) and 3.12) must not be interviewed in the absence of an independent person capable of interpreting or without that assistance.

C:13.6 An interpreter should also be called if a juvenile is interviewed and their parent or guardian, present as the appropriate adult, appears to have a hearing or speech impediment, unless the interview is urgent and paragraphs 11.1 or 11.18(c) apply.

Note: paragraph 1.5A extends the requirement in this paragraph to interviews of 17-year-old suspects.

C:13.7 The interviewer shall make sure the interpreter is allowed to read the interview record and certify its accuracy in the event of the interpreter being called to give evidence. If the interview is audibly recorded or visually recorded, the arrangements in Code E or F apply.

(d) *Additional rules for detained persons*

C:13.8 [*Not used.*]

C:13.9 If paragraph 6.1 applies and the detainee cannot communicate with the solicitor because of language, hearing or speech difficulties, an interpreter must be called. A police officer or any other police staff may not be used for this purpose.

C:13.10 After the custody officer has determined that a detainee requires an interpreter (see para. 3.5(c)(ii)) and following the initial action in paragraphs 3.1 to 3.5, arrangements must also be made for an interpreter to:

- explain the grounds and reasons for any authorisation for their continued detention, before or after charge and any information about the authorisation given to them by the authorising officer and which is recorded in the custody record (see paras 15.3, 15.4 and 15.16(a) and (b));

- be present at the magistrates' court for the hearing of an application for a warrant of further detention or any extension or further extension of such warrant to explain any grounds and reasons for the application and any information about the authorisation of their further detention given to them by the court (see PACE, ss.43 and 44 and paras 15.2 and 15.16(c)), and

- explain any offence with which the detainee is charged or for which they are informed they may be prosecuted and any other information about the offence given to them by or on behalf of the custody officer (see paras 16.1 and 16.3).

C:13.10A If a detainee complains that they are not satisfied with the quality of interpretation, the custody officer or (as the case may be) the interviewer, is responsible for deciding whether a different interpreter should be called in accordance with the procedures set out in the arrangements made by the chief officer (see para. 13.1A).

(e) *Translations of essential documents*

C:13.10B Written translations, oral translations and oral summaries of essential documents in a language the detainee understands shall be provided in accordance with Annex M (translations of documents and records).

C:13.10C If a detainee complains that they are not satisfied with the quality of the translation, the custody officer or (as the case may be) the interviewer, is responsible for deciding whether a further translation should be provided in accordance with the procedures set out in the arrangements made by the chief officer (see para. 13.1A).

(f) *Decisions not to provide interpretation and translation.*

C:13.10D If a suspect challenges a decision:

- made by the custody officer or (as the case may be) by the interviewer, in accordance with this code (see paras 3.5(c)(ii) and 3.21) that they do not require an interpreter; or
- made in accordance with paragraphs 13.10A, 13.10B or 13.10C not to provide a different interpreter or another translation or not to translate a requested document,

the matter shall be reported to an inspector to deal with as a complaint for the purposes of paragraph 9.2 or paragraph 12.9 if the challenge is made during an interview.

(g) *Documentation*

C:13.11 The following must be recorded in the custody record or, as applicable, the interview record:

- (a) action taken to call an interpreter;
- (b) action taken when a detainee is not satisfied about the standard of interpretation or translation provided (see paras 13.10A and 13.10C);
- (c) when an urgent interview is carried out in accordance with paragraph 13.2 or 13.5 in the absence of an interpreter;
- (d) when a detainee has been assisted by an interpreter for the purpose of providing or being given information or being interviewed;
- (e) action taken in accordance with Annex M when:
  - a written translation of an essential document is provided;
  - an oral translation or oral summary of an essential document is provided instead of a written translation and the authorising officer's reason(s) why this would not prejudice the fairness of the proceedings (see Annex M, para. 3);
  - a suspect waives their right to a translation of an essential document (see Annex M, para. 4);
  - when representations that a document which is not included in the table is essential and that a translation should be provided are refused and the reason for the refusal (see Annex M, para. 8).

Notes for guidance

C:13A *Chief officers have discretion when determining the individuals or organisations they use to provide interpretation and translation services for their forces provided that these are compatible with the requirements of the directive. One example which chief officers may wish to consider is the Ministry of Justice framework agreement for interpretation and translation services.*

C:13B *A procedure for determining whether a person needs an interpreter might involve a telephone interpreter service or using cue cards or similar visual aids which enable the detainee to indicate their ability to speak and understand English and their preferred language. This could be confirmed through an interpreter who could also assess the extent to which the person can speak and understand English.*

C:13C *There should also be a procedure for determining whether a suspect who requires an interpreter requires assistance in accordance with paragraph 3.20 to help them check and, if applicable, sign any documentation.*

C:14 Questioning—special restrictions

C:14.1 If a person is arrested by one police force on behalf of another and the lawful period of **A-83** detention in respect of that offence has not yet commenced in accordance with PACE, s.41, no questions may be put to them about the offence while they are in transit between the forces except to clarify any voluntary statement they make.

C:14.2 If a person is in police detention at a hospital, they may not be questioned without the agreement of a responsible doctor. See *Note 14A.*

Note for guidance

C:14A *If questioning takes place at a hospital under paragraph 14.2, or on the way to or from a hospital, the* **A-84** *period of questioning concerned counts towards the total period of detention permitted.*

C:15 Reviews and extensions of detention

(a) *Persons detained under PACE*

A-85   C:15.0 The requirement in paragraph 3.4(b) that documents and materials essential to challenging the lawfulness of the detainee's arrest and detention must be made available to the detainee or their solicitor, applies for the purposes of this section as follows:

> (a) the officer reviewing the need for detention without charge (PACE, s.40), or (as the case may be) the officer considering the need to extend detention without charge from 24 to 36 hours (PACE, s.42), is responsible, in consultation with the investigating officer, for deciding which documents and materials are essential and must be made available;
>
> (b) when paragraph 15.7A applies (application for a warrant of further detention or extension of such a warrant), the officer making the application is responsible for deciding which documents and materials are essential and must be made available before the hearing. See *Note 3ZA*.

C:15.1 The review officer is responsible under PACE, s.40, for periodically determining if a person's detention, before or after charge, continues to be necessary. This requirement continues throughout the detention period and, except as in paragraph 15.10, the review officer must be present at the police station holding the detainee. See *Notes 15A and 15B*.

C:15.2 Under PACE, s.42, an officer of superintendent rank or above who is responsible for the station holding the detainee may give authority any time after the second review to extend the maximum period the person may be detained without charge by up to 12 hours. Further detention without charge may be authorised only by a magistrates' court in accordance with PACE, ss.43 and 44. See *Notes 15C, 15D and 15E*.

C:15.2A An authorisation under section 42(1) of PACE extends the maximum period of detention permitted before charge for indictable offences from 24 hours to 36 hours. Detaining a juvenile or mentally vulnerable person for longer than 24 hours will be dependent on the circumstances of the case and with regard to the person's:

> (a) special vulnerability;
>
> (b) the legal obligation to provide an opportunity for representations to be made prior to a decision about extending detention;
>
> (c) the need to consult and consider the views of any appropriate adult; and
>
> (d) any alternatives to police custody.

Note: paragraph 1.5A extends sub-paragraph (c) to 17-year-old detainees.

C:15.3 Before deciding whether to authorise continued detention the officer responsible under paragraph 15.1 or 15.2 shall give an opportunity to make representations about the detention to:

> (a) the detainee, unless in the case of a review as in paragraph 15.1, the detainee is asleep;
>
> (b) the detainee's solicitor if available at the time; and
>
> (c) the appropriate adult if available at the time.

Note: paragraph 1.5A extends the requirement in sub-paragraph (c) to 17-year-old detainees. See *Note 15CA*.

C:15.3A Other people having an interest in the detainee's welfare may also make representations at the authorising officer's discretion.

C:15.3B Subject to paragraph 15.10, the representations may be made orally in person or by telephone or in writing. The authorising officer may, however, refuse to hear oral representations from the detainee if the officer considers them unfit to make representations because of their condition or behaviour. See *Note 15C*.

C:15.3C The decision on whether the review takes place in person or by telephone or by video conferencing (see *Note 15G*) is a matter for the review officer. In determining the form the review may take, the review officer must always take full account of the needs of the person in custody. The benefits of carrying out a review in person should always be considered, based on the individual circumstances of each case with specific additional consideration if the person is:

> (a) a juvenile (and the age of the juvenile); or (note: para. 1.5A extends this sub-paragraph to 17-year-old detainees)
>
> (b) suspected of being mentally vulnerable; or
>
> (c) in need of medical attention for other than routine minor ailments; or
>
> (d) subject to presentational or community issues around their detention.

A-86   C:15.4 Before conducting a review or determining whether to extend the maximum period of detention without charge, the officer responsible must make sure the detainee is reminded of their entitlement to free legal advice, see paragraph 6.5, unless in the case of a review the person is asleep.

C:15.5 If, after considering any representations, the review officer under paragraph 15.1 decides to keep the detainee in detention or the superintendent under paragraph 15.2 extends the maximum period for which they may be detained without charge, then any comment made by the detainee shall be recorded. If applicable, the officer shall be informed of the comment as soon as practicable. See also paragraphs 11.4 and 11.13.

C:15.6 No officer shall put specific questions to the detainee:

- regarding their involvement in any offence; or
- in respect of any comments they may make:
  - when given the opportunity to make representations; or
  - in response to a decision to keep them in detention or extend the maximum period of detention.

Such an exchange could constitute an interview as in paragraph 11.1A and would be subject to the associated safeguards in section 11 and, in respect of a person who has been charged, paragraph 16.5. See also paragraph 11.13.

C:15.7 A detainee who is asleep at a review, see paragraph 15.1, and whose continued detention is authorised must be informed about the decision and reason as soon as practicable after waking.

C:15.7A When an application is made to a magistrates' court under PACE, s.43, for a warrant of further detention to extend detention without charge of a person arrested for an indictable offence, or under section 44, to extend or further extend that warrant, the detainee:

(a) must be brought to court for the hearing of the application;

(b) is entitled to be legally represented if they wish, in which case, Annex B cannot apply;

(c) must be given a copy of the information which supports the application and states:

  (i) the nature of the offence for which the person to whom the application relates has been arrested;

  (ii) the general nature of the evidence on which the person was arrested;

  (iii) what inquiries about the offence have been made and what further inquiries are proposed;

  (iv) the reasons for believing continued detention is necessary for the purposes of the further inquiries.

Note: a warrant of further detention can only be issued or extended if the court has reasonable grounds for believing that the person's further detention is necessary for the purpose of obtaining evidence of an indictable offence for which the person has been arrested and that the investigation is being conducted diligently and expeditiously.

See paragraph 15.0(b).

C:15.8 [*Not used.*]

(b) *Review of detention by telephone and video conferencing facilities*

C:15.9 PACE, s.40A, provides that the officer responsible under section 40 for reviewing the deten- **A-87** tion of a person who has not been charged, need not attend the police station holding the detainee and may carry out the review by telephone.

C:15.9A PACE, s.45A(2), provides that the officer responsible under section 40 for reviewing the detention of a person who has not been charged, need not attend the police station holding the detainee and may carry out the review by video conferencing facilities. (See *Note 15G.*)

C:15.9B A telephone review is not permitted where facilities for review by video conferencing exist and it is practicable to use them.

C:15.9C The review officer can decide at any stage that a telephone review or review by video conferencing should be terminated and that the review will be conducted in person. The reasons for doing so should be noted in the custody record. See *Note 15F.*

C:15.10 When a review is carried out by telephone or by video conferencing facilities, an officer at the station holding the detainee shall be required by the review officer to fulfil that officer's obligations under PACE, s.40, and this code by:

(a) making any record connected with the review in the detainee's custody record;

(b) if applicable, making the record in (a) in the presence of the detainee; and

(c) for a review by telephone, giving the detainee information about the review.

C:15.11 When a review is carried out by telephone or by video conferencing facilities, the requirement in paragraph 15.3 will be satisfied:

(a) if facilities exist for the immediate transmission of written representations to the review officer, *e.g.* fax or email message, by allowing those who are given the opportunity to make representations, to make their representations:

  (i) orally by telephone or (as the case may be) by means of the video conferencing facilities; or

(ii) in writing using the facilities for the immediate transmission of written representations; and

(b) in all other cases, by allowing those who are given the opportunity to make representations, to make their representations orally by telephone or by means of the video conferencing facilities.

(c) *Documentation*

C:15.12 It is the officer's responsibility to make sure all reminders given under paragraph 15.4 are noted in the custody record.

C:15.13 The grounds for, and extent of, any delay in conducting a review shall be recorded.

C:15.14 When a review is carried out by telephone or video conferencing facilities, a record shall be made of:

(a) the reason the review officer did not attend the station holding the detainee;

(b) the place the review officer was;

(c) the method representations, oral or written, were made to the review officer, see paragraph 15.11.

C:15.15 Any written representations shall be retained.

C:15.16 A record shall be made as soon as practicable of:

(a) the outcome of each review of detention before or after charge, and if paragraph 15.7 applies, of when the person was informed and by whom;

(b) the outcome of any determination under PACE, s.42, by a superintendent whether to extend the maximum period of detention without charge beyond 24 hours from the relevant time; if an authorisation is given, the record shall state the number of hours and minutes by which the detention period is extended or further extended;

(c) the outcome of each application under PACE, s.43, for a warrant of further detention or under section 44, for an extension or further extension of that warrant; if a warrant for further detention is granted under section 43 or extended or further extended under 44, the record shall state the detention period authorised by the warrant and the date and time it was granted or (as the case may be) the period by which the warrant is extended or further extended.

Note: any period during which a person is released on bail does not count towards the maximum period of detention without charge allowed under PACE, ss.41 to 44.

Notes for guidance

A-88

C:15A *Review officer for the purposes of:*

• *PACE, ss.40, 40A and 45A means, in the case of a person arrested but not charged, an officer of at least inspector rank not directly involved in the investigation and, if a person has been arrested and charged, the custody officer.*

C:15B *The detention of persons in police custody not subject to the statutory review requirement in paragraph 15.1 should still be reviewed periodically as a matter of good practice. Such reviews can be carried out by an officer of the rank of sergeant or above. The purpose of such reviews is to check the particular power under which a detainee is held continues to apply, any associated conditions are complied with and to make sure appropriate action is taken to deal with any changes. This includes the detainee's prompt release when the power no longer applies, or their transfer if the power requires the detainee be taken elsewhere as soon as the necessary arrangements are made. Examples include persons:*

(a) *arrested on warrant because they failed to answer bail to appear at court;*

(b) *arrested under the Bail Act 1976, s.7(3), for breaching a condition of bail granted after charge;*

(c) *in police custody for specific purposes and periods under the Crime (Sentences) Act 1997, Sched. 1;*

(d) *convicted, or remand prisoners, held in police stations on behalf of the Prison Service under the Imprisonment (Temporary Provisions) Act 1980, s.6;*

(e) *being detained to prevent them causing a breach of the peace;*

(f) *detained at police stations on behalf of Immigration Enforcement (formerly the UK Immigration Service);*

(g) *detained by order of a magistrates' court under the Criminal Justice Act 1988, s.152 (as amended by the Drugs Act 2005, s.8) to facilitate the recovery of evidence after being charged with drug possession or drug trafficking and suspected of having swallowed drugs.*

The detention of persons remanded into police detention by order of a court under the Magistrates' Courts Act 1980, s.128, is subject to a statutory requirement to review that detention. This is to make sure the detainee is taken back to court no later than the end of the period authorised by the court or when the need for their detention by police ceases, whichever is the sooner.

C:15C *In the case of a review of detention, but not an extension, the detainee need not be woken for the review. However, if the detainee is likely to be asleep, e.g. during a period of rest allowed as in paragraph 12.2, at the latest time a review or authorisation to extend detention may take place, the officer should, if the legal obligations and time constraints permit, bring forward the procedure to allow the detainee to make representations. A detainee not asleep during the review must be present when the grounds for their continued detention are recorded and must at the same time be informed of those grounds unless the review officer considers the person is incapable of understanding what is said, violent or likely to become violent or in urgent need of medical attention.*

C:15CA *In paragraph 15.3(b) and (c), "available" includes being contactable in time to enable them to make representations remotely by telephone or other electronic means or in person by attending the station. Reasonable efforts should therefore be made to give the solicitor and appropriate adult sufficient notice of the time the decision is expected to be made so that they can make themselves available.*

C:15D *An application to a magistrates' court under PACE, s.43 or 44, for a warrant of further detention or its extension should be made between 10am and 9pm, and if possible during normal court hours. It will not usually be practicable to arrange for a court to sit specially outside the hours of 10am to 9pm. If it appears a special sitting may be needed outside normal court hours but between 10am and 9pm, the clerk to the justices should be given notice and informed of this possibility, while the court is sitting if possible.*

C:15E *In paragraph 15.2, the officer responsible for the station holding the detainee includes a superintendent or above who, in accordance with their force operational policy or police regulations, is given that responsibility on a temporary basis whilst the appointed long-term holder is off duty or otherwise unavailable.*

C:15F *The provisions of PACE, s.40A, allowing telephone reviews do not apply to reviews of detention after charge by the custody officer. When video conferencing is not required, they allow the use of a telephone to carry out a review of detention before charge. The procedure under PACE, s.42, must be done in person.*

C:15G *Video conferencing facilities means any facilities (whether a live television link or other facilities) by means of which the review can be carried out with the review officer, the detainee concerned and the detainee's solicitor all being able to both see and to hear each other. The use of video conferencing facilities for decisions about detention under section 45A of PACE is subject to regulations made by the Secretary of State being in force.*

C:16 Charging detained persons

(a) *Action*

C:16.1 When the officer in charge of the investigation reasonably believes there is sufficient **A-89** evidence to provide a realistic prospect of conviction for the offence (see paragraph 11.6), they shall without delay, and subject to the following qualification, inform the custody officer who will be responsible for considering whether the detainee should be charged. See *Notes 11B* and *16A*. When a person is detained in respect of more than one offence it is permissible to delay informing the custody officer until the above conditions are satisfied in respect of all the offences, but see paragraph 11.6. If the detainee is a juvenile, mentally disordered or otherwise mentally vulnerable, any resulting action shall be taken in the presence of the appropriate adult if they are present at the time.

Note: paragraph 1.5A requires someone to fulfil the role of the appropriate adult to be present when the action applies to a 17-year-old detainee.

See *Notes 16B* and *16C*.

C:16.1A Where guidance issued by the Director of Public Prosecutions under PACE, s.37A, is in force the custody officer must comply with that guidance in deciding how to act in dealing with the detainee. See *Notes 16AA* and *16AB*.

C:16.1B Where in compliance with the DPP's guidance the custody officer decides that the case should be immediately referred to the CPS to make the charging decision, consultation should take place with a crown prosecutor as soon as is reasonably practicable. Where the crown prosecutor is unable to make the charging decision on the information available at that time, the detainee may be released without charge and on bail (with conditions if necessary) under section 37(7)(a). In such circumstances, the detainee should be informed that they are being released to enable the Director of Public Prosecutions to make a decision under section 37B.

C:16.2 When a detainee is charged with or informed they may be prosecuted for an offence, see *Note 16B*, they shall, unless the restriction on drawing adverse inferences from silence applies, see Annex C, be cautioned as follows:

"You do not have to say anything. But it may harm your defence if you do not mention now something which you later rely on in court. Anything you do say may be given in evidence.".

Where the use of the Welsh language is appropriate, a constable may provide the caution directly in Welsh in the following terms:

"Does dim rhaid i chi ddweud dim byd. Ond gall niweidio eich amddiffyniad os na fyddwch chi'n sôn, yn awr, am rywbeth y byddwch chi'n dibynnu arno nes ymlaen yn y llys. Gall unrhyw beth yr ydych yn ei ddweud gael ei

roi fel tystiolaeth.".

Annex C, paragraph 2, sets out the alternative terms of the caution to be used when the restriction on drawing adverse inferences from silence applies.

C:16.3 When a detainee is charged they shall be given a written notice showing particulars of the offence and, subject to paragraph 2.6A, the officer's name and the case reference number. As far as possible the particulars of the charge shall be stated in simple terms, but they shall also show the precise offence in law with which the detainee is charged. The notice shall begin:

"You are charged with the offence(s) shown below." Followed by the caution.

If the detainee is a juvenile, mentally disordered or otherwise mentally vulnerable, a copy of the notice should also be given to the appropriate adult.

Note: paragraph 1.5A provides that a copy of the notice should be given to the person called to fulfil the role of the appropriate adult when a 17-year-old detainee is charged.

C:16.4 If, after a detainee has been charged with or informed they may be prosecuted for an offence, an officer wants to tell them about any written statement or interview with another person relating to such an offence, the detainee shall either be handed a true copy of the written statement or the content of the interview record brought to their attention. Nothing shall be done to invite any reply or comment except to:

    (a) caution the detainee, *"You do not have to say anything, but anything you do say may be given in evidence.";*

        where the use of the Welsh Language is appropriate, caution the detainee in the following terms:

        "Does dim rhaid i chi ddweud dim byd, ond gall unrhyw beth yr ydych yn ei ddweud gael ei roi fel tystiolaeth."; and

    (b) remind the detainee about their right to legal advice.

C:16.4A If the detainee:

    • cannot read, the document may be read to them;

    • is a juvenile, mentally disordered or otherwise mentally vulnerable, the appropriate adult shall also be given a copy, or the interview record shall be brought to their attention.

Note: paragraph 1.5A requires a copy of the record to be given to, or brought to the attention of, the person called to fulfil the role of the appropriate adult for a 17-year-old detainee.

C:16.5 A detainee may not be interviewed about an offence after they have been charged with, or informed they may be prosecuted for it, unless the interview is necessary:

    • to prevent or minimise harm or loss to some other person, or the public;

    • to clear up an ambiguity in a previous answer or statement;

    • in the interests of justice for the detainee to have put to them, and have an opportunity to comment on, information concerning the offence which has come to light since they were charged or informed they might be prosecuted.

Before any such interview, the interviewer shall:

    (a) caution the detainee, *"You do not have to say anything, but anything you do say may be given in evidence.";*

        where the use of the Welsh language is appropriate, the interviewer shall caution the detainee: *"Does dim rhaid i chi ddweud dim byd, ond gall unrhyw beth yr ydych yn ei ddweud gael ei roi fel tystiolaeth.";*

    (b) remind the detainee about their right to legal advice.

See *Note 16B*.

C:16.6 The provisions of paragraphs 16.2 to 16.5 must be complied with in the appropriate adult's presence if they are already at the police station. If they are not at the police station then these provisions must be complied with again in their presence when they arrive unless the detainee has been released. See *Note 16C*.

Note: Paragraph 1.5A extends the requirement in this paragraph to 17-year-old detainees.

C:16.7 When a juvenile is charged with an offence and the custody officer authorises their continued detention after charge, the custody officer must make arrangements for the juvenile to be taken into the care of a local authority to be detained pending appearance in court unless the custody officer certifies in accordance with PACE, s.38(6), that:

    (a) for any juvenile, it is impracticable to do so; or

    (b) in the case of a juvenile of at least 12 years old, no secure accommodation is available and other accommodation would not be adequate to protect the public from serious harm from that juvenile. See *Note 16D*.

Note: the 16-year-old maximum age limit for transfer to local authority accommodation, the power of the local authority to detain the person transferred and take over responsibility for that person from the police are determined by section 38 of PACE. For this reason, this paragraph and *Note 16D* do <u>not</u> apply to detainees who appear to have attained the age of 17 (see para. 1.5A(a)).

C:16.7A The requirement in paragraph 3.4(b) that documents and materials essential to effectively challenging the lawfulness of the detainee's arrest and detention must be made available to the detainee and, if they are represented, their solicitor, applies for the purposes of this section and a person's detention after charge. This means that the custody officer making the bail decision (PACE, s.38) or reviewing the need for detention after charge (PACE, s.40), is responsible for determining what, if any, documents or materials are essential and must be made available to the detainee or their solicitor. See *Note 3ZA.*

(b) *Documentation*

C:16.8 A record shall be made of anything a detainee says when charged.

C:16.9 Any questions put in an interview after charge and answers given relating to the offence shall be recorded in full during the interview on forms for that purpose and the record signed by the detainee or, if they refuse, by the interviewer and any third parties present. If the questions are audibly recorded or visually recorded the arrangements in Code E or F apply.

C:16.10 If arrangements for a juvenile's transfer into local authority care as in paragraph 16.7 are not made, the custody officer must record the reasons in a certificate which must be produced before the court with the juvenile. See *Note 16D.*

Notes for guidance

C:16A *The custody officer must take into account alternatives to prosecution under the Crime and Disorder Act* **A-91** *1998 applicable to persons under 18, and in national guidance on the cautioning of offenders applicable to persons aged 18 and over.*

C:16AA *When a person is arrested under the provisions of the Criminal Justice Act 2003 which allow a person to be re-tried after being acquitted of a serious offence which is a qualifying offence specified in Schedule 5 to that Act and not precluded from further prosecution by virtue of section 75(3) of that Act the detention provisions of PACE are modified and make an officer of the rank of superintendent or above who has not been directly involved in the investigation responsible for determining whether the evidence is sufficient to charge.*

C:16AB *Where guidance issued by the Director of Public Prosecutions under section 37B is in force, a custody officer who determines in accordance with that guidance that there is sufficient evidence to charge the detainee, may detain that person for no longer than is reasonably necessary to decide how that person is to be dealt with under PACE, s.37(7)(a) to (d), including, where appropriate, consultation with the duty prosecutor. The period is subject to the maximum period of detention before charge determined by PACE, ss.41 to 44. Where in accordance with the guidance the case is referred to the CPS for decision, the custody officer should ensure that an officer involved in the investigation sends to the CPS such information as is specified in the guidance.*

C:16B *The giving of a warning or the service of the notice of intended prosecution required by the Road Traffic Offenders Act 1988, s.1 does not amount to informing a detainee they may be prosecuted for an offence and so does not preclude further questioning in relation to that offence.*

C:16C *There is no power under PACE to detain a person and delay action under paragraphs 16.2 to 16.5 solely to await the arrival of the appropriate adult. Reasonable efforts should therefore be made to give the appropriate adult sufficient notice of the time the decision (charge etc.) is to be implemented so that they can be present. If the appropriate adult is not, or cannot be, present at that time, the detainee should be released on bail to return for the decision to be implemented when the adult is present, unless the custody officer determines that the absence of the appropriate adult makes the detainee unsuitable for bail for this purpose. After charge, bail cannot be refused, or release on bail delayed, simply because an appropriate adult is not available, unless the absence of that adult provides the custody officer with the necessary grounds to authorise detention after charge under PACE, s.38.*

C:16D *Except as in paragraph 16.7, neither a juvenile's behaviour nor the nature of the offence provides grounds for the custody officer to decide it is impracticable to arrange the juvenile's transfer to local authority care. Impracticability concerns the transport and travel requirements and the lack of secure accommodation which is provided for the purposes of restricting liberty does not make it impracticable to transfer the juvenile. The availability of secure accommodation is only a factor in relation to a juvenile aged 12 or over when other local authority accommodation would not be adequate to protect the public from serious harm from them. The obligation to transfer a juvenile to local authority accommodation applies as much to a juvenile charged during the daytime as to a juvenile to be held overnight, subject to a requirement to bring the juvenile before a court under PACE, s.46.*

This note does not apply to 17-year-old detainees (see para. 16.7).

C:17 Testing persons for the presence of specified Class A drugs

(a) *Action*

C:17.1 This section of Code C applies only in selected police stations in police areas where the provisions for drug testing under section 63B of PACE (as amended by section 5 of the Criminal Justice Act 2003 and section 7 of the Drugs Act 2005) are in force and in respect of which the Secretary of State has given a notification to the relevant chief officer of police that arrangements for the taking of samples have been made. Such a notification will cover either a police area as a whole or particular stations within a police area. The notification indicates whether the testing applies to those arrested or charged or under the age of 18 as the case may be and testing can only take place in respect of the persons so indicated in the notification. Testing cannot be carried out unless the relevant notification has been given and has not been withdrawn. See *Note 17F.*

C:17.2 A sample of urine or a non-intimate sample may be taken from a person in police detention for the purpose of ascertaining whether they have any specified Class A drug in their body only where they have been brought before the custody officer and:

(a) either the arrest condition, see paragraph 17.3, or the charge condition, see paragraph 17.4, is met;

(b) the age condition, see paragraph 17.5, is met;

(c) the notification condition is met in relation to the arrest condition, the charge condition, or the age condition, as the case may be (testing on charge and/or arrest must be specifically provided for in the notification for the power to apply; in addition, the fact that testing of under 18s is authorised must be expressly provided for in the notification before the power to test such persons applies); see paragraph 17.1; and

(d) a police officer has requested the person concerned to give the sample (the request condition).

C:17.3 The arrest condition is met where the detainee:

(a) has been arrested for a trigger offence, see *Note 17E*, but not charged with that offence; or

(b) has been arrested for any other offence but not charged with that offence and a police officer of inspector rank or above, who has reasonable grounds for suspecting that their misuse of any specified Class A drug caused or contributed to the offence, has authorised the sample to be taken.

C:17.4 The charge condition is met where the detainee:

(a) has been charged with a trigger offence; or

(b) has been charged with any other offence and a police officer of inspector rank or above, who has reasonable grounds for suspecting that the detainee's misuse of any specified Class A drug caused or contributed to the offence, has authorised the sample to be taken.

C:17.5 The age condition is met where:

(a) in the case of a detainee who has been arrested but not charged as in paragraph 17.3, they are aged 18 or over;

(b) in the case of a detainee who has been charged as in paragraph 17.4, they are aged 14 or over.

C:17.6 Before requesting a sample from the person concerned, an officer must:

(a) inform them that the purpose of taking the sample is for drug testing under PACE; this is to ascertain whether they have a specified Class A drug present in their body;

(b) warn them that if, when so requested, they fail without good cause to provide a sample they may be liable to prosecution;

(c) where the taking of the sample has been authorised by an inspector or above in accordance with paragraph 17.3(b) or 17.4(b) above, inform them that the authorisation has been given and the grounds for giving it;

(d) remind them of the following rights, which may be exercised at any stage during the period in custody:

(i) the right to have someone informed of their arrest [see section 5];

(ii) the right to consult privately with a solicitor and that free independent legal advice is available [see section 6]; and

(iii) the right to consult these codes of practice [see section 3].

C:17.7 In the case of a person who has not attained the age of 17—

(a) the making of the request for a sample under paragraph 17.2(d) above;

(b) the giving of the warning and the information under paragraph 17.6 above; and

(c) the taking of the sample,

may not take place except in the presence of an appropriate adult. See *Note 17G.*

Note: paragraph 1.5A requires someone to fulfil the role of the appropriate adult to be present if the person to be tested appears to be under the age of 18.

C:17.8 Authorisation by an officer of the rank of inspector or above within paragraph 17.3(b) or 17.4(b) may be given orally or in writing but, if it is given orally, it must be confirmed in writing as soon as practicable.

C:17.9 If a sample is taken from a detainee who has been arrested for an offence but not charged with that offence as in paragraph 17.3, no further sample may be taken during the same continuous period of detention. If during that same period the charge condition is also met in respect of that detainee, the sample which has been taken shall be treated as being taken by virtue of the charge condition, see paragraph 17.4, being met.

C:17.10 A detainee from whom a sample may be taken may be detained for up to six hours from the time of charge if the custody officer reasonably believes the detention is necessary to enable a sample to be taken. Where the arrest condition is met, a detainee whom the custody officer has decided to release on bail without charge may continue to be detained, but not beyond 24 hours from the relevant time (as defined in section 41(2) of PACE), to enable a sample to be taken.

C:17.11 A detainee in respect of whom the arrest condition is met, but not the charge condition, see paragraphs 17.3 and 17.4, and whose release would be required before a sample can be taken had they not continued to be detained as a result of being arrested for a further offence which does not satisfy the arrest condition, may have a sample taken at any time within 24 hours after the arrest for the offence that satisfies the arrest condition.

(b) *Documentation*

C:17.12 The following must be recorded in the custody record:
- (a) if a sample is taken following authorisation by an officer of the rank of inspector or above, the authorisation and the grounds for suspicion;
- (b) the giving of a warning of the consequences of failure to provide a sample;
- (c) the time at which the sample was given; and
- (d) the time of charge or, where the arrest condition is being relied upon, the time of arrest and, where applicable, the fact that a sample taken after arrest but before charge is to be treated as being taken by virtue of the charge condition, where that is met in the same period of continuous detention. See paragraph 17.9.

(c) *General*

C:17.13 A sample may only be taken by a prescribed person. See *Note 17C*.

C:17.14 Force may not be used to take any sample for the purpose of drug testing.

C:17.15 The terms "Class A drug" and "misuse" have the same meanings as in the Misuse of Drugs Act 1971. "Specified" (in relation to a Class A drug) and "trigger offence" have the same meanings as in Part III of the Criminal Justice and Court Services Act 2000.

C:17.16 Any sample taken:
- (a) may not be used for any purpose other than to ascertain whether the person concerned has a specified Class A drug present in his body; and
- (b) can be disposed of as clinical waste unless it is to be sent for further analysis in cases where the test result is disputed at the point when the result is known, including on the basis that medication has been taken, or for quality assurance purposes.

(d) *Assessment of misuse of drugs*

C:17.17 Under the provisions of Part 3 of the Drugs Act 2005, where a detainee has tested positive for a specified Class A drug under section 63B of PACE a police officer may, at any time before the person's release from the police station, impose a requirement on the detainee to attend an initial assessment of their drug misuse by a suitably qualified person and to remain for its duration. Where such a requirement is imposed, the officer must, at the same time, impose a second requirement on the detainee to attend and remain for a follow-up assessment. The officer must inform the detainee that the second requirement will cease to have effect if, at the initial assessment they are informed that a follow-up assessment is not necessary. These requirements may only be imposed on a person if:
- (a) they have reached the age of 18;
- (b) notification has been given by the Secretary of State to the relevant chief officer of police that arrangements for conducting initial and follow-up assessments have been made for those from whom samples for testing have been taken at the police station where the detainee is in custody.

C:17.18 When imposing a requirement to attend an initial assessment and a follow-up assessment the police officer must:

(a) inform the person of the time and place at which the initial assessment is to take place;

(b) explain that this information will be confirmed in writing; and

(c) warn the person that they may be liable to prosecution if they fail without good cause to attend the initial assessment and remain for its duration and if they fail to attend the follow-up assessment and remain for its duration (if so required).

C:17.19 Where a police officer has imposed a requirement to attend an initial assessment and a follow-up assessment in accordance with paragraph 17.17, he must, before the person is released from detention, give the person notice in writing which:

(a) confirms their requirement to attend and remain for the duration of the assessments; and

(b) the information and repeats the warning referred to in paragraph 17.18.

C:17.20 The following must be recorded in the custody record:

(a) that the requirement to attend an initial assessment and a follow-up assessment has been imposed; and

(b) the information, explanation, warning and notice given in accordance with paragraphs 17.17 and 17.19.

C:17.21 Where a notice is given in accordance with paragraph 17.19, a police officer can give the person a further notice in writing which informs the person of any change to the time or place at which the initial assessment is to take place and which repeats the warning referred to in paragraph 17.18(c).

C:17.22 Part 3 of the Drugs Act 2005 also requires police officers to have regard to any guidance issued by the Secretary of State in respect of the assessment provisions.

Notes for guidance

C:17A *When warning a person who is asked to provide a urine or non-intimate sample in accordance with paragraph 17.6(b), the following form of words may be used:*

"You do not have to provide a sample, but I must warn you that if you fail or refuse without good cause to do so, you will commit an offence for which you may be imprisoned, or fined, or both".

Where the Welsh language is appropriate, the following form of words may be used:

"*Does dim rhaid i chi roi sampl, ond mae'n rhaid i mi eich rhybuddio y byddwch chin cyflawni trosedd os byddwch chi'n methu neu yn gwrthod gwneud hynny heb reswm da, ac y gellir, oherwydd hynny, eich carcharu, eich dirwyo, neu'r ddau.*"

C:17B *A sample has to be sufficient and suitable. A sufficient sample is sufficient in quantity and quality to enable drug-testing analysis to take place. A suitable sample is one which by its nature, is suitable for a particular form of drug analysis.*

C:17C *A prescribed person in paragraph 17.13 is one who is prescribed in regulations made by the Secretary of State under section 63B(6) of the Police and Criminal Evidence Act 1984. [The regulations are currently contained in regulation S.I. 2001 No. 2645, the Police and Criminal Evidence Act 1984 (Drug Testing Persons in Police Detention) (Prescribed Persons) Regulations 2001.]*

C:17D *Samples, and the information derived from them, may not be subsequently used in the investigation of any offence or in evidence against the persons from whom they were taken.*

C:17E *Trigger offences are:*

1. *Offences under the following provisions of the Theft Act 1968:*

section 1	*(theft)*
section 8	*(robbery)*
section 9	*(burglary)*
section 10	*(aggravated burglary)*
section 12	*(taking a motor vehicle or other conveyance without authority)*
section 12A	*(aggravated vehicle-taking)*
section 22	*(handling stolen goods)*
section 25	*(going equipped for stealing, etc.).*

2. *Offences under the following provisions of the Misuse of Drugs Act 1971, if committed in respect of a specified Class A drug:*

section 4	*(restriction on production and supply of controlled drugs)*

section 5(2)   *(possession of a controlled drug)*

section 5(3)   *(possession of a controlled drug with intent to supply).*

3. *Offences under the following provisions of the Fraud Act 2006:*

section 1   *(fraud)*

section 6   *(possession etc. of articles for use in frauds)*

section 7   *(making or supplying articles for use in frauds).*

3A. *An offence under section 1(1) of the Criminal Attempts Act 1981 if committed in respect of an offence under:*

(a) any of the following provisions of the Theft Act 1968:

section 1   *(theft)*

section 8   *(robbery)*

section 9   *(burglary)*

section 22   *(handling stolen goods)*

(b) section 1 of the Fraud Act 2006 (fraud).

4. *Offences under the following provisions of the Vagrancy Act 1824:*

section 3   *(begging)*

section 4   *(persistent begging).*

C:17F *The power to take samples is subject to notification by the Secretary of State that appropriate arrangements for the taking of samples have been made for the police area as a whole or for the particular police station concerned for whichever of the following is specified in the notification:*

(a) *persons in respect of whom the arrest condition is met;*

(b) *persons in respect of whom the charge condition is met;*

(c) *persons who have not attained the age of 18.*

Note: notification is treated as having been given for the purposes of the charge condition in relation to a police area, if testing (on charge) under section 63B(2) of PACE was in force immediately before section 7 of the Drugs Act 2005 was brought into force; and for the purposes of the age condition, in relation to a police area or police station, if immediately before that day, notification that arrangements had been made for the taking of samples from persons under the age of 18 (those aged 14-17) had been given and had not been withdrawn.

C:17G *Appropriate adult in paragraph 17.7 means the person's—*

(a) *parent or guardian or, if they are in the care of a local authority or voluntary organisation, a person representing that authority or organisation; or*

(b) *a social worker of a local authority; or*

(c) *if no person falling within (a) or (b) above is available, any responsible person aged 18 or over who is not a police officer or a person employed by the police.*

Note: paragraph 1.5A extends this note to the person called to fulfil the role of the appropriate adult for a 17-year-old detainee for the purposes of paragraph 17.7.

ANNEX A

Intimate and strip searches

A Intimate search

C:1. An intimate search consists of the physical examination of a person's body orifices other than **A-92** the mouth. The intrusive nature of such searches means the actual and potential risks associated with intimate searches must never be underestimated.

(a) Action

C:2. Body orifices other than the mouth may be searched only: **A-93**

(a) if authorised by an officer of inspector rank or above who has reasonable grounds for believing that the person may have concealed on themselves:

(i) anything which they could and might use to cause physical injury to themselves or others at the station; or

(ii) a Class A drug which they intended to supply to another or to export;

and the officer has reasonable grounds for believing that an intimate search is the only means of removing those items; and

(b) if the search is under paragraph 2(a)(ii) (a drug offence search), the detainee's appropriate consent has been given in writing.

C:2A. Before the search begins, a police officer or designated detention officer, must tell the detainee:

    (a) that the authority to carry out the search has been given;

    (b) the grounds for giving the authorisation and for believing that the article cannot be removed without an intimate search.

        Note: paragraph 1.5A of this code requires someone to fulfil the role of the appropriate adult to be present when a 17-year-old is told about the authority and grounds for an intimate search.

C:2B. Before a detainee is asked to give appropriate consent to a search under paragraph 2(a)(ii) (a drug offence search) they must be warned that if they refuse without good cause their refusal may harm their case if it comes to trial, see *Note A6*. This warning may be given by a police officer or member of police staff. In the case of juveniles, mentally vulnerable or mentally disordered suspects the seeking and giving of consent must take place in the presence of the appropriate adult. A juvenile's consent is only valid if their parent's or guardian's consent is also obtained unless the juvenile is under 14, when their parent's or guardian's consent is sufficient in its own right. A detainee who is not legally represented must be reminded of their entitlement to have free legal advice, see Code C, paragraph 6.5, and the reminder noted in the custody record.

        Note: paragraph 1.5A of this code requires someone to fulfil the role of the appropriate adult to be present when the warning is given to a 17-year-old and their consent to a drug offence search is sought and given but the consent of their parent or guardian is not required.

C:3. An intimate search may only be carried out by a registered medical practitioner or registered nurse, unless an officer of at least inspector rank considers this is not practicable and the search is to take place under paragraph 2(a)(i), in which case a police officer may carry out the search. See *Notes A1 to A5.*

C:3A. Any proposal for a search under paragraph 2(a)(i) to be carried out by someone other than a registered medical practitioner or registered nurse must only be considered as a last resort and when the authorising officer is satisfied the risks associated with allowing the item to remain with the detainee outweigh the risks associated with removing it. See *Notes A1 to A5.*

C:4. An intimate search under:

- paragraph 2(a)(i) may take place only at a hospital, surgery, other medical premises or police station;
- paragraph 2(a)(ii) may take place only at a hospital, surgery or other medical premises and must be carried out by a registered medical practitioner or a registered nurse.

C:5. An intimate search at a police station of a juvenile or mentally disordered or otherwise mentally vulnerable person may take place only in the presence of an appropriate adult of the same sex (see Annex L), unless the detainee specifically requests a particular adult of the opposite sex who is readily available. In the case of a juvenile, the search may take place in the absence of the appropriate adult only if the juvenile signifies in the presence of the appropriate adult they do not want the adult present during the search and the adult agrees. A record shall be made of the juvenile's decision and signed by the appropriate adult.

        Note: paragraph 1.5A of this code extends the requirement in this paragraph to an intimate search of a 17-year-old.

C:6. When an intimate search under paragraph 2(a)(i) is carried out by a police officer, the officer must be of the same sex as the detainee (see Annex L). A minimum of two people, other than the detainee, must be present during the search. Subject to paragraph 5, no person of the opposite sex who is not a medical practitioner or nurse shall be present, nor shall anyone whose presence is unnecessary. The search shall be conducted with proper regard to the sensitivity and vulnerability of the detainee.

(b) Documentation

A-94 C:7. In the case of an intimate search, the following shall be recorded as soon as practicable in the detainee's custody record:

    (a) for searches under paragraphs 2(a)(i) and (ii);

- the authorisation to carry out the search;
- the grounds for giving the authorisation;
- the grounds for believing the article could not be removed without an intimate search;
- which parts of the detainee's body were searched;
- who carried out the search;
- who was present;

- the result;
(b) for searches under paragraph 2(a)(ii):
    - the giving of the warning required by paragraph 2B;
    - the fact that the appropriate consent was given or (as the case may be) refused, and if refused, the reason given for the refusal (if any).
C:8. If an intimate search is carried out by a police officer, the reason why it was impracticable for a registered medical practitioner or registered nurse to conduct it must be recorded.

B *Strip search*

C:9. A strip search is a search involving the removal of more than outer clothing. In this code, outer clothing includes shoes and socks. **A-95**

(a) Action

C:10. A strip search may take place only if it is considered necessary to remove an article which a detainee would not be allowed to keep and the officer reasonably considers the detainee might have concealed such an article. Strip searches shall not be routinely carried out if there is no reason to consider that articles are concealed. **A-96**

The conduct of strip searches

C:11. When strip searches are conducted:
(a) a police officer carrying out a strip search must be the same sex as the detainee (see Annex L);
(b) the search shall take place in an area where the detainee cannot be seen by anyone who does not need to be present, nor by a member of the opposite sex (see Annex L) except an appropriate adult who has been specifically requested by the detainee;
(c) except in cases of urgency, where there is risk of serious harm to the detainee or to others, whenever a strip search involves exposure of intimate body parts, there must be at least two people present other than the detainee, and if the search is of a juvenile or mentally disordered or otherwise mentally vulnerable person, one of the people must be the appropriate adult; except in urgent cases as above, a search of a juvenile may take place in the absence of the appropriate adult only if the juvenile signifies in the presence of the appropriate adult that they do not want the adult to be present during the search and the adult agrees; a record shall be made of the juvenile's decision and signed by the appropriate adult; the presence of more than two people, other than an appropriate adult, shall be permitted only in the most exceptional circumstances (note: para. 1.5A of this code extends the requirement in this sub-paragraph to a strip search of a 17-year-old);
(d) the search shall be conducted with proper regard to the sensitivity and vulnerability of the detainee in these circumstances and every reasonable effort shall be made to secure the detainee's co-operation and minimise embarrassment; detainees who are searched shall not normally be required to remove all their clothes at the same time, *e.g.* a person should be allowed to remove clothing above the waist and redress before removing further clothing;
(e) if necessary to assist the search, the detainee may be required to hold their arms in the air or to stand with their legs apart and bend forward so a visual examination may be made of the genital and anal areas provided no physical contact is made with any body orifice;
(f) if articles are found, the detainee shall be asked to hand them over; if articles are found within any body orifice other than the mouth, and the detainee refuses to hand them over, their removal would constitute an intimate search, which must be carried out as in Part A;
(g) a strip search shall be conducted as quickly as possible, and the detainee allowed to dress as soon as the procedure is complete.

(b) Documentation

C:12. A record shall be made on the custody record of a strip search including the reason it was considered necessary, those present and any result. **A-97**

Notes for guidance

A-98   C:A1 *Before authorising any intimate search, the authorising officer must make every reasonable effort topersuade the detainee to hand the article over without a search. If the detainee agrees, a registered medical practitioner or registered nurse should whenever possible be asked to assess the risks involved and, if necessary, attend to assist the detainee.*

C:A2 *If the detainee does not agree to hand the article over without a search, the authorising officer must carefully review all the relevant factors before authorising an intimate search. In particular, the officer must consider whether the grounds for believing an article may be concealed are reasonable.*

C:A3 *If authority is given for a search under paragraph 2(a)(i), a registered medical practitioner or registered nurse shall be consulted whenever possible. The presumption should be that the search will be conducted by the registered medical practitioner or registered nurse and the authorising officer must make every reasonable effort to persuade the detainee to allow the medical practitioner or nurse to conduct the search.*

C:A4 *A constable should only be authorised to carry out a search as a last resort and when all other approaches have failed. In these circumstances, the authorising officer must be satisfied the detainee might use the article for one or more of the purposes in paragraph 2(a)(i) and the physical injury likely to be caused is sufficiently severe to justify authorising a constable to carry out the search.*

C:A5 *If an officer has any doubts whether to authorise an intimate search by a constable, the officer should seek advice from an officer of superintendent rank or above.*

C:A6 *In warning a detainee who is asked to consent to an intimate drug offence search, as in paragraph 2B, the following form of words may be used:*

"You do not have to allow yourself to be searched, but I must warn you that if you refuse without good cause, your refusal may harm your case if it comes to trial.".

Where the use of the Welsh language is appropriate, the following form of words may be used:

"Nid oes rhaid i chi roi caniatâd i gael eich archwilio, ond mae'n rhaid i mi eich rhybuddio os gwrthodwch heb reswm da, y gallai eich penderfyniad i wrthod wneud niwed i'ch achos pe bai'n dod gerbron llys.".

ANNEX B

Delay in notifying arrest or allowing access to legal advice

A Persons detained under PACE

A-99   C:1. The exercise of the rights in section 5 or section 6, or both, may be delayed if the person is in police detention, as in PACE, section 118(2), in connection with an indictable offence, has not yet been charged with an offence and an officer of superintendent rank or above, or inspector rank or above only for the rights in section 5, has reasonable grounds for believing their exercise will:

    (i) lead to:

        • interference with, or harm to, evidence connected with an indictable offence; or

        • interference with, or physical harm to, other people; or

    (ii) lead to alerting other people suspected of having committed an indictable offence but not yet arrested for it; or

    (iii) hinder the recovery of property obtained in consequence of the commission of such an offence.

C:2. These rights may also be delayed if the officer has reasonable grounds to believe that:

    (i) the person detained for an indictable offence has benefited from their criminal conduct (decided in accordance with Part 2 of the Proceeds of Crime Act 2002); and

    (ii) the recovery of the value of the property constituting that benefit will be hindered by the exercise of either right.

C:3. Authority to delay a detainee's right to consult privately with a solicitor may be given only if the authorising officer has reasonable grounds to believe the solicitor the detainee wants to consult will, inadvertently or otherwise, pass on a message from the detainee or act in some other way which will have any of the consequences specified under paragraphs 1 or 2. In these circumstances, the detainee must be allowed to choose another solicitor. See *Note B3.*

C:4. If the detainee wishes to see a solicitor, access to that solicitor may not be delayed on the grounds they might advise the detainee not to answer questions or the solicitor was initially asked to attend the police station by someone else. In the latter case, the detainee must be told the solicitor has come to the police station at another person's request, and must be asked to sign the custody record to signify whether they want to see the solicitor.

C:5. The fact the grounds for delaying notification of arrest may be satisfied does not automatically mean the grounds for delaying access to legal advice will also be satisfied.

C:6. These rights may be delayed only for as long as grounds exist and in no case beyond 36 hours after the relevant time as in PACE, s.41. If the grounds cease to apply within this time, the detainee must, as soon as practicable, be asked if they want to exercise either right, the custody record must be noted accordingly, and action taken in accordance with the relevant section of the code.

C:7. A detained person must be permitted to consult a solicitor for a reasonable time before any court hearing.

B [*Not used.*]

C *Documentation*

C:13. The grounds for action under this annex shall be recorded and the detainee informed of them as soon as practicable. **A-100**

C:14. Any reply given by a detainee under paragraphs 6 or 11 must be recorded and the detainee asked to endorse the record in relation to whether they want to receive legal advice at this point.

D *Cautions and special warnings*

C:15. When a suspect detained at a police station is interviewed during any period for which access to legal advice has been delayed under this annex, the court or jury may not draw adverse inferences from their silence.

Notes for guidance

C:B1 *Even if Annex B applies in the case of a juvenile, or a person who is mentally disordered or otherwise* **A-101** *mentally vulnerable, action to inform the appropriate adult and the person responsible for a juvenile's welfare if that is a different person, must nevertheless be taken as in paragraph 3.13 and 3.15.*

Note: paragraph 1.5A of this code extends this note to 17-year-old detainees.

C:B2 *In the case of Commonwealth citizens and foreign nationals, see Note 7A.*

C:B3 *A decision to delay access to a specific solicitor is likely to be a rare occurrence and only when it can be shown the suspect is capable of misleading that particular solicitor and there is more than a substantial risk that the suspect will succeed in causing information to be conveyed which will lead to one or more of the specified consequences.*

ANNEX C

Restriction on drawing adverse inferences from silence and terms of the caution when the restriction applies

(a) *The restriction on drawing adverse inferences from silence*

C:1. The Criminal Justice and Public Order Act 1994, ss.34, 36 and 37 as amended by the Youth **A-102** Justice and Criminal Evidence Act 1999, s.58 describe the conditions under which adverse inferences may be drawn from a person's failure or refusal to say anything about their involvement in the offence when interviewed, after being charged or informed they may be prosecuted. These provisions are subject to an overriding restriction on the ability of a court or jury to draw adverse inferences from a person's silence. This restriction applies:

    (a) to any detainee at a police station, see *Note 10C*, who, before being interviewed, see section 11, or being charged or informed they may be prosecuted, see section 16, has:

        (i) asked for legal advice, see section 6, paragraph 6.1;

        (ii) not been allowed an opportunity to consult a solicitor, including the duty solicitor, as in this code; and

        (iii) not changed their mind about wanting legal advice, see section 6, paragraph 6.6(d);

          – [note the condition in (ii) will

            – apply when a detainee who has asked for legal advice is interviewed before speaking to a solicitor as in section 6, paragraph 6.6(a) or (b);

            – not apply if the detained person declines to ask for the duty solicitor, see section 6, paragraphs 6.6(c) and (d)];

    (b) to any person charged with, or informed they may be prosecuted for, an offence who:

        (i) has had brought to their notice a written statement made by another person or the content of an interview with another person which relates to that offence, see section 16, paragraph 16.4;

        (ii) is interviewed about that offence, see section 16, paragraph 16.5; or

(iii) makes a written statement about that offence, see Annex D paragraphs 4 and 9.

(b) *Terms of the caution when the restriction applies*

C:2. When a requirement to caution arises at a time when the restriction on drawing adverse inferences from silence applies, the caution shall be:

"You do not have to say anything, but anything you do say may be given in evidence.".

Where the use of the Welsh language is appropriate, the caution may be used directly in Welsh in the following terms:

"Does dim rhaid i chi ddweud dim byd, ond gall unrhyw beth yr ydych chi'n ei ddweud gael ei roi fel tystiolaeth.".

C:3. Whenever the restriction either begins to apply or ceases to apply after a caution has already been given, the person shall be re-cautioned in the appropriate terms. The changed position on drawing inferences and that the previous caution no longer applies shall also be explained to the detainee in ordinary language. See *Note C2.*

Notes for guidance

C:C1 *The restriction on drawing inferences from silence does not apply to a person who has not been detained and who therefore cannot be prevented from seeking legal advice if they want to, see paragraphs 10.2 and 3.15.*

C:C2 *The following is suggested as a framework to help explain changes in the position on drawing adverse inferences if the restriction on drawing adverse inferences from silence:*

(a) *begins to apply:*

"The caution you were previously given no longer applies. This is because after that caution:

(i) *you asked to speak to a solicitor but have not yet been allowed an opportunity to speak to a solicitor;" see paragraph 1(a); or*

"(ii) *you have been charged with/informed you may be prosecuted." See paragraph 1(b).*

"This means that from now on, adverse inferences cannot be drawn at court and your defence will not be harmed just because you choose to say nothing. Please listen carefully to the caution I am about to give you because it will apply from now on. You will see that it does not say anything about your defence being harmed.";

(b) *ceases to apply before or at the time the person is charged or informed they may be prosecuted, see paragraph 1(a);*

"The caution you were previously given no longer applies. This is because after that caution you have been allowed an opportunity to speak to a solicitor. Please listen carefully to the caution I am about to give you because it will apply from now on. It explains how your defence at court may be affected if you choose to say nothing.".

ANNEX D

Written statements under caution

(a) *Written by a person under caution*

A-103   C:1. A person shall always be invited to write down what they want to say.

C:2. A person who has not been charged with, or informed they may be prosecuted for, any offence to which the statement they want to write relates, shall:

(a) unless the statement is made at a time when the restriction on drawing adverse inferences from silence applies, see Annex C, be asked to write out and sign the following before writing what they want to say:

"I make this statement of my own free will. I understand that I do not have to say anything but that it may harm my defence if I do not mention when questioned something which I later rely on in court. This statement may be given in evidence.";

(b) if the statement is made at a time when the restriction on drawing adverse inferences from silence applies, be asked to write out and sign the following before writing what they want to say;

"I make this statement of my own free will. I understand that I do not have to say anything. This statement may be given in evidence.".

C:3. When a person, on the occasion of being charged with or informed they may be prosecuted for any offence, asks to make a statement which relates to any such offence and wants to write it they shall:

(a) unless the restriction on drawing adverse inferences from silence, see Annex C, applied when they were so charged or informed they may be prosecuted, be asked to write out and sign the following before writing what they want to say:

"*I make this statement of my own free will. I understand that I do not have to say anything but that it may harm my defence if I do not mention when questioned something which I later rely on in court. This statement may be given in evidence.*";

(b) if the restriction on drawing adverse inferences from silence applied when they were so charged or informed they may be prosecuted, be asked to write out and sign the following before writing what they want to say:

"*I make this statement of my own free will. I understand that I do not have to say anything. This statement may be given in evidence.*".

C:4. When a person who has already been charged with or informed they may be prosecuted for any offence asks to make a statement which relates to any such offence and wants to write it, they shall be asked to write out and sign the following before writing what they want to say:

"*I make this statement of my own free will. I understand that I do not have to say anything. This statement may be given in evidence.*".

C:5. Any person writing their own statement shall be allowed to do so without any prompting except a police officer or police staff may indicate to them which matters are material or question any ambiguity in the statement.

(b) *Written by a police officer or other police staff*

C:6. If a person says they would like someone to write the statement for them, a police officer, or **A-104** other police staff shall write the statement.

C:7. If the person has not been charged with, or informed they may be prosecuted for, any offence to which the statement they want to make relates they shall, before starting, be asked to sign, or make their mark, to the following:

(a) unless the statement is made at a time when the restriction on drawing adverse inferences from silence applies, see Annex C:

"*I, ..., wish to make a statement. I want someone to write down what I say. I understand that I do not have to say anything but that it may harm my defence if I do not mention when questioned something which I later rely on in court. This statement may be given in evidence.*";

(b) if the statement is made at a time when the restriction on drawing adverse inferences from silence applies:

"*I, ..., wish to make a statement. I want someone to write down what I say. I understand that I do not have to say anything. This statement may be given in evidence.*".

C:8. If, on the occasion of being charged with or informed they may be prosecuted for any offence, the person asks to make a statement which relates to any such offence they shall before starting be asked to sign, or make their mark to, the following:

(a) unless the restriction on drawing adverse inferences from silence applied, see Annex C, when they were so charged or informed they may be prosecuted:

"*I, ..., wish to make a statement. I want someone to write down what I say. I understand that I do not have to say anything but that it may harm my defence if I do not mention when questioned something which I later rely on in court. This statement may be given in evidence.*";

(b) if the restriction on drawing adverse inferences from silence applied when they were so charged or informed they may be prosecuted:

"*I, ..., wish to make a statement. I want someone to write down what I say. I understand that I do not have to say anything. This statement may be given in evidence.*".

C:9. If, having already been charged with or informed they may be prosecuted for any offence, a person asks to make a statement which relates to any such offence they shall before starting, be asked to sign, or make their mark to:

"*I, ..., wish to make a statement. I want someone to write down what I say. I understand that I do not have to say anything. This statement may be given in evidence.".*

C:10. The person writing the statement must take down the exact words spoken by the person making it and must not edit or paraphrase it. Any questions that are necessary, *e.g.* to make it more intelligible, and the answers given must be recorded at the same time on the statement form.

C:11. When the writing of a statement is finished the person making it shall be asked to read it and to make any corrections, alterations or additions they want. When they have finished reading they shall be asked to write and sign or make their mark on the following certificate at the end of the statement:

"I have read the above statement, and I have been able to correct, alter or add anything I wish. This statement is true. I have made it of my own free will.".

C:12. If the person making the statement cannot read, or refuses to read it, or to write the above mentioned certificate at the end of it or to sign it, the person taking the statement shall read it to them and ask them if they would like to correct, alter or add anything and to put their signature or make their mark at the end. The person taking the statement shall certify on the statement itself what has occurred.

ANNEX E

Summary of provisions relating to mentally disordered and otherwise mentally vulnerable people

A-105

C:1. If an officer has any suspicion, or is told in good faith, that a person of any age may be mentally disordered or otherwise mentally vulnerable, or mentally incapable of understanding the significance of questions or their replies that person shall be treated as mentally disordered or otherwise mentally vulnerable for the purposes of this code. See paragraph 1.4 and *Note E4.*

C:2. In the case of a person who is mentally disordered or otherwise mentally vulnerable, "the appropriate adult" means:

    (a) a relative, guardian or other person responsible for their care or custody;

    (b) someone experienced in dealing with mentally disordered or mentally vulnerable people but who is not a police officer or employed by the police;

    (c) failing these, some other responsible adult aged 18 or over who is not a police officer or employed by the police.

See paragraph 1.7(b) and *Note 1D.*

C:3. If the custody officer authorises the detention of a person who is mentally vulnerable or appears to be suffering from a mental disorder, the custody officer must as soon as practicable inform the appropriate adult of the grounds for detention and the person's whereabouts, and ask the adult to come to the police station to see them. If the appropriate adult:

    • is already at the station when information is given as in paragraphs 3.1 to 3.5 the information must be given in their presence;

    • is not at the station when the provisions of paragraph 3.1 to 3.5 are complied with these provisions must be complied with again in their presence once they arrive.

See paragraphs 3.15 to 3.17.

C:4. If the appropriate adult, having been informed of the right to legal advice, considers legal advice should be taken, the provisions of section 6 apply as if the mentally disordered or otherwise mentally vulnerable person had requested access to legal advice. See paragraph 3.19 and *Note E1.*

C:5. The custody officer must make sure a person receives appropriate clinical attention as soon as reasonably practicable if the person appears to be suffering from a mental disorder or in urgent cases immediately call the nearest appropriate healthcare professional or an ambulance. It is not intended these provisions delay the transfer of a detainee to a place of safety under the Mental Health Act 1983, s.136, if that is applicable. If an assessment under that Act is to take place at a police station, the custody officer must consider whether an appropriate healthcare professional should be called to conduct an initial clinical check on the detainee. See paragraph 9.5 and 9.6.

C:6. It is imperative a mentally disordered or otherwise mentally vulnerable person detained under the Mental Health Act 1983, s.136, be assessed as soon as possible. A police station should only be used as a place of safety as a last resort but if that assessment is to take place at the police station, an approved social worker and registered medical practitioner shall be called to the station as soon as possible to carry it out. Once the detainee has been assessed and suitable arrangements been made for their treatment or care, they can no longer be detained under section 136. A detainee should be immediately discharged from detention if a registered medical practitioner having examined them, concludes they are not mentally disordered within the meaning of the Act. See paragraph 3.16.

C:7. If a mentally disordered or otherwise mentally vulnerable person is cautioned in the absence of the appropriate adult, the caution must be repeated in the appropriate adult's presence. See paragraph 10.12.

C:8. A mentally disordered or otherwise mentally vulnerable person must not be interviewed or asked to provide or sign a written statement in the absence of the appropriate adult unless the provisions of paragraphs 11.1 or 11.18 to 11.20 apply. Questioning in these circumstances may not continue in the absence of the appropriate adult once sufficient information to avert the risk has been obtained. A record shall be made of the grounds for any decision to begin an interview in these circumstances. See paragraphs 11.1, 11.15 and 11.18 to 11.20.

C:9. If the appropriate adult is present at an interview, they shall be informed they are not expected to act simply as an observer and the purposes of their presence are to:

- advise the interviewee;
- observe whether or not the interview is being conducted properly and fairly;
- facilitate communication with the interviewee.

See paragraph 11.17.

C:10. If the detention of a mentally disordered or otherwise mentally vulnerable person is reviewed by a review officer or a superintendent, the appropriate adult must, if available at the time, be given an opportunity to make representations to the officer about the need for continuing detention. See paragraph 15.3. **A-106**

C:11. If the custody officer charges a mentally disordered or otherwise mentally vulnerable person with an offence or takes such other action as is appropriate when there is sufficient evidence for a prosecution this must be carried out in the presence of the appropriate adult if they are at the police station. A copy of the written notice embodying any charge must also be given to the appropriate adult. See paragraphs 16.1 to 16.4A.

C:12. An intimate or strip search of a mentally disordered or otherwise mentally vulnerable person may take place only in the presence of the appropriate adult of the same sex, unless the detainee specifically requests the presence of a particular adult of the opposite sex. A strip search may take place in the absence of an appropriate adult only in cases of urgency when there is a risk of serious harm to the detainee or others. See Annex A, paragraphs 5 and 11(c).

C:13. Particular care must be taken when deciding whether to use any form of approved restraints on a mentally disordered or otherwise mentally vulnerable person in a locked cell. See paragraph 8.2.

Notes for guidance

C:E1 *The purpose of the provision at paragraph 3.19 is to protect the rights of a mentally disordered or otherwise mentally vulnerable detained person who does not understand the significance of what is said to them. If the detained person wants to exercise the right to legal advice, the appropriate action should be taken and not delayed until the appropriate adult arrives. A mentally disordered or otherwise mentally vulnerable detained person should always be given an opportunity, when an appropriate adult is called to the police station, to consult privately with a solicitor in the absence of the appropriate adult if they want.* **A-107**

C:E2 *Although people who are mentally disordered or otherwise mentally vulnerable are often capable of providing reliable evidence, they may, without knowing or wanting to do so, be particularly prone in certain circumstances to provide information that may be unreliable, misleading or self-incriminating. Special care should always be taken when questioning such a person, and the appropriate adult should be involved if there is any doubt about a person's mental state or capacity. Because of the risk of unreliable evidence, it is important to obtain corroboration of any facts admitted whenever possible.*

C:E3 *Because of the risks referred to in Note E2, which the presence of the appropriate adult is intended to minimise, officers of superintendent rank or above should exercise their discretion to authorise the commencement of an interview in the appropriate adult's absence only in exceptional cases, if it is necessary to avert an immediate risk of serious harm. See paragraphs 11.1, 11.18 to 11.20.*

C:E4 *There is no requirement for an appropriate adult to be present if a person is detained under section 136 of the Mental Health Act 1983 for assessment.*

ANNEX F

[*Not used.*] **A-108**

ANNEX G

Fitness to be interviewed

C:1. This annex contains general guidance to help police officers and health care professionals assess whether a detainee might be at risk in an interview. **A-109**

C:2. A detainee may be at risk in an interview if it is considered that:

(a) conducting the interview could significantly harm the detainee's physical or mental state;

    (b) anything the detainee says in the interview about their involvement or suspected involvement in the offence about which they are being interviewed **might** be considered unreliable in subsequent court proceedings because of their physical or mental state.

   C:3. In assessing whether the detainee should be interviewed, the following must be considered:

    (a) how the detainee's physical or mental state might affect their ability to understand the nature and purpose of the interview, to comprehend what is being asked and to appreciate the significance of any answers given and make rational decisions about whether they want to say anything;

    (b) the extent to which the detainee's replies may be affected by their physical or mental condition rather than representing a rational and accurate explanation of their involvement in the offence;

    (c) how the nature of the interview, which could include particularly probing questions, might affect the detainee.

A-110

   C:4. It is essential health care professionals who are consulted consider the functional ability of the detainee rather than simply relying on a medical diagnosis, *e.g.* it is possible for a person with severe mental illness to be fit for interview.

   C:5. Health care professionals should advise on the need for an appropriate adult to be present, whether reassessment of the person's fitness for interview may be necessary if the interview lasts beyond a specified time, and whether a further specialist opinion may be required.

   C:6. When health care professionals identify risks they should be asked to quantify the risks. They should inform the custody officer:

- whether the person's condition:
  - is likely to improve;
  - will require or be amenable to treatment; and
- indicate how long it may take for such improvement to take effect.

   C:7. The role of the health care professional is to consider the risks and advise the custody officer of the outcome of that consideration. The health care professional's determination and any advice or recommendations should be made in writing and form part of the custody record.

   C:8. Once the health care professional has provided that information, it is a matter for the custody officer to decide whether or not to allow the interview to go ahead and if the interview is to proceed, to determine what safeguards are needed. Nothing prevents safeguards being provided in addition to those required under the code. An example might be to have an appropriate health care professional present during the interview, in addition to an appropriate adult, in order constantly to monitor the person's condition and how it is being affected by the interview.

ANNEX H

Detained person: observation list

A-111

   C:1. If any detainee fails to meet any of the following criteria, an appropriate health care professional or an ambulance must be called.

   C:2. When assessing the level of rousability, consider:

    Rousability—can they be woken?

- go into the cell
- call their name
- shake gently

    Response to questions—can they give appropriate answers to questions such as:

- What's your name?
- Where do you live?
- Where do you think you are?

    Response to commands—can they respond appropriately to commands such as:

- Open your eyes!
- Lift one arm, now the other arm!

   C:3. Remember to take into account the possibility or presence of other illnesses, injury, or mental condition; a person who is drowsy and smells of alcohol may also have the following:

- Diabetes
- Epilepsy
- Head injury
- Drug intoxication or overdose
- Stroke

ANNEX I

[*Not used.*]

ANNEX J

[*Not used.*]

ANNEX K

X-rays and ultrasound scans

(a) *Action*

C:1. PACE, s.55A allows a person who has been arrested and is in police detention to have an **A-111a**
x-ray taken of them or an ultrasound scan to be carried out on them (or both) if:
  (a) authorised by an officer of inspector rank or above who has reasonable grounds for
       believing that the detainee:
       (i) may have swallowed a Class A drug; and
       (ii) was in possession of that Class A drug with the intention of supplying it to another or
            to export; and
  (b) the detainee's appropriate consent has been given in writing.

C:2. Before an x-ray is taken or an ultrasound scan carried out, a police officer or designated
detention officer must tell the detainee:
  (a) that the authority has been given; and
  (b) the grounds for giving the authorisation.

Note: paragraph 1.5A in this code requires someone to fulfil the role of the appropriate adult to
be present when a 17-year-old is told about the authority and grounds for an x-ray and ultrasound
scan.

C:3. Before a detainee is asked to give appropriate consent to an x-ray or an ultrasound scan, they
must be warned that if they refuse without good cause their refusal may harm their case if it comes
to trial, see *Notes K1* and *K2*. This warning may be given by a police officer or member of police staff.
In the case of juveniles, mentally vulnerable or mentally disordered suspects the seeking and giving
of consent must take place in the presence of the appropriate adult. A juvenile's consent is only valid
if their parent's or guardian's consent is also obtained unless the juvenile is under 14, when their
parent's or guardian's consent is sufficient in its own right. A detainee who is not legally represented
must be reminded of their entitlement to have free legal advice, see Code C, paragraph 6.5, and the
reminder noted in the custody record.

Note: paragraph 1.5A in this code requires someone to fulfil the role of the appropriate adult to
be present when the warning is given to a 17-year-old and their consent to an x-ray or ultrasound
scan is sought and given but the consent of their parent or guardian is not required.

C:4. An x-ray may be taken, or an ultrasound scan may be carried out, only by a registered medical practitioner or registered nurse, and only at a hospital, surgery or other medical premises.

(b) *Documentation*

C:5. The following shall be recorded as soon as practicable in the detainee's custody record:
  (a) the authorisation to take the x-ray or carry out the ultrasound scan (or both);
  (b) the grounds for giving the authorisation;
  (c) the giving of the warning required by paragraph 3; and
  (d) the fact that the appropriate consent was given or (as the case may be) refused, and if
       refused, the reason given for the refusal (if any); and
  (e) if an x-ray is taken or an ultrasound scan carried out:
       • where it was taken or carried out;
       • who took it or carried it out;
       • who was present;
       • the result.

Notes for guidance

C:K1 *If authority is given for an x-ray to be taken or an ultrasound scan to be carried out (or both),* **A-111b**
consideration should be given to asking a registered medical practitioner or registered nurse to explain to the
detainee what is involved and to allay any concerns the detainee might have about the effect which taking an x-ray
or carrying out an ultrasound scan might have on them. If appropriate consent is not given, evidence of the

explanation may, if the case comes to trial, be relevant to determining whether the detainee had a good cause for refusing.

C:K2 *In warning a detainee who is asked to consent to an x-ray being taken or an ultrasound scan being carried out (or both), as in paragraph 3, the following form of words may be used:*

"You do not have to allow an x-ray of you to be taken or an ultrasound scan to be carried out on you, but I must warn you that if you refuse without good cause, your refusal may harm your case if it comes to trial.".

Where the use of the Welsh language is appropriate, the following form of words may be provided in Welsh:

"Does dim rhaid i chi ganiatáu cymryd sgan uwchsain neu belydr-x (neu'r ddau) arnoch, ond mae'n rhaid i mi eich rhybuddio os byddwch chin gwrthod gwneud hynny heb reswm da, fe allai hynny niweidio eich achos pe bai'n dod gerbron llys.".

ANNEX L

Establishing gender of persons for the purpose of searching

A-111c   C:1. 1. Certain provisions of this and other PACE codes explicitly state that searches and other procedures may only be carried out by, or in the presence of, persons of the same sex as the person subject to the search or other procedure. See *Note L1*.

C:2. All searches and procedures must be carried out with courtesy, consideration and respect for the person concerned. Police officers should show particular sensitivity when dealing with transgender individuals (including transsexual persons) and transvestite persons (see *Notes L2, L3* and *L4*).

(a) *Consideration*

A-111d   C:3. In law, the gender (and accordingly the sex) of an individual is their gender as registered at birth unless they have been issued with a gender recognition certificate (GRC) under the Gender Recognition Act 2004 (GRA), in which case the person's gender is their acquired gender. This means that if the acquired gender is the male gender, the person's sex becomes that of a man and, if it is the female gender, the person's sex becomes that of a woman and they must be treated as their acquired gender.

C:4. When establishing whether the person concerned should be treated as being male or female for the purposes of these searches and procedures, the following approach which is designed to minimise embarrassment and secure the person's co-operation should be followed:

    (a) the person must not be asked whether they have a GRC (see paragraph 8);

    (b) if there is no doubt as to as to whether the person concerned should be treated as being male or female, they should be dealt with as being of that sex;

    (c) if at any time (including during the search or carrying out the procedure) there is doubt as to whether the person should be treated, or continue to be treated, as being male or female:

        (i) the person should be asked what gender they consider themselves to be; if they express a preference to be dealt with as a particular gender, they should be asked to indicate and confirm their preference by signing the custody record or, if a custody record has not been opened, the search record or the officer's notebook; subject to (ii) below, the person should be treated according to their preference;

        (ii) if there are grounds to doubt that the preference in (i) accurately reflects the person's predominant lifestyle, for example, if they ask to be treated as a woman but documents and other information make it clear that they live predominantly as a man, or vice versa, they should be treated according to what appears to be their predominant lifestyle and not their stated preference;

        (iii) if the person is unwilling to express a preference as in (i) above, efforts should be made to determine their predominant lifestyle and they should be treated as such; for example, if they appear to live predominantly as a woman, they should be treated as being female; or

        (iv) if none of the above apply, the person should be dealt with according to what reasonably appears to have been their sex as registered at birth.

C:5. Once a decision has been made about which gender an individual is to be treated as, each officer responsible for the search or procedure should where possible be advised before the search or procedure starts of any doubts as to the person's gender and the person informed that the doubts have been disclosed. This is important so as to maintain the dignity of the person and any officers concerned.

(b) *Documentation*

C:6. The person's gender as established under paragraph 4(c)(i) to (iv) above must be recorded in **A-111e** the person's custody record or, if a custody record has not been opened, on the search record or in the officer's notebook.

C:7. Where the person elects which gender they consider themselves to be under paragraph 4(b)(i) but, following 4(b)(ii) is not treated in accordance with their preference, the reason must be recorded in the search record, in the officer's notebook or, if applicable, in the person's custody record.

(c) *Disclosure of information*

C:8. Section 22 of the GRA defines any information relating to a person's application for a GRC or **A-111f** to a successful applicant's gender before it became their acquired gender as "protected information". Nothing in this annex is to be read as authorising or permitting any police officer or any police staff who has acquired such information when acting in their official capacity to disclose that information to any other person in contravention of the GRA. Disclosure includes making a record of "protected information" which is read by others.

Notes for guidance

C:L1 *Provisions to which paragraph 1 applies include:* **A-111g**

- *in Code C; paragraph 4.1 and Annex A, paragraphs 5, 6 and 11 (searches, strip and intimate searches of detainees under sections 54 and 55 of PACE);*
- *in Code A; paragraphs 2.8 and 3.6 and Note 4;*
- *in Code D; paragraph 5.5 and Note 5F (searches, examinations and photographing of detainees under section 54A of PACE) and paragraph 6.9 (taking samples);*
- *in Code H; paragraph 4.1 and Annex A, paragraphs 6, 7 and 12 (searches, strip and intimate searches under sections 54 and 55 of PACE of persons arrested under section 41 of the Terrorism Act 2000).*

C:L2 *While there is no agreed definition of transgender (or trans), it is generally used as an umbrella term to describe people whose gender identity (self-identification as being a woman, man, neither or both) differs from the sex they were registered as at birth. The term includes, but is not limited to, transsexual people.*

C:L3 *Transsexual means a person who is proposing to undergo, is undergoing or has undergone a process (or part of a process) for the purpose of gender reassignment, which is a protected characteristic under the Equality Act 2010 (see paragraph 1.0) by changing physiological or other attributes of their sex. This includes aspects of gender such as dress and title. It would apply to a woman making the transition to being a man and a man making the transition to being a woman, as well as to a person who has only just started out on the process of gender reassignment and to a person who has completed the process. Both would share the characteristic of gender reassignment with each having the characteristics of one sex, but with certain characteristics of the other sex.*

C:L4 *Transvestite means a person of one gender who dresses in the clothes of a person of the opposite gender. However, a transvestite does not live permanently in the gender opposite to their birth sex.*

C:L5 *Chief officers are responsible for providing corresponding operational guidance and instructions for the deployment of transgender officers and staff under their direction and control to duties which involve carrying out, or being present at, any of the searches and procedures described in paragraph 1. The guidance and instructions must comply with the Equality Act 2010 and should therefore complement the approach in this annex.*

ANNEX M

Documents and records to be translated

C:1. For the purposes of Directive 2010/64/EU of the European Parliament and of the Council of **A-111h** 20 October 2010 and this code, essential documents comprise records required to be made in accordance with this code which are relevant to decisions to deprive a person of their liberty, to any charge and to any record considered necessary to enable a detainee to defend themselves in criminal proceedings and to safeguard the fairness of the proceedings. Passages of essential documents which are not relevant need not be translated. See *Note M1*.

C:2. The table below lists the documents considered essential for the purposes of this code and when (subject to paras 3 to 7) written translations must be created and provided.

Table of essential documents:

A-111i

	Essential documents for the purposes of this code	When translation to be created	When translation to be provided.
(i)	The grounds for each of the following authorisations to keep the person in custody as they are described and referred to in the custody record: (a) authorisation for detention before and after charge given by the custody o cer and by the review officer, see Code C, paras 3.4 and 15.16(a); (b) authorisation to extend detention without charge beyond 24 hours given by a superintendent, see Code C, para. 15.16(b); (c) a warrant of further detention issued by a magistrates' court and any extension(s) of the warrant, see Code C, para. 15.16(c); (d) an authority to detain in accordance with the directions in a warrant of arrest issued in connection with criminal proceedings including the court issuing the warrant.	As soon as practicable after each authorisation has been recorded in the custody record.	As soon as practicable after the translation has been created, whilst the person is detained or after they have been released (see *Note M3*).
(ii)	Written notice showing particulars of the offence charged required by Code C, para. 16.3, or the offence for which the suspect has been told they may be prosecuted.	As soon as practicable after the person has been charged or reported.	
(iii)	Written interview records: Code C:11.11, 13.3, 13.4 & Code E4.7 Written statement under caution: Code C, Annex D.	To be created contemporaneously by the interpreter for the person to check and sign.	As soon as practicable after the person has been charged or told they may be prosecuted.

C:3. The custody officer may authorise an oral translation or oral summary of documents (i) to (ii) in the table (but not (iii)) to be provided (through an interpreter) instead of a written translation. Such an oral translation or summary may only be provided if it would not prejudice the fairness of the proceedings by in any way adversely affecting or otherwise undermining or limiting the ability of the suspect in question to understand their position and to communicate effectively with police officers, interviewers, solicitors and appropriate adults with regard to their detention and the investigation of the offence in question and to defend themselves in the event of criminal proceedings. The quantity and complexity of the information in the document should always be considered and specific additional consideration given if the suspect is mentally disordered or otherwise mentally vulnerable or is a juvenile or a 17-year-old (see Code C, para. 1.5A). The reason for the decision must be recorded (see para. 13.11(e))

C:4. Subject to paragraphs 5 to 7 below, a suspect may waive their right to a written translation of the essential documents described in the table but only if they do so voluntarily after receiving legal advice or having full knowledge of the consequences and give their unconditional and fully informed consent in writing (see para. 9).

C:5. The suspect may be asked if they wish to waive their right to a written translation and before giving their consent, they must be reminded of their right to legal advice and asked whether they wish to speak to a solicitor.

C:6. No police officer or police staff should do or say anything with the intention of persuading a suspect who is entitled to a written translation of an essential document to waive that right. See *Notes M2* and *M3*.

C:7. For the purpose of the waiver:

(a) the consent of a person who is mentally disordered or otherwise mentally vulnerable person is only valid if the information about the circumstances under which they can waive the right and the reminder about their right to legal advice mentioned in paragraphs 3 to 5 and their consent is given in the presence of the appropriate adult (note: para. 1.5A in Code C requires someone to fulfil the role of the appropriate adult to be present when a 17-year-old is given the information and reminder mentioned in sub-para. (a) above and gives their consent to waive their right; the consent of their parent or guardian is not required);

(b) the consent of a juvenile is only valid if their parent's or guardian's consent is also obtained unless the juvenile is under 14, when their parent's or guardian's consent is sufficient in its own right and the information and reminder mentioned in sub-paragraph (a) above and their consent is also given in the presence of the appropriate adult (who may or may not be a parent or guardian).

C:8. The detainee, their solicitor or appropriate adult may make representations to the custody officer that a document which is not included in the table is essential and that a translation should be provided. The request may be refused if the officer is satisfied that the translation requested is not essential for the purposes described in paragraph 1 above.

C:9. If the custody officer has any doubts about—

• providing an oral translation or summary of an essential document instead of a written translation (see para. 3),

• whether the suspect fully understands the consequences of waiving their right to a written translation of an essential document (see para. 4), or

• about refusing to provide a translation of a requested document (see para. 7),

the officer should seek advice from an inspector or above.

Documentation

C:10. Action taken in accordance with this annex shall be recorded in the detainee's custody **A-111j** record or interview record as appropriate (see Code C, para. 13.11(e)).

Notes for guidance

C:M1 *It is not necessary to disclose information in any translation which is capable of undermining or* **A-111k** *otherwise adversely affecting any investigative processes, for example, by enabling the suspect to fabricate an innocent explanation or to conceal lies from the interviewer.*

C:M2 *No police officer or police staff shall indicate to any suspect, except to answer a direct question, whether the period for which they are liable to be detained or if not detained, the time taken to complete the interview, might be reduced:*

• *if they do not ask for legal advice before deciding whether they wish to waive their right to a written translation of an essential document; or*

• *if they decide to waive their right to a written translation of an essential document.*

C:M3 *There is no power under PACE to detain a person or to delay their release solely to create and provide a written translation of any essential document.*

(5) Identification

The text that follows is of the version of the code that came into force on March 7, 2011: see **A-112** *ante*, Appendix A-1.

In connection with Code D, see also §§ 14-39 *et seq.* (application of code), §§ 14-45 *et seq.* (identification procedures), § 14-54 (group identification, confrontation and video identification), §§ 14-57 *et seq.* (effect of breaches), §§ 14-60 *et seq.* (photographs), § 14-62 (video recordings), and § 15-199 (photographs) in the main work.

D. CODE OF PRACTICE FOR THE IDENTIFICATION OF PERSONS BY POLICE OFFICERS

Commencement—Transitional arrangements

A-113   This code has effect in relation to any identification procedure carried out after midnight on 6 March 2011.

D:1 Introduction

A-114   D:1.1 This code of practice concerns the principal methods used by police to identify people in connection with the investigation of offences and the keeping of accurate and reliable criminal records. The powers and procedures in this code must be used fairly, responsibly, with respect for the people to whom they apply and without unlawful discrimination. The Equality Act 2010 makes it unlawful for police officers to discriminate against, harass or victimise any person on the grounds of the "protected characteristics" of age, disability, gender reassignment, race, religion or belief, sex and sexual orientation, marriage and civil partnership, pregnancy and maternity when using their powers. When police forces are carrying out their functions they also have a duty to have regard to the need to eliminate unlawful discrimination, harassment and victimisation and to take steps to foster good relations.

D:1.2 In this code, identification by an eye-witness arises when a witness who has seen the offender committing the crime and is given an opportunity to identify a person suspected of involvement in the offence in a video identification, identification parade or similar procedure. These eyewitness identification procedures (see Part A of section 3 below) are designed to:

- test the witness's ability to identify the suspect as the person they saw on a previous occasion;
- provide safeguards against mistaken identification.

While this code concentrates on visual identification procedures, it does not preclude the police making use of aural identification procedures such as a "voice identification parade", where they judge that appropriate.

D:1.2A In this code, separate provisions in Part B of section 3 below apply when any person, including a police officer, is asked if they recognise anyone they see in an image as being someone they know and to test their claim that they recognise that person as someone who is known to them. Except where stated, these separate provisions are not subject to the eye-witnesses identification procedures described in paragraph 1.2.

D:1.3 Identification by fingerprints applies when a person's fingerprints are taken to:

- compare with fingerprints found at the scene of a crime;
- check and prove convictions;
- help to ascertain a person's identity.

D:1.3A Identification using footwear impressions applies when a person's footwear impressions are taken to compare with impressions found at the scene of a crime.

D:1.4 Identification by body samples and impressions includes taking samples such as blood or hair to generate a DNA profile for comparison with material obtained from the scene of a crime, or a victim.

D:1.5 Taking photographs of arrested people applies to recording and checking identity and locating and tracing persons who:

- are wanted for offences;
- fail to answer their bail.

D:1.6 Another method of identification involves searching and examining detained suspects to find, *e.g.*, marks such as tattoos or scars which may help establish their identity or whether they have been involved in committing an offence.

D:1.7 The provisions of the Police and Criminal Evidence Act 1984 (PACE) and this code are designed to make sure fingerprints, samples, impressions and photographs are taken, used and retained, and identification procedures carried out, only when justified and necessary for preventing, detecting or investigating crime. If these provisions are not observed, the application of the relevant procedures in particular cases may be open to question.

D:2 General

A-115   D:2.1 This code must be readily available at all police stations for consultation by:

- police officers and police staff;
- detained persons;
- members of the public.

D:2.2 The provisions of this code:

- include the Annexes;
- do not include the *Notes for guidance*.

D:2.3 Code C, paragraph 1.4, regarding a person who may be mentally disordered or otherwise mentally vulnerable and the *Notes for guidance* applicable to those provisions apply to this code.

D:2.4 Code C, paragraph 1.5, regarding a person who appears to be under the age of 17 applies to this code.

D:2.5 Code C, paragraph 1.6, regarding a person who appears to be blind, seriously visually impaired, deaf, unable to read or speak or has difficulty communicating orally because of a speech impediment applies to this code.

D:2.6 In this code: **A-116**
- "appropriate adult" means the same as in Code C, paragraph 1.7;
- "solicitor" means the same as in Code C, paragraph 6.12;
  and the *Notes for guidance* applicable to those provisions apply to this code;
- where a search or other procedure under this code may only be carried out or observed by a person of the same sex as the person to whom the search or procedure applies, the gender of the detainee and other persons present should be established and recorded in line with Annex F of Code A.

D:2.7 References to custody officers include those performing the functions of custody officer, see paragraph 1.9 of Code C.

D:2.8 When a record of any action requiring the authority of an officer of a specified rank is made under this code, subject to paragraph 2.18, the officer's name and rank must be recorded.

D:2.9 When this code requires the prior authority or agreement of an officer of at least inspector or superintendent rank, that authority may be given by a sergeant or chief inspector who has been authorised to perform the functions of the higher rank under PACE, s.107.

D:2.10 Subject to paragraph 2.18, all records must be timed and signed by the maker.

D:2.11 Records must be made in the custody record, unless otherwise specified. References to **A-117** "pocket book" include any official report book issued to police officers or police staff.

D:2.12 If any procedure in this code requires a person's consent, the consent of a:
- mentally disordered or otherwise mentally vulnerable person is only valid if given in the presence of the appropriate adult;
- juvenile is only valid if their parent's or guardian's consent is also obtained unless the juvenile is under 14, when their parent's or guardian's consent is sufficient in its own right. If the only obstacle to an identification procedure in section 3 is that a juvenile's parent or guardian refuses consent or reasonable efforts to obtain it have failed, the identification officer may apply the provisions of paragraph 3.21. See *Note 2A*.

D:2.13 If a person is blind, seriously visually impaired or unable to read, the custody officer or identification officer shall make sure their solicitor, relative, appropriate adult or some other person likely to take an interest in them and not involved in the investigation is available to help check any documentation. When this code requires written consent or signing, the person assisting may be asked to sign instead, if the detainee prefers. This paragraph does not require an appropriate adult to be called solely to assist in checking and signing documentation for a person who is not a juvenile, or mentally disordered or otherwise mentally vulnerable (see *Note 2B* and Code C, paragraph 3.15).

D:2.14 If any procedure in this code requires information to be given to or sought from a suspect, it must be given or sought in the appropriate adult's presence if the suspect is mentally disordered, otherwise mentally vulnerable or a juvenile. If the appropriate adult is not present when the information is first given or sought, the procedure must be repeated in the presence of the appropriate adult when they arrive. If the suspect appears deaf or there is doubt about their hearing or speaking ability or ability to understand English, and effective communication cannot be established, the information must be given or sought through an interpreter.

D:2.15 Any procedure in this code involving the participation of a suspect who is mentally disordered, otherwise mentally vulnerable or a juvenile must take place in the presence of the appropriate adult. See Code C, paragraph 1.4.

D:2.15A Any procedure in this code involving the participation of a witness who is or appears to be mentally disordered, otherwise mentally vulnerable or a juvenile should take place in the presence of a pre-trial support person unless the witness states that they do not want a support person to be present. A support person must not be allowed to prompt any identification of a suspect by a witness. See *Note 2AB*.

D:2.16 References to:
- "taking a photograph", include the use of any process to produce a single, still or moving, visual image;

- "photographing a person", should be construed accordingly;
- "photographs", "films", "negatives" and "copies" include relevant visual images recorded, stored, or reproduced through any medium;
- "destruction" includes the deletion of computer data relating to such images or making access to that data impossible.

D:2.17 Except as described, nothing in this code affects the powers and procedures:

(i) for requiring and taking samples of breath, blood and urine in relation to driving offences, etc, when under the influence of drink, drugs or excess alcohol under the:
- Road Traffic Act 1988, ss.4 to 11;
- Road Traffic Offenders Act 1988, ss.15 and 16;
- Transport and Works Act 1992, ss.26 to 38;

(ii) under the Immigration Act 1971, Sched. 2, para. 18, for taking photographs and fingerprints from persons detained under that Act, Schedule 2, paragraph 16 (administrative controls as to control on entry etc.); for taking fingerprints in accordance with the Immigration and Asylum Act 1999, ss.141 and 142(3), or other methods for collecting information about a person's external physical characteristics provided for by regulations made under that Act, section 144;

(iii) under the Terrorism Act 2000, Sched. 8, for taking photographs, fingerprints, skin impressions, body samples or impressions from people:
- arrested under that Act, section 41,
- detained for the purposes of examination under that Act, Schedule 7, and to whom the code of practice issued under that Act, Schedule 14, paragraph 6, applies ("the terrorism provisions"); see *Note 2C*;

(iv) for taking photographs, fingerprints, skin impressions, body samples or impressions from people who have been:
- arrested on warrants issued in Scotland, by officers exercising powers under the Criminal Justice and Public Order Act 1994, s.136(2);
- arrested or detained without warrant by officers from a police force in Scotland exercising their powers of arrest or detention under the Criminal Justice and Public Order Act 1994, s.137(2) (cross border powers of arrest etc.).

Note: in these cases, police powers and duties and the person's rights and entitlements whilst at a police station in England and Wales are the same as if the person had been arrested in Scotland by a Scottish police officer.

D:2.18 Nothing in this code requires the identity of officers or police staff to be recorded or disclosed:

(a) in the case of enquiries linked to the investigation of terrorism;
(b) if the officers or police staff reasonably believe recording or disclosing their names might put them in danger.

In these cases, they shall use warrant or other identification numbers and the name of their police station. See *Note 2D*.

A-118   D:2.19 In this code:

(a) "designated person" means a person other than a police officer, designated under the Police Reform Act 2002, Pt 4, who has specified powers and duties of police officers conferred or imposed on them;
(b) any reference to a police officer includes a designated person acting in the exercise or performance of the powers and duties conferred or imposed on them by their designation.

D:2.20 If a power conferred on a designated person:

(a) allows reasonable force to be used when exercised by a police officer, a designated person exercising that power has the same entitlement to use force;
(b) includes power to use force to enter any premises, that power is not exercisable by that designated person except:
  (i) in the company, and under the supervision, of a police officer; or
  (ii) for the purpose of:
    - saving life or limb; or
    - preventing serious damage to property.

D:2.21 Nothing in this code prevents the custody officer, or other officer given custody of the detainee, from allowing police staff who are not designated persons to carry out individual procedures or tasks at the police station if the law allows. However, the officer remains responsible for making sure the procedures and tasks are carried out correctly in accordance with the codes of practice. Any such person must be:

(a) a person employed by a police authority maintaining a police force and under the control and direction of the chief officer of that force;

(b) employed by a person with whom a police authority has a contract for the provision of services relating to persons arrested or otherwise in custody.

D:2.22 Designated persons and other police staff must have regard to any relevant provisions of the codes of practice.

Notes for guidance

D:2A *For the purposes of paragraph 2.12, the consent required from a parent or guardian may, for a juvenile* **A-119** *in the care of a local authority or voluntary organisation, be given by that authority or organisation. In the case of a juvenile, nothing in paragraph 2.12 requires the parent, guardian or representative of a local authority or voluntary organisation to be present to give their consent, unless they are acting as the appropriate adult under paragraphs 2.14 or 2.15. However, it is important that a parent or guardian not present is fully informed before being asked to consent. They must be given the same information about the procedure and the juvenile's suspected involvement in the offence as the juvenile and appropriate adult. The parent or guardian must also be allowed to speak to the juvenile and the appropriate adult if they wish. Provided the consent is fully informed and is not withdrawn, it may be obtained at any time before the procedure takes place.*

D:2AB *The Youth Justice and Criminal Evidence Act 1999 guidance "Achieving Best Evidence in Criminal Proceedings" indicates that a pre-trial support person should accompany a vulnerable witness during any identification procedure unless the witness states that they do not want a support person to be present. It states that this support person should not be (or not be likely to be) a witness in the investigation.*

D:2B *People who are seriously visually impaired or unable to read may be unwilling to sign police documents. The alternative, i.e. their representative signing on their behalf, seeks to protect the interests of both police and suspects.*

D:2C *Photographs, fingerprints, samples and impressions may be taken from a person detained under the terrorism provisions to help determine whether they are, or have been, involved in terrorism, as well as when there are reasonable grounds for suspecting their involvement in a particular offence.*

D:2D *The purpose of paragraph 2.18(b) is to protect those involved in serious organised crime investigations or arrests of particularly violent suspects when there is reliable information that those arrested or their associates may threaten or cause harm to the officers. In cases of doubt, an officer of inspector rank or above should be consulted.*

D:3 Identification and recognition of suspects

(a) *Identification of a suspect by an eye-witness*

D:3.0 This part applies when an eye-witness has seen the offender committing the crime or in any **A-120** other circumstances which tend to prove or disprove the involvement of the person they saw in the crime, for example, close to the scene of the crime, immediately before or immediately after it was committed. It sets out the procedures to be used to test the ability of that eye-witness to identify a person suspected of involvement in the offence as the person they saw on the previous occasion. Except where stated, this part does not apply to the procedures described in Part B and *Note 3AA*.

D:3.1 A record shall be made of the suspect's description as first given by a potential witness. This record must:

(a) be made and kept in a form which enables details of that description to be accurately produced from it, in a visible and legible form, which can be given to the suspect or the suspect's solicitor in accordance with this code; and

(b) unless otherwise specified, be made before the witness takes part in any identification procedures under paragraphs 3.5 to 3.10, 3.21 or 3.23.

A copy of the record shall where practicable, be given to the suspect or their solicitor before any procedures under paragraphs 3.5 to 3.10, 3.21 or 3.23 are carried out. See *Note 3E*.

(a) Cases when the suspect's identity is not known

D:3.2 In cases when the suspect's identity is not known, a witness may be taken to a particular neighbourhood or place to see whether they can identify the person they saw on a previous occasion. Although the number, age, sex, race, general description and style of clothing of other people present at the location and the way in which any identification is made cannot be controlled, the principles applicable to the formal procedures under paragraphs 3.5 to 3.10 shall be followed as far as practicable. For example:

(a) where it is practicable to do so, a record should be made of the witness's description of the suspect, as in paragraph 3.1(a), before asking the witness to make an identification;

(b) care must be taken not to direct the witness's attention to any individual unless, taking into account all the circumstances, this cannot be avoided; however, this does not prevent a witness being asked to look carefully at the people around at the time or to look towards a group or in a particular direction, if this appears necessary to make sure that the witness does not overlook a possible suspect simply because the witness is looking in the opposite direction and also to enable the witness to make comparisons between any suspect and others who are in the area; see *Note 3F*;

(c) where there is more than one witness, every effort should be made to keep them separate and witnesses should be taken to see whether they can identify a person independently;

(d) once there is sufficient information to justify the arrest of a particular individual for suspected involvement in the offence, *e.g.*, after a witness makes a positive identification, the provisions set out from paragraph 3.4 onwards shall apply for any other witnesses in relation to that individual;

(e) the officer or police staff accompanying the witness must record, in their pocket book, the action taken as soon as, and in as much detail, as possible. The record should include: the date, time and place of the relevant occasion the witness claims to have previously seen the suspect; where any identification was made; how it was made and the conditions at the time (*e.g.* the distance the witness was from the suspect, the weather and light); if the witness's attention was drawn to the suspect; the reason for this; and anything said by the witness or the suspect about the identification or the conduct of the procedure.

D:3.3 A witness must not be shown photographs, computerised or artist's composite likenesses or similar likenesses or pictures (including "E-fit" images) if the identity of the suspect is known to the police and the suspect is available to take part in a video identification, an identification parade or a group identification. If the suspect's identity is not known, the showing of such images to a witness to obtain identification evidence must be done in accordance with Annex E.

(b) Cases when the suspect is known and available

A-121   D:3.4 If the suspect's identity is known to the police and they are available, the identification procedures set out in paragraphs 3.5 to 3.10 may be used. References in this section to a suspect being "known" mean there is sufficient information known to the police to justify the arrest of a particular person for suspected involvement in the offence. A suspect being "available" means they are immediately available or will be within a reasonably short time and willing to take an effective part in at least one of the following which it is practicable to arrange:

• video identification;
• identification parade; or
• group identification.

Video identification

D:3.5 A "video identification" is when the witness is shown moving images of a known suspect, together with similar images of others who resemble the suspect. Moving images must be used unless:

• the suspect is known but not available (see paragraph 3.21 of this code); or
• in accordance with paragraph 2A of Annex A of this code, the identification officer does not consider that replication of a physical feature can be achieved or that it is not possible to conceal the location of the feature on the image of the suspect.

The identification officer may then decide to make use of video identification but using **still** images.

D:3.6 Video identifications must be carried out in accordance with Annex A.

Identification parade

D:3.7 An "identification parade" is when the witness sees the suspect in a line of others who resemble the suspect.

D:3.8 Identification parades must be carried out in accordance with Annex B.

Group identification

D:3.9 A "group identification" is when the witness sees the suspect in an informal group of people.

D:3.10 Group identifications must be carried out in accordance with Annex C.

Arranging identification procedures

D:3.11 Except for the provisions in paragraph 3.19, the arrangements for, and conduct of, the identification procedures in paragraphs 3.5 to 3.10 and circumstances in which an identification procedure must be held shall be the responsibility of an officer not below inspector rank who is not involved with the investigation, "the identification officer". Unless otherwise specified, the identification officer may allow another officer or police staff, see paragraph 2.21, to make arrangements for, and conduct, any of these identification procedures. In delegating these procedures, the identification officer must be able to supervise effectively and either intervene or be contacted for advice. No officer or any other person involved with the investigation of the case against the suspect, beyond the extent required by these procedures, may take any part in these procedures or act as the identification officer. This does not prevent the identification officer from consulting the officer in charge of the investigation to determine which procedure to use. When an identification procedure is required, in the interest of fairness to suspects and witnesses, it must be held as soon as practicable.

Circumstances in which an eye-witness identification procedure must be held

D:3.12 Whenever: **A-122**

    (i) an eye witness has identified a suspect or purported to have identified them prior to any identification procedure set out in paragraphs 3.5 to 3.10 having been held; or

    (ii) there is a witness available who expresses an ability to identify the suspect, or where there is a reasonable chance of the witness being able to do so, and they have not been given an opportunity to identify the suspect in any of the procedures set out in paragraphs 3.5 to 3.10,

and the suspect disputes being the person the witness claims to have seen, an identification procedure shall be held unless it is not practicable or it would serve no useful purpose in proving or disproving whether the suspect was involved in committing the offence, for example:

    • where the suspect admits being at the scene of the crime and gives an account of what took place and the eye-witness does not see anything which contradicts that;

    • when it is not disputed that the suspect is already known to the witness who claims to have recognised them when seeing them commit the crime.

D:3.13 An eye-witness identification procedure may also be held if the officer in charge of the investigation considers it would be useful.

Selecting an identification procedure

D:3.14 If, because of paragraph 3.12, an identification procedure is to be held, the suspect shall initially be offered a video identification unless:

    (a) a video identification is not practicable; or

    (b) an identification parade is both practicable and more suitable than a video identification; or

    (c) paragraph 3.16 applies.

The identification officer and the officer in charge of the investigation shall consult each other to determine which option is to be offered. An identification parade may not be practicable because of factors relating to the witnesses, such as their number, state of health, availability and travelling requirements. A video identification would normally be more suitable if it could be arranged and completed sooner than an identification parade. Before an option is offered the suspect must also be reminded of their entitlement to have free legal advice, see Code C, paragraph 6.5.

D:3.15 A suspect who refuses the identification procedure first offered shall be asked to state their reason for refusing and may get advice from their solicitor and/or if present, their appropriate adult. The suspect, solicitor and/or appropriate adult shall be allowed to make representations about why another procedure should be used. A record should be made of the reasons for refusal and any representations made. After considering any reasons given, and representations made, the identification officer shall, if appropriate, arrange for the suspect to be offered an alternative which the officer considers suitable and practicable. If the officer decides it is not suitable and practicable to offer an alternative identification procedure, the reasons for that decision shall be recorded.

D:3.16 A group identification may initially be offered if the officer in charge of the investigation considers it is more suitable than a video identification or an identification parade and the identification officer considers it practicable to arrange.

Notice to suspect

D:3.17 Unless paragraph 3.20 applies, before a video identification, an identification parade or **A-123** group identification is arranged, the following shall be explained to the suspect:

    (i) the purposes of the video identification, identification parade or group identification;

    (ii) their entitlement to free legal advice; see Code C, paragraph 6.5;

    (iii) the procedures for holding it, including their right to have a solicitor or friend present;

    (iv) that they do not have to consent to or co-operate in a video identification, identification parade or group identification;

    (v) that if they do not consent to, and co-operate in, a video identification, identification parade or group identification, their refusal may be given in evidence in any subsequent trial and police may proceed covertly without their consent or make other arrangements to test whether a witness can identify them, see paragraph 3.21;

    (vi) whether, for the purposes of the video identification procedure, images of them have previously been obtained, see paragraph 3.20, and if so, that they may co-operate in providing further, suitable images to be used instead;

    (vii) if appropriate, the special arrangements for juveniles;

    (viii) if appropriate, the special arrangements for mentally disordered or otherwise mentally vulnerable people;

    (ix) that if they significantly alter their appearance between being offered an identification procedure and any attempt to hold an identification procedure, this may be given in evidence if the case comes to trial, and the identification officer may then consider other forms of identification, see paragraph 3.21 and *Note 3C*;

    (x) that a moving image or photograph may be taken of them when they attend for any identification procedure;

    (xi) whether, before their identity became known, the witness was shown photographs, a computerised or artist's composite likeness or similar likeness or image by the police, see *Note 3B*;

    (xii) that if they change their appearance before an identification parade, it may not be practicable to arrange one on the day or subsequently and, because of the appearance change, the identification officer may consider alternative methods of identification, see *Note 3C*;

    (xiii) that they or their solicitor will be provided with details of the description of the suspect as first given by any witnesses who are to attend the video identification, identification parade, group identification or confrontation, see paragraph 3.1.

D:3.18 This information must also be recorded in a written notice handed to the suspect. The suspect must be given a reasonable opportunity to read the notice, after which, they should be asked to sign a second copy to indicate if they are willing to co-operate with the making of a video or take part in the identification parade or group identification. The signed copy shall be retained by the identification officer.

D:3.19 The duties of the identification officer under paragraphs 3.17 and 3.18 may be performed by the custody officer or other officer not involved in the investigation if:

    (a) it is proposed to release the suspect in order that an identification procedure can be arranged and carried out and an inspector is not available to act as the identification officer, see paragraph 3.11, before the suspect leaves the station; or

    (b) it is proposed to keep the suspect in police detention whilst the procedure is arranged and carried out and waiting for an inspector to act as the identification officer, see paragraph 3.11, would cause unreasonable delay to the investigation.

The officer concerned shall inform the identification officer of the action taken and give them the signed copy of the notice. See *Note 3C*.

D:3.20 If the identification officer and officer in charge of the investigation suspect, on reasonable grounds that if the suspect was given the information and notice as in paragraphs 3.17 and 3.18, they would then take steps to avoid being seen by a witness in any identification procedure, the identification officer may arrange for images of the suspect suitable for use in a video identification procedure to be obtained before giving the information and notice. If suspect's [*sic*] images are obtained in these circumstances, the suspect may, for the purposes of a video identification procedure, co-operate in providing new images which if suitable, would be used instead, see paragraph 3.17(vi).

(c) Cases when the suspect is known but not available

A-124   D:3.21 When a known suspect is not available or has ceased to be available, see paragraph 3.4, the identification officer may make arrangements for a video identification (see Annex A). If necessary, the identification officer may follow the video identification procedures but using still images. Any suitable moving or still images may be used and these may be obtained covertly if necessary. Alternatively, the identification officer may make arrangements for a group identification. See *Note 3D*. These provisions may also be applied to juveniles where the consent of their parent or guardian is either refused or reasonable efforts to obtain that consent have failed (see paragraph 2.12).

    D:3.22 Any covert activity should be strictly limited to that necessary to test the ability of the witness to identify the suspect.

D:3.23 The identification officer may arrange for the suspect to be confronted by the witness if none of the options referred to in paragraphs 3.5 to 3.10 or 3.21 are practicable. A "confrontation" is when the suspect is directly confronted by the witness. A confrontation does not require the suspect's consent. Confrontations must be carried out in accordance with Annex D.

D:3.24 Requirements for information to be given to, or sought from, a suspect or for the suspect to be given an opportunity to view images before they are shown to a witness, do not apply if the suspect's lack of co-operation prevents the necessary action.

(d) Documentation

D:3.25 A record shall be made of the video identification, identification parade, group identification or confrontation on forms provided for the purpose. **A-125**

D:3.26 If the identification officer considers it is not practicable to hold a video identification or identification parade requested by the suspect, the reasons shall be recorded and explained to the suspect.

D:3.27 A record shall be made of a person's failure or refusal to co-operate in a video identification, identification parade or group identification and, if applicable, of the grounds for obtaining images in accordance with paragraph 3.20.

(e) Showing films and photographs of incidents and information released to the media

D:3.28 Nothing in this code inhibits showing films, photographs or other images to the public **A-126** through the national or local media, or to police officers for the purposes of recognition and tracing suspects. However, when such material is shown to obtain evidence of recognition, the procedures in Part B will apply. See *Note 3AA*.

D:3.29 When a broadcast or publication is made, see paragraph 3.28, a copy of the relevant material released to the media for the purposes of recognising or tracing the suspect, shall be kept. The suspect or their solicitor shall be allowed to view such material before any eye-witness identification procedures under paragraphs 3.5 to 3.10, 3.21 or 3.23 of Part A are carried out, provided it is practicable and would not unreasonably delay the investigation. Each eye-witness involved in the procedure shall be asked, after they have taken part, whether they have seen any film, photograph or image relating to the offence or any description of the suspect which has been broadcast or published in any national or local media or on any social networking site and if they have, they should be asked to give details of the circumstances, such as the date and place as relevant. Their replies shall be recorded. This paragraph does not affect any separate requirement under the Criminal Procedure and Investigations Act 1996 to retain material in connection with criminal investigations.

(f) Destruction and retention of photographs taken or used in eye-witness identification procedures

D:3.30 PACE, s.64A, see paragraph 5.12, provides powers to take photographs of suspects and allows these photographs to be used or disclosed only for purposes related to the prevention or detection of crime, the investigation of offences or the conduct of prosecutions by, or on behalf of, police or other law enforcement and prosecuting authorities inside and outside the United Kingdom or the enforcement of a sentence. After being so used or disclosed, they may be retained but can only be used or disclosed for the same purposes.

D:3.31 Subject to paragraph 3.33, the photographs (and all negatives and copies), of suspects not taken in accordance with the provisions in paragraph 5.12 which are taken for the purposes of, or in connection with, the identification procedures in paragraphs 3.5 to 3.10, 3.21 or 3.23 must be destroyed unless the suspect:

   (a) is charged with, or informed they may be prosecuted for, a recordable offence;
   (b) is prosecuted for a recordable offence;
   (c) is cautioned for a recordable offence or given a warning or reprimand in accordance with the Crime and Disorder Act 1998 for a recordable offence; or
   (d) gives informed consent, in writing, for the photograph or images to be retained for purposes described in paragraph 3.30.

D:3.32 When paragraph 3.31 requires the destruction of any photograph, the person must be given an opportunity to witness the destruction or to have a certificate confirming the destruction if they request one within five days of being informed that the destruction is required.

D:3.33 Nothing in paragraph 3.31 affects any separate requirement under the Criminal Procedure and Investigations Act 1996 to retain material in connection with criminal investigations.

(b) *Evidence of recognition by showing films, photographs and other images*

A-126a   D:3.34 This part of this section applies when, for the purposes of obtaining evidence of recognition, any person, including a police officer:

(a) views the image of an individual in a film, photograph or any other visual medium; and

(b) is asked whether they recognise that individual as someone who is known to them.

See *Notes 3AA* and *3G*.

D:3.35 The films, photographs and other images shall be shown on an individual basis to avoid any possibility of collusion and to provide safeguards against mistaken recognition (see *Note 3G*), the showing shall as far as possible follow the principles for video identification if the suspect is known, see Annex A, or identification by photographs if the suspect is not known, see Annex E.

D:3.36 A record of the circumstances and conditions under which the person is given an opportunity to recognise the individual must be made and the record must include:

(a) whether the person knew or was given information concerning the name or identity of any suspect;

(b) what the person has been told *before* the viewing about the offence, the person(s) depicted in the images or the offender and by whom;

(c) how and by whom the witness was asked to view the image or look at the individual;

(d) whether the viewing was alone or with others and if with others, the reason for it;

(e) the arrangements under which the person viewed the film or saw the individual and by whom those arrangements were made;

(f) whether the viewing of any images was arranged as part of a mass circulation to police and the public or for selected persons;

(g) the date time and place images were viewed or further viewed or the individual was seen;

(h) the times between which the images were viewed or the individual was seen;

(i) how the viewing of images or sighting of the individual was controlled and by whom;

(j) whether the person was familiar with the location shown in any images or the place where they saw the individual and if so, why;

(k) whether or not on this occasion, the person claims to recognise any image shown, or any individual seen, as being someone known to them, and if they do:

(i) the reason;

(ii) the words of recognition;

(iii) any expressions of doubt;

(iv) what features of the image or the individual triggered the recognition.

D:3.37 The record under paragraph 3.36 may be made by:

• the person who views the image or sees the individual and makes the recognition;

• the officer or police staff in charge of showing the images to the person or in charge of the conditions under which the person sees the individual.

Notes for guidance

A-127   D:3AA *The eye-witness identification procedures in Part A should not be used to test whether a witness can recognise a person as someone they know and would be able to give evidence of recognition along the lines that "On (describe date, time location) I saw an image of an individual who I recognised as AB." In these cases, the procedures in Part B shall apply.*

D:3A *Except for the provisions of Annex E, paragraph 1, a police officer who is a witness for the purposes of this part of the code is subject to the same principles and procedures as a civilian witness.*

D:3B *When a witness attending an identification procedure has previously been shown photographs, or been shown or provided with computerised or artist's composite likenesses, or similar likenesses or pictures, it is the officer in charge of the investigation's responsibility to make the identification officer aware of this.*

D:3C *The purpose of paragraph 3.19 is to avoid or reduce delay in arranging identification procedures by enabling the required information and warnings, see sub-paragraphs 3.17(ix) and 3.17(xii), to be given at the earliest opportunity.*

D:3D *Paragraph 3.21 would apply when a known suspect deliberately makes themselves "unavailable" in order to delay or frustrate arrangements for obtaining identification evidence. It also applies when a suspect refuses or fails to take part in a video identification, an identification parade or a group identification, or refuses or fails to take part in the only practicable options from that list. It enables any suitable images of the suspect, moving or still, which are available or can be obtained, to be used in an identification procedure. Examples include images from custody and other CCTV systems and from visually recorded interview records, see Code F, Note for Guidance 2D.*

D:3E *When it is proposed to show photographs to a witness in accordance with Annex E, it is the responsibility of the officer in charge of the investigation to confirm to the officer responsible for supervising and directing the showing, that the first description of the suspect given by that witness has been recorded. If this description has not been recorded, the procedure under Annex E must be postponed. See Annex E, paragraph 2.*

D:3F *The admissibility and value of identification evidence obtained when carrying out the procedure under paragraph 3.2 may be compromised if:*

(a) *before a person is identified, the witness's attention is specifically drawn to that person; or*

(b) *the suspect's identity becomes known before the procedure.*

D:3G *The admissibility and value of evidence of recognition obtained when carrying out the procedures in Part B may be compromised if before the person is recognised, the witness who has claimed to know them is given or is made, or becomes aware of, information about the person which was not previously known to them personally but which they have purported to rely on to support their claim that the person is in fact known to them.*

D:4 Identification by fingerprints and footwear impressions

(a) *Taking fingerprints in connection with a criminal investigation*

(a) General

D:4.1 References to "fingerprints" means any record, produced by any method, of the skin pattern and other physical characteristics or features of a person's: **A-128**

(i) fingers; or

(ii) palms.

(b) Action

D:4.2 A person's fingerprints may be taken in connection with the investigation of an offence only with their consent or if paragraph 4.3 applies. If the person is at a police station consent must be in writing.

D:4.3 PACE, s.61, provides powers to take fingerprints without consent from any person over the age of ten years:

(a) under section 61(3), from a person detained at a police station in consequence of being arrested for a recordable offence, see *Note 4A*, if they have not had their fingerprints taken in the course of the investigation of the offence unless those previously taken fingerprints are not a complete set or some or all of those fingerprints are not of sufficient quality to allow satisfactory analysis, comparison or matching;

(b) under section 61(4), from a person detained at a police station who has been charged with a recordable offence, see *Note 4A*, or informed they will be reported for such an offence if they have not had their fingerprints taken in the course of the investigation of the offence unless those previously taken fingerprints are not a complete set or some or all of those fingerprints are not of sufficient quality to allow satisfactory analysis, comparison or matching;

(c) under section 61(4A), from a person who has been bailed to appear at a court or police station if the person:

(i) has answered to bail for a person whose fingerprints were taken previously and there are reasonable grounds for believing they are not the same person; or

(ii) who has answered to bail claims to be a different person from a person whose fingerprints were previously taken;

and in either case, the court or an officer of inspector rank or above, authorises the fingerprints to be taken at the court or police station (an inspector's authority may be given in writing or orally and confirmed in writing, as soon as practicable);

(ca) under section 61(5A) from a person who has been arrested for a recordable offence and released if the person:

(i) is on bail and has not had their fingerprints taken in the course of the investigation of the offence; or

(ii) has had their fingerprints taken in the course of the investigation of the offence, but they do not constitute a complete set or some, or all, of the fingerprints are not of sufficient quality to allow satisfactory analysis, comparison or matching;

(cb) under section 61(5B) from a person not detained at a police station who has been charged with a recordable offence or informed they will be reported for such an offence if they have not had their fingerprints taken in the course of the investigation or their fingerprints have been taken in the course of the investigation of the offence, but they do not constitute a complete set or some, or all, of the fingerprints are not of sufficient quality to allow satisfactory analysis, comparison or matching;

(d) under section 61(6), from a person who has been:
  (i) convicted of a recordable offence;
  (ii) given a caution in respect of a recordable offence which, at the time of the caution, the person admitted; or
  (iii) warned or reprimanded under the Crime and Disorder Act 1998, s.65, for a recordable offence, if, since their conviction, caution, warning or reprimand their fingerprints have not been taken or their fingerprints which have been taken since then do not constitute a complete set or some, or all, of the fingerprints are not of sufficient quality to allow satisfactory analysis, comparison or matching, and in either case, an officer of inspector rank or above, is satisfied that taking the fingerprints is necessary to assist in the prevention or detection of crime and authorises the taking;
(e) under section 61(6A) from a person a constable reasonably suspects is committing or attempting to commit, or has committed or attempted to commit, any offence if either:
  • the person's name is unknown and cannot be readily ascertained by the constable; or
  • the constable has reasonable grounds for doubting whether a name given by the person is their real name; note: fingerprints taken under this power are not regarded as having been taken in the course of the investigation of an offence; [see *Note 4C*];
(f) under section 61(6D) from a person who has been convicted outside England and Wales of an offence which if committed in England and Wales would be a qualifying offence as defined by PACE, s.65A [see *Note 4AB*] if:
  (i) the person's fingerprints have not been taken previously under this power or their fingerprints have been so taken on a previous occasion but they do not constitute a complete set or some, or all, of the fingerprints are not of sufficient quality to allow satisfactory analysis, comparison or matching; and
  (ii) a police officer of inspector rank or above is satisfied that taking fingerprints is necessary to assist in the prevention or detection of crime and authorises them to be taken.

D:4.4 PACE, s.63A(4), and Sched. 2A, provide powers to:
(a) make a requirement (in accordance with Annex G) for a person to attend a police station to have their fingerprints taken in the exercise of certain powers in paragraph 4.3 above when that power applies at the time the fingerprints would be taken in accordance with the requirement; those powers are:
  (i) section 61(5A)—persons arrested for a recordable offence and released, see paragraph 4.3(ca): the requirement may not be made more than six months from the day the investigating officer was informed that the fingerprints previously taken were incomplete or below standard;
  (ii) section 61(5B)—persons charged etc. with a recordable offence, see paragraph 4.3(cb): the requirement may not be made more than six months from:
    • the day the person was charged or reported if fingerprints have not been taken since then; or
    • the day the investigating officer was informed that the fingerprints previously taken were incomplete or below standard;
  (iii) section 61(6)—person convicted, cautioned, warned or reprimanded for a recordable offence in England and Wales, see paragraph 4.3(d): where the offence for which the person was convicted etc is also a qualifying offence (see *Note 4AB*), there is no time limit for the exercise of this power; where the conviction etc. is for a recordable offence which is *not* a qualifying offence, the requirement may not be made more than two years from:
    • the day the person was convicted, cautioned, warned or reprimanded, or the day Schedule 2A comes into force (if later), if fingerprints have not been taken since then; or
    • the day an officer from the force investigating the offence was informed that the fingerprints previously taken were incomplete or below standard or the day Schedule 2A comes into force (if later);
  (v) [*sic*] section 61(6D)—a person who has been convicted of a qualifying offence (see *Note 4AB*) outside England and Wales, see paragraph 4.3(g): there is no time limit for making the requirement;
  note: a person who has had their fingerprints taken under any of the powers in section 61 mentioned in paragraph 4.3 on two occasions in relation to any offence may not be required under Schedule 2A to attend a police station for their fingerprints to be taken again under section 61 in relation to that offence, unless authorised by an officer of

inspector rank or above; the fact of the authorisation and the reasons for giving it must be recorded as soon as practicable;

    (b) arrest, without warrant, a person who fails to comply with the requirement.

D:4.5 A person's fingerprints may be taken, as above, electronically.

D:4.6 Reasonable force may be used, if necessary, to take a person's fingerprints without their consent under the powers as in paragraphs 4.3 and 4.4.

D:4.7 Before any fingerprints are taken:

    (a) without consent under any power mentioned in paragraphs 4.3 and 4.4 above, the person must be informed of:

        (i) the reason their fingerprints are to be taken;

        (ii) the power under which they are to be taken; and

        (iii) the fact that the relevant authority has been given if any power mentioned in paragraph 4.3(c), (d) or (f) applies;

    (b) with or without consent at a police station or elsewhere, the person must be informed:

        (i) that their fingerprints may be subject of a speculative search against other fingerprints, see *Note 4B*; and

        (ii) that their fingerprints may be retained in accordance with Annex F, Part (a) unless they were taken under the power mentioned in paragraph 4.3(e) when they must be destroyed after they have being [*sic*] checked (see *Note 4C*).

(c) Documentation

D:4.8A A record must be made as soon as practicable after the fingerprints are taken, of:

- the matters in paragraph 4.7(a)(i) to (iii) and the fact that the person has been informed of those matters; and
- the fact that the person has been informed of the matters in paragraph 4.7(b)(i) and (ii).

The record must be made in the person's custody record if they are detained at a police station when the fingerprints are taken.

D:4.8 If force is used, a record shall be made of the circumstances and those present.

D:4.9 [*Not used.*]

(b) *Taking fingerprints in connection with immigration enquiries*

Action

D:4.10 A person's fingerprints may be taken and retained for the purposes of immigration law **A-129** enforcement and control in accordance with powers and procedures other than under PACE and for which the UK Border Agency (not the police) are responsible. Details of these powers and procedures which are under the Immigration Act 1971, Sched. 2 and Immigration and Asylum Act 1999, s.141, including modifications to the *PACE Codes of Practice* are contained in Chapter 24 of the operational instructions and guidance manual which is published by the UK Border Agency (see *Note 4D*).

D:4.11–15 [*Not used.*]

(c) *Taking footwear impressions in connection with a criminal investigation*

(a) Action

D:4.16 Impressions of a person's footwear may be taken in connection with the investigation of an offence only with their consent or if paragraph 4.17 applies. If the person is at a police station consent must be in writing.

D:4.17 PACE, s.61A, provides power for a police officer to take footwear impressions without consent from any person over the age of ten years who is detained at a police station:

    (a) in consequence of being arrested for a recordable offence, see *Note 4A*; or if the detainee has been charged with a recordable offence, or informed they will be reported for such an offence; and

    (b) the detainee has not had an impression of their footwear taken in the course of the investigation of the offence unless the previously taken impression is not complete or is not of sufficient quality to allow satisfactory analysis, comparison or matching (whether in the case in question or generally).

D:4.18 Reasonable force may be used, if necessary, to take a footwear impression from a detainee without consent under the power in paragraph 4.17.

D:4.19 Before any footwear impression is taken with, or without, consent as above, the person must be informed:

    (a) of the reason the impression is to be taken;

    (b) that the impression may be retained and may be subject of a speculative search against other impressions, see *Note 4B*, unless destruction of the impression is required in accordance with Annex F, Part (a); and

    (c) that if their footwear impressions are required to be destroyed, they may witness their destruction as provided for in Annex F, Part (a).

(b) Documentation

D:4.20 A record must be made as soon as possible, of the reason for taking a person's footwear impressions without consent. If force is used, a record shall be made of the circumstances and those present.

D:4.21 A record shall be made when a person has been informed under the terms of paragraph 4.19(b), of the possibility that their footwear impressions may be subject of a speculative search.

Notes for guidance

D:4A *References to "recordable offences" in this code relate to those offences for which convictions, cautions, reprimands and warnings may be recorded in national police records: see PACE, s.27(4). The recordable offences current at the time when this code was prepared, are any offences which carry a sentence of imprisonment on conviction (irrespective of the period, or the age of the offender or actual sentence passed) as well as the non-imprisonable offences under the Vagrancy Act 1824, ss.3 and 4 (begging and persistent begging), the Street Offences Act 1959, s.1 (loitering or soliciting for purposes of prostitution), the Road Traffic Act 1988, s.25 (tampering with motor vehicles), the Criminal Justice and Public Order Act 1994, s.167 (touting for car hire services) and others listed in the National Police Records (Recordable Offences) Regulations 2000 as amended.*

D:4AB *A qualifying offence is one of the offences specified in PACE, s.65A. These indictable offences which concern the use or threat of violence or unlawful force against persons, sexual offences and offences against children include, for example, murder, manslaughter, false imprisonment, kidnapping and other offences such as:*

    • *sections 4, 16, 18, 20 to 24 or 47 of the Offences Against the Person Act 1861;*

    • *sections 16 to 18 of the Firearms Act 1968;*

    • *sections 9 or 10 of the Theft Act 1968 or under section 12A of that Act involving an accident which caused a person's death;*

    • *section 1 of the Criminal Damage Act 1971 required to be charged as arson;*

    • *section 1 of the Protection of Children Act 1978 and;*

    • *sections 1 to 19, 25, 26, 30 to 41, 47 to 50, 52, 53, 57 to 59, 61 to 67, 69 and 70 of the Sexual Offences Act 2003.*

D:4B *Fingerprints, footwear impressions or a DNA sample (and the information derived from it) taken from a person arrested on suspicion of being involved in a recordable offence, or charged with such an offence, or informed they will be reported for such an offence, may be subject of a speculative search. This means the fingerprints, footwear impressions or DNA sample may be checked against other fingerprints, footwear impressions and DNA records held by, or on behalf of, the police and other law enforcement authorities in, or outside, the UK, or held in connection with, or as a result of, an investigation of an offence inside or outside the UK. Fingerprints, footwear impressions and samples taken from a person suspected of committing a recordable offence but not arrested, charged or informed they will be reported for it, may be subject to a speculative search only if the person consents in writing. The following is an example of a basic form of words:*

> *"I consent to my fingerprints, footwear impressions and DNA sample and information derived from it being retained and used only for purposes related to the prevention and detection of a crime, the investigation of an offence or the conduct of a prosecution either nationally or internationally.*
>
> *I understand that my fingerprints, footwear impressions or DNA sample may be checked against other fingerprint, footwear impressions and DNA records held by or on behalf of relevant law enforcement authorities, either nationally or internationally.*
>
> *I understand that once I have given my consent for my fingerprints, footwear impressions or DNA sample to be retained and used I cannot withdraw this consent."*

See Annex F regarding the retention and use of fingerprints and footwear impressions taken with consent for elimination purposes.

D:4C *The power under section 61(6A) of PACE described in paragraph 4.3(e) allows fingerprints of a suspect who has not been arrested to be taken in connection with any offence (whether recordable or not) using a mobile device and then checked on the street against the database containing the national fingerprint collection. Fingerprints taken under this power cannot be retained after they have been checked. The results may make an arrest for the suspected offence based on the name condition unnecessary (see code G, paragraph 2.9(a)) and enable the offence to be disposed of without arrest, for example, by summons/charging by post, penalty notice or words of advice. If arrest for a non-recordable offence is necessary for any other reasons, this power may also be exercised at the station. Before the power is exercised, the officer should:*

- *inform the person of the nature of the suspected offence and why they are suspected of committing it;*
- *give them a reasonable opportunity to establish their real name before deciding that their name is unknown and cannot be readily ascertained or that there are reasonable grounds to doubt that a name they have given is their real name;*
- *as applicable, inform the person of the reason why their name is not known and cannot be readily ascertained or of the grounds for doubting that a name they have given is their real name, including, for example, the reason why a particular document the person has produced to verify their real name, is not sufficient.*

D:4D *Powers to take fingerprints without consent for immigration purposes are given to police and immigration officers under the:*

(a) *Immigration Act 1971, Sched. 2, para. 18(2), when it is reasonably necessary for the purposes of identifying a person detained under the Immigration Act 1971, Sched. 2, para. 16 (detention of person liable to examination or removal), and*

(b) *Immigration and Asylum Act 1999, s.141(7) when a person:*
- *fails without reasonable excuse to produce, on arrival, a valid passport with a photograph or some other document satisfactorily establishing their identity and nationality;*
- *is refused entry to the UK but is temporarily admitted if an immigration officer reasonably suspects the person might break a residence or reporting condition;*
- *is subject to directions for removal from the UK;*
- *has been arrested under the Immigration Act 1971, Sched. 2, para. 17;*
- *has made a claim for asylum;*
- *is a dependant of any of the above.*

The Immigration and Asylum Act 1999, s.142(3), also gives police and immigration officers power to arrest without warrant a person who fails to comply with a requirement imposed by the Secretary of State to attend a specified place for fingerprinting.

D:5 Examinations to establish identity and the taking of photographs

(a) *Detainees at police stations*

(a) Searching or examination of detainees at police stations

D:5.1 PACE, s.54A(1), allows a detainee at a police station to be searched or examined or both, to **A-130** establish:

(a) whether they have any marks, features or injuries that would tend to identify them as a person involved in the commission of an offence and to photograph any identifying marks, see paragraph 5.5; or

(b) their identity, see *Note 5A.*

A person detained at a police station to be searched under a stop and search power, see Code A, is not a detainee for the purposes of these powers.

D:5.2 A search and/or examination to find marks under section 54A(1)(a) may be carried out without the detainee's consent, see paragraph 2.12, only if authorised by an officer of at least inspector rank when consent has been withheld or it is not practicable to obtain consent, see *Note 5D.*

D:5.3 A search or examination to establish a suspect's identity under section 54A(1)(b) may be carried out without the detainee's consent, see paragraph 2.12, only if authorised by an officer of at least inspector rank when the detainee has refused to identify themselves or the authorising officer has reasonable grounds for suspecting the person is not who they claim to be.

D:5.4 Any marks that assist in establishing the detainee's identity, or their identification as a person involved in the commission of an offence, are identifying marks. Such marks may be photographed with the detainee's consent, see paragraph 2.12; or without their consent if it is withheld or it is not practicable to obtain it, see *Note 5D.*

D:5.5 A detainee may only be searched, examined and photographed under section 54A, by a police officer of the same sex.

D:5.6 Any photographs of identifying marks, taken under section 54A, may be used or disclosed only for purposes related to the prevention or detection of crime, the investigation of offences or the conduct of prosecutions by, or on behalf of, police or other law enforcement and prosecuting authorities inside, and outside, the UK. After being so used or disclosed, the photograph may be retained but must not be used or disclosed except for these purposes, see *Note 5B.*

D:5.7 The powers, as in paragraph 5.1, do not affect any separate requirement under the Criminal Procedure and Investigations Act 1996 to retain material in connection with criminal investigations.

D:5.8 Authority for the search and/or examination for the purposes of paragraphs 5.2 and 5.3

may be given orally or in writing. If given orally, the authorising officer must confirm it in writing as soon as practicable. A separate authority is required for each purpose which applies.

D:5.9 If it is established a person is unwilling to co-operate sufficiently to enable a search and/or examination to take place or a suitable photograph to be taken, an officer may use reasonable force to:

> (a) search and/or examine a detainee without their consent; and
> (b) photograph any identifying marks without their consent.

D:5.10 The thoroughness and extent of any search or examination carried out in accordance with the powers in section 54A must be no more than the officer considers necessary to achieve the required purpose. Any search or examination which involves the removal of more than the person's outer clothing shall be conducted in accordance with Code C, Annex A, paragraph 11.

D:5.11 An intimate search may not be carried out under the powers in section 54A.

(b) Photographing detainees at police stations and other persons elsewhere than at a police station

A-131   D:5.12 Under PACE, s.64A, an officer may photograph:

> (a) any person whilst they are detained at a police station; and
> (b) any person who is elsewhere than at a police station and who has been:
>> (i) arrested by a constable for an offence;
>> (ii) taken into custody by a constable after being arrested for an offence by a person other than a constable;
>> (iii) made subject to a requirement to wait with a community support officer under paragraph 2(3) or (3B) of Schedule 4 to the Police Reform Act 2002;
>> (iiia) given a direction by a constable under section 27 of the Violent Crime Reduction Act 2006;
>> (iv) given a penalty notice by a constable in uniform under Chapter 1 of Part 1 of the Criminal Justice and Police Act 2001, a penalty notice by a constable under section 444A of the Education Act 1996, or a fixed penalty notice by a constable in uniform under section 54 of the Road Traffic Offenders Act 1988;
>> (v) given a notice in relation to a relevant fixed penalty offence (within the meaning of paragraph 1 of Schedule 4 to the Police Reform Act 2002) by a community support officer by virtue of a designation applying that paragraph to him;
>> (vi) given a notice in relation to a relevant fixed penalty offence (within the meaning of paragraph 1 of Schedule 5 to the Police Reform Act 2002) by an accredited person by virtue of accreditation specifying that that paragraph applies to him; or
>> (vii) given a direction to leave and not return to a specified location for up to 48 hours by a police constable (under section 27 of the Violent Crime Reduction Act 2006).

D:5.12A Photographs taken under PACE, s.64A:

> (a) may be taken with the person's consent, or without their consent if consent is withheld or it is not practicable to obtain their consent, see *Note 5E*; and
> (b) may be used or disclosed only for purposes related to the prevention or detection of crime, the investigation of offences or the conduct of prosecutions by, or on behalf of, police or other law enforcement and prosecuting authorities inside and outside the United Kingdom or the enforcement of any sentence or order made by a court when dealing with an offence. After being so used or disclosed, they may be retained but can only be used or disclosed for the same purposes. See *Note 5B*.

D:5.13 The officer proposing to take a detainee's photograph may, for this purpose, require the person to remove any item or substance worn on, or over, all, or any part of, their head or face. If they do not comply with such a requirement, the officer may remove the item or substance.

D:5.14 If it is established the detainee is unwilling to co-operate sufficiently to enable a suitable photograph to be taken and it is not reasonably practicable to take the photograph covertly, an officer may use reasonable force, see *Note 5F*:

> (a) to take their photograph without their consent; and
> (b) for the purpose of taking the photograph, remove any item or substance worn on, or over, all, or any part of, the person's head or face which they have failed to remove when asked.

D:5.15 For the purposes of this code, a photograph may be obtained without the person's consent by making a copy of an image of them taken at any time on a camera system installed anywhere in the police station.

(c) Information to be given

A-132   D:5.16 When a person is searched, examined or photographed under the provisions as in paragraph 5.1 and 5.12, or their photograph obtained as in paragraph 5.15, they must be informed of the:

    (a) purpose of the search, examination or photograph;

    (b) grounds on which the relevant authority, if applicable, has been given; and

    (c) purposes for which the photograph may be used, disclosed or retained.

This information must be given before the search or examination commences or the photograph is taken, except if the photograph is:

    (i) to be taken covertly;

    (ii) obtained as in paragraph 5.15, in which case the person must be informed as soon as practicable after the photograph is taken or obtained.

(d) Documentation

D:5.17 A record must be made when a detainee is searched, examined, or a photograph of the person, or any identifying marks found on them, are [*sic*] taken. The record must include the:

    (a) identity, subject to paragraph 2.18, of the officer carrying out the search, examination or taking the photograph;

    (b) purpose of the search, examination or photograph and the outcome;

    (c) detainee's consent to the search, examination or photograph, or the reason the person was searched, examined or photographed without consent;

    (d) giving of any authority as in paragraphs 5.2 and 5.3, the grounds for giving it and the authorising officer.

D:5.18 If force is used when searching, examining or taking a photograph in accordance with this section, a record shall be made of the circumstances and those present.

(b) *Persons at police stations not detained*

D:5.19 When there are reasonable grounds for suspecting the involvement of a person in a **A-133** criminal offence, but that person is at a police station *voluntarily* and not detained, the provisions of paragraphs 5.1 to 5.18 should apply, subject to the modifications in the following paragraphs.

D:5.20 References to the "person being detained" and to the powers mentioned in paragraph 5.1 which apply only to detainees at police stations shall be omitted.

D:5.21 Force may not be used to:

    (a) search and/or examine the person to:

        (i) discover whether they have any marks that would tend to identify them as a person involved in the commission of an offence; or

        (ii) establish their identity, see *Note 5A*;

    (b) take photographs of any identifying marks, see paragraph 5.4; or

    (c) take a photograph of the person.

D:5.22 Subject to paragraph 5.24, the photographs of persons or of their identifying marks which are not taken in accordance with the provisions mentioned in paragraphs 5.1 or 5.12, must be destroyed (together with any negatives and copies) unless the person:

    (a) is charged with, or informed they may be prosecuted for, a recordable offence;

    (b) is prosecuted for a recordable offence;

    (c) is cautioned for a recordable offence or given a warning or reprimand in accordance with the Crime and Disorder Act 1998 for a recordable offence; or

    (d) gives informed consent, in writing, for the photograph or image to be retained as in paragraph 5.6.

D:5.23 When paragraph 5.22 requires the destruction of any photograph, the person must be given an opportunity to witness the destruction or to have a certificate confirming the destruction provided they so request the certificate within five days of being informed the destruction is required.

D:5.24 Nothing in paragraph 5.22 affects any separate requirement under the Criminal Procedure and Investigations Act 1996 to retain material in connection with criminal investigations.

Notes for guidance

D:5A *The conditions under which fingerprints may be taken to assist in establishing a person's identity, are* **A-134** *described in section 4.*

D:5B *Examples of purposes related to the prevention or detection of crime, the investigation of offences or the conduct of prosecutions include:*

    (a) *checking the photograph against other photographs held in records or in connection with, or as a result of, an investigation of an offence to establish whether the person is liable to arrest for other offences;*

(b) *when the person is arrested at the same time as other people, or at a time when it is likely that other people will be arrested, using the photograph to help establish who was arrested, at what time and where;*

(c) *when the real identity of the person is not known and cannot be readily ascertained or there are reasonable grounds for doubting a name and other personal details given by the person are their real name and personal details; in these circumstances, using or disclosing the photograph to help to establish or verify their real identity or determine whether they are liable to arrest for some other offence, e.g. by checking it against other photographs held in records or in connection with, or as a result of, an investigation of an offence;*

(d) *when it appears any identification procedure in section 3 may need to be arranged for which the person's photograph would assist;*

(e) *when the person's release without charge may be required, and if the release is:*

(i) *on bail to appear at a police station, using the photograph to help verify the person's identity when they answer their bail and if the person does not answer their bail, to assist in arresting them; or*

(ii) *without bail, using the photograph to help verify their identity or assist in locating them for the purposes of serving them with a summons to appear at court in criminal proceedings;*

(f) *when the person has answered to bail at a police station and there are reasonable grounds for doubting they are the person who was previously granted bail, using the photograph to help establish or verify their identity;*

(g) *when the person arrested on a warrant claims to be a different person from the person named on the warrant and a photograph would help to confirm or disprove their claim;*

(h) *when the person has been charged with, reported for, or convicted of, a recordable offence and their photograph is not already on record as a result of (a) to (f) or their photograph is on record but their appearance has changed since it was taken and the person has not yet been released or brought before a court.*

D:5C *There is no power to arrest a person convicted of a recordable offence solely to take their photograph. The power to take photographs in this section applies only where the person is in custody as a result of the exercise of another power, e.g. arrest for fingerprinting under PACE, s.27.*

D:5D *Examples of when it would not be practicable to obtain a detainee's consent, see paragraph 2.12, to a search, examination or the taking of a photograph of an identifying mark include:*

(a) *when the person is drunk or otherwise unfit to give consent;*

(b) *when there are reasonable grounds to suspect that if the person became aware a search or examination was to take place or an identifying mark was to be photographed, they would take steps to prevent this happening, e.g. by violently resisting, covering or concealing the mark etc and it would not otherwise be possible to carry out the search or examination or to photograph any identifying mark;*

(c) *in the case of a juvenile, if the parent or guardian cannot be contacted in sufficient time to allow the search or examination to be carried out or the photograph to be taken.*

D:5E *Examples of when it would not be practicable to obtain the person's consent, see paragraph 2.12, to a photograph being taken include:*

(a) *when the person is drunk or otherwise unfit to give consent;*

(b) *when there are reasonable grounds to suspect that if the person became aware a photograph, suitable to be used or disclosed for the use and disclosure described in paragraph 5.6, was to be taken, they would take steps to prevent it being taken, e.g. by violently resisting, covering or distorting their face etc, and it would not otherwise be possible to take a suitable photograph;*

(c) *when, in order to obtain a suitable photograph, it is necessary to take it covertly; and*

(d) *in the case of a juvenile, if the parent or guardian cannot be contacted in sufficient time to allow the photograph to be taken.*

D:5F *The use of reasonable force to take the photograph of a suspect elsewhere than at a police station must be carefully considered. In order to obtain a suspect's consent and co-operation to remove an item of religious headwear to take their photograph, a constable should consider whether in the circumstances of the situation the removal of the headwear and the taking of the photograph should be by an officer of the same sex as the person. It would be appropriate for these actions to be conducted out of public view.*

D:6 Identification by body samples and impressions

(a) *General*

D:6.1 References to: **A-135**

(a) an "intimate sample" mean a dental impression or sample of blood, semen or any other tissue fluid, urine, or pubic hair, or a swab taken from any part of a person's genitals or from a person's body orifice other than the mouth;

(b) a "non-intimate sample" means:

    (i) a sample of hair, other than pubic hair, which includes hair plucked with the root, see Note 6A;

    (ii) a sample taken from a nail or from under a nail;

    (iii) a swab taken from any part of a person's body other than a part from which a swab taken would be an intimate sample;

    (iv) saliva;

    (v) a skin impression which means any record, other than a fingerprint, which is a record, in any form and produced by any method, of the skin pattern and other physical characteristics or features of the whole, or any part of, a person's foot or of any other part of their body.

(b) *Action*

(a) Intimate samples

D:6.2 PACE, s.62, provides that intimate samples may be taken under: **A-136**

(a) section 62(1), from a person in police detention only:

    (i) if a police officer of inspector rank or above has reasonable grounds to believe such an impression or sample will tend to confirm or disprove the suspect's involvement in a recordable offence, see *Note 4A*, and gives authorisation for a sample to be taken; and

    (ii) with the suspect's written consent;

(b) section 62(1A), from a person not in police detention but from whom two or more non-intimate samples have been taken in the course of an investigation of an offence and the samples, though suitable, have proved insufficient if:

    (i) a police officer of inspector rank or above authorises it to be taken; and

    (ii) the person concerned gives their written consent; see *Notes 6B* and *6C*;

(c) section 62(2A), from a person convicted outside England and Wales of an offence which if committed in England and Wales would be qualifying offence [*sic*] as defined by PACE, s.65A (see *Note 4AB*) from whom two or more non-intimate samples taken under section 63(3E) (see paragraph 6.6(h)) have proved insufficient if:

    (i) a police officer of inspector rank or above is satisfied that taking the sample is necessary to assist in the prevention or detection of crime and authorises it to be taken; and

    (ii) the person concerned gives their written consent.

D:6.2A PACE, s.63A(4), and Sched. 2A, provide powers [*sic*] to:

(a) [*sic*] make a requirement (in accordance with Annex G) for a person to attend a police station to have an intimate sample taken in the exercise of one of the following powers in paragraph 6.2 when that power applies at the time the sample is to be taken in accordance with the requirement or after the person's arrest if they fail to comply with the requirement:

    (i) section 62(1A)—persons from whom two or more non-intimate samples have been taken and proved to be insufficient, see paragraph 6.2(b); there is no time limit for making the requirement;

    (ii) section 62(2A)—persons convicted outside England and Wales from whom two or more non-intimate samples taken under section 63(3E) (see paragraph 6.6(h)) have proved insufficient, see paragraph 6.2(c); there is no time limit for making the requirement.

D:6.3 Before a suspect is asked to provide an intimate sample, they must be:

(a) informed:

    (i) of the reason, including the nature of the suspected offence (except if taken under paragraph 6.2(c) from a person convicted outside England and Wales;

    (ii) that authorisation has been given and the provisions under which given;

    (iii) that a sample taken at a police station may be subject of a speculative search;

(b) warned that if they refuse without good cause their refusal may harm their case if it comes to trial, see *Note 6D*. If the suspect is in police detention and not legally represented, they must also be reminded of their entitlement to have free legal advice, see Code C, paragraph 6.5, and the reminder noted in the custody record. If paragraph 6.2(b) applies and the person is attending a station voluntarily, their entitlement to free legal advice as in Code C, paragraph 3.21 shall be explained to them.

D:6.4 Dental impressions may only be taken by a registered dentist. Other intimate samples, except for samples of urine, may only be taken by a registered medical practitioner or registered nurse or registered paramedic.

(b) Non-intimate samples

D:6.5 A non-intimate sample may be taken from a detainee only with their written consent or if paragraph 6.6 applies.

D:6.6 A non-intimate sample may be taken from a person without the appropriate consent in the following circumstances:

(a) under section 63(2A) from a person who is in police detention as a consequence of being arrested for a recordable offence and who has not had a non-intimate sample of the same type and from the same part of the body taken in the course of the investigation of the offence by the police or they have had such a sample taken but it proved insufficient;

(b) under section 63(3) from a person who is being held in custody by the police on the authority of a court if an officer of at least the rank of inspector authorises it to be taken; an authorisation may be given:

(i) if the authorising officer has reasonable grounds for suspecting the person of involvement in a recordable offence and for believing that the sample will tend to confirm or disprove that involvement; and

(ii) in writing or orally and confirmed in writing, as soon as practicable; but an authorisation may not be given to take from the same part of the body a further non-intimate sample consisting of a skin impression unless the previously taken impression proved insufficient;

(c) under section 63(3ZA) from a person who has been arrested for a recordable offence and released if the person:

(i) is on bail and has not had a sample of the same type and from the same part of the body taken in the course of the investigation of the offence; or

(ii) has had such a sample taken in the course of the investigation of the offence, but it proved unsuitable or insufficient;

(d) under section 63(3A), from a person (whether or not in police detention or held in custody by the police on the authority of a court) who has been charged with a recordable offence or informed they will be reported for such an offence if the person:

(i) has not had a non-intimate sample taken from them in the course of the investigation of the offence;

(ii) has had a sample so taken, but it proved unsuitable or insufficient, see *Note 6B*; or

(iii) has had a sample taken in the course of the investigation of the offence and the sample has been destroyed and in proceedings relating to that offence there is a dispute as to whether a DNA profile relevant to the proceedings was derived from the destroyed sample;

(e) under section 63(3B), from a person who has been:

(i) convicted of a recordable offence;

(ii) given a caution in respect of a recordable offence which, at the time of the caution, the person admitted; or

(iii) warned or reprimanded under the Crime and Disorder Act 1998, s.65, for a recordable offence,

if, since their conviction, caution, warning or reprimand a non-intimate sample has not been taken from them or a sample which has been taken since then has proved to be unsuitable or insufficient and in either case, an officer of inspector rank or above, is satisfied that taking the fingerprints [*sic*] is necessary to assist in the prevention or detection of crime and authorises the taking;

(f) under section 63(3C) from a person to whom section 2 of the Criminal Evidence (Amendment) Act 1997 applies (persons detained following acquittal on grounds of insanity or finding of unfitness to plead);

(g) under section 63(3E) from a person who has been convicted outside England and Wales of an offence which if committed in England and Wales would be a qualifying offence as defined by PACE, s.65A (see *Note 4AB*) if:

    (i) a non-intimate sample has not been taken previously under this power or unless a sample was so taken but was unsuitable or insufficient; and

    (ii) a police officer of inspector rank or above is satisfied that taking a sample is necessary to assist in the prevention or detection of crime and authorises it to be taken.

D:6.6A PACE, s.63A(4), and Sched. 2A, provide powers to:

(a) make a requirement (in accordance with Annex G) for a person to attend a police station to have a non-intimate sample taken in the exercise of one of the following powers in paragraph 6.6 when that power applies at the time the sample would be taken in accordance with the requirement:

    (i) section 63(3ZA)—persons arrested for a recordable offence and released, see paragraph 6.6(c); the requirement may not be made more than six months from the day the investigating officer was informed that the sample previously taken was unsuitable or insufficient;

    (ii) section 63(3A)—persons charged etc. with a recordable offence, see paragraph 6.6(d); the requirement may not be made more than six months from:

- the day the person was charged or reported if a sample has not been taken since then; or
- the day the investigating officer was informed that the sample previously taken was unsuitable or insufficient;

    (iii) section 63(3B)—person convicted, cautioned, warned or reprimanded for a recordable offence in England and Wales, see paragraph 6.6(e); where the offence for which the person was convicted etc is also a qualifying offence (see *Note 4AB*), there is no time limit for the exercise of this power; where the conviction etc was for a recordable offence that is not a qualifying offence, the requirement may not be made more than two years from:

- the day the person was convicted, cautioned, warned or reprimanded, or the day Schedule 2A comes into force (if later), if a samples [*sic*] has not been taken since then; or
- the day an officer from the force investigating the offence was informed that the sample previously taken was unsuitable or insufficient or the day Schedule 2A comes into force (if later);

    (iv) section 63(3E)—a person who has been convicted of qualifying offence (see *Note 4AB*) outside England and Wales, see paragraph 6.6(h); there is no time limit for making the requirement;

    note: a person who has had a non-intimate sample taken under any of the powers in section 63 mentioned in paragraph 6.6 on two occasions in relation to any offence may not be required under Schedule 2A to attend a police station for a sample to be taken again under section 63 in relation to that offence, unless authorised by an officer of inspector rank or above; the fact of the authorisation and the reasons for giving it must be recorded as soon as practicable;

(b) arrest, without warrant, a person who fails to comply with the requirement.

D:6.7 Reasonable force may be used, if necessary, to take a non-intimate sample from a person without their consent under the powers mentioned in paragraph 6.6.

D:6.8 Before any non-intimate sample is taken:

(a) without consent under any power mentioned in paragraphs 6.6 and 6.6A, the person must be informed of:

    (i) the reason for taking the sample;

    (ii) the power under which the sample is to be taken;

    (iii) the fact that the relevant authority has been given if any power mentioned in paragraph 6.6(b), (e) or (h) applies;

(b) with or without consent at a police station or elsewhere, the person must be informed:

    (i) that their sample or information derived from it may be subject of a speculative search against other samples and information derived from them, see *Note 6E*; and

    (ii) that their sample and the information derived from it may be retained in accordance with Annex F, Part (a).

D:6.9 When clothing needs to be removed in circumstances likely to cause embarrassment to the person, no person of the opposite sex who is not a registered medical practitioner or registered health care professional shall be present (unless in the case of a juvenile, mentally disordered or mentally vulnerable person, that person specifically requests the presence of an appropriate adult of the opposite sex who is readily available), nor shall anyone whose presence is unnecessary. However, in the case of a juvenile, this is subject to the overriding proviso that such a removal of clothing may take place in the absence of the appropriate adult only if the juvenile signifies in their presence, that they prefer the adult's absence and they agree.

(c) Documentation

D:6.10 A record must be made as soon as practicable after the sample is taken of:
- the matters in paragraph 6.8(a)(i) to (iii) and the fact that the person has been informed of those matters; and
- the fact that the person has been informed of the matters in paragraph 6.8(b)(i) and (ii).

D:6.10A If force is used, a record shall be made of the circumstances and those present.

D:6.11 A record must be made of a warning given as required by paragraph 6.3.

Notes for guidance

A-138   D:6A *When hair samples are taken for the purpose of DNA analysis (rather than for other purposes such as making a visual match), the suspect should be permitted a reasonable choice as to what part of the body the hairs are taken from. When hairs are plucked, they should be plucked individually, unless the suspect prefers otherwise and no more should be plucked than the person taking them reasonably considers necessary for a sufficient sample.*

(a) *An insufficient sample is one which is not sufficient either in quantity or quality to provide information for a particular form of analysis, such as DNA analysis. A sample may also be insufficient if enough information cannot be obtained from it by analysis because of loss, destruction, damage or contamination of the sample or as a result of an earlier, unsuccessful attempt at analysis.*

(b) *An unsuitable sample is one which, by its nature, is not suitable for a particular form of analysis.*

D:6C *Nothing in paragraph 6.2 prevents intimate samples being taken for elimination purposes with the consent of the person concerned but the provisions of paragraph 2.12 relating to the role of the appropriate adult, should be applied. Paragraph 6.2(b) does not, however, apply where the non-intimate samples were previously taken under the Terrorism Act 2000, Sched. 8, para. 10.*

D:6D *In warning a person who is asked to provide an intimate sample as in paragraph 6.3, the following form of words may be used:*

"*You do not have to provide this sample/allow this swab or impression to be taken, but I must warn you that if you refuse without good cause, your refusal may harm your case if it comes to trial.*"

D:6E *Fingerprints or a DNA sample and the information derived from it taken from a person arrested on suspicion of being involved in a recordable offence, or charged with such an offence, or informed they will be reported for such an offence, may be subject of a speculative search. This means they may be checked against other fingerprints and DNA records held by, or on behalf of, the police and other law enforcement authorities in or outside the UK or held in connection with, or as a result of, an investigation of an offence inside or outside the UK. Fingerprints and samples taken from any other person, e.g. a person suspected of committing a recordable offence but who has not been arrested, charged or informed they will be reported for it, may be subject to a speculative search only if the person consents in writing to their fingerprints being subject of such a search. The following is an example of a basic form of words:*

"*I consent to my fingerprints/DNA sample and information derived from it being retained and used only for purposes related to the prevention and detection of a crime, the investigation of an offence or the conduct of a prosecution either nationally or internationally.*

I understand that this sample may be checked against other fingerprint/DNA records held by or on behalf of relevant law enforcement authorities, either nationally or internationally.

I understand that once I have given my consent for the sample to be retained and used I cannot withdraw this consent."

See Annex F regarding the retention and use of fingerprints and samples taken with consent for elimination purposes.

D:6F *Samples of urine and non-intimate samples taken in accordance with sections 63B and 63C of PACE may not be used for identification purposes in accordance with this code. See Code C note for guidance 17D.*

ANNEX A

Video identification

(a) *General*

D:1 The arrangements for obtaining and ensuring the availability of a suitable set of images to be **A-139** used in a video identification must be the responsibility of an identification officer, who has no direct involvement with the case.

D:2 The set of images must include the suspect and at least eight other people who, so far as possible, resemble the suspect in age, general appearance and position in life. Only one suspect shall appear in any set unless there are two suspects of roughly similar appearance, in which case they may be shown together with at least twelve other people.

D:2A If the suspect has an unusual physical feature, *e.g.* a facial scar, tattoo or distinctive hairstyle or hair colour which does not appear on the images of the other people that are available to be used, steps may be taken to:

(a) conceal the location of the feature on the images of the suspect and the other people; or

(b) replicate that feature on the images of the other people.

For these purposes, the feature may be concealed or replicated electronically or by any other method which it is practicable to use to ensure that the images of the suspect and other people resemble each other. The identification officer has discretion to choose whether to conceal or replicate the feature and the method to be used. If an unusual physical feature has been described by the witness, the identification officer should, if practicable, have that feature replicated. If it has not been described, concealment may be more appropriate.

D:2B If the identification officer decides that a feature should be concealed or replicated, the reason for the decision and whether the feature was concealed or replicated in the images shown to any witness shall be recorded.

D:2C If the witness requests to view an image where an unusual physical feature has been concealed or replicated without the feature being concealed or replicated, the witness may be allowed to do so.

D:3 The images used to conduct a video identification shall, as far as possible, show the suspect and other people in the same positions or carrying out the same sequence of movements. They shall also show the suspect and other people under identical conditions unless the identification officer reasonably believes:

(a) because of the suspect's failure or refusal to co-operate or other reasons, it is not practicable for the conditions to be identical; and

(b) any difference in the conditions would not direct a witness's attention to any individual image.

D:4 The reasons identical conditions are not practicable shall be recorded on forms provided for the purpose.

D:5 Provision must be made for each person shown to be identified by number.

D:6 If police officers are shown, any numerals or other identifying badges must be concealed. If a prison inmate is shown, either as a suspect or not, then either all, or none of, the people shown should be in prison clothing.

D:7 The suspect or their solicitor, friend, or appropriate adult must be given a reasonable op- **A-140** portunity to see the complete set of images before it is shown to any witness. If the suspect has a reasonable objection to the set of images or any of the participants, the suspect shall be asked to state the reasons for the objection. Steps shall, if practicable, be taken to remove the grounds for objection. If this is not practicable, the suspect and/or their representative shall be told why their objections cannot be met and the objection, the reason given for it and why it cannot be met shall be recorded on forms provided for the purpose.

D:8 Before the images are shown in accordance with paragraph 7, the suspect or their solicitor shall be provided with details of the first description of the suspect by any witnesses who are to attend the video identification. When a broadcast or publication is made, as in paragraph 3.28, the suspect or their solicitor must also be allowed to view any material released to the media by the police for the purpose of recognising or tracing the suspect, provided it is practicable and would not unreasonably delay the investigation.

D:9 The suspect's solicitor, if practicable, shall be given reasonable notification of the time and place the video identification is to be conducted so a representative may attend on behalf of the suspect. The suspect may not be present when the images are shown to the witness(es). In the absence of the suspect's solicitor, the viewing itself shall be recorded on video. No unauthorised people may be present.

(b) *Conducting the video identification*

A-141   D:10 The identification officer is responsible for making the appropriate arrangements to make sure, before they see the set of images, witnesses are not able to communicate with each other about the case, see any of the images which are to be shown, see, or be reminded of, any photograph or description of the suspect or be given any other indication as to the suspect's identity, or overhear a witness who has already seen the material. There must be no discussion with the witness about the composition of the set of images and they must not be told whether a previous witness has made any identification.

D:11 Only one witness may see the set of images at a time. Immediately before the images are shown, the witness shall be told that the person they saw on a specified earlier occasion may, or may not, appear in the images they are shown and that if they cannot make a positive identification, they should say so. The witness shall be advised that at any point, they may ask to see a particular part of the set of images or to have a particular image frozen for them to study. Furthermore, it should be pointed out to the witness that there is no limit on how many times they can view the whole set of images or any part of them. However, they should be asked not to make any decision as to whether the person they saw is on the set of images until they have seen the whole set at least twice.

D:12 Once the witness has seen the whole set of images at least twice and has indicated that they do not want to view the images, or any part of them, again, the witness shall be asked to say whether the individual they saw in person on a specified earlier occasion has been shown and, if so, to identify them by number of the image. The witness will then be shown that image to confirm the identification, see paragraph 17.

D:13 Care must be taken not to direct the witness's attention to any one individual image or give any indication of the suspect's identity. Where a witness has previously made an identification by photographs, or a computerised or artist's composite or similar likeness, the witness must not be reminded of such a photograph or composite likeness once a suspect is available for identification by other means in accordance with this code. Nor must the witness be reminded of any description of the suspect.

D:14 After the procedure, each witness shall be asked whether they have seen any broadcast or published films or photographs, or any descriptions of suspects relating to the offence and their reply shall be recorded.

(c) *Image security and destruction*

D:15 Arrangements shall be made for all relevant material containing sets of images used for specific identification procedures to be kept securely and their movements accounted for. In particular, no-one involved in the investigation shall be permitted to view the material prior to it being shown to any witness.

D:16 As appropriate, paragraph 3.30 or 3.31 applies to the destruction or retention of relevant sets of images.

(d) *Documentation*

D:17 A record must be made of all those participating in, or seeing, the set of images whose names are known to the police.

D:18 A record of the conduct of the video identification must be made on forms provided for the purpose. This shall include anything said by the witness about any identifications or the conduct of the procedure and any reasons it was not practicable to comply with any of the provisions of this code governing the conduct of video identifications.

ANNEX B

Identification parades

(a) *General*

A-142   D:1 A suspect must be given a reasonable opportunity to have a solicitor or friend present, and the suspect shall be asked to indicate on a second copy of the notice whether or not they wish to do so.

D:2 An identification parade may take place either in a normal room or one equipped with a screen permitting witnesses to see members of the identification parade without being seen. The procedures for the composition and conduct of the identification parade are the same in both cases, subject to paragraph 8 (except that an identification parade involving a screen may take place only when the suspect's solicitor, friend or appropriate adult is present or the identification parade is recorded on video).

D:3 Before the identification parade takes place, the suspect or their solicitor shall be provided with details of the first description of the suspect by any witnesses who are attending the identification parade. When a broadcast or publication is made as in paragraph 3.28, the suspect or their solicitor should also be allowed to view any material released to the media by the police for the purpose of recognising or tracing the suspect, provided it is practicable to do so and would not unreasonably delay the investigation.

(b) *Identification parades involving prison inmates*

D:4 If a prison inmate is required for identification, and there are no security problems about the person leaving the establishment, they may be asked to participate in an identification parade or video identification.

D:5 An identification parade may be held in a Prison Department establishment but shall be conducted, as far as practicable under normal identification parade rules. Members of the public shall make up the identification parade unless there are serious security, or control, objections to their admission to the establishment. In such cases, or if a group or video identification is arranged within the establishment, other inmates may participate. If an inmate is the suspect, they are not required to wear prison clothing for the identification parade unless the other people taking part are other inmates in similar clothing, or are members of the public who are prepared to wear prison clothing for the occasion.

(c) *Conduct of the identification parade*

D:6 Immediately before the identification parade, the suspect must be reminded of the procedures   **A-143**
governing its conduct and cautioned in the terms of Code C, paragraphs 10.5 or 10.6, as appropriate.

D:7 All unauthorised people must be excluded from the place where the identification parade is held.

D:8 Once the identification parade has been formed, everything afterwards, in respect of it, shall take place in the presence and hearing of the suspect and any interpreter, solicitor, friend or appropriate adult who is present (unless the identification parade involves a screen, in which case everything said to, or by, any witness at the place where the identification parade is held, must be said in the hearing and presence of the suspect's solicitor, friend or appropriate adult or be recorded on video).

D:9 The identification parade shall consist of at least eight people (in addition to the suspect) who, so far as possible, resemble the suspect in age, height, general appearance and position in life. Only one suspect shall be included in an identification parade unless there are two suspects of roughly similar appearance, in which case they may be paraded together with at least twelve other people. In no circumstances shall more than two suspects be included in one identification parade and where there are separate identification parades, they shall be made up of different people.

D:10 If the suspect has an unusual physical feature, *e.g.*, a facial scar, tattoo or distinctive hairstyle or hair colour which cannot be replicated on other members of the identification parade, steps may be taken to conceal the location of that feature on the suspect and the other members of the identification parade if the suspect and their solicitor, or appropriate adult, agree. For example, by use of a plaster or a hat, so that all members of the identification parade resemble each other in general appearance.

D:11 When all members of a similar group are possible suspects, separate identification parades shall be held for each unless there are two suspects of similar appearance when they may appear on the same identification parade with at least twelve other members of the group who are not suspects. When police officers in uniform form an identification parade any numerals or other identifying badges shall be concealed.

D:12 When the suspect is brought to the place where the identification parade is to be held, they shall be asked if they have any objection to the arrangements for the identification parade or to any of the other participants in it and to state the reasons for the objection. The suspect may obtain advice from their solicitor or friend, if present, before the identification parade proceeds. If the suspect has a reasonable objection to the arrangements or any of the participants, steps shall, if practicable, be taken to remove the grounds for objection. When it is not practicable to do so, the suspect shall be told why their objections cannot be met and the objection, the reason given for it and why it cannot be met, shall be recorded on forms provided for the purpose.

D:13 The suspect may select their own position in the line, but may not otherwise interfere with the order of the people forming the line. When there is more than one witness, the suspect must be told, after each witness has left the room, that they can, if they wish, change position in the line. Each position in the line must be clearly numbered, whether by means of a number laid on the floor in front of each identification parade member or by other means.

D:14 Appropriate arrangements must be made to make sure, before witnesses attend the identifica-   **A-144**
tion parade, they are not able to:

    (i) communicate with each other about the case or overhear a witness who has already seen the identification parade;

    (ii) see any member of the identification parade;

    (iii) see, or be reminded of, any photograph or description of the suspect or be given any other indication as to the suspect's identity; or

    (iv) see the suspect before or after the identification parade.

D:15 The person conducting a witness to an identification parade must not discuss with them the composition of the identification parade and, in particular, must not disclose whether a previous witness has made any identification.

D:16 Witnesses shall be brought in one at a time. Immediately before the witness inspects the identification parade, they shall be told the person they saw on a specified earlier occasion may, or may not, be present and if they cannot make a positive identification, they should say so. The witness must also be told they should not make any decision about whether the person they saw is on the identification parade until they have looked at each member at least twice.

D:17 When the officer or police staff (see paragraph 3.11) conducting the identification procedure is satisfied the witness has properly looked at each member of the identification parade, they shall ask the witness whether the person they saw on a specified earlier occasion is on the identification parade and, if so, to indicate the number of the person concerned, see paragraph 28.

D:18 If the witness wishes to hear any identification parade member speak, adopt any specified posture or move, they shall first be asked whether they can identify any person(s) on the identification parade on the basis of appearance only. When the request is to hear members of the identification parade speak, the witness shall be reminded that the participants in the identification parade have been chosen on the basis of physical appearance only. Members of the identification parade may then be asked to comply with the witness's request to hear them speak, see them move or adopt any specified posture.

D:19 If the witness requests that the person they have indicated remove anything used for the purposes of paragraph 10 to conceal the location of an unusual physical feature, that person may be asked to remove it.

D:20 If the witness makes an identification after the identification parade has ended, the suspect and, if present, their solicitor, interpreter or friend shall be informed. When this occurs, consideration should be given to allowing the witness a second opportunity to identify the suspect.

D:21 After the procedure, each witness shall be asked whether they have seen any broadcast or published films or photographs or any descriptions of suspects relating to the offence and their reply shall be recorded.

D:22 When the last witness has left, the suspect shall be asked whether they wish to make any comments on the conduct of the identification parade.

(d) *Documentation*

D:23 A video recording must normally be taken of the identification parade. If that is impracticable, a colour photograph must be taken. A copy of the video recording or photograph shall be supplied, on request, to the suspect or their solicitor within a reasonable time.

D:24 As appropriate, paragraph 3.30 or 3.31, should apply to any photograph or video taken as in paragraph 23.

D:25 If any person is asked to leave an identification parade because they are interfering with its conduct, the circumstances shall be recorded.

D:26 A record must be made of all those present at an identification parade whose names are known to the police.

D:27 If prison inmates make up an identification parade, the circumstances must be recorded.

D:28 A record of the conduct of any identification parade must be made on forms provided for the purpose. This shall include anything said by the witness or the suspect about any identifications or the conduct of the procedure, and any reasons it was not practicable to comply with any of this code's provisions.

ANNEX C

Group identification

(a) *General*

D:1 The purpose of this annex is to make sure, as far as possible, group identifications follow the   **A-146**
principles and procedures for identification parades so the conditions are fair to the suspect in the
way they test the witness's ability to make an identification.

D:2 Group identifications may take place either with the suspect's consent and co-operation or
covertly without their consent.

D:3 The location of the group identification is a matter for the identification officer, although the
officer may take into account any representations made by the suspect, appropriate adult, their solicitor or friend.

D:4 The place where the group identification is held should be one where other people are either
passing by or waiting around informally, in groups such that the suspect is able to join them and be
capable of being seen by the witness at the same time as others in the group. For example people
leaving an escalator, pedestrians walking through a shopping centre, passengers on railway and bus
stations, waiting in queues or groups or where people are standing or sitting in groups in other
public places.

D:5 If the group identification is to be held covertly, the choice of locations will be limited by the
places where the suspect can be found and the number of other people present at that time. In these
cases, suitable locations might be along regular routes travelled by the suspect, including buses or
trains or public places frequented by the suspect.

D:6 Although the number, age, sex, race and general description and style of clothing of other   **A-147**
people present at the location cannot be controlled by the identification officer, in selecting the location the officer must consider the general appearance and numbers of people likely to be present. In
particular, the officer must reasonably expect that over the period the witness observes the group,
they will be able to see, from time to time, a number of others whose appearance is broadly similar to
that of the suspect.

D:7 A group identification need not be held if the identification officer believes, because of the
unusual appearance of the suspect, none of the locations it would be practicable to use, satisfy the
requirements of paragraph 6 necessary to make the identification fair.

D:8 Immediately after a group identification procedure has taken place (with or without the
suspect's consent), a colour photograph or video should be taken of the general scene, if practicable,
to give a general impression of the scene and the number of people present. Alternatively, if it is
practicable, the group identification may be video recorded.

D:9 If it is not practicable to take the photograph or video in accordance with paragraph 8, a
photograph or film of the scene should be taken later at a time determined by the identification officer if the officer considers it practicable to do so.

D:10 An identification carried out in accordance with this code remains a group identification even
though, at the time of being seen by the witness, the suspect was on their own rather than in a
group.

D:11 Before the group identification takes place, the suspect or their solicitor shall be provided
with details of the first description of the suspect by any witnesses who are to attend the identification.
When a broadcast or publication is made, as in paragraph 3.28, the suspect or their solicitor should
also be allowed to view any material released by the police to the media for the purposes of recognising or tracing the suspect, provided that it is practicable and would not unreasonably delay the
investigation.

D:12 After the procedure, each witness shall be asked whether they have seen any broadcast or
published films or photographs or any descriptions of suspects relating to the offence and their reply
recorded.

(b) *Identification with the consent of the suspect*

D:13 A suspect must be given a reasonable opportunity to have a solicitor or friend present. They   **A-148**
shall be asked to indicate on a second copy of the notice whether or not they wish to do so.

D:14 The witness, the person carrying out the procedure and the suspect's solicitor, appropriate
adult, friend or any interpreter for the witness, may be concealed from the sight of the individuals in
the group they are observing, if the person carrying out the procedure considers this assists the
conduct of the identification.

D:15 The person conducting a witness to a group identification must not discuss with them the
forthcoming group identification and, in particular, must not disclose whether a previous witness has
made any identification.

D:16 Anything said to, or by, the witness during the procedure about the identification should be
said in the presence and hearing of those present at the procedure.

D:17 Appropriate arrangements must be made to make sure, before witnesses attend the group
identification, they are not able to:

(i) communicate with each other about the case or overhear a witness who has already been given an opportunity to see the suspect in the group;

(ii) see the suspect; or

(iii) see, or be reminded of, any photographs or description of the suspect or be given any other indication of the suspect's identity.

D:18 Witnesses shall be brought one at a time to the place where they are to observe the group. Immediately before the witness is asked to look at the group, the person conducting the procedure shall tell them that the person they saw may, or may not, be in the group and that if they cannot make a positive identification, they should say so. The witness shall be asked to observe the group in which the suspect is to appear. The way in which the witness should do this will depend on whether the group is moving or stationary.

Moving group

A-149

D:19 When the group in which the suspect is to appear is moving, *e.g.* leaving an escalator, the provisions of paragraphs 20 to 24 should be followed.

D:20 If two or more suspects consent to a group identification, each should be the subject of separate identification procedures. These may be conducted consecutively on the same occasion.

D:21 The person conducting the procedure shall tell the witness to observe the group and ask them to point out any person they think they saw on the specified earlier occasion.

D:22 Once the witness has been informed as in paragraph 21 the suspect should be allowed to take whatever position in the group they wish.

D:23 When the witness points out a person as in paragraph 21 they shall, if practicable, be asked to take a closer look at the person to confirm the identification. If this is not practicable, or they cannot confirm the identification, they shall be asked how sure they are that the person they have indicated is the relevant person.

D:24 The witness should continue to observe the group for the period which the person conducting the procedure reasonably believes is necessary in the circumstances for them to be able to make comparisons between the suspect and other individuals of broadly similar appearance to the suspect as in paragraph 6.

Stationary groups

A-150

D:25 When the group in which the suspect is to appear is stationary, *e.g.* people waiting in a queue, the provisions of paragraphs 26 to 29 should be followed.

D:26 If two or more suspects consent to a group identification, each should be subject to separate identification procedures unless they are of broadly similar appearance when they may appear in the same group. When separate group identifications are held, the groups must be made up of different people.

D:27 The suspect may take whatever position in the group they wish. If there is more than one witness, the suspect must be told, out of the sight and hearing of any witness, that they can, if they wish, change their position in the group.

D:28 The witness shall be asked to pass along, or amongst, the group and to look at each person in the group at least twice, taking as much care and time as possible according to the circumstances, before making an identification. Once the witness has done this, they shall be asked whether the person they saw on the specified earlier occasion is in the group and to indicate any such person by whatever means the person conducting the procedure considers appropriate in the circumstances. If this is not practicable, the witness shall be asked to point out any person they think they saw on the earlier occasion.

D:29 When the witness makes an indication as in paragraph 28, arrangements shall be made, if practicable, for the witness to take a closer look at the person to confirm the identification. If this is not practicable, or the witness is unable to confirm the identification, they shall be asked how sure they are that the person they have indicated is the relevant person.

All cases

A-151

D:30 If the suspect unreasonably delays joining the group, or having joined the group, deliberately conceals themselves [*sic*] from the sight of the witness, this may be treated as a refusal to co-operate in a group identification.

D:31 If the witness identifies a person other than the suspect, that person should be informed what has happened and asked if they are prepared to give their name and address. There is no obligation upon any member of the public to give these details. There shall be no duty to record any details of any other member of the public present in the group or at the place where the procedure is conducted.

D:32 When the group identification has been completed, the suspect shall be asked whether they wish to make any comments on the conduct of the procedure.

D:33 If the suspect has not been previously informed, they shall be told of any identifications made by the witnesses.

(c) *Identification without the suspect's consent*

D:34 Group identifications held covertly without the suspect's consent should, as far as practicable, **A-152** follow the rules for conduct of group identification by consent.

D:35 A suspect has no right to have a solicitor, appropriate adult or friend present as the identification will take place without the knowledge of the suspect.

D:36 Any number of suspects may be identified at the same time.

(d) *Identifications in police stations*

D:37 Group identifications should only take place in police stations for reasons of safety, security or because it is not practicable to hold them elsewhere.

D:38 The group identification may take place either in a room equipped with a screen permitting witnesses to see members of the group without being seen, or anywhere else in the police station that the identification officer considers appropriate.

D:39 Any of the additional safeguards applicable to identification parades should be followed if the identification officer considers it is practicable to do so in the circumstances.

(e) *Identifications involving prison inmates*

D:40 A group identification involving a prison inmate may only be arranged in the prison or at a **A-153** police station.

D:41 When a group identification takes place involving a prison inmate, whether in a prison or in a police station, the arrangements should follow those in paragraphs 37 to 39. If a group identification takes place within a prison, other inmates may participate. If an inmate is the suspect, they do not have to wear prison clothing for the group identification unless the other participants are wearing the same clothing.

(f) *Documentation*

D:42 When a photograph or video is taken as in paragraph 8 or 9, a copy of the photograph or video shall be supplied on request to the suspect or their solicitor within a reasonable time.

D:43 Paragraph 3.30 or 3.31, as appropriate, shall apply when the photograph or film taken in accordance with paragraph 8 or 9 includes the suspect.

D:44 A record of the conduct of any group identification must be made on forms provided for the purpose. This shall include anything said by the witness or suspect about any identifications or the conduct of the procedure and any reasons why it was not practicable to comply with any of the provisions of this code governing the conduct of group identifications.

ANNEX D

Confrontation by a witness

D:1 Before the confrontation takes place, the witness must be told that the person they saw may, **A-154** or may not, be the person they are to confront and that if they are not that person, then the witness should say so.

D:2 Before the confrontation takes place the suspect or their solicitor shall be provided with details of the first description of the suspect given by any witness who is to attend. When a broadcast or publication is made, as in paragraph 3.28, the suspect or their solicitor should also be allowed to view any material released to the media for the purposes of recognising or tracing the suspect, provided it is practicable to do so and would not unreasonably delay the investigation.

D:3 Force may not be used to make the suspect's face visible to the witness.

D:4 Confrontation must take place in the presence of the suspect's solicitor, interpreter or friend unless this would cause unreasonable delay.

D:5 The suspect shall be confronted independently by each witness, who shall be asked "Is this the person?". If the witness identifies the person but is unable to confirm the identification, they shall be asked how sure they are that the person is the one they saw on the earlier occasion.

D:6 The confrontation should normally take place in the police station, either in a normal room or one equipped with a screen permitting a witness to see the suspect without being seen. In both cases, the procedures are the same except that a room equipped with a screen may be used only when the suspect's solicitor, friend or appropriate adult is present or the confrontation is recorded on video.

D:7 After the procedure, each witness shall be asked whether they have seen any broadcast or published films or photographs or any descriptions of suspects relating to the offence and their reply shall be recorded.

ANNEX E

Showing photographs

(a) *Action*

A-155   D:1 An officer of sergeant rank or above shall be responsible for supervising and directing the showing of photographs. The actual showing may be done by another officer or police staff, see paragraph 3.11.

D:2 The supervising officer must confirm the first description of the suspect given by the witness has been recorded before they are shown the photographs. If the supervising officer is unable to confirm the description has been recorded they shall postpone showing the photographs.

D:3 Only one witness shall be shown photographs at any one time. Each witness shall be given as much privacy as practicable and shall not be allowed to communicate with any other witness in the case.

D:4 The witness shall be shown not less than twelve photographs at a time, which shall, as far as possible, all be of a similar type.

D:5 When the witness is shown the photographs, they shall be told the photograph of the person they saw may, or may not, be amongst them and if they cannot make a positive identification, they should say so. The witness shall also be told they should not make a decision until they have viewed at least twelve photographs. The witness shall not be prompted or guided in any way but shall be left to make any selection without help.

D:6 If a witness makes a positive identification from photographs, unless the person identified is otherwise eliminated from enquiries or is not available, other witnesses shall not be shown photographs. But both they, and the witness who has made the identification, shall be asked to attend a video identification, an identification parade or group identification unless there is no dispute about the suspect's identification.

A-156   D:7 If the witness makes a selection but is unable to confirm the identification, the person showing the photographs shall ask them how sure they are that the photograph they have indicated is the person they saw on the specified earlier occasion.

D:8 When the use of a computerised or artist's composite or similar likeness has led to there being a known suspect who can be asked to participate in a video identification, appear on an identification parade or participate in a group identification, that likeness shall not be shown to other potential witnesses.

D:9 When a witness attending a video identification, an identification parade or group identification has previously been shown photographs or computerised or artist's composite or similar likeness (and it is the responsibility of the officer in charge of the investigation to make the identification officer aware that this is the case), the suspect and their solicitor must be informed of this fact before the identification procedure takes place.

D:10 None of the photographs shown shall be destroyed, whether or not an identification is made, since they may be required for production in court. The photographs shall be numbered and a separate photograph taken of the frame or part of the album from which the witness made an identification as an aid to reconstituting it.

(b) *Documentation*

A-157   D:11 Whether or not an identification is made, a record shall be kept of the showing of photographs on forms provided for the purpose. This shall include anything said by the witness about any identification or the conduct of the procedure, any reasons it was not practicable to comply with any of the provisions of this code governing the showing of photographs and the name and rank of the supervising officer.

D:12 The supervising officer shall inspect and sign the record as soon as practicable.

ANNEX F

Fingerprints, footwear impressions and samples—destruction and speculative searches

(a) *Fingerprints, footwear impressions and samples taken in connection with a criminal investigation from a
person suspected of committing the offence under investigation*

D:1 The retention and destruction of fingerprints, footwear impressions and samples taken in con-   **A-158**
nection with a criminal investigation from a person suspected of committing the offence under
investigation is subject to PACE, s.64.

(b) *Fingerprints, footwear impressions and samples taken in connection with a criminal investigation from a
person not suspected of committing the offence under investigation*

D:2 When fingerprints, footwear impressions or DNA samples are taken from a person in connection with an investigation and the person is not suspected of having committed the offence, see *Note
F1*, they must be destroyed as soon as they have fulfilled the purpose for which they were taken
unless:

    (a) they were taken for the purposes of an investigation of an offence for which a person has
       been convicted; and

    (b) fingerprints, footwear impressions or samples were also taken from the convicted person
       for the purposes of that investigation.

However, subject to paragraph 2, the fingerprints, footwear impressions and samples, and the
information derived from samples, may not be used in the investigation of any offence or in evidence
against the person who is, or would be, entitled to the destruction of the fingerprints, footwear
impressions and samples, see *Note F2*.

D:3 The requirement to destroy fingerprints, footwear impressions and DNA samples, and
information derived from samples, and restrictions on their retention and use in paragraph 1 do not
apply if the person gives their written consent for their fingerprints, footwear impressions or sample
to be retained and used after they have fulfilled the purpose for which they were taken, see *Note F1*.

D:4 When a person's fingerprints, footwear impressions or sample are to be destroyed:

    (a) any copies of the fingerprints and footwear impressions must also be destroyed;

    (b) the person may witness the destruction of their fingerprints, footwear impressions or cop-
       ies if they ask to do so within five days of being informed destruction is required;

    (c) access to relevant computer fingerprint data shall be made impossible as soon as it is
       practicable to do so and the person shall be given a certificate to this effect within three
       months of asking; and

    (d) neither the fingerprints, footwear impressions, the sample, or any information derived
       from the sample, may be used in the investigation of any offence or in evidence against
       the person who is, or would be, entitled to its destruction.

D:5 Fingerprints, footwear impressions or samples, and the information derived from samples,
taken in connection with the investigation of an offence which are not required to be destroyed, may
be retained after they have fulfilled the purposes for which they were taken but may be used only for
purposes related to the prevention or detection of crime, the investigation of an offence or the
conduct of a prosecution in, as well as outside, the UK and may also be subject to a speculative
search. This includes checking them against other fingerprints, footwear impressions and DNA
records held by, or on behalf of, the police and other law enforcement authorities in, as well as
outside, the UK.

(b) [sic] *Fingerprints taken in connection with Immigration Service enquiries*

    D:6 See paragraph 4.10.   **A-159**

Notes for guidance

    D:F1 *Fingerprints, footwear impressions and samples given voluntarily for the purposes of elimination play an*   **A-160**
*important part in many police investigations. It is, therefore, important to make sure innocent volunteers are not
deterred from participating and their consent to their fingerprints, footwear impressions and DNA being used for
the purposes of a specific investigation is fully informed and voluntary. If the police or volunteer seek to have the
fingerprints, footwear impressions or samples retained for use after the specific investigation ends, it is important
the volunteer's consent to this is also fully informed and voluntary.*

    Examples of consent for:
      • *DNA/fingerprints/footwear impressions—to be used only for the purposes of a specific investigation;*
      • *DNA/fingerprints/footwear impressions—to be used in the specific investigation and retained by the
        police for future use.*

To minimise the risk of confusion, each consent should be physically separate and the volunteer should be asked to sign **each consent**.

   (a) *DNA:*

      (i) *DNA sample taken for the purposes of elimination or as part of an intelligence-led screening and to be used only for the purposes of that investigation and destroyed afterwards:*

      "I consent to my DNA/mouth swab being taken for forensic analysis. I understand that the sample will be destroyed at the end of the case and that my profile will only be compared to the crime stain profile from this enquiry. I have been advised that the person taking the sample may be required to give evidence and/or provide a written statement to the police in relation to the taking of it.".

      (ii) *DNA sample to be retained on the National DNA database and used in the future:*

      "I consent to my DNA sample and information derived from it being retained and used only for purposes related to the prevention and detection of a crime, the investigation of an offence or the conduct of a prosecution either nationally or internationally.

      I understand that this sample may be checked against other DNA records held by, or on behalf of, relevant law enforcement authorities, either nationally or internationally.

      I understand that once I have given my consent for the sample to be retained and used I cannot withdraw this consent.".

   (b) *Fingerprints:*

      (i) *Fingerprints taken for the purposes of elimination or as part of an intelligence-led screening and to be used only for the purposes of that investigation and destroyed afterwards:*

      "I consent to my fingerprints being taken for elimination purposes. I understand that the fingerprints will be destroyed at the end of the case and that my fingerprints will only be compared to the fingerprints from this enquiry. I have been advised that the person taking the fingerprints may be required to give evidence and/or provide a written statement to the police in relation to the taking of it.".

      (ii) *Fingerprints to be retained for future use:*

      "I consent to my fingerprints being retained and used only for purposes related to the prevention and detection of a crime, the investigation of an offence or the conduct of a prosecution either nationally or internationally.

      I understand that my fingerprints may be checked against other records held by, or on behalf of, relevant law enforcement authorities, either nationally or internationally.

      I understand that once I have given my consent for my fingerprints to be retained and used I cannot withdraw this consent.".

   (c) *Footwear impressions:*

      (i) *Footwear impressions taken for the purposes of elimination or as part of an intelligence-led screening and to be used only for the purposes of that investigation and destroyed afterwards:*

      "I consent to my footwear impressions being taken for elimination purposes. I understand that the footwear impressions will be destroyed at the end of the case and that my footwear impressions will only be compared to the footwear impressions from this enquiry. I have been advised that the person taking the footwear impressions may be required to give evidence and/or provide a writtens statement to the police in relation to the taking of it.".

      (ii) *Footwear impressions to be retained for future use:*

      "I consent to my footwear impressions being retained and used only for purposes related to the prevention and detection of a crime, the investigation of an offence or the conduct of a prosecution, either nationally or internationally.

      I understand that my footwear impressions may be checked against other records held by, or on behalf of, relevant law enforcement authorities, either nationally or internationally.

      I understand that once I have given my consent for my footwear impressions to be retained and used I cannot withdraw this consent.".

A-161   D:F2 *The provisions for the retention of fingerprints, footwear impressions and samples in paragraph 1 allow for all fingerprints, footwear impressions and samples in a case to be available for any subsequent miscarriage of justice investigation.*

ANNEX G

Requirement for a person to attend a police station for fingerprints and samples

D:1 A requirement under Schedule 2A for a person to attend a police station to have fingerprints **A-161a**
or samples taken:

    (a) must give the person a period of at least seven days within which to attend the police station; and

    (b) may direct them to attend at a specified time of day or between specified times of day.

D:2 When specifying the period and times of attendance, the officer making the requirements must consider whether the fingerprints or samples could reasonably be taken at a time when the person is required to attend the police station for any other reason. See *Note G1.*

D:3 An officer of the rank of inspector or above may authorise a period shorter than 7 days if there is an urgent need for person's fingerprints or sample for the purposes of the investigation of an offence. The fact of the authorisation and the reasons for giving it must be recorded as soon as practicable.

D:4 The constable making a requirement and the person to whom it applies may agree to vary it so as to specify any period within which, or date or time at which, the person is to attend. However, variation shall not have effect for the purposes of enforcement, unless it is confirmed by the constable in writing.

Notes for guidance

D:G1 *The specified period within which the person is to attend need not fall within the period allowed (if ap-* **A-161b**
plicable) for making the requirement.

D:G2 *To justify the arrest without warrant of a person who fails to comply with a requirement, (see paragraph 4.4(b) above), the officer making the requirement, or confirming a variation, should be prepared to explain how, when and where the requirement was made or the variation was confirmed and what steps were taken to ensure the person understood what to do and the consequences of not complying with the requirement.*

(6) Tape-recording of interviews

The text that follows is of the version of the code that came into force on February 2, 2016: see **★A-162**
ante, Appendix A-1.

For further details of the application of the code, and as to commencement of the governing legislation, see § 15-174 in the main work.

E. CODE OF PRACTICE ON AUDIO RECORDING INTERVIEWS WITH SUSPECTS

Commencement—transitional arrangements

This code applies to interviews carried out after 00.00 on [on February 2, 2016] notwithstanding **A-162a**
that the interview may have commenced before that time.

E:1 General

E:1.0 The procedures in this code must be used fairly, responsibly, with respect for the people to **A-163**
whom they apply and without unlawful discrimination. Under the Equality Act 2010, s.149, when police officers are carrying out their functions, they also have a duty to have due regard to the need to eliminate unlawful discrimination, harassment and victimisation, to advance equality of opportunity between people who share a relevant protected characteristic and people who do not share it, and to take steps to foster good relations between those persons. See *Note 1B.*

E:1.1 This code of practice must be readily available for consultation by:

    • police officers;

    • police staff;

    • detained persons;

    • members of the public.

E:1.2 The *Notes for Guidance* included are not provisions of this code.

E:1.3 Nothing in this code shall detract from the requirements of Code C, the code of practice for the detention, treatment and questioning of persons by police officers.

E:1.4 The interviews to which this code applies are described in section 3.

E:1.5 The term:

    • "appropriate adult" has the same meaning as in Code C, para. 1.7, and in the case of a 17-year-old suspect, includes the person called to fulfil that role in accordance with paragraph 1.5A of Code C;

- "solicitor" has the same meaning as in Code C, para. 6.12;
- "interview" has the same meaning as in Code C, para. 11.1A.

E:1.5A Recording of interviews shall be carried out openly to instil confidence in its reliability as an impartial and accurate record of the interview.

★**A-164**   E:1.6 In this code:

(aa) "recording media" means any removable, physical audio recording medium (such as magnetic tape, optical disc or solid state memory) which can be played and copied;

(a) "designated person" means a person other than a police officer, designated under the Police Reform Act 2002, Pt 4, who has specified powers and duties of police officers conferred or imposed on them;

(b) any reference to a police officer includes a designated person acting in the exercise or performance of the powers and duties conferred or imposed on them by their designation; and

(c) "secure digital network" is a computer network system which enables an original interview recording to be stored as a digital multi media file or a series of such files, on a secure file server which is accredited by the National Accreditor for Police Information Systems in accordance with the UK Government Protective Marking Scheme. (See section 7 of this code.).

E:1.7 Sections 2 to 6 of this code set out the procedures and requirements which apply to all audio recorded interviews which are audio together with the provisions which apply only to interviews which are audio recorded using removable media. Section 7 sets out the provisions which apply to interviews which are audio recorded using a secure digital network and specifies the provisions in sections 2 to 6 which do not apply to secure digital network recording. The annex to this code sets out the terms and conditions of the exemption from the requirement to audio record interviews about indictable offences referred to in paragraph 3.1(a)(iii).

★**A-165**   E:1.8 Nothing in this code prevents the custody officer, or other officer given custody of the detainee, from allowing police staff who are not designated persons to carry out individual procedures or tasks at the police station if the law allows. However, the officer remains responsible for making sure the procedures and tasks are carried out correctly in accordance with this code. Any such police staff must be:

(a) a person employed by a police force and under the control and direction of the chief officer of that force; or

(b) employed by a person with whom a police force has a contract for the provision of services relating to persons arrested or otherwise in custody.

E:1.9 Designated persons and other police staff must have regard to any relevant provisions of the codes of practice.

E:1.10 References to pocket book [*sic*] include any official report book issued to police officers or police staff.

E:1.11 References to a custody officer include those performing the functions of a custody officer as in paragraph 1.9 of Code C.

E:1.12 In the application of this code to the conduct and recording of an interview of a suspect who has not been arrested:

(a) references to the "custody officer" include references to an officer of the rank of sergeant or above who is not directly involved in the investigation of the offence(s);

(b) if the interview takes place elsewhere than at a police station, references to "interview room" include any place or location which the interviewer is satisfied will enable the interview to be conducted and recorded in accordance with this code and where the suspect is present voluntarily (see Note 1A); and

(c) provisions in addition to those which expressly apply to these interviews shall be followed insofar as they are relevant and can be applied in practice.

Notes for guidance

E:1A *An interviewer who is not sure, or has any doubt, about the suitability of a place or location of an interview to be carried out elsewhere than at a police station, should consult an officer of the rank of sergeant or above for advice.*

E:1B *In paragraph 1.0, the "relevant protected characteristics" are: age, disability, gender reassignment, pregnancy and maternity, race, religion/belief, sex and sexual orientation.*

E:2 Recording and sealing master recordings

E:2.1 [*Not used.*]

E:2.2 One recording, the master recording, will be sealed in the suspect's presence. A second recording will be used as a working copy. The master recording is any of the recordings made by a multi-deck/drive machine or the only recording made by a single deck/drive machine. The working copy is one of the other recordings made by a multi-deck/drive machine or a copy of the master recording made by a single deck/drive machine. (See *Note 2A*.)

[This paragraph does not apply to interviews recorded using a secure digital network, see paras 7.4 to 7.6.]

E:2.3 Nothing in this code requires the identity of officers or police staff conducting interviews to be recorded or disclosed:

(a) [*not used*];

(b) if the interviewer reasonably believes recording or disclosing their name might put them in danger.

In these cases interviewers should use warrant or other identification numbers and the name of their police station. Such instances and the reasons for them shall be recorded in the custody record or the interviewer's pocket book. See *Note 2C*.

Notes for guidance

E:2A *The purpose of sealing the master recording before it leaves the suspect's presence is to establish their* **A-167** *confidence that the integrity of the recording is preserved. If a single deck/drive machine is used the working copy of the master recording must be made in the suspect's presence and without the master recording leaving their sight. The working copy shall be used for making further copies if needed.*

E:2B [*Not used.*]

E:2C *The purpose of paragraph 2.3(b) is to protect those involved in serious organised crime investigations or arrests of particularly violent suspects when there is reliable information that those arrested or their associates may threaten or cause harm to those involved. In cases of doubt, an officer of inspector rank or above should be consulted.*

E:3 Interviews to be audio recorded

E:3.1 Subject to paragraph 3.4, audio recording shall be used for any interview:

★**A-168**

(a) with a person cautioned under Code C, section 10 in respect of any indictable offence, which includes any offence triable either way, except when:

   (i) that person has been arrested and the interview takes place elsewhere than at a police station in accordance with Code C, paragraph 11.1 for which a written record would be required;

   (ii) the conditions in paragraph 3.3A are satisfied and authority not to audio record the interview is given by:
   - the custody officer in the case of a detained suspect, or
   - an officer of the rank of sergeant or above in the case of a suspect who has not been arrested and to whom paragraphs 3.21 and 3.22 of Code C (persons attending a police station or elsewhere voluntarily) apply; or

   (iii) the conditions in Part 1 of the annex to this code are satisfied, in which case the interview must be conducted and recorded in writing, in accordance with section 11 of Code C (see *Note 3A*);

(b) which takes place as a result of an interviewer exceptionally putting further questions to a suspect about an indictable offence after they have been charged with, or told they may be prosecuted for, that offence, see Code C, para. 16.5 and *Note 3E*;

(c) when an interviewer wants to tell a person, after they have been charged with, or informed they may be prosecuted for, an indictable offence, about any written statement or interview with another person, see Code C, para. 16.4 and *Note 3F*.

See *Note 3D*.

E:3.2 The Terrorism Act 2000 and the Counter-Terrorism Act 2008 make separate provisions for a code of practice for the video recording with sound of:

- interviews of persons detained under section 41 of, or Schedule 7 to, the 2000 Act; and
- post-charge questioning of persons authorised under section 22 or 23 of the 2008 Act.

The provisions of this code do not apply to such interviews. (See *Note 3C*.)

E:3.3 [*Not used.*]

E:3.3A The conditions referred to in paragraph 3.1(a)(ii) are:

(a) it is not reasonably practicable to audio record, or as the case may be, continue to audio record, the interview because of equipment failure or the unavailability of a suitable interview room or recording equipment; and

(b) the authorising officer considers, on reasonable grounds, that the interview or continuation of the interview should not be delayed until the failure has been rectified or until a suitable room or recording equipment becomes available.

In these cases:

- the interview must be recorded or continue to be recorded in writing in accordance with Code C, section 11; and
- the authorising officer shall record the specific reasons for not audio recording and the interviewer is responsible for ensuring that the written interview record shows the date and time of the authority, the authorising officer and where the authority is recorded. (See *Note 3B*.)

E:3.4 If a detainee refuses to go into or remain in a suitable interview room, see Code C, paragraph 12.5, and the custody officer considers, on reasonable grounds, that the interview should not be delayed the interview may, at the custody officer's discretion, be conducted in a cell using portable recording equipment or, if none is available, recorded in writing as in Code C, section 11. The reasons for this shall be recorded in accordance with Code C, para. 12.11.

E:3.5 The whole of each interview shall be audio recorded, including the taking and reading back of any statement.

E:3.6 A sign or indicator which is visible to the suspect must show when the recording equipment is recording.

Notes for guidance

★**A-169**   E:3A *Nothing in this code is intended to preclude audio recording at police discretion of interviews at police stations or elsewhere with people cautioned in respect of offences not covered by paragraph 3.1, or responses made by persons after they have been charged with, or told they may be prosecuted for, an offence, provided this code is complied with.*

E:3B *A decision made in accordance with paragraphs 3.1(a)(ii) and 3.3A not to audio record an interview for any reason may be the subject of comment in court. The authorising offcer should be prepared to justify that decision.*

E:3C *If, during the course of an interview under this code, it becomes apparent that the interview should be conducted under the terrorism code for the video recording with sound of interviews, the interview should only continue in accordance with that code.*

E:3D *Attention is drawn to the provisions set out in Code C about the matters to be considered when deciding whether a detained person is fit to be interviewed.*

E:3E *Code C sets out the circumstances in which a suspect may be questioned about an offence after being charged with it.*

E:3F *Code C sets out the procedures to be followed when a person's attention is drawn after charge, to a statement made by another person. One method of bringing the content of an interview with another person to the notice of a suspect may be to play them a recording of that interview.*

E:4 The interview

(a) *General*

A-170   E:4.1 The provisions of Code C:

- sections 10 and 11, and the applicable *Notes for Guidance* apply to the conduct of interviews to which this code applies;
- paragraphs 11.7 to 11.14 apply only when a written record is needed.

E:4.2 Code C, paragraphs 10.10, 10.11 and Annex C describe the restriction on drawing adverse inferences from an arrested suspect's failure or refusal to say anything about their involvement in the offence when interviewed or after being charged or informed they may be prosecuted, and how it affects the terms of the caution and determines if and by whom a special warning under sections 36 and 37 of the Criminal Justice and Public Order Act 1994 can be given.

(b) *Commencement of interviews*

E:4.3 When the suspect is brought into the interview room the interviewer shall, without delay but in the suspect's sight, load the recorder with new recording media and set it to record. The recording media must be unwrapped or opened in the suspect's presence.

[This paragraph does not apply to interviews recorded using a secure digital network, see paras 7.4 and 7.5.]

E:4.4 The interviewer should tell the suspect about the recording process and point out the sign or indicator which shows that the recording equipment is activated and recording. See paragraph 3.6. The interviewer shall:

(a) explain that the interview is being audibly recorded;

(b) subject to paragraph 2.3, give their name and rank and that of any other interviewer present;

(c) ask the suspect and any other party present, *e.g.* the appropriate adult, a solicitor or interpreter, to identify themselves;

(d) state the date, time of commencement and place of the interview; and

(e) state the suspect will be given a notice about what will happen to the recording. [This sub-paragraph does not apply to interviews recorded using a secure digital network, see paras 7.4 and 7.6 to 7.7.]

See *Note 4A*.

E:4.4A Any person entering the interview room after the interview has commenced shall be invited by the interviewer to identify themselves for the purpose of the audio recording and state the reason why they have entered the interview room.

E:4.5 The interviewer shall:

• caution the suspect, see Code C, section 10; and

• if they are detained, remind them of their entitlement to free legal advice, see Code C, para. 11.2; or

• if they are not detained under arrest, explain this and their entitlement to free legal advice, see Code C, para. 3.21.

E:4.6 The interviewer shall put to the suspect any significant statement or silence, see Code C, paragraph 11.4.

(c) *Interviews with suspects who appear to have a hearing impediment*

E:4.7 If the suspect appears to have a hearing impediment, the interviewer shall make a written **A-171** note of the interview in accordance with Code C, at the same time as audio recording it in accordance with this code. (See *Notes 4B* and *4C*.)

(d) *Objections and complaints by the suspect*

E:4.8 If the suspect or an appropriate adult on their behalf objects to the interview being audibly recorded either at the outset, during the interview or during a break, the interviewer shall explain that the interview is being audibly recorded and that this code requires the objections to be recorded on the audio recording. When any objections have been audibly recorded or the suspect or appropriate adult have refused to have their objections recorded, the interviewer shall say they are turning off the recorder, give their reasons and turn it off. The interviewer shall then make a written record of the interview as in Code C, section 11. If, however, the interviewer reasonably considers they may proceed to question the suspect with the audio recording still on, the interviewer may do so. This procedure also applies in cases where the suspect has previously objected to the interview being visually recorded, see Code F, para. 4.8, and the investigating officer has decided to audibly record the interview. (See *Note 4D*.)

E:4.9 If in the course of an interview a complaint is made by or on behalf of the person being questioned concerning the provisions of this or any other codes, or it comes to the interviewer's notice that the person may have been treated improperly, the interviewer shall act as in Code C, para. 12.9. (See *Notes 4E* and *4F*.)

E:4.10 If the suspect indicates they want to tell the interviewer about matters not directly connected with the offence of which they are suspected and they are unwilling for these matters to be audio recorded, the suspect should be given the opportunity to tell the interviewer about these matter [*sic*] after the conclusion of the formal interview.

(e) *Changing recording media*

E:4.11 When the recorder shows the recording media only has a short time left to run, the interviewer shall so inform the person being interviewed and round off that part of the interview. If the interviewer leaves the room for a second set of recording media, the suspect shall not be left unattended. The interviewer will remove the recording media from the recorder and insert the new recording media which shall be unwrapped or opened in the suspect's presence. The recorder should be set to record on the new media. To avoid confusion between the recording media, the interviewer shall mark the media with an identification number immediately after it is removed from the recorder.

[This paragraph does not apply to interviews recorded using a secure digital network as this does not use removable media, see paras 1.6(c), 7.4 and 7.14 to 7.15.]

(f) *Taking a break during interview*

A-172   E:4.12 When a break is taken, the fact that a break is to be taken, the reason for it and the time shall be recorded on the audio recording.

E:4.12A When the break is taken and the interview room vacated by the suspect, the recording media shall be removed from the recorder and the procedures for the conclusion of an interview followed, see paragraph 4.18.

E:4.13 When a break is a short one and both the suspect and an interviewer remain in the interview room, the recording may be stopped. There is no need to remove the recording media and when the interview recommences the recording should continue on the same recording media. The time the interview recommences shall be recorded on the audio recording.

E:4.14 After any break in the interview the interviewer must, before resuming the interview, remind the person being questioned of their right to legal advice if they have not exercised it and that they remain under caution or, if there is any doubt, give the caution in full again. (See *Note 4G.*)

[Paragraphs 4.12 to 4.14 do not apply to interviews recorded using a secure digital network, see paras 7.4 and 7.8 to 7.10.]

(g) *Failure of recording equipment*

E:4.15 If there is an equipment failure which can be rectified quickly, *e.g.* by inserting new recording media, the interviewer shall follow the appropriate procedures as in paragraph 4.11. When the recording is resumed the interviewer shall explain what happened and record the time the interview recommences. If, however, it will not be possible to continue recording on that recorder and no replacement recorder is readily available, the interview may continue without being audibly recorded. If this happens, the interviewer shall seek the authority as in paragraph 3.3 of the custody officer, or as applicable, a sergeant or above. (See *Note 4H.*)

[This paragraph does not apply to interviews recorded using a secure digital network, see paras 7.4 and 7.11.]

(h) *Removing recording media from the recorder*

E:4.16 Recording media which is removed from the recorder during the interview shall be retained and the procedures in paragraph 4.18 followed.

[This paragraph does not apply to interviews recorded using a secure digital network as this does not use removable media, see 1.6(c), 7.4 and 7.14 to 7.15.]

(i) *Conclusion of interview*

E:4.17 At the conclusion of the interview, the suspect shall be offered the opportunity to clarify anything they have said and asked if there is anything they want to add.

E:4.18 At the conclusion of the interview, including the taking and reading back of any written statement, the time shall be recorded and the recording shall be stopped. The interviewer shall seal the master recording with a master recording label and treat it as an exhibit in accordance with force standing orders. The interviewer shall sign the label and ask the suspect and any third party present during the interview to sign it. If the suspect or third party refuse to sign the label an officer of at least the rank of inspector, or if not available the custody officer, or if the suspect has not been arrested, a sergeant, shall be called into the interview room and asked, subject to paragraph 2.3, to sign it.

E:4.19 The suspect shall be handed a notice which explains:
- how the audio recording will be used;
- the arrangements for access to it;
- that if they are charged or informed they will be prosecuted, a copy of the audio recording will be supplied as soon as practicable or as otherwise agreed between the suspect and the police or on the order of the court.

[Paragraphs 4.17 to 4.19 do not apply to interviews recorded using a secure digital network, see paras 7.4 and 7.12 to 7.13.]

Notes for guidance

E:4A *For the purpose of voice identification the interviewer should ask the suspect and any other people present* **A-173**
to identify themselves.

E:4B *This provision is to give a person who is deaf or has impaired hearing equivalent rights of access to the*
full interview record as far as this is possible using audio recording.

E:4C *The provisions of Code C on interpreters for suspects who do not appear to speak or understand English,*
or who appear to have a hearing or speech impediment, continue to apply.

E:4D *The interviewer should remember that a decision to continue recording against the wishes of the suspect*
may be the subject of comment in court.

E:4E *If the custody officer, or in the case of a person who has not been arrested, a sergeant, is called to deal*
with the complaint, the recorder should, if possible, be left on until the officer has entered the room and spoken to
the person being interviewed. Continuation or termination of the interview should be at the interviewer's discretion
pending action by an inspector under Code C, para. 9.2.

E:4F *If the complaint is about a matter not connected with this code or Code C, the decision to continue is at* **A-174**
the interviewer's discretion. When the interviewer decides to continue the interview, they shall tell the suspect that
at the conclusion of the interview, the complaint will be brought to the attention of the custody officer, or in the
case of a person who has not been arrested, a sergeant. When the interview is concluded the interviewer must, as
soon as practicable, inform the custody officer or, as the case may be, the sergeant, about the existence and nature
of the complaint made.

E:4G *In considering whether to caution again after a break, the interviewer should bear in mind that they may*
have to satisfy a court that the person understood that they were still under caution when the interview resumed.
The interviewer should also remember that it may be necessary to show to the court that nothing occurred during a
break or between interviews which influenced the suspect's recorded evidence. After a break or at the beginning of
a subsequent interview, the interviewer should consider summarising on the record the reason for the break and
confirming this with the suspect.

E:4H *Where the interview is being recorded and the media or the recording equipment fails, the interviewer*
should stop the interview immediately. Where part of the interview is unaffected by the error and is still accessible
on the media, that part shall be copied and sealed in the suspect's presence as a master copy and the interview
recommenced using new equipment/media as required. Where the content of the interview has been lost in its
entirety, the media should be sealed in the suspect's presence and the interview begun again. If the recording
equipment cannot be fixed or no replacement is immediately available, the interview should be recorded in accord-
ance with Code C, section 11.

E:5 After the interview

E:5.1 The interviewer shall make a note in their pocket book that the interview has taken place **A-175**
and that it was audibly recorded, the time it commenced, its duration and date and identification
number of the master recording.

E:5.2 If no proceedings follow in respect of the person whose interview was recorded, the recording media must be kept securely as in paragraph 6.1 and *Note 6A.*

[This section (paras 5.1, 5.2 and Note 5A) does not apply to interviews recorded using a secure
digital network, see paras 7.4 and 7.14 to 7.15.]

Note for guidance

E:5A *Any written record of an audio recorded interview should be made in accordance with current national* **A-176**
guidelines for police officers, police staff and CPS prosecutors concerned with the preparation, processing and
submission of prosecution files.

E:6 Master recording security

(a) *General*

E:6.1 The officer in charge of each police station at which interviews with suspects are recorded or **A-177**
as the case may be, where recordings of interviews carried out elsewhere than at a police station are
held, shall make arrangements for master recordings to be kept securely and their movements accounted for on the same basis as material which may be used for evidential purposes, in accordance
with force standing orders. (See *Note 6A.*)

(b) *Breaking master recording seal for criminal proceedings*

E:6.2 A police officer has no authority to break the seal on a master recording which is required for criminal trial or appeal proceedings. If it is necessary to gain access to the master recording, the police officer shall arrange for its seal to be broken in the presence of a representative of the Crown Prosecution Service. The defendant or their legal adviser should be informed and given a reasonable opportunity to be present. If the defendant or their legal representative is present they shall be invited to re-seal and sign the master recording. If either refuses or neither is present this should be done by the representative of the Crown Prosecution Service. (See *Notes 6B* and *6C*.)

(c) *Breaking master recording seal: other cases*

E:6.3 The chief officer of police is responsible for establishing arrangements for breaking the seal of the master copy where no criminal proceedings result, or the criminal proceedings to which the interview relates have been concluded and it becomes necessary to break the seal. These arrangements should be those which the chief officer considers are reasonably necessary to demonstrate to the person interviewed and any other party who may wish to use or refer to the interview record that the master copy has not been tampered with and that the interview record remains accurate. (See *Note 6D*.)

E:6.3A Subject to paragraph 6.3C, a representative of each party must be given a reasonable opportunity to be present when the seal is broken and the master recording copied and resealed.

E:6.3B If one or more of the parties is not present when the master copy seal is broken because they cannot be contacted or refuse to attend or paragraph 6.6 applies, arrangements should be made for an independent person such as a custody visitor, to be present. Alternatively, or as an additional safeguard, arrangement should be made for a film or photographs to be taken of the procedure.

E:6.3C Paragraph 6.3A does not require a person to be given an opportunity to be present when:

(a) it is necessary to break the master copy seal for the proper and effective further investigation of the original offence or the investigation of some other offence; and

(b) the officer in charge of the investigation has reasonable grounds to suspect that allowing an opportunity might prejudice any such an investigation or criminal proceedings which may be brought as a result or endanger any person. (See *Note 6E*.)

(d) *Documentation*

E:6.4 When the master recording seal is broken, a record must be made of the procedure followed, including the date, time, place and persons present.

[This section (paras 6.1 to 6.4 and *Notes 6A* to *6E*) does not apply to interviews recorded using a secure digital network, see paras 7.4 and 7.14 to 7.15.]

Notes for guidance

E:6A *This section is concerned with the security of the master recording sealed at the conclusion of the interview. Care must be taken of working recordings because their loss or destruction may lead unnecessarily to the need to access master recordings.*

E:6B *If the master recording has been delivered to the Crown Court for their keeping after committal for trial the crown prosecutor will apply to the chief clerk of the Crown Court centre for the release of the recording for unsealing by the crown prosecutor.*

E:6C *Reference to the Crown Prosecution Service or to the crown prosecutor in this part of the code should be taken to include any other body or person with a statutory responsibility for the proceedings for which the police recorded interview is required.*

E:6D *The most common reasons for needing access to master copies that are not required for criminal proceedings arise from civil actions and complaints against police and civil actions between individuals arising out of allegations of crime investigated by police.*

E:6E *Paragraph 6.3C could apply, for example, when one or more of the outcomes or likely outcomes of the investigation might be: (i) the prosecution of one or more of the original suspects; (ii) the prosecution of someone previously not suspected, including someone who was originally a witness; and (iii) any original suspect being treated as a prosecution witness and when premature disclosure of any police action, particularly through contact with any parties involved, could lead to a real risk of compromising the investigation and endangering witnesses.*

E:7 Recording of interviews by secure digital network

E:7.1 A secure digital network does not use removable media and this section specifies the provisions which will apply when a secure digital network is used.

E:7.2 [*Not used.*]

E:7.3 The following requirements are solely applicable to the use of a secure digital network for the recording of interviews.

(a) *Application of sections 1 to 6 of Code E*

E:7.4 Sections 1 to 6 of Code E above apply except for the following paragraphs:
- paragraph 2.2 under "Recording and sealing of master recordings";
- paragraph 4.3 under "(b) Commencement of interviews";
- paragraph 4.4 (e) under "(b) Commencement of interviews";
- paragraphs 4.11 to 4.19 under "(e) Changing recording media", "(f) Taking a break during interview", "(g) Failure of recording equipment", "(h) Removing recording media from the recorder" and (i) "Conclusion of the interview"; and
- paragraphs 6.1 to 6.4 and *Notes 6A* to *6C* under "Media security".

(b) *Commencement of interviews*

E:7.5 When the suspect is brought into the interview room, the interviewer shall without delay and in the sight of the suspect, switch on the recording equipment and enter the information necessary to log on to the secure network and start recording.

E:7.6 The interviewer must then inform the suspect that the interview is being recorded using a secure digital network and that recording has commenced.

E:7.7 In addition to the requirements of paragraph 4.4(a) to (d) above, the interviewer must inform the person that:
- they will be given access to the recording of the interview in the event that they are charged or informed that they will be prosecuted but if they are not charged or informed that they will be prosecuted they will only be given access as agreed with the police or on the order of a court; and
- they will be given a written notice at the end of the interview setting out their rights to access the recording and what will happen to the recording.

(c) *Taking a break during interview*

E:7.8 When a break is taken, the fact that a break is to be taken, the reason for it and the time shall be recorded on the audio recording. The recording shall be stopped and the procedures in paragraphs 7.12 and 7.13 for the conclusion of an interview followed.

E:7.9 When the interview recommences the procedures in paragraphs 7.5 to 7.7 for commencing an interview shall be followed to create a new file to record the continuation of the interview. The time the interview recommences shall be recorded on the audio recording.

E:7.10 After any break in the interview the interviewer must, before resuming the interview, remind the person being questioned that they remain under caution or, if there is any doubt, give the caution in full again. (See *Note 4G.*)

(d) *Failure of recording equipment*

E:7.11 If there is an equipment failure which can be rectified quickly, *e.g.* by commencing a new secure digital network recording, the interviewer shall follow the appropriate procedures as in paragraphs 7.8 to 7.10. When the recording is resumed the interviewer shall explain what happened and record the time the interview recommences. If, however, it is not possible to continue recording on the secure digital network the interview should be recorded on removable media as in paragraph 4.3 unless the necessary equipment is not available. If this happens the interview may continue without being audibly recorded and the interviewer shall seek the authority of the custody officer or a sergeant as in paragraph 3.3(a) or (b). (See *Note 4H.*)

(e) *Conclusion of interview*

E:7.12 At the conclusion of the interview, the suspect shall be offered the opportunity to clarify anything he or she has said and asked if there is anything they want to add.

E:7.13 At the conclusion of the interview, including the taking and reading back of any written statement:
(a) the time shall be orally recorded;

(b) the suspect shall be handed a notice (see *Note 7A*) which explains:
- how the audio recording will be used,
- the arrangements for access to it,
- that if they are charged or informed that they will be prosecuted, they will be given access to the recording of the interview either electronically or by being given a copy on removable recording media, but if they are not charged or informed that they will prosecuted, they will only be given access as agreed with the police or on the order of a court;

(c) the suspect must be asked to confirm that he or she has received a copy of the notice at sub-paragraph (b) above; if the suspect fails to accept or to acknowledge receipt of the notice, the interviewer will state for the recording that a copy of the notice has been provided to the suspect and that he or she has refused to take a copy of the notice or has refused to acknowledge receipt;

(d) the time shall be recorded and the interviewer shall notify the suspect that the recording is being saved to the secure network. The interviewer must save the recording in the presence of the suspect. The suspect should then be informed that the interview is terminated.

(f) *After the interview*

E:7.14 The interviewer shall make a note in their pocket book that the interview has taken place and that it was audibly recorded, the time it commenced, its duration and date and the identification number of the original recording.

E:7.15 If no proceedings follow in respect of the person whose interview was recorded, the recordings must be kept securely as in paragraphs 7.16 and 7.17. (See *Note 5A*.)

(g) *Security of secure digital network interview records*

E:7.16 Interview record files are stored in read only format on non-removable storage devices, for example, hard disk drives, to ensure their integrity. The recordings are first saved locally to a secure non-removable device before being transferred to the remote network device. If for any reason the network connection fails, the recording remains on the local device and will be transferred when the network connections are restored.

E:7.17 Access to interview recordings, including copying to removable media, must be strictly controlled and monitored to ensure that access is restricted to those who have been given specific permission to access for specified purposes when this is necessary. For example, police officers and CPS lawyers involved in the preparation of any prosecution case, persons interviewed if they have been charged or informed they may be prosecuted and their legal representatives.

Note for guidance

A-179g   E:7A *The notice at paragraph 7.13 above should provide a brief explanation of the secure digital network and how access to the recording is strictly limited. The notice should also explain the access rights of the suspect, his or her legal representative, the police and the prosecutor to the recording of the interview. Space should be provided on the form to insert the date and the file reference number for the interview.*

ANNEX

Paragraph 3.1(a)(iii) - exemption from the requirement to audio record interviews for indictable offences - conditions

[See *Notes A1*, *A2* and *A3*.]

Part 1: Four specified indictable offence types – four conditions

★A-179h   E:1. The first condition is that the person has not been arrested.

E:2. The second condition is that the interview takes place elsewhere than at a police station (see *Note A4*).

E:3. The third condition is that the indictable offence in respect of which the person has been cautioned is one of the following:

(a) possession of a controlled drug, contrary to section 5(2) of the Misuse of Drugs Act 1971 if the drug is cannabis as defined by that Act but it is not cannabis oil (see *Note A5*);

(b) possession of a controlled drug, contrary to section 5(2) of the Misuse of Drugs Act 1971 if the drug is khat as defined by that Act (see *Note A5*);

(c) retail theft (shoplifting), contrary to section 1 of the Theft Act 1968 (see *Note A6*); and

(d) criminal damage to property, contrary to section 1(1) of the Criminal Damage Act 1971
(see *Note A6*),

and in this paragraph, the reference to each of the above offences applies to an attempt to commit
that offence, as defined by section 1 of the Criminal Attempts Act 1981.

E:4. The fourth condition is that:

(a) where the person has been cautioned in respect of an offence described in paragraph 3(a)
(possession of cannabis) or paragraph 3(b) (possession of khat), the requirements of
paragraphs 5 and 6 are satisfied; or

(b) where the person has been cautioned in respect of an offence described in paragraph 3(c)
(retail theft), the requirements of paragraphs 5 and 7 are satisfied; or

(c) where the person has been cautioned in respect of an offence described in paragraph 3(d)
(criminal damage), the requirements of paragraphs 5 and 8 are satisfied.

E:5. The requirements of this paragraph that apply to all four offences described in paragraph 3
are that:

(i) the person suspected of committing the offence:
- appears to be aged 18 or over;
- does not require an appropriate adult (see paragraph 1.5 of this code);
- appears to be able to appreciate the significance of questions and their answers;
- does not appear to be unable to understand what is happening because of the effects
of drink, drugs or illness, ailment or condition; and
- does not require an interpreter in accordance with Code C, section 13;

(ii) it appears that the commission of the offence:
- has not resulted in any injury to any person;
- has not involved any realistic threat or risk of injury to any person; and
- has not caused any substantial financial or material loss to the private property of any
individual;

(iii) in accordance with Code G (arrest), the person's arrest is not necessary in order to
investigate the offence; and

(iv) the person is not being interviewed about any other offence.

See *Notes A3* and *A8*.

E:6. The requirements of this paragraph that apply to the offences described in paragraph 3(a)
(possession of cannabis) and paragraph 3(b) (possession of khat) are that a police officer who is
experienced in the recognition of the physical appearance, texture and smell of cannabis or (as the
case may be) khat, is able to say that the substance which has been found in the suspect's possession
by that officer or, as the case may be, by any other officer not so experienced and trained:

(i) is a controlled drug being either cannabis which is not cannabis oil or khat; and

(ii) the quantity of the substance found is consistent with personal use by the suspect and
does not provide any grounds to suspect an intention to supply others.

See *Note A5*.

E:7. The requirements of this paragraph that apply to the offence described in paragraph 3(c)
(retail theft), are that it appears to the officer:

(i) that the value of the property stolen does not exceed £100 inclusive of VAT;

(ii) that the stolen property has been recovered and remains fit for sale unless the items
stolen comprised drink or food and have been consumed; and

(iii) that the person suspected of stealing the property is not employed (whether paid or not)
by the person, company or organisation to which the property belongs.

See *Note A3*.

E:8. The requirements of this paragraph that apply to the offence described in paragraph 3(d)
(criminal damage), are that it appears to the officer:

(i) that the value of the criminal damage does not exceed £300; and

(ii) that the person suspected of damaging the property is not employed (whether paid or
not) by the person, company or organisation to which the property belongs.

See *Note A3*.

Part 2: Other provisions applicable to all interviews to which this annex applies

E:9. Subject to paragraph 10, the provisions of paragraphs 3.21 and 3.22 of Code C (persons at-   ★**A-179i**
tending a police station or elsewhere voluntarily) regarding the suspect's right to free legal advice
and the other rights and entitlements that apply to all voluntary interviews, irrespective of where
they take place, will apply to any interview to which this annex applies. See *Note A7*.

E:10. If it appears to the interviewing officer that before the conclusion of an interview, any of the requirements in paragraphs 5 to 8 of Part 1 that apply to the offence in question described in paragraph 3 of Part 1 have ceased to apply, this annex shall cease to apply. The person being interviewed must be so informed and a break in the interview must be taken. The reason must be recorded in the interview record and the continuation of the interview shall be audio recorded in accordance with sections 1 to 7 of this code. For the purpose of the continuation, the provisions of paragraphs 4.3 and 7.5 (commencement of interviews) shall apply. See *Note A8*.

Notes for guidance

★**A-179j** E:A1 *This annex sets out conditions and requirements of the limited exemption referred to in paragraph 3.1(a)(iii), from the requirement to make an audio recording of an interview about an indictable offence, including offences triable either way.*

E:A2 *The purpose of the exemption is to support the policy which gives police in England and Wales options for dealing with low-level offences quickly and non-bureaucratically in a proportionate manner. Guidance for police about these options is available at: https://www.app.college.police.uk/app-content/prosecution-and-case-management/justiceoutcomes/.*

E:A3 *A decision in relation to a particular offence that the conditions and requirements in this annex for an audio-recording exemption are satisfied is an operational matter for the interviewing officer according to all the particular circumstances of the case. These circumstances include the outcome of the officer's investigation at that time and any other matters that are relevant to the officer's consideration as to how to deal with the matter.*

E:A4 *An interviewer who is not sure, or has any doubt, about the suitability of a place or location for carrying out an interview elsewhere than at a police station, should consult an officer of the rank of sergeant or above for advice. (Repeated from Note 1A).*

E:A5 *Under the Misuse of Drugs Act 1971 as at the date this code comes into force:*

    (a) *cannabis includes any part of the cannabis plant but not mature stalks and seeds separated from the plant, cannabis resin and cannabis oil, but paragraph 3(a) does not apply to the possession of cannabis oil; and*

    (b) *khat includes the leaves, stems and shoots of the plant.*

E:A6 *The power to issue a penalty notice for disorder (PND) for an offence contrary to section 1 of the Theft Act 1968 applies when the value of the goods stolen does not exceed £100 inclusive of VAT. The power to issue a PND for an offence contrary to section 1(1) of the Criminal Damage Act 1971 applies when the value of the damage does not exceed £300.*

E:A7 *The interviewing officer is responsible for ensuring compliance with the provisions of Code C applicable to the conduct and recording of voluntary interviews to which this annex applies. These include the right to free legal advice and the provision of a notice explaining the arrangements (see Code C, para. 3.21 and section 6), the provision of information about the offence before the interview (see Code C, para. 11.1A) and the right to interpretation and translation (see Code C, section 13).*

E:A8 *The requirements in paragraph 5 of Part 1 will cease to apply if, for example during the course of an interview, as a result of what the suspect says or other information which comes to the interviewing officer's notice:*

    • *it appears that the suspect:*

      ~ *is aged under 18;*

      ~ *does require an appropriate adult;*

      ~ *is unable to appreciate the significance of questions and their answers;*

      ~ *is unable to understand what is happening because of the effects of drink, drugs or illness, ailment or condition; or*

      ~ *requires an interpreter; or*

    • *the police officer decides that the suspect's arrest is now necessary (see Code G).*

(7) Visual recording of interviews

A-180 The text that follows is of the version of the code that came into force on October 27, 2013: see *ante*, Appendix A-1.

As at February 26, 2016, there was no requirement on any police force to make visual recordings of interviews, but police officers who choose to make such recordings will still be required to have regard to the provisions of this code.

F. CODE OF PRACTICE ON VISUAL RECORDINGS WITH SOUND OF INTERVIEWS WITH SUSPECTS

Commencement—transitional arrangements

The contents of this code should be considered if an interviewer decides to make a visual record- **A-180a** ing with sound of an interview with a suspect after 00.00 on 27 October 2013. There is no statutory requirement under *PACE* to visually record interviews.

F:1 General

F:1.0 The procedures in this code must be used fairly, responsibly, with respect for the people to **A-181** whom they apply and without unlawful discrimination. Under the Equality Act 2010, section 149, when police officers are carrying out their functions, they also have a duty to have due regard to the need to eliminate unlawful discrimination, harassment and victimisation, to advance equality of opportunity between people who share a relevant protected characteristic and people who do not share it, and to take steps to foster good relations between those persons. [See *Note 1C*.]

F:1.1 This code of practice must be readily available for consultation by police officers and other police staff, detained persons and members of the public.

F:1.2 The notes for guidance included are not provisions of this code. They form guidance to police officers and others about its application and interpretation.

F:1.3 Nothing in this code shall be taken as detracting in any way from the requirements of the Code of Practice for the Detention, Treatment and Questioning of Persons by Police Officers (Code C). [See *Note 1A*.]

F:1.4 The interviews to which this code applies are described in section 3.

F:1.5 In this code, the term "appropriate adult", "solicitor" and "interview" have the same meaning as those set out in Code C and in the case of a 17-year-old suspect, "appropriate adult" includes the person called to fulfil that role in accordance with paragraph 1.5A of Code C. The corresponding provisions and *Notes for Guidance* in Code C applicable to those terms shall also apply where appropriate.

F:1.5A The visual recording of interviews shall be carried out openly to instil confidence in its reliability as an impartial and accurate record of the interview.

F:1.6 Any reference in this code to visual recording shall be taken to mean visual recording with sound and in this code:

(aa) "recording media" means any removable, physical audio recording medium (such as magnetic tape, optical disc or solid state memory) which can be played and copied;

(a) "designated person" means a person other than a police officer, designated under the Police Reform Act 2002, Pt 4, who has specified powers and duties of police officers conferred or imposed on them;

(b) any reference to a police officer includes a designated person acting in the exercise or performance of the powers and duties conferred or imposed on them by their designation;

(c) "secure digital network" is a computer network system which enables an original interview recording to be stored as a digital multi media file or a series of such files, on a secure file server which is accredited by the National Accreditor for Police Information Systems in accordance with the UK Government Protective Marking Scheme. See paragraph 1.6A and section 7 of this code.

F:1.6A Section 7 below sets out the provisions which apply to interviews visually recorded using a secure digital network by reference to Code E and by excluding provisions of sections 1 to 6 of this code which relate or apply only to removable media.

F:1.7 References to "pocket book" in this code include any official report book issued to police officers.

F:1.8 In the application of this code to the conduct and visual recording of an interview of a suspect who has not been arrested:

(a) references to the "custody officer" include references to an officer of the rank of sergeant or above who is not directly involved in the investigation of the offence(s);

(b) if the interview takes place elsewhere than at a police station, references to "interview room" include any place or location which the interviewer is satisfied will enable the interview to be conducted and recorded in accordance with this code and where the suspect is present voluntarily [see *Note 1B*]; and

(c) provisions in addition to those which expressly apply to these interviews shall be followed insofar as they are relevant and can be applied in practice.

Notes for guidance

F:1A *As in paragraph 1.9 of Code C, references to custody officers include those carrying out the functions of a custody officer.*

F:1B *An interviewer who is not sure, or has any doubt, about the suitability of a place or location of an interview to be carried out elsewhere than at a police station, should consult an officer of the rank of sergeant or above for advice.*

F:1C *In paragraph 1.0, "relevant protected characteristic" includes: age, disability, gender reassignment, pregnancy and maternity, race, religion/belief, sex and sexual orientation.*

F:2 Recording and sealing of master recordings

A-182

F:2.1 [*Not used.*]

F:2.2 The camera(s) shall be placed in the interview room so as to ensure coverage of as much of the room as is practicably possible whilst the interviews are taking place. [See *Note 2A.*]

F:2.3 When the recording medium is placed in the recorder and it is switched on to record, the correct date and time, in hours, minutes and seconds will be superimposed automatically, second by second, during the whole recording, see *Note 2B*. See section 7 regarding the use of a secure digital network to record the interview.

F:2.4 One recording, referred to in this code as the master recording copy, will be sealed before it leaves the presence of the suspect. A second recording will be used as a working copy. [See *Notes 2C* and *2D*.]

F:2.5 Nothing in this code requires the identity of an officer or police staff to be recorded or disclosed:

    (a) [*not used*];

    (b) if the interviewer reasonably believes that recording or disclosing their name might put them in danger.

In these cases, the interviewer will have their back to the camera and shall use their warrant or other identification number and the name of the police station to which they are attached. Such instances and the reasons for them shall be recorded in the custody record or the interviewer's pocket book. [See *Note 2E*.]

Notes for guidance

A-183

F:2A *Interviewers will wish to arrange that, as far as possible, visual recording arrangements are unobtrusive. It must be clear to the suspect, however, that there is no opportunity to interfere with the recording equipment or the recording media.*

F:2B *In this context, the recording medium should be capable of having an image of the date and time superimposed as the interview is recorded.*

F:2C *The purpose of sealing the master recording before it leaves the presence of the suspect is to establish their confidence that the integrity of the recording is preserved.*

F:2D *The visual recording of the interview may be used for identification procedures in accordance with paragraph 3.21 or Annex E of Code D.*

F:2E *The purpose of the [sic] paragraph 2.5(b) is to protect police officers and others involved in the investigation of serious organised crime or the arrest of particularly violent suspects when there is reliable information that those arrested or their associates may threaten or cause harm to the officers, their families or their personal property. In cases of doubt, an officer of inspector rank should be consulted.*

F:3 Interviews to be visually recorded

A-184

F:3.1 Subject to paragraph 3.2 below, when an interviewer is deciding whether to make a visual recording, these are the areas where it might be appropriate:

    (a) with a suspect in respect of an indictable offence (including an offence triable either way) [see *Notes 3A* and *3B*];

    (b) which takes place as a result of an interviewer exceptionally putting further questions to a suspect about an offence described in sub-paragraph (a) above after they have been charged with, or informed they may be prosecuted for, that offence [see *Note 3C*];

    (c) in which an interviewer wishes to bring to the notice of a person, after that person has been charged with, or informed they may be prosecuted for an offence described in subparagraph (a) above, any written statement made by another person, or the content of an interview with another person [see *Note 3D*];

    (d) with, or in the presence of, a deaf or deaf/blind or speech impaired person who uses sign language to communicate;

(e) with, or in the presence of anyone who requires an "appropriate adult"; or

(f) in any case where the suspect or their representative requests that the interview be recorded visually.

F:3.2 The Terrorism Act 2000 and the Counter-Terrorism Act 2008 make separate provisions for **A-185** a code of practice for the video recording with sound of:

- interviews of persons detained under section 41 of, or Schedule 7 to, the 2000 Act; and
- post-charge questioning of persons authorised under section 22 or 23 of the 2008 Act.

The provisions of this code do not therefore apply to such interviews. [See *Note 3E*.]

F:3.3 Following a decision by an interviewer to visually record any interview mentioned in paragraph 3.1 above, the custody officer in the case of a detained person, or a sergeant in the case of a suspect who has not been arrested, may authorise the interviewer not to make a visual record and for the purpose of this code (F), the provisions of Code E, paras 3.1, 3.2, 3.3, 3.3A and 3.4 shall apply as appropriate. However, authority not to make a visual recording does not detract in any way from the requirement for audio recording. This would require a further authorisation not to make in accordance with Code E. [See *Note 3F*.]

F:3.4 [*Not used*.]

F:3.5 The whole of each interview shall be recorded visually, including the taking and reading back of any statement.

F:3.6 A sign or indicator which is visible to the suspect must show when the visual recording equipment is recording.

Notes for guidance

F:3A *Nothing in the code is intended to preclude visual recording at police discretion of interviews at police* **A-186** *stations or elsewhere with people cautioned in respect of offences not covered by paragraph 3.1, or responses made by persons after they have been charged with or informed they may be prosecuted for, an offence, provided that this code is complied with.*

F:3B *Attention is drawn to the provisions set out in Code C about the matters to be considered when deciding whether a detained person is fit to be interviewed.*

F:3C *Code C sets out the circumstances in which a suspect may be questioned about an offence after being charged with it.*

F:3D *Code C sets out the procedures to be followed when a person's attention is drawn after charge, to a statement made by another person. One method of bringing the content of an interview with another person to the notice of a suspect may be to play them a recording of that interview.*

F:3E *If during the course of an interview under this code, it becomes apparent that the interview should be conducted under the terrorism code for the video recording with sound of interviews, the interview should only continue in accordance with that code.*

F:3F *A decision not to record an interview visually for any reason may be the subject of comment in court. The authorising officer should therefore be prepared to justify their decision in each case.*

F:4 The interview

(a) *General*

F:4.1 The provisions of Code C in relation to cautions and interviews and the Notes for Guidance **A-187** applicable to those provisions shall apply to the conduct of interviews to which this code applies.

F:4.2 Particular attention is drawn to those parts of Code C that describe the restrictions on drawing adverse inferences from an arrested suspect's failure or refusal to say anything about their involvement in the offence when interviewed, or after being charged or informed they may be prosecuted and how those restrictions affect the terms of the caution and determine whether a special warning under sections 36 and 37 of the Criminal Justice and Public Order Act 1994 can be given.

(b) *Commencement of interviews*

F:4.3 When the suspect is brought into the interview room the interviewer shall without delay, but **A-188** in sight of the suspect, load the recording equipment and set it to record. The recording media must be unwrapped or otherwise opened in the presence of the suspect. [See *Note 4A*.]

F:4.4 The interviewer shall then tell the suspect formally about the visual recording and point out the sign or indicator which shows that the recording equipment is activated and recording. See paragraph 3.6. The interviewer shall:

(a) explain that the interview is being visually recorded;

(b) subject to paragraph 2.5, give their name and rank, and that of any other interviewer present;

(c) ask the suspect and any other party present (*e.g.* the appropriate adult, a solicitor or interpreter) to identify themselves;

(d) state the date, time of commencement and place of the interview; and

(e) state that the suspect will be given a notice about what will happen to the recording.
[See *Note 4AA.*]

F:4.4A Any person entering the interview room after the interview has commenced shall be invited by the interviewer to identify themselves for the purpose of the recording and state the reason why they have entered the interview room.

F:4.5 The interviewer shall then caution the suspect, see Code C, section 10, and:

• if they are detained, remind them of their entitlement to free legal advice, see Code C, para. 11.2, or

• if they are not detained under arrest, explain this and their entitlement to free legal advice, see Code C, para. 3.21.

F:4.6 The interviewer shall then put to the suspect any significant statement or silence, see Code C, para. 11.4.

(c) *Interviews with suspects who appear to require an interpreter*

A-189   F:4.7 The provisions of Code C on interpreters for suspects who do not appear to speak or understand English, or who appear to have a hearing or speech impediment, continue to apply.

(d) *Objections and complaints by the suspect*

A-190   F:4.8 If the suspect or an appropriate adult on their behalf, objects to the interview being visually recorded either at the outset or during the interview or during a break in the interview, the interviewer shall explain that the interview is being visually recorded and that this code requires the objections to be recorded on the visual recording. When any objections have been recorded or the suspect or the appropriate adult have refused to have their objections recorded, the interviewer shall say that they are turning off the visual recording, give their reasons and turn it off. If a separate audio recording is being maintained, the interviewer shall ask the person to record the reasons for refusing to agree to the interview being visually recorded. Paragraph 4.8 of Code E will apply if the person also objects to the interview being audio recorded. If the interviewer reasonably considers they may proceed to question the suspect with the visual recording still on, the interviewer may do so. [See *Note 4G.*]

F:4.9 If in the course of an interview a complaint is made by the person being questioned, or on their behalf, concerning the provisions of this or any other code, or it comes to the interviewer's notice that the person may have been treated improperly, then the interviewer shall act as in Code C, para. 12.9. [See *Notes 4B* and *4C.*]

F:4.10 If the suspect indicates that they wish to tell the interviewer about matters not directly connected with the offence of which they are suspected and that they are unwilling for these matters to be visually recorded, the suspect should be given the opportunity to tell the interviewer about these matters after the conclusion of the formal interview.

(e) *Changing the recording media*

A-191   F:4.11 In instances where the recording medium is not of sufficient length to record all of the interview with the suspect, further certified recording medium will be used. When the recording equipment indicates that the recording medium has only a short time left to run, the interviewer shall advise the suspect and round off that part of the interview. If the interviewer wishes to continue the interview but does not already have further certified recording media with him, they shall obtain a set. The suspect should not be left unattended in the interview room. The interviewer will remove the recording media from the recording equipment and insert the new ones which have been unwrapped or otherwise opened in the suspect's presence. The recording equipment shall then be set to record. Care must be taken, particularly when a number of sets of recording media have been used, to ensure that there is no confusion between them. This could be achieved by marking the sets of recording media with consecutive identification numbers.

(f) *Taking a break during the interview*

A-192   F:4.12 When a break is taken, the fact that a break is to be taken, the reason for it and the time shall be recorded on the visual record.

F:4.12A When the break is taken and the interview room vacated by the suspect, the recording media shall be removed from the recorder and the procedures for the conclusion of an interview followed. (See para. 4.18.)

F:4.13 When a break is a short one and both the suspect and an interviewer remain in the interview room, the recording may be stopped. There is no need to remove the recording media and when the interview recommences the recording should continue on the same recording media. The time at which the interview recommences shall be recorded.

F:4.14 After any break in the interview the interviewer must, before resuming the interview, remind the person being questioned of their right to legal advice if they have not exercised it and that they remain under caution or, if there is any doubt, give the caution in full again. [See *Notes 4D* and *4E.*]

(g) *Failure of recording equipment*

F:4.15 If there is a failure of equipment which can be rectified quickly, the appropriate procedures **A-193** set out in paragraph 4.12 shall be followed. When the recording is resumed the interviewer shall explain what has happened and record the time the interview recommences. If, however, it is not possible to continue recording on that particular recorder and no alternative equipment is readily available, the interview may continue without being recorded visually. In such circumstances, the procedures set out in paragraph 3.3 of this code for seeking the authority of the custody officer or a sergeant will be followed. [See *Note 4F.*]

(h) *Removing used recording media from recording equipment*

F:4.16 Where used recording media are removed from the recording equipment during the **A-194** course of an interview, they shall be retained and the procedures set out in paragraph 4.18 below followed.

(i) *Conclusion of interview*

F:4.17 Before the conclusion of the interview, the suspect shall be offered the opportunity to **A-195** clarify anything he or she has said and asked if there is anything that they wish to add.

F:4.18 At the conclusion of the interview, including the taking and reading back of any written statement, the time shall be recorded and the recording equipment switched off. The master recording shall be removed from the recording equipment, sealed with a master recording label and treated as an exhibit in accordance with the force standing orders. The interviewer shall sign the label and also ask the suspect and any third party present during the interview to sign it. If the suspect or third party refuses to sign the label, an officer of at least the rank of inspector, or if one is not available, the custody officer or, if the suspect has not been arrested, a sergeant, shall be called into the interview room and asked, subject to paragraph 2.5, to sign it.

F:4.19 The suspect shall be handed a notice which explains the use which will be made of the recording and the arrangements for access to it. The notice will also advise the suspect that a copy of the tape shall be supplied as soon as practicable if the person is charged or informed that he will be prosecuted.

Notes for guidance

F:4AA *For the purpose of voice identification the interviewer should ask the suspect and any other people* **A-196** *present to identify themselves.*

F:4A *The interviewer should attempt to estimate the likely length of the interview and ensure that an appropriate quantity of certified recording media and labels with which to seal the master copies are available in the interview room.*

F:4B *Where the custody officer, or in the case of a person who has not been arrested, a sergeant, is called to deal with the complaint, wherever possible the recorder should be left to run until the officer has entered the interview room and spoken to the person being interviewed. Continuation or termination of the interview should be at the discretion of the interviewer pending action by an inspector under Code C, para.9.2.*

F:4C *Where the complaint is about a matter not connected with this code or Code C, the decision to continue with the interview is at the interviewer's discretion. Where the interviewer decides to continue with the interview, the person being interviewed shall be told that at the conclusion of the interview, the complaint will be brought to the attention of the custody officer, or in the case of a person who has not been arrested, a sergeant. When the interview is concluded, the interviewer must, as soon as practicable, inform the custody officer or the sergeant of the existence and nature of the complaint made.*

F:4D *In considering whether to caution again after a break, the interviewer should bear in mind that they may have to satisfy a court that the person understood that they were still under caution when the interview resumed.*

F:4E *The officer should bear in mind that it may be necessary to satisfy the court that nothing occurred during a break in an interview or between interviews which influenced the suspect's recorded evidence. On the recommencement of an interview, the interviewer should consider summarising on the record the reason for the break and confirming this with the suspect.*

F:4F *Where the interview is being recorded and the media or the recording equipment fails, the interviewer should stop the interview immediately. Where part of the interview is unaffected by the error and is still accessible on the media, that part shall be copied and sealed in the suspect's presence as a master copy and the interview recommenced using new equipment/media as required. Where the content of the interview has been lost in its entirety, the media should be sealed in the suspect's presence and the interview begun again. If the recording equipment cannot be fixed or no replacement is immediately available, the interview should be audio recorded in accordance with Code E.*

F:4G *The interviewer should be aware that a decision to continue recording against the wishes of the suspect may be the subject of comment in court.*

F:5 After the interview

A-197

F:5.1 The interviewer shall make a note in his or her pocket book of the fact that the interview has taken place and has been recorded, its time, duration and date and the identification number of the master copy of the recording media.

F:5.2 Where no proceedings follow in respect of the person whose interview was recorded, the recording media must nevertheless be kept securely in accordance with paragraph 6.1 and *Note 6A.*

Note for guidance

F:5A *Any written record of a recorded interview shall be made in accordance with current national guidelines for police officers, police staff and CPS prosecutors concerned with the preparation, processing and submission of files.*

F:6 Master recording security

(a) *General*

A-198

F:6.1 The officer in charge of the police station at which interviews with suspects are recorded or as the case may be, where recordings of interviews carried out elsewhere than at a police station are held, shall make arrangements for the master copies to be kept securely and their movements accounted for on the same basis as other material which may be used for evidential purposes, in accordance with force standing orders. [See *Note 6A.*]

(b) *Breaking master recording seal for criminal proceedings*

A-199

F:6.2 A police officer has no authority to break the seal on a master copy which is required for criminal trial or appeal proceedings. If it is necessary to gain access to the master copy, the police officer shall arrange for its seal to be broken in the presence of a representative of the Crown Prosecution Service. The defendant or their legal adviser shall be informed and given a reasonable opportunity to be present. If the defendant or their legal representative is present they shall be invited to reseal and sign the master copy. If either refuses or neither is present, this shall be done by the representative of the Crown Prosecution Service. [See *Notes 6B* and *6C.*]

(c) *Breaking master recording seal: other cases*

A-200

F:6.3 The chief officer of police is responsible for establishing arrangements for breaking the seal of the master copy where no criminal proceedings result, or the criminal proceedings, to which the interview relates, have been concluded and it becomes necessary to break the seal. These arrangements should be those which the chief officer considers are reasonably necessary to demonstrate to the person interviewed and any other party who may wish to use or refer to the interview record that the master copy has not been tampered with and that the interview record remains accurate. [See *Note 6D.*]

F:6.4 Subject to paragraph 6.6, a representative of each party must be given a reasonable opportunity to be present when the seal is broken and the master recording copied and re-sealed.

F:6.5 If one or more of the parties is not present when the master copy seal is broken because they cannot be contacted or refuse to attend or paragraph 6.6 applies, arrangements should be made for an independent person such as a custody visitor, to be present. Alternatively, or as an additional safeguard, arrangement should be made for a film or photographs to be taken of the procedure.

F:6.6 Paragraph 6.4 does not require a person to be given an opportunity to be present when:

    (a) it is necessary to break the master copy seal for the proper and effective further investigation of the original offence or the investigation of some other offence; and

    (b) the officer in charge of the investigation has reasonable grounds to suspect that allowing an opportunity might prejudice any such an investigation or criminal proceedings which may be brought as a result or endanger any person. [See *Note 6E.*]

(d) *Documentation*

F:6.7 When the master copy seal is broken, copied and re-sealed, a record must be made of the **A-201** procedure followed, including the date time and place and persons present.

Notes for guidance

F:6A *This section is concerned with the security of the master recordings which will have been sealed at the* **A-202** *conclusion of the interview. Care should, however, be taken of working recordings since their loss or destruction may lead unnecessarily to the need to have access to master copies.*

F:6B *If the master recording has been delivered to the Crown Court for their keeping after committal for trial the crown prosecutor will apply to the chief clerk of the Crown Court centre for its release for unsealing by the crown prosecutor.*

F:6C *Reference to the Crown Prosecution Service or to the crown prosecutor in this part of the code shall be taken to include any other body or person with a statutory responsibility for prosecution for whom the police conduct any recorded interviews.*

F:6D *The most common reasons for needing access to master recordings that are not required for criminal proceedings arise from civil actions and complaints against police and civil actions between individuals arising out of allegations of crime investigated by police.*

F:6E *Paragraph 6.6 could apply, for example, when one or more of the outcomes or likely outcomes of the investigation might be: (i) the prosecution of one or more of the original suspects; (ii) the prosecution of someone previously not suspected, including someone who was originally a witness; and (iii) any original suspect being treated as a prosecution witness and when premature disclosure of any police action, particularly through contact with any parties involved, could lead to a real risk of compromising the investigation and endangering witnesses.*

F:7 Visual recording of interviews by secure digital network

F:7.1 This section applies if an officer wishes to make a visual recording with sound of an interview **A-202a** mentioned in section 3 of this code using a secure digital network which does not use removable media (see paragraph 1.6(c) above).

F:7.3 [*sic*] The provisions of sections 1 to 6 of this code which relate or apply only to removable media will not apply to a secure digital network recording.

F:7.4 The statutory requirement and provisions for the audio recording of interviews using a secure digital network set out in section 7 of Code E should be applied to the visual recording with sound of interviews mentioned in section 3 of this code as if references to audio recordings of interviews include visual recordings with sound.

(8) **Statutory power of arrest**

The first version of Code G came into force on January 1, 2006, to coincide with the com- **A-203** mencement of the substantial changes to the provisions of the PACE Act 1984 relating to the powers of arrest of police constables. As from that date, all offences became arrestable offences, but the lawfulness of an arrest by a constable for an offence became dependent on the constable having "reasonable grounds for believing that for any of the reasons mentioned in subsection (5) [of section 24] it is necessary to arrest the person in question". For the substituted section 24, see § 15-131 in the main work.

A revised code G came into force on November 12, 2012 (see *ante*, A-1).

G. CODE OF PRACTICE FOR THE STATUTORY POWER OF ARREST BY POLICE OFFICERS

Commencement

This code applies to any arrest made by a police officer after 00.00 on 12 November 2012. **A-203a**

G:1 Introduction

G:1.1 This code of practice deals with statutory power of police to arrest a person who is involved, **A-204** or suspected of being involved, in a criminal offence. The power of arrest must be used fairly, responsibly, with respect for people suspected of committing offences and without unlawful discrimination. The Equality Act 2010 makes it unlawful for police officers to discriminate against, harass or victimise any person on the grounds of the "protected characteristics" of age, disability, gender reassignment, race, religion or belief, sex and sexual orientation, marriage and civil partnership, pregnancy and maternity when using their powers. When police forces are carrying out their functions they also have a duty to have regard to the need to eliminate unlawful discrimination, harassment and victimisation and to take steps to foster good relations.

G:1.2 The exercise of the power of arrest represents an obvious and significant interference with the right to liberty and security under Article 5 of the European Convention on Human Rights set out in Part I of Schedule 1 to the Human Rights Act 1998.

G:1.3 The use of the power must be fully justified and officers exercising the power should consider if the necessary objectives can be met by other, less intrusive means. Absence of justification for exercising the power of arrest may lead to challenges should the case proceed to court. It could also lead to civil claims against police for unlawful arrest and false imprisonment. When the power of arrest is exercised it is essential that it is exercised in a non-discriminatory and proportionate manner which is compatible with the right to liberty under Article 5. See *Note 1B*.

G:1.4 Section 24 of the Police and Criminal Evidence Act 1984 (as substituted by section 110 of the Serious Organised Crime and Police Act 2005) provides the statutory power for a constable to arrest without warrant for all offences. If the provisions of the Act and this code are not observed, both the arrest and the conduct of any subsequent investigation may be open to question.

G:1.5 This code of practice must be readily available at all police stations for consultation by police officers and police staff, detained persons and members of the public.

G:1.6 The notes for guidance are not provisions of this code.

G:2 Elements of arrest under section 24 PACE

A-205   G:2.1 A lawful arrest requires two elements:

a person's involvement or suspected involvement or attempted involvement in the commission of a criminal offence; and

reasonable grounds for believing that the person's arrest is necessary.

Both elements must be satisfied, and it can never be necessary to arrest a person unless there are reasonable grounds to suspect them of committing an offence.

G:2.2 The arrested person must be informed that they have been arrested, even if this fact is obvious, and of the relevant circumstances of the arrest in relation to both the above elements. The custody officer must be informed of these matters on arrival at the police station. See paragraphs 2.9, 3.3 and *Note 3* and Code C, para. 3.4.

(a) *"Involvement in the commission of an offence"*

A-206   G:2.3 A constable may arrest without warrant in relation to any offence (see *Notes 1* and *1A*) anyone:

- who is about to commit an offence or is in the act of committing an offence;
- whom the officer has reasonable grounds for suspecting is about to commit an offence or to be committing an offence;
- whom the officer has reasonable grounds to suspect of being guilty of an offence which he or she has reasonable grounds for suspecting has been committed;
- anyone [*sic*] who is guilty of an offence which has been committed or anyone whom the officer has reasonable grounds for suspecting to be guilty of that offence.

G:2.3A There must be some reasonable, objective grounds for the suspicion, based on known facts and information which are relevant to the likelihood the offence has been committed and the person liable to arrest committed it. See *Notes 2* and *2A*.

(b) *Necessity criteria*

A-207   G:2.4 The power of arrest is only exercisable if the constable has reasonable grounds for believing that it is necessary to arrest the person. The statutory criteria for what may constitute necessity are set out in paragraph 2.9 and it remains an operational decision at the discretion of the constable to decide:

- which one or more of the necessity criteria (if any) applies to the individual; and
- if any of the criteria do apply, whether to arrest, grant street bail after arrest, report for summons or for charging by post, issue a penalty notice or take any other action that is open to the officer.

G:2.5 In applying the criteria, the arresting officer has to be satisfied that at least one of the reasons supporting the need for arrest is satisfied.

G:2.6 Extending the power of arrest to all offences provides a constable with the ability to use that power to deal with any situation. However, applying the necessity criteria requires the constable to examine and justify the reason or reasons why a person needs to be arrested or (as the case may be) further arrested, for an offence for the custody officer to decide whether to authorise their detention for that offence. See *Note 2C*.

G:2.7 The criteria in paragraph 2.9 below which are set out in section 24 of PACE, as substituted by section 110 of the Serious Organised Crime and Police Act 2005, are exhaustive. However, the circumstances that may satisfy those criteria remain a matter for the operational discretion of individual officers. Some examples are given to illustrate what those circumstances might be and what officers might consider when deciding whether arrest is necessary.

G:2.8 In considering the individual circumstances, the constable must take into account the situation of the victim, the nature of the offence, the circumstances of the suspect and the needs of the investigative process.

G:2.9 When it is practicable to tell a person why their arrest is necessary (as required by paragraphs **A-208** 2.2, 3.3 and *Note 3*), the constable should outline the facts, information and other circumstances which provide the grounds for believing that their arrest is necessary and which the officer considers satisfy one or more of the statutory criteria in sub-paragraphs (a) to (f), namely:

(a) to enable the name of the person in question to be ascertained (in the case where the constable does not know, and cannot readily ascertain, the person's name, or has reasonable grounds for doubting whether a name given by the person as his name is his real name):

an officer might decide that a person's name cannot be readily ascertained if they fail or refuse to give it when asked, particularly after being warned that failure or refusal is likely to make their arrest necessary (see *Note 2D*); grounds to doubt a name given may arise if the person appears reluctant or hesitant when asked to give their name or to verify the name they have given;

where mobile fingerprinting is available and the suspect's name cannot be ascertained or is doubted, the officer should consider using the power under section 61(6A) of PACE (see Code D, para. 4.3(e)) to take and check the fingerprints of a suspect as this may avoid the need to arrest solely to enable their name to be ascertained;

(b) correspondingly as regards the person's address:

an officer might decide that a person's address cannot be readily ascertained if they fail or refuse to give it when asked, particularly after being warned that such a failure or refusal is likely to make their arrest necessary (see *Note 2D*); grounds to doubt an address given may arise if the person appears reluctant or hesitant when asked to give their address or is unable to provide verifiable details of the locality they claim to live in;

when considering reporting to consider summons or charging by post as alternatives to arrest, an address would be satisfactory if the person will be at it for a sufficiently long period for it to be possible to serve them with the summons or requisition and charge; or, that some other person at that address specified by the person will accept service on their behalf; when considering issuing a penalty notice, the address should be one where the person will be in the event of enforcement action if the person does not pay the penalty or is convicted and fined after a court hearing;

(c) to prevent the person in question:

(i) causing physical injury to himself or any other person; this might apply where the suspect has already used or threatened violence against others and it is thought likely that they may assault others if they are not arrested (see *Note 2D*);

(ii) suffering physical injury; this might apply where the suspect's behaviour and actions are believed likely to provoke, or have provoked, others to want to assault the suspect unless the suspect is arrested for their own protection (see *Note 2D*);

(iii) causing loss or damage to property; this might apply where the suspect is a known persistent offender with a history of serial offending against property (theft and criminal damage) and it is thought likely that they may continue offending if they are not arrested;

(iv) committing an offence against public decency (only applies where members of the public going about their normal business cannot reasonably be expected to avoid the person in question); this might apply when an offence against public decency is being committed in a place to which the public have access and is likely to be repeated in that or some other public place at a time when the public are likely to encounter the suspect (see *Note 2D*);

(v) causing an unlawful obstruction of the highway; this might apply to any offence where its commission causes an unlawful obstruction which it is believed may continue or be repeated if the person is not arrested, particularly if the person has been warned that they are causing an obstruction (see *Note 2D*);

(d) to protect a child or other vulnerable person from the person in question; this might apply when the health (physical or mental) or welfare of a child or vulnerable person is likely to be harmed or is at risk of being harmed, if the person is not arrested in cases where it is not practicable and appropriate to make alternative arrangements to prevent the suspect from having any harmful or potentially harmful contact with the child or vulnerable person;

(e) to allow the prompt and effective investigation of the offence or of the conduct of the person in question (see *Note 2E*); this may arise when it is thought likely that unless the person is arrested and then either taken in custody to the police station or granted "street bail" to attend the station later (see *Note 2J*), further action considered necessary to properly investigate their involvement in the offence would be frustrated, unreasonably delayed or otherwise hindered and therefore be impracticable; examples of such actions include:

(i) interviewing the suspect on occasions when the person's voluntary attendance is not considered to be a practicable alternative to arrest, because for example:
- it is thought unlikely that the person would attend the police station voluntarily to be interviewed;
- it is necessary to interview the suspect about the outcome of other investigative action for which their arrest is necessary, see (ii) to (v) below;
- arrest would enable the special warning to be given in accordance with Code C, paras 10.10 and 10.11 when the suspect is found:
  - in possession of incriminating objects, or at a place where such objects are found;
  - at or near the scene of the crime at or about the time it was committed;
- the person has made false statements and/or presented false evidence;
- it is thought likely that the person:
  - may steal or destroy evidence;
  - may collude or make contact with, co-suspects or conspirators;
  - may intimidate or threaten or make contact with, witnesses;
(see *Notes 2F* and *2G*);

(ii) when considering arrest in connection with the investigation of an indictable offence (see *Note 6*), there is a need:
- to enter and search without a search warrant any premises occupied or controlled by the arrested person or where the person was when arrested or immediately before arrest;
- to prevent the arrested person from having contact with others;
- to detain the arrested person for more than 24 hours before charge;

(iii) when considering arrest in connection with any recordable offence and it is necessary to secure or preserve evidence of that offence by taking fingerprints, footwear impressions or samples from the suspect for evidential comparison or matching with other material relating to that offence, for example, from the crime scene (see *Note 2H*);

(iv) when considering arrest in connection with any offence and it is necessary to search, examine or photograph the person to obtain evidence (see *Note 2H*);

(v) when considering arrest in connection with an offence to which the statutory Class A drug testing requirements in Code C, section 17, apply, to enable testing when it is thought that drug misuse might have caused or contributed to the offence (see *Note 2I*);

(f) to prevent any prosecution for the offence from being hindered by the disappearance of the person in question; this may arise when it is thought that:
- if the person is not arrested they are unlikely to attend court if they are prosecuted;
- the address given is not a satisfactory address for service of a summons or a written charge and requisition to appear at court because the person will not be at it for a sufficiently long period for the summons or charge and requisition to be served and no other person at that specified address will accept service on their behalf.

G:3 Information to be given on arrest

(a) Cautions—when a caution must be given

A-209   G:3.1 Code C, paras 10.1 and 10.2, set out the requirement for a person whom there are grounds to suspect of an offence (see *Note 2*) to be cautioned before being questioned or further questioned about an offence.

G:3.2 [*Not used.*]

G:3.3 A person who is arrested, or further arrested, must be informed at the time if practicable, or if not, as soon as it becomes practicable thereafter, that they are under arrest and of the grounds and reasons for their arrest (see paragraphs [*sic*] 2.2 and *Note 3*).

G:3.4 A person who is arrested, or further arrested, must be cautioned unless:

  (a) it is impracticable to do so by reason of their condition or behaviour at the time;

  (b) they have already been cautioned immediately prior to arrest as in paragraph 3.1.

(b) *Terms of the caution (taken from Code C, section 10)*

G:3.5 The caution, which must be given on arrest, should be in the following terms: **A-210**

"*You do not have to say anything. But it may harm your defence if you do not mention when questioned something which you later rely on in court. Anything you do say may be given in evidence.*".

Where the use of the Welsh language is appropriate, a constable may provide the caution directly in Welsh in the following terms:

"*Does dim rhaid i chi ddweud dim byd. Ond gall niweidio eich amddiffyniad os na fyddwch chi'n sôn, wrth gael eich holi, am rywbeth y byddwch chi'n dibynnu arno nes ymlaen yn y Llys. Gall unrhyw beth yr ydych yn ei ddweud gael ei roi fel tystiolaeth.*".

See *Note 4*.

G:3.6 Minor deviations from the words of any caution given in accordance with this code do not constitute a breach of this code, provided the sense of the relevant caution is preserved. See *Note 5*.

G:3.7 *Not used.*

G:4 Records of arrest

(a) *General*

G:4.1 The arresting officer is required to record in his pocket book or by other methods used for   **A-211** recording information:

  • the nature and circumstances of the offence leading to the arrest;

  • the reason or reasons why arrest was necessary;

  • the giving of the caution; and

  • anything said by the person at the time of arrest.

G:4.2 Such a record should be made at the time of the arrest unless impracticable to do. If not made at that time, the record should then be completed as soon as possible thereafter.

G:4.3 On arrival at the police station or after being first arrested at the police station, the arrested person must be brought before the custody officer as soon as practicable and a custody record must be opened in accordance with section 2 of Code C. The information given by the arresting officer on the circumstances and reason or reasons for arrest shall be recorded as part of the custody record. Alternatively, a copy of the record made by the officer in accordance with paragraph 4.1 above shall be attached as part of the custody record. See paragraph 2.2 and Code C, paras 3.4 and 10.3.

G:4.4 The custody record will serve as a record of the arrest. Copies of the custody record will be provided in accordance with paragraphs 2.4 and 2.4A of Code C and access for inspection of the original record in accordance with paragraph 2.5 of Code C.

(b) *Interviews and arrests*

G:4.5 Records of interviews, significant statements or silences will be treated in the same way as set out in sections 10 and 11 of Code C and in Codes E and F (audio and visual recording of interviews).

Notes for guidance

G:1 *For the purposes of this code, "offence" means any statutory or common law offence for which a person may*   **A-212** *be tried by a magistrates' court or the Crown Court and punished if convicted.* [The note then gives examples of statutory and common law offences.]

G:1A *This code does not apply to powers of arrest conferred on constables under any arrest warrant, for example, a warrant issued under the Magistrates' Courts Act 1980, ss.1 or 13, or the Bail Act 1976, s.7(1), or to the powers of constables to arrest without warrant other than under section 24 of PACE for an offence. These other powers to arrest without warrant do not depend on the arrested person committing any specific offence and include:*

  • *PACE, s.46A, arrest of person who fails to answer police bail to attend police station or is suspected of breaching any condition of that bail for the custody officer to decide whether they should be kept in* police detention which applies whether or not the person commits an offence under section 6 of the Bail Act 1976 (e.g. failing without reasonable cause to surrender to custody);

- Bail Act 1976, s.7(3), arrest of person bailed to attend court who is suspected of breaching, or is believed likely to breach, any condition of bail to take them to court for bail to be re-considered;
- Children and Young Persons Act 1969, s.32(1A) (absconding) – arrest to return the person to the place where they are required to reside;
- Immigration Act 1971, Sched. 2, to arrest a person liable to examination to determine their right to remain in the U.K.;
- Mental Health Act 1983, s.136 to remove person suffering from mental disorder to place of safety for assessment;
- Prison Act 1952, s.49, arrest to return person unlawfully at large to the prison, etc., where they are liable to be detained;
- Road Traffic Act 1988, s.6D, arrest of driver following the outcome of a preliminary roadside test requirement to enable the driver to be required to provide an evidential sample;
- common law power to stop or prevent a breach of the peace—after arrest a person aged 18 or over may be brought before a justice of the peace court to show cause why they should not be bound over to keep the peace – not criminal proceedings.

G:1B *Juveniles should not be arrested at their place of education unless this is unavoidable. When a juvenile is arrested at their place of education, the principal or their nominee must be informed (from Code C, Note 11D).*

G:2 *Facts and information relevant to a person's suspected involvement in an offence should not be confined to those which tend to indicate the person has committed or attempted to commit the offence. Before making a decision to arrest, a constable should take account of any facts and information that are available, including claims of innocence made by the person, that might dispel the suspicion.*

G:2A *Particular examples of facts and information which might point to a person's innocence and may tend to dispel suspicion include those which relate to the statutory defence provided by the Criminal Law Act 1967, s.3(1) which allows the use of reasonable force in the prevention of crime or making an arrest and the common law of self-defence. This may be relevant when a person appears, or claims, to have been acting reasonably in defence of themselves or others or to prevent their property or the property of others from being stolen, destroyed or damaged, particularly if the offence alleged is based on the use of unlawful force, e.g. a criminal assault. When investigating allegations involving the use of force by school staff, the power given to all school staff under the Education and Inspections Act 2006, s.93, to use reasonable force to prevent their pupils from committing any offence, injuring persons, damaging property or prejudicing the maintenance of good order and discipline may be similarly relevant. The Association of Chief Police Officers and the Crown Prosecution Service have published joint guidance to help the public understand the meaning of reasonable force and what to expect from the police and CPS in cases which involve claims of self-defence. Separate advice for school staff on their powers to use reasonable force is available from the Department for Education.*

G:2B *If a constable who is dealing with an allegation of crime and considering the need to arrest becomes an investigator for the purposes of the Code of Practice under the Criminal Procedure and Investigations Act 1996, the officer should, in accordance with paragraph 3.5 of that code, "pursue all reasonable lines of inquiry, whether these point towards or away from the suspect. What is reasonable in each case will depend on the particular circumstances."*

G:2C *For a constable to have reasonable grounds for believing it necessary to arrest, he or she is not required to be satisfied that there is no viable alternative to arrest. However, it does mean that in all cases, the officer should consider that arrest is the practical, sensible and proportionate option in all the circumstances at the time the decision is made. This applies equally to a person in police detention after being arrested for an offence who is suspected of involvement in a further offence and the necessity to arrest them for that further offence is being considered.*

G:2D *Although a warning is not expressly required, officers should if practicable, consider whether a warning which points out their offending behaviour, and explains why, if they do not stop, the resulting consequences may make their arrest necessary. Such a warning might:*

- *if heeded, avoid the need to arrest, or*
- *if it is ignored, support the need to arrest and also help prove the mental element of certain offences, for example, the person's intent or awareness, or help to rebut a defence that they were acting reasonably.*

A person who is warned that they may be liable to arrest if their real name and address cannot be ascertained, should be given a reasonable opportunity to establish their real name and address before deciding that either or both are unknown and cannot be readily ascertained or that there are reasonable grounds to doubt that a name and address they have given is their real name and address. They should be told why their name is not known and cannot be readily ascertained and (as the case may be) of the grounds for doubting that a name and address they have given is their real name and address, including, for example, the reason why a particular document the person has produced to verify their real name and/or address, is not sufficient.

G:2E *The meaning of "prompt" should be considered on a case by case basis taking account of all the circumstances. It indicates that the progress of the investigation should not be delayed to the extent that it would adversely affect the effectiveness of the investigation. The arresting officer also has discretion to release the arrested person on "street bail" as an alternative to taking the person directly to the station (see Note 2J).*

G:2F *An officer who believes that it is necessary to interview the person suspected of committing the offence must then consider whether their arrest is necessary in order to carry out the interview. The officer is not required to interrogate the suspect to determine whether they will attend a police station voluntarily to be interviewed but they must consider whether the suspect's voluntary attendance is a practicable alternative for carrying out the interview. If it is, then arrest would not be necessary. Conversely, an officer who considers this option but is not satisfied that it is a practicable alternative, may have reasonable grounds for deciding that the arrest is necessary at the outset "on the street". Without such considerations, the officer would not be able to establish that arrest was necessary in order to interview.*

Circumstances which suggest that a person's arrest "on the street" would not be necessary to interview them might be where the officer:

- *is satisfied as to their identity and address and that they will attend the police station voluntarily to be interviewed, either immediately or by arrangement at a future date and time; and*
- *is not aware of any other circumstances which indicate that voluntary attendance would not be a practicable alternative (see paragraph 2.9(e)(i) to (v)).*

When making arrangements for the person's voluntary attendance, the officer should tell the person:

- *that to properly investigate their suspected involvement in the offence they must be interviewed under caution at the police station, but in the circumstances their arrest for this purpose will not be necessary if they attend the police station voluntarily to be interviewed;*
- *that if they attend voluntarily, they will be entitled to free legal advice before, and to have a solicitor present at, the interview;*
- *that the date and time of the interview will take account of their circumstances and the needs of the investigation; and*
- *that if they do not agree to attend voluntarily at a time which meets the needs of the investigation, or having so agreed, fail to attend, or having attended, fail to remain for the interview to be completed, their arrest will be necessary to enable them to be interviewed.*

G:2G *When the person attends the police station voluntarily for interview by arrangement as in Note 2F above, their arrest on arrival at the station prior to interview would only be justified if:*

- *new information coming to light after the arrangements were made indicates that from that time, voluntary attendance ceased to be a practicable alternative and the person's arrest became necessary; and*
- *it was not reasonably practicable for the person to be arrested before they attended the station.*

If a person who attends the police station voluntarily to be interviewed decides to leave before the interview is complete, the police would at that point be entitled to consider whether their arrest was necessary to carry out the interview. The possibility that the person might decide to leave during the interview is therefore not a valid reason for arresting them before the interview has commenced (see Code C, para. 3.21).

G:2H *The necessity criteria do not permit arrest solely to enable the routine taking, checking (speculative searching) and retention of fingerprints, samples, footwear impressions and photographs when there are no prior grounds to believe that checking and comparing the fingerprints, etc., or taking a photograph would provide relevant evidence of the person's involvement in the offence concerned or would help to ascertain or verify their real identity.*

G:2I *The necessity criteria do not permit arrest for an offence solely because it happens to be one of the statutory drug testing "trigger offences" (see Code C, Note 17E) when there is no suspicion that Class A drug misuse might have caused or contributed to the offence.*

G:2J *Having determined that the necessity criteria have been met and having made the arrest, the officer can then consider the use of street bail on the basis of the effective and efficient progress of the investigation of the offence in question. It gives the officer discretion to compel the person to attend a police station at a date/ time that best suits the overall needs of the particular investigation. Its use is not confined to dealing with child care issues or allowing officers to attend to more urgent operational duties and granting street bail does not retrospectively negate the need to arrest.*

G:3 *An arrested person must be given sufficient information to enable them to understand they have been deprived of their liberty and the reason they have been arrested, as soon as practicable after the arrest, e.g. when a person is arrested on suspicion of committing an offence they must be informed of the nature of the suspected offence and when and where it was committed. The suspect must also be informed of the reason or reasons why arrest is considered necessary. Vague or technical language should be avoided. When explaining why one or more of the arrest criteria apply, it is not necessary to disclose any specific details that might undermine or otherwise adversely affect any investigative processes. An example might be the conduct of a formal interview when prior disclosure of such details might give the suspect an opportunity to fabricate an innocent explanation or to otherwise conceal lies from the interviewer.*

G:4 *Nothing in this code requires a caution to be given or repeated when informing a person not under arrest they may be prosecuted for an offence. However, a court will not be able to draw any inferences under the Criminal Justice and Public Order Act 1994, s.34, if the person was not cautioned.*

G:5 *If it appears a person does not understand the caution, the person giving it should explain it in their own words.*

G:6 *Certain powers available as the result of an arrest - for example, entry and search of premises, detention without charge beyond 24 hours, holding a person incommunicado and delaying access to legal advice - only apply in respect of indictable offences and are subject to the specific requirements on authorisation as set out in PACE and the relevant code of practice.*

(9) Detention treatment and questioning of terrorist suspects

A-213   The Police and Criminal Evidence Act 1984 (Code of Practice C and Code of Practice H) Order 2006 (S.I. 2006 No. 1938) provided for a revised Code C, and for a new Code H (on detention, treatment and questioning by police officers of persons under section 41 of, and Schedule 8 to, the Terrorism Act 2000), to come into operation on July 25, 2006. The new codes were consequential upon the commencement of the provisions of the Terrorism Act 2006, which were concerned with the 28-day detention of those arrested under section 41 of the 2000 Act. Whereas Code C had previously regulated the detention, treatment and questioning of those detained following arrest under section 41, from that date onwards these matters were regulated by Code H. Code C was revised so as to remove references to detention under the 2000 Act. The new Code H largely mirrored the provisions of Code C, but with various differences.

A revised Code H came into force on July 10, 2012, and a further revision came into force on October 27, 2013. The text that follows is that of a yet further revision that came into force on June 2, 2014 (see *ante*, A-1).

H. CODE OF PRACTICE IN CONNECTION WITH THE DETENTION, TREATMENT AND QUESTIONING BY POLICE OFFICERS OF PERSONS UNDER SECTION 41 OF, AND SCHEDULE 8 TO, THE TERRORISM ACT 2000

Commencement—transitional arrangements

A-214   This code applies to people in police detention after 00.00 on 2 June 2014, notwithstanding that their period of detention may have commenced before that time.

H:1 General

A-214a   H:1.0 *[Identical to C1:0.]*

H:1.1 This code of practice applies to, and only to:

(a) persons in police detention after being arrested under section 41 of the Terrorism Act 2000 (TACT) and detained under section 41 of, or Schedule 8 to that Act and not charged; and

(b) detained persons in respect of whom an authorisation has been given under section 22 of the Counter-Terrorism Act 2008 (post-charge questioning of terrorist suspects) to interview them in which case, section 15 of this code will apply.

H:1.2 The provisions in *PACE* Code C apply when a person:

(a) is in custody otherwise than as a result of being arrested under section 41 of TACT or detained for examination under Schedule 7 to TACT (see paragraph 1.4);

(b) is charged with an offence; or

(c) is being questioned about any offence after being charged with that offence without an authorisation being given under section 22 of the Counter-Terrorism Act 2008.

See *Note 1N.*

H:1.3 In this code references to an offence and to a person's involvement or suspected involvement in an offence where the person has not been charged with an offence, include being concerned, or suspected of being concerned, in the commission, preparation or instigation of acts of terrorism.

H:1.4 The code of practice issued under paragraph 6 of Schedule 14 to TACT applies to persons detained for examination under Schedule 7 to TACT. See *Note 1N.*

H:1.5 All persons in custody must be dealt with expeditiously, and released as soon as the need for detention no longer applies.

H:1.6 There is no provision for bail under TACT before or after charge. See *Note 1N.*

H:1.7 An officer must perform the assigned duties in this code as soon as practicable. An officer will not be in breach of this code if delay is justifiable and reasonable steps are taken to prevent unnecessary delay. The custody record shall show when a delay has occurred and the reason. See *Note 1H.*

H:1.8–1.10 [*Identical to C:1.2 to C:1.4, respectively.*]

H:1.11 For the purposes of this code, a juvenile is any person under the age of 17. If anyone appears to be under 17, and there is no clear evidence that they are 17 or over, they shall be treated as a juvenile for the purposes of this code.

H:1.11A If anyone appears to have attained the age of 17 and to be under the age of 18, they shall in the absence of clear evidence that they are older, be treated as a 17-year-old for the purposes of this code and the provisions and *Notes for Guidance* which in accordance with paragraph 1.11 apply to a juvenile and the way they are to be treated shall also apply to them, except for the purposes of the statutory provisions in section 65(1) of PACE (appropriate consent) which by virtue of paragraph 15 of Schedule 8 to the Terrorism Act 2000, applies to the powers in paragraphs 10 to 14 of that schedule to take fingerprints, intimate and non-intimate samples. For these powers, the statutory requirement for appropriate consent for a person who has not attained the age of 17 to be given by them and their parent or guardian shall not apply to a person who appears to have attained the age of 17 and whose consent alone is sufficient. (See *Notes 1O* and *1P.*)

H:1.12 [*Identical to C:1.6.*]

H:1.13 [*Identical to C:1.7, save for reference to "paragraph 1.11A" in lieu of reference to "paragraph 1.5A".*]

H:1.14 [*Identical to C:1.8.*]

H:1.15 [*Identical to C:1.9.*]

H:1.16 When this code requires the prior authority or agreement of an officer of at least inspector or superintendent rank, that authority may be given by a sergeant or chief inspector authorised by section 107 of PACE to perform the functions of the higher rank under TACT.

H:1.17 In this code:

- (a) "designated person" means a person other than a police officer, designated under the Police Reform Act 2002, Pt 4, who has specified powers and duties of police officers conferred or imposed on them;
- (b) reference to a police officer includes a designated person acting in the exercise or performance of the powers and duties conferred or imposed on them by their designation;
- (c) where a search or other procedure to which this code applies may only be carried out or observed by a person of the same sex as the detainee, the gender of the detainee and other parties present should be established and recorded in line with Annex I of this code.

H:1.18 [*Identical to C:1.14.*]

H:1.19 [*Identical to C:1.15.*]

H:1.20 Designated persons and other police staff must have regard to any relevant provisions of this code.

H:1.21 [*Identical to C:1.17.*]

Notes for guidance

H:1A *Although certain sections of this code apply specifically to people in custody at police stations, those there* **A-214b** *voluntarily to assist with an investigation should be treated with no less consideration, e.g. offered refreshments at appropriate times, and enjoy an absolute right to obtain legal advice or communicate with anyone outside the police station.*

H:1AA [*Identical to C:1AA.*]

H:1B *A person, including a parent or guardian, should not be an appropriate adult if they:*

- *are:*
  - *suspected of involvement in the offence or involvement in the commission, preparation or instigation of acts of terrorism;*
  - *the victim;*
  - *a witness;*
  - *involved in the investigation;*
- *received admissions prior to attending to act as the appropriate adult.*

Note: if a juvenile's parent is estranged from the juvenile, they should not be asked to act as the appropriate adult if the juvenile expressly and specifically objects to their presence.

Note: Paragraph 1.11A applies this note to 17-year-old detainees.

H:1C *If a juvenile admits an offence to, or in the presence of, a social worker or member of a youth offending team other than during the time that person is acting as the juvenile's appropriate adult, another appropriate adult should be appointed in the interest of fairness.*

Note: Paragraph 1.11A applies this note to 17-year-old detainees.

H:1D–1G [*Identical to C:1D–G.*]

H:1H *Paragraph 1.7 is intended to cover delays which may occur in processing detainees* e.g. *if:*

- *a large number of suspects are brought into the station simultaneously to be placed in custody;*
- *interview rooms are all being used;*
- *there are difficulties contacting an appropriate adult, solicitor or interpreter.*

H:1I–1K [*Identical to C:1I to C:1K, respectively.*]

H:1L *If a person is moved from a police station to receive medical treatment, or for any other reason, the period of detention is still calculated from the time of arrest under section 41 of TACT (or, if a person was being detained under TACT, Sched. 7, when arrested, from the time at which the examination under Schedule 7 began).*

H:1M *Under paragraph 1 of Schedule 8 to TACT, all police stations are designated for detention of persons arrested under section 41 of TACT. Paragraph 4 of Schedule 8 requires that the constable who arrests a person under section 41 takes him as soon as practicable to the police station which the officer considers is "most appropriate".*

H:1N *The powers under Part IV of PACE to detain and release on bail (before or after charge) a person arrested under section 24 of PACE for any offence (see PACE Code G (Arrest)) do not apply to persons whilst they are detained under the terrorism powers following their arrest/detention under section 41 of, or Schedule 7 to, TACT. If when the grounds for detention under these powers cease the person is arrested under section 24 of PACE for a specific offence, the detention and bail provisions of PACE will apply and must be considered from the time of that arrest.*

H:1O *Paragraph 1.11A does not amend the provisions in any enactment which expressly refer and apply to persons under the age of 17. Until amended by Parliament, these statutory provisions alone do not extend to persons who have attained the age of 17.*

H:1P *The purpose of paragraph 1.11A is to extend the safeguards for juveniles to 17-year-olds unless this is precluded by any statutory provisions. The exception identifies section 65 of PACE which by virtue of paragraph 15 of Schedule 8 to the Terrorism Act 2000, is applied to the powers under that schedule to take fingerprints and samples. All other safeguards in this code are extended and the requirements which are indicated in the relevant provisions and Notes for Guidance are as follows:*

(a) *under paragraph 3.15 of this code, to identify and inform someone responsible for the welfare of a 17-year-old which is in addition to their right in section 5 of this code not to be held incommunicado;*

(b) *under paragraph 3.16 of this code to notify a person who has statutory responsibility under a court order to supervise or monitor a 17-year-old;*

(c) *under paragraph 8.9 with regard to cell accommodation and keeping 17-year-old detainees separate from adults;*

(d) *to call a person described by paragraph 1.13(a) to fulfil the role of the appropriate adult for the purposes of this or any other code to support and assist a 17-year-old:*

    (i) *by being present when:*

- *they are informed of their rights and entitlements and the grounds for their detention (see paras 3.17 and 3.18);*
- *they are cautioned or given a special warning (see paras 10.10 and 10.11A);*
- *they are being interviewed unless paragraph 11.11 of this code allows the interview to go ahead without the adult being present;*
- *an intimate search is carried out (see Annex A, paras 3 and 6);*
- *a strip search is carried out (see Annex A, para. 12);*

    (ii) *by allowing:*

- *the adult to inspect their custody record and to have a copy of their record (see paras 2.5, 2.6 and 2.7);*
- *a 17-year-old to consult the adult in private (see para. 3.19);*
- *the adult to request legal advice on their behalf to advise and assist them (see paras 3.20, 6.6 and 11.10).*

H:2 Custody records

H:2.1 When a person is:

- brought to a police station following arrest under TACT, s.41;
- arrested under TACT, s.41 at a police station having attended there voluntarily;
- brought to a police station and there detained to be questioned in accordance with an authorisation under section 22 of the Counter-Terrorism Act 2008 (post-charge questioning) (see *Notes 15A* and *15B*); or

- at a police station and there detained when authority for post-charge questioning is given under section 22 of the Counter-Terrorism Act 2008 (see *Notes 15A* and *15B*),

they should be brought before the custody officer as soon as practicable after their arrival at the station or, if appropriate, following the authorisation of post-charge questioning or following arrest after attending the police station voluntarily: see *Note 3H*. A person is deemed to be "at a police station" for these purposes if they are within the boundary of any building or enclosed yard which forms part of that police station.

H:2.2 A separate custody record must be opened as soon as practicable for each person described in paragraph 2.1. All information recorded under this code must be recorded as soon as practicable in the custody record unless otherwise specified. Any audio or video recording made in the custody area is not part of the custody record.

H:2.3 If any action requires the authority of an officer of a specified rank, this must be noted in the custody record, subject to paragraph 2.8.

H:2.3A If a person is arrested under TACT, s.41, and taken to a police station as a result of a search in the exercise of any stop and search power to which PACE Code A (stop and search) or the "search powers code" issued under TACT applies, the officer carrying out the search is responsible for ensuring that the record of that stop and search is made as part of the person's custody record. The custody officer must then ensure that the person is asked if they want a copy of the search record and if they do, that they are given a copy as soon as practicable. The person's entitlement to a copy of the search record which is made as part of their custody record is in addition to, and does not affect, their entitlement to a copy of their custody record or any other provisions of section 2 (custody records) of this code. See Code A, para. 4.2B, and the TACT search powers code para. 5.3.5.

H:2.4 [*Identical to C:2.3.*]

H:2.5 The detainee's solicitor and appropriate adult must be permitted to inspect the whole of the detainee's custody record as soon as practicable after their arrival at the station and at any other time on request whilst the person is detained. This includes the following specific records relating to the reasons for the detainee's arrest and detention and the offence concerned to which paragraph 3.1(b) refers:

- (a) the information about the circumstances and reasons for the detainee's arrest as recorded in the custody record in accordance with paragraph 3.4; this applies to any further reasons which come to light and are recorded whilst the detainee is detained;
- (b) the record of the grounds for each authorisation to keep the person in custody; the authorisations to which this applies are the same as those described in paragraph 2 of Annex M [*sic*] of this code.

Access to the records in sub-paragraphs (a) and (b) is in addition to the requirements in paragraphs 3.4(b), 11.1 and 14.0 (to make certain documents and materials available and to provide information about the reasons for arrest and detention) and in paragraph 14.4A to provide written information about the grounds for continued detention when an application for a warrant of further detention (or for an extension of such a warrant) is made.

Access to the custody record for the purposes of this paragraph must be arranged and agreed with the custody officer and may not unreasonably interfere with the custody officer's duties or the justifiable needs of the investigation. A record shall be made when access is allowed and whether it includes the records described in sub-paragraphs (a) and (b) above.

Note: paragraph 1.11A extends this paragraph to the person called to fulfil the role of the appropriate adult for a 17-year-old detainee.

H:2.6 [*Identical to C:2.4A, save for reference to "paragraph 1.11A" in lieu of reference to "paragraph 1.5A".*]

H:2.7 The detainee, appropriate adult or legal representative shall be permitted to inspect the original custody record once the detained person is no longer being held under the provisions of TACT, s.41, and Sched. 8, or being questioned after charge as authorised under section 22 of the Counter-Terrorism Act 2008 (see section 15), provided they give reasonable notice of their request. Any such inspection shall be noted in the custody record.

Note: paragraph 1.11A extends this paragraph to the person called to fulfil the role of the appropriate adult for a 17-year-old detainee.

H:2.8 All entries in custody records must be timed and identified by the maker. Nothing in this code requires the identity of officers or other police staff to be recorded or disclosed in the case of enquiries linked to the investigation of terrorism. In these cases, they shall use their warrant or other identification numbers and the name of their police station: see *Note 2A*. Records entered on computer shall be timed and contain the operator's identification.

H:2.9 [*Identical to C:2.7.*]

Note for guidance

A-215a   H:2A *The purpose of paragraph 2.8 is to protect those involved in terrorist investigations or arrests of terrorist suspects from the possibility that those arrested, their associates or other individuals or groups may threaten or cause harm to those involved.*

H:3 Initial action

(a) *Detained persons—normal procedure*

A-215b   H:3.1 When a person to whom paragraph 2.1 applies is at a police station, the custody officer must make sure the person is told clearly about:

(a) the following continuing rights which may be exercised at any stage during the period in custody:

(i) their right to consult privately with a solicitor and that free independent legal advice is available as in section 6;

(ii) their right to have someone informed of their arrest as in section 5;

(iii) the right to consult this code of practice (see *Note 3D*); and

(iv) if applicable, their right to interpretation and translation (see para. 3.14) and their right to communicate with their high commission, embassy or consulate (see para. 3.14A);

(b) their right to be informed about why they have been arrested and detained on suspicion of being involved in the commission, preparation or instigation of acts of terrorism in accordance with paragraphs 2.5, 3.4(a) and 11.1A of this code.

H:3.2 The detainee must also be given a written notice, which contains information:

(a) setting out:

(i) their rights under paragraphs 3.1, 3.14 and 3.14A;

(ii) the arrangements for obtaining legal advice, see section 6;

(iii) their right to a copy of the custody record as in paragraph 2.6;

(iv) their right to remain silent as set out in the caution in the terms prescribed in section 10;

(v) their right to have access to records and documents which are essential to effectively challenging the lawfulness of their arrest and detention as required in accordance with paragraphs 3.4(b) and 14.0 of this code;

(vi) the maximum period for which they may be kept in police detention without being charged, when detention must be reviewed and when release is required;

(vii) their right to medical assistance in accordance with section 9 of this code;

(viii) their right, if they are prosecuted, to have access to the evidence in the case before their trial in accordance with the Criminal Procedure and Investigations Act 1996, the Attorney General's Guidelines on Disclosure, the common law and the Criminal Procedure Rules;

(b) briefly setting out their other entitlements while in custody, by:

(i) mentioning:

– the provisions relating to the conduct of interviews;

– the circumstances in which an appropriate adult should be available to assist the detainee and their statutory rights to make representations whenever the need for their detention is reviewed;

(ii) listing the entitlements in this code, concerning:

– reasonable standards of physical comfort;

– adequate food and drink;

– access to toilets and washing facilities, clothing, medical attention, and exercise when practicable.

See *Note 3A*.

H:3.2A The detainee must be given an opportunity to read the notice and shall be asked to sign the custody record to acknowledge receipt of these notices. Any refusal must be recorded on the custody record.

H:3.3 [*Not used.*]

H:3.3A [*Identical to C:3.3A.*]

H:3.4

(a) The custody officer shall:

• record that the person was arrested under section 41 of TACT and the reason(s) for the arrest on the custody record (see para. 10.2 and *Note 3G*);

- note on the custody record any comment the detainee makes in relation to the arresting officer's account but shall not invite comment; if the arresting officer is not physically present when the detainee is brought to a police station, the arresting officer's account must be made available to the custody officer remotely or by a third party on the arresting officer's behalf;
- note any comment the detainee makes in respect of the decision to detain them but shall not invite comment;
- not put specific questions to the detainee regarding their involvement in any offence (see para. 1.3), nor in respect of any comments they may make in response to the arresting officer's account or the decision to place them in detention (see paras 14.1 and 14.2 and *Notes 3H, 14A* and *14B*); such an exchange is likely to constitute an interview as in paragraph 11.1 and require the associated safeguards in section 11.

Note: this sub-paragraph also applies to any further reasons and grounds for detention which come to light whilst the person is detained.

See paragraph 11.8A in respect of unsolicited comments.

If the first review of detention is carried out at this time, see paragraphs 14.1 and 14.2, and Part II of Schedule 8 to the Terrorism Act 2000 in respect of action by the review officer.

(b) Any available documents and materials which are essential to effectively challenging the lawfulness the detainee's arrest and detention must be made available to the detainee or their solicitor. Documents and material will be "essential" for this purpose if they are capable of undermining the reasons and grounds which make the detainee's arrest and detention necessary. The decision about whether particular documents or materials must made [*sic*] available for the purpose of this requirement rests with the officer responsible under Schedule 8 to the Terrorism Act 2000 for determining whether detention is necessary, in consultation with the investigating officer who has the knowledge of the documents and materials in a particular case necessary to inform that decision (see *Note 3G*). A note should be made in the detainee's custody record of the fact that documents or materials have been made available under this sub-paragraph and when. The investigating officer should make a separate note of what is made available in a particular case. This sub-paragraph also applies for the purposes of section 14 (reviews and extensions of detention under the Terrorism Act 2000). See *Note 3ZA* and paragraph 14.0.

H:3.5 The custody officer or other custody staff as directed by the custody officer shall:

(a) ask the detainee, whether at this time, they:
   (i) would like legal advice, see paragraph 6.4;
   (ii) want someone informed of their detention, see section 5;

(b) ask the detainee to sign the custody record to confirm their decisions in respect of (a);

(c) determine whether the detainee:
   (i) is, or might be, in need of medical treatment or attention, see section 9;
   (ii) requires:
      - an appropriate adult (see paras 1.10, 1.11A, and 3.15);
      - help to check documentation (see para. 3.21);
      - an interpreter (see para. 3.14 and *Note 13B*).

(d) record the decision in respect of (c).

Where any duties under this paragraph have been carried out by custody staff at the direction of the custody officer, the outcomes shall, as soon as practicable, be reported to the custody officer who retains overall responsibility for the detainee's care and safe custody and ensuring it complies with this code. See *Note 3I*.

H:3.6 When these needs are determined, the custody officer is responsible for initiating an assessment to consider whether the detainee is likely to present specific risks to custody staff, any individual who may have contact with the detainee (*e.g.* legal advisers, medical staff), or themselves. Such assessments should always include a check on the Police National Computer, to be carried out as soon as practicable, to identify any risks highlighted in relation to the detainee. Although such assessments are primarily the custody officer's responsibility, it will be necessary to obtain information from other sources, especially the investigation team (see *Note 3E*), the arresting officer or an appropriate healthcare professional (see paragraph 9.15). Reasons for delaying the initiation or completion of the assessment must be recorded.

H:3.7 [*Identical to C:3.7.*]

H:3.8 Risk assessments must follow a structured process which clearly defines the categories of risk to be considered and the results must be incorporated in the detainee's custody record. The custody officer is responsible for making sure those responsible for the detainee's custody are appropriately briefed about the risks. The content of any risk assessment and any analysis of the level of risk relating to the person's detention is not required to be shown or provided to the detainee or any person acting on behalf of the detainee. If no specific risks are identified by the assessment, that should be noted in the custody record. See *Note 3F* and paragraph 9.15.

H:3.8A The content of any risk assessment and any analysis of the level of risk relating to the person's detention is not required to be shown or provided to the detainee or any person acting on behalf of the detainee. But information should not be withheld from any person acting on the detainee's behalf, for example, an appropriate adult, solicitor or interpreter, if to do so might put that person at risk.

H:3.9 Custody officers are responsible for implementing the response to any specific risk assessment, which should include for example:

- reducing opportunities for self harm;
- calling a health care professional;
- increasing levels of monitoring or observation;
- reducing the risk to those who come into contact with the detainee.

See *Note 3F*.

H:3.10, 3.11 *[Identical to C:3.10 and C:3.11, respectively.]*

H:3.12 A constable, prison officer or other person authorised by the Secretary of State may take any steps which are reasonably necessary for—

(a) photographing the detained person,

(b) measuring the person, or

(c) identifying the person.

H:3.13 Paragraph 3.12 concerns the power in TACT, Sched. 8, para. 2. The power in TACT, Sched. 8, para. 2, does not cover the taking of fingerprints, intimate samples or non-intimate samples, which is covered in TACT, Sched. 8, paras 10–15.

(b) *Detained persons—special groups*

H:3.14 *[Identical to C:3.12, save for reference to "Annex K" in lieu of reference to "Annex M".]*

H:3.14A *[Identical to C:3.12A.]*

H:3.15, 3.16 *[Identical to C:3.13 and C:3.14 respectively, save for references to "paragraph 1.11A" in lieu of references to "paragraph 1.5A".]*

H:3.17 *[Identical to C:3.15, save for references to "paragraph 3.15" and "paragraph 1.11A" in lieu of references to "paragraph 3.13" and "paragraph 1.5A" respectively.]*

H:3.18–3.20 *[Identical to C:3.17 to C:3.19 respectively, save for references to "paragraph 1.11A" in lieu of references to "paragraph 1.5A".]*

H:3.21 *[Identical to C:3.20, save for reference to "paragraph 3.17" in lieu of reference to "paragraph 3.15".]*

(d) [sic] *Documentation*

H:3.22 The grounds for a person's detention shall be recorded, in the person's presence if practicable.

H:3.23 Action taken under paragraphs 3.14 to 3.22 shall be recorded.

(e) *Requirements for suspects to be informed of certain rights*

H:3.24 The provisions of this section identify the information which must be given to suspects who have been arrested under section 41 of the Terrorism Act and cautioned in accordance with section 10 of this code. It includes information required by EU Directive 2012/13 on the right to information in criminal proceedings. If a complaint is made by or on behalf of such a suspect that the information and (as the case may be) access to records and documents has not been provided as required, the matter shall be reported to an inspector to deal with as a complaint for the purposes of paragraph 9.3, or paragraph 12.10 if the challenge is made during an interview. This would include, for example:

- not informing them of their rights (see para. 3.1);
- not giving them a copy of the notice (see para. 3.2(a));
- not providing an opportunity to read the notice (see para. 3.2A);
- not providing the required information (see paras 3.2(a), 3.14(b) and, 3.14A);
- not allowing access to the custody record (see para. 2.5);
- not providing a translation of the notice (see para. 3.14(c) and (d)).

Notes for guidance

H:3ZA *For the purposes of paragraphs 3.4(b) and 14.0:*   **A-216**

> (a) *investigating officers are responsible for bringing to the attention of the officer who is responsible for authorising the suspect's detention or (as the case may be) continued detention, any documents and materials in their possession or control which appear to undermine the need to keep the suspect in custody; in accordance with Part II of Schedule 8 to the Terrorism Act 2000, this officer will be either the inspector or superintendent reviewing the need for detention; this officer is then responsible for determining which, if any, of those documents and materials are capable of undermining the need to detain the suspect and must therefore be made available to the suspect or their solicitor;*

> (b) *the way in which documents and materials are "made available", is a matter for the investigating officer to determine on a case by case basis and having regard to the nature and volume of the documents and materials involved; for example, they may be made available by supplying a copy or allowing supervised access to view; however, for view only access, it will be necessary to demonstrate that sufficient time is allowed for the suspect and solicitor to view and consider the documents and materials in question.*

H:3A *[Identical to C:3A.]*

H:3B *[Not used.]*

H:3C *[Identical to C:3C.]*

H:3D *The right to consult this or other relevant codes of practice does not entitle the person concerned to delay unreasonably any necessary investigative or administrative action whilst they do so. Examples of action which need not be delayed unreasonably include:*

> • *searching detainees at the police station;*

> • *taking fingerprints or non-intimate samples without consent for evidential purposes.*

H:3E *The investigation team will include any officer involved in questioning a suspect, gathering or analysing evidence in relation to the offences of which the detainee is suspected of having committed. Should a custody officer require information from the investigation team, the first point of contact should be the officer in charge of the investigation.*

H:3F *Home Office Circular 32/2000 provides more detailed guidance on risk assessments and identifies key risk areas which should always be considered.*

H:3G *Arrests under TACT, s.41, can only be made where an officer has reasonable grounds to suspect that the individual concerned is a "terrorist". This differs from the PACE power of arrest in that it need not be linked to a specific offence. There may also be circumstances where an arrest under TACT is made on the grounds of sensitive information which cannot be disclosed. In such circumstances, the grounds for arrest may be given in terms of the interpretation of a "terrorist" set out in TACT, s.40(1)(a) or (b).*

H:3H *For the purpose of arrests under TACT, s.41, the review officer is responsible for authorising detention (see paragraphs 14.1 and 14.2, and Notes for Guidance 14A and 14B). The review officer's role is explained in TACT, Sched. 8, Pt II. A person may be detained after arrest pending the first review, which must take place as soon as practicable after the person's arrest.*

H:3I *A custody officer or other officer who, in accordance with this code, allows or directs the carrying out of any task or action relating to a detainee's care, treatment, rights and entitlements by another officer or any police staff must be satisfied that the officer or police staff concerned are suitable, trained and competent to carry out the task or action in question.*

H:4 Detainee's property

(a) *Action*

H:4.1 The custody officer is responsible for: **A-216a**

> (a) ascertaining what property a detainee:
>> (i) has with them when they come to the police station, either on first arrival at the police station or any subsequent arrivals at a police station in connection with that detention;
>> (ii) might have acquired for an unlawful or harmful purpose while in custody;
> (b) the safekeeping of any property taken from a detainee which remains at the police station.

The custody officer may search the detainee or authorise their being searched to the extent they consider necessary, provided a search of intimate parts of the body or involving the removal of more than outer clothing is only made as in Annex A. A search may only be carried out by an officer of the same sex as the detainee. See *Note 4A* and Annex I.

H:4.2, 4.3 *[Identical to C:4.2 and C:4.3, respectively.]*

(b) *Documentation*

H:4.4 It is a matter for the custody officer to determine whether a record should be made of the property a detained person has with him or had taken from him on arrest [see *Note 4D*]. Any record made is not required to be kept as part of the custody record but the custody record should be noted as to where such a record exists. Whenever a record is made the detainee shall be allowed to check and sign the record of property as correct. Any refusal to sign shall be recorded.

H:4.5 [*Identical to C:4.5.*]

Notes for guidance

H:4A–4C [*Identical to C:4A to C:4C, respectively.*]

H:4D *Section 43(2) of TACT allows a constable to search a person who has been arrested under section 41 to discover whether they have anything in their possession that may constitute evidence that they are a terrorist.*

H:5 Right not to be held incommunicado

(a) *Action*

H:5.1 Any person to whom this code applies who is held in custody at a police station or other premises may, on request, have one named person who is a friend, relative or a person known to them who is likely to take an interest in their welfare informed at public expense of their whereabouts as soon as practicable. If the person cannot be contacted the detainee may choose up to two alternatives. If they cannot be contacted, the person in charge of detention or the investigation has discretion to allow further attempts until the information has been conveyed. See *Notes 5D* and *5E*.

H:5.2 [*Identical to C:5.2.*]

H:5.3 The above right may be exercised each time a detainee is taken to another police station or returned to a police station having been previously transferred to prison. This code does not afford such a right to a person on transfer to a prison, where a detainee's rights will be governed by prison rules [see paragraph 14.8].

H:5.4 If the detainee agrees, they may at the custody officer's discretion receive visits from friends, family or others likely to take an interest in their welfare, or in whose welfare the detainee has an interest. Custody officers should liaise closely with the investigation team [see *Note 3E*] to allow risk assessments to be made where particular visitors have been requested by the detainee or identified themselves to police. In circumstances where the nature of the investigation means that such requests cannot be met, consideration should be given, in conjunction with a representative of the relevant scheme, to increasing the frequency of visits from independent visitor schemes. See *Notes 5B* and *5C*.

H:5.5 [*Identical to C:5.5, save for reference to "Note 5E" in lieu of reference to "Note 5D".*]

H:5.6 The detainee shall be given writing materials, on request, and allowed to telephone one person for a reasonable time, see *Notes 5A* and *5F*. Either or both these privileges may be denied or delayed if an officer of inspector rank or above considers sending a letter or making a telephone call may result in any of the consequences in Annex B, paras 1 and 2, particularly in relation to the making of a telephone call in a language which an officer listening to the call [see paragraph 5.7] does not understand. See *Note 5G*.

Nothing in this paragraph permits the restriction or denial of the rights in paragraphs 5.1 and 6.1.

H:5.7 Before any letter or message is sent, or telephone call made, the detainee shall be informed that what they say in any letter, call or message (other than in a communication to a solicitor) may be read or listened to and may be given in evidence. A telephone call may be terminated if it is being abused [see *Note 5G*]. The costs can be at public expense at the custody officer's discretion.

H:5.8 [*Identical to C:5.7A.*]

(b) *Documentation*

H:5.9 A record must be kept of any:

   (a) request made under this section and the action taken;
   (b) letters, messages or telephone calls made or received or visit received;
   (c) refusal by the detainee to have information about them given to an outside enquirer, or any refusal to see a visitor. The detainee must be asked to countersign the record accordingly and any refusal recorded.

Notes for guidance

H:5A *A person may request an interpreter to interpret a telephone call or translate a letter.*

H:5B *At the custody officer's discretion (and subject to the detainee's consent), visits should be allowed when possible, subject to sufficient personnel being available to supervise a visit and any possible hindrance to the investigation. Custody officers should bear in mind the exceptional nature of prolonged TACT detention and consider the potential benefits that visits may bring to the health and welfare of detainees who are held for extended periods.*

H:5C *Official visitors should be given access following consultation with the officer who has overall responsibility for the investigation provided the detainee consents, and they do not compromise safety or security or unduly delay or interfere with the progress of an investigation. Official visitors should still be required to provide appropriate identification and subject to any screening process in place at the place of detention. Official visitors may include:*

- *an accredited faith representative;*
- *Members of either House of Parliament;*
- *public officials needing to interview the prisoner in the course of their duties;*
- *other persons visiting with the approval of the officer who has overall responsibility for the investigation;*
- *consular officials visiting a detainee who is a national of the country they represent subject to section 7 of this code.*

Visits from appropriate members of the Independent Custody Visitors Scheme should be dealt with in accordance with the separate Code of Practice on Independent Custody Visiting.

H:5D *If the detainee does not know anyone to contact for advice or support or cannot contact a friend or relative, the custody officer should bear in mind any local voluntary bodies or other organisations that might be able to help. Paragraph 6.1 applies if legal advice is required.*

H:5E *In some circumstances it may not be appropriate to use the telephone to disclose information under paragraphs 5.1 and 5.5.*

H:5F *The telephone call at paragraph 5.6 is in addition to any communication under paragraphs 5.1 and 6.1. Further calls may be made at the custody officer's discretion.*

H:5G *The nature of terrorism investigations means that officers should have particular regard to the possibility of suspects attempting to pass information which may be detrimental to public safety, or to an investigation.*

H:6 Right to legal advice

(a) *Action*

H:6.1 Unless Annex B applies, all detainees must be informed that they may at any time consult **A-217b** and communicate privately with a solicitor, whether in person, in writing or by telephone, and that free independent legal advice is available from the duty solicitor. Where an appropriate adult is in attendance, they must also be informed of this right. See paragraph 3.1, *Note 11, Notes 6B and 6J.*

H:6.2 A poster advertising the right to legal advice must be prominently displayed in the charging area of every police station. See *Note 6G.*

H:6.3 [*Identical to C:6.4.*]

H:6.4 The exercise of the right of access to legal advice may be delayed exceptionally only as in Annex B. Whenever legal advice is requested, and unless Annex B applies, the custody officer must act without delay to secure the provision of such advice. If, on being informed or reminded of this right, the detainee declines to speak to a solicitor in person, the officer should point out that the right includes the right to speak with a solicitor on the telephone (see paragraph 5.6). If the detainee continues to waive this right the officer should ask them why and any reasons should be recorded on the custody record or the interview record as appropriate. Reminders of the right to legal advice must be given as in paragraphs 3.5, 11.3 and 5 of Annex K [*sic*] of this code and *PACE* Code D on the Identification of Persons by Police Officers, paragraphs 3.17(ii) and 6.3. Once it is clear a detainee does not want to speak to a solicitor in person or by telephone they should cease to be asked their reasons. See *Note 6J.*

H:6.5 An officer of the rank of commander or assistant chief constable or above may give a direction under TACT, Sched. 8, para. 9, that a detainee may only consult a solicitor within the sight and hearing of a qualified officer. Such a direction may only be given if the officer has reasonable grounds to believe that if it were not, it may result in one of the consequences set out in TACT, Sched. 8, para. 8(4) or (5)(c). See Annex B, para. 3, and *Note 6I.* A "qualified officer" means a police officer who:

(a) is at least the rank of inspector;

(b) is of the uniformed branch of the force of which the officer giving the direction is a member; and

(c) in the opinion of the officer giving the direction, has no connection with the detained person's case.

Officers considering the use of this power should first refer to Home Office *Circular 40/2003*.

H:6.6 [*Identical to C:6.5A, save for reference to "paragraph 1.11A" in lieu of reference to "paragraph 1.5A".*]

H:6.7 A detainee who wants legal advice may not be interviewed or continue to be interviewed until they have received such advice unless:

    (a) [*identical to C:6.6(a)*];

    (b) [*identical to C:6.6(b)*];

    (c) [*identical to C:6.6(c)*];

    (d) the detainee changes their mind, about wanting legal advice or (as the case may be) about wanting a solicitor present at the interview, and states that they no longer wish to speak to a solicitor; in these circumstances the interview may be started or continued without delay provided that:

        (i) an officer of inspector rank or above:

- speaks to the detainee to enquire about the reasons for their change of mind (see *Note 6J*); and
- makes, or directs the making of, reasonable efforts to ascertain the solicitor's expected time of arrival and to inform the solicitor that the suspect has stated that they wish to change their mind and the reason (if given);

        (ii) the detainee's reason for their change of mind (if given) and the outcome of the action in (i) are recorded in the custody record;

        (iii) the detainee, after being informed of the outcome of the action in (i) above, confirms in writing that they want the interview to proceed without speaking or further speaking to a solicitor or (as the case may be) without a solicitor being present and do not wish to wait for a solicitor by signing an entry to this effect in the custody record;

        (iv) an officer of inspector rank or above is satisfied that it is proper for the interview to proceed in these circumstances and:

- gives authority in writing for the interview to proceed and if the authority is not recorded in the custody record, the officer must ensure that the custody record shows the date and time of authority and where it is recorded; and
- takes or directs the taking of, reasonable steps to inform the solicitor that the authority has been given and the time when the interview is expected to commence and records or causes to be recorded, the outcome of this action in the custody record;

        (v) when the interview starts and the interviewer reminds the suspect of their right to legal advice (see paragraph 11.3) and the code of practice issued under paragraph 3 of Schedule 8 to the Terrorism Act 2000 for the video recording with sound of interviews, the interviewer shall then ensure that the following is recorded in the interview record made in accordance with that code:

- confirmation that the detainee has changed their mind about wanting legal advice or (as the case may be) about wanting a solicitor present and the reasons for it if given;
- the fact that authority for the interview to proceed has been given and, subject to paragraph 2.8, the name of the authorising officer;
- that if the solicitor arrives at the station before the interview is completed, the detainee will be so informed without delay and a break will be taken to allow them to speak to the solicitor if they wish, unless paragraph 6.7(a) applies; and
- that at any time during the interview, the detainee may again ask for legal advice and that if they do, a break will be taken to allow them to speak to the solicitor, unless paragraph 6.7(a), (b) or (c) applies.

        Note: in these circumstances the restriction on drawing adverse inferences from silence in Annex C will not apply because the detainee is allowed an opportunity to consult a solicitor if they wish.

H:6.8 If paragraph 6.7(a) applies, where the reason for authorising the delay ceases to apply, there may be no further delay in permitting the exercise of the right in the absence of a further authorisation unless paragraph 6.7(b), (c) or (d) applies. If paragraph 6.7(b)(i) applies, once sufficient information has been obtained to avert the risk, questioning must cease until the detainee has received legal advice unless paragraph 6.7(a), (b)(ii), (c) or (d) applies.

H:6.9 [*Identical to C:6.8, save for reference to "paragraph 6.7" in lieu of reference to "paragraph 6.6".*]

H:6.10 The solicitor may only be required to leave the interview if their conduct is such that the interviewer is unable properly to put questions to the suspect. See *Notes 6C* and *6D*.

H:6.11 [*Identical to C:6.10, save for reference to "Note 6D" in lieu of reference to "Note 6E".*]

H:6.12 [*Identical to C:6.11.*]

H: 6.13 [*Identical to C:6.12.*]

H:6.14 [*Identical to C:6.12A, save for references to "Note 6C" and to "paragraphs 6.7 to 6.11" in lieu of references to "Note 6D" and "paragraphs 6.6. to 6.10".*]

H:6.15 In exercising their discretion under paragraph 6.14, the officer should take into account in particular:
- whether:
  - the identity and status of an accredited or probationary representative have been satisfactorily established;
  - they are of suitable character to provide legal advice,
- any other matters in any written letter of authorisation provided by the solicitor on whose behalf the person is attending the police station. See *Note 6E*.

H:6.16 If the inspector refuses access to an accredited or probationary representative or a decision is taken that such a person should not be permitted to remain at an interview, the inspector must notify the solicitor on whose behalf the representative was acting and give them an opportunity to make alternative arrangements. The detainee must be informed and the custody record noted.

H:6.17 If a solicitor arrives at the station to see a particular person, that person must, unless Annex B applies, be so informed whether or not they are being interviewed and asked if they would like to see the solicitor. This applies even if the detainee has declined legal advice or, having requested it, subsequently agreed to be interviewed without receiving advice. The solicitor's attendance and the detainee's decision must be noted in the custody record.

(b) *Documentation*

H:6.18, 6.19 [*Identical to C:6.16 and C:6.17, respectively.*]

Notes for guidance

H:6ZA *No police officer or police staff shall indicate to any suspect, except to answer a direct question, that* **A-218**
period for which they are liable to be detained, or the time taken to complete the interview, might be reduced:
- *if they do not ask for legal advice or do not want a solicitor present when they are interviewed; or*
- *if after asking for legal advice, they change their mind about wanting it or or (as the case may be) wanting a solicitor present when they are interviewed and agree to be interviewed without waiting for a solicitor.*

H:6A *In considering if paragraph 6.7(b) applies, the officer should, if practicable, ask the solicitor for an estimate of how long it will take to come to the station and relate this to the time detention is permitted, the time of day (i.e. whether the rest period under paragraph 12.2 is imminent) and the requirements of other investigations. If the solicitor is on their way or is to set off immediately, it will not normally be appropriate to begin an interview before they arrive. If it appears necessary to begin an interview before the solicitor's arrival, they should be given an indication of how long the police would be able to wait so there is an opportunity to make arrangements for someone else to provide legal advice. Nothing within this section is intended to prevent police from ascertaining immediately after the arrest of an individual whether a threat to public safety exists (see paragraph 11.2).*

H:6B *A detainee has a right to free legal advice and to be represented by a solicitor. This note for guidance explains the arrangements which enable detainees to whom this code applies to obtain legal advice. An outline of these arrangements is also included in the Notice of Rights and Entitlements given to detainees in accordance with paragraph 3.2.*

The detainee can ask for free advice from a solicitor they know or if they do not know a solicitor or the solicitor they know cannot be contacted, from the duty solicitor.

To arrange free legal advice, the police should telephone the Defence Solicitor Call Centre (DSCC). The call centre will contact either the duty solicitor or the solicitor requested by the detainee as appropriate.

When a detainee wants to pay for legal advice themselves:
- *the DSCC will contact a solicitor of their choice on their behalf;*
- *they should be given an opportunity to consult a specific solicitor or another solicitor from that solicitor's firm; if this solicitor is not available, they may choose up to two alternatives; if these alternatives are not available, the custody officer has discretion to allow further attempts until a solicitor has been contacted and agreed to provide advice;*
- *they are entitled to a private consultation with their chosen solicitor on the telephone or the solicitor may decide to come to the police station;*
- *if their chosen solicitor cannot be contacted, the DSCC may still be called to arrange free legal advice.*

Apart from carrying out duties necessary to implement these arrangements, an officer must not advise the suspect about any particular firm of solicitors.

H:6C [*Identical to C:6D.*]

H:6D [*Identical to C:6E.*]

H:6E [*Identical to C:6F.*]

H:6F [*Identical to C:6G, save for reference to "paragraph 6.7(b)" in lieu of reference to "paragraph 6.6(b)".*]

H:6G [*Identical to C:6H.*]

H:6H [*Not used.*]

H:6I *Whenever a detainee exercises their right to legal advice by consulting or communicating with a solicitor, they must be allowed to do so in private. This right to consult or communicate in private is fundamental. Except as allowed by the Terrorism Act 2000, Sched. 8, para. 9, if the requirement for privacy is compromised because what is said or written by the detainee or solicitor for the purpose of giving and receiving legal advice is overheard, listened to, or read by others without the informed consent of the detainee, the right will effectively have been denied. When a detainee speaks to a solicitor on the telephone, they should be allowed to do so in private unless a direction under Schedule 8, paragraph 9 of the Terrorism Act 2000 has been given or this is impractical because of the design and layout of the custody area, or the location of telephones. However, the normal expectation should be that facilities will be available, unless they are being used, at all police stations to enable detainees to speak in private to a solicitor either face to face or over the telephone.*

H:6J [*Identical to C:6K.*]

H:7 Citizens of independent Commonwealth countries or foreign nationals

A-218a   [*Identical to C:7 (apart from use of "are" instead of "is" in paragraph 7.4).*]

H:8 Conditions of detention

(a) *Action*

A-218b   H:8.1, 8.2 [*Identical to C:8.1, save for omission of reference to Note 8C, and C:8.2, respectively.*]

H:8.3 [*Identical to C:8.3, save for omission of reference to Note 8A.*]

H:8.4, 8.5 [*Identical to C:8.4 and C:8.5, respectively.*]

H:8.6 At least two light meals and one main meal should be offered in any 24-hour period. See *Note 8B.* Drinks should be provided at meal times and upon reasonable request between meals. Whenever necessary, advice shall be sought from the appropriate health care professional, see *Note 9A,* on medical and dietary matters. As far as practicable, meals provided shall offer a varied diet and meet any specific dietary needs or religious beliefs the detainee may have. Detainees should also be made aware that the meals offered meet such needs. The detainee may, at the custody officer's discretion, have meals supplied by their family or friends at their expense. See *Note 8A.*

H:8.7 Brief outdoor exercise shall be offered daily if practicable. Where facilities exist, indoor exercise shall be offered as an alternative if outside conditions are such that a detainee cannot be reasonably expected to take outdoor exercise (*e.g.*, in cold or wet weather) or if requested by the detainee or for reasons of security. See *Note 8C.*

H:8.8 Where practicable, provision should be made for detainees to practice [*sic*] religious observance. Consideration should be given to providing a separate room which can be used as a prayer room. The supply of appropriate food and clothing, and suitable provision for prayer facilities, such as uncontaminated copies of religious books, should also be considered. See *Note 8D.*

H:8.9 A juvenile shall not be placed in a cell unless no other secure accommodation is available and the custody officer considers it is not practicable to supervise them if they are not placed in a cell or that a cell provides more comfortable accommodation than other secure accommodation in the station. A juvenile may not be placed in a cell with a detained adult.

Note: paragraph 1.11A extends these requirements to 17-year-old detainees.

H:8.10 Police stations should keep a reasonable supply of reading material available for detainees, including but not limited to, the main religious texts. See *Note 8D.* Detainees should be made aware that such material is available and reasonable requests for such material should be met as soon as practicable unless to do so would:

(i) interfere with the investigation; or

(ii) prevent or delay an officer from discharging his statutory duties, or those in this code.

If such a request is refused on the grounds of (i) or (ii) above, this should be noted in the custody record and met as soon as possible after those grounds cease to apply.

(b) *Documentation*

H:8.11, 8.12 [*Identical to C:8.9 and C:8.11, respectively.*]

Notes for guidance

H:8A *In deciding whether to allow meals to be supplied by family or friends, the custody officer is entitled to* **A-219** *take account of the risk of items being concealed in any food or package and the officer's duties and responsibilities under food handling legislation. If an officer needs to examine food or other items supplied by family and friends before deciding whether they can be given to the detainee, he should inform the person who has brought the item to the police station of this and the reasons for doing so.*

H:8B [*Identical to C:8B.*]

H:8C *In light of the potential for detaining individuals for extended periods of time, the overriding principle should be to accommodate a period of exercise, except where to do so would hinder the investigation, delay the detainee"s release or charge, or it is declined by the detainee.*

H:8D *Police forces should consult with representatives of the main religious communities to ensure the provision for religious observance is adequate, and to seek advice on the appropriate storage and handling of religious texts or other religious items.*

H:9 Care and treatment of detained persons

(a) *General*

H:9.1 Notwithstanding other requirements for medical attention as set out in this section, detainees **A-219a** who are held for more than 96 hours must be visited by an appropriate healthcare professional at least once every 24 hours.

H:9.2, 9.3 [*Identical to C:9.1, save for omission of reference to Note 8C, and C:9.2, respectively.*]

H:9.4 [*Identical to C:9.3, save for references to "Note 9C", "paragraph 9.15" and "Note 9G" in lieu of references to "Note 9CA", "paragraph 9.13" and "Note 9H", respectively.*]

H:9.5 [*Identical to C:9.4.*]

(b) *Clinical treatment and attention*

H:9.6, 9.7, 9.8 [*Identical to C:9.5, C:9.5A and C: 9.5B, respectively.*]

H:9.9 [*Identical to C:9.7, save for reference to "Note 9D" in lieu of reference to "Note 9E".*]

H:9.10 [*Identical to C:9.8.*]

H:9.11 [*Identical to C:9.9, save for reference to "paragraph 9.12" in lieu of reference to "paragraph 9.10".*]

H:9.12 No police officer may administer or supervise the self-administration of medically prescribed controlled drugs of the types and forms listed in the Misuse of Drugs Regulations 2001, Sched. 2 or 3. A detainee may only self-administer such drugs under the personal supervision of the registered medical practitioner authorising their use or other appropriate healthcare professional. The custody officer may supervise the self-administration of, or authorise other custody staff to supervise the self-administration of, drugs listed in Schedule 4 or 5 if the officer has consulted the appropriate healthcare professional authorising their use and both are satisfied self-administration will not expose the detainee, police officers or anyone else to the risk of harm or injury.

H:9.13 When appropriate healthcare professionals administer drugs or authorise the use of other medications, or consult with the custody officer about allowing self-administration of drugs listed in Schedule 4 or 5, it must be within current medicines legislation and the scope of practice as determined by their relevant regulatory body.

H:9.14 [*Identical to C:9.12, save for reference to "paragraph 9.6" in lieu of reference to "paragraph 9.5".*]

H:9.15 [*Identical to C:9.13.*]

H:9.16 [*Identical to C:9.14, save for reference to "Note 9E" in lieu of reference to "Note 9F".*]

(c) *Documentation*

H:9.17 [*Identical to C:9.15, save for references to "paragraph 9.3", "paragraph 9.6", "paragraph 9.10", "Note 9F", "Notes 9D and 9E" and "Note 9G" in lieu of references to "paragraph 9.2", "paragraph 9.5", "paragraph 9.8", "Note 9G", "Notes 9E and 9F" and "Note 9H", respectively.*]

H:9.18 [*Identical to C:9.16, save for reference to "Note 9F" in lieu of reference to "Note 9G".*]

H:9.19 [*Identical to C:9.17.*]

Notes for guidance

A-219b   H:9A, 9B [*Identical to C:9A and C:9B (save for reference to "paragraph 1.11A" in lieu of reference to "paragraph 1:5A"), respectively.*]

H:9C [*Identical to C:9C, save for reference to "Paragraph 9.6" in lieu of reference to "Paragraph 9.5".*]

H:9D, 9E [*Identical to C:9E and C:9F, respectively.*]

H:9F [*Identical to C:9G, save for reference to "Paragraphs 9.17 and 9.18" in lieu of reference to "Paragraphs 9.15 and 9.16".*]

H:9G [*Identical to C:9H.*]

H:10 Cautions

(a) *When a caution must be given*

A-220   H:10.1 A person whom there are grounds to suspect of an offence, see *Note 10A*, must be cautioned before any questions about an offence, or further questions if the answers provide the grounds for suspicion, are put to them if either the suspect's answers or silence (*i.e.* failure or refusal to answer or answer satisfactorily) may be given in evidence to a court in a prosecution.

H:10.2 A person who is arrested, or further arrested, must be informed at the time if practicable or, if not, as soon as it becomes practicable thereafter, that they are under arrest and of the grounds and reasons for their arrest, see paragraph 3.4, *Note 3G* and *Note 10B*.

H:10.3 [*Effectively identical to C:10.4.*]

(b) *Terms of the cautions*

H:10.4 The caution which must be given:

  (a) on arrest;
  (b) on all other occasions before a person is charged or informed they may be prosecuted; see PACE, Code C, section 16; and
  (c) before post-charge questioning under section 22 of the Counter-Terrorism Act 2008 (see section 15.9);

should, unless the restriction on drawing adverse inferences from silence applies, see Annex C, be in the following terms:

  "You do not have to say anything. But it may harm your defence if you do not mention when questioned something which you later rely on in court. Anything you do say may be given in evidence.".

Where the use of the Welsh language is appropriate, a constable may provide the caution directly in Welsh in the following terms:

  "Does dim rhaid i chi ddweud dim byd. Ond gall niweidio eich amddiffyniad os na fyddwch chi'n sôn, wrth gael eich holi, am rywbeth y byddwch chi'n dibynnu arno nes ymlaen yn y Llys. Gall unrhyw beth yr ydych yn ei ddweud gael ei roi fel tystiolaeth.".

See *Note 10F*.

H:10.5 [*Identical to C:10.6.*]

H:10.6 [*Identical to C:10.7, save for reference to "Note 10C" in lieu of reference to "Note 10D".*]

H:10.7 [*Identical to C:10.8, save for reference to "Note 10D" in lieu of reference to "Note 10E".*]

H: 10.8 [*Identical to C:10.9, but the words following "statutory requirement" have been omitted.*]

(c) *Special warnings under the Criminal Justice and Public Order Act 1994, sections 36 and 37*

H:10.9 [*Identical to C:10.10, save for references to "Note 10E" and "paragraph 10.10" in lieu of references to "Note 10F" and "paragraph 10.11", respectively.*]

H:10.10 [*Identical to C:10.11.*]

(d) *Juveniles and persons who are mentally disordered or otherwise mentally vulnerable*

H:10.10A [*Identical to C:10.11A, save for reference to "paragraph 10.10" in lieu of reference to "paragraph 10.11".*]

H:10.11 [*Identical to C:10.12.*]

H:10.11A Paragraph 1.11A extends the requirements in paragraphs 10.10A and 10.11 to 17-year-old detainees.

(e) *Documentation*

H:10.12 [*Identical to C:10.13.*]

Notes for guidance

H:10A [*Identical to C:10A.*]
H:10B [*Identical to C:10B, save for inclusion of reference to "Note 3G" after the word "committed".*]
H:10C–10F [*Identical to C:10D to C:10G.*]

H:11 Interviews—general

(a) *Action*

H:11.1 An interview in this code is the questioning of a person arrested on suspicion of being a terrorist which, under paragraph 10.1, must be carried out under caution. Before a person is interviewed they and, if they are represented, their solicitor must be informed of the grounds for arrest, and given sufficient information to enable them to understand the nature of their suspected involvement in the commission, preparation or instigation of acts of terrorism (see para. 3.4(a)) in order to allow for the effective exercise of the rights of the defence. However, whilst the information must always be sufficient information for the person to understand the nature of their suspected involvement in the commission, preparation or instigation of acts of terrorism, this does not require the disclosure of details at a time which might prejudice the investigation (see *Notes 3G* and *11ZA*). The decision about what needs to be disclosed for the purpose of this requirement therefore rests with the investigating officer who has sufficient knowledge of the case to make that decision. The officer who discloses the information shall make a record of the information disclosed and when it was disclosed. This record may be made in the interview record, in the officer's pocket book or other form provided for this purpose.

H:11.2 Following the arrest of a person under section 41 TACT, that person must not be interviewed about the relevant offence except at a place designated for detention under Schedule 8, paragraph 1, of the Terrorism Act 2000, unless the consequent delay would be likely to:

(a) lead to:
- interference with, or harm to, evidence connected with an offence;
- interference with, or physical harm to, other people; or
- serious loss of, or damage to, property;

(b) lead to alerting other people suspected of committing an offence but not yet arrested for it; or

(c) hinder the recovery of property obtained in consequence of the commission of an offence.

Interviewing in any of these circumstances shall cease once the relevant risk has been averted or the necessary questions have been put in order to attempt to avert that risk.

H:11.3 Immediately prior to the commencement or re-commencement of any interview at a designated place of detention, the interviewer should remind the suspect of their entitlement to free legal advice and that the interview can be delayed for legal advice to be obtained, unless one of the exceptions in paragraph 6.7 applies. It is the interviewer's responsibility to make sure all reminders are recorded in the interview record.

H:11.4, 11.5 [*Identical to C:11.4 and C:11.4A.*]
H:11.6 [*Identical to C:11.5, save for reference "paragraph 10.8" in lieu of reference to "paragraph 10.9".*]
H:11.7 [*Identical to C:11.6, but with the omission of the final sub-paragraph of that paragraph.*]

(b) *Interview records*

H:11.8 Interviews of a person detained under section 41 of, or Schedule 8 to, TACT must be video recorded with sound in accordance with the code of practice issued under paragraph 3 of Schedule 8 to the Terrorism Act 2000, or in the case of post-charge questioning authorised under section 22 of the Counter-Terrorism Act 2008, the code of practice issued under section 25 of that Act.

H:11.8A [*Identical to C:11.13.*]

(c) *Juveniles and mentally disordered or otherwise mentally vulnerable people*

H:11.9 [*Identical to C:11.15, save for reference to "paragraphs 11.2, 11.11 to 11.13" in lieu of reference to "paragraphs 11.1, 11.18 to 11.20", and to "paragraph 1.11A" in lieu of reference to "paragraph 1.5A".*]

H:11.10 If an appropriate adult is present at an interview, they shall be informed:
- that they are not expected to act simply as an observer; and

- that the purpose of their presence is to:
  - advise the person being interviewed;
  - observe whether the interview is being conducted properly and fairly;
  - facilitate communication with the person being interviewed.

The appropriate adult may be required to leave the interview if their conduct is such that the interviewer is unable properly to put questions to the suspect. This will include situations where the appropriate adult's approach or conduct prevents or unreasonably obstructs proper questions being put to the suspect or the suspect's responses being recorded. If the interviewer considers an appropriate adult is acting in such a way, they will stop the interview and consult an officer not below superintendent rank, if one is readily available, and otherwise an officer not below inspector rank not connected with the investigation. After speaking to the appropriate adult, the officer consulted will decide if the interview should continue without the attendance of that appropriate adult. If they decide it should not, another appropriate adult should be obtained before the interview continues, unless the provisions of paragraph 11.11 below apply.

(d) *Vulnerable suspects—urgent interviews at police stations*

H:11.11–11.13 [*Identical to C:11.18 to C:11.20, save for references to "paragraph 11.2(a) to (c)", "paragraph 1.11A", "paragraph 3.14" and "paragraph 11.11", in lieu of references to "paragraph 11.1(a) to (c)", "paragraph 1.5A", paragraph "3.12" and "paragraph 11.18", respectively.*]

Notes for guidance

A-221   H:11ZA *The requirement in paragraph 11.1A for a suspect to be given sufficient information about the nature of their suspected involvement in the commission, preparation or instigation of acts of terrorism applies prior to the interview and whether or not they are legally represented. What is sufficient will depend on the circumstances of the case, but it should normally include, as a minimum, enough to avoid suspects being confused or unclear about what they are supposed to have done and to help an innocent suspect to clear the matter up more quickly.*

H:11A–11C [*Identical to C:11A (save for an erroneous reference to para. 3.4 of code of practice under 1996 Act) to C:11C (save for reference to "paragraph 1.11A" in lieu of reference to "paragraph 1.5A"), respectively.*]

H:11B *The Criminal Procedure and Investigations Act 1996 Code of Practice, paragraph 3.4 states 'In conducting an investigation, the investigator should pursue all reasonable lines of enquiry, whether these point towards or away from the suspect. What is reasonable will depend on the particular circumstances.' Interviewers should keep this in mind when deciding what questions to ask in an interview.*

H:11C *Although juveniles or people who are mentally disordered or otherwise mentally vulnerable are often capable of providing reliable evidence, they may, without knowing or wishing to do so, be particularly prone in certain circumstances to provide information that may be unreliable, misleading or self-incriminating. Special care should always be taken when questioning such a person, and the appropriate adult should be involved if there is any doubt about a person's age, mental state or capacity. Because of the risk of unreliable evidence it is also important to obtain corroboration of any facts admitted whenever possible. Paragraph 1.11A extends this note to 17-year-old suspects.*

H:11D *Consideration should be given to the effect of extended detention on a detainee and any subsequent information they provide, especially if it relates to information on matters that they have failed to provide previously in response to similar questioning: see Annex G.*

H:11E [*Identical to C:11E.*]

H:12 Interviews in police stations

(a) *Action*

A-221a   H:12.1 If a police officer wants to interview or conduct enquiries which require the presence of a detainee, the custody officer is responsible for deciding whether to deliver the detainee into the officer's custody. An investigating officer who is given custody of a detainee takes over responsibility for the detainee's care and treatment for the purposes of this code until they return the detainee to the custody officer when they must report the manner in which they complied with the code whilst having custody of the detainee.

H:12.2 Except as below, in any period of 24 hours a detainee must be allowed a continuous period of at least 8 hours for rest, free from questioning, travel or any interruption in connection with the investigation concerned. This period should normally be at night or other appropriate time which takes account of when the detainee last slept or rested. If a detainee is arrested at a police station after going there voluntarily, the period of 24 hours runs from the time of their arrest (or, if a person was being detained under TACT, Sched. 7, when arrested, from the time at which the examination under Schedule 7 began) and not the time of arrival at the police station. The period may not be interrupted or delayed, except:

   (a) when there are reasonable grounds for believing not delaying or interrupting the period
would:

     (i) involve a risk of harm to people or serious loss of, or damage to, property;

     (ii) delay unnecessarily the person's release from custody; or

     (iii) otherwise prejudice the outcome of the investigation;

   (b) at the request of the detainee, their appropriate adult or legal representative;

   (c) when a delay or interruption is necessary in order to:

     (i) comply with the legal obligations and duties arising under section 14; or

     (ii) to take action required under section 9 or in accordance with medical advice.

If the period is interrupted in accordance with (a), a fresh period must be allowed. Interruptions
under (b) and (c), do not require a fresh period to be allowed.

H:12.3 [*Identical to C:12.3, save that there is no reference to "Annex G" and the references to "paragraph
11.18" and "paragraphs 11.18 to 11.20" are replaced by references to "paragraph 11.11" and "paragraphs
11.11 to 11.13".*]

H:12.4 [*Identical to C:12.4.*]

H:12.5 A suspect whose detention without charge has been authorised under TACT, Sched. 8,
because the detention is necessary for an interview to obtain evidence of the offence for which they
have been arrested, may choose not to answer questions but police do not require the suspect's
consent or agreement to interview them for this purpose. If a suspect takes steps to prevent
themselves being questioned or further questioned, *e.g.* by refusing to leave their cell to go to a suitable interview room or by trying to leave the interview room, they shall be advised their consent or
agreement to interview is not required. The suspect shall be cautioned as in section 10, and informed
if they fail or refuse to co-operate, the interview may take place in the cell and that their failure or
refusal to co-operate may be given in evidence. The suspect shall then be invited to co-operate and
go into the interview room.

H:12.6 People being questioned or making statements shall not be required to stand.

H:12.7 Before the interview commences each interviewer shall, subject to the qualification at
paragraph 2.8, identify themselves and any other persons present to the interviewee.

H:12.8 [*Effectively identical to C:12.8.*]

H:12.9 During extended periods where no interviews take place, because of the need to gather
further evidence or analyse existing evidence, detainees and their legal representative shall be
informed that the investigation into the relevant offence remains ongoing. If practicable, the detainee
and legal representative should also be made aware in general terms of any reasons for long gaps
between interviews. Consideration should be given to allowing visits, more frequent exercise, or for
reading or writing materials to be offered: see paragraph 5.4, section 8 and *Note 12C*.

H:12.10 [*Identical to C:12.9.*]

(b) *Documentation*

H:12.11-12.15 [*Identical to C:12.10 to C:12.14, respectively.*]

Notes for guidance

H:12A *It is not normally necessary to ask for a written statement if the interview was recorded in accordance*   **A-221b**
*with the code of practice issued under TACT, Sched. 8, para. 3. Statements under caution should normally be
taken in these circumstances only at the person's express wish. A person may however be asked if they want to make
such a statement.*

H:12B [*Identical to C:12B.*]

H:12C *Consideration should be given to the matters referred to in paragraph 12.9 after a period of over 24
hours without questioning. This is to ensure that extended periods of detention without an indication that the
investigation remains ongoing do not contribute to a deterioration of the detainee's well-being.*

H:13 Interpreters

(a) *General*

H:13.1 Chief officers are responsible for making arrangements to provide appropriately qualified
independent persons to act as interpreters and to provide translations of essential documents for
detained suspects who, in accordance with paragraph 3.5(c)(ii), the custody officer has determined
require an interpreter.

If the suspect has a hearing or speech impediment, references to "interpreter" and "interpretation" in this code include appropriate assistance necessary to establish effective communication with
that person. See paragraph 13.1C if the detainee is in Wales.

H:13.1A *[Identical to C:13.1A, save for reference to "Annex K" in lieu of reference to "Annex M".]*

H:13.1B *[Identical to C:13.1B.]*

H:13.1C *[Identical to C:13.1C, save for reference to paragraph "3.14" in lieu of reference to paragraph "3.12".]*

(b) *Interviewing suspects—foreign languages*

H:13.2 Unless paragraphs 11.2 or 11.11(c) apply, a suspect who for the purposes of this code requires an interpreter because they do not appear to speak or understand English (see paras 3.5(c)(ii) and 3.14) must not be interviewed in the absence of a person capable of interpreting.

H:13.3 An interpreter should also be called if a juvenile is interviewed and their parent or guardian, present as the appropriate adult, does not appear to speak or understand English, unless the interview is urgent and paragraphs 11.2 or 11.11(c) apply.

Note: paragraph 1.11A extends the requirement in this paragraph to interviews of 17-year-old suspects.

H:13.4 *[Identical to C:13.4.]*

(c) *Interviewing suspects who have a hearing or speech impediment*

H:13.5 *[Identical to C:13.5, save for reference to paragraph "3.14" in lieu of reference to paragraph "3.12".]*

H:13.6 An interpreter should also be called if a juvenile is interviewed and their parent or guardian present as the appropriate adult appears to have a hearing or speech impediment, unless the interview is urgent and paragraphs 11.2 or 11.11(c) apply.

Note: paragraph 1.11A extends the requirement in this paragraph to interviews of 17-year-old suspects.

H:13.7 *[Not used.]*

(d) *Additional rules for detained persons*

H:13.8 *[Not used.]*

H:13.9 *[Identical to C:13.9.]*

H:13.10 After the custody officer has determined that a detainee requires an interpreter (see para. 3.5(c)(ii)) and following the initial action in paragraphs 3.1 to 3.5, arrangements must also be made for an interpreter to explain:

- the grounds and reasons for any authorisation of their detention under the provisions of the Terrorism Act 2000 or the Counter Terrorism Act 2008 (post-charge questioning) to which this code applies, and
- any information about the authorisation given to them by the authorising officer or (as the case may be) the court and which is recorded in the custody record.

See sections 14 and 15 of this code.

H:13.10A *[Identical to C:13.10A.]*

(e) *Translations of essential documents*

H:13.10B *[Identical to C:13.10B, save for reference to "Annex K" in lieu of reference to "Annex M".]*

H:13.10C *[Identical to C:13.10C.]*

(f) *Decisions not to provide interpretation and translation.*

H:13.10D If a suspect challenges a decision:

- made by the custody officer in accordance with this code (see para. 3.5(c)(ii)) that they do not require an interpreter, or
- made in accordance with paragraphs 13.10A, 13.10B or 13.10C not to provide a different interpreter or another translation or not to translate a requested document,

the matter shall be reported to an inspector to deal with as a complaint for the purposes of paragraph 9.3 or 12.10 if the challenge is made during an interview.

(g) *Documentation*

H:13.11 *[Identical to C:13.11, save for references to "Annex K" in lieu of references to "Annex M".]*

Notes for guidance

H:13A–13C [*Identical to C:13A to C:13C, respectively.*]

H:14 Reviews and extensions of detention under the Terrorism Act 2000

(a) *General*

H:14.0 The requirement in paragraph 3.4(b) that documents and materials essential to challeng- **A-222** ing the lawfulness of the detainee's arrest and detention must be made available to the detainee or their solicitor, applies for the purposes of this section as follows:

(a) the officer reviewing the need for detention (TACT, Sched. 8) is responsible, in consultation with the investigating officer, for deciding which documents and materials are essential and must be made available;

(b) when an application is to be made for a warrant as described in paragraph 14.3, the person making the application is responsible for deciding which documents and materials are essential and must be made available before the hearing. See *Note 3ZA*.

H:14.1 The powers and duties of the review officer are in the Terrorism Act 2000, Sched. 8, Pt II. See *Notes 14A* and *14B*. A review officer should carry out their duties at the police station where the detainee is held, and be allowed such access to the detainee as is necessary to exercise those duties.

H:14.2 For the purposes of reviewing a person's detention, no officer shall put specific questions to the detainee:

- regarding their involvement in any offence; or
- in respect of any comments they may make:
  - when given the opportunity to make representations; or
  - in response to a decision to keep them in detention or extend the maximum period of detention.

Such an exchange could constitute an interview as in paragraph 11.1 and would be subject to the associated safeguards in section 11.

H:14.3 If detention is necessary for longer than 48 hours from the time of arrest or, if a person was being detained under TACT, Sched. 7, from the time at which the examination under Schedule 7 began), a police officer of at least superintendent rank, or a crown prosecutor may apply for a warrant of further detention or for an extension or further extension of such a warrant under paragraph 29 or (as the case may be) 36 of Part III of Schedule 8 to the Terrorism Act 2000. See paragraph 14.0(b) and *Note 14C*.

H:14.4 When an application is made for a warrant as described in paragraph 14.3, the detained person and their representative must be informed of their rights in respect of the application. These include:

(i) the right to a written notice of the application (see para. 14.4 [*sic*]);

(ii) the right to make oral or written representations to the judicial authority/High Court judge about the application;

(iii) the right to be present and legally represented at the hearing of the application, unless specifically excluded by the judicial authority/High Court judge;

(iv) their right to free legal advice (see section 6 of this code).

H:14.4A TACT, Sched. 8, para. 31, requires the notice of the application for a warrant of further detention to be provided before the judicial hearing of the application for that warrant and that the notice must include:

(a) notification that the application for a warrant has been made;

(b) the time at which the application was made;

(c) the time at which the application is to be heard;

(d) the grounds on which further detention is sought.

A notice must also be provided each time an application is made to extend or further extend an existing warrant.

(b) *Transfer of persons detained for more than 14 days to prison*

H:14.5 If the *Detention of Terrorists Suspects (Temporary Extension) Bill* is enacted and in force, a High Court judge may extend or further extend a warrant of further detention to authorise a person to be detained beyond a period of 14 days from the time of their arrest (or if they were being detained under TACT, Sched. 7, from the time at which their examination under Schedule 7 began). The provisions of Annex J will apply when a warrant of further detention is so extended or further extended.

H:14.6–14.10 [*Not used.*]

(c) Documentation

H:14.11 It is the responsibility of the officer who gives any reminders as at paragraph 14.4, to ensure that these are noted in the custody record, as well any comments made by the detained person upon being told of those rights.

H:14.12 The grounds for, and extent of, any delay in conducting a review shall be recorded.

H:14.13 Any written representations shall be retained.

H:14.14 A record shall be made as soon as practicable about the outcome of each review and, if applicable, the grounds on which the review officer authorises continued detention. A record shall also be made as soon as practicable about the outcome of an application for a warrant of further detention or its extension.

H:14.15 [*Not used.*]

Notes for guidance

H:14A *TACT, Sched. 8, Pt II, sets out the procedures for review of detention up to 48 hours from the time of arrest under TACT, s.41 (or if a person was being detained under TACT, Sched. 7, from the time at which the examination under Schedule 7 began). These include provisions for the requirement to review detention, postponing a review, grounds for continued detention, designating a review officer, representations, rights of the detained person and keeping a record. The review officer's role ends after a warrant has been issued for extension of detention under Part III of Schedule 8.*

H:14B *A review officer may authorise a person's continued detention if satisfied that detention is necessary—*

    (a) *to obtain relevant evidence whether by questioning the person or otherwise;*

    (b) *to preserve relevant evidence;*

    (c) *while awaiting the result of an examination or analysis of relevant evidence;*

    (d) *for the examination or analysis of anything with a view to obtaining relevant evidence;*

    (e) *pending a decision to apply to the Secretary of State for a deportation notice to be served on the detainee, the making of any such application, or the consideration of any such application by the Secretary of State;*

    (f) *pending a decision to charge the detainee with an offence.*

H:14C *Applications for warrants to extend detention beyond 48 hours, may be made for periods of 7 days at a time (initially under TACT, Sched. 8, para. 29, and extensions thereafter under TACT, Sched. 8, para. 36), up to a maximum period of 14 days (or 28 days if the Detention of Terrorists Suspects (Temporary Extension) Bill is enacted and in force) from the time of their arrest (or if they were being detained under TACT, Sched. 7, from the time at which their examination under Schedule 7 began). Applications may be made for shorter periods than 7 days, which must be specified. The judicial authority or High Court judge may also substitute a shorter period if they feel a period of 7 days is inappropriate.*

H:14D *Unless Note 14F applies, applications for warrants that would take the total period of detention up to 14 days or less should be made to a judicial authority, meaning a District Judge (Magistrates' Court) designated by the Lord Chief Justice to hear such applications.*

H:14E *If by virtue of the relevant provisions described in Note 14C being enacted the maximum period of detention is extended to 28 days, any application for a warrant which would take the period of detention beyond 14 days from the time of arrest (or if a person was being detained under TACT, Sched. 7, from the time at which the examination under Schedule 7 began), must be made to a High Court Judge.*

H:14F *If, when the Detention of Terrorists Suspects (Temporary Extension) Bill is enacted and in force, an application is made to a High Court judge for a warrant which would take detention beyond 14 days and the High Court judge instead issues a warrant for a period of time which would not take detention beyond 14 days, further applications for extension of detention must also be made to a High Court judge, regardless of the period of time to which they refer.*

H:14G [*Not used.*]

H:14H *An officer applying for an order under TACT, Sched. 8, para. 34, to withhold specified information on which they intend to rely when applying for a warrant of further detention or the extension or further extension of such a warrant, may make the application for the order orally or in writing. The most appropriate method of application will depend on the circumstances of the case and the need to ensure fairness to the detainee.*

H:14I *After hearing any representations by or on behalf of the detainee and the applicant, the judicial authority or High Court judge may direct that the hearing relating to the extension of detention under Part III of Schedule 8 is to take place using video conferencing facilities. However, if the judicial authority requires the detained person to be physically present at any hearing, this should be complied with as soon as practicable. Paragraph 33(4) to (9) of TACT, Sched. 8, govern the hearing of applications via video-link or other means.*

H:14J [*Not used.*]

H:14K [*Not used.*]

H:15 Charging and post-charge questioning in terrorism cases

(a) *Charging*

H:15.1 Charging of detained persons is covered by PACE and guidance issued under PACE by the   **A-222b**
Director of Public Prosecutions. Decisions to charge persons to whom this code (H) applies, the
charging process and related matters are subject to section 16 of PACE Code C.

(b) *Post-charge questioning*

H:15.2 Under section 22 of the Counter-Terrorism Act 2008, a judge of the Crown Court may   **A-222c**
authorise the questioning of a person about an offence for which they have been charged, informed
that they may be prosecuted or sent for trial, if the offence:
- is a terrorism offence as set out in section 27 of the Counter-Terrorism Act 2008; or
- is an offence which appears to the judge to have a terrorist connection (see *Note 15C*).

The decision on whether to apply for such questioning will be based on the needs of the
investigation. There is no power to detain a person solely for the purposes of post-charge questioning.
A person can only be detained whilst being so questioned (whether at a police station or in prison) if
they are already there in lawful custody under some existing power. If at a police station the contents
of sections 8 and 9 of this code must be considered the minimum standards of treatment for such
detainees.

H:15.3 The Crown Court judge may authorise the questioning if they are satisfied that:
- further questioning is necessary in the interests of justice;
- the investigation for the purposes of which the further questioning is being proposed is
  being conducted diligently and expeditiously; and
- the questioning would not interfere unduly with the preparation of the person's defence
  to the charge or any other criminal charge that they may be facing.

See *Note 15E*.

H:15.4 The judge authorising questioning may specify the location of the questioning.

H:15.5 The judge may only authorise a period up to a maximum of 48 hours before further
authorisation must be sought. The 48 hour period would run continuously from the commencement
of questioning. This period must include breaks in questioning in accordance with paragraphs 8.6
and 12.2 of this code (see *Note 15B*).

H:15.6 Nothing in this code shall be taken to prevent a suspect seeking a voluntary interview with
the police at any time.

H:15.7 For the purposes of this section, any reference in sections 6, 10, 11, 12 and 13 of this code
to:
- "suspect" means the person in respect of whom an authorisation has been given under
  section 22 of the Counter-Terrorism Act 2008 (post-charge questioning of terrorist
  suspects) to interview them;
- "interview" means post-charge questioning authorised under section 22 of the
  CounterTerrorism Act 2008;
- "offence" means an offence for which the person has been charged, informed that they
  may be prosecuted or sent for trial and about which the person is being questioned; and
- "place of detention" means the location of the questioning specified by the judge (see
  paragraph 15.4),

and the provisions of those sections apply (as appropriate), to such questioning (whether at a police
station or in prison) subject to the further modifications in the following paragraphs:

Right to legal advice

H:15.8 In section 6 of this code, for the purposes of post-charge questioning:
- access to a solicitor may not be delayed under Annex B; and
- paragraph 6.5 (direction that a detainee may only consult a solicitor within the sight and
  hearing of a qualified officer) does not apply.

Cautions

H:15.9 In section 10 of this code, unless the restriction on drawing adverse inferences from
silence applies (see paragraph 15.10), for the purposes of post-charge questioning, the caution must
be given in the following terms before any such questions are asked:

"You do not have to say anything. But it may harm your defence if you do not mention when questioned
something which you later rely on in court. Anything you do say may be given in evidence.".

Where the use of the Welsh language is appropriate, a constable may provide the caution directly in Welsh in the following terms:

"*Does dim rhaid i chi ddweud dim byd. Ond gall niweidio eich amddiffyniad os na fyddwch chi'n sôn, yn awr, am rywbeth y byddwch chi'n dibynnu arno nes ymlaen yn y llys. Gall unrhyw beth yr ydych yn ei ddweud gael ei roi fel tystiolaeth.*".

H:15.10 The only restriction on drawing adverse inferences from silence, see Annex C, applies in those situations where a person has asked for legal advice and is questioned before receiving such advice in accordance with paragraph 6.7(b).

Interviews

H:15.11 In section 11, for the purposes of post-charge questioning, whenever a person is questioned, they must be informed of the offence for which they have been charged or informed that they may be prosecuted, or that they have been sent for trial and about which they are being questioned.

H:15.12 Paragraph 11.2 (place where questioning may take place) does not apply to postcharge questioning.

Recording post-charge questioning

H:15.13 All interviews must be video recorded with sound in accordance with the separate code of practice issued under section 25 of the Counter-Terrorism Act 2008 for the video recording with sound of post-charge questioning authorised under section 22 of the Counter-Terrorism Act 2008 (see paragraph 11.8).

Notes for guidance

H:15A *If a person is detained at a police station for the purposes of post-charge questioning, a custody record must be opened in accordance with section 2 of this code. The custody record must note the power under which the person is being detained, the time at which the person was transferred into police custody, their time of arrival at the police station and their time of being presented to the custody officer.*

H:15B *The custody record must note the time at which the interview process commences. This shall be regarded as the relevant time for any period of questioning in accordance with paragraph 15.5 of this code.*

H:15C *Where reference is made to "terrorist connection" in paragraph 15.2, this is determined in accordance with section 30 of the Counter-Terrorism Act 2008. Under section 30 of that Act a court must in certain circumstances determine whether an offence has a terrorist connection. These are offences under general criminal law which may be prosecuted in terrorism cases (for example explosives-related offences and conspiracy to murder). An offence has a terrorist connection if the offence is, or takes place in the course of, an act of terrorism or is committed for the purposes of terrorism (section 98 of the Act). Normally the court will make the determination during the sentencing process, however for the purposes of post-charge questioning, a Crown Court judge must determine whether the offence could have a terrorist connection.*

H:15D *The powers under section 22 of the Counter-Terrorism Act 2008 are separate from and additional to the normal questioning procedures within this code. Their overall purpose is to enable the further questioning of a terrorist suspect after charge. They should not therefore be used to replace or circumvent the normal powers for dealing with routine questioning.*

H:15E *Post-charge questioning has been created because it is acknowledged that terrorist investigations can be large and complex and that a great deal of evidence can come to light following the charge of a terrorism suspect. This can occur, for instance, from the translation of material or as the result of additional investigation. When considering an application for post-charge questioning, the police must "satisfy" the judge on all three points under paragraph 15.3. This means that the judge will either authorise or refuse an application on the balance of whether the conditions in paragraph 15.3 are all met. It is important therefore, when making the application, to consider the following questions:*

- *What further evidence is the questioning expected to provide?*
- *Why was it not possible to obtain this evidence before charge?*
- *How and why was the need to question after charge first recognised?*
- *How is the questioning expected to contribute further to the case?*
- *To what extent could the time and place for further questioning interfere with the preparation of the person's defence (for example if authorisation is sought close to the time of a trial)?*
- *What steps will be taken to minimise any risk that questioning might interfere with the preparation of the person's defence?*

This list is not exhaustive but outlines the type of questions that could be relevant to any asked by a judge in considering an application.

H:16 Testing persons for the presence of specified Class A drugs

H:16.1 The provisions for drug testing under section 63B of PACE (as amended by section 5 of **A-223**
the Criminal Justice Act 2003 and section 7 of the Drugs Act 2005), do not apply to persons to whom
this code applies. Guidance on these provisions can be found in section 17 of PACE Code C.

ANNEX A

Intimate and strip searches

A *Intimate search*

H:1. [*Identical to Code C, Annex A, para. 1.*]　　　　　　　　　　　**A-223a**

(a) Action

H:2. Body orifices other than the mouth may be searched if authorised by an officer of inspector
rank or above who has reasonable grounds for believing that the person may have concealed on
themselves anything which they could and might use to cause physical injury to themselves or others
at the station and the officer has reasonable grounds for believing that an intimate search is the only
means of removing those items.

H:3. [*Identical to Code C, Annex A, para. 2A, save for reference to "paragraph 1.11A" in lieu of reference to
"paragraph 1.5A".*]

H:4. An intimate search may only be carried out by a registered medical practitioner or registered
nurse, unless an officer of at least inspector rank considers this is not practicable, in which case a
police officer may carry out the search. See *Notes A1 to A5*.

H:5. Any proposal for a search under paragraph 2 to be carried out by someone other than a
registered medical practitioner or registered nurse must only be considered as a last resort and when
the authorising officer is satisfied the risks associated with allowing the item to remain with the
detainee outweigh the risks associated with removing it. See *Notes A1 to A5*.

H:6. An intimate search at a police station of a juvenile or mentally disordered or otherwise
mentally vulnerable person may take place only in the presence of an appropriate adult of the same
sex (see Annex I), unless the detainee specifically requests a particular adult of the opposite sex who
is readily available. In the case of a juvenile the search may take place in the absence of the appropriate adult only if the juvenile signifies in the presence of the appropriate adult they do not want the
adult present during the search and the adult agrees. A record shall be made of the juvenile's decision and signed by the appropriate adult.

Note: paragraph 1.11A of this code extends the requirement in this paragraph to an intimate
search of a 17-year-old.

H:7. When an intimate search under paragraph 2 is carried out by a police officer, the officer must
be of the same sex as the detainee (see Annex I). A minimum of two people, other than the detainee,
must be present during the search. Subject to paragraph 6, no person of the opposite sex who is not
a medical practitioner or nurse shall be present, nor shall anyone whose presence is unnecessary.
The search shall be conducted with proper regard to the sensitivity and vulnerability of the detainee.

(b) Documentation

H:8. In the case of an intimate search under paragraph 2, the following shall be recorded as soon
as practicable, in the detainee's custody record:

- the authorisation to carry out the search;
- the grounds for giving the authorisation;
- the grounds for believing the article could not be removed without an intimate search;
- which parts of the detainee's body were searched;
- who carried out the search;
- who was present;
- the result.

H:9. [*Identical to Code C, Annex A, para. 8.*]

B *Strip search*

H:10. [*Identical to Code C, Annex A, para. 9.*]

(a) Action

H:11. [*Identical to Code C, Annex A, para. 10.*]

The conduct of strip searches

H:12. [*Identical to Code C, Annex A, para. 11, save for references to "Annex I" in lieu of references to "Annex L", and reference to "paragraph 1.11A" in lieu of reference to "paragraph 1.5A".*]

(b) Documentation

H:13. [*Identical to Code C, Annex A, para. 12.*]

Notes for guidance

A-223b

H:A1 [*Identical to Code C, Annex A, A1.*]

H:A2 [*Identical to Code C, Annex A, A2.*]

H:A3 [*Identical to Code C, Annex A, A3, save for reference to "paragraph 2" in lieu of reference to "paragraph 2(a)(i)".*]

H:A4 [*Identical to Code C, Annex A, A4, save for reference to "paragraph 2" in lieu of reference to "paragraph 2(a)(i)".*]

H:A5 [*Identical to Code C, Annex A, A5.*]

ANNEX B

Delay in notifying arrest or allowing access to legal advice for persons detained under the Terrorism Act 2000

A-224

H:1. The rights as in sections 5 or 6, may be delayed if the person is detained under the Terrorism Act 2000, s.41, has not yet been charged with an offence and an officer of superintendent rank or above has reasonable grounds for believing the exercise of either right will have one of the following consequences:

  (a) interference with or harm to evidence of a serious offence;
  (b) interference with or physical injury to any person;
  (c) the alerting of persons who are suspected of having committed a serious offence but who have not been arrested for it;
  (d) the hindering of the recovery of property obtained as a result of a serious offence or in respect of which a forfeiture order could be made under section 23;
  (e) interference with the gathering of information about the commission, preparation or instigation of acts of terrorism;
  (f) the alerting of a person and thereby making it more difficult to prevent an act of terrorism; or
  (g) the alerting of a person and thereby making it more difficult to secure a person's apprehension, prosecution or conviction in connection with the commission, preparation or instigation of an act of terrorism.

H:2. These rights may also be delayed if the officer has reasonable grounds for believing that:

  (a) the detained person has benefited from his criminal conduct (to be decided in accordance with Part 2 of the Proceeds of Crime Act 2002); and
  (b) the recovery of the value of the property constituting the benefit will be hindered by—
   (i) informing the named person of the detained person's detention (in the case of an authorisation under paragraph 8(1)(a) of Schedule 8 to TACT); or
   (ii) the exercise of the right under paragraph 7 (in the case of an authorisation under paragraph 8(1)(b) of Schedule 8 to TACT).

H:3. Authority to delay a detainee's right to consult privately with a solicitor may be given only if the authorising officer has reasonable grounds to believe the solicitor the detainee wants to consult will, inadvertently or otherwise, pass on a message from the detainee or act in some other way which will have any of the consequences specified under paragraph 8 of Schedule 8 to the Terrorism Act 2000. In these circumstances, the detainee must be allowed to choose another solicitor. See *Note B3*.

H:4. [*Identical to Code C, Annex B, para. 4.*]

H:5. [*Identical to Code C, Annex B, para. 5.*]

H:6. These rights may be delayed only for as long as is necessary but not beyond 48 hours from the time of arrest (or if a person was being detained under TACT, Sched. 7, from the time at which the examination under Schedule 7 began). If the above grounds cease to apply within this time the detainee must as soon as practicable be asked if they wish to exercise either right, the custody record noted accordingly, and action taken in accordance with the relevant section of this code.

H:7. A person must be allowed to consult a solicitor for a reasonable time before any court hearing.

Documentation

H:8. [*Identical to Code C, Annex B, para. 13.*]

H:9. [*Identical to Code C, Annex B, para. 14, save for reference to "paragraph 6" in lieu of reference to "paragraphs 6 or 11".*]

Cautions and special warnings

H:10. [*Identical to Code C, Annex B, para. 15.*]

Notes for guidance

H:B1 [*Identical to Code C, Annex B, B1, save for reference to "paragraph 3.15 and 3.17" in lieu of reference to "paragraph 3.13 and 3.15" and reference to "paragraph 1.11A" in lieu of reference to "paragraph 1.5A".*] **A-224a**

H:B2 [*Identical to Code C, Annex B, B2.*]

H:B3 [*Identical to Code C, Annex B, B3.*]

ANNEX C

Restriction on drawing adverse inferences from silence and terms of the caution when the restriction applies

(a) *The restriction on drawing adverse inferences from silence*

H:1. The Criminal Justice and Public Order Act 1994, ss.34, 36 and 37 as amended by the Youth **A-224b**
Justice and Criminal Evidence Act 1999, s.58 describe the conditions under which adverse inferences may be drawn from a person's failure or refusal to say anything about their involvement in the offence when interviewed, after being charged or informed they may be prosecuted. These provisions are subject to an overriding restriction on the ability of a court or jury to draw adverse inferences from a person's silence. This restriction applies:

  (a) to any detainee at a police station who, before being interviewed, see section 11 or being charged or informed they may be prosecuted, see section 15, has:

   (i) asked for legal advice, see section 6, paragraph 6.1;

   (ii) not been allowed an opportunity to consult a solicitor, including the duty solicitor, as in this code; and

   (iii) not changed their mind about wanting legal advice, see section 6, paragraph 6.7(d);
   Note the condition in (ii) will:

     – apply when a detainee who has asked for legal advice is interviewed before speaking to a solicitor as in section 6, paragraph 6.6(a) or (b);

     – not apply if the detained person declines to ask for the duty solicitor, see section 6, paragraphs 6.7(b) and (c);

  (b) to any person who has been charged with, or informed they may be prosecuted for, an offence who:

   (i) has had brought to their notice a written statement made by another person or the content of an interview with another person which relates to that offence, see PACE Code C, section 16, paragraph 16.4;

   (ii) is interviewed about that offence, see *PACE* Code C, section 16, paragraph 16.5; or

   (iii) makes a written statement about that offence, see Annex D, paragraphs 4 and 9, unless post-charge questioning has been authorised in accordance with section 22 of the Counter-Terrorism Act 2008, in which case the restriction will apply only if the person has asked for legal advice, see section 6, paragraph 6.1, and is questioned before receiving such advice in accordance with paragraph 6.7(b). See paragraph 15.11.

(b) *Terms of the caution when the restriction applies*

H:2. [*Identical to Code C, Annex C, para. 2.*]

H:3. [*Identical to Code C, Annex C, para. 3, save for reference to "Note C1" in lieu of reference to "Note C2".*]

Notes for guidance

A-225   H:C1 *[Identical to Code C, Annex C, C2.]*

ANNEX D

Written statements under caution

A-225a   *[Identical to Annex D to Code C.]*

ANNEX E

Summary of provisions relating to mentally disordered and otherwise mentally vulnerable people

A-225b   H:1. *[Identical to Code C, Annex E, para. 1, save for reference to "paragraph 1.10" in lieu of reference to "paragraph 1.4" and absence of any reference to Note E4.]*

H:2. *[Identical to Code C, Annex E, para. 2, save for reference to "paragraph 1.13(b)" in lieu of reference to "paragraph 1.7(b)".]*

H:3. If the detention of a person who is mentally vulnerable or appears to be suffering from a mental disorder is authorised by the review officer (see paragraphs 14.1 and 14.2 and *Notes for Guidance 14A and 14B*), the custody officer must as soon as practicable inform the appropriate adult of the grounds for detention and the person's whereabouts, and ask the adult to come to the police station to see them. If the appropriate adult:

- is already at the station when information is given as in paragraphs 3.1 to 3.5 the information must be given in their presence
- is not at the station when the provisions of paragraph 3.1 to 3.5 are complied with these provisions must be complied with again in their presence once they arrive.

See paragraphs 3.15 to 3.16.

H:4. *[Identical to Code C, Annex E, para. 4, save for reference to "paragraph 3.20" in lieu of reference to "paragraph 3.19".]*

H:5. *[Identical to Code C, Annex E, para. 5, save for reference to "paragraph 9.6 and 9.8" in lieu of reference to "paragraph 9.5 and 9.6".]*

H:6. If a mentally disordered or otherwise mentally vulnerable person is cautioned in the absence of the appropriate adult, the caution must be repeated in the appropriate adult's presence. See paragraph 10.11.

H:7. A mentally disordered or otherwise mentally vulnerable person must not be interviewed or asked to provide or sign a written statement in the absence of the appropriate adult unless the provisions of paragraphs 11.2 or 11.11 to 11.13 apply. Questioning in these circumstances may not continue in the absence of the appropriate adult once sufficient information to avert the risk has been obtained. A record shall be made of the grounds for any decision to begin an interview in these circumstances. See paragraphs 11.2, 11.9 and 11.11 to 11.13.

H:8. If the appropriate adult is present at an interview, they shall be informed they are not expected to act simply as an observer and the purposes of their presence are to:

- advise the interviewee;
- observe whether or not the interview is being conducted properly and fairly;
- facilitate communication with the interviewee.

See paragraph 11.10.

H:9. If the custody officer charges a mentally disordered or otherwise mentally vulnerable person with an offence or takes such other action as is appropriate when there is sufficient evidence for a prosecution this must be carried out in the presence of the appropriate adult if they are at the police station. A copy of the written notice embodying any charge must be given to the appropriate adult. See *PACE* Code C, section 16.

H:10. *[Identical to Code C, Annex E, para. 12, save for reference to "paragraphs 6 and 12(c)" in lieu of reference to "paragraphs 5 and 11(c)".]*

H:11. *[Identical to Code C, Annex E, para. 13.]*

Notes for guidance

A-226   H:E1 *[Identical to Code C, Annex E, E1, save for reference to "paragraph 3.20" in lieu of reference to "paragraph 3.19".]*

H:E2 *[Identical to Code C, Annex E, E2.]*

H:E3 *[Identical to Code C, Annex E, E3, save for reference to "paragraphs 11.2, 11.11 to 11.13" in lieu of reference to "paragraphs 11.1, 11.18 to 11.20".]*

ANNEX F

[*Not used.*]

ANNEX G

Fitness to be interviewed

[*Identical to Annex G to Code C.*]

ANNEX H

Detained person: observation list

[*Identical to Annex H to Code C.*]

ANNEX I

Establishing gender of persons for the purpose of searching

[*Identical to Annex L to Code C, save that the references to notes are to Note I1, I2 and so on, rather than to Note L1, L2 and so on.*]

ANNEX J

Transfer of persons detained for more than 14 days to prison

H:1. When a warrant of further detention is extended or further extended by a High Court judge to authorise a person's detention beyond a period of 14 days from the time of their arrest (or if they were being detained under TACT, Sched. 7, from the time at which their examination under Schedule 7 began), the person must be transferred from detention in a police station to detention in a designated prison as soon as is practicable after the warrant is issued, unless:

    (a) the detainee specifically requests to remain in detention at a police station and that request can be accommodated; or

    (b) there are reasonable grounds to believe that transferring the detainee to a prison would:

        (i) significantly hinder a terrorism investigation;

        (ii) delay charging of the detainee or their release from custody; or

        (iii) otherwise prevent the investigation from being conducted diligently and expeditiously.

Any grounds in (b)(i) to (iii) above which are relied upon for not transferring the detainee to prison must be presented to the senior judge as part of the application for the extension or further extension of the warrant. See *Note J1*.

H:2 If at any time during which a person remains in detention at a police station under the warrant, the grounds at (b)(i) to (iii) cease to apply, the person must be transferred to a prison as soon as practicable.

H:3 Police should maintain an agreement with the National Offender Management Service (NOMS) that stipulates named prisons to which individuals may be transferred under this paragraph. This should be made with regard to ensuring detainees are moved to the most suitable prison for the purposes of the investigation and their welfare, and should include provision for the transfer of male, female and juvenile detainees. Police should ensure that the governor of a prison to which they intend to transfer a detainee is given reasonable notice of this. Where practicable, this should be no later than the point at which a warrant is applied for that would take the period of detention beyond 14 days.

H:4 Following a detainee's transfer to a designated prison, their detention will be governed by the terms of Schedule 8 to TACT 2000 and the Prison Rules and this code of practice will not apply during any period that the person remains in prison detention. The code will once more apply if the person is transferred back from prison detention to police detention. In order to enable the governor to arrange for the production of the detainee back into police custody, police should give notice to the governor of the relevant prison as soon as possible of any decision to transfer a detainee from prison back to a police station. Any transfer between a prison and a police station should be conducted by police and this code will be applicable during the period of transit. See *Note 2J*. A detainee should only remain in police custody having been transferred back from a prison, for as long as is necessary for the purpose of the investigation.

H:5 The investigating team and custody officer should provide as much information as necessary to enable the relevant prison authorities to provide appropriate facilities to detain an individual. This should include, but not be limited to:

    (i) medical assessments;

    (ii) security and risk assessments;

    (iii) details of the detained person's legal representatives;

    (iv) details of any individuals from whom the detained person has requested visits, or who have requested to visit the detained person.

H:6 Where a detainee is to be transferred to prison, the custody officer should inform the detainee's legal adviser beforehand that the transfer is to take place (including the name of the prison). The custody officer should also make all reasonable attempts to inform:

- family or friends who have been informed previously of the detainee's detention; and
- the person who was initially informed of the detainee's detention in accordance with paragraph 5.1.

H:7 Any decision not to transfer a detained person to a designated prison under paragraph 1, must be recorded, along with the reasons for this decision. If a request under paragraph 1(a) is not accommodated, the reasons for this should also be recorded.

Notes for guidance

A-230

    H:J1 *Transfer to prison is intended to ensure that individuals who are detained for extended periods of time are held in a place designed for longer periods of detention than police stations. Prison will provide detainees with a greater range of facilities more appropriate to longer detention periods.*

    H:J2 *This code will only apply as is appropriate to the conditions of detention during the period of transit. There is obviously no requirement to provide such things as bed linen or reading materials for the journey between prison and police station.*

ANNEX K

Documents and records to be translated

A-230a

    H:1. [*Identical to Code C, Annex M, para. 1.*]

    H:2. The documents considered essential for the purposes of this code and for which (subject to paragraphs 3 to 7) written translations must be created are the records made in accordance with this code of the grounds and reasons for any authorisation of a suspect's detention under the provisions of the Terrorism Act 2000 or the Counter Terrorism Act 2008 (post-charge questioning) to which this code applies as they are described and referred to in the suspect's custody record. Translations should be created as soon as practicable after the authorisation has been recorded and provided as soon as practicable thereafter, whilst the person is detained or after they have been released (see *Note K3*).

    H:3. [*Identical to Code C, Annex M, para. 3, save for reference to "Code H, paragraph 1.11A" in lieu of reference to "Code C, paragraph 1.5A".*]

    H:4. [*Identical to Code C, Annex M, para. 4 (but note that there is no table in Annex K (unlike Annex M to Code C)).*]

    H:5. [*Identical to Code C, Annex M, para. 5.*]

    H:6. [*Identical to Code C, Annex M, para. 6, save for reference to "Notes K2 and K3" in lieu of reference to "Notes M2 and M3".*]

    H:7. For the purpose of the waiver:

    (a) the consent of a person who is mentally disordered or otherwise mentally vulnerable person is only valid if the information about the circumstances under which they can waive the right and the reminder about their right to legal advice mentioned in paragraphs 3 to 5 and their consent is given in the presence of the appropriate adult, and the appropriate adult also agrees;

    (b) the consent of a juvenile is only valid if their parent's or guardian's consent is also obtained unless the juvenile is under 14, when their parent's or guardian's consent is sufficient in its own right and the information and reminder mentioned in sub-paragraph (a) above and their consent is also given in the presence of the appropriate adult (who may or may not be a parent or guardian).

Note: paragraph 1.11A in Code C [*sic*] requires someone to fulfil the role of the appropriate adult to be present when a 17-year-old is given the information and reminder mentioned in sub paragraph (a) above and gives their consent to waive their right. The consent of their parent or guardian is not required.

    H:8. [*Identical to Code C, Annex M, para. 8 (but note that there is no table in Annex K (unlike Annex M to Code C)).*]

    H:9. [*Identical to Code C, Annex M, para. 9.*]

Documentation

H:10. [*Identical to Code C, Annex M, para. 10, save for reference to "Code H" in lieu of reference to "Code C".*]

Note for guidance

H:K1–K3 [*Identical to Code C, Annex M, M1–M3, save for reference to 2000 Act in lieu of reference to 1984 Act.*]

B. Under the Criminal Procedure and Investigations Act 1996

(1) As to the recording and retention by the police of material obtained during an investigation and its supply to the prosecutor

Introduction

Pursuant to sections 23 and 25 of the 1996 Act (§§ 12-97, 12-98 in the main work), the Secretary **A-231** of State has prepared and published three codes of practice governing the action the police must take in recording and retaining material obtained in the course of a criminal investigation and regulating its supply to the prosecutor for a decision on disclosure.

The first code came into force on the day appointed for the purpose of Part I of the 1996 Act, namely April 1, 1997 (S.I. 1997 No. 1033). A second code came into force on April 4, 2005: Criminal Procedure and Investigations Act 1996 (Code of Practice) Order 2005 (S.I. 2005 No. 985). The third code (set out *post*) came into force on March 19, 2015: Criminal Procedure and Investigations Act 1996 (Code of Practice) Order 2015 (S.I. 2015 No. 861).

In connection with this code, see also § 12-96 in the main work (meaning of "investigation").

As to the significance of the code of practice in relation to material held overseas, outside the European Union, by entities not subject to the jurisdiction of the United Kingdom, see *R. v. Flook* [2010] 1 Cr.App.R. 30, CA (§ 12-53 in the main work).

CRIMINAL PROCEDURE AND INVESTIGATIONS ACT 1996 CODE OF PRACTICE UNDER PART II

Preamble

This code of practice is issued under Part II of the Criminal Procedure and Investigations Act **A-232** 1996 ("the Act"). It sets out the manner in which police officers are to record, retain and reveal to the prosecutor material obtained in a criminal investigation and which may be relevant to the investigation, and related matters.

1. Introduction

1.1 This code of practice applies in respect of criminal investigations conducted by police officers **A-232a** which begin on or after the day on which this code comes into effect. Persons other than police officers who are charged with the duty of conducting an investigation as defined in the Act are to have regard to the relevant provisions of the code, and should take these into account in applying their own operating procedures.

1.2 This code does not apply to persons who are not charged with the duty of conducting an investigation as defined in the Act.

1.3 Nothing in this code applies to material intercepted in obedience to a warrant issued under section 2 of the Interception of Communications Act 1985 or section 5 of the Regulation of Investigatory Powers Act 2000, or to any copy of that material as defined in section 10 of the 1985 Act or section 15 of the 2000 Act.

1.4 This code extends only to England and Wales.

2. Definitions

2.1 In this code: **A-233**
- a criminal investigation is an investigation conducted by police officers with a view to it being ascertained whether a person should be charged with an offence, or whether a person charged with an offence is guilty of it. This will include:
  - investigations into crimes that have been committed;
  - investigations whose purpose is to ascertain whether a crime has been committed, with a view to the possible institution of criminal proceedings; and

- investigations which begin in the belief that a crime may be committed, for example when the police keep premises or individuals under observation for a period of time, with a view to the possible institution of criminal proceedings;
- charging a person with an offence includes prosecution by way of summons or postal requisition;
- an investigator is any police officer involved in the conduct of a criminal investigation. All investigators have a responsibility for carrying out the duties imposed on them under this code, including in particular recording information, and retaining records of information and other material;
- the officer in charge of an investigation is the police officer responsible for directing a criminal investigation. He is also responsible for ensuring that proper procedures are in place for recording information, and retaining records of information and other material, in the investigation;
- the disclosure officer is the person responsible for examining material retained by the police during the investigation; revealing material to the prosecutor during the investigation and any criminal proceedings resulting from it, and certifying that he has done this; and disclosing material to the accused at the request of the prosecutor;
- the prosecutor is the authority responsible for the conduct, on behalf of the Crown, of criminal proceedings resulting from a specific criminal investigation;
- material is material of any kind, including information and objects, which is obtained or inspected in the course of a criminal investigation and which may be relevant to the investigation. This includes not only material coming into the possession of the investigator (such as documents seized in the course of searching premises) but also material generated by him (such as interview records);
- material may be relevant to the investigation if it appears to an investigator, or to the officer in charge of an investigation, or to the disclosure officer, that it has some bearing on any offence under investigation or any person being investigated, or on the surrounding circumstances of the case, unless it is incapable of having any impact on the case;
- sensitive material is material, the disclosure of which, the disclosure officer believes, would give rise to a real risk of serious prejudice to an important public interest;
- references to prosecution disclosure are to the duty of the prosecutor under sections 3 and 7A of the Act to disclose material which is in his possession or which he has inspected in pursuance of this code, and which might reasonably be considered capable of undermining the case against the accused, or of assisting the case for the accused;
- references to the disclosure of material to a person accused of an offence include references to the disclosure of material to his legal representative;
- references to police officers and to the chief officer of police include those employed in a police force as defined in section 3(3) of the Prosecution of Offences Act 1985.

As to the meaning of "criminal investigation", see *DPP v. Metten*, unreported, January 22, 1999, DC (§ 12-96 in the main work).

3. General responsibilities

A-234   3.1 The functions of the investigator, the officer in charge of an investigation and the disclosure officer are separate. Whether they are undertaken by one, two or more persons will depend on the complexity of the case and the administrative arrangements within each police force. Where they are undertaken by more than one person, close consultation between them is essential to the effective performance of the duties imposed by this code.

3.2 In any criminal investigation, one or more deputy disclosure officers may be appointed to assist the disclosure officer, and a deputy disclosure officer may perform any function of a disclosure officer as defined in paragraph 2.1.

3.3 The chief officer of police for each police force is responsible for putting in place arrangements to ensure that in every investigation the identity of the officer in charge of an investigation and the disclosure officer is recorded. The chief officer of police for each police force shall ensure that disclosure officers and deputy disclosure officers have sufficient skills and authority, commensurate with the complexity of the investigation, to discharge their functions effectively. An individual must not be appointed as disclosure officer, or continue in that role, if that is likely to result in a conflict of interest, for instance, if the disclosure officer is the victim of the alleged crime which is the subject of the investigation. The advice of a more senior officer must always be sought if there is doubt as to whether a conflict of interest precludes an individual acting as disclosure officer. If thereafter the doubt remains, the advice of a prosecutor should be sought.

3.4 The officer in charge of an investigation may delegate tasks to another investigator, to civilians employed by the police force, or to other persons participating in the investigation under arrangements for joint investigations, but he remains responsible for ensuring that these have been carried out and for accounting for any general policies followed in the investigation. In particular, it is an essential part of his duties to ensure that all material which may be relevant to an investigation is retained, and either made available to the disclosure officer or (in exceptional circumstances) revealed directly to the prosecutor.

3.5 In conducting an investigation, the investigator should pursue all reasonable lines of inquiry, whether these point towards or away from the suspect. What is reasonable in each case will depend on the particular circumstances. For example, where material is held on computer, it is a matter for the investigator to decide which material on the computer it is reasonable to inquire into, and in what manner.

3.6 If the officer in charge of an investigation believes that other persons may be in possession of material that may be relevant to the investigation, and if this has not been obtained under paragraph 3.5 above, he should ask the disclosure officer to inform them of the existence of the investigation and to invite them to retain the material in case they receive a request for its disclosure. The disclosure officer should inform the prosecutor that they may have such material. However, the officer in charge of an investigation is not required to make speculative enquiries of other persons; there must be some reason to believe that they may have relevant material. That reason may come from information provided to the police by the accused or from other inquiries made or from some other source.

3.7 If, during a criminal investigation, the officer in charge of an investigation or disclosure officer for any reason no longer has responsibility for the functions falling to him, either his supervisor or the police officer in charge of criminal investigations for the police force concerned must assign someone else to assume that responsibility. That person's identity must be recorded, as with those initially responsible for these functions in each investigation.

As to the meaning of "criminal investigation", see *DPP v. Metten*, unreported, January 22, 1999, DC (§ 12-96 in the main work).

Where, in the run-up to an election, there was an arrangement that a local electoral office would notify the police of any suspected fraudulent applications for postal votes, where that office submitted 1,600 suspected fraudulent applications to the police (out of a total of 10,000 applications), where the criminal investigation that ensued resulted in the prosecution of the appellants for conspiracy to defraud the electoral officer, and where complaint was made about the non-disclosure of the 8,400 postal vote applications that had been examined by the electoral office, but had not been submitted to the police, there was no duty of disclosure on the electoral office as either a delegate of the investigator or as a joint investigator within paragraph 3.4; the role of the electoral office was in the nature of an examination by a complainant of suspicious documents subsequently handed to the police, comparable to that of a bank handing over suspicious cheques to the police: *R. v. Khan* [2011] L.S. Gazette, October 20, 23, CA ([2011] EWCA Crim. 2240).

4. Recording of information

4.1 If material which may be relevant to the investigation consists of information which is not recorded in any form, the officer in charge of an investigation must ensure that it is recorded in a durable or retrievable form (whether in writing, on video or audio tape, or on computer disk). **A-235**

4.2 Where it is not practicable to retain the initial record of information because it forms part of a larger record which is to be destroyed, its contents should be transferred as a true record to a durable and more easily-stored form before that happens.

4.3 Negative information is often relevant to an investigation. If it may be relevant it must be recorded. An example might be a number of people present in a particular place at a particular time who state that they saw nothing unusual.

4.4 Where information which may be relevant is obtained, it must be recorded at the time it is obtained or as soon as practicable after that time. This includes, for example, information obtained in house-to-house enquiries, although the requirement to record information promptly does not require an investigator to take a statement from a potential witness where it would not otherwise be taken.

5. Retention of material

(a) Duty to retain material

5.1 The investigator must retain material obtained in a criminal investigation which may be **A-236** relevant to the investigation. Material may be photographed, video-recorded, captured digitally or otherwise retained in the form of a copy rather than the original at any time, if the original is perishable; the original was supplied to the investigator rather than generated by him and is to be returned to its owner; or the retention of a copy rather than the original is reasonable in all the circumstances.

5.2 Where material has been seized in the exercise of the powers of seizure conferred by the Police and Criminal Evidence Act 1984, the duty to retain it under this code is subject to the provisions on the retention of seized material in section 22 of that Act.

5.3 If the officer in charge of an investigation becomes aware as a result of developments in the case that material previously examined but not retained (because it was not thought to be relevant) may now be relevant to the investigation, he should, wherever practicable, take steps to obtain it or ensure that it is retained for further inspection or for production in court if required.

5.4 The duty to retain material includes in particular the duty to retain material falling into the following categories, where it may be relevant to the investigation:

- crime reports (including crime report forms, relevant parts of incident report books or police officer's notebooks);
- custody records;
- records which are derived from tapes of telephone messages (for example, 999 calls) containing descriptions of an alleged offence or offender;
- final versions of witness statements (and draft versions where their content differs from the final version), including any exhibits mentioned (unless these have been returned to their owner on the understanding that they will be produced in court if required);
- interview records (written records, or audio or video tapes, of interviews with actual or potential witnesses or suspects);
- communications between the police and experts such as forensic scientists, reports of work carried out by experts, and schedules of scientific material prepared by the expert for the investigator, for the purposes of criminal proceedings;
- records of the first description of a suspect by each potential witness who purports to identify or describe the suspect, whether or not the description differs from that of subsequent descriptions by that or other witnesses;
- any material casting doubt on the reliability of a witness.

5.5 The duty to retain material, where it may be relevant to the investigation, also includes in particular the duty to retain material which may satisfy the test for prosecution disclosure in the Act, such as:

- information provided by an accused person which indicates an explanation for the offence with which he has been charged;
- any material casting doubt on the reliability of a confession;
- any material casting doubt on the reliability of a prosecution witness.

5.6 The duty to retain material falling into these categories does not extend to items which are purely ancillary to such material and possess no independent significance (for example, duplicate copies of records or reports).

(b) Length of time for which material is to be retained

A-236a

5.7 All material which may be relevant to the investigation must be retained until a decision is taken whether to institute proceedings against a person for an offence.

5.8 If a criminal investigation results in proceedings being instituted, all material which may be relevant must be retained at least until the accused is acquitted or convicted or the prosecutor decides not to proceed with the case.

5.9 Where the accused is convicted, all material which may be relevant must be retained at least until:

- the convicted person is released from custody, or discharged from hospital, in cases where the court imposes a custodial sentence or a hospital order;
- six months from the date of conviction, in all other cases.

If the court imposes a custodial sentence or hospital order and the convicted person is released from custody or discharged from hospital earlier than six months from the date of conviction, all material which may be relevant must be retained at least until six months from the date of conviction.

5.10 If an appeal against conviction is in progress when the release or discharge occurs, or at the end of the period of six months specified in paragraph 5.9, all material which may be relevant must be retained until the appeal is determined. Similarly, if the Criminal Cases Review Commission is considering an application at that point in time, all material which may be relevant must be retained at least until the Commission decides not to refer the case to the court.

6. Preparation of material for prosecutor

(a) Introduction

6.1 The officer in charge of the investigation, the disclosure officer or an investigator may seek **A-237** advice from the prosecutor about whether any particular item of material may be relevant to the investigation.

6.2 Material which may be relevant to an investigation, which has been retained in accordance with this code, and which the disclosure officer believes will not form part of the prosecution case, must be listed on a schedule. This process will differ depending on whether the case is likely to be heard in the magistrates' court or the Crown Court.

(b) Magistrates' Court

Anticipated guilty pleas

6.3 If the accused is charged with a summary offence or an either-way offence that is likely to **A-237a** remain in the magistrates' court, and it is considered that he is likely to plead guilty (*e.g.* because he has admitted the offence), a schedule or streamlined disclosure certificate is not required. However, the common law duty to disclose material which may assist the defence at bail hearings or in the early preparation of their case remains, and where there is such material the certification on the Police Report (MG5/SDF) must be completed. Where there is no such material, a certificate to that effect must be completed in like form to that attached at the Annex.

6.4 If, contrary to the expectation of a guilty plea being entered, the accused pleads not guilty at the first hearing, the disclosure officer must ensure that the streamlined disclosure certificate is prepared and submitted as soon as is reasonably practicable after that happens.

Anticipated not guilty pleas

6.5 If the accused is charged with a summary offence or an either-way offence that is likely to **A-237b** remain in the magistrates' court, and it is considered that he is likely to plead not guilty, a streamlined disclosure certificate must be completed in like form to that attached at the Annex.

Material which may assist the defence

6.6 In every case, irrespective of the anticipated plea, if there is material known to the disclosure **A-237c** officer that might assist the defence with the early preparation of their case or at a bail hearing (for example, a key prosecution witness has relevant previous convictions or a witness has withdrawn his or her statement), a note must be made on the MG5 (or other format agreed under the National File Standards). The material must be disclosed to the prosecutor who will disclose it to the defence if he thinks it meets this common law test.

No undermining or assisting material and sensitive material – magistrates' court cases

6.7 If there is no material which might fall to be disclosed as undermining the prosecution case or **A-237d** assisting the defence, the officer should complete the appropriate entry on the streamlined disclosure certificate. If there is any sensitive unused material the officer should complete a sensitive material schedule (MG6D or similar) and attach it to the prosecution file. In exceptional circumstances, when its existence is so sensitive that it cannot be listed, it should be revealed to the prosecutor separately.

(c) Crown Court

6.8 For cases to be held in the Crown Court, the unused material schedules (MG6 series) are used. **A-237e**
6.9 The disclosure officer must ensure that a schedule is prepared in the following circumstances:
- the accused is charged with an offence which is triable only on indictment;
- the accused is charged with an offence which is triable either way, and it is considered that the case is likely to be tried on indictment.

6.10 Material which the disclosure officer does not believe is sensitive must be listed on a schedule of non-sensitive material. The schedule must include a statement that the disclosure officer does not believe the material is sensitive.

Way in which material is to be listed on schedule

6.11 For indictable only cases or either-way cases sent to the Crown Court, schedules MG6 C, D **A-237f** and E should be completed to facilitate service of the MG6C with the prosecution case, wherever possible. The disclosure officer should ensure that each item of material is listed separately on the schedule, and is numbered consecutively. The description of each item should make clear the nature of the item and should contain sufficient detail to enable the prosecutor to decide whether he needs to inspect the material before deciding whether or not it should be disclosed.

6.12 In some enquiries it may not be practicable to list each item of material separately. For example, there may be many items of a similar or repetitive nature. These may be listed in a block and described by quantity and generic title.

6.13 Even if some material is listed in a block, the disclosure officer must ensure that any items among that material which might satisfy the test for prosecution disclosure are listed and described individually.

(d) Sensitive material – Crown Court

A-237g
6.14 Any material which is believed to be sensitive either must be listed on a schedule of sensitive material or, in exceptional circumstances where its existence is so sensitive that it cannot be listed, it should be revealed to the prosecutor separately. If there is no sensitive material, the disclosure officer must record this fact on a schedule of sensitive material, or otherwise so indicate.

6.15 Subject to paragraph 6.16 below, the disclosure officer must list on a sensitive schedule any material the disclosure of which he believes would give rise to a real risk of serious prejudice to an important public interest, and the reason for that belief. The schedule must include a statement that the disclosure officer believes the material is sensitive. Depending on the circumstances, examples of such material may include the following among others:

- material relating to national security;
- material received from the intelligence and security agencies;
- material relating to intelligence from foreign sources which reveals sensitive intelligence gathering methods;
- material given in confidence;
- material relating to the identity or activities of informants, or undercover police officers, or witnesses, or other persons supplying information to the police who may be in danger if their identities are revealed;
- material revealing the location of any premises or other place used for police surveillance, or the identity of any person allowing a police officer to use them for surveillance;
- material revealing, either directly or indirectly, techniques and methods relied upon by a police officer in the course of a criminal investigation, for example covert surveillance techniques, or other methods of detecting crime;
- material whose disclosure might facilitate the commission of other offences or hinder the prevention and detection of crime;
- material upon the strength of which search warrants were obtained;
- material containing details of persons taking part in identification parades;
- material supplied to an investigator during a criminal investigation which has been generated by an official of a body concerned with the regulation or supervision of bodies corporate or of persons engaged in financial activities, or which has been generated by a person retained by such a body;
- material supplied to an investigator during a criminal investigation which relates to a child or young person and which has been generated by a local authority social services department, an Area Child Protection Committee or other party contacted by an investigator during the investigation;
- material relating to the private life of a witness.

6.16 In exceptional circumstances, where an investigator considers that material is so sensitive that its revelation to the prosecutor by means of an entry on the sensitive schedule is inappropriate, the existence of the material must be revealed to the prosecutor separately. This will apply only where compromising the material would be likely to lead directly to the loss of life, or directly threaten national security.

6.17 In such circumstances, the responsibility for informing the prosecutor lies with the investigator who knows the detail of the sensitive material. The investigator should act as soon as is reasonably practicable after the file containing the prosecution case is sent to the prosecutor. The investigator must also ensure that the prosecutor is able to inspect the material so that he can assess whether it is disclosable and, if so, whether it needs to be brought before a court for a ruling on disclosure.

7. Revelation of material to prosecutor

A-238
7.1 Certain unused material must be disclosed to the accused at common law if it would assist the defence with the early preparation of their case or at a bail hearing. This material may consist of

items such as a previous relevant conviction of a key prosecution witness or the withdrawal of support for the prosecution by a witness. This material must be revealed to the prosecutor for service on the defence with the initial details of the prosecution case.

7.1A In anticipated not guilty plea cases for hearing in the magistrates' court the disclosure officer must give the streamlined disclosure certificate to the prosecutor at the same time as he gives the prosecutor the file containing the material for the prosecution case.

7.1B In cases sent to the Crown Court, wherever possible, the disclosure officer should give the schedules concerning unused material to the prosecutor at the same time as the prosecution file in preparation for the first hearing and any case management that the judge may wish to conduct at that stage.

7.2 The disclosure officer should draw the attention of the prosecutor to any material an investigator has retained (including material to which paragraph 6.13 applies) which may satisfy the test for prosecution disclosure in the Act, and should explain why he has come to that view.

N.B. The reference to paragraph 6.13 (a leftover from the previous version of the code) should have been updated to refer to paragraph 6.16.

7.3 At the same time as complying with the duties in paragraphs 7.1 and 7.2, the disclosure officer must give the prosecutor a copy of any material which falls into the following categories (unless such material has already been given to the prosecutor as part of the file containing the material for the prosecution case):

- information provided by an accused person which indicates an explanation for the offence with which he has been charged;
- any material casting doubt on the reliability of a confession;
- any material casting doubt on the reliability of a prosecution witness;
- any other material which the investigator believes may satisfy the test for prosecution disclosure in the Act;

7.4 If the prosecutor asks to inspect material which has not already been copied to him, the disclosure officer must allow him to inspect it. If the prosecutor asks for a copy of material which has not already been copied to him, the disclosure officer must give him a copy. However, this does not apply where the disclosure officer believes, having consulted the officer in charge of the investigation, that the material is too sensitive to be copied and can only be inspected.

7.5 If material consists of information which is recorded other than in writing, whether it should be given to the prosecutor in its original form as a whole, or by way of relevant extracts recorded in the same form, or in the form of a transcript, is a matter for agreement between the disclosure officer and the prosecutor.

8. Subsequent action by disclosure officer

8.1 At the time when a streamlined disclosure certificate is prepared for magistrates' court cases, or **A-239** a schedule of non-sensitive material is prepared for Crown Court cases, the disclosure officer may not know exactly what material will form the case against the accused. In addition, the prosecutor may not have given advice about the likely relevance of particular items of material. Once these matters have been determined, the disclosure officer must give the prosecutor, where necessary, an amended certificate or schedule listing any additional material:

- which may be relevant to the investigation;
- which does not form part of the case against the accused;
- which is not already listed on the schedule; and
- which he believes is not sensitive,

unless he is informed in writing by the prosecutor that the prosecutor intends to disclose the material to the defence.

8.2 Section 7A of the Act imposes a continuing duty on the prosecutor, for the duration of criminal proceedings against the accused, to disclose material which satisfies the test for disclosure (subject to public interest considerations). To enable him to do this, any new material coming to light should be treated in the same way as the earlier material.

8.3 In particular, after a defence statement has been given, or details of the issues in dispute have been recorded on the effective trial preparation form, the disclosure officer must look again at the material which has been retained and must draw the attention of the prosecutor to any material which might reasonably be considered capable of undermining the case for the prosecution against the accused or of assisting the case for the accused; and he must reveal it to him in accordance with paragraphs 7.4 and 7.5 above.

9. Certification by disclosure officer

9.1 The disclosure officer must certify to the prosecutor that, to the best of his knowledge and **A-240** belief, all relevant material which has been retained and made available to him has been revealed to the prosecutor in accordance with this code. He must sign and date the certificate. It will be necessary to certify not only at the time when the schedule and accompanying material is submitted to the prosecutor, and when relevant material which has been retained is reconsidered after the accused has given a defence statement, but also whenever a schedule is otherwise given or material is otherwise revealed to the prosecutor.

10. Disclosure of material to accused

A-240a   10.1 Other than early disclosure under common law, in the magistrates' court the streamlined certificate at the Annex (and any relevant unused material to be disclosed under it) must be disclosed to the accused either:

- at the hearing where a not guilty plea is entered, or
- as soon as possible following a formal indication from the accused or representative that a not guilty plea will be entered at the hearing.

10.1A If material has not already been copied to the prosecutor, and he requests its disclosure to the accused on the ground that:

- it satisfies the test for prosecution disclosure, or
- the court has ordered its disclosure after considering an application from the accused,

the disclosure officer must disclose it to the accused.

10.2 If material has been copied to the prosecutor, and it is to be disclosed, whether it is disclosed by the prosecutor or the disclosure officer is a matter of agreement between the two of them.

10.3 The disclosure officer must disclose material to the accused either by giving him a copy or by allowing him to inspect it. If the accused person asks for a copy of any material which he has been allowed to inspect, the disclosure officer must give it to him, unless in the opinion of the disclosure officer that is either not practicable (for example because the material consists of an object which cannot be copied, or because the volume of material is so great), or not desirable (for example because the material is a statement by a child witness in relation to a sexual offence).

10.4 If material which the accused has been allowed to inspect consists of information which is recorded other than in writing, whether it should be given to the accused in its original form or in the form of a transcript is a matter for the discretion of the disclosure officer. If the material is transcribed, the disclosure officer must ensure that the transcript is certified to the accused as a true record of the material which has been transcribed.

10.5 If a court concludes that an item of sensitive material satisfies the prosecution disclosure test and that the interests of the defence outweigh the public interest in withholding disclosure, it will be necessary to disclose the material if the case is to proceed. This does not mean that sensitive documents must always be disclosed in their original form: for example, the court may agree that sensitive details still requiring protection should be blocked out, or that documents may be summarised, or that the prosecutor may make an admission about the substance of the material under section 10 of the Criminal Justice Act 1967.

ANNEX

A-241   The annex to the code is not set out in this work.

(2) As to the practice for arranging and conducting interviews of witnesses notified by the accused

Introduction

A-241a   As from May 1, 2010, a new code of practice entitled "Code of Practice for Arranging and Conducting Interviews of Witnesses Notified by the Accused", which was prepared under section 21A of the CPIA 1996, was brought into force by the Criminal Procedure and Investigations Act 1996 (Code of Practice for Interviews of Witnesses Notified by Accused) Order 2010 (S.I. 2010 No. 1223).

CODE OF PRACTICE FOR ARRANGING AND CONDUCTING INTERVIEWS OF WITNESSES NOTIFIED BY THE ACCUSED

Preamble

This code of practice is issued under section 21A of the Criminal Procedure and Investigations Act   **A-241b** 1996 ("the Act"). It sets out guidance that police officers and other persons charged with investigating offences must follow if they arrange or conduct interviews of proposed witnesses whose details are disclosed to the prosecution by an accused person pursuant to the disclosure provisions in Part I of the Act.

Introduction

1.1 Part I of the Act sets out rules governing disclosure of information in the course of criminal   **A-241c** proceedings by both the prosecution and persons accused of offences to which that Part of the Act applies.

1.2. Sections 5 and 6 of the Act provide for accused persons to give defence statements to the prosecution and to the court and section 6A sets out what those defence statements must contain. Section 6A(2) requires that any defence statement that discloses an alibi must give particulars of it, including prescribed details of any witness who the accused believes is able to give evidence in support of the alibi and any information the accused has which may assist in identifying or finding such a witness.

1.3. Section 6C of the Act requires the accused to give to the prosecutor and the court a notice indicating whether he intends to call any witnesses at trial and giving details of those witnesses.

1.4. This code of practice sets out guidance that police officers and other persons charged with investigating offences must have regard to when they are arranging and conducting interviews of proposed witnesses identified in a defence statement given under section 6A(2) of the Act or a notice given under section 6C of the Act.

Definitions

2. In this code:—   **A-241d**

   – *the accused* means a person mentioned in section 1(1) or (2) of the Act;

   – "an appropriate person" means:

     (a) in the case of a witness under the age of 18:

       (i) the parent, guardian or, if the witness is in local authority or voluntary organisation care, or is otherwise being looked after under the Children Act 1989, a person representing that authority or organisation; or

       (ii) a social worker of a local authority; or

       (iii) failing these, some other responsible person aged 18 or over who is not a police officer or employed by the police; and

     (b) in the case of a witness who is mentally disordered or mentally vulnerable:

       (i) a relative, guardian or other person responsible for the witness's care or custody; or

       (ii) someone experienced in dealing with mentally disordered or mentally vulnerable people but who is not a police officer or employed by the police; or

       (iii) failing these, some other responsible person aged 18 or over who is not a police officer or employed by the police.

   – *an investigator* is a police officer or any other person charged with the duty of investigating offences.

   – *a witness* is a potential witness identified by an accused person either:

     – in a defence statement under section 6A(2) of the Act as being a witness that he believes is able to give evidence in support of an alibi disclosed in the statement; or

     – in a notice given to the court and the prosecutor under section 6C of the Act as being a person that he intends to call as a witness at his trial.

Arrangement of the interview

Information to be provided to the witness before any interview may take place

3.1. If an investigator wishes to interview a witness, the witness must be asked whether he consents   **A-241e** to being interviewed and informed that:

   • an interview is being requested following his identification by the accused as a proposed witness under section 6A(2) or section 6C of the Act;

   • he is not obliged to attend the proposed interview;

   • he is entitled to be accompanied by a solicitor at the interview (but nothing in this code of

315

practice creates any duty on the part of the Legal Services Commission to provide fund-ing for any such attendance); and

- a record will be made of the interview and he will subsequently be sent a copy of the record.

3.2. If the witness consents to being interviewed, the witness must be asked:

- whether he wishes to have a solicitor present at the interview;
- whether he consents to a solicitor attending the interview on behalf of the accused, as an observer; and
- whether he consents to a copy of the record being sent to the accused. If he does not consent, the witness must be informed that the effect of disclosure requirements in criminal proceedings may nevertheless require the prosecution to disclose the record to the accused (and any co-accused) in the course of the proceedings.

Information to be provided to the accused before any interview may take place

A-241f   4.1. The investigator must notify the accused or, if the accused is legally represented in the proceedings, the accused's representatives:

- that the investigator requested an interview with the witness;
- whether the witness consented to the interview; and
- if the witness consented to the interview, whether the witness also consented to a solicitor attending the interview on behalf of the accused, as an observer.

4.2. If the accused is not legally represented in the proceedings, and if the witness consents to a solicitor attending the interview on behalf of the accused, the accused must be offered the op-portunity, a reasonable time before the interview is held, to appoint a solicitor to attend it.

Identification of the date, time and venue for the interview

A-241g   5. The investigator must nominate a reasonable date, time and venue for the interview and notify the witness of them and any subsequent changes to them.

Notification to the accused's solicitor of the date, time and venue of the interview

A-241h   6. If the witness has consented to the presence of the accused's solicitor, the accused's solicitor must be notified that the interview is taking place, invited to observe, and provided with reasonable notice of the date, time and venue of the interview and any subsequent changes.

Conduct of the interview

The investigator conducting the interview

A-241i   7. The identity of the investigator conducting the interview must be recorded. That person must have sufficient skills and authority, commensurate with the complexity of the investigation, to discharge his functions effectively. That person must not conduct the interview if that is likely to result in a conflict of interest, for instance, if that person is the victim of the alleged crime which is the subject of the proceedings. The advice of a more senior officer must always be sought if there is doubt as to whether a conflict of interest precludes an individual conducting the interview. If thereafter the doubt remains, the advice of a prosecutor must be sought.

Attendance of the accused's solicitor

A-241j   8.1. The accused's solicitor may only attend the interview if the witness has consented to his pres-ence as an observer. Provided that the accused's solicitor was given reasonable notice of the date, time and place of the interview, the fact that the accused's solicitor is not present will not prevent the interview from being conducted. If the witness at any time withdraws consent to the accused's solici-tor being present at the interview, the interview may continue without the presence of the accused's solicitor.

8.2. The accused's solicitor may attend only as an observer.

Attendance of the witness's solicitor

A-241k   9. Where a witness has indicated that he wishes to appoint a solicitor to be present, that solicitor must be permitted to attend the interview.

Attendance of any other appropriate person

10. A witness under the age of 18 or a witness who is mentally disordered or otherwise mentally **A-241l** vulnerable must be interviewed in the presence of an appropriate person.

Recording of the interview

11.1. An accurate record must be made of the interview, whether it takes place at a police station **A-241m** or elsewhere. The record must be made, where practicable, by audio recording or by visual recording with sound, or otherwise in writing. Any written record must be made and completed during the interview, unless this would not be practicable or would interfere with the conduct of the interview, and must constitute either a verbatim record of what has been said or, failing this, an account of the interview which adequately and accurately summarises it. If a written record is not made during the interview it must be made as soon as practicable after its completion. Written interview records must be timed and signed by the maker.

11.2 A copy of the record must be given, within a reasonable time of the interview, to:
    (a) the witness; and
    (b) if the witness consents, to the accused or the accused's solicitor.

II. ATTORNEY-GENERAL'S GUIDELINES

A. DISCLOSURE

Introduction

On December 3, 2013, the Attorney-General published revised guidelines on disclosure, replac- **A-242** ing the 2005 guidelines, and also the supplementary guidelines on digital material issued in 2011, which are now annexed to the new guidelines. The new guidelines should be read together with the revised protocol on the disclosure of unused material in criminal cases (*post*, Appendix N-52 *et seq.*), and are not designed to be a substitute for a thorough understanding of the relevant legislation, codes of practice, case law and procedure. They have immediate effect (para. 73).

Paragraphs 1 to 3 emphasise the importance of disclosure and a "timely dialogue between the prosecution, defence and the court", and are a shortened version of the introductory section to the 2005 guidelines. Paragraphs 4 to 14 relate to general principles and incorporate most of the corresponding section in the 2005 guidelines, but also stress the role the defence have to play in ensuring that the prosecution are directed towards appropriate material, the importance of communication within the prosecution team and the role of the reviewing lawyer. Paragraphs 15 to 27 relate to the duties on investigators and disclosure officers, incorporating a shortened version of the corresponding section in the 2005 guidelines. They underline that thought must be given to defining and limiting the scope of investigations under the guidance of the reviewing lawyer and prosecutor where appropriate, the need to keep full records of meetings and decisions taken and that, whilst there will be some cases where detailed examination of all material seized will be necessary, there will be others where this is impossible. Paragraphs 28 to 34 set out the disclosure duties on prosecutors, again incorporating a shortened version of the corresponding section in the 2005 guidelines, and also highlighting that prosecutors should challenge the lack of, or inadequate, defence statements in writing, copying the document to the court. Paragraphs 35 to 37 set out the disclosure duties on prosecution advocates, incorporating a shortened version of the corresponding section in the 2005 guidelines, and make clear the duty to keep disclosure under review, whenever possible in consultation with the reviewing prosecutor. Paragraphs 39 to 43 deal with the defence, and emphasise the importance of early and meaningful defence engagement and defence statements, including in the magistrates' courts.

Paragraphs 44 to 47 relate to disclosure obligations in magistrates' courts where a not guilty plea is entered. Paragraphs 48 and 49 relate to the Crown Court, particularly cases which involve digital material. Paragraphs 50 to 52 deal with large and complex cases in the Crown Court. Paragraphs 53 to 55 relate to material held by government departments and third parties and paragraphs 56 and 57 to material held by other domestic bodies. Both largely replicate the corresponding sections in the 2005 guidelines. Paragraphs 59 to 64 concern material held overseas (and correspond to paras 58-63 of the 2011 supplementary guidelines on digital material). Paragraphs 65 to 69 deal with applications for non-disclosure in the public interest and largely reproduce the corresponding section in the 2005 guidelines. Finally, paragraphs 70 to 72 ("other disclosure", "material relevant to sentence" and "post-conviction") correspond to the sections relating to material relevant to sentence and the post-conviction period in the 2005 guidelines.

As to the significance of the guidelines in relation to material held overseas, outside the European Union, by entities not subject to the jurisdiction of the United Kingdom, see *R. v. Flook* [2010] 1 Cr.App.R. 30, CA (§§ 12-53, 12-101 in the main work).

★ The 2013 guidelines (including the annex (*post*, A-262 *et seq.*)) were given extensive consideration in *R. v. R.* (*ante*, § 12-59).

Foreword

A-242a We are pleased to publish a revised judicial protocol and revised guidance on the disclosure of unused material in criminal cases. Proper disclosure of unused material, made through a rigorous and carefully considered application of the law, remains a crucial part of a fair trial, and essential to avoiding miscarriages of justice. These new documents are intended to clarify the procedures to be followed and to encourage the active participation of all parties.

They have been prepared following the recommendations of Lord Justice Gross in his September 2011 "Review of Disclosure in Criminal Proceedings" and take account of Lord Justice Gross and Lord Justice Treacy's "Further review of disclosure in criminal proceedings: sanctions for disclosure failure", published in November 2012.

There are important roles for the prosecution, the defence and the court in ensuring that disclosure is conducted properly, including on the part of the investigating, case progression and disclosure officers, as well as the lawyers and advocates. Lord Justice Gross particularly recommended that the guidance on disclosure of unused material in criminal cases should be consolidated and abbreviated. Given all of those involved in this process have separate constitutional roles, the judiciary and the Attorney-General have worked together to produce complementary guidance that is shorter than the previous iterations, but remains comprehensive. The two documents are similarly structured for ease of reference and should be read together.

The Rt. Hon. Dominic Grieve Q.C. M.P., Attorney General

The Rt. Hon. The Lord Thomas, Lord Chief Justice of England and Wales

Introduction

A-243 These guidelines are issued by the Attorney General for investigators, prosecutors and defence practitioners on the application of the disclosure regime contained in the Criminal Procedure and Investigations Act 1996 ("CPIA"). The guidelines emphasise the importance of prosecution-led disclosure and the importance of applying the CPIA regime in a "thinking manner", tailored, where appropriate, to the type of investigation or prosecution in question.

The guidelines do not contain the detail of the disclosure regime; they outline the high level principles which should be followed when the disclosure regime is applied.

These guidelines replace the existing Attorney General's Guidelines on Disclosure issued in 2005 and the Supplementary Guidelines on Digital Material issued in 2011, which is an annex to the general guidelines.

The guidelines are intended to operate alongside the Judicial Protocol on the Disclosure of Unused Material in Criminal Cases. They are not designed to be an unequivocal statement of the law at any one time, nor are they a substitute for a thorough understanding of the relevant legislation, codes of practice, case law and procedure.

Readers should note that a review of disclosure in the magistrates' courts is currently being undertaken by H.H.J. Kinch Q.C. and the Chief Magistrate, on behalf of Lord Justice Gross, the Senior Presiding Judge. Amendments may therefore be made to these documents following the recommendations of that review, and in accordance with other forthcoming changes to the criminal justice system.

The importance of disclosure

A-244 1. The statutory framework for criminal investigations and disclosure is contained in the Criminal Procedure and Investigations Act 1996 (the CPIA) and the *CPIA Code of Practice*. The CPIA aims to ensure that criminal investigations are conducted in a fair, objective and thorough manner, and requires prosecutors to disclose to the defence material which has not previously been disclosed to the accused and which might reasonably be considered capable of undermining the case for the prosecution against the accused or of assisting the case for the accused. The CPIA requires a timely dialogue between the prosecution, defence and the court to enable the prosecution properly to identify such material.

2. Every accused person has a right to a fair trial, a right long embodied in our law and guaranteed

by Article 6 of the European Convention on Human Rights (ECHR). A fair trial is the proper object and expectation of all participants in the trial process. Fair disclosure to the accused is an inseparable part of a fair trial. A fair trial should not require consideration of irrelevant material and should not involve spurious applications or arguments which serve to divert the trial process from examining the real issues before the court.

3. Properly applied, the CPIA should ensure that material is not disclosed which overburdens the participants in the trial process, diverts attention from the relevant issues, leads to unjustifiable delay, and is wasteful of resources. Consideration of disclosure issues should be an integral part of a good investigation and not something that exists separately.

Disclosure: general principles

4. Disclosure refers to providing the defence with copies of, or access to, any prosecution material **A-245** which might reasonably be considered capable of undermining the case for the prosecution against the accused, or of assisting the case for the accused, and which has not previously been disclosed (s.3 CPIA).

5. Prosecutors will only be expected to anticipate what material might undermine their case or strengthen the defence in the light of information available at the time of the disclosure decision, and they may take into account information revealed during questioning.

6. In deciding whether material satisfies the disclosure test, consideration should be given amongst other things to:
    a. the use that might be made of it in cross-examination;
    b. its capacity to support submissions that could lead to:
      (i) the exclusion of evidence;
      (ii) a stay of proceedings, where the material is required to allow a proper application to be made;
      (iii) a court or tribunal finding that any public authority had acted incompatibly with the accused's rights under the ECHR;
    c. its capacity to suggest an explanation or partial explanation of the accused's actions;
    d. the capacity of the material to have a bearing on scientific or medical evidence in the case.

7. It should also be borne in mind that while items of material viewed in isolation may not be reasonably considered to be capable of undermining the prosecution case or assisting the accused, several items together can have that effect.

8. Material relating to the accused's mental or physical health, intellectual capacity, or to any ill treatment which the accused may have suffered when in the investigator's custody is likely to fall within the test for disclosure set out in paragraph 4 above.

9. Disclosure must not be an open-ended trawl of unused material. A critical element to fair and proper disclosure is that the defence play their role to ensure that the prosecution are directed to material which might reasonably be considered capable of undermining the prosecution case or assisting the case for the accused. This process is key to ensuring prosecutors make informed determinations about disclosure of unused material. The defence statement is important in identifying the issues in the case and why it is suggested that the material meets the test for disclosure.

10. Disclosure should be conducted in a thinking manner and never be reduced to a box-ticking exercise[1]; at all stages of the process, there should be consideration of **why** the CPIA disclosure regime requires a particular course of action and what should be done to achieve that aim.

11. There will always be a number of participants in prosecutions and investigations: senior investigation officers, disclosure officers, investigation officers, reviewing prosecutors, leading counsel, junior counsel, and sometimes disclosure counsel. Communication within the "prosecution team" is vital to ensure that all matters which could have a bearing on disclosure issues are given sufficient attention by the right person. This is especially so given many reviewing lawyers will be unable to sit behind the trial advocate throughout the trial. In practice, this is likely to mean that a full log of disclosure decisions (with reasons) must be kept on the file and made available as appropriate to the prosecution team.

12. The role of the reviewing lawyer will be central to ensuring all members of the prosecution team are aware of, and carry out, their duties and role(s). Where this involves counsel or more than one reviewing lawyer, this should be done by giving clear written instructions and record keeping.

13. The centrality of the reviewing lawyer does not mean that he or she has to do all the work personally; on the contrary, it will often mean effective delegation. Where the conduct of a prosecution is assigned to more than one prosecutor, steps must be taken to ensure that all involved in the case properly record their decisions. Subsequent prosecutors must be able to see and understand previous disclosure decisions before carrying out their continuous review function.

---

[1] *R. v. Olu, Wilson and Brooks* [2010] EWCA Crim. 2975, [2011] 1 Cr.App.R. 33, CA (at [42]).

14. Investigators must always be alive to the potential need to reveal and prosecutors to the potential need to disclose material, in the interests of justice and fairness in the particular circumstances of any case, after the commencement of proceedings but before their duty arises under the Act. For instance, disclosure ought to be made of significant information that might affect a bail decision. This is likely to depend on what the defence chooses to reveal at that stage.

Investigators and disclosure officers

A-246

15. Investigators and disclosure officers must be fair and objective and must work together with prosecutors to ensure that disclosure obligations are met. Investigators and disclosure officers should be familiar with the CPIA Code of Practice, in particular their obligations to **retain** and **record** relevant material, to **review** it and to **reveal** it to the prosecutor.

16. Whether a case is a summary only matter or a long and complex trial on indictment, it is important that investigators and disclosure officers should approach their duties in a "thinking manner" and not as a box ticking exercise. Where necessary, the reviewing lawyer should be consulted. It is important that investigators and disclosure officers are deployed on cases which are commensurate with their training, skills and experience. The conduct of an investigation provides the foundation for the entire case, and may even impact the conduct of linked cases. It is vital that there is always consideration of disclosure matters at the outset of an investigation, regardless of its size.

17. A fair investigation involves the pursuit of material following all reasonable lines of enquiry, whether they point towards or away from the suspect. What is "reasonable" will depend on the context of the case. A fair investigation does not mean an endless investigation: investigators and disclosure officers must give thought to defining, and thereby limiting, the scope of their investigations, seeking the guidance of the prosecutor where appropriate.

18. Where there are a number of disclosure officers assigned to a case, there should be a lead disclosure officer who is the focus for enquiries and whose responsibility it is to ensure that the investigator's disclosure obligations are complied with. Where appropriate, regular case conferences and other meetings should be held to ensure prosecutors are apprised of all relevant developments in investigations. Full records should be kept of such meetings.

19. The *CPIA Code of Practice* encourages investigators and disclosure officers to seek advice from prosecutors about whether any particular item of material may be relevant to the investigation, and if so, how. Investigators and disclosure officers should record key decisions taken on these matters and be prepared to account for their actions later. An identical approach is not called for in each and every case.

20. Investigators are to approach their task seeking to establish what actually happened. They are to be fair and objective.

21. Disclosure officers (or their deputies) must inspect, view, listen to or search all relevant material that has been retained by the investigator and the disclosure officer must provide a personal declaration to the effect that this task has been undertaken. In some cases, a detailed examination of all material seized may be required. In others, however, a detailed examination of every item of material seized would be virtually impossible: see the **Annex**.

22. Prosecutors only have knowledge of matters which are revealed to them by investigators and disclosure officers, and the schedules are the written means by which that revelation takes place. Whatever the approach taken by investigators or disclosure officers to examining the material gathered or generated in the course of an investigation, it is crucial that disclosure officers record their reasons for a particular approach in writing.

23. In meeting the obligations in paragraph 6.9 and 8.1 of the code, schedules must be completed in a form which not only reveals sufficient information to the prosecutor, but which demonstrates a transparent and thinking approach to the disclosure exercise, to command the confidence of the defence and the court. Descriptions on non-sensitive schedules must be clear and accurate, and must contain sufficient detail to enable the prosecutor to make an informed decision on disclosure. The use of abbreviations and acronyms can be problematic and lead to difficulties in appreciating the significance of the material.

24. Sensitive schedules must contain sufficiently clear descriptions to enable the prosecutor to make an informed decision as to whether or not the material itself should be viewed, to the extent possible without compromising the confidentiality of the information.

25. It may become apparent to an investigator that some material obtained in the course of an investigation, either because it was considered to be potentially relevant, or because it was inextricably linked to material that was relevant, is, in fact, incapable of impact. It is not necessary to retain such material, although the investigator should err on the side of caution in reaching that conclusion and should be particularly mindful of the fact that some investigations continue over some time and that what is incapable of impact may change over time. The advice of the prosecutor should be sought where appropriate.

26. Disclosure officers must specifically draw material to the attention of the prosecutor for consideration where they have any doubt as to whether it might reasonably be considered capable of undermining the prosecution case or of assisting the case for the accused.

27. Disclosure officers must seek the advice and assistance of prosecutors when in doubt as to their responsibility as early as possible. They must deal expeditiously with requests by the prosecutor for further information on material, which may lead to disclosure.

Prosecutors

28. Prosecutors are responsible for making proper disclosure in consultation with the disclosure officer. The duty of disclosure is a continuing one and disclosure should be kept under review. In addition, prosecutors should ensure that advocates in court are properly instructed as to disclosure issues. Prosecutors must also be alert to the need to provide advice to, and where necessary probe actions taken by, disclosure officers to ensure that disclosure obligations are met. There should be no aspects of an investigation about which prosecutors are unable to ask probing questions. **A-247**

29. Prosecutors must review schedules prepared by disclosure officers thoroughly and must be alert to the possibility that relevant material may exist which has not been revealed to them or material included which should not have been. If no schedules have been provided, or there are apparent omissions from the schedules, or documents or other items are inadequately described or are unclear, the prosecutor must at once take action to obtain properly completed schedules. Likewise schedules should be returned for amendment if irrelevant items are included. If prosecutors remain dissatisfied with the quality or content of the schedules they must raise the matter with a senior investigator to resolve the matter satisfactorily.

30. Where prosecutors have reason to believe that the disclosure officer has not discharged the obligation in paragraph 21 to inspect, view, listen to or search relevant material, they must at once raise the matter with the disclosure officer and request that it be done. Where appropriate the matter should be raised with the officer in the case or a senior officer.

31. Prosecutors should copy the defence statement to the disclosure officer and investigator as soon as reasonably practicable and prosecutors should advise the investigator if, in their view, reasonable and relevant lines of further enquiry should be pursued. If the defence statement does point to other reasonable lines of enquiry, further investigation is required and evidence obtained as a result of these enquiries may be used as part of the prosecution case or to rebut the defence.

32. It is vital that prosecutors consider defence statements thoroughly. Prosecutors cannot comment upon, or invite inferences to be drawn from, failures in defence disclosure otherwise than in accordance with section 11 of the CPIA. Prosecutors may cross-examine the accused on differences between the defence case put at trial and that set out in his or her defence statement. In doing so, it may be appropriate to apply to the judge under section 6E of the CPIA for copies of the statement to be given to a jury, edited if necessary to remove inadmissible material. Prosecutors should examine the defence statement to see whether it points to other lines of enquiry.

33. Prosecutors should challenge the lack of, or inadequate, defence statements in writing, copying the document to the court and the defence and seeking directions from the court to require the provision of an adequate statement from the defence.

34. If the material does not fulfil the disclosure test there is no requirement to disclose it. For this purpose, the parties' respective cases should not be restrictively analysed but must be carefully analysed to ascertain the specific facts the prosecution seek to establish and the specific grounds on which the charges are resisted.

Prosecution advocates

35. Prosecution advocates should ensure that all material which ought to be disclosed under the Act is disclosed to the defence. However, prosecution advocates cannot be expected to disclose material if they are not aware of its existence. As far as is possible, prosecution advocates must place themselves in a fully informed position to enable them to make decisions on disclosure. **A-248**

36. Upon receipt of instructions, prosecution advocates should consider as a priority all the information provided regarding disclosure of material. Prosecution advocates should consider, in every case, whether they can be satisfied that they are in possession of all relevant documentation and that they have been fully instructed regarding disclosure matters. If as a result the advocate considers that further information or action is required, written advice should promptly be provided setting out the aspects that need clarification or action.

37. The prosecution advocate must keep decisions regarding disclosure under review until the conclusion of the trial, whenever possible in consultation with the reviewing prosecutor. The prosecution advocate must in every case specifically consider whether he or she can satisfactorily discharge the duty of continuing review on the basis of the material supplied already, or whether it is necessary

to inspect further material or to reconsider material already inspected. Prosecution advocates must not abrogate their responsibility under the CPIA by disclosing material which does not pass the test for disclosure, set out in paragraph 4, above.

38. There remains no basis in practice or law for counsel to counsel disclosure.

Defence

A-249

39. Defence engagement must be early and meaningful for the CPIA regime to function as intended. Defence statements are an integral part of this and are intended to help focus the attention of the prosecutor, court and co-defendants on the relevant issues in order to identify exculpatory unused material. Defence statements should be drafted in accordance with the relevant provisions of the CPIA.

40. Defence requests for further disclosure should ordinarily only be answered by the prosecution if the request is relevant to and directed to an issue identified in the defence statement. If it is not, then a further or amended defence statement should be sought by the prosecutor and obtained before considering the request for further disclosure.

41. In some cases that involve extensive unused material that is within the knowledge of a defendant, the defence will be expected to provide the prosecution and the court with assistance in identifying material which is suggested to pass the test for disclosure.

42. The prosecution's continuing duty to keep disclosure under review is crucial, and particular attention must be paid to understanding the significance of developments in the case on the unused material and earlier disclosure decisions. Meaningful defence engagement will help the prosecution to keep disclosure under review. The continuing duty of review for prosecutors is less likely to require the disclosure of further material to the defence if the defence have clarified and articulated their case, as required by the CPIA.

43. In the magistrates' courts, where the provision of a defence statement is not mandatory, early identification of the material issues by the defence, whether through a defence statement, case management form or otherwise, will help the prosecution to focus its preparation of the case and allow any defence disclosure queries to be dealt with promptly and accurately.

Magistrates' courts (including the youth court)

A-250

44. The majority of criminal cases are heard in the magistrates' court. The requirement for the prosecution to provide initial disclosure only arises after a not guilty plea has been entered but prosecutors should be alert to the possibility that material may exist which should be disclosed to the defendant prior to the CPIA requirements applying to the case.[2]

45. Where a not guilty plea is entered in the magistrates' court, prosecutors should ensure that any issues of dispute which are raised are noted on the file. They should also seek to obtain a copy of any Magistrates' Court Trial Preparation Form. Consideration of the issues raised in court and on the trial preparation form will assist in deciding what material undermines the prosecution case or assists the defendant.

46. Where a matter is set down for trial in the magistrates' court, prosecutors should ensure that the investigator is requested to supply any outstanding disclosure schedules as a matter of urgency. Prosecutors should serve initial disclosure in sufficient time to ensure that the trial date is effective.

47. There is no requirement for a defence statement to be served in the magistrates' court but it should be noted that if none is given the court has no power to hear an application for further prosecution disclosure under section 8 of the CPIA and the Criminal Procedure Rules.

Cases in the Crown Court

A-251

48. The exponential increase in the use of technology in society means that many routine Crown Court cases are increasingly likely to have to engage with digital material of some form. It is not only in large and complex cases that there may be large quantities of such material. Where such investigations involve digital material, it will be virtually impossible for investigators (or prosecutors) to examine every item of such material individually and there should be no expectation that such material will be so examined. Having consulted with the prosecution as appropriate, disclosure officers should determine what their approach should be to the examination of the material. Investigators or disclosure officers should decide how best to pursue a reasonable line of enquiry in relation to the relevant digital material, and ensure that the extent and manner of the examination are commensurate with the issues in the case.

49. Consideration should be given to any local or national agreements in relation to disclosure in "Early Guilty Plea Scheme" cases.

---

[2] See for example *R. v. DPP, ex p. Lee* [1999] 2 Cr.App.R. 304, DC.

Large and complex cases in the Crown Court

50. The particular challenges presented by large and complex criminal prosecutions require an **A-252** approach to disclosure which is specifically tailored to the needs of such cases. In these cases more than any other is the need for careful thought to be given to prosecution-led disclosure matters from the very earliest stage. It is essential that the prosecution takes a grip on the case and its disclosure requirements from the very outset of the investigation, which must continue throughout all aspects of the case preparation.

Disclosure management documents

51. Accordingly, investigations and prosecutions of large and complex cases should be carefully **A-253** defined and accompanied by a clear investigation and prosecution strategy. The approach to disclosure in such cases should be outlined in a document which should be served on the defence and the court at an early stage. Such documents, sometimes known as disclosure management documents, will require careful preparation and presentation, tailored to the individual case. They may include:

    a. where prosecutors and investigators operate in an integrated office, an explanation as to how the disclosure responsibilities have been managed;

    b. a brief summary of the prosecution case and a statement outlining how the prosecutor's general approach will comply with the CPIA regime, these guidelines and the Judicial Protocol on the Disclosure of Unused Material in Criminal Cases;

    c. the prosecutor's understanding of the defence case, including information revealed during interview;

    d. an outline of the prosecution's general approach to disclosure, which may include detail relating to:

        (i) digital material: explaining the method and extent of examination, in accordance with the **Annex** to these guidelines;

        (ii) video footage;

        (iii) linked investigations: explaining the nexus between investigations, any memoranda of understanding or disclosure agreements between investigators;

        (iv) third party and foreign material, including steps taken to obtain the material;

        (v) reasonable lines of enquiry: a summary of the lines pursued, particularly those that point away from the suspect, or which may assist the defence;

        (vi) credibility of a witness: confirmation that witness checks, including those of professional witnesses have, or will be, carried out.

52. Thereafter the prosecution should follow the disclosure management document. They are living documents and should be amended in light of developments in the case; they should be kept up to date as the case progresses. Their use will assist the court in its own case management and will enable the defence to engage from an early stage with the prosecution's proposed approach to disclosure.

Material not held by the prosecution

Involvement of other agencies: material held by other government departments and third parties

53. Where it appears to an investigator, disclosure officer or prosecutor that a government depart- **A-254** ment or other Crown body has material that may be relevant to an issue in the case, reasonable steps should be taken to identify and consider such material. Although what is reasonable will vary from case to case, the prosecution should inform the department or other body of the nature of its case and of relevant issues in the case in respect of which the department or body might possess material, and ask whether it has any such material.

54. It should be remembered that investigators, disclosure officers and prosecutors cannot be regarded to be in constructive possession of material held by government departments or Crown bodies simply by virtue of their status as government departments or Crown bodies.

55. Where, after reasonable steps have been taken to secure access to such material, access is denied, the investigator, disclosure officer or prosecutor should consider what if any further steps might be taken to obtain the material or inform the defence. The final decision on any further steps will be for the prosecutor.

Third party material: other domestic bodies

56. There may be cases where the investigator, disclosure officer or prosecutor believes that a third **A-255** party (for example, a local authority, a social services department, a hospital, a doctor, a school, a

provider of forensic services) has material or information which might be relevant to the prosecution case. In such cases, investigators, disclosure officers and prosecutors should take reasonable steps to identify, secure and consider material held by any third party where it appears to the investigator, disclosure officer or prosecutor that (a) such material exists and (b) that it may be relevant to an issue in the case.

57. If the investigator, disclosure officer or prosecutor seeks access to the material or information but the third party declines or refuses to allow access to it, the matter should not be left. If despite any reasons offered by the third party it is still believed that it is reasonable to seek production of the material or information, and the requirements of section 2 of the Criminal Procedure (Attendance of Witnesses) Act 1965 or as appropriate section 97 of the Magistrates' Courts Act 1980 are satisfied (or any other relevant power), then the prosecutor or investigator should apply for a witness summons causing a representative of the third party to produce the material to the court.

58. Sometimes, for example through multi-agency working arrangements, investigators, disclosure officers or prosecutors may become aware of the content or nature of material held by a third party. Consultation with the relevant third party must always take place before disclosure is made; there may be public interest reasons to apply to the court for an order for non-disclosure in the public interest, in accordance with the procedure outlined in paragraph 65 and following.

International matters

A-256   59. The obligations under the CPIA Code to pursue all reasonable lines of enquiry apply to material held overseas.

60. Where it appears that there is relevant material, the prosecutor must take reasonable steps to obtain it, either informally or making use of the powers contained in the Crime (International Co-operation) Act 2003 and any EU and international conventions. See CPS Guidance "Obtaining Evidence and Information from Abroad".

61. There may be cases where a foreign state or a foreign court refuses to make the material available to the investigator or prosecutor. There may be other cases where the foreign state, though willing to show the material to investigators, will not allow the material to be copied or otherwise made available and the courts of the foreign state will not order its provision.

62. It is for these reasons that there is no absolute duty on the prosecutor to disclose relevant material held overseas by entities not subject to the jurisdiction of the courts in England and Wales. However consideration should be given to whether the type of material believed to be held can be provided to the defence.

63. The obligation on the investigator and prosecutor under the CPIA is to take reasonable steps. Where investigators are allowed to examine files of a foreign state but are not allowed to take copies or notes or list the documents held, there is no breach by the prosecution in its duty of disclosure by reason of its failure to obtain such material, provided reasonable steps have been taken to try and obtain the material. Prosecutors have a margin of consideration as to what steps are appropriate in the particular case but prosecutors must be alive to their duties and there may be some circumstances where these duties cannot be met. Whether the prosecutor has taken reasonable steps is for the court to determine in each case if the matter is raised.

64. In these circumstances it is important that the position is clearly set out in writing so that the court and the defence know what the position is. Investigators and prosecutors must record and explain the situation and set out, insofar as they are permitted by the foreign state, such information as they can and the steps they have taken.

Applications for non-disclosure in the public interest

A-257   65. The CPIA allows prosecutors to apply to the court for an order to withhold material which would otherwise fall to be disclosed if disclosure would give rise to a real risk of serious prejudice to an important public interest. Before making such an application, prosecutors should aim to disclose as much of the material as they properly can (for example, by giving the defence redacted or edited copies or summaries). Neutral material or material damaging to the defendant need not be disclosed and there is no need to bring it to the attention of the court. Only in truly borderline cases should the prosecution seek a judicial ruling on whether material in its possession should be disclosed.

66. Prior to the hearing, the prosecutor and the prosecution advocate must examine all material which is the subject matter of the application and make any necessary enquiries of the investigator. The investigator must be frank with the prosecutor about the full extent of the sensitive material. Prior to or at the hearing, the court must be provided with full and accurate information about the material.

67. The prosecutor (or representative) and/or investigator should attend such applications. Section 16 of the CPIA allows a person claiming to have an interest in the sensitive material to apply to the court for the opportunity to be heard at the application.

68. The principles set out at paragraph 36 of *R. v. H.* [2004] 2 A.C. 134, [2004] UKHL 3, should be applied rigorously, firstly by the prosecutor and then by the court considering the material. It is essential that these principles are scrupulously adhered to, to ensure that the procedure for examination of material in the absence of the accused is compliant with Article 6.

69. If prosecutors conclude that a fair trial cannot take place because material which satisfies the test for disclosure cannot be disclosed, and that this cannot be remedied by the above procedure; how the case is presented; or by any other means, they should not continue with the case.

Other disclosure

70. Disclosure of any material that is made outside the ambit of CPIA will attract confidentiality by virtue of *Taylor v. Serious Fraud Office* [1999] 2 A.C. 177, HL.   **A-258**

Material relevant to sentence

71. In all cases the prosecutor must consider disclosing in the interests of justice any material which is relevant to sentence (*e.g.* information which might mitigate the seriousness of the offence or assist the accused to lay blame in part upon a co-accused or another person).   **A-259**

Post-conviction

72. Where, after the conclusion of the proceedings, material comes to light, that might cast doubt upon the safety of the conviction, the prosecutor must consider disclosure of such material.   **A-260**

Applicability of these guidelines

73. These guidelines shall have immediate effect.   **A-261**

Annex: Attorney General's Guidelines on Disclosure: Supplementary Guidelines on Digitally Stored Material (2011)

A1. The guidelines are intended to supplement the Attorney General's Guidelines on Disclosure.   **A-262**

A2. As a result of the number of cases now involving digitally stored material and the scale of the digital material that may be involved, more detailed guidance is considered to be needed. The objective of these guidelines is to set out how material satisfying the tests for disclosure can best be identified and disclosed to the defence without imposing unrealistic or disproportionate demands on the investigator and prosecutor.

A3. The approach set out in these guidelines is in line with existing best practice, in that:

    a. investigating and prosecuting agencies, especially in large and complex cases, will apply their respective case management and disclosure strategies and policies and be transparent with the defence and the courts about how the prosecution has approached complying with its disclosure obligations in the context of the individual case; and,

    b. the defence will be expected to play their part in defining the real issues in the case. In this context, the defence will be invited to participate in defining the scope of the reasonable searches that may be made of digitally stored material by the investigator to identify material that might reasonably be expected to undermine the prosecution case or assist the defence.

A4. Only if this approach is followed can the courts be in a position to use their case management powers effectively and to determine applications for disclosure fairly.

A5. The Attorney General's Guidelines are not detailed operational guidelines. They are intended to set out a common approach to be adopted in the context of digitally stored material.

Types of digital material

A6. Digital material falls into two categories: the first category is material which is created natively within an electronic environment (*e.g.* email, office files, system files, digital photographs, audio, etc.); the second category is material which has been digitised from an analogue form (*e.g.* scanned copy of a document, scanned photograph, a faxed document). Irrespective of the way in which technology changes, the categorisation of digital material will remain the same.   **A-263**

A7. Digital material is usually held on one of the three types of media. Optical media (*e.g.* CD, DVD, Blu-ray) and solid-state media (*e.g.* removable memory cards, solid-state music players or mobile devices, etc.) cater for usually lower volume storage. Magnetic media (*e.g.* disk drives and back up tapes) usually cater for high volume storage.

General principles for investigators

A-264   A8. The general principles[3] to be followed by investigators in handling and examining digital material are:

a. no action taken by investigators or their agents should change data held on a computer or storage media which may subsequently be relied upon in court;

b. in circumstances where a person finds it necessary to access original data held on computer or storage media, that person must be competent to do so and be able to give evidence explaining the relevance and implications of their actions;

c. an audit trail or other record of all processes applied to computer-based electronic evidence should be created and preserved; an independent third party should be able to examine those processes (see further the sections headed "Record keeping" and "Scheduling" below); and

d. the person in charge of the investigation has overall responsibility for ensuring that the law and these principles are followed.

A9. Where an investigator has reasonable grounds for believing that digital material may contain material subject to legal professional privilege, very strong legal constraints apply. No digital material may be seized which an investigator has reasonable grounds for believing to be subject to legal privilege, other than where the provisions of the Criminal Justice and Police Act 2001 apply. Strict controls need to be applied where privileged material is seized. See the more detailed section on legal professional privilege starting at paragraph A28, below.

Seizure, relevance and retention

A-265   A10. The legal obligations are to be found in a combination of the Police and Criminal Evidence Act 1984 (PACE), the Criminal Justice and Police Act 2001 (CJPA 2001) and the Criminal Procedure and Investigations Act 1996 (the CPIA 1996).

A11. These guidelines also apply to digital material seized or imaged under other statutory provisions. For example, the Serious Fraud Office has distinct powers of seizure under warrant obtained under section 2(4) of the Criminal Justice Act 1987. In cases concerning indecent images of children and obscene material, special provisions apply to the handling, storage and copying of such material. Practitioners should refer to specific guidance on the application of those provisions.

Seizure

A-266   A12. Before searching a suspect's premises where digital evidence is likely to be found, consideration must be given to what sort of evidence is likely to be found and in what volume, whether it is likely to be possible to view and copy, if relevant, the material at the location (it is not uncommon with the advent of cloud computing for digital material to be hosted by a third party) and to what should be seized. Business and commercial premises will often have very substantial amounts of digital material stored on computers and other media. Investigators will need to consider the practicalities of seizing computer hard drives and other media, the effect this may have on the business and, where it is not feasible to obtain an image of digital material, the likely timescale for returning seized items.

A13. In deciding whether to seize and retain digital material it is important that the investigator either complies with the procedure under the relevant statutory authority, relying either on statutory powers or a search warrant, or obtains the owner's consent. In particular, investigators need to be aware of the constraints applying to legally privileged material.

A14. A computer hard drive or single item of media, such as a back up tape, is a single storage entity. This means that if any digital material found on the hard drive or other media can lawfully be seized the computer hard drive or single item of media may, if appropriate, be seized or imaged. In some circumstances investigators may wish to image specific folders, files or categories of data where it is feasible to do so without seizing the hard drive or other media, or instead of taking an image of all data on the hard drive or other media. In practice, the configuration of most systems means that data may be contained across a number of hard drives and more than one hard drive or item of media may be required in order to access the information sought.

A15. Digital material must not be seized if an investigator has reasonable grounds for believing it is subject to legal professional privilege, other than where sections 50 or 51 of the CJPA 2001 apply. If such material is seized it must be isolated from other seized material and any other investigation material in the possession of the investigating authority.

---

[3] Based on: Association of Chief Police Officers: Good Practice Guide for Computer Based Electronic Evidence Version 0.1.4.

The Police and Criminal Evidence Act 1984

A16. PACE 1984 provides powers to seize and retain anything for which the search has been **A-267** authorised or after arrest, other than items attracting legal professional privilege.[4] In addition, there is a general power to seize anything which is on the premises if there are reasonable grounds to believe that it has been obtained in the commission of an offence, or that it is evidence and that it is necessary to seize it to prevent it being concealed, lost, altered or destroyed.[5] There is another related power to require information which is stored in any electronic form and is accessible from the premises to be produced in a form in which it can be taken away and in which it is visible and legible or from which it can readily be produced in a visible and legible form.[6]

A17. An image (a forensically sound copy) of the digital material may be taken at the location of the search. Where the investigator makes an image of the digital material at the location, the original need not be seized. Alternatively, when originals are taken, investigators must be prepared to copy or image the material for the owners when reasonably practicable in accordance with PACE 1984, Code B 7.17.

A18. Where it is not possible or reasonably practicable to image the computer or hard drive, it will need to be removed from the location or premises for examination elsewhere. This allows the investigator to seize and sift material for the purpose of identifying that which meets the tests for retention in accordance with the 1984 PACE.[7]

The Criminal Justice and Police Act 2001

A19. The additional powers of seizure in sections 50 and 51 of the CJPA 2001 Act [*sic*] only extend **A-268** the scope of existing powers of search and seizure under the PACE and other specified statutory authorities[8] where the relevant conditions and circumstances apply.

A20. Investigators must be careful only to exercise powers under the CJPA 2001 when it is necessary and not to remove any more material than is justified. The removal of large volumes of material, much of which may not ultimately be retainable, may have serious consequences for the owner of the material, particularly when they are involved in business or other commercial activities.

A21. A written notice must be given to the occupier of the premises where items are seized under sections 50 and 51.[9]

A22. Until material seized under the CJPA 2001 has been examined, it must be kept securely and separately from any material seized under other powers. Any such material must be examined as soon as reasonably practicable to determine which elements may be retained and which should be returned. Regard must be had to the desirability of allowing the person from whom the property was seized — or a person with an interest in the property — an opportunity of being present or represented at the examination.

Retention

A23. Where material is seized under the powers conferred by PACE the duty to retain it under **A-269** the code of practice issued under the CPIA is subject to the provisions on retention under section 22 of PACE. Material seized under sections 50 and 51 of the CJPA 2001 may be retained or returned in accordance with sections 53–58 of that Act.

A24. Retention is limited to evidence and relevant material (as defined in the code of practice issued under the CPIA). Where either evidence or relevant material is inextricably linked to nonrelevant material which is not reasonably practicable to separate, that material can also be retained. Inextricably linked material is material that is not reasonably practicable to separate from other linked material without prejudicing the use of that other material in any investigation or proceedings.

A25. However, inextricably linked material must not be examined, imaged, copied or used for any purpose other than for providing the source of or the integrity of the linked material.

A26. There are four categories of material that may be retained:

    a. material that is evidence or potential evidence in the case; where material is retained for evidential purposes there will be a strong argument that the whole thing (or an authenticated image or copy) should be retained for the purpose of proving provenance and continuity;

---

[4] By warrant under s.8, and Sched. 1 and s.18.
[5] S.19.
[6] S.20.
[7] Special provision exists for investigations conducted by Her Majesty's Revenue and Customs in the application of their powers under PACE — see s.114(2)(b) — and the CJPA 2001.
[8] Sched. 1 to the CJPA 2001.
[9] S.52.

    b. where evidential material has been retained, inextricably linked non-relevant material which is not reasonably practicable to separate can also be retained (PACE, Code B, para. 7);

    c. an investigator should retain material that is relevant to the investigation and required to be scheduled as unused material; this is broader than but includes the duty to retain material which may satisfy the test for prosecution disclosure; the general duty to retain relevant material is set out in the CPIA code at paragraph 5; or

    d. material which is inextricably linked to relevant unused material which of itself may not be relevant material; such material should be retained (PACE, Code B, para. 7).

A27. The balance of any digital material should be returned in accordance with sections 53–55 of the CJPA 2001 if seized under that Act.

Legal professional privilege (LPP)

A-270   A28. No digital material may be seized which an investigator has reasonable grounds for believing to be subject to LPP, other than under the additional powers of seizure in the CJPA 2001.

A29. The CJPA 2001 enables an investigator to seize relevant items which contain LPP material where it is not reasonably practicable on the search premises to separate LPP material from non-LPP material.

A30. Where LPP material or material suspected of containing LPP is seized, it must be isolated from the other material which has been seized in the investigation. The mechanics of securing property vary according to the circumstances; "bagging up", *i.e.* placing materials in sealed bags or containers, and strict subsequent control of access, is the appropriate procedure in many cases.

A31. Where material has been identified as potentially containing LPP it must be reviewed by a lawyer independent of the prosecuting authority. No member of the investigative or prosecution team involved in either the current investigation or, if the LPP material relates to other criminal proceedings, in those proceedings should have sight of or access to the LPP material.

A32. If the material is voluminous, search terms or other filters may have to be used to identify the LPP material. If so this will also have to be done by someone independent and not connected with the investigation.

A33. It is essential that anyone dealing with LPP material maintains proper records showing the way in which the material has been handled and those who have had access to it as well as decisions taken in relation to that material.

A34. LPP material can only be retained in specific circumstances in accordance with section 54 of the CJPA 2001, *i.e.* where the property which comprises the LPP material has been lawfully seized and it is not reasonably practicable for the item to be separated from the rest of the property without prejudicing the use of the rest of the property. LPP material which cannot be retained must be returned as soon as practicable after the seizure without waiting for the whole examination of the seized material.

Excluded and special procedure material

A-271   A35. Similar principles to those that apply to LPP material apply to excluded or special procedure material, as set out in section 55 of the CJPA 2001.[10]

Encryption

A-272   A36. Part III of the Regulation of Investigatory Powers Act 2000 (RIPA) and the *Investigation of Protected Electronic Information Code of Practice* govern encryption. See the CPS's Guidance RIPA, Part III.

A37. RIPA enables specified law enforcement agencies to compel individuals or companies to provide passwords or encryption keys for the purpose of rendering protected material readable. Failure to comply with RIPA, Part III orders is a criminal offence. The code of practice provides guidance when exercising powers under RIPA, to require disclosure of protected electronic data in an intelligible form or to acquire the means by which protected electronic data may be accessed or put in an intelligible form.

Sifting/examination

A-273   A38. In complying with its duty of disclosure, the prosecution should follow the procedure as outlined below.

A39. Where digital material is examined, the extent and manner of inspecting, viewing or listening will depend on the nature of the material and its form.

---

[10] Special provision exists for investigations conducted by Her Majesty's Revenue and Customs in the application of their powers under PACE — see s.114(2)(b) — and the CJPA.

A40. It is important for investigators and prosecutors to remember that the duty under the CPIA code of practice is to "pursue all reasonable lines of enquiry including those that point away from the suspect". Lines of enquiry, of whatever kind, should be pursued only if they are reasonable in the context of the individual case. It is not the duty of the prosecution to comb through all the material in its possession – *e.g.* every word or byte of computer material – on the look out for anything which might conceivably or speculatively assist the defence. The duty of the prosecution is to disclose material which might reasonably be considered capable of undermining its case or assisting the case for the accused which they become aware of, or to which their attention is drawn.

A41. In some cases the sift may be conducted by an investigator/disclosure officer manually assessing the content of the computer or other digital material from its directory and determining which files are relevant and should be retained for evidence or unused material.

A42. In other cases such an approach may not be feasible. Where there is an enormous volume of material it is perfectly proper for the investigator/disclosure officer to search it by sample, key words, or other appropriate search tools or analytical techniques to locate relevant passages, phrases and identifiers.

A43. In cases involving very large quantities of data, the person in charge of the investigation will develop a strategy setting out how the material should be analysed or searched to identify categories of data. Where search tools are used to examine digital material it will usually be appropriate to provide the accused and his or her legal representative with a copy of reasonable search terms used, or to be used, and invite them to suggest any further reasonable search terms. If search terms are suggested which the investigator or prosecutor believes will not be productive – for example because of the use of common words that are likely to identify a mass of irrelevant material, the investigator or prosecutor is entitled to open a dialogue with the defence representative with a view to agreeing sensible refinements. The purpose of this dialogue is to ensure that reasonable and proportionate searches can be carried out.

A44. It may be necessary to carry out sampling and searches on more than one occasion, especially as there is a duty on the prosecutor to keep duties of disclosure under review. To comply with this duty it may be appropriate (and should be considered) where further evidence or unused material is obtained in the course of the investigation; the defence statement is served on the prosecutor; the defendant makes an application under section 8 of the CPIA for disclosure; or the defendant requests that further sampling or searches be carried out (provided it is a reasonable line of enquiry).

Record keeping

A45. A record or log must be made of all digital material seized or imaged and subsequently retained as relevant to the investigation.   **A-274**

A46. In cases involving very large quantities of data where the person in charge of the investigation has developed a strategy setting out how the material should be analysed or searched to identify categories of data, a record should be made of the strategy and the analytical techniques used to search the data. The record should include details of the person who has carried out the process and the date and time it was carried out. In such cases the strategy should record the reasons why certain categories have been searched for (such as names, companies, dates, etc).

A47. In any case it is important that any searching or analytical processing of digital material, as well as the data identified by that process, is properly recorded. So far as practicable, what is required is a record of the terms of the searches or processing that has been carried out. This means that in principle the following details may be recorded:

    a. a record of all searches carried out, including the date of each search and the person(s) who conducted it;

    b. a record of all search words or terms used on each search; however where it is impracticable to record each word or terms (such as where Boolean searches or search strings or conceptual searches are used) it will usually be sufficient to record each broad category of search;

    c. a log of the key judgements made while refining the search strategy in the light of what is found, or deciding not to carry out further searches; and

    d. where material relating to a "hit" is not examined, the decision not to examine should be explained in the record of examination or in a statement; for instance, a large number of "hits" may be obtained in relation to a particular search word or term, but material relating to the "hits" is not examined because they do not appear to be relevant to the investigation; any subsequent refinement of the search terms and further hits should also be noted and explained as above.

A48. Just as it is not necessary for the investigator or prosecutor to produce records of every search made of hard copy material, it is not necessary to produce records of what may be many hundreds of searches or analyses that have been carried out on digitally stored material, simply to demonstrate that these have been done. It should be sufficient for the prosecution to explain how the disclosure exercise has been approached and to give the accused or suspect's legal representative an opportunity to participate in defining the reasonable searches to be made, as described in the section on sifting/examination.

Scheduling

A-275   A49. The disclosure officer should ensure that scheduling of relevant material is carried out in accordance with the CPIA code of practice. This requires each item of unused material to be listed separately on the unused material schedule and numbered consecutively. The description of each item should make clear the nature of the item and should contain sufficient detail to enable the prosecutor to decide whether he needs to inspect the material before deciding whether or not it should be disclosed (see para. A24).

A50. In some enquiries it may not be practicable to list each item of material separately. If so, these may be listed in a block and described by quantity and generic title. Even if the material is listed in a block, the search terms used and any items of material which might satisfy the disclosure test are listed and described separately. In practical terms this will mean, where appropriate, cross referencing the schedules to your disclosure management document.

A51. The remainder of any computer hard drive/media containing material which is not responsive to search terms or other analytical technique or not identified by any "hits", and material identified by "hits" but not examined, is unused material and should be recorded (if appropriate by a generic description) and retained.

A52. Where continuation sheets of the unused material schedule are used, or additional schedules are sent subsequently, the item numbering must be, where possible, sequential to all other items on earlier schedules.

Third party material

A-275a   A53. Third party material is material held by a person, organisation, or government department other than the investigator and prosecutor within the UK or outside the UK.

Within the UK

A-275b   A54. The CPIA code and the AG's Guidelines make clear the obligation on the prosecution to pursue all reasonable lines of enquiry in relation to material held by third parties within the UK.

A55. If as a result of the duty to pursue all reasonable lines of enquiry, the investigator or prosecutor obtains or receives the material from the third party, then it must be dealt with in accordance with the CPIA, *i.e.* the prosecutor must disclose material if it meets the disclosure tests, subject to any public interest immunity claim. The person who has an interest in the material (the third party) may make representations to the court concerning public interest immunity (see s.16 of the CPIA 1996).

A56. Material not in the possession of an investigator or prosecutor falls outside the CPIA. In such cases the Attorney General's Guidelines on Disclosure prescribe the approach to be taken to disclosure of material held by third parties as does the judicial disclosure protocol.

B. ACCEPTANCE OF PLEAS

Introduction

A-276   The Attorney-General issued revised guidelines on the acceptance of pleas, which came into force on December 1, 2009. The principal changes were to Part C (basis of plea). Paragraph C.1 now makes it clear that in multi-handed cases, any bases of plea must be factually consistent with each other. Paragraph C.2 now states that a defence advocate must reduce an acceptable basis of plea to writing in all cases save for those in which the defendant has indicated that the guilty plea has been or will be tendered on the basis of the prosecution case (previously this was not necessary in cases where the issue was "simple"). Paragraph C.4 now additionally provides that, where the basis of plea differs in its implications for sentencing or the making of ancillary orders from the case originally outlined by the prosecution, the prosecution advocate must ensure that such differences are accurately reflected in the written record prior to showing it to the prosecuting authority. New paragraph C.6 provides that in all cases where it is likely to assist the court where the sentencing issues are complex or unfamiliar, the prosecution must add to the written outline of the case served upon the court a summary of the key considerations, taking the form of brief notes on (a) any statutory limitations, (b) any relevant sentencing authorities or guidelines, (c) the scope for any ancillary orders, and (d) the age of the defendant and information regarding any outstanding offences. Paragraph C.7 was new and clarifies that the prosecution are able to provide further written information where they think that it is likely to assist the judge or where the judge requests it. Old paragraph C.7 became new paragraph C.8, and was amended to ensure that the procedure to be followed where the prosecution advocate takes issue with all or part of the written basis of plea is in line with the then consolidated criminal practice direction. Old paragraph C.8 is now paragraph C.11. For the relevant provisions of *Criminal Practice Direction VII (Sentence) B*, see § 4-175 in the main work; and *post*, Appendix B-149 *et seq.*

ATTORNEY-GENERAL'S GUIDELINES ON THE ACCEPTANCE OF PLEAS AND THE PROSECUTOR'S ROLE IN THE SENTENCING EXERCISE

A. Foreword

A:1. Prosecutors have an important role in protecting the victim's interests in the criminal justice **A-277** process, not least in the acceptance of pleas and the sentencing exercise. The basis of plea, particularly in a case that is not contested, is the vehicle through which the victim's voice is heard. Factual inaccuracies in pleas in mitigation cause distress and offence to victims, the families of victims and witnesses. This can take many forms but may be most acutely felt when the victim is dead and the family hears inaccurate assertions about the victim's character or lifestyle. Prosecution advocates are reminded that they are required to adhere to the standards set out in the Victim's Charter, which places the needs of the victim at the heart of the criminal justice process, and that they are subject to a similar obligation in respect of the Code of Practice for Victims of Crime.

A:2. The principle of fairness is central to the administration of justice. The implementation of Human Rights Act 1998 [*sic*] in October 2000 incorporated into domestic law the principle of fairness to the accused articulated in the European Convention on Human Rights. Accuracy and reasonableness of plea plays an important part in ensuring fairness both to the accused and to the victim.

A:3. The Attorney General's Guidelines on the Acceptance of Pleas issued on December 7, 2000 highlighted the importance of transparency in the conduct of justice. The basis of plea agreed by the parties in a criminal trial is central to the sentencing process. An illogical or unsupported basis of plea can lead to an unduly lenient sentence being passed and has a consequential effect where consideration arises as to whether to refer the sentence to the Court of Appeal under section 36 of the Criminal Justice Act 1988.

A:4. These Guidelines, which replace the Guidelines issued in October 2005, give guidance on how prosecutors should meet these objectives of protection of victims' interests and of securing fairness and transparency in the process. They take into account paragraphs IV.45.4 and following of the consolidated criminal practice direction, amended May 2009, and the guidance issued by the Court of Appeal (Criminal) Division [*sic*] in *R. v. Beswick* [1996] 1 Cr.App.R. 343, *R. v. Tolera* [1999] 1 Cr.App.R. 25 and *R. v. Underwood* [2005] 1 Cr.App.R 13. They complement the Bar Council Guidance on Written Standards for the Conduct of Professional Work issued with the 7th edition of the Code of Conduct for the Bar of England and Wales and the Law Society's Professional Conduct Rules. When considering the acceptance of a guilty plea prosecution advocates are also reminded of the need to apply "The Farquharson Guidelines on The Role and Responsibilities of the Prosecution Advocate".

A:5. The Guidelines should be followed by all prosecutors and those persons designated under section 7 of the Prosecution of Offences Act 1985 (designated caseworkers) and apply to prosecutions conducted in England and Wales.

B. General Principles

B:1. Justice in this jurisdiction, save in the most exceptional circumstances, is conducted in public. **A-278** This includes the acceptance of pleas by the prosecution and sentencing.

B:2. The Code for Crown Prosecutors governs the prosecutor's decision-making prior to the commencement of the trial hearing and sets out the circumstances in which pleas to a reduced number of charges, or less serious charges, can be accepted.

B:3. When a case is listed for trial and the prosecution form the view that the appropriate course is to accept a plea before the proceedings commence or continue, or to offer no evidence on the indictment or any part of it, the prosecution should whenever practicable speak to the victim or the victim's family, so that the position can be explained. The views of the victim or the family may assist in informing the prosecutor's decision as to whether it is the [*sic*] public interest, as defined by the Code for Crown Prosecutors, to accept or reject the plea. The victim or victim's family should then be kept informed and decisions explained once they are made at court.

B:4. The appropriate disposal of a criminal case after conviction is as much a part of the criminal justice process as the trial of guilt or innocence. The prosecution advocate represents the public interest, and should be ready to assist the court to reach its decision as to the appropriate sentence. This will include drawing the court's attention to:

— any victim personal statement or other information available to the prosecution advocate as to the impact of the offence on the victim;

— where appropriate, to any evidence of the impact of the offending on a community;

— any statutory provisions relevant to the offender and the offences under consideration;

— any relevant sentencing guidelines and guideline cases; and

— the aggravating and mitigating factors of the offence under consideration.

The prosecution advocate may also offer assistance to the court by making submissions, in the light of all these factors, as to the appropriate sentencing range.

In all cases, it is the prosecution advocate's duty to apply for appropriate ancillary orders, such as anti-social behaviour orders and confiscation orders. When considering which ancillary orders to apply for, prosecution advocates must always have regard to the victim's needs, including the question of his or her future protection.

C. The Basis of Plea

A-279

C:1. The basis of a guilty plea must not be agreed on a misleading or untrue set of facts and must take proper account of the victim's interests. An illogical or insupportable basis of plea will inevitably result in the imposition of an inappropriate sentence and is capable of damaging public confidence in the criminal justice system. In cases involving multiple defendants the bases of plea for each defendant must be factually consistent with each other.

C:2. When the defendant indicates an acceptable plea, the defence advocate should reduce the basis of the plea to writing. This must be done in all cases save for those in which the defendant has indicated that the guilty plea has been or will be tendered on the basis of the prosecution case.

C:3. The written basis of plea must be considered with great care, taking account of the position of any other relevant defendant where appropriate. The prosecution should not lend itself to any agreement whereby a case is presented to the sentencing judge on a misleading or untrue set of facts or on a basis that is detrimental to the victim's interests. There will be cases where a defendant seeks to mitigate on the basis of assertions of fact which are outside the scope of the prosecution's knowledge. A typical example concerns the defendant's state of mind. If a defendant wishes to be sentenced on this basis, the prosecution advocate should invite the judge not to accept the defendant's version unless he or she gives evidence on oath to be tested in cross-examination. Paragraph IV.45.14 of the consolidated criminal practice direction states that in such circumstances the defence advocate should be prepared to call the defendant and, if the defendant is not willing to testify, subject to any explanation that may be given, the judge may draw such inferences as appear appropriate.

C:4. The prosecution advocate should show the prosecuting authority any written record relating to the plea and agree with them the basis on which the case will be opened to the court. If, as may well be the case, the basis of plea differs in its implications for sentencing or the making of ancillary orders from the case originally outlined by the prosecution, the prosecution advocate must ensure that such differences are accurately reflected in the written record prior to showing it to the prosecuting authority.

C:5. It is the responsibility of the prosecution advocate thereafter to ensure that the defence advocate is aware of the basis on which the plea is accepted by the prosecution and the way in which the prosecution case will be opened to the court.

C:6. In all cases where it is likely to assist the court where the sentencing issues are complex or unfamiliar the prosecution must add to the written outline of the case which is served upon the court a summary of the key considerations. This should take the form of very brief notes on:

— any relevant statutory limitations;

— the names of any relevant sentencing authorities or guidelines;

— the scope for any ancillary orders (*e.g.* concerning anti-social behaviour, confiscation or deportation will need to be considered).

The outline should also include the age of the defendant and information regarding any outstanding offences.

C:7. It remains open to the prosecutor to provide further written information (for example to supplement and update the analysis at later stages of the case) where he or she thought that likely to assist the court, or if the judge requests it.

C:8. When the prosecution advocate has agreed the written basis of plea submitted by the defence advocate, he or she should endorse the document accordingly. If the prosecution advocate takes issue with all or part of the written basis of plea, the procedure set out in the consolidated criminal practice direction (and in Part 37.10(5) of the Criminal Procedure Rules) should be followed. The defendant's basis of plea must be set out in writing identifying what is in dispute; the court may invite the parties to make representations about whether the dispute is material to sentence; and if the court decides that it is a material dispute, the court will invite further representations or evidence as it may require and decide the dispute in accordance with the principles set out in *R. v. Newton*, 77 Cr.App.R.13, CA. The signed original document setting out the disputed factual matters should be made available to the trial judge and thereafter lodged with the court papers, as it will form part of the record of the hearing.

C:9. Where the basis of plea cannot be agreed and the discrepancy between the two accounts is such as to have a potentially significant effect on the level of sentence, it is the duty of the defence advocate so to inform the court before the sentencing process begins. There remains an overriding duty on the prosecution advocate to ensure that the sentencing judge is made aware of the discrepancy and of the consideration which must be given to holding a *Newton* hearing to resolve the issue. The court should be told where a derogatory reference to a victim, witness or third party is not accepted, even though there may be no effect on sentence.

C:10. As emphasised in paragraph IV.45.10 of the consolidated criminal practice direction, whenever an agreement as to the basis of plea is made between the prosecution and defence, any such agreement will be subject to the approval of the trial judge, who may of his or her own motion disregard the agreement and direct that a *Newton* hearing should be held to determine the proper basis on which sentence should be passed.

C:11. Where a defendant declines to admit an offence that he or she previously indicated should be taken into consideration, the prosecution advocate should indicate to the defence advocate and the court that, subject to further review, the offence may now form the basis of a new prosecution.

D. Sentence Indications

D:1. Only in the Crown Court may sentence indications be sought. Advocates there are reminded **A-280** that indications as to sentence should not be sought from the trial judge unless issues between the prosecution and defence have been addressed and resolved. Therefore, in difficult or complicated cases, no less than seven days notice in writing of an intention to seek an indication should normally be given to the prosecution and the court. When deciding whether the circumstances of a case require such notice to be given, defence advocates are reminded that prosecutors should not agree a basis of plea unless and until the necessary consultation has taken place first with the victim and/or the victim's family and second, in the case of an independent prosecution advocate, with the prosecuting authority.

D:2. If there is no final agreement about the plea to the indictment, or the basis of plea, and the defence nevertheless proceeds to seek an indication of sentence, which the judge appears minded to give, the prosecution advocate should remind him or her of the guidance given in *R. v. Goodyear (Karl)* [2005] EWCA 888 [*sic*] that normally speaking an indication of sentence should not be given until the basis of the plea has been agreed or the judge has concluded that he or she can properly deal with the case without the need for a trial of the issue.

D:3. If an indication is sought, the prosecution advocate should normally enquire whether the judge is in possession of or has access to all the evidence relied on by the prosecution, including any victim personal statement, as well as any information about relevant previous convictions recorded against the defendant.

D:4. Before the judge gives the indication, the prosecution advocate should draw the judge's attention to any minimum or mandatory statutory sentencing requirements. Where the prosecution advocate would be expected to offer the judge assistance with relevant guideline cases or the views of the Sentencing Guidelines Council, he or she should invite the judge to allow them to do so. Where it applies, the prosecution advocate should remind the judge that the position [*sic*] of the Attorney General to refer any sentencing decision as unduly lenient is unaffected. In any event, the prosecution advocate should not say anything which may create the impression that the sentence indication has the support or approval of the Crown.

E. Pleas in Mitigation

E:1. The prosecution advocate must challenge any assertion by the defence in mitigation which is **A-281** derogatory to a person's character (for instance, because it suggests that his or her conduct is or has been criminal, immoral or improper) and which is either false or irrelevant to proper sentencing considerations. If the defence advocate persists in that assertion, the prosecution advocate should invite the court to consider holding a *Newton* hearing to determine the issue.

E:2. The defence advocate must not submit in mitigation anything that is derogatory to a person's character without giving advance notice in writing so as to afford the prosecution advocate the opportunity to consider their position under paragraph E:1. When the prosecution advocate is so notified they must take all reasonable steps to establish whether the assertions are true. Reasonable steps will include seeking the views of the victim. This will involve seeking the views of the victim's family if the victim is deceased, and the victim's parents or legal guardian where the victim is a child. Reasonable steps may also include seeking the views of the police or other law enforcement authority, as appropriate. An assertion which is derogatory to a person's character will rarely amount to mitigation unless it has a causal connection to the circumstances of the offence or is otherwise relevant to proper sentencing considerations.

E:3. Where notice has not been given in accordance with paragraph E:2, the prosecution advocate must not acquiesce in permitting mitigation which is derogatory to a person's character. In such circumstances, the prosecution advocate should draw the attention of the court to the failure to give advance notice and seek time, and if necessary, an adjournment to investigate the assertion in the same way as if proper notice had been given. Where, in the opinion of the prosecution advocate, there are substantial grounds for believing that such an assertion is false or irrelevant to sentence, he or she should inform the court of their opinion and invite the court to consider making an order under section 58(8) of the Criminal Procedure and Investigations Act 1996, preventing publication of the assertion.

E:4. Where the prosecution advocate considers that the assertion is, if true, relevant to sentence, or the court has so indicated, he or she should seek time, and if necessary an adjournment, to establish whether the assertion is true. If the matter cannot be resolved to the satisfaction of the parties, the prosecution advocate should invite the court to consider holding a *Newton* hearing to determine the issue.

C. JURY CHECKS

Introduction

A-282   For the background to these guidelines, see § 4-275 in the main work. They were updated in November 2012.

Attorney-General's Guidelines: Jury checks, unreported, November 27, 2012

A-283   1. The principles which are generally to be observed are:

  (a) that members of a jury should be selected at random from the panel,

  (b) the Juries Act 1974 identifies those classes of persons who alone are either disqualified from or ineligible for service on a jury; no other class of person may be treated as disqualified or ineligible,

  (c) the correct way for the Crown to seek to exclude a member of the panel from sitting as a juror is by the exercise in open court of the right to request a stand by or, if necessary, to challenge for cause.

2. Parliament has provided safeguards against jurors who may be corrupt or biased. In addition to the provision for majority verdicts, there is the sanction of a criminal offence for a disqualified person to serve on a jury. The omission of a disqualified person from the panel is a matter for court officials—they will check criminal records for the purpose of ascertaining whether or not a potential juror is a disqualified person.

A-284   3. There are, however, certain exceptional types of case of public importance for which the provisions as to majority verdicts and the disqualification of jurors may not be sufficient to ensure the proper administration of justice. In such cases it is in the interests of both justice and the public that there should be further safeguards against the possibility of bias and in such cases checks which go beyond the investigation of criminal records may be necessary.

4. These classes of case may be defined broadly as (a) cases in which national security is involved and part of the evidence is likely to be heard *in camera*, and (b) security and terrorist cases in which a juror's extreme beliefs could prevent a fair trial.

5. The particular aspects of these cases which may make it desirable to seek extra precautions are:

  (a) in security cases a danger that a juror, either voluntarily or under pressure, may make an improper use of evidence which, because of its sensitivity, has been given in camera,

  (b) in both security and terrorist cases the danger that a juror's personal beliefs are so biased as to go beyond normally reflecting the broad spectrum of views and interests in the community to reflect the extreme views of sectarian interest or pressure group to a degree which might interfere with his fair assessment of the facts of the case or lead him to exert improper pressure on his fellow jurors.

A-285   6. In order to ascertain whether in exceptional circumstances of the above nature either of these factors might seriously influence a potential juror's impartial performance of his duties or his respecting the secrecy of evidence given *in camera*, it may be necessary to conduct a limited investigation of the panel. In general, such further investigation beyond one of criminal records made for disqualifications may only be made with the records of the police. However, a check may, additionally, be made against the records of the Security Service. No checks other than on these sources and no general inquiries are to be made save to the limited extent that they may be needed to confirm the identity of a juror about whom the initial check has raised serious doubts.

7. No further investigation, as described in paragraph 6 above, should be made save with the personal authority of the Attorney-General on the application of the Director of Public Prosecutions and such checks are hereafter referred to as "authorised checks". When a chief officer of police or the prosecutor has reason to believe that it is likely that an authorised check may be desirable and proper in accordance with these guidelines, he should refer the matter to the Director of Public Prosecutions. In those cases in which the Director of Public Prosecutions believes authorised checks are both proportionate and necessary, the Director will make an application to the Attorney-General.

8. The Director of Public Prosecutions will provide the Attorney-General with all relevant information in support of the requested authorised checks. The Attorney-General will consider personally the request and, if appropriate, authorise the check.

9. The result of any authorised check will be sent to the Director of Public Prosecutions. The Director will then decide, having regard to the matters set out in paragraph 5 above, what information ought to be brought to the attention of prosecuting counsel. The Director will also provide the Attorney-General with the result of the authorised check.

10. Although the right of stand by and the decision to authorise checks are wholly within the **A-286** discretion of the Attorney-General, when the Attorney-General has agreed to an authorised check being conducted, the Director of Public Prosecutions will write to the presiding judge for the area to advise him that this is being done.

11. No right of stand by should be exercised by counsel for the Crown on the basis of information obtained as a result of an authorised check save with the personal authority of the Attorney-General and unless the information is such as, having regard to the facts of the case and the offences charged, to afford strong reason for believing that a particular juror might be a security risk, be susceptible to improper approaches or be influenced in arriving at a verdict for the reasons given above.

12. Information revealed in the course of an authorised check must be considered in line with the normal rules on disclosure.

13. A record is to be kept by the Director of Public Prosecutions of the use made by counsel of the information passed to him and of the jurors stood by or challenged by the parties to the proceedings. A copy of this record is to be forwarded to the Attorney-General for the sole purpose of enabling him to monitor the operation of these guidelines.

14. No use of the information obtained as a result of an authorised check is to be made except as **A-287** may be necessary in direct relation to or arising out of the trial for which the check was authorised. The information may, however, be used for the prevention of crime or as evidence in a future criminal prosecution, save that material obtained from the Security Service may only be used in those circumstances with the authority of the Security Service.

D. Prosecution's Right of Stand By

For the background to these guidelines, see §§ 4-304, 4-305 in the main work. They were **A-288** updated in November, 2012.

Attorney-General's Guidelines on the Exercise by the Crown of its Right of Stand By, unreported, November 27, 2012

1. Although the law has long recognised the right of the Crown to exclude a member of a jury **A-289** panel from sitting as a juror by the exercise in open court of the right to request a stand by or, if necessary, by challenge for cause, it has been customary for those instructed to prosecute on behalf of the Crown to assert that right only sparingly and in exceptional circumstances. It is generally accepted that the prosecution should not use its right in order to influence the overall composition of a jury or with a view to tactical advantage.

2. The approach outlined above is founded on the principles that:

    (a) the members of a jury should be selected at random from the panel subject to any rule of law as to right of challenge by the defence, and

    (b) the Juries Act 1974 identifies those classes of persons who alone are disqualified from or ineligible for service on a jury. No other class of person may be treated as disqualified or ineligible.

3. The enactment by Parliament of section 118 of the Criminal Justice Act 1988 abolishing the right of defendants to remove jurors by means of peremptory challenge makes it appropriate that the Crown should assert its right to stand by only on the basis of clearly defined and restrictive criteria. Derogation from the principle that members of a jury should be selected at random should be permitted only where it is essential.

4. Primary responsibility for ensuring that an individual does not serve on a jury if he is not competent to discharge properly the duties of a juror rests with the appropriate court officer and, ultimately the trial judge. Current legislation provides, in sections 9 to 10 of the Juries Act 1974, fairly wide discretion to excuse, defer or discharge jurors.

5. The circumstances in which it would be proper for the Crown to exercise its right to stand by a member of a jury panel are:

> (a) where a jury check authorised in accordance with the Attorney-General's guidelines on jury checks reveals information justifying exercise of the right to stand by in accordance with paragraph 11 of the guidelines ... and the Attorney-General personally authorises the exercise of the right to stand by; or

> (b) where a person is about to be sworn as a juror who is manifestly unsuitable and the defence agree that, accordingly, the exercise by the prosecution of the right to stand by would be appropriate. An example of the sort of exceptional circumstances which might justify stand by is where it becomes apparent that, despite the provisions mentioned in paragraph 4 above, a juror selected for service to try a complex case is in fact illiterate.

E. CONSPIRACY TO DEFRAUD

A-290 The Attorney-General has issued guidance to prosecuting authorities in relation to charging a common law conspiracy to defraud instead of a substantive offence, contrary to the Fraud Act 2006, or a statutory conspiracy to commit a substantive offence, contrary to section 1 of the CLA 1977 (§ 33-2 in the main work); the prosecutor should consider (i) whether the conduct alleged falls within the ambit of a statutory offence, and (ii) whether such a charge or charges would adequately reflect the gravity of the alleged offending; as to (i), non-exhaustive examples of circumstances falling outside of the range of statutory offences, but within the ambit of the common law offence, are: (a) the dishonest obtaining of land or other property which cannot be stolen; (b) the dishonest infringement of another's right (*e.g.* the dishonest exploitation of another's patent); (c) an agreement involving an intention that the final offence be committed by someone outside the conspiracy; and (d) an agreement where the conspirators cannot be proved to have had the necessary degree of knowledge for the substantive offence to be perpetrated; as to (ii), prosecution for the common law offence may be more effective where the interests of justice can only be served by presenting an overall picture which could not be achieved by charging a series of substantive offences or statutory conspiracies (because of a large number of counts and/or the possibility of severed trials and evidence on one count being deemed inadmissible on another); where a case lawyer proposes to charge the common law offence, he must consider, and set out in the review note, how much such a charge would add to the amount of evidence likely to be called by the parties, the justification for using the charge, and why specific statutory offences are inadequate or otherwise inappropriate; a supervising lawyer experienced in fraud cases must also specifically approve the charge: *Attorney-General's guidance on the use of the common law offence of conspiracy to defraud*, unreported, January 9, 2007.

F. PROSECUTOR'S ROLE IN APPLICATIONS FOR WITNESS ANONYMITY ORDERS

A-291 On July 21, 2008, the Attorney-General issued guidelines on the overarching principles which a prosecutor must consider when deciding whether to apply for witness anonymity orders under the Criminal Evidence (Witness Anonymity) Act 2008 (now the Coroners and Justice Act 2009, ss.86–97 (§§ 8-151 *et seq.* in the main work)).

The guidance is in four parts (Part A (foreword), Part B (prosecutor's duties), Part C (applications by defendants) and Part D (appointment and role of special counsel)), and, to a large extent, highlights various provisions of the Act and restates elementary aspects of fairness at trial. Paragraph A2 makes clear that, given that the defendant's right to confront and challenge those who accuse him is an important aspect of a fair trial, making a witness anonymity order is a serious step which must only be taken where there are genuine grounds to believe that the conditions set out in the Act have been satisfied, which must be evaluated with care on the facts of each case. Paragraph B3 sets out the prosecutor's role, which prosecutors must approach in light of their overriding duties to be fair, independent and objective, and which includes a duty: (a) to examine with care and probe where appropriate, the material provided in support of the application and the evidential basis for it, and (b) to put before the court and to disclose to the defendant all material relevant to the application and the defence, including material which may undermine or qualify the prosecution case. Any such material is particularly relevant if credibility is in issue, for example, if there is a known link between the witness and defendant or a co-accused. Paragraph B4 explains that applications should only be authorised by prosecutors of an appropriately senior level. Paragraph D5 explains that a prosecutor making an application for an order must always be prepared to assist the court to consider whether the circumstances are such that exceptionally the appointment of special counsel may be called for, and, where appropriate, should draw to the attention of the court any aspect of the application which may be relevant to such appointment. Where the court decides to invite the Attorney-General to appoint special counsel, the prosecutor should (regardless of any steps taken by the court or any defendant) ensure that the Attorney-General's office is promptly notified and receives all information needed to take a decision as to whether to make such appointment. If special counsel is appointed, the prosecutor should then provide special counsel with open material made available to the accused regarding the application, and any other open material requested by special counsel. Closed or unredacted material which has been provided to the court should only be given to special counsel after open material has been provided and after special counsel has subsequently sought instructions from the defendant and his legal representative.

G. Plea Discussions in Cases of Serious or Complex Fraud

(1) Guidelines

On March 18, 2009, the Attorney-General issued guidelines setting out the process by which a   **A-292** prosecutor may discuss allegations of serious or complex fraud with a person whom he is prosecuting or expecting to prosecute.

ATTORNEY GENERAL'S GUIDELINES ON PLEA DISCUSSIONS IN CASES OF SERIOUS OR COMPLEX FRAUD

A. Foreword

A:1 These guidelines set out a process by which a prosecutor may discuss an allegation of serious   **A-293** or complex fraud with a person who he or she is prosecuting or expects to prosecute, or with that person's legal representative. They come into force on the 5th day of May 2009 and apply to plea discussions initiated on or after that date.

A:2 The guidelines will be followed by all prosecutors in England and Wales when conducting plea discussions in cases of serious or complex fraud. For the purposes of the guidelines, fraud means any financial, fiscal or commercial misconduct or corruption which is contrary to the criminal law. Fraud may be serious or complex if at least two of the following factors are present:

- the amount obtained or intended to be obtained is alleged to exceed £500,000;
- there is a significant international dimension;
- the case requires specialised knowledge of financial, commercial, fiscal or regulatory matters such as the operation of markets, banking systems, trusts or tax regimes;
- the case involves allegations of fraudulent activity against numerous victims;
- the case involves an allegation of substantial and significant fraud on a public body;
- the case is likely to be of widespread public concern;
- the alleged misconduct endangered the economic well-being of the United Kingdom, for example by undermining confidence in financial markets.

Taking account of these matters, it is for the prosecutor to decide whether or not a case is one of fraud, and whether or not it is serious or complex.

A:3 The decision whether a person should be charged with a criminal offence rests with the prosecutor. In selecting the appropriate charge or charges, the prosecutor applies principles set out in the Code for Crown Prosecutors ("the code"). Charges should reflect the seriousness and extent of the offending, give the court adequate sentencing powers and enable the case to be presented in a clear and simple way. The code also states that prosecutors should not go ahead with more charges to encourage a defendant to plead guilty to a few; equally, prosecutors should not charge a more serious offence to encourage a defendant to plead to a less serious one.

A:4 Once proceedings are instituted, the accused may plead guilty to all of the charges selected. If the defendant will plead guilty to some, but not all, of the charges or to a different, possibly less serious charge, the code states that a prosecutor is entitled to accept such pleas if he or she assesses that the court could still pass an adequate sentence. In taking these decisions the prosecutor also applies the Attorney General's Guidelines on the Acceptance of Pleas and the Prosecutor's Role in the Sentencing Exercise ("the acceptance of pleas guidelines") [*ante*, A-259 *et seq.*].

A:5 The purpose of plea discussions is to narrow the issues in the case with a view to reaching a just outcome at the earliest possible time, including the possibility of reaching an agreement about acceptable pleas of guilty and preparing a joint submission as to sentence.

A:6 The potential benefits of plea discussions are that:
- early resolution of the case may reduce the anxiety and uncertainty for victims and witnesses, and provide earlier clarity for accused persons who admit their guilt (subject to the court's power to reject the agreement);
- the issues in dispute may be narrowed so that even if the case proceeds to trial, it can be managed more efficiently in accordance with rule 3.2 of the Criminal Procedure Rules 2005. If pleas are agreed, litigation can be kept to a minimum.

A:7 Where plea discussions take place prior to the commencement of proceedings, the charges brought by the prosecutor will reflect those agreed, rather than those that the prosecutor would necessarily have preferred if no agreement had been reached. Also, any criminal investigation may not be complete when these discussions take place. For these reasons it is important that the procedures followed should command public and judicial confidence; that any agreement reached is reasonable, fair and just; that there are safeguards to ensure that defendants are not under improper pressure to make admissions; and that there are proper records of discussions that have taken place.

A:8 The guidelines are not intended to prevent or discourage existing practices by which prosecutors and prosecuting advocates discuss cases with defence legal representatives after charge, in order to narrow the issues or to agree a basis of plea. Neither do they affect the existing practice of judicial sentence indications at the plea and case management hearing or later in accordance with the guidance in *R. v. Goodyear* [2005] 2 Cr.App.R. 20 (§ 5-110 in the main work) (see also the acceptance of pleas guidelines). They complement, and do not detract from or replace, the code and the acceptance of pleas guidelines, or any other relevant guidance such as the Prosecutor's Pledge, the Victim's Charter and the Code of Practice for Victims of Crime.

A:9 Where a plea agreement is reached, it remains entirely a matter for the court to decide how to deal with the case.

B. General Principles

B:1 In conducting plea discussions and presenting a plea agreement to the court, the prosecutor must act openly, fairly and in the interests of justice.

B:2 Acting in the interests of justice means ensuring that the plea agreement reflects the seriousness and extent of the offending, gives the court adequate sentencing powers, and enables the court, the public and the victims to have confidence in the outcome. The prosecutor must consider carefully the impact of a proposed plea or basis of plea on the community and the victim, and on the prospects of successfully prosecuting any other person implicated in the offending. The prosecutor must not agree to a reduced basis of plea which is misleading, untrue or illogical.

B:3 Acting fairly means respecting the rights of the defendant and of any other person who is being or may be prosecuted in relation to the offending. The prosecutor must not put improper pressure on a defendant in the course of plea discussions, for example by exaggerating the strength of the case in order to persuade the defendant to plead guilty, or to plead guilty on a particular basis.

B:4 Acting openly means being transparent with the defendant, the victim and the court. The prosecutor must:
- ensure that a full and accurate record of the plea discussions is prepared and retained;
- ensure that the defendant has sufficient information to enable him or her to play an informed part in the plea discussions;
- communicate with the victim before accepting a reduced basis of plea, wherever it is practicable to do so, so that the position can be explained; and
- ensure that the plea agreement placed before the court fully and fairly reflects the matters agreed. The prosecutor must not agree additional matters with the defendant which are not recorded in the plea agreement and made known to the court.

C. Initiating Plea Discussions

When and with whom discussions should be initiated and conducted

C:1 Where he or she believes it advantageous to do so, the prosecutor may initiate plea discussions **A-295** with any person who is being prosecuted or investigated with a view to prosecution in connection with a serious or complex fraud, and who is legally represented. The prosecutor will not initiate plea discussions with a defendant who is not legally represented. If the prosecutor receives an approach from such a defendant, he or she may enter into discussions if satisfied that it is appropriate to do so.

C:2 Where proceedings have not yet been instituted, the prosecutor should not initiate plea discussions until he or she and the investigating officer are satisfied that the suspect's criminality is known. This will not usually be the case until after the suspect has been interviewed under caution.

C:3 The prosecutor should be alert to any attempt by the defendant to use plea discussions as a means of delaying the investigation or prosecution, and should not initiate or continue discussions where the defendant's commitment to the process is in doubt. The prosecutor should ensure that the position is preserved during plea discussions by, for example, restraining assets in anticipation of the making of a confiscation order. Where a defendant declines to take part in plea discussions, the prosecutor should not make a second approach unless there is a material change in circumstances.

Invitation letter

C:4 In order to initiate the plea discussions, the prosecutor will send the defendant's representatives a letter which:

- asks whether the defence wish to enter into discussions in accordance with these guidelines; and
- sets a deadline for a response from the defence.

Terms and conditions letter

C:5 Where the defence agree to engage in plea discussions, the prosecutor should send them a letter setting out the way in which the discussions will be conducted. This letter should deal with:

- the confidentiality of information provided by the prosecutor and defendant in the course of the plea discussions;
- the use which may be made by the prosecutor of information provided by the defendant; and
- the practical means by which the discussions will be conducted.

Confidentiality and use of information

C:6 In relation to confidentiality, the prosecutor will indicate that he or she intends to provide an undertaking to the effect that the fact that the defendant has taken part in the plea discussions, and any information provided by the defence in the course of the plea discussions will be treated as confidential and will not be disclosed to any other party other than for the purposes of the plea discussions and plea agreement (applying these guidelines), or as required by law. The undertaking will make it clear that the law in relation to the disclosure of unused material may require the prosecutor to provide information about the plea discussions to another defendant in criminal proceedings.

C:7 The prosecutor will require the defendant's legal representative to provide an undertaking to the effect that information provided by the prosecutor in the course of the plea discussions will be treated as confidential and will not be disclosed to any other party, other than for the purposes of the plea discussion and plea agreement or as required by law.

C:8 In relation to the use of information, the prosecutor will indicate that he or she intends to undertake not to rely upon the fact that the defendant has taken part in the plea discussions, or any information provided by the defendant in the course of the discussions, as evidence in any prosecution of that defendant for the offences under investigation, should the discussions fail. However, this undertaking will make it clear that the prosecutor is not prevented from:

- relying upon a concluded and signed plea agreement as confession evidence or as admissions;
- relying upon any evidence obtained from enquiries made as a result of the provision of information by the defendant;
- relying upon information provided by the defendant as evidence against him or her in any prosecution for an offence other than the fraud which is the subject of the plea discussion and any offence which is consequent upon it, such as money laundering; and
- relying upon information provided by the defendant in a prosecution of any other person for any offence (so far as the rules of evidence allow).

C:9 In exceptional circumstances the prosecutor may agree to different terms regarding the confidentiality and use of information. However, the prosecutor must not surrender the ability to rely upon a concluded and signed plea agreement as evidence against the defendant. The prosecutor may reserve the right to bring other charges (additional to those to which the defendant has indicated a willingness to plead guilty) in specific circumstances, for example if substantial new information comes to light at a later stage, the plea agreement is rejected by the court, or the defendant fails to honour the agreement.

C:10 Until the issues of confidentiality and use of information have been agreed to the satisfaction of both parties, and the agreement reflected in signed undertakings, the prosecutor must not continue with the substantive plea discussions.

D. Conducting Plea Discussions

Statement of case

A-296

D:1 Where plea discussions take place prior to proceedings being instituted, the prosecutor will provide a statement of case to the defence. This is a written summary of the nature of the allegation against the suspect and the evidence which has been obtained, or is expected to be obtained, to support it. The statement of case should include a list of the proposed charges. Material in support of the statement of case may also be provided, whether or not in the form of admissible evidence. However, the prosecutor is not obliged to reveal to the suspect all of the information or evidence supporting his case, provided that this does not mislead the suspect to his or her prejudice.

D:2 Where plea discussions are initiated after proceedings have been commenced, but before the prosecutor has provided the defence with a case summary or opening note, the prosecutor may provide a statement of case to assist the defendant in understanding the evidence and identifying the issues.

Unused material

D:3 These guidelines do not affect the prosecutor's existing duties in relation to the disclosure of unused material. Where plea discussions take place prior to the institution of proceedings, the prosecutor should ensure that the suspect is not misled as to the strength of the prosecution case. It will not usually be necessary to provide copies of unused material in order to do this.

Conducting and recording the discussions

D:4 Having provided the defence with the statement of case and supporting material, the parties will then be in a position to conduct the plea discussion proper. Whether this is done by correspondence, by face-to-face meetings or by a combination of the two is a matter for the parties to decide in the individual case.

D:5 It is essential that a full written record is kept of every key action and event in the discussion process, including details of every offer or concession made by each party, and the reasons for every decision taken by the prosecutor. Meetings between the parties should be minuted and the minutes agreed and signed. Particular care should be taken where the defendant is not legally represented. The prosecutor should only meet with a defendant who is not legally represented if the defendant agrees to the meeting being recorded, or to the presence of an independent third party.

Queen's evidence

D:6 If the defendant offers at any stage to provide information, or to give evidence about the criminal activities of others, any such offer will be dealt with in accordance with sections 71 to 75 of the Serious Organised Crime and Police Act 2005 ("SOCPA"), the judgment of the Court of Appeal in *R. v. P.*; *R. v. Blackburn* [2008] 2 Cr.App.R.(S.) 5 (§ 5-137 in the main work) and the guidance agreed and issued by the Director of Public Prosecutions, the Director of the Serious Fraud Office and the Director of Revenue and Customs Prosecutions.

Discussion of pleas

D:7 In deciding whether or not to accept an offer by the defendant to plead guilty, the prosecutor will follow sections 7 and 10 of the code relating to the selection of charges and the acceptance of guilty pleas. The prosecutor should ensure that:

- the charges reflect the seriousness and extent of the offending;
- they give the court adequate powers to sentence and impose appropriate post-conviction orders;
- they enable the case to be presented in a clear and simple way (bearing in mind that many cases of fraud are necessarily complex);

- the basis of plea enables the court to pass a sentence that matches the seriousness of the offending, particularly if there are aggravating features;
- the interests of the victim, and where possible any views expressed by the victim, are taken into account when deciding whether it is in the public interest to accept the plea; and
- the investigating officer is fully appraised of developments in the plea discussions and his or her views are taken into account.

D:8 In reaching an agreement on pleas, the parties should resolve any factual issues necessary to allow the court to sentence the defendant on a clear, fair and accurate basis. Before agreeing to proposed pleas, the prosecutor should satisfy him or herself that the full code test as set out in the code will be made out in respect of each charge. In considering whether the evidential stage of the test will be met, the prosecutor should assume that the offender will sign a plea agreement amounting to an admission to the charge.

Discussion of sentence

D:9 Where agreement is reached as to pleas, the parties should discuss the appropriate sentence with a view to presenting a joint written submission to the court. This document should list the aggravating and mitigating features arising from the agreed facts, set out any personal mitigation available to the defendant, and refer to any relevant sentencing guidelines or authorities. In the light of all of these factors, it should make submissions as to the applicable sentencing range in the relevant guideline. The prosecutor must ensure that the submissions are realistic, taking full account of all relevant material and considerations.

D:10 The prosecutor should bear in mind all of the powers of the court, and seek to include in the joint submission any relevant ancillary orders. It is particularly desirable that measures should be included that achieve redress for victims (such as compensation orders) and protection for the public (such as directors' disqualification orders, serious crime prevention orders or financial reporting orders).

D:11 Due regard should be had to the court's asset recovery powers and the desirability of using these powers both as a deterrent to others and as a means of preventing the defendant from benefiting from the proceeds of crime or funding future offending. The Proceeds of Crime Act 2002 requires the Crown Court to proceed to the making of a confiscation order against a convicted defendant who has benefited from his criminal conduct where the prosecutor asks the court to do so, or the court believes that it is appropriate to do so. Fraud is an acquisitive crime, and the expectation in a fraud case should be that a confiscation order will be sought by the prosecutor reflecting the full benefit to the defendant. However, in doing so it is open to the prosecutor to take a realistic view of the likely approach of the court to the determination of any points in dispute (such as the interest of a third party in any property).

D:12 In the course of the plea discussions the prosecutor must make it clear to the defence that the joint submission as to sentence (including confiscation) is not binding on the court.

Liaison with another prosecutor or regulator

D:13 The prosecutor may become aware that another prosecuting authority or regulatory body (either in England and Wales or elsewhere) has an interest in the defendant. The prosecutor should liaise with the other agency, in accordance with the Prosecutors' Convention and any other relevant agreement or guidance. The other agency may wish to take part in the plea discussions, or they may authorise the prosecutor to discuss with the defendant the matters which they are interested in, with a view to resolving all matters in one plea agreement. The prosecutor should warn the defendant that a plea agreement will not bind any other agency which is not a party to it.

E. The Written Plea Agreement

E:1 All matters agreed between the prosecutor and the defence must be reduced to writing as a **A-297** plea agreement and signed by both parties. The plea agreement will include:

- a list of the charges;
- a statement of the facts; and
- a declaration, signed by the defendant personally, to the effect that he or she accepts the stated facts and admits he or she is guilty of the agreed charges.

E:2 Any agreement under the SOCPA regarding the giving of assistance to the prosecutor by the defendant should be in a separate document accompanying the plea agreement.

E:3 Once a plea agreement is signed in a case where proceedings have not yet been commenced, the prosecutor will review the case in accordance with the code and, assuming the evidential stage of the full code test is satisfied on the basis of the signed plea agreement and the other available evidence, will arrange for proceedings to be instituted by summons or charge.

E:4 In advance of the defendant's first appearance in the Crown Court, the prosecutor should send the court sufficient material to allow the judge to understand the facts of the case and the history of the plea discussions, to assess whether the plea agreement is fair and in the interests of justice, and to decide the appropriate sentence. This will include:

- the signed plea agreement;
- a joint submission as to sentence and sentencing considerations;
- any relevant sentencing guidelines or authorities;
- all of the material provided by the prosecution to the defendant in the course of the plea discussions;
- any material provided by the defendant to the prosecution, such as documents relating to personal mitigation; and
- the minutes of any meetings between the parties and any correspondence generated in the plea discussions.

E:5 It will then be for the court to decide how to deal with the plea agreement. In particular, the court retains an absolute discretion as to whether or not it sentences in accordance with the joint submission from the parties.

F. Failure of Plea Discussions

A-298

F:1 There are several circumstances in which plea discussions may result in an outcome other than the defendant pleading guilty in accordance with a plea agreement. The prosecutor or the defendant may break off the discussions. They may be unable to reach an agreement. They may reach an agreement, but intervening events may lead the prosecutor to decide that proceedings should not be instituted. Proceedings may be instituted but the court may reject the plea agreement. The defendant may decline to plead guilty in accordance with the plea agreement, either as a result of a sentence indication given under the procedure set out in *R. v. Goodyear*, or for some other reason.

F:2 If any of these situations arises, the prosecutor may wish for further enquiries to be made with a view to bringing or completing proceedings against the defendant. If proceedings have already been instituted, the prosecutor will use the appropriate means to delay them - either discontinuing under section 23 or 23A of the Prosecution of Offences Act 1985 or (if the indictment has already been preferred) applying for an adjournment or stay of the proceedings. The prosecutor and the defendant's representatives will continue to be bound by the preliminary undertakings made in relation to the confidentiality and use of information provided in the course of the plea discussions.

F:3 Where plea discussions have broken down for any reason, it will be rare that the prosecutor will wish to re-open them, but he or she may do so if there is a material change in circumstances which warrants it.

(2) Practice

A-299

See paragraphs 15 to 27 of *Criminal Practice Direction VII (Sentencing) B, post*, Appendix B-154 *et seq.*

(3) Authorities

A-300

As to the limitations on prosecuting authorities' power to enter into agreements (with overseas authorities or a potential accused) as to how a case should be disposed of, see *R. v. Innospec Ltd*, § 1-369 in the main work. As to this case, see also § 5-804 in the main work.

In *R. v. Dougall* [2011] 1 Cr.App.R.(S.) 37, CA, it was said that a joint submission as to sentence pursuant to the Attorney-General's Guidelines on Plea Discussions in Cases of Serious or Complex Fraud, *ante*, should recognise that it is the court alone that decides on sentence, should avoid advocacy of a particular outcome, and should confine itself to the appropriate range within which it is said the sentence should fall. As to this case, see also § 5-138 in the main work.

H. Asset Recovery Powers of Prosecuting Authorities

A-301

The Attorney-General and the Home Secretary have issued joint guidance under section 2A of the PCA 2002 to the National Crime Agency, the DPP, the Director of Revenue and Customs Prosecutions, the Director of the Serious Fraud Office and the DPP for Northern Ireland directing them to consider using their civil asset recovery powers under the 2002 Act wherever proceeds of crime have been identified but it is not feasible to secure a conviction, or a conviction has been secured but no confiscation order made (para. 2). They must also consider whether the public interest might be better served by using these powers, rather than by instituting a criminal investigation or prosecution, whilst applying the principle that a criminal disposal will generally make the best contribution to the reduction of crime (para. 3). Paragraph 4 states that the factors listed in the Code for Crown Prosecutors (*post*, Appendix E-6) as being relevant to the question whether a prosecution would be in the public interest might also be relevant when considering at any stage whether or not the civil recovery powers should be used; but it is emphasised that a potential defendant should not be able to escape an appropriate prosecution by the simple device of agreeing to a civil recovery order. Paragraph 5 contains a non-exhaustive list of circumstances in which use of the powers might be appropriate because it is not feasible to secure a conviction and paragraph 6 contains an equivalent list for where a conviction is feasible but where the public interest might be better served by use of these powers. Paragraph 8 sets out the ways in which the relevant authorities should seek to minimise any potential prejudice to a related or potential criminal investigation or proceedings, including through the disclosure of relevant information. Paragraph 9 confirms that the guidance does not prohibit (i) a criminal investigation being carried out by a law enforcement authority at the same time as a civil recovery and/or a tax investigation; (ii) civil recovery and/or tax proceedings being instituted where a criminal investigation by a law enforcement authority is being carried out at the same time into unrelated criminality (subjectto the duty set out in para. 8, *ante*); or (iii) criminal proceedings being instituted or carried on by a prosecuting authority at the same time as a civil recovery and/or tax investigation is being carried out. However, paragraph 10 prohibits in all circumstances criminal and civil/tax proceedings being carried on at the same time in relation to the same criminality. Where criminal proceedings have been stayed by a court, or cannot progress (*e.g.* because the defendant has absconded), they are not being "carried on" for the purposes of this prohibition. Paragraph 11 sets out the circumstances in which a relevant authority may agree to accept a reduced sum in satisfaction of a civil recovery claim. For the full text of the guidance, see http://www.attorneygen eral.gov.uk/Publications/Pages/AttorneyGeneralsGuidelines.aspx.

APPENDIX B
Criminal Practice Directions

I. CRIMINAL PRACTICE DIRECTIONS (2015)

CPD I General Matters A

A.1 [*Recites power to make practice directions (Courts Act 2003, s.74).*] **B-1**

A.2 These practice directions replace the *Criminal Practice Directions* (2013) [2013] 1 W.L.R. 3164 (as amended).

A.3 Annexes D and E to the *Consolidated Criminal Practice Direction* [2002] 1 W.L.R. 2870, as amended, which set out forms for use in connection with the Criminal Procedure Rules, remain in force. See also para. I 5A of these practice directions.

A.4 These practice directions supplement ... the Criminal Procedure Rules, and include other directions about practice and procedure in the courts to which they apply. They are to be known as the *Criminal Practice Directions* 2015. They come into force on 5th October, 2015. They apply to all cases in all the criminal courts of England and Wales from that date.

A.5, A.6 [*Brief explanation of layout.*]

CPD I General Matters 1A: The Overriding Objective

1A.1 The presumption of innocence and an adversarial process are essential features of English **B-2** and Welsh legal tradition and of the defendant's right to a fair trial. But it is no part of a fair trial that questions of guilt and innocence should be determined by procedural manoeuvres. On the contrary, fairness is best served when the issues between the parties are identified as early and as clearly as possible. As Lord Justice Auld noted, a criminal trial is not a game under which a guilty defendant should be provided with a sporting chance. It is a search for truth in accordance with the twin principles that the prosecution must prove its case and that a defendant is not obliged to inculpate himself, the object being to convict the guilty and acquit the innocent.

1A.2 Further, it is not just for a party to obstruct or delay the preparation of a case for trial in order to secure some perceived procedural advantage, or to take unfair advantage of a mistake by someone else. If courts allow that to happen it damages public confidence in criminal justice. The rules and the practice directions, taken together, make it clear that courts must not allow it to happen.

CPD I General Matters 3A: Case Management

3A.1 CrimPR 1.1(2)(e) requires that cases be dealt with efficiently and expeditiously. CrimPR 3.2 **B-3** requires the court to further the overriding objective by actively managing the case, for example:

  a) when dealing with an offence which is triable only on indictment the court must ask the defendant whether he or she intends to plead guilty at the Crown Court (CrimPR 9.7(5));

  b) on a guilty plea, the court must pass sentence at the earliest opportunity, in accordance with CrimPR 24.11(9)(a) (magistrates' courts) and 25.16(7)(a) (the Crown Court).

3A.2 Given these duties, magistrates' courts and the Crown Court therefore will proceed as described in paragraphs 3A.3 to 3A.28 below. The parties will be expected to have prepared in accordance with CrimPR 3.3(1) to avoid unnecessary and wasted hearings. They will be expected to have communicated with each other by the time of the first hearing; to report to the court on that communication at the first hearing; and to continue thereafter to communicate with each other and with the court officer, in accordance with CrimPR 3.3(2).

3A.3 There is a Preparation for Effective Trial form for use in the magistrates' courts, and a Plea and Trial Preparation Hearing form for use in the Crown Court, each of which must be used as appropriate in connection with CrimPR, Pt 3: see para. 5A.2 ... . Versions of those forms in pdf and Word, together with guidance notes, are available on the Criminal Procedure Rules pages of the Ministry of Justice website.

Case progression and trial preparation in magistrates' courts

3A.4 CrimPR 8.3 [§ 12-144 in the main work] applies in all cases and requires the prosecutor to **B-4** serve:

  i. a summary of the circumstances of the offence;

  ii. any account given by the defendant in interview, whether contained in that summary or in another document;

iii. any written witness statement or exhibit that the prosecutor then has available and considers material to plea or to the allocation of the case for trial or sentence;

iv. a list of the defendant's criminal record, if any; and

v. any available statement of the effect of the offence on a victim, a victim's family or others.

The details must include sufficient information to allow the defendant and the court at the first hearing to take an informed view:

i. on plea;

ii. on venue for trial (if applicable);

iii. for the purposes of case management; or

iv. for the purposes of sentencing (including committal for sentence, if applicable).

Defendant in custody

B-5

3A.5 If the defendant has been detained in custody after being charged with an offence which is indictable only or triable either way, at the first hearing a magistrates' court will proceed at once with the allocation of the case for trial, where appropriate, and, if so required, with the sending of the defendant to the Crown Court for trial. The court will be expected to ask for and record any indication of plea and issues for trial to assist the Crown Court.

3A.6 If the offence charged is triable only summarily, or if at that hearing the case is allocated for summary trial, the court will forthwith give such directions as are necessary, either (on a guilty plea) to prepare for sentencing, or for a trial.

Defendant on bail

B-6

3A.7 If the defendant has been released on bail after being charged, the case must be listed for the first hearing 14 days after charge, or the next available court date thereafter when the prosecutor anticipates a guilty plea which is likely to be sentenced in the magistrates' court. In cases where there is an anticipated not guilty plea or the case is likely to be sent or committed to the Crown Court for either trial or sentence, then it must be listed for the first hearing 28 days after charge or the next available court date thereafter.

Guilty plea in the magistrates' courts

B-7

3A.8 Where a defendant pleads guilty or indicates a guilty plea in a magistrates' court the court should consider whether a pre-sentence report – a stand down report if possible – is necessary.

Guilty plea in the Crown Court

B-8

3A.9 Where a magistrates' court is considering committal for sentence or the defendant has indicated an intention to plead guilty in a matter which is to be sent to the Crown Court, the magistrates' court should request the preparation of a pre-sentence report for the Crown Court's use if the magistrates' court considers that:

(a) there is a realistic alternative to a custodial sentence; or

(b) the defendant may satisfy the criteria for classification as a dangerous offender; or

(c) there is some other appropriate reason for doing so.

3A.10 When a magistrates' court sends a case to the Crown Court for trial and the defendant indicates an intention to plead guilty at the Crown Court, then that magistrates' court must set a date for a Plea and Trial Preparation Hearing at the Crown Court, in accordance with CrimPR 9.7(5)(a)(i) [§ 1-117g in the main work].

Case sent for Crown Court trial: no indication of guilty plea

B-9

3A.11 In any case sent to the Crown Court for trial, other than one in which the defendant indicates an intention to plead guilty, the magistrates' court must set a date for a Plea and Trial Preparation Hearing, in accordance with CrimPR 9.7(5)(a)(ii). The Plea and Trial Preparation Hearing must be held within 28 days of sending, unless the standard directions of the presiding judges of the circuit direct otherwise. Paragraph 3A.16 below additionally applies to the arrangements for such hearings. A magistrates' court may give other directions appropriate to the needs of the case, in accordance with CrimPR 3.5(3) [§ 4-116 in the main work], and in accordance with any standard directions issued by the presiding judges of the circuit.

Defendant on bail: anticipated not guilty plea

B-10

3A.12 Where the defendant has been released on bail after being charged, and where the prosecutor does not anticipate a guilty plea at the first hearing in a magistrates' court, then it is essential that the initial details of the prosecution case that are provided for that first hearing are sufficient to assist the court, in order to identify the real issues and to give appropriate directions for an effective trial (regardless of whether the trial is to be heard in the magistrates' court or the Crown Court). In these circumstances, unless there is good reason not to do so, the prosecution should make available the following material in advance of the first hearing in the magistrates' court:

> (a) a summary of the circumstances of the offence(s) including a summary of any account given by the defendant in interview;
>
> (b) statements and exhibits that the prosecution has identified as being of importance for the purpose of plea or initial case management, including any relevant CCTV that would be relied upon at trial and any streamlined forensic report;
>
> (c) details of witness availability, as far as they are known at that hearing;
>
> (d) defendant's criminal record;
>
> (e) victim personal statements if provided;
>
> (f) an indication of any medical or other expert evidence that the prosecution is likely to adduce in relation to a victim or the defendant;
>
> (g) any information as to special measures, bad character or hearsay, where applicable.

3A.13 In addition to the material required by CrimPR, Pt 8, the information required by the Preparation for Effective Trial form must be available to be submitted at the first hearing, and the parties must complete that form, in accordance with the guidance published with it. Where there is to be a contested trial in a magistrates' court, that form includes directions and a timetable that will apply in every case unless the court otherwise orders.

3A.14 Nothing in paragraph 3A.12-3A.13 shall preclude the court from taking a plea pursuant to CrimPR 3.9(2)(b) [§ 4-117 in the main work] at the first hearing and for the court to case manage as far as practicable under Part 3 CrimPR.

Exercise of magistrates' court's powers

3A.15 In accordance with CrimPR 9.1, sections 49, 51(13) and 51A(11) of the CDA 1998 [§§ 1-25, **B-11** 1-26 in the main work], and sections 17E, 18(5) and 24D of the MCA 1980 [§§ 1-92 *et seq.* in the main work] a single justice can:

> a) allocate and send for trial;
>
> b) take an indication of a guilty plea (but not pass sentence);
>
> c) take a not guilty plea and give directions for the preparation of trial including:
>> i. timetable for the proceedings;
>> ii. the attendance of the parties;
>> iii. the service of documents;
>> iv. the manner in which evidence is to be given.

Case progression and trial preparation in the Crown Court

Plea and Trial Preparation Hearing

3A.16 In a case in which a magistrates' court has directed a Plea and Trial Preparation Hearing, **B-12** the period which elapses between sending for trial and the date of that hearing must be consistent within each circuit. In every case, the time allowed for the conduct of the Plea and Trial Preparation Hearing must be sufficient for effective trial preparation. It is expected in every case that an indictment will be lodged at least 7 days in advance of the hearing. Please see the Note to the Practice Direction.

3A.17 In a case in which the defendant, not having done so before, indicates an intention to plead guilty to his representative after being sent for trial but before the Plea and Trial Preparation Hearing, the defence representative will notify the Crown Court and the prosecution forthwith. The court will ensure there is sufficient time at the Plea and Trial Preparation Hearing for sentence and a judge should at once request the preparation of a pre-sentence report if it appears to the court that either:

> (a) there is a realistic alternative to a custodial sentence; or
>
> (b) the defendant may satisfy the criteria for classification as a dangerous offender; or
>
> (c) there is some other appropriate reason for doing so.

3A.18 If at the Plea and Trial Preparation Hearing the defendant pleads guilty and no presentence report has been prepared, if possible the court should obtain a stand down report.

3A.19 Where the defendant was remanded in custody after being charged and was sent for trial without initial details of the prosecution case having been served, then at least 7 days before the Plea and Trial Preparation Hearing the prosecutor should serve, as a minimum, the material identified in paragraph 3A.12 above. If at the Plea and Trial Preparation Hearing the defendant does not plead guilty, the court will be expected to identify the issues in the case and give appropriate directions for an effective trial. Please see the Note to the Practice Direction.

3A.20 At the Plea and Trial Preparation Hearing, in addition to the material required by paragraph 3A.12 above, the prosecutor must serve sufficient evidence to enable the court to case manage effectively without the need for a further case management hearing, unless the case falls within paragraph 3A.21. In addition, the information required by the Plea and Trial Preparation Hearing form must be available to the court at that hearing, and it must have been discussed between the parties in advance. The prosecutor must provide details of the availability of likely prosecution witnesses so that a trial date can immediately be arranged if the defendant does not plead guilty.

Further case management hearing

B-13   3A.21 In accordance with CrimPR 3.13(1)(c) [§ 4-120a in the main work], after the Plea and Trial Preparation Hearing there will be no further case management hearing before the trial unless:

> (i) a condition listed in that rule is met; and
> (ii) the court so directs, in order to further the overriding objective.

The directions to be given at the Plea and Trial Preparation Hearing therefore may include a direction for a further case management hearing, but usually will do so only in one of the following cases:

> (a) Class 1 cases;
> (b) Class 2 cases which carry a maximum penalty of 10 years or more;
> (c) cases involving death by driving (whether dangerous or careless), or death in the workplace;
> (d) cases involving a vulnerable witness;
> (e) cases in which the defendant is a child or otherwise under a disability, or requires special assistance;
> (f) cases in which there is a corporate or unrepresented defendant;
> (g) cases in which the expected trial length is such that a further case management hearing is desirable and any case in which the trial is likely to last longer than four weeks;
> (h) cases in which expert evidence is to be introduced;
> (i) cases in which a party requests a hearing to enter a plea;
> (j) cases in which an application to dismiss or stay has been made;
> (k) cases in which arraignment has not taken place, whether because of an issue relating to fitness to plead, or abuse of process or sufficiency of evidence, or for any other reason;
> (l) cases in which there are likely to be linked criminal and care directions in accordance with the 2013 Protocol.

3A.22 If a further case management hearing is directed, a defendant in custody will not usually be expected to attend in person, unless the court otherwise directs.

Compliance hearing

B-14   3A.23 If a party fails to comply with a case management direction, that party may be required to attend the court to explain the failure. Unless the court otherwise directs a defendant in custody will not usually be expected to attend. See paras 3A.26-3A.28 below.

Conduct of case progression hearings

B-15   3A.24 As far as possible, case progression should be managed without a hearing in the courtroom, using electronic communication in accordance with CrimPR 3.5(2)(d) [§ 4-116 in the main work]. Court staff should be nominated to conduct case progression as part of their role, in accordance with CrimPR 3.4(2) [§ 4-115 in the main work]. To aid effective communication the prosecution and defence representative should notify the court and provide details of who shall be dealing with the case at the earliest opportunity.

Completion of effective trial monitoring form

B-16   3A.25 It is imperative that the Effective Trial Monitoring form (as devised and issued by Her Majesty's Courts and Tribunals Service) is accurately completed by the parties for all cases that have been listed for trial. Advocates must engage with the process by providing the relevant details and completing the form.

Compliance courts

B-17   3A.26 To ensure effective compliance with directions of the courts made in accordance with the

Criminal Procedure Rules and the overriding objective, courts should maintain a record whenever a party to the proceedings has failed to comply with a direction made by the court. The parties may have to attend a hearing to explain any lack of compliance.

3A.27 These hearings may be conducted by live link facilities or via other electronic means, as the court may direct.

3A.28 It will be for the presiding judges, resident judge and justices' clerks to decide locally how often compliance courts should be held, depending on the scale and nature of the problem at each court centre.

Note to the practice direction

In 3A.16 and 3A.19 the reference to "at least 7 days" in advance of the hearing is necessitated by **B-18** the fact that, for the time being, different circuits have different timescales for the Plea and Trial Preparation Hearing. Had this not been so, the paragraphs would have been drafted forward from the date of sending rather than backwards from the date of the Plea and Trial Preparation Hearing.

CPD I General Matters 3B: Pagination and Indexing of Served Evidence

3B.1 The following directions apply to matters before the Crown Court, where— **B-19**
    (a) there is an application to prefer a bill of indictment in relation to the case;
    (b) a person is sent for trial under section 51 of the CDA 1998 ... , to the service of copies of the documents containing the evidence on which the charge or charges are based under paragraph 1 of Schedule 3 to that Act; or
    (c) a defendant wishes to serve evidence.
3B.2 A party who serves documentary evidence in the Crown Court should:
    (a) paginate each page in any bundle of statements and exhibits sequentially;
    (b) provide an index to each bundle of statements produced including the following information:
        (i) the name of the case;
        (ii) the author of each statement;
        (iii) the start page number of the witness statement;
        (iv) the end page number of the witness statement;
    (c) provide an index to each bundle of documentary and pictorial exhibits produced, including the following information:
        (i) the name of the case;
        (ii) the exhibit reference;
        (iii) a short description of the exhibit;
        (iv) the start page number of the exhibit;
        (v) the end page number of the exhibit;
        (vi) where possible, the name of the person producing the exhibit should be added.
3B.3 Where additional documentary evidence is served, a party should paginate following on from the last page of the previous bundle or in a logical and sequential manner. A party should also provide notification of service of any amended index.

3B.4 The prosecution must ensure that the running total of the pages of prosecution evidence is easily identifiable on the most recent served bundle of prosecution evidence.

3B.5 For the purposes of these directions, the number of pages of prosecution evidence served on the court includes all (a) witness statements; (b) documentary and pictorial exhibits; (c) records of interviews with the defendant; and (d) records of interviews with other defendants which form part of the served prosecution documents or which are included in any notice of additional evidence, but does not include any document provided on CD-ROM or by other means of electronic communication.

CPD I General Matters 3C: Abuse of Process Stay Applications

3C.1 In all cases where a defendant in the Crown Court proposes to make an application to stay **B-20** an indictment on the ground of abuse of process, written notice of such application must be given to the prosecuting authority and to any co-defendant as soon as practicable after the defendant becomes aware of the grounds for doing so and not later than 14 days before the date fixed or warned for trial ("the relevant date"). Such notice must (a) give the name of the case and the indictment number; (b) state the fixed date or the warned date as appropriate; (c) specify the nature of the application; (d) set out in numbered sub-paragraphs the grounds on which the application is to be made; (e) be copied to the chief listing officer at the court centre where the case is due to be heard.

3C.2 Any co-defendant who wishes to make a like application must give a like notice not later than seven days before the relevant date, setting out any additional grounds relied upon.

3C.3 In relation to such applications, the following automatic directions shall apply: (a) the advocate for the applicant(s) must lodge with the court and serve on all other parties a skeleton argument in support of the application, at least five clear working days before the relevant date; if reference is to be made to any document not in the existing trial documents, a paginated and indexed bundle of such documents is to be provided with the skeleton argument; (b) the advocate for the prosecution must lodge with the court and serve on all other parties a responsive skeleton argument at least two clear working days before the relevant date, together with a supplementary bundle if appropriate.

3C.4 All skeleton arguments must specify any propositions of law to be advanced (together with the authorities relied on in support, with paragraph references to passages relied upon), and, where appropriate, include a chronology of events and a list of *dramatis personae*. In all instances where reference is made to a document, the reference in the trial documents or supplementary bundle is to be given.

3C.5 The above time limits are minimum time limits. In appropriate cases the court will order longer lead times. To this end in all cases where defence advocates are, at the time of the preliminary hearing or as soon as practicable after the case has been sent, considering the possibility of an abuse of process application, this must be raised with the judge dealing with the matter, who will order a different timetable if appropriate, and may wish, in any event, to give additional directions about the conduct of the application. If the trial judge has not been identified, the matter should be raised with the resident judge.

CPD I General Matters 3D: Vulnerable People in the Courts

3D.1 In respect of eligibility for special measures, "vulnerable" and "intimidated" witnesses are defined in sections 16 and 17 of the YJCEA 1999 ...; "vulnerable" includes those under 18 years of age and people with a mental disorder or learning disability; a physical disorder or disability; or who are likely to suffer fear or distress in giving evidence because of their own circumstances or those relating to the case.

3D.2 However, many other people giving evidence in a criminal case, whether as a witness or defendant, may require assistance: the court is required to take "every reasonable step" to encourage and facilitate the attendance of witnesses and to facilitate the participation of any person, including the defendant (r.3.9(3)(a) and (b) [§ 4-117 in the main work]). This includes enabling a witness or defendant to give their best evidence, and enabling a defendant to comprehend the proceedings and engage fully with his defence. The pre-trial and trial process should, so far as necessary, be adapted to meet those ends. Regard should be had to the welfare of a young defendant as required by section 44 of the CYPA 1933 [§ 5-64 in the main work], and generally to Parts 1 and 3 of the Criminal Procedure Rules ... .

3D.3 Under Part 3 of the rules, the court must identify the needs of witnesses at an early stage (r.3.2(2)(b)) and may require the parties to identify arrangements to facilitate the giving of evidence and participation in the trial (r.3.11(c)(iv) and (v), [§ 4-118 in the main work]). There are various statutory special measures that the court may utilise to assist a witness in giving evidence. Part 18 of the rules [§§ 8-110 *et seq.* in the main work] gives the procedures to be followed. Courts should note the "primary rule" which requires the court to give a direction for a special measure to assist a child witness or qualifying witness and that in such cases an application to the court is not required (r.18.9).

3D.4 Court of Appeal decisions on this subject include ... *R. v. Cox* [§ 4-86 in the main work], *R. v. Wills* [§ 8-217a in the main work], and *R. v. E.* [§ 8-217a in the main work].

3D.5 In *R. v. Wills*, the court endorsed the approach taken by the report of the Advocacy Training Council (ATC) *"Raising the Bar: the Handling of Vulnerable Witnesses, Victims and Defendants in Court"* (20ll). The report includes and recommends the use of "toolkits" to assist advocates as they prepare to question vulnerable people at court: http://www.advocacytrainingcouncil.org/vulnerable-witnesses/r aising-the-bar.

3D.6 Further toolkits are available through the advocate's gateway which is managed by the ATC's management committee: http://www.theadvocatesgateway.org/.

3D.7 These toolkits represent best practice. Advocates should consult and follow the relevant guidance whenever they prepare to question a young or otherwise vulnerable witness or defendant. Judges may find it helpful to refer advocates to this material and to use the toolkits in case management.

3D.8 "Achieving Best Evidence in Criminal Proceedings" (Ministry of Justice 2011) [§ 8-91 in the main work] describes best practice in preparation for the investigative interview and trial: http://www. cps.gov.uk/publications/docs/best_evidence_in_criminal_proceedings.pdf.

CPD I General Matters 3E: Ground Rules Hearings to Plan the Questioning of a Vulnerable Witness or Defendant

3E.1 The judiciary is responsible for controlling questioning. Over-rigorous or repetitive cross-examination of a child or vulnerable witness should be stopped. Intervention by the judge, magistrates or intermediary (if any) is minimised if questioning, taking account of the individual's communication needs, is discussed in advance and ground rules are agreed and adhered to. **B-22**

3E.2 Discussion of ground rules is required in all intermediary trials where they must be discussed between the judge or magistrates, advocates and intermediary before the witness gives evidence. The intermediary must be present but is not required to take the oath (the intermediary's declaration is made just before the witness gives evidence).

3E.3 Discussion of ground rules is good practice, even if no intermediary is used, in all young witness cases and in other cases where a witness or defendant has communication needs. Discussion before the day of trial is preferable to give advocates time to adapt their questions to the witness's needs. It may be helpful for a trial practice note of boundaries to be created at the end of the discussion. The judge may use such a document in ensuring that the agreed ground rules are complied with.

3E.4 All witnesses, including the defendant and defence witnesses, should be enabled to give the best evidence they can. In relation to young and/or vulnerable people, this may mean departing radically from traditional cross-examination. The form and extent of appropriate cross-examination will vary from case to case. For adult non-vulnerable witnesses an advocate will usually put his case so that the witness will have the opportunity of commenting upon it and/or answering it. When the witness is young or otherwise vulnerable, the court may dispense with the normal practice and impose restrictions on the advocate "putting his case" where there is a risk of a young or otherwise vulnerable witness failing to understand, becoming distressed or acquiescing to leading questions. Where limitations on questioning are necessary and appropriate, they must be clearly defined. The judge has a duty to ensure that they are complied with and should explain them to the jury and the reasons for them. If the advocate fails to comply with the limitations, the judge should give relevant directions to the jury when that occurs and prevent further questioning that does not comply with the ground rules settled upon in advance. Instead of commenting on inconsistencies during cross-examination, following discussion between the judge and the advocates, the advocate or judge may point out important inconsistencies after (instead of during) the witness's evidence. The judge should also remind the jury of these during summing up. The judge should be alert to alleged inconsistencies that are not in fact inconsistent, or are trivial.

3E.5 If there is more than one defendant, the judge should not permit each advocate to repeat the questioning of a vulnerable witness. In advance of the trial, the advocates should divide the topics between them, with the advocate for the first defendant leading the questioning, and the advocate(s) for the other defendant(s) asking only ancillary questions relevant to their client's case, without repeating the questioning that has already taken place on behalf of the other defendant(s).

3E.6 In particular in a trial of a sexual offence, "body maps" should be provided for the witness's use. If the witness needs to indicate a part of the body, the advocate should ask the witness to point to the relevant part on the body map. In sex cases, judges should not permit advocates to ask the witness to point to a part of the witness's own body. Similarly, photographs of the witness's body should not be shown around the court while the witness is giving evidence.

CPD I General Matters 3F: Intermediaries

3F.1 Intermediaries are communication specialists (not supporters or expert witnesses) whose role is to facilitate communication between the witness and the court, including the advocates. Intermediaries are independent of the parties and owe their duty to the court (see *Registered Intermediaries Procedural Guidance Manual*, Ministry of Justice, 2012): http://www.cps.gov.uk/publicatio ns/docs/RI_ProceduralGuidanceManual_2012.pdf **B-23**

3F.2 Intermediaries for witnesses, with the exception of defendants, are one of the special measures available under the YJCEA 1999 and Part 18 of the Criminal Procedure Rules.

3F.3 There is currently no statutory provision in force for intermediaries for defendants. Section 104 of the Coroners and Justice Act 2009 ... creates a new section 33BA of the YJCEA 1999 [§ 8-101 in the main work]. This will provide an intermediary to an eligible defendant only while giving evidence. A court may use its inherent powers to appoint an intermediary to assist the defendant's communication at trial (either solely when giving evidence or throughout the trial) and, where necessary, in preparation for trial: *R. (A.S.) v. Great Yarmouth Youth Court* [2012] Crim. L.R. 478 ; *R. v. H. (Special measures)* [§ 8-72 in the main work]; *R. (C.) v. Sevenoaks Youth Court* [§§ 4-162, 8-72 in the main work]; *R. (D.) v. Camberwell Green Youth Court* [§§ 8-72, 8-80 in the main work]; *R. (T.P.) v. West London Youth Court* [§§ 4-86, 4-162 in the main work].

3F.4 Ministry of Justice regulation only applies to registered intermediaries appointed for prosecution and defence witnesses through its witness intermediary scheme. All defendant intermediaries — professionally qualified or otherwise — are "non-registered" in this context, even though they may be a registered intermediary in respect of witnesses. Even where a judge concludes he has a common law power to direct the provision of an intermediary, the direction will be ineffective if no intermediary can be identified for whom funding would be available.

3F.5 Assessment should be considered if a child or young person under 18 seems unlikely to be able to recognise a problematic question or, even if able to do so, may be reluctant to say so to a questioner in a position of authority. Studies suggest that the majority of young witnesses, across all age groups, fall into one or other of these categories. For children aged 11 years and under in particular, there should be a presumption that an intermediary assessment is appropriate. Once the child's individual requirements are known and discussed at the ground rules hearing, the intermediary may agree that his or her presence is not needed for the trial.

3F.6 In the absence of an intermediary for the defendant, trials should not be stayed where an asserted unfairness can be met by the trial judge adapting the trial process with appropriate and necessary caution (*R. v. Cox, ante*). This includes setting ground rules for all witness testimony to help the defendant follow proceedings; for example, directing that all witness evidence be adduced by simple questions, with witnesses asked to answer in short sentences; and short periods of evidence, followed by breaks to enable the defendant to relax and for counsel to summarise the evidence for him and to take further instructions.

Photographs of court facilities

B-24

3F.7 Resident judges in the Crown Court or the chief clerk or other responsible person in the magistrates' courts should, in consultation with HMCTS managers responsible for court security matters, develop a policy to govern under what circumstances photographs or other visual recordings may be made of court facilities, such as a live link room, to assist vulnerable or child witnesses to familiarise themselves with the setting, so as to be enabled to give their best evidence. For example, a photograph may provide a helpful reminder to a witness whose court visit has taken place sometime earlier. Resident judges should tend to permit photographs to be taken for this purpose by intermediaries or supporters, subject to whatever restrictions the resident judge or responsible person considers to be appropriate, having regard to the security requirements of the court.

CPD I General Matters 3G: Vulnerable Defendants

Before the trial, sentencing or appeal

B-25

3G.1 If a vulnerable defendant, especially one who is young, is to be tried jointly with one who is not, the court should consider at the plea and case management hearing, or at a case management hearing in a magistrates' court, whether the vulnerable defendant should be tried on his own, but should only so order if satisfied that a fair trial cannot be achieved by use of appropriate special measures or other support for the defendant. If a vulnerable defendant is tried jointly with one who is not, the court should consider whether any of the modifications set out in this direction should apply in the circumstances of the joint trial and, so far as practicable, make orders to give effect to any such modifications.

3G.2 It may be appropriate to arrange that a vulnerable defendant should visit, out of court hours and before the trial, sentencing or appeal hearing, the courtroom in which that hearing is to take place so that he can familiarise him or herself with it.

3G.3 Where an intermediary is being used to help the defendant to communicate at court, the intermediary should accompany the defendant on his or her pre-trial visit. The visit will enable the defendant to familiarise him or herself with the layout of the court, and may include matters such as: where the defendant will sit, either in the dock or otherwise; court officials (what their roles are and where they sit); who else might be in the court, for example those in the public gallery and press box; the location of the witness box; basic court procedure; and the facilities available in the court.

3G.4 If the defendant's use of the live link is being considered, he or she should have an opportunity to have a practice session.

3G.5 If any case against a vulnerable defendant has attracted or may attract widespread public or media interest, the assistance of the police should be enlisted to try and ensure that the defendant is not, when attending the court, exposed to intimidation, vilification or abuse. Section 41 of the CJA

1925 prohibits the taking of photographs of defendants and witnesses (among others) in the court building or in its precincts, or when entering or leaving those precincts. A direction reminding media representatives of the prohibition may be appropriate. The court should also be ready at this stage, if it has not already done so, where relevant to make a reporting restriction under section 39 of the CYPA 1933 or, on an appeal to the Crown Court from a youth court, to remind media representatives of the application of section 49 of that Act.

3G.6 The provisions of the practice direction accompanying Part 6 should be followed.

The trial, sentencing or appeal hearing

3G.7 Subject to the need for appropriate security arrangements, the proceedings should, if **B-26** practicable, be held in a courtroom in which all the participants are on the same or almost the same level.

3G.8 Subject again to the need for appropriate security arrangements, a vulnerable defendant, especially if he is young, should normally, if he wishes, be free to sit with members of his family or others in a like relationship, and with some other suitable supporting adult such as a social worker, and in a place which permits easy, informal communication with his legal representatives. The court should ensure that a suitable supporting adult is available throughout the course of the proceedings.

3G.9 It is essential that at the beginning of the proceedings, the court should ensure that what is to take place has been explained to a vulnerable defendant in terms he or she can understand and, at trial in the Crown Court, it should ensure in particular that the role of the jury has been explained. It should remind those representing the vulnerable defendant and the supporting adult of their responsibility to explain each step as it takes place and, at trial, explain the possible consequences of a guilty verdict and credit for a guilty plea. The court should also remind any intermediary of the responsibility to ensure that the vulnerable defendant has understood the explanations given to him/her. Throughout the trial the court should continue to ensure, by any appropriate means, that the defendant understands what is happening and what has been said by those on the bench, the advocates and witnesses.

3G.10 A trial should be conducted according to a timetable which takes full account of a vulnerable defendant's ability to concentrate. Frequent and regular breaks will often be appropriate. The court should ensure, so far as practicable, that the whole trial is conducted in clear language that the defendant can understand and that evidence in chief and cross-examination are conducted using questions that are short and clear. The conclusions of the "ground rules" hearing should be followed, and advocates should use and follow the "toolkits" as discussed above (*Criminal Practice Direction I (General matters) 3D [ante,* B-21]).

3G.11 A vulnerable defendant who wishes to give evidence by live link, in accordance with section 33A of the YJCEA 1999 [§ 8-99 in the main work], may apply for a direction to that effect; the procedure in rules 18.14 to 18.17 [§ 8-123 of the main work] should be followed. Before making such a direction, the court must be satisfied that it is in the interests of justice to do so and that the use of a live link would enable the defendant to participate more effectively as a witness in the proceedings. The direction will need to deal with the practical arrangements to be made, including the identity of the person or persons who will accompany him or her.

3G.12 In the Crown Court, the judge should consider whether robes and wigs should be worn, and should take account of the wishes of both a vulnerable defendant and any vulnerable witness. It is generally desirable that those responsible for the security of a vulnerable defendant who is in custody, especially if he or she is young, should not be in uniform, and that there should be no recognisable police presence in the courtroom save for good reason.

3G.13 The court should be prepared to restrict attendance by members of the public in the courtroom to a small number, perhaps limited to those with an immediate and direct interest in the outcome. The court should rule on any challenged claim to attend. However, facilities for reporting the proceedings (subject to any restrictions under s.39 or 49 of the CYPA 1933) must be provided. The court may restrict the number of reporters attending in the courtroom to such number as is judged practicable and desirable. In ruling on any challenged claim to attend in the courtroom for the purpose of reporting, the court should be mindful of the public's general right to be informed about the administration of justice.

3G.14 Where it has been decided to limit access to the courtroom, whether by reporters or generally, arrangements should be made for the proceedings to be relayed, audibly and if possible visually, to another room in the same court complex to which the media and the public have access if it appears that there will be a need for such additional facilities. Those making use of such a facility should be reminded that it is to be treated as an extension of the courtroom and that they are required to conduct themselves accordingly.

CPD I General Matters 3H: Wales and the Welsh Language: Devolution Issues

[*See § 4-64 in the main work.*] **B-27**

CPD I General Matters 3J: Wales and the Welsh Language: Applications for Evidence to be Given in Welsh

B-28   3J.1 If a defendant in a court in England asks to give or call evidence in the Welsh language, the case should not be transferred to Wales. In ordinary circumstances, interpreters can be provided on request.

CPD I General Matters 3K: Wales and the Welsh Language: Use of the Welsh Language in Courts in Wales

B-29   3K.1 The purpose of this direction is to reflect the principle of the Welsh Language Act 1993 that, in the administration of justice in Wales, the English and Welsh languages should be treated on a basis of equality.

General

B-30   3K.2 It is the responsibility of the legal representatives in every case in which the Welsh language may be used by any witness or party, or in any document which may be placed before the court, to inform the court of that fact, so that appropriate arrangements can be made for the listing of the case.

3K.3 Any party or witness is entitled to use Welsh in a magistrates' court in Wales without giving prior notice. Arrangements will be made for hearing such cases in accordance with the "Magistrates' Courts' Protocol for Listing Cases where the Welsh Language is used" (January 2008) which is available on the judiciary's website: http://www.judiciary.gov.uk/NR/exeres/57AD4763-F265-47B9-8A35-0442E08160E6. See also r.24.14.

3K.4 If the possible use of the Welsh language is known at the time of sending or appeal to the Crown Court, the court should be informed immediately after sending or when the notice of appeal is lodged. Otherwise, the court should be informed as soon as the possible use of the Welsh language becomes known.

3K.5 If costs are incurred as a result of failure to comply with these directions, a wasted costs order may be made against the defaulting party and / or his legal representatives.

3K.6 The law does not permit the selection of jurors in a manner which enables the court to discover whether a juror does or does not speak Welsh, or to secure a jury whose members are bilingual, to try a case in which the Welsh language may be used.

Preliminary and plea and case management hearings

B-31   3K.7 An advocate in a case in which the Welsh language may be used must raise that matter at the preliminary and/or the plea and case management hearing and endorse details of it on the advocates' questionnaire, so that appropriate directions may be given for the progress of the case.

Listing

B-32   3K.8 The listing officer, in consultation with the resident judge, should ensure that a case in which the Welsh language may be used is listed—

(a) wherever practicable before a Welsh speaking judge, and

(b) in a court in Wales with simultaneous translation facilities.

Interpreters

B-33   3K.9 Whenever an interpreter is needed to translate evidence from English into Welsh or from Welsh into English, the court listing officer in whose court the case is to be heard shall contact the Welsh Language Unit who will ensure the attendance of an accredited interpreter.

Jurors

B-34   3K.10 The jury bailiff, when addressing the jurors at the start of their period of jury service, shall inform them that each juror may take an oath or affirm in Welsh or English as he wishes.

3K.11 After the jury has been selected to try a case, and before it is sworn, the court officer swearing in the jury shall inform the jurors in open court that each juror may take an oath or affirm in Welsh or English as he wishes. A juror who takes the oath or affirms in Welsh should not be asked to repeat it in English.

3K.12 Where Welsh is used by any party or witness in a trial, an accredited interpreter will provide simultaneous translation from Welsh to English for the jurors who do not speak Welsh. There is no provision for the translation of evidence from English to Welsh for a Welsh speaking juror.

3K.13 The jury's deliberations must be conducted in private with no other person present and therefore no interpreter may be provided to translate the discussion for the benefit of one or more of the jurors.

Witnesses

3K.14 When each witness is called, the court officer administering the oath or affirmation shall inform the witness that he may be sworn or affirm in Welsh or English, as he wishes. A witness who takes the oath or affirms in Welsh should not be asked to repeat it in English. **B-35**

Opening / closing of Crown Courts

3K.15 Unless it is not reasonably practicable to do so, the opening and closing of the court should be performed in Welsh and English. **B-36**

Role of liaison judge

3K.16 If any question or problem arises concerning the implementation of these directions, contact should in the first place be made with the liaison judge for the Welsh language through the Wales Circuit Office: HMCTS WALES / GLITEM CYMRU,3rd Floor, Churchill House / 3ydd Llawr Ty Churchill,Churchill Way / Fford Churchill,Cardiff / Caerdydd,CF10 2HH029 2067 8300 **B-37**

CPD I General Matters 3L: Security of Prisoners at Court

3L.1 High-risk prisoners identified to the court as presenting a significant risk of escape, violence in court or danger to those in the court and its environs, and to the public at large, will as far as possible, have administrative and remand appearances listed for disposal by way of live link. They will have priority for the use of video equipment. **B-38**

3L.2 In all other proceedings that require the appearance in person of a high-risk prisoner, the proceedings will be listed at an appropriately secure court building and in a court with a secure (enclosed or ceiling-high) dock.

3L.3 Where a secure dock or live link is not available the court will be asked to consider an application for additional security measures, which may include: (a) the use of approved restraints (but see below at para. 3L.6); (b) the deployment of additional escort staff; (c) securing the court room for all or part of the proceedings; (d) in exceptional circumstances, moving the hearing to a prison.

3L.4 National Offender Management Service ("NOMS") will be responsible for providing the assessment of the prisoner and it is accepted that this may change at short notice. NOMS must provide notification to the listing officer of all Category A prisoners, those on the escape list and restricted status prisoners or other prisoners who have otherwise been assessed as presenting a significant risk of violence or harm. There is a presumption that all prisoners notified as high-risk will be allocated a hearing by live link and/or secure dock facilities. Where the court cannot provide a secure listing, the reasons should be provided to the establishment so that alternative arrangements can be considered.

Applications for use of approved restraints

3L.5 It is the duty of the court to decide whether a prisoner who appears before them should appear in restraints or not. Their decision must comply with the requirements of the ECHR, particularly Article 3, which prohibits degrading treatment: see *Raninen v. Finland*, 26 E.H.R.R. 563. **B-39**

3L.6 No prisoner should be handcuffed in court unless there are reasonable grounds for apprehending that he will be violent or will attempt to escape. If an application is made, it must be entertained by the court and a ruling must be given. The defence should be given the opportunity to respond to the application: proceeding in the absence of the defendant or his representative may give rise to an issue under Article 6.1 of the Convention [§ 16-72 in the main work]: *R. v. Rollinson*, 161 J.P. 107. If an application is to be made *ex parte* then that application should be made *inter partes* and the defence should be given an opportunity to respond.

Additional security measures

3L.7 It may be in some cases that additional dock officers are deployed to mitigate the risk that a prisoner presents. When the nature of the risk is so serious that increased deployment will be insufficient or would in itself be so obtrusive as to prejudice a fair trial, then the court may be required to consider the following measures: (a) reconsider the case for a live link hearing, including transferring the case to a court where the live link is available; (b) transfer the case to an appropriately secure court; (c) the use of approved restraints on the prisoner for all or part of the proceedings; (d) securing the court room for all or part of the proceedings; and (e) the use of (armed) police in the court building. **B-40**

3L.8 The establishment seeking the additional security measures will submit a court management directions form setting out the evidence of the prisoner's identified risk of escape or violence and requesting the court's approval of security measures to mitigate that risk. This must be sent to the listing officer along with current, specific and credible evidence that the security measures are both necessary and proportionate to the identified risk and that the risk cannot be managed in any other way.

3L.9 If the court is asked to consider transfer of the case, then this must be in accordance with *Criminal Practice Direction XIII (Listing) F*, paras 11-13 [*post*, B-222]. The listing officer will liaise with the establishment, prosecution and the defence to ensure the needs of the witnesses are taken into account.

3L.10 The judge who has conduct of the case must deal with any application for the use of restraints or any other security measure and will hear representations from the Crown Prosecution Service and the defence before proceeding. The application will only be granted if: (a) there are good grounds for believing that the prisoner poses a significant risk of trying to escape from the court (beyond the assumed motivation of all prisoners to escape) and/or risk of serious harm towards those persons in court or the public generally should an escape attempt be successful; and (b) where there is no other viable means of preventing escape or serious harm.

High-risk prisoners giving evidence from the witness box

B-41

3L.11 High-risk prisoners giving evidence from the witness box may pose a significant security risk. In circumstances where such prisoners are required to move from a secure dock to an insecure witness box, an application may be made for the court to consider the use of additional security measures including: (a) the use of approved restraints; (b) the deployment of additional escort staff or police in the courtroom or armed police in the building (the decision to deploy an armed escort is for the chief inspector of the relevant borough: the decision to allow the armed escort in or around the court room is for the senior presiding judge [see *Criminal Practice Direction I (General matters) 3M*]); (c) securing the courtroom for all or part of the proceedings; (d) giving evidence from the secure dock; and (e) use of live link if the prisoner is not the defendant.

CPD I General Matters 3M: Procedure for Application for Armed Police Presence in Crown Courts and Magistrates' Court Buildings

B-42

[*Not set out in this work.*]

CPD I General Matters 5A: Forms

B-43

5A.1 The forms at Annex D to the *Consolidated Criminal Practice Direction* [2002] 1 W.L.R. 2870, or forms to that effect, are to be used in the criminal courts, in accordance with rule 5.1.

5A.2 The forms at Annex E to that practice direction, the case management forms, must be used in the criminal courts, in accordance with rule 3.11(1) [now r.5.1].

5A.3 The table at the beginning of each of those annexes lists the forms and:

(a) shows the rule in connection with which each applies;

(b) describes each form.

5A.4 The forms may be amended or withdrawn from time to time, or new forms added, under the authority of the Lord Chief Justice.

CPD I General Matters 5B: Access to Information Held by the Court

B-44

5B.1 Open justice, as Toulson L.J. ... reiterated in ... *R. (Guardian News and Media Ltd) v. City of Westminster Magistrates' Court (Article 19 intervening)*; *Guardian News and Media Ltd v. Government of the United States of America* [§ 2-133 in the main work], is a "principle at the heart of our system of justice and vital to the rule of law." There are exceptions but these "have to be justified by some even more important principle." However, the practical application of that undisputed principle, and the proper balancing of conflicting rights and principles, call for careful judgments to be made. The following is intended to provide some assistance to courts making decisions when asked to provide the public, including journalists, with access to or copies of information and documents held by the court. It is not a prescriptive list, as the court will have to consider all the circumstances of each individual case.

5B.2 It remains the responsibility of the recipient of information or documents to ensure that they comply with any and all restrictions such as reporting restrictions (see Pt 16 and the accompanying practice direction).

5B.3 For the purposes of this direction, the word document includes images in photographic, digital including DVD format, video, CCTV or any other form.

5B.4 Certain information can and should be provided to the public on request, unless there are restrictions, such as reporting restrictions, imposed in that particular case. Rule 5.8(4) and (6) read together specify the information that the court officer will supply to the public; an oral application is acceptable and no reason need be given for the request. There is no requirement for the court officer to consider the non-disclosure provisions of the Data Protection Act 1998 as the exemption under section 35 applies to all disclosure made under "any enactment ... or by the order of a court", which includes under the Criminal Procedure Rules.

5B.5 If the information sought is not listed at rule 5.8(6), rule 5.8(7) will apply, and the provision of information is at the discretion of the court. The following guidance is intended to assist the court in exercising that discretion.

5B.6 A request for access to documents used in a criminal case should first be addressed to the party who presented them to the court. Prosecuting authorities are subject to the Freedom of Information Act 2000 and the Data Protection Act 1998 and their decisions are susceptible to review.

5B.7 If the request is from a journalist or media organisation, note that there is a protocol between ACPO, the CPS and the media entitled "Publicity and the Criminal Justice System": http://www.cps.gov.uk/publications/agencies/mediaprotocol.html. There is additionally a protocol made under rule 5.8(5)(b) between the media and HMCTS: http://www.newspapersoc.org.uk/sites/default/files/Docs/Protocol-for-Sharing-Court-Registers-and-Court-Lists-with-Local-Newspapers_September-2011.doc. This practice direction does not affect the operation of those protocols. Material should generally be sought under the relevant protocol before an application is made to the court.

5B.8 An application to which rule 5.8(7) applies must be made in accordance with rule 5.8; it must be in writing, unless the court permits otherwise, and "must explain for what purpose the information is required." A clear, detailed application, specifying the name and contact details of the applicant, whether or not he ... represents a media organisation, and setting out the reasons for the application and to what use the information will be put, will be of most assistance to the court. Applicants should state if they have requested the information under a protocol and include any reasons given for the refusal. Before considering such an application, the court will expect the applicant to have given notice of the request to the parties.

5B.9 The court will consider each application on its own merits. The burden of justifying a request for access rests on the applicant. Considerations to be taken into account will include: (i) whether or not the request is for the purpose of contemporaneous reporting; a request after the conclusion of the proceedings will require careful scrutiny by the court; (ii) the nature of the information or documents being sought; (iii) the purpose for which they are required; (iv) the stage of the proceedings at the time when the application is made; (v) the value of the documents in advancing the open justice principle, including enabling the media to discharge its role, which has been described as a "public watchdog", by reporting the proceedings effectively; (vi) any risk of harm which access to them may cause to the legitimate interests of others; and (vii) any reasons given by the parties for refusing to provide the material requested and any other representations received from the parties. Further, all of the principles below are subject to any specific restrictions in the case. Courts should be aware that the risk of providing a document may reduce after a particular point in the proceedings, and when the material requested may be made available.

Documents read aloud in their entirety

5B.10 If a document has been read aloud to the court in its entirety, it should usually be provided **B-45** on request, unless to do so would be disruptive to the court proceedings or place an undue burden on the court, the advocates or others. It may be appropriate and convenient for material to be provided electronically, if this can be done securely.

5B.11 Documents likely to fall into this category are: (i) opening notes; (ii) statements agreed under section 9 of the CJA 1967 [§ 10-14 in the main work], including experts' reports, if read in their entirety; (iii) admissions made under section 10 of the CJA 1967 [§ 10-7 in the main work].

Documents treated as read aloud in their entirety

5B.12 A document treated by the court as if it had been read aloud in public, though in fact it has **B-46** been neither read nor summarised aloud, should generally be made available on request. The burden on the court, the advocates or others in providing the material should be considered, but the presumption in favour of providing the material is greater when the material has only been treated as having been read aloud. Again, subject to security considerations, it may be convenient for the material to be provided electronically.

5B.13 Documents likely to fall into this category include: (i) skeleton arguments; (ii) written submissions.

Documents read aloud in part or summarised aloud

B-47

5B.14 Open justice requires only access to the part of the document that has been read aloud. If a member of the public requests a copy of such a document, the court should consider whether it is proportionate to order one of the parties to produce a suitably redacted version. If not, access to the document is unlikely to be granted; however, open justice will generally have been satisfied by the document having been read out in court.

5B.15 If the request comes from an accredited member of the press (see *Access by reporters* below), there may be circumstances in which the court orders that a copy of the whole document be shown to the reporter, or provided, subject to the condition that those matters that had not been read out to the court may not be used or reported. A breach of such an order would be treated as a contempt of court.

5B.16 Documents in this category are likely to include section 9 statements that are edited.

Jury bundles and exhibits (including video footage shown to the jury)

B-48

5B.17 The court should consider:

   (i) whether access to the specific document is necessary to understand or effectively to report the case;

   (ii) the privacy of third parties, such as the victim (in some cases, the reporting restriction imposed by s.1 of the Judicial Proceedings (Regulation of Reports) Act 1926 will apply (indecent or medical matter));

   (iii) whether the reporting of anything in the document may be prejudicial to a fair trial in this or another case, in which case whether it may be necessary to make an order under section 4(2) of the Contempt of Court Act 1981 [§ 28-65 in the main work].

The court may order one of the parties to provide a copy of certain pages (or parts of the footage), but these should not be provided electronically.

Statements of witnesses who give oral evidence

B-49

5B.18 A witness statement does not become evidence unless it is agreed under section 9 of the CJA 1967 [§ 10-14 in the main work] and presented to the court. Therefore the statements of witnesses who give oral evidence, including ABE interview and transcripts and experts' reports, should not usually be provided. Open justice is generally satisfied by public access to the court.

Confidential documents

B-50

5B.19 A document the content of which, though relied upon by the court, has not been communicated to the public or reporters, nor treated as if it had been, is likely to have been supplied in confidence and should be treated accordingly. This will apply even if the court has made reference to the document or quoted from the document. There is most unlikely to be a sufficient reason to displace the expectation of confidentiality ordinarily attaching to a document in this category, and it would be exceptional to permit the inspection or copying by a member of the public or of the media of such a document. The rights and legitimate interests of others are likely to outweigh the interests of open justice with respect these documents.

5B.20 Documents in this category are likely to include: (i) pre-sentence reports; (ii) medical reports; (iii) victim personal statements; (iv) reports and summaries for confiscation.

Prohibitions against the provision of information

B-51

5B.21 Statutory provisions may impose specific prohibitions against the provision of information. Those most likely to be encountered are listed in the note to rule 5.8 and include the Rehabilitation of Offenders Act 1974 [§§ 13-120 *et seq.* in the main work], section 18 of the CPIA 1996 ("unused material" disclosed by the prosecution) [§ 12-91 in the main work], sections 33, 34 and 35 of the LASPOA 2012 (privileged information furnished to the Legal Aid Agency) and reporting restrictions generally.

5B.22 Reports of allocation or sending proceedings are restricted by section 52A of the CDA 1998 [§ 1-32 in the main work], so that only limited information, as specified in the statute, may be reported, whether it is referred to in the courtroom or not. The magistrates' court has power to order that the restriction shall not apply; if any defendant objects the court must apply the interests of justice test as specified in section 52A. The restriction ceases to apply either after all defendants indicate a plea of guilty, or after the conclusion of the trial of the last defendant to be tried. If the case does not result in a guilty plea, a finding of guilt or an acquittal, the restriction does not lift automatically and an application must be made to the court.

5B.23 Extradition proceedings have some features in common with committal proceedings, but no automatic reporting restrictions apply.

5B.24 Public interest immunity and the rights of a defendant, witnesses and victims under Article 6 and 8 of the ECHR [§§ 16-72, 16-137 in the main work] may also restrict the power to release material to third parties.

Other documents

5B.25 The following table indicates the considerations likely to arise on an application to inspect **B-52** or copy other documents.

Document	Considerations
Charge sheet/ Indictment	The alleged offence(s) will have been read aloud in court, and their terms must be supplied under rule 5.8(4).
Material disclosed under CPIA 1996	To the extent that the content is deployed at trial, it becomes public at that hearing. Otherwise, it is a criminal offence for it to be disclosed: s.18 of the 1996 Act.
Written notices, applications, replies (including any application for representation)	To the extent that evidence is introduced, or measures taken, at trial, the content becomes public at that hearing. A statutory prohibition against disclosure applies to an application for representation: ss.33, 34 and 35 of the LASPOA 2012
Sentencing remarks	Sentencing remarks should usually be provided to the accredited press, if the judge was reading from a prepared script which was handed out immediately afterwards; if not, then permission for a member of the accredited press to obtain a transcript should usually be given (see also paras 26 and 29 below).
Official recordings/transcript	Rule 5.5

Access by reporters

5B.26 Under Part 5 of the rules, the same procedure applies for applications for access to informa- **B-53** tion by reporters as to other members of the public. However, if the application is made by legal representatives instructed by the media, or by an accredited member of the media, who is able to produce in support of the application a valid press card (http://www.ukpresscardauthority.co.uk/) then there is a greater presumption in favour of providing the requested material, in recognition of the press' role as "public watchdog" in a democratic society (*Observer and Guardian v. U.K.*, 14 E.H.R.R. 153). The general principle in those circumstances is that the court should supply documents and information unless there is a good reason not to in order to protect the rights or legitimate interests of others and the request will not place an undue burden on the court (*R. (Guardian News and Media Ltd) v. City of Westminster Magistrates' Court (Article 19 intervening), ante* (at [87])). Subject to that, the paragraphs above relating to types of documents should be followed.

5B.27 Court staff should usually verify the authenticity of cards, checking the expiry date on the card and where necessary may consider telephoning the number on the reverse of the card to verify the card holder. Court staff may additionally request sight of other identification if necessary to ensure that the card holder has been correctly identified. The supply of information under rule 5.8(7) is at the discretion of the court, and court staff must ensure that they have received a clear direction from the court before providing any information or material under rule 5.8(7) to a member of the public, including to the accredited media or their legal representatives.

5B.28 Opening notes and skeleton arguments or written submissions, once they have been placed before the court, should usually be provided to the media. If there is no opening note, permission for the media to obtain a transcript of the prosecution opening should usually be given (see *post*). It may be convenient for copies to be provided electronically by counsel, provided that the documents are kept suitably secure. The media are expected to be aware of the limitations on the use to which such material can be put, for example that legal argument held in the absence of the jury must not be reported before the conclusion of the trial.

5B.29 The media should also be able to obtain transcripts of hearings held in open court directly from the transcription service provider, on payment of any required fee. The service providers commonly require the judge's authorisation before they will provide a transcript, as an additional verification to ensure that the correct material is released and reporting restrictions are noted. However, responsibility for compliance with any restriction always rests with the person receiving the information or material: see *Criminal Practice Direction I (General Matters) 6B*.

5B.30 It is not for the judge to exercise an editorial judgment about "the adequacy of the material already available to the paper for its journalistic purpose" (*R. (Guardian News and Media Ltd) v. City of Westminster Magistrates' Court (Article 19 intervening), ante* (at [82])), but the responsibility for complying with the Contempt of Court Act 1981 and any and all restrictions on the use of the material rests with the recipient.

CPD I General Matters: 5C Issue of Medical Certficates

B-54

5C.1 Doctors will be aware that medical notes are normally submitted by defendants in criminal proceedings as justification for not answering bail. Medical notes may also be submitted by witnesses who are due to give evidence and jurors.

5C.2 If a medical certificate is accepted by the court, this will result in cases (including contested hearings and trials) being adjourned rather than the court issuing a warrant for the defendant's arrest without bail. Medical certificates will also provide the defendant with sufficient evidence to defend a charge of failure to surrender to bail.

5C.3 However, a court is not absolutely bound by a medical certificate. The medical practitioner providing the certificate may be required by the court to give evidence. Alternatively the court may exercise its discretion to disregard a certificate which it finds unsatisfactory: *R. v. Ealing Magistrates' Court, ex p. Burgess,* 165 J.P. 82, D. C.

5C.4 Circumstances where the court may find a medical certificate unsatisfactory include:

(a) where the certificate indicates that the defendant is unfit to attend work (rather than to attend court);

(b) where the nature of the defendant's ailment (*e.g.* a broken arm) does not appear to be capable of preventing his attendance at court;

(c) where the defendant is certified as suffering from stress/anxiety/depression and there is no indication of the defendant recovering within a realistic timescale.

5C.5 It therefore follows that the minimum standards a medical certificate should set out are:

(a) the date on which the medical practitioner examined the defendant;

(b) the exact nature of the defendant's ailments

(c) if it is not self-evident, why the ailment prevents the defendant attending court;

(d) an indication as to when the defendant is likely to be able to attend court, or a date when the current certificate expires.

5C.6 Medical practitioners should be aware that when issuing a certificate to a defendant in criminal proceedings they make themselves liable to being summonsed to court to give evidence about the content of the certificate, and they may be asked to justify their statements.

CPD I General Matters 6A: Unofficial Sound Recording of Proceedings

B-55

6A.1 [*Summarises s.9(1)(a)–(c) and (4) of the Contempt of Court Act 1981 (§ 28-74 in the main work).*]

6A.2 The discretion given to the court to grant, withhold or withdraw leave to use equipment for recording sound or to impose conditions as to the use of the recording is unlimited, but the following factors may be relevant to its exercise:

(a) the existence of any reasonable need on the part of the applicant for leave, whether a litigant or a person connected with the press or broadcasting, for the recording to be made;

(b) the risk that the recording could be used for the purpose of briefing witnesses out of court;

(c) any possibility that the use of the recorder would disturb the proceedings or distract or worry any witnesses or other participants.

6A.3 Consideration should always be given whether conditions as to the use of a recording made pursuant to leave should be imposed. The identity and role of the applicant for leave and the nature of the subject-matter of the proceedings may be relevant to this.

6A.4 The particular restriction imposed by section 9(1)(b) applies in every case, but may not be present to the mind of every applicant to whom leave is given. It may, therefore, be desirable on occasion for this provision to be drawn to the attention of those to whom leave is given.

6A.5 The transcript of a permitted recording is intended for the use of the person given leave to make it and is not intended to be used as, or to compete with, the official transcript mentioned in section 9(4).

6A.6 [*See § 28-74 in the main work.*]

CPD I General Matters 6B: Restrictions on Reporting Proceedings

B-56

6B.1 Open justice is an essential principle in the criminal courts but the principle is subject to some statutory restrictions. These restrictions are either automatic or discretionary. Guidance is provided in the joint publication, *Reporting Restrictions in the Criminal Courts* issued by the Judicial College, the Newspaper Society, the Society of Editors and the Media Lawyers Association. The current version is the fourth edition and has been updated to be effective from May 2015.

6B.2 Where a restriction is automatic no order can or should be made in relation to matters falling within the relevant provisions. However, the court may, if it considers it appropriate to do so, give a reminder of the existence of the automatic restriction. The court may also discuss the scope of the restriction and any particular risks in the specific case in open court with representatives of the press present. Such judicial observations cannot constitute an order binding on the editor or the reporter although it is anticipated that a responsible editor would consider them carefully before deciding what should be published. It remains the responsibility of those reporting a case to ensure that restrictions are not breached.

6B.3 Before exercising its discretion to impose a restriction the court must follow precisely the statutory provisions under which the order is to be made, paying particular regard to what has to be established, by whom and to what standard.

6B.4 Without prejudice to the above paragraph, certain general principles apply to the exercise of the court's discretion:

(a) the court must have regard to Parts 6 [§§ 4-47 *et seq.* in the main work] and 18 [§§ 8-110 *et seq.* in the main work] of the Criminal Procedure Rules;

(b) the court must keep in mind the fact that every order is a departure from the general principle that proceedings shall be open and freely reported;

(c) before making any order the court must be satisfied that the purpose of the proposed order cannot be achieved by some lesser measure, *e.g.* the grant of special measures, screens or the clearing of the public gallery (usually subject to a representative/s of the media remaining);

(d) the terms of the order must be proportionate so as to comply with Article 10 [of the] ECHR (freedom of expression) [§ 16-157 in the main work];

(e) no order should be made without giving other parties to the proceedings and any other interested party, including any representative of the media, an opportunity to make representations;

(f) any order should provide for any interested party who has not been present or represented at the time of the making of the order to have permission to apply within a limited period, *e.g.* 24 hours;

(g) the wording of the order is the responsibility of the judge or bench making the order; it must be in precise terms and, if practicable, agreed with the advocates.

(h) the order must be in writing and must state:

(i) the power under which it is made;

(ii) its precise scope and purpose; and

(iii) the time at which it shall cease to have effect, if appropriate;

(i) the order must specify, in every case, whether or not the making or terms of the order may be reported or whether this itself is prohibited; such a report could cause the very mischief which the order was intended to prevent.

6B.5 A series of template orders have been prepared by the Judicial College and are available as an appendix to the Crown Court Bench Book Companion; these template orders should generally be used.

6B.6 A copy of the order should be provided to any person known to have an interest in reporting the proceedings and to any local or national media who regularly report proceedings in the court.

6B.7 Court staff should be prepared to answer any enquiry about a specific case; but it is and will remain the responsibility of anyone reporting a case to ensure that no breach of any order occurs and the onus rests on such person to make enquiry in case of doubt.

CPD I General Matters 6C: Use of Live Text-based Forms of Communication (including Twitter) from Court for the Purposes of Fair and Accurate Reporting

6C.1 This part clarifies the use which may be made of live text-based communications, such as **B-57** mobile email, social media (including Twitter) and internet-enabled laptops in and from courts throughout England and Wales. For the purpose of this part these means of communication are referred to, compendiously, as "live text-based communications". It is consistent with the legislative structure which:

(a) prohibits:

(i) the taking of photographs in court (s.41 of the CJA 1925);

       (ii) the use of sound recording equipment in court unless the leave of the judge has first been obtained (s.9 of the Contempt of Court Act 1981 [§ 28-74 in the main work]); and

    (b) requires compliance with the strict prohibition rules created by sections 1, 2 and 4 of the Contempt of Court Act 1981 [§§ 28-55 *et seq.* in the main work] in relation to the reporting of court proceedings.

General principles

B-58   6C.2 The judge has an overriding responsibility to ensure that proceedings are conducted consistently, with the proper administration of justice, and to avoid any improper interference with its processes.

6C.3 A fundamental aspect of the proper administration of justice is the principle of open justice. Fair and accurate reporting of court proceedings forms part of that principle. The principle is, however, subject to well-known statutory and discretionary exceptions. Two such exceptions are the prohibitions, set out in paragraph 6C.1(a), on photography in court and on making sound recordings of court proceedings.

6C.4 The statutory prohibition on photography in court, by any means, is absolute. There is no judicial discretion to suspend or dispense with it. Any equipment which has photographic capability must not have that function activated.

6C.5 Sound recordings are also prohibited unless, in the exercise of its discretion, the court permits such equipment to be used. In criminal proceedings, some of the factors relevant to the exercise of that discretion are contained in paragraph 6A.2. The same factors are likely to be relevant when consideration is being given to the exercise of this discretion in civil or family proceedings.

Use of live text-based communications: general considerations

B-59   6C.6 The normal, indeed almost invariable, rule has been that mobile phones must be turned off in court. There is however no statutory prohibition on the use of live text-based communications in open court.

6C.7 Where a member of the public, who is in court, wishes to use live text-based communications during court proceedings an application for permission to activate and use, in silent mode, a mobile phone, small laptop or similar piece of equipment, solely in order to make live text-based communications of the proceedings will need to be made. The application may be made formally or informally (for instance by communicating a request to the judge through court staff).

6C.8 It is presumed that a representative of the media or a legal commentator using live text-based communications from court does not pose a danger of interference to the proper administration of justice in the individual case. This is because the most obvious purpose of permitting the use of live text-based communications would be to enable the media to produce fair and accurate reports of the proceedings. As such, a representative of the media or a legal commentator who wishes to use live text-based communications from court may do so without making an application to the court.

6C.9 When considering, either generally on its own motion, or following a formal application or informal request by a member of the public, whether to permit live text-based communications, and if so by whom, the paramount question for the judge will be whether the application may interfere with the proper administration of justice.

6C.10 In considering the question of permission, the factors listed in paragraph 6A.2 are likely to be relevant.

6C.11 Without being exhaustive, the danger to the administration of justice is likely to be at its most acute in the context of criminal trials e.g., where witnesses who are out of court may be informed of what has already happened in court and so coached or briefed before they then give evidence, or where information posted on, for instance, Twitter about inadmissible evidence may influence members of the jury. However, the danger is not confined to criminal proceedings; in civil and sometimes family proceedings, simultaneous reporting from the courtroom may create pressure on witnesses, by distracting or worrying them.

6C.12 It may be necessary for the judge to limit live text-based communications to representatives of the media for journalistic purposes but to disallow its use by the wider public in court. That may arise if it is necessary, for example, to limit the number of mobile electronic devices in use at any given time because of the potential for electronic interference with the court's own sound recording equipment, or because the widespread use of such devices in court may cause a distraction in the proceedings.

6C.13 Subject to these considerations, the use of an unobtrusive, hand-held, silent piece of modern equipment, for the purposes of simultaneous reporting of proceedings to the outside world as they unfold in court, is generally unlikely to interfere with the proper administration of justice.

6C.14 Permission to use live text-based communications from court may be withdrawn by the court at any time.

CPD II Preliminary Proceedings 8A: Defendant's Record

Copies of record

8A.1 The defendant's record (previous convictions, cautions, reprimands, etc) may be taken into **B-60** account when the court decides not only on sentence but also, for example, about bail, or when allocating a case for trial. It is therefore important that up to date and accurate information is available. Previous convictions must be provided as part of the initial details of the prosecution case under Part 8 of the rules [§§ 12-142 *et seq.* in the main work].

8A.2 The record should usually be provided in the following format:

Personal details and summary of convictions and cautions — Police National Computer ["PNC"] Court / Defence / Probation Summary Sheet;

Previous convictions — PNC Court / Defence / Probation printout, supplemented by Form MG16 if the police force holds convictions not shown on PNC;

Recorded cautions — PNC Court / Defence / Probation printout, supplemented by Form MG17 if the police force holds cautions not shown on PNC.

8A.3 The defence representative should take instructions on the defendant's record and if the defence wish to raise any objection to the record, this should be made known to the prosecutor immediately.

8A.4 It is the responsibility of the prosecutor to ensure that a copy of the defendant's record has been provided to the probation service.

8A.5 Where following conviction a custodial order is made, the court must ensure that a copy is attached to the order sent to the prison.

Additional information

8A.6 In the Crown Court, the police should also provide brief details of the circumstances of the **B-61** last three similar convictions and / or of convictions likely to be of interest to the court, the latter being judged on a case-by-case basis.

8A.7 Where the current alleged offence could constitute a breach of an existing sentence such as a suspended sentence, community order or conditional discharge, and it is known that that sentence is still in force then details of the circumstances of the offence leading to the sentence should be included in the antecedents. The detail should be brief and include the date of the offence.

8A.8 On occasions the PNC printout provided may not be fully up to date. It is the responsibility of the prosecutor to ensure that all of the necessary information is available to the court and the probation service and provided to the defence. Oral updates at the hearing will sometimes be necessary, but it is preferable if this information is available in advance.

CPD II Preliminary Proceedings 9A: Allocation (Mode of Trial)

9A.1 Courts must follow the Sentencing Council's guideline on allocation (mode of trial) when **B-62** deciding whether or not to send defendants charged with "either-way" offences for trial in the Crown Court under section 51(1) of the CDA 1998 [§ 1-25 in the main work]. The guideline refers to the factors to which a court must have regard in accordance with section 19 of the MCA 1980. Section 19(2)(a) [§ 1-96 in the main work] permits reference to previous convictions of the defendant.

9A.2 The allocation guideline lists four factors, a) to d), that the court must also have regard to. No examples or guidance are given, however, the following could be a consideration when applying the factors: that where cases involve complex questions of fact or difficult questions of law, including difficult issues of disclosure of sensitive material, the court should consider sending for trial.

9A.3 Certain general observations can also be made:

(a) the court should never make its decision on the grounds of convenience or expedition; and

(b) the fact that the offences are alleged to be specimens is a relevant consideration (although it has to be borne in mind that difficulties can arise in sentencing in relation to specimen counts: see *R. v. Clark* [1996] 2 Cr.App.R. 282, CA, *R. v. Canavan*; *R. v. Kidd*; *R. v. Shaw* [1998] 1 Cr.App.R. 79, CA, and *R. v. Oakes* [2013] 2 Cr.App.R.(S.) 22, CA (see case of *R. v. Restivo*)); the fact that the defendant will be asking for other offences to be taken into consideration, if convicted, is not.

CPD II Preliminary Proceedings 10A: Settling the Indictment

10A.1 CrimPR 10.1 requires the prosecutor to serve a draft indictment not more than 28 days **B-63** after service of the evidence in a case sent for trial, after the sending of the defendant for trial, or after one of the other events listed in that rule. CrimPR 10.2(5) provides that an indictment may contain any count charging substantially the same offence as one sent for trial and any other count based on the prosecution evidence already served which the Crown Court has jurisdiction to try. Where the prosecutor intends to include in the draft indictment counts which differ materially from, or are additional to, those on which the defendant was sent for trial then the defendant should be given as much notice as possible, usually by service of a draft indictment, or a provisional draft indictment, at the earliest possible opportunity.

10A.2 There is no rule of law or practice which prohibits two indictments being in existence at the same time for the same offence against the same person and on the same facts. But the court will not allow the prosecution to proceed on both indictments. They cannot be tried together and the court will require the prosecution to elect the one on which the trial will proceed. Where different defendants have been separately sent for trial for offences which can lawfully be charged in the same indictment then it is permissible to join in one indictment counts based on the separate sendings for trial even if an indictment based on one of them already has been signed. Where necessary the court should be invited to exercise its powers of amendment under section 5 of the Indictments Act 1915.

10A.3 Save in the special circumstances described in the following paragraphs of this Practice Direction, it is undesirable that a large number of counts should be contained in one indictment. Where defendants on trial have a variety of offences alleged against them then, in the interests of effective case management, it is the court's responsibility to exercise its powers in accordance with the overriding objective set out in CrimPR, Pt 1. The prosecution may be required to identify a selection of counts on which the trial should proceed, leaving a decision to be taken later whether to try any of the remainder. Where an indictment contains substantive counts and one or more related conspiracy counts, the court will expect the prosecution to justify the joinder. Failing justification, the prosecution should be required to choose whether to proceed on the substantive counts or on the conspiracy counts. In any event, if there is a conviction on any counts that are tried, then those that have been postponed can remain on the file marked "not to be proceeded with without the leave of the court or the Court of Appeal". In the event that a conviction is later quashed on appeal, the remaining counts can be tried. Where necessary the court has power to order that an indictment be severed.

Multiple offending: trial by jury and then by judge alone

B-64

10A.4 Under sections 17 to 21 of the Domestic Violence, Crime and Victims Act 2004 [§§ 4-338 *et seq.* in the main work], the court may order that the trial of certain counts will be by jury in the usual way and, if the jury convicts, that other associated counts will be tried by judge alone. The use of this power is likely to be appropriate where justice cannot be done without charging a large number of separate offences and the allegations against the defendant appear to fall into distinct groups by reference to the identity of the victim, by reference to the dates of the offences, or by some other distinction in the nature of the offending conduct alleged.

10A.5 In such a case, it is essential to make clear from the outset the association asserted by the prosecutor between those counts to be tried by a jury and those counts which it is proposed should be tried by judge alone, if the jury convict on the former. A special form of indictment is prescribed for this purpose.

10A.6 An order for such a trial may be made only at a preparatory hearing. It follows that where the prosecutor intends to invite the court to order such a trial it will normally be appropriate to proceed as follows. The draft indictment served under rule 10.1 [§ 1-299 in the main work] should be in the form appropriate to such a trial. It should be accompanied by an application under rule 3.15 for a preparatory hearing. This will ensure that the defendant is aware at the earliest possible opportunity of what the prosecution propose and of the proposed association of counts in the indictment. It is undesirable for a draft indictment in the usual form to be served where the prosecutor expects to apply for a two stage trial and hence, of necessity, for permission to amend the indictment at a later stage in order that it may be in the special form.

10A.7 On receipt of a draft two part indictment, a Crown Court officer should sign it at the end of Part Two. At the start of the preparatory hearing, the defendant should be arraigned on all counts in Part One of the indictment. Arraignment on Part Two need not take place until after there has been either a guilty plea to, or finding of guilt on, an associated count in Part One of the indictment.

10A.8 If the prosecution application is successful, the prosecutor should prepare an abstract of the indictment, containing the counts from Part One only, for use in the jury trial. Preparation of such an abstract does not involve "amendment" of the indictment. It is akin to where a defendant pleads guilty to certain counts in an indictment and is put in the charge of the jury on the remaining counts only.

10A.9 If the prosecution application for a two stage trial is unsuccessful, the prosecutor may apply to amend the indictment to remove from it any counts in Part Two which would make jury trial on the whole indictment impracticable and to revert to a standard form of indictment. It will be a matter for the court whether arraignment on outstanding counts takes place at the preparatory hearing, or at a future date.

Multiple offending: count charging more than one incident

10A.10 CrimPR 10.2(2) allows a single count to allege more than one incident of the commission **B-65** of an offence in certain circumstances. Each incident must be of the same offence. The circumstances in which such a count may be appropriate include, but are not limited to, the following:

> (a) the victim on each occasion was the same, or there was no identifiable individual victim as, for example, in a case of the unlawful importation of controlled drugs or of money laundering;
>
> (b) the alleged incidents involved a marked degree of repetition in the method employed or in their location, or both;
>
> (c) the alleged incidents took place over a clearly defined period, typically (but not necessarily) no more than about a year;
>
> (d) in any event, the defence is such as to apply to every alleged incident without differentiation. Where what is in issue differs between different incidents, a single "multiple incidents" count will not be appropriate, though it may be appropriate to use two or more such counts according to the circumstances and to the issues raised by the defence.

10A.11 Even in circumstances such as those set out above, there may be occasions on which a prosecutor chooses not to use such a count, in order to bring the case within section 75(3)(a) of the PCA 2002 (criminal lifestyle established by conviction of three or more offences in the same proceedings [§ 5-906 in the main work]): for example, because section 75(2)(c) of that Act does not apply (criminal lifestyle established by an offence committed over a period of at least six months). Where the prosecutor proposes such a course, it is unlikely that CrimPR, Pt 1 (the overriding objective) will require an indictment to contain a single "multiple incidents" count in place of a larger number of counts, subject to the general principles set out at paragraph 10A.3.

10A.12 For some offences, particularly sexual offences, the penalty for the offence may have changed during the period over which the alleged incidents took place. In such a case, additional "multiple incidents" counts should be used so that each count only alleges incidents to which the same maximum penalty applies.

10A.13 In other cases, such as sexual or physical abuse, a complainant may be in a position only to give evidence of a series of similar incidents without being able to specify when or the precise circumstances in which they occurred. In these cases, a "multiple incidents" count may be desirable. If on the other hand, the complainant is able to identify particular incidents of the offence by reference to a date or other specific event, but alleges that in addition there were other incidents which the complainant is unable to specify, then it may be desirable to include separate counts for the identified incidents and a "multiple incidents" count or counts alleging that incidents of the same offence occurred "many" times. Using a "multiple incidents" count may be an appropriate alternative to using "specimen" counts in some cases where repeated sexual or physical abuse is alleged. The choice of count will depend on the particular circumstances of the case and should be determined bearing in mind the implications for sentencing set out in *R. v. Canavan*; *R. v. Kidd*; *R. v. Shaw* [1998] 1 Cr.App.R. 79, CA.

CPD II Preliminary Proceedings 10B: Voluntary Bills of Indictment

10B.1 Section 2(2)(b) of the Administration of Justice (Miscellaneous Provisions) Act 1933 [§ 1-277 **B-66** in the main work] and paragraph 2(6) of Schedule 3 to the CDA 1998 [§ 1-36 in the main work] allow the preferment of a bill of indictment by the direction or with the consent of a judge of the High Court. Bills so preferred are known as "voluntary bills".

10B.2 Applications for such consent must not only comply with each paragraph of the Indictments (Procedure) Rules 1971 (S.I. 1971 No. 2084) [§§ 1-302 *et seq.* in the main work], but must also be accompanied by: (a) a copy of any charges on which the defendant has been sent for trial; (b) a copy of any charges on which his or her sending for trial was refused by the magistrates' court; (c) a copy of any existing indictment which has been preferred in consequence of his or her sending; (d) a summary of the evidence or other document which (i) identifies the counts in the proposed indictment on which he or she has been sent for trial (or which are substantially the same as charges on which he or she has been so sent), and (ii) in relation to each other count in the proposed indictment, identifies the pages in the accompanying statements and exhibits where the essential evidence said to support that count is to be found.

10B.3 These requirements should be complied with in relation to each defendant named in the indictment for which consent is sought, whether or not it is proposed to prefer any new count against him or her.

10B.4 The preferment of a voluntary bill is an exceptional procedure. Consent should only be granted where good reason to depart from the normal procedure is clearly shown and only where the interests of justice, rather than considerations of administrative convenience, require it.

10B.5 Neither the 1933 Act nor the 1971 rules expressly require a prosecuting authority applying for consent to the preferment of a voluntary bill to give notice of the application to the prospective defendant, nor to serve on him or her a copy of documents delivered to the judge; nor is it expressly required that the prospective defendant have any opportunity to make any submissions to the judge, whether in writing or orally.

10B.6 However, the Attorney-General previously issued guidance to prosecutors on the procedures to be adopted in seeking judicial consent to the preferment of voluntary bills. Those procedures remain applicable and prosecutors should: (a) on making an application for consent to preferment of a voluntary bill, give notice to the prospective defendant that such application has been made; (b) at about the same time, serve on the prospective defendant a copy of all the documents delivered to the judge (save to the extent that they have already been served on him or her); (c) inform the prospective defendant that he or she may make submissions in writing to the judge, provided that he or she does so within nine working days of the giving of notice under (a) above.

10B.7 Prosecutors must follow these procedures unless there are good reasons for not doing so, in which case prosecutors must inform the judge that the procedures have not been followed and seek leave to dispense with all or any of them. Judges should not give leave to dispense unless good reasons are shown.

10B.8 A judge to whom application for consent to the preferment of a voluntary bill is made will, of course, wish to consider carefully the documents submitted by the prosecutor and any written submissions made by the prospective defendant, and may properly seek any necessary amplification. The judge may invite oral submissions from either party, or accede to a request for an opportunity to make oral submissions, if the judge considers it necessary or desirable to receive oral submissions in order to make a sound and fair decision on the application. Any such oral submissions should be made on notice to the other party and in open court.

CPD III Custody and Bail 14A: Bail before Sending for Trial

B-67

14A.1 Before the Crown Court can deal with an application under rule 14.8 [§ 3-125 in the main work] by a defendant after a magistrates' court has withheld bail, it must be satisfied that the magistrates' court has issued a certificate, under section 5(6A) of the Bail Act 1976 [§ 3-28 in the main work], that it heard full argument on the application for bail before it refused the application. The certificate of full argument is produced by the magistrates' court's computer system, Libra, as part of the GENORD (General Form of Order). Two hard copies are produced, one for the defence and one for the prosecution. Some magistrates' courts may also produce a manual certificate which will usually be available from the justices' legal adviser at the conclusion of the hearing; the GENORD may not be produced until the following day. Under rule 14.4(4) [§ 3-121 in the main work], the magistrates' court officer will provide the defendant with a certificate that the court heard full argument. However, it is the responsibility of the defence, as the applicant in the Crown Court, to ensure that a copy of the certificate ... is provided to the Crown Court as part of the application (r.14.8(3)(e)). The applicant's solicitors should attach a copy of the certificate to the bail application form. If the certificate is not enclosed with the application form, it will be difficult to avoid some delay in listing.

Venue

B-68

14A.2 Applications should be made to the court to which the defendant will be, or would have been, sent for trial. In the event of an application in a purely summary case, it should be made to the Crown Court centre which normally receives class 3 work. The hearing will be listed as a chambers matter unless a judge has directed otherwise.

CPD III Custody and Bail 14B: Bail: Failure to Surrender and Trials in Absence

B-69

14B.1 The failure of defendants to comply with the terms of their bail by not surrendering, or not doing so at the appointed time, undermines the administration of justice and disrupts proceedings. The resulting delays impact on victims, witnesses and other court users and also waste costs. A defendant's failure to surrender affects not only the case with which he ... is concerned, but also the court's ability to administer justice more generally, by damaging the confidence of victims, witnesses and the public in the effectiveness of the court system and the judiciary. It is, therefore, most important that defendants who are granted bail appreciate the significance of the obligation to surrender to custody in accordance with the terms of their bail and that courts take appropriate action, if they fail to do so.

14B.2 A defendant who will be unable for medical reasons to attend court in accordance with his ... bail must obtain a certificate from his ... general practitioner or another appropriate medical practitioner such as the doctor with care of the defendant at a hospital. This should be obtained in advance of the hearing and conveyed to the court through the defendant's legal representative. In order to minimise the disruption to the court and to others, particularly witnesses if the case is listed for trial, the defendant should notify the court through his legal representative as soon as his inability to attend court becomes known.

14B.3 Guidance has been produced by the British Medical Association and the CPS on the roles and responsibilities of medical practitioners when issuing medical certificates in criminal proceedings. Judges and magistrates should seek to ensure that this guidance is followed. However, it is a matter for each individual court to decide whether, in any particular case, the issued certificate should be accepted. Without a medical certificate or if an unsatisfactory certificate is provided, the court is likely to consider that the defendant has failed to surrender to bail.

14B.4 If a defendant fails to surrender ...there are at least four courses of action for the courts to consider taking:—

    (a) imposing penalties for the failure to surrender [*see the definitive sentencing guideline,* post, *K-107* et seq.];

    (b) revoking bail or imposing more stringent conditions;

    (c) conducting trials in the absence of the defendant; and

    (d) ordering that some or all of any sums of money lodged with the court as a security or pledged by a surety as a condition on the grant of bail be forfeit.

CPD III Custody and Bail 14C: Penalties for Failure to Surrender

Initiating proceedings—bail granted by a police officer

14C.1 When a person has been granted bail by a police officer to attend court and subsequently **B-70** fails to surrender ..., the decision whether to initiate proceedings for a section 6(1) or ... (2) [§ 3-31 in the main work] offence will be for the police/prosecutor and proceedings are commenced in the usual way.

14C.2 The offence in this form is a summary offence .... The offence should be dealt with on the first appearance after arrest, unless an adjournment is necessary, as it will be relevant in considering whether to grant bail again.

Initiating proceedings—bail granted by a court

14C.3 Where a person has been granted bail by a court and subsequently fails to surrender on ar- **B-71** rest that person should normally be brought as soon as appropriate before the court at which the proceedings in respect of which bail was granted are to be heard. (There is no requirement to lay an information within the time limit for a Bail Act offence where bail was granted by the court.)

14C.4 Given that bail was granted by a court, it is more appropriate that the court itself should initiate the proceedings by its own motion although the prosecutor may invite the court to take proceedings, if the prosecutor considers proceedings are appropriate.

Timing of disposal

14C.5 Courts should not, without good reason, adjourn the disposal of a section 6(1) or ... (2) ... **B-72** offence ... until the conclusion of the proceedings in respect of which bail was granted but should deal with defendants as soon as is practicable. In deciding what is practicable, the court must take into account when the proceedings in respect of which bail was granted are expected to conclude, the seriousness of the offence for which the defendant is already being prosecuted, the type of penalty that might be imposed for the Bail Act offence and the original offence, as well as any other relevant circumstances.

14C.6 If the Bail Act offence is adjourned alongside the substantive proceedings, then it is still necessary to consider imposing a separate penalty at the trial. In addition, bail should usually be revoked in the meantime. Trial in the absence of the defendant is not a penalty for the Bail Act offence and a separate penalty may be imposed for the Bail Act offence.

Conduct of proceedings

14C.7 Proceedings under section 6 ... may be conducted either as a summary offence or as a **B-73** criminal contempt of court. Where proceedings are commenced by the police or prosecutor, the prosecutor will conduct the proceedings and, if the matter is contested, call the evidence. Where the court initiates proceedings, with or without an invitation from the prosecutor, the court may expect the assistance of the prosecutor, such as in cross-examining the defendant, if required.

14C.8 The burden of proof is on the defendant to prove that he had reasonable cause for his failure to surrender ... (s.6(3)).

14C.9, 14C.10 [*Sentencing for a Bail Act offence: see post, Appendix K-107 et seq.*]

CPD III Custody and Bail 14D: Relationship between the Bail Act Offence and Further Remands on Bail or in Custody

B-74   14D.1 The court at which the defendant is produced should, where practicable and legally permissible, arrange to have all outstanding cases brought before it (including those from different courts) for the purpose of progressing matters and dealing with the question of bail. This is likely to be practicable in the magistrates' court where cases can easily be transferred from one magistrates' court to another. Practice is likely to vary in the Crown Court. If the defendant appears before a different court, for example because he is charged with offences committed in another area, and it is not practicable for all matters to be concluded by that court then the defendant may be remanded on bail or in custody, if appropriate, to appear before the first court for the outstanding offences to be dealt with.

14D.2 When a defendant has been convicted of a Bail Act offence, the court should review the remand status of the defendant, including the conditions of that bail, in respect of all outstanding proceedings against the defendant.

14D.3 Failure by the defendant to surrender or a conviction for failing to surrender to bail in connection with the main proceedings will be significant factors weighing against the re-granting of bail.

14D.4 Whether or not an immediate custodial sentence has been imposed for the Bail Act offence, the court may, having reviewed the defendant's remand status, also remand the defendant in custody in the main proceedings.

CPD III Custody and Bail 14E: Trials in Absence

B-75   14E.1 A defendant has a right, in general, to be present and to be represented at his trial. However, a defendant may choose not to exercise those rights, such as by voluntarily absenting himself and failing to instruct his lawyers adequately so that they can represent him.

14E.2 The court has a discretion as to whether a trial should take place or continue in the defendant's absence and must exercise its discretion with due regard for the interests of justice. The overriding concern must be to ensure that such a trial is as fair as circumstances permit and leads to a just outcome. If the defendant's absence is due to involuntary illness or incapacity it would very rarely, if ever, be right to exercise the discretion in favour of commencing or continuing the trial.

14E.3, 14E.4 [*See § 3-225a in the main work.*]

CPD III Custody and Bail 14F: Forfeiture of Monies Lodged as Security or Pledged by a Surety/ Estreatment of Recognizances

B-76   14F.1 A surety undertakes to forfeit a sum of money if the defendant fails to surrender as required. Considerable care must be taken to explain that obligation and the consequences before a surety is taken. This system ... has great antiquity. It is immensely valuable. A court concerned that a defendant will fail to surrender will not normally know that defendant personally, nor indeed much about him. When members of the community who do know the defendant say they trust him to surrender and are prepared to stake their own money on that trust, that can have a powerful influence on the decision of the court as to whether or not to grant bail. There are two important side-effects. The first is that the surety will keep an eye on the defendant, and report to the authorities if there is a concern that he will abscond. In those circumstances, the surety can withdraw. The second is that a defendant will be deterred from absconding by the knowledge that if he does so then his family or friends who provided the surety will lose their money. In the experience of the courts, it is comparatively rare for a defendant to fail to surrender when meaningful sureties are in place.

14F.2 Any surety should have the opportunity to make representations to the defendant to surrender himself, in accordance with their obligations.

14F.3 The court should not wait or adjourn a decision on estreatment of sureties or securities until such time, if any, that the bailed defendant appears before the court. It is possible that any defendant who apparently absconds may have a defence of reasonable cause to the allegation of failure to surrender. If that happens, then any surety or security estreated would be returned. The reason for proceeding is that the defendant may never surrender, or may not surrender for many years. The court should still consider the sureties' obligations if that happens. Moreover, the longer the matter is delayed the more probable it is that the personal circumstances of the sureties will change.

14F.4 The court should follow the procedure at rule 14.15 of the Criminal Procedure Rules [§ 3-132 in the main work]. Before the court makes a decision, it should give the sureties the opportunity to make representations, either in person, through counsel or by statement.

14F.5 The court has discretion to forfeit the whole sum, part only of the sum, or to remit the sum. The starting point is that the surety is forfeited in full. It would be unfortunate if this valuable method of allowing a defendant to remain at liberty were undermined. Courts would have less confidence in the efficacy of sureties. It is also important to note that a defendant who absconds without in any way forewarning his sureties does not thereby release them from any or all of their responsibilities. Even if a surety does his best, he remains liable for the full amount, except at the discretion of the court. However, all factors should be taken into account and the following are noted for guidance only:

(i) the presence or absence of culpability is a factor, but is not in itself a reason to reduce or set aside the obligations entered into by the surety;

(ii) the means of a surety, and in particular changed means, are relevant;

(iii) the court should forfeit no more than is necessary, in public policy, to maintain the integrity and confidence of the system of taking sureties.

CPD III Custody and Bail 14G: Bail during Trial

14G.1 The following should be read subject to the Bail Act 1976. **B-77**

14G.2 Once a trial has begun the further grant of bail, whether during the short adjournment or overnight, is in the discretion of the trial judge or trial bench. It may be a proper exercise of this discretion to refuse bail during the short adjournment if the accused cannot otherwise be segregated from witnesses and jurors.

14G.3 An accused who was on bail while on remand should not be refused bail during the trial unless, in the opinion of the court, there are positive reasons to justify this refusal. Such reasons might include:

(a) that a point has been reached where there is a real danger that the accused will abscond, either because the case is going badly for him, or for any other reason;

(b) that there is a real danger that he may interfere with witnesses, jurors or co-defendants.

14G.4 Once the jury has returned a guilty verdict or a finding of guilt has been made, a further renewal of bail should be decided in the light of the gravity of the offence, any friction between codefendants and the likely sentence to be passed in all the circumstances of the case.

CPD III Custody and Bail 14H: Crown Court Judge's Certificaton of Fitness to Appeal and Applications to the Crown Court for Bail Pending Appeal

14H.1 The trial or sentencing judge may grant a certificate of fitness for appeal (see, *e.g.*, ss.1(2)(b) **B-78** and 11(1A) of the CAA 1968 [§§ 7-37, 7-125 in the main work]); the judge ... should only certify cases in exceptional circumstances. The ... judge should use the Criminal Appeal Office Form C (Crown Court Judge's Certificate of fitness for appeal) which is available to court staff on the HMCTS intranet.

14H.2 The judge may well think it right to encourage the defendant's advocate to submit to the court, and serve on the prosecutor, before the hearing of the application, a draft of the grounds of appeal which he will ask the judge to certify on Form C.

14H.3 The first question for the judge is then whether there exists a particular and cogent ground of appeal. If there is no such ground, there can be no certificate; and if there is no certificate there can be no bail. A judge should not grant a certificate with regard to sentence merely in the light of mitigation to which he has, in his opinion, given due weight, nor in regard to conviction on a ground where he considers the chance of a successful appeal is not substantial. The judge should bear in mind that, where a certificate is refused, application may be made to the Court of Appeal for leave to appeal and for bail; it is expected that certificates will only be granted in exceptional circumstances.

14H.4 Defence advocates should note that the effect of a grant of a certificate is to remove the need for leave to appeal to be granted by the Court of Appeal. It does not in itself commence the appeal. The completed Form C will be sent by the Crown Court to the Criminal Appeal Office; it is not copied to the parties. The procedures in Part 39 of the Criminal Procedure Rules [§§ 7-380 *et seq.* in the main work] should be followed.

14H.5 Bail pending appeal ... may be granted by the ... judge if they have certified the case as fit for appeal (see s.81(1)(f) and (1B) of the Senior Courts Act 1981 [§ 7-175 in the main work]). Bail can only be granted in the Crown Court within 28 days of the conviction or sentence which is to be the subject of the appeal and may not be granted if an application for bail has already been made to the Court of Appeal. The procedure for bail to be granted by a judge of the Crown Court pending an appeal is governed by Part 14 of the Criminal Procedure Rules [§§ 3-118 *et seq.* in the main work]. The ... judge should use the Criminal Appeal Office Form BC (Crown Court Judge's Order granting bail) which is available to court staff on the HMCTS intranet.

14H.6 The length of the period which might elapse before the hearing of any appeal is not relevant to the grant of a certificate; but, if the judge does decide to grant a certificate, it may be one factor in the decision whether or not to grant bail. If bail is granted, the judge should consider imposing a condition of residence in line with the practice in the Court of Appeal.

CPD IV Disclosure 15A: Disclosure of Unused Material

B-79   [*See §§ 12-48 and 12-101 in the main work.*]

CPD V Evidence 16A: Evidence by Written Statement

B-80   16A.1 Where the prosecution proposes to tender written statements in evidence under section 9 of the CJA 1967 [§ 10-14 in the main work], it will frequently be necessary for certain statements to be edited. This will occur either because a witness has made more than one statement whose contents should conveniently be reduced into a single, comprehensive statement, or where a statement contains inadmissible, prejudicial or irrelevant material. Editing of statements must be done by a crown prosecutor (or by a legal representative, if any, of the prosecutor if the case is not being conducted by the CPS) and not by a police officer.

Composite statements

B-81   16A.2 A composite statement giving the combined effect of two or more earlier statements must be prepared in compliance with the requirements of section 9 of the 1967 Act and must then be signed by the witness.

Editing single statements

B-82   16A.3 There are two acceptable methods of editing single statements. They are:
(a) by marking copies of the statement in a way which indicates the passages on which the prosecution will not rely; this merely indicates that the prosecution will not seek to adduce the evidence so marked; the original signed statement to be tendered to the court is not marked in any way; the marking on the copy statement is done by lightly striking out the passages to be edited, so that what appears beneath can still be read, or by bracketing, or by a combination of both; it is not permissible to produce a photocopy with the deleted material obliterated, since this would be contrary to the requirement that the defence and the court should be served with copies of the signed original statement; whenever the striking out / bracketing method is used, it will assist if the following words appear at the foot of the frontispiece or index to any bundle of copy statements to be tendered: "*The prosecution does not propose to adduce evidence of those passages of the attached copy statements which have been struck out and / or bracketed (nor will it seek to do so at the trial unless a notice of further evidence is served).*";
(b) by obtaining a fresh statement, signed by the witness, which omits the offending material, applying the procedure for composite statements above.

16A.4 In most cases where a single statement is to be edited, the striking out/bracketing method will be the more appropriate, but the taking of a fresh statement is preferable in the following circumstances. (a) When a police (or other investigating) officer's statement contains details of interviews with more suspects than are eventually charged, a fresh statement should be prepared and signed omitting all details of interview with those not charged except, in so far as it is relevant, for the bald fact that a certain named person was interviewed at a particular time, date and place. (b) When a suspect is interviewed about more offences than are eventually made the subject of charges, a fresh statement should be prepared and signed, omitting all questions and answers about the uncharged offences unless either they might appropriately be taken into consideration, or evidence about those offences is admissible on the charges preferred. It may, however, be desirable to replace the omitted questions and answers with a phrase such as: "After referring to some other matters, I then said ... ", so as to make it clear that part of the interview has been omitted. (c) A fresh statement should normally be prepared and signed if the only part of the original on which the prosecution is relying is only a small proportion of the whole, although it remains desirable to use the alternative method if there is reason to believe that the defence might itself wish to rely, in mitigation or for any other purpose, on at least some of those parts which the prosecution does not propose to adduce. (d) When the passages contain material which the prosecution is entitled to withhold from disclosure to the defence.

16A.5 Prosecutors should also be aware that, where statements are to be tendered under section 9 of the 1967 Act in the course of *summary* proceedings, there will be a need to prepare fresh statements excluding inadmissible or prejudicial material, rather than using the striking out or bracketing method.

16A.6 Whenever a fresh statement is taken from a witness and served in evidence, the earlier, unedited statement(s) becomes unused material and should be scheduled and reviewed for disclosure to the defence in the usual way.

CPD V Evidence 16B: Video Recorded Evidence in Chief

16B.1 [*Recites the relevant provisions (s.27 of the 1999 Act (§ 8-89 in the main work) and Pt 18 of the 2014 rules (§§ 8-110* et seq. *in the main work)).*] **B-83**

16B.2 Where a court, on application by a party to the proceedings or of its own motion, grants leave to admit a video recording in evidence under section 27(1) ..., it may direct that any part of the recording be excluded (s.27(2) and (3)). When such direction is given, the party who made the application to admit the video recording must edit the recording in accordance with the judge's directions and send a copy of the edited recording to the appropriate officer of the Crown Court and to every other party to the proceedings.

16B.3 Where a video recording is to be adduced during proceedings before the Crown Court, it should be produced and proved by the interviewer, or any other person who was present at the interview with the witness at which the recording was made. The applicant should ensure that such a person will be available for this purpose, unless the parties have agreed to accept a written statement in lieu of attendance by that person.

16B.4 Once a trial has begun, if, by reason of faulty or inadequate preparation or for some other cause, the procedures set out above have not been properly complied with and an application is made to edit the video recording, thereby necessitating an adjournment for the work to be carried out, the court may, at its discretion, make an appropriate award of costs.

CPD V Evidence 16C: Evidence of Audio and Video Recorded Interviews

16C.1 The interrogation of suspects is primarily governed by Code C [*ante*, Appendix A-39 *et seq.*] **B-84** ... Under that code, interviews must normally be contemporaneously recorded. Under ... Code E [*ante*, Appendix A-162 *et seq.*], interviews conducted at a police station concerning an indictable offence must normally be audio-recorded. In practice, most interviews are audio-recorded under Code E, or video-recorded under Code F, and it is best practice to do so. The questioning of terrorism suspects is governed ... by Code H [*ante*, Appendix A-213 *et seq.*].

16C.2 Where a record of the interview is to be prepared, this should be in accordance with the current national guidelines, as envisaged by Note 5A of Code E.

16C.3 If the prosecution wishes to rely on the defendant's interview in evidence, the prosecution should seek to agree the record with the defence. Both parties should have received a copy of the audio or video recording, and can check the record against the recording. The record should be edited (see below) if inadmissible matters are included within it and, in particular if the interview is lengthy, the prosecution should seek to shorten it by editing or summary.

16C.4 If the record is agreed there is usually no need for the audio or video recording to be played in court. It is a matter for the discretion of the ... judge, but usual practice is for edited copies of the record to be provided to the court, and to the jury if there is one, and for the prosecution advocate to read the interview with the interviewing officer or the officer in the case, as part of the officer's evidence in chief, the officer reading the interviewer and the advocate reading the defendant and defence representative. In the magistrates' court, the Bench sometimes retire to read the interview themselves, and the document is treated as if it had been read aloud in court. This is permissible, but rule 24.5 should be followed.

16C.5 Where the prosecution intends to adduce the interview in evidence, and agreement between the parties has not been reached about the record, sufficient notice must be given to allow consideration of any amendment to the record, or the preparation of any transcript of the interview, or any editing of a recording for the purpose of playing it in court. To that end, the following practice should be followed:

 (a) where the defence is unable to agree a record of interview or transcript (where one is already available) the prosecution should be notified at latest at the Plea and Case Management Hearing ("PCMH"), with a view to securing agreement to amend; the notice should specify the part to which objection is taken, or the part omitted which the defence consider should be included; a copy of the notice should be supplied to the court within the period specified above; the PCMH form inquires about the admissibility of the defendant's interview and shortening by editing or summarising for trial;

(b) if agreement is not reached and it is proposed that the audio or video recording or part of it be played in court, notice should be given to the prosecution by the defence as ordered at the PCMH, in order that the advocates for the parties may agree those parts of the audio or video recording that should not be adduced and that arrangements may be made, by editing or in some other way, to exclude that material; a copy of the notice should be supplied to the court;

(c) notice of any agreement reached should be supplied to the court by the prosecution, as soon as is practicable.

16C.6 Alternatively, if, the prosecution advocate proposes to play the audio or video recording or part of it, the prosecution should at latest at the PCMH, notify the defence and the court. The defence should notify the prosecution and the court within 14 days of receiving the notice, if they object to the production of the audio or video recording on the basis that a part of it should be excluded. If the objections raised by the defence are accepted, the prosecution should prepare an edited recording, or make other arrangements to exclude the material part; and should notify the court of the arrangements made.

16C.7 If the defendant wishes to have the audio or video recording or any part of it played to the court, the defence should provide notice to the prosecution and the court at latest at the PCMH. The defence should also, at that time, notify the prosecution of any proposals to edit the recording and seek the prosecution's agreement to those amendments.

16C.8 Whenever editing or amendment of a record of interview or of an audio or video recording or of a transcript takes place, the following general principles should be followed:

(i) where a defendant has made a statement which includes an admission of one or more other offences, the portion relating to other offences should be omitted unless it is or becomes admissible in evidence;

(ii) where the statement of one defendant contains a portion which exculpates him ... and partly implicates a co-defendant in the trial, the defendant making the statement has the right to insist that everything relevant which is exculpatory goes before the jury; in such a case the judge must be consulted about how best to protect the position of the co-defendant.

16C.9 If it becomes necessary for either party to access the master copy of the audio or video recording, they should give notice to the other party and follow the procedure in ... Code E at section 6.

16C.10 If there is a challenge to the integrity of the master recording, notice and particulars should be given to the court and to the prosecution by the defence as soon as is practicable. The court may then, at its discretion, order a case management hearing or give such other directions as may be appropriate.

16C.11 If an audio or video recording is to be adduced during proceedings before the Crown Court, it should be produced and proved in a witness statement by the interviewing officer or any other officer who was present at the interview at which the recording was made. The prosecution should ensure that the witness is available to attend court if required by the defence in the usual way.

16C.12 It is the responsibility of the prosecution to ensure that there is a person available to operate any audio or video equipment needed during the course of the proceedings. Subject to their other responsibilities, the court staff may be able to assist.

16C.13 If either party wishes to present audio or video evidence, that party must ensure, in advance of the hearing, that the evidence is in a format that is compatible with the court's equipment, and that the material to be used does in fact function properly in the relevant court room.

16C.14 In order to avoid the necessity for the court to listen to or watch lengthy or irrelevant material before the relevant part of a recording is reached, counsel shall indicate to the equipment operator those parts of a recording which it may be necessary to play. Such an indication should, so far as possible, be expressed in terms of the time track or other identifying process used by the interviewing police force and should be given in time for the operator to have located those parts by the appropriate point in the trial.

16C.15 Once a trial has begun, if, by reason of faulty preparation or for some other cause, the procedures above have not been properly complied with, and an application is made to amend the record of interview or transcript or to edit the recording, as the case may be, thereby making necessary an adjournment for the work to be carried out, the court may make at its discretion an appropriate award of costs.

16C.16 Where a case is listed for hearing on a date which falls within the time limits set out above, it is the responsibility of the parties to ensure that all the necessary steps are taken to comply with this Practice Direction within such shorter period as is available.

CPD V Evidence 17A: Wards of Court and Children Subject to Current Family Proceedings

B-85

17A.1 Where police wish to interview a child who is subject to current family proceedings, leave of the Family Court is only required where such an interview may lead to a child disclosing information confidential to those proceedings and not otherwise available to the police under Working Together to Safeguard Children (March 2013), a guide to inter-agency working to safeguard and promote the welfare of children: www.workingtogetheronline.co.uk/chapters/contents.html.

17A.2 Where exceptionally the child to be interviewed or called as a witness in criminal proceedings is a ward of court then the leave of the court which made the wardship order will be required.

17A.3 Any application for leave in respect of any such child must be made to the court in which the relevant family proceedings are continuing and must be made on notice to the parents, any actual carer (*e.g.* relative or foster parent) and, in care proceedings, to the local authority and the guardian. In private proceedings the family court reporter (if appointed) should be notified.

17A.4 If the police need to interview the child without the knowledge of another party (usually a parent or carer), they may make the application for leave without giving notice to that party.

17A.5 Where leave is given the order should ordinarily give leave for any number of interviews that may be required. However, anything beyond that actually authorised will require a further application.

17A.6 Exceptionally the police may have to deal with complaints by or allegations against such a child immediately without obtaining the leave of the court as, for example:

    (a) a serious offence against a child (like rape) where immediate medical examination and collection of evidence is required; or

    (b) where the child is to be interviewed as a suspect.

When any such action is necessary, the police should, in respect of each and every interview, notify the parents and other carer (if any) and the family court reporter (if appointed). In care proceedings the local authority and guardian should be notified. The police must comply with all relevant codes of practice when conducting any such interview.

17A.7 The Family Court should be appraised of the position at the earliest reasonable opportunity by one of the notified parties and should thereafter be kept informed of any criminal proceedings.

17A.8 No evidence or document in the family proceedings or information about the proceedings should be disclosed into criminal proceedings without the leave of the Family Court.

CPD V Evidence 18A: Measures to Assist a Witness or Defendant to Give Evidence

18A.1 For special measures applications, the procedures at Part 18 [§§ 8-110 *et seq.* in the main **B-86** work] should be followed. However, assisting a vulnerable witness to give evidence is not merely a matter of ordering the appropriate measure. Further directions about vulnerable people in the courts, ground rules hearings and intermediaries are given in the practice direction accompanying Part 3 [*ante*, B-3 *et seq.*].

18A.2 Special measures need not be considered or ordered in isolation. The needs of the individual witness should be ascertained, and a combination of special measures may be appropriate. For example, if a witness who is to give evidence by live link wishes, screens can be used to shield the live link screen from the defendant and the public, as would occur if screens were being used for a witness giving evidence in the court room.

CPD V Evidence 18B: Witnesses Giving Evidence by Live Link

18B.1 A special measures direction for the witness to give evidence by live link may also provide **B-87** for a specified person to accompany the witness (r.18.10(f)). In determining who this should be, the court must have regard to the wishes of the witness. The presence of a supporter is designed to provide emotional support to the witness, helping reduce the witness's anxiety and stress and contributing to the ability to give best evidence. It is preferable for the direction to be made well before the trial begins and to ensure that the designated person is available on the day of the witness's testimony so as to provide certainty for the witness.

18B.2 An increased degree of flexibility is appropriate as to who can act as supporter. This can be anyone known to and trusted by the witness who is not a party to the proceedings and has no detailed knowledge of the evidence in the case. The supporter may be a member of the witness service but need not be an usher or court official. Someone else may be appropriate.

18B.3 The usher should continue to be available both to assist the witness and the witness supporter, and to ensure that the court's requirements are properly complied with in the live link room.

18B.4 In order to be able to express an informed view about special measures, the witness is entitled to practise speaking using the live link (and to see screens in place). Simply being shown the room and equipment is inadequate for this purpose.

18B.5 If, with the agreement of the court, the witness has chosen not to give evidence by live link but to do so in the court room, it may still be appropriate for a witness supporter to be selected in the same way, and for the supporter to sit alongside the witness while the witness is giving evidence.

CPD V Evidence 18C: Visually Recorded Interviews: Memory Refreshing and Watching at a Different Time from the Jury

B-88
18C.1 Witnesses are entitled to refresh their memory from their statement or visually recorded interview. The court should enquire at the PCMH or other case management hearing about arrangements for memory refreshing. The witness's first viewing of the visually recorded interview can be distressing or distracting. It should not be seen for the first time immediately before giving evidence. Depending upon the age and vulnerability of the witness several competing issues have to be considered and it may be that the assistance of the intermediary is needed to establish exactly how memory refreshing should be managed.

18C.2 If the interview is ruled inadmissible, the court must decide what constitutes an acceptable alternative method of memory refreshing.

18C.3 Decisions about how, when and where refreshing should take place should be court-led and made on a case-by-case basis in respect of each witness. General principles to be addressed include:

(i) the venue for viewing; the delicate balance between combining the court familiarisation visit and watching the DVD, and having them on two separate occasions, needs to be considered in respect of each witness as combining the two may lead to "information overload"; refreshing need not necessarily take place within the court building but may be done, for example, at the police ABE suite;

(ii) requiring that any viewing is monitored by a person (usually the officer in the case) who will report to the court about anything said by the witness;

(iii) whether it is necessary for the witness to see the DVD more than once for the purpose of refreshing; the court will need to ask the advice of the intermediary, if any, with respect to this;

(iv) arrangements, if the witness will not watch the DVD at the same time as the trial bench or judge and jury, for the witness to watch it before attending to be cross-examined (depending upon their ability to retain information this may be the day before).

18C.4 There is no legal requirement that the witness should watch the interview at the same time as the trial bench or jury. Increasingly, this is arranged to occur at a different time, with the advantages that breaks can be taken as needed without disrupting the trial, and cross-examination starts while the witness is fresh. An intermediary may be present to facilitate communication but should not act as the independent person designated to take a note and report to the court if anything is said. Where the viewing takes place at a different time from that of the jury, the witness is sworn just before cross-examination, asked if he or she has watched the interview and if its contents are "true" (or other words tailored to the witness's understanding).

CPD V Evidence 18D: Witness Anonymity Orders

B-89
18D.1 [*Recites that this direction supplements the Coroners and Justice Act 2009, s.87 (§ 8-157 in the main work) and rr.18.18-18.22 (§§ 8-127 et seq. in the main work).*]

18D.2 As the Court of Appeal stated in *R. v. Mayers* [§§ 8-170 *et seq.* in the main work] and emphasised again in *R. v. Donovan and Kafunda* [§ 8-172 in the main work], "a witness anonymity order is to be regarded as a special measure of the last practicable resort". In making such an application, the prosecution's obligations of disclosure "go much further than the ordinary duties of disclosure" (*R. v. Mayers*); reference should be made to the Judicial Protocol on Disclosure (*post*, Appendix N-52 *et seq.*): see the practice direction accompanying Part 15 [§§ 12-48, 12-101 in the main work].

Case management

B-90
18D.3 Where such an application is proposed, with the parties' active assistance the court should set a realistic timetable, in accordance with the duties imposed by rules 3.2 and 3.3. Where possible, the trial judge should determine the application, and any hearing should be attended by the parties' trial advocates.

Service of evidence and disclosure of prosecution material pending an application

B-91
18D.4 Where the prosecutor proposes an application for a witness anonymity order it is not necessary for that application to have been determined before the proposed evidence is served. In most cases an early indication of what that evidence will be if an order is made will be consistent with a party's duties under rules 1.2 and 3.3 [§§ 4-114, 4-115 in the main work]. The prosecutor should serve with the other prosecution evidence a witness statement setting out the proposed evidence,

redacted in such a way as to prevent disclosure of the witness' identity, as permitted by section 87(4) ... . Likewise the prosecutor should serve with other prosecution material disclosed under the CPIA 1996 any such material appertaining to the witness, similarly redacted.

The application

18D.5 An application for a witness anonymity order should be made as early as possible and **B-92** within the period for which rule 18.3 provides. The application, and any hearing of it, must comply with the requirements of that rule and with those of rule 18.19. In accordance with rules 1.2 and 3.3, the applicant must provide the court with all available information relevant to the considerations to which the Act requires a court to have regard.

Response to the application

18D.6 A party upon whom an application for a witness anonymity order is served must serve a **B-93** response in accordance with rule 18.22. That period may be extended or shortened in the court's discretion: r.18.5.

18D.7 To avoid the risk of injustice, a respondent, whether the prosecution or a defendant, must actively assist the court. If not already done, a respondent defendant should serve a defence statement under section 5 or 6 of the CPIA 1996 [§§ 12-62, 12-63 in the main work], so that the court is fully informed of what is in issue. When a defendant makes an application for a witness anonymity order the prosecutor should consider the continuing duty to disclose material under section 7A of the CPIA 1996 [§ 12-74 in the main work]; therefore a prosecutor's response should include confirmation that that duty has been considered. Great care should be taken to ensure that nothing disclosed contains anything that might reveal the witness' identity. A respondent prosecutor should provide the court with all available information relevant to the considerations to which the Act requires a court to have regard, whether or not that information falls to be disclosed under the 1996 Act.

Determination of the application

18D.8 All parties must have an opportunity to make oral representations to the court on an ap- **B-94** plication for a witness anonymity order: s.87(6) ... . However, a hearing may not be needed if none is sought: r.18.18(1)(a). Where, for example, the witness is an investigator who is recognisable by the defendant but known only by an assumed name, and there is no likelihood that the witness' credibility will be in issue, then the court may indicate a provisional decision and invite representations within a defined period, usually 14 days, including representations about whether there should be a hearing. In such a case, where the parties do not object the court may make an order without a hearing. Or where the court provisionally considers an application to be misconceived, an applicant may choose to withdraw it without requiring a hearing. Where the court directs a hearing of the application then it should allow adequate time for service of the representations in response.

18D.9 The hearing of an application for a witness anonymity order usually should be in private: r.18.18(1)(a). The court has power to hear a party in the absence of a defendant and that defendant's representatives: s.87(7) ... and r.18.18(1)(b). In the Crown Court, a recording of the proceedings will be made, in accordance with rule 5.5 [§ 2-181 in the main work]. The Crown Court officer must treat such a recording in the same way as the recording of an application for a public interest ruling. It must be kept in secure conditions, and the arrangements made by the Crown Court officer for any transcription must impose restrictions that correspond with those under rule 5.5(2).

18D.10 Where confidential supporting information is presented to the court before the last stage of the hearing, the court may prefer not to read that information until that last stage.

18D.11 The court may adjourn the hearing at any stage, and should do so if its duty under rule 3.2 [§ 4-115 in the main work] so requires.

18D.12 On a prosecutor's application, the court is likely to be assisted by the attendance of a senior investigator or other person of comparable authority who is familiar with the case.

18D.13 During the last stage of the hearing it is essential that the court test thoroughly the information supplied in confidence in order to satisfy itself that the conditions prescribed by the Act are met. At that stage, if the court concludes that this is the only way in which it can satisfy itself as to a relevant condition or consideration, exceptionally it may invite the applicant to present the proposed witness to be questioned by the court. Any such questioning should be carried out at such a time, and the witness brought to the court in such a way, as to prevent disclosure of his ... identity.

18D.14 The court may ask the Attorney-General to appoint special counsel to assist. However, it must be kept in mind that, "Such an appointment will always be exceptional, never automatic; a course of last and never first resort. It should not be ordered unless and until the trial judge is satisfied that no other course will adequately meet the overriding requirement of fairness to the defendant": *R. v. H.* [§ 12-109 in the main work]. Whether to accede to such a request is a matter for the Attorney-General, and adequate time should be allowed for the consideration of such a request.

18D.15 The Court of Appeal in *R. v. Mayers* emphasised that all three conditions, A, B and C, must be met before the jurisdiction to make a witness anonymity order arises. Each is mandatory. Each is distinct. The court also noted that if there is more than one anonymous witness in a case any link, and the nature of any link, between the witnesses should be investigated: "questions of possible improper collusion between them, or cross-contamination of one another, should be addressed."

18D.16 Following a hearing the court should announce its decision ... in the parties' presence and in public: r.18.4(2). The court should give such reasons as it is possible to give without revealing the witness' identity. In the Crown Court, the court will be conscious that reasons given in public may be reported and reach the jury. Consequently, the court should ensure that nothing in its decision or its reasons could undermine any warning it may give jurors under section 90(2) [§ 8-160 in the main work] ... . A record of the reasons must be kept. In the Crown Court, the announcement of those reasons will be recorded.

Order

B-95

18D.17 Where the court makes a witness anonymity order, it is essential that the measures to be taken are clearly specified in a written record of that order approved by the court and issued on its behalf. An order made in a magistrates' court must be recorded in the court register, in accordance with rule 5.4 [§ 2-180 in the main work].

18D.18 Self-evidently, the written record of the order must not disclose the identity of the witness to whom it applies. However, it is essential that there be maintained some means of establishing a clear correlation between witness and order, and especially where in the same proceedings witness anonymity orders are made in respect of more than one witness, specifying different measures in respect of each. Careful preservation of the application for the order, including the confidential part, ordinarily will suffice for this purpose.

Discharge or variation of the order

B-96

18D.19 Section 91 [§ 8-161 in the main work] ... allows the court to discharge or vary a witness anonymity order: on application, if there has been a material change of circumstances since the order was made or since any previous variation of it; or on its own initiative. Rule 18.21 allows the parties to apply for the variation of a pre-trial direction where circumstances have changed.

18D.20 The court should keep under review the question of whether the conditions for making an order are met. In addition, consistently with the parties' duties under rules 1.2 and 3.3 [§§ 4-114, 4-115 in the main work], it is incumbent on each, and in particular on the applicant for the order, to keep the need for it under review.

18D.21 Where the court considers the discharge or variation of an order, the procedure that it adopts should be appropriate to the circumstances. As a general rule, that procedure should approximate to the procedure for determining an application for an order. The court may need to hear further representations by the applicant for the order in the absence of a respondent defendant and that defendant's representatives.

Retention of confidential material

B-97

18D.22 If retained by the court, confidential material must be stored in secure conditions by the court officer. Alternatively, subject to such directions as the court may give, such material may be committed to the safe-keeping of the applicant or any other appropriate person in exercise of the powers conferred by rule 18.6. If the material is released to any such person, the court should ensure that it will be available to the court at trial.

CPD V Evidence 19A: Expert Evidence

B-98

19A.1 Expert opinion evidence is admissible in criminal proceedings at common law if, in summary, (i) it is relevant to a matter in issue in the proceedings; (ii) it is needed to provide the court with information likely to be outside the court's own knowledge and experience; and (iii) the witness is competent to give that opinion.

19A.2 [*Summarises the CJA 1988, s.30 [§ 10-35 in the main work], and the Criminal Procedure Rules 2015, Pt 19 [§§ 10-39 et seq. in the main work].*]

19A.3 [*Refers to the non-implementation of a Law Commission proposal for the enactment of a statutory test for admissibility.*] The common law, therefore, remains the source of the criteria by reference to which the court must assess the admissibility and weight of such evidence; and rule 19.4 ... lists those matters with which an expert's report must deal, so that the court can conduct an adequate such assessment.

19A.4 In ... [*R. v. Dlugosz; R. v. Pickering; R. v. S. (M.D.)* [2013] 1 Cr.App.R. 32], the Court of Appeal observed (at [11]): "It is essential to recall the principle which is applicable, namely in determining the issue of admissibility, the court must be satisfied that there is a sufficiently reliable scientific basis for the evidence to be admitted. If there is then the court leaves the opposing views to be tested before the jury." Nothing at common law precludes assessment by the court of the reliability of an expert opinion by reference to substantially similar factors to those the Law Commission recommended as conditions of admissibility, and courts are encouraged actively to enquire into such factors.

19A.5 Therefore factors which the court may take into account in determining the reliability of expert opinion, and especially of expert scientific opinion, include:

    (a) the extent and quality of the data on which the expert's opinion is based, and the validity of the methods by which they were obtained;

    (b) if the expert's opinion relies on an inference from any findings, whether the opinion properly explains how safe or unsafe the inference is (whether by reference to statistical significance or in other appropriate terms);

    (c) if the expert's opinion relies on the results of the use of any method (for instance, a test, measurement or survey), whether the opinion takes proper account of matters, such as the degree of precision or margin of uncertainty, affecting the accuracy or reliability of those results;

    (d) the extent to which any material upon which the expert's opinion is based has been reviewed by others with relevant expertise (for instance, in peer-reviewed publications), and the views of those others on that material;

    (e) the extent to which the expert's opinion is based on material falling outside the expert's own field of expertise;

    (f) the completeness of the information which was available to the expert, and whether the expert took account of all relevant information in arriving at the opinion (including information as to the context of any facts to which the opinion relates);

    (g) if there is a range of expert opinion on the matter in question, where in the range the expert's own opinion lies and whether the expert's preference has been properly explained; and

    (h) whether the expert's methods followed established practice in the field and, if they did not, whether the reason for the divergence has been properly explained.

19A.6 In addition, in considering reliability, and especially the reliability of expert scientific opinion, the court should be astute to identify potential flaws in such opinion which detract from its reliability, such as:

    (a) being based on a hypothesis which has not been subjected to sufficient scrutiny (including, where appropriate, experimental or other testing), or which has failed to stand up to scrutiny;

    (b) being based on an unjustifiable assumption;

    (c) being based on flawed data;

    (d) relying on an examination, technique, method or process which was not properly carried out or applied, or was not appropriate for use in the particular case; or

    (e) relying on an inference or conclusion which has not been properly reached.

CPD V Evidence 21A: Spent Convictions

21A.1 The effect of section 4(1) of the Rehabilitation of Offenders Act 1974 [§ 13-125 in the main **B-99** work] is that a person who has become a rehabilitated person for the purpose of the Act in respect of a conviction ... shall be treated for all purposes in law as a person who has not committed, or been charged with or prosecuted for, or convicted of or sentenced for, the offence or offences which were the subject of that conviction.

21A.2 Section 4(1) ... does not apply, however, to evidence given in criminal proceedings: s.7(2)(a) [§ 13-133 in the main work]. During the trial of a criminal charge, reference to previous convictions (and therefore to spent convictions) can arise in a number of ways. The most common is when a bad character application is made under the CJA 2003. When considering bad character applications ... regard should always be had to the general principles of the [1974 Act].

21A.3 On conviction, the court must be provided with a statement of the defendant's record for the purposes of sentence. The record supplied should contain all previous convictions, but those which are spent should, so far as practicable, be marked as such. No one should refer in open court to a spent conviction without the authority of the judge, which authority should not be given unless the interests of justice so require. When passing sentence the judge should make no reference to a spent conviction unless it is necessary to do so for the purpose of explaining the sentence to be passed.

CPD VI Trial 24A: Role of the Justices' Clerk/Legal Adviser

B-100   *[Not set out in this work.]*

CPD VI Trial 26A: Juries: Introduction

B-101   *[See § 4-266 in the main work.]*

CPD VI Trial 26B: Juries: Preliminary Matters Arising before Jury Service Commences

B-102   26B.1 The effect of section 321 of the CJA 2003 was to remove certain categories of persons from those previously ineligible for jury service (the judiciary and others concerned with the administration of justice) and certain other categories ceased to be eligible for excusal as of right (such as Members of Parliament and medical professionals). The normal presumption is that everyone, unless ineligible or disqualified, will be required to serve when summoned to do so.

26B.2 *[Power of jury summoning officer to defer or excuse individuals in accordance with the guidance at § 4-284 in the main work.]*

26B.3 *[Appeal from summoning officer's refusal to excuse or postpone jury service: see § 4-289 in the main work.]*

26B.4 *[Provision of further relevant information to jurors by the court officer/]*

CPD VI Trial 26C: Juries: Eligibility

English language ability

B-103   26C.1 Under the Juries Act 1974, s.10 [§ 4-291 in the main work], a person summoned for jury service who applies for excusal on the grounds of insufficient understanding of English may, where necessary, be brought before the judge.

26C.2 The court may exercise its power to excuse any person from jury service for lack of capacity to act effectively as a juror because of an insufficient understanding of English.

26C.3 The judge has the discretion to stand down jurors who are not competent to serve by reason of a personal disability: *R. v. Mason* [§ 4-275 in the main work]; *R. v. Jalil* [§ 4-292 in the main work].

Jurors with professional and public service commitments

B-104   26C.4 The legislative change in the CJA 2003 means that more individuals are eligible to serve as jurors, including those previously excused as of right or ineligible. Judges need to be vigilant to the need to exercise their discretion to adjourn a trial, excuse or discharge a juror should the need arise.

26C.5 Whether or not an application has already been made to the jury summoning officer for deferral or excusal, it is also open to the person summoned to apply to the court to be excused. Such applications must be considered with common sense and according to the interests of justice. An explanation should be required for an application being much later than necessary.

Serving police officers, prison officers or employees of prosecuting agencies

B-105   26C.6 A judge should always be made aware at the stage of jury selection if any juror in waiting is in these categories. The juror summons warns jurors in these categories that they will need to alert court staff.

26C.7 In the case of police officers an inquiry by the judge will have to be made to assess whether a police officer may serve as a juror. Regard should be had to: whether evidence from the police is in dispute in the case and the extent to which that dispute involves allegations made against the police; whether the potential juror knows or has worked with the officers involved in the case; whether the potential juror has served or continues to serve in the same police units within the force as those dealing with the investigation of the case or is likely to have a shared local service background with police witnesses in a trial.

26C.8 In the case of a serving prison officer summoned to a court, the judge will need to inquire whether the individual is employed at a prison linked to that court or is likely to have special knowledge of any person involved in a trial.

26C.9 The judge will need to ensure that employees of prosecuting authorities do not serve on a trial prosecuted by the prosecuting authority by which they are employed. They can serve on a trial prosecuted by another prosecuting authority: *R. v. Abdroikov* [§ 4-293 in the main work]; *Hanif v. U.K.* [§ 7-89 in the main work]; *R. v. L. (L.)* [§ 4-293 in the main work]. Similarly, a serving police officer can serve where there is no particular link between the court and the station where the police officer serves.

26C.10 Potential jurors falling into these categories should be excused from jury service unless there is a suitable alternative court/trial to which they can be transferred.

CPD VI Trial 26D: Juries: Precautionary Measures before Swearing

26D.1 There should be a consultation with the advocates as to the questions, if any, it may be ap- **B-106**
propriate to ask potential jurors. Topics to be considered include: (a) the availability of jurors for the duration of a trial that is likely to run beyond the usual period for which jurors are summoned; (b) whether any juror knows the defendant or parties to the case; (c) whether potential jurors are so familiar with any locations that feature in the case that they may have, or come to have, access to information not in evidence; (d) in cases where there has been any significant local or national publicity, whether any questions should be asked of potential jurors.

26D.2 Judges should however exercise caution. At common law a judge has a residual discretion to discharge a particular juror who ought not to be serving, but this discretion can only be exercised to prevent an individual juror who is not competent from serving. It does not include a discretion to discharge a jury drawn from particular sections of the community or otherwise to influence the overall composition of the jury. However, if there is a risk that there is widespread local knowledge of the defendant or a witness in a particular case, the judge may, after hearing submissions from the advocates, decide to exclude jurors from particular areas to avoid the risk of jurors having or acquiring personal knowledge of the defendant or a witness.

Length of trial

26D.3 Where the length of the trial is estimated to be significantly longer than the normal period **B-107**
of jury service, it is good practice for the trial judge to enquire whether the potential jurors on the jury panel foresee any difficulties with the length and if the judge is satisfied that the jurors' concerns are justified, he may say that they are not required for that particular jury. This does not mean that the judge must excuse the juror from sitting at that court altogether, as it may well be possible for the juror to sit on a shorter trial at the same court.

Juror with potential connection to the case or parties

26D.4 Where a juror appears on a jury panel, it will be appropriate for a judge to excuse the **B-108**
juror from that particular case where the potential juror is personally concerned with the facts of the particular case, or is closely connected with a prospective witness. Judges need to exercise due caution as noted above.

CPD VI Trial 26E: Juries: Swearing in Jurors

Swearing jury for trial

26E.1 All jurors shall be sworn or affirm. All jurors shall take the oath or affirmation in open court **B-109**
in the presence of one another. If, as a result of the juror's delivery of the oath or affirmation, a judge has concerns that a juror has such difficulties with language comprehension or reading ability that might affect that juror's capacity to undertake his or her duties, bearing in mind the likely evidence in the trial, the judge should make appropriate inquiry of that juror.

Form of oath or affirmation

26E.2 Each juror should have the opportunity to indicate to the court the Holy Book on which he **B-110**
or she wishes to swear. The precise wording will depend on his or her faith as indicated to the court.

26E.3 Any person who prefers to affirm shall be permitted to make a solemn affirmation instead. The wording of the affirmation is: "I do solemnly, sincerely and truly declare and affirm that I will faithfully try the defendant and give a true verdict according to the evidence."

CPD VI Trial 26G: Juries: Preliminary Instructions to Jurors

26G.1 After the jury has been sworn and the defendant has been put in charge the judge will want **B-111**
to give directions to the jury on a number of matters.

26G.2 Jurors can be expected to follow the instructions diligently. As the Privy Council stated in *Taylor (Bonnett) v. The Queen* [2013] 2 Cr.App.R. 18:

> "The assumption must be that the jury understood and followed the direction that they were given: ... the experience of trial judges is that juries perform their duty according to law. ... [T]he law proceeds on the footing that the jury, acting in accordance with the instructions given to them

by the trial judge, will render a true verdict in accordance with the evidence. To conclude otherwise would be to underrate the integrity of the system of trial by jury and the effect on the jury of the instructions by the trial judge."

At the start of the trial

B-112   26G.3 Trial judges should instruct the jury on general matters which will include the time estimate for the trial and normal sitting hours. The jury will always need clear guidance on the following:

    (i) the need to try the case only on the evidence and remain faithful to their oath or affirmation;

    (ii) the prohibition on internet searches for matters related to the trial, issues arising or the parties;

    (iii) the importance of not discussing any aspect of the case with anyone outside their own number or allowing anyone to talk to them about it, whether directly, by telephone, through internet facilities such as Facebook or Twitter or in any other way;

    (iv) the importance of taking no account of any media reports about the case;

    (v) the collective responsibility of the jury; as Lord Judge C.J. made clear in *R. v. Thompson* [2010] 2 Cr.App.R. 27: "[T]here is a collective responsibility for ensuring that the conduct of each member is consistent with the jury oath and that the directions of the trial judge about the discharge of their responsibilities are followed. The collective responsibility of the jury for its own conduct must be regarded as an integral part of the trial itself.";

    (vi) the need to bring any concerns, including concerns about the conduct of other jurors, to the attention of the judge at the time, and not to wait until the case is concluded; the point should be made that, unless that is done while the case is continuing, it may not be possible to deal with the problem at all.

Subsequent reminder of the jury instructions

B-113   26G.4 Judges should consider reminding jurors of these instructions as appropriate at the end of each day and in particular when they separate after retirement.

CPD VI Trial 26H: Juries: Discharge of a Juror for Personal Reasons

B-114   26H.1 Where a juror unexpectedly finds him or herself in difficult professional or personal circumstances during the course of the trial, the juror should be encouraged to raise such problems with the trial judge. This might apply, for example, to a parent whose childcare arrangements unexpectedly fail, or a worker who is engaged in the provision of services the need for which can be critical, or a Member of Parliament who has deferred their jury service to an apparently more convenient time, but is unexpectedly called back to work for a very important reason. Such difficulties would normally be raised through a jury note in the normal manner.

26H.2 In such circumstances, the judge must exercise his or her discretion according to the interests of justice and the requirements of each individual case. The judge must decide for him or herself whether the juror has presented a sufficient reason to interfere with the course of the trial. If the juror has presented a sufficient reason, in longer trials it may well be possible to adjourn for a short period in order to allow the juror to overcome the difficulty.

26H.3 In shorter cases, it may be more appropriate to discharge the juror and to continue the trial with a reduced number of jurors. The power to do this is implicit in section 16(1) of the Juries Act 1974 [§ 4-311 in the main work]. In unusual cases (such as an unexpected emergency arising overnight) a juror need not be discharged in open court. The good administration of justice depends on the cooperation of jurors, who perform an essential public service. All such applications should be dealt with sensitively and sympathetically and the trial judge should always seek to meet the interests of justice without unduly inconveniencing any juror.

CPD VI Trial 26J: Juries: Views

B-115   26J.1 In each case in which it is necessary for the jury to view a location, the judge should produce ground rules for the view, after discussion with the advocates. The rules should contain details of what the jury will be shown and in what order and who, if anyone, will be permitted to speak and what will be said. The rules should also make provision for the jury to ask questions and receive a response from the judge, following submissions from the advocates, while the view is taking place.

CPD VI Trial 26K: Juries: Directions to Jury before Retirement

B-116   26K.1 At the conclusion of the summing up, a number of directions are required. In particular it is important that judges direct the jury:

(i) that their verdict must be unanimous in respect of each count and each defendant;

(ii) not to think about "majority verdicts" unless and until given further directions;

(iii) that they will need to select one of their number to chair their discussions and speak on their behalf.

CPD VI Trial 26L: Juries: Jury Access to Exhibits and Evidence in Retirement

26L.1 At the end of the summing up it is also important that the judge informs the jury that any **B-117** exhibits they wish to have will be made available to them.

26L.2 Judges should invite submissions from the advocates as to what material the jury should retire with and what material before them should be removed, such as the transcript of an ABE interview (which should usually be removed from the jury as soon as the recording has been played.)

26L.3 Judges will also need to inform the jury of the opportunity to view certain audio, DVD or CCTV evidence that has been played (excluding, for example ABE interviews). If possible, it may be appropriate for the jury to be able to view any such material in the jury room alone, such as on a sterile laptop, so that they can discuss it freely; this will be a matter for the judge's discretion, following discussion with counsel.

CPD VI Trial 26M: Juries: Jury Irregularities

26M.1 [*Introductory.*] **B-118**

26M.2 A jury irregularity is anything that may prevent one or more jurors from remaining faithful to their oath or affirmation to "faithfully try the defendant and give a true verdict according to the evidence." Jury irregularities take many forms. Some are clear-cut such as a juror conducting research about the case or an attempt to suborn or intimidate a juror. Others are less clear-cut – for example, when there is potential bias or friction between jurors.

26M.3 A jury irregularity may involve contempt of court and / or the commission of an offence by or in relation to a juror.

26M.4 Under the previous version of this practice direction, the Crown Court required approval from the Vice-President of the Court of Appeal (Criminal Division) (CACD) prior to providing a juror's details to the police for the purposes of an investigation into a jury irregularity. Such approval is no longer required. Provision of a juror's details to the police is now a matter for the Crown Court.

Jury irregularity during trial

26M.5 A jury irregularity that comes to light during a trial may impact on the conduct of the trial. **B-119** It may also involve contempt of court and / or the commission of an offence by or in relation to a juror. *The primary concern of the judge should be the impact on the trial.*

26M.6 A jury irregularity should be drawn to the attention of the judge in the absence of the jury as soon as it becomes known.

26M.7 When the judge becomes aware of a jury irregularity, the judge should follow the procedure set out below:

STEP 1: Consider isolating juror(s)

STEP 2: Consult with advocates

STEP 3: Consider appropriate provisional measures (which may include surrender / seizure of electronic communications devices and taking defendant into custody)

STEP 4: Seek to establish basic facts of jury irregularity

STEP 5: Further consult with advocates

STEP 6: Decide what to do in relation to conduct of trial

STEP 7: Consider ancillary matters (contempt in face of court and / or commission of criminal offence)

STEP 1: Consider isolating juror(s)

26M.8 The judge should consider whether the juror(s) concerned should be isolated from the rest **B-120** of the jury, particularly if the juror(s) may have conducted research about the case.

26M.9 If two or more jurors are concerned, the judge should consider whether they should also be isolated from each other, particularly if one juror has made an accusation against another.

STEP 2: Consult with advocates

26M.10 The judge should consult with the advocates and invite submissions about appropriate **B-121** provisional measures (Step 3) and how to go about establishing the basic facts of the jury irregularity (Step 4).

26M.11 The consultation should be conducted

- in open court;
- in the presence of the defendant; and
- with all parties represented

unless there is good reason not to do so.

26M.12 If the jury irregularity involves a suspicion about the conduct of the defendant or another party, there may be good reason for the consultation to take place in the absence of the defendant or the other party. There may also be good reason for it to take place in private. If so, the proper location is in the court room, with DARTS recording, rather than in the judge's room.

26M.13 If the jury irregularity relates to the jury's deliberations, the judge should warn all those present that it is an offence to disclose, solicit or obtain information about a jury's deliberations (s.20D(1) of the Juries Act 1974 [§ 28-41d in the main work] – see paras 26M.35 to 26M.38 regarding the offence and exceptions). This would include disclosing information about the jury's deliberations divulged in court during consultation with the advocates (Step 2 and Step 5) or when seeking to establish the basic facts of the jury irregularity (Step 4). The judge should emphasise that the advocates, court staff and those in the public gallery would commit the offence by explaining to another what is said in court about the jury's deliberations.

STEP 3: Consider appropriate provisional measures

B-122   26M.14 The judge should consider appropriate provisional measures which may include surrender / seizure of electronic communications devices and taking the defendant into custody.

Surrender / seizure of electronic communications devices

B-123   26M.15 The judge should consider whether to make an order under section 15A(1) of the Juries Act 1974 [§ 4-325b in the main work] requiring the juror(s) concerned to surrender electronic communications devices, such as mobile telephones or smart phones.

26M.16 Having made an order for surrender, the judge may require a court security officer to search a juror to determine whether the juror has complied with the order. Section 54A of the Courts Act 2003 contains the court security officer's powers of search and seizure.

26M.17 Section 15A(5) of the Juries Act 1974 provides that it is contempt of court for a juror to fail to surrender an electronic communications device in accordance with an order for surrender (see paras 26M.29 to 26M.30 regarding the procedure for dealing with such a contempt).

26M.18 Any electronic communications device surrendered or seized under these provisions should be kept safe by the court until returned to the juror or handed to the police as evidence.

Taking defendant into custody

B-124   26M.19 If the defendant is on bail, and the jury irregularity involves a suspicion about the defendant's conduct, the judge should consider taking the defendant into custody. If that suspicion involves an attempt to suborn or intimidate a juror, the defendant should be taken into custody.

STEP 4: Seek to establish basic facts of jury irregularity

B-125   26M.20 The judge should seek to establish the basic facts of the jury irregularity for the purpose of determining how to proceed in relation to the conduct of the trial. The judge's enquiries may involve having the juror(s) concerned write a note of explanation and / or questioning the juror(s). The judge may enquire whether the juror(s) feel able to continue and remain faithful to their oath or affirmation. If there is questioning, each juror should be questioned separately, in the absence of the rest of the jury, unless there is good reason not to do so.

26M.21 In accordance with paragraphs 26M.10 to 26M.13, the enquiries should be conducted in open court; in the presence of the defendant; and with all parties represented unless there is good reason not to do so.

STEP 5: Further consult with advocates

B-126   26M.22 The judge should further consult with the advocates and invite submissions about how to proceed in relation to the conduct of the trial and what should be said to the jury (Step 6).

26M.23 In accordance with paragraphs 26M.10 to 26M.13, the consultation should be conducted in open court; in the presence of the defendant; and with all parties represented unless there is good reason not to do so.

STEP 6: Decide what to do in relation to conduct of trial

26M.24 When deciding how to proceed, the judge may take time to reflect. **B-127**

26M.25 Considerations may include the stage the trial has reached. The judge should be alert to attempts by the defendant or others to thwart the trial. In cases of potential bias, the judge should consider whether a fair minded and informed observer would conclude that there was a real possibility that the juror(s) or jury would be biased (*Porter v. Magill* [2002] 2 AC 357, HL).

26M.26 In relation to the conduct of the trial, there are three possibilities:

1. Take no action and continue with the trial

   If so, the judge should consider what, if anything, to say to the jury. For example, the judge may reassure the jury nothing untoward has happened or remind them their verdict is a decision of the whole jury and that they should try to work together. Anything said should be tailored to the circumstances of the case.

2. Discharge the juror(s) concerned and continue with the trial

   If so, the judge should consider what to say to the discharged juror(s) and the jurors who remain. All jurors should be warned not to discuss what has happened.

3. Discharge the whole jury

   If so, the judge should consider what to say to the jury and they should be warned not to discuss what has happened.

If the judge is satisfied that jury tampering has taken place, depending on the circumstances, the judge may continue the trial without a jury (s.46(3) of the CJA 2003 [§ 4-333 in the main work]) or order a new trial without a jury (s.46(5) of the CJA 2003). Alternatively, the judge may re-list the trial. If there is a real and present danger of jury tampering in the new trial, the prosecution may apply for a trial without a jury (s.44 of the CJA 2003 [§ 4-330 in the main work]).

STEP 7: Consider ancillary matters

26M.27 A jury irregularity may also involve contempt in the face of the court and / or the commission of a criminal offence. The possibilities include the following: **B-128**

- contempt in the face of the court by a juror;
- an offence by a juror or a non-juror under the Juries Act 1974 (ss.20-20D [§§ 28-41 *et seq.* in the main work]);
- an offence by juror or a non-juror other than under the Juries Act 1974 (examples are given).

Contempt in the face of the court by a juror

26M.28 If a juror commits contempt in the face of the court, the juror's conduct may also **B-129** constitute an offence. If so, the judge should decide whether to deal with the juror summarily under the procedure for contempt in the face of the court or refer the matter to the Attorney-General's office or the police (see paras 26M.31 and 26M.33).

26M.29 In the case of a *minor and clear* contempt in the face of the court, the judge may deal with the juror summarily. The judge should follow the procedure in CrimPR 48.5 to 48.8 [§ 28-105 *et seq.* in the main work]. The judge should also have regard to the practice direction regarding contempt of court issued in March 2015 (*Practice Direction: Committal for Contempt of Court – Open Court*) [§ 28-129a in the main work], which emphasises the principle of open justice in relation to proceedings for contempt before all courts.

26M.30 If a juror fails to comply with an order for surrender of an electronic communications device (see paras 26M.15 to 26M.18), the judge should deal with the juror summarily following the procedure for contempt in the face of the court.

Offence by a juror or non-juror under the Juries Act 1974

26M.31 If it appears that an offence under the Juries Act 1974 may have been committed by a **B-130** juror or non-juror (and the matter has not been dealt with summarily under the procedure for contempt in the face of the court), *the judge* should contact the Attorney-General's office to consider a police investigation, setting out the position neutrally. The officer in the case should not be asked to investigate. Contact details for the Attorney-General's office are set out at the end of this practice direction.

26M.32 If relevant to an investigation, any electronic communications device surrendered or seized pursuant to an order for surrender should be passed to the police as soon as practicable.

Offence by a juror or non-juror other than under the Juries Act 1974

26M.33 If it appears that an offence, other than an offence under the Juries Act 1974, may have **B-131** been committed by a juror or non-juror (and the matter has not been dealt with summarily under the procedure for contempt in the face of the court), *the judge or a member of court staff* should contact the police setting out the position neutrally. The officer in the case should not be asked to investigate.

26M.34 If relevant to an investigation, any electronic communications device surrendered or seized pursuant to an order for surrender should be passed to the police as soon as practicable.

Other matters to consider

• **Jury deliberations**

B-132   26M.35 In light of the offence of disclosing, soliciting or obtaining information about a jury's deliberations (s.20D(1) of the Juries Act 1974 [§ 28-40d in the main work]), great care is required if a jury irregularity relates to the jury's deliberations.

26M.36 During the trial, there are exceptions to this offence that enable the judge (and only the judge) to:

- seek to establish the basic facts of a jury irregularity involving the jury's deliberations (Step 4); and
- disclose information about the jury's deliberations to the Attorney-General's office if it appears that an offence may have been committed (Step 7).

26M.37 With regard to seeking to establish the basic facts of a jury irregularity involving the jury's deliberations (Step 4), it is to be noted that during the trial it is not an offence for the judge to disclose, solicit or obtain information about the jury's deliberations for the purposes of dealing with the case (ss.20E(2)(a) and 20G(1) of the Juries Act 1974 [§§ 28-41e, 28-41g in the main work]).

26M.38 With regard to disclosing information about the jury's deliberations to the Attorney-General's Office if it appears that an offence may have been committed (Step 7), it is to be noted that during the trial:

- it is not an offence for the judge to disclose information about the jury's deliberations for the purposes of an investigation by a relevant investigator into whether an offence or contempt of court has been committed by or in relation to a juror (s.20E(2)(b) of the Juries Act 1974); and
- a relevant investigator means a police force or the Attorney-General (s.20E(5) of the Juries Act 1974).

• **Minimum number of jurors**

B-133   26M.39 If it is decided to discharge one or more jurors (Step 6), a minimum of nine jurors must remain if the trial is to continue (s.16(1) of the Juries Act 1974 [§ 4-311 in the main work]).

• **Preparation of statement by judge**

B-134   26M.40 If a jury irregularity occurs, and the trial continues, the judge should have regard to the remarks of Lord Hope in *R. v. Connors and Mirza* [2004] 1 A.C. 1118, HL (at [127], [128]), and consider whether to prepare a statement that could be used in an application for leave to appeal or an appeal relating to the jury irregularity.

Jury irregularity after jury discharged

B-135   26M.41 A jury irregularity that comes to light after the jury has been discharged may involve the commission of an offence by or in relation to a juror. It may also provide a ground of appeal.

26M.42 A jury irregularity after the jury has been discharged may come to the attention of the:

- trial judge or court
- Registrar of Criminal Appeals (the Registrar)
- prosecution
- defence.

• **Role of the trial judge or court**

B-136   26M.43 The judge has no jurisdiction in relation to a jury irregularity that comes to light after the jury has been discharged (*R. v. Thompson* [2010] 2 Cr.App.R. 27, CA). The jury will be deemed to have been discharged when all verdicts on all defendants have been delivered or when the jury has been discharged from giving all verdicts on all defendants.

26M.44 The judge will be functus officio in relation to a jury irregularity that comes to light during an adjournment between verdict and sentence. The judge should proceed to sentence unless there is good reason not to do so.

26M.45 In practice, a jury irregularity often comes to light when the judge or court receives a communication from a former juror.

26M.46 If a jury irregularity comes to the attention of a judge or court after the jury has been discharged, and regardless of the result of the trial, the judge or a member of court staff should contact the Registrar setting out the position neutrally. Any communication from a former juror should be forwarded to the Registrar.

Contact details for the Registrar are set out at the end of this practice direction.

• **Role of the Registrar**

26M.47 If a jury irregularity comes to the attention of the Registrar after the jury has been **B-137** discharged, and regardless of the result of the trial, the Registrar should consider if it appears that an offence may have been committed by or in relation to a juror. The Registrar should also consider if there may be a ground of appeal.

26M. 48 When deciding how to proceed, particularly in relation to a communication from a former juror, the Registrar may seek the direction of the Vice-President of the Court of Appeal (Criminal Division) (CACD) or another judge of the CACD in accordance with instructions from the Vice-President.

26M.49 If it appears that an offence may have been committed by or in relation to a juror, the Registrar should contact the private office of the Director of Public Prosecutions to consider a police investigation.

26M.50 If there may be a ground of appeal, the Registrar should inform the defence.

26M.51 If a communication from a former juror is not of legal significance, the Registrar should respond explaining that no action is required. An example of such a communication is if it is restricted to a general complaint about the verdict from a dissenting juror or an expression of doubt or second thoughts.

• **Role of the prosecution**

26M.52 If a jury irregularity comes to the attention of the prosecution after the jury has been **B-138** discharged, which may provide a ground of appeal, they should notify the defence in accordance with their duties to act fairly and assist in the administration of justice (*R. v. Makin* [2004] EWCA Crim. 1607, (2004) 148 S.J. 821).

• **Role of the defence**

26M.53 If a jury irregularity comes to the attention of the defence after the jury has been **B-139** discharged, which provides an arguable ground of appeal, an application for leave to appeal may be made.

Other matters to consider

• **Jury deliberations**

26M.54 In light of the offence of disclosing, soliciting or obtaining information about a jury's **B-140** deliberations (s.20D(1) of the Juries Act 1974 [§ 28-41d in the main work]), great care is required if a jury irregularity relates to the jury's deliberations.

26M.55 After the jury has been discharged, there are exceptions to this offence that enable a judge, a member of court staff, the Registrar, the prosecution and the defence to disclose information about the jury's deliberations if it appears that an offence may have been committed by or in relation to a juror or if there may be a ground of appeal.

26M.56 For example, it is to be noted that:
- after the jury has been discharged, it is not an offence for a person to disclose information about the jury's deliberations to defined persons if the person reasonably believes that an offence or contempt of court may have been committed by or in relation to a juror or the conduct of a juror may provide grounds of appeal (s.20F(1), (2) of the Juries Act 1974 [§ 28-41f in the main work]);
- the defined persons to whom such information may be disclosed are a member of a police force, a judge of the CACD, the Registrar, a judge where the trial took place or a member of court staff where the trial took place who would reasonably be expected to disclose the information only to one of the aforementioned defined persons (s.20F(2) of the Juries Act 1974);
- after the jury has been discharged, it is not an offence for a judge of the CACD or the Registrar to disclose information about the jury's deliberations for the purposes of an

investigation by a relevant investigator into whether an offence or contempt of court has been committed by or in relation to a juror or the conduct of a juror may provide grounds of appeal (s.20F(4) of the Juries Act 1974);

- a relevant investigator means a police force, the Attorney-General, the Criminal Cases Review Commission (CCRC) or the CPS (s.20F(10) of the Juries Act 1974).

• **Investigation by the Criminal Cases Review Commission (CCRC)**

B-141   26M.57 If an application for leave to appeal, or an appeal, includes a ground of appeal relating to a jury irregularity, the Registrar may refer the case to the full court to decide whether to direct the CCRC to conduct an investigation under section 23A of the CAA 1968.

26M.58 If the court directs the CCRC to conduct an investigation, directions should be given as to the scope of the investigation.

Contact details

B-142   *Attorney General's Office*
Contempt.SharedMailbox@attorneygeneral.gsi.gov.uk
Telephone: 020 7271 2492
The Registrar
penny.donnelly@hmcts.x.gsi.gov.uk (Secretary) or
criminalappealoffice.generaloffice@hmcts.gsi.gov.uk
Telephone: 020 7947 6103 (Secretary) or 020 7947 6011

CPD VI Trial 26N: Open Justice

B-143   26N.1 There must be freedom of access between advocate and judge. Any discussion must, however, be between the judge and the advocates on both sides. If an advocate is instructed by a solicitor who is in court, he or she, too, should be allowed to attend the discussion. This freedom of access is important because there may be matters calling for communication or discussion of such a nature that the advocate cannot, in the client's interest, mention them in open court, *e.g.* the advocate, by way of mitigation, may wish to tell the judge that reliable medical evidence shows that the defendant is suffering from a terminal illness and may not have long to live. It is imperative that, so far as possible, justice must be administered in open court. Advocates should, therefore, only ask to see the judge when it is felt to be really necessary. The judge must be careful only to treat such communications as private where, in the interests of justice, this is necessary. Where any such discussion takes place it should be recorded, preferably by audio recording.

CPD VI Trial 26P: Defendant's Right to Give or not to Give Evidence

B-144   26P.1 At the conclusion of the evidence for the prosecution, section 35(2) of the CJPOA 1994 [§ 4-377 in the main work] requires the court to satisfy itself that the defendant is aware that the stage has been reached at which evidence can be given for the defence and that the defendant's failure to give evidence, or if he does so his failure to answer questions, without a good reason, may lead to inferences being drawn against him.

If the accused is legally represented

B-145   26P.2 After the close of the prosecution case, if the defendant's representative requests a brief adjournment to advise his client on this issue the request should, ordinarily, be granted. When appropriate the judge should, in the presence of the jury, inquire of the representative in these terms:

"Have you advised your client that the stage has now been reached at which he may give evidence and, if he chooses not to do so or, having been sworn, without good cause refuses to answer any question, the jury may draw such inferences as appear proper from his failure to do so?"

26P.3 If the representative replies to the judge that the defendant has been so advised, then the case shall proceed. If counsel replies that the defendant has not been so advised, then the judge shall direct the representative to advise his client of the consequences and should adjourn briefly for this purpose, before proceeding further.

If the defendant is not legally represented

B-146   26P.4 If the defendant is not represented, the judge shall, at the conclusion of the evidence for the prosecution, in the absence of the jury, indicate what he will say to him in the presence of the jury and ask if he understands and whether he would like a brief adjournment to consider his position.

26P.5 When appropriate, and in the presence of the jury, the judge should say to the defendant:

"You have heard the evidence against you. Now is the time for you to make your defence. You may give evidence on oath, and be cross-examined like any other witness. If you do not give evidence or, having been sworn, without good cause refuse to answer any question the jury may draw such inferences as appear proper. That means they may hold it against you. You may also call any witness or witnesses whom you have arranged to attend court or lead any agreed evidence. Afterwards you may also, if you wish, address the jury. But you cannot at that stage give evidence. Do you now intend to give evidence?"

CPD VI Trial 26Q: Majority Verdicts

26Q.1 It is very important that all those trying indictable offences should, so far as possible, adopt   **B-147** a uniform practice when complying with section 17 of the Juries Act 1974 [§ 4-509 in the main work], both in directing the jury in summing-up and also in receiving the verdict or giving further directions after retirement. So far as the summing-up is concerned, it is inadvisable for the judge, and indeed for advocates, to attempt an explanation of the section for fear that the jury will be confused. Before the jury retires, however, the judge should direct the jury in some such words as the following:

"As you may know, the law permits me, in certain circumstances, to accept a verdict which is not the verdict of you all. Those circumstances have not as yet arisen, so that when you retire I must ask you to reach a verdict upon which each one of you is agreed. Should, however, the time come when it is possible for me to accept a majority verdict, I will give you a further direction."

26Q.2 Thereafter the practice should be as follows. Should the jury return *before* two hours and ten minutes since the last member of the jury left the jury box to go to the jury room (or such longer time as the judge thinks reasonable) has elapsed (see s.17(4)), they should be asked: (a) "Have you reached a verdict upon which you are all agreed? Please answer Yes or No"; (b) (i) if unanimous, "What is your verdict?"; (ii) if not unanimous, the jury should be sent out again for further deliberation with a further direction to arrive if possible at a unanimous verdict.

26Q.3 Should the jury return (whether for the first time or subsequently) or be sent for *after* the two hours and ten minutes (or the longer period) has elapsed, questions (a) and (b)(i) in the paragraph above should be put to them and, if it appears that they are not unanimous, they should be asked to retire once more and told that they should continue to endeavour to reach a unanimous verdict but that, if they cannot, the judge will accept a majority verdict as in section 17(1).

26Q.4 When the jury finally return, they should be asked: (a) "Have at least ten (or nine as the case may be) of you agreed upon your verdict?"; (b) if "Yes", "What is your verdict? Please answer only Guilty or Not Guilty"; (c) (i) if "Not Guilty", accept the verdict without more ado; (ii) if "Guilty", "Is that the verdict of you all or by a majority?"; (d) if "Guilty" by a majority, "How many of you agreed to the verdict and how many dissented?"

26Q.5 At whatever stage the jury return, before question (a) is asked, the senior officer of the court present shall state in open court, for each period when the jury was out of court for the purpose of considering their verdict(s), the time at which the last member of the jury left the jury box to go to the jury room and the time of their return to the jury box; and will additionally state in open court the total of such periods.

26Q.6 The reason why section 17(3) is confined to a majority verdict of guilty, and for the somewhat complicated procedure set out above, is to prevent it being known that a verdict of "Not Guilty" is a majority verdict. If the final direction continues to require the jury to arrive, if possible, at a unanimous verdict and the verdict is received as specified, it will not be known for certain that the acquittal is not unanimous.

26Q.7 Where there are several counts (or alternative verdicts) left to the jury the above practice will, of course, need to be adapted to the circumstances. The procedure will have to be repeated in respect of each count (or alternative verdict), the verdict being accepted in those cases where the jury are unanimous and the further direction being given in cases in which they are not unanimous.

26Q.8 Should the jury in the end be unable to agree on a verdict by the required majority, the judge in his discretion will either ask them to deliberate further, or discharge them

26Q.9 Section 17 will, of course, apply also to verdicts other than "Guilty" or "Not Guilty", *e.g.* to special verdicts under the Criminal Procedure (Insanity) Act 1964, following a finding by the judge that the defendant is unfit to be tried, and special verdicts on findings of fact. Accordingly in such cases the questions to jurors will have to be suitably adjusted.

CPD VII Sentencing A: Pleas of Guilty in the Crown Court

A.1 Prosecutors and prosecution advocates should be familiar with and follow the Attorney-   **B-148**

General's Guidelines on the Acceptance of Pleas and the Prosecutor's Role in the Sentencing Exercise [*ante*, Appendix A-277 *et seq.*].

CPD VII Sentencing B: Determining the Factual Basis of Sentence

Where a guilty plea is offered to less than the whole indictment and the prosecution is minded to accept pleas tendered to some counts or to lesser alternative counts.

B-149   B.1 [*Introductory.*]

B.2-4 [*See § 4-175 in the main work.*]

Where a guilty plea is offered on a limited basis

B-150   B.6 A defendant may put forward a plea of guilty without accepting all of the facts as alleged by the prosecution. The basis of plea offered may seek to limit the facts or the extent of the offending for which the defendant is to be sentenced. Depending on the view taken by the prosecution, and the content of the offered basis, the case will fall into one of [four] categories... .

(a) A plea of guilty upon a basis of plea agreed by the prosecution and defence

B-151   B.7 The prosecution may reach an agreement with the defendant as to the factual basis on which the defendant will plead guilty, often known as an "agreed basis of plea". It is always subject to the approval of the court, which will consider whether it adequately and appropriately reflects the evidence as disclosed on the papers, whether it is fair and whether it is in the interests of justice.

B.8 *R. v. Underwood* [§§ 5-95 *et seq.* in the main work] outlines the principles to be applied where the defendant admits that he ... is guilty, but disputes the basis of offending alleged by the prosecution:

>   (a) the prosecution may accept and agree the defendant's account of the disputed facts or reject it in its entirety, or in part; if the prosecution accepts the defendant's basis of plea, it must ensure that the basis of plea is factually accurate and enables the sentencing judge to impose a sentence appropriate to reflect the justice of the case;
>   (b) in resolving any disputed factual matters, the prosecution must consider its primary duty to the court and must not agree with or acquiesce in an agreement which contains material factual disputes;
>   (c) if the prosecution does accept the defendant's basis of plea, it must be reduced to writing, be signed by advocates for both sides, and made available to the judge prior to the prosecution's opening;
>   (d) an agreed basis of plea that has been reached between the parties should not contain matters which are in dispute and any aspects upon which there is not agreement should be clearly identified;
>   (e) on occasion, the prosecution may lack the evidence positively to dispute the defendant's account, for example, where the defendant asserts a matter outside the knowledge of the prosecution; simply because the prosecution does not have evidence to contradict the defendant's assertions does not mean those assertions should be agreed; in such a case, the prosecution should test the defendant's evidence and submissions by requesting a *Newton* hearing [§ 5-99 in the main work], following the procedure set out below.
>   (f) if it is not possible for the parties to resolve a factual dispute when attempting to reach a plea agreement under this part, it is the responsibility of the prosecution to consider whether the matter should proceed to trial, or to invite the court to hold a *Newton* hearing as necessary.

B.9 *R. v. Underwood* emphasises that, whether or not pleas have been "agreed", the judge is not bound by any such agreement and is entitled of his ... own motion to insist that any evidence relevant to the facts in dispute (or upon which the judge requires further evidence for whatever reason) should be called. Any view formed by the prosecution on a proposed basis of plea is deemed to be conditional on the judge's acceptance of the basis of plea.

B.10 A judge is not entitled to reject a defendant's basis of plea absent a *Newton* hearing unless it is determined by the court that the basis is manifestly false and as such does not merit examination by way of the calling of evidence or alternatively the defendant declines the opportunity to engage in ... the *Newton* hearing whether by giving evidence on his own behalf or otherwise.

(b) A plea of guilty on a basis signed by the defendant but in respect of which there is no or only partial agreement by the prosecution

B-152   B.11 Where the defendant pleads guilty, but disputes the basis of offending alleged by the prosecution and agreement as to that has not been reached, the following procedure should be followed:

    (a) the defendant's basis of plea must be set out in writing, identifying what is in dispute and must be signed by the defendant;

    (b) the prosecution must respond in writing setting out their alternative contentions and indicating whether or not they submit that a *Newton* hearing is necessary;

    (c) the court may invite the parties to make representations about whether the dispute is material to sentence; and

    (d) if the court decides that it is a material dispute, the court will invite such further representations or evidence as it may require and resolve the dispute in accordance with the principles set out in *R. v. Newton*.

B.12 Where the disputed issue arises from facts which are within the exclusive knowledge of the defendant and the defendant is willing to give evidence in support of his case, the defence advocate should be prepared to call the defendant. If the defendant is not willing to testify, and subject to any explanation which may be given, the judge may draw such inferences as appear appropriate.

B.13 The decision whether or not a *Newton* hearing is required is one for the judge. Once the decision has been taken that there will be a *Newton* hearing, evidence is called by the parties in the usual way and the criminal burden and standard of proof applies. Whatever view has been taken by the prosecution, the prosecutor should not leave the questioning to the judge, but should assist the court by exploring the issues which the court wishes to have explored. The rules of evidence should be followed as during a trial, and the judge should direct himself appropriately as the tribunal of fact. Paragraphs 6 to 10 of *Underwood* provide additional guidance regarding the ... procedure.

(c) A plea of guilty on a basis that contains within it matters that are purely mitigation and which do not amount to a contradiction of the prosecution case

B.14 A basis of plea should not normally set out matters of mitigation but there may be   **B-153** circumstances where it is convenient and sensible for the document ... to deal with facts closely aligned to the circumstances of the offending which amount to mitigation and which may need to be resolved prior to sentence. The resolution of these matters does not amount to a *Newton* hearing properly so defined and in so far as facts fall to be established the defence will have to discharge the civil burden in order to do so. The scope of the evidence required to resolve issues that are purely matters of mitigation is for the court to determine.

(d) Cases involving serious fraud – a plea of guilty upon a basis of plea agreed by the prosecution and defence accompanied by joint submissions as to sentence

B.15 This section applies when the prosecution and the defendant(s) to a matter before the   **B-154** Crown Court involving allegations of serious or complex fraud have agreed a basis of plea and seek to make submissions to the court regarding sentence.

B.16 Guidance for prosecutors regarding the operation of this procedure is set out in the Attorney-General's Guidelines on Plea Discussions in Cases of Serious or Complex Fraud [*ante*, Appendix A-293 *et seq.*], ... and is referred to in this direction as the "Attorney-General's Plea Discussion Guidelines".

B.17 In this part—

    (a) "a plea agreement" means a written basis of plea agreed between the prosecution and defendant(s) in accordance with the principles set out in *R. v. Underwood* [see § 5-95 in the main work, and *ante*, Appendix A-277], supported by admissible documentary evidence or admissions under section 10 of the CJA 1967;

    (b) "a sentencing submission" means sentencing submissions made jointly by the prosecution and defence as to the appropriate sentencing authorities and applicable sentencing range in the relevant sentencing guideline relating to the plea agreement;

    (c) "serious or complex fraud" includes, but is not limited to, allegations of fraud where two or more of the following are present [list as per the guidelines, *ante*, Appendix A-293]:

Procedure

B.18 The procedure regarding agreed bases of plea outlined above [§§ 5-95 *et seq.* in the main   **B-155** work], applies with equal rigour to the acceptance of pleas under this procedure. However, because under this procedure the parties will have been discussing the plea agreement and the charges from a much earlier stage, it is vital that the judge is fully informed of all relevant background to the discussions, charges and the eventual basis of plea.

B.19 Where the defendant has not yet appeared before the Crown Court, the prosecutor must send full details of the plea agreement and sentencing submission(s) to the court, at least 7 days in advance of the defendant's first appearance. Where the defendant has already appeared before the Crown Court, the prosecutor must notify the court as soon as is reasonably practicable that a plea agreement and sentencing submissions under the Attorney-General's Plea Discussion Guidelines are to be submitted. The court should set a date for the matter to be heard, and the prosecutor must send full details of the plea agreement and sentencing submission(s) to the court as soon as practicable, or in accordance with the directions of the court.

B.20 The provision to the judge of full details of the plea agreement requires sufficient information to be provided to allow the judge to understand the facts of the case and the history of the plea discussions, to assess whether the plea agreement is fair and in the interests of justice, and to decide the appropriate sentence. This will include, but is not limited to: (i) the plea agreement; (ii) the sentencing submission(s); (iii) all of the material provided by the prosecution to the defendant in the course of the plea discussions; (iv) relevant material provided by the defendant, for example documents relating to personal mitigation; and (v) the minutes of any meetings between the parties and any correspondence generated in the plea discussions. The parties should be prepared to provide additional material at the request of the court.

B.21 The court should at all times have regard to the length of time that has elapsed since the date of the occurrence of the events giving rise to the plea discussions, the time taken to interview the defendant, the date of charge and the prospective trial date (if the matter were to proceed to trial) so as to ensure that its consideration of the plea agreement and sentencing submissions does not cause any unnecessary further delay.

Status of plea agreement and joint sentencing submissions

B-156

B.22 Where a plea agreement and joint sentencing submissions are submitted, it remains entirely a matter for the court to decide how to deal with the case. The judge retains the absolute discretion to refuse to accept the plea agreement and to sentence otherwise than in accordance with the sentencing submissions made under the Attorney-General's Plea Discussion Guidelines.

B.23 Sentencing submissions should draw the court's attention to any applicable range in any relevant guideline, and to any ancillary orders that may be applicable. Sentencing submissions should not include a specific sentence or agreed range other than the ranges set out in sentencing guidelines or authorities.

B.24 Prior to pleading guilty in accordance with the plea agreement, the defendant(s) may apply to the court for an indication of the likely maximum sentence [in accordance with *R. v. Goodyear*, as to which, see § 5-110 in the main work].

B.25 In the event that the judge indicates a sentence or passes a sentence which is not within the submissions made on sentencing, the plea agreement remains binding.

B.26 If the defendant does not plead guilty in accordance with the plea agreement or if a defendant who has pleaded guilty in accordance with a plea agreement successfully applies to withdraw his plea under rule 25.5 of the Criminal Procedure Rules [§ 4-254 in the main work], the signed plea agreement may be treated as confession evidence, and may be used against the defendant at a later stage in these or any other proceedings. Any credit for a timely guilty plea may be lost. The court may exercise its discretion under section 78 of the PACE Act 1984 [§ 15-401 in the main work] to exclude any such evidence … .

B.27 Where a defendant has failed to plead guilty in accordance with a plea agreement, the case is unlikely to be ready for trial immediately. The prosecution may have been commenced earlier than it otherwise would have been, in reliance upon the defendant's agreement to plead guilty. This is likely to be a relevant consideration for the court in deciding whether or not to grant an application to adjourn or stay the proceedings to allow the matter to be prepared for trial in accordance with the protocol on the Control and Management of Heavy Fraud and other Complex Criminal Cases, or as required.

CPD VII Sentencing C: Indications of Sentence: R v Goodyear

B-157

C.1–8 [*See § 5-111 in the main work.*]

CPD VII Sentencing D: Facts to be Stated on Pleas of Guilty

B-158

D.1 [*See § 5-108 in the main work.*]

CPD VII Sentencing E: Concurrent and Consecutive Sentences

B-159

E.1 Where a court passes on a defendant more than one term of imprisonment the court should state in the presence of the defendant whether the terms are to be concurrent or consecutive. Should this not be done the court clerk should ask the court, before the defendant leaves the court, to do so.

E.2 If a defendant is, at the time of sentence, already serving two or more consecutive terms of imprisonment and the court intends to increase the total period of imprisonment, it should use the expression "consecutive to the total period of imprisonment to which you are already subject" rather than "at the expiration of the term of imprisonment you are now serving", as the defendant may not then be serving the last of the terms to which he is already subject.

E.3 [*Refers to the Sentencing Council's guideline (*post, *Appendix K-280 et seq.).*]

CPD VII Sentencing F: Victim Personal Statements

F.1 Victims of crime are invited to make a statement, known as a victim personal statement **B-160** ("VPS"). The statement gives victims a formal opportunity to say how a crime has affected them. It may help to identify whether they have a particular need for information, support and protection. The court will take the statement into account when determining sentence. In some circumstances, it may be appropriate for relatives of a victim to make a VPS, for example where the victim has died as a result of the relevant criminal conduct. The revised *Code of Practice for Victims of Crime*, published on 29 October 2013, gives further information about victims' entitlements within the criminal justice system, and the duties placed on criminal justice agencies when dealing with victims of crime.

F.2 When a police officer takes a statement from a victim, the victim should be told about the scheme and given the chance to make a VPS. The decision about whether or not to make a VPS is entirely a matter for the victim; no pressure should be brought to bear on their decision, and no conclusion should be drawn if they choose not to make such a statement. A VPS or a further VPS may be made (in proper s.9 form, see below) at any time prior to the disposal of the case. It will not normally be appropriate for a VPS to be made after the disposal of the case; there may be rare occasions between sentence and appeal when a further VPS may be necessary, for example, when the victim was injured and the final prognosis was not available at the date of sentence. However, VPS after disposal should be confined to presenting up-to-date factual material, such as medical information, and should be used sparingly.

F.3 If the court is presented with a VPS the following approach, subject to the further guidance given by the Court of Appeal in *R. v. Perkins* [§ 5-106 in the main work], should be adopted:

    (a) the VPS and any evidence in support should be considered and taken into account by the court, prior to passing sentence;

    (b) evidence of the effects of an offence on the victim contained in the VPS or other statement, must be in proper form, that is a witness statement made under section 9 of the CJA 1967 or an expert's report; and served in good time on the defendant's solicitor or the defendant, if he or she is not represented; except where inferences can properly be drawn from the nature of or circumstances surrounding the offence, a sentencing court must not make assumptions unsupported by evidence about the effects of an offence on the victim; the maker of a VPS may be cross-examined on its content;

    (c) at the discretion of the court, the VPS may also be read aloud or played in open court, in whole or in part, or it may be summarised; if the VPS is to be read aloud, the court should also determine who should do so; in making these decisions, the court should take account of the victim's preferences, and follow them unless there is good reason not to do so; examples of this include the inadmissibility of the content or the potentially harmful consequences for the victim or others; court hearings should not be adjourned solely to allow the victim to attend court to read the VPS; for the purposes of *CPD I (General matters) 5B* (access to information held by the court) [*ante*, B-44 *et seq.*] a VPS that is read aloud or played in open court in whole or in part should be considered as such, and no longer treated as a confidential document;

    (d) in all cases it will be appropriate for a VPS to be referred to in the course of the sentencing hearing and/or in the sentencing remarks;

    (e) the court must pass what it judges to be the appropriate sentence having regard to the circumstances of the offence and of the offender, taking into account, so far as the court considers it appropriate, the impact on the victim; the opinions of the victim or the victim's close relatives as to what the sentence should be are therefore not relevant, unlike the consequences of the offence on them; victims should be advised of this; if, despite the advice, opinions as to sentence are included in the statement, the court should pay no attention to them.

CPD VII Sentencing G: Families Bereaved by Homicide and Other Criminal Conduct

G.1–3 [*See § 5-104 in the main work.*] **B-161**

CPD VII Sentencing H: Community Impact Statements

H.1 A community impact statement may be prepared by the police to make the court aware of **B-162** particular crime trends in the local area and the impact of these on the local community.

H.2 Such statements must be in proper form, that is a witness statement made under section 9 of the CJA 1967 or an expert's report; and served in good time upon the defendant's solicitor or the defendant, if he is not represented.

H.3 The community impact statement and any evidence in support should be considered and taken into account by the court, prior to passing sentence. The statement should be referred to in the course of the sentencing hearing and/or in the sentencing remarks. Subject to the court's discretion, the contents of the statement may be summarised or read out in open court.

H.4 The court must pass what it judges to be the appropriate sentence having regard to the circumstances of the offence and of the offender, taking into account, so far as the court considers it appropriate, the impact on the local community. Opinions as to what the sentence should be are therefore not relevant. If, despite the advice, opinions as to sentence are included in the statement, the court should pay no attention to them.

H.5 Except where inferences can properly be drawn from the nature of or circumstances surrounding the offence, a sentencing court must not make assumptions unsupported by evidence about the effects of an offence on the local community.

H.6 It will not be appropriate for a community impact statement to be made after disposal of the case but before an appeal.

CPD VII Sentencing I: Impact Statements for Businesses

B-163   I.1 Individual victims of crime are invited to make a statement, known as a victim personal statement ("VPS") ... If the victim, or one of the victims, is a business or enterprise (including charities but excluding public sector bodies), of any size, a nominated representative may make an impact statement for business ("ISB"). The ISB gives a formal opportunity for the court to be informed how a crime has affected a business. The court will take the statement into account when determining sentence. This does not prevent individual employees from making a VPS about the impact of the same crime on them as individuals. Indeed the ISB should be about the impact on the business exclusively, and the impact on any individual included within a VPS.

I.2 When a police officer takes statements about the alleged offence, he or she should also inform the business about the scheme. An ISB may be made to the police at that time, or the ISB template may be downloaded from www.police.uk, completed and e-mailed or posted to the relevant police contact. Guidance on how to complete the form is available on www.police.uk and on the CPS website. There is no obligation on any business to make an ISB.

I.3 An ISB or an updated ISB may be made (in proper s.9 form, see below) at any time prior to the disposal of the case. It will not be appropriate for an ISB to be made after disposal of the case but before an appeal.

I.4 A business wishing to make an ISB should consider carefully who to nominate as the representative to make the statement on its behalf. A person making an ISB on behalf of a business, the nominated representative, must be authorised to do so on behalf of the business, either by nature of their position within the business, such as a director or owner, or by having been suitably authorised, such as by the owner or board of directors. The nominated representative must also be in a position to give admissible evidence about the impact of the crime on the business. This will usually be through first-hand personal knowledge, or using business documents (as defined in s.117 of the CJA 2003 [§ 11-26 in the main work]). The most appropriate person will vary depending on the nature of the crime, and the size and structure of the business and may for example include a manager, director, chief executive or shop owner.

I.5 If the nominated representative leaves the business before the case comes to court, he or she will usually remain the representative, as the ISB made by him or her will still provide the best evidence of the impact of the crime, and he or she could still be asked to attend court. Nominated representatives should be made aware of the on-going nature of the role at the time of making the ISB.

I.6 If necessary a further ISB may be provided to the police if there is a change in circumstances. This could be made by an alternative nominated representative. However, the new ISB will usually supplement, not replace, the original ISB and again must contain admissible evidence. The prosecutor will decide which ISB to serve on the defence as evidence, and any ISB that is not served in evidence will be included in the unused material and considered for disclosure to the defence.

I.7 The ISB must be made in proper form, that is as a witness statement made under section 9 of the CJA 1967 or an expert's report; and served in good time on the defendant's solicitor or the defendant, if he or she is not represented. The maker of an ISB can be cross-examined on its content.

I.8 The ISB and any evidence in support should be considered and taken into account by the court, prior to passing sentence. The statement should be referred to in the course of the sentencing hearing and/or in the sentencing remarks. Subject to the court's discretion, the contents of the statement may be summarised or read out in open court; the views of the business should be taken into account in reaching a decision.

I.9 The court must pass what it judges to be the appropriate sentence having regard to the circumstances of the offence and of the offender, taking into account, so far as the court considers it appropriate, the impact on the victims, including any business victim. Opinions as to what the sentence should be are therefore not relevant. If, despite the advice, opinions as to sentence are included in the statement, the court should pay no attention to them.

I.10 Except where inferences can properly be drawn from the nature of or circumstances surrounding the offence, a sentencing court must not make assumptions unsupported by evidence about the effects of an offence on a business.

CPD VII Sentencing J: Binding Over Orders and Conditional Discharges

J.1 [*Introductory.*] **B-164**

Binding over to keep the peace

J.2 Before imposing a binding over order, the court must be satisfied so that it is sure that a **B-165** breach of the peace involving violence, or an imminent threat of violence, has occurred or that there is a real risk of violence in the future. Such violence may be perpetrated by the individual who will be subject to the order or by a third party as a natural consequence of the individual's conduct.

J.3 In light of the judgment in *Hashman and Harrup v. U.K.* [§§ 16-37, 16-166 in the main work], courts should no longer bind an individual over "to be of good behaviour". Rather than binding an individual over to "keep the peace" in general terms, the court should identify the specific conduct or activity from which the individual must refrain.

Written order

J.4 When making an order binding an individual over to refrain from specified types of conduct **B-166** or activities, the details of that conduct or those activities should be specified by the court in a written order, served on all relevant parties. The court should state its reasons for the making of the order, its length and the amount of the recognizance. The length of the order should be proportionate to the harm sought to be avoided and should not generally exceed 12 months.

Evidence

J.5 Sections 51 to 57 of the MCA 1980 set out the jurisdiction of the magistrates' court to hear an **B-167** application made on complaint and the procedure which is to be followed. This includes a requirement under section 53 to hear evidence and the parties, before making any order. This practice should be applied to all cases in the magistrates' court and the Crown Court where the court is considering imposing a binding over order. The court should give the individual who would be subject to the order and the prosecutor the opportunity to make representations, both as to the making of the order and as to its terms. The court should also hear any admissible evidence the parties wish to call and which has not already been heard in the proceedings. Particularly careful consideration may be required where the individual who would be subject to the order is a witness in the proceedings.

J.6 Where there is an admission which is sufficient to found the making of a binding over order and/or the individual consents to the making of the order, the court should nevertheless hear sufficient representations and, if appropriate, evidence, to satisfy itself that an order is appropriate in all the circumstances and to be clear about the terms of the order.

J.7 Where there is an allegation of breach of a binding over order and this is contested, the court should hear representations and evidence, including oral evidence, from the parties before making a finding. If unrepresented and no opportunity has been given previously the court should give a reasonable period for the person said to have breached the binding over order to find representation.

Burden and standard of proof

J.8 The court should be satisfied so that it is sure of the matters complained of before a binding **B-168** over order may be imposed. Where the procedure has been commenced on complaint, the burden of proof rests on the complainant. In all other circumstances, the burden of proof rests upon the prosecution.

J.9 Where there is an allegation of breach of a binding over order, the court should be satisfied on the balance of probabilities that the defendant is in breach before making any order for forfeiture of a recognizance. The burden of proof shall rest on the prosecution.

Recognizance

B-169   J.10 The court must be satisfied on the merits of the case that an order for binding over is appropriate and should announce that decision before considering the amount of the recognizance. If unrepresented, the individual who is made subject to the binding over order should be told he has a right of appeal from the decision.

J.11 When fixing the amount of recognizance, courts should have regard to the individual's financial resources and should hear representations from the individual or his legal representatives regarding finances.

J.12 A recognizance is made in the form of a bond giving rise to a civil debt on breach of the order.

Refusal to enter into a recognizance

B-170   J.13 If there is any possibility that an individual will refuse to enter a recognizance, the court should consider whether there are any appropriate alternatives to a binding over order (for example, continuing with a prosecution). Where there are no appropriate alternatives and the individual continues to refuse to enter into the recognizance, the court may commit the individual to custody. In the magistrates' court, the power to do so will derive from section 1(7) of the Justices of the Peace Act 1968 or, more rarely, from section 115(3) of the MCA 1980, and the court should state which power it is acting under; in the Crown Court, this is a common law power.

J.14 Before the court exercises a power to commit the individual to custody, the individual should be given the opportunity to see a duty solicitor or another legal representative and be represented in proceedings if the individual so wishes. Public funding should generally be granted to cover representation. In the Crown Court this rests with the judge who may grant a representation order.

J.15 In the event that the individual does not take the opportunity to seek legal advice, the court shall give the individual a final opportunity to comply with the request and shall explain the consequences of a failure to do so.

Antecedents

B-171   J.16 Courts are reminded of ... section 7(5) of the Rehabilitation of Offenders Act 1974 [§ 13-133 in the main work] which excludes from a person's antecedents any order of the court "with respect to any person otherwise than on a conviction".

Binding over to come up for judgment

B-172   J.17 If the Crown Court is considering binding over an individual to come up for judgment, the court should specify any conditions with which the individual is to comply in the meantime and not specify that the individual is to be of good behaviour.

J.18 The Crown Court should, if the individual is unrepresented, explain the consequences of a breach of the binding over order in these circumstances.

Binding over of parent or guardian

B-173   J.19 [See § 5-1281 in the main work.]

Security for good behaviour

B-174   J.20 [See § 5-174a in the main work.]

CPD VII Sentencing K: Committal for Sentence

B-175   K.1 CrimPR 28.10 applies when a case is committed to the Crown Court for sentence and specifies the information and documentation that must be provided by the magistrates' court. On a committal for sentence any reasons given by the magistrates for their decision should be included with the documents. All of these documents should be made available to the judge in the Crown Court if the judge requires them, in order to decide before the hearing questions of listing or representation or the like. They will also be available to the court during the hearing if it becomes necessary or desirable for the court to see what happened in the lower court.

CPD VII Sentencing L: Imposition of Life Sentences

B-176   L.1 Section 82A of the PCC(S)A 2000 [§ 5-531 in the main work] empowers a judge when passing a sentence of life imprisonment, where such a sentence is not fixed by law, to specify by order such part of the sentence ("the relevant part") as shall be served before the prisoner may require the Secretary of State to refer his case to the Parole Board. This is applicable to defendants under the age of 18 years as well as to adult defendants.

L.2 Thus the life sentence falls into two parts: (a) the relevant part, which consists of the period of detention imposed for punishment and deterrence, taking into account the seriousness of the offence, and (b) the remaining part of the sentence, during which the prisoner's detention will be governed by considerations of risk to the public.

L.3 The judge is not obliged by statute to make use of the provisions of section 82A when passing a life sentence. However, the judge should do so, save in the very exceptional case where the judge considers that the offence is so serious that detention for life is justified by the seriousness of the offence alone, irrespective of the risk to the public. In such a case, the judge should state this in open court when passing sentence.

L.4 In cases where the judge is to specify the relevant part of the sentence under section 82A, the judge should permit the advocate for the defendant to address the court as to the appropriate length of the relevant part. Where no relevant part is to be specified, the advocate for the defendant should be permitted to address the court as to the appropriateness of this course of action.

L.5 In specifying the relevant part of the sentence, the judge should have regard to the specific terms of section 82A and should indicate the reasons for reaching his decision as to the length of the relevant part.

CPD VII Sentencing M: Mandatory Life Sentences

M.1 The purpose of this section is to give practical guidance as to the procedure for passing a **B-177** mandatory life sentence under [the CJA 2003, s.269, and Sched. 21 [§§ 5-403, 5-425 *et seq.* in the main work]. This direction also gives guidance as to the transitional arrangements under section 276 of, and Schedule 22 to, the Act. It clarifies the correct approach to looking at the practice of the Secretary of State prior to December, 2002, for the purposes of Schedule 22 ..., in the light of the judgment in *R. v. Sullivan; R. v. Gibbs; R. v. Elener (Barry) and Elener (Derek)* [2005] 1 Cr.App.R. 3, CA.

M.2 Section 269 came into force on 18 December 2003. Under section 269, all courts passing a mandatory life sentence must either announce in open court the minimum term the prisoner must serve before the Parole Board can consider release on licence under the provisions of section 28 of the C(S)A 1997 [§ 5-423 in the main work] ..., or announce that the seriousness of the offence is so exceptionally high that the early release provisions should not apply at all (a "whole life order").

M.3 In setting the minimum term, the court must set the term it considers appropriate taking into account the seriousness of the offence. In considering the seriousness of the offence, the court must have regard to the general principles set out in Schedule 21 ... and any guidelines relating to offences in general which are relevant to the case and not incompatible with the provisions of Schedule 21. Although it is necessary to have regard to such guidance, it is always permissible not to apply the guidance if a judge considers there are reasons for not following it. It is always necessary to have regard to the need to do justice in the particular case. However, if a court departs from any of the starting points given in Schedule 21, the court is under a duty to state its reasons for doing so (s.270(2)(b) [§ 5-420 in the main work]).

M.4 Schedule 21 states that the first step is to choose one of five starting points: "whole life", 30 years, 25 years, 15 years or 12 years. Where the 15 year starting point has been chosen, judges should have in mind that this starting point encompasses a very broad range of murders. [In] *Sullivan*, the court found it should not be assumed that Parliament intended to raise all minimum terms that would previously have had a lower starting point, to 15 years.

M.5–M.11 [*Summarise Sched. 21.*]

M.12 The second step after choosing a starting point is to take account of any aggravating or mitigating factors which would justify a departure from the starting point. Additional aggravating factors ... are listed at paragraph 10 of Schedule 21. Examples of mitigating factors are listed at paragraph 11 .... Taking into account the aggravating and mitigating features, the court may add to or subtract from the starting point to arrive at the appropriate punitive period.

M.13 The third step is that the court should consider the effect of section 143(2) of the Act [§ 5-67 in the main work] in relation to previous convictions; section 143(3) of the Act where the offence was committed whilst the offender was on bail; and section 144 of the Act [§ 5-107 in the main work] where the offender has pleaded guilty (para. 12). The court should then take into account what credit the offender would have received for a remand in custody under section 240 or 240ZA [§ 5-643 in the main work] of the Act and/or for a remand on bail subject to a qualifying curfew condition under section 240A [§ 5-645 in the main work], but for the fact that the mandatory sentence is one of life imprisonment. Where the offender has been thus remanded in connection with the offence or a related offence, the court should have in mind that no credit will otherwise be given for this time when the prisoner is considered for early release. The appropriate time to take it into account is when setting the minimum term. The court should make any appropriate subtraction from the punitive period it would otherwise impose, in order to reach the minimum term.

M.14 Following these calculations, the court should have arrived at the appropriate minimum term to be announced in open court. As paragraph 9 of Schedule 21 makes clear, the judge retains ultimate discretion and the court may arrive at any minimum term from any starting point.

CPD VII Sentencing N: Transitional Arrangements for Sentences Where the Offence was Committed before 18 December 2003

B-178

N.1 Where the court is passing a sentence of mandatory life imprisonment for an offence committed before 18 December 2003, the court should take a fourth step in determining the minimum term in accordance with section 276 and Schedule 22 ... .

N.2 The purpose of those provisions is to ensure that the sentence does not breach the principle of non-retroactivity by ensuring that a lower minimum term would not have been imposed for the offence when it was committed. Before setting the minimum term the court must check whether the proposed term is greater than that which the Secretary of State would probably have notified under the practice followed by the Secretary of State before December 2002.

N.3 The decision in *Sullivan* [*ante*] ... gives detailed guidance as to the correct approach to this practice and judges passing mandatory life sentences where the murder was committed prior to 18 December 2003 are well advised to read that judgment before proceeding.

N.4 The practical result of that judgment is that in sentences where the murder was committed before 31st May 2002, the best guide to what would have been the practice of the Secretary of State is the letter sent to judges by Lord Bingham C.J. on 10th February 1997, the relevant parts of which are set out below.

N.5 The practice of Lord Bingham, as set out in his letter ... was to take 14 years as the period actually to be served for the "average", "normal" or "unexceptional" murder. Examples of factors he outlined as capable, in appropriate cases, of mitigating the normal penalty were:

> youth;
>
> age (where relevant to physical capacity on release or the likelihood of the defendant dying in prison);
>
> intellectual disability or mental disorder;
>
> provocation (in a non-technical sense), or an excessive response to a personal threat;
>
> the absence of an intention to kill;
>
> spontaneity and lack of premeditation (beyond that necessary to constitute the offence: *e.g.* a sudden response to family pressure or to prolonged and eventually insupportable stress);
>
> mercy killing;
>
> a plea of guilty, or hard evidence of remorse or contrition.

N.6 Lord Bingham then listed the following factors as likely to call for a sentence more severe than the norm:

> evidence of a planned, professional, revenge or contract killing;
>
> the killing of a child or a very old or otherwise vulnerable victim;
>
> evidence of sadism, gratuitous violence, or sexual maltreatment, humiliation or degradation before the killing;
>
> killing for gain (in the course of burglary, robbery, blackmail, insurance fraud, *etc.*);
>
> multiple killings;
>
> the killing of a witness or potential witness to defeat the ends of justice;
>
> the killing of those doing their public duty (policemen, prison officers, postmasters, firemen, judges, *etc*);
>
> terrorist or politically motivated killings;
>
> the killing of those doing their public duty (policemen, prison officers, postmasters, firemen, judges, etc);
>
> terrorist or politically motivated killings;
>
> the use of firearms or other dangerous weapons, whether carried for defensive or offensive reasons;
>
> a substantial record of serious violence;
>
> macabre attempts to dismember or conceal the body.

N.7 Lord Bingham further stated that the fact that a defendant was under the influence of drink or drugs at the time of the killing is so common he would be inclined to treat it as neutral. But in the not unfamiliar case in which a couple, inflamed by drink, indulge in a violent quarrel in which one dies, often against a background of long-standing drunken violence, then he would tend to recommend a term somewhat below the norm.

N.8 Lord Bingham went on to say that given the intent necessary for proof of murder, the consequences of taking life and the understandable reaction of relatives to the deceased, a substantial term will almost always be called for, save perhaps in a truly venial case of mercy killing. While a recommendation of a punitive term longer than, say, 30 years will be very rare indeed, there should not be any upper limit. Some crimes will certainly call for terms very well in excess of the norm.

N.9 For the purposes of sentences where the murder was committed after 31 May 2002 and before 18 December 2003, the judge should apply the practice statement handed down on 31 May 2002 reproduced at paras N.10 to N.20 below.

N.10 This statement replaces the previous single normal tariff of 14 years by substituting a higher and a normal starting point of respectively 16 (comparable to 32 years) and 12 years (comparable to 24 years). These starting points have then to be increased or reduced because of aggravating or mitigating factors such as those referred to below. It is emphasised that they are no more than starting points.

The normal starting point of 12 years

N.11 Cases falling within this starting point will normally involve the killing of an adult victim, **B-179** arising from a quarrel or loss of temper between two people known to each other. It will not have the characteristics referred to in paragraph N.13. Exceptionally, the starting point may be reduced because of the sort of circumstances described in the next paragraph.

N.12 The normal starting point can be reduced because the murder is one where the offender's culpability is significantly reduced, for example, because: (a) the case came close to the borderline between murder and manslaughter; or (b) the offender suffered from mental disorder, or from a mental disability which lowered the degree of his criminal responsibility for the killing, although not affording a defence of diminished responsibility; or (c) the offender was provoked (in a non-technical sense), such as by prolonged and eventually unsupportable stress; or (d) the case involved an over reaction in self-defence; or (e) the offence was a mercy killing. These factors could justify a reduction to 8/9 years (equivalent to 16/18 years).

The higher starting point of 15/16 years

N.13 The higher starting point will apply to cases where the offender's culpability was exception- **B-180** ally high or the victim was in a particularly vulnerable position. Such cases will be characterised by a feature which makes the crime especially serious, such as: (a) the killing was "professional" or a contract killing; (b) the killing was politically motivated; (c) the killing was done for gain (in the course of a burglary, robbery *etc.*); (d) the killing was intended to defeat the ends of justice (as in the killing of a witness or potential witness); (e) the victim was providing a public service; (f) the victim was a child or was otherwise vulnerable; (g) the killing was racially aggravated; (h) the victim was deliberately targeted because of his or her religion or sexual orientation; (i) there was evidence of sadism, gratuitous violence or sexual maltreatment, humiliation or degradation of the victim before the killing; (j) extensive and/or multiple injuries were inflicted on the victim before death; (k) the offender committed multiple murders.

Variation of the starting point

N.14 Whichever starting point is selected in a particular case, it may be appropriate for the trial **B-181** judge to vary the starting point upwards or downwards, to take account of aggravating or mitigating factors, which relate to either the offence or the offender, in the particular case.

N.15 Aggravating factors relating to the offence can include: (a) the fact that the killing was planned; (b) the use of a firearm; (c) arming with a weapon in advance; (d) concealment of the body, destruction of the crime scene and/or dismemberment of the body; (e) particularly in domestic violence cases, the fact that the murder was the culmination of cruel and violent behaviour by the offender over a period of time.

N.16 Aggravating factors relating to the offender will include the offender's previous record and failures to respond to previous sentences, to the extent that this is relevant to culpability rather than to risk.

N.17 Mitigating factors relating to the offence will include: (a) an intention to cause grievous bodily harm, rather than to kill; (b) spontaneity and lack of pre-meditation.

N.18 Mitigating factors relating to the offender may include: (a) the offender's age; (b) clear evidence of remorse or contrition; (c) a timely plea of guilt.

Very serious cases

N.19 A substantial upward adjustment may be appropriate in the most serious cases, for example, **B-182** those involving a substantial number of murders, or if there are several factors identified as attracting the higher starting point present. In suitable cases, the result might even be a minimum term of 30 years (equivalent to 60 years) which would offer little or no hope of the offender's eventual release. In cases of exceptional gravity, the judge, rather than setting a whole life minimum term, can state that there is no minimum period which could properly be set in that particular case.

N.20 Among the categories of case referred to in paragraph N.13 some offences may be especially grave. These include cases where the victim was performing his duties as a prison officer at the time of the crime or the offence was a terrorist or sexual or sadistic murder or involved a young child. In such a case, a term of 20 years and upwards could be appropriate.

N.21 In following this guidance, judges should bear in mind the conclusion of the court in *Sullivan* [*ante*] that the general effect of both these statements is the same. While Lord Bingham does not identify as many starting points, it is open to the judge to come to exactly the same decision irrespective of which was followed. Both pieces of guidance give the judge a considerable degree of discretion.

CPD VII Sentencing P: Procedure for Announcing the Minimum Term in Open Court

B-183
P.1 Having gone through the three or four steps outlined above, the court is then under a duty, under section 270 of the Act [§ 5-420 in the main work], to state in open court, in ordinary language, its reasons for deciding on the minimum term or for passing a whole life order.

P.2 In order to comply with this duty, the court should state clearly the minimum term it has determined. In doing so, it should state which of the starting points it has chosen and its reasons for doing so. Where the court has departed from that starting point due to mitigating or aggravating features, it must state the reasons for that departure and any aggravating or mitigating features which have led to that departure. At that point, the court should also declare how much, if any, time is being deducted for time spent in custody and/or on bail subject to a qualifying curfew condition. The court must then explain that the minimum term is the minimum amount of time the prisoner will spend in prison, from the date of sentence, before the Parole Board can order early release. If it remains necessary for the protection of the public, the prisoner will continue to be detained after that date. The court should also state that where the prisoner has served the minimum term and the Parole Board has decided to direct release, the prisoner will remain on licence for the rest of his life and may be recalled to prison at any time.

P.3 Where the offender was 21 or over when he committed the offence and the court considers that the seriousness of the offence is so exceptionally high that a 'whole life order' is appropriate, the court should state clearly its reasons for reaching this conclusion. It should also explain that the early release provisions will not apply.

CPD VII Sentencing Q: Financial, Etc. Information Required for Sentencing

B-184
Q.1 These directions supplement CrimPR 24.11 and 25.16 [§ 5-11a in the main work], which set out the procedure to be followed where a defendant pleads guilty, or is convicted, and is to be sentenced. They are not concerned exclusively with corporate defendants, or with offences of an environmental, public health, health and safety or other regulatory character, but the guidance which they contain is likely to be of particular significance in such cases.

Q.2 The rules set out the prosecutor's responsibilities in all cases. Where the offence is of a character, or is against a prohibition, with which the sentencing court is unlikely to be familiar, those responsibilities are commensurately more onerous. The court is entitled to the greatest possible assistance in identifying information relevant to sentencing.

Q.3 In such a case, save where the circumstances are very straightforward, it is likely that justice will best be served by the submission of the required information in writing: see *R. v. Friskies Petcare (U.K.) Ltd* [2000] 2 Cr.App.R.(S.) 401, CA. Though it is the prosecutor's responsibility to the court to prepare any such document, if the defendant pleads guilty, or indicates a guilty plea, then it is very highly desirable that such sentencing information should be agreed between the parties and jointly submitted. If agreement cannot be reached in all particulars, then the nature and extent of the disagreement should be indicated. If the court concludes that what is in issue is material to sentence, then it will give directions for resolution of the dispute, whether by hearing oral evidence or by other means. In every case, when passing sentence the sentencing court must make clear on what basis sentence is passed: in fairness to the defendant, and for the information of any other person, or court, who needs or wishes to understand the reasons for sentence.

Q.4 If so directed by or on behalf of the court, a defendant must supply accurate information about financial circumstances. In fixing the amount of any fine the court must take into account, amongst other considerations, the financial circumstances of the offender (whether an individual or other person) as they are known or as they appear to be. Before fixing the amount of fine when the defendant is an individual, the court must inquire into his financial circumstances. Where the defendant is an individual the court may make a financial circumstances order in respect of him. This means an order in which the court requires an individual to provide a statement as to his financial means, within a specified time. It is an offence, punishable with imprisonment, to fail to comply with such an order or for knowingly/recklessly furnishing a false statement or knowingly failing to disclose a material fact. The provisions of section 20A of the CJA 1991 apply to any person (thereby including a corporate organisation) and place the offender under a statutory duty to provide the court with a statement as to his financial means in response to an official request. There are offences for non-compliance, false statements or non-disclosure. It is for the court to decide how much information is required, having regard to relevant sentencing guidelines or guideline cases. However, by reference to those same guidelines and cases the parties should anticipate what the court will require, and prepare accordingly. In complex cases, and in cases involving a corporate defendant, the information required will be more extensive than in others. In the case of a corporate defendant, that information usually will include details of the defendant's corporate structure; annual profit and loss accounts, or extracts; annual balance sheets, or extracts; details of shareholders' receipts; and details of the remuneration of directors or other officers.

Q.5 [*Quotes extensively from the judgment in R. v. F. Howe & Son (Engineers) Ltd (as to which, see § 5-684a in the main work).*]

Q.6 In the case of an individual, the court is likewise entitled to conclude that the defendant is able to pay any fine imposed unless the defendant has supplied financial information to the contrary. It is the defendant's responsibility to disclose to the court such information relevant to his or her financial position as will enable it to assess what he or she reasonably can afford to pay. If necessary, the court may compel the disclosure of an individual defendant's financial circumstances. In the absence of such disclosure, or where the court is not satisfied that it has been given sufficient reliable information, the court will be entitled to draw reasonable inferences as to the offender's means from evidence it has heard and from all the circumstances of the case.

CPD IX Appeal 34A: Appeals to the Crown Court

34A.1 CrimPR 34.4 [§ 2-120 in the main work] applies when a defendant appeals to the Crown **B-184a** Court against conviction or sentence and specifies the information and documentation that must be provided by the magistrates' court.

34A.2 On an appeal against conviction, the reasons given by the magistrates for their decision should not be included with the documents; the appeal hearing is not a review of the magistrates' court's decision but a re-hearing.

34A.3 On an appeal against sentence, the magistrates' court's reasons and factual finding leading to the finding of guilt should be included, but any reasons for the sentence imposed should be omitted as the Crown Court will be conducting a fresh sentencing exercise.

CPD IX Appeal 39A: Appeals Against Conviction and Sentence—the Provision of Notice to the Prosecution

39A.1 When an appeal notice served under rule 39.2 [§ 7-381 in the main work] is received by the **B-185** Registrar of Criminal Appeals, the registrar will notify the relevant prosecution authority, giving the case name, reference number and the trial or sentencing court.

39A.2 If the court or the registrar directs, or invites, the prosecution authority to serve a respondent's notice under rule 39.6 [§ 7-202 in the main work], prior to the consideration of leave, the registrar will also at that time serve on the prosecution authority the appeal notice containing the grounds of appeal and the transcripts, if available. If the prosecution authority is not directed or invited to serve a respondent's notice but wishes to do so, the authority should request the grounds of appeal and any existing transcript from the Criminal Appeal Office. Any respondent's notice received prior to the consideration of leave will be made available to the single judge.

39A.3 The Registrar of Criminal Appeals will notify the relevant prosecution authority in the event that:

    (a) leave to appeal against conviction or sentence is granted by the single judge; or

    (b) the single judge or the registrar refers an application for leave to appeal against conviction or sentence to the full court for determination; or

    (c) there is to be a renewed application for leave to appeal against sentence only.

If the prosecution authority has not yet been served with the appeal notice and transcript, the registrar will serve these with the notification, and if leave is granted, the registrar will also serve the authority with the comments of the single judge.

39A.4 The prosecution should notify the registrar without delay if they wish to be represented at the hearing. The prosecution should note that the registrar will not delay listing to await a response from the prosecution as to whether they wish to attend. Prosecutors should note that occasionally, for example, where the single judge fixes a hearing date at short notice, the case may be listed very quickly.

39A.5 If the prosecution wishes to be represented at any hearing, the notification should include details of counsel instructed and a time estimate. An application by the prosecution to remove a case from the list for counsel's convenience, or to allow further preparation time, will rarely be granted.

39A.6 There may be occasions when the Court of Appeal ... will grant leave to appeal to an unrepresented applicant and proceed forthwith with the appeal in the absence of the appellant and counsel. The prosecution should not attend any hearing at which the appellant is unrepresented (*Nasteska v. The former Yugoslav Republic of Macedonia (Application No.23152/05)*). As a court of review, the Court of Appeal ... would expect the prosecution to have raised any specific matters of relevance with the sentencing judge in the first instance.

CPD IX Appeal 39B: Listing of Appeals Against Conviction and Sentence in the Court of Appeal Criminal Division (CACD)

B-186

39B.1 Arrangements for the fixing of dates for the hearing of appeals will be made by the Criminal Appeal Office Listing Officer, under the superintendence of the Registrar of Criminal Appeals who may give such directions as he deems necessary.

39B.2 Where possible, regard will be had to an advocate's existing commitments. However, in relation to the listing of appeals, the Court of Appeal takes precedence over all lower courts, including the Crown Court. Wherever practicable, a lower court will have regard to this principle when making arrangements to release an advocate to appear in the Court of Appeal. In case of difficulty the lower court should communicate with the Registrar. In general an advocate's commitment in a lower court will not be regarded as a good reason for failing to accept a date proposed for a hearing in the Court of Appeal.

39B.3 Similarly when the Registrar directs that an appellant should appear by video link, the prison must give precedence to video-links to the Court of Appeal over video-links to the lower courts, including the Crown Court.

39B.4 The copy of the Criminal Appeal Office summary provided to advocates will contain the summary writer's time estimate for the whole hearing including delivery of judgment. It will also contain a time estimate for the judges' reading time of the core material. The listing officer will rely on those estimates, unless the advocate for the appellant or the Crown provides different time estimates to the listing officer, in writing, within 7 days of the receipt of the summary by the advocate. Where the time estimates are considered by an advocate to be inadequate, or where the estimates have been altered because, for example, a ground of appeal has been abandoned, it is the duty of the advocate to inform the court promptly, in which event the Registrar will reconsider the time estimates and inform the parties accordingly.

39B.5 [*Provides for the following target times to run from receipt of an appeal by the listing officer as being ready for hearing: in the case of sentence appeals, 14 days from receipt by listing officer to fixing a hearing date, and 14 days from fixing the date to the date of hearing; in the case of conviction appeals, the corresponding times would be 21 and 42 days respectively; and, where a witness is to attend, the times would be 28 and 52 days respectively; where legal vacations impinge on those periods, they might be extended, and where expedition was required they might be abridged; and, for these purposes, "appeal" includes an application for leave to appeal which requires an oral hearing.*]

CPD IX Appeal 39C: Appeal Notices Containing Grounds of Appeal

B-187

39C.1 The requirements for the service of notices of appeal and the time limits for doing so are as set out in Part 39 of the Criminal Procedure Rules [§§ 7-380 *et seq.*]. The court must be provided with an appeal notice as a single document which sets out the grounds of appeal. Advocates should not provide the court with an advice addressed to lay or professional clients. Any appeal notice or grounds of appeal served on the court will usually be provided to the respondent.

39C.2 Advocates should not settle grounds unless they consider that they are properly arguable. Grounds should be carefully drafted; the court is not assisted by grounds of appeal which are not properly set out and particularised. Should leave to amend the grounds be granted, it is most unlikely that further grounds will be entertained.

CPD IX Appeal 39D: Respondents' Notices

B-188

[*See § 7-202 in the main work.*]

CPD IX Appeal 39E: Loss of Time

B-189

39E.1 Both the court and the single judge have power, in their discretion ... to direct that part of the time during which an applicant is in custody after lodging his notice of application for leave to appeal should not count towards sentence. Those contemplating an appeal should seek advice and should remember that a notice of appeal without grounds is ineffective and that grounds should be substantial and particularised and not a mere formula. When leave to appeal has been refused by the single judge, it is often of assistance to consider the reasons given by the single judge before making a decision whether to renew the application. Where an application devoid of merit has been refused by the single judge he may indicate that the full court should consider making a direction for loss of time on renewal of the application. However, the full court may make such a direction whether or not such an indication has been given by the single judge.

39E.2 Applicants and counsel are reminded of the warning given ... in *R. v. Hart; R. v. George; R. v. Clarke; R. v. Brown* [§ 7-228 in the main work].

CPD IX Appeal 39F: Skeleton Arguments

39F.1 Advocates should always ensure that the court, and any other party as appropriate, has a **B-190** single document containing all of the points that are to be argued. The appeal notice must comply with the requirements of Part 68. In cases of an appeal against conviction, advocates must serve a skeleton argument when the appeal notice does not sufficiently outline the grounds of the appeal, particularly in cases where a complex or novel point of law has been raised. In an appeal against sentence it may be helpful for an advocate to serve a skeleton argument when a complex issue is raised.

39F.2 The appellant's skeleton argument, if any, must be served no later than 21 days before the hearing date, and the respondent's skeleton argument, if any, no later than 14 days before the hearing date, unless otherwise directed by the court.

39F.3 A skeleton argument, if provided, should contain a numbered list of the points the advocate intends to argue, grouped under each ground of appeal, and stated in no more than one or two sentences. It should be as succinct as possible. Advocates should ensure that the correct Criminal Appeal Office number and the date on which the document was served appears at the beginning of any document and that their names are at the end.

CPD IX Appeal 39G: Criminal Appeal Office Summaries

39G.1 To assist the court the Criminal Appeal Office prepares summaries of the cases coming **B-191** before it. These are entirely objective and do not contain any advice about how the court should deal with the case or any view about its merits. They consist of two parts.

39G.2 Part I, which is provided to all of the advocates in the case, generally contains (a) particulars of the proceedings in the Crown Court, including representation and details of any co-accused, (b) particulars of the proceedings in the Court of Appeal (Criminal Division), (c) the facts of the case, as drawn from the transcripts, appeal notice, respondent's notice, witness statements and/or the exhibits, (d) the submissions and rulings, summing up and sentencing remarks. Should an advocate not want any factual material in his advice taken into account this should be stated in the advice.

39G.3 The contents of the summary are a matter for the professional judgment of the writer, but an advocate wishing to suggest any significant alteration to Part I should write to the Registrar of Criminal Appeals. If the registrar does not agree, the summary and the letter will be put to the court for decision. The court will not generally be willing to hear oral argument about the content of the summary.

39G.4 Advocates may show Part I of the summary to their professional or lay clients (but to no one else) if they believe it would help to check facts or formulate arguments, but summaries are not to be copied or reproduced without the permission of the Criminal Appeal Office; permission for this will not normally be given in cases involving children or sexual offences or where the Crown Court has made an order restricting reporting.

39G.5 Unless a judge of the High Court or the Registrar of Criminal Appeals gives a direction to the contrary in any particular case involving material of an explicitly salacious or sadistic nature, Part I will also be supplied to appellants who seek to represent themselves before the full court or who renew to the full court their applications for leave to appeal against conviction or sentence.

39G.6 Part II, which is supplied to the court alone, contains (a) a summary of the grounds of appeal and (b) in appeals against sentence (and applications for such leave), summaries of the antecedent histories of the parties and of any relevant pre-sentence, medical or other reports.

39G.7 All of the source material is provided to the court and advocates are able to draw attention to anything in it which may be of particular relevance.

CPD IX Appeal 44A: References to the European Court of Justice

44A.1 Further to rule 44.3 of the Criminal Procedure Rules [§ 2-189 in the main work], the order **B-192** containing the reference shall be filed with the Senior Master of the Queen's Bench Division of the High Court for onward transmission to the Court of Justice of the European Union. The order should be marked for the attention of Mrs Isaac and sent to the Senior Master, c/o Queen's Bench Division Associates Dept, Room WG03, Royal Courts of Justice, Strand, London, WC2A 2LL.

44A.2 There is no longer a requirement that the relevant court file be sent to the Senior Master. The parties should ensure that all appropriate documentation is sent directly to the European Court at the following address: The Registrar, Court of Justice of the European Union, Kirchberg, L-2925 Luxemburg.

44A.3 There is no prescribed form for use but the following details must be included in the back sheet to the order: (i) solicitor's full address; (ii) solicitor's and court references; (iii) solicitor's e-mail address.

44A.4 The European Court of Justice regularly updates its recommendation to national courts and tribunals in relation to the initiation of preliminary ruling proceedings. The current recommendation is 2012/C338/01: http://eurlex.europa.eu/LexUriServ/LexUriServ.do?uri=OJ:C:2012:338:0001:0006:EN:PDF.

44A.5 The referring court may request the Court of Justice of the European Union to apply its urgent preliminary ruling procedure where the referring court's proceedings relate to a person in custody. For further information see Council Decision 2008/79/EC [2008] OJ L24/42: http://eurlex.eu ropa.eu/LexUriServ/LexUriServ.do?uri=OJ:L:2008:024:0042:0043:EN:PDF.

44A.6 Any such request must be made in a document separate from the order or in a covering letter and must set out: (i) the matters of fact and law which establish the urgency; (ii) the reasons why the urgent preliminary ruling procedure applies; and (iii) in so far as possible, the court's view on the answer to the question referred to the Court of Justice of the European Union for a preliminary ruling.

44A.7 Any request to apply the urgent preliminary ruling procedure should be filed with the Senior Master as described above.

CPD XI Other Proceedings 47A: Investigation Orders and Warrants

B-193   47A.1 Powers of entry, search and seizure, and powers to obtain banking and other confidential information, are among the most intrusive that investigators can exercise. Every application must be carefully scrutinised with close attention paid to what the relevant statutory provision requires of the applicant and to what it permits. CrimPR, Pt 47 [§§ 15-272 *et seq.* in the main work] must be followed, and the accompanying forms must be used. These are designed to prompt applicants, and the courts, to deal with all of the relevant criteria.

47A.2 The issuing of a warrant or the making of such an order is never to be treated as a formality and it is therefore essential that the judge or magistrate considering the application is given, and must take, sufficient time for the purpose. The prescribed forms require the applicant to provide a time estimate, and listing officers and justices' legal advisers should take account of these.

47A.3 Applicants for orders and warrants owe the court duties of candour and truthfulness. On any application made without notice to the respondent, and so on all applications for search warrants, the duty of frank and complete disclosure is especially onerous. The applicant must draw the court's attention to any information that is unfavourable to the application. The existence of unfavourable information will not necessarily lead to the application being refused; it will be a matter for the court what weight to place on each piece of information.

47A.4 Where an applicant supplements an application with additional oral or written information, on questioning by the court or otherwise, it is essential that the court keeps an adequate record. What is needed will depend upon the circumstances. The rules require that a record of the 'gist' be retained. The purpose of such a record is to allow the sufficiency of the court's reasons for its decision subsequently to be assessed. The gravity of such decisions requires that their exercise should be susceptible to scrutiny and to explanation by reference to all of the information that was taken into account.

47A.5 The forms that accompany CrimPR, Pt 47 provide for the most frequently encountered applications. However, there are some hundreds of powers of entry, search and seizure, supplied by a corresponding number of legislative provisions. In any criminal matter, if there is no form designed for the particular warrant or order sought, the forms should still be used, as far as is practicable, and adapted as necessary. The applicant should pay particular attention to the specific legislative requirements for the granting of such an application to ensure that the court has all of the necessary information, and, if the court might be unfamiliar with the legislation, should provide a copy of the relevant provisions. Applicants must comply with the duties of candour and truthfulness, and include in their application the declarations required by the Rules and must make disclosure of any unfavourable information to the court.

CPD XI Other Proceedings 48A: Contempt in the Face of the Magistrates' Court

48A [*Refers to Contempt of Court Act 1981, s.12 [§28-81in the main work]; advises that, in the majority of* **B-194** *cases, an apology and a promise as to future conduct should be enough to secure a person's release; but there are likely to be cases where the nature and seriousness of the conduct will require the court to consider using its powers under s.12(2) to fine or commit to custody; before imposing a penalty, the court should offer the offender a further opportunity to apologise, and should follow the procedure in rule 48.8(4) of the Criminal Procedure Rules (§28-108in the main work); in deciding how to deal with the offender, regard should be had to the period during which he has been detained, whether the conduct was admitted and its seriousness; and period of committal should be as short as possible commensurate with the interests of preserving good order in the administration of justice.*]

CPD XII General Application A: Court Dress

A.1 In magistrates' courts advocates appear without robes or wigs. In all other courts, Queen's **B-195** Counsel wear a short wig and a silk (or stuff) gown over a court coat with bands, junior counsel wear a short wig and stuff gown with bands. Solicitors and other advocates authorised under the Courts and Legal Services Act 1990 [now the Legal Services Act 2007] wear a black solicitor's gown with bands; they may wear short wigs in circumstances where they would be worn by Queen's counsel or junior counsel.

A.2 [*High Court judges.*]

CPD XII General Application B: Modes of Address and Titles of Judges and Magistrates

Modes of address

B.1 The following judges, when sitting in court, should be addressed as "My Lord" or "My Lady", **B-196** as the case may be, whatever their personal status:
  (a) judges of the Court of Appeal and of the High Court;
  (b) any circuit judge sitting as a judge of the Court of Appeal (Criminal Division) or the High Court under section 9(1) of the Senior Courts Act 1981;
  (c) any judge sitting at the Central Criminal Court;
  (d) any senior circuit judge who is an Honorary Recorder.

B.2 Subject to the paragraph above, circuit judges, qualifying judge advocates, recorders and deputy circuit judges should be addressed as "Your Honour" when sitting in court.

District judges (magistrates' courts) should be addressed as "Sir [or Madam]" or "Judge" when sitting in Court.

Magistrates in court should be addressed through the Chairperson as "Sir [or Madam]" or collectively as "Your Worships".

B.3 [*Description in cause lists.*] **B-197**

CPD XII General application C: Availability of Judgments Given in the Court of Appeal and the High Court

[*See § 7-33 in the main work*] **B-198**

CPD XII General Application D: Citation of Authority and Provision of Copies of Judgments to the Court

D.1 This practice direction applies to all criminal matters before the Court of Appeal (Criminal **B-199** Division), the Crown Court and the magistrates' courts. In relation to those matters only, *Practice Direction (Citation of Authorities)* [2012] 1 W.L.R. 780 is hereby revoked.

Citation of authority

D.2 In *R. v. Erskine*; *R. v. Williams* [2009] 2 Cr.App.R. 29, CA, Lord Judge C.J. stated: **B-200**

  "75. The essential starting point, relevant to any appeal against conviction or sentence, is that, adapting the well-known aphorism of Viscount Falkland in 1641: if it is not necessary to refer to a previous decision of the court, it is necessary not to refer to it. Similarly, if it is not necessary to include a previous decision in the bundle of authorities, it is necessary to exclude it. That approach will be rigidly enforced.
  76. It follows that when the advocate is considering what authority, if any, to cite for a proposition, only an authority which establishes the principle should be cited. Reference should not be made to authorities which do no more than either (a) illustrate the principle or (b) restate it.

78. Advocates must expect to be required to justify the citation of each authority relied on or included in the bundle. The court is most unlikely to be prepared to look at an authority which does no more than illustrate or restate an established proposition.

80. ... In particular, in sentencing appeals, where a definitive Sentencing Guidelines Council guideline is available there will rarely be any advantage in citing an authority reached before the issue of the guideline, and authorities after its issue which do not refer to it will rarely be of assistance. In any event, where the authority does no more than uphold a sentence imposed at the Crown Court, the advocate must be ready to explain how it can assist the court to decide that a sentence is manifestly excessive or wrong in principle."

D.3 Advocates should only cite cases when it is necessary to do so; when the case identifies or represents a principle or the development of a principle. In sentencing appeals, other cases are rarely helpful, providing only an illustration, and this is especially true if there is a sentencing guideline. Unreported cases should only be cited in exceptional circumstances, and the advocate must expect to explain why such a case has been cited.

D.4 Advocates should not assume that because a case cited to the court is not referred to in the judgment the court has not considered it; it is more likely that the court was not assisted by it.

D.5 When an authority is to be cited, whether in written or oral submissions, the advocate should always provide the neutral citation followed by the law report reference.

D.6 The following practice should be followed: (i) where a judgment is reported in the ... Law Reports (A.C., Q.B., Ch., Fam.) ... or the Criminal Appeal Reports or the Criminal Appeal Reports (Sentencing) one of those two series of reports must be cited; either is equally acceptable; however, where a judgment is reported in the Criminal Appeal Reports or the Criminal Appeal Reports (Sentencing) that reference must be given in addition to any other reference; other series of reports and official transcripts ... may only be used when a case is not reported, or not yet reported, in the ... Law Reports or the Criminal Appeal Reports or the Criminal Appeal Reports (Sentencing); (ii) if a judgment is not reported in the ... Law Reports, the Criminal Appeal Reports or the Criminal Appeal Reports (Sentencing), but it is reported in an authoritative series of reports which contains a headnote and is made by individuals [*sic*] holding a Senior Courts qualification (for the purposes of s.115 of the Courts and Legal Services Act 1990 [now the Legal Services Act 2007]), that report should be cited; (iii) where a judgment is not reported in any of the reports referred to above, but is reported in other reports, they may be cited; (iv) where a judgment has not been reported, reference may be made to the official transcript if that is available, not the handed-down text of the judgment, as this may have been subject to late revision after the text was handed down; official transcripts may be obtained from, for instance, BAILLI (http://www.bailii.org/).

D.7 In the majority of cases, it is expected that all references will be to the ... Law Reports and the Criminal Appeal Reports or the Criminal Appeal Reports (Sentencing); it will be rare for there to be a need to refer to any other reports. An unreported case should not be cited unless it contains a relevant statement of legal principle not found in reported authority, and it is expected that this will only occur in exceptional circumstances.

Provision of copies of judgments to the court

B-201

D.8 The paragraphs below specify whether or not copies should be provided to the court. Authorities should not be included for propositions not in dispute. If more than one authority is to be provided, the copies should be presented in paginated and tagged bundles.

D.9 If required, copies of judgments should be provided either by way of a photocopy of the published report or by way of a copy of a reproduction of the judgment in electronic form that has been authorised by the publisher of the relevant series, but in any event: (i) the report must be presented to the court in an easily legible form (a 12-point font is preferred but a 10 or 11-point font is acceptable), and (ii) the advocate presenting the report must be satisfied that it has not been reproduced in a garbled form from the data source. In any case of doubt the court will rely on the printed text of the report (unless the editor of the report has certified that an electronic version is more accurate because it corrects an error contained in an earlier printed text of the report).

D.10 If such a copy is unavailable, a printed transcript such as from BAILLI may be included.

Provision of copies to the Court of Appeal (Criminal Division)

B-202

D.11 Advocates must provide to the Registrar of Criminal Appeals, with their appeal notice, respondent's notice or skeleton argument, a list of authorities upon which they wish to rely in their written or oral submissions. The list ... should contain the name of the applicant, appellant or respondent and the Criminal Appeal Office number where known. The list should include reference to the relevant paragraph numbers in each authority. An updated list can be provided if a new authority is issued, or in response to a respondent's notice or skeleton argument. From time to time, the registrar may issue guidance as to the style or content of lists of authorities, including a suggested format; this guidance should be followed by all parties. The latest guidance is available from the Criminal Appeal Office.

D.12 If the case cited is reported in the ... Law Reports, the Criminal Appeal Reports or the Criminal Appeal Reports (Sentencing), the law report reference must be given after the neutral citation, and the relevant paragraphs listed, but copies should not be provided to the court.

D.13 If, exceptionally, reference is made to a case that is not reported in [those reports], three copies must be provided to the registrar with the list of authorities and the relevant appeal notice or respondent's notice (or skeleton argument, if provided). The relevant passages of the authorities should be marked or sidelined.

Provision of copies to the Crown Court and the magistrates' courts

D.14 When the court is considering routine applications, it may be sufficient for the court to be **B-203** referred to the applicable legislation or to one of the practitioner texts. However, it is the responsibility of the advocate to ensure that the court is provided with the material that it needs properly to consider any matter.

D.15 If it would assist the court to consider any authority, the directions at paragraphs D.2 to D.7 above relating to citation will apply and a list of authorities should be provided.

D.16 Copies should be provided by the party seeking to rely upon the authority in accordance with rule 25.12. This rule is applicable in the magistrates' courts, and in relation to the provision of authorities, should also be followed in the Crown Court since courts often do not hold library stock. Advocates should comply with paragraphs D.8 to D.10 relating to the provision of copies to the court.

CPD XII General Application E: Preparation of Judgments: Neutral Citation

[*Preparation of judgments; neutral citation.*] **B-204**

CPD XII General Application F: Citation of Hansard

F.1 Where any party intends to refer to the reports of parliamentary proceedings as reported in **B-205** the Official Reports of either House of Parliament ("Hansard") in support of any such argument as is permitted by the decisions in *Pepper v. Hart* [1993] A.C. 593, HL, and *Pickstone v. Freemans Plc* [1989] A.C. 66, HL, or otherwise he must, unless the court otherwise directs, serve upon all other parties and the court copies of any such extract together with a brief summary of the argument intended to be based upon such extract. No other report of parliamentary proceedings may be cited.

F.2 Unless the court otherwise directs, service of the extract and summary of the argument shall be effected not less than five clear working days before the first day of the hearing, whether or not it has a fixed date. Advocates must keep themselves informed as to the state of the lists where no fixed date has been given. Service on the court shall be effected by sending three copies to the Registrar of Criminal Appeals, Royal Courts of Justice, Strand, London WC2A 2LL or to the court manager of the relevant Crown Court centre, as appropriate. If any party fails to do so the court may make such order (relating to costs or otherwise) as is in all the circumstances appropriate.

CPD XIII Listing A: Judicial Responsibility for Listing and Key Principles

Listing as a judicial responsibility and function

A.1 Listing is a judicial responsibility and function. The purpose is to ensure that all cases are **B-206** brought to a hearing or trial in accordance with the interests of justice, that the resources available for criminal justice are deployed as effectively as possible, and that cases are heard by an appropriate judge or bench with the minimum of delay.

A.2 The agreement reached between the Lord Chief Justice and the Secretary of State for Constitutional Affairs and Lord Chancellor set out in a statement to the House of Lords on 26 January 2004 ("the Concordat"), states that judges, working with HMCTS, are responsible for deciding on the assignment of cases to particular courts and the listing of those cases before particular judges. Therefore:

    (a) The presiding judges of each circuit have the overall responsibility for listing at all courts, Crown and magistrates', on their circuit.

    (b) Subject to the supervision of the presiding judges, the resident judge at each Crown Court has the general responsibility within his or her court centre for the allocation of criminal judicial work, to ensure the just and efficient despatch of the business of the court or group of courts. This includes overseeing the deployment of allocated judges at the court or group, including the distribution of work between all the judges allocated to that court. A resident judge must appoint a deputy or deputies to exercise his or her functions when he or she is absent from his or her court centre. See also para. A.5.

(c) The listing officer in the Crown Court is responsible for carrying out the day-to-day operation of listing practice under the direction of the resident judge. The listing officer at each Crown Court centre has one of the most important functions at that Crown Court and makes a vital contribution to the efficient running of that Crown Court and to the efficient operation of the administration of criminal justice.

(d) In the magistrates' courts, the Judicial Business Group, subject to the supervision of the presiding judges of the circuit, is responsible for determining the listing practice in that area. The day-to-day operation of that listing practice is the responsibility of the justices' clerk with the assistance of the listing officer.

Key principles of listing

B-207   A.3 When setting the listing practice, the resident judge or the Judicial Business Group should take into account principles (a)–(j).

(a) Ensure the timely trial of cases and resolution of other issues (such as confiscation) so that justice is not delayed. The following factors are relevant. (i) In general, each case should be tried within as short a time of its arrival in the court as is consistent with the interests of justice, the needs of victims and witnesses, and with the proper and timely preparation by the prosecution and defence of their cases in accordance with the directions and timetable set. (ii) Priority should be accorded to the trial of young defendants, and cases where there are vulnerable or young witnesses. In *R. v. Barker (Steven), The Times,* February 5, 2010, CA, Lord Judge C.J. highlighted "the importance to the trial and investigative process of keeping any delay in a case involving a child complainant to an irreducible minimum". (iii) Custody time limits ("CTLs") should be observed: see CPD Listing F. (iv) Every effort must be made to avoid delay in cases in which the defendant is on bail.

(b) Ensure that in the magistrates' court unless impracticable, non-custody anticipated guilty plea cases are listed 14 days after charge, and non-custody anticipated not guilty pleas are listed 28 days after charge.

(c) Provide, when possible, for certainty and/or as much advance notice as possible, of the trial date; and take all reasonable steps to ensure that the trial date remains fixed.

(d) Ensure that a judge or bench with any necessary authorisation and of appropriate experience is available to try each case and, wherever desirable and practicable, there is judicial continuity, including in relation to post-trial hearings.

(e) Strike an appropriate balance in the use of resources, by taking account of: (i) the efficient deployment of the judiciary in the Crown Court and the magistrates' courts taking into account relevant sitting requirements for magistrates (see Annex 1 for information to support judicial deployment in the magistrates' courts); (ii) the proper use of the courtrooms available at the court; (iii) the provision in long and/or complex cases for adequate reading time for the judiciary; (iv) the facilities in the available courtrooms, including the security needs (such as a secure dock), size and equipment, such as video and live link facilities; (v) the proper use of those who attend the Crown Court as jurors; (vi) the availability of legal advisers in the magistrates' courts; (vii) the need to return those sentenced to custody as soon as possible after the sentence is passed, and to facilitate the efficient operation of the prison escort contract.

(f) Provide where practicable: (i) the defendant and the prosecution with the advocate of their choice where this does not result in any delay to the trial of the case; and, (ii) for the efficient deployment of advocates, lawyers and associate prosecutors of the CPS, and other prosecuting authorities, and of the resources available to the independent legal profession, for example by trying to group certain cases together.

(g) Meet the need for special security measures for category A and other high-risk defendants.

(h) Ensure that proper time (including judicial reading time) is afforded to hearings in which the court is exercising powers that impact on the rights of individuals, such as applications for investigative orders or warrants.

(i) Consider the significance of ancillary proceedings, such as confiscation hearings, and the need to deal with such hearings promptly and, where possible, for such hearings to be conducted by the trial judge.

(j) Provide for government initiatives or projects approved by the Lord Chief Justice.

A.4 Although the listing practice at each Crown Court centre and magistrates' court will take these principles into account, the listing practice adopted will vary from court to court depending particularly on the number of courtrooms and the facilities available, the location and the workload, its volume and type.

Discharge of judicial responsibilities

A.5 The resident judge of each court is responsible for: (i) ensuring that good practice is **B-208** implemented throughout the court, such that all hearings commence on time; (ii) ensuring that the causes of trials that do not proceed on the date originally fixed are examined to see if there is any systemic issue; (iii) monitoring the general performance of the court and the listing practices; (iv) monitoring the timeliness of cases and reporting any cases of serious concern to the presiding judge; (v) maintaining and reviewing annually a list of recorders, qualifying judge advocates and deputy circuit judges authorised to hear appeals from the magistrates' courts unless such a list is maintained by the presiding judge.

A.6 The Judicial Business Group for each clerkship subject to the overall jurisdiction of the presiding judge is responsible for: (i) monitoring the workload and anticipated changes which may impact on listing policies; (ii) ensuring that any listing practice meets the needs of the system as a whole.

CPD XIII Listing B: Classification

B.1 The classification structure outlined below is solely for the purposes of trial in the Crown **B-209** Court. The structure has been devised to accommodate practical administrative functions and is not intended to reflect a hierarchy of the offences therein. Offences are classified as follows:

Class 1: A:

(i) Murder; (ii) attempted murder; (iii) manslaughter; (iv) infanticide; (v) child destruction (section 1(1) of the Infant Life (Preservation) Act 1929); (vi) abortion (section 58 of the Offences against the Person Act 1861); (vii) assisting a suicide; (viii) cases including section 5 of the Domestic Violence, Crime and Victims Act 2004, as amended (if a fatality has resulted); (ix) soliciting, inciting, encouraging or assisting, attempting or conspiring to commit any of the above offences or assisting an offender having committed such an offence.

Class 1: B:

(i) Genocide; (ii) torture, hostage-taking and offences under the War Crimes Act 1991; (iii) offences under sections 51 and 52 of the International Criminal Court Act 2001; (iv) an offence under section 1 of the Geneva Conventions Act 1957; (v) terrorism offences (where offence charged is indictable only and took place during an act of terrorism or for the purposes of terrorism as defined in s.1 of the Terrorism Act 2000); (vi) piracy, under the Merchant Shipping and Maritime Security Act 1997; (vii) treason; (viii) an offence under the Official Secrets Acts; (ix) incitement to disaffection; (x) soliciting, inciting, encouraging or assisting, attempting or conspiring to commit any of the above offences or assisting an offender having committed such an offence.

Class 1: C:

(i) Prison mutiny, under the Prison Security Act 1992; (ii) riot in the course of serious civil disturbance; (iii) serious gang related crime resulting in the possession or discharge of firearms, particularly including a campaign of firebombing or extortion, especially when accompanied by allegations of drug trafficking on a commercial scale; (iv) complex sexual offence cases in which there are many complainants (often under age, in care or otherwise particularly vulnerable) and/or many defendants who are alleged to have systematically groomed and abused them, often over a long period of time; (v) cases involving people trafficking for sexual, labour or other exploitation and cases of human servitude; (vi) soliciting, inciting, encouraging or assisting, attempting or conspiring to commit any of the above offences or assisting an offender having committed such an offence.

Class 1: D:

(i) Causing death by dangerous driving; (ii) causing death by careless driving; (iii) causing death by unlicensed, disqualified or uninsured driving; (iv) any health and safety case resulting in a fatality or permanent serious disability; (v) any other case resulting in a fatality or permanent serious disability; (vi) soliciting, inciting, encouraging or assisting, attempting or conspiring to commit any of the above offences or assisting an offender having committed such an offence.

Class 2: A:

(i) Arson with intent to endanger life or reckless as to whether life was endangered; (ii) cases in which explosives, firearms or imitation firearms are used or carried or possessed; (iii) kidnapping or false imprisonment (without intention to commit a sexual offence but charged on the same indictment as a serious offence of violence such as under section 18 or section 20 of the Offences against the Person Act 1861); (iv) cases in which the defendant is a police officer, member of the legal profession or a high profile or public figure; (v) cases in which the complainant or an important witness is a high profile or public figure; (vi) riot otherwise than in the course of serious civil disturbance; (vii) child cruelty; (viii) cases including section 5 of the Domestic Violence, Crime and Victims Act 2004, as amended (if no fatality has resulted); (ix) soliciting, inciting, encouraging or assisting, attempting or conspiring to commit any of the above offences or assisting an offender having committed such an offence.

Class 2: B:

(i) Any sexual offence, with the exception of those included in Class 1C; (ii) kidnapping or false imprisonment (with intention to commit a sexual offence or charged on the same indictment as a sexual offence); (iii) soliciting, inciting, encouraging or assisting, attempting or conspiring to commit any of the above offences or assisting an offender having committed such an offence.

Class 2: C:

(i) Serious, complex fraud; (ii) serious and/or complex money laundering; (iii) serious and/or complex bribery; (iv) corruption; (v) complex cases in which the defendant is a corporation (including cases for sentence as well as for trial); (vi) any case in which the defendant is a corporation with a turnover in excess of £1 billion (including cases for sentence as well as for trial); (vii) soliciting, inciting, encouraging or assisting, attempting or conspiring to commit any of the above offences or assisting an offender having committed such an offence.

Class 3: All other offences not listed in the classes above.

Deferred prosecution agreements

B-210   B.2 Cases coming before the court under section 45 of, and Schedule 17 to, the Crime and Courts Act 2013 must be referred to the President of the Queen's Bench Division who will allocate the matter to a judge from a list of judges approved by the Lord Chief Justice. Only the allocated judge may thereafter hear any matter or make any decision in relation to that case.

Criminal Cases Review Commission

B-211   B.3 Where the Criminal Cases Review Commission refers a case upon conviction from the magistrates' courts to the Crown Court, this shall be dealt with at a Crown Court centre designated by the senior presiding judge.

CPD XIII Listing C: Referral of Cases in the Crown Court to the Resident Judge and to the Presiding Judges

B-212   C.1 This practice direction specifies: (a) cases which must be referred to a presiding judge for release; and (b) cases which must be referred to the resident judge before being assigned to a judge, recorder or qualifying judge advocate to hear. It is applicable to all Crown Courts, but its application may be modified by the senior presiding judge or the presiding judges, with the approval of the senior presiding judge, through the provision of further specific guidance to resident judges in relation to the allocation and management of the work at their court.

C.2 This practice direction does not prescribe the way in which the resident judge gives directions as to listing policy to the listing officer; its purpose is to ensure that there is appropriate judicial control over the listing of cases. However, the resident judge must arrange with the listing officers a satisfactory means of ensuring that all cases listed at their court are listed before judges, recorders or qualifying judge advocates of suitable seniority and experience, subject to the requirements of this practice direction. The resident judge should ensure that listing officers are made aware of the contents and importance of this practice direction, and that listing officers develop satisfactory procedures for referral of cases to him or her.

C.3 In order to assist the resident judge and the listing officer, all cases sent to the Crown Court should where possible include a brief case summary prepared by the prosecution. The prosecutor should ensure that any factors that make the case complex, or would lead it to be referred to the resident judge or a presiding judge are highlighted. The defence may also send submissions to the court, again highlighting any areas of complexity or any other factors that might assist in the case being allocated to an appropriate judge.

Cases in the Crown Court to be referred to the resident judge

C.4 All cases in Class 1A, 1B, 1C, 1D, 2A and 2C must be referred to the resident judge as must **B-213**
any case which appears to raise particularly complex, sensitive or serious issues.

C.5 Resident judges should give guidance to the judges and staff of their respective courts as to
which Class 2B cases should be referred to them following consultation with the senior presiding
judge. This will include any cases that may be referred to the presiding judge, see below. Class 2B
cases to be referred to the resident judge are likely to be identified by the list officer, or by the judge
at the first hearing in the Crown Court.

C.6 Once a case has been referred to the resident judge, the resident judge should refer the case
to the presiding judge, following the guidance below, or allocate the case to an appropriate category
of judge, and if possible to a named judge.

Cases in the Crown Court to be referred to a presiding judge

C.7 All cases in Class 1A, 1B and 1C must be referred by the resident judge to a presiding judge, **B-214**
as must a case in any class which is: (i) an usually grave or complex case or one in which a novel and
important point of law is to be raised; (ii) a case where it is alleged that the defendant caused more
than one fatality; (iii) a non-fatal case of baby shaking where serious injury resulted; (iv) a case where
the defendant is a police officer, or a member of the legal profession or a high profile figure; (v) a
case which for any reason is likely to attract exceptional media attention; (vi) a case where a large
organisation or corporation may, if convicted, be ordered to pay a very large fine; (vii) any case likely
to last more than three months.

C.8 Resident judges are encouraged to refer any other case if they think it is appropriate to do so.

C.9 Presiding judges and resident judges should agree a system for the referral of cases to the
presiding judge, ideally by electronic means. The system agreed should include provision for the
resident judge to provide the presiding judge with a brief summary of the case, a clear recommendation by the resident judge about the judges available to try the case and any other comments. A written record of the decision and brief reasons for it must be made and retained.

C.10 Once a case has been referred to the presiding judge, the presiding judge may retain the
case for trial by a High Court judge, or release the case back to the resident judge, either for trial by
a named judge, or for trial by an identified category of judges, to be allocated by the resident judge.

CPD XIII Listing D: Authorisation of Judges

D.1 Judges must be authorised by the Lord Chief Justice before they may hear certain types of **B-215**
case.

D.2 Judges (other than High Court judges) to hear Class 1A cases must be authorised to hear such
cases. Any judge previously granted a "Class 1" or "murder" authorisation is authorised to hear Class
1A cases. Judges previously granted an "attempted murder" (including soliciting, incitement or
conspiracy thereof) authorisation can only deal with these cases within Class 1A.

D.3 Judges (other than High Court judges) to hear sexual offences cases in Class 1C or any case
within Class 2B must be authorised to hear such cases. Any judge previously granted a "Class 2" or
"serious sex offences" authorisation is authorised to hear sexual offences cases in Class 1C or 2B. It is
a condition of the authorisation that it does not take effect until the judge has attended the relevant
Judicial College course; the resident judge should check in the case of newly authorised judges that
they have attended the course. Judges who have been previously authorised to try such cases should
make every effort to ensure their training is up-to-date and maintained by by attending the serious
sexual offences seminar at least once every three years. See Annex 2 for guidance in dealing with
sexual offences in the youth court.

D.4 Cases in the magistrates' courts involving the imposition of very large fines:

(i) where a defendant appears before a magistrates' court for an either way offence, to which CPD
XIII, Annex 3 applies the case must be dealt with by a district judge (magistrates' courts) who has
been authorised to deal with such cases by the Chief Magistrate;

(ii) the authorised district judge (magistrates' courts) must first consider whether such cases should
be allocated to the Crown Court or, where the defendant pleads guilty, committed for sentence
under section 3 of the PCC(S)A 2000 [§ 5-25 in the main work], and must do so when the district
judge (magistrates' courts) considers the offence or combination of offences so serious that the Crown
Court should deal with the defendant had they been convicted on indictment;

(iii) if an authorised district judge (magistrates' courts) decides not to commit such a case the
reasons must be recorded in writing to be entered onto the court register.

CPD XIII Listing E: Allocation of Business within the Crown Court

E.1 Cases in Class 1A may only be tried by: (i) a High Court judge, or (ii) a circuit judge, or **B-216** deputy High Court judge, authorised to try such cases and provided that the presiding judge has released the case for trial by such a judge.

E.2 Cases in Class 1B may only be tried by: (i) a High Court judge, or (ii) a circuit judge, or a deputy High Court judge, provided that the presiding judge has released the case for trial by such a judge.

E.3 Cases in Class 1C may only be tried by: (i) a High Court judge, or (ii) a circuit judge, or a deputy High Court judge, or deputy circuit judge, authorised to try such cases (if the case requires the judge to be authorised to hear sexual offences cases), provided that the presiding judge has released the case for trial by such a judge, or, if the case is a sexual offence, the presiding judge has assigned the case to that named judge. See also *CPD XIII Listing* C.10.

E.4 Cases in Class 1D and 2A may be tried by: (i) a High Court judge, or (ii) a circuit judge, or deputy High Court judge, or deputy circuit judge, or a recorder or a qualifying judge advocate, provided that either the presiding judge has released the case or the resident judge has allocated the case for trial by such a judge; with the exception that Class 2A(i) cases may not be tried by a recorder or qualifying judge advocate.

E.5 Cases in Class 2B may be tried by: (i) a High Court judge, or (ii) a circuit judge, or deputy High Court judge, or deputy circuit judge, or a recorder or a qualifying judge advocate, authorised to try such cases and provided that either the presiding judge has released the case or the resident judge has allocated the case for trial by such a judge.

E.6 Cases in Class 2C may be tried by: (i) a High Court judge, or (ii) a circuit judge, or deputy High Court judge, or deputy circuit judge, or a recorder or a qualifying judge advocate, with suitable experience (for example, with company accounts or other financial information) and provided that either the presiding judge has released the case or the resident judge has allocated the case for trial by such a judge.

E.7 Cases in Classes 1D, 2A and 2C will usually be tried by a circuit judge.

E.8 Cases in Class 3 may be tried by a High Court judge, or a circuit judge, a deputy circuit judge, a recorder or a qualifying judge advocate. A case in Class 3 shall not be listed for trial by a High Court judge except with the consent of a presiding judge.

E.9 If a case has been allocated to a judge, recorder or qualifying judge advocate, the preliminary hearing should be conducted by the allocated judge if practicable, and if not, if possible by a judge of at least equivalent standing. PCMHs should only be heard by recorders or qualifying judge advocates with the approval of the resident judge.

E.10 For cases in Class 1A, 1B or 1C, or any case that has been referred to the presiding judge, the preliminary hearing and PCMH must be conducted by a High Court judge; by a circuit judge; or by a judge authorised by the presiding judges to conduct such hearings. In the event of a guilty plea before such an authorised judge, the case will be adjourned for sentencing and will immediately be referred to the presiding judge who may retain the case for sentence by a High Court judge, or release the case back to the resident judge, either for sentence by a named judge, or for sentence by an identified category of judges, to be allocated by the resident judge.

E.11 Appeals from decisions of magistrates' courts shall be heard by: (i) a resident judge, or (ii) a circuit judge, nominated by the resident judge, who regularly sits at the Crown Court centre, or (iii) a recorder or qualifying judge advocate or a deputy circuit judge listed by the presiding judge to hear such appeals; or, if there is no such list nominated by the resident judge to hear such appeals; (iv) and, no less than two and no more than four justices of the peace, none of whom took part in the decision under appeal; (v) where no circuit judge or recorder or qualifying judge advocate satisfying the requirements above is available, by a circuit judge, recorder, qualifying judge advocate or deputy circuit judge selected by the resident judge to hear a specific case or cases listed on a specific day.

E.12 Allocation or committal for sentence following breach (such as a matter in which a community order has been made, or a suspended sentence passed), should, where possible, be listed before the judge who originally dealt with the matter or, if not, before a judge of the same or higher level.

E.13 Applications for removal of a driving disqualification should be made to the location of the Crown Court where the order of disqualification was made. Where possible, the matter should be listed before the judge who originally dealt with the matter or, if not, before a judge of the same or higher level.

CPD XIII Listing F: Listing of Trials, Custody Time Limits and Transfer of Cases

Estimates of trial length

B-217

F.1 Under the regime set out in the Crim PR, the parties will be expected to provide an accurate estimate of the length of trial at the hearing where the case is to be managed based on a detailed estimate of the time to be taken with each witness to be called, and accurate information about the availability of witnesses.

F.2 At the hearing the judge will ask the prosecution to clarify any custody time limit ("CTL") dates. The court clerk must ensure the CTL date is marked clearly on the court file or electronic file. When a case is subject to a CTL all efforts must be made at the first hearing to list the case within the CTL and the judge should seek to ensure this. Further guidance on listing CTL cases can be found below.

Cases that should usually have fixed trial dates

F.3 The cases where fixtures should be given will be set out in the listing practice applicable at the **B-218** court, but should usually include the following: (i) cases in classes 1A, 1B, 1C, 2B and 2C; (ii) cases involving vulnerable and intimidated witnesses (including domestic violence cases), whether or not special measures have been ordered by the court; (iii) cases where the witnesses are under 18 or have to come from overseas; (iv) cases estimated to last more than a certain time—the period chosen will depend on the size of the centre and the available judges; (v) cases where a previous fixed hearing has not been effective; (vi) retrials; and, (vii) cases involving expert witnesses.

Custody time limits

F.4 Every effort must be made to list cases for trial within the CTL limits set by Parliament. The **B-219** guiding principles are: (i) At the first hearing in the Crown Court, prosecution will inform the court when the CTL lapses. The CTL may only be extended in accordance with section 22 of the Prosecution of Offences Act 1985 [§ 1-342 in the main work], and the Prosecution of Offences (Custody Time Limits) Regulations 1987 (S.I. 1987 No. 299) [*ibid.*, §§ 3-79 *et seq.*]. (iii) If suitable, given priority and listed on a date not less than two weeks before the CTL expires, the case may be placed in a warned list. (iv) The CTL must be kept under continual review by the parties, HMCTS and the resident judge. (v) If the CTL is at risk of being exceeded, an additional hearing should take place and should be listed before the resident judge or trial judge or other judge nominated by the resident judge. (vi) An application to extend the CTL in any case listed outside the CTL must be considered by the court whether or not it was listed with the express consent of the defence. (vii) Any application to extend CTLs must be considered as a matter of urgency. The reasons for needing the extension must be ascertained and fully explained to the court. (viii) Where courtroom or judge availability is an issue, the court must itself list the case to consider the extension of any CTL. The delivery director of the circuit must provide a statement setting out in detail what has been done to try to accommodate the case within the CTL. (ix) Where courtroom or judge availability is not in issue, but all parties and the court agree that the case will not be ready for trial before the expiration of the CTL, a date may be fixed outside the CTL. This may be done without prejudice to any application to extend the CTLs or with the express consent of the defence; this must be noted on the papers.

F.5 As legal argument may delay the swearing in of a jury, it is desirable to extend the CTL to a date later than the first day of the trial.

Retrials ordered by the Court of Appeal

F.6 The Crown Court must comply with the directions of the Court of Appeal and cannot vary **B-220** those directions without reference to the Court of Appeal.

F.7 In cases where a retrial is ordered by the Court of Appeal the CTL is 112 days starting from the date that the new indictment is preferred, ie from the date that the indictment is delivered to the Crown Court. Court centres should check that CREST has calculated the dates correctly and that it has not used 182 days on cases that have previously been "sent".

Changes to the date of fixed cases

F.8 Once a trial date or window is fixed, it should not be vacated or moved without good reason. **B-221** Under the Crim PR, parties are expected to be ready by the trial date.

F.9 The listing officer may, in circumstances determined by the resident judge, agree to the movement of the trial to a date to which the defence and prosecution both consent, provided the timely hearing of the case is not delayed. The prosecution will be expected to have consulted the witnesses before agreeing to any change.

F.10 In all other circumstances, requests to adjourn or vacate fixtures or trial windows must be referred to the resident judge for his or her personal attention; the resident judge may delegate the decision to a named deputy.

Transferring cases to another court

F.11 Transfer between courts on the same circuit must be agreed by the resident judges of each **B-222** court, subject to guidance from the presiding judges of the circuit.

F.12 Transfer of trials between circuits must be agreed between the presiding judges and delivery directors of the respective circuits.

F.13 Transfers may be agreed either in specific cases or in accordance with general principles agreed between those cited above.

CPD XIII Listing G: Listing of Hearings other than Trials

B-223

G.1 In addition to trials, the court's listing practice will have to provide court time for shorter matters, such as those listed below. These hearings are important, often either for setting the necessary case management framework for the proper and efficient preparation of cases for trial, or for determining matters that affect the rights of individuals. They must be afforded the appropriate level of resource that they require to be considered properly, and this may include judicial reading time as well as an appropriate length of hearing.

G.2 The applicant is responsible for notifying the court, and the other party if appropriate, and ensuring that the papers are served in good time, including a time estimate for judicial reading time and for the hearing. The applicant must endeavour to complete the application within the time estimate provided unless there are exceptional circumstances.

G.3 Hearings other than trials include the following: (i) applications for search warrants and production orders, sufficient reading time must be provided: see G.8 below; (ii) bail applications; (iii) applications to vacate or adjourn hearings; (iv) applications for dismissal of charges; (v) preliminary hearings; (vi) preparatory hearings; (vii) plea and case management hearings; (viii) applications for disclosure of further unused material under section 8 of the CPIA 1996 [§ 12-76 in the main work]; (ix) case progression or case management hearings; (x) applications in respect of sentence indications not sought at the PCMH; (xi) sentences; (xii) civil applications under the Anti-social Behaviour, Crime and Policing Act 2014; (xiii) appeals from the magistrates' court: it is essential in all cases where witnesses are likely to be needed on the appeal to check availability before a date is fixed.

G.4 Short hearings should not generally be listed before a judge such that they may delay the start or continuation of a trial at the Crown Court. It is envisaged that any such short hearing will be completed by 10.30 am or start after 4.30 pm.

G.5 Each Crown Court equipped with a video link with a prison must have in place arrangements for the conduct of PCMHs, other pre-trial hearings and sentencing hearings by video link.

Notifying sureties of hearing dates

B-224

G.6 Where a surety has entered into a recognisance in the magistrates' court in respect of a case allocated or sent to the Crown Court and where the bail order or recognisance refers to attendance at the first hearing in the Crown Court, the defendant should be reminded by the listing officer that the surety should attend the first hearing in the Crown Court in order to provide further recognisance. If attendance is not arranged, the defendant may be remanded in custody pending the recognisance being provided.

G.7 The court should also notify sureties of the dates of the hearing at the Crown Court at which the defendant is ordered to appear in as far in advance as possible: see the observations of Parker L.J. in *R. v. Reading Crown Court, ex p. Bello*, 92 Cr.App.R. 303, CA (Civ. Div.) [§ 3-192 in the main work].

Applications for production orders and search warrants

B-225

G.8 The use of production orders and search warrants involve the use of intrusive state powers that affect the rights and liberties of individuals. It is the responsibility of the court to ensure that those powers are not abused. To do so, the court must be presented with a properly completed application, on the appropriate form, which includes a summary of the investigation to provide the context for the order, a clear explanation of how the statutory requirements are fulfilled, and full and frank disclosure of anything that might undermine the basis for the application. Further directions on the proper making and consideration of such applications will be provided by practice direction. However, the complexity of the application must be taken into account in listing it such that the judge is afforded appropriate reading time and the hearing is given sufficient time for the issues to be considered thoroughly, and a short judgment given.

Confiscation and related hearings

B-226

G.9 Applications for restraint orders should be determined by the resident judge, or a judge nominated by the resident judge, at the Crown Court location at which they are lodged.

G.10 In order to prevent possible dissipation of assets of significant value, applications under the

PCA 2002 should be considered urgent when lists are being fixed. In order to prevent potential prejudice, applications for the variation and discharge of orders, for the appointment of receivers, and applications to punish alleged breaches of orders as a contempt of court should similarly be treated as urgent and listed expeditiously.

Confiscation hearings

G.11 It is important that confiscation hearings take place in good time after the defendant is **B-227** convicted or sentenced.

CPD XIII Listing: Annex 1 General Principles for the Deployment of the Judiciary in the Magistrates' Court

This distils the full deployment guidance issued in November 2012. The relevant sections dealing **B-228** specifically with the allocation of work within the magistrates' court have been incorporated into this practice direction. It does not seek to replace the guidance in its entirety.

Presumptions

1 The presumptions which follow are intended to provide an acceptable and flexible framework **B-229** establishing the deployment of the district judges (magistrates' courts) and magistrates. The system must be capable of adaptation to meet particular needs, whether of locality or caseload. In any event, the presumptions which follow are illustrative not exhaustive.

2 District judges (magistrates' courts) should generally (not invariably) be deployed in accordance with the following presumptions ("the presumptions"): (a) Cases involving complex points of law and evidence; (b) cases involving complex procedural issues; (c) long cases (included on grounds of practicality); (d) interlinked cases (given the need for consistency, together with their likely complexity and novelty); (e) cases for which armed police officers are required in court, such as high end firearms cases; (f) a share of the more routine business of the court, including case management and pre-trial reviews, (for a variety of reasons, including the need for district judges (magistrates' courts) to have competence in all areas of work and the desirability of an equitable division of work between magistrates and district judges (magistrates' courts), subject always to the interests of the administration of justice); (g) where appropriate, in supporting the training of magistrates; (h) occasionally, in mixed benches of district judges (magistrates' courts) and magistrates (with a particular view both to improving the case management skills of magistrates and to improving the culture of collegiality); (i) in the short-term tackling of particular local backlogs ("backlog busting"), sometimes in combination with magistrates from the local or (with the senior presiding judge's approval) adjoining benches.

3 In accordance with current arrangements certain classes of cases necessarily require district judges (magistrates' courts) and have therefore been excluded from the above presumptions; these are as follows: (a) extradition; (b) terrorism; (c) prison adjudications; (d) sex cases in the youth court as per Annex 2; (e) cases where the defendant is likely to be sentenced to a very large fine: see Annex 3; (f) the special jurisdiction of the Chief Magistrate.

4 In formulating the presumptions, the following considerations have been taken into account.

  (a) The listing of cases is here, as elsewhere, a judicial function: see *CPD XIII Listing A*, para. 10. In the magistrates' courts the Judicial Business Group, subject to the supervision of the presiding judges of the circuit, is responsible for determining the day-to-day listing practice in that area. The day-to-day operation of that listing practice is the responsibility of the justices' clerk with the assistance of the listing officer.

  (b) Equally, providing the training of magistrates is a responsibility of justices' clerks.

  (c) It is best not to treat "high profile" cases as a separate category but to consider their listing in the light of the principles and presumptions. The circumstances surrounding high profile cases do not permit ready generalisation, save that they are likely to require especially sensitive handling. Listing decisions involving such cases will often benefit from good communication at a local level between the justices' clerk, the district judge (magistrates' courts) and the bench chairman.

  (d) Account must be taken of the need to maintain the competences of all members of the judiciary sitting in the magistrates' court.

CPD XIII Listing: Annex 2 Sexual Offences in the Youth Court

Introduction

1 This annex sets out the procedure to be applied in the youth court in all cases involving allega- **B-230** tions of sexual offences which are capable of being sent for trial at the Crown Court under the grave

crime provisions.

2 This applies to all cases involving such charges, irrespective of the gravity of the allegation, the age of the defendant and/or the antecedent history of the defendant. (So, for example, every allegation of sexual touching, under s.3 of the SOA 2003, is covered by this protocol.)

3 This does not alter the test (set out in the Sentencing Guidelines Council's definitive guideline, entitled "*Overarching Principles—Sentencing Youths*" [*post*, Appendix K-240 *et seq.*]) that the youth court must apply when determining whether a case is a "grave crime".

4 In the Crown Court, cases involving allegations of sexual offences frequently involve complex and sensitive issues and only those circuit judges and recorders who have been specifically authorised and who have attended the appropriate Judicial College course may try this type of work.

5 A number of district judges (magistrates' courts) have now undertaken training in dealing with these difficult cases and have been specifically authorised to hear cases involving serious sexual offences which fall short of requiring to be sent to the Crown Court ("an authorised district judge (magistrates' courts)"). As such, a procedure similar to that of the Crown Court will now apply to allegations of sexual offences in the youth court.

Procedure

B-231

6 The determination of venue in the youth court is governed by section 51 of the CDA 1998 [§ 1-25 in the main work], which provides that the youth must be tried summarily unless charged with such a grave crime that long-term detention is a realistic possibility (s.24(1) of the MCA 1980 [*ibid.*, § 1-110]), or that one of the other exceptions to this presumption arises.

7 Wherever possible such cases should be listed before an authorised district judge (magistrates' courts), to decide whether the case falls within the grave crime provisions and should therefore be sent for trial. If jurisdiction is retained and the allegation involves actual, or attempted, penetrative activity, the case must be tried by an authorised district judge (magistrates' courts). In all other cases, the authorised district judge (magistrates' courts) must consider whether the case is so serious and/or complex that it must be tried by an authorised district judge (magistrates' courts), or whether the case can be heard by any district judge (magistrates' courts) or any youth court bench.

8 If it is not practicable for an authorised district judge (magistrates' courts) to determine venue, any district judge (magistrates' courts) or any youth court bench may consider that issue. If jurisdiction is retained, appropriate directions may be given but the case papers, including a detailed case summary and a note of any representations made by the parties, must be sent to an authorised district judge (magistrates' courts) to consider. As soon as possible the authorised district judge (magistrates' courts) must decide whether the case must be tried by an authorised district judge (magistrates' courts) or whether the case is suitable to be heard by any district judge (magistrates' courts) or any youth court bench; however, if the case involves actual, or alleged, penetrative activity, the trial must be heard by an authorised district judge (magistrates' courts).

9 Once an authorised district judge (magistrates' courts) has decided that the case is one which must be tried by an authorised district judge (magistrates' courts), and in all cases involving actual or alleged penetrative activity, all further procedural hearings should, so far as practicable, be heard by an authorised district judge (magistrates' courts).

10 All cases which are remitted for sentence from the Crown Court to the youth court should be listed for sentence before an authorised district judge (magistrates' courts).

Arrangements for an authorised district judge (magistrates' courts) to be appointed

B-232

11 Where a case is to be tried by an authorised district judge (magistrates' courts) but no such judge is available, the bench legal adviser should contact the Chief Magistrate's office for an authorised district judge (magistrates' courts) to be assigned.

CPD Listing: Annex 3 Cases Involving Very Large Fines in the Magistrates' Court

B-233

1 [*Applies following commencement of LASPOA 2012, s.85 (§ 1-125 in the main work).*]

2 An authorised district judge (magistrates' courts) must deal with any allocation decision, trial and sentencing hearing in the following types of cases which are triable either way: (a) cases involving death or significant, life changing injury or a high risk of death or significant, life-changing injury; (b) cases involving substantial environmental damage or polluting material of a dangerous nature; (c) cases where major adverse effect on human health or quality of life, animal health or flora has resulted; (d) cases where major costs through clean-up, site restoration or animal rehabilitation have been incurred; (e) cases where the defendant corporation has a turnover in excess of £10m but does not exceed £250m, and has acted in a deliberate, reckless or negligent manner; (f) cases where the defendant corporation has a turnover in excess of £250m; (g) cases where the court will be expected to analyse complex company accounts; (h) high profile cases or ones of an exceptionally sensitive

nature.

3 The prosecution agency must notify the justices' clerk where practicable of any case of the type mentioned in paragraph 2 ..., no less than seven days before the first hearing to ensure that an authorised district judge (magistrates' courts) is available at the first hearing.

4 The justices' clerk shall contact the office of the Chief Magistrate to ensure that an authorised district judge (magistrates' courts) can be assigned to deal with such a case if there is not such a person available in the courthouse. The justices' clerk shall also notify a presiding judge of the circuit that such a case has been listed.

5 Where an authorised district judge (magistrates' courts) is not appointed at the first hearing the court shall adjourn the case. The court shall ask the accused for an indication of his plea, but shall not allocate the case nor, if the accused indicates a guilty plea, sentence him, commit him for sentence, ask for a pre-sentence report or give any indication as to likely sentence that will be imposed. The justices' clerk shall ensure an authorised district judge (magistrates' courts) is appointed for the following hearing and notify the presiding judge of the circuit that the case has been listed.

6 When dealing with sentence, section 3 of the PCC(S)A 2000 [§ 5-25 in the main work] can be invoked where, despite the magistrates' court having maximum fine powers available to it, the offence or combination of offences make it so serious that the Crown Court should deal with it as though the person had been convicted on indictment.

7 An authorised district judge (magistrates' courts) should consider allocating the case to the Crown Court or committing the accused for sentence.

CPD Listing: Annex 4 The Management of Terrorism Cases

Application

1 This annex applies to "terrorism cases". For the purposes of this annex a case is a "terrorism   **B-234** case" where:

- (a) one of the offences charged against any of the defendants is indictable only and it is alleged by the prosecution that there is evidence that it took place during an act of terrorism or for the purposes of terrorism as defined in section 1 of the Terrorism Act 2000; this may include, but is not limited to:
  - (i) murder;
  - (ii) manslaughter;
  - (iii) an offence under section 18 of the Offences against the Person Act 1861 (wounding with intent);
  - (iv) an offence under section 23 or 24 of that Act (administering poison etc);
  - (v) an offence under section 28 or 29 of that Act (explosives);
  - (vi) an offence under section 2, 3 or 5 of the Explosive Substances Act 1883 (causing explosions);
  - (vii) an offence under section 1 (2) of the Criminal Damage Act 1971 (endangering life by damaging property);
  - (viii) an offence under section 1 of the Biological Weapons Act 1974 (biological weapons);
  - (ix) an offence under section 2 of the Chemical Weapons Act 1996 (chemical weapons);
  - (x) an offence under section 56 of the Terrorism Act 2000 (directing a terrorist organisation);
  - (xi) an offence under section 59 of that Act (inciting terrorism overseas);
  - (xii) offences under (v), (vii) and (viii) above given jurisdiction by virtue of section 62 of that Act (terrorist bombing overseas); and
  - (xiii) an offence under section 5 of the Terrorism Act 2006 (preparation of terrorism acts);
- (b) one of the offences charged is indictable only and includes an allegation by the prosecution of serious fraud that took place during an act of terrorism or for the purposes of terrorism as defined in section 1 of the Terrorism Act 2000 and the prosecutor gives a notice under section 51B of the CDA 1998 (notices in serious or complex fraud cases) [§ 1-27 in the main work]:
- (c) one of the offences charged is indictable only, which includes an allegation that a defendant conspired, incited or attempted to commit an offence under sub-paragraphs (1)(a) or (b) above; or
- (d) it is a case (which can be indictable only or triable either way) that a judge of the terrorism cases list (see paragraph 2(a) below) considers should be a terrorism case.

In deciding whether a case not covered by sub-paragraphs (1)(a), (b) or (c) above should be a terrorism case, the judge may hear representations from the CPS.

The terrorism cases list

B-235   2 (a) All terrorism cases, wherever they originate in England and Wales, will be managed in a list known as the "terrorism cases list" by such judges of the High Court as are nominated by the President of the Queen's Bench Division.

         (b) Such cases will be tried, unless otherwise directed by the President of the Queen's Bench Division, by a judge of the High Court as nominated by the President of the Queen's Bench Division.

3 The judges managing the terrorism cases referred to in paragraph 2(a) will be supported by the London and South Eastern Regional Co-ordinator's Office (the "Regional Co-ordinator's Office"). An official of that office or an individual nominated by that office will act as the case progression officer for cases in that list for the purposes of rule 3.4 of the Criminal Procedure Rules [§ 4-115 in the main work].

Procedure after charge

B-236   4 Immediately after a person has been charged in a terrorism case, anywhere in England and Wales, a representative of the CPS will notify the person on the 24-hour rota for special jurisdiction matters at Westminster Magistrates' Court of the following information:

         (a) the full name of each defendant and the name of his solicitor of other legal representative, if known;

         (b) the charges laid;

         (c) the name and contact details of the crown prosecutor with responsibility for the case, if known; and

         (d) confirmation that the case is a terrorism case.

5 The person on the 24-hour rota will then ensure that all terrorism cases wherever they are charged in England and Wales are listed before the Chief Magistrate or other District Judge designated under the Terrorism Act 2000. Unless the Chief Magistrate or other District Judge designated under the Terrorism Act 2000 directs otherwise, the first appearance of all defendants accused of terrorism offences will be listed at Westminster Magistrates' Court.

6 In order to comply with section 46 of the PACE Act 1984 [§ 3-164 in the main work], if a defendant in a terrorism case is charged at a police station within the local justice area in which Westminster Magistrates' Court is situated, the defendant must be brought before Westminster Magistrates' Court as soon as is practicable and in any event not later than the first sitting after he is charged with the offence. If a defendant in a terrorism case is charged in a police station outside the local justice area in which Westminster Magistrates' Court is situated, unless the Chief Magistrate or other designated judge directs otherwise, the defendant must be removed to that area as soon as is practicable. He must then be brought before [that court] as soon as is practicable after his arrival in the area and in any event not later than the first sitting of [that court] after his arrival in that area.

7 As soon as is practicable after charge a representative of the CPS will also provide the Regional Listing Co-ordinator's Office with the information listed in paragraph 4 above.

8 The Regional Co-ordinator's Office will then ensure that the Chief Magistrate and the Legal Aid Agency have the same information.

Cases to be sent to the Crown Court under section 51 of the Crime and Disorder Act 1998 [§ 1-25 in the main work]

B-237   9 The court should ordinarily direct that the plea and trial preparation hearing should take place about 14 days after charge.

10 The sending magistrates' court should contact the Regional Listing Co-ordinator's Office who will be responsible for notifying the magistrates' court as to the relevant Crown Court to which to send the case.

11 In all terrorism cases, the magistrates' court case progression form for cases sent to the Crown Court under section 51 of the [1998 Act] should not be used. Instead of the automatic directions set out in that form, the magistrates' court shall make the following directions to facilitate the preliminary hearing at the Crown Court:

         (a) three days prior to the preliminary hearing in the terrorism cases list, the prosecution must serve upon each defendant and the Regional Listing Co-ordinator:

            (i) a preliminary summary of the case;

  (ii) the names of those who are to represent the prosecution, if known;

  (iii) an estimate of the length of the trial;

  (iv) a suggested provisional timetable which should generally include:

- the general nature of further enquiries being made by the prosecution,
- the time needed for the completion of such enquiries,
- the time required by the prosecution to review the case,
- a timetable for the phased service of the evidence,
- the time for the provision by the Attorney-General for his consent if necessary,
- the time for service of the detailed defence case statement,
- the date for the case management hearing, and
- the estimated trial date;

  (v) a preliminary statement of the possible disclosure issues setting out the nature and scale of the problem, including the amount of unused material, the manner in which the prosecution seeks to deal with these matters and a suggested timetable for discharging their statutory duty; and

  (vi) any information relating to bail and custody time limits;

  (b) one day prior to the preliminary hearing in the terrorist cases list, each defendant must serve in writing on the Regional Listing Co-ordinator and the prosecution:

  (i) the proposed representation;

  (ii) observations on the timetable; and

  (iii) an indication of plea and the general nature of the defence.

Cases to be sent to the Crown Court after the prosecutor gives notice under section 51D of the Crime and Disorder Act 1998 [§ 1-29 in the main work]

12 If a terrorism case is to be sent to the Crown Court after the prosecutor gives a notice under **B-238** section 51B of the CDA 1998 [§ 1-27 in the main work] the magistrates' court should proceed as in paragraphs 9–11 above.

13 When a terrorism case is so sent the case will go into the terrorism list and be managed by a judge as described in paragraph 2(a) above.

The preliminary hearing at the Crown Court

14 At the plea and trial preparation hearing, the judge will determine whether the case is one to **B-239** remain in the terrorism list and if so, give directions setting the provisional timetable.

15 The Legal Aid Agency must attend the hearing by an authorised officer to assist the court.

Use of video links

16 Unless a judge otherwise directs, all Crown Court hearings prior to the trial will be conducted **B-240** by video link for all defendants in custody.

Security

17 The police service and the prison service will provide the Regional Listing Co-ordinator's Of- **B-241** fice with an initial joint assessment of the security risks associated with any court appearance by the defendants within 14 days of charge. Any subsequent changes in circumstances or the assessment of risk which have the potential to impact upon the choice of trial venue will be notified to the Regional Listing Co-ordinator's Office immediately.

CPD Listing: Annex 5 Management of Cases from the Organised Crime Division of the Crown Prosecution Service

1 The Organised Crime Division (OCD) of the CPS is responsible for prosecution of cases from the **B-242** National Crime Agency (NCA). Typically, these cases involve more than one defendant, are voluminous and raise complex and specialised issues of law. It is recognised that if not closely managed, such cases have the potential to cost vast amounts of public money and take longer than necessary.

2 This annex applies to all cases handled by the OCD.

Designated court centres

3 Subject to the overriding discretion of the presiding judges of the circuit, OCD cases should **B-243** normally be heard at Designated Court Centres (DCC). The process of designating court centres for

this purpose has taken into account geographical factors and the size, security and facilities of those court centres. The designated court centres are:

    (a) Northern Circuit: Manchester, Liverpool and Preston;
    (b) North Eastern Circuit: Leeds, Newcastle and Sheffield;
    (c) Western Circuit: Bristol and Winchester;
    (d) South Eastern Circuit (not including London): Reading, Luton, Chelmsford, Ipswich, Maidstone, Lewes and Hove;
    (e) South Eastern Circuit (London only): Southwark, Blackfriars, Kingston, Woolwich, Croydon and the Central Criminal Court;
    (f) Midland Circuit: Birmingham, Leicester and Nottingham;
    (g) Wales Circuit: Cardiff, Swansea and Mold.

Selection of designated court centres

B-244   4 If arrests are made in different parts of the country and the OCD seeks to have all defendants tried by one Crown Court, the OCD will, at the earliest opportunity, write to the relevant court cluster manager with a recommendation as to the appropriate designated court centre, requesting that the decision be made by the relevant presiding judges. In the event that the designated court centre within one region is unable to accommodate a case, for example, as a result of a custody time limit expiry date, consideration may be given to transferring the case to a DCC in another region with the consent of the relevant presiding judges.

5 There will be a single point of contact person at the OCD for each HMCTS region, to assist listing co-ordinators.

6 The single contact person for each HMCTS region will be the relevant cluster manager, with the exception of the South Eastern Circuit, where the appropriate person will be the Regional Listing Co-ordinator.

Designation of the trial judge

B-245   7 The trial judge will be assigned by the Presiding Judge at the earliest opportunity, and in accordance with *CPD XIII Listing E* [*ante*, B-216]. Where the trial judge is unable to continue with the case, all further pre-trial hearings should be by a single judge until a replacement has been assigned.

Procedure after charge

B-246   8 Within 24 hours of the laying of a charge, a representative of the OCD will notify the relevant cluster manager of the following information to enable an agreement to be reached between that cluster manager and the reviewing CPS lawyer before the first appearance as to the DCC to which the case should be sent:

    (a) the full name of each defendant and the name of his legal representatives, if known;
    (b) the charges laid; and
    (c) the name and contact details of the crown prosecutor with responsibility for the case.

Exceptions

B-247   9 Where it is not possible to have a case dealt with at a DCC, the OCD should liaise closely with the relevant cluster manager and the presiding judges to ensure that the cases are sent to the most appropriate court centre. This will, among other things, take into account the location of the likely source of the case, convenience of the witnesses, travelling distance for OCD staff and facilities at the court centres.

10 In the event that it is allocated to a non-designated court centre, the OCD should be permitted to make representations in writing to the presiding judges within 14 days as to why the venue is not suitable. The presiding judges will consider the reasons and, if necessary, hold a hearing. The CPS may renew their request at any stage where further reasons come to light that may affect the original decision on venue.

11 Nothing in this annex should be taken to remove the right of the defence to make representations as to the venue.

II. CRIMINAL COSTS PRACTICE DIRECTIONS (2015)

Part 1: General

Scope

B-248   1.1.1 [*Recital of power to make practice directions.*]

1.1.2 [*Revocation of 2013 costs practice direction ([2013] 1 W.L.R. 3255).*]

1.1.3 This practice direction has effect in magistrates' courts, the Crown Court, the High Court and the Court of Appeal (Criminal Division) where the court, in the exercise of its discretion, considers an award of costs in criminal proceedings or deals with criminal legal aid and recovery of defence costs orders. [It] is to be known as the Practice Direction (Costs in Criminal Proceedings) 2015. It comes into force on October 5, 2015.

1.1.4 [*Introductory.*]

The power to award costs

1.2.1 The powers enabling the court to award costs in criminal proceedings are primarily contained in Part II of the Prosecution of Offences Act 1985 ("the Act") (ss.16–19B), the Access to Justice Act 1999 and the LASPOA 2012 (in relation to funded clients) and in regulations made under those Acts including the Costs in Criminal Cases (General) Regulations 1986 (S.I. 1986 No. 1335) [§§ 6-54 *et seq.* in the main work], as amended ("the General Regulations"). References in this direction to sections and regulations by number alone are to the sections and regulations so numbered in the Act and the General Regulations unless otherwise stated. Schedule 1 below sets out details of the relevant regulations. **B-249**

1.2.2 [*Summary of ss.16–19B of the 1985 Act, and of regs 3A–31 of S.I. 1986 No. 1335 (§§ 6-3 et seq., §§ 6-58 et seq. in the main work).*]

1.2.3 The Senior Courts also have the power under their inherent jurisdiction over officers of the court to order a solicitor personally to pay costs thrown away. The inherent jurisdiction of the court should be invoked only to avoid a clear injustice (*Symbol Park Lane Ltd v. Steggles* [1985] 1 W.L.R. 668, CA (Civ. Div.)). Where the legislature has stepped in with particular legislation in a particular area (*e.g.* the wasted costs provisions) then, within that particular area, the existing inherent jurisdiction will be ousted or curtailed, at any rate in so far as the particular legislation is negative in character (*Shiloh Spinners Ltd v. Harding* [1973] A.C. 691, HL; *Harrison v. Tew* [1990] 2 A.C. 523, HL). Given the present provisions relating to costs, the exercise of the inherent jurisdiction will occur only in the rarest of circumstances.

1.2.4 Where the court orders a defendant to pay costs to the prosecutor; orders one party to pay costs to another party or a third party to pay costs; disallows or orders a legal or other representative to meet any wasted costs; or makes a defendant's costs order other than for the full amount; the order for costs must specify the sum to be paid or disallowed. Where the court is required to specify the amount of costs to be paid it cannot delegate the decision, but may require the appropriate officer of the court to make enquires to inform the court as to the costs incurred, and may adjourn the proceedings for enquiries to be made if necessary. The rules provide that a party who has incurred wasted costs should provide assistance to the court as to the amount involved: Criminal Procedure Rules, r.45.8(5), 45.9(5).

Extent of orders for costs from central funds

1.3.1 Where a court orders that the costs of a defendant, appellant or private prosecutor should be paid from central funds, the order will be for such amount as the court considers sufficient reasonably to compensate the party for expenses incurred by him in the proceedings; unless the court considers that there are circumstances that make it inappropriate to allow the full amount in which event it will allow such lesser sum as it considers just and reasonable. This will include the costs incurred in the proceedings in the lower courts unless for good reason the court directs that such costs are not included in the order, but it cannot include expenses incurred which do not directly relate to the proceedings themselves, such as loss of earnings. Where the party in whose favour the costs order is made is legally aided, he will only recover his personal costs: see s.21(4A)(a) of the Act. Schedule 2 below sets out the extent of availability of costs from central funds and the relevant statutory authority. **B-250**

1.3.2 If a defendant's costs order includes legal costs (sums paid for advocacy, litigation services or experts' fees) the order must include a statement to that effect.

Amount of costs to be paid

1.4.1 If the court does not fix the amount of costs to be paid out of central funds, the costs will be determined in accordance with the General Regulations by the appropriate authority. The appropriate authority will calculate the amount payable in respect of legal costs at such rates and scales as are prescribed by the Lord Chancellor. Where the court makes a defendant's costs order, or an order in favour of a private prosecutor, but is of the opinion there are circumstances which make it inappropriate that the person in whose favour the order is made should recover the full amount of the costs, the court may assess the lesser amount that would in its opinion be just and reasonable, and **B-251** specify that amount in the order. If the court is not in a position to specify the amount payable, the judge may make remarks which the appropriate authority will take into account as a relevant circumstance when determining the costs payable.

1.4.2 In respect of proceedings commenced on or after 1 October 2012 legal costs (sums paid for advocacy, litigation services or experts' fees) may only be included in a defendant's costs order to a defendant who is an individual and only in proceedings in a magistrates' court, appeals against conviction or sentence from a magistrates' court to the Crown Court, relevant Crown Court proceedings after 27 January 2014 (as to which see para 1.4.3 below) and appeals to the Court of Appeal (i) against a verdict of not guilty by reason of insanity (ii) against a finding under the Criminal Procedure (Insanity) Act 1964 that the appellant is under a disability or that he did the act or made the omission charged or (iii) under section 16A of the CAA 1968 (appeals against order made in cases of insanity or unfitness to plead).

1.4.3 After 27 January 2014 legal costs may be included in a defendant's costs order, provided that the defendant is an individual, in relevant proceedings in the Crown Court if the Director of Legal Aid Casework has made a determination of financial ineligibility in relation to that defendant. The relevant proceedings are those in which the accused has been sent by a magistrates' court to the Crown Court for trial, where a bill of indictment has been preferred (under s.2(2)(b) of the Administration of Justice (Miscellaneous Provisions) Act 1933 [§ 1-277 in the main work]) or following an order for a retrial made by the Court of Appeal or the Supreme Court.

1.4.4 Where legal costs may be allowed, if the court fixes the amount to be paid to a defendant under section 16(6C) of the Act or under sections 62A(4) or 135A(4) of the Extradition Act 2003 it must calculate any amounts to be allowed in respect of legal costs in accordance with rates and scales prescribed by the Lord Chancellor.

1.4.5 Rules 45.2(6) and (7) of the Criminal Procedure Rules ("CrimPR") contain general rules about the amount of an award of costs that apply subject to any statutory limitation.

Criminal Procedure Rules

1.5.1 [*Summary of rr.33.47–33.50 (§§ 5-986 et seq. in the main work) and of Pt 45 (ibid., §§ 6-108 et seq.).*]

1.5.2 The procedure for the assessment of costs under CrimPR 45.11 applies where the court makes an award between parties in one of the cases listed in rule 45.11(1). The assessment of an award of costs out of central funds is governed by substantially similar procedures under (i) the General Regulations or (ii) the Serious Crime Act 2007 (Appeals under Section 24) Order 2008 (S.I. 2008 No. 1863) [§§ 7-338 *et seq.* in the main work].

PART 2: COSTS OUT OF CENTRAL FUNDS

In a magistrates' court

2.1.1 Where an information laid before a justice of the peace charging a person with an offence is not proceeded with or a magistrates' court dealing summarily with an offence dismisses the information the court may make a defendant's costs order. An order under section 16 of the Act may also be made in relation to breach of bind-over proceedings in a magistrates' court or the Crown Court: regulation 14(4) of the General Regulations. Whether to make such an order is a matter in the discretion of the court in the light of the circumstances of each particular case. A defendant's costs order should normally be made unless there are positive reasons for not doing so, for example, where the defendant's own conduct has brought suspicion on himself and has misled the prosecution into thinking that the case against him was stronger than it was. Where the defendant has been acquitted on some counts but convicted on others the court may make an order that only part of the costs be paid: see paras 2.2.1 and.2.2.2 below. The court when declining to make a costs order should explain, in open court, that the reason for not making an order does not involve any suggestion that the defendant is guilty of any criminal conduct but the order is refused because of the positive reason that should be identified (*Hussain v. U.K.* (2006) 43 E.H.R.R. 22). Where the court considers that it would be inappropriate that the defendant should recover all of the costs properly incurred, either the amount allowed must be specified in the order or the court may describe to the appropriate authority the reduction required.

2.1.2 In respect of proceedings in a magistrates' court commenced on or after 1 October 2012 legal costs (sums paid for advocacy, litigation services or experts' fees) may only be allowed to a defendant who is an individual. Where legal costs may be allowed, if the court fixes the amount to be paid under section 16(6C) of the Act or under sections 62A(4) or 135A(4) of the Extradition Act 2003 it must calculate any amounts allowed in respect of legal costs in accordance with the rates and scales prescribed by the Lord Chancellor. If the court does not fix the amount of costs to be paid out of central funds, the costs will be determined by the appropriate authority in accordance with the General Regulations and any legal costs allowed will be calculated at the prescribed rates and scales.

In the Crown Court

2.2.1 Where a person is not tried for an offence for which he has been indicted, or in respect of **B-254** which proceedings against him have been sent for trial or transferred for trial, or has been acquitted on any count in the indictment, the court may make a defendant's costs order in his favour. Whether to make such an order is a matter for the discretion of the court in the light of the circumstances of the particular case. A defendant's costs order should normally be made whether or not an order for costs between the parties is made, unless there are positive reasons for not doing so, for example, where the defendant's own conduct has brought suspicion on himself and has misled the prosecution into thinking that the case against him was stronger than it was. [*Identical to penultimate sentence in para. 2.1.1.*] Where the court considers that it would be inappropriate that the defendant should recover all of the costs properly incurred, either the lesser amount must be specified in the order, or the court must describe to the appropriate authority the reduction required.

2.2.2 Where a person is convicted of some count(s) in the indictment and acquitted on other(s) the court may exercise its discretion to make a defendant's costs order but may order that only a proportion of the costs incurred be paid. The court should make whatever order seems just having regard to the relative importance of the charges and the conduct of the parties generally. The proportion of costs allowed must be specified in the order.

2.2.3 The Crown Court may make a defendant's costs order in favour of a successful appellant: see section 16(3) of the Act.

2.2.4 In respect of proceedings in the Crown Court commenced on or after 1 October 2012 legal costs ... may only be allowed under a defendant's costs order to a defendant who is an individual and only (1) in respect of appeals against conviction or sentence from a magistrates' court; or (2) after 27 January 2014 in other relevant Crown Court proceedings provided that the Director of Legal Aid Casework has made a determination of financial ineligibility in relation to the defendant. The relevant proceedings are those in which the accused has been sent by a magistrates' court to the Crown Court for trial, where a bill of indictment has been preferred (under s.2(2)(b) of the Administration of Justice (Miscellaneous Provisions) Act 1933 [§ 1-277 in the main work]) or following an order for a retrial made by the Court of Appeal or the Supreme Court. Where legal costs may be allowed, if the court fixes the amount to be paid under section 16(6C) of the Act it must calculate any amounts allowed in respect of legal costs in accordance with the rates and scales prescribed by the Lord Chancellor. [*Identical to last sentence of para. 2.1.2.*]

In the High Court

2.3.1 The Divisional Court of the Queen's Bench Division may make a defendant's costs order on **B-255** determining proceedings in a criminal cause or matter: see s.16(5)(a) of the Act.

In the Court of Appeal (Criminal Division)

2.4.1, 2.4.2 [*Set out the powers of the court to make an order for costs out of central funds under the 1985* **B-256** *Act, the CJA 1972 and the CJA 1988.*]

2.4.3 In considering whether to make such an order the court will have in mind the principles applied by the Crown Court in relation to acquitted defendants: see paras. 2.2.1 and 2.2.2 above.

2.4.4 In respect of appeals where the application for leave to appeal is made or notice of appeal given on or after 1 October 2012 legal costs ... may only be allowed under a defendant's costs order to a defendant who is an individual and only in appeals (i) against a verdict of not guilty by reason of insanity (ii) against a finding under the Criminal Procedure (Insanity) Act 1964 that the appellant is under a disability or that he did the act or made the omission charged or (iii) under section 16A of the CAA 1968 (appeal against order made in cases of insanity or unfitness to plead). If the court does not fix the amount of costs to be paid out of central funds, the costs will be determined in accordance with the General Regulations by the appropriate authority. The appropriate authority will calculate the amount payable in respect of legal costs at such rates and scales as are prescribed by the Lord Chancellor.

Costs of witness, interpreter or medical evidence

2.5.1 The costs of attendance of a witness required by the accused, a private prosecutor or the **B-257** court, or of an interpreter required because of the accused's lack of English or an intermediary under section 29 of the YJCEA 1999, or of an oral report by a medical practitioner are allowed out of central funds unless the court directs otherwise: see reg. 16(1) of the General Regulations. In the case of a witness if, and only if, the court makes such a direction can the expense of the witness be claimed as a disbursement for the purposes of criminal legal aid. A witness includes any person properly attending to give evidence whether or not he gives evidence or is called, but it does not include a character witness unless the court has certified that the interests of justice require his attendance: see s.21(1) of the Act.

2.5.2 The Crown Court may order the payment out of central funds of such sums as appear to be sufficient reasonably to compensate any medical practitioner for the expenses, trouble or loss of time properly incurred in preparing and making a report on the mental condition of a person accused of murder: see s.34(5) of the Mental Health (Amendment) Act 1982 [§ 6-99 in the main work].

Private prosecutor's costs from central funds

B-258

2.6.1 There is no power to order the payment of costs out of central funds of any prosecutor who is a public authority, a person acting on behalf of a public authority, or acting as an official appointed by a public authority as defined in the Act. In the limited number of cases in which a prosecutor's costs may be awarded out of central funds, an application is to be made by the prosecution in each case. An order should be made save where there is good reason for not doing so, for example, where proceedings have been instituted or continued without good cause. This provision applies to proceedings in respect of an indictable offence or proceedings before the High Court in respect of a summary offence. Regulation 14(1) of the General Regulations extends it to certain committals for sentence from a magistrates' court.

2.6.2 Where the court is of the opinion that there are circumstances which make it inappropriate to award the full amount of costs out of central funds, the order must be for the payment of such lesser amount as is just and reasonable. Where the court considers it appropriate to do so, and the prosecutor agrees the amount, it must fix the amount. Otherwise it must make an order for such costs as are just and reasonable, describing in the order any reduction in the amount of costs required, and the costs will, be determined by the appropriate authority in accordance with the General Regulations.

2.6.3 For the purposes of an order under section 17 of the Act the costs of the prosecutor are taken to include the expense of compensating any witness for the expenses, travel and loss of time properly incurred in or incidental to his attendance.

2.6.4 If there has been misconduct a private prosecutor should not be awarded costs out of central funds (*R. v. Esher and Walton JJ., ex p. Victor Value & Co Ltd* (1967) 111 S.J. 473, DC).

2.6.5 Where the conduct of a private prosecution is taken over by the CPS the power of the court to order payment of prosecution costs out of central funds extends only to the period prior to the intervention of the CPS.

Procedure

B-259

2.7.1 CrimPR 45.4, and the general rules in the first section of CrimPR, Pt 45, apply to the exercise of the court's powers to award costs out of central funds.

PART 3: AWARDS OF COSTS AGAINST DEFENDANTS

B-260

3.1 [*Summary of s.18(1) of 1985 Act (§ 6-26 in the main work).*]

3.2 [*Summary of s.18(4), (5) of 1985 Act (§ 6-26 in the main work).*]

3.3 [*Summary of s.18(2), (6) of 1985 Act (§ 6-26 in the main work).*]

3.4 An order should be made where the court is satisfied that the defendant or appellant has the means and the ability to pay. The order is not intended to be in the nature of a penalty which can only be satisfied on the defendant's release from prison. An order should not be made on the assumption that a third party might pay. Whilst the court should take into account any debt of the appellant or defendant, where the greater part of those debts relates to the offence itself, the court may still make an order for costs.

3.5 Where co-defendants are husband and wife, the couple's means should not be taken together. Where there are multiple defendants the court may make joint and several orders, but the costs ordered to be paid by an individual should be related to the costs in or about the prosecution of that individual. In a multi-handed case where some defendants have insufficient means to pay their share of the costs, it is not right for that share to be divided among the other defenders [*sic*].

3.6 The prosecution should serve upon the defence, at the earliest time, full details of its costs so as to give the defendant a proper opportunity to make representations upon them if appropriate. If a defendant wishes to dispute all or any of the prosecution's claim for costs, the defendant should, if possible, give proper notice to the prosecution of the objections proposed to be made or at least make it plain to the court precisely what those objections are. There is no provision for assessment of prosecution costs in a criminal case, such disputes have to be resolved by the court, which must specify the amount to be paid (see *R. v. Associated Octel Ltd* [§ 6-34 in the main work]).

3.7 The principles to be applied in deciding on the amount of costs are those set out by the Court of Appeal in *Neville v Gardner Merchant* [§ 6-34 in the main work]. The court when awarding prosecution costs may award costs in respect of time spent in bringing the offences to light, even if the necessary investigation was carried out, for example, by an environmental health official. Generally it will not be just or reasonable to order a defendant to pay costs of investigation which the prosecutor itself will not satisfy. In *R. v. Balshaw* [§ 6-34 in the main work] the Court of Appeal considered the circumstances in which the CPS may be able to recover costs associated with the investigation incurred by the police. The Divisional Court has held that there is a requirement that any sum ordered to be paid by way of costs should not ordinarily be greatly at variance with any fine imposed. Where substantial research is required in order to counter possible defences, the court may also award costs in respect of that work if it considers it to be justified.

3.8 The High Court is not covered by section 18 of the Act but it has complete discretion over all costs between the parties in relation to proceedings before it (Senior Courts Act 1981, s.51).

3.9 An order under section 18 of the Act includes the cost of advice, assistance or representation provided under the criminal legal aid provisions: see s.21(4A)(b) of the Act.

3.10 CrimPR 45.5, 45.6 and the general rules in the first section of CrimPR, Pt 45, apply to the exercise of the court's powers to award costs against a defendant on conviction, sentence or appeal.

PART 4: OTHER COSTS ORDERS

Costs incurred as a result of unnecessary or improper act or omission

4.1.1 A magistrates' court, the Crown Court and the Court of Appeal (Criminal Division) may **B-261** order the payment of any costs incurred as a result of any unnecessary or improper act or omission by or on behalf of any party to the proceedings as distinct from his legal representative: s.19 of the Act and reg. 3 of the General Regulations. The court may find it helpful to adopt a three stage approach. (a) Has there been an unnecessary or improper, act or omission? (b) As a result have any costs been incurred by another party? (c) If the answers to (a) and (b) are "yes", should the court exercise its discretion to order the party responsible to meet the whole or any part of the relevant costs, and if so what specific sum is involved? CrimPR 45.8 sets out the procedure. A form of application is set out in Schedule 5 to this practice direction.

4.1.2 The court must hear the parties and may then order that all or part of the costs so incurred by one party shall be paid to him by the other party.

4.1.3 Before making such an order the court may take into account any other order as to costs and the order must specify the amount of the costs to be paid. The court is entitled to take such an order into account when making any other order as to costs in the proceedings: reg. 3(2)–(4) of the General Regulations. The order can extend to legal aid costs incurred on behalf of any party: s.21(4A)(b) of the Act.

4.1.4 In a magistrates' court no order may be made which requires a convicted person under 17 to pay an amount by way of costs which exceeds the amount of any fine imposed upon him: reg. 3(5) of the General Regulations.

4.1.5 Such an order is appropriate only where the failure is that of the defendant or of the prosecutor. Where the failure is that of a legal representative(s), paragraphs 4.2 and 4.5 (below) may be more suitable.

Costs against legal representatives - wasted costs

4.2.1 Section 19A of the Act allows a magistrates' court, the Crown Court or the Court of Appeal **B-262** (Criminal Division) to disallow or order the legal or other representative to meet the whole or any part of the wasted costs. The order can be made against any person exercising a right of audience or a right to conduct litigation (in the sense of acting for a party to the proceedings). "Wasted costs" are costs incurred by a party (which includes a legally aided party) as a result of any improper, unreasonable or negligent act or omission on the part of any representative or his employee, or which, in the light of any such act or omission occurring after they were incurred, the court considers it unreasonable to expect that party to pay: s.19A(3) of the Act; s.89(8) of the PCA 2002 [§ 5-921 in the main work]. CrimPR 45.9 sets out the procedure. A form of application is set out in Schedule 5 to this practice direction.

4.2.2 The judge has a much greater and more direct responsibility for costs in criminal proceedings than in civil and should keep the question of costs in the forefront of his mind at every stage of the case and ought to be prepared to take the initiative himself without any prompting from the parties.

4.2.3 Regulation 3B of the General Regulations requires the court to specify the amount of the wasted costs and before making the order to allow the legal or other representative and any party to the proceedings to make representations. In making the order the court may take into account any other orders for costs and may take the wasted costs order into account when making any other order as to costs. The court should also give reasons for making the order and must notify any interested party (which includes the Legal Aid Agency and central funds determining authorities) of the order and the amount.

4.2.4 Judges contemplating making a wasted costs order should bear in mind the guidance given by the Court of Appeal in *In re A. Barrister (Wasted Costs Order) (No 1 of 1991)* [1993] Q.B. 293. The guidance, which is set out below, is to be considered together with all the statutory and other rules and recommendations set out by Parliament and in this practice direction.

(i) There is a clear need for any judge or court intending to exercise the wasted costs jurisdiction to formulate carefully and concisely the complaint and grounds upon which such an order may be sought. These measures are draconian and, as in contempt proceedings, the grounds must be clear and particular.

(ii) Where necessary a transcript of the relevant part of the proceedings under discussion should be available and in accordance with the rules a transcript of any wasted cost [*sic*] hearing must be made.

(iii) A defendant involved in a case where such proceedings are contemplated should be present if, after discussion with an advocate, it is thought that his interest may be affected and he should certainly be present and represented if the matter might affect the course of his trial. CrimPR 45.2(1) requires that the court must not make a costs order unless each party, and any other person affected, (a) is present, or (b) has had an opportunity to attend or to make representations.

(iv) A three stage test or approach is recommended when a wasted costs order is contemplated. (a) Has there been an improper, unreasonable or negligent act or omission? (b) As a result have any costs been incurred by a party? (c) If the answers to (a) and (b) are "yes", should the court exercise its discretion to disallow or order the representative to meet the whole or any part of the relevant costs, and if so what specific sum is involved?

(v) It is inappropriate to propose any settlement that the representative might forgo fees. The complaint should be formally stated by the judge and the representative invited to make his own comments. After any other party has been heard the judge should give his formal ruling. Discursive conversations may be unfair and should certainly not take place.

(vi) The judge must specify the sum to be allowed or ordered. Alternatively the relevant available procedure should be substituted should it be impossible to fix the sum: see para 4.2.7 below.

4.2.5 The Court of Appeal has given further guidance in *In re P. (A Barrister)(Wasted Costs Order)* [2002] 1 Cr.App.R. 19 as follows:

(i) the primary object is not to punish but to compensate, albeit as the order is sought against a non party, it can from that perspective be regarded as penal;

(ii) the jurisdiction is a summary jurisdiction to be exercised by the court which has "tried the case in the course of which the misconduct was committed";

(iii) fairness is assured if the lawyer alleged to be at fault has sufficient notice of the complaint made against him and a proper opportunity to respond to it;

(iv) because of the penal element a mere mistake is not sufficient to justify an order: there must be a more serious error;

(v) although the trial judge can decline to consider an application in respect of costs, for example on the ground that he or she is personally embarrassed by an appearance of bias, it will only be in exceptional circumstances that it will be appropriate to pass the matter to another judge, and the fact that, in the proper exercise of his judicial function, a judge has expressed views in relation to the conduct of a lawyer against whom an order is sought, does not of itself normally constitute bias or the appearance of bias so as to necessitate a transfer;

(vi) the normal civil standard of proof applies but if the allegation is one of serious misconduct or crime clear evidence will be required to meet that standard.

4.2.6 Though the court cannot delegate its decision to the appropriate authority, it may require the appropriate officer of the court to make enquiries and inform the court as to the likely amount of costs incurred. By CrimPR 45.9(5), the court is entitled to the assistance in this respect of the party who incurred the costs concerned.

4.2.7 The court may postpone the making of a wasted costs order to the end of the case if it appears more appropriate to do so, for example, because the likely amount is not readily available, there is a possibility of conflict between the legal representatives as to the apportionment of blame, or the legal representative concerned is unable to make full representations because of a possible conflict with the duty to the client.

4.2.8 A wasted costs order should normally be made regardless of the fact that the client of the legal representative concerned is legally aided. However where the court is minded to disallow substantial legal aid costs, it may, instead of making a wasted costs order, make observations to the determining authority that work may have been unreasonably done: see para 4.3 below. This practice should only be adopted where the extent and amount of the costs wasted is not entirely clear.

Appeals against wasted costs orders

4.2.9 A party against whom a wasted costs order has been made may appeal against that order. In the case of an order made by a magistrates' court, appeal is to the Crown Court, and CrimPR, Pt 34 [§§ 2-117 *et seq.* in the main work] sets out the procedure. In the case of an order made at first instance by the Crown Court, the appeal is to the Court of Appeal and the procedure is set out in CrimPR, Pt 39 [§§ 7-380 *et seq.* in the main work]. In both cases the time limit for appeal is 21 days from the date of the order. **B-263**

4.2.10 Having heard the submissions, the appeal court may affirm, vary or revoke the order as it thinks fit and must notify its decision to the appellant, any interested party and the court which made the order.

Disallowance of criminal legal aid costs

4.3.1 Where it appears to any judge of the Crown Court or the Court of Appeal (Criminal Division), sitting in proceedings for which legal aid has been granted, that work may have been unreasonably done, e.g. if the represented person's case may have been conducted unreasonably so as to incur unjustifiable expense, or costs may have been wasted by failure to conduct the proceedings with reasonable competence or expedition, the judge may make observations to that effect for the attention of the appropriate authority. The judge or the court, as the case may be, should specify as precisely as possible the item, or items, which the determining officer should consider or investigate on the determination of the costs payable pursuant to the representation order. The precise terms of the observations must be entered in the court record. **B-264**

4.3.2 Article [*sic*] 26 of the Criminal Legal Aid (Remuneration) Regulations 2013 [*post*, Appendix G-32] permits the appropriate officer to reduce any fee which would otherwise be payable by such proportion as the officer considers reasonable in the light of any adverse comments made by the court. The power to make adverse comments co-exists with the power to disallow fees when making a wasted costs order. Article [*sic*] 27 of the 2013 regulations [*post*, Appendix G-33] allows the determining officer to disallow the amount of the wasted costs order from the amount otherwise payable to the litigator or advocate and allows for deduction of a greater amount if appropriate.

4.3.3 Where the judge or the court has in mind making observations under paragraph 4.3 the litigator or advocate whose fees or expenses might be affected must be informed of the precise terms thereof and of his right to make representations to the appropriate authority and be given a reasonable opportunity to show cause why the observations or direction should not be made.

4.3.4 Where such observations or directions are made the appropriate authority must afford an opportunity to the litigator or advocate whose fees might be affected to make representations in relation to them.

4.3.5 Whether or not observations under paragraph 4.3.1 have been made the appropriate authority may consult the judge or the court on any matter touching the allowance or disallowance of fees and expenses, but if the observations then made are to the effect mentioned in paragraph 4.3.1, the appropriate authority should afford an opportunity to the litigator or advocate concerned to make representations in relation to them.

Very High Cost Cases

4.4.1 In proceedings which are classified as a very high cost case ("VHCC") as defined by regulation 2 of the Criminal Legal Aid (Remuneration) Regulations 2013 [*post*, Appendix G-7], the judge or court should, at the earliest opportunity, ask the representative of the legally aided party whether they have notified the Lord Chancellor of the case in accordance with regulation 12 of those regulations [*post*, Appendix G-18a]. If they have not they should be warned that they may not be able to recover their costs. **B-265**

Wasted costs orders in the High Court

4.5.1 In the High Court (Divisional Court) where the court is considering whether to make an **B-266** order under section 51(6) of the Senior Courts Act 1981 (a wasted costs order or disallowing wasted costs) it will do so in accordance with CPR, r.46.8 which contains similar provisions as to giving the legal representative a reasonable opportunity to attend a hearing to give reasons why the court should not make such an order.

Awards of costs against solicitors under the court's inherent jurisdiction

B-267   4.6.1 In addition to the power under regulation 3 of the General Regulations to order that costs improperly incurred be paid by a party to the proceedings and the power to make wasted costs orders under section 19A of the Act, the Senior Courts (which includes the Crown Court) may, in the exercise of its inherent jurisdiction over officers of the court, order a solicitor personally to pay costs thrown away by reason of a serious breach on the part of the solicitor of his duty to the court.

4.6.2 No such order may be made unless reasonable notice has been given to the solicitor of the matter alleged against him and he is given a reasonable opportunity of being heard in reply.

4.6.3 This power should be used only in exceptional circumstances not covered by the statutory powers: see para 1.2.3.

Award of costs against third parties

B-268   4.7.1 The [*sic*] magistrates' court, the Crown Court and the Court of Appeal may make a third party costs order if there has been serious misconduct (whether or not constituting a contempt of court) by a third party and the court considers it appropriate, having regard to that misconduct, to make a third party costs order against him. A "third party costs order" is an order for the payment of costs incurred by a party to criminal proceedings by a person who is not a party to those proceedings ("the third party"): s.19B of the 1985 Act and regs 3E to 3I of the General Regulations. CrimPR, 45.10 sets out the procedure.

4.7.2 The court may make a third party costs order at any time during or after the criminal proceedings, but should only make such an order during the proceedings if it decides that there are good reasons to do so.

4.7.3 The court must notify the parties and the third party of those reasons and allow any of them to make representations.

4.7.4 A third party costs order may be made on the application of any party, or on the court's own initiative, but not in any other circumstances. Before making an order the court must allow the third party, and any other party, to make representations and may hear evidence.

4.7.5 When the court is making a third party costs order, it may take into account any other order as to costs in respect of the criminal proceedings, and may take the third party costs order into account when making any other order for costs in respect of those proceedings.

4.7.6 The order must specify the amount of costs to be paid, and the court must notify the third party and any interested party of the order and the amount ordered to be paid.

4.7.7 If the court is considering making a third party costs order on its own initiative the appropriate officer should serve notice in writing on the third party and any other parties. Where a party applies for such an order the application must be in writing, and must contain the names and addresses of the applicant, the other parties and the third party against whom the order is sought, together with a summary of the facts upon which the applicant intends to rely, including in particular details of the alleged misconduct of the third party.

4.7.8 At the hearing of the application the court may proceed in the absence of the third party, and of any other party if satisfied that that party has been duly served with the notice by the appropriate officer, and with a copy of the application. The power to make a third party costs order extends to making such an order against a government department where there has been serious misconduct, including deliberate or negligent failure to attend to one's duties, or falling below a proper standard in that regard, but there is a higher threshold for liability than for a wasted costs order (*R. v. Ahmati*, unreported, July 7, 2006 ([2006] EWCA Crim. 1826)).

Appeals against third party costs orders

B-269   4.7.9 A third party against whom a third party costs order has been made may appeal against that order. In the case of an order made by a magistrates' court, appeal is to the Crown Court, and CrimPR, Pt 34 [§ 2-117 *et seq.* in the main work] sets out the procedure. In the case of an order made at first instance by the Crown Court, the appeal is to the Court of Appeal and the procedure is set out in CrimPR, Pt 39 [§§ 7-380 *et seq.* in the main work]. In both cases the time limit for appeal is 21 days from the date of the order.

4.7.10 [*Identical to para. 4.2.10.*]

Part 5: Assessment of Costs

Assessment of defence costs out of central funds

5.1.1 Where a legally aided defendant wishes to claim out of pocket expenses or costs for work **B-270** which has not been done under the representation order, the assessment of those costs should be carried out at the same time as the assessment of his solicitor's costs under the representation order and the solicitors should ensure that the two claims are submitted together for assessment (*R. (Brewer) v. Supreme Court Costs Office* [2007] Costs L.R. 20, DC).

Appeals to a costs judge

5.2.1 Under regulation 9 of the General Regulations, or under CrimPR 45.11(7), a party dissatis- **B-271** fied with a costs assessment may apply to the relevant authority for a review of that assessment. Under regulation 10 of the General Regulations, or under CrimPR 45.12, appeal against a decision on such a review lies to the senior costs judge of the Senior Courts Costs Office. Written notice of appeal must be given within 21 days of receipt of the reasons for the decision, or within such longer time as a costs judge may direct.

5.2.2 The notice of appeal should be in the form set out in Schedule 3 below (adapted where appropriate) setting out in separate numbered paragraphs each fee or item of costs or disbursement in respect of which the appeal is brought, showing the amount claimed for the item, the amount determined and the grounds of objection to the decision on the assessment or determination.

5.2.3 Advocates and litigators must provide detailed grounds of objection in respect of each item in accordance with regulation 10(2) of the General Regulations, CrimPR 45.12(2)(b) and regulation 29(5) of the Criminal Legal Aid (Remuneration) Regulations 2013 [*post*, Appendix G-35]. Reference to accompanying correspondence or documents is insufficient and will result in the appeal being dismissed.

5.2.4 The appeal must be accompanied by a cheque for the appropriate fee made payable to "H.M. Paymaster General". The notice must state whether the appellant wishes to appear or to be represented, or whether he will accept a decision given in his absence.

The following documents should be forwarded with the notice of appeal:

(a) a legible copy of the bill of costs (with any supporting submissions) showing the allowance made;

(b) a copy of the advocate's fee claim and any fee note, together with any note or memorandum by the advocate submitted to the determining authority;

(c) a copy of the original determination of costs and a copy of the redetermination;

(d) a copy of the appellant's representations made to the determining authority on seeking redetermination;

(e) the written reasons of the determining officer;

(f) a copy of the representation order and any authorities given under it.

Supporting papers

5.3.1 Appellants who do not intend to appear at the hearing of their appeal should lodge all **B-272** relevant supporting papers with the documents listed above. Appellants who do wish to attend the hearing of their appeal should not lodge their supporting papers until directed to do so by the Senior Courts Costs Office.

5.3.2 Appellants are reminded that it is their responsibility to procure the lodgment of the relevant papers, even if they are in the possession of the Crown Court or other persons. Appeals may be listed for dismissal if the relevant papers are not lodged when required.

5.3.3 Delays frequently arise in dealing with appeals by advocates because the relevant papers have been returned by the court to the litigator whose file may not be readily available or who may have destroyed the papers. These problems would be avoided if the advocate were, immediately on lodging with the court a request for redetermination, to ask instructing litigators to retain the relevant papers.

5.3.4 In complex or multi-handed appeals guidance should be sought from the Clerk of Appeals before lodging a large volume of papers to avoid duplication and unnecessary reading by the Costs Judge.

Time limits

5.4.1 Appellants who are likely to be unable to lodge an appeal within the time limits should make **B-273** an application prior to the expiry of the time limit seeking a reasonable extension with brief reasons for the request.

5.4.2 Appellants who have not been able to lodge an appeal within the time limits, and who have failed to make application before those time limits have expired, should make application to the costs judge for leave to appeal out of time in writing setting out in full the circumstances relied upon.

5.4.3 If the application is refused on the papers it may be renewed to a costs judge at an oral hearing. Such oral hearings should not be necessary if a full explanation is given in writing in the initial request for extension of time.

5.4.4 Appeals should not be delayed because certain relevant documents are not available. An accompanying note setting out the missing documents and an undertaking to lodge within a specified period, normally not exceeding 28 days, should be sent with the notice of appeal.

Appeals to the High Court

B-274   5.5.1 An appellant desiring to appeal to a High Court judge from a decision of the costs judge should, within 21 days of the decision, request the costs judge to certify that a point of principle of general importance (specifying the same) is involved. The appeal can proceed only if such a certificate is granted. Such an appeal is instituted by appellant's notice under CPR, Pt 52 in the Queen's Bench Division within 21 days of the receipt of the costs judge's certificate. The times may be extended by a costs judge or a High Court judge as the case may be.

5.5.2 The appellant's notice must contain full particulars of the item or items, or the amount allowed in respect of which the appeal is brought. After issue of the notice the appellant must forthwith lodge with the clerk of appeals at the Senior Courts Costs Office all the documents used on the appeal to the costs judge.

5.5.3 The appellant's notice should be served in accordance with the provisions of CPR, Pt 6 and the practice direction thereto. It is no longer necessary to endorse an estimate of the length of hearing on the appellant's notice. The clerk of appeals will obtain from the judge a date for hearing and will notify the parties.

5.5.4 The appeal, which is final, will be heard by a judge of the Queen's Bench Division who will normally sit with two assessors, one of whom will be a costs judge and the other a practising litigator or advocate.

5.5.5 After the appeal has been heard and determined the clerk will obtain the documents together with a sealed copy of any order of the judge which may have been drawn up and will notify the court concerned of the result of the appeal.

PART 6: CONTRIBUTION ORDERS AND RECOVERY OF DEFENCE COSTS ORDERS

Contribution orders in the Crown Court

B-275   6.1.1 In proceedings to which the Criminal Legal Aid (Contribution Orders) Regulations 2013 (S.I. 2013 No. 483) [§§ 6-322 *et seq.* in the main work] apply, namely proceedings in the Crown Court, the represented defendant may be liable to make payments under an income contribution order. If the defendant is convicted or if the representation order is withdrawn, the defendant may be required to pay the whole or part of the cost of the representation under a capital contribution order.

6.1.2 If the trial judge considers that there are exceptional reasons, a defendant who is acquitted may nevertheless be required to pay the whole or part of the costs of the representation in the Crown Court: reg. 25(b).

6.1.3 Where a defendant is convicted of one or more, but not all, offences he may apply in writing to the trial judge (or a judge nominated for that purpose by the resident judge) for an order that he pay a proportion only of the costs of the representation in the Crown Court on the ground that it would be manifestly unreasonable that he pay the whole amount: reg. 26. An application must be made within 21 days of the date on which the individual is dealt with. The judge may refuse the application or make an order specifying the proportion of costs which the defendant must pay.

Recovery of defence costs orders on appeals

B-276   6.2.1 Recovery of defence costs orders ("RDCOs") are created and regulated by the Criminal Legal Aid (Recovery of Defence Costs Orders) Regulations 2013 (S.I. 2013 No. 511) [§§ 6-299 *et seq.* in the main work]. They may be made in proceedings in any court other than the magistrates' court or the Crown Court.

6.2.2 Where an individual receives criminal legal aid in respect of proceedings, the court before which the proceedings are heard (other than a magistrates' court or the Crown Court) must make an order requiring him to pay some or all of the costs of any representation, except for the following:

- where the defendant has appeared in the magistrates' court and/or the Crown Court only;
- where the court has allowed the appeals of the defendant in respect of every conviction, unless the court considers it reasonable in all the circumstances to make an order; or
- where the defendant does not have capital exceeding £3,000 or equity in the main dwelling exceeding £100,000 or gross annual income exceeding £22,325; or
- where the defendant is in receipt of a qualifying benefit; or
- where the d defendant is under the age of 18 on the date on which his application for legal aid was determined; or
- where it would not be reasonable to make an order on the basis of the information and evidence available; or
- where in the exceptional circumstances of the case an order would involve undue financial hardship: Criminal Legal Aid (Recovery of Defence Costs Orders) Regulations 2003, regs 6-11.

6.2.3 Where the court exercises its discretion on the basis of reasonableness or undue financial hardship it must give reasons for reaching that decision: reg. 11.

6.2.4 Subject to the exceptions set out above, the court must make an RDCO and must give reasons for the terms of the order: reg. 5.

6.2.5 The court (or the registrar of the Supreme Court or the Registrar of Criminal Appeals, as the case may be) must assess the financial resources of the defendant (including the resources of the defendant's partner unless the partner has a contrary interest) or refer the matter to the Director of Legal Aid Casework for assessment. When determining the amount, other than in exceptional circumstances, the court shall not take into account:

- the first £3,000 of available capital,
- the first £100,000 of equity in the main dwelling, or
- gross annual income of less than £22,235: reg. 15.

    These limits are prescribed and are subject to regular amendment.

6.2.6 The court may ask the defendant's litigator to provide an estimate of the total costs which are likely to be incurred under the representation order. It should be borne in mind that whilst the litigator may have little difficulty in producing an estimate of the costs incurred up until the point of request, this estimate may not be accurate. In a very high cost case which has been managed under contract, the litigator will be able to provide accurate figures of all costs incurred to date and to say what costs have been agreed as reasonable for the next stage of the case. Where an RDCO is made based on this estimate the defendant's litigator must inform the Lord Chancellor if it subsequently transpires that the costs incurred were lower than the amount ordered to be paid under an RDCO. In these circumstances, where the defendant has paid the amount ordered, the balance will be repaid to him: reg. 19.

6.2.7 The defendant is obliged to provide such details or evidence of his means as is required by the court. At the end of the case where the court is considering whether to make an RDCO or what order to make, it may adjourn the making of the order and order that any further information which is required should be provided: reg. 16. This power may be used where further information has come to light during the case about the defendant's means.

6.2.8 Where information required under the Regulations is not provided the court may nevertheless make an RDCO for the full cost of the representation incurred under the representation order or such proportion of the cost as the court considers reasonable: reg. 17.

6.2.9 Where it appears to the court that the defendant has transferred any financial resources to another person, directly or indirectly deprived themselves of any resources, or converted any resources into resources which are to be disregarded under the regulations, the court must treat such financial resources as part of the defendant's financial resources or as not so converted. Where it appears to the court that another person has been substantially maintaining the defendant or the defendant's partner or that any of the financial resources of another person have been made available to the defendant or the defendant's partner, the court may assess the amount of the maintenance or the resources made available and treat such amounts as the resources of the defendant: reg. 14.

Part 7: Costs in Restraint, Confiscation or Receivership Proceedings

The order for costs

7.1.1 This part of the practice direction applies where the Crown Court is deciding whether to **B-277** make an order for costs in relation to restraint proceedings or receivership proceedings brought under the PCA 2002. (Confiscation proceedings are treated for costs purposes as part of the criminal trial.) The court has discretion as to: whether costs are payable by one party to another; the amount of those costs; and, when they are to be paid. The general rule is that if the court decides to make an order about costs the unsuccessful party will be ordered to pay the costs of the successful party but the court may make a different order: CrimPR 33.47(3)

7.1.2 Attention is drawn to the fact that in receivership proceedings the rules provide that the Crown Court may make orders in respect of security to be given by a receiver to cover his liability for his acts and omissions as a receiver: CrimPR 33.60. The court may also make orders in relation to determining the remuneration of the receiver: CrimPR 33.61. (Para. 7.3 below deals with determination of the remuneration of a receiver.)

7.1.3 In deciding what if any order to make about costs the court is required to have regard to all the circumstances including the conduct of all the parties and whether a party has succeeded on part of an application, even if that party has not been wholly successful.

7.1.4 The rules set out the type of order which the court may make (the list is not exclusive):

    (a) a proportion of another party's costs;

    (b) a stated amount in respect of another party's costs;

    (c) costs from or until a certain date only;

    (d) costs incurred before proceedings have begun;

    (e) costs relating to particular steps taken in the proceedings;

    (f) costs relating only to a distinct part of the proceedings; and

    (g) interest on costs from or until a certain date including a date before the making of an order.

7.1.5 The court is required, where it is practicable, to award a proportion (*e.g.* a percentage) of the costs, or costs between certain dates, rather than making an order relating only to a distinct part or issue in the proceedings. The latter type of order makes it extremely difficult for the costs to be assessed.

7.1.6 Where the court orders a party to pay costs it may, in addition, order an amount to be paid on account by one party to another before the costs are assessed. Where the court makes such an order, the order should state the amount to be paid and the date on or before which payment is to be made.

Assessment of costs

B-278

7.2.1 Where the Crown Court makes an order for costs in restraint, or receivership, proceedings it may make an assessment of the costs itself there and then (a summary assessment), or order assessment of the costs under CrimPR 45.11: CrimPR 33.48(1). If the court neither makes an assessment of the costs nor orders assessment as specified above, the order for costs will be treated as an order for the amount of costs to be decided by assessment under rule 45.11 unless the order otherwise provides.

7.2.2 Whenever the court awards costs to be assessed it should consider whether to exercise the power to order the paying party to pay such sum of money as it thinks just, on account of those costs.

7.2.3 In carrying out the assessment of costs the court or the assessing authority is required to allow only costs which are proportionate to the matters in issue, and to resolve any doubt which it may have, as to whether the costs were reasonably incurred or were reasonable and proportionate in amount, in favour of the paying party.

7.2.4 The court or assessing authority carrying out the assessment should have regard to all the circumstances in deciding whether costs were proportionately or reasonably incurred or proportionate and reasonable in amount. Effect must be given to any orders for costs which have already been made. The court or the assessing authority should also have regard to:

    (a) the conduct of all the parties, including in particular conduct before as well as during the proceedings;

    (b) the amount or value of any property involved;

    (c) the importance of the matter to all the parties;

    (d) the particular complexity of the matter or the difficulty or novelty of the questions raised;

    (e) the skill, effort, specialised knowledge and responsibility involved;

    (f) the time spent on the case; and

    (g) the place where and the circumstances in which work or any part of it was done.

7.2.5 In applying the test of proportionality regard should be had to the objective of dealing with cases justly. Dealing with a case justly includes, so far as practicable, dealing with it in ways which are proportionate to:

    (i) the amount of money involved;

    (ii) the importance of the case;

    (iii) the complexity of the issues; and

    (iv) the financial position of each party.

        The relationship between the total of the costs incurred and the financial value of the claim may not be a reliable guide.

7.2.6 In any proceedings there will be costs which will inevitably be incurred and which are necessary for the successful conduct of the case. Litigators are not required to conduct litigation at rates which are uneconomic, thus in a modest claim the proportion of costs is likely to be higher than in a large claim and may even equal or possibly exceed the amount in dispute.

7.2.7 Where a hearing takes place, the time taken by the court in dealing with a particular issue may not be an accurate guide to the amount of time properly spent by the legal or other representatives in preparing for the trial of that issue.

7.2.8 The Criminal Procedure Rules do not apply to the assessment of costs in proceedings to the extent that section 26 of the LASPOA 2012 (costs in civil proceedings) applies and statutory instruments made under that Act make different provision.

Remuneration of a receiver

7.3.1 A receiver may only charge for his services if the Crown Court so directs and specifies the basis on which the receiver is to be remunerated: CrimPR 33.61(2). The Crown Court (unless it orders otherwise) is required to award such sum as is reasonable and proportionate in all the circumstances. In arriving at the figure for remuneration the court should take into account: **B-279**

    (a) the time properly given by the receiver and his staff to the receivership;

    (b) the complexity of the receivership;

    (c) any responsibility of an exceptional kind or degree which falls on the receiver in consequence of the receivership;

    (d) the effectiveness with which the receiver appears to be carrying out or to have carried out his duties; and

    (e) the value and nature of the subject matter of the receivership.

7.3.2 The Crown Court may instead of determining the receiver's remuneration itself refer it to be ascertained by the assessing authority of the Crown Court. In these circumstances CrimPR 45.11 to 45.13 (which deal with review by the assessing authority, further review by a costs judge and appeal to a High Court judge) have effect.

Procedure on appeal to the Court of Appeal

    The costs of and incidental to all proceedings on an appeal to the criminal division of the Court of Appeal against orders made in restraint proceedings, or appeals against or relating to the making of receivership orders, are in the discretion of the court: PCA 2002, s.89(4) [§ 5-921 in the main work]. **B-280**

7.4.1 The court has full power to determine by whom and to what extent the costs are to be paid.

7.4.2 In any such proceedings the court may disallow or (as the case may be) order the legal or other representative concerned to meet the whole of any wasted costs or such part of them as may be determined in accordance with the Criminal Procedure Rules. (As to wasted costs orders, see Pt 4 above.)

7.4.3 These provisions have retrospective effect in relation to proceedings on appeals in respect of offences committed or alleged to have been committed on or after 24 March 2003: Courts Act 2003, s.94(3).

PART 8: ADVICE ON APPEAL TO THE COURT OF APPEAL (CRIMINAL DIVISION)

8.1 In all cases the procedure set out in "A Guide to Proceedings in the Court of Appeal (Criminal Division)" published by the Criminal Appeal Office with the approval of the Lord Chief Justice [*post*, Appendix J] should be followed. **B-281**

8.2 This procedure requires that immediately following the conclusion of a case, legal representatives should see the defendant, and the advocate should express orally his final view as to the prospects of a successful appeal (whether against conviction or sentence or both). Litigators should not wait to be asked for advice by the defendant. In simple cases this will involve little or no expense. If the procedure is not followed and the work has not been done with due care, fees may be reduced accordingly. If there are no reasonable grounds of appeal, that should be confirmed in writing and a copy provided then or as soon as practicable thereafter, to the defendant by the litigator. Where the advocate's immediate and final view is that there are no reasonable grounds of appeal, no additional fee will normally be allowed. If there are reasonable grounds, grounds of appeal should be drafted, signed and sent to the instructing litigator as soon as possible. Litigators should immediately send a copy of the documents received from the advocate to the defendant. Provision for advice or assistance on appeal is included in the trial representation order issued by the Crown Court.

8.3 Notice and grounds (Form NG and the advocate's advice) should be lodged at the Crown Court (where the trial was conducted) within 28 days from the date of the conviction in the case of an application for leave to appeal against conviction and within 28 days from the date of sentence in the case of an application for leave to appeal against sentence. On a reference by the CCRC, Form NG and grounds should be served on the Registrar not more than 56 days after the Registrar has served notice that the CCRC has referred a conviction and not more than 28 days in the case of a sentence referral.

8.4 When (a) positive advice on appeal has been given; and (b) notice and grounds have been lodged with the Crown Court on the strength of that advice, the Registrar of Criminal Appeals is the authority for decisions about representation orders, in accordance with the principle that the court before which there are proceedings is the court with power to grant a right to representation. The Crown Court should not determine the fees in respect of the work in connection with the advice, notice and grounds unless the litigator confirms that the notice and grounds were not given on the litigator's or the advocate's advice. Where no notice of application is given, either because of unfavourable advice or despite favourable advice, the appropriate authority is the appropriate officer for the Crown Court.

8.5 If it appears that the defendant was never given advice, the Crown Court should direct the litigators' attention to this fact and if there is no satisfactory explanation as to why no advice was sent, the determining officer should bear this in mind when determining the litigator's costs and should draw the litigator's attention to the above mentioned guide.

8.6 Prior to the service of the notice and grounds of appeal, the Registrar of Criminal Appeals has no power to grant a representation order.

8.7 The Crown Court can only amend a representation order in favour of fresh legal representatives if advice on appeal has not been given by trial legal representatives and it is necessary and reasonable for another legal representative to be instructed.

PART 9: VAT

B-282   [*Not set out in this work*].

APPENDIX C
The Duties of Advocates

I. CODE OF CONDUCT

The first edition of the Bar Standards Board Handbook came into force on January 6, 2014. It **C-1** contains (in Part 2) the ninth edition of the Code of Conduct for the Bar of England and Wales. Part 1 of the handbook is an introduction. Parts 3 and 4 contain the scope of practice rules and the qualification rules. Part 5 comprises the enforcement regulations and Part 6 provides for the interpretation of terms used throughout the handbook.

Within the code, there are "core duties", "outcomes", "rules" and "guidance". The significance of each is explained in the introductory section of the handbook. Thus the core duties (italicised words and expressions are defined in Part 6)—

> "underpin the entire regulatory framework and set the mandatory standards that all *BSB regulated persons* are required to meet. They also define the core elements of professional conduct. Disciplinary proceedings may be taken against a *BSB regulated person* if the *Bar Standards Board* believes there has been a breach by that person of the Core Duties set out in this *Handbook* and that such action would be in accordance with the *Enforcement Policy*."

The outcomes—

> "explain the reasons for the regulatory scheme and what it is designed to achieve. They are derived from the *regulatory objectives* as defined in the *LSA* and the risks which must be managed if those objectives are to be achieved. They are not themselves mandatory rules, but they are factors which *BSB regulated persons* should have in mind when considering how the Core Duties, Conduct Rules or Qualification Rules (as appropriate) should be applied in particular circumstances. The *Bar Standards Board* will take into account whether or not an Outcome has, or might have been, adversely affected when considering how to respond to alleged breaches of the Core Duties, Conduct Rules or Qualification Rules."

The conduct rules (*i.e.* those in the code of conduct)—

> "supplement the Core Duties and are mandatory. Disciplinary proceedings may be taken against a *BSB regulated person* if the *Bar Standards Board* believes there has been a breach by that person of the Conduct Rules set out in Part 2 of this *Handbook* and that it would be in accordance with the *Enforcement policy* to take such action. However, the Conduct Rules are not intended to be exhaustive. In any situation where no specific Rule applies, reference should be made to the Core Duties. In situations where specific Rules do apply, it is still necessary to consider the Core Duties, since compliance with the Rules alone will not necessarily be sufficient to comply with the Core Duties."

The guidance is self-explanatory, its principal purpose being to assist in the interpretation of the core duties and rules.

The code of conduct itself is divided into four sections: A - Application, B - The Core Duties, C **C-2** - The Conduct Rules, and D - Rules Applying to Particular Groups of Regulated Persons. The conduct rules are themselves divided into five sections, *viz.* C1 "You and the court", C2 "Behaving ethically", C3 "You and your client", C4 "You and your regulator" and C5 "You and your practice". So far as practice in court is concerned, the most important rules are contained in section C1. These, together with the core duties, are set in full, *post.* The handbook runs to a total of 277 pages and space precludes the inclusion of more detail. However it should be noted that C2 (behaving ethically) contains provisions relating to honesty, integrity and independence, referral fees, undertakings, discrimination and foreign work, and that C3 (you and your client) has rules relating to "best interests of each client, provision of a competent standard of work, and confidentiality", "not misleading clients and potential clients", "personal responsibility", "accepting instructions", "defining terms or basis on which instructions are accepted", "returning instructions", "requirement not to discriminate", "the 'cab-rank rule'" and the "quality assurance scheme for advocates rules".

Core duties

CD1	You must observe your duty to the court in the administration of justice.
CD2	You must act in the best interests of each client.
CD3	You must act with honesty and integrity.
CD4	You must maintain your independence.
CD5	You must not behave in a way which is likely to diminish the trust and confidence which the public places in you or in the profession.
CD6	You must keep the affairs of each client confidential.
CD7	You must provide a competent standard of work and service to each client.
CD8	You must not discriminate unlawfully against any person.
CD9	You must be open and co-operative with your regulators.
CD10	You must take reasonable steps to manage your practice, or carry out your role within your practice, competently and in such a way as to achieve compliance with your legal and regulatory obligations.

Guidance to the core duties

gC1 The Core Duties are not presented in order of precedence, subject to the following:

.1 CD1 overrides any other core duty, if and to the extent the two are inconsistent. Rules C3.5 and C4 deal specifically with the relationship between CD1, CD2 and CD6 and you should refer to those rules and to the related Guidance;

.2 in certain other circumstances set out in this Code of Conduct one Core Duty overrides another. Specifically, Rule C16 provides that CD2 (as well as being subject to CD1) is subject to your obligations under CD3, CD4 and CD8.

gC2 Your obligation to take reasonable steps to manage your *practice*, or carry out your role within your *practice*, competently and in such a way as to achieve compliance with your legal and regulatory obligations (CD10) includes an obligation to take all reasonable steps to mitigate the effects of any breach of those legal and regulatory obligations once you become aware of the same.

The Conduct Rules

C.1 You and the court

Outcomes

oC1 The *court* is able to rely on information provided to it by those conducting litigation and by advocates who appear before it.

oC2 The proper administration of justice is served.

oC3 The interests of *clients* are protected to the extent compatible with outcomes oC1 and oC2 and the Core Duties.

oC4 Both those who appear before the *court* and *clients* understand clearly the extent of the duties owed to the *court* by advocates and those conducting litigation and the circumstances in which duties owed to *clients* will be overridden by the duty owed to the *court*.

oC5 *The public* has confidence in the administration of justice and in those who serve it.

Rules

rC3 You owe a duty to the *court* to act with independence in the interests of justice. This duty overrides any inconsistent obligations which you may have (other than obligations under the criminal law). It includes the following specific obligations which apply whether you are acting as an advocate or are otherwise involved in the conduct of litigation in whatever role (with the exception of Rule C3.1 below, which applies when acting as an advocate):

.1 you must not knowingly or recklessly mislead or attempt to mislead the *court*;

.2 you must not abuse your role as an advocate;

.3 you must take reasonable steps to avoid wasting the *court's* time;

.4 you must take reasonable steps to ensure that the *court* has before it all relevant decisions and legislative provisions;

.5 you must ensure that your ability to act independently is not compromised.

rC4 Your duty to act in the best interests of each *client* is subject to your duty to the *court*.

rC5 Your duty to the *court* does not require you to act in breach of your duty to keep the affairs of each *client* confidential.

Not misleading the court

rC6 Your duty not to mislead the *court* or to permit the *court* to be misled will include the follow-   **C-7**
ing obligations:

     .1 you must not:

         .a make submissions, representations or any other statement; or

         .b ask questions which suggest facts to witnesses

         which you know, or are instructed, are untrue or misleading.

     .2 you must not call witnesses to give evidence or put affidavits or witness statements to the *court* which you know, or are *instructed*, are untrue or misleading, unless you make clear to the *court* the true position as known by or instructed to you.

Not abusing your role as an advocate

rC7 Where you are acting as an advocate, your duty not to abuse your role includes the following   **C-8**
obligations:

     .1 you must not make statements or ask questions merely to insult, humiliate or annoy a witness or any other person;

     .2 you must not make a serious allegation against a witness whom you have had an opportunity to cross-examine unless you have given that witness a chance to answer the allegation in cross-examination;

     .3 you must not make a serious allegation against any person, or suggest that a person is guilty of a crime with which your *client* is charged unless:

         .a you have reasonable grounds for the allegation; and

         .b the allegation is relevant to your *client's* case or the credibility of a witness; and

         .c where the allegation relates to a third party, you avoid naming them in open *court* unless this is reasonably necessary.

     .4 you must not put forward to the *court* a personal opinion of the facts or the law unless you are invited or required to do so by the *court* or by law.

Guidance

Guidance on Rules C3 - C6 and relationship to CD1 and CD2

gC3 Rules C3 - C6 set out some specific aspects of your duty to the *court* (CD1). See CD1 and as-   **C-9**
sociated Guidance at gC1.

gC4 Knowingly misleading the *court* includes inadvertently misleading the *court* if you later realise that you have misled the *court*, and you fail to correct the position. Recklessness means being indifferent to the truth, or not caring whether something is true or false. The duty continues to apply for the duration of the case.

gC5 Your duty under Rule C3.3 includes drawing to the attention of the *court* any decision or provision which may be adverse to the interests of your *client*. It is particularly important where you are appearing against a litigant who is not legally represented.

gC6 You are obliged by CD2 to promote and to protect your *client's* interests so far as that is consistent with the law and with your overriding duty to the *court* under CD1. Your duty to the *court* does not prevent you from putting forward your *client's* case simply because you do not believe that the facts are as your *client* states them to be (or as you, on your *client's* behalf, state them to be), as long as any positive case you put forward accords with your *instructions* and you do not mislead the *court*. Your role when acting as an advocate or conducting litigation is to present your *client's* case, and it is not for you to decide whether your *client's* case is to be believed.

gC7 For example, you are entitled and it may often be appropriate to draw to the witness's attention other evidence which appears to conflict with what the witness is saying and you are entitled to indicate that a *court* may find a particular piece of evidence difficult to accept. But if the witness maintains that the evidence is true, it should be recorded in the witness statement and you will not be misleading the *court* if you call the witness to confirm their witness statement. Equally, there may be circumstances where you call a hostile witness whose evidence you are instructed is untrue. You will not be in breach of Rule C6 if you make the position clear to the *court*. See further the guidance at gC14.

gC8 As set out in Rule C4, your duty to the *court* does not permit or require you to disclose confidential information which you have obtained in the course of your *instructions* and which your *client* has not authorised you to disclose to the *court*. However, Rule C6 requires you not knowingly to mislead the *court* or to permit the *court* to be misled. There may be situations where you have obligations under both these rules.

gC9 Rule C3.5 makes it clear that your duty to act in the best interests of your *client* is subject to your duty to the *court*. For example, if your *client* were to tell you that he had committed the crime with which he was charged, in order to be able to ensure compliance with Rule C4 on the one hand and Rule C3 and Rule C6 on the other:

    .1 you would not be entitled to disclose that information to the *court* without your *client's* consent; and

    .2 you would not be misleading the *court* if, after your *client* had entered a plea of "not guilty", you were to test in cross-examination the reliability of the evidence of the prosecution witnesses and then address the jury to the effect that the prosecution had not succeeded in making them sure of your *client's* guilt.

gC10 However, you would be misleading the *court* and would therefore be in breach of Rules C3 and C6 if you were to set up a positive case inconsistent with the confession, as for example by:

    .1 suggesting to prosecution witnesses, calling your *client* or your witnesses to show; or submitting to the *jury*, that your *client* did not commit the crime; or

    .2 suggesting that someone else had done so; or

    .3 putting forward an alibi.

gC11 If there is a risk that the *court* will be misled unless you disclose confidential information which you have learned in the course of your *instructions*, you should ask the client for permission to disclose it to the *court*. If your *client* refuses to allow you to make the disclosure you must cease to act, and return your *instructions*: see Rules C25 to C27 below. In these circumstances you must not reveal the information to the *court*.

gC12 For example, if your *client* tells you that he has previous *convictions* of which the prosecution is not aware, you may not disclose this without his consent. However, in a case where mandatory sentences apply, the non-disclosure of the previous *convictions* will result in the *court* failing to pass the sentence that is required by law. In that situation, you must advise your *client* that if consent is refused to your revealing the information you will have to cease to act. In situations where mandatory sentences do not apply, and your *client* does not agree to disclose the previous *convictions*, you can continue to represent your *client* but in doing so must not say anything that misleads the *court*. This will constrain what you can say in mitigation. For example, you could not advance a positive case of previous good character knowing that there are undisclosed prior *convictions*. Moreover, if the *court* asks you a direct question you must not give an untruthful answer and therefore you would have to withdraw if, on your being asked such a question, your *client* still refuses to allow you to answer the question truthfully. You should explain this to your *client*.

gC13 Similarly, if you become aware that your *client* has a document which should be disclosed but has not been disclosed, you cannot continue to act unless your *client* agrees to the disclosure of the document. In these circumstances you must not reveal the existence or contents of the document to the *court*.

[The next paragraph is C-20.]

II. BAR COUNCIL GUIDANCE

Written standards of work

C-20   The Bar Council issued written standards for the conduct of professional work together with the eighth edition of the code of conduct. They did not form part of the code, but paragraph 701(d) obliged a barrister "to have regard to any relevant written standards." They can still be found on the website of the Bar Standards Board, but it does not appear that they are intended to have any continuing effect as there is a statement at the top of the page to the effect that, as from January 6, 2014, barristers should refer to the board's handbook (as to which, see *ante*, C-1) for rules and guidance on their conduct as such.

[The next paragraph is C-45.]

Criticism of previous counsel

In consequence of observations made by the Court of Appeal in *R. v. Clarke and Jones, The* **C-45** *Times,* August 19, 1994, and *R. v. Bowler, The Times,* May 9, 1995, the following guidance was approved by Lord Taylor C.J. and the Bar Council. It is still to be found on the website of the Bar Council, but it is emphasised there that it is not "guidance" for the purposes of the Bar Standards Board's handbook (as to which, see *ante,* C-1)), and it is accompanied by a disclaimer to the effect that it does not constitute legal advice and a statement to the effect that it was prepared by the Bar Council to assist barristers on matters of professional conduct and ethics.

1. Allegations against former counsel may receive substantial publicity whether accepted or rejected by the court. Counsel should not settle or sign grounds of appeal unless he is satisfied that they are reasonable, have some real prospect of success and are such that he is prepared to argue before the court (Guide to Proceedings in the Court of Appeal Criminal Division, para. A2-6 [*post,* Appendix J-5]). When such allegations are properly made however, in accordance with the Code of Conduct counsel newly instructed must promote and protect fearlessly by all proper and lawful means his lay client's best interests without regard to others, including fellow members of the legal profession (Code, para. 303(a)).

2. When counsel newly instructed is satisfied that such allegations are made, and a waiver of privilege is necessary, he should advise the lay client fully about the consequences of waiver and should obtain a waiver of privilege in writing signed by the lay client relating to communications with, instructions given to and advice given by former counsel. The allegations should be set out in the Grounds of Application for Leave of Appeal. Both waiver and grounds should be lodged without delay; the grounds may be perfected if necessary in due course.

3. On receipt of the waiver and grounds, the Registrar of Criminal Appeals will send both to former counsel with an invitation on behalf of the court to respond to the allegations made.

4. If former counsel wishes to respond and considers the time for doing so insufficient, he should ask the Registrar for further time. The court will be anxious to have full information and to give counsel adequate time to respond.

5. The response should be sent to the Registrar. On receipt, he will send it to counsel newly instructed who may reply to it. The grounds and the responses will go before the single judge.

6. The Registrar may have received grounds of appeal direct from the applicant, and obtained a waiver of privilege before fresh counsel is assigned. In those circumstances, when assigning counsel, the Registrar will provide copies of the waiver, the grounds of appeal and any response from former counsel.

7. This guidance covers the formal procedures to be followed. It is perfectly proper for counsel newly instructed to speak to former counsel as a matter of courtesy before grounds are lodged to inform him of the position.

As to the need to follow the Bar Council's guidance, see *R. v. Nasser, The Times,* February 19, 1998, CA.

Preparation of defence statements

As to guidance regarding the duties of counsel in relation to the preparation of defence state- **C-46** ments, see § 12-122 in the main work.

III. MISCELLANEOUS AUTHORITIES ON DUTIES OF ADVOCATES

(1) Return of brief or instructions

Members of the criminal bar have a personal responsibility for compliance with provisions of **C-47** the Code of Conduct relating to the return of instructions, of which their clerks should be aware. It is open to a court concerned with a problem caused by a late return of a brief to send a complaint to the Professional Conduct Committee of the Bar Council: *R. v. Sutton JJ., ex p. DPP,* 95 Cr.App.R. 180, DC, *per* Brooke J., at p. 186 (decided in relation to paragraphs 507 and 508 of the fifth edition of the Code of Conduct).

The absence of what counsel would regard as sufficient time for preparation does not constitute an exception to the cab-rank rule requiring him to act for his client: see *R. v. Ulcay* (§ 4-67 in the main work).

(2) Duty not to accept certain instructions

C-48   Counsel should not appear for the prosecution in a case where the defendant is a person he has previously represented; para. 501(f) of the Code of Conduct for the Bar (6th ed.) referred to the risk that the barrister might have consential information or special knowledge disadvantageous to the defendant, his former client; it is contrary to the spirit of the code that a barrister should put himself in a position where such a risk might be perceived: *R. v. Dann* [1997] Crim.L.R. 46, CA. As to *Dann*, see further *Re T. and A. (Children) (Risk of Disclosure)* [2002] 1 F.L.R. 859, CA (Civ.Div.).

(3) Duty in relation to the giving of advice and taking of instructions

C-48a   Although not laid down in prescriptive form in the codes of conduct governing barristers and solicitors, solicitors and counsel should make a brief note of the advice given and the instructions received in conference on important issues as to the conduct of the defence (such as discussions relating to strategy, including as to whether the defendant should give evidence); such a note would be to the benefit of the client, in that it will serve to ensure that he has been given the appropriate advice; it would also serve to protect the advocate and his instructing solicitors from criticism based on assertions made after the event by a dissatisfied client: *R. v. Anderson, The Times*, December 23, 2010, CA.

(4) Duty of counsel to acquaint themselves with the terms of the indictment

C-49   See *R. v. Peckham*, 25 Cr.App.R. 125, CCA (prosecution), and *R. v. Olivo*, 28 Cr.App.R. 173, CCA (defence).

(5) Duty concerning recent legislation

C-50   In *R. v. Isaacs, The Times*, February 9, 1990, the Court of Appeal said that when presenting cases at first instance or in appellate courts, counsel have a positive duty to inform the court of all relevant commencement dates of recent legislation.

(6) Duty of counsel to inform themselves of the sentencing powers of the court

C-51   The Court of Appeal has repeatedly emphasised the duty of both counsel to inform themselves before the commencement of proceedings in the Crown Court of the sentencing powers of the court, including powers in relation to ancillary orders, such as costs, compensation, etc. The starting point is *R. v. Clarke (R.W.W.)*, 59 Cr.App.R. 298, CA. Lawton L.J. concluded the judgment of the court with the following general observations and guidance. His Lordship's remarks are even more apposite today than when they were made: legislation in relation to sentence has become ever more complex. Sections 28 and 29 of the MCA 1952 were replaced by sections 37 and 38 respectively of the MCA 1980, which have themselves since been subject to extensive amendment. Section 37 was eventually repealed by the CDA 1998, and section 38 was repealed and replaced by section 3 of the PCC(S)A 2000.

> "We adjudge that counsel as a matter of professional duty to the Court, and in the case of defending counsel to their client, should always before starting a criminal case satisfy themselves as to what the maximum sentence is. There can be no excuse for counsel not doing this and they should remember that the performance of this duty is particularly important in a case where a man has been committed to the Crown Court for sentencing pursuant to the provisions of sections 28 and 29 of the Magistrates' Courts Act 1952, and section 56 of the Criminal Justice Act 1967. Those statutory provisions are pregnant with dangers for court and for counsel and above all for accused persons...
> Secondly, those who administer the Crown Court should act as follows. Before the Crown Court came into existence..., it was the practice of many clerks of assize and many clerks of the peace to make a note on the documents put before the trial judge of the maximum sentence which could be passed and of the paragraphs in *Archbold's Criminal Pleading, Evidence and Practice* which dealt with the offence. In some Crown Courts this former practice has been followed. On the other hand it is clear from this case and from inquiries which we have made that it is not

always followed. It should be; and it is particularly important that it should be when judges are asked to deal with cases committed for sentence under the statutory provisions to which I have already referred" (at pp. 301–302).

A reminder of the duty of counsel for both sides to ensure that sentences imposed, and orders made, are within the powers of the court, and to invite the court to vary a sentence if on subsequent consideration it appears to be unlawful, was given in *R. v. Komsta and Murphy*, 12 Cr.App.R.(S.) 63. Turner J. commented that it could not be too clearly understood that there was positive obligation on counsel, both for the prosecution and the defence, to ensure that no order was made that the court had no power to make. The PCC(S)A 2000, s. 155(1) (see § 5-1289 in the main work) allowed the Crown Court to alter or vary any sentence or order, within the period of 28 [now 56] days of the making of the order. If it appeared to either counsel that the order was one which the court had no power to make, counsel should not hesitate to invite the court to exercise such powers.

See also *R. v. Richards*, *The Times*, April 1, 1993, CA, *R. v. Hartrey* [1993] Crim.L.R. 230, CA, *R. v. Johnstone (D.)*, *The Times*, June 18, 1996, CA, *R. v. Bruley* [1996] Crim.L.R. 913, CA, *R. v. McDonnell* [1996] Crim.L.R. 914, CA, *R. v. Street*, 161 J.P. 28, CA, *R. v. Blight* [1999] Crim.L.R. 426, CA and, most recently, *R. v. Cain* [2007] 2 Cr.App.R.(S.) 25, CA. In *Blight*, it was said that counsel do not discharge their duty simply by having a copy of *Archbold* "to hand"; it is the duty of both counsel to be aware in advance of the powers of the court so that any error may be recited immediately; as to the defence counsel, it was said to be very difficult to see how mitigation can be done properly without having in the very front of the mind the powers within which the judge must exercise his duty. In *R. v. Cain*, it was said that defence advocates should ascertain and be prepared to assist the judge with any relevant legal restrictions on sentence, and the prosecution advocate should ensure that the sentencer does not, through inadvertence, impose an unlawful sentence; in particular, prosecution advocates should always be ready to assist the court by drawing attention to any statutory provisions that govern the court's sentencing powers and to any sentencing guidelines or guideline decisions of the Court of Appeal.

In *R. v. Reynolds* [2007] 2 Cr.App.R.(S.) 87, CA, it was said that prosecuting and defence **C-52** advocates must ensure that they are fully aware of the potential impact of the provisions of the dangerous offender provisions in Chapter 5 of Part 12 of the CJA 2003 (§§ 5-495 *et seq.* in the main work), that they are able to assist the sentencer in that respect and are alert to any mistakes made in passing sentence so that any problem can be resolved before it is too late.

(7) Defendant absconding

See generally, §§ 3-222 *et seq.* in the main work, and *R. v. Shaw*, 70 Cr.App.R. 313, CA (§ 7-87 **C-53** in the main work).

(8) Defendant not giving evidence

In *R. v. Bevan*, 98 Cr.App.R. 354, CA, it was held that where a defendant decides not to give **C-54** evidence, it should be the invariable practice of counsel to record that decision and to cause the defendant to sign that record, indicating clearly first, that he has, of his own free will, decided not to give evidence and, secondly, that he has so decided bearing in mind the advice given to him by counsel. In the light of section 35 of the CJPOA 1994 (§ 4-377 in the main work), the advice of the Court of Appeal in *Bevan* is likely to become of greater importance than at the time of the decision. As to this, see also *Ebanks (Kurt) v. The Queen* [2006] 1 W.L.R. 1827, PC (§ 4-382 in the main work).

(9) Duties in relation to cross-examination

See §§ 8-216, 8-219 *et seq.* in the main work and, in relation to defence counsel's duty when **C-55** cross-examining a co-defendant, see *R. v. Fenlon*, 71 Cr.App.R. 307, CA, see § 8-297 in the main work.

(10) Duties in relation to the summing up

See §§ 4-433 *et seq.* in the main work. **C-56**

(11) Duties in relation to appeal

As to the duty to advise in relation to the possibility of an appeal against conviction or sentence, **C-57** see §§ 7-165 *et seq.* in the main work.

As to counsel's general duty in relation to the drafting of grounds of appeal, see § 7-168 in the main work. As to criticism of former counsel, see § 7-83 in the main work and *ante*, and C-45, *ante*.

As to the duty of counsel for the prosecution, see § 7-201 in the main work.

The duty of a barrister to present his client's case before the Court of Appeal could not extend to advancing the client's assertion, unsubstantiated by any evidence, that the trial judge was corrupt or biased. A barrister's duty in such circumstances is either to decline to comply with the instructions or to withdraw from the case: *Thatcher v. Douglas, The Times*, January 8, 1996, CA (Civ. Div.).

(12) Duties of prosecuting counsel

C-58   Apart from the matters mentioned above, see also (a) *The Role and Responsibilities of the Prosecution Advocate, post*, E-15 *et seq.*; (b) *R. v. Herbert*, 94 Cr.App.R. 230, CA (§ 4-173 in the main work) and *R. v. Richards and Stober*, 96 Cr.App.R. 258, CA (§ 19-103 in the main work), in relation to "plea-bargaining" and the acceptance of pleas, with particular reference to cases where there are two or more defendants; (c) §§ 4-342 *et seq.* in the main work, in relation to the opening of a case generally, and *R. v. Hobstaff*, 14 Cr.App.R.(S.) 605, CA, in relation to opening the facts on a plea of guilty; and (d) the Attorney-General's guidelines on the acceptance of pleas and the prosecutor's role in the sentencing exercise (*ante*, Appendix A-276 *et seq.*).

(13) Advocate as witness

C-59   In *R. v. Jacquith (or Jaquith) and Emode* [1989] Crim.L.R. 508 and 563, CA, junior counsel for one defendant has been called on his behalf to rebut a suggestion of recent invention made against him. The Court of Appeal said that the evidence on this point was admissible but it was very undesirable for counsel to give evidence on this point in court. In addition to the effect on the jury it caused embarrassment and difficulty to other members of the Bar who had to set about cross-examining a colleague.

May L.J. said that the suggestion had been made that the court give some indication of its views concerning evidence given by counsel and also where a client alleged an attempt to pervert the court of justice by a co-defendant. their Lordships considered, however, that the right course would be to list points for consideration by the Bar Council and the Law Society. It was not sought to lay these maters down as ones of principle; their Lordships merely thought they deserved consideration.

1. No advocate should ever give evidence if that could possibly be avoided. 2. Where it was not possible for an advocate to avoid giving evidence, he should take no further part in the case. It necessarily followed that, if he was not being led, the trial must stop and a retrial be ordered. 3. There was a duty on counsel to anticipate circumstances in which he might be called upon to give evidence. Experienced counsel ought to be able to anticipate whether such a situation might arise. Where such a situation was anticipated, or envisaged even as a possibility, he should withdraw from the case. 4. Where it came to the notice of a legal adviser, through an accused person, that one of his co-defendants had attempted to pervert the court of justice, there was a duty on the legal adviser, usually the instructing solicitor, to take a detailed proof at once to provide a record and for further investigation. 5. Where the giving of evidence by an advocate caused real embarrassment or inhibition or difficulty regarding cross-examination by other advocates, the judge should exercise his discretion to discharge the jury and order a retrial.

(14) Co-habiting counsel

C-60   It is generally undesirable for husband and wife, or other partners living together, to appear as counsel on opposite sides in the same criminal matter since it might give rise to an apprehension that the proper conduct of the case had been in some way affected by that personal relationship: *R. v. Batt, The Times*, May 30, 1996, CA. See also *Re L. (Minors) (Care Proceedings: Solicitors)* [2001] 1 W.L.R. 100, Fam D. (Wilson J.).

APPENDIX D
Forms for use at Plea and Trial Preparation Hearings

PTPH – INTRODUCTION AND GUIDANCE

PLEA AND TRIAL PREPARATION HEARINGS

Introduction and Guidance

Why the Change?

There has been a widely held perception that Preliminary Hearings in cases where not guilty pleas are expected have been held too early in the process for the court to give more than perfunctory orders and that Plea and Case Management Hearings are either unnecessary or not held at a time when active case management could be most effective. The result has been a multiplicity of hearings.

There have also been differing local practices and protocols, and differing methods of recording court orders. The result has been failings of compliance when orders made have not always been communicated clearly to those who must act upon them.

The new Plea and Trial Preparation Hearing (PTPH) and related procedures will provide a single national process to be used in all Crown Courts. It builds on the Transforming Summary Justice initiative in the Magistrates' Courts.

The PTPH:

- Takes place a little later in the process than Preliminary Hearings, either 21 or 28 days after sending (depending on Circuit) unless, in individual cases, the Resident Judge orders otherwise;
- Occurs after the prosecution will have provided available information about the case and obtained details of the availability of likely prosecution witnesses. In many cases this should be sufficient to enable the court to case manage effectively without the need for a Further Case Management Hearing (FCMH) before trial.
- Presumes that the parties will have communicated with each other prior to the PTPH and will continue to do so thereafter.

What the PTPH should achieve

An effective PTPH will

- arraign the defendant unless there is good reason not to;
- set the trial date;
- identify, so far as can be determined at that stage, the issues for trial;
- provide a timetable for the necessary pre-trial preparation and give appropriate directions for an effective trial;
- make provision for any Further Case Management hearing that is actually required to take place at the time when it can be of maximum effectiveness.

Engagement between the parties and with the court should ensure that these elements can be achieved.

PTPH – Introduction and Guidance – October 2015 - Page 1 of 6

PTPH – INTRODUCTION AND GUIDANCE

Why the form? **The form must be used for all cases sent to the Crown Court after ??????? 2015 where not guilty pleas are anticipated** unless expressly exempted by the CrimPR or CrimPD. In most cases the prosecution should prepare and circulate a copy tailored to the number of defendants and populated with the prosecution Information no less than 7 days prior to the PTPH.

The form is intended to:

- gather necessary information from the parties;
- monitor the extent to which the prosecution provide information prior to the PTPH;
- allow the court to make, record <u>and distribute</u> clear orders timetabling the preparation of the case for trial. This is particularly important as it will address the need for those who have to act upon the orders to know exactly what the judge ordered.
- allow the court to provide for further hearings when they are going to be necessary and most useful.

The form is to be regarded as the primary record of orders made. After the hearing the court will make copies available to the parties (either electronically or on paper) including to the named Officer in the Case. Case Progression Officers must ensure that they obtain a copy and, if the OIC's details have not been provided, ensure that the OIC receives one.

Completing the Form The blank form (PTPH NG1) will be available on paper and in pdf and Word formats on the Criminal Procedure Rules pages of the Ministry of Justice website.

It is accepted that in many instances the form will be completed as a paper document but parties are encouraged to complete and distribute it electronically where possible. At this stage the form will often be completed partly electronically and partly on paper and so drop down menus or other similar devices have been avoided.

If it is completed on paper please keep in mind that the document will be scanned for distribution.

Contact Information The provision of contact information is vital to allow proper communication between participants. The form expressly reminds participants of their duties under the CrimPR. Individual names are required but it is acceptable to provide group email addresses provided they are properly monitored and acted upon. Parties must ensure effective cover for sickness or absence.

What the Prosecution will serve prior to the PTPH The usefulness of the PTPH depends on:

- The lodging no less than seven days prior to the PTPH of a draft indictment; and
- service prior to the hearing of the principal parts of the prosecution case then available. The summary required will, in police cases, usually be the MG5. The prosecution

PTPH – Introduction and Guidance – October 2015 - Page 2 of 6

PTPH – INTRODUCTION AND GUIDANCE

material is to be served:
- If the defendant is on bail – by the sending hearing in the Magistrates' Court;
- If the defendant is in custody – no less than seven days before the PTPH.

Details of what is expected to be served are set out in the CrimPD 3A.12 and 3A.20 and a breakdown appears in the form so that compliance can be monitored.

There may be good reasons why the prosecution has not served all the materials listed prior to the PTPH but the court will usually expect to proceed with the hearing rather than adjourn it.

When will a further hearing be required?

After the PTPH there will be no Further Case Management Hearing (FCMH) before the trial unless:
- The court is informed that a guilty plea is to be entered;
- It is necessary to give directions for an effective trial; or
- A Ground Rules hearing is required - CrimPR 3.9(7);

And the court directs a FCMH is necessary to further the overriding objective.

At the PTPH the court may order a FCMH but usually will do so only in one of the following cases:
- Class 1 cases[1];
- Class 2 cases which carry a maximum penalty of 10 years or more;
- Cases involving death by driving (whether dangerous or careless), or death in the workplace;
- Cases involving a vulnerable witness;
- Cases in which the defendant is a child or otherwise under a disability, or requires special assistance;
- Cases in which there is a corporate defendant or an unrepresented defendant;
- Cases in which the expected length of the trial is such that a FCMH is desirable and any case in which the trial is likely to last longer than four weeks;
- Cases in which expert evidence is to be introduced;
- Cases in which there are likely to be linked criminal and care directions in accordance with the 2013 Protocol.

The Court may also order a FCMH:
- Where the defendant requests a hearing to enter a guilty plea;
- Cases in which an application to dismiss or stay has been made;
- Cases in which arraignment has not taken place for any reason.

See CrimPD I. 3A.21

---

[1] For classification of cases see Criminal Practice Direction XIII Listing B: Classification.

PTPH – INTRODUCTION AND GUIDANCE

The Defendant will not usually be required to attend FCMHs unless a good reason is provided or statute requires it. Unless a good reason is provided a defendant in custody will not be produced, nor will an interpreter be booked for a Defendant on bail who wishes to attend. In contrast a Defendant is required to attend a Ground Rules Hearing.

The Court's Directions

The form includes standard directions. These have been approved by the Lord Chief Justice and will apply unless the Court expressly orders otherwise.

Directions are numbered and a two or three letter code appears alongside the directions as a visual prompt, and, following the re-numbering exercise this year, there are references to the Criminal Procedure Rules 2015.

In individual cases the court may revise the standard directions or make other bespoke orders as necessary. However the form is designed so that the numbering of standard orders will not alter.

It is accepted that individual courts have developed systems that have, for them, worked well and may find that not all of the elements of their current systems are present in this form. However the use of a national form with standard directions will greatly assist both prosecution and defence in developing systems to respond to them. This is why local forms and protocols can no longer continue to be used.

Four Stages

In most cases the court will be able to set just four dates for the parties to complete their pre-trial preparation and therefore the Judge or court will need only to insert the dates for the four stages and delete any orders that are not required. The draft orders have been grouped in a way intended to facilitate such an approach.

The setting of a multiplicity of dates is recognised as the enemy of compliance but where necessary individual dates can be set.

The four stages are:

- **Stage 1** – for the service of the bulk of prosecution materials. This date will ordinarily be 50 days (custody cases) or 70 days (bail cases) after the sending. This is in line with the timetable for the service of the prosecution case provided in the Crime and Disorder Act (Services of Prosecution Evidence) Regulations 2005. The court does not have power to abridge this time (without consent) but does have power to extend it.
- **Stage 2** – for the service of the defence response. This date will ordinarily be 28 days after Stage 1 reflecting the time provided for the service of a Defence Statement
- **Stage 3** – for the prosecution response to the Defence Statement and other defence items. This date will ordinarily be 14 or 28 days after Stage 2 depending on the anticipated date of trial.
- **Stage 4** - for the defence to provide final materials or make applications that will commonly arise out of prosecution disclosure.

PTPH – INTRODUCTION AND GUIDANCE

In cases involving witnesses aged under 10 a different timetable will
be required to conform to the Protocol to Expedite Cases of 19th Jan
2015.

**Non-
contentious
orders**

There will be considerable savings of resources for all parties if non-
contentious orders, such as some special measures orders, are made
at the PTPH without further formality.

**Standard
Witness List**

In many cases it will be possible for the defence to provide details of
witness requirements at the PTPH and should expect to do so.
In other cases that will not be possible and therefore a defendant's full
witness requirements (with considered estimates of the time required)
will have to be given at a later stage. The new Standard Witness List
must be used to notify witness requirements. Unless otherwise
ordered it must be served by the defence on the prosecution at Stage
2 - the same time that the Defence Statement is due (whether or not a
Defence Statement is also actually served).
Where a full Standard Witness List cannot be completed at the PTPH
the defence should complete the section "Witness Requirements
Known at PTPH".

**Compliance
And
Compliance
Courts**

Parties are expected to comply with the timetables set. If,
exceptionally, an element required by a particular stage is not
available that is not to be regarded as a reason for not serving the
remainder.
If a party had been directed to serve, for example, a special measures
application by a certain date but later decides not to pursue such an
application it is not necessary to file any formal notice that the matter
will not be pursued.
Parties are reminded that all participants have a duty to prepare and
conduct the case in accordance with the overriding objective; to
comply with the Criminal Procedure Rules, Practice Directions and
directions of the Court; and at once to inform the court and all parties
of any significant failure (CrimPR1.2)
If a party fails to comply with a case management direction then that
party may be required to attend the court to explain the failure. Unless
otherwise directed a defendant and other parties to the case will not
usually be expected to attend such a hearing (CrimPD I 3A.23; 26-28)

**Administrative
Directions**

Where further directions are required pre-trial and the parties have not
succeeded in resolving matters between themselves, the court will
usually expect to give administrative directions without the need for an
oral hearing.

**What if the
Defendant
decides to**

The form is intended for those who will be pleading not guilty.
If, after sending, the defendant decides to plead guilty the defendant
should not wait for the PTPH but instead inform the court and, if so
advised, apply for the preparation of a Fast Delivery Format Pre-

PTPH – Introduction and Guidance – October 2015 - Page 5 of 6

PTPH – INTRODUCTION AND GUIDANCE

plead guilty? sentence report, or a full Pre-sentence report and/or a DRR assessment. In each case reasons why a report is justified are required. The court will consider that request administratively and may adjourn the case for a Plea and Sentence hearing on a date by which any report that has been ordered will be available. A court ordering the preparation of a Pre-sentence Report will usually direct a "Fast Delivery Style" report unless good reason for a full report has been identified.

The future The introduction of the PTPH and this form is a step towards electronic case management and the electronic monitoring of compliance which will be possible with the introduction of the Common Platform. This will have huge advantages for all. The use of a single national process with largely standard directions is essential to the future development of systems for the court, prosecution and defence that work one with another.

Improving the Form Court users who would like to propose adjustments to the form or to suggest additional, or re-phrased, standard directions are encouraged to make suggestions to info@..........................

Signed: Lord Chief Justice

Senior Presiding Judge

President

Date:

PLEA AND TRIAL PREPARATION
HEARING FORM

This form must be completed for all cases sent to the Crown Court after ....2015 where a trial is anticipated
unless the case is expressly exempted by the CrimPR or CrimPD.
THIS FORM IS TO BE REGARDED AS THE PRIMARY RECORD OF ORDERS MADE.
After the hearing the court will make available copies of the completed form to the parties (whether completed
electronically or on paper) and Case Progression Officers and OICs must ensure that they receive and act upon it. Any
additional written orders of the court must be attached or incorporated.

PART 1 – PRE-HEARING INFORMATION to be completed by the parties

Crown Court at: T: PTI URN:

	Defendant	DOB	Principal Charge(s)	Remand Status	Custody Time Limit	Elected Trial?
D1				☐ Unconditional Bail ☐ Conditional Bail ☐ Custody ☐ Youth Det. Remand		☐

	Defence to set out, so far as known, the real issues in the case. CrimPR 3.2;3.3;3.11	Are the conclusions of any served Streamlined Forensics Report (SFR) admitted as fact. If not identify the disputed issues concerning that conclusion? CrimPR 19.3
D1		☐YES ☐NO Disputed Issues:

Other Proceedings:		
Are there any associated CRIMINAL proceedings?	☐	Particulars:
Are there any linked FAMILY proceedings?	☐	Particulars:

PLEA AND TRIAL PREPARATION HEARING FORM – Page 1 of 9

Contact Information and Duties:
The parties must provide the information required below at the PTPH or if not then available it must be provided to the court and other parties in writing within 14 days. The court and other parties must be informed of any change and effective cover must be provided for sickness or absence. The names of individuals must be given but it is acceptable to provide group email addresses provided that they are effectively monitored and acted upon.

If the prosecution or defence have not allocated a trial advocate then the advocate at a hearing or, the prosecution Reviewing Lawyer or the defence solicitor is required to respond to issues in place of the trial advocate.

Parties are reminded that:
All participants have a duty to prepare and conduct the case in accordance with the overriding objective; to comply with the CrimPR, practice directions and directions of the court; and at once to inform the court and all parties of any significant failure - CrimPR1.2.

Prosecution and Defence Case Progression Officers are reminded of their duties to monitor compliance with directions; make sure the court is kept informed of events that may affect the progress of the case; make sure that he or she can be contacted promptly about the case during ordinary business hours; act promptly and reasonably in response to communications about the case and, if he or she will be unavailable appoint a substitute to fulfil his or her duties and inform the other Case Progression Officers - CrimPR3.4.

Parties must actively assist the court to fulfil the overriding objective and engage with other parties to further the overriding objective without or if necessary with a direction - CrimPR3.3. Provided they promptly inform the court Case Progression Officer parties may agree to vary a time limit fixed by a direction if the variation will not affect the date of any hearing that has been fixed or significantly affect the progress of the case in any other way -CrimPR 3.7

Court Case Progression	Name:	Phone:	Email:
Case Progression Officer:			

Prosecution Information	Name:	Phone:	Email:
Advocate at PTPH			
Advocate for trial			
Reviewing Lawyer			
Case Progression Officer (usually Paralegal)			
Officer in the Case (or equivalent)			

Defence Information		Name and Address for Service:	Phone:	Email for service:
D1	Defence Solicitors			☐ Secure ☐ Not Secure
	Case Progression Officer			☐ Secure ☐ Not Secure
	Funding	Private Funding ☐; Legal Rep applied for ☐; OR Legal Rep Order granted ☐		
		Name:	Phone:	Email:
	Advocate at PTPH			
	Advocate for trial			

PLEA AND TRIAL PREPARATION HEARING FORM – Page 2 of 9

State of Preparation at PTPH

PROSECUTION		Served	If not yet served they can be served by:
IND	Draft Indictment	☐	
SUM	Summary of circumstances of the offence(s) and of any account given by defendant(s) in interview (this may be in Form MG5).	☐	
EVI	Statements identified by prosecution as being of importance for the purpose of plea and initial case management.	☐	
EVI	Exhibits identified by prosecution as being of importance for the purpose of plea and initial case management.	☐	
TV	Relevant CCTV that would be relied upon by prosecution at trial.	☐	
EXP	Streamlined Forensic Report(s) or indication of scientific evidence that the prosecution is likely to introduce.	☐	
EXP	Indication of medical evidence that the prosecution is likely to introduce.	☐	
EXP	Indication of other expert evidence that the prosecution is likely to introduce.	☐	
BC	Indication of bad character evidence to be relied on.	☐	
HS	Indication of any hearsay evidence to be relied on.	☐	
SM	Indication of special measures to be sought.	☐	
CRO	Defendant's criminal record if any.	☐	
VPS	Victim Personal Statement if any.	☐	

DEFENCE			Particulars
ABU FTP	Are there preliminary issues such as Abuse of Process or Fitness to Plead?	☐	
DMS	Is an application for Dismissal anticipated after time for service elapse?	☐	
SEV	Is an application for Severance anticipated? CrimPR 3.21	☐	
ARR	Can the defendant be arraigned at PTPH? If not set out the reason.	☐	
ALT	Is the defendant willing to offer a plea to another offence and/or a plea on a limited basis?	☐	
DS	Is a Defence Statement available at this stage?	☐	

THIRD PARTY DISCLOSURE			Particulars
TPD	Is it believed that any third party holds potentially disclosable material?	☐	
TPD	Will the prosecution be making enquiries to review that material?	☐	

PLEA AND TRIAL PREPARATION HEARING FORM – Page 3 of 9

WITNESS REQUIREMENTS KNOWN AT PTPH

List the prosecution witnesses who, at the time of the PTPH, it can be predicted will be required to give live evidence. You do not need to fill out this part if you are able to fill out the Standard Witness Table at the PTPH

Name of witness	Page No.	Required by:	Relevant disputed issue.	Mark if availability known?
				☐
				☐
				☐
				☐
				☐
				☐
				☐
				☐
				☐

PART 2 – PLEA AND TRIAL PREPARATION HEARING ORDERS
to be completed by the court.

PLEAS

1	Pleas entered at PTPH:	
2	Reason if not arraigned at PTPH:	
3	Judicial warnings Given ☑	☐ Credit for Plea
		☐ Warning that failure to provide a sufficiently detailed Defence Statement may count against the Defendant
		☐ (Bail) Failure to attend is a separate offence
		☐ (Bail) Trial in absence – advocates may withdraw
	Notes:	

TRIAL	Date:		☑ Facilities required:	☺ Time Estimate
4		☐ Fixture ☐ Fixed Floater ☐ Warned List commencing.	☐ CCTV ☐ Live Link ☐ Satellite Link from: ☐ Interpreter for defendant(s) (language):	days weeks

FURTHER MANAGEMENT IF REQUIRED	Date:		☺ Time Estimate
5	**Pre-Arraignment Further Case Management Hearing to resolve ☑:** ☐ Abuse of Process; ☐ Fitness to Plead; ☐ Dismissal applications; ☐ Joinder/Severance.		☐ Defendant not required ☐ Defendant must attend ☐ Application/skeleton and reports by: ☐ Response by:	Minutes Hours
6	**Further Case Management Hearing** (including Preparatory Hearing or Pre-Trial Hearing).		☐ Defendant not required ☐ Defendant must attend	Minutes Hours
7	**Pre-Trial Review.** The PTR may be vacated on <u>all</u> parties informing the Court CPO in writing that they are fully trial ready and no orders are required.		☐ Defendant not required ☐ Defendant must attend	Minutes Hours
8	**Ground Rules Hearing**		Defendant must attend	Minutes Hours

PLEA AND TRIAL PREPARATION HEARING FORM – Page 5 of 9

ORDERS THAT CAN BE MADE AT PTPH WITHOUT FURTHER FORMALITY			
9	SM	Special measures orders that can be made at PTPH – CrimPR 18	Special measures granted for the following witnesses: [ ]ABE evidence] [ ]Live link] [ ]Screens] [ ]ABE evidence] [ ]Live link] [ ]Screens] [ ]ABE evidence] [ ]Live link] [ ]Screens]
10	SAT	Satellite/Live Link	Live Link order made for the following witnesses (particulars of link to be provided not less than three weeks before trial CrimPD 18.23-4): for Live link from for Live link from for Live link from
11	WIT	Young or vulnerable witnesses – CrimPR 18 & 3.9(7)	Young or vulnerable witnesses to which an Advocates' Gateway toolkit applies are to be examined and cross-examined in accordance with that toolkit unless that is superseded by specific ground rules.
12	EXP	Expert witnesses – CrimPR 19	Expert witnesses of comparable disciplines must liaise and serve on the parties and the Court a statement of the points on which they agree and disagree with reasons no less than 14 days prior to the trial.
13		Other:	
14		Other:	

STAGE 1 - UNLESS INDIVIDUAL DATES ARE PROVIDED THE PROSECUTION SHALL SERVE THE FOLLOWING BY:		Date:		
Ordinarily 50 days (custody cases) or 70 days (bail cases) after sending.				
		ITEM	*Date :*	*Additional requirements/particulars/directions if any:*
15	EVI	Service of prosecution case.		As required by Crime and Disorder Act (Service of Prosecution Evidence) Regulations 2005 Regs. 2 & 3 (70 days or 50 days after sending). To include making available ABE transcripts and recordings.
16	DCL	Initial disclosure (if not yet served).		
17	TV	CCTV relied upon.		To be served in format compatible with systems available at court. Otherwise party to provide system.
18	IV	Written record of defendant's taped Interview(s) (ROTI).		The parties are expected to engage pre-trial to agree a summary or editing.
19	IV	Audio recording of defendant's tape interviews(s).		
20	999	999 call transcript(s) and recording(s).		
21	TEL	Telephone records to be relied upon.		
22	FOR	Full forensic science statements that can be served by Stage 1.		Full forensic statements will only be ordered if the defendant has identified what conclusion in a Streamlined Report is not admitted and what are the disputed issues concerning that conclusion – CrimPR 19.3.
23	BC	Bad character notice(s) CrimPR 21		To include, if to be relied upon, evidence of facts of bad character.
24	HSY	Hearsay application(s) CrimPR 20		
25	SM	Special measures application(s) CrimPR 18		

PLEA AND TRIAL PREPARATION HEARING FORM – Page 6 of 9

26		Other:		
27		Other:		

THIRD PARTY DISCLOSURE: It is ordered:			*Date:*
28	TPD	Prosecution shall either make requests to third party, OR notify defence in writing that it does not intend to make any application for Third Party Disclosure (TPD) by:	
29	TPD	If the prosecution is to pursue TPD then the prosecution must serve a report in writing on the outcome of efforts to identify potentially disclosable materials held by third parties and any ongoing enquiries not yet completed by:	
30		Other:	

STAGE 2 - UNLESS INDIVIDUAL DATES ARE PROVIDED IT IS ORDERED THAT THE DEFENCE SHALL SERVE THE FOLLOWING BY: Ordinarily 28 days after Stage 1.				**DATE:**
		ITEM	*Date:*	*Additional requirements/particulars/directions:*
31	DS	Defence Statement.		To include particulars of alibi; and requests for disclosure.
32	WIT	Final list of prosecution witnesses required to give live evidence; defence witnesses and interpreter requirements.		To be submitted in the Standard Witness Table with time estimates.
33	SM	Special measures application for defendant or defence witnesses.		Any reply from prosecution or other party to be served within 14 days.
34	ABE	List of editing requests or objections to ABE interview recording.		
35	IV	List of editing requests for the Defendant's ROTI (if any).		
36	BC	Response to prosecution bad character Notice(s) - CrimPR 21.		
37	HSY	Response to prosecution hearsay application(s) – CrimPR 20.		
38	SM	Response to prosecution special measures application(s) - CrimPR 18.		
39	EXP	Defence expert evidence to be relied upon - CrimPR 19.		
40		Other:		
41		Other:		

STAGE 3 – UNLESS INDIVIDUAL DATES ARE PROVIDED IT IS ORDERED THAT THE PROSECUTION SHALL SERVE THE FOLLOWING BY: Ordinarily 14 or 28 days after Stage 2				**DATE:**
		ITEM	*Date for Service*	*Additional requirements/particulars/directions:*
42	DCL	Further disclosure.		Items required to be disclosed under CPIA resulting from or requested by the Defence Statement.
43	EVI	Further evidence to be relied upon that could not be served by Stage 1.		

PLEA AND TRIAL PREPARATION HEARING FORM – Page 7 of 9

44	**FOR**	Full forensic science statements that could not be served by Stage 1.		Full statements will only be ordered if the defendant has identified what conclusion in a Streamlined Report is not admitted and what are the disputed issues concerning that conclusion – CrimPR 19.3
45	**EXP**	Expert medical evidence.		
46	**EXP**	Psychiatric evidence.		
47	**EXP**	Other (specify) expert evidence.		
48	**SAT**	Satellite/Live link application(s) CrimPD 18.23-24		
49	**TEL**	Cell site analysis.		
50	**INT**	Intermediary report(s) with draft specific Ground Rules if required. CrimPR 18 & 3.9(7)		For Witness:
51		Other:		
52		Other:		

STAGE 4 – UNLESS INDIVIDUAL DATES ARE GIVEN IT IS ORDERED THAT THE DEFENCE SHALL SERVE THE FOLLOWING BY: Ordinarily 14 or 28 days after Stage 3.				DATE:
		ITEM	*Date:*	*Additional requirements/particulars/directions:*
53	**DCL**	Complaint about prosecution non-disclosure		To comply with s.8 CPIA and CrimPR 15.5.
54	**DCL**	Application(s) for witness summons for Third Party Disclosure if the prosecution indicates at PTPH that it will not be pursuing any TPD issues OR any Defendant is dissatisfied with the outcome of prosecution enquiries.		To comply with CrimPR 17.5
55	**EXP**	Defence expert evidence to be relied upon that could not be served by Stage 2 - CrimPR 19		
56	**BC**	s.100 or 101 bad character of non-defendant application - CrimPR 21		Any reply from prosecution or other party to be served within 14 days
57	**SXB**	s.41 Evidence of sexual behaviour application - CrimPR 22		Any reply from prosecution or other party to be served within 14 days
58	**SM**	Response to prosecution intermediary Report(s) - CrimPR 18		
59	**INT**	Intermediary report for defendant or defence witnesses with draft Ground Rules		Any reply from prosecution or other party to be served within 14 days
60	**SAT**	Satellite/Live link application(s) CrimPD 18.23-24		
61		Other:		
62		Other.		

PLEA AND TRIAL PREPARATION HEARING FORM – Page 8 of 9

ADDITIONAL ORDERS:	*Date:*
62	
63	
64	

D-3

Crown Court at:		T:		PTI URN:	

The Queen v.	

STANDARD WITNESS TABLE

DEFENCE: The Defence must use this form to notify witness requirements. It must be served on the Prosecution and the Court no later than the date set for the provision of the Defence Statement (whether a Defence Statement is also provided or not). The Defence must give to the Prosecution and the Court the name, address, and date of birth of each proposed Defence witness so far as is known together with the other information specified in s.6C CPIA 1996 and such information must be provided at the same time as this form.

PROSECUTION: The Prosecution must then complete time estimates, consider if it is necessary to revise the trial time estimate, and serve on all parties and the Court.

The attendance of any witness is subject to the Judge's direction.

Unless the Court otherwise directs the Parties must limit their examinations to time estimates given.

DATE INFORMATION PROVIDED:	Date:
By the Defence:	
By the Prosecution:	

TIME ESTIMATES

The Time Estimate given at the PTPH (to include time for jury retirement) was:	days
In the light of the full witness requirements the time estimate needs to be revised to:	Days OR No Change

WITNESSES FOR THE PROSECUTION

Name of Witness	Page No.	Required by:	Relevant disputed issue.	⏱ Time Estimate	
				Examination by Prosecution	Cross-examination

STANDARD WITNESS TABLE – Page 1 of 2

WITNESSES FOR THE FIRST DEFENDANT					
Name of Witness	*Date of Birth*	*Will Special Measures be applied for/required?*	*Interpreter required. State language*	⏱ *Time Estimate*	
				Examination by calling party	Notes
The Defendant (if called)	✕				

STANDARD WITNESS TABLE – Page 2 of 2

APPENDIX E
Crown Prosecution Service

I. CODE FOR CROWN PROSECUTORS

A. Introduction

The Crown Prosecution Service is the principal public prosecuting authority for England and **E-1** Wales and is headed by the Director of Public Prosecutions, who is to discharge his functions under the superintendence of the Attorney-General (Prosecution of Offences Act 1985, s.3(1)). The Attorney-General is accountable to Parliament for the Service.

The Crown Prosecution Service is a national organisation consisting of 42 areas. Each area is headed by a Chief Crown Prosecutor and corresponds to a single police force area, with one for London. It was set up in 1986 to prosecute cases investigated by the police.

Although the Crown Prosecution Service works closely with the police, it is independent of them. The independence of crown prosecutors is of fundamental constitutional importance. Casework decisions taken with fairness, impartiality and integrity help deliver justice for victims, witnesses, defendants and the public.

The Crown Prosecution Service co-operates with the investigating and prosecuting agencies of other jurisdictions.

The Director of Public Prosecutions is responsible for issuing a Code for Crown Prosecutors under section 10 of the Prosecution of Offences Act 1985, giving guidance on the general principles to be applied when making decisions about prosecutions. This is the seventh edition of the code and replaces all earlier versions. It was issued on January 28, 2013.

B. The Code

1. Introduction

1.1 The Code for Crown Prosecutors (the code) is issued by the Director of Public Prosecutions **E-2** (DPP) under section 10 of the Prosecution of Offences Act 1985. This is the seventh edition of the code and replaces all earlier versions.

1.2 The DPP is the head of the Crown Prosecution Service (CPS), which is the principal public prosecution service for England and Wales. The DPP operates independently, under the superintendence of the Attorney-General who is accountable to Parliament for the work of the CPS.

1.3 The code gives guidance to prosecutors on the general principles to be applied when making decisions about prosecutions. The code is issued primarily for prosecutors in the CPS, but other prosecutors follow the code either through convention or because they are required to do so by law.

1.4 In this code, the term "suspect" is used to describe a person who is not yet the subject of formal criminal proceedings; the term "defendant" is used to describe a person who has been charged or summonsed; and the term "offender" is used to describe a person who has admitted his or her guilt to a police officer or other investigator or prosecutor, or who has been found guilty in a court of law.

2. General Principles

2.1 The decision to prosecute or to recommend an out-of-court disposal is a serious step that af- **E-3** fects suspects, victims, witnesses and the public at large and must be undertaken with the utmost care.

2.2 It is the duty of prosecutors to make sure that the right person is prosecuted for the right offence and to bring offenders to justice wherever possible. Casework decisions taken fairly, impartially and with integrity help to secure justice for victims, witnesses, defendants and the public. Prosecutors must ensure that the law is properly applied; that relevant evidence is put before the court; and that obligations of disclosure are complied with.

2.3 Although each case must be considered on its own facts and on its own merits, there are general principles that apply in every case.

2.4 Prosecutors must be fair, independent and objective. They must not let any personal views about the ethnic or national origin, gender, disability, age, religion or belief, political views, sexual orientation, or gender identity of the suspect, victim or any witness influence their decisions. Neither must prosecutors be affected by improper or undue pressure from any source. Prosecutors must always act in the interests of justice and not solely for the purpose of obtaining a conviction.

2.5 The CPS is a public authority for the purposes of current, relevant equality legislation. Prosecutors are bound by the duties set out in this legislation.

2.6 Prosecutors must apply the principles of the European Convention on Human Rights, in accordance with the Human Rights Act 1998, at each stage of a case. Prosecutors must also comply with any guidelines issued by the Attorney-General; with the *Criminal Procedure Rules* currently in force; and have regard to the obligations arising from international conventions. They must follow the policies and guidance of the CPS issued on behalf of the DPP and available for the public to view on the CPS website.

3. THE DECISION WHETHER TO PROSECUTE

E-4

3.1 In more serious or complex cases, prosecutors decide whether a person should be charged with a criminal offence and, if so, what that offence should be. They make their decisions in accordance with this code and the DPP's guidance on charging. The police apply the same principles in deciding whether to start criminal proceedings against a person in those cases for which they are responsible.

3.2 The police and other investigators are responsible for conducting enquiries into any alleged crime and for deciding how to deploy their resources. This includes decisions to start or continue an investigation and on the scope of the investigation. Prosecutors often advise the police and other investigators about possible lines of inquiry and evidential requirements, and assist with pre-charge procedures. In large scale investigations the prosecutor may be asked to advise on the overall investigation strategy, including decisions to refine or narrow the scope of the criminal conduct and the number of suspects under investigation. This is to assist the police and other investigators to complete the investigation within a reasonable period of time and to build the most effective prosecution case. However, prosecutors cannot direct the police or other investigators.

3.3 Prosecutors should identify and, where possible, seek to rectify evidential weaknesses, but, subject to the threshold test (see section 5), they should swiftly stop cases which do not meet the evidential stage of the full code test (see section 4) and which cannot be strengthened by further investigation, or where the public interest clearly does not require a prosecution (see section 4). Although prosecutors primarily consider the evidence and information supplied by the police and other investigators, the suspect or those acting on his or her behalf may also submit evidence or information to the prosecutor via the police or other investigators, prior to charge, to help inform the prosecutor's decision.

3.4 Prosecutors must only start or continue a prosecution when the case has passed both stages of the full code test (see section 4). The exception is when the threshold test (see section 5) may be applied where it is proposed to apply to the court to keep the suspect in custody after charge, and the evidence required to apply the full code test is not yet available.

3.5 Prosecutors should not start or continue a prosecution which would be regarded by the courts as oppressive or unfair and an abuse of the court's process.

3.6 Prosecutors review every case they receive from the police or other investigators. Review is a continuing process and prosecutors must take account of any change in circumstances that occurs as the case develops, including what becomes known of the defence case. Wherever possible, they should talk to the investigator when thinking about changing the charges or stopping the case. Prosecutors and investigators work closely together, but the final responsibility for the decision whether or not a case should go ahead rests with the CPS.

3.7 Parliament has decided that a limited number of offences should only be taken to court with the agreement of the DPP. These are called consent cases. In such cases the DPP, or prosecutors acting on his or her behalf, apply the code in deciding whether to give consent to a prosecution. There are also certain offences that should only be taken to court with the consent of the Attorney-General. Prosecutors must follow current guidance when referring any such cases to the Attorney-General. Additionally, the Attorney-General will be kept informed of certain cases as part of his or her superintendence of the CPS and accountability to Parliament for its actions.

4. THE FULL CODE TEST

E-5

4.1 The full code test has two stages: (i) the evidential stage; followed by (ii) the public interest stage.

4.2 In most cases, prosecutors should only decide whether to prosecute after the investigation has been completed and after all the available evidence has been reviewed. However there will be cases where it is clear, prior to the collection and consideration of all the likely evidence, that the public interest does not require a prosecution. In these instances, prosecutors may decide that the case should not proceed further.

4.3 Prosecutors should only take such a decision when they are satisfied that the broad extent of the criminality has been determined and that they are able to make a fully informed assessment of the public interest. If prosecutors do not have sufficient information to take such a decision, the investigation should proceed and a decision taken later in accordance with the full code test set out in this section.

The evidential stage

4.4 Prosecutors must be satisfied that there is sufficient evidence to provide a realistic prospect of **E-6** conviction against each suspect on each charge. They must consider what the defence case may be, and how it is likely to affect the prospects of conviction. A case which does not pass the evidential stage must not proceed, no matter how serious or sensitive it may be.

4.5 The finding that there is a realistic prospect of conviction is based on the prosecutor's objective assessment of the evidence, including the impact of any defence and any other information that the suspect has put forward or on which he or she might rely. It means that an objective, impartial and reasonable jury or bench of magistrates or judge hearing a case alone, properly directed and acting in accordance with the law, is more likely than not to convict the defendant of the charge alleged. This is a different test from the one that the criminal courts themselves must apply. A court may only convict if it is sure that the defendant is guilty.

4.6 When deciding whether there is sufficient evidence to prosecute, prosecutors should ask themselves the following:

Can the evidence be used in court?

Prosecutors should consider whether there is any question over the admissibility of certain evidence. In doing so, prosecutors should assess:

    (a) the likelihood of that evidence being held as inadmissible by the court; and

    (b) the importance of that evidence in relation to the evidence as a whole.

Is the evidence reliable?

Prosecutors should consider whether there are any reasons to question the reliability of the evidence, including its accuracy or integrity.

Is the evidence credible?

Prosecutors should consider whether there are any reasons to doubt the credibility of the evidence.

The public interest stage

4.7 In every case where there is sufficient evidence to justify a prosecution, prosecutors must go **E-7** on to consider whether a prosecution is required in the public interest.

4.8 It has never been the rule that a prosecution will automatically take place once the evidential stage is met. A prosecution will usually take place unless the prosecutor is satisfied that there are public interest factors tending against prosecution which outweigh those tending in favour. In some cases the prosecutor may be satisfied that the public interest can be properly served by offering the offender the opportunity to have the matter dealt with by an out-of-court disposal rather than bringing a prosecution.

4.9 When deciding the public interest, prosecutors should consider each of the questions set out below in paragraphs 4.12(a) to (g) so as to identify and determine the relevant public interest factors tending for and against prosecution. These factors, together with any public interest factors set out in relevant guidance or policy issued by the DPP, should enable prosecutors to form an overall assessment of the public interest.

4.10 The explanatory text below each question in paragraphs 4.12(a) to (g) provides guidance to prosecutors when addressing each particular question and determining whether it identifies public interest factors for or against prosecution. The questions identified are not exhaustive, and not all the questions may be relevant in every case. The weight to be attached to each of the questions, and the factors identified, will also vary according to the facts and merits of each case.

4.11 It is quite possible that one public interest factor alone may outweigh a number of other factors which tend in the opposite direction. Although there may be public interest factors tending against prosecution in a particular case, prosecutors should consider whether nonetheless a prosecution should go ahead and those factors put to the court for consideration when sentence is passed.

4.12 Prosecutors should consider each of the following questions:

(a) *How serious is the offence committed?*

The more serious the offence, the more likely it is that a prosecution is required. When deciding the level of seriousness of the offence committed, prosecutors should include amongst the factors for consideration the suspect's culpability and the harm to the victim by asking themselves the questions at (b) and (c).

(b) *What is the level of culpability of the suspect?*

The greater the suspect's level of culpability, the more likely it is that a prosecution is required. Culpability is likely to be determined by the suspect's level of involvement; the extent to which the offending was premeditated and/or planned; whether they have previous criminal convictions and/or out-of-court disposals and any offending whilst on bail or whilst subject to a court order; whether the offending was or is likely to be continued, repeated or escalated; and the suspect's age or maturity (see paragraph (d) below for suspects under 18). Prosecutors should also have regard when considering culpability as to whether the suspect is, or was at the time of the offence, suffering from any significant mental or physical ill-health as in some circumstances this may mean that it is less likely that a prosecution is required. However, prosecutors will also need to consider how serious the offence was, whether it is likely to be repeated and the need to safeguard the public or those providing care to such persons.

(c) *What are the circumstances of and the harm caused to the victim?*

The circumstances of the victim are highly relevant. The greater the vulnerability of the victim, the more likely it is that a prosecution is required. This includes where a position of trust or authority exists between the suspect and victim. A prosecution is also more likely if the offence has been committed against a victim who was at the time a person serving the public. Prosecutors must also have regard to whether the offence was motivated by any form of discrimination against the victim's ethnic or national origin, gender, disability, age, religion or belief, sexual orientation or gender identity; or the suspect demonstrated hostility towards the victim based on any of those characteristics. The presence of any such motivation or hostility will mean that it is more likely that prosecution is required. In deciding whether a prosecution is required in the public interest, prosecutors should take into account the views expressed by the victim about the impact that the offence has had. In appropriate cases, this may also include the views of the victim's family. Prosecutors also need to consider if a prosecution is likely to have an adverse effect on the victim's physical or mental health, always bearing in mind the seriousness of the offence. If there is evidence that prosecution is likely to have an adverse impact on the victim's health it may make a prosecution less likely, taking into account the victim's views. However, the CPS does not act for victims or their families in the same way as solicitors act for their clients, and prosecutors must form an overall view of the public interest.

(d) *Was the suspect under the age of 18 at the time of the offence?*

The criminal justice system treats children and young people differently from adults and significant weight must be attached to the age of the suspect if they are a child or young person under 18. The best interests and welfare of the child or young person must be considered including whether a prosecution is likely to have an adverse impact on his or her future prospects that is disproportionate to the seriousness of the offending. Prosecutors must have regard to the principal aim of the youth justice system which is to prevent offending by children and young people. Prosecutors must also have regard to the obligations arising under the United Nations 1989 Convention on the Rights of the Child. As a starting point, the younger the suspect, the less likely it is that a prosecution is required. However, there may be circumstances which mean that notwithstanding the fact that the suspect is under 18, a prosecution is in the public interest. These include where the offence committed is serious, where the suspect's past record suggests that there are no suitable alternatives to prosecution, or where the absence of an admission means that out-of-court disposals which might have addressed the offending behaviour are not available.

(e) *What is the impact on the community?*

The greater the impact of the offending on the community, the more likely it is that a prosecution is required. In considering this question, prosecutors should have regard to how community is an inclusive term and is not restricted to communities defined by location.

(f) *Is prosecution a proportionate response?*

Prosecutors should also consider whether prosecution is proportionate to the likely outcome, and in so doing the following may be relevant to the case under consideration:

- the cost to the CPS and the wider criminal justice system, especially where it could be regarded as excessive when weighed against any likely penalty (prosecutors should not decide the public interest on the basis of this factor alone; it is essential that regard is also given to the public interest factors identified when considering the other questions in paragraphs 4.12(a) to (g), but cost is a relevant factor when making an overall assessment of the public interest);
- cases should be capable of being prosecuted in a way that is consistent with principles of effective case management; for example, in a case involving multiple suspects, prosecution might be reserved for the main participants in order to avoid excessively long and complex proceedings.

(g) *Do sources of information require protecting?*

In cases where public interest immunity does not apply, special care should be taken when proceeding with a prosecution where details may need to be made public that could harm sources of information, international relations or national security. It is essential that such cases are kept under continuing review.

5. The Threshold Test

5.1 The threshold test may only be applied where the suspect presents a substantial bail risk and **E-8** not all the evidence is available at the time when he or she must be released from custody unless charged.

When the threshold test may be applied

5.2 Prosecutors must determine whether the following conditions are met: **E-8a**
- (a) there is insufficient evidence currently available to apply the evidential stage of the full code test; and
- (b) there are reasonable grounds for believing that further evidence will become available within a reasonable period; and
- (c) the seriousness or the circumstances of the case justifies the making of an immediate charging decision; and
- (d) there are continuing substantial grounds to object to bail in accordance with the Bail Act 1976 and in all the circumstances of the case it is proper to do so.

5.3 Where any of the above conditions is not met, the threshold test cannot be applied and the suspect cannot be charged. The custody officer must determine whether the person may continue to be detained or be released on bail, with or without conditions.

5.4 There are two parts to the evidential consideration of the threshold test.

The first part of the threshold test—is there reasonable suspicion?

5.5 Prosecutors must be satisfied that there is at least a reasonable suspicion that the person to be charged has committed the offence.

5.6 In determining this, prosecutors must consider the evidence then available. This may take the form of witness statements, material or other information, provided the prosecutor is satisfied that:
- (a) it is relevant; and
- (b) it is capable of being put into an admissible format for presentation in court; and
- (c) it would be used in the case.

5.7 If satisfied on this the prosecutor should then consider the second part of the threshold test.

The second part of the threshold test – can further evidence be gathered to provide a realistic prospect of conviction?

5.8 Prosecutors must be satisfied that there are reasonable grounds for believing that the continuing investigation will provide further evidence, within a reasonable period of time, so that all the evidence together is capable of establishing a realistic prospect of conviction in accordance with the full code test.

5.9 The further evidence must be identifiable and not merely speculative.

5.10 In reaching this decision prosecutors must consider:
- (a) the nature, extent and admissibility of any likely further evidence and the impact it will have on the case;
- (b) the charges that all the evidence will support;
- (c) the reasons why the evidence is not already available;

(d) the time required to obtain the further evidence and whether any consequential delay is reasonable in all the circumstances.

5.11 If both parts of the threshold test are satisfied, prosecutors must apply the public interest stage of the full code test based on the information available at that time.

Reviewing the threshold test

E-9   5.12 A decision to charge under the threshold test must be kept under review. The evidence must be regularly assessed to ensure that the charge is still appropriate and that continued objection to bail is justified. The full code test must be applied as soon as is reasonably practicable and in any event before the expiry of any applicable custody time limit.

6. SELECTION OF CHARGES

E-10   6.1 Prosecutors should select charges which:
  (a) reflect the seriousness and extent of the offending supported by the evidence;
  (b) give the court adequate powers to sentence and impose appropriate post-conviction orders; and
  (c) enable the case to be presented in a clear and simple way.

6.2 This means that prosecutors may not always choose or continue with the most serious charge where there is a choice.

6.3 Prosecutors should never go ahead with more charges than are necessary just to encourage a defendant to plead guilty to a few. In the same way, they should never go ahead with a more serious charge just to encourage a defendant to plead guilty to a less serious one.

6.4 Prosecutors should not change the charge simply because of the decision made by the court or the defendant about where the case will be heard.

6.5 Prosecutors must take account of any relevant change in circumstances as the case progresses after charge.

7. OUT-OF-COURT DISPOSALS

E-11   7.1 An out-of-court disposal may take the place of a prosecution in court if it is an appropriate response to the offender and/or the seriousness and consequences of the offending.

7.2 Prosecutors must follow any relevant guidance when asked to advise on or authorise a simple caution, a conditional caution, any appropriate regulatory proceedings, a punitive or civil penalty, or other disposal. They should ensure that the appropriate evidential standard for the specific out-of-court disposal is met including, where required, a clear admission of guilt, and that the public interest would be properly served by such a disposal.

8. MODE OF TRIAL

E-12   8.1 Prosecutors must have regard to the current guidelines on sentencing and allocation when making submissions to the magistrates' court about where the defendant should be tried.

8.2 Speed must never be the only reason for asking for a case to stay in the magistrates' court. But prosecutors should consider the effect of any likely delay if a case is sent to the Crown Court, and the possible effect on any victim or witness if the case is delayed.

Venue for trial in cases involving youths

8.3 Prosecutors must bear in mind that youths should be tried in the youth court wherever possible. It is the court which is best designed to meet their specific needs. A trial of a youth in the Crown Court should be reserved for the most serious cases or where the interests of justice require a youth to be jointly tried with an adult.

9. ACCEPTING GUILTY PLEAS

E-12a   9.1 Defendants may want to plead guilty to some, but not all, of the charges. Alternatively, they may want to plead guilty to a different, possibly less serious, charge because they are admitting only part of the crime.

9.2 Prosecutors should only accept the defendant's plea if they think the court is able to pass a sentence that matches the seriousness of the offending, particularly where there are aggravating features. Prosecutors must never accept a guilty plea just because it is convenient.

9.3 In considering whether the pleas offered are acceptable, prosecutors should ensure that the interests and, where possible, the views of the victim, or in appropriate cases the views of the victim's family, are taken into account when deciding whether it is in the public interest to accept the plea. However, the decision rests with the prosecutor.

9.4 It must be made clear to the court on what basis any plea is advanced and accepted. In cases where a defendant pleads guilty to the charges but on the basis of facts that are different from the prosecution case, and where this may significantly affect sentence, the court should be invited to hear evidence to determine what happened, and then sentence on that basis.

9.5 Where a defendant has previously indicated that he or she will ask the court to take an offence into consideration when sentencing, but then declines to admit that offence at court, prosecutors will consider whether a prosecution is required for that offence. Prosecutors should explain to the defence advocate and the court that the prosecution of that offence may be subject to further review, in consultation with the police or other investigators wherever possible.

9.6 Particular care must be taken when considering pleas which would enable the defendant to avoid the imposition of a mandatory minimum sentence. When pleas are offered, prosecutors must also bear in mind the fact that ancillary orders can be made with some offences but not with others.

10. Reconsidering a Prosecution Decision

10.1 People should be able to rely on decisions taken by the CPS. Normally, if the CPS tells a **E-12b** suspect or defendant that there will not be a prosecution, or that the prosecution has been stopped, the case will not start again. But occasionally there are reasons why the CPS will overturn a decision not to prosecute or to deal with the case by way of an out-of-court disposal or when it will restart the prosecution, particularly if the case is serious.

10.2 These reasons include:

(a) cases where a new look at the original decision shows that it was wrong and, in order to maintain confidence in the criminal justice system, a prosecution should be brought despite the earlier decision;

(b) cases which are stopped so that more evidence which is likely to become available in the fairly near future can be collected and prepared; in these cases, the prosecutor will tell the defendant that the prosecution may well start again;

(c) cases which are stopped because of a lack of evidence but where more significant evidence is discovered later; and

(d) cases involving a death in which a review following the findings of an inquest concludes that a prosecution should be brought, notwithstanding any earlier decision not to prosecute.

© Crown Copyright 2013

C. Authorities

Charging of youths

Whereas the code for crown prosecutors requires consideration to be given to the interests of a **E-12c** child or young person when deciding whether it is in the public interest to prosecute (see now para. 4.12(d), *ante*, E-7), there is no requirement that a crown prosecutor should obtain a risk assessment from the youth offending services or that he should contact the potential defendant's school: *R. (A.) v. South Yorkshire Police and CPS*, 171 J.P. 465, DC.

In *D. and B. v. Commr of Police for the Metropolis, CPS, Croydon JJ.* [2008] A.C.D. 47, DC, it was held that it was permissible for a crown prosecutor to decide that the combination of the seriousness of an offence and the public interest warranted prosecution, despite the fact that the particular circumstances of the offence would normally, in accordance with the guidance issued under section 65 of the CDA 1998, be such as to justify only a final warning.

Charging victims of human trafficking

What follows will have to be considered in the light of the defence provided by section 45 of **E-12d** the Modern Slavery Act 2015 (§ 19-464 in the main work).

Where it is possible that a defendant or potential defendant is a victim of human trafficking, a prosecutor should take cognisance of the CPS guidance on (i) the prosecution of defendants charged with immigration offences who might be victims of trafficking, and (ii) the prosecution of young offenders charged with offences who might be such victims; in particular, under (i), when deciding whether to prosecute, or to continue to prosecute, a "credible trafficked victim" for immigration offences, prosecutors should consider whether this would serve the public interest; and under (ii), a case should be discontinued on evidential grounds where there is clear evidence that a youth has a credible defence of duress, but, if the evidence is less certain, further details should be sought from the police and youth offender teams; the defence, on the other hand, should make inquiries wherever there is credible material showing that the defendant might have been a trafficked victim, especially if the client is young; as a signatory to the Council of Europe Convention on Action against Trafficking in Human Beings, the United Kingdom is required to identify and protect victims of trafficking, and, whereas the CPS guidance supports the purpose of the convention, a trial which had failed to have proper regard to it was not fair, either under the principles of the common law or under the principles enshrined in the ECHR: *R. v. O.*, *The Times*, October 2, 2008, CA ([2008] EWCA Crim. 2835).

R. v. O. and the issues arising from it were further considered in *R. v. M. (L.)*, *B. (M.) and G. (D.)*; *R. v. Tabot*; *R. v. Tijani* [2011] 1 Cr.App.R. 12, CA. It was held that one way in which the duty under Article 26 of the Council of Europe Convention (to avoid the imposition of penalties on victims of human trafficking for their involvement in unlawful activities to the extent that they were compelled to become so involved) is met in England and Wales, is by means of the guidance given to prosecutors considering whether charges should be brought against those who are or may be victims of trafficking (the court pointed out that whilst the guidance is now set out in the context of immigration offences only, it should be taken to apply whatever the nature of the allegation). The effect of the CPS's guidance, according to the court, is to require of prosecutors a three-stage exercise, asking, first, whether there is reason to believe that the person has been trafficked, secondly, whether there is clear evidence of a common law defence (in which case, any proceedings will be discontinued on evidential grounds) and, thirdly, where there is no such evidence, but the offence may have been committed as a result of compulsion arising from the trafficking, whether the public interest requires a prosecution. It was said that Article 26 does not require a blanket immunity from prosecution for trafficked victims, and that there will normally be no reason not to prosecute a victim of trafficking if the offence appears to have been committed out-with any reasonable nexus of compulsion occasioned by the trafficking. The court said that material considerations for the prosecutor when deciding whether to pursue a prosecution will be the gravity of the offence, the degree of continuing compulsion and the alternatives reasonably available to the defendant. As to this case, see also § 17-119 in the main work.

R. v. O. and *R. v. M. (L.)*, *B. (M.) and G. (D.)*; *R. v. Tabot*; *R. v. Tijani* were further considered in *R. v. N. (A.)*; *R. v. Le* [2012] 1 Cr.App.R. 35, CA. It was held that: (i) implementation of Article 26 is normally achieved by the proper exercise of the prosecutorial discretion which enables the Crown, however strong the evidence, to decide that it would be inappropriate to prosecute, or to continue with the prosecution of, a defendant who is unable to advance duress as a defence, but who falls within the protective ambit of that article; this requires a judgment to be made in the light of all the available evidence; the responsibility is not that of the court but of the prosecution; but the court may intervene if its process is abused by using the "ultimate sanction" of a stay; the burden of establishing an improper exercise of the discretion rests on the defendant; that the context is the United Kingdom's convention obligation does not involve the creation of any new principles; apart from the specific jurisdiction to stay proceedings, the court may also, in the exercise of its sentencing responsibilities, implement Article 26 in the language of the article itself, by discharging the defendant absolutely or conditionally; (ii) the only publication likely to be relevant to an inquiry into an alleged abuse is the CPS's guidance on human trafficking and smuggling as it was in force at the time when the relevant decisions were made; unless it is to be argued that the guidance itself is open to question because it has failed to keep itself regularly updated in light of developing knowledge, for the purposes of the court considering an alleged abuse for which the prosecution are responsible, it is that guidance that should be the starting, and in the overwhelming majority of cases, the finishing point; (iii) expert evidence is unlikely to assist on the issue of the correctness of the decision to prosecute; (iv) a defendant has one opportunity to give his instructions to his legal advisers; it is only most exceptionally that the court would, on appeal, consider it appropriate to allow a defendant to advance fresh instructions about the facts; and there is no special category of exceptionality in the context of Article 26; and (v) an abuse argument founded on the convention that is advanced long after conviction is most unlikely to succeed on the basis that subsequent events show that, if the decision whether to prosecute were to be taken now, the result might have been different from the decision actually taken in the light of the standards and guidance existing at the time it was taken.

These issues were further considered in *R. v. L. (C.)*; *R. v. N. (H.V.)*; *R. v. N. (T.H.)*; *R. v. T. (H.D.) (Children's Commr for England and Equality and Human Rights Commission Intervening)* [2013] 2 Cr.App.R. 23, CA. It was held that: (i) whereas Article 8 of European Parliament and Council Directive 2011/36/EU obliges member states to "take the necessary measures to ensure that competent national authorities are entitled not to prosecute or impose penalties on victims of trafficking ... for their involvement in criminal activities which they have been compelled to commit as a direct consequence of being subjected" to trafficking, the courts will give effect to this obligation by reviewing decisions to prosecute, staying inappropriate prosecutions and discharging defendants where prosecution was appropriate but punishment inappropriate; as to the review of the decision to prosecute, this is no mere *Wednesbury* review (*Associated Picture Houses Ltd v. Wednesbury Corporation* [1948] 1 K.B. 223, CA); the court must reach its own conclusion on the evidence presented to it; (ii) if it is found that the defendant is a victim of trafficking, the next question is the extent to which the offences with which he is charged were integral to, or consequent on, the exploitation of which he was the victim; in some cases the facts will show that he was under levels of compulsion that mean that, in reality, culpability was extinguished; if so, a stay is likely to be granted; in other cases, more likely in the case of a defendant who is no longer a child (18 plus), culpability may be diminished but nevertheless be significant; for these individuals, prosecution may well be appropriate, with due allowance to be made in any sentencing decision for their diminished culpability; in yet other cases, the fact that the defendant was a victim of trafficking will provide no more than a colourable excuse for criminality that is unconnected to and does not arise from their victimisation; (iii) as to the question whether the defendant was indeed a victim of trafficking, where there has been a referral to one of the two competent authorities (the U.K. Border Agency and the U.K. Human Tracking Centre), if their conclusion is that the defendant is a victim of trafficking, the court is likely to adopt that view although it is not bound by it, as it is the court that has the ultimate responsibility for making the decision with all the relevant evidence bearing on the issues of trafficking, exploitation, age and culpability being addressed; while there is no obligation to seek assistance from experts in the field, the court may adjourn for further information on the subject, and indeed may require the assistance of various authorities; and (iv) where the defendant is under 18, his best interests are not the only consideration, but they are a primary consideration; and where there is any doubt about whether or not the defendant is under that age, "due inquiry" must be made (CYPA 1933, s.99(1) (§ 19-412 in the main work)); this requires much more than superficial observation of the defendant in the dock; the court must be provided with all the relevant evidence that bears on the issue of age; if, at the end of the inquiry, his age remains in doubt and there are reasons to believe that he is under the age of 18, he must be presumed to be under that age.

The full code test/evidential stage

When applying the "realistic prospect of conviction" test, a prosecutor should adopt a "merits based" approach, imagining himself to be the fact finder and asking himself, whether, on balance, the evidence is sufficient to merit a conviction, taking into account what he knows about the defence case, rather than a predictive "bookmaker's" approach, based on past experience of similar cases; questions of how a jury are likely to see a case are not relevant at this stage but at a later stage, under the public interest test in paragraphs 5.6 to 5.13 of the code: *R. (F.B.) v. DPP* [2009] 1 Cr.App.R. 38, DC. As to this case, see also §§ 1-337, 16-48 in the main work.

E-12e

II. LEGAL GUIDANCE AND CHARGING STANDARDS

Apart from the code for crown prosecutors, the CPS has prepared legal guidance to prosecutors and caseworkers in relation to many criminal offences and procedural issues. It has never been suggested that such guidance has the force of law, or even parity of standing with the code. It is merely, in the words of the CPS website (where it is available to the public), "an aid to guide crown prosecutors and associate prosecutors in the use of their discretion in making decisions in cases", which "does not create any rights enforceable at law, in any legal proceedings", and is subject to the principles as set out in the code for crown prosecutors.

E-13

Incorporated within the guidance are various "charging standards" for various offences or groups of offences, such as offences against the person, driving offences, drug offences, public

E-14

order offences and theft. They contain a mixture of propositions of law (as to the ingredients of the various offences, maximum penalties, available alternative verdicts, etc.) and guidance as to the various factors that should be taken into consideration in deciding which offence to charge. The standards emphasise that they:

(a) are not to be used in the determination of any pre-charge decision, such as the decision to arrest;

(b) do not override any guidance issued on the use of appropriate alternative forms of disposal short of charge, such as cautioning;

(c) do not override the principles set out in the code for crown prosecutors;

(d) do not override the need for consideration to be given in every case as to whether a charge or prosecution is in the public interest;

(e) do not override particular policy guidance involving hate crimes; and

(f) do not remove the need for each case to be considered on its individual merits or fetter the discretion of the police to charge and the CPS to prosecute the most appropriate of-fence depending on the particular facts of the case in question.

The following recitation of general charging principles is common to all the standards:

(a) the charge or charges preferred should accurately reflect the extent of the defendant's involvement and responsibility, thereby allowing the courts the discretion to sentence appropriately;

(b) the choice of charges should ensure the clear and simple presentation of the case, particularly where there is more than one defendant;

(c) it is wrong to encourage a defendant to plead guilty to a few charges by selecting more charges than are necessary;

(d) it is wrong to select a more serious charge which is not supported by the evidence in order to encourage a plea of guilty to a lesser allegation.

III. THE ROLE AND RESPONSIBILITIES OF THE PROSECUTION ADVOCATE

Foreword

E-15   The prosecution advocate plays an important public role and as such may be considered a cornerstone of an open and fair criminal justice system. The principles so well articulated by Farquharson L.J. and his committee as to the role of the prosecution advocate have served us well since they were published in 1986. However, the time has come for new guidance which, whilst building on the established principles, reflects the changes that have occurred in the criminal courts, at the Bar and within the Crown Prosecution Service over recent years.

I welcome and commend the new Guidelines which, whilst not legally binding unless expressly approved by the Court of Appeal, nonetheless provide important practical guidance for practitioners involved in the prosecution process.

Lord Woolf C.J.

Introduction

E-16   The work undertaken in 1986 by the committee chaired by Farquharson L.J. has, for over 15 years, provided valuable guidance as to role [*sic*] of the prosecution advocate and their relationship with the Crown Prosecution Service (CPS).

However, the ever-evolving criminal justice system, changes at the Bar and developments in the CPS brought about by the implementation of Sir Iain Glidewell's Review, mean that the environment in which we all operate has radically changed since the original report was published.

Whilst the principles established by Farquharson L.J.'s committee have been enormously helpful and will continue to apply, the time has come for new guidance that reflects the changes and emphasises the new relationship that is developing between CPS Areas and the local Bar.

The new Guidelines have therefore been developed to take account of the changes and are the result of the Bar and CPS working in partnership and in consultation with the judiciary, Bar Council and Law Society.

We commend the Guidelines as providing valuable guidance and a framework within which the Bar and the CPS can work effectively together.

Lord Goldsmith Q.C., Attorney General

David Calvert-Smith Q.C., Director of Public Prosecutions

1. Pre-trial preparation

Farquharson

(a) *It is the duty of prosecution counsel to read the Instructions delivered to him expeditiously and to advise or* **E-17** *confer with those instructing him on all aspects of the case well before its commencement.*

1.1 The Crown Prosecution Service (CPS) will deliver instructions at a stage in the proceedings **E-18** that allows sufficient time for the prosecution advocate adequately to consider, prepare and advise on the evidence before the court hearing or draft/agree the indictment.

1.2 Where a CPS higher court advocate represents the prosecution at a Plea and Directions Hearing (PDH), the CPS will deliver instructions to the trial advocate no later than 10 working days after the date of the PDH.

1.3 The CPS will deliver instructions which:

    i. address the issues in the case including any strategic decisions that have been or may need to be made;

    ii. identify relevant case law;

    iii. explain the basis and rationale of any decision made in relation to the disclosure of unused material;

    iv. where practical, provide specific guidance or indicate parameters on acceptable plea(s); and

    v. where a case is an appeal either to the Crown Court from the magistrates' court or is before the Court of Appeal, Divisional Court or House of Lords, address the issues raised in the notice of appeal, case stated, application for judicial review or petition.

Action on receipt of instructions

1.4 On receipt of instructions the prosecution advocate will consider the papers and advise the **E-19** CPS, ordinarily in writing, or orally in cases of urgency where:

    i. the prosecution advocate forms a different view to that expressed by the CPS (or where applicable a previous prosecution advocate) on acceptability of plea;

    ii. the indictment as preferred requires amendment;

    iii. additional evidence is required;

    iv. there is an evidential deficiency (which cannot be addressed by the obtaining of further evidence) and, applying the Code for Crown Prosecutors, there is no longer a realistic prospect of conviction; or the prosecution advocate believes that it is not in the public interest to continue the prosecution;

    v. in order to expedite and simplify proceedings certain formal admissions should be made;

    vi. the prosecution advocate, having reviewed previous disclosure decisions, disagrees with a decision that has been made; or is not satisfied that he or she is in possession of all relevant documentation; or considers that he or she has not been fully instructed regarding disclosure matters;

    vii. a case conference is required (particularly where there is a sensitive issue, *e.g.* informant/ PII/ disclosure etc);

    viii. the presentation of the case to the court requires special preparation of material for the jury or presentational aids.

1.5 The prosecution advocate will endeavour to respond within five working days of receiving **E-20** instructions, or within such period as may be specified or agreed where the case is substantial or the issues complex.

1.6 Where the prosecution advocate is to advise on a specific aspect of the case other than 1.4 (i-viii), the advocate should contact the CPS and agree a realistic timescale within which advice is to be provided.

1.7 The prosecution advocate will inform the CPS without delay where the advocate is unlikely to be available to undertake the prosecution or advise within the relevant timescale.

1.8 When returning a brief, the advocate originally instructed must ensure that the case is in good order and should discuss outstanding issues or potential difficulties with the advocate receiving the brief. Where the newly instructed advocate disagrees with a decision or opinion reached by the original advocate, the CPS should be informed so that the matter can be discussed.

Case summaries

E-21

1.9 When a draft case summary is prepared by the CPS, the prosecution advocate will consider the summary and either agree the contents or advise the CPS of any proposed amendment.

1.10 In cases where the prosecution advocate is instructed to settle the case summary or schedules, the document(s) will be prepared and submitted to the CPS without delay.

Case management plan

E-22

1.11 On receipt of a case management plan the prosecution advocate, having considered the papers, will contact the Crown Prosecutor within seven days, or such period as may be specified or agreed where the case is substantial or the issues complex, to discuss and agree the plan. The plan will be maintained and regularly reviewed to reflect the progress of the case.

Keeping the prosecution advocate informed

E-23

1.12 The CPS will inform the prosecution advocate of developments in the case without delay and, where a decision is required which may materially affect the conduct and presentation of the case, will consult with the prosecution advocate prior to that decision.

1.3 Where the CPS is advised by the defence of a plea(s) of guilty or there are developments which suggest that offering no evidence on an indictment or count therein is an appropriate course, the matter should always be discussed with the prosecution advocate without delay unless to do so would be wholly impracticable.

Victims and witnesses

E-24

1.14 When a decision whether or not to prosecute is based on the public interest, the CPS will always consider the consequences of that decision for the victim and will take into account any views expressed by the victim or the victim's family.

1.15 The prosecution advocate will follow agreed procedures and guidance on the care and treatment of victims and witnesses, particularly those who may be vulnerable or have special needs.

Appeals

E-25

1.16 Where the prosecution advocate forms a different view to that expressed by the CPS on the conduct/approach to the appeal, the advocate should advise the CPS within FIVE working days of receiving instructions or such period as may be specified or agreed where the case is substantial or the issues complex.

PDH and other preliminary hearings

E-26

1.17 The principles and procedures applying to trials as set out in the following paragraphs will be equally applicable where the prosecution advocate is conducting a PDH or other preliminary hearing.

2. Withdrawal of instructions

Farquharson

E-27

(b) *A solicitor who has briefed counsel to prosecute may withdraw his instructions before the commencement of the trial up to the point when it becomes impracticable to do so, if he disagrees with the advice given by Counsel or for any other proper professional reason.*

2.1 The CPS will consult and take all reasonable steps to resolve any issue or disagreement and will only consider withdrawing instructions from a prosecution advocate as a last resort.

2.2 If the prosecution advocate disagrees with any part of his or her instructions the advocate should contact the responsible Crown Prosecutor to discuss the matter. Until the disagreement has been resolved the matter will remain confidential and must not be discussed by the prosecution advocate with any other party to the proceedings.

"Proper professional reason"

E-28

2.3 The prosecution advocate will keep the CPS informed of any personal concerns, reservations or ethical issues that the advocate considers have the potential to lead to possible conflict with his or her instructions.

2.4 Where the CPS identifies the potential for professional embarrassment or has concerns about the prosecution advocate's ability or experience to present the case effectively to the court, the CPS reserves the right to withdraw instructions.

Timing

2.5 It is often difficult to define when, in the course of a prosecution it becomes impracticable to **E-29** withdraw instructions as circumstances will vary according to the case. The nature of the case, its complexity, witness availability and the view of the court will often be factors that will influence the decision.

2.6 In the majority of prosecutions it will not be practicable to withdraw instructions once the judge has called the case before the court as a preliminary step to the swearing of the jury.

2.7 If instructions are withdrawn, the prosecution advocate will be informed in writing and reasons will be given.

2.8 Instructions may only be withdrawn by or with the consent of the Chief Crown Prosecutor, Assistant Chief Crown Prosecutor, Head of a CPS Trials Unit or, in appropriate cases, Head of a CPS Criminal Justice Unit.

2.9 In relation to cases prosecuted by the CPS Casework Directorate, the decision may only be taken by the Director Casework or Head of Division.

3. Presentation and conduct

Farquharson

(c) *While he remains instructed it is for counsel to take all necessary decisions in the presentation and general* **E-30** *conduct of the prosecution.*

3.1 The statement at 3(c) applies when the prosecution advocate is conducting the trial, PDH or any other preliminary hearing, but is subject to the principles and procedures relating to matters of policy set out in section 4 below.

Disclosure of material

3.2 Until the conclusion of the trial the prosecution advocate and CPS have a continuing duty to **E-31** keep under review decisions regarding disclosure. The prosecution advocate should in every case specifically consider whether he or she can satisfactorily discharge the duty of continuing review on the basis of the material supplied already, or whether it is necessary to inspect further material or to reconsider material already inspected.

3.3 Disclosure of material must always follow the established law and procedure. Unless consultation is impracticable or cannot be achieved without a delay to the hearing, it is desirable that the CPS, and where appropriate the disclosure officer are consulted over disclosure decisions.

4. Policy decisions

Farquharson

(d) *Where matters of policy[1] fall to be decided after the point indicated in (b) above (including offering no* **E-32** *evidence on the indictment or on a particular count, or on the acceptance of pleas to lesser counts), it is the duty of Counsel to consult his Instructing Solicitor/Crown Prosecutor whose views at this stage are of crucial importance.*

(e) *In the rare case where counsel and his instructing solicitor are unable to agree on a matter of policy, it is, subject to (g) below, for prosecution counsel to make the necessary decisions.*

Policy issues arising at trial

4.1 The prosecution advocate should alert the CPS at the first opportunity if a matter of policy is **E-33** likely to arise.

4.2 The prosecution advocate must not give an indication or undertaking which binds the prosecution without first discussing the issue with the CPS.

CPS representation at Crown Court

4.3 Whenever possible, an experienced Crown Prosecutor will be available at the Crown Court to **E-34** discuss and agree any issue involving the conduct or progress of the case.

---

[1] "Policy" decisions should be understood as referring to non-evidential decisions on: the acceptance of pleas of guilty to lesser counts or groups of counts or available alternatives; offering no evidence on particular counts; consideration of a retrial; whether to lodge an appeal; certification of a point of law; and the withdrawal of the prosecution as a whole.

4.4 When it is not possible to provide a Crown Prosecutor at court, an experienced caseworker will attend and facilitate communication between the prosecution advocate and the Crown Prosecutor having responsibility for the case.

4.5 In exceptional circumstances where it is not possible to contact a Crown Prosecutor, the prosecution advocate should ask the court to adjourn the hearing for a realistic period in order to consult with the CPS. Where an adjournment is refused, the prosecution advocate may make the decision but should record his or her reasons in writing.

Referral to senior CPS representative

E-35

4.6 Where an issue remains unresolved following consultation with a Crown Prosecutor; or where the case/issue under consideration is substantial, sensitive or complex; or the prosecution advocate disagrees with the advice of the Crown Prosecutor, the matter may be referred to the Chief Crown Prosecutor, the Director Casework or to a senior Crown Prosecutor with delegated authority to act on their behalf.

4.7 In order to ensure consultation takes place at the highest level appropriate to the circumstances and nature of the case, the court should be asked to adjourn if necessary. When an adjournment is sought, the facts leading to the application should be placed before the court only in so far as they are relevant to that application.

4.8 Where a Chief Crown Prosecutor has been directly involved in the decision making process and the issue remains unresolved, the matter may be referred to the Director of Public Prosecutions.

Farquharson

E-36

(f) *Where counsel has taken a decision on a matter of policy with which his Instructing Solicitor has not agreed, then it would be appropriate for the Attorney General to require Counsel to submit to him a written report of all the circumstances, including his reasons for disagreeing with those who instruct him.*

4.9 It will only be in exceptional circumstances that the Attorney General will require a written report. The prosecution advocate will first discuss the decision with the Chief Crown Prosecutor or the Director, Casework. Where, by agreement, the issue remains one that either party considers should be drawn to the attention of the Director of Public Prosecutions the prosecution advocate will, on request, provide a written report for submission to the Director of Public Prosecutions. If he considers it appropriate to do so, the Director of Public Prosecutions may refer the matter to the Attorney General.

4.10 Where there has been a disagreement on a matter of policy, provided that the CPS is satisfied that the prosecution advocate followed the principles set out in this document, the professional codes of conduct and was not *Wednesbury* unreasonable, the CPS will not apply sanctions in respect of any future work solely as a result of the decision in a particular case.

5. Change of advice

Farquharson

E-37

(g) *When counsel has had the opportunity to prepare his brief and to confer with those instructing him, but at the last moment before trial unexpectedly advises that the case should not proceed or that pleas to lesser offences should be accepted, and his Instructing Solicitor does not accept such advice, counsel should apply for an adjournment if instructed so to do.*

E-38

5.1 The CPS and the prosecution advocate should agree a period of adjournment that would allow a newly instructed advocate to prepare for trial. The period should be realistic and acknowledge that in such circumstances a case conference will usually be required.

5.2 The facts leading to the application for the adjournment should be placed before the court only in so far as they are relevant to that application.

6. Prosecution advocate's role in decision making at trial

Farquharson

E-39

(h) *Subject to the above, it is for prosecution counsel to decide whether to offer no evidence on a particular count or on the indictment as a whole and whether to accept pleas to a lesser count or counts.*

6.1 The prosecution advocate may ask the defence advocate as to whether a plea will be forthcoming but at this initial stage should not suggest or indicate a plea that might be considered acceptable to the prosecution before a plea is offered.

6.2 Where the defence advocate subsequently offers details of a plea, the prosecution advocate may discuss the matter with a view to establishing an acceptable plea that reflects the defendant's criminality and provides the court with sufficient powers to sentence appropriately.

Responsibility of prosecution advocate to consult

6.3 Where the prosecution advocate forms the view that the appropriate course is to accept a plea **E-40** before proceedings commence or continue, or to offer no evidence on the indictment or any part of it, the prosecution advocate should:

> i. whenever practicable, speak with the victim or victim's family attending court to explain the position;
>
> ii. ensure that the interests of the victim or any views expressed by the victim or victim's family are taken into account as part of the decision making process; and
>
> iii. keep the victim or victim's family attending court informed and explain decisions as they are made.

6.4 Where appropriate the prosecution advocate may seek an adjournment of the court hearing in order to facilitate discussion with the victim or victim's family.

6.5 The prosecution advocate should always comply with paragraph 6.3 and, where practicable, discuss the matter with the CPS before informing the defence advocate or the court that a plea is acceptable.

6.6 Where the defendant indicates an acceptable plea, unless the issue is simple, the defence should reduce the basis of the plea to writing. The prosecution advocate should show the CPS any written record relating to the plea and agree with the CPS the basis on which the case will be opened to the court.

6.7 It is the responsibility of the prosecution advocate to ensure that the defence advocate is aware of the basis on which the plea is accepted by the prosecution and the way in which the prosecution case will be opened to the court.

6.8 It will not be necessary for the prosecution advocate to consult the CPS where the plea or course of action accords with the written instructions received from the CPS, although paragraph 6.3 may still apply.

Prosecution advocate's role in sentencing

6.9 The prosecution advocate should always draw the court's attention to any matters, including **E-41** aggravating or mitigating features, that might affect sentence. Additionally, the advocate should be in a position to assist the court, if requested, with any statutory provisions or sentencing guidelines and should always draw attention to potential sentencing errors.

6.10 Where a discussion on plea and sentence takes place, the prosecution advocate must adhere to the Attorney General's Guidelines on the Acceptance of Pleas published on 7 December 2000.

7. Seeking judicial approval

Farquharson

(i) *If prosecution counsel invites the Judge to approve the course he is proposing to take, then he must abide by* **E-42** *the judge's decision.*

7.1 A discussion with the judge about the acceptability of a plea or conduct of the case should be held in the presence of the defendant unless exceptional circumstances apply.[2]

7.2 In exceptional circumstances, where the prosecution advocate considers it appropriate to communicate with the judge or seek the judge's view in chambers, the CPS should be consulted before such a step is taken.

7.3 Where discussions take place in chambers it is the responsibility of the prosecution advocate to remind the judge, if necessary, that an independent record must always be kept.

7.4 The prosecution advocate should also make a full note of such an event, recording all decisions and comments. This note should be made available to the CPS.

Farquharson

(j) *If prosecution counsel does not invite the judge's approval of his decision it is open to the judge to express* **E-43**

---

[2] For the purposes of these guidelines, "exceptional circumstances" would include the following:

> (i) Where there is material or information which should not be made public, *e.g.* a police text, or for some other compelling reason such as a defendant or witness suffering, unkown to them, from a serious or terminal illness; or
>
> (ii) There are sensitivities surrounding a prosecution decision or proposed action which need to be explained in chambers with a view to obtaining judicial approval. Such approval may be given in open court where it is necessary to explain a prosecution decision or action in order to maintain public confidence in the criminal justice system.

his dissent with the course proposed and invite counsel to reconsider the matter with those instructing him, but having done so, the final decision remains with counsel.

7.5 Where a judge expresses a view based on the evidence or public interest, the CPS will carry out a further review of the case.

7.6 The prosecution advocate will inform the CPS in a case where the judge has expressed a dissenting view and will agree the action to be taken. Where there is no CPS representative at court, the prosecution advocate will provide a note of the judge's comments.

7.7 The prosecution advocate will ensure that the judge is aware of all factors that have a bearing on the prosecution decision to adopt a particular course. Where there is a difference of opinion between the prosecution advocate and the CPS the judge will be informed as to the nature of the disagreement.

Farquharson

E-44
(k) *In an extreme case where the judge is of the opinion that the course proposed by counsel would lead to serious injustice, he may decline to proceed with the case until counsel has consulted with either the Director or the Attorney General as may be appropriate.*

7.8 As a preliminary step, the prosecution advocate will discuss the judge's observations with the Chief Crown Prosecutor in an attempt to resolve the issue. Where the issue remains unresolved the Director of Public Prosecutions will be consulted. In exceptional circumstances the Director of Public Prosecutions may consult the Attorney General.

E-45
Note: These Guidelines are subject to the Code of Conduct of the Bar of England and Wales (barrister advocates) and The Law Society's The Guide to the Professional Conduct of Solicitors (solicitor advocates). Whilst reference is made in the guidelines to the CPS and levels of authority within the Service, the guidelines may be adopted as best practice, with consequential amendments to levels of authority, by other prosecuting authorities.

These Guidelines may be amended at any time and copyright is waived.

These Guidelines are also available on the CPS Website: www.cps.gov.uk.

APPENDIX F
Interpretation Act 1978

General provisions as to enactment and operation

Words of enactment

1. Every section of an Act takes effect as a substantive enactment without introductory words.   **F-1**

Amendment or repeal in same Session

2. Any Act may be amended or repealed in the Session of Parliament in which it is passed.   **F-2**

Judicial notice

3. Every Act is a public Act to be judicially noticed as such, unless the contrary is expressly   **F-3**
provided by the Act.

Time of commencement

4. An Act or provision of an Act comes into force—   **F-4**

    (a) where provision is made for it to come into force on a particular day, at the beginning of
that day;

    (b) where no provision is made for its coming into force, at the beginning of the day on which
the Act receives the Royal Assent.

Interpretation and construction

Definitions

5. In any Act, unless the contrary intention appears, words and expressions listed in Schedule 1 to   **F-5**
this Act are to be construed according to that Schedule.

Gender and number

6. In any Act, unless the contrary intention appears,—   **F-6**

    (a) words importing the masculine gender include the feminine;

    (b) words importing the feminine gender include the masculine;

    (c) words in the singular include the plural and words in the plural include the singular.

References to service by post

7. Where an Act authorises or requires any document to be served by post (whether the expres-   **F-7**
sion "serve" or the expression "give" or "send" or any other expression is used) then, unless the
contrary intention appears, the service is deemed to be effected by properly addressing, prepaying
and posting a letter containing the document and, unless the contrary is proved, to have been effected at the time at which the letter would be delivered in the ordinary course of post.

References to distance

8. In the measurement of any distance for the purposes of an Act, that distance shall, unless the   **F-8**
contrary intention appears, be measured in a straight line on a horizontal plane.

References to time of day

9. Subject to section 3 of the Summer Time Act 1972 (construction of references to points of time   **F-9**
during the period of summer time), whenever an expression of time occurs in an Act, the time
referred to shall, unless it is otherwise specifically stated, be held to be Greenwich mean time.

References to Sovereign

10. In any Act a reference to the Sovereign reigning at the time of the passing of the Act is to be   **F-10**
construed, unless the contrary intention appears, as a reference to the Sovereign for the time being.

Construction of subordinate legislation

11. Where an Act confers power to make subordinate legislation, expressions used in that legisla-   **F-11**
tion have, unless the contrary intention appears, the meaning which they bear in the Act.

Statutory powers and duties

Continuity of powers and duties

12.—(1) Where an Act confers a power or imposes a duty it is implied, unless the contrary inten-   **F-12**
tion appears, that the power may be exercised, or the duty is to be performed, from time to time as
occasion requires.

(2) Where an Act confers a power or imposes a duty on the holder of an office as such, it is
implied, unless the contrary intention appears, that the power may be exercised, or the duty is to be
performed, by the holder for the time being of the office.

Anticipatory exercise of powers

13. Where an Act which (or any provision of which) does not come into force immediately on its   **F-13**

passing confers power to make subordinate legislation, or to make appointments, give notices, prescribe forms or do any other thing for the purposes of the Act, then, unless the contrary intention appears, the power may be exercised, and any instrument made thereunder may be made so as to come into force, at any time after the passing of the Act so far as may be necessary or expedient for the purpose—

    (a) of bringing the Act or any provision of the Act into force; or

    (b) of giving full effect to that Act or any such provision at or after the time when it comes into force.

Implied power to amend

F-14   **14.** Where an Act confers power to make—

    (a) rules, regulations or byelaws; or

    (b) Orders in Council, orders or other subordinate legislation to be made by statutory instrument,

it implies, unless the contrary intention appears, a power exercisable in the same manner and subject to the same conditions or limitations, to revoke, amend or re-enact any instrument made under the power.

Power to include sunset and review provisions in subordinate legislation

F-14a   **14A.**—(1) This section applies where an Act confers a power or a duty on a person to make subordinate legislation except to the extent that—

    (a) the power or duty is exercisable by the Scottish Ministers, or

    (b) the power or duty is exercisable by any other person within devolved competence (within the meaning of the Scotland Act 1998).

    (2) The subordinate legislation may include—

    (a) provision requiring the person to review the effectiveness of the legislation within a specified period or at the end of a specified period;

    (b) provision for the legislation to cease to have effect at the end of a specified day or a specified period;

    (c) if the power or duty is being exercised to amend other subordinate legislation, provision of the kind mentioned in paragraph (a) or (b) in relation to that other legislation.

    (3) The provision that may be made by virtue of subsection (2)(a) includes provision requiring the person to consider whether the objectives which it was the purpose of the legislation to achieve remain appropriate and, if so, whether they could be achieved in another way.

    (4) Subordinate legislation including provision of a kind mentioned in subsection (2) may make such provision generally or only in relation to specified provisions of the legislation or specified cases or circumstances.

    (5) Subordinate legislation including provision of a kind mentioned in subsection (2) may make transitional, consequential, incidental or supplementary provision or savings in connection with such provision.

    (6) In this section "specified" means specified in the subordinate legislation.

[This section was inserted by the Enterprise and Regulatory Reform Act 2013, s.59(1) and (2).]

Repealing enactments

Repeal of repeal

F-15   **15.** Where an Act repeals a repealing enactment, the repeal does not revive any enactment previously repealed unless words are added reviving it.

General savings

F-16   **16.**—(1) Without prejudice to section 15, where an Act repeals an enactment, the repeal does not, unless the contrary intention appears,—

    (a) revive anything not in force or existing at the time at which the repeal takes effect;

    (b) affect the previous operation of the enactment repealed or anything duly done or suffered under that enactment;

    (c) affect any right, privilege, obligation or liability acquired, accrued or incurred under that enactment;

    (d) affect any penalty, forfeiture or punishment incurred in respect of any offence committed against that enactment;

    (e) affect any investigation, legal proceeding or remedy in respect of any such right, privilege, obligation, liability, penalty, forfeiture or punishment;

and any such investigation, legal proceeding or remedy may be instituted, continued or enforced, and any such penalty, forfeiture or punishment may be imposed, as if the repealing Act had not been passed.

(2) This section applies to the expiry of a temporary enactment as if it were repealed by an Act.

[Considered in *R. v. West London Stipendiary Magistrate, ex p. Simeon* [1983] A.C. 234, HL. See also *Hough v. Windus* (1884) 12 Q.B.D. 224, and *R. v. Fisher (Charles)* [1969] 1 W.L.R. 8, CA.]

Repeal and re-enactment

17.—(1) Where an Act repeals a previous enactment and substitutes provisions for the enactment **F-17** repealed, the repealed enactment remains in force until the substitute provisions come into force.

(2) Where an Act repeals and re-enacts, with or without modification, a previous enactment then, unless the contrary intention appears,—

    (a) any reference in any other enactment to the enactment so repealed shall be construed as a reference to the provision re-enacted;

    (b) in so far as any subordinate legislation made or other thing done under the enactment so repealed, or having effect as if so made or done, could have been made or done under the provision re-enacted, it shall have effect as if made or done under that provision.

Miscellaneous

Duplicated offences

18. Where an act or omission constitutes an offence under two or more Acts, or both under an Act **F-18** and at common law, the offender shall, unless the contrary intention appears, be liable to be prosecuted and punished under either or any of those Acts or at common law, but shall not be liable to be punished more than once for the same offence.

See in the main work, § 4-189.

Citation of other Acts

19. Where an Act cites another Act by year, statute, session or chapter, or a section or other por- **F-19** tion of another Act by number or letter, the reference shall, unless the contrary intention appears, be read as referring—

    (a) in the case of Acts included in any revised edition of the statutes printed by authority, to that edition;

    (b) in the case of Acts not so included but included in the edition prepared under the direction of the Record Commission, to that edition;

    (c) in any other case, to the Acts printed by the Queen's Printer, or under the superintendence or authority of Her Majesty's Stationery Office.

(2) An Act may continue to be cited by the short title authorised by any enactment notwithstanding the repeal of that enactment.

References to other enactments

20.—(1) Where an Act describes or cites a portion of an enactment by referring to words, sections **F-20** or other parts from or to which or from and to which the portion extends, the portion described or cited includes the words, sections or other parts referred to unless the contrary intention appears.

(2) Where an Act refers to an enactment, the reference unless the contrary intention appears, is a reference to that enactment as amended, and includes a reference thereto as extended or applied, by or under any other enactment, including any other provision of that Act.

References to EU instruments

20A. Where an Act passed after the commencement of this section refers to a EU instrument that **F-20a** has been amended, extended or applied by another such instrument, the reference, unless the contrary intention appears, is a reference to that instrument as so amended, extended or applied.

[This section was inserted by the Legislative and Regulatory Reform Act 2006, s.25(1). It is printed as amended by the European Union (Amendment) Act 2008, s.3, and Sched., Pt 2.]

Supplementary

Interpretation, etc.

F-21   **21.**—(1) In this Act "Act" includes a local and personal or private Act; and "subordinate legislation" means Orders in Council, orders, rules, regulations, schemes, warrants, byelaws and other
instruments made or to be made under any Act.

(2) This Act binds the Crown.

Application to Acts and Measures

F-22   **22.**—(1) This Act applies to itself, to any Act passed after the commencement of this Act (subject, in
the case of section 20A, to the provision made in that section) and, to the extent specified in Part I of
Schedule 2, to Acts passed before the commencement of this Act.

(2) In any of the foregoing provisions of this Act a reference to an Act is a reference to an Act to
which that provision applies; but this does not affect the generality of references to enactments or of
the references in section 19(1) to other Acts.

(3) This Act applies to Measures of the General Synod of the Church of England (and, so far as it
relates to Acts passed before the commencement of this Act, to Measures of the Church Assembly
passed after May 28, 1925) as it applies to Acts.

[This section is printed as amended by the Legislative and Regulatory Reform Act 2006,
s.25(2).]

Application to other instruments

F-23   **23.**—(1) The provisions of this Act, except sections 1 to 3 and 4(b), apply, so far as applicable and
unless the contrary intention appears, to subordinate legislation made after the commencement of
this Act and, to the extent specified in Part II of Schedule 2, to subordinate legislation made before
the commencement of this Act, as they apply to Acts.

(2) In the application of this Act to Acts passed or subordinate legislation made after the commencement of this Act, all references to an enactment include an enactment comprised in subordinate
legislation whenever made, and references to the passing or repeal of an enactment are to be
construed accordingly.

(3) Sections 9 and 19(1) also apply to deeds and other instruments and documents as they apply to
Acts and subordinate legislation; and in the application of section 17(2)(a) to Acts passed or
subordinate legislation made after the commencement of this Act, the reference to any other enactment includes any deed or other instrument or document.

(4) Subsections (1) and (2) of this section do not apply to Orders in Council made under section 5
of the Statutory Instruments Act 1946, section 1(3) of the Northern Ireland (Temporary Provisions)
Act 1972 or Schedule 1 to the Northern Ireland Act 1974.

F-23a   **23A.** [*Acts of the Scottish Parliament,*] etc.

F-23b   **23B.** [*Measures and Acts of the National Assembly for Wales,*] etc.

F-24   **24.** [*Application to Northern Ireland.*]

Repeals and savings

F-25   **25.**—(1) The enactments described in Schedule 3 are repealed to the extent specified in the third
column of that Schedule.

(2) Without prejudice to section 17(2)(a), a reference to the Interpretation Act 1889, to any provision of that Act or to any other enactment repealed by this Act whether occurring in another Act, in
subordinate legislation, in Northern Ireland legislation or in any deed or other instrument or document, shall be construed as referring to this Act, or to the corresponding provision of this Act, as it
applies to Acts passed at the time of the reference.

(3) The provisions of this Act relating to Acts passed after any particular time do not affect the
construction of Acts passed before that time, though continued or amended by Acts passed thereafter.

F-26   **26.** [*Commencement.*]

F-27   **27.** [*Short title.*]

SCHEDULES

SCHEDULE 1

Words and Expressions Defined

F-28   *Note*: The years or dates which follow certain entries in this Schedule are relevant for the purposes
of paragraph 4 of Schedule 2 (application to existing enactments).

Definitions

... .

"Bank of England" means, as the context requires, the Governor and Company of the Bank of England or the bank of the Governor and Company of the Bank of England.

... .

"British Islands" means the United Kingdom, the Channel Islands and the Isle of Man. [1889]

"British possession" means any part of Her Majesty's dominions outside the United Kingdom; and where parts of such dominions are under both a central and local legislature, all parts under the central legislature are deemed, for the purposes of this definition, to be one British possession. [1889]

... .

"Central funds", in an enactment providing in relation to England and Wales for the payment of costs out of central funds, means money provided by Parliament.

... .

"Civil partnership" means a civil partnership which exists under or by virtue of the Civil Partnership Act 2004 (and any reference to a civil partner is to be read accordingly).

[This definition is inserted by the Civil Partnership Act 2004, s.261(1), and Sched. 27, para. 59.]

"Colonial legislature", and "legislature" in relation to a British possession, mean the authority, other than the Parliament of the United Kingdom or Her Majesty in Council, competent to make laws for the possession. [1889]

"Colony" means any part of Her Majesty's dominions outside the British Islands except—

> (a) countries having fully responsible status within the Commonwealth;
>
> (b) territories for whose external relations a country other than the United Kingdom is responsible;
>
> (c) associated states; and where parts of such dominions are under both a central and a local legislature, all parts under the central legislature are deemed for the purposes of this definition to be one colony. [1889]

"Commencement", in relation to an Act or enactment, means the time when the Act or enactment comes into force.

"The EU", or "the EU Treaties" and other expressions defined by section 1 of and Schedule 1 to the European Communities Act 1972 have the meanings prescribed by that Act.

[This definition is printed as amended by the European Union (Amendment) Act 2008, s.3, and Sched., Pt 2.]

... .

"Consular officer" has the meaning assigned by Article 1 of the Vienna Convention set out in Schedule 1 to the Consular Relations Act 1968.

... .

"County Court" means—

> (a) in relation to England and Wales, the County Court established under section A1 of the County Courts Act 1984;
>
> (b) [*Northern Ireland*].

[This definition is printed as amended by the County Courts Act 1984, Sched. 2; and the Crime and Courts Act 2013, s.17(5), and Sched. 9. para. 94.]

"Court of Appeal" means—

> (a) in relation to England and Wales, Her Majesty's Court of Appeal in England;
>
> (b) in relation to Northern Ireland, Her Majesty's Court of Appeal in Northern Ireland.

"Court of summary jurisdiction", "summary conviction" and "Summary Jurisdiction Acts", in relation to Northern Ireland, have the same meanings as in Measures of the Northern Ireland Assembly and Acts of the Parliament of Northern Ireland.

"Crown Court" means—

> (a) in relation to England and Wales, the Crown Court constituted by section 4 of the Courts Act 1971;
>
> (b) [*Northern Ireland*].

... .

"EEA agreement" means the agreement on the European Economic Area signed at Oporto on 2nd

May 1992, together with the Protocol adjusting that Agreement signed at Brussels on 17th March 1993, as modified or supplemented from time to time. [The date of the coming into force of this paragraph.]

"EEA state", in relation to any time, means—

    (a) a state which at that time is a member State; or

    (b) any other state which at that time is a party to the EEA agreement. [The date of the coming into force of this paragraph.]

[These two definitions were inserted, as from January 8, 2007, by the Legislative and Regulatory Reform Act 2006, s.26(1).]

"England" means, subject to any alteration of boundaries under Part IV of the Local Government Act 1972, the area consisting of the counties established by section 1 of that Act, Greater London and the Isles of Scilly. [1st April 1974]

  ... .

"Governor-General" includes any person who for the time being has the powers of the Governor-General, and "Governor", in relation to any British possession, includes the officer for the time being administering the government of that possession. [1889]

"Her Majesty's Revenue and Customs" has the meaning given by section 4 of the Commissioners for Revenue and Customs Act 2005.

[This definition was inserted by the Commissioners for Revenue and Customs Act 2005, s.4(3).]

"High Court" means—

    (a) in relation to England and Wales, Her Majesty's High Court of Justice in England;

    (b) in relation to Northern Ireland, Her Majesty's High Court of Justice in Northern Ireland.

  ... .

"Land" includes buildings and other structures, land covered with water, and any estate, interest, easement, servitude or right in or over land. [1st January 1979]

  ... .

"Local policing body" has the meaning given by section 101(1) of the Police Act 1996.

[This definition was inserted by the Police Reform and Social Responsibility Act 2011, s.97(1) and (2).]

"London borough" means a borough described in Schedule 1 to the London Government Act 1963, "inner London borough" means one of the boroughs so described and numbered from 1 to 12 and "outer London borough" means one of the boroughs so described and numbered 13 to 32, subject (in each case) to any alterations made under Part IV of the Local Government Act 1972 or Part II of the Local Government Act 1992.

[This definition is printed as amended by the Local Government Act 1992, s.27(1), and Sched. 3, para. 21.]

"Lord Chancellor" means the Lord High Chancellor of Great Britain.

"Magistrates' court" has the meaning assigned to it—

    (a) in relation to England and Wales, by section 148 of the Magistrates' Courts Act 1980;

    (b) [*Northern Ireland*].

[This definition is printed as amended by the MCA 1980, s.154, and Sched. 7, para. 169.]

"Month" means calendar month. [1850]

  ... .

"Oath" and "affidavit" include affirmation and declaration, and "swear" includes affirm and declare.

"Officer of Revenue and Customs" has the meaning given by section 2(1) of the Commissioners for Revenue and Customs Act 2005.

[This definition was inserted by the Commissioners for Revenue and Customs Act 2005, s.2(7).]

"Ordnance Map" means a map made under powers conferred by the Ordnance Survey Act 1841 or the Boundary Survey (Ireland) Act 1854.

"Parliamentary Election" means the election of a Member to serve in Parliament for a constituency. [1889]

"Person" includes a body of persons corporate or unincorporate. [1889]

"Police and crime commissioner" means a police and crime commissioner established under section 1 of the Police Reform and Social Responsibility Act 2011.

[This definition was inserted by the Police Reform and Social Responsibility Act 2011, s.97(1) and (3).]

"Police area" ... and other expressions relating to the police have the meaning or effect described—
(a) in relation to England and Wales, by section 101(1) of the Police Act 1996; ...

[This definition is printed as amended by the Police Act 1996, Sched. 7, para. 32; the Police Reform and Social Responsibility Act 2011, s.97(1) and (4); and the Police and Fire Reform (Scotland) Act 2012 (Consequential Provisions and Modifications) Order 2013 (S.I. 2013 No. 602).]

"The Privy Council" means the Lords and others of Her Majesty's Most Honourable Privy Council.

"Registered" in relation to nurses, midwives and health visitors, means registered in the register maintained by the United Kingdom Central Council for Nursing, Midwifery and Health Visiting by virtue of qualifications in nursing, midwifery or health visiting, as the case may be.

[This definition was inserted by the Nurses, Midwives and Health Visitors Act 1979, s.23(4), and Sched. 7, para. 30.]

"Registered medical practitioner" means a fully registered person within the meaning of the Medical Act 1983 who holds a licence to practise under that Act. [1st January 1979]

[This definition is printed as amended by the Medical Act 1983, s.56(1), and Sched. 5, para. 18; and the Medical Act 1983 (Amendment) Order 2002 (S.I 2002 No. 3135), Sched.1, para. 10.]

"Rules of Court" in relation to any court means rules made by the authority having power to make rules or orders regulating the practice and procedure of that court, and in Scotland includes Acts of Adjournal and Acts of Sederunt; and the power of the authority to make rules of court (as above defined) includes power to make such rules for the purpose of any Act which directs or authorises anything to be done by rules of court. [1889]

"Secretary of State" means one of Her Majesty's Principal Secretaries of State.

"Senior Courts" means the Senior Courts of England and Wales.

[This definition was inserted by the Constitutional Reform Act 2005, s.59(5), and Sched. 11, para. 24.]

"Sent for trial" means, in relation to England and Wales, sent by a magistrates' court to the Crown Court for trial pursuant to section 51 or 51A of the Crime and Disorder Act 1998.

[This definition was inserted by the CJA 2003, s.41, and Sched. 3, para. 49(b).]

... .

"The standard scale", with reference to a fine or penalty for an offence triable only summarily,—
(a) in relation to England and Wales, has the meaning given by section 37 of the Criminal Justice Act 1982;
(b) [*Scotland*];
(c) [*Northern Ireland*].

[This definition was inserted by the CJA 1988, s.170(1), and Sched. 15, para. 58(a). (For s.37 of the 1982 Act, see the main work, § 5-683.)]

"Statutory declaration" means a declaration made by virtue of the Statutory Declarations Act 1835.

"Statutory maximum", with reference to a fine or penalty on summary conviction for an offence—
(a) in relation to England and Wales, means the prescribed sum within the meaning of section 32 of the Magistrates' Courts Act 1980;
(b) [*Scotland*]; and
(c) [*Northern Ireland*].

[This definition was inserted by the CJA 1988, s.170(1), and Sched. 15, para. 58(b). (For s.32 of the 1980 Act, see the main work, § 1-125.)]

"Supreme Court" means the Supreme Court of the United Kingdom.

[This definition is printed as amended by the Constitutional Reform Act 2005, s.59(5), and Sched. 11, para. 24.]

"The Treasury" means the Commissioners of Her Majesty's Treasury.

"United Kingdom" means Great Britain and Northern Ireland. [12th April 1927]

"Wales" means the combined area of the counties which were created by section 20 of the Local

Government Act 1972, as originally enacted, but subject to any alteration made under section 73 of that Act (consequential alteration of boundary following alteration of watercourse) [1st April 1974]

[This definition was substituted by the Local Government (Wales) Act 1994, Sched. 2, para. 9.]

. . . .

"Writing" includes typing, printing, lithography, photography and other modes of representing or reproducing words in avisible form, and expressions referring to writing are construed accordingly.

Construction of certain expressions relating to offences

In relation to England and Wales—
    (a) "indictable offence" means an offence which, if committed by an adult, is triable on indictment, whether it is exclusively so triable or triable either way;
    (b) "summary offence" means an offence which, if committed by an adult, is triable only summarily;
    (c) "offence triable either way" means an offence, other than an offence triable on indictment only by virtue of Part V of the Criminal Justice Act 1988 which, if committed by an adult, is triable either on indictment or summarily;
and the terms "indictable", "summary" and "triable either way", in their application to offences are to be construed accordingly.

In the above definitions references to the way or ways in which an offence is triable are to be construed without regard to the effect, if any, of section 22 of the Magistrates' Courts Act 1980 on the mode of trial in a particular case.

[This para. is printed as amended by the MCA 1980, Sched. 7; and the CJA 1988, Sched. 15, para. 59.]

Construction of certain references to relationships

In relation to England and Wales—
    (a) references (however expressed) to any relationship between two persons;
    (b) references to a person whose father and mother were or were not married to each other at the time of his birth; and
    (c) references cognate with references falling within paragraph (b) above,
shall be construed in accordance with section 1 of the Family Law Reform Act 1987. [The date of the coming into force of that section.]

[This para. was added by Schedule 2 to the Family Law Reform Act 1987.]

Construction of certain expressions relating to the police: Scotland

In relation to Scotland—
    (a) references to a police force include references to the Police Service of Scotland;
    (b) references to a chief officer of police include references to the chief constable of the Police Service of Scotland;
    (c) "police authority" means the Scottish Police Authority;
    (d) the "police area" of the Police Service of Scotland is Scotland and references to a police force or police authority for any area include references to the Police Service of Scotland or, as the case may be, the Scottish Police Authority;
    (e) references to a constable or chief constable of, or appointed for, any area are to be construed as references to a constable or, as the case may be, the chief constable of, or appointed for, the Police Service of Scotland.

[This para. was added by the Police and Fire Reform (Scotland) Act 2012 (Consequential Provisions and Modifications) Order 2013 (S.I. 2013 No. 602).]

NOTE: the definitions of the following expressions have been omitted: "Associated state", "Bank of Ireland", "Building regulations", "Charity Commissioners", "Comptroller and Auditor General", "Consular officer", "The Corporation Tax Acts", "Crown Estate Commissioners", "Financial year", "The Income Tax Acts", "Lands Clauses Act", "National Debt Commissioners",

"Northern Ireland legislation", "Sewerage undertaker", "Sheriff", "The Tax Acts" and "Water undertaker".

SCHEDULE 2

APPLICATION OF ACT TO EXISTING ENACTMENTS

PART I

ACTS

1. The following provisions of this Act apply to Acts whenever passed:— **F-29**

> Section 6(a) and (c) so far as applicable to enactments relating to offences punishable on indictment or on summary conviction
> Section 9
> Section 10
> Section 11 so far as it relates to subordinate legislation made after the year 1889
> Section 14A
> Section 18
> Section 19(2).

[Para. 1 is printed as amended by the Enterprise and Regulatory Reform Act 2013, s.59(1) and (3).]

2. The following apply to Acts passed after the year 1850:—

> Section 1
> Section 2
> Section 3
> Section 6(a) and (c) so far as not applicable to such Acts by virtue of paragraph 1
> Section 15
> Section 17(1).

3. The following apply to Acts passed after the year 1889:—

> Section 4
> Section 7
> Section 8
> Section 12
> Section 13
> Section 14 so far as it relates to rules, regulations or byelaws
> Section 16(1)
> Section 17(2)(a)
> Section 19(1)
> Section 20(1).

4.—(1) Subject to the following provisions of this paragraph—

> (a) paragraphs of Schedule 1 at the end of which a year or date is specified or described apply, so far as applicable, to Acts passed on or after the date, or after the year, so specified or described; and
> (b) paragraphs of that Schedule at the end of which no year or date is specified or described apply, so far as applicable, to Acts passed at any time.

(2) The definition of "British Islands", in its application to Acts passed after the establishment of the Irish Free State but before the commencement of this Act, includes the Republic of Ireland.

(3) The definition of "colony", in its application to an Act passed at any time before the commencement of this Act, includes—

> (a) any colony within the meaning of section 18(3) of the Interpretation Act 1889 which was excluded, but in relation only to Acts passed at a later time, by any enactment repealed by this Act;
> (b) any country or territory which ceased after that time to be part of Her Majesty's dominions but subject to a provision for the continuation of existing law as if it had not so ceased;

and paragraph (b) of the definition does not apply.

(4) The definition of "Lord Chancellor" does not apply to Acts passed before 1st October 1921 in which that expression was used in relation to Ireland only.

(5) The definition of "person", so far as it includes bodies corporate, applies to any provision of an Act whenever passed relating to an offence punishable on indictment or on summary conviction.

(6) This paragraph applies to the National Health Service Reorganisation Act 1973 and the Water Act 1973 as if they were passed after 1st April 1974.

[Para. 4 is printed as amended by the Family Law Reform Act 1987, Scheds 2 and 4.]

5. The following definitions shall be treated as included in Schedule 1 for the purposes specified in this paragraph—

 (a) in any Act passed before 1st April 1974, a reference to England includes Berwick upon Tweed and Monmouthshire and, in the case of an Act passed before the Welsh Language Act 1967, Wales;

 (b) in any Act passed before the commencement of this Act and after the year 1850, "land" includes messuages, tenements and hereditaments, houses and buildings of any tenure;

 (c) [*Scotland*].

PART II

SUBORDINATE LEGISLATION

F-30 6. Sections 4(a), 9 and 19(1), and so much of Schedule 1 as defines the following expressions, namely—

 England;
 Local land charges register and appropriate local land charges register;
 in relation to Scotland, expressions relating to the police;
 United Kingdom;
 Wales;

apply to subordinate legislation made at any time before the commencement of this Act as they apply to Acts passed at that time.

[Para. 6 is printed as amended by the British Nationality Act 1981, Sched. 9; and the Police and Fire Reform (Scotland) Act 2012 (Consequential Provisions and Modifications) Order 2013 (S.I. 2013 No. 602).]

7. The definition in Schedule 1 of "county court", in relation to England and Wales, applies to Orders in Council made after the year 1846.

APPENDIX G
Guidelines on Claims for Fees under a Crown Court Representation Order and in the Court of Appeal

A. Summary of Source Material

Legislation

As from April 2, 2001 the relevant provisions of the Legal Aid in Criminal and Care Proceedings (Costs) Regulations 1989 (S.I. 1989 No. 343), as amended, were superseded, virtually unamended, by the Criminal Defence Service (Funding) Order 2001 (S.I. 2001 No. 855) ("the Funding Order 2001"). This was significantly amended by a series of amending orders until it was revoked and replaced, in relation to representation orders granted on or after April 30, 2007, by the Criminal Defence Service (Funding) Order 2007 (S.I. 2007 No. 1174). The 2007 order was itself amended on many occasions over the following six years, until it lapsed on April 1, 2013, with the commencement of the repeal of its enabling legislation by the LASPOA 2012, s.39(1), and Sched. 5, para. 39. Full details of all the amending instruments for both the 2001 order and the 2007 order may be found in the second supplement to the 2013 edition of this work, together with the full text of the 2007 order (as amended). **G-1**

The Criminal Legal Aid (Remuneration) Regulations 2013 (S.I. 2013 No. 435) (set out in full, *post*, G-6 *et seq.*) came into force on April 1, 2013. The substance of the 2013 regulations is almost identical to that of the 2007 order as it read at the time it lapsed, and many, if not all, the authorities that related to the 2007 order at that time will simply carry across. Where they are referred to *post* in this appendix, references to provisions of the former legislation have simply been updated to refer to the corresponding provision of the 2013 regulations.

As to the transitional arrangements in connection with the repeal of the relevant provisions of the Access to Justice Act 1999 and the commencement of the relevant provisions of the 2012 Act, see *ante*, § 6-173.

A challenge to the 8.75 per cent reduction in litigators' fees effected by amendments to Schedules 2, 3 and 4 to S.I. 2013 No. 435 (*ante*) in the Criminal Legal Aid (Remuneration) (Amendment) Regulations 2014 (S.I. 2013 No. 415) (as to which, see *post*, G-71, G-71a, G-72, G-72a, G-73, G-75a, G-80, G-86, G-92a) was rejected in *R. (London Criminal Courts Solicitors' Association) v. Lord Chancellor* [2015] Costs L.R. 7, QBD (Burnett J.).

Recent amendments

S.I. 2013 No. 435 (*ante*) was amended by two further instruments in the second half of 2015. **★G-1a** The first of these was the Criminal Legal Aid (Remuneration etc.) (Amendment) Regulations 2015 (S.I. 2015 No. 1369). Part 2 (reg. 3) and Schedules 1 to 3 amended the principal regulations so as further to reduce the fees payable to litigators under Schedules 2 (graduated fee scheme for Crown Court work), 3 (proceedings in the Court of Appeal) and 4 (advice and assistance, representation in a magistrates' court, and certain other work). The remainder of the amendments (in Pt 3 (regs 4-7, and Scheds 4 to 13)) were originally due to come into force on January 11, 2016. However, this was first delayed to April 1, 2016, by amendments effected by the Criminal Legal Aid (Remuneration etc.) (Amendment) (No. 2) Regulations 2015 (S.I. 2015 No. 2049). Then, on January 28, 2016, the Justice Secretary announced in a ministerial statement that it is no longer intended to bring these amendments into force and that the July, 2015, decrease in fees would be suspended for one year from April 1, 2016. It was not made apparent how this was to be achieved, but it would appear that at least one further amending instrument will be required prior to April 1, 2016.

The amendments made by Part 2 apply to matters in which a determination under section 13 (advice and assistance for individuals in custody (§ 6-209 in the main work)), 15 (advice and assistance for criminal proceedings (*ibid.*, § 6-211)) or 16 (representation for criminal proceedings (*ibid.*, § 6-212)) of the 2012 Act was made after June 30, 2015 (reg. 2(1)). Part 2 came into force on July 1, 2015.

The second measure was the Civil and Criminal Legal Aid (Amendment) (No. 2) Regulations 2015 (S.I. 2015 No. 1678). The majority of the amendments were overdue amendments that were consequential on the abolition of committals and transfers for trial. The remainder were consequential on new rules on preparation for trial in the Crown Court under the Criminal Procedure Rules 2015 (S.I. 2015 No. 1490). In particular, certain references to a plea and case management hearing (no longer mandatory) have been omitted, with the regulations now making provision by reference to the occurrence, or result, of the first hearing at which the assisted person enters a plea instead. According to the explanatory memorandum "This reflects the fact that for purposes of remuneration ..., it is the type of plea which is relevant, not the name of the hearing at which it is entered."

There is transitional provision in relation to committal proceedings that have been discontinued or withdrawn, in relation to committals and transfers that occurred before the abolition of committals and transfers and in relation to payment for preparation of a plea and case management hearing questionnaire where no oral hearing takes place. These regulations came into force in stages on October 5, 2015, and November 1, 2015.

In the text of S.I. 2013 No. 435 that follows (*post*, G-6 *et seq.*), all the above amendments save those that were to have been made by Part 3 of S.I. 2015 No. 1369 have been taken in. Any practitioner who wishes to refer to the text as it would have been amended should consult the first supplement to this edition.

The current regimes

G-2 Apart from a handful of historical cases which will be governed by the former provisions for *ex post facto* taxation (as to which see Appendix G-200 *et seq.* in the supplements to the 2010 edition of this work), advocates' fees in the Crown Court effectively fall into one of two regimes:

   (i) *Graduated fees.* These were first introduced in 1997 for trials lasting up to 10 days, appeals and other minor Crown Court business: Legal Aid in Criminal and Care Proceedings (Costs) Regulations 1989 (S.I. 1989 No. 343), Sched. 3. The scheme was then extended to cover trials of up to 25 days and, as from 2005, of trials up to 40 days. As from April 30, 2007, it was intended that the scheme would cover all Crown Court work save for those cases contracted under the Very High Costs Case provisions: Criminal Defence Service (Funding) Order 2007 (S.I. 2007 No. 1174), art. 3(6A), and Sched. 1, para. 2(1). The 2007 scheme is sometimes referred to as the Revised Advocacy Graduated Fee Scheme (RAGFS). The details were contained in Schedule 1 to the 2007 order, which replaced Schedule 4 to the Criminal Defence Service (Funding) Order 2001 (S.I. 2001 No. 855). The 2007 scheme (as amended) is now to be found in Schedule 1 to the Criminal Legal Aid (Remuneration) Regulations 2013 (S.I. 2013 No. 435).

   (ii) *Very High Cost Cases (VHCC).* This regime came into effect on October 29, 2001. All cases estimated to last more than 24 days are capable of being subject to a VHCC contract. As to the current VHCC regime, see *post*, G-181 *et seq.*

Notes for guidance

(a) Graduated fees

G-3 The Ministry of Justice's *Graduated Fee Scheme Guidance (GFSG)* is updated at regular intervals. In addition, guidance notes have been issued by the Criminal Bar Association, and are available on both the Criminal Bar Association's and the Courts Service's National Taxing Team's websites. The GFSG includes references to costs judges' decisions which are given and commonly referred to and indexed by their "X" references. For convenience these references are used hereafter. The guidance may be cited by advocates when asking for a re-determination: GFSG, Preface. However, while interesting and instructive, it is simply the department's gloss on the wording of the regulations, and does not bind costs judges: *R. v. Phillips*, X1, SCTO 594/97.

The Bar Council has also introduced a *Graduated Fee Payment Protocol*. This is an essential part of the mechanism by which advocates will be remunerated in future, and sets out arrangements to ensure that substitute advocates are paid by instructed advocates. The protocol falls outside the immediate scope of this work. It is available on both the Bar Council's and the Criminal Bar Association's websites.

(b) Very High Cost Cases

Very High Cost Cases are governed by the Very High Cost (Crime) Cases Arrangements 2013 **G-4**
(see *post*, G-181 *et seq.*). Additional guidance is contained in the 2013 VHCC Guidance (published by the Legal Aid Agency, an executive agency of the Ministry of Justice).

Contract Appeals Committee decisions

Summaries of decisions of the Contract Appeals Committee have been collated and appear on **G-5**
the website of the Legal Aid Agency's section of the Ministry of Justice's website.

B. The Remuneration Regulations

Criminal Legal Aid (Remuneration) Regulations 2013 (S.I. 2013 No. 435)

Citation and commencement

1. These Regulations may be cited as the Criminal Legal Aid (Remuneration) Regulations 2013 **G-6**
and shall come into force on 1st April 2013.

Interpretation

2.—(1) In these Regulations—   **G-7**

"the Act" means the Legal Aid, Sentencing and Punishment of Offenders Act 2012;

"advocate" means a barrister, a solicitor advocate or a solicitor who is exercising their automatic rights of audience in the Crown Court;

"appropriate officer" means—

    (a) in the case of proceedings in the civil division of the Court of Appeal, the head of the civil appeals office;

    (b) in the case of proceedings in the criminal division of the Court of Appeal, the registrar of criminal appeals;

    (c) in the case of proceedings in the Crown Court, the Lord Chancellor;

    (d) in respect of advice or assistance as to an appeal from the Crown Court to the Court of Appeal (except in the case of an appeal under section 9(11) of the Criminal Justice Act 1987 (preparatory hearings)) where, on the advice of any representative instructed, notice of appeal is given, or application for leave to appeal is made, whether or not such appeal is later abandoned, the registrar of criminal appeals;

    (e) in respect of advice or assistance as to an appeal to the Courts-Martial Appeal Court, the registrar of criminal appeals;

    (f) in respect of advice or assistance as to an appeal from the Court of Appeal to the Supreme Court, where the appeal is not lodged with the Supreme Court, the registrar of criminal appeals; and

    (g) in any other case, the Lord Chancellor,

and, in any case, includes an officer designated by the person who is the appropriate officer by virtue of paragraphs (a) to (g) to act on his behalf for the purposes of these Regulations;

"assisted person" means an individual in whose favour a section 16 determination has been made;

"fee earner" means a litigator, or person employed by a litigator, who undertakes work on a case;

"instructed advocate" means—

    (a) where the section 16 determination provides for representation by a single advocate, the first barrister or solicitor advocate instructed in the case, who has primary responsibility for the case; or

    (b) where the section 16 determination provides for representation by more than one advocate, each of—

        (i) the leading instructed advocate; and

(ii) the led instructed advocate;

"leading instructed advocate" means the first leading barrister or solicitor advocate instructed in the case who has primary responsibility for those aspects of a case undertaken by a leading advocate;

"led instructed advocate" means the first led barrister or solicitor advocate instructed in the case who has primary responsibility for those aspects of the case undertaken by a led advocate;

"litigator" means the person referred to in the representation order as representing an assisted person, being a solicitor, firm of solicitors or other appropriately qualified person.

"main hearing" means—

     (a) in relation to a case which goes to trial, the trial;

     (b) in relation to a guilty plea (within the meaning of Schedule 1), the hearing at which pleas are taken or, where there is more than one such hearing, the last such hearing;

     (c) in relation to a cracked trial (within the meaning of Schedule 1), the hearing at which—

         (i) the case becomes a cracked trial by meeting the conditions in the definition of a cracked trial, whether or not any pleas were taken at that hearing; or

         (ii) a formal verdict of not guilty was entered as a result of the prosecution offering no evidence, whether or not the parties attended the hearing;

     (d) in relation to an appeal against conviction or sentence in the Crown Court, the hearing of the appeal;

     (e) in relation to proceedings arising out of a committal for sentence in the Crown Court, the sentencing hearing; and

     (f) in relation to proceedings arising out of an alleged breach of an order of the Crown Court, the hearing at which those proceedings are determined;

"related proceedings" means—

     (a) two or more sets of proceedings involving the same defendant which are prepared, heard or dealt with together; or

     (b) proceedings involving more than one defendant which arise out of the same incident, so that the defendants are charged, tried or disposed of together;

"relevant order" means whichever of the 2015 Duty Provider Crime Contract or the 2015 Own Client Crime Contract governs the provision of advice and assistance made available under sections 13 or 15 of the Act, for which remuneration is claimed;

"representation order" means a document which records a section 16 determination;

"representative" means a litigator or an advocate including, where appropriate, an instructed advocate or trial advocate;

"section 16 determination" means a determination made under section 16 of the Act that an individual qualities for representation for the purposes of criminal proceedings;

"senior solicitor" means a solicitor who, in the judgement of the appropriate officer, has the skill, knowledge and experience to deal with the most difficult and complex cases;

"solicitor advocate" means a solicitor who has obtained a higher courts advocacy qualification in accordance with regulations and rules of conduct of the Law Society;

"solicitor, legal executive or fee earner of equivalent experience" means a solicitor, Fellow of the Institute of Legal Executives or equivalent senior fee earner who, in the judgement of the appropriate officer, has good knowledge and experience of the conduct of criminal cases;

"trainee solicitor or fee earner of equivalent experience" means a trainee solicitor or other fee earner who is not a Fellow of the Institute of Legal Executives, who, in the judgement of the appropriate officer, carries out the routine work on a case;

"trial advocate" means, unless otherwise provided, an advocate instructed pursuant to a section 16 determination to represent the assisted person at the main hearing in any case;

"Very High Cost Case" means a case in which a section 16 determination has been made and which the Director classifies as a Very High Cost Case on the grounds that—

     (a) in relation to fees claimed by litigators—

         (i) if the case were to proceed to trial, the trial would in the opinion of the Director be likely to last for more than 40 days and the Director considers that there are no exceptional circumstances which make it unsuitable to be dealt with under an individual case contract for Very High Cost Cases made by the Lord Chancellor under section 2(1) of the Act; or

         (ii) if the case were to proceed to trial, the trial would in the opinion of the Director be likely to last no fewer than 25 and no more than 40 days and the Director considers that there are circumstances which make it suitable to be dealt with

under an individual case contract for Very High Cost Cases made by the Lord
Chancellor under section 2(1) of the Act;

(b) in relation to fees claimed by advocates, if the case were to proceed to trial, the trial
would in the opinion of the Director be likely to last for more than 60 days and the
Director considers that there are no exceptional circumstances which make it unsuitable to be dealt with under an individual case contract for Very High Cost Cases
made by the Lord Chancellor under section 2(1) of the Act;

"Very High Cost Case contract" means the 2013 VHCC contract between the Lord Chancellor
and a representative for the provision of representation under section 16 of the Act (criminal
legal aid).

(2) The fees and rates set out in the Schedules to these Regulations are exclusive of value added
tax.

(3) A function of the Lord Chancellor or Director under these Regulations may be exercised by, or
by an employee of, a person authorised for that purpose by the Lord Chancellor or Director
respectively.

[This regulation is printed as amended (insertion of definition of "Very High Cost Case
contract") by the Criminal Legal Aid (Remuneration) (Amendment) Regulations 2013 (S.I. 2013
No. 2803), reg. 3(1) and (3). The amendment applies in relation to fees for work undertaken on
or after December 2, 2013: *ibid.*, reg. 4. It is also printed as further amended by the Criminal
Legal Aid (Remuneration) (Amendment) Regulations 2015 (S.I. 2015 No. 882), reg. 2(1) and (2)
(insertion of definitions of "main hearing" and "trial advocate", and inclusion of words "or trial
advocate" at the end of the definition of "representative"). The amendments apply to criminal
proceedings in the Crown Court in which a determination under the LASPOA 2012, s.16 (§ 6-212
in the main work) is made on or after May 5, 2015.]

Scope
  3.—(1) Regulations 5(2), 10 and 14(1) apply to proceedings in magistrates' courts and to proceed-   **G-8**
ings in the Crown Court.

(2) Regulation 8 and Schedule 4 apply to proceedings in magistrates' courts, to proceedings in the
County Court, to proceedings in the Crown Court and to proceedings in the High Court.

(3) Regulations 16 and 31 and Schedule 5 apply to proceedings in magistrates' courts, to proceedings in the Crown Court and to proceedings in the Court of Appeal.

(4) Regulations 4, 5(1) and (3) to (8), 13, 14(2) to (9), 15, 17 to 24 and 28 to 30 and Schedules 1
and 2 apply to proceedings in the Crown Court only.

(5) Regulations 9, 11 and 25 to 27, apply to proceedings in the Crown Court and to proceedings
in the Court of Appeal.

(6) Regulation 6 and Schedule 3 apply to proceedings in the Court of Appeal only.

(7) Regulation 7 applies to proceedings in the Supreme Court only.

(8) With the exception of regulations 12 and 12A and paragraphs 13(8) and (9) of Schedule 2 and
Schedule 6, these regulations do not apply to Very High Cost Cases.

(9) For the purpose of these regulations, any reference to the Court of Appeal includes as appropriate a reference to—

(a)   the criminal division of the Court of Appeal;
(b)   the civil division of the Court of Appeal;
(c)   the Courts-Martial Appeal Court; and
(d)   a Divisional Court of the High Court.

[This regulation is printed as amended (insertion of references to reg. 12A and Sched. 6) by
the Criminal Legal Aid (Remuneration) (Amendment) Regulations 2013 (S.I. 2013 No. 2803),
reg. 3(1) and (4). The amendment applies in relation to fees for work undertaken on or after
December 2, 2013: *ibid.*, reg. 4. It is also printed as further amended by the Civil and Criminal
Legal Aid (Remuneration) (Amendment) Regulations 2015 (S.I. 2015 No. 325), reg. 3(1) and (2).]

[The next paragraph is G-10.]

Claims for fees by advocates—Crown Court
  4.—(1) Claims for fees by a trial advocate in proceedings in the Crown Court must be made and   **G-10**
determined in accordance with the provisions of Schedule 1 to these Regulations.

(2) A claim for fees under this regulation and Schedule 1 must be made by each trial advocate.

(3) Subject to regulation 31, a claim by a trial advocate for fees in respect of work done pursuant to a section 16 determination must not be entertained unless the trial advocate submits it within three months of the conclusion of the proceedings to which it relates.

(4) A trial advocate must submit a claim for fees to the appropriate officer in such form and manner as the appropriate officer may direct.

(5) A trial advocate must supply such further information and documents as the appropriate officer may require.

(6) Where a confiscation hearing under Part 2 of the Proceeds of Crime Act 2002 (confiscation: England and Wales), section 2 of the Drug Trafficking Act 1994 (confiscation orders) or section 71 of the Criminal Justice Act 1988 (confiscation orders) is to be held more than 28 days after—

    (a)   the conclusion of the trial to which the section 16 determination relates; or

    (b)   the entering of a guilty plea,

a trial advocate may submit any claim for fees in respect of the trial or guilty plea as soon as the trial has concluded or the guilty plea has been entered.

(7) Where the section 16 determination provides for representation by—

    (a)   a single advocate other than a QC; or

    (b)   two or more advocates other than QC,

and a QC agrees to appear as the single advocate or as a leading junior, that QC must be treated for all the purposes of these Regulations as having been instructed in relation to that determination, and the remuneration of that QC must be determined as if the advocate were not a QC.

(8) In this regulation, where the main hearing is a trial, "trial advocate" means an advocate who—

    (a)   is instructed pursuant to a section 16 determination to represent the assisted person at the trial, and

    (b)   attends the first day of the trial.

[This regulation is printed as amended, with effect from May 5, 2015, by the Criminal Legal Aid (Remuneration) (Amendment) Regulations 2015 (S.I. 2015 No. 882), reg. 2(3)(a), (4)(a), (5)(a), (6)(a) and (7). For the transitional provision, see *ante*, G-7.]

Claims for fees and disbursements by litigators—Crown Court

G-11   **5.**—(1) Claims for fees by litigators in proceedings in the Crown Court must be made and determined in accordance with the provisions of Schedule 2 to these Regulations.

(2) Claims for disbursements by litigators in proceedings in the Crown Court or in proceedings in a magistrates' court which are subsequently sent for trial to the Crown Court must be made and determined in accordance with the provisions of regulations 14 to 17.

(3) Subject to regulation 31, a claim by a litigator for fees in respect of work done pursuant to a section 16 determination must not be entertained unless the litigator submits it within three months of the conclusion of the proceedings to which it relates.

(4) Subject to paragraph (5), a claim by a litigator for fees in proceedings in the Crown Court must be submitted to the appropriate officer in such form and manner as the appropriate officer may direct and must be accompanied by the representation order and any receipts or other documents in support of any disbursement claimed.

(5) A claim under paragraph 20 or 26 of Schedule 2 to these Regulations must—

    (a)   summarise the items of work done by a fee earner in respect of which fees are claimed according to the classes specified in paragraph 26(2) of Schedule 2;

    (b)   state, where appropriate, the dates on which the items of work were done, the time taken, the sums claimed and whether the work was done for more than one assisted person;

    (c)   specify, where appropriate, the level of fee earner who undertook each of the items of work claimed; and

    (d)   give particulars of any work done in relation to more than one indictment or a retrial.

(6) Where the litigator claims that paragraph 29 of Schedule 2 applies in relation to an item of work, the litigator must give full particulars in support of the claim.

(7) The litigator must specify any special circumstances which the litigator considers should be drawn to the attention of the appropriate officer.

(8) The litigator must supply such further information and documents as the appropriate officer may require.

[This regulation is printed as amended by S.I. 2015 No. 1678 (as to which, see *ante*, G-1a).]

[The next paragraph is G-13.]

Proceedings in the Court of Appeal

6. Claims for fees by representatives in proceedings in the Court of Appeal must be made and   **G-13**
determined in accordance with the provisions of Schedule 3 to these Regulations.

Proceedings in the Supreme Court

7.—(1) In proceedings in the Supreme Court, the fees payable to a representative in respect of   **G-14**
advice and assistance or representation made available to an individual in accordance with sections
15 or 16 of the Act must be determined by such officer as may be prescribed by order of the Supreme
Court.

(2) Subject to paragraph (1), these Regulations do not apply to proceedings in the Supreme Court.

Claims for fees for certain categories of work to which the Standard Crime Contract applies

8.—(1) This regulation applies to—   **G-15**

    (a) advice and assistance provided pursuant to a determination made under section 13 or sec-
tion 15 of the Act;

    (b) representation in proceedings in a magistrates' court pursuant to a section 16
determination;

    (c) representation pursuant to a section 16 determination in proceedings prescribed as criminal
proceedings under section 14(h) of the Act; and

    (d) representation in appeals by way of case stated to the High Court.

(2) Claims for fees in cases to which this regulation applies must—

    (a) be made and determined in accordance with the 2010 Standard Crime Contract; and

    (b) be paid in accordance with the rates set out in Schedule 4.

(3) In this regulation and in Schedule 4, "2010 Standard Crime Contract" means the contract so
named between the Lord Chancellor and a person with whom the Lord Chancellor has made an arrangement under section 2(1) of the Act for the provision of advice, assistance and representation
made available under sections 13, 15 and 16 of the Act.

Payments from other sources

9. Where representation is provided in respect of any proceedings, the representative, whether   **G-16**
acting pursuant to a section 16 determination or otherwise, must not receive or be a party to the
making of any payment for work done in connection with those proceedings, except such payments
as may be made—

    (a) by the Lord Chancellor; or

    (b) in respect of any expenses or fees incurred in—

        (i) preparing, obtaining or considering any report, opinion or further evidence, whether
provided by an expert witness or otherwise; or

        (ii) obtaining any transcripts or recordings,

where an application under regulation 13 for an authority to incur such fees or expenses has been
refused by a committee appointed under arrangements made by the Lord Chancellor to deal with,
amongst other things, appeals of, or review of, assessment of costs.

In connection with regulation 9, see *R. v. Banfield, ante*, § 7-165.

Cases sent for trial to the Crown Court

10.—(1) Where a case is sent for trial to the Crown Court, the payment in relation to work carried   **G-17**
out in the magistrates' court is included within the applicable fee payable under Schedule 1 or
Schedule 2.

(2) Paragraph (1) does not apply where the case is remitted to a magistrates' court.

[This regulation is printed as amended by S.I. 2015 No. 1678 (*ante*, G-1a).]

Proceedings for contempt

11. Where representation is provided in proceedings referred to in section 14(g) of the Act   **G-18**
(proceedings for contempt in the face of a court), the Lord Chancellor may only pay remuneration
for services in accordance with Schedules 1, 2 and 3.

Notification of Very High Cost Cases

12.—(1) A litigator who has conduct of a case which is, or is likely to be classified as, a Very High   **G-18a**
Cost Case, must notify the Lord Chancellor in writing as soon as practicable.

(2) Where a litigator fails to comply with this regulation without good reason, and as a result there is a loss to public funds, the Lord Chancellor may refuse payment of the litigator's costs up to the extent of such loss.

(3) The Lord Chancellor must not refuse payment under paragraph (2) unless the litigator has been given a reasonable opportunity to show why the payment should not be refused.

Fees in Very High Cost Cases

12A. Where services consisting of representation made available under section 16 of the Act (criminal legal aid) are provided in a case which is the subject of a Very High Cost Case contract, fees for that case must be paid—

    (a) in accordance with the terms of that contract; and

    (b) at the rates set out for the appropriate category and level of representative set out in Schedule 6 to these Regulations.

[This regulation was inserted by the Criminal Legal Aid (Remuneration) (Amendment) Regulations 2013 (S.I. 2013 No. 2803), reg. 3(1) and (5). It applies in relation to fees for work undertaken on or after December 2, 2013: *ibid.*, reg. 4.]

Authorisation of expenditure

G-18b   **13.**—(1) Where it appears to a litigator necessary for the proper conduct of proceedings in the Crown Court for costs to be incurred in relation to representation by taking any of the following steps—

    (a) obtaining a written report or opinion of one or more experts;

    (b) employing a person to provide a written report or opinion (otherwise than as an expert);

    (c) obtaining any transcripts or recordings; or

    (d) performing an act which is either unusual in its nature or involves unusually large expenditure,

the litigator may apply to the Lord Chancellor for prior authority to do so.

(2) Where the Lord Chancellor authorises the taking of any step referred to in paragraph (1), the Lord Chancellor shall also authorise the maximum to be paid in respect of that step.

(3) A representative assigned to an assisted person in any proceedings in the Crown Court may apply to the Lord Chancellor for prior authority for the incurring of travelling and accommodation expenses in order to attend at the main hearing in those proceedings.

[This regulation is printed as amended, with effect from May 5, 2015, by the Criminal Legal Aid (Remuneration) (Amendment) Regulations 2015 (S.I. 2015 No. 882), reg. 2(8). For the transitional provision, see *ante*, G-7.]

The following authorities were decided under the corresponding provisions in earlier legal aid legislation: see, in particular, regulation 54 of the Legal Aid in Criminal and Care Proceedings (General) Regulations 1989 (S.I. 1989 No. 344).

In *R. v. Silcott, Braithwaite and Raghip, The Times*, December 9, 1991, the Court of Appeal said that all members of the legal profession were under a duty not to involve the legal aid fund in unnecessary expenditure. If an expert consulted by the defence was hostile to the accused's case or his solicitor considered the opinion to be wrong or defective it was most unlikely that legal aid authority would be given on application by the solicitor to consult more than one expert and certainly no more than two. In the instant case, the opinions of two experts had been obtained on behalf of one defendant. They were adverse to the defendant. Neither expert was called, but both changed their views in the light of the opinion of a third expert, who had been consulted after the trial's conclusion. This demonstrated that a third opinion had been necessary in the interests of justice. "Expert shopping" was to be discouraged, but there were exceptional cases where the need for a further expert opinion could be demonstrated. In such cases counsel should be asked to advise on evidence in support of an extension of the legal aid certificate, if he thought it right to do so. The courts and those responsible for the legal aid fund must rely on proper professional standards being observed by all the lawyers concerned.

A judge has no power to authorise the incurring of costs under a legal aid order for an expert witness, although he may express his opinion as to the desirability of legal aid being so extended: *R. v. Donnelly* [1998] Crim.L.R. 131, CA.

G-19   **14.**—(1) A litigator may submit a claim to the appropriate officer for payment of a disbursement for which the litigator has incurred liability in proceedings in the Crown Court, or in proceedings in a magistrates' court which are subsequently sent for trial to the Crown Court, in accordance with the provisions of this regulation.

(2) A claim for payment under paragraph (1) may be made where—

    (a)   a litigator has obtained prior authority to incur expenditure of £100 or more under regulation 13; and

    (b)   the litigator has incurred such a liability.

(3) Without prejudice to regulation 17(4) and (5) a claim for payment under paragraph (1) must not exceed the maximum amount authorised under the prior authority.

(4) A claim for payment under paragraph (1) may be made at any time before the litigator submits a claim for fees under regulation 5.

(5) A claim for payment under paragraph (1) must be submitted to the appropriate officer in such form and manner as the appropriate officer may direct and must be accompanied by the authority to incur expenditure and any invoices or other documents in support of the claim.

(6) Subject to regulation 16, the appropriate officer must allow the disbursement subject to the limit in paragraph (3) if it appears to have been reasonably incurred in accordance with the prior authority.

(7) The appropriate officer must notify the litigator and, where the disbursement claimed includes the fees or charges of any person, may notify that person of the appropriate officer's decision.

(8) Where the appropriate officer allows the disbursement, the appropriate officer must notify the litigator and, where the disbursement includes the fees or charges of any person, may notify that person, of the amount payable, and must authorise payment to the litigator accordingly.

(9) Regulations 28 to 30 do not apply to a payment under this regulation.

[This regulation is printed as amended by S.I. 2015 No. 1678 (*ante*, G-1a).]

Interim disbursements and final determination of fees

15.—(1) On a final determination of fees, regulations 5(2) and 17 apply notwithstanding that a **G-20** payment has been made under regulation 14.

(2) Where the amount found to be due under regulation 17 in respect of a disbursement is less than the amount paid under regulation 14 ("the interim payment"), the appropriate officer must deduct the difference from the sum otherwise payable to the litigator on the determination of fees, and where the amount due under regulation 17 exceeds the interim payment, the appropriate officer must add the difference to the amount otherwise payable to the litigator.

Expert services

16.—(1) Subject to paragraph (2), the Lord Chancellor may provide for the payment of expert **G-20a** services only at the fixed fees or at rates not exceeding the rates set out in Schedule 5.

(2) The appropriate officer may, in relation to a specific claim, increase the fixed fees or rates set out in Schedule 5 if that officer considers it reasonable to do so in exceptional circumstances.

(3) For the purposes of paragraph (2), exceptional circumstances are where the expert's evidence is key to the client's case and either—

    (a)   the complexity of the material is such that an expert with a high level of seniority is required; or

    (b)   the material is of such a specialised and unusual nature that only very few experts are available to provide the necessary evidence.

Determination of litigators' disbursements

17.—(1) Subject to paragraphs (2) to (5), the appropriate officer must allow such disbursements **G-21** claimed under regulation 5(2) as appear to the appropriate officer to have been reasonably incurred.

(2) If the disbursements claimed are abnormally large by reason of the distance of the court or the assisted person's residence or both from the litigator's place of business, the appropriate officer may limit reimbursement of the disbursements to what otherwise would, having regard to all the circumstances, be a reasonable amount.

(3) No question as to the propriety of any step or act in relation to which prior authority has been obtained under regulation 13 may be raised on any determination of disbursements, unless the litigator knew or ought reasonably to have known that the purpose for which the authority was given had failed or had become irrelevant or unnecessary before the disbursements were incurred.

(4) Where disbursements are reasonably incurred in accordance with and subject to the limit imposed by a prior authority given under regulation 13, no question may be raised on any determina-

tion of fees as to the amount of the payment to be allowed for the step or act in relation to which the authority was given.

(5) Where disbursements are incurred in taking any steps or doing any act for which authority may be given under regulation 13, without such authority having been given or in excess of any fee so authorised, payment in respect of those disbursements may nevertheless be allowed on a determination of disbursements payable under regulation 5.

(6) Paragraph (7) applies where the Lord Chancellor receives a request for funding of an expert service of a type not listed in Schedule 5.

(7) In considering the rate at which to fund the expert service the Lord Chancellor—

(a)   must have regard to the rates set out in Schedule 5; and

(b)   may require more than one quotation for provision of the service to be submitted to the Lord Chancellor.

Interim payment of litigators' fees

G-21a   17A.—(1) A litigator may make a claim to the appropriate officer for an interim payment of the litigator's fees, in relation to proceedings in the Crown Court, in accordance with this regulation.

(2) Subject to paragraphs (3) to (6), a litigator may make a claim for an interim payment under this regulation in relation to one or more of the following stages in the proceedings—

(a)   after the first hearing at which the assisted person enters a plea of not guilty;

(b)   where representation is transferred to the litigator following the ordering of a retrial, after the date for the retrial has been set; and

(c)   after commencement of a trial which is listed for 10 days or more.

(3) A litigator may not make a claim for an interim payment under paragraph (2)(a) or (b) in relation to a case committed or sent for trial to the Crown Court on the election of a defendant where the magistrates' court has determined the case to be suitable for summary trial.

(4) Subject to paragraphs (5) and (6), a litigator may make only one claim in relation to each of the stages in the proceedings set out in paragraph (2).

(5) A litigator may not make a claim for an interim payment under paragraph (2)(a) or (b) at the same time as, or after, that litigator has made a claim for an interim payment under paragraph (2)(c).

(6) A litigator may not make a claim for an interim payment under paragraph (2)(c) if the trial in question is a retrial and the litigator was the litigator for the first or a previous trial.

(7) A litigator may not make a claim for an interim payment at the same time as, or after, that litigator has made a claim under regulation 5.

(8) A litigator must make a claim for an interim payment to the appropriate officer in such form and manner as the appropriate officer may direct.

(9) A litigator must supply such information and documents as the appropriate officer may require to determine the claim for interim payment.

(10) Where a claim for an interim payment is made in accordance with this regulation, the appropriate officer must authorise payment.

(11) Where the claim is made under paragraph (2)(a) the amount of the interim payment is the sum of—

(a)   the fee which, on a final determination of fees, would be paid to the litigator if paragraph 13 of Schedule 2 and the scenario "Before trial transfer (original litigator)" set out in the table following that paragraph applied; and

(b)   any additional payments which, on a final determination of fees, would be paid to the litigator under paragraph 12 of Schedule 2.

(12) Where the claim is made under paragraph (2)(b), the amount of the interim payment is the sum of—

(a)   the fee which, on a final determination of fees, would be paid to the litigator under paragraph 13 of Schedule 2 and the scenario "Transfer before cracked retrial (new litigator)" set out in the table following that paragraph; and

(b)   any additional payments which, on a final determination of fees, would be paid to the litigator under paragraph 12 of Schedule 2.

(13) Where the claim is made under paragraph (2)(c), the amount of the interim payment is—

(a)   the sum of—

(i)   the fee determined in accordance with paragraph (14) on the basis that the trial length is one day; and

(ii)   any additional payments which, on a final determination of fees, must be paid to the litigator under paragraph 12 of Schedule 2;

(b)   less any amount paid to the litigator, in the proceedings in question, for a claim under paragraph (2)(a) or (b).

(14) The fee referred to in paragraph (13)(a)(i) is—

    (a) where the number of pages of prosecution evidence is less than or equal to the PPE Cut-off specified in the table following paragraph 5(2) of Schedule 2, the basic fee specified in the table following paragraph 7(2) of that Schedule;

    (b) where the pages of prosecution evidence exceeds the PPE Cut-off specified in the table following paragraph 5(2) of Schedule 2, the final fee as calculated in accordance with paragraph 9(2) of that Schedule.

(15) For purposes of paragraphs (11) to (14)—

    (a) the number of defendants;

    (b) the number of pages of prosecution evidence served on the court; and

    (c) the offence with which the assisted person is charged are determined as at the date of the claim for the interim payment.

(16) Where a litigator has received a hardship payment under regulation 21, the amount of that hardship payment must be deducted from any interim payment payable to that litigator under this regulation.

(17) Where a litigator has already received one or more interim payments under this regulation, the amount to be deducted under paragraph (16) excludes any hardship payment already deducted from any earlier interim payment.

(18) Regulations 28 to 30 do not apply to a payment under this regulation.

(19) In this regulation, "PPE Cut-off" has the meaning given in Schedule 2.

[This regulation was inserted by the Criminal Legal Aid (Remuneration) (Amendment) (No. 2) Regulations 2014 (S.I. 2014 No. 2422), reg. 2(3), and Sched., with effect from October 2, 2014. The amendments made by those regulations apply to criminal proceedings in which a determination under the LASPOA 2012, s.16 (§ 6-212 in the main work) was made on or after October 2 2014: reg. 3. It is printed as further amended by S.I. 2015 No. 1678 (*ante*, G-1a).]

Interim payments in cases awaiting determination of fees

18.—(1) The appropriate officer must authorise an interim payment in respect of a claim for fees   **G-22** in proceedings in the Crown Court in accordance with this regulation.

(2) Entitlement to a payment arises in respect of a claim for fees by a trial advocate, where—

    (a) the graduated fee claimed in accordance with Schedule 1 is £4,000 or more (exclusive of value added tax); and

    (b) the claim for fees is for less than the amount mentioned in sub-paragraph (a) but is related to any claim for fees falling under sub-paragraph (a).

(3) For the purposes of this regulation, the following claims for fees are related to each other—

    (a) the claims of trial advocates acting in the same proceedings for a defendant; and

    (b) the claims of any instructed advocate acting for any assisted person in related proceedings.

(4) Entitlement to a payment under paragraph (1) does not arise until three months have elapsed from the earlier of—

    (a) the date on which the claim for fees is received by the appropriate officer for determination, except that where there are related claims for fees, the date on which the last claim is received by the appropriate officer; or

    (b) three months after the conclusion of the last of any related proceedings.

(5) A trial advocate may submit a claim for an interim payment under this regulation where—

    (a) no payment has been made under paragraph (1); and

    (b) six months have elapsed from the conclusion of the proceedings against the assisted person.

(6) Subject to regulation 31, payment must not be made under this regulation unless the trial advocate has submitted a claim for fees in accordance with regulation 4(3).

(7) In this regulation, where the main hearing is a trial, "trial advocate" means an advocate who—

    (a) is instructed pursuant to a section 16 determination to represent the assisted person at the trial, and

    (b) attends the first day of the trial.

[This regulation is printed as amended, with effect from May 5, 2015, by the Criminal Legal Aid (Remuneration) (Amendment) Regulations 2015 (S.I. 2015 No. 882), reg. 2(3)(b), (4)(b), (5)(b) and (9). For the transitional provision, see *ante*, G-7.]

Amount of interim payments in cases awaiting determination of fees

19.—(1) Where entitlement to an interim payment arises under regulation 18, the amount payable   **G-23** is 40% of the total claim for fees, less any sum already paid.

(2) Regulations 28 to 30 do not apply to an interim payment under this regulation.

Staged payments in long Crown Court proceedings

G-24   **20.**—(1) An instructed advocate may submit a claim to the appropriate officer for a staged payment of the instructed advocate's fees in relation to proceedings in the Crown Court.

(2) Where a claim is submitted in accordance with this regulation, a staged payment must be allowed where the appropriate officer is satisfied—

> (a) that the claim relates to fees for a period of preparation of 100 hours or more, for which the instructed advocate will, subject to final determination of the fees payable, be entitled to be paid in accordance with Schedule 1; and
>
> (b) that the period from sending for trial (or from the date of the section 16 determination, if later) to the conclusion of the Crown Court proceedings is likely to exceed 12 months, having regard, amongst other matters, to the number of defendants, the anticipated pleas and the weight and complexity of the case.

(3) In this regulation, "preparation" means—

> (a) reading the papers in the case;
>
> (b) contact with prosecutors;
>
> (c) written or oral advice on plea;
>
> (d) researching the law, preparation for examination of witnesses and preparation of oral submissions;
>
> (e) viewing exhibits or undisclosed material at police stations;
>
> (f) written advice on evidence;
>
> (g) preparation of written submissions, notices or other documents for use at the trial;
>
> (h) attendance at views at the scene of the alleged offence,

and is limited to preparation done before the trial, except in proceedings in which a preparatory hearing has been ordered under section 8 of the Criminal Justice Act 1987 (commencement of trial and arraignment), in which case it is limited to preparation done before the date on which the jury is sworn (or on which it became certain, by reason of pleas of guilty or otherwise, that the matter would not proceed to trial).

(4) The amount allowed for preparation falling within paragraph (3) must be determined by reference to the number of hours of preparation which it appears to the appropriate officer, without prejudice to the final determination of the fees payable, has been reasonably done, multiplied by the hourly rate for special preparation as set out in the table following paragraph 24 of Schedule 1, as appropriate to the category of advocate.

(5) A claim for staged payment of fees under this regulation must be made to the appropriate officer in such form and manner as the appropriate officer may direct, including such case plan as the appropriate officer may require for the purposes of paragraph (2)(a).

(6) An instructed advocate may claim further staged payments in accordance with this regulation in respect of further periods of preparation exceeding 100 hours which were not included in an earlier claim.

(7) Regulations 28 to 30 do not apply to a payment under this regulation.

[This regulation is printed as amended by S.I. 2015 No. 1678 (*ante*, G-1a).]

[The next paragraph is G-26.]

Hardship payments

G-26   **21.**—(1) Subject to paragraphs (5) and (6), the appropriate officer may allow a hardship payment to a representative in the circumstances set out in paragraph (2).

(2) Those circumstances are that the representative—

> (a) represents the assisted person in proceedings in the Crown Court;
>
> (b) applies for such payment, in such form and manner as the appropriate officer may direct, not less than six months after the representative was first instructed in those proceedings, or in related proceedings if the representative was instructed in those proceedings earlier than in the proceedings to which the application relates;
>
> (c) is unlikely to receive final payment in respect of the proceedings, as determined under Schedule 1 or 2, within the three months following the application for the hardship payment; and
>
> (d) satisfies the appropriate officer that, by reason of the circumstance in sub-paragraph (c), the representative is likely to suffer financial hardship.

(3) Every application for a hardship payment by an advocate must be accompanied by such information and documents as the appropriate officer may require as evidence of—

    (a) the work done by the advocate in relation to the proceedings up to the date of the application; and

    (b) the likelihood of financial hardship.

(4) Every application for a hardship payment by a litigator must be accompanied by such information and documents as the appropriate officer may require as evidence of—

    (a) the Class of Offence with which the assisted person is charged, in accordance with Part 7 of Schedule 1;

    (b) the length of trial, where appropriate;

    (c) the number of pages of prosecution evidence, determined in accordance with paragraph 1(2) of Schedule 2;

    (d) the total number of defendants in the proceedings who are represented by the litigator;

    (e) the likelihood of financial hardship.

(5) The amount of any hardship payment is at the discretion of the appropriate officer, but must not exceed such sum as would be reasonable remuneration for the work done by the representative in the proceedings up to the date of the application.

(6) A hardship payment must not be made if it appears to the appropriate officer that the sum which would be reasonable remuneration for the representative, or the sum required to relieve the representative's financial hardship, is less than £5,000 (excluding value added tax).

(7) Subject to paragraphs (9) and (10) where the appropriate officer allows a hardship payment under paragraph (1), the appropriate officer must authorise payment accordingly.

(8) Where the application for a hardship payment is made by an advocate other than a trial advocate, and the appropriate officer allows a hardship payment under paragraph (1)—

    (a) payment must be made to the—

        (i) appropriate trial advocate who attends the first day of trial, where the trial has commenced;

        (ii) appropriate trial advocate, where a trial has not commenced, or

        (iii) appropriate instructed advocate, where there is no trial advocate, and;

    (b) the appropriate officer must notify the advocate who made the application that payment has been made to the appropriate trial advocate or the appropriate instructed advocate.

(9) Where a litigator has received an interim payment under regulation 17A, the amount of that interim payment must be deducted from any hardship payment payable to that litigator under this regulation.

(10) Where a litigator has already received one or more hardship payments under this regulation, the amount deducted under paragraph (9) excludes any interim payment already deducted from any earlier hardship payment.

(11) In paragraph (8)—

"appropriate instructed advocate" means—

        (a) where the section 16 determination provides for representation by a single advocate, the instructed advocate, or

        (b) where the section 16 determination provides for representation by more than one advocate, the leading instructed advocate or the led instructed advocate, as appropriate, and

"appropriate trial advocate" means—

        (a) where the section 16 determination provides for representation by a single advocate, the trial advocate, or

        (b) where the section 16 determination provides for representation by more than one advocate, the leading trial advocate or the led trial advocate, as appropriate.

[This regulation is printed as amended by S.I. 2014 No. 2422 (*ante*, G-21a). For the transitional provision, see *ante*, G-21a. It is printed as further amended, with effect from May 5, 2015, by the Criminal Legal Aid (Remuneration) (Amendment) Regulations 2015 (S.I. 2015 No. 882), reg. 2(3)(c) and (10) (for transitional provision, see *ante*, G-7).]

Computation of final claim where an interim payment has been made

22.—(1) At the conclusion of a case in which one or more payments have been made to an **G-27** instructed advocate, a trial advocate or a litigator under regulations 17A to 21, the trial advocate or litigator must submit a claim under regulation 4 or 5 for the determination of the overall remuneration, whether or not such a claim will result in any payment additional to those already made.

(2) In the determination of the amount payable to a trial advocate or litigator under regulation 4 or 5—

    (a) the appropriate officer must deduct the amount of any payment made under regulations 17A to 21 in respect of the same case from the amount that would otherwise be payable; and

    (b) if the amount of the interim payment is greater than the amount that would otherwise be payable, the appropriate officer may recover the amount of the difference, either by way of repayment by the trial advocate or litigator or by way of deduction from any other amount that may be due to the trial advocate or litigator.

(3) In this regulation, where the main hearing is a trial, "trial advocate" means an advocate who—

    (a) is instructed pursuant to a section 16 determination to represent the assisted person at the trial, and

    (b) attends the first day of the trial.

[This regulation is printed as amended by S.I. 2014 No. 2422 (*ante*, G-21a). For the transitional provision, see *ante*, G-21a. It is also printed as further amended, with effect from May 5, 2015, by the Criminal Legal Aid (Remuneration) (Amendment) Regulations 2015 (S.I. 2015 No. 882), reg. 2(3)(d), (6)(b) and (11). For the transitional provision, see *ante*, G-7.]

Payment of fees to advocates—Crown Court

G-28
    23.—(1) Having determined the fees payable to each trial advocate, in accordance with Schedule 1, the appropriate officer must notify each trial advocate of the fees payable and authorise payment accordingly.

(2) Where, as a result of any redetermination or appeal made or brought pursuant to regulations 28 to 30, the fees payable under paragraph (1) are altered—

    (a) if they are increased, the appropriate officer must authorise payment of the increase; or

    (b) if they are decreased, the trial advocate must repay the amount of such decrease.

(3) Where the payment of any fees of a trial advocate is ordered under regulation 29(12) or regulation 30(8), the appropriate officer must authorise payment.

(4) In this regulation, where the main hearing is a trial, "trial advocate" means an advocate who—

    (a) is instructed pursuant to a section 16 determination to represent the assisted person at the trial, and

    (b) attends the first day of the trial.

[This regulation is printed as amended, with effect from May 5, 2015, by the Criminal Legal Aid (Remuneration) (Amendment) Regulations 2015 (S.I. 2015 No. 882), reg. 2(3)(e), (5)(c), (6)(c) and (12). For the transitional provision, see *ante*, G-7.]

Payment of fees to litigators—Crown Court

G-29
    24.—(1) Having determined the fees payable to a litigator in accordance with Schedule 2, the appropriate officer must authorise payment accordingly.

(2) Where the appropriate officer determines that the fees payable under paragraph (1) are greater than or less than the amount claimed by the litigator under regulation 5(1), the appropriate officer must notify the litigator of the amount the appropriate officer has determined to be payable.

(3) Where, as a result of any redetermination or appeal made or brought pursuant to regulations 28 to 30, the fees payable under paragraph (1) are altered—

    (a) if they are increased, the appropriate officer must authorise payment of the increase; or

    (b) if they are decreased, the litigator must repay the amount of such decrease.

(4) Where the payment of any fees of the litigator is ordered under regulation 29(12) or regulation 30(8), the appropriate officer must authorise payment.

[The next paragraph is G-31.]

Recovery of overpayments

G-31
    25.—(1) This regulation applies where a representative is entitled to be paid a certain sum ("the amount due") by virtue of the provisions of Schedule 1, 2 or 3 and, for whatever reason, the representative is paid an amount greater than that sum.

(2) Where this regulation applies, the appropriate officer may—

    (a) require immediate repayment of the amount in excess of the amount due ("the excess amount"); or

(b) deduct the excess amount from any other sum which is or becomes payable to the representative by virtue of the provisions of Schedule 1, 2 or 3,

and where sub-paragraph (a) applies the representative must repay the excess amount to the appropriate officer.

(3) The appropriate officer may proceed under paragraph (2)(b) without first proceeding under paragraph (2)(a).

(4) Paragraph (2) applies notwithstanding that the representative to whom the excess amount was paid is exercising, or may exercise, a right under regulations 28 to 30.

(5) In this regulation, where the main hearing is a trial, "trial advocate" means, for the purposes of the meaning of "representative", the advocate who—

(a) is instructed pursuant to a section 16 determination to represent the assisted person at the trial, and

(b) attends the first day of the trial.

[This regulation is printed as amended, with effect from May 5, 2015, by the Criminal Legal Aid (Remuneration) (Amendment) Regulations 2015 (S.I. 2015 No. 882), reg. 2(13). For the transitional provision, see *ante*, G-7.]

Adverse observations

26.—(1) Where in any proceedings to which Schedule 1, 2 or 3 applies, the court makes adverse **G-32** observations concerning a representative's conduct of the proceedings, the appropriate officer may reduce any fee which would otherwise be payable in accordance with Schedule 1, 2 or 3 by such proportion as the appropriate officer considers reasonable.

(2) Before reducing the fee payable to a representative in accordance with the provisions of paragraph (1), the appropriate officer must give the representative the opportunity to make representations about whether it is appropriate to reduce the fee and the extent to which the fee should be reduced.

Wasted costs orders

27.—(1) Subject to paragraph (2), where the court has disallowed the whole or any part of any **G-33** wasted costs under section 19A of the Prosecution of Offences Act 1985 (costs against legal representatives *etc*), the appropriate officer, in determining fees in respect of work done by the representative against whom the wasted costs order was made, may deduct the amount in the wasted costs order from the amount otherwise payable in accordance with these Regulations.

(2) Where the appropriate officer, in accordance with this regulation, is minded to disallow any amount of a claim for work done to which the wasted costs order relates, the appropriate officer must disallow that amount or the amount of the wasted costs order, whichever is the greater.

Redetermination of fees by appropriate officer

28.—(1) Where— **G-34**

(a) an advocate in proceedings in the Crown Court is dissatisfied with the decision not to allow any of the following fees, or with the number of hours allowed in the calculation of such a fee, namely—

(i) a special preparation fee under paragraph 17 of Schedule 1; or

(ii) a wasted preparation fee under paragraph 18 of Schedule 1; or

(b) a trial advocate in proceedings in the Crown Court is dissatisfied with—

(i) the decision not to allow an hourly fee in respect of attendance at conferences or views at the scene of the alleged offence under paragraph 19 of Schedule 1, or with the number of hours allowed in the calculation of such a fee;

(ii) the calculation by the appropriate officer of the fee payable to the trial advocate in accordance with Schedule 1; or

(iii) the decision of the appropriate officer under paragraph 3(3) of Schedule 1 (reclassification of an offence not specifically listed in the relevant Table of Offences and so deemed to fall within Class H); or

(c) a litigator is dissatisfied with—

(i) the calculation by the appropriate officer of the fee payable to the litigator in accordance with Schedule 2; or

(ii) the decision of the appropriate officer under paragraph 3(3) of Schedule 2 (reclassification of an offence not specifically listed in the relevant Table of Offences and so deemed to fall within Class H),

the advocate, trial advocate or litigator, as the case may be, may apply to the appropriate officer to redetermine those fees, to review that decision or to reclassify the offence, as appropriate.

(2) An application under paragraph (1) may not challenge the quantum of any of the fees set out in Schedule 1 or Schedule 2.

(3) Subject to regulation 31, an application under paragraph (1), or paragraph 11(1) of Schedule 3, must be made—

    (a) within 21 days of the receipt of the fees payable under regulation 23, regulation 24 or paragraph 10 of Schedule 3, as appropriate;

    (b) by giving notice in writing to the appropriate officer, specifying the matters in respect of which the application is made and the grounds of objection; and

    (c) in such form and manner as the appropriate officer may direct.

(4) The notice of application must be accompanied by the information and documents supplied under regulation 4, regulation 5 or Schedule 3, as appropriate.

(5) The notice of application must state whether the applicant wishes to appear or to be represented and, if the applicant so wishes, the appropriate officer must notify the applicant of the hearing date and time.

(6) The applicant must supply such further information and documents as the appropriate officer may require.

(7) The appropriate officer must, in the light of the objections made by the applicant or on behalf of the applicant—

    (a) redetermine the fees, whether by way of confirmation, or increase or decrease in the amount previously determined;

    (b) confirm the classification of the offence within Class H; or

    (c) reclassify the offence,

as the case may be, and must notify the applicant of his decision.

(8) Where the applicant so requests, the appropriate officer must give reasons in writing for the appropriate officer's decision.

(9) Subject to regulation 31, any request under paragraph (8) must be made within 21 days of receiving notification of the appropriate officer's decision under paragraph (7).

(10) In this regulation, where the main hearing is a trial, "trial advocate" means an advocate who—

    (a) is instructed pursuant to a section 16 determination to represent the assisted person at the trial, and

    (b) attends the first day of the trial.

[This regulation is printed as amended, with effect from May 5, 2015, by the Criminal Legal Aid (Remuneration) (Amendment) Regulations 2015 (S.I. 2015 No. 882), reg. 2(14) (for transitional provision, see *ante*, G-7).]

Appeals to a costs judge

G-35   **29.**—(1) Where the appropriate officer has given his reasons for his decision under regulation 28(8), a representative who is dissatisfied with that decision may appeal to a costs judge.

(2) Subject to regulation 31, an appeal under paragraph (1) or paragraph 11(2) of Schedule 3 must be instituted within 21 days of the receipt of the appropriate officer's reasons, by giving notice in writing to the Senior Costs Judge.

(3) The appellant must send a copy of any notice of appeal given under paragraph (2) to the appropriate officer.

(4) The notice of appeal must be accompanied by—

    (a) a copy of any written representations given under regulation 28(3);

    (b) the appropriate officer's reasons for the appropriate officer's decision given under regulation 28(8); and

    (c) the information and documents supplied to the appropriate officer under regulation 28.

(5) The notice of appeal must—

    (a) be in such form as the Senior Costs Judge may direct;

    (b) specify separately each item appealed against, showing (where appropriate) the amount claimed for the item, the amount determined and the grounds of the objection to the determination; and

    (c) state whether the appellant wishes to appear or to be represented or whether the appellant will accept a decision given in the appellant's absence.

(6) The Senior Costs Judge may, and if so directed by the Lord Chancellor either generally or in a particular case must, send to the Lord Chancellor a copy of the notice of appeal together with copies of such other documents as the Lord Chancellor may require.

(7) With a view to ensuring that the public interest is taken into account, the Lord Chancellor may arrange for written or oral representations to be made on the Lord Chancellor's behalf and, if the Lord Chancellor intends to do so, the Lord Chancellor must inform the Senior Costs Judge and the appellant.

(8) Any written representations made on behalf of the Lord Chancellor under paragraph (7) must be sent to the Senior Costs Judge and the appellant and, in the case of oral representations, the Senior Costs Judge and the appellant must be informed of the grounds on which such representations will be made.

(9) The appellant must be permitted a reasonable opportunity to make representations in reply.

(10) The costs judge must inform the appellant (or the person representing him) and the Lord Chancellor, where representations have been or are to be made on the Lord Chancellor's behalf, of the date of any hearing and, subject to the provisions of this regulation, may give directions as to the conduct of the appeal.

(11) The costs judge may consult the trial judge or the appropriate officer and may require the appellant to provide any further information which the costs judge requires for the purpose of the appeal and, unless the costs judge otherwise directs, no further evidence may be received on the hearing of the appeal and no ground of objection may be raised which was not raised under regulation 28.

(12) The costs judge has the same powers as the appropriate officer under these Regulations and, in the exercise of such powers, may alter the redetermination of the appropriate officer in respect of any sum allowed, whether by increasing or decreasing it, as the costs judge thinks fit.

(13) The costs judge must communicate his decision and the reasons for it in writing to the appellant, the Lord Chancellor and the appropriate officer.

(14) Where the costs judge increases the sums redetermined under regulation 28, the costs judge may allow the appellant a sum in respect of part or all of any reasonable costs incurred by the appellant in connection with the appeal (including any fee payable in respect of an appeal).

Appeals to the High Court

30.—(1) A representative who is dissatisfied with the decision of a costs judge on an appeal under **G-36** regulation 29 may apply to a costs judge to certify a point of principle of general importance.

(2) Subject to regulation 31, an application under paragraph (1) or paragraph 11(3) of Schedule 3 must be made within 21 days of receiving notification of a costs judge's decision under regulation 29(13).

(3) Where a costs judge certifies a point of principle of general importance the appellant may appeal to the High Court against the decision of a costs judge on an appeal under regulation 29, and the Lord Chancellor must be a respondent to such an appeal.

(4) Subject to regulation 31, an appeal under paragraph (3) must be instituted within 21 days of receiving notification of a costs judge's certificate under paragraph (1).

(5) Where the Lord Chancellor is dissatisfied with the decision of a costs judge on an appeal under regulation 29, the Lord Chancellor may, if no appeal has been made by an appellant under paragraph (3), appeal to the High Court against that decision, and the appellant must be a respondent to the appeal.

(6) Subject to regulation 31, an appeal under paragraph (5) must be instituted within 21 days of receiving notification of the costs judge's decision under regulation 29(13).

(7) An appeal under paragraph (3) or (5) must—

    (a) be brought in the Queen's Bench Division;

    (b) subject to paragraph (4), follow the procedure set out in Part 52 of the Civil Procedure Rules 1998; and

    (c) be heard and determined by a single judge whose decision will be final.

(8) The judge has the same powers as the appropriate officer and a costs judge under these Regulations and may reverse, affirm or amend the decision appealed against or make such other order as the judge thinks fit.

Time limits

31.—(1) Subject to paragraph (2), the time limit within which any act is required or authorised to **G-37** be done under these Regulations may, for good reason, be extended—

    (a) in the case of acts required or authorised to be done under regulations 29 or 30, by a costs judge or the High Court as the case may be; and

    (b) in the case of acts required or authorised to be done by a representative under any other regulation, by the appropriate officer.

(2) Where a representative without good reason has failed (or, if an extension were not granted, would fail) to comply with a time limit, the appropriate officer, a costs judge or the High Court, as the case may be, may, in exceptional circumstances, extend the time limit and must consider whether it is reasonable in the circumstances to reduce the fees payable to the representative under regulations 4, 5 or 6, provided that the fees must not be reduced unless the representative has been allowed a reasonable opportunity to show cause orally or in writing why the fees should not be reduced.

(3) A representative may appeal to a costs judge against a decision made under this regulation by an appropriate officer and such an appeal must be instituted within 21 days of the decision being given by giving notice in writing to the Senior Costs Judge specifying the grounds of appeal.

(4) In this regulation, where the main hearing is a trial, "trial advocate" means, for the purposes of the meaning of "representative", the advocate who—

    (a) is instructed pursuant to a section 16 determination to represent the assisted person at the trial, and

    (b) attends the first day of the trial.

[This regulation is printed as amended, with effect from May 5, 2015, by the Criminal Legal Aid (Remuneration) (Amendment) Regulations 2015 (S.I. 2015 No. 882), reg. 2(15). For the transitional provision, see *ante*, G-7.]

[The next paragraph is G-39.]

Regulation 4   SCHEDULE 1

ADVOCATES' GRADUATED FEE SCHEME

PART 1

DEFINITIONS AND SCOPE

Interpretation

G-39   1.—(1) In this Schedule—

"case" means proceedings in the Crown Court against any one assisted person—

    (a) on one or more counts of a single indictment;

    (b) arising out of a single notice of appeal against conviction or sentence, or a single committal for sentence, whether on one or more charges; or

    (c) arising out of a single alleged breach of an order of the Crown Court,

    and a case falling within paragraph (c) must be treated as a separate case from the proceedings in which the order was made;

"cracked trial" means a case on indictment in which—

    (a) the assisted person enters a plea of not guilty to one or more counts at the first hearing at which he or she enters a plea and

        (i) the case does not proceed to trial (whether by reason of pleas of guilty or for other reasons) or the prosecution offers no evidence; and

        (ii) either—

            (aa) in respect of one or more counts to which the assisted person pleaded guilty, the assisted person did not so plead at the first hearing at which he or she entered a plea; or

            (bb) in respect of one or more counts which did not proceed, the prosecution did not, before or at the first hearing at which the assisted person entered a plea, declare an intention of not proceeding with them; or

    (b) the case is listed for trial without a hearing at which the assisted persons enters a plea;

"excluded hearing" means—

    (a) the first hearing at which the assisted person enters a plea;

    (b) any hearing which forms part of the main hearing, or

    (c) any hearing for which a fee is payable under a provision of this Schedule other than paragraph 12(2);

"guilty plea" means a case on indictment which—

    (a) is disposed of without a trial because the assisted person pleaded guilty to one or more counts; and

(b) is not a cracked trial;

"Newton hearing" means a hearing at which evidence is heard for the purpose of determining the sentence of a convicted person in accordance with the principles of *R. v. Newton* (1982) 77 Cr.App.R. 13;

"standard appearance" means an appearance by the trial advocate or substitute advocate in any of the following hearings unless it is an excluded hearing—

    (a) a plea and case management hearing;

    (b) a pre-trial review;

    (ba) a pre-trial preparation hearing;

    (bb) a case management hearing;

    (c) the hearing of a case listed for plea which is adjourned for trial;

    (d) any hearing (except a trial, the first hearing at which the assisted person enters a plea or a hearing referred to in paragraph 2(1)(b)) which is listed but cannot proceed because of the failure of the assisted person or a witness to attend, the unavailability of a pre-sentence report or other good reason;

    (e) custody time limit applications;

    (f) bail and other applications (except where any such applications take place in the course of a hearing referred to in paragraph 2(1)(b));

    (g) the hearing of the case listed for mention only, including applications relating to the date of the trial (except where an application takes place in the course of a hearing referred to in paragraph 2(1)(b));

    (h) a sentencing hearing other than one falling within paragraph 2(1)(b)(ii), paragraph 15(1) or paragraph 34;

    (i) a preliminary hearing; or

    (j) a hearing, whether contested or not, relating to breach of bail, failure to surrender to bail or execution of a bench warrant,

provided that a fee is not payable elsewhere under this Schedule in respect of the hearing;

"substitute advocate" means an advocate who is not an instructed advocate or the trial advocate but who undertakes work on the case; ... .

(2) For the purposes of this Schedule, the number of pages of prosecution evidence served on the court must be determined in accordance with sub-paragraphs (3) to (5).

(3) The number of pages of prosecution evidence includes all—

    (a) witness statements;

    (b) documentary and pictorial exhibits;

    (c) records of interviews with the assisted person; and

    (d) records of interviews with other defendants,

which form part of the served prosecution documents or which are included in any notice of additional evidence.

(4) Subject to sub-paragraph (5), a document served by the prosecution in electronic form is included in the number of pages of prosecution evidence.

(5) A documentary or pictorial exhibit which—

    (a) has been served by the prosecution in electronic form; and

    (b) has never existed in paper form,

is not included within the number of pages of prosecution evidence unless the appropriate officer decides that it would be appropriate to include it in the pages of prosecution evidence taking into account the nature of the document and any other relevant circumstances.

(6) In proceedings on indictment in the Crown Court initiated otherwise than by sending for trial, the appropriate officer must determine the number of pages of prosecution evidence in accordance with sub-paragraphs (2) to (5) or as nearly in accordance with those sub-paragraphs as possible as the nature of the case permits.

(7) A reference to the Table of Offences in this Schedule is to the Table of Offences in Part 7 and a reference to a Class of Offence in this Schedule is to the Class in which that offence is listed in the Table of Offences.

[This paragraph is printed as amended, with effect from May 5, 2015, by the Criminal Legal Aid (Remuneration) (Amendment) Regulations 2015 (S.I. 2015 No. 882), reg. 2(16)(a). For the transitional provision, see *ante*, G-7. It is printed as further amended by S.I. 2015 No. 1678 (*ante*, G-1a).]

Application

2.—(1) Subject to sub-paragraphs (2) to (11), this Schedule applies to—   **G-40**

    (a) every case on indictment; and

    (b) the following proceedings in the Crown Court—

        (i) an appeal against conviction or sentence;

        (ii) a sentencing hearing following a committal for sentence to the Crown Court; and

        (iii) proceedings arising out of an alleged breach of an order of the Crown Court (whether or not this Schedule applies to the proceedings in which the order was made).

(2) Sub-paragraphs (3) and (4) apply where, following a trial, an order is made for a new trial and the same trial advocate appears at both trials where—

    (a) the defendant is an assisted person at both trials; or

    (b) the defendant is an assisted person at the new trial only; or

    (c) the new trial is a cracked trial or guilty plea.

(3) Subject to sub-paragraph (4), in respect of a new trial, or if the trial advocate so elects, in respect of the first trial, the graduated fee payable to the trial advocate must be calculated in accordance with Part 2 or Part 3, as appropriate, except that the fee must be reduced by—

    (a) 30%, where the new trial started within one month of the conclusion of the first trial;

    (b) 20%, where the new trial did not start within one month of the conclusion of the first trial;

    (c) 40%, where the new trial becomes a cracked trial or guilty plea within one month of the conclusion of the first trial; or

    (d) 25% where the new trial becomes a cracked trial or guilty plea more than one month after the conclusion of the first trial.

(4) Where—

    (a) in relation to the first trial, the case was sent for trial to the Crown Court on the election of a defendant where the magistrates' court had determined the case to be suitable for summary trial; and

    (b) the new trial becomes a cracked trial or guilty plea,

the fee payable to the trial advocate must be

        (i) the graduated fee calculated in accordance with Part 2, in respect of the first trial; and

        (ii) the fixed fee set out in paragraph 10 in respect of the new trial.

(5) Sub-paragraphs (6) and (7) apply in the circumstances set out in sub-paragraph (2) but where a different trial advocate appears for the assisted person at each trial.

(6) Subject to sub-paragraph (7), in respect of each trial, the graduated fee payable to the trial advocate must be calculated in accordance with Part 2 or Part 3 as appropriate.

(7) Where—

    (a) in relation to the first trial, the case was sent for trial to the Crown Court on the election of a defendant where the magistrates' court had determined the case to be suitable for summary trial; and

    (b) the new trial becomes a cracked trial or guilty plea,

the fee payable to the trial advocate at the first trial must be the graduated fee, calculated in accordance with Part 2 and the fee payable to the trial advocate at the new trial must be the fixed fee set out in paragraph 10.

(8) Where following a case on indictment a *Newton* hearing takes place—

    (a) for the purposes of this Schedule the case is to be treated as having gone to trial;

    (b) the length of the trial is to be taken to be the combined length of the main hearing and the *Newton* hearing;

    (c) the provisions of this Schedule relating to cracked trials and guilty pleas do not apply; and

    (d) no fee is payable under paragraph 15 in respect of the *Newton* hearing.

(10) Where, at any time after proceedings are sent for trial to the Crown Court they are—

    (a) discontinued by a notice served under section 23A of the Prosecution of Offences Act 1985 (discontinuance of proceedings after accused has been sent for trial), or

    (b) dismissed pursuant to paragraph 2 of Schedule 3 to the Crime and Disorder Act 1998 (applications for dismissal),

the provisions of paragraph 22 apply.

(11) For the purposes of this Schedule, a case on indictment which discontinues at or before the first hearing at which the assisted person enters a plea otherwise than—

    (a) by reason of a plea of guilty being entered; or

    (b) in accordance with sub-paragraph (10),

must be treated as a guilty plea.

[Para. 2 is printed as amended by S.I. 2015 No. 1678 (*ante*, G-1a).]

Class of offences

3.—(1) For the purposes of this Schedule—   **G-41**

(a)   every indictable offence falls within the Class under which it is listed in the Table of Offences and, subject to sub-paragraph (2), indictable offences not specifically so listed are deemed to fall within Class H;

(b)   conspiracy to commit an indictable offence contrary to section 1 of the Criminal Law Act 1977 (the offence of conspiracy), incitement to commit an indictable offence and attempts to commit an indictable offence contrary to section 1 of the Criminal Attempts Act 1981 (attempting to commit an offence) fall within the same Class as the substantive offence to which they relate;

(c)   where the Table of Offences specifies that the Class within which an offence falls depends on whether the value involved exceeds a stated limit, the value must be presumed not to exceed that limit unless the advocate making the claim under regulation 4 proves otherwise to the satisfaction of the appropriate officer;

(d)   where more than one count of the indictment is for an offence in relation to which the Class depends on the value involved, that value must be taken to be the total value involved in all those offences, but where two or more counts relate to the same property, the value of that property must be taken into account once only;

(e)   where an entry in the Table of Offences specifies an offence as being contrary to a statutory provision, then subject to any express limitation in the entry that entry includes every offence contrary to that statutory provision whether or not the words of description in the entry are appropriate to cover all such offences;

(f)   where in a case on indictment there is a hearing to determine the question of whether an assisted person is unfit to plead or unfit to stand trial, the trial advocate must elect whether that hearing falls within the same Class as the indictable offence to which it relates or within Class D; and

(g)   where in a case on indictment a restriction order is made under section 41 of the Mental Health Act 1983 (power of higher courts to restrict discharge from hospital), the offence falls within Class A, regardless of the Class under which the offence would be listed in the Table of Offences but for this paragraph.

(2) Where an advocate in proceedings in the Crown Court is dissatisfied with the classification within Class H of an indictable offence not listed in the Table of Offences, the advocate may apply to the appropriate officer when lodging the claim for fees to reclassify the offence.

(3) The appropriate officer must, in light of the objections made by the advocate—

(a)   confirm the classification of the offence within Class H; or

(b)   reclassify the offence,

and must notify the advocate of the decision.

As to this paragraph, see *post*, G-119.

PART 2

GRADUATED FEES FOR TRIAL

Calculation of graduated fees

4. The amount of the graduated fee for a single trial advocate representing one assisted person be-   **G-42** ing tried on one indictment in the Crown Court in a trial lasting one to 40 days must be calculated in accordance with the following formula—

$$G = B + (d \times D) + (e \times E) + (w \times W)$$

Where—

• **G** is the amount of the graduated fee;

• **B** is the basic fee specified in the table following paragraph 5 as appropriate to the offence for which the assisted person is tried and the category of trial advocate;

• **d** is the number of days or parts of a day on which the advocate attends at court by which the trial exceeds 2 days but does not exceed 40 days;

• **D** is the fee payable in respect of daily attendance at court for the number of days by which the trial exceeds 2 days but does not exceed 40 days, as appropriate to the offence for which the assisted person is tried and the category of trial advocate;

• **e** is the number of pages of prosecution evidence excluding the first 50, up to a maximum of 10,000;

• **E** is the evidence uplift specified in the table following paragraph 5 as appropriate to the offence for which the assisted person is tried and the category of trial advocate;

• **w** is the number of prosecution witnesses excluding the first 10;

517

- **W** is the witness uplift specified in the table following paragraph 5 as appropriate to the offence for which the assisted person is tried and the category of trial advocate.

Table of fees

G-43

5. For the purposes of paragraph 4 the basic fee (B), the daily attendance fee (D), the evidence uplift (E) and the witness uplift (W) appropriate to any offence are those specified in the table following this paragraph in accordance with the Class within which that offence falls.

TABLE OF FEES AND UPLIFTS

Class of Offence	Basic Fee (B) (£)	Daily attendance fee (D) (£)	Evidence uplift (E) (£)	Witness uplift (W) (£)
QC				
A	2,856	979	1.63	6.53
B	2,529	857	1.63	6.53
C	1,968	816	1.63	6.53
D	2,284	816	1.63	6.53
E	1,514	612	1.63	6.53
F	1,514	612	1.63	6.53
G	1,514	612	1.63	6.53
H	1,903	816	1.63	6.53
I	2,122	816	1.63	6.53
J	2,856	979	1.63	6.53
K	2,856	979	1.63	6.53
Leading Junior				
A	2,142	734	1.23	4.9
B	1,897	643	1.23	4.9
C	1,476	612	1.23	4.9
D	1,714	612	1.23	4.9
E	1,136	459	1.23	4.9
F	1,136	459	1.23	4.9
G	1,136	459	1.23	4.9
H	1,427	612	1.23	4.9
I	1,592	612	1.23	4.9
J	2,142	734	1.23	4.9
K	2,142	734	1.23	4.9
Led Junior				
A	1,632	490	0.81	3.26
B	1,265	428	0.81	3.26
C	898	408	0.81	3.26
D	1,125	408	0.81	3.26
E	694	306	0.81	3.26
F	694	306	0.81	3.26
G	694	306	0.81	3.26
H	816	408	0.81	3.26
I	979	408	0.81	3.26
J	1,632	490	0.81	3.26
K	1,428	490	0.81	3.26
Junior alone				
A	1,632	530	0.98	4.9

Class of Offence	Basic Fee (B) (£)	Daily attendance fee (D) (£)	Evidence uplift (E) (£)	Witness uplift (W) (£)
B	1,305	469	0.98	4.9
C	898	408	0.98	4.9
D	1,125	408	0.98	4.9
E	653	326	0.98	4.9
F	694	326	0.98	4.9
G	694	326	0.98	4.9
H	816	408	0.98	4.9
I	979	408	0.98	4.9
J	1,632	530	0.98	4.9
K	1,632	530	0.98	4.9

PART 3

GRADUATED FEES FOR GUILTY PLEAS AND CRACKED TRIALS

Scope of Part 3

6.—(1) Subject to sub-paragraph (2) and to paragraph 22, this Part does not apply to a case sent **G-44** for trial to the Crown Court on the election of a defendant where the magistrates' court has determined the case to be suitable for a summary trial.

(2) This Part applies in all cases where the trial is a cracked trial because the prosecution offer no evidence on all counts against a defendant and the judge directs that a not guilty verdict be entered.

[This paragraph was substituted by S.I. 2014 No. 2422 (*ante*, G-21a). For the transitional provision, see *ante*, G-21a. It is printed as amended by S.I. 2015 No. 1678 (*ante*, G-1a).]

Calculation of graduated fees in guilty pleas and cracked trials

7.—(1) The amount of the graduated fee for a single trial advocate representing one assisted **G-44a** person in a guilty plea or cracked trial is—

    (a) where the case is a guilty plea or a trial which cracks in the first third—
        (i) the basic fee specified in Table A following paragraph 8 as appropriate to the offence with which the assisted person is charged, and the category of trial advocate; and
        (ii) the evidence uplift, as appropriate to the number of pages of prosecution evidence, calculated in accordance with that table; and

    (b) where the case is a trial which cracks in the second or last third—
        (i) the basic fee specified in Table B following paragraph 8 as appropriate to the offence with which the assisted person is charged and the category of trial advocate; and
        (ii) the evidence uplift, as appropriate to the number of pages of prosecution evidence, calculated in accordance with that table.

(2) Where—

    (a) the trial of a case does not commence on the date first fixed; or
    (b) the case is not taken and disposed of from the first warned list in which it is entered,

the basic fee and evidence uplift for the offence are those specified for the last third in Table B following paragraph 8.

(3) In this paragraph, and in the tables following paragraph 8, references to the first, second and last third are references to the first, second and last third—

    (a) where a case is first listed for trial on a fixed date, of the period of time beginning with the day after the date on which the case is so listed and ending with the day before the date so fixed;
    (b) where the case is first placed in a warned list, of the period of time beginning with the day after the date on which the case is so placed and ending with the day before the date of the start of that warned list,

and where the number of days in this period of time cannot be divided by three equally, any days remaining after such division must be added to the last third.

(4) Where a graduated fee is calculated in accordance with this Part for the purposes of paragraph 2(3), the fee must be calculated as if the trial had cracked in the last third.

Tables of fees

8. Subject to paragraph 7, the basic fee and evidence uplift appropriate to any offence are specified **G-45**

519

in the tables following this paragraph in accordance with the Class within which that offence falls, the category of trial advocate and whether the case is a guilty plea, a trial which cracks in the first third or a trial which cracks in the second or last third.

TABLE A: FEES AND UPLIFTS IN GUILTY PLEAS AND TRIALS WHICH CRACK IN THE FIRST THIRD

Class of Offence	Basic fee (£)	Evidence uplift per page of prosecution evidence (pages 1 to 1,000) (£)	Evidence uplift per page of prosecution evidence (1,001 to 10,000) (£)
QC			
A	1,714	2.85	1.43
B	1,305	1.8	0.9
C	1,224	1.28	0.64
D	1,305	2.85	1.43
E	1,081	0.92	0.46
F	1,081	1.2	0.61
G	1,081	1.2	0.61
H	1,224	1.65	0.82
I	1,224	1.61	0.8
J	1,714	2.85	1.43
K	1,714	1.59	0.8
Leading Junior			
A	1,285	2.15	1.07
B	979	1.35	0.67
C	918	0.96	0.48
D	979	2.15	1.07
E	811	0.69	0.35
F	811	0.9	0.46
G	811	0.9	0.46
H	918	1.24	0.61
I	918	1.21	0.6
J	1,285	2.15	1.07
K	1,285	1.19	0.6
Led Junior			
A	857	1.43	0.72
B	653	0.9	0.45
C	612	0.64	0.32
D	653	1.43	0.72
E	541	0.46	0.23
F	541	0.61	0.3
G	541	0.61	0.3
H	612	0.83	0.42
I	612	0.8	0.4
J	857	1.43	0.72
K	857	0.8	0.4
Junior Alone			
A	979	1.19	0.59
B	694	0.81	0.41
C	449	0.6	0.3

Class of Offence	Basic fee (£)	Evidence uplift per page of prosecution evidence (pages 1 to 1,000) (£)	Evidence uplift per page of prosecution evidence (1,001 to 10,000) (£)
D	694	1.19	0.59
E	408	0.35	0.17
F	408	0.54	0.27
G	408	0.54	0.27
H	490	0.54	0.28
I	571	0.42	0.22
J	979	1.19	0.59
K	979	1.02	0.51

TABLE B: FEES AND UPLIFTS IN TRIALS WHICH CRACK IN THE SECOND OR FINAL THIRD

Class of Offence	Basic Fee (£)	Evidence uplift per page of prosecution evidence (pages 1 to 250) (£)	Evidence up lift per page of prosecutionevidence (pages 251-1000) (£)	Evidence uplift per page of prosecution evidence (pages 1,001 to 10,000) (£)
QC				
A	2,324	5.07	1.27	1.68
B	1,743	3.2	0.8	1.06
C	1,520	2.27	0.57	0.75
D	1,743	5.07	1.27	1.68
E	1,232	1.63	0.41	0.54
F	1,232	2.14	0.54	0.71
G	1,232	2.14	0.54	0.71
H	1,540	2.93	0.73	0.96
I	1,598	2.87	0.71	0.94
J	2,324	5.07	1.27	1.68
K	2,324	2.83	0.71	0.94
Leading Junior				
A	1,744	3.8	0.95	1.26
B	1,307	2.4	0.6	0.8
C	1,140	1.7	0.43	0.56
D	1,307	3.8	0.95	1.26
E	924	1.22	0.31	0.41
F	924	1.6	0.41	0.53
G	924	1.6	0.41	0.53
H	1,155	2.2	0.54	0.72
I	1,198	2.14	0.53	0.71
J	1,744	3.8	0.95	1.26
K	1,744	2.13	0.53	0.71
Led Junior				
A	1162	2.54	0.64	0.84
B	871	1.6	0.4	0.53
C	760	1.14	0.28	0.37
D	871	2.54	0.64	0.84
E	616	0.82	0.2	0.27

Class of Offence	Basic Fee (£)	Evidence uplift per page of prosecution evidence (pages 1 to 250) (£)	Evidence up lift per page of prosecutionevidence (pages 251-1000) (£)	Evidence uplift per page of prosecution evidence (pages 1,001 to 10,000) (£)
F	616	1.07	0.27	0.36
G	616	1.07	0.27	0.36
H	770	1.46	0.37	0.48
I	798	1.43	0.36	0.48
J	1162	2.54	0.64	0.84
K	1162	1.42	0.36	0.47
Junior alone				
A	1307	4.52	2.1	0.69
B	908	3.11	1.45	0.48
C	581	2.31	1.07	0.36
D	808	4.52	2.1	0.69
E	508	1.34	0.63	0.2
F	508	2.08	0.96	0.32
G	508	2.08	0.96	0.32
H	618	2.08	0.97	0.32
I	726	1.63	0.76	0.25
J	1307	4.52	2.1	0.69
K	1234	3.91	1.82	0.60

PART 4

FIXED FEE FOR GUILTY PLEAS AND CRACKED TRIALS

Scope of Part 4

G-46
9.—(1) Subject to sub-paragraph (2), this Part applies to a case sent for trial to the Crown Court on the election of a defendant where the magistrates' court has determined the case to be suitable for summary trial.

(2) This Part does not apply where the trial is a cracked trial because the prosecution offer no evidence on all counts against a defendant and the judge directs that a not guilty verdict be entered.

[This paragraph was substituted by S.I. 2014 No. 2422 (*ante*, G-21a). For the transitional provision, see *ante*, G-21a. It is printed as amended by S.I. 2015 No. 1678 (*ante*, G-1a).]

Fixed fee for guilty pleas or cracked trials

10. The fee payable to an advocate in relation to a guilty plea or cracked trial to which this Part applies is £194 per proceedings.

PART 5

FIXED FEES

General provisions

G-46a
11.—(1) All work undertaken by an advocate in a case to which Part 4 applies is included within the fee set out in paragraph 10 except for attendance at a confiscation hearing to which paragraph 14 applies.

(2) Except as provided under this Part, all work undertaken by an advocate in a case to which Part 3 applies is included within the basic fee (B) specified in the table following paragraph 5, or that following paragraph 8, as appropriate to—

(a) the offence for which the assisted person is tried;

(b) the category of advocate; and

(c) whether the case is a cracked trial, guilty plea or trial.

Fees for standard appearance

G-47
12.—(1) The fee payable in respect of—

(a) an appearance by the trial advocate or substitute advocate at the first hearing at which the assisted person enters a plea; and

(b) up to four standard appearances by the trial advocate or substitute advocate,

is included within the basic fee (B) specified in the table following paragraph 5, or that following paragraph 8, as appropriate to the offence for which the assisted person is tried and the category of trial advocate.

(2) The fee payable in respect of an appearance by the trial advocate or substitute advocate at a standard appearance not included in sub-paragraph (1) is specified in the table following paragraph 24 as appropriate to the category of trial advocate or substitute advocate.

(4) This paragraph does not apply to a standard appearance which is or forms part of the main hearing in a case or to a hearing for which a fee is payable elsewhere under this Schedule.

[Para. 12 is printed as amended by S.I. 2015 No. 1678 (*ante*, G-1a).]

As to whether any appearances can be remunerated under paragraph 12(2) where no basic fee is payable, see *R. v. Metcalf* and *R. v. Muoka, post*, G-129.

Fees for abuse of process, disclosure, admissibility and withdrawal of plea hearings

13.—(1) This paragraph applies to—

G-48

(a) the hearing of an application to stay the case on indictment or any count on the ground that the proceedings constitute an abuse of the process of the court;

(b) any hearing relating to the question of whether any material should be disclosed by the prosecution to the defence or the defence to the prosecution (whether or not any claim to public interest immunity is made);

(c) the hearing of an application under section 2(1) of the Criminal Procedure (Attendance of Witnesses) Act 1965 (issue of witness summons on application to Crown Court) for disclosure of material held by third parties;

(d) any hearing relating to the question of the admissibility as evidence of any material; and

(e) the hearing of an application to withdraw a plea of guilty where the application is—

(i) made by an advocate other than the advocate who appeared at the hearing at which the plea of guilty was entered; and

(ii) unsuccessful.

(2) Where a hearing to which this paragraph applies is held on any day of the main hearing of a case on indictment, no separate fee is payable in respect of attendance at the hearing, but the hearing is included in the length of the main hearing for the purpose of calculating the fees payable.

(3) Where a hearing to which this paragraph applies is held prior to the first or only day of the main hearing, it is not included in the length of the main hearing for the purpose of calculating the fees payable and the trial advocate or substitute advocate must be remunerated for attendance at such a hearing—

(a) in respect of any day where the hearing begins before and ends after the luncheon adjournment, at the daily rate set out in the table following paragraph 24 as appropriate to the category of trial advocate or substitute advocate; or

(b) in respect of any day where the hearing begins and ends before the luncheon adjournment, or begins after the luncheon adjournment, at the half-daily rate set out in the table following paragraph 24 as appropriate to the category of trial advocate or substitute advocate.

Fees for confiscation hearings

14.—(1) This paragraph applies to—

G-49

(a) a hearing under Part 2 of the Proceeds of Crime Act 2002 (confiscation: England and Wales);

(b) a hearing under section 2 of the Drug Trafficking Act 1994 (confiscation orders); and

(c) a hearing under section 71 of the Criminal Justice Act 1988 (confiscation orders).

(2) A hearing to which this paragraph applies is not included in the length of the main hearing or of any sentencing hearing for the purpose of calculating the fees payable, and the trial advocate or substitute advocate must be remunerated in respect of such a hearing—

(a) where the number of pages of evidence is fewer than 51, for attendance—

(i) in respect of any day when the hearing begins before and ends after the luncheon adjournment, at the daily rate set out in the first section of the table following this sub-paragraph; or

(ii) in respect of any day when the hearing begins and ends before the luncheon adjournment, or begins after the luncheon adjournment, at the half-daily rate set out in the first section of that table, as appropriate to the category of trial advocate or substitute advocate;

(b) where the number of pages of evidence is between 51 and 1000—

    (i) at the rates for the relevant number of pages set out in the second section of the table following this sub-paragraph; and

    (ii) where the hearing lasts for more than one day, for attendance on subsequent days or half-days at the daily rate or half-daily rate set out in the first section of that table, as appropriate to the category of trial advocate or substitute advocate; or

(c) where the number of pages of evidence exceeds 1000—

    (i) at the rates for 751 to 1000 pages set out in the second section of the table following this sub-paragraph;

    (ii) with such fee as the appropriate officer considers reasonable for preparation in respect of the pages in excess of 1000, at the hourly rates for preparation set out in the third section of that table; and

    (iii) where the hearing lasts for more than one day, for attendance on subsequent days or half-days at the daily rate or half-daily rate set out in the first section of that table, as appropriate to the category of trial advocate or substitute advocate.

FEES FOR CONSFISCATION HEARINGS

	Fee for QC (£)	Fee for leading junior (£)	Fee for junior alone (£)	Fee for led junior (£)
1. Daily and half-daily rates				
Half-daily rate	260	195	130	130
Daily rate	497	346	238	238
2. Pages of evidence				
51-250	649	541	433	324
251–500	973	811	649	486
501–750	1,298	1,081	865	649
751–1000	1,946	1,622	1,298	973
3. Preparation				
Hourly rates	74	56	39	39

(3) In sub-paragraph (2) "evidence" means—

(a) the statement of information served under section 16 of the Proceeds of Crime Act 2002 and relied on by the prosecution for the purposes of a hearing under Part 2 of that Act, or a similar statement served and so relied on for the purposes of a hearing under section 2 of the Drug Trafficking Act 1994 or under section 71 of the Criminal Justice Act 1988 and, in each case, any attached annexes and exhibits;

(b) any other document which—

    (i) is served as a statement or an exhibit for the purposes of the trial;

    (ii) is specifically referred to in, but not served with, a statement mentioned in paragraph (a); and

    (iii) the prosecution state that they intend to rely on in the hearing; and

(c) any written report of an expert obtained with the prior authority of the Lord Chancellor under regulation 13 or allowed by the appropriate officer under these Regulations, and any attached annexes and exhibits, other than documents contained in such annexes or exhibits which have also been served under paragraph (a) or (b) or which consist of financial records or similar data.

Fees for sentencing hearings

G-50   15.—(1) This paragraph applies to a sentencing hearing following a case on indictment to which this Schedule applies, where sentence has been deferred under section 1 of the Powers of Criminal Courts (Sentencing) Act 2000 (deferment of sentence).

(2) The fee payable to an advocate for appearing at a hearing to which this paragraph applies is that set out in the table following paragraph 24 as appropriate to the category of trial advocate or substitute advocate and the circumstances of the hearing.

Fees for ineffective trials

G-51   16. The fee set out in the table following paragraph 24 as appropriate to the category of trial advocate is payable in respect of each day on which the case was listed for trial but did not proceed on the day for which it was listed, for whatever reason.

Fees for special preparation

17.—(1) This paragraph applies where, in any case on indictment in the Crown Court in respect **G-52** of which a graduated fee is payable under Part 2 or Part 3—

- (a) it has been necessary for an advocate to do work by way of preparation substantially in excess of the amount normally done for cases of the same type because the case involves a very unusual or novel point of law or factual issue;
- (b) the number of pages of prosecution evidence, as defined in paragraph 1(2), exceeds 10,000 and the appropriate officer considers it reasonable to make a payment in excess of the graduated fee payable under this Schedule; or
- (c) a documentary or pictorial exhibit is served by the prosecution in electronic form where—
  - (i) the exhibit has never existed in paper form; and
  - (ii) the appropriate officer—
    - (aa) does not consider it appropriate to include the exhibit in the pages of prosecution evidence; and
    - (bb) considers it reasonable to make a payment in respect of the exhibit in excess of the graduated fee.

(2) Where this paragraph applies, a special preparation fee may be paid, in addition to the graduated fee payable under Part 2 or Part 3.

(3) The amount of the special preparation fee must be calculated—

- (a) where sub-paragraph (1)(a) applies, from the number of hours preparation in excess of the amount the appropriate officer considers reasonable for cases of the same type;
- (b) where sub-paragraph (1)(b) applies, from the number of hours which the appropriate officer considers reasonable to read the excess pages; and
- (c) where sub-paragraph (1)(c) applies, from the number of hours which the appropriate officer considers reasonable to view the prosecution evidence,

and in each case using the hourly fee rates set out in the table following paragraph 24 as appropriate to the category of trial advocate.

(4) Any claim for a special preparation fee under this paragraph must be made by a trial advocate, whether or not the trial advocate did the work claimed for.

(5) A trial advocate claiming a special preparation fee must supply such information and documents as may be required by the appropriate officer in support of the claim.

(6) In determining a claim under this paragraph, the appropriate officer must take into account all the relevant circumstances of the case, including, where special preparation work has been undertaken by more than one advocate, the benefit of such work to the trial advocate.

(7) In sub-paragraphs (4) and (5), where the main hearing is a trial, "trial advocate" means the advocate who—

- (a) is instructed pursuant to a section 16 determination to represent the assisted person at the trial, and
- (b) attends the first day of the trial.

[This paragraph is printed as amended, with effect from May 5, 2015, by the Criminal Legal Aid (Remuneration) (Amendment) Regulations 2015 (S.I. 2015 No. 882), reg. 2(3)(f), (4)(c), (6)(d), and (16)(b). For the transitional provision, see *ante*, G-7.]

Fees for wasted preparation

18.—(1) A wasted preparation fee may be claimed where a trial advocate in any case to which this **G-53** paragraph applies is prevented from representing the assisted person in the main hearing by any of the following circumstances—

- (a) the trial advocate is instructed to appear in other proceedings at the same time as the main hearing in the case and has been unable to secure a change of date for either the main hearing or the other proceedings;
- (b) the date fixed for the main hearing is changed by the court despite the trial advocate's objection;
- (c) the trial advocate has withdrawn from the case with the leave of the court because of the trial advocate's professional code of conduct or to avoid embarrassment in the exercise of the trial advocate's profession;
- (d) the trial advocate has been dismissed by the assisted person or the litigator; or
- (e) the trial advocate is obliged to attend at any place by reason of a judicial office held by the trial advocate or other public duty.

(2) This paragraph applies to every case on indictment to which this Schedule applies provided that—

> (a) the case goes to trial, and the trial lasts for five days or more; or
>
> (b) the case is a cracked trial, and the number of pages of prosecution evidence exceeds 150.

(3) The amount of the wasted preparation fee must be calculated from the number of hours of preparation reasonably carried out by the trial advocate, using the hourly fee rates set out in the table following paragraph 24 as appropriate to the category of trial advocate, but no such fee is payable unless the number of hours of preparation is eight or more.

(4) Any claim for a wasted preparation fee under this paragraph must be made by a trial advocate, whether or not the trial advocate did the work claimed for.

(5) A trial advocate claiming a wasted preparation fee must supply such information and documents as may be required by the appropriate officer as proof of the circumstances in which the advocate was prevented from representing the assisted person and of the number of hours of preparation.

(6) In sub-paragraphs (4) and (5), where the main hearing is a trial, "trial advocate" means an advocate who—

> (a) is instructed pursuant to a section 16 determination to represent the assisted person at the trial, and
>
> (b) attends the first day of the trial.

[This paragraph is printed as amended, with effect from May 5, 2015, by the Criminal Legal Aid (Remuneration) (Amendment) Regulations 2015 (S.I. 2015 No. 882), reg. 2(4)(c), (6)(d) and (16)(c). For the transitional provision, see *ante*, G-7.]

Fees for conferences and views

G-54   19.—(1) This paragraph applies to the following types of work—

> (a) attendance by the trial advocate at pre-trial conferences with prospective or actual expert witnesses not held at court;
>
> (b) attendance by the trial advocate at views at the scene of the alleged offence;
>
> (c) attendance by the trial advocate at pre-trial conferences with the assisted person not held at court;
>
> (d) reasonable travelling time by the trial advocate for the purpose of attending a view at the scene of the alleged offence; or
>
> (e) reasonable travelling time by the trial advocate for the purpose of attending a pre-trial conference with the assisted person or prospective or actual expert witness, where the appropriate officer is satisfied that the assisted person or prospective or actual expert witness was unable or could not reasonably have been expected to attend a conference at the trial advocate's chambers or office.

(2) The fees payable in respect of attendance at the first three pre-trial conferences or views, as set out in sub-paragraph (1)(a) to (c), are included in the basic fee (B) specified in the table following paragraph 5, or that following paragraph 8, as appropriate to the offence for which the assisted person is tried, the category of trial advocate and whether the case is a guilty plea, cracked trial or trial, provided that the trial advocate satisfies the appropriate officer that the work was reasonably necessary.

(3) The fee specified in the table following paragraph 24 as appropriate to the category of trial advocate is payable in the following circumstances, provided that the trial advocate satisfies the appropriate officer that the work was reasonably necessary—

> (a) for trials lasting not less than 21 and not more than 25 days, and cracked trials where it was accepted by the court at the first hearing at which the assisted person entered a plea that the trial would last not less than 21 days and not more than 25 days, one further pre-trial conference or view not exceeding two hours;
>
> (b) for trials lasting not less than 26 and not more than 35 days, and cracked trials where it was accepted by the court at the first hearing at which the assisted person entered a plea that the trial would last not less than 26 days and not more than 35 days, two further pre-trial conferences or views each not exceeding two hours; and
>
> (c) for trials lasting not less than 36 days, and cracked trials where it was accepted by the court at the first hearing at which the assisted person entered a plea that the trial would last not less than 36 days and not more than 40 days, three further pre-trial conferences or views each not exceeding two hours.

(4) Travel expenses must be paid for all conferences and views set out in sub-paragraph (1)(a) to (c), provided that the trial advocate satisfies the appropriate officer that they were reasonably incurred.

(5) Travelling time must be paid for all conferences and views set out in sub-paragraph (1)(a) to (c), provided that the trial advocate satisfies the appropriate officer that it was reasonable.

[Para. 19 is printed as amended by S.I. 2015 No. 1678 (*ante*, G-1a).]

Fees for appeals, committals for sentence and breach hearings

20.—(1) Subject to sub-paragraphs (4) and (5) and paragraph 26 the fee payable to a trial advocate **G-55** in any of the hearings referred to in paragraph 2(1)(b) is the fixed fee specified in the table following paragraph 24.

(2) Where a hearing referred to in paragraph 2(1)(b) is listed but cannot proceed because of the failure of the assisted person or a witness to attend, the unavailability of a pre-sentence report, or other good reason, the fee payable to the advocate is the fixed fee specified in the table following paragraph 24.

(3) Where—

(a)　a bail application;

(b)　a mention hearing; or

(c)　any other application,

takes place in the course of a hearing referred to in paragraph 2(1)(b), the fee payable to the advocate is the fixed fee specified in the table following paragraph 24.

(4) Where it appears to the appropriate officer that the fixed fee allowed under sub-paragraph (1) would be inappropriate taking into account all of the relevant circumstances of the case the appropriate officer may instead allow fees of such amounts as appear to the appropriate officer to be reasonable remuneration for the relevant work in accordance with sub-paragraph (5).

(5) The appropriate officer may allow any of the following classes of fees to an advocate in respect of work allowed by the appropriate officer under this paragraph—

(a)　a fee for preparation including, where appropriate, the first day of the hearing including, where they took place on that day—

    (i)　short conferences;

    (ii)　consultations;

    (iii)　applications and appearances (including bail applications);

    (iv)　views at the scene of the alleged offence; and

    (v)　any other preparation;

(b)　a refresher fee for any day or part of a day for which a hearing continued, including, where they took place on that day—

    (i)　short conferences;

    (ii)　consultations;

    (iii)　applications and appearances (including bail applications);

    (iv)　views at the scene of the alleged offence; and

    (v)　any other preparation; and

(c)　subsidiary fees for—

    (i)　attendance at conferences, consultations and views at the scene of the alleged offence not covered by paragraph (a) or (b);

    (ii)　written advice on evidence, plea, appeal, case stated or other written work; and

    (iii)　attendance at applications and appearances (including bail applications and adjournments for sentence) not covered by paragraph (a) or (b).

Fees for contempt proceedings

21.—(1) Subject to sub-paragraph (2), remuneration for advocates in proceedings referred to in **G-55a** section 14(g) of the Act in the Crown Court must be at the rates specified in the table following this sub-paragraph.

Category of advocate	Payment rates (£ per day)
QC	300
Leading junior	225
Led junior or junior acting alone	150

(2) Where an advocate and a litigator are instructed in proceedings referred to in section 14(g) of the Act, remuneration must be at the rates specified in the table following this sub-paragraph, as appropriate to the category of advocate.

Category of advocate	Payment rates (£ per day)
QC	175

Category of advocate	Payment rates (£ per day)
Leading junior	125
Led junior or junior acting alone	100

Discontinuance or dismissal of proceedings

G-56 22.—(1) This paragraph applies to proceedings which are sent for trial in the Crown Court.

(2) Where proceedings referred to in sub-paragraph (1) are discontinued by a notice served under section 23A of the Prosecution of Offences Act 1985 (discontinuance of proceedings after accused has been sent for trial) at any time before the prosecution serves its evidence in accordance with the Crime and Disorder Act 1998 (Service of Prosecution Evidence) Regulations 2005 the advocate must be paid 50% of the basic fee (B) for a guilty plea, as specified in the table following paragraph 8 as appropriate to the offence for which the assisted person is charged and the category of advocate.

(3) Where proceedings referred to in sub-paragraph (1) are discontinued by a notice served under section 23A of the Prosecution of Offences Act 1985 (discontinuance of proceedings after accused has been sent for trial) at any time after the prosecution serves its evidence in accordance with the Crime and Disorder Act 1998 (Service of Prosecution Evidence) Regulations 2005, the advocate must be paid a graduated fee calculated in accordance with paragraph 7, as appropriate for representing an assisted person in a guilty plea.

(5) Where, at or before the first hearing at which the assisted person enters a plea—

(a) the prosecution offers no evidence and the assisted person is discharged; or

(b) the case is remitted to the magistrates' court in accordance with paragraph 10(3)(a), 13(2) or 15(3)(a) of Schedule 3 to the Crime and Disorder Act 1998,

the advocate instructed in the proceedings must be paid a graduated fee calculated in accordance with paragraph 7, as appropriate for representing an assisted person in a guilty plea.

(6) Where an application for dismissal is made under paragraph 2 of Schedule 3 to the Crime and Disorder Act 1998, the advocate must be remunerated for attendance at the hearing of the application for dismissal—

(a) in respect of any day where the hearing begins before and ends after the luncheon adjournment, at the daily rate set out in the table following paragraph 24 as appropriate to the category of advocate; or

(b) in respect of any day where the hearing begins and ends before the luncheon adjournment, or begins after the luncheon adjournment, at the half-daily rate set out in that table as appropriate to the category of advocate,

provided that a fee is not payable elsewhere under this Schedule in respect of any day of the hearing.

(7) Where an application for dismissal is made under paragraph 2 of Schedule 3 to the Crime and Disorder Act 1998, and—

(a) the charge, or charges, are dismissed and the assisted person is discharged; or

(b) the case is remitted to the magistrates' court in accordance with paragraph 10(3)(a), 13(2) or 15(3)(a) of Schedule 3 to the Crime and Disorder Act 1998,

in respect of the first day of the hearing of the application to dismiss, the advocate instructed in the proceedings must be paid a graduated fee calculated in accordance with paragraph 7, as appropriate for representing an assisted person in a guilty plea.

(8) Where an advocate represents more than one assisted person in proceedings referred to in sub-paragraph (1), the advocate must be paid a fixed fee of 20% of—

(a) the fee specified in sub-paragraph (2) where that sub-paragraph applies; or

(b) the basic fee (B) specified in the table following paragraph 8 where sub-paragraph (3), (4) or (5) applies, as appropriate for the circumstances set out in the relevant sub-paragraph,

in respect of each additional assisted person the advocate represents.

[Para. 22 is printed as amended by S.I. 2015 No. 1678 (*ante*, G-1a).]

Noting brief fees

G-57 23. The fee payable to an advocate retained solely for the purpose of making a note of any hearing must be the daily fee set out in the table following paragraph 24.

Fixed fees

G-57a 24. The table following this paragraph sets out the fixed fees payable in relation to the category of work specified in the first column of the table.

FIXED FEES

Category of work	Paragraph providing for fee	Fee for QC £	Fee for leading junior £	Fee for led junior or junior alone £
Standard appearance	9(2)	173 per day	130 per day	87 per day
Abuse of process hearing	10(1)(a)	260 Half day	195 Half day	130 Half day
		497 Full day	346 Full day	238 Full day
Hearings relating to disclosure	10(1)(b) and (c)	260 Half day	195 Half day	130 Half day
		497 Full day	346 Full day	238 Full day
Hearings relating to the admissibility of evidence	10(1)(d)	260 Half day	195 Half day	130 Half day
		497 Full day	346 Full day	238 Full day
Hearings on withdrawal of guilty plea	10(1)(e)	260 Half day	195 Half day	130 Half day
		497 Full day	346 Full day	238 Full day
Deferred sentencing hearing	12(1)(a)	324 per day	238 per day	173 per day
Ineffective trial payment	13	281 per day	195 per day	130 per day
Special preparation	14	74 per hour	56 per hour	39 per hour
Wasted preparation	15	74 per hour	56 per hour	39 per hour
Conferences and views	16	74 per hour	56 per hour	39 per hour
Appeals to the Crown Court against conviction	17(1)	260 per day	195 per day	130 per day
Appeals to the Crown Court against sentence	17(1)	216 per day	151 per day	108 per day
Proceedings relating to breach of an order of the Crown Court	17(1)	216 per day	151 per day	108 per day
Committal for sentence	17(1)	260 per day	195 per day	130 per day
Adjourned appeals, committals for sentence and breach hearings	17(2)	173 per day	130 per day	87 per day
Bail applications, mentions and other applications in appeals, committals for sentence and breach hearings	17(3)	173 per day	130 per day	87 per day
Second and subsequent days of an application to dismiss	18(6)	260 Half day	195 Half day	130 Half day
		497 Full day	346 Full day	238 Full day
Noting brief	19	—	—	108 per day

Category of work	Paragraph providing for fee	Fee for QC £	Fee for leading junior £	Fee for led junior or junior alone £
Hearing for mitigation of sentence	29	260 per day	173 per day	108 per day

[The table is printed as amended by S.I. 2015 No. 1678 (*ante*, G-1a).]

PART 6

MISCELLANEOUS

Identity of instructed advocate

G-58   25.—(1) Where an instructed advocate is appointed before the first hearing at which the assisted person enters a plea, the instructed advocate must notify the Court in writing as soon as the appointment is made and, where appropriate, must confirm whether the instructed advocate is the leading instructed advocate or the led instructed advocate.

(2) Where the section 16 determination provides for representation by a single advocate and no instructed advocate has been notified to the Court in accordance with sub-paragraph (1)—

    (a) the barrister or solicitor advocate who attends the first hearing at which the assisted person enters a plea is deemed to be the instructed advocate; and

    (b) the Court must make a written record of this fact.

(3) Where the section 16 determination provides for representation by a single advocate and no barrister or solicitor advocate attends the first hearing at which the assisted person enters a plea—

    (a) the barrister or solicitor advocate who attends the next hearing in the case is deemed to be the instructed advocate; and

    (b) the Court must make a written record of this fact.

(4) Where the section 16 determination provides for representation by more than one advocate, and no leading instructed advocate has been notified to the Court in accordance with sub-paragraph (1), the leading advocate who attends—

    (a) the first hearing at which the assisted person enters a plea; or

    (b) where no leading advocate attends the first hearing at which the assisted person enters a plea, the next hearing in the case attended by a leading advocate,

is deemed to be the leading instructed advocate, and the Court must make a written record of this fact.

(5) Where the section 16 determination provides for representation by more than one advocate, and no led instructed advocate has been notified to the Court in accordance with sub-paragraph (1), the led advocate who attends—

    (a) the first hearing at which the assisted person enters a plea; or

    (b) where no led advocate attends the first hearing at which the assisted person enters a plea, the next hearing in the case attended by a led advocate,

is deemed to be the led instructed advocate, and the Court must make a written record of this fact.

(6) Where a section 16 determination is amended after the first hearing at which the assisted person enters a plea to provide for representation by more than one advocate—

    (a) the additional instructed advocate must notify the Court in writing of the additional instructed advocate's appointment within 7 days of the date on which the section 16 determination is amended; and

    (b) each instructed advocate must notify the Court whether that instructed advocate is the leading instructed advocate or the led instructed advocate.

(7) Where no additional instructed advocate has been notified to the Court in accordance with sub-paragraph (6)(a), the advocate who attends the next hearing in the case is deemed to be an instructed advocate and the Court must record in writing whether that instructed advocate is the leading instructed advocate or the led instructed advocate, as appropriate to the circumstances of the case.

(8) Where—

    (a) a case ceases to be a Very High Cost Case (in relation to fees claimed by advocates); and

    (b) none of sub-paragraphs (1) to (7) applies,

the instructed advocate must notify the Court in writing of the instructed advocate's appointment within 7 days of the case ceasing to be a Very High Cost Case.

(9) The Court must attach—

    (a) any notice received under sub-paragraph (1), (6) or (8); and

    (b) any record made by it under sub-paragraph (2), (3), (4), (5) or (7), to the representation order.

(10) An instructed advocate must remain as instructed advocate at all times, except where—

    (a) a date for trial is fixed at or before the first hearing at which the assisted person enters a plea and the instructed advocate is unable to conduct the trial due to the instructed advocate's other pre-existing commitments;

    (b) the instructed advocate is dismissed by the assisted person or the litigator; or

    (c) the instructed advocate is required to withdraw because of his professional code of conduct.

(11) Where, in accordance with sub-paragraph (10), an instructed advocate withdraws, the instructed advocate must—

    (a) immediately notify the court of the withdrawal—

        (i) in writing; or

        (ii) where the withdrawal takes place at a hearing, orally; and

    (b) within 7 days of the date of the withdrawal, notify the court in writing of the identity of a replacement instructed advocate, who must fulfil all the functions of an instructed advocate in accordance with these Regulations.

(12) This paragraph does not apply to a claim for fees under paragraph 32, 33 or 34.

[Para. 25 is printed as amended by S.I. 2015 No. 1678 (*ante*, G-1a).]

Payment of fees to trial advocate

26.—(1) In accordance with regulation 23 the appropriate officer must notify each trial advocate of **G-59** the total fees payable and authorise payment to the trial advocate accordingly.

(2) Payment of the fees in accordance with sub-paragraph (1) must be made to each trial advocate.

(3) Where the section 16 determination provides for representation by a single advocate, the trial advocate is responsible for arranging payment of fees to the instructed advocate and any substitute advocate who has undertaken work on the case.

(4) Where there are two trial advocates for an assisted person, payment must be made to each trial advocate individually, and—

    (a) the leading trial advocate is responsible for arranging payment of fees to the instructed advocate and any substitute advocate who have undertaken work on the case of a type for which a leading advocate is responsible; and

    (b) the led trial advocate is responsible for arranging payment of fees to the instructed advocate and any substitute advocate who have undertaken work on the case of a type for which a led advocate is responsible.

(4A) In this paragraph, where the main hearing is a trial, "trial advocate" means an advocate who—

    (a) is instructed pursuant to a section 16 determination to represent the assisted person at the trial, and

    (b) attends the first day of the trial.

(5) This paragraph does not apply to a claim for fees under paragraph 32, 33 or 34.

[This paragraph is printed as amended, with effect from May 5, 2015, by the Criminal Legal Aid (Remuneration) (Amendment) Regulations 2015 (S.I. 2015 No. 882), reg. 2(5)(d) and (16)(d). For the transitional provision, see *ante*, G-7.]

Additional charges and additional cases

27.—(1) Where an assisted person is charged with more than one offence on one indictment, the **G-60** fee payable to the trial advocate under this Schedule must be based on whichever of those offences the trial advocate selects.

(2) Where two or more cases to which this Schedule applies involving the same trial advocate are heard concurrently (whether involving the same or different assisted persons)—

    (a) the trial advocate must select one case ("the principal case"), which must be treated for the purposes of remuneration in accordance with this Schedule;

    (b) in respect of the main hearing in each of the other cases the trial advocate must be paid a fixed fee of 20% of—

        (i) the basic fee (B) specified in the table following paragraph 5 or that following paragraph 8, as appropriate, for the principal case, where that is a case falling within paragraph 2(1)(a); or

        (ii) the fixed fee for the principal case, where that is a case falling within paragraph 2(1)(b) or paragraph 10.

(3) Nothing in sub-paragraphs (4) to (6) permits a fixed fee under Part 5, other than one to which paragraph 14 applies, to be paid in a case to which Part 4 applies.

(4) Where a trial advocate or substitute advocate appears at a hearing specified in paragraph 12,

13, 14, 15 or 16, forming part of two or more cases involving different assisted persons, the trial advocate or substitute advocate must be paid—

    (a) in respect of the first such case, the fixed fee for that hearing specified in the table following paragraph 24; and

    (b) in respect of each of the other cases, 20% of that fee.

(5) Subject to sub-paragraphs (1) to (4), where a trial advocate or substitute advocate appears at a hearing forming part of two or more cases, the trial advocate or substitute advocate must be paid the fixed fee for that hearing specified in the table following paragraph 24 in respect of one such case, without any increase in respect of the other cases.

(6) Where a trial advocate selects—

    (a) one offence, in preference to another offence, under sub-paragraph (1); or

    (b) one case as the principal case, in preference to another case, under sub-paragraph (2),

that selection does not affect the trial advocate's right to claim any of the fees set out in the table following paragraph 24 to which the trial advocate would otherwise have been entitled.

Multiple advocates

G-61

28. Where a section 16 determination provides for representation by three advocates in a case the provisions of this Schedule apply, and the fees payable to the led juniors in accordance with Part 2 or Part 3 are payable to each led junior who is instructed in the case.

Non-local appearances

G-62

29. Where an advocate is instructed to appear in a court which is not within 40 kilometres of the advocate's office or chambers, the appropriate officer may allow an amount for travelling and other expenses incidental to that appearance, provided that the amount must not be greater than the amount, if any, which would be payable to a trial advocate from the nearest local Bar or the nearest advocate's office (whichever is the nearer) unless the advocate instructed to appear has obtained prior approval under regulation 13 for the incurring of such expenses or can justify the attendance having regard to all the relevant circumstances of the case.

Trials lasting over 40 days

G-63

30. Where a trial exceeds 40 days, the trial advocate must be paid a fee as set out in the table following this paragraph, as appropriate to the category of trial advocate and the Class of Offence, for each day by which the trial exceeds 40 days on which the trial advocate attends at court.

DAILY RATES PAYABLE WHERE A TRIAL LASTS OVER 40 DAYS

Class of Offence	Daily rate payable for days 41 to 50 (£)	Daily rate payable for days 51 and over (£)
QC		
A–K	387	414
Leading Junior		
A–K	331	356
Led Junior		
A–K	221	237
Junior Acting Alone		
A	266	285
B	247	265
C	247	265
D	266	285
E	225	241
F	225	241
G	225	241
H	247	265
I	247	265
J	266	285
K	266	285

Assisted person unfit to plead or stand trial

31. Where in any case a hearing is held to determine the question of whether the assisted person **G-64** is unfit to plead or to stand trial (a "fitness hearing")—

   (a) if a trial on indictment is held, or continues, at any time thereafter, the length of the fitness hearing is included in determining the length of the trial for the calculation of the graduated fee in accordance with Part 2 or Part 3;

   (b) if a trial on indictment is not held, or does not continue, thereafter by reason of the assisted person being found unfit to plead or to stand trial, the trial advocate must be paid—

      (i) a graduated fee calculated in accordance with paragraph 4 as appropriate to the combined length of—

        (aa) the fitness hearing; and

        (bb) any hearing under section 4A of the Criminal Procedure (Insanity) Act 1964 (finding that the accused did the act or made the omission charged against him); or

      (ii) a graduated fee calculated in accordance with paragraph 7 as appropriate for representing an assisted person in a cracked trial,

     whichever the trial advocate elects; and

   (c) if at any time the assisted person pleads guilty to the indictable offence, the trial advocate must be paid either—

      (i) a graduated fee calculated in accordance with paragraph 4 as appropriate to the length of the fitness hearing; or

      (ii) a graduated fee calculated in accordance with paragraph 7 as appropriate for representing an assisted person in a guilty plea,

     whichever the trial advocate elects.

Cross examination of witness

32.—(1) Where in any case on indictment an advocate is retained solely for the purpose of cross- **G-65** examining a witness under section 38 of the Youth Justice and Criminal Evidence Act 1999 (defence representation for purposes of cross-examination), the advocate must be paid a graduated fee calculated in accordance with paragraph 4.

(2) For the purposes of this paragraph the daily attendance fee (D) is as set out in the table following paragraph 5 as appropriate to the number of days of attendance at court by the advocate.

Provision of written or oral advice

33.—(1) Where in any case on indictment an advocate is assigned pursuant to a section 16 **G-66** determination solely for the purpose of providing written or oral advice, the advocate must be paid for the reasonable number of hours of preparation for that advice using the hourly fee rates for special preparation set out in the table following paragraph 24 as appropriate to the category of trial advocate.

(2) An advocate claiming a fee for advice under this paragraph may apply to the appropriate officer to redetermine the fee under regulation 28 and the advocate must supply such information and documents as may be required by the appropriate officer as proof of the number of hours of preparation.

Mitigation of sentence

34.—(1) Where in any case on indictment an advocate is assigned pursuant to a section 16 **G-67** determination to appear at a sentencing hearing solely for the purpose of applying to the court to mitigate the assisted person's sentence, the advocate must be paid in respect of that appearance the fee specified in the table following paragraph 24 together with a fee calculated from the reasonable number of hours of preparation for that appearance using the hourly fee rates for special preparation set out in the table following paragraph 24 as appropriate to the category of trial advocate.

(2) An advocate claiming an hourly preparation fee under this paragraph may apply to the appropriate officer to redetermine such hourly fee under regulation 28 and the advocate must supply such information and documents as may be required by the appropriate officer as proof of the number of hours of preparation.

Table of offences

At the end of Schedule 1 to the regulations (in Pt 7), there is a table of offences. For the effect **G-68** thereof, see *post*, G-119, G-168 *et seq.*

Regulation 5   SCHEDULE 2

LITIGATORS' GRADUATED FEE SCHEME

PART 1

DEFINITION AND SCOPE

Interpretation

G-69   1.—(1) In this Schedule—

"case" means proceedings in the Crown Court against any one assisted person—

    (a) on one or more counts of a single indictment;

    (b) arising out of a single notice of appeal against conviction or sentence, or a single committal for sentence, whether on one or more charges; or

    (c) arising out of a single alleged breach of an order of the Crown Court,

    and a case falling within paragraph (c) must be treated as a separate case from the proceedings in which the order was made;

"cracked trial" means a case on indictment in which—

    (a) the assisted person enters a plea of not guilty to one or more counts at the first hearing at which he or she enters a plea and

        (i) the case does not proceed to trial (whether by reason of pleas of guilty or for other reasons) or the prosecution offers no evidence; and

        (ii) either—

            (aa) in respect of one or more counts to which the assisted person pleaded guilty, the assisted person did not so plead at the first hearing at which he or she entered a plea; or

            (bb) in respect of one or more counts which did not proceed, the prosecution did not, before or at the first hearing at which the assisted person entered a plea, declare an intention of not proceeding with them; or

    (b) the case is listed for trial without a hearing at which the assisted persons enters a plea;

"guilty plea" means a case on indictment which—

    (a) is disposed of without a trial because the assisted person pleaded guilty to one or more counts; and

    (b) is not a cracked trial;

"main hearing" means—

    (a) in relation to a case which goes to trial, the trial;

    (b) in relation to a guilty plea, the hearing at which pleas are taken or, where there is more than one such hearing, the last such hearing;

    (c) in relation to a cracked trial, the hearing at which—

        (i) the case becomes a cracked trial by meeting the conditions in the definition of a cracked trial, whether or not any pleas were taken at that hearing; or

        (ii) a formal verdict of not guilty was entered as a result of the prosecution offering no evidence, whether or not the parties attended the hearing;

    (d) in relation to an appeal against conviction or sentence in the Crown Court, the hearing of the appeal;

    (e) in relation to proceedings arising out of a committal for sentence in the Crown Court, the sentencing hearing; and

    (f) in relation to proceedings arising out of an alleged breach of an order of the Crown Court, the hearing at which those proceedings are determined;

"Newton hearing" means a hearing at which evidence is heard for the purpose of determining the sentence of a convicted person in accordance with the principles of *R. v. Newton* (1982) 77 Cr.App.R. 13;

"PPE Cut-off" means the minimum number of pages of prosecution evidence for use in calculating the fee payable to a litigator under this Schedule, as set out in the tables following paragraph 5(1) and (2).

(2) For the purposes of this Schedule, the number of pages of prosecution evidence served on the court must be determined in accordance with sub-paragraphs (3) to (5).

(3) The number of pages of prosecution evidence includes all—

    (a) witness statements;

    (b) documentary and pictorial exhibits;

    (c) records of interviews with the assisted person; and

    (d) records of interviews with other defendants,

which form part of the served prosecution documents or which are included in any notice of additional evidence.

(4) Subject to sub-paragraph (5), a document served by the prosecution in electronic form is included in the number of pages of prosecution evidence.

(5) A documentary or pictorial exhibit which—

    (a) has been served by the prosecution in electronic form; and

    (b) has never existed in paper form,

is not included within the number of pages of prosecution evidence unless the appropriate officer decides that it would be appropriate to include it in the pages of prosecution evidence taking into account the nature of the document and any other relevant circumstances.

(6) In proceedings on indictment in the Crown Court initiated otherwise than by sending for trial, the appropriate officer must determine the number of pages of prosecution evidence in accordance with sub-paragraphs (2) to (5) or as nearly in accordance with those sub-paragraphs as possible as the nature of the case permits.

(7) A reference to the Table of Offences in this Schedule is to the Table of Offences in Part 7 of Schedule 1 and a reference to a Class of Offence in this Schedule is to the Class in which that offence is listed in the Table of Offences.

[Para. 1 is printed as amended by S.I. 2015 No. 1678 (*ante*, G-1a).]

Application

    2.—(1) Subject to sub-paragraphs (2) to (7), this Schedule applies to— **G-69a**

    (a) every case on indictment;

    (b) the following proceedings in the Crown Court—

        (i)   an appeal against conviction or sentence from the magistrates' court;

        (ii)   a sentencing hearing following a committal for sentence to the Crown Court;

        (iii) proceedings arising out of an alleged breach of an order of the Crown Court (whether or not this Schedule applies to the proceedings in which the order was made);

    (c) a sentencing hearing following a case on indictment to which this Schedule applies, where sentence has been deferred under section 1 of the Powers of Criminal Courts (Sentencing) Act 2000 (deferment of sentence);

    (d) any other post-sentence hearing.

    (3) Where, at any time after proceedings are sent for trial to the Crown Court they are—

    (a) discontinued by a notice served under section 23A of the Prosecution of Offences Act 1985 (discontinuance of proceedings after accused has been sent for trial); or

    (b) dismissed pursuant to paragraph 2 of Schedule 3 to the Crime and Disorder Act 1998 (applications for dismissal),

the provisions of paragraphs 21 and 22 apply.

    (4) Where, following a case on indictment, a *Newton* hearing takes place—

    (a) for the purposes of this Schedule the case is to be treated as having gone to trial;

    (b) the length of the trial is to be taken to be the combined length of the main hearing and the *Newton* hearing; and

    (c) the provisions of this Schedule relating to cracked trials and guilty pleas will not apply.

    (5) For the purposes of this Schedule, a case on indictment which discontinues at or before the first hearing at which the assisted person enters a plea otherwise than—

    (a) by reason of a plea of guilty being entered; or

    (b) in accordance with sub-paragraph (3),

must be treated as a guilty plea.

    (6) For the purposes of this Schedule, where a trial that is not a Very High Cost Case (in relation to fees claimed by litigators) lasts over 200 days, it must be treated as if it had lasted 200 days.

    (7) For the purposes of this Schedule, where the number of pages of prosecution evidence in a case which is not a Very High Cost Case (in relation to fees claimed by litigators) exceeds—

    (a) the PPE Cut-off figure specified in the table following paragraph 5(2) as appropriate to the offence for which the assisted person is to be tried and the length of trial; and

    (b) 10,000,

the case must be treated as though it had 10,000 pages of prosecution evidence.

[Para. 2 is printed as amended by S.I. 2015 No. 1678 (*ante*, G-1a).]

Class of offences

    3.—(1) For the purposes of this Schedule— **G-70**

    (a) every indictable offence falls within the Class under which it is listed in the Table of Offences and, subject to sub-paragraph (2), indictable offences not specifically so listed are deemed to fall within Class H;

   (b) conspiracy to commit an indictable offence contrary to section 1 of the Criminal Law Act 1977 (the offence of conspiracy), incitement to commit an indictable offence and attempts to commit an indictable offence contrary to section 1 of the Criminal Attempts Act 1981 (attempting to commit an offence) fall within the same Class as the substantive offence to which they relate;

   (c) where the Table of Offences specifies that the Class within which an offence falls depends on whether the value involved exceeds a stated limit, the value must be presumed not to exceed that limit unless the litigator making the claim under regulation 5 proves otherwise to the satisfaction of the appropriate officer;

   (d) where more than one count of the indictment is for an offence in relation to which the Class depends on the value involved, that value must be taken to be the total value involved in all those offences, but where two or more counts relate to the same property, the value of that property must be taken into account once only;

   (e) where an entry in the Table of Offences specifies an offence as being contrary to a statutory provision, then subject to any express limitation in the entry that entry includes every offence contrary to that statutory provision whether or not the words of description in the entry are appropriate to cover all such offences;

   (f) where in a case on indictment there is a hearing to determine the question of whether an assisted person is unfit to plead or unfit to stand trial, the litigator must elect whether that hearing falls within the same Class as the indictable offence to which it relates or within Class D;

   (g) where in a case on indictment a restriction order is made under section 41 of the Mental Health Act 1983 (power of higher courts to restrict discharge from hospital), the offence falls within Class A, regardless of the Class under which the offence would be listed in the Table of Offences, but for this paragraph.

(2) Where a litigator in proceedings in the Crown Court is dissatisfied with the classification within Class H of an indictable offence not listed in the Table of Offences, the litigator may apply to the appropriate officer, when lodging the claim for fees, to reclassify the offence.

(3) The appropriate officer must, in light of the objections made by the litigator—

   (a) confirm the classification of the offence within Class H; or

   (b) reclassify the offence,

and must notify the litigator of the decision.

As to this paragraph, see *post*, G-119.

PART 2

GRADUATED FEES FOR GUILTY PLEAS, CRACKED TRIALS AND TRIALS

Scope

G-70a   4.—(1) Subject to sub-paragraph (2) and to paragraph 21, this Part does not apply to a guilty plea or cracked trial in a case sent for trial to the Crown Court on the election of a defendant where the magistrates' court has determined the case to be suitable for summary trial.

(2) This Part applies in all cases where the trial is a cracked trial because the prosecution offer no evidence on all counts against a defendant and the judge directs that a not guilty verdict be entered.

[This paragraph was substituted by S.I. 2014 No. 2422 (*ante*, G-21a). For the transitional provision, see *ante*, G-21a. It is printed as amended by S.I. 2015 No. 1678 (*ante*, G-1a).]

Pages of prosecution evidence

G-70b   5.—(1) For the purposes of this Part, the PPE Cut-off figures in a cracked trial or guilty plea are specified in the table following this sub-paragraph, as appropriate to the offence with which the assisted person is charged.

PPE CUT-OFF FIGURES IN CRACKED TRIALS AND GUILTY PLEAS

	Class of offence										
Type of case	*A*	*B*	*C*	*D*	*E*	*F*	*G*	*H*	*I*	*J*	*K*
Cracked trial or guilty plea	80	70	40	80	40	50	50	40	40	80	120

(2) For the purposes of this Part, the PPE Cut-off figures in a trial are specified in the table following this sub-paragraph, as appropriate to the offence for which the assisted person is tried and the

length of trial.

PPE Cut-off figures in trials

Trial length in days	PPE Cut off A	PPE Cut off B	PPE Cut off C	PPE Cut off D	PPE Cut off E	PPE Cut off F	PPE Cut off G	PPE Cut off H	PPE Cut off I	PPE Cut off J	PPE Cut off K
1	80	70	40	80	40	50	50	40	40	80	120
2	80	70	40	80	40	50	50	40	40	80	120
3	95	105	81	95	120	138	138	122	134	95	186
4	126	139	120	126	158	173	173	157	185	126	252
5	156	170	157	156	195	206	206	191	232	156	314
6	186	203	193	186	229	240	240	225	281	186	372
7	218	238	230	218	265	276	276	260	329	218	433
8	257	274	267	257	301	310	310	301	376	257	495
9	293	306	301	293	333	342	342	338	420	293	550
10	330	338	339	330	365	373	373	374	464	330	606
11	367	370	378	367	399	405	405	412	509	367	663
12	404	402	417	404	433	437	437	449	554	404	721
13	440	434	455	440	467	470	470	486	598	440	779
14	477	465	493	477	500	501	501	523	642	477	836
15	514	497	531	514	532	533	533	559	686	514	894
16	551	535	569	551	565	564	564	596	730	551	951
17	587	573	607	587	598	596	596	637	774	587	1,007
18	624	611	646	624	646	627	627	687	818	624	1,063
19	661	649	684	661	696	659	659	736	862	661	1,119
20	697	687	722	697	746	690	690	786	907	697	1,174
21	742	722	753	742	787	720	720	826	943	742	1,230
22	786	757	785	786	828	752	752	867	980	786	1,286
23	830	792	819	830	868	784	784	908	1,017	830	1,341
24	874	826	857	874	908	816	816	948	1,053	874	1,396
25	917	860	894	917	948	848	848	988	1,088	917	1,451
26	961	895	931	961	988	880	880	1,028	1,124	961	1,505

Trial length in days	PPE Cut off A	PPE Cut off B	PPE Cut off C	PPE Cut off D	PPE Cut off E	PPE Cut off F	PPE Cut off G	PPE Cut off H	PPE Cut off I	PPE Cut off J	PPE Cut off K
27	1,005	935	967	1,005	1,028	912	912	1,068	1,160	1,005	1,560
28	1,049	975	1,004	1,049	1,068	944	944	1,107	1,196	1,049	1,615
29	1,099	1,016	1,041	1,099	1,108	976	976	1,147	1,231	1,099	1,670
30	1,150	1,057	1,077	1,150	1,148	1,007	1,007	1,187	1,267	1,150	1,725
31	1,200	1,098	1,114	1,200	1,188	1,039	1,039	1,226	1,303	1,200	1,780
32	1,251	1,138	1,151	1,251	1,228	1,070	1,070	1,266	1,349	1,251	1,835
33	1,301	1,179	1,187	1,301	1,268	1,102	1,102	1,307	1,394	1,301	1,889
34	1,352	1,220	1,224	1,352	1,308	1,133	1,133	1,357	1,439	1,352	1,944
35	1,402	1,261	1,262	1,402	1,347	1,165	1,165	1,407	1,485	1,402	1,999
36	1,453	1,302	1,303	1,453	1,435	1,196	1,196	1,457	1,530	1,453	2,054
37	1,503	1,348	1,345	1,503	1,526	1,228	1,228	1,507	1,575	1,503	2,109
38	1,554	1,395	1,386	1,554	1,617	1,259	1,259	1,557	1,621	1,554	2,164
39	1,604	1,441	1,428	1,604	1,708	1,291	1,291	1,607	1,666	1,604	2,219
40	1,652	1,484	1,444	1,652	1,745	1,314	1,314	1,629	1,704	1,652	2,271
41	1,700	1,527	1,461	1,700	1,782	1,338	1,338	1,651	1,742	1,700	2,324
42	1,748	1,570	1,477	1,748	1,820	1,361	1,361	1,673	1,780	1,748	2,377
43	1,796	1,613	1,494	1,796	1,857	1,384	1,384	1,695	1,818	1,796	2,430
44	1,844	1,656	1,511	1,844	1,895	1,410	1,410	1,716	1,856	1,844	2,483
45	1,892	1,699	1,527	1,892	1,932	1,440	1,440	1,738	1,894	1,892	2,536
46	1,939	1,742	1,544	1,939	1,970	1,470	1,470	1,760	1,932	1,939	2,589
47	1,987	1,785	1,560	1,987	2,007	1,501	1,501	1,782	1,970	1,987	2,642
48	2,039	1,828	1,577	2,039	2,045	1,531	1,531	1,804	2,008	2,039	2,695
49	2,091	1,871	1,594	2,091	2,082	1,561	1,561	1,826	2,046	2,091	2,749
50	2,144	1,914	1,610	2,144	2,120	1,591	1,591	1,848	2,084	2,144	2,802
51	2,196	1,957	1,627	2,196	2,158	1,622	1,622	1,870	2,122	2,196	2,855
52	2,249	2,000	1,644	2,249	2,195	1,652	1,652	1,892	2,160	2,249	2,908
53	2,301	2,043	1,660	2,301	2,233	1,682	1,682	1,914	2,198	2,301	2,962
54	2,354	2,086	1,677	2,354	2,271	1,712	1,712	1,936	2,236	2,354	3,015

Trial length in days	PPE Cut off A	PPE Cut off B	PPE Cut off C	PPE Cut off D	PPE Cut off E	PPE Cut off F	PPE Cut off G	PPE Cut off H	PPE Cut off I	PPE Cut off J	PPE Cut off K
55	2,406	2,129	1,694	2,406	2,308	1,743	1,743	1,958	2,275	2,406	3,068
56	2,459	2,172	1,710	2,459	2,346	1,773	1,773	1,980	2,313	2,459	3,121
57	2,512	2,215	1,727	2,512	2,384	1,803	1,803	2,002	2,351	2,512	3,175
58	2,564	2,258	1,744	2,564	2,422	1,833	1,833	2,024	2,389	2,564	3,228
59	2,617	2,301	1,760	2,617	2,459	1,864	1,864	2,046	2,427	2,617	3,281
60	2,669	2,345	1,777	2,669	2,497	1,894	1,894	2,068	2,465	2,669	3,335
61	2,722	2,388	1,794	2,722	2,535	1,924	1,924	2,090	2,503	2,722	3,388
62	2,775	2,431	1,811	2,775	2,572	1,959	1,959	2,112	2,542	2,775	3,442
63	2,827	2,474	1,827	2,827	2,610	2,020	2,020	2,134	2,580	2,827	3,495
64	2,880	2,517	1,844	2,880	2,648	2,081	2,081	2,156	2,618	2,880	3,549
65	2,933	2,561	1,861	2,933	2,686	2,141	2,141	2,178	2,656	2,933	3,602
66	2,985	2,604	1,877	2,985	2,723	2,202	2,202	2,200	2,694	2,985	3,656
67	3,038	2,647	1,894	3,038	2,761	2,263	2,263	2,222	2,776	3,038	3,709
68	3,091	2,690	1,911	3,091	2,799	2,323	2,323	2,244	2,865	3,091	3,763
69	3,144	2,734	1,927	3,144	2,836	2,384	2,384	2,266	2,954	3,144	3,816
70	3,196	2,777	1,944	3,196	2,874	2,445	2,445	2,288	3,043	3,196	3,870
71	3,249	2,820	1,961	3,249	2,912	2,506	2,506	2,310	3,132	3,249	3,923
72	3,302	2,864	1,978	3,302	2,950	2,566	2,566	2,332	3,221	3,302	3,977
73	3,355	2,907	1,994	3,355	2,987	2,627	2,627	2,354	3,310	3,355	4,031
74	3,407	2,950	2,016	3,407	3,025	2,688	2,688	2,376	3,399	3,407	4,084
75	3,460	2,994	2,040	3,460	3,063	2,749	2,749	2,398	3,488	3,460	4,138
76	3,513	3,037	2,064	3,513	3,101	2,809	2,809	2,420	3,577	3,513	4,192
77	3,566	3,080	2,089	3,566	3,138	2,870	2,870	2,442	3,666	3,566	4,245
78	3,619	3,124	2,113	3,619	3,176	2,931	2,931	2,464	3,755	3,619	4,299
79	3,672	3,167	2,137	3,672	3,214	2,992	2,992	2,486	3,844	3,672	4,353
80	3,724	3,211	2,161	3,724	3,251	3,052	3,052	2,508	3,933	3,724	4,406
81	3,777	3,254	2,185	3,777	3,289	3,113	3,113	2,530	4,023	3,777	4,460
82	3,830	3,297	2,210	3,830	3,327	3,174	3,174	2,552	4,112	3,830	4,514

Trial length in days	PPE Cut off A	PPE Cut off B	PPE Cut off C	PPE Cut off D	PPE Cut off E	PPE Cut off F	PPE Cut off G	PPE Cut off H	PPE Cut off I	PPE Cut off J	PPE Cut off K
83	3,883	3,341	2,234	3,883	3,365	3,235	3,235	2,575	4,201	3,883	4,568
84	3,936	3,384	2,258	3,936	3,402	3,295	3,295	2,597	4,290	3,936	4,622
85	3,989	3,428	2,282	3,989	3,440	3,356	3,356	2,619	4,379	3,989	4,675
86	4,042	3,471	2,307	4,042	3,478	3,417	3,417	2,641	4,469	4,042	4,729
87	4,095	3,515	2,331	4,095	3,516	3,478	3,478	2,663	4,558	4,095	4,783
88	4,148	3,558	2,355	4,148	3,553	3,539	3,539	2,685	4,647	4,148	4,837
89	4,201	3,602	2,379	4,201	3,591	3,599	3,599	2,707	4,737	4,201	4,891
90	4,254	3,645	2,404	4,254	3,629	3,660	3,660	2,729	4,826	4,254	4,945
91	4,307	3,689	2,428	4,307	3,666	3,721	3,721	2,751	4,915	4,307	4,999
92	4,360	3,733	2,452	4,360	3,704	3,782	3,782	2,774	5,005	4,360	5,053
93	4,413	3,776	2,477	4,413	3,742	3,843	3,843	2,796	5,094	4,413	5,107
94	4,466	3,820	2,501	4,466	3,780	3,903	3,903	2,818	5,183	4,466	5,161
95	4,519	3,863	2,525	4,519	3,817	3,964	3,964	2,840	5,273	4,519	5,215
96	4,572	3,907	2,549	4,572	3,855	4,025	4,025	2,862	5,362	4,572	5,269
97	4,625	3,951	2,574	4,625	3,893	4,086	4,086	2,884	5,452	4,625	5,323
98	4,679	3,994	2,598	4,679	3,930	4,147	4,147	2,906	5,541	4,679	5,377
99	4,732	4,038	2,622	4,732	3,968	4,207	4,207	2,929	5,631	4,732	5,431
100	4,785	4,082	2,647	4,785	4,006	4,268	4,268	2,951	5,720	4,785	5,485
101	4,838	4,125	2,671	4,838	4,044	4,329	4,329	2,973	5,810	4,838	5,539
102	4,891	4,169	2,695	4,891	4,081	4,390	4,390	2,995	5,899	4,891	5,593
103	4,944	4,213	2,720	4,944	4,119	4,451	4,451	3,032	5,989	4,944	5,647
104	4,997	4,257	2,744	4,997	4,157	4,512	4,512	3,073	6,079	4,997	5,702
105	5,051	4,300	2,768	5,051	4,195	4,573	4,573	3,114	6,168	5,051	5,756
106	5,104	4,344	2,793	5,104	4,232	4,633	4,633	3,155	6,258	5,104	5,810
107	5,157	4,388	2,817	5,157	4,270	4,694	4,694	3,196	6,348	5,157	5,864
108	5,210	4,432	2,841	5,210	4,308	4,755	4,755	3,237	6,437	5,210	5,918
109	5,264	4,475	2,866	5,264	4,345	4,816	4,816	3,278	6,527	5,264	5,973
110	5,317	4,519	2,890	5,317	4,383	4,877	4,877	3,319	6,617	5,317	6,027

Trial length in days	PPE Cut off A	PPE Cut off B	PPE Cut off C	PPE Cut off D	PPE Cut off E	PPE Cut off F	PPE Cut off G	PPE Cut off H	PPE Cut off I	PPE Cut off J	PPE Cut off K
111	5,370	4,563	2,914	5,370	4,421	4,938	4,938	3,361	6,706	5,370	6,081
112	5,423	4,607	2,939	5,423	4,459	4,999	4,999	3,402	6,796	5,423	6,135
113	5,477	4,650	2,963	5,477	4,496	5,059	5,059	3,443	6,886	5,477	6,189
114	5,530	4,694	2,987	5,530	4,534	5,120	5,120	3,484	6,976	5,530	6,244
115	5,583	4,738	3,012	5,583	4,572	5,181	5,181	3,525	7,066	5,583	6,298
116	5,637	4,782	3,036	5,637	4,610	5,242	5,242	3,566	7,155	5,637	6,352
117	5,690	4,826	3,060	5,690	4,647	5,303	5,303	3,607	7,245	5,690	6,406
118	5,743	4,869	3,085	5,743	4,685	5,364	5,364	3,648	7,335	5,743	6,460
119	5,797	4,913	3,109	5,797	4,723	5,425	5,425	3,689	7,425	5,797	6,514
120	5,850	4,957	3,133	5,850	4,760	5,486	5,486	3,730	7,515	5,850	6,569
121	5,904	5,001	3,158	5,904	4,798	5,547	5,547	3,771	7,605	5,904	6,623
122	5,956	5,044	3,182	5,956	4,836	5,607	5,607	3,812	7,693	5,956	6,677
123	6,009	5,088	3,206	6,009	4,874	5,668	5,668	3,853	7,782	6,009	6,731
124	6,061	5,131	3,230	6,061	4,911	5,729	5,729	3,895	7,871	6,061	6,785
125	6,114	5,175	3,254	6,114	4,949	5,789	5,789	3,936	7,959	6,114	6,839
126	6,167	5,218	3,278	6,167	4,987	5,850	5,850	3,977	8,048	6,167	6,892
127	6,219	5,261	3,302	6,219	5,025	5,911	5,911	4,017	8,137	6,219	6,945
128	6,272	5,304	3,326	6,272	5,062	5,971	5,971	4,058	8,225	6,272	6,999
129	6,324	5,347	3,350	6,324	5,100	6,032	6,032	4,098	8,314	6,324	7,052
130	6,377	5,390	3,374	6,377	5,138	6,093	6,093	4,139	8,403	6,377	7,106
131	6,430	5,433	3,398	6,430	5,175	6,153	6,153	4,179	8,491	6,430	7,159
132	6,482	5,476	3,422	6,482	5,213	6,214	6,214	4,219	8,580	6,482	7,212
133	6,535	5,520	3,446	6,535	5,251	6,274	6,274	4,260	8,669	6,535	7,266
134	6,588	5,563	3,470	6,588	5,289	6,335	6,335	4,300	8,757	6,588	7,319
135	6,640	5,606	3,494	6,640	5,326	6,396	6,396	4,341	8,846	6,640	7,373
136	6,693	5,649	3,518	6,693	5,364	6,456	6,456	4,381	8,935	6,693	7,426
137	6,745	5,692	3,542	6,745	5,402	6,517	6,517	4,422	9,023	6,745	7,479
138	6,798	5,735	3,566	6,798	5,439	6,578	6,578	4,462	9,112	6,798	7,533

Trial length in days	PPE Cut off A	PPE Cut off B	PPE Cut off C	PPE Cut off D	PPE Cut off E	PPE Cut off F	PPE Cut off G	PPE Cut off H	PPE Cut off I	PPE Cut off J	PPE Cut off K
139	6,851	5,778	3,590	6,851	5,477	6,638	6,638	4,503	9,201	6,851	7,586
140	6,903	5,821	3,614	6,903	5,515	6,699	6,699	4,543	9,289	6,903	7,639
141	6,956	5,864	3,638	6,956	5,553	6,760	6,760	4,584	9,378	6,956	7,693
142	7,008	5,908	3,662	7,008	5,590	6,820	6,820	4,624	9,467	7,008	7,746
143	7,061	5,951	3,686	7,061	5,628	6,881	6,881	4,664	9,555	7,061	7,800
144	7,114	5,994	3,709	7,114	5,666	6,942	6,942	4,705	9,644	7,114	7,853
145	7,166	6,037	3,733	7,166	5,704	7,002	7,002	4,745	9,733	7,166	7,906
146	7,219	6,080	3,757	7,219	5,741	7,063	7,063	4,786	9,821	7,219	7,960
147	7,272	6,123	3,781	7,272	5,779	7,124	7,124	4,826	9,910	7,272	8,013
148	7,324	6,166	3,805	7,324	5,817	7,184	7,184	4,867	9,999	7,324	8,067
149	7,377	6,209	3,829	7,377	5,854	7,245	7,245	4,907	10,087	7,377	8,120
150	7,429	6,252	3,853	7,429	5,892	7,305	7,305	4,948	10,176	7,429	8,173
151	7,482	6,296	3,877	7,482	5,930	7,366	7,366	4,988	10,265	7,482	8,227
152	7,535	6,339	3,901	7,535	5,968	7,427	7,427	5,029	10,353	7,535	8,280
153	7,587	6,382	3,925	7,587	6,005	7,487	7,487	5,069	10,442	7,587	8,333
154	7,640	6,425	3,949	7,640	6,043	7,548	7,548	5,110	10,531	7,640	8,387
155	7,692	6,468	3,973	7,692	6,081	7,609	7,609	5,150	10,619	7,692	8,440
156	7,745	6,511	3,997	7,745	6,119	7,669	7,669	5,190	10,708	7,745	8,494
157	7,798	6,554	4,021	7,798	6,156	7,730	7,730	5,231	10,797	7,798	8,547
158	7,850	6,597	4,045	7,850	6,194	7,791	7,791	5,271	10,885	7,850	8,600
159	7,903	6,641	4,069	7,903	6,232	7,851	7,851	5,312	10,974	7,903	8,654
160	7,956	6,684	4,093	7,956	6,269	7,912	7,912	5,352	11,063	7,956	8,707
161	8,008	6,727	4,117	8,008	6,307	7,973	7,973	5,393	11,151	8,008	8,760
162	8,061	6,770	4,141	8,061	6,345	8,033	8,033	5,433	11,240	8,061	8,814
163	8,113	6,813	4,165	8,113	6,383	8,094	8,094	5,474	11,329	8,113	8,867
164	8,166	6,856	4,189	8,166	6,420	8,155	8,155	5,514	11,417	8,166	8,921
165	8,219	6,899	4,213	8,219	6,458	8,215	8,215	5,555	11,506	8,219	8,974
166	8,271	6,942	4,237	8,271	6,496	8,276	8,276	5,595	11,595	8,271	9,027

Trial length in days	PPE Cut off A	PPE Cut off B	PPE Cut off C	PPE Cut off D	PPE Cut off E	PPE Cut off F	PPE Cut off G	PPE Cut off H	PPE Cut off I	PPE Cut off J	PPE Cut off K
167	8,324	6,985	4,261	8,324	6,534	8,337	8,337	5,636	11,683	8,324	9,081
168	8,376	7,029	4,285	8,376	6,571	8,397	8,397	5,676	11,772	8,376	9,134
169	8,429	7,072	4,309	8,429	6,609	8,458	8,458	5,716	11,861	8,429	9,188
170	8,482	7,115	4,333	8,482	6,647	8,518	8,518	5,757	11,949	8,482	9,241
171	8,534	7,158	4,357	8,534	6,684	8,579	8,579	5,797	12,038	8,534	9,294
172	8,587	7,201	4,380	8,587	6,722	8,640	8,640	5,838	12,127	8,587	9,348
173	8,639	7,244	4,404	8,639	6,760	8,700	8,700	5,878	12,215	8,639	9,401
174	8,692	7,287	4,428	8,692	6,798	8,761	8,761	5,919	12,304	8,692	9,454
175	8,745	7,330	4,452	8,745	6,835	8,822	8,822	5,959	12,393	8,745	9,508
176	8,797	7,373	4,476	8,797	6,873	8,882	8,882	6,000	12,481	8,797	9,561
177	8,850	7,417	4,500	8,850	6,911	8,943	8,943	6,040	12,570	8,850	9,615
178	8,903	7,460	4,524	8,903	6,948	9,004	9,004	6,081	12,659	8,903	9,668
179	8,955	7,503	4,548	8,955	6,986	9,064	9,064	6,121	12,747	8,955	9,721
180	9,008	7,546	4,572	9,008	7,024	9,125	9,125	6,162	12,836	9,008	9,775
181	9,060	7,589	4,596	9,060	7,062	9,186	9,186	6,202	12,925	9,060	9,828
182	9,113	7,632	4,620	9,113	7,099	9,246	9,246	6,242	13,013	9,113	9,881
183	9,166	7,675	4,644	9,166	7,137	9,307	9,307	6,283	13,102	9,166	9,935
184	9,218	7,718	4,668	9,218	7,174	9,368	9,368	6,323	13,191	9,218	9,988
185	9,271	7,762	4,692	9,271	7,211	9,428	9,428	6,364	13,279	9,271	10,042
186	9,323	7,805	4,716	9,323	7,248	9,489	9,489	6,404	13,368	9,323	10,095
187	9,376	7,848	4,740	9,376	7,285	9,549	9,549	6,445	13,457	9,376	10,148
188	9,429	7,891	4,764	9,429	7,322	9,610	9,610	6,485	13,545	9,429	10,202
189	9,481	7,934	4,788	9,481	7,360	9,671	9,671	6,526	13,634	9,481	10,255
190	9,534	7,977	4,812	9,534	7,397	9,731	9,731	6,566	13,723	9,534	10,309
191	9,587	8,020	4,836	9,587	7,434	9,792	9,792	6,607	13,811	9,587	10,362
192	9,639	8,063	4,860	9,639	7,471	9,853	9,853	6,647	13,900	9,639	10,415
193	9,692	8,106	4,884	9,692	7,508	9,913	9,913	6,687	13,988	9,692	10,469
194	9,744	8,150	4,908	9,744	7,545	9,974	9,974	6,728	14,077	9,744	10,522

Trial length in days	PPE Cut off A	PPE Cut off B	PPE Cut off C	PPE Cut off D	PPE Cut off E	PPE Cut off F	PPE Cut off G	PPE Cut off H	PPE Cut off I	PPE Cut off J	PPE Cut off K
195	9,797	8,193	4,932	9,797	7,582	10,035	10,035	6,768	14,166	9,797	10,575
196	9,850	8,236	4,956	9,850	7,620	10,095	10,095	6,809	14,254	9,850	10,629
197	9,902	8,279	4,980	9,902	7,657	10,156	10,156	6,849	14,343	9,902	10,682
198	9,955	8,322	5,004	9,955	7,694	10,217	10,217	6,890	14,432	9,955	10,736
199	10,007	8,365	5,028	10,007	7,731	10,277	10,277	6,930	14,520	10,007	10,789
200	10,060	8,408	5,051	10,060	7,768	10,338	10,338	6,971	14,609	10,060	10,842

Cracked trial or guilty plea where the number of pages of prosecution evidence is less than or equal to the PPE Cut-off

★G-70c   6.—(1) Where in a cracked trial or guilty plea the number of pages of prosecution evidence is less than or equal to the PPE Cut-off specified in the table following paragraph 5(1) as appropriate to the Class of Offence with which the assisted person is charged, the total fee payable to the litigator is—

    (a)   the basic fee, calculated in accordance with the table following sub-paragraph (2) of this paragraph;

    (b)   the defendant uplift, if any, calculated in accordance with the table following paragraph 12; and

    (c)   the adjustment for transfers and retrials, if any, calculated in accordance with paragraph 13.

(2) For the purposes of sub-paragraph (1), the basic fee appropriate to a cracked trial or a guilty plea is specified in the table following this sub-paragraph, in accordance with the type of case and Class of Offence with which the assisted person is charged.

BASIC FEES FOR CRACKED TRIALS AND GUILTY PLEAS (£)

Type of case	Class of Offence										
	A	*B*	*C*	*D*	*E*	*F*	*G*	*H*	*I*	*J*	*K*
Cracked trial	904.58	707.32	524.83	859.35	233.03	224.23	224.23	237.00	253.67	904.58	773.86
Guilty plea	680.39	556.11	442.91	646.36	184.70	195.81	195.81	190.97	174.60	680.39	640.84

[The table following para. 6(2) is printed as substituted by the Criminal Legal Aid (Remuneration) (Amendment) Regulations 2014 (S.I. 2014 No. 415). The amendments made by S.I. 2014 No. 415 apply to matters in which a determination under section 13 (advice or assistance for individuals in custody (as to which, see § 6-209 in the main work)), 15 (advice or assistance for criminal proceedings (§ 6-211 in the main work)) or 16 representation for criminal proceedings (§ 6-212 in the main work)) of the LASPOA 2012 is made on or after March 20, 2014: S.I. 2014 No. 415, reg. 3.]

Trial where the number of pages of prosecution evidence is less than or equal to the PPE Cut-off

G-71   7.—(1) Where in a trial the number of pages of prosecution evidence is less than or equal to the PPE Cut-off specified in the table following paragraph 5(2) as appropriate to the offence for which the assisted person is tried and the length of trial, the total fee payable to the litigator is—

    (a)   the basic fee, calculated in accordance with the table following sub-paragraph (2);

    (b)   the length of trial proxy, if any, calculated in accordance with the table following subparagraph (3);

    (c)   the defendant uplift, if any, calculated in accordance with the table following paragraph 12; and

    (d)   the adjustment for transfers and retrials, if any, calculated in accordance with paragraph 13.

(2) For the purposes of sub-paragraph (1), the basic fee appropriate to a trial is specified in the table following this sub-paragraph, in accordance with the offence for which the assisted person is tried.

Type of case	Class of Offence										
	A	B	C	D	E	F	G	H	I	J	K
Trial	1,326.86	992.41	668.67	1,260.51	318.90	323.31	323.31	323.44	323.17	1,326.86	932.88

(3) For the purposes of sub-paragraph (1), the length of trial proxy is specified in the table following this sub-paragraph, in accordance with the offence for which the assisted person is tried and the length of trial.

Trial Length in Days	Trial length proxy A	Trial length proxy B	Trial length proxy C	Trial length proxy D	Trial length proxy E	Trial length proxy F	Trial length proxy G	Trial length proxy H	Trial length proxy I	Trial length proxy J	Trial length proxy K
1	0	0	0	0	0	0	0	0	0	0	0
2	0	0	0	0	0	0	0	0	0	0	0
3	228.33	409.46	391.03	216.92	647.86	583.09	583.09	636.22	779.69	228.33	519.07
4	695.97	795.30	762.47	661.17	934.54	812.58	812.58	912.99	1,194.26	695.97	1,031.25
5	1,140.22	1,161.86	1,115.32	1,083.22	1,206.86	1,030.60	1,030.60	1,175.92	1,588.10	1,140.22	1,517.83
6	1,592.29	1,533.35	1,465.74	1,512.69	1,462.04	1,253.49	1,253.49	1,436.68	1,989.58	1,592.29	1,971.90
7	2,037.74	1,900.64	1,818.19	1,935.86	1,731.77	1,476.26	1,476.26	1,699.29	2,384.72	2,037.74	2,453.09
8	2,483.19	2,267.90	2,170.65	2,359.04	2,001.51	1,695.43	1,695.43	1,961.89	2,779.86	2,483.19	2,934.27
9	2,903.03	2,598.44	2,487.85	2,757.88	2,244.26	1,892.71	1,892.71	2,198.24	3,140.36	2,903.03	3,367.34
10	3,322.86	2,929.00	2,805.06	3,156.71	2,487.04	2,089.97	2,089.97	2,434.58	3,500.86	3,322.86	3,800.40
11	3,745.81	3,259.99	3,130.87	3,558.52	2,740.96	2,292.87	2,292.87	2,677.41	3,868.71	3,745.81	4,252.92
12	4,165.90	3,590.57	3,456.83	3,957.61	2,994.95	2,495.77	2,495.77	2,919.95	4,236.85	4,165.90	4,705.71
13	4,585.99	3,921.14	3,775.38	4,356.69	3,248.60	2,697.85	2,697.85	3,157.22	4,598.55	4,585.99	5,158.52
14	5,006.08	4,251.73	4,093.92	4,755.79	3,494.44	2,896.17	2,896.17	3,394.49	4,960.24	5,006.08	5,611.30
15	5,426.17	4,582.31	4,412.47	5,154.86	3,739.54	3,094.48	3,094.48	3,631.77	5,321.93	5,426.17	6,064.06
16	5,846.26	4,912.89	4,731.01	5,553.95	3,984.64	3,292.81	3,292.81	3,869.04	5,683.61	5,846.26	6,516.10
17	6,266.35	5,243.48	5,049.56	5,953.04	4,229.74	3,491.14	3,491.14	4,106.31	6,045.30	6,266.35	6,956.09
18	6,686.44	5,574.05	5,368.10	6,352.12	4,474.84	3,689.46	3,689.46	4,343.58	6,406.99	6,686.44	7,396.08
19	7,106.53	5,904.63	5,686.64	6,751.21	4,719.94	3,887.78	3,887.78	4,580.85	6,768.68	7,106.53	7,836.07
20	7,526.62	6,235.22	6,005.19	7,150.29	4,965.04	4,086.10	4,086.10	4,818.12	7,130.38	7,526.62	8,276.07
21	7,954.72	6,540.58	6,266.94	7,556.98	5,167.59	4,248.35	4,248.35	5,013.25	7,427.59	7,954.72	8,716.07
22	8,382.73	6,845.91	6,528.74	7,963.59	5,370.14	4,410.68	4,410.68	5,208.48	7,724.82	8,382.73	9,156.06
23	8,803.51	7,151.22	6,790.58	8,363.34	5,566.65	4,573.01	4,573.01	5,403.71	8,022.08	8,803.51	9,596.05
24	9,224.28	7,449.61	7,052.41	8,763.08	5,763.19	4,735.34	4,735.34	5,598.94	8,316.07	9,224.28	10,036.05
25	9,645.08	7,747.99	7,312.87	9,162.81	5,959.71	4,897.65	4,897.65	5,791.01	8,606.36	9,645.08	10,476.05
26	10,065.85	8,046.37	7,568.78	9,562.57	6,156.23	5,059.98	5,059.98	5,981.58	8,896.66	10,065.85	10,916.05
27	10,486.62	8,344.75	7,824.70	9,962.30	6,352.76	5,222.31	5,222.31	6,172.14	9,186.95	10,486.62	11,356.03

Trial Length in Days	Trial length proxy A	Trial length proxy B	Trial length proxy C	Trial length proxy D	Trial length proxy E	Trial length proxy F	Trial length proxy G	Trial length proxy H	Trial length proxy I	Trial length proxy J	Trial length proxy K
28	10,907.41	8,643.14	8,080.61	10,362.04	6,549.29	5,384.63	5,384.63	6,362.71	9,477.25	10,907.41	11,796.03
29	11,328.19	8,941.52	8,336.53	10,761.78	6,745.80	5,545.06	5,545.06	6,553.26	9,767.55	11,328.19	12,236.02
30	11,748.97	9,239.89	8,592.43	11,161.52	6,942.33	5,704.56	5,704.56	6,743.81	10,057.85	11,748.97	12,676.02
31	12,169.75	9,538.28	8,848.35	11,561.26	7,138.86	5,864.07	5,864.07	6,934.38	10,348.14	12,169.75	13,116.02
32	12,590.52	9,836.66	9,104.26	11,961.00	7,335.38	6,023.56	6,023.56	7,124.94	10,638.44	12,590.52	13,556.00
33	13,011.31	10,135.04	9,360.18	12,360.74	7,531.90	6,183.06	6,183.06	7,315.51	10,928.73	13,011.31	13,996.00
34	13,432.09	10,433.42	9,616.08	12,760.49	7,728.43	6,342.57	6,342.57	7,506.06	11,219.03	13,432.09	14,436.00
35	13,852.86	10,731.81	9,872.00	13,160.23	7,924.95	6,502.06	6,502.06	7,696.62	11,509.34	13,852.86	14,876.00
36	14,273.65	11,030.18	10,127.91	13,559.96	8,121.47	6,661.57	6,661.57	7,887.18	11,799.63	14,273.65	15,315.98
37	14,694.43	11,328.57	10,383.83	13,959.71	8,318.00	6,821.07	6,821.07	8,077.75	12,089.92	14,694.43	15,755.98
38	15,115.20	11,626.95	10,639.74	14,359.45	8,514.53	6,980.56	6,980.56	8,268.31	12,380.22	15,115.20	16,195.98
39	15,535.99	11,925.33	10,895.65	14,759.18	8,711.04	7,140.07	7,140.07	8,458.87	12,670.52	15,535.99	16,635.98
40	15,932.57	12,198.37	10,997.20	15,135.94	8,789.83	7,257.98	7,257.98	8,541.27	12,912.50	15,932.57	17,056.83
41	16,331.30	12,473.49	11,099.87	15,514.74	8,870.71	7,376.13	7,376.13	8,624.67	13,155.90	16,331.30	17,480.81
42	16,730.13	12,748.68	11,202.58	15,893.63	8,951.62	7,494.28	7,494.28	8,708.10	13,399.36	16,730.13	17,904.93
43	17,129.07	13,023.98	11,305.29	16,272.62	9,032.58	7,612.44	7,612.44	8,791.54	13,642.87	17,129.07	18,329.19
44	17,528.11	13,299.35	11,408.02	16,651.70	9,113.57	7,730.60	7,730.60	8,875.00	13,886.42	17,528.11	18,753.59
45	17,927.23	13,574.81	11,510.77	17,030.87	9,194.58	7,848.78	7,848.78	8,958.49	14,130.05	17,927.23	19,178.13
46	18,326.47	13,850.35	11,613.54	17,410.15	9,275.65	7,966.96	7,966.96	9,041.98	14,373.70	18,326.47	19,602.83
47	18,725.78	14,125.97	11,716.34	17,789.50	9,356.75	8,085.15	8,085.15	9,125.50	14,617.42	18,725.78	20,027.65
48	19,125.22	14,401.69	11,819.15	18,168.96	9,437.88	8,203.34	8,203.34	9,209.04	14,861.20	19,125.22	20,452.62
49	19,524.73	14,677.48	11,921.98	18,548.50	9,519.05	8,321.54	8,321.54	9,292.59	15,105.01	19,524.73	20,877.73
50	19,924.34	14,953.36	12,024.83	18,928.13	9,600.24	8,439.75	8,439.75	9,376.17	15,348.88	19,924.34	21,302.99
51	20,324.06	15,229.33	12,127.71	19,307.86	9,681.49	8,557.96	8,557.96	9,459.76	15,592.81	20,324.06	21,728.39
52	20,723.88	15,505.37	12,230.59	19,687.68	9,762.77	8,676.20	8,676.20	9,543.37	15,836.77	20,723.88	22,153.92
53	21,123.79	15,781.51	12,333.50	20,067.61	9,844.08	8,794.42	8,794.42	9,627.00	16,080.79	21,123.79	22,579.61
54	21,523.80	16,057.73	12,436.43	20,447.60	9,925.43	8,912.66	8,912.66	9,710.65	16,324.87	21,523.80	23,005.43
55	21,923.90	16,334.03	12,539.37	20,827.69	10,006.81	9,030.90	9,030.90	9,794.31	16,568.99	21,923.90	23,431.39

Trial Length in Days	Trial length proxy A	Trial length proxy B	Trial length proxy C	Trial length proxy D	Trial length proxy E	Trial length proxy F	Trial length proxy G	Trial length proxy H	Trial length proxy I	Trial length proxy J	Trial length proxy K
56	22,324.10	16,610.42	12,642.35	21,207.90	10,088.23	9,149.15	9,149.15	9,878.00	16,813.18	22,324.10	23,857.51
57	22,724.39	16,886.88	12,745.33	21,588.18	10,169.68	9,267.41	9,267.41	9,961.69	17,057.40	22,724.39	24,283.76
58	23,124.79	17,163.44	12,848.34	21,968.55	10,251.14	9,385.68	9,385.68	10,045.41	17,301.69	23,124.79	24,710.14
59	23,525.29	17,440.09	12,951.37	22,349.03	10,332.61	9,503.95	9,503.95	10,129.16	17,546.02	23,525.29	25,136.69
60	23,925.87	17,716.81	13,054.41	22,729.58	10,414.07	9,622.23	9,622.23	10,212.91	17,790.40	23,925.87	25,563.37
61	24,326.57	17,993.61	13,157.48	23,110.24	10,495.53	9,740.52	9,740.52	10,296.69	18,034.84	24,326.57	25,990.18
62	24,727.35	18,270.52	13,260.56	23,490.98	10,577.00	9,858.81	9,858.81	10,380.50	18,279.33	24,727.35	26,417.14
63	25,128.24	18,547.49	13,363.66	23,871.83	10,658.46	9,977.10	9,977.10	10,464.31	18,523.87	25,128.24	26,844.25
64	25,529.21	18,824.55	13,466.80	24,252.76	10,739.92	10,095.42	10,095.42	10,548.14	18,768.44	25,529.21	27,271.50
65	25,930.29	19,101.70	13,569.94	24,633.77	10,821.38	10,213.73	10,213.73	10,631.99	19,013.09	25,930.29	27,698.89
66	26,331.47	19,378.94	13,673.10	25,014.90	10,902.84	10,332.05	10,332.05	10,715.86	19,257.79	26,331.47	28,126.41
67	26,732.74	19,656.25	13,776.28	25,396.11	10,984.30	10,450.38	10,450.38	10,799.75	19,502.52	26,732.74	28,554.08
68	27,134.11	19,933.66	13,879.49	25,777.41	11,065.76	10,568.72	10,568.72	10,883.66	19,747.32	27,134.11	28,981.90
69	27,535.58	20,211.14	13,982.70	26,158.79	11,147.22	10,687.07	10,687.07	10,967.58	19,992.17	27,535.58	29,409.86
70	27,937.14	20,488.71	14,085.94	26,540.28	11,228.68	10,805.42	10,805.42	11,051.53	20,237.06	27,937.14	29,837.96
71	28,338.81	20,766.36	14,189.21	26,921.87	11,310.14	10,923.78	10,923.78	11,135.50	20,482.01	28,338.81	30,266.21
72	28,740.57	21,044.11	14,292.48	27,303.54	11,391.60	11,042.15	11,042.15	11,219.47	20,727.01	28,740.57	30,694.60
73	29,142.42	21,321.94	14,395.79	27,685.31	11,473.06	11,160.52	11,160.52	11,303.47	20,972.06	29,142.42	31,123.12
74	29,544.37	21,599.84	14,499.10	28,067.16	11,554.52	11,278.90	11,278.90	11,387.49	21,217.17	29,544.37	31,551.79
75	29,946.43	21,877.84	14,602.44	28,449.10	11,635.98	11,397.28	11,397.28	11,471.53	21,462.33	29,946.43	31,980.60
76	30,348.57	22,155.91	14,705.80	28,831.15	11,717.44	11,515.67	11,515.67	11,555.59	21,707.52	30,348.57	32,409.55
77	30,750.83	22,434.08	14,809.18	29,213.28	11,798.90	11,634.08	11,634.08	11,639.65	21,952.78	30,750.83	32,838.65
78	31,153.16	22,712.32	14,912.58	29,595.51	11,880.36	11,752.48	11,752.48	11,723.75	22,198.09	31,153.16	33,267.89
79	31,555.61	22,990.65	15,015.99	29,977.84	11,961.82	11,870.90	11,870.90	11,807.86	22,443.46	31,555.61	33,697.27
80	31,958.15	23,269.07	15,119.43	30,360.24	12,043.28	11,989.32	11,989.32	11,892.00	22,688.86	31,958.15	34,126.79
81	32,360.78	23,547.57	15,222.88	30,742.75	12,124.74	12,107.75	12,107.75	11,976.15	22,934.32	32,360.78	34,556.45
82	32,763.51	23,826.16	15,326.36	31,125.34	12,206.21	12,226.19	12,226.19	12,060.30	23,179.84	32,763.51	34,986.25
83	33,166.34	24,104.83	15,429.85	31,508.04	12,287.67	12,344.62	12,344.62	12,144.50	23,425.40	33,166.34	35,416.20

Trial Length in Days	Trial length proxy A	Trial length proxy B	Trial length proxy C	Trial length proxy D	Trial length proxy E	Trial length proxy F	Trial length proxy G	Trial length proxy H	Trial length proxy I	Trial length proxy J	Trial length proxy K
84	33,569.27	24,383.58	15,533.36	31,890.81	12,369.13	12,463.09	12,463.09	12,228.69	23,671.02	33,569.27	35,846.30
85	33,972.30	24,662.42	15,636.89	32,273.69	12,450.59	12,581.54	12,581.54	12,312.92	23,916.68	33,972.30	36,276.53
86	34,375.42	24,941.34	15,740.46	32,656.66	12,532.06	12,700.00	12,700.00	12,397.16	24,162.41	34,375.42	36,706.91
87	34,778.64	25,220.35	15,844.03	33,039.72	12,613.52	12,818.47	12,818.47	12,481.43	24,408.19	34,778.64	37,137.42
88	35,181.97	25,499.45	15,947.61	33,422.87	12,694.98	12,936.96	12,936.96	12,565.70	24,654.00	35,181.97	37,568.08
89	35,585.39	25,778.62	16,051.22	33,806.12	12,776.44	13,055.44	13,055.44	12,650.00	24,899.88	35,585.39	37,998.89
90	35,988.89	26,057.88	16,154.85	34,189.44	12,857.90	13,173.93	13,173.93	12,734.30	25,145.80	35,988.89	38,429.84
91	36,392.51	26,337.23	16,258.51	34,572.88	12,939.36	13,292.43	13,292.43	12,818.64	25,391.78	36,392.51	38,860.92
92	36,796.20	26,616.65	16,362.18	34,956.41	13,020.82	13,410.94	13,410.94	12,902.99	25,637.81	36,796.20	39,292.14
93	37,200.02	26,896.17	16,465.86	35,340.01	13,102.28	13,529.46	13,529.46	12,987.36	25,883.89	37,200.02	39,723.52
94	37,603.91	27,175.77	16,569.57	35,723.72	13,183.74	13,647.98	13,647.98	13,071.75	26,130.02	37,603.91	40,155.04
95	38,007.92	27,455.46	16,673.30	36,107.52	13,265.20	13,766.50	13,766.50	13,156.17	26,376.20	38,007.92	40,586.68
96	38,412.02	27,735.23	16,777.05	36,491.42	13,346.66	13,885.04	13,885.04	13,240.58	26,622.44	38,412.02	41,018.49
97	38,816.21	28,015.09	16,880.82	36,875.40	13,428.12	14,003.58	14,003.58	13,325.00	26,868.72	38,816.21	41,450.43
98	39,220.50	28,295.03	16,984.61	37,259.48	13,509.58	14,122.14	14,122.14	13,409.42	27,115.05	39,220.50	41,882.51
99	39,624.89	28,575.05	17,088.41	37,643.64	13,591.04	14,240.70	14,240.70	13,493.83	27,361.45	39,624.89	42,314.74
100	40,029.37	28,855.15	17,192.23	38,027.90	13,672.50	14,359.26	14,359.26	13,578.25	27,607.87	40,029.37	42,747.09
101	40,433.96	29,135.35	17,296.08	38,412.26	13,753.96	14,477.83	14,477.83	13,662.67	27,854.38	40,433.96	43,179.61
102	40,838.64	29,415.61	17,399.94	38,796.71	13,835.42	14,596.40	14,596.40	13,747.08	28,100.91	40,838.64	43,612.26
103	41,243.42	29,695.97	17,503.84	39,181.25	13,916.88	14,714.99	14,714.99	13,831.50	28,347.50	41,243.42	44,045.06
104	41,648.29	29,976.42	17,607.73	39,565.89	13,998.34	14,833.58	14,833.58	13,915.92	28,594.15	41,648.29	44,477.99
105	42,053.27	30,256.96	17,711.62	39,950.60	14,079.80	14,952.18	14,952.18	14,000.33	28,840.85	42,053.27	44,911.07
106	42,458.34	30,537.56	17,815.51	40,335.42	14,161.27	15,070.79	15,070.79	14,084.75	29,087.59	42,458.34	45,344.19
107	42,863.51	30,818.24	17,919.40	40,720.33	14,242.73	15,189.41	15,189.41	14,169.17	29,334.39	42,863.51	45,777.31
108	43,268.78	31,098.90	18,023.30	41,105.34	14,324.19	15,308.02	15,308.02	14,253.58	29,581.24	43,268.78	46,210.44
109	43,674.14	31,379.58	18,127.20	41,490.43	14,405.66	15,426.66	15,426.66	14,338.01	29,828.15	43,674.14	46,643.55
110	44,079.59	31,660.24	18,231.09	41,875.61	14,487.12	15,545.29	15,545.29	14,422.42	30,075.09	44,079.59	47,076.68
111	44,485.16	31,940.91	18,334.98	42,260.91	14,568.58	15,663.94	15,663.94	14,506.83	30,322.10	44,485.16	47,509.79

Trial Length in Days	Trial length proxy A	Trial length proxy B	Trial length proxy C	Trial length proxy D	Trial length proxy E	Trial length proxy F	Trial length proxy G	Trial length proxy H	Trial length proxy I	Trial length proxy J	Trial length proxy K
112	44,890.81	32,221.58	18,438.87	42,646.27	14,650.04	15,782.58	15,782.58	14,591.26	30,569.15	44,890.81	47,942.92
113	45,296.56	32,502.24	18,542.77	43,031.74	14,731.50	15,901.24	15,901.24	14,675.67	30,816.27	45,296.56	48,376.04
114	45,702.41	32,782.92	18,646.67	43,417.29	14,812.96	16,019.91	16,019.91	14,760.08	31,063.43	45,702.41	48,809.16
115	46,108.36	33,063.58	18,750.56	43,802.94	14,894.42	16,138.58	16,138.58	14,844.51	31,310.63	46,108.36	49,242.29
116	46,514.41	33,344.26	18,854.45	44,188.68	14,975.88	16,257.25	16,257.25	14,928.92	31,557.89	46,514.41	49,675.40
117	46,920.55	33,624.92	18,958.34	44,574.52	15,057.34	16,375.94	16,375.94	15,013.33	31,805.21	46,920.55	50,108.53
118	47,326.79	33,905.59	19,062.24	44,960.45	15,138.80	16,494.63	16,494.63	15,097.76	32,052.57	47,326.79	50,541.65
119	47,733.12	34,186.26	19,166.14	45,346.46	15,220.26	16,613.33	16,613.33	15,182.17	32,299.99	47,733.12	50,974.77
120	48,139.56	34,466.92	19,270.03	45,732.58	15,301.72	16,732.04	16,732.04	15,266.58	32,547.45	48,139.56	51,407.90
121	48,546.09	34,747.60	19,373.92	46,118.79	15,383.18	16,850.75	16,850.75	15,351.01	32,794.97	48,546.09	51,841.01
122	48,946.61	35,028.26	19,477.81	46,499.28	15,464.64	16,968.95	16,968.95	15,435.42	33,039.03	48,946.61	52,274.14
123	49,347.12	35,308.94	19,581.71	46,879.78	15,546.10	17,087.15	17,087.15	15,519.83	33,283.08	49,347.12	52,707.25
124	49,747.64	35,586.31	19,684.09	47,260.26	15,627.56	17,205.35	17,205.35	15,604.26	33,527.14	49,747.64	53,139.54
125	50,148.15	35,862.77	19,786.42	47,640.75	15,709.02	17,323.56	17,323.56	15,688.67	33,771.20	50,148.15	53,566.16
126	50,548.67	36,139.22	19,888.75	48,021.25	15,790.48	17,441.75	17,441.75	15,773.03	34,015.25	50,548.67	53,992.79
127	50,949.20	36,415.68	19,991.09	48,401.74	15,871.94	17,559.95	17,559.95	15,856.19	34,259.31	50,949.20	54,419.42
128	51,349.71	36,692.14	20,093.43	48,782.23	15,953.40	17,678.16	17,678.16	15,939.35	34,503.37	51,349.71	54,846.03
129	51,750.22	36,968.60	20,195.76	49,162.72	16,034.87	17,796.36	17,796.36	16,022.49	34,747.42	51,750.22	55,272.67
130	52,150.74	37,245.05	20,298.09	49,543.21	16,116.33	17,914.55	17,914.55	16,105.64	34,991.48	52,150.74	55,699.29
131	52,551.25	37,521.51	20,400.44	49,923.70	16,197.79	18,032.76	18,032.76	16,188.79	35,235.54	52,551.25	56,125.91
132	52,951.78	37,797.98	20,502.77	50,304.19	16,279.25	18,150.96	18,150.96	16,271.95	35,479.60	52,951.78	56,552.54
133	53,352.30	38,074.43	20,605.10	50,684.68	16,360.72	18,269.15	18,269.15	16,355.10	35,723.66	53,352.30	56,979.16
134	53,752.81	38,350.88	20,707.43	51,065.17	16,442.18	18,387.35	18,387.35	16,438.25	35,967.71	53,752.81	57,405.79
135	54,153.32	38,627.35	20,809.78	51,445.66	16,523.64	18,505.56	18,505.56	16,521.39	36,211.77	54,153.32	57,832.41
136	54,553.84	38,903.81	20,912.12	51,826.15	16,605.10	18,623.76	18,623.76	16,604.54	36,455.83	54,553.84	58,259.03
137	54,954.36	39,180.26	21,014.45	52,206.64	16,686.56	18,741.95	18,741.95	16,687.70	36,699.89	54,954.36	58,685.67
138	55,354.88	39,456.72	21,116.78	52,587.13	16,768.02	18,860.16	18,860.16	16,770.85	36,943.95	55,354.88	59,112.28
139	55,755.39	39,733.18	21,219.12	52,967.62	16,849.48	18,978.37	18,978.37	16,854.00	37,188.01	55,755.39	59,538.91

Trial Length in Days	Trial length proxy A	Trial length proxy B	Trial length proxy C	Trial length proxy D	Trial length proxy E	Trial length proxy F	Trial length proxy G	Trial length proxy H	Trial length proxy I	Trial length proxy J	Trial length proxy K
140	56,155.91	40,009.65	21,321.46	53,348.11	16,930.94	19,096.56	19,096.56	16,937.15	37,432.07	56,155.91	59,965.54
141	56,556.42	40,286.09	21,423.79	53,728.60	17,012.40	19,214.76	19,214.76	17,020.29	37,676.12	56,556.42	60,392.15
142	56,956.94	40,562.56	21,526.12	54,109.09	17,093.86	19,332.97	19,332.97	17,103.45	37,920.18	56,956.94	60,818.79
143	57,357.47	40,839.02	21,628.46	54,489.59	17,175.32	19,451.17	19,451.17	17,186.61	38,164.24	57,357.47	61,245.41
144	57,757.98	41,115.48	21,730.80	54,870.08	17,256.78	19,569.36	19,569.36	17,269.75	38,408.29	57,757.98	61,672.03
145	58,158.49	41,391.93	21,833.13	55,250.56	17,338.24	19,687.56	19,687.56	17,352.90	38,652.35	58,158.49	62,098.66
146	58,559.01	41,668.39	21,935.46	55,631.06	17,419.70	19,805.77	19,805.77	17,436.05	38,896.41	58,559.01	62,525.28
147	58,959.52	41,944.86	22,037.80	56,011.55	17,501.16	19,923.96	19,923.96	17,519.21	39,140.46	58,959.52	62,951.91
148	59,360.05	42,221.31	22,140.14	56,392.05	17,582.62	20,042.16	20,042.16	17,602.36	39,384.52	59,360.05	63,378.53
149	59,760.57	42,497.76	22,242.47	56,772.53	17,664.08	20,160.37	20,160.37	17,685.50	39,628.58	59,760.57	63,805.15
150	60,161.08	42,774.23	22,344.80	57,153.02	17,745.54	20,278.57	20,278.57	17,768.65	39,872.63	60,161.08	64,231.79
151	60,561.59	43,050.69	22,447.14	57,533.52	17,827.00	20,396.76	20,396.76	17,851.80	40,116.69	60,561.59	64,658.40
152	60,962.11	43,327.14	22,549.48	57,914.01	17,908.46	20,514.97	20,514.97	17,934.96	40,360.75	60,962.11	65,085.03
153	61,362.63	43,603.60	22,651.81	58,294.50	17,989.93	20,633.18	20,633.18	18,018.11	40,604.80	61,362.63	65,511.66
154	61,763.15	43,880.06	22,754.14	58,674.99	18,071.39	20,751.37	20,751.37	18,101.26	40,848.86	61,763.15	65,938.27
155	62,163.67	44,156.52	22,856.48	59,055.48	18,152.85	20,869.57	20,869.57	18,184.40	41,092.92	62,163.67	66,364.91
156	62,564.18	44,432.97	22,958.82	59,435.98	18,234.32	20,987.77	20,987.77	18,267.55	41,336.97	62,564.18	66,791.53
157	62,964.69	44,709.43	23,061.15	59,816.46	18,315.78	21,105.98	21,105.98	18,350.71	41,581.03	62,964.69	67,218.15
158	63,365.21	44,985.90	23,163.48	60,196.96	18,397.24	21,224.17	21,224.17	18,433.86	41,825.09	63,365.21	67,644.78
159	63,765.74	45,262.35	23,265.83	60,577.45	18,478.70	21,342.37	21,342.37	18,517.01	42,069.14	63,765.74	68,071.40
160	64,166.25	45,538.81	23,368.17	60,957.94	18,560.16	21,460.58	21,460.58	18,600.16	42,313.20	64,166.25	68,498.03
161	64,566.77	45,815.27	23,470.50	61,338.43	18,641.62	21,578.77	21,578.77	18,683.30	42,557.26	64,566.77	68,924.65
162	64,967.28	46,091.73	23,572.83	61,718.92	18,723.08	21,696.97	21,696.97	18,766.46	42,801.31	64,967.28	69,351.27
163	65,367.79	46,368.18	23,675.17	62,099.42	18,804.54	21,815.18	21,815.18	18,849.62	43,045.37	65,367.79	69,777.91
164	65,768.32	46,644.64	23,777.51	62,479.91	18,886.00	21,933.38	21,933.38	18,932.76	43,289.43	65,768.32	70,204.52
165	66,168.84	46,921.11	23,879.84	62,860.39	18,967.46	22,051.57	22,051.57	19,015.91	43,533.48	66,168.84	70,631.15
166	66,569.35	47,197.57	23,982.17	63,240.89	19,048.92	22,169.78	22,169.78	19,099.06	43,777.54	66,569.35	71,057.78
167	66,969.86	47,474.01	24,084.51	63,621.38	19,130.38	22,287.98	22,287.98	19,182.22	44,021.60	66,969.86	71,484.39

Trial Length in Days	Trial length proxy A	Trial length proxy B	Trial length proxy C	Trial length proxy D	Trial length proxy E	Trial length proxy F	Trial length proxy G	Trial length proxy H	Trial length proxy I	Trial length proxy J	Trial length proxy K
168	67,370.38	47,750.48	24,186.85	64,001.87	19,211.84	22,406.18	22,406.18	19,265.37	44,265.66	67,370.38	71,911.03
169	67,770.90	48,026.94	24,289.18	64,382.36	19,293.30	22,524.38	22,524.38	19,348.52	44,509.72	67,770.90	72,337.65
170	68,171.42	48,303.40	24,391.51	64,762.85	19,374.76	22,642.58	22,642.58	19,431.66	44,753.78	68,171.42	72,764.27
171	68,571.94	48,579.85	24,493.85	65,143.34	19,456.22	22,760.78	22,760.78	19,514.81	44,997.83	68,571.94	73,190.90
172	68,972.45	48,856.31	24,596.19	65,523.83	19,537.68	22,878.98	22,878.98	19,597.97	45,241.89	68,972.45	73,617.52
173	69,372.96	49,132.78	24,698.52	65,904.32	19,619.14	22,997.18	22,997.18	19,681.12	45,485.95	69,372.96	74,044.15
174	69,773.48	49,409.23	24,800.85	66,284.81	19,700.60	23,115.39	23,115.39	19,764.27	45,730.01	69,773.48	74,470.77
175	70,174.01	49,685.68	24,903.19	66,665.30	19,782.06	23,233.58	23,233.58	19,847.41	45,974.07	70,174.01	74,897.39
176	70,574.52	49,962.15	25,005.53	67,045.79	19,863.53	23,351.78	23,351.78	19,930.56	46,218.13	70,574.52	75,324.03
177	70,975.04	50,238.61	25,107.86	67,426.28	19,944.99	23,469.99	23,469.99	20,013.72	46,462.18	70,975.04	75,750.64
178	71,375.55	50,515.06	25,210.19	67,806.77	20,026.45	23,588.19	23,588.19	20,096.87	46,706.24	71,375.55	76,177.27
179	71,776.06	50,791.52	25,312.53	68,187.26	20,107.91	23,706.38	23,706.38	20,180.02	46,950.30	71,776.06	76,603.90
180	72,176.59	51,067.98	25,414.87	68,567.75	20,189.38	23,824.59	23,824.59	20,263.17	47,194.35	72,176.59	77,030.51
181	72,577.11	51,344.44	25,517.21	68,948.24	20,270.84	23,942.79	23,942.79	20,346.32	47,438.41	72,577.11	77,457.15
182	72,977.62	51,620.89	25,619.54	69,328.73	20,352.30	24,060.98	24,060.98	20,429.48	47,682.47	72,977.62	77,883.77
183	73,378.14	51,897.36	25,721.87	69,709.23	20,432.59	24,179.19	24,179.19	20,512.63	47,926.52	73,378.14	78,310.39
184	73,778.65	52,173.82	25,824.22	70,089.72	20,512.82	24,297.39	24,297.39	20,595.77	48,170.58	73,778.65	78,737.02
185	74,179.17	52,450.27	25,926.55	70,470.20	20,593.06	24,415.59	24,415.59	20,678.92	48,414.64	74,179.17	79,163.64
186	74,579.69	52,726.73	26,028.88	70,850.70	20,673.30	24,533.79	24,533.79	20,762.07	48,658.69	74,579.69	79,590.27
187	74,980.21	53,003.19	26,131.22	71,231.19	20,753.54	24,651.99	24,651.99	20,845.23	48,902.75	74,980.21	80,016.89
188	75,380.72	53,279.65	26,233.56	71,611.69	20,833.78	24,770.20	24,770.20	20,928.38	49,146.81	75,380.72	80,443.51
189	75,781.23	53,556.10	26,335.89	71,992.17	20,914.02	24,888.39	24,888.39	21,011.53	49,390.86	75,781.23	80,870.15
190	76,181.75	53,832.56	26,438.22	72,372.66	20,994.26	25,006.59	25,006.59	21,094.67	49,634.92	76,181.75	81,296.76
191	76,582.28	54,109.03	26,540.56	72,753.16	21,074.50	25,124.80	25,124.80	21,177.82	49,878.98	76,582.28	81,723.39
192	76,982.79	54,385.49	26,642.90	73,133.65	21,154.74	25,243.00	25,243.00	21,260.98	50,123.03	76,982.79	82,150.02
193	77,383.31	54,661.93	26,745.23	73,514.14	21,234.98	25,361.19	25,361.19	21,344.13	50,367.09	77,383.31	82,576.63
194	77,783.82	54,938.40	26,847.56	73,894.63	21,315.22	25,479.40	25,479.40	21,427.28	50,611.15	77,783.82	83,003.27
195	78,184.33	55,214.86	26,949.90	74,275.12	21,395.46	25,597.60	25,597.60	21,510.43	50,855.20	78,184.33	83,429.89

Trial Length in Days	Trial length proxy A	Trial length proxy B	Trial length proxy C	Trial length proxy D	Trial length proxy E	Trial length proxy F	Trial length proxy G	Trial length proxy H	Trial length proxy I	Trial length proxy J	Trial length proxy K
196	78,584.86	55,491.32	27,052.24	74,655.62	21,475.70	25,715.79	25,715.79	21,593.57	51,099.26	78,584.86	83,856.51
197	78,985.38	55,767.77	27,154.57	75,036.10	21,555.94	25,833.99	25,833.99	21,676.73	51,343.32	78,985.38	84,283.14
198	79,385.89	56,044.23	27,256.90	75,416.60	21,636.18	25,952.20	25,952.20	21,759.89	51,587.37	79,385.89	84,709.76
199	79,786.41	56,320.70	27,359.24	75,797.09	21,716.42	26,070.40	26,070.40	21,843.03	51,831.43	79,786.41	85,136.39
200	80,186.92	56,597.15	27,461.58	76,177.58	21,796.66	26,188.59	26,188.59	21,926.18	52,075.49	80,186.92	85,563.01

[The tables following sub-paras 7(2) and (3) are printed as substituted by the Criminal Legal Aid (Remuneration etc.) (Amendment) Regulations 2015 (S.I. 2015 No. 1369). The substituted tables apply to matters in which a relevant determination (*i.e.* one under s.13, 15 or 16 of the LASPOA 2012 (as to which, see §§ 6-209 *et seq.* in the main work)) was made on or after July 1, 2015.]

Cracked trials and guilty pleas where the number of pages of prosecution evidence exceeds the PPE cut-off

8.—(1) Where in a cracked trial or guilty plea the number of pages of prosecution evidence **G-72** exceeds the PPE Cut-off specified in the table following paragraph 5(1) as appropriate to the offence with which the assisted person is charged, the total fee payable to the litigator is—

(a) the final fee, calculated in accordance with sub-paragraph (2) of this paragraph;

(b) the defendant uplift, if any, calculated in accordance with the table following paragraph 12; and

(c) the adjustment for transfers and retrials, if any, calculated in accordance with paragraph 13.

(2) For the purposes of sub-paragraph (1), the final fee payable to a litigator in a cracked trial or guilty plea is calculated in accordance with the following formula—

$$F = I + (D \times i)$$

Where—

• **F** is the amount of the final fee;

• **I** is the initial fee specified in the tables following this paragraph, as appropriate to the type of case, the offence with which the assisted person is charged and the number of pages of prosecution evidence;

• **D** is the difference between—

(i) the number of pages of prosecution evidence in the case; and

(ii) the lower number in the PPE range as specified in the tables following this paragraph, as appropriate to the type of case, the offence with which the assisted person is charged and the number of pages of prosecution evidence in the case;

• **i** is the incremental fee per page of prosecution evidence specified in the tables following this paragraph, as appropriate to the type of case, the offence with which the assisted person is charged and the number of pages of prosecution evidence in the case.

TABLE OF FINAL FEES IN CRACKED TRIALS

Class of Offence	PPE Range	Initial fee (£)	Incremental fee per page of prosecution evidence (£)
A and J	0–79	904.58	0
A and J	80–249	904.58	10.70
A and J	250–999	2,722.89	6.71
A and J	1000–2799	7,757.90	3.92
A and J	2800–4599	14,820.75	3.92
A and J	4600–6399	21,883.61	3.11
A and J	6400–8199	27,490.35	3.11
A and J	8200–9999	33,097.09	3.11
A and J	10,000	38,700.71	0
B	0–69	709.15	0
B	70–249	709.15	7.83
B	250–999	2,117.67	3.66
B	1000–2799	4,864.56	2.44
B	2800–4599	9,255.51	2.44
B	4600–6399	13,646.46	2.05
B	6400–8199	17,338.49	2.05
B	8200–9999	21,030.50	2.05
B	10,000	24,720.46	0

Class of Offence	PPE Range	Initial fee (£)	Incremental fee per page of prosecution evidence (£)
C	0–39	524.84	0
C	40–249	524.84	3.92
C	250–999	1,348.77	2.25
C	1000–2799	3,033.06	1.43
C	2800–4599	5,607.48	1.43
C	4600–6399	8,181.89	1.43
C	6400–8199	10,756.31	1.43
C	8200–9999	13,330.74	1.43
C	10,000	15,903.73	0
D	0–79	859.35	0
D	80–249	859.35	10.14
D	250–999	2,582.50	6.11
D	1000–2799	7,163.76	3.61
D	2800–4599	13,655.74	3.61
D	4600–6399	20,147.71	2.96
D	6400–8199	25,474.79	2.96
D	8200–9999	30,801.87	2.96
D	10,000	36,125.98	0
E	0–39	233.03	0
E	40–249	233.03	4.60
E	250–999	1,199.43	1.46
E	1000–2799	2,291.54	0.61
E	2800–4599	3,390.26	0.61
E	4600–6399	4,488.97	0.61
E	6400–8199	5,587.69	0.61
E	8200–9999	6,686.41	0.61
E	10,000	7,784.51	0
F and G	0–49	224.22	0
F and G	50–249	224.22	4.42
F and G	250–999	1,107.53	1.79
F and G	1000–2799	2,450.39	0.70
F and G	2800–4599	3,704.67	0.70
F and G	4600–6399	4,958.94	0.70
F and G	6400–8199	6,213.21	0.70
F and G	8200–9999	7,467.49	0.70
F and G	10,000	8,721.06	0
H	0–39	237.00	0
H	40–249	237.00	4.26
H	250–999	1,131.61	1.56
H	1000–2799	2,298.20	0.70
H	2800–4599	3,550.79	0.70
H	4600–6399	4,803.37	0.70
H	6400–8199	6,055.96	0.70

Class of Offence	PPE Range	Initial fee (£)	Incremental fee per page of prosecution evidence (£)
H	8200–9999	7,308.55	0.70
H	10,000	8,560.44	0
I	0–39	253.68	0
I	40–249	253.68	5.92
I	250–999	1,496.80	2.31
I	1000–2799	3,231.91	0.90
I	2800–4599	4,847.36	0.90
I	4600–6399	6,462.79	0.90
I	6400–8199	8,078.23	0.90
I	8200–9999	9,693.67	0.90
I	10,000	11,308.20	0
K	0–119	773.86	0
K	120–249	773.86	6.55
K	250–999	1,624.85	5.02
K	1000–2799	5,388.98	4.39
K	2800–4599	13,299.04	4.39
K	4600–6399	21,209.12	3.75
K	6400–8199	27,954.29	3.75
K	8200–9999	34,699.46	3.75
K	10,000	41,440.89	0

TABLE OF FINAL FEES IN GUILTY PLEAS

Class of Offence	PPE Range	Initial fee (£)	Incremental fee per page of prosecution evidence (£)
A and J	0–79	680.39	0
A and J	80–399	680.39	5.62
A and J	400–999	2,478.29	2.96
A and J	1000–2799	4,256.09	1.89
A and J	2800–4599	7,666.89	1.89
A and J	4600–6399	11,077.68	1.12
A and J	6400–8199	13,090.60	1.12
A and J	8200–9999	15,103.53	1.12
A and J	10,000	17,115.33	0
B	0–69	556.11	0
B	70–399	556.11	4.52
B	400–999	2,046.59	2.28
B	1000–2799	3,411.75	1.45
B	2800–4599	6,025.92	1.45
B	4600–6399	8,640.11	1.06
B	6400–8199	10,555.35	1.06
B	8200–9999	12,470.60	1.06
B	10,000	14,384.78	0
C	0–39	442.91	0

Class of Offence	PPE Range	Initial fee (£)	Incremental fee per page of prosecution evidence (£)
C	40–399	442.91	2.66
C	400–999	1,401.88	1.46
C	1000–2799	2,276.27	0.79
C	2800–4599	3,699.93	0.79
C	4600–6399	5,123.61	0.79
C	6400–8199	6,547.28	0.79
C	8200–9999	7,970.95	0.79
C	10,000	9,393.82	0
D	0–79	646.36	0
D	80–399	646.36	5.23
D	400–999	2,320.66	2.75
D	1000–2799	3,968.37	1.71
D	2800–4599	7,046.20	1.71
D	4600–6399	10,124.03	1.06
D	6400–8199	12,036.98	1.06
D	8200–9999	13,949.91	1.06
D	10,000	15,861.79	0
E	0–39	184.70	0
E	40–399	184.70	2.92
E	400–999	1,237.24	1.25
E	1000–2799	1,989.07	0.46
E	2800–4599	2,819.70	0.46
E	4600–6399	3,650.33	0.46
E	6400–8199	4,480.96	0.46
E	8200–9999	5,311.59	0.46
E	10,000	6,141.75	0
F and G	0–49	195.81	0
F and G	50–399	195.81	2.83
F and G	400–999	1,187.73	0.99
F and G	1000–2799	1,781.21	0.32
F and G	2800–4599	2,354.07	0.32
F and G	4600–6399	2,926.93	0.32
F and G	6400–8199	3,499.78	0.32
F and G	8200–9999	4,072.64	0.32
F and G	10,000	4,645.18	0
H	0–39	190.97	0
H	40–399	190.97	2.79
H	400–999	1,196.59	0.99
H	1000–2799	1,790.74	0.32
H	2800–4599	2,359.85	0.32
H	4600–6399	2,928.98	0.32
H	6400–8199	3,498.10	0.32
H	8200–9999	4,067.22	0.32

Class of Offence	PPE Range	Initial fee (£)	Incremental fee per page of prosecution evidence (£)
H	10,000	4,636.00	0
I	0–39	174.60	0
I	40–399	174.60	3.12
I	400–999	1,298.52	1.36
I	1000–2799	2,116.29	0.51
I	2800–4599	3,033.02	0.51
I	4600–6399	3,949.75	0.51
I	6400–8199	4,866.48	0.51
I	8200–9999	5,783.22	0.51
I	10,000	6,699.45	0
K	0–119	640.84	0
K	120–399	640.84	5.26
K	400–999	2,113.13	2.93
K	1000–2799	3,869.24	2.73
K	2800–4599	8,775.55	2.73
K	4600–6399	13,681.86	2.08
K	6400–8199	17,423.28	2.08
K	8200–9999	21,164.71	2.08
K	10,000	24,904.04	0

Trials where the number of pages of prosecution evidence exceeds the PPE Cut-off

9.—(1) Where in a trial the number of pages of prosecution evidence exceeds the PPE Cut-off **G-72a** figure specified in the table following paragraph 5(2) as appropriate to the offence for which the assisted person is tried and the length of trial, the total fee payable to the litigator is—

    (a) the final fee, calculated in accordance with sub-paragraph (2) of this paragraph;

    (b) the defendant uplift, if any, calculated in accordance with the table following paragraph 12; and

    (c) the adjustment for transfers and retrials, if any, calculated in accordance with paragraph 13.

(2) For the purposes of sub-paragraph (1), the final fee is calculated in accordance with the following formula—

$$F = I + (D \times i)$$

Where—

- **F** is the amount of the final fee;
- **I** is the initial fee specified in the table following this paragraph as appropriate to the offence for which the assisted person is tried and the number of pages of prosecution evidence;
- **D** is the difference between—
  - (i) the number of pages of prosecution evidence in the case; and
  - (ii) the lower number in the PPE range as specified in the table following this paragraph, as appropriate to the offence for which the assisted person is tried and the number of pages of prosecution evidence in the case;
- **i** is the incremental fee per page of prosecution evidence specified in the table following this paragraph, as appropriate to the offence for which the assisted person is tried and the number of pages of prosecution evidence in the case.

TABLE OF FINAL FEES IN TRIALS

Offence Class	PPE Range	Initial Fee	Incremental fee per page
A and J	0–79	1,467.58	0
A and J	80–209	1,467.58	16.58

Offence Class	PPE Range	Initial Fee	Incremental fee per page
A and J	210–699	3,622.54	12.66
A and J	700–1049	9,824.91	10.62
A and J	1050–1999	13,543.42	9.21
A and J	2000–3599	22,295.42	8.42
A and J	3600–5199	35,767.03	8.42
A and J	5200–6799	49,238.64	8.42
A and J	6800–8399	62,710.26	8.42
A and J	8400–9999	76,181.87	8.42
A and J	10,000	89,645.06	0
B	0–69	1,097.66	0
B	70–199	1,097.66	12.81
B	200–499	2,762.60	11.44
B	500–899	6,195.38	9.63
B	900–1299	10,048.21	8.09
B	1300–1999	13,285.03	7.09
B	2000–3299	18,249.51	7.09
B	3300–4999	27,469.24	7.09
B	5000–5999	39,525.82	7.09
B	6000–7999	46,617.93	7.09
B	8000–8999	60,802.14	7.09
B	9000–9999	67,894.24	7.09
B	10,000	74,979.26	0
C	0–39	739.59	0
C	40–299	739.59	10.57
C	300–799	3,486.54	9.23
C	800–1249	8,101.74	7.73
C	1250–1999	11,578.09	6.83
C	2000–3199	16,700.93	4.72
C	3200–4559	22,368.79	4.72
C	4560–5919	28,792.38	4.72
C	5920–7279	35,215.96	4.72
C	7280–8639	41,639.54	4.72
C	8640–9999	48,063.12	4.72
C	10,000	54,482.00	0
D	0–79	1,394.20	0
D	80–209	1,394.20	15.75
D	210–699	3,441.41	12.03
D	700–1049	9,333.67	10.09
D	1050–1999	12,866.25	8.75
D	2000–3599	21,180.65	8.00
D	3600–5199	33,978.67	8.00
D	5200–6799	46,776.70	8.00
D	6800–8399	59,574.74	8.00
D	8400–9999	72,372.77	8.00
D	10,000	85,162.80	0

Offence Class	PPE Range	Initial Fee	Incremental fee per page
E	0–39	352.72	0
E	40–69	352.72	9.52
E	70–129	638.20	8.57
E	130–599	1,152.58	8.29
E	600–1349	5,049.74	5.44
E	1350–2999	9,131.96	2.39
E	3000–4749	13,072.77	2.39
E	4750–6499	17,252.41	2.39
E	6500–8249	21,432.04	2.39
E	8250–9999	25,611.69	2.39
E	10,000	29,788.93	0
F and G	0–49	357.60	0
F and G	50–229	357.60	7.31
F and G	230–699	1,673.21	6.96
F and G	700–1399	4,946.64	5.60
F and G	1400–1949	8,865.80	4.32
F and G	1950–3549	11,242.37	2.16
F and G	3550–5149	14,691.41	2.16
F and G	5150–6749	18,140.45	2.16
F and G	6750–8349	21,589.49	2.16
F and G	8350–9999	25,038.53	2.16
F and G	10,000	28,593.21	0
H	0–39	357.75	0
H	40–249	357.75	8.60
H	250–619	2,162.92	7.15
H	620–1299	4,807.79	5.31
H	1300–2999	8,418.74	4.21
H	3000–4999	15,583.59	2.27
H	5000–5999	20,129.84	2.27
H	6000–6999	22,402.90	2.27
H	7000–7999	24,676.03	2.27
H	8000–8999	26,949.15	2.27
H	9000–9999	29,222.28	2.27
H	10,000	31,493.13	0
I	0–39	357.44	0
I	40–369	357.44	9.14
I	370–799	3,373.66	9.09
I	800–1299	7,282.43	8.99
I	1300–2699	11,779.02	7.08
I	2700–4199	21,697.63	3.04
I	4200–5359	26,264.52	3.04
I	5360–6519	29,796.25	3.04
I	6520–7679	33,327.97	3.04
I	7680–8839	36,859.71	3.04
I	8840–9999	40,391.43	3.04

Offence Class	PPE Range	Initial Fee	Incremental fee per page
I	10,000	43,920.11	0
K	0–119	1,031.82	0
K	120–734	1,031.82	8.66
K	735-1289	6,356.06	8.72
K	1290–2399	11,193.67	8.87
K	2400–4499	21,042.53	8.84
K	4500–7999	39,605.74	8.84
K	8000–8399	70,544.40	8.84
K	8400–8799	74,080.24	8.84
K	8800–9199	77,616.08	8.84
K	9200–9599	81,151.94	8.84
K	9600–9999	84,687.78	8.84
K	10,000	88,214.79	0

[The table in para. 9 is printed as substituted by the Criminal Legal Aid (Remuneration) (Amendment) Regulations 2014 (S.I. 2014 No. 415). As to its application, see *ante*, G-70c.]

PART 3

FIXED FEE FOR GUILTY PLEAS AND CRACKED TRIALS

Scope of Part 3

G-73   10.—(1) Subject to sub-paragraph (2), this Part applies to a case sent for trial to the Crown Court on the election of a defendant where the magistrates' court has determined the case to be suitable for summary trial.

(2) This Part does not apply where the trial is a cracked trial because the prosecution offer no evidence on all counts against a defendant and the judge directs that a not guilty verdict be entered.

[This paragraph was substituted by S.I. 2014 No. 2422 (*ante*, G-21a). For the transitional provision, see *ante*, G-21a. It is printed as amended by S.I. 2015 No. 1678 (*ante*, G-1a).]

Fixed fee for guilty pleas or cracked trials

11. The fee payable to a litigator in relation to a guilty plea or cracked trial to which this Part applies is £298.65 per proceedings.

[Para. 11 is printed as amended by S.I. 2015 No. 1369 (*ante*, G-1a, G-15). The amendment applies to matters in which a relevant determination (*i.e.* one under s.13, 15 or 16 of the LASPOA 2012 (as to which, see §§ 6-209 *et seq.* in the main work)) was made on or after July 1, 2015.]

PART 4

DEFENDANT UPLIFTS, RETRIALS AND TRANSFERS

Defendant uplifts

G-73a   12.—(1) The defendant uplift payable to a litigator is calculated in accordance with the table following this paragraph.

(2) Only one defendant uplift is payable in each case.

(3) In the table following this paragraph, the total fee means—

(a) in a cracked trial or guilty plea where the number of pages of prosecution evidence does not exceed the PPE Cut-off specified in the table following paragraph 5(1), the basic fee specified in the table following paragraph 6(2);

(b) in a trial where the number of pages of prosecution evidence does not exceed the PPE Cut-off specified in the table following paragraph 5(2), the basic fee specified in the table following paragraph 7(2) plus the length of trial proxy specified in the table following paragraph 7(3);

(c) in a cracked trial or guilty plea where the number of pages of prosecution evidence exceeds the PPE Cut-off specified in the table following paragraph 5(1), the final fee, as calculated in accordance with paragraph 8(2); and

(d) in a trial where the number of pages of prosecution evidence exceeds the PPE Cut-off specified in the table following paragraph 5(2), the final fee, as calculated in accordance with paragraph 9(2);

(e)   where appropriate, the fee set out in paragraph 11.

(4) In a case where the representation of one defendant would attract a fixed fee under Part 3 and the representation of one or more of the other defendants would attract a graduated fee under Part 2, the total fee is the fee falling within whichever of paragraphs (a) to (d) of sub-paragraph (3) is appropriate.

DEFENDANT UPLIFTS

Total number of defendants represented by litigator	Percentage uplift to total fee
2–4	20%
5+	30%

Retrials and transfers

13.—(1) Where following a trial an order is made for a retrial and the same litigator acts for the   **G-73b** assisted person at both trials the fee payable to that litigator is—

(a)   in respect of the first trial, a fee calculated in accordance with the provisions of this Schedule; and

(b)   in respect of the retrial, 25% of the fee, as appropriate to the circumstances of the retrial, in accordance with the provisions of this Schedule.

(2) Where—

(a)   a case is transferred to a new litigator; or

(b)   a retrial is ordered and a new litigator acts for the assisted person at the retrial,

the fee payable to the original litigator and the new litigator is a percentage of the total fee, calculated in accordance with the table following this paragraph, as appropriate to the circumstances and timing of the retrial, transfer or withdrawal of the section 16 determination.

(3) In sub-paragraph (2), "transfer" includes the making of a section 16 determination in favour of an individual who, immediately before the making of the section 16 determination—

(a)   had represented themselves; or

(b)   had been represented (otherwise than pursuant to a section 16 determination) by the litigator named in the order,

and for the purposes of that sub-paragraph the litigator is to be treated as a new litigator.

(4) For the purposes of sub-paragraph (2), a case is not transferred to a new litigator where—

(a)   a firm of solicitors is named as litigator in the representation order and the solicitor or other appropriately qualified person with responsibility for the case moves to another firm;

(b)   a firm of solicitors is named as litigator in the representation order and the firm changes (whether by merger or acquisition or in some other way), but so that the new firm remains closely related to the firm named in the order; or

(c)   a solicitor or other appropriately qualified person is named as litigator in the representation order and responsibility for the case is transferred to another solicitor or appropriately qualified person in the same firm or a closely related firm.

(5) For the purposes of sub-paragraph (2), where a case which has been transferred to a new litigator is transferred again, that new litigator—

(a)   must be treated as the original litigator, where the transfer takes place at any time before the trial or any retrial;

(b)   must be treated as a new litigator, where the transfer takes place during the trial or any retrial; and

(c)   must not receive any fee, where the transfer takes place after the trial or any retrial but before the sentencing hearing.

(6) Where a section 16 determination is withdrawn before the case ends, a litigator must receive a percentage of the total fee, in accordance with the table following this paragraph, as appropriate to the circumstances and timing of a transfer.

(7) In the table following this paragraph, the total fee means—

(a)   in a cracked trial or guilty plea in a case to which Part 2 applies, where the number of pages of prosecution evidence is less than or equal to the PPE Cut-off specified in the table following paragraph 5(1), the basic fee as set out in the table following paragraph 6(2);

(b)   in a trial where the number of pages of prosecution evidence is less than or equal to the PPE Cut-off specified in the table following paragraph 5(2), the basic fee specified in the table following paragraph 7(2) plus the length of trial proxy specified in the table following paragraph 7(3);

(c)   in a cracked trial or guilty plea in a case to which Part 2 applies, where the number of pages of prosecution evidence exceeds the PPE Cut-off specified in the table following paragraph 5(1), the final fee as calculated in accordance with paragraph 8(2);

(d) in a trial where the number of pages of prosecution evidence exceeds the PPE Cut-off specified in the table following paragraph 5(2), the final fee, as calculated in accordance with paragraph 9(2);

(e) in a cracked trial or guilty plea in a case to which Part 3 applies, the fixed fee set out in paragraph 11.

(8) Where a case becomes a Very High Cost Case after a section 16 determination has been made and is transferred from the litigator named on the representation order to a new litigator—

(a) the original litigator must be remunerated in accordance with the individual Very High Cost Case contract entered into by that litigator; and

(b) the new litigator must be remunerated in accordance with the individual Very High Cost Case contract entered into by that litigator.

(9) Where a case becomes a Very High Cost Case after a section 16 determination has been made and the section 16 determination is withdrawn before the end of the case, the litigator must be remunerated in accordance with the table following this paragraph as appropriate to the circumstances and timing of the withdrawal.

(10) Sub-paragraph (11) applies where—

(a) the case is a case to which Part 3 would apply if it resulted in a cracked trial or guilty plea; and

(b) at the time the case is transferred to a new litigator in accordance with sub-paragraph (2) it is not known whether the case would result in a cracked trial or guilty plea or whether it would proceed to trial.

(11) Where this sub-paragraph applies—

(a) for the purpose of a claim by the original litigator at the time of the transfer of the case, "total fee" in the table following this paragraph, means the fixed fee set out in paragraph 11;

(b) the original litigator may, if the case proceeds to trial, claim the difference between the payment received at the time of transfer of the case and the payment that would have been due at that time if that payment had been based on the case proceeding to trial.

(12) A litigator may not be treated both as an original litigator and as a new litigator in a case.

RETRIALS AND TRANSFERS

Scenario	Percentage of the total fee	Case type used to determine total fee	Claim period
Cracked trial before retrial, where there is no change of litigator	25%	Cracked trial	—
Retrial, where there is no change of litigator	25%	Trial	—
Up to and including plea and case management hearing transfer (original litigator)	25%	Cracked trial	—
Transfer at or before the first hearing at which the assisted person enters a plea — guilty plea (new litigator)	100%	Guilty plea	—
Transfer at or before the first hearing at which the assisted person enters a plea — cracked trial (new litigator)	100%	Cracked trial	—
Transfer at or before the first hearing at which the assisted person enters a plea — trial (new litigator)	100%	Trial	—
Before trial transfer (original litigator)	75%	Cracked trial	—
Before trial transfer — cracked trial (new litigator)	100%	Cracked trial	—

Scenario	Percentage of the total fee	Case type used to determine total fee	Claim period
Before trial transfer — trial (new litigator)	100%	Trial	—
During trial transfer (original litigator)	100%	Trial	Claim up to and including the day before the transfer
During trial transfer (new litigator)	50%	Trial	Claim for the full trial length
Transfer after trial or guilty plea and before sentencing hearing (original litigator)	100%	Trial, cracked trial or guilty plea as appropriate	Claim for the full trial length, excluding the length of the sentencing hearing
Transfer after trial or guilty plea and before sentencing hearing (new litigator)	10%	Trial	Claim for one day, or for the length of the sentencing hearing if longer than one day
Transfer before retrial (original litigator)	25%	Cracked trial	—
Transfer before cracked retrial (new litigator)	50%	Cracked trial	
Transfer before retrial (new litigator)	50%	Trial	Claim for the full retrial length
Transfer during retrial (original litigator)	25%	Trial	Claim up to and including the day before the transfer
Transfer during retrial (new litigator)	50%	Trial	Claim for the full retrial length
Transfer after retrial or cracked retrial and before sentencing hearing (original litigator)	25%	Trial or cracked trial as appropriate	Claim for the full retrial length, excluding the length of the sentencing hearing
Transfer after retrial or cracked retrial and before sentencing hearing (new litigator)	10%	Trial	Claim for one day, or for the length of the sentencing hearing if longer than one day

[Para. 13 is printed as amended by S.I. 2015 No. 1678 (*ante*, G-1a).]

PART 5

FIXED FEES

General provisions

14.—(1) All work undertaken by a litigator in a case to which Part 3 applies is included within the **G-74** fee set out in paragraph 11 except for a defendant uplift as provided for in paragraph 22.

(2) Except as provided under this Part, remuneration for all work undertaken by a litigator in a case to which Part 2 applies is included within the fee set out in Part 2 in this Schedule as appropriate to—

    (a) the offence for which the assisted person is charged or tried;

    (b) whether the case is a cracked trial, guilty plea or trial; and

    (c) the number of pages of prosecution evidence.

Fees for appeals and committals for sentence hearings

15. The fee payable to a litigator instructed in— **G-74a**

    (a) an appeal against conviction from a magistrates' court;

    (b) an appeal against sentence from a magistrates' court; or

    (c) a sentencing hearing following a committal for sentence to the Crown Court,

is that set out in the table following paragraph 19.

Fees for hearing subsequent to sentence

G-74b
16.—(1) The fee payable to a litigator instructed in relation to a hearing under an enactment listed in sub-paragraph (2) is that set out in the table following paragraph 19.

(2) The enactments are—

    (a) section 1CA of the Crime and Disorder Act 1998 (variation and discharge of orders under section 1C);

    (b) section 155 of the Powers of Criminal Courts (Sentencing) Act 2000 (alteration of Crown Court sentence);

    (c) section 74 of the Serious Organised Crime and Police Act 2005 (assistance by defendant: review of sentence).

Fees for contempt proceedings

G-75
17.—(1) This paragraph applies to proceedings referred to in section 14(g) of the Act in the Crown Court.

(2) Where, in proceedings to which this paragraph applies, the contempt is alleged to have been committed by a person other than a defendant in a case to which this Schedule applies, remuneration for litigators must be at the rate set out in the table following paragraph 19.

(3) Where, in proceedings to which this paragraph applies, the contempt is alleged to have been committed by the defendant in a case to which this Schedule applies, all work undertaken by the litigator is included within—

    (a) the fee payable under Part 2 of this Schedule, or

    (b) in proceedings under paragraph 15 or paragraph 18, the fixed fee set out in the table following paragraph 19.

Fees for alleged breaches of a Crown Court order

G-75a
18.—(1) This paragraph applies to proceedings in the Crown Court against one assisted person arising out of a single alleged breach of an order of the Crown Court.

(3) The fee payable to the litigator in respect of the proceedings to which this paragraph applies is that set out in the table following paragraph 19.

Fixed Fees

19. The table following this paragraph sets out the fixed fees payable in relation to the category of work specified in the first column of the table.

Types of proceedings	Paragraph providing for fee	Fee payable — (£ per proceedings)
Appeal against sentence from a magistrates' court	15	140.42
Appeal against conviction from a magistrates' court	15	315.96
Committal for sentence	15	210.64
Hearing subsequent to sentence	16	140.42
Contempt proceedings (where contempt is alleged to have been committed by a person other than the defendant)	17(2)	105.32
Alleged breach of a Crown Court order	18(2)	70.22

[The table in para. 19 is printed as substituted by S.I. 2015 No. 1369 (*ante*, G-1a, G-15). The substitution applies to matters in which a relevant determination (*i.e.* one under s.13, 15 or 16 of the LASPOA 2012 (as to which, see §§ 6-209 *et seq.* in the main work)) was made on or after July 1, 2015.]

Fees for special preparation

G-76
20.—(1) This paragraph applies in any case on indictment in the Crown Court—

    (a) where a documentary or pictorial exhibit is served by the prosecution in electronic form and—

        (i) the exhibit has never existed in paper form; and

        (ii) the appropriate officer does not consider it appropriate to include the exhibit in the pages of prosecution evidence; or

    (b) in respect of which a fee is payable under Part 2 (other than paragraph 7), where the number of pages of prosecution evidence, as so defined, exceeds 10,000, and the appropriate officer considers it reasonable to make a payment in excess of the fee payable under Part 2.

(2) Where this paragraph applies, a special preparation fee may be paid, in addition to the fee payable under Part 2.

(3) The amount of the special preparation fee must be calculated from the number of hours which the appropriate officer considers reasonable—

    (a) where sub-paragraph (1)(a) applies, to view the prosecution evidence; and

    (b) where sub-paragraph (1)(b) applies, to read the excess pages,

and in each case using the rates specified in the table following paragraph 27.

(4) A litigator claiming a special preparation fee must supply such information and documents as may be required by the appropriate officer in support of the claim.

(5) In determining a claim under this paragraph, the appropriate officer must take into account all the relevant circumstances of the case.

Discontinuance or dismissal of proceedings

21.—(1) This paragraph applies to proceedings which are sent for trial to the Crown Court.   **G-76a**

(2) Where proceedings to which this paragraph applies are discontinued by a notice served under section 23A of the Prosecution of Offences Act 1985 (discontinuance of proceedings after accused has been sent for trial) at any time before the prosecution serves its evidence in accordance with the Crime and Disorder Act 1998 (Service of Prosecution Evidence) Regulations 2005 the litigator must be paid 50% of the basic fee for a guilty plea, as specified in the table following paragraph 6, as appropriate to the offence for which the assisted person is charged.

(3) Where proceedings to which this paragraph applies are discontinued by a notice served under section 23A of the Prosecution of Offences Act 1985 (discontinuance of proceedings after accused has been sent for trial) at any time after the prosecution serves its evidence in accordance with the Crime and Disorder Act 1998 (Service of Prosecution Evidence) Regulations 2005, the litigator must be paid a fee calculated in accordance with paragraph 6, or, where appropriate, paragraph 8, as appropriate for representing an assisted person in a guilty plea.

(4) Where an application for dismissal is made under paragraph 2 of Schedule 3 to the Crime and Disorder Act 1998, section 6 of the Criminal Justice Act 1987 or paragraph 5 of Schedule 6 to the Criminal Justice Act 1991, and—

    (a) the charge, or charges are dismissed and the assisted person is discharged; or

    (b) the case is remitted to the magistrates' court in accordance with paragraph 10(3)(a), 13(2) or 15(3)(a) of Schedule 3 to the Crime and Disorder Act 1998,

the litigator instructed in the proceedings must be paid a fee calculated in accordance with paragraph 6, or where appropriate, paragraph 8, as appropriate for representing an assisted person in a guilty plea.

(6) Where, at or before the first hearing at which the assisted person enters a plea–

    (a) the prosecution offers no evidence and the assisted person is discharged; or

    (b) the case is remitted to the magistrates' court in accordance with paragraph 10(3)(a), 13(2) or 15(3)(a) of Schedule 3 to the Crime and Disorder Act 1998,

the litigator must be paid a fee calculated in accordance with paragraph 6 or where appropriate paragraph 8, as appropriate for representing an assisted person in a guilty plea.

[Para. 21 is printed as amended by S.I. 2015 No. 1678 (*ante*, G-1a).]

Defendant uplifts

22.—(1) Where a litigator represents more than one assisted person in proceedings referred to in **G-77** paragraph 21(2), (3), (4) or (5), a defendant uplift is payable.

(2) The defendant uplift must be calculated in accordance with the table following this paragraph.

(3) In the table following this paragraph, the total fee means—

    (a) the fee specified in sub-paragraph (2) of paragraph 21 where that sub-paragraph applies;

    (b) the basic fee (B) specified in the table following paragraph 6, or, where appropriate, the initial fee specified in paragraph 8, where paragraph 21(3), (4) or (5) applies, as appropriate for the circumstances set out in that sub-paragraph; or

    (c) where appropriate the fee set out in paragraph 11.

(4) In a case where the representation of one defendant would attract a fixed fee under Part 3 and the representation of one or more of the other defendants would attract a graduated fee under Part 2, the total fee in the table following this paragraph means the fee falling within sub-paragraph (3)(b).

DEFENDANT UPLIFTS

Total number of defendants represented by litigator	Percentage uplift to total fee
2–4	20%
5+	30%

Warrant for arrest

G-77a

23.—(1) This paragraph applies where—

    (a) the assisted person fails to attend a hearing;

    (b) at that hearing the court issues a warrant for the arrest of the assisted person, pursuant to section 7(1) of the Bail Act 1976 ("the warrant"); and

    (c) the case does not proceed in the absence of the assisted person.

(2) Where in a case on indictment the warrant is not executed within three months of the date on which it was issued, the fee payable to the litigator is—

    (a) where the warrant is issued at or before the first hearing at which the assisted person enters a plea, the fee payable for a guilty plea in accordance with paragraph 6 or where appropriate paragraph 8;

    (b) where the warrant is issued after the first hearing at which the assisted person enters a plea but before the trial, the fee payable for a cracked trial in accordance with paragraph 6 or where appropriate paragraph 8, as appropriate to the Class of Offence with which the assisted person is charged; and

    (c) where the warrant is issued during the trial, and the trial is aborted as a result, the fee payable for a trial as if the trial had ended on the day the warrant was issued.

(3) Where the warrant is issued during the course of proceedings referred to in paragraph 15 or 18 the fee payable to the litigator is the fee set out in the table following paragraph 19, as appropriate to the type of proceedings.

(4) Sub-paragraph (5) applies where—

    (a) a fee has been paid, or is payable, to the litigator in accordance with sub-paragraph (2);

    (b) the warrant is executed within 15 months of the date on which it was issued;

    (c) the case proceeds after the warrant has been executed; and

    (d) the litigator submits a claim for fees for the determination of the litigator's overall remuneration in the case, in accordance with regulation 5.

(5) Where this sub-paragraph applies—

    (a) the appropriate officer must deduct the amount paid or payable in accordance with sub-paragraph (2) from the amount payable to the litigator on the final determination of fees in the case; and

    (b) if the fee paid or payable in accordance with sub-paragraph (2) is greater than the amount payable to the litigator on the final determination of fees in the case, the appropriate officer may recover the amount of the difference by way of repayment by the litigator.

[Para. 23 is printed as amended by S.I. 2015 No. 1678 (*ante*, G-1a).]

PART 6

MISCELLANEOUS

Additional charges

G-78

24.—(1) Where an assisted person is charged with more than one offence on one indictment, the fee payable to the litigator under this Schedule must be based on whichever of those offences the litigator selects.

(2) Where a litigator selects one offence, in preference to another offence, under sub-paragraph (1) that selection does not affect the litigator's right to claim any of the fees provided for in Part 5 of this Schedule to which the litigator would otherwise have been entitled.

Assisted person unfit to plead or stand trial

★G-78a

25. Where in any case a hearing is held to determine the question of whether the assisted person is unfit to plead or to stand trial (a "fitness hearing")—

    (a) if a trial on indictment is held, or continues, at any time thereafter, the length of the fitness hearing is included in determining the length of the trial for the calculation of the fee in accordance with Part 2;

    (b) if a trial on indictment is not held, or does not continue, thereafter by reason of the assisted person being found unfit to plead or to stand trial, the litigator must be paid—

        (i) a fee calculated in accordance with paragraph 7 or where appropriate paragraph 9, as appropriate to the combined length of—

      (aa) the fitness hearing; and

      (bb) any hearing under section 4A of the Criminal Procedure (Insanity) Act 1964 (finding that the accused did the act or made the omission charged against him); or

    (ii) a fee calculated in accordance with paragraph 6, or where appropriate paragraph 8, as appropriate, for representing an assisted person in a cracked trial,

whichever the litigator elects; and

(c) if at any time the assisted person pleads guilty to the indictable offence, the litigator must be paid either—

    (i) a fee calculated in accordance with paragraph 7 or, where appropriate, paragraph 9, as appropriate to the length of the fitness hearing; or

    (ii) a fee calculated in accordance with paragraph 6 or, where appropriate, paragraph 8, as appropriate for representing an assisted person in a guilty plea,

whichever the litigator elects.

Fees for confiscation proceedings

26.—(1) This paragraph applies to— **G-79**

(a) proceedings under Part 2 of the Proceeds of Crime Act 2002 (confiscation: England and Wales);

(b) proceedings under section 2 of the Drug Trafficking Act 1994 (confiscation orders); and

(c) proceedings under section 71 of the Criminal Justice Act 1988 (confiscation orders).

(2) Where this paragraph applies, the appropriate officer may allow work done in the following classes by a litigator—

(a) preparation, including taking instructions, interviewing witnesses, ascertaining the prosecution case, preparing and perusing documents, dealing with letters and telephone calls, instructing an advocate and expert witnesses, conferences, consultations and work done in connection with advice on appeal;

(b) attending at court where an advocate is instructed, including conferences with the advocate at court;

(c) travelling and waiting; and

(d) writing routine letters and dealing with routine telephone calls.

(3) The appropriate officer must consider the claim, any further particulars, information or documents submitted by the litigator under regulation 5 and any other relevant information and must allow such work as appears to him to have been reasonably done in the proceedings.

(4) Subject to sub-paragraph (3), the appropriate officer must allow fees under this paragraph in accordance with paragraph 27.

(5) The appropriate officer must allow fees in accordance with paragraphs 27 to 29 as appropriate to such of the following grades of fee earner as the appropriate officer considers reasonable—

(a) senior solicitor;

(b) solicitor, legal executive or fee earner of equivalent experience; or

(c) trainee or fee earner of equivalent experience.

Prescribed fee rates

27. Subject to paragraphs 28 and 29, for proceedings in the Crown Court to which paragraph 26 **G-80** applies the appropriate officer must allow fees for work under paragraph 26(2) at the following prescribed rates—

Class of work	Grade of fee earner	Rate	Variations
Preparation	Senior solicitor	£43.73 per hour	£45.99 per hour for a fee hour earner whose office is situated within the City of London or a London borough
	Solicitor, legal executive or fee earner of equivalent experience	£37.13 per hour	£38.98 per hour for a fee earner whose office is situated within the City of London or a London borough
	Trainee or fee earner of equivalent experience	£24.54 per hour	£28.05 per hour for a fee earner whose office is situated within the

Class of work	Grade of fee earner	Rate	Variations
			City of London or a London borough
Attendance at court where more than one representative instructed	Senior solicitor	£34.86 per hour	
	Solicitor, legal executive or fee earner of equivalent experience	£28.05 per hour	
	Trainee or fee earner of equivalent experience	£16.91 per hour	
Travelling and waiting	Senior solicitor	£20.42 per hour	
	Solicitor, legal executive or fee earner of equivalent experience	£20.42 per hour	
	Trainee or fee earner of equivalent experience	£10.31 per hour	
Writing routine letters and dealing with routine telephone calls		£2.85 per item	£2.97 per item for a fee earner whose office is situated within the City of London or a London borough.

[The table in para. 27 is printed as substituted by S.I. 2015 No. 1369 (*ante*, G-1a, G-15). The substitution applies to matters in which a relevant determination (*i.e.* one under s.13, 15 or 16 of the LASPOA 2012 (as to which, see §§ 6-209 *et seq.* in the main work)) was made on or after July 1, 2015.]

Allowing fees at less than the prescribed rates

G-81   28. In respect of any item of work, the appropriate officer may allow fees at less than the relevant prescribed rate specified in paragraph 27 where it appears to the appropriate officer reasonable to do so having regard to the competence and despatch with which the work was done.

Allowing fees at more than the prescribed rates

G-81a   29.—(1) Upon a determination the appropriate officer may, subject to the provisions of this paragraph, allow fees at more than the relevant prescribed rate specified in paragraph 27 for preparation, attendance at court where more than one representative is instructed, routine letters written and routine telephone calls, in respect of offences in Class A, B, C, D, G, I, J or K in the Table of Offences.

(2) The appropriate officer may allow fees at more than the prescribed rate where it appears to the appropriate officer, taking into account all the relevant circumstances of the case, that—

(a)   the work was done with exceptional competence, skill or expertise;

(b)   the work was done with exceptional despatch; or

(c)   the case involved exceptional complexity or other exceptional circumstances.

(3) Paragraph 3 of Schedule 1 applies to litigators in respect of proceedings in the Crown Court as it applies to advocates.

(4) Where the appropriate officer considers that any item or class of work should be allowed at more than the prescribed rate, the appropriate officer must apply to that item or class of work a percentage enhancement in accordance with the following provisions of this paragraph.

(5) In determining the percentage by which fees should be enhanced above the prescribed rate the appropriate officer must have regard to—

(a)   the degree of responsibility accepted by the fee earner;

(b)   the care, speed and economy with which the case was prepared; and

(c)   the novelty, weight and complexity of the case.

(6) The percentage above the relevant prescribed rate by which fees for work may be enhanced must not exceed 100%.

(7) The appropriate officer may have regard to the generality of proceedings to which these Regulations apply in determining what is exceptional within the meaning of this paragraph.

In *R. v. Farrell and Selby* [2007] Costs L.R. 495, it was held in relation to the provisions of **G-81b** paragraph 4 of Part 1 of Schedule 2 to the Criminal Defence Service (Funding) Order 2001 (S.I. 2001 No. 855) for paying enhanced rates to solicitors, (i) it was open to a determining officer to apply different rates of enhancement to different items of work; since a determining officer was required, in deciding on the rate of enhancement, to have regard, *inter alia*, to the "degree of responsibility accepted by the solicitor and his staff", it was permissible for a determining officer to apply a lesser rate of enhancement to work of a routine nature done by Grade B fee earners than that applied to the senior fee earners to whom they reported; (ii) when enhancement was appropriate, a determining officer should first assess what enhanced rate would have been applied if legal aid had been granted prior to October 1, 1994 (the date of commencement of the revised rules as to enhancement introduced by the Legal Aid in Criminal and Care Proceedings (Costs) (Amendment) (No. 3) Regulations 1994 (S.I. 1994 No. 2218)), *viz.* the hourly broad average direct cost rate plus an appropriate uplift for care and conduct, and then he should adjust the resulting figure upwards to allow for subsequent inflation; he should then decide on a rate of enhancement such as would match this figure; where, however, the figure exceeded the maximum enhanced rate under the 2001 order, then the determining officer should apply the maximum enhanced rate. Since the provisions under consideration corresponded to those of paragraph 6 of Schedule 2 to the Criminal Defence Service (Funding) Order 2007 (S.I. 2007 No. 1174) (prior to amendment), it could safely be taken that this decision carried across to that order (prior to amendment) with the effect—as in this case—that, wherever enhanced rates are appropriate, the rate of enhancement is always going to be 100 per cent because the 1994 hourly direct cost plus uplift for care and attention, plus uplift for inflation is always going to exceed twice the current hourly rates, which have remained unchanged for many years. This was confirmed in *R. v. Bowles* [2007] Costs L.R. 514. Whilst the provision for payment at enhanced rates under the 2013 regulations relates only to fees payable under paragraph 26, the provisions of paragraph 29 correspond to paragraph 6 of the unamended Schedule 2, and it would appear that the decision in *Farrell and Selby* will carry across to this paragraph in the same way that it carried across to paragraph 6.

Regulation 6   SCHEDULE 3

PROCEEDINGS IN THE COURT OF APPEAL

General provisions
1.—(1) The provisions of this Schedule apply to proceedings in the Court of Appeal.   **G-82**
(2) In determining fees the appropriate officer must, subject to the provisions of this Schedule—
  (a) take into account all the relevant circumstances of the case including the nature, importance, complexity or difficulty of the work and the time involved; and
  (b) allow a reasonable amount in respect of all work actually and reasonably done.

Claims for fees and disbursements by litigators
2.—(1) Subject to regulation 31, no claim by a litigator for fees and disbursements in respect of work done in proceedings in the Court of Appeal pursuant to a section 16 determination must be entertained unless the litigator submits it within three months of the conclusion of the proceedings to which it relates.
(2) Subject to sub-paragraph (3), a claim for fees in proceedings in the Court of Appeal must be submitted to the appropriate officer in such form and manner as the appropriate officer may direct and must be accompanied by the representation order and any receipts or other documents in support of any disbursement claimed.
(3) A claim must—
  (a) summarise the items of work done by a fee earner in respect of which fees are claimed according to the classes specified in paragraph 3(1);
  (b) state, where appropriate, the dates on which the items of work were done, the time taken, the sums claimed and whether the work was done for more than one assisted person;
  (c) specify, where appropriate, the level of fee earner who undertook each of the items of work claimed;
  (d) give particulars of any work done in relation to more than one indictment or a retrial; and
  (e) specify any disbursements claimed, the circumstances in which they were incurred and the amounts claimed in respect of them.

(4) Where the litigator claims that paragraph 8(1) applies in relation to an item of work, the litigator must give full particulars in support of the claim.

(5) The litigator must specify any special circumstances which the litigator considers should be drawn to the attention of the appropriate officer.

(6) The litigator must supply such further information and documents as the appropriate officer may require.

(7) Where a retrospective section 16 determination has been made under regulations made under section 19 of the Act in respect of any proceedings where an appellant has been successful on appeal and granted a defendant's costs order under section 16(4) of the Prosecution of Offences Act 1985 (defence costs), the litigator must certify that no claim for fees incurred before the retrospective section 16 determination was made has been or will be made from central funds in relation to that work.

Determination of litigators' fees

G-83
3.—(1) The appropriate officer may allow work done in the following classes by fee earners—

(a) preparation, including taking instructions, interviewing witnesses, ascertaining the prosecution case, advising on plea and mode of trial, preparing and perusing documents, dealing with letters and telephone calls which are not routine, preparing for advocacy, instructing an advocate and expert witnesses, conferences, consultations, views and work done in connection with advice on appeal;

(b) advocacy, including applications for bail and other applications to the court;

(c) attending at court where an advocate is assigned, including conferences with the advocate at court;

(d) travelling and waiting; and

(e) writing routine letters and dealing with routine telephone calls.

(2) The appropriate officer must consider the claim, any further information or documents submitted by the fee earner under paragraph 2 and any other relevant information and must allow—

(a) such work as appears to the appropriate officer to have been reasonably done pursuant to the section 16 determination (including any representation or advice which is deemed to be work done pursuant to that determination) by a fee earner, classifying such work according to the classes specified in sub-paragraph (1) as the appropriate officer considers appropriate; and

(b) such time in each class of work allowed by him (other than routine letters written and routine telephone calls) as the appropriate officer considers reasonable.

(3) The fees allowed in accordance with this Schedule are those appropriate to such of the following grades of litigator as the appropriate officer considers reasonable—

(a) senior solicitor;

(b) solicitor, legal executive or fee earner of equivalent experience; or

(c) trainee or fee earner of equivalent experience.

Determination of litigators' disbursements

G-84
4. The appropriate officer must allow such disbursements claimed under paragraph 2 as appear to the appropriate officer to have been reasonably incurred, provided that—

(a) if they are abnormally large by reason of the distance of the court or the assisted person's residence or both from the litigator's place of business, the appropriate officer may limit reimbursement of the disbursements to what otherwise would, having regard to all the circumstances, be a reasonable amount; and

(b) the cost of a transcript, or any part thereof, of the proceedings in the court from which the appeal lies obtained otherwise than through the registrar must not be allowed except where the appropriate officer considers that it is reasonable in all the circumstances for such disbursement to be allowed.

Claims for fees by advocates

5.—(1) Subject to regulation 31, a claim by an advocate for fees for work done in proceedings in the Court of Appeal pursuant to a section 16 determination must not be entertained unless the advocate submits it within three months of the conclusion of the proceedings to which the section 16 determination relates.

(2) Where the advocate claims that paragraph 9(4) applies in relation to an item of work the advocate must give full particulars in support of his claim.

(3) Subject to sub-paragraph (4), a claim for fees by an advocate in proceedings in the Court of Appeal must be submitted to the appropriate officer in such form and manner as the appropriate officer may direct.

(4) A claim must—

    (a) summarise the items of work done by an advocate in respect of which fees are claimed according to the classes specified in paragraph 6(2);

    (b) state, where appropriate, the dates on which the items of work were done, the time taken, the sums claimed and whether the work was done for more than one assisted person; and

    (c) give particulars of any work done in relation to more than one indictment or a retrial.

(5) The advocate must specify any special circumstances which the advocate considers should be drawn to the attention of the appropriate officer.

(6) The advocate must supply such further information and documents as the appropriate officer may require.

Determination of advocate's fees

6.—(1) The appropriate officer must consider the claim, any further particulars and information **G-85** submitted by an advocate under paragraph 5 and any other relevant information and must allow such work as appears to the appropriate officer to have been reasonably done.

(2) The appropriate officer may allow any of the following classes of fee to an advocate in respect of work allowed by him under this paragraph—

    (a) a basic fee for preparation including preparation for a pre-trial review and, where appropriate, the first day's hearing including, where they took place on that day, short conferences, consultations, applications and appearances (including bail applications), views and any other preparation;

    (b) a refresher fee for any day or part of a day during which a hearing continued, including, where they took place on that day, short conferences, consultations, applications and appearances (including bail applications), views at the scene of the alleged offence and any other preparation;

    (c) subsidiary fees for—

        (i) attendance at conferences, consultations and views at the scene of the alleged offence not covered by paragraph (a) or (b);

        (ii) written advice on evidence, plea or appeal or other written work; and

        (iii) attendance at pre-trial reviews, applications and appearances (including bail applications and adjournments for sentence) not covered by paragraph (a) or (b).

(3) Where a section 16 determination provides for representation by—

    (a) a single advocate other than a QC; or

    (b) two advocates other than QC,

and a QC agrees to appear as the single advocate or as a leading junior, that QC must be treated for all the purposes of this Schedule as having been instructed pursuant to that section 16 determination, and the remuneration of the QC must be determined as if the advocate were not a QC.

In connection with this paragraph, see *R. v. Bromige, post*, G-160.

Litigators' fees for proceedings in the Court of Appeal

7.—(1) For proceedings in the Court of Appeal the appropriate officer must allow fees for work by **G-86** litigators at the following prescribed rates

Class of work	Grade of fee earner	Rate	Variations
Preparation	Senior solicitor	£43.73 per hour	£45.99 per hour for a litigator whose office is situated within the City of London or a London borough
	Solicitor, legal executive or fee earner of equivalent experience	£37.13 per hour	£38.98 per hour for a litigator whose office is situated within the City of London or a London borough
	Trainee or fee earner of equivalent experience	£24.54 per hour	£28.05 per hour for a litigator whose office is situated within the City of London or a London borough
Advocacy	Senior solicitor	£52.80 per hour	

Class of work	Grade of fee earner	Rate	Variations
	Solicitor	£46.20 per hour	
Attendance at court where more than one representative assigned	Senior solicitor	£34.86 per hour	
	Solicitor, legal executive or fee earner of equivalent experience	£28.05 per hour	
	Trainee or fee earner of equivalent experience	£16.91 per hour	
Travelling and waiting	Senior solicitor	£20.42 per hour	
	Solicitor, legal executive or fee earner of equivalent experience	£20.42 per hour	
	Trainee or fee earner of equivalent experience	£10.31 per hour	
Routine letters written and routine telephone calls		£2.85 per item	£2.97 per item for a litigator whose office is situated within the City of London or a London borough.

(2) In respect of any item of work, the appropriate officer may allow fees at less than the relevant prescribed rate specified in the table following sub-paragraph (1) where it appears to the appropriate officer reasonable to do so having regard to the competence and despatch with which the work was done.

[The table in para. 7 is printed as substituted by S.I. 2015 No. 1369 (*ante*, G-1a,G-15). The substitution applies to matters in which a relevant determination (*i.e.* one under s.13, 15 or 16 of the LASPOA 2012 (as to which, see §§ 6-209 *et seq*. in the main work)) was made on or after July 1, 2015.]

Allowance of litigators' fees at more than the prescribed rate

G-87   8.—(1) Upon a determination of fees the appropriate officer may, subject to the provisions of this paragraph, allow fees at more than the relevant prescribed rate specified in paragraph 7 for preparation, advocacy, attendance at court where more than one representative is assigned, routine letters written and routine telephone calls, in respect of offences in Class A, B, C, D, G, I, J or K in the Table of Offences in Part 7 of Schedule 1.

(2) The appropriate officer may allow fees at more than the prescribed rate where it appears to the appropriate officer, taking into account all the relevant circumstances of the case, that—

    (a) the work was done with exceptional competence, skill or expertise;

    (b) the work was done with exceptional despatch; or

    (c) the case involved exceptional complexity or other exceptional circumstances.

(3) Paragraph 3 of Schedule 1 applies to litigators in respect of proceedings in the Court of Appeal as it applies to advocates.

(4) Where the appropriate officer considers that any item or class of work should be allowed at more than the prescribed rate, the appropriate officer must apply to that item or class of work a percentage enhancement in accordance with the following provisions of this paragraph.

(5) In determining the percentage by which fees should be enhanced above the prescribed rate the appropriate officer may have regard to—

    (a) the degree of responsibility accepted by the fee earner;

    (b) the care, speed and economy with which the case was prepared; and

    (c) the novelty, weight and complexity of the case.

(6) The percentage above the relevant prescribed rate by which fees for work may be enhanced must not exceed 100%.

(7) The appropriate officer may have regard to the generality of proceedings to which these Regulations apply in determining what is exceptional within the meaning of this paragraph.

Advocates' fees for proceedings in the Court of Appeal

9.—(1) Subject to sub-paragraph 9(4), for proceedings in the Court of Appeal the appropriate of- **G-88**
ficer must allow fees for work by advocates at the following prescribed rates—

JUNIOR COUNSEL

Type of proceedings	*Basic fee*	*Full day refresher*	*Subsidiary fees*		
			Attendance at consultation, conferences and views	*Written work*	*Attendance at pretrial reviews, applications and other appearances*
All appeals	Maximum amount: £545.00 per case	Maximum amount: £178.75 per day	£33.50 per hour, minimum amount: £16.75	Maximum amount: £58.25 per item	Maximum amount: £110 per appearance

QC

Type of proceedings	*Basic fee*	*Full day refresher*	*Subsidiary fees*		
			Attendance at consultation, conferences and views	*Written work*	*Attendance at pretrial reviews, applications and other appearances*
All appeals	Maximum amount: £5,400.00 per case	Maximum amount: £330.50 per day	£62.50 per hour, minimum amount: £32.00	Maximum amount: £119.50 per item	Maximum amount: £257.50 per appearance

(2) Where an hourly rate is specified in the table following sub-paragraph (1), the appropriate officer must determine any fee for such work in accordance with that hourly rate, provided that the fee determined must not be less than the minimum amount specified.

(3) Where a refresher fee is claimed in respect of less than a full day, the appropriate officer must allow such fee as appears to the appropriate officer reasonable having regard to the fee which would be allowable for a full day.

(4) Where it appears to the appropriate officer, taking into account all the relevant circumstances of the case, that owing to the exceptional circumstances of the case the amount payable by way of fees in accordance with the table following sub-paragraph (1) would not provide reasonable remuneration for some or all of the work the appropriate officer has allowed, the appropriate officer may allow such amounts as appear to the appropriate officer to be reasonable remuneration for the relevant work.

[The next paragraph is G-91.]

Payment of fees

10.—(1) Having determined the fees payable to a representative in accordance with the terms of **G-91**
this Schedule, the appropriate officer must notify the representative of the fees payable and authorise payment accordingly.

(2) Where, as a result of any redetermination or appeal made or brought pursuant to paragraph 11, the fees payable under paragraph (1) are altered—

    (a) if they are increased, the appropriate officer must authorise payment of the increase; and

    (b) if they are decreased, the representative must repay the amount of such decrease.

(3) Where the payment of any fees of the representative is ordered under regulation 29(12) or regulation 30(8), the appropriate officer must authorise payment.

Redeterminations and appeals

11.—(1) Where a representative is dissatisfied with— **G-92**

    (a) the fees determined in accordance with the provisions of this Schedule; or

    (b) the decision of the appropriate officer under paragraph 3(3) of Schedule 1,

he may apply to the appropriate officer to redetermine those fees or reclassify the offence, in accordance with the provisions of regulation 28(3) to (9).

(2) Where—
> (a) a representative has made an application to the appropriate officer under sub-paragraph (1); and
> (b) the appropriate officer has given his reasons for a decision under regulation 28(7),

a representative who is dissatisfied with that decision may appeal to a costs judge, in accordance with the provisions of regulation 29(2) to (14).

(3) A representative who is dissatisfied with the decision of a costs judge on an appeal under subparagraph (2) may apply to a costs judge to certify a point of principle of general importance, and the provisions of regulation 30(2) to (8) apply.

Regulation 8   SCHEDULE 4

RATES PAYABLE FOR THE CLAIMS SPECIFIED IN REGULATION 8

G-92a   [*Sets out the rates payable for proceedings in a magistrates' court and certain other work to which the 2015 Duty Provider Contract or the 2015 Own Client Contract applies. It has been amended by the Criminal Legal Aid (Remuneration) (Amendment) Regulations 2013 (S.I. 2013 No. 2803), the Criminal Legal Aid (Remuneration) (Amendment) Regulations 2014 (S.I. 2014 No. 415), the Civil and Criminal Legal Aid (Remuneration) Regulations 2015 (S.I. 2015 No. 325), and the Criminal Legal Aid (Remuneration etc.) (Amendment) Regulations 2015 (S.I. 2015 No. 1369).*]

Regulation 16   SCHEDULE 5

EXPERTS' FEES AND RATES

G-92b

Expert	Non-London – hourly rate unless stated to be a fixed fee	London – hourly rate unless stated to be a fixed fee
A&E consultant	£100.80	£108
Accident reconstruction	£72	£54.40
Accountant	£64	£64
Accountant (general staff)	£40	£40
Accountant (manager)	£86.40	£86.40
Accountant (partner)	£115.20	£115.20
Anaesthetist	£108	£72
Architect	£79.20	£72
Back calculations	£144 fixed fee	£151.20 fixed fee
Benefit expert	£72	£72
Cardiologist	£115.20	£72
Cell telephone site analysis	£72	£72
Child psychiatrist	£108	£72
Child psychologist	£100.80	£72
Computer expert	£72	£72
Consultant engineer	£72	£54.40
Dentist	£93.60	£72
Dermatologist	£86.40	£72
Disability consultant	£54.40	£54.40
DNA (testing of sample)	£252 per test	£252 per test
DNA (preparation of report)	£72	£72
Doctor (GP)	£79.20	£72
Drug expert	£72	£72
Employment consultant	£54.40	£54.40
Enquiry agent	£25.60	£18.40
ENT surgeon	£100.80	£72
Facial mapping	£108	£72
Fingerprint expert	£72	£37.60

Expert	Non-London – hourly rate unless stated to be a fixed fee	London – hourly rate unless stated to be a fixed fee
Fire investigation	£72	£54.40
Firearm expert	£72	£72
Forensic scientist	£90.40	£72
General surgeon	£108	£72
Geneticist	£86.40	£72
GP (records report)	£50.40 fixed fee	£72 fixed fee
Gynaecologist	£108	£72
Haematologist	£97.60	£72
Handwriting expert	£72	£72
Interpreter	£28	£25
Lip reader/Signer	£57.60	£32.80
Mediator	£100.80	£100.80
Medical consultant	£108	£72
Medical microbiologist	£108	£72
Medical report	£79.20	£72
Meteorologist	£100.80	£144 fixed fee
Midwife	£72	£72
Neonatologist	£108	£72
Neurologist	£122.40	£72
Neuropsychiatrist	£126.40	£72
Neuroradiologist	£136.80	£72
Neurosurgeon	£136.80	£72
Nursing expert	£64.80	£64.80
Obstetrician	£108	£72
Occupational therapist	£54.40	£54.40
Oncologist	£112	£72
Orthopaedic surgeon	£115.20	£72
Paediatrician	£108	£72
Pathologist	£122.40	£432 fixed fee
Pharmacologist	£97.60	£72
Photographer	£25.60	£18.40
Physiotherapist	£64.80	£64.80
Plastic surgeon	£108	£72
Process server	£25.60	£18.40
Psychiatrist	£108	£72
Psychologist	£93.60	£72
Radiologist	£108	£72
Rheumatologist	£108	£72
Risk assessment expert	£50.40	£50.40
Speech therapist	£79.20	£72
Surgeon	£108	£72
Surveyor	£40	£40
Telecoms expert	£72	£72
Toxicologist	£108	£72

Expert	Non-London – hourly rate unless stated to be a fixed fee	London – hourly rate unless stated to be a fixed fee
Urologist	£108	£72
Vet	£72	£72
Voice recognition	£93.60	£72

[Schedule 5 is printed as substituted by the Criminal Legal Aid (Remuneration) (Amendment) Regulations 2013 (S.I. 2013 No. 2803), reg. 3(1) and (7), and Sched. 1.]

SCHEDULE 6

FEES IN VERY HIGH COST CASES

PART 1

INTERPRETATION AND APPLICATION

Interpretation

G-92c   1.—(1) In this Schedule—

(a) a reference to a level is a reference to that level as defined in the Very High Cost Case contract;

(b) a reference to a category is a reference to that category as defined in that contract;

(c) the standard rates apply to work as described in the Very High Cost Case contract Guide; and

(d) the preliminary hearing, half day and full day rates apply as described in the Very High Cost Case contract Guide.

(2) In this Part—

(a) "Task List" has the meaning given in the Very High Cost Case contract;

(b) "parties" means the representative who has signed the Very High Cost Case contract and the Lord Chancellor.

(3) In Table 2, a junior may be either a barrister or a solicitor-advocate.

Application

G-92d   2.—(1) This paragraph makes provision in relation to the application of this Schedule to work done in a case which is the subject of a Very High Cost Case contract signed by the parties before 2nd December 2013.

(2) Part 2 of this Schedule applies to work done pursuant to any Task List agreed between the parties before 2nd December 2013.

(3) Subject to sub-paragraph (4), Part 3 of this Schedule applies to work done pursuant to any Task List agreed between the parties on or after 2nd December 2013.

(4) Part 2 of this Schedule applies to work done in a case in which—

(a) the court has set a trial date before 2nd December 2013; and

(b) that trial date is on or before 31st March 2014.

(5) For the purpose of sub-paragraph (4), any adjournment or postponement of a trial which takes place after the trial date is set must be disregarded.

3. Part 3 of this Schedule applies to work done in a case which is the subject of a Very High Cost Case contract signed by the parties on or after 2nd December 2013.

PART 2

TABLE 1: PREPARATION (HOURLY RATES)

G-92e

	Category 1 (£)	Category 2 (£)	Category 3 (£)	Category 4 (£)	Standard Rates (£)
Litigator					
Level A	145.00	113.00	91.00	91.00	55.75
Level B	127.00	100.00	79.00	79.00	47.25
Level C	84.00	65.00	51.00	51.00	34.00
Pupil/junior	45.00	36.00	30.00	30.00	
Barrister					

	Category 1 (£)	Category 2 (£)	Category 3 (£)	Category 4 (£)	Standard Rates (£)
QC	145.00	113.00	91.00	91.00	
Leading junior	127.00	100.00	79.00	79.00	
Led junior	91.00	73.00	61.00	61.00	
Junior alone	100.00	82.00	70.00	70.00	
2nd Led junior	63.00	50.00	43.00	43.00	
Solicitor Advocate					
Leading level A	145.00	113.00	91.00	91.00	
Led level A	127.00	100.00	79.00	79.00	
Leading level B	127.00	100.00	79.00	79.00	
Led level B	104.00	86.00	66.00	66.00	
Level A alone	131.00	109.00	88.00	88.00	
Level B alone	113.00	95.00	75.00	75.00	
Second advocate	63.00	50.00	43.00	43.00	

TABLE 2: ADVOCACY RATES

G-92f

	Preliminary hearing (£)	Half day (£)	Full day (£)
QC	113.00	238.00	476.00
Leading junior	86.00	195.00	390.00
Led junior	58.00	126.00	252.00
Junior alone	67.00	143.00	285.00
2nd Led junior	34.00	64.00	128.00
Noting junior	29.00	55.00	109.00

TABLE 3: ATTENDANCE AT COURT WITH ADVOCATE (HOURLY RATES FOR LITIGATORS)

G-92g

	£
Level A	42.25
Level B	34.00
Level C	20.50

TABLE 4: TRAVELLING, WAITING AND MILEAGE

G-92h

	£
Travelling (hourly rates)	25.00 (up to a maximum of 4 hours in one day)
Waiting (hourly rates)	25.00
Mileage	00.45 per mile

PART 3

TABLE 1: PREPARATION (HOURLY RATES)

G-92i

	Category 1 (£)	Category 2 (£)	Category 3 (£)	Category 4 (£)	Standard Rates (£)
Litigator					
Level A	101.50	79.10	63.70	63.70	39.03
Level B	88.90	70.00	55.30	55.30	33.08

	Category 1 (£)	Category 2 (£)	Category 3 (£)	Category 4 (£)	Standard Rates (£)
Level C	58.80	45.50	35.70	35.70	24.50
Pupil/junior	31.50	25.20	21.00	21.00	
Barrister					
QC	101.50	79.10	63.70	63.70	
Leading junior	88.90	70.00	55.30	55.30	
Led junior	63.70	51.10	42.70	42.70	
Junior alone	70.00	57.40	49.00	49.00	
2nd Led junior	44.10	35.00	30.10	30.10	
Solicitor Advocate					
Leading level A	101.50	79.10	63.70	63.70	
Led level A	88.90	70.00	55.30	55.30	
Leading level B	88.90	70.00	55.30	55.30	
Led level B	72.80	60.20	46.20	46.20	
Level A alone	91.70	76.30	61.60	61.60	
Level B alone	79.10	66.50	52.50	52.50	
Second advocate	44.10	35.00	30.10	30.10	

TABLE 2: ADVOCACY RATES

G-92j

	Preliminary hearing (£)	Half day (£)	Full day (£)
QC	79.10	166.60	333.20
Leading junior	60.20	136.50	273.00
Led junior	40.60	88.20	176.40
Junior alone	46.90	100.10	199.50
2nd Led junior	23.80	44.80	89.60
Noting junior	20.30	38.50	76.30

TABLE 3: ATTENDANCE AT COURT WITH ADVOCATE (HOURLY RATES FOR LITIGATORS)

G-92k

	£
Level A	29.58
Level B	23.80
Level C	14.35

TABLE 4: TRAVELLING, WAITING AND MILEAGE

G-92l

	£
Travelling (hourly rates)	25.00 (up to a maximum of 4 hours in one day)
Waiting (hourly rates)	25.00
Mileage	00.45 per mile

[Schedule 6 was inserted by the Criminal Legal Aid (Remuneration) (Amendment) Regulations 2013 (S.I. 2013 No. 2803), reg. 3(1) and (8), and Sched. 2. It applies in relation to fees for work undertaken on or after December 2, 2013: *ibid.*, reg. 4.]

C. REPRESENTATION ORDERS

G-93   Representatives are entitled to claim and be remunerated only for work done in respect of

Crown Court proceedings in accordance with the provisions of the schedules to the remuneration regulations: S.I. 2013 No. 435, regs 4, 5 and 9.

Existence of a valid representation order

Payment can only be made for work done under a representation order. There is no power **G-94** under the legislation to make a payment in respect of work actually and reasonably undertaken by counsel in the genuine but mistaken belief that the appropriate order was in existence.

Solicitors are obliged to enclose a copy of the representation order with counsel's instructions, and to inform counsel of any subsequent amendments: *General Criminal Contract: Contract Specification*, Part B, para. 5.4. It is, however, incumbent upon counsel to check whether the appropriate order exists. If it is not with his instructions, then it is his duty, if he seeks to look to the legal aid fund thereafter for remuneration, to see that the appropriate authority is obtained and supplied to him: *Hunt v. East Dorset Health Authority* [1992] 1 W.L.R. 785 at 788 (Hobhouse J.); and *R. v. Welsby* [1998] 1 Cr.App.R. 197, Crown Court (Ebsworth J.) (counsel has a professional duty to ensure that he is covered by appropriate certificate).

Determining the effective date of a representation order

The effective date of a representation order for the purposes of determining which regulations **G-95** apply is the date upon which representation was first granted to counsel's instructing solicitors and not the date of the later representation order under which they instructed counsel: *R. v. Hadley* [2005] Costs L.R. 548.

Orders made ultra vires

Representation orders assigning solicitors or counsel which are made *ultra vires* are invalid, and **G-96** work done under such an order cannot be remunerated. However, where it is possible to construe an order as *intra vires*, that construction should be adopted: *R. v. O'Brien and Oliffe*, 81 Cr.App.R. 25 at 30 (Hobhouse J.). There is no power to backdate a representation order: *R. v. Welsby, ante*; *R. v. Conroy* [2004] Costs L.R. 182.

Representation by an advocate

As to when a representation order may include representation by one or more advocates or by **G-97** a Queen's Counsel, see regulations 16 to 20 of the Criminal Legal Aid (Determinations by a Court and Choice of Representative) Regulations 2013 (S.I. 2013 No. 614) (*ante*, §§ 6-263f *et seq.*).

It is submitted that a leading junior would not be entitled to any remuneration where he acts under a certificate granted for Queen's Counsel. A leading junior who acted under an unamended legal aid certificate granted to cover Queen's Counsel was not covered by the certificate and could not be remunerated under the order or by a defendant's costs order under section 16 of the Prosecution of Offences Act 1985: *R. v. Liverpool Crown Court, ex p. The Lord Chancellor, The Times*, April 22, 1993, DC. However, a Queen's Counsel must be remunerated at the appropriate rate for junior counsel where he agrees to act as a sole advocate or as a leading junior: S.I. 2013 No. 435, reg. 4(7).

[The next paragraph is G-100.]

Orders for Queen's Counsel acting alone

Where prior authority has been obtained to instruct a Queen's Counsel alone, the propriety of **G-100** the order may not be challenged on the determination of Queen's Counsel's fees unless the solicitor knew or ought reasonably to have known that the purpose for which the authority had been given had failed or become irrelevant or unnecessary before the fees were incurred: S.I. 2013 No. 435, reg. 17(3).

Work done under the order

The work claimed for must have been done under the order. Work done before the date of **G-101** commencement of the representation order cannot be claimed or allowed: *R. v. Clarke* (1991)

Costs L.R. 496. An order cannot be backdated in respect of proceedings in the Crown Court: *R. v. North Staffordshire JJ., ex p. O'Hara* [1994] C.O.D. 248, DC; *R. v. Welsby* [1998] 1 Cr.App.R. 197, Crown Court (Ebsworth J.).

"Topping up"

G-102   An assisted person's solicitor or advocate is prohibited from receiving or being party to the making of any payment for work done in connection with the proceedings in respect of which the representation order was made other than payments by the Lord Chancellor or in respect of various specified disbursements: S.I. 2013 No. 435, reg. 9. These provisions are designed to prevent "topping" up of fees, rather than to prevent counsel from receiving payment for private fees incurred before the representation order was granted or *ex gratia* payments from solicitors who wrongly instructed counsel in the mistaken belief that he was covered by a representation order. However, once a representation order has been granted, the prohibition applies to all solicitors and advocates and not merely those persons acting under the representation order: *R. v. Grant* [2006] Costs L.R. 173.

D. Reasonable Remuneration

G-103   The basic principle of remuneration under the former *ex post facto* regime was that counsel should receive reasonable remuneration for work actually and reasonably undertaken by him. Assessment of the work undertaken and the remuneration claimed was made in each case after the event by experienced officers appointed by the Lord Chancellor's department and subject to the appellate and expert supervision of costs judges and the High Court.

G-104   Graduated fees are calculated by reference to pre-determined fixed fees. Although allowances are made for different classes of case and for the length and size of each case, the scheme necessarily embraces a "swings and roundabouts" principle. Save in exceptional cases, graduated fees draw no distinction between straightforward and complex cases of the same length, class and size.

When they were introduced in 1997, it was intended that they would be cost neutral. The extension of fees to cover 25 to 40 day cases represented a diminution in fees for defence work, balanced by an increase in the fees of prosecution counsel who are now subject to a similar scheme. The further extension of the scheme in 2007 to all trials on indictment save for those covered by VHCC contracts was a far remove from its original ambit, and may give rise to some serious underfunding of cases or aspects of cases.

Very High Cost Cases are remunerated by an hourly preparation fee and refreshers which fall within prescribed bands. The categorisation of the class of case, rates of remuneration, refreshers and the number of hours of preparation allowed to counsel must be agreed before the work is undertaken.

E. Interim Fees and other Pre-assessment Payments

(1) Staged payments for preparation in long cases

G-105   Where the period from sending to the Crown Court to the conclusion of the proceedings is likely to exceed 12 months, a legal representative may apply for staged payments (*i.e.* interim fees for the preparation of a case) in respect of each period of preparation of 100 hours or more undertaken before trial or, in serious fraud cases, before the empanelling of a jury. Preparation in this context is widely defined and includes, *inter alia*, conferences with the defendant, written advice on evidence or plea, legal research and preparation for oral or written submissions: S.I. 2013 No. 435, reg. 20.

[The next paragraph is G-110.]

(2) Interim payment of expenses

G-110   A litigator may make a claim for an interim payment of disbursements in accordance with the provisions of regulation 14 of S.I. 2013 No. 435.

(3) Interim payment pending determination

Entitlement

G-111   In certain circumstances, an advocate may claim an interim payment of 40 per cent of the total claim less any sum already paid: S.I. 2013 No. 435, reg. 19(1). Such payments may only be made where, (a) the basic fee claimed by counsel, or the total costs claimed by a solicitor in a related claim, or the basic fee claimed by counsel in a related claim, exceeds £4,000 (exclusive of VAT); and (b) three months have elapsed from either the date on which the bill is ready to tax or, if earlier, three months after the conclusion of the last of any related proceedings. A bill is deemed to be ready to tax on the date of receipt of the last bill in a related claim. Related claims are claims for costs of solicitors and counsel in the same proceedings acting for the same defendant or acting in related proceedings. Related proceedings are those involving the same defendant which are prepared, heard, or dealt with together, or proceedings involving more than one defendant arising out of the same incident so that the defendants are charged, tried, or disposed of together: S.I. 2013 No. 435, reg. 18.

There is no right of re-determination or appeal against the interim award: S.I. 2013 No. 435, reg. 19(2).

Claims

An advocate may submit a claim for interim payment where, (a) he is entitled to such payment; **G-112** (b) no payment has been made; (c) six months have elapsed since the conclusion of the proceedings against the defendant he represented; and (d) counsel has submitted a proper claim under regulation 4(3) (three-month time limit for the submission of claims): S.I. 2013 No. 435, reg. 18(2)–(6).

(4) Hardship payments

A discretionary hardship payment may be made on proof of the likelihood of financial hardship. **G-113** The proof required is left to the discretion of taxing officers. Counsel are advised to contact their circuit representative, before submitting a claim, to determine the form of proof likely to be acceptable. The sum paid cannot exceed the amount which is likely to be eventually paid, but payment will not be made for sums less than £5,000. Claims may only be made, (a) at least six months after the legal representative was first instructed, and (b) where final payment is unlikely to be made within the next three months by reason of which the applicant is likely to suffer financial hardship: S.I. 2013 No. 435, reg. 21.

(5) Obligations to submit claims

Any person who has received a staged, interim or hardship payment must submit a claim **G-114** under the appropriate regulation for final determination of his overall remuneration: S.I. 2013 No. 435, reg. 22(1). Any such payment will be set off against the overall remuneration on final determination and excess payments can be recovered: *ibid.*, reg. 22(2).

F. GRADUATED FEES

(1) Introduction

As to the introduction of the scheme for graduated fees, see *ante*, G-2. **G-115**

The scheme determines the taxation and payment of fees for advocacy and preparation in something of a mechanistic or formulaic way: *Meeke and Taylor v. Secretary of State for Constitutional Affairs* [2006] Costs L.R. 1. It is a comprehensive scheme which must be applied by examining the particular wording of the legislation: *R. v. Kemp*, X15 363/99. There is no "equity" in the regulations; they have to be construed and given effect however hard the result might be: *R. v. Riddell*, X3, SCCO 319/98, even where payment is morally due: see *R. v. Dhaliwal* [2004] Costs L.R. 689. Conversely, as was pointed out in *R. v. Chubb* [2002] Costs L.R. 333:

> "As has often been said, when the graduated fee system was introduced, it was on a principle which was expressed as being 'swings and roundabouts'. It is perfectly reasonable where the system operates against the Lord Chancellor's Department, that an appeal should be launched. There are many occasions, in my experience, when the graduated fee system has operated very much to the disadvantage of members of the bar and there is no reason why the bar should not take advantage when it operates in their favour."

References within this section to paragraphs are references to paragraphs in Schedule 1 to S.I. 2013 No. 435 (unless otherwise stated).

[The next paragraph is G-118.]

(2) Cases on indictment

Scheduled offences

G-118   A "case" includes proceedings in the Crown Court against any one assisted person on one or more counts of a single indictment: S.I. 2013 No. 435, Sched. 1, para. 1(1). Where counts or defendants are severed and dealt with separately, then each separate indictment is a separate case. Conversely, indictments which are joined should be treated as one case: GFSG: A1, A2: *R. v. Chubb* [2002] Costs L.R. 333. A "case" should not be confused with a trial; there may be two trials in one case: *R. v. Bond* [2005] Costs L.R. 533.

All cases on indictment now fall within the scheme unless specifically excluded: S.I. 2013 No. 435, Sched. 1, para. 2. As to pre-indictment hearings, see *post*, G-121a.

In *R. v. Hussain* [2011] Costs L.R. 689, after one defendant was committed for trial and a plea and case management hearing was conducted in relation to a single-count indictment, a second defendant was committed for trial, as a result of which a second indictment was preferred which included the allegation against the first defendant in the single-count indictment, and the defendants were in due course tried on the second indictment. It was held that: (i) whereas paragraph 1(1) of Schedule 2 to S.I. 2013 No. 435 (*ante*, G-69) provides that "'case' means proceedings in the Crown Court against any one assisted person—(a) on one or more counts of a single indictment ...", there were two "cases"; (ii) in respect of the second indictment, the solicitors were entitled to a graduated fee for trial, together with the appropriate uplift for representing more than one defendant; and (iii) in respect of the first indictment, they were entitled to a graduated fee for a cracked trial. The costs judge observed that whilst it might be thought that the solicitors had obtained something of a windfall for, in layman's terms, this was really only one case, the regulations must be applied mechanistically.

Table of offences

G-119   The table of offences in Schedule 1 to S.I. 2013 No. 435 contains offences listed by statute with a description set out only for convenience. The statutory reference includes every offence contrary to that reference, whether or not the description of the offence is apt to describe the offence actually charged: S.I. 2013 No. 435, Sched. 1, para. 3(1)(e). Cases which do not appear in the table of offences are deemed to fall within Class H: S.I. 2013 No. 435, Sched. 1, para. 3(1)(a). An advocate who is dissatisfied with that deemed classification may apply to the appropriate officer to reclassify the offence: S.I. 2013 No. 435, Sched. 1, para. 3(2).

The offences are divided into the following classes:

Class A	Homicide and related grave offences
Class B	Offences involving serious violence or damage and serious drug offences
Class C	Lesser offences involving violence or damage, and less serious drug offences
Class D	Sexual offences and offences against children
Class E	Burglary and going equipped
Class F	Other offences of dishonesty including those where the value does not exceed £30,000
Class G	Other more serious offences of dishonesty including those where the value exceeds £30,000 but does not exceed £100,000
Class H	Miscellaneous lesser offences
Class I	Offences against public justice and similar offences

Class J	Serious sexual offences
Class K	The most serious offences of dishonesty and other offences where the value exceeds £100,000

Where counts of differing classes appear in the same indictment, the fee is based upon the class selected by the advocate: S.I. 2013 No. 435, Sched. 1, para. 27(1). Once counsel has chosen which count to use as the basis of a claim, that choice is irrevocable: *R. v. Buoniauto*, X25, SCCO 483/2000. Where an indictment is drafted in such a way that the offence charged could fall into either of two different classes in the table of offences, the advocate may choose the class to which the case is to be assigned for the purpose of calculating the fees payable: *Lord Chancellor v. Ahmed* [2014] Costs L.R. 21, QBD (Andrews J.). Where two or more advocates appear for the same defendant, the grounds of each claim must be the same: *R. v. Powell*, X8, SCTO 336/98.

The offences are summarised and listed alphabetically by statute: *post*, G-168 *et seq.*

Conspiracy, incitement or attempt to commit an offence fall within the same class as the substantive offence: S.I. 2013 No. 435, Sched. 1, para. 3(1)(b). Conspiracy to defraud at common law does not appear in the table of offences. It will accordingly fall within Class H: S.I. 2013 No. 435, Sched. 1, para. 3(1)(a). Where the appropriate class depends upon a value, the lower value is presumed unless the claimant "proves otherwise to the satisfaction of the appropriate authority": S.I. 2013 No. 435, Sched. 1, para. 3(1)(c). This may be done by extracts from the indictment or witness statements. Values relating to offences taken into consideration should be excluded from the computation: GFSG: E10. The proof required is proof on a balance of probabilities, and the appropriate officer must take a common sense approach in deciding whether the burden has been discharged: *R. v. Garness* [2014] Costs L.R. 201. **G-120**

In *R. v. O'Donnell and Fawley* [2012] Costs L.R. 431, it was held that the scheme is mechanistic and that there is no discretion for the court to say that, because the defendants may have been shown to have committed offences in a different class, which would attract a higher fee, it is permissible to reclassify the offence actually charged accordingly.

The calculation of values

The property values of each count falling within the same class may be aggregated, provided the same property is not counted twice: S.I. 2013 No. 435, Sched. 1, para. 3(1)(d). However, offences taken into consideration are excluded from the calculation, even where it is agreed that the counts on the indictment are to be treated merely as sample counts: *R. v. Knight*, X35, SCCO 34/2003. **G-121**

In *R. v. Wei* [2010] Costs L.R. 846, it was held that "value", for the purposes of paragraph 3 of Schedule 2 to S.I. 2013 No. 435 and the table of offences in Part 7 of Schedule 1 (*ante*, G-68, G-70; *post*, G-168 *et seq.*), must, in the context of an offence of dishonesty, such as possession of articles for use in fraud, mean the value of the dishonest enterprise, and not the value of the particular articles. The court said that the obvious intention was to provide greater remuneration for more complex and lengthy cases within the confines of the formulaic graduated fee system.

Preliminary hearings

In *Lord Chancellor v. Shapiro* [2010] Costs L.R. 769, QBD (Sweeney J.), it was held that for a first hearing in the Crown Court of a case sent for trial under section 51 of the CDA 1998 (§ 1-25 in the main work) to fall within the graduated fee scheme there must be an indictment in existence at the time. It was said that since the order makes no specific provision for such hearings, it follows that they fall to be remunerated as part of the basic fee if there is an indictment in existence at the time, and, if there is not, there is no provision for payment; in particular, the order making no provision for *ex post facto* taxation (except in strictly limited circumstances), there is no power to make a payment on an *ex post facto* basis. For criticism of this decision, see the commentary in CLW/10/38/8. **G-121a**

Pleas and directions hearings and pre-trial reviews

Pleas and directions hearings are not defined under the regulations. Accordingly if a matter is listed as a pleas and directions hearing, it will be so treated. There is nothing to prevent a pleas **G-122** and directions hearing from being adjourned, or there being more than one or even a series of such hearings: *R. v. Beecham*, X11, QBD (Ebsworth J.). However, the listing of the case is not necessarily determinative. For example, although a case may be listed as a pleas and directions hearing, if a defendant pleads at that hearing and is sentenced, it cannot be said that a pleas and directions hearing has taken place: *R. v. Johnson*, SCCO 51/06. Pleas and directions hearings (other than those which form part of the main hearing) and pre-trial reviews are payable at a fixed rate. Any pre-trial hearings to determine, for example, the admissibility of evidence, fall outside the main hearing and are remunerated as standard appearance fees: *R. v. Rahman*, X21, SCCO 119/2000; *R. v. Carter*, X18, SCCO 384/99.

Fees for oral hearings which fall within the definition of a standard appearance are deemed to be included in the basic fee: see *post*, G-129. Case management hearings which are not standard appearances are remunerated according to the fees set out in the table following paragraph 24: S.I. 2013 No. 435, Sched. 1, para. 12(2). As to standard appearances, see *post*, G-129.

The start of the main hearing

G-123   In *Lord Chancellor v. Ian Henery Solicitors Ltd* [2012] Costs L.R. 205, QBD (Spencer J.), it was held that when considering the question whether, and if so on what date, a case has proceeded to trial, the following principles apply: (i) whether or not a jury have been sworn is not conclusive; (ii) there can be no doubt that a trial will have begun if the jury have been sworn, the case has been opened, and evidence has been called; (iii) a trial will also have begun if the jury have been sworn and the case has been opened to any extent, even if only for a few minutes (*Meeke and Taylor v. Secretary of State for Constitutional Affairs* [2006] Costs L.R. 1, QBD (David Clarke J.)); (iv) a trial will not have begun, even if the jury have been sworn (and whether or not the defendant has been put in the charge of the jury), if there has been no trial in a meaningful sense, *e.g.* because, before the case can be opened, the defendant pleads guilty (*R. v. Brook* [2004] Costs L.R. 178, *R. v. Baker and Fowler* [2004] Costs L.R. 693, and *R. v. Sanghera* [2008] Costs L.R. 823); (v) a trial will have begun, even if there has been no empanelment of a jury, if submissions have begun in a continuous process resulting in the empanelling of a jury, the opening of the case, and the leading of evidence (considering *R. v. Wembo* [2011] Costs L.R. 926, *R. v. Bullingham* [2011] Costs L.R. 1078, and an unreported decision of Mitting J. in December, 2005, in the case of *R. v. Smith*); (vi) if, in accordance with modern practice in long cases, a jury have been selected but not sworn, then provided the court is dealing with substantial matters of case management it may well be that the trial has begun in a meaningful sense; and (vii) where there is likely to be any difficulty in deciding whether a trial has begun, and if so when it began, the judge should be prepared, upon request, to indicate his view on the matter for the benefit of the parties and the determining officer, in the light of these principles.

In *R. v. Budai* [2011] Costs L.R. 1073, the costs judge acknowledged the principle in (v), *ante*, but held that this did not cover a case where, on the day listed for trial, all that was done was that interpreters were sworn, a potential panel of 18 jurors was selected (prior to their being sent away until the following day to assess their availability for a lengthy trial) and there was a direction made regarding the amendment of the indictment. On the other side of the line are *R. v. Wembo, ante* (where, immediately prior to a jury being empanelled, counsel had attended two days of hearings that related to a witness anonymity order, those days had formed part of the trial for the purposes of calculating the graduated fee); and *R. v. Bullingham, ante* (where a jury had not been empanelled, but the judge directed that there should be a *voire dire* to determine the admissibility of evidence which the prosecution wanted to open to the jury, and there was such a *voire dire* at which evidence was called, the trial started with the giving of that direction even though the effect of the ruling on the *voire dire* was that the prosecution decided to accept pleas to lesser offences in consequence of which the defendant pleaded guilty and there was no requirement for a jury). The reasoning in *Bullingham* was expressly approved in *Lord Chancellor v. Ian Henery Solicitors Ltd, ante*, but it is submitted that the result is difficult to justify, not least for its failure to give effect to the obvious purpose of paragraph 13 of Schedule 1 (*ante*, § G-48), which the costs judge did not even refer to. Sub-paragraph (1)(d) expressly contemplates that a hearing as to the admissibility of evidence may take place before the main hearing of a case (trial or cracked trial), and if it does, it is to be remunerated in accordance with that paragraph. The decision of the costs judge effectively emasculates this by converting the admissibility hearing into the main hearing. See also the commentary in CLW/12/01/14.

The start of a preparatory hearing is the commencement of the trial for the purposes of the regulations: *R. v. Jones*, X17, SCCO 527/99: GFSG: B8, B8A.

Calculating the length of the main hearing

Length of the main hearing means the number of days of the main hearing together with the **G-124** number of days of any *Newton* hearing in relation to the assisted person whose trial is under consideration: S.I. 2013 No. 435, reg. 2(1), and Sched. 1, para. 2(8). Thus, where counsel successfully submits that there is no case to answer, the main hearing ceases, despite the fact that the trial may continue against the co-defendants: *Secretary of State for Constitutional Affairs v. Stork*, *The Times*, October 7, 2005, QBD (Gray J.). This can lead to harsh anomalies, as where a defendant pleads guilty shortly after a jury have been sworn during an estimated three-week trial; despite preparation for a three-week trial, counsel will be remunerated as for a one day trial: *Meeke and Taylor v. Secretary of State for Constitutional Affairs, ante.* Non-sitting days cannot be included: *R. v. Nassir*, X13, SCCO 703/98. Where a jury are sworn, but discharged the same day for some reason other than the private or professional convenience of counsel, with a new jury sworn the following day, there may be sufficient continuity to conclude that the trial did in fact proceed, and start of the trial is the date on which the first jury were sworn: *R. v. Gussman*, X14, SCTO 40/99, but part of a day counts as a whole day: S.I. 2013 No. 435, Sched. 1, para. 4. Applications relating to abuse of process, disclosure and witness summonses are to be treated as part of the main hearing where they are heard during the main hearing: S.I. 2013 No. 435, Sched. 1, para. 13(2). The length of a fitness hearing which precedes a trial on indictment must also be included in determining the length of the trial: S.I. 2013 No. 435, Sched. 1, para. 31(a). Confiscation proceedings are excluded from the computation: S.I. 2013 No. 435, Sched. 1, para. 14(2).

Where, during the currency of a trial, there had been a day when one juror could not attend, but the judge had directed all counsel to attend in order that agreement should be reached as to how to reduce one section of the evidence, counsel was not entitled to count that day as a day of the trial; although the judge had indicated he would be available in case there was some issue on which agreement could not be reached, it had not been necessary to involve the judge and the case had not been called on in court; counsel was, however, entitled to a non-effective hearing fee for that day (under Sched. 1, para. 16 (*ante*, G-51)); the case was listed for that day, counsel had been obliged to attend, but in fact the trial did not proceed on that day: *R. v. Budai, ante.*

Fees for contested trials

The calculation of any graduated fee involves arcane formulae: S.I. 2013 No. 435, Sched. 1, **G-125** para. 4. To calculate the correct fee, the appropriate figures should be substituted from the tables of fees and uplifts: S.I. 2013 No. 435, Sched. 1, para. 5.

[The next paragraph is G-129.]

Standard appearances

Standard appearances are defined in S.I. 2013 No. 435 as appearances which do not form part **G-129** of the main hearing, and constitute (i) plea and case management hearings; (ii) pre-trial reviews and pre-trial preparation hearings; (iii) the hearing of a case listed for plea which is adjourned for trial; (iv) custody time limit, bail and other applications; (v) mentions, including applications relating to the date of trial; (vi) a sentencing hearing other than one following a committal for sentence to the Crown Court, or one where sentence has been deferred under the PCC(S)A 2000, s.1, or one where the advocate has been instructed solely for the purposes of entering a plea in mitigation under paragraph 34 of Schedule 1; (vii) a hearing, whether contested or not, relating to breach of bail, failure to surrender to bail or execution of a bench warrant; and (viii) any hearing (except a trial, the first hearing at which the assisted person enters a plea, appeal against conviction or sentence, sentencing hearing following a committal for sentence to the Crown Court, or proceedings arising out of an alleged breach of an order of the Crown Court) which is listed but cannot proceed because of the failure of the assisted person or a witness to attend, the unavailability of a pre-sentence report or other good reason: Sched. 1, para. 1(1). Under S.I.

2013 No. 435, an advocate's fees payable for the first plea and case management hearing or pre-trial review and up to four standard appearances are deemed to be included in the basic fee and are not subject to separate remuneration: Sched. 1, para. 12 (*ante*, G-47). The fifth and subsequent standard appearances are remunerated as set out in the table following paragraph 24: *ibid.*, para. 12(2).

Where an advocate made three appearances at non-effective hearings, the first two of which had been listed as a plea and case management hearing and the third of which had been listed for an anticipated plea of guilty to be taken, where the third hearing was ineffective because the defendant had absconded, and where a bench warrant had been issued which remained outstanding, paragraph 12(1) did not apply as no basic fee had become payable (and thus it did not prevent payment in respect of the three appearances); payment could be made under paragraph 12(2); there was no authority in the legislation for a statement in the graduated fee scheme guidance that suggested that no fee could be paid so long as a bench warrant was outstanding: *R. v. Metcalf* [2010] Costs L.R. 646; and, to similar effect, see *R. v. Muoka* [2013] Costs L.R. 523.

Trial of Bail Act offences

G-130   The trial of any Bail Act 1976 offence in the Crown Court entitles counsel who attends to apply for a new "trial" fee for the contested trial or plea: *R. v. Shaw* [2005] Costs L.R. 326; *R. v. Despres* [2005] Costs L.R. 750.

Sendings to the Crown Court

G-131   Where cases are sent to the Crown Court under the CDA 1998, s.51, and are discontinued before the prosecution serve their evidence, the advocate is entitled to 50 per cent of the fee calculated on the basis of a guilty plea: S.I. 2013 No. 435, Sched. 1, para. 22(2), together with an additional 20 per cent of that fee for each additional person represented: para. 22(8)(a). Once the prosecution have served their evidence, discontinuance, the offering of no evidence at a pleas and case management hearing, or the remitting of the case to the magistrates' court at such hearing because the indictment contains no indictable offence, is treated for the purposes of calculating the relevant fee as if each was a guilty plea: *ibid.*, para. 22(3) and (5). An advocate representing more than one person in the latter circumstances is entitled to 20 per cent of the appropriate basic fee for each additional person he represents: para. 22(8)(b).

Dismissal hearings

G-132   Where a successful application for dismissal is made under the CDA 1998, Sched. 3, para. 2, with the result that the case is dismissed or remitted back to the magistrates' court, the fee is calculated as if the matter had been disposed of by a guilty plea, together with an attendance fee based upon the total number of days and half days occupied by the hearing: S.I. 2013 No. 435, Sched. 1, para. 22(6) and (7). A full day's hearing is any court day which begins before and ends after the luncheon adjournment: para. 22(6)(a). An advocate representing more than one person in such circumstances is entitled to 20 per cent of the appropriate basic fee for each additional person he represents: para. 22(8)(b).

Transfers

G-133   A case will be "transferred" to a new litigator for the purposes of paragraph 13(2)(a) of Schedule 2 to the Criminal Legal Aid (Remuneration) Regulations 2013 (S.I. 2013 No. 435) (*ante*, G-73b) where the representation order has been amended to substitute the new litigator and the new litigator has agreed to accept the instructions and has carried out a conflicts check; an amended representation order will not be effective to transfer a case to a new litigator who has not carried out a conflicts check because it is incumbent upon any firm of solicitors to carry out such a check before accepting instructions and, therefore, in such circumstances, it cannot be said that the new litigator has been "instructed" until that duty has been discharged: *Tuckers Solicitors v. Lord Chancellor* [2014] Costs L.R. 29, QBD (Andrews J.) (considering a corresponding provision in the Criminal Defence Service (Funding) Order 2007 (S.I. 2007 No. 1174), and observing that, in practice, it would be desirable if, when the Crown Court sends information to the putative new litigator, it were to include the indictment, witness list and, if available, the case summary, rather than leaving it to the former solicitors to do so).

In *R. v. Rayan* [2010] Costs L.R. 969, it was held that, for the purposes of paragraph 13(2) of Schedule 2 to S.I. 2013 No. 435 (*ante*, G-73b), which provides that where a case is transferred from one litigator to another, the original litigator is entitled to 25 per cent of the cracked trial fee where the transfer took place "up to and including plea and case management hearing" or a fee of 75 per cent of the cracked trial fee for a "before trial transfer", the reference to a "plea and case management hearing" must be taken to be a reference to an effective such hearing. An effective hearing, it was held, requires there to have been a plea, and for case management directions of sufficient substance to have been made such that the hearing could be described as a plea and case management hearing.

Retrials

A standard graduated fee is paid for retrials, where the same advocate appears, subject to the   **G-134** following discounts based upon the time elapsed from the conclusion of the first trial to the start of the retrial: S.I. 2013 No. 435, para. 2(3):

30 per cent	retrial starts within one month
20 per cent	retrial starts after one month
40 per cent	retrial is cracked or becomes a guilty plea within one month
25 per cent	retrial is cracked or becomes a guilty plea after one month.

No discounts are applied where the advocate who conducts the retrial is not the advocate who conducted the original trial: *ibid.*, para. 2(5) and (6).

In *R. v. Connors* [2014] Costs L.R. 942 it was held that under the graduated fee scheme for advocates as set out in Schedule 1 to the Criminal Defence Service (Funding) Order 2007 (S.I. 2007 No. 1174), where there is a trial followed by a retrial with the same advocate acting in both trials, the advocate does not have to wait until the conclusion of the second trial to claim payment for the first trial. Furthermore, an advocate need not wait until the conclusion of the second trial before electing to have the reduced fee applied to the first trial under paragraph 2(4) of Schedule 1 to the 2007 order (now under Sched. 1, para. 2(2) and (3), to S.I. 2013 No. 435 (*ante*, G-40)). If it turned out that there should have been a greater reduction than the one actually applied, the Legal Aid Agency could recoup any excess payment via article 26 of the 2007 order (now via reg. 25 of S.I. 2013 No. 435 (Appendix G-31)): *ibid.*

Where the case was sent to the Crown Court on the election of the defendant where the magistrates' court had determined the case to be suitable for summary trial, and the new trial becomes a cracked trial or guilty plea, the advocate will receive a graduated fee for the first trial and a fixed fee for the second trial: S.I. 2013 No. 435, Sched. 1, para. 2(4). This also applies where the trial advocate is different at the second trial: S.I. 2013 No. 435, Sched. 1, para. 2(5) and (7).

Where a defence advocate was initially retained privately but, the jury at the first trial having   **G-134a** been unable to agree on a verdict, was then instructed for the retrial under a representation order, the defendant having run out of money, and where the defendant was acquitted at the retrial with a defendant's costs order being made in his favour, no payment could be made under the defendant's costs order out of central funds in respect of work done in preparation for the retrial between the date of the first trial and the grant of the representation order; the graduated fee payable for a retrial under the Criminal Defence Service (Funding) Order 2001 (S.I. 2001 No. 855) was intended to allow for all preparation carried out for that retrial; to have authorised the payment would have resulted in a double payment out of public funds effectively in respect of the same work: *R. v. Long* [2009] Costs L.R. 151. The result would be the same under S.I. 2013 No. 435.

In *Lord Chancellor v. Purnell and McCarthy* [2010] Costs L.R. 81, QBD (Sir Christopher Holland), where a full trial had been conducted in which the jury had acquitted the defendant on the main charge of murder, but had been unable to agree on an alternative charge of manslaughter and on another count of violent disorder, where a date for a retrial had been fixed, where the prosecution eventually decided to offer no evidence, and where it was clear that counsel had not, meanwhile, been standing by awaiting a decision by the prosecution whether to proceed (it was not the case that the matter had been adjourned after trial to allow the prosecution time to decide whether they intended to proceed further) but, on the contrary, had begun preparing for the retrial, it was held that counsel were entitled to a graduated fee for a "cracked trial". They had every reason to expect and prepare for a retrial, as the case was serious and had so far featured a finding by at least three jurors that manslaughter had been proved against the defendant to the criminal standard. Under the 2001 order, there was no provision for any percentage reduction of the fee in such cases. This, however, has since been remedied: see now S.I. 2013 No. 435, Sched. 1, para. 2(2) and (3) (*ante*, G-40).

In *R. v. Seivwright* [2011] Costs L.R. 327, it was held that paragraph 13(1) of Schedule 2 to S.I. 2013 No. 435 (*ante*, G-73b) applies only where the retrial follows a trial and an order has been made for a retrial following appeal or where a jury have failed to reach a verdict, and that "retrial" for this purpose means a new trial which is not part of the same procedural and temporal matrix as the first trial. It was said that whilst this conclusion might be thought to conflict with the Litigator Graduated Fee Scheme Guidance published by the Legal Services Commission, that was merely guidance and not a source of law that was binding. On the facts, it was held that where the trial had commenced on a Monday, the jury had been discharged on the Thursday, the matter was listed for mention on the Friday when it was agreed that a new jury would be empanelled on the following Monday, and where they were so empanelled, there was but one trial.

In *R. v. Nettleton* [2014] Costs L.R. 387, it was held that where the question arises whether "an order [was] made for a retrial", this is not to be confined to cases where one jury are discharged following a disagreement and an order for a new trial is made before a different jury, but it does not extend to every interruption to the trial process, even if it involves the discharge of one jury and the empanelment of a fresh jury. The question is whether the new proceeding was part of the same procedural and temporal matrix as the prior proceeding (see *Seivwright*, *ante*). If there is a continuous process, even a long gap will not necessarily render the second proceeding a "retrial", and the fact that additional evidence has been served by the prosecution, including from one or more new witnesses, will not *per se* render the new proceeding a retrial. In this case, it was held that it was clear that there had been a trial and a retrial where the jury at the original hearing had been discharged following the arrest of the judge, and there had then been a four-month gap before the second proceeding began with a new judge, new jury and, in the case of some defendants, new counsel.

Guilty pleas

G-135   S.I. 2013 No. 435 defines a guilty plea as a case on indictment which is disposed of without trial because of the guilty plea, and is not a cracked trial: Sched. 1, para. 1(1). Cases which result in a *Newton* hearing are excluded: *ibid.*, para. 2(8)(c); and see *post*, G-147.

The graduated fee for guilty pleas is calculated by reference to the basic fee, together with the appropriate evidence uplift per page as set out in the table of fees and uplifts: S.I. 2013 No. 435, Sched. 1, paras 7 and 8 (and Table A).

Graduated fees for guilty pleas under Part 3 of Schedule 1 to S.I. 2013 No. 435 no longer apply to cases committed to the Crown Court on the election of the defendant where the magistrates' court determined that the case was suitable for summary trial: S.I. 2013 No. 435, Sched. 1, para. 6.

In *R. v. Agbobu* [2009] Costs L.R. 374, it was held that even though a case may not be a "guilty plea" within the definition in paragraph 1(1) of Schedule 2 to S.I. 2013 No. 435 (*ante*, G-69), paragraph 21(4) of Part 3 of that schedule (*ante*, G-76a) nevertheless provides that "where an application for dismissal is made ... and—(a) the charge, or charges are dismissed and the assisted person is discharged; ... the litigator instructed in the proceedings must be paid a fee calculated in accordance with paragraph 6, or where appropriate, paragraph 8, as appropriate for representing an assisted person in a guilty plea". Accordingly, the fee payable for a litigator representing a defendant against whom charges were dismissed was that payable for a guilty plea and not a cracked trial.

Cracked trials

G-136   A cracked trial is a case on indictment in which (a) the assisted person enters a plea of not guilty to one or more counts at the first hearing at which he or she enters a plea and (i) the case does not proceed to trial (whether by reason of pleas of guilty or for other reasons) or the prosecution offer no evidence; and (ii) either (aa) in respect of one or more counts to which the assisted person pleaded guilty, he did not so plead at the first hearing at which he entered a plea; or (bb) in respect of one or more counts which did not proceed, the prosecution did not, before or at the first hearing at which the assisted person entered a plea, declare an intention of not proceeding with them; or (b) the case is listed for trial without hearing at which the assisted persons enters a plea: S.I. 2013 No. 435, Sched. 1, para. 1(1) (the definition is defective in that in (b) there is no reference to the case not proceeding to trial (read literally it would cover cases that go to trial where no plea and case management hearing took place)). The rationale for the cracked trial fee is that it provides some element of compensation for the loss of refreshers and trial length increments which otherwise would have been payable: *R. v. Frampton* [2005] Costs L.R. 527. Graduated fees for guilty pleas under Part 3 of Schedule 1 to S.I. 2013 No. 435 no longer apply to cases committed to the Crown Court on the election of the defendant where the magistrates' court determined that the case was suitable for summary trial: S.I. 2013 No. 435, Sched. 1, para. 6.

The essence of a cracked trial is that after the conclusion of a pleas and directions hearing there are still counts on which the prosecution and defence do not agree so that a trial remains a real possibility: *R. v. Minster*, X23, SCTO 647/99; *R. v. Mohammed*, X27, SCCO 210/2000. A case listed for a plea and directions hearing is ultimately defined by what actually happens at that hearing. If a defendant pleads guilty at what is listed as a plea and directions hearing, the plea obviates the need for such a hearing. Accordingly, an advocate is entitled to a fee for a cracked trial: *R. v. Johnson* [2006] Costs L.R. 852 (*sed quaere*, as this flies in the face of the definition of a "cracked trial": see (a), *ante*). Where an indictment containing two counts was listed for trial following a plea and directions hearing, but the defendant pleaded guilty to one count, which was acceptable to the prosecution, whereupon the case was put back for sentence, and where, at the adjourned hearing, a formal not guilty verdict was entered on the other count and where the defendant was represented by different counsel on the two occasions, it was counsel who represented him on the first occasion who was entitled to the "cracked trial" fee as what happened on that occasion came within the definition of a "cracked trial" (*viz.* case was one in which a plea and directions hearing took place, the case did not proceed to trial, but the guilty plea was not entered at that hearing): *R. v. Johnson (Craig)* [2007] Costs L.R. 316. Once a meaningful trial has started, a change of plea cannot convert the trial into a cracked trial: *R. v. Maynard*, X19, SCCO 461/99; *R. v. Karra*, X19A, SCCO 375/99; and *Meeke and Taylor v. Secretary of State for Constitutional Affairs* [2006] Costs L.R. 1, QBD (David Clarke J.). Where a jury were discharged on the second day of a trial on a three count indictment, and on the following working day the prosecution added a new lesser count, and, before a new jury were sworn, the defendant offered sufficient pleas to the indictment, counsel was entitled to a fee for the first (abortive) trial, and a cracked trial fee for the later hearing at which pleas were tendered: *Frampton, ante*.

Cracked trial fees do not apply where a person pleads not guilty at a pleas and directions hearing, but later the same day changes his plea; a guilty plea fee is appropriate: *R. v. Baxter*, X22, SCCO 375/99.

The fee for a cracked trial is calculated by reference to when the case cracked, *i.e.* in the first, second or third part of a period calculated from the date when the court first fixed the date of trial or first ordered that the case should be placed into a warned list, to the date of that first fixture or the date of the start of that warned list. The fact that the fixture might later be broken, or the case moved to another warned list is immaterial and does not affect the calculation. Where the number of days in the period cannot be equally divided by three, the remainder is simply added to the last third of the period: S.I. 2013 No. 435, Sched. 1, paras 7 and 8. The fee is payable to the advocate who appeared at the hearing where pleas were entered or the last such hearing if there was more than one: *R. v. Faulkner*, X33, SCCO 201/02.

In *R. v. Carty* [2009] Costs L.R. 500, it was held that where the prosecution of one of several defendants was stayed, the case fell within the definition of a "cracked trial". The fact that the defendant's advocate had not been present on the occasion of the stay (which had been ordered at a hearing when the principal defendant, being before the court on a separate indictment, had then entered acceptable pleas to the indictment in question) did not preclude payment. Moreover, since 1996, there had been an administrative practice which permitted the prosecution to offer no evidence and an acquittal to be pronounced in open court without the legal representatives being present, and paragraph F.11 of the Graduated Fee Guidance Manual permitted a cracked trial fee to be paid in such circumstances. For this purpose, there was no reason to differentiate between a cracked trial arising from the prosecution offering no evidence and one arising from a stay.

In *R. v. Harris* [2009] Costs L.R. 507, where the defendant had pleaded guilty at a pleas and directions hearing to various offences, but where his "benefit" for the purpose of confiscation proceedings under the CJA 1988 had not yet been agreed, and where sentence and those proceedings had therefore been adjourned, the matter was held not to fall within the definition of a "cracked trial" in paragraph 9(3) of Schedule 4 to the Criminal Defence Service (Funding) Order 2001 (S.I. 2001 No. 855) (which corresponds to the current definition), and the hearing at which the confiscation order was eventually made was said not to fall within the definition of a *Newton* hearing (*R. v. Newton*, 77 Cr.App.R. 13, CA) under paragraph 1(1) (corresponding to the definition in para. 1(1) of Sched. 1 to S.I. 2013 No. 435) for the purposes of paragraph 2(6) (see now para. 2(6) of Sched. 1 to S.I. 2013 No. 435, *ante*, G-40). The prosecution had accepted the basis of the defendant's guilty plea, but in the knowledge that it would take further time, and in all likelihood another hearing, to work out the defendant's benefit. The matter, therefore, fell within the definition of "guilty plea" under paragraph 9(5).

As to the distinction between a "trial" and a "cracked trial", see also *ante*, G-123.

Calculating the pages of prosecution evidence

G-137   Prosecution evidence includes all witness statements, documentary and pictorial exhibits and records of interview with any defendant served on the defence pursuant to the Crime and Disorder Act 1998 (Service of Prosecution Evidence) Regulations 2005 (S.I. 2005 No. 902) (§§ 1-47, 1-48 in the main work), or included in any notice of additional evidence, and now includes documents served in electronic form, except for a documentary or pictorial exhibit which has never existed in paper form, unless the appropriate officer decides that it would be appropriate to include it in the page count taking into account the nature of the document and any other relevant circumstances: S.I. 2013 No. 435, Sched. 1, para. 1(2) to (5), and Sched. 2, para. 1(2) to (5). The first 50 pages must be excluded for the purposes of the calculation: S.I. 2013 No. 435, Sched. 1, para. 4. Additional documents cannot be included in the computation unless accompanied by a written notice of additional evidence: *R. v. Sturdy*, X9, December 18, 1998, SCTO 714/98; *R. v. Gkampos* [2011] Costs L.R. 142 (pages of antecedent materials relating to the defendant); and *R. v. Ward* [2012] Costs L.R. 605; but see *R. v. Qu* [2012] Costs L.R. 599 (evidence served by prosecution during trial and on which they intended to rely to be included in page count, though not accompanied by formal notice of additional evidence (see CLW/12/26/12 for the suggestion that the costs judge arrived at the correct result, but not necessarily for the right reasons)). Where one or more notices of additional evidence have been served, a page count should include the contents of all such notices, unless all sides are agreed that service of a particular notice was an administrative error; and it is irrelevant when a notice was served, or whether it was requested by the defence or prosecution: *R. v. Taylor* [2005] Costs L.R. 712 (notice served on day jury retired). A prosecution notice of intention to adduce bad character evidence does not fall within the term "any notice of additional evidence": *R. v. McCall* [2011] Costs L.R. 914 (but for a critique of the reasoning, see CLW/11/40/5). Where the Crown have exhibited and served tapes of interview, and defence counsel considers that a transcript of the interview is necessary, the pages of transcript should be included in the computation: *R. v. Brazier*, X5, SCTO 810/97. Taxing officers have been directed to include the fullest transcript produced, together with the version in the transfer bundle (if shorter), and also to include any video evidence transcripts requested by the judge: GFSG A4, A4A. Taxing officers have been directed to exclude title and separator pages: GFSG: A4A; and any additional edited versions of transcripts placed before a jury: GFSG: A5. Fax front sheets which are no more than title pages, duplicate witness statements, whether typed or hand-written, and very short lists of (*e.g.* two) exhibits should not be counted: *R. v. El Treki*, X26, SCCO 431/2000. And nor should pages comprising admissions and a jury bundle consisting of, *inter alia*, an index and details of the defendants: *R. v. Wei* [2010] Costs L.R. 846. No allowance is made for small or large typefaces or for line spacing. Unused material is also excluded.

Whereas paragraph 1(3) of Schedule 2 to S.I. 2013 No. 435 (*ante*, G-69) lists the documents that may be included when calculating the "pages of prosecution evidence" for the purposes of determining a litigator's fee under the graduated fee scheme, the list is to be taken to be exhaustive, notwithstanding that it does not include documents which will have to be read in most cases or even referred to in court (such as the indictment, custody records, correspondence, crime reports, and unused material): *R. v. Tucker* [2010] Costs L.R. 850.

In *R. v. Jalibaghodelehzi* [2014] Costs L.R. 781, it was held that when deciding whether a documentary or pictorial exhibit fell within paragraph 1(2C) of Schedule 1 to the Criminal Defence Service (Funding) Order 2007 (S.I. 2007 No. 1174) (see now the corresponding provision in paragraph 1(5) of Schedules 1 and 2 to S.I. 2013 No. 435 (*ante*, G-39, G-69)), such exhibits should be included if they required a similar degree of consideration to evidence served on paper. Thus, if thousands of pages of raw telephone data were served and the task of the defence lawyers was simply to see whether their client's mobile phone number appeared anywhere (a task more easily done by electronic search), it would be difficult to conclude that the pages should be treated as part of the page count. However, if the evidence served electronically was an important part of the prosecution case, it would be difficult to conclude that the pages should not be included in the page count.

A submission that *R. v. Jalibaghodelehzi* (*ante*) was wrongly decided was rejected in *R. v. Napper* [2014] Costs L.R. 947. In that case it was held that any documentary or pictorial exhibit served electronically is to be included in the page count where it previously existed in paper form. Where it had not previously existed in paper form, or it was impossible to determine whether it had previously existed in paper form, then determining officers are required to consider the nature of the documents and all the relevant circumstances, including the significance of the documents in the case as a whole. The court said that the task of a determining officer under paragraph 1(2C) of Schedule 1 to the 2007 order (*ante*) was not merely to make a determination as to whether such evidence would in practice have been served in paper form prior to the amendments made by the Criminal Defence Service (Funding) (Amendment) Order 2012 (S.I. 2012 No. 750). However, where the litigator and the advocate are one and the same person, this is a circumstance to be taken into account. It was stated that in such a case, if it is appropriate to include exhibits falling within paragraph (2C) in the page count for the purposes of calculating the litigator's fee, it will not be appropriate to include them again when calculating the fee payable under Schedule 1.

R. v. Jalibaghodelehzi and *R. v. Napper* (*ante*) were approved and followed in *R. v. Dodd* [2014] Costs L.R. 1131; and the factual narrative revealed in *R. v. Sana* [2014] Costs L.R. 1143, suggests that, in that case at least, the Legal Aid Agency had accepted and applied the approach in *R. v. Jalibaghodelehzi* and *R. v. Napper*. In *R. v. Furniss* [2015] Costs L.R. 151, Crown Court at Nottingham, Haddon-Cave J. (i) approved *R. v. Jalibaghodelehzi*, (ii) said that cell site, telephone, and similar material served by the prosecution in digital form must be included as pages of prosecution evidence for graduated fee purposes, irrespective of how important or central it is to the prosecution case (thus going further than the costs judges in *R. v. Jalibaghodelehzi, R. v. Napper* and *R. v. Dodd*), and (iii) opined that the page-count limit of 10,000 pages in the graduated fee scheme for advocates constituted an artificial cap on their remuneration irrespective of the work actually done, and that, whilst it was possible to divine a pragmatic reason for a rough-and-ready cap where the actual page count was not significantly above the maximum (say 20–30 per cent), where it vastly exceeded 10,000 pages, such a restriction was manifestly disproportionate and could not rationally have been intended to apply. However, it appears that no argument to the contrary was advanced (and certainly none on behalf of the Lord Chancellor), and it is submitted that his Lordship's remarks (which included gratuitous suggestions as to the computation of the page count in confiscation proceedings and as to costs against the Legal Aid Agency on an indemnity basis if advocates have to bring further appeals on these points to costs judges), made in the context of a Crown Court trial and wholly outside the legislative framework for the determination of legal aid fees, are of doubtful authoritative status (as to which, see the commentary in CLW/15/05/8).

It was held in *R. v. Thompson* [2015] Costs L.R. 173 that *R. v. Furniss* (*ante*) is binding on costs judges. However, it was further held that *Furniss* was only concerned with cases in which the representation order was granted before April 1, 2012 (the date on which the amendments to the Criminal Defence Service (Funding) Order 2007 (S.I. 2007 No. 1174) effected by the Criminal

Defence Service (Funding) (Amendment) Order 2012 (S.I. 2012 No. 750), came into force), and that where a representation order was granted before that date (as in the instant case), costs judges had no discretion to include the material referred to in *Furniss* in the page count. In the instant appeal, the Lord Chancellor did not appear but made a written submission in which he pointed out that, on any view, *Furniss* did not apply to the case, and more generally, he took issue with the status of *Furniss*.

In *R. v Manning*, unreported, April 3, 2015, Crown Court at Manchester (H.H. Judge Mansell Q.C.), the judge found that *R. v. Furniss* was not only not binding on the Crown Court, but that the reasoning was flawed for the reasons given in the commentary in CLW/15/05/8. The judge further found that it is no part of the function of a trial judge to dictate to the prosecution how to serve their evidence or to direct them to make agreements with the defence so as to affect the calculation of defence graduated fees (or to dictate to the determining officer how fees are to be calculated under the Criminal Legal Aid (Remuneration) Regulations 2013 (S.I. 2013 No. 435) (*ante*, G-6 *et seq.*) in any given case).

★   The most recent addition to this saga is *R. v. Jagelo*, unreported, January 6, 2016, in which Costs Judge Rowley held that *Furniss* is not binding on costs judges, and that the provision for the graduated fee payable for a given case to be supplemented by a payment under the special preparation arrangements where the number of pages exceeded 10,000 was compatible with the right of a defendant, under Article 6(3)(c) of the ECHR (§ 16-72 in the main work), to receive representation that was adequately remunerated, such that there was no need to read down paragraph 2(7) of Schedule 2 (*ante*, G-69a) to remove or restrict the cap; the special preparation process is neither arbitrary nor irrational in principle.

The decisions of the costs judges in *R. v. O'Cuneff* [2010] Costs L.R. 476, *R. v. Burbidge* [2010] Costs L.R. 639, and *R. v. Ibefune*, unreported, June 24, 2010, evidence a conflict as between them and the Legal Services Commission as to the weight to be given to the number of pages of prosecution evidence agreed between the parties and the Crown Court at the end of the case. The commission's stance of not accepting this figure without additional objective evidence has now, however, been fully vindicated by *Criminal Practice Direction I (General matters) 3B* (*ante*, Appendix B-19). This inserts new requirements relating to the pagination and indexing of served evidence (as to which, see § 4-344 in the main work). It was plainly no coincidence that, in doing so, the practice direction adopted the (then) definition of "pages of prosecution evidence" contained in the Criminal Defence Service (Funding) Order 2007 (S.I. 2007 No. 1174). Compliance with the requirements of the new provisions by the prosecution will supply the commission (and costs judges) with an objective measure of the number of pages of prosecution evidence.

In *R. v. Greenwood* [2010] Costs L.R. 268, it was held that whereas paragraph 13(2) of Schedule 2 to S.I. 2013 No. 435 (*ante*, G-73b) provides that "where …a case is transferred to a new litigator … the fee payable to the original litigator and the new litigator is a percentage of the total fee, calculated in accordance with the table following this paragraph, as appropriate to the circumstances and timing of the … transfer", and whereas the table provides that where a case is transferred prior to the plea and case management hearing the original litigator should receive 25 per cent of a cracked trial fee, in calculating that fee, the number of pages of prosecution evidence should be taken to be the number of such pages served on the court as at the date of transfer.

Images and photographs

G-138   See now paragraphs 1(2) to (5) of Schedules 1 and 2 to S.I. 2013 No. 435. For authorities on the former provision, which will still apply where the representation order was granted before April 1, 2012, see *R. v. Rigelsford* [2006] Costs L.R. 518, and *R. v. Austin* [2006] Costs L.R. 857.

Fees for leading and junior counsel

G-139   Under S.I. 2013 No. 435, fees payable to Queen's Counsel, leading juniors and led juniors are not directly related, and are calculated from the relevant tables: see, for example, the tables following paragraphs 5 and 8 of Schedule 1. Where two or more led juniors are instructed in the same case, each is paid as if they were the sole junior: Sched. 1, para. 28.

G-140   In *R. v. Newport* [2009] Costs L.R. 983, where two juniors appeared for the defendant when the representation order authorised instruction of junior counsel and Queen's Counsel, it was held that whilst a strict approach would lead to the conclusion that the leading junior was entitled to no payment, such an outcome would be unjust. Justice demanded that some payment should be made, especially given that the representation order had contemplated payment of two counsel. However, it was said that payment should be at the rate applicable to a leading junior. As to this case, see also *post*, G-269.

Advocates instructed for limited purposes

Advocates retained for a limited purpose are remunerated according to the specific provisions **G-141** of S.I. 2013 No. 435. The limited purposes are:

    (a) the cross-examination of witnesses under the YJCEA 1999, s.38, which is remunerated as if for trial, save that the daily attendance fee is calculated by reference to the number of days the advocate actually attended court, instead of the number of days of the trial itself: S.I. 2013 No. 435, Sched. 1, para. 32;

    (b) the provision of written or oral advice: see *post*, G-160;

    (c) mitigation of sentence on indictment, which is remunerated as for a sentencing hearing together with a fee based on the fixed hourly special preparation rate according to the "reasonable number of hours" taken: S.I. 2013 No. 435, Sched. 1, para. 34(1); and an advocate who is discontented with the fee paid may seek a redetermination: para. 34(2).

[The next paragraph is G-143.]

Instructed and substitute advocates

An instructed advocate is the first advocate instructed in the case who has primary responsibil- **G-143** ity for the case, or, where a representation order provides for more than one advocate, it means both the first advocate instructed who has primary responsibility for those aspects of a case undertaken by a leading advocate and the first advocate instructed who has primary responsibility for those aspects of a case undertaken by a led advocate: S.I. 2013 No. 435, reg. 2(1).

The new scheme (RAGFS) places great emphasis on continuity of representation. It seeks to achieve this partly by identifying an "instructed advocate" who is responsible for advocacy services and partly by paying the total fee for advocacy to the instructed advocate. An instructed advocated remains an instructed advocate at all times, although provision is made for the instructed advocate to be changed, where, for example, he is unable to conduct the trial because of a clash of commitments, is dismissed by the client, or professionally embarrassed: see Sched. 1, para. 25(10). If the instructed advocate cannot attend a preliminary hearing, and sends a substitute advocate, he nevertheless remains responsible both for the conduct of the case and the ultimate payment of the substitute advocate.

Instructed advocates appointed before the pleas and directions hearing must in writing inform the court of their appointment as soon as they are appointed, otherwise the advocate who attends the pleas and directions hearing will be deemed to be the instructed advocate. If no advocate attends the plea and directions hearing, the advocate who attends the next hearing will be deemed to be and will be recorded by the court as the instructed advocate: see Sched. 1, para. 25(1)–(6). Where the representation order is amended after a plea and case management hearing to include a second advocate, each advocate must notify the court in writing whether they are the led or leading advocate. Where no additional instructed advocate is notified to the court in writing within seven days of the plea and case management hearing, the advocate to appear at the next hearing is deemed to be the instructed advocate and the court will record in writing whether he is the leading instructed advocate or the led instructed advocate, as appropriate to the circumstances of the case: *ibid.*, para. 25(7).

To give effect to the scheme, emphasise the continuity of representation, and ensure that all substitute advocates are paid for any RAGFS work they undertake, the Bar Council has introduced a *Graduated Fee Payment Protocol*. The protocol is an essential part of the mechanism by which advocates will be remunerated in future, but it falls outside the immediate scope of this work. It is available on both the Bar Council's and the Criminal Bar Association's websites.

Sentencing hearings in cases on indictment

Any person appearing at a sentencing hearing in a case on indictment is entitled to a fixed fee **G-144** where sentence has been deferred: S.I. 2013 No. 435, Sched. 1, para. 15.

A contested application for an anti-social behaviour order at a sentencing hearing does not attract a separate or additional fee: *R. v. Brinkworth* [2006] Costs L.R. 512.

Under S.I. 2013 No. 435, an advocate instructed solely for the purpose of mitigation shall be paid the fee payable under paragraph 15 together with a fee calculated by reference to the reasonable number of hours of preparation for that appearance multiplied by the hourly rate set out in the table following paragraph 24 which is appropriate to the category of trial advocate: Sched. 1, para. 34(1). The advocate may apply for redetermination of such fee and shall supply such information and documents as may be required by the appropriate officer as proof of the number of hours of preparation: *ibid.*, para. 34(2).

Fitness hearings

G-145   A fitness hearing is a hearing to determine whether a defendant is fit to plead or stand trial: S.I. 2013 No. 435, Sched. 1, para. 31. If there is a trial on indictment at any time thereafter, the length of the fitness hearing shall be included in determining the length of the trial: *ibid.*, para. 31(a). Where a person pleads guilty at any time after a fitness hearing is held, the advocate may elect to be paid either as if the fitness hearing was a trial or for the guilty plea: *ibid.*, para. 31(c). Where a person is found to be unfit, the trial advocate may elect to treat the fitness hearing either as a trial or as a cracked trial: *ibid.*, para. 31(b).

Cross-examination of vulnerable witnesses

G-146   Where an advocate is retained solely for the purpose of cross-examining a vulnerable witness under section 38 of the YJCEA 1999, the graduated fee shall be assessed as though the matter was a trial, with the length of trial uplift and refresher calculated by reference to the number of days the advocate attended court: S.I. 2013 No. 435, Sched. 1, para. 32.

Newton hearings

G-147   Where a *Newton* hearing takes place following a trial on indictment the provisions relating to cracked trials, guilty pleas and sentencing hearings do not apply. The hearing is remunerated as for a contested trial. For the purposes of computation, the length of the *Newton* hearing is added to the main hearing: S.I. 2013 No. 435, Sched. 1, para. 2(8). Thus the main hearing starts on the day the plea is entered, even if this occurred during a pleas and directions hearing: *R. v. Gemeskel*, X2, SCTO 180/98. The advocate who attended the main hearing should claim the whole fee and remunerate the other advocate (if any) who attended the *Newton* hearing: GFSG: B12, 13.

Where a *Newton* hearing does not take place because the basis of plea was subsequently agreed, the case reverts to a guilty plea or cracked trial as appropriate: *R. v. Riddell*, X3, SCTO 318/98. If the hearing is aborted, the usual rules apply: see *post*, G-162, and *R. v. Ayres* [2002] Costs L.R. 330.

In *R. v. Newton*, 77 Cr.App.R. 13, the Court of Appeal clearly envisaged circumstances in which a sentencing judge could reach a conclusion without hearing evidence. However, the regulations define a *Newton* hearing as one at which evidence is heard for the purpose of determining the sentence of a convicted person in accordance with the *Newton* principles. Accordingly, a *Newton* hearing at which no evidence is called can only be remunerated by a standard appearance fee as it is not a *Newton* hearing for the purposes of the regulations: *R. v. Hunter-Brown*, X29, SCCO, 164/2001.

Where a *Newton* hearing is held on a committal for sentence, the only fee payable under Schedule 2 to S.I. 2013 No. 435 is the fixed fee payable for a committal for sentence: *R. v. Holden* [2010] Costs L.R. 851.

Adverse judicial comment and reduction of graduated or fixed fees

G-148   Where a trial judge makes adverse observations concerning an advocate's conduct of a graduated or fixed fee case, the appropriate authority may reduce the fee by such proportion as it "considers reasonable", having first given the advocate the opportunity to make representations about the extent of the reduction: S.I. 2013 No. 435, reg. 26. See also *post*, G-220.

(3) Additional fees

Confiscation proceedings

G-149   Hearings under section 2 of the DTA 1994, section 71 of the CJA 1988 or Part 2 of the PCA

2002 are excluded from the length computation of the main hearing and are remunerated separately as work for which a daily or half-daily fee is payable: S.I. 2013 No. 435, Sched. 1, para. 14(1) and (2). Entitlement to the daily fee arises where the hearing begins before but ends after the luncheon adjournment; a half-daily fee is paid where the hearing ends before or begins after the luncheon adjournment: S.I. 2013 No. 435, Sched. 1, para. 14(2). The appropriate rates are set out in the table following paragraph 14(2).

Abuse of process, disclosure and witness summonses' etc.

Applications relating to abuse of process, disclosure or witness summonses heard before the main hearing are paid at the daily rates set out in the table following paragraph 24: S.I. 2013 No. 435, Sched. 1, para. 13(2). As to remuneration for such applications where they take place as part of the main hearing, see *ante*, G-124. A hearing merely relating to the failure of the prosecution to comply with an earlier disclosure order attracts only a standard appearance fee: GFSG: 12. **G-150**

In respect of representation orders granted on or after April 30, 2007, these provisions were extended to include applications relating to the admissibility of evidence, and an unsuccessful application to withdraw a guilty plea made by an advocate other than the advocate who appeared at the hearing where the plea was tendered: see now S.I. 2013 No. 435, Sched. 1, para. 13(1)(d) and (e).

[The next paragraph is G-152.]

Conferences and views

The first three pre-trial conferences or views are not separately remunerated; the fees are deemed to be included in the basic fee: Sched. 1, para. 19(2). Thereafter, the permitted number of further conferences or views (each not exceeding two hours) is as follows: **G-152**

1 conference	trials of more than 20 but less than 26 days
2 conferences	trials of more than 25 days but less than 36 days
3 conferences	trials of more than 35 days

The number of further conferences allowed in respect of cracked trials is similar, save that the anticipated length of trial is that accepted by the court at the plea and case management hearing (save that, on a literal reading of the legislation, three conferences will only be paid for where it was accepted that the trial would last not more than 40 days): Sched. 1, para. 19(3).

Conferences include conferences with expert witnesses: S.I. 2013 No. 435, Sched. 1, para. 19(1)(a). Travel expenses and the time taken in travelling, including time taken to travel to a conference with a defendant who could not reasonably be expected to attend counsel's chambers, are remunerated at the specified hourly rate: *ibid*., para. 19(5). Where such fees are allowed, reasonable travelling expenses may also be claimed: *ibid*., para. 19(4). The local bar rule has no application to such fees: *R. v. Carlyle* [2002] Costs L.R. 192. **G-153**

[The next paragraph is G-156.]

Special preparation

Special preparation is preparation substantially in excess of the amount normally done for cases of the type in question and undertaken because the case involves "a very unusual or novel point of law or factual issue": S.I. 2013 No. 435, Sched. 1, para. 17(1)(a). "Very" qualifies both "unusual" and "novel" and the phrase "very unusual or novel" qualifies both the expressions "point of law" and "factual issue": *Meeke and Taylor v. Secretary of State for Constitutional Affairs* [2006] Costs L.R. 1, QBD (David Clarke J.). Remuneration is calculated at an hourly rate for "the number of hours preparation in excess of the amount the appropriate officer considers reasonable for cases of the same type": S.I. 2013 No. 435, Sched. 1, para. 17(3)(a); and with no enhancement under paragraph 29 of Schedule 2: *Lord Chancellor v. McLarty & Co. Solicitors* [2012] Costs L.R. 190, QBD (Burnett J.). **G-156**

What falls to be compensated is the extra work caused by the unusual or novel point by comparison with the sort of case involved without the unusual or novel point; as the term is used in relation to the quantification of fees, "type" in this context should be defined as an indication of weight; but the exercise does not include any consideration of the reasonableness of the time claimed; thus, once the determining officer has resolved that the case qualifies for a special preparation fee, he must assess the number of hours worked in excess of the norm and compensate for those hours at the prescribed hourly rate: *R. v. Goodwin* [2008] Costs L.R. 497.

R. v. Goodwin, ante, was considered in *R. v. Kholi* [2010] Costs L.R. 982, in which it was held that under paragraph 52(i) of the Guidance Manual for the CPS Graduated Fee Scheme (which is in materially identical terms to para. 17(1)(a) of Sched. 1 to S.I. 2013 No. 435 (*ante,* G-53)), it is only those hours of work attributable to the unusual or novel point of law or factual issue which was involved, which fall to be remunerated as special preparation; it is not the case that all time spent by the advocate in preparation over and above the norm for the type of case should be so remunerated.

The concept of "normal preparation" done for a case of the same type is wholly artificial. Other than in routine cases of burglary and theft, in virtually all other crimes in the criminal calendar, the circumstances vary infinitely: *R. v. Briers* [2005] Costs L.R. 146. The test is "What is the normal preparation for this offence?" not "What is the normal preparation for a case exhibiting these particular facts": *Briers, ante; R. v. Ward-Allen* [2005] Costs L.R. 745.

It is for counsel to differentiate between what he considers to be the normal preparation for a case of that type and the actual preparation that he has carried out: *Briers, ante; R. v. Marandola* [2006] Costs L.R. 184.

Very unusual or novel points of law have an obvious meaning, namely a point of law which either has never been raised or decided (novel) or which is outwith the usual professional experience (very unusual): *R. v. Ward-Allen, ante.* Some further assistance can be found in *Perry v. Lord Chancellor, The Times,* May 26, 1994, although it should be noted that that case was not concerned with these regulations.

Very unusual or novel factual issues have a similar meaning, namely a factual issue which either has never been raised or which is outwith the usual professional experience: *R. v. Ward-Allen, ante.* Such issues might cover extremely rare medical conditions, such as Munchausen's Syndrome by Proxy or "pubic symphysitis dysfunction", the exceptional, if not unique, nature of which was held in *R. v. Bishop* [2008] Costs L.R. 808, to justify a special preparation fee where it had contributed to prosecution material of over 600 pages (not served as part of the page count); novel issues might, for example have included DNA fingerprinting when it was introduced, but it would not qualify now. A case involving "shaken baby syndrome" does not necessarily attract a special preparation fee, unless there are additional medical complications: *R. v. Khair* [2005] Costs L.R. 542. A special preparation fee was allowed in *R. v. Thompson* [2006] Costs L.R. 668 where the defendant was accused of murdering her husband 10 years earlier. Counsel had to consider not only pathology and toxicology reports, but also a psychiatric profile on the husband prepared by a psychiatrist who had never met him, and issues arising in diabetology and physiology. Transcripts of the original coroner's inquest and the defendant's previous trials for theft and attempted murder of another husband were also served.

The novelty of the bad character provisions of the CJA 2003 did not provide grounds for claiming a special preparation fee; the criminal law is constantly changing: *R. v. Christie* [2010] 4 Costs L.R. 634.

A special preparation fee would be reasonable where counsel had to check a sample of over 33,000 original photographs of which the prosecution had only copied a representative fraction for use at trial: *R. v. Rigelsford* [2006] Costs L.R. 523; and see *ante,* G-138. But the mere fact that preparation properly undertaken for a complex three-week rape trial was "wasted" because the defendant decided to plead guilty during the prosecution opening did not justify a special preparation fee: *Meeke and Taylor v. Secretary of State for Constitutional Affairs, ante.*

A large quantity of unused material does not of itself give rise to a novel or unusual factual issue even where it is accepted that detailed examination of the material was necessary: *R. v. Lawrence* [2007] Costs L.R. 138; and even where the trial judge has extended a representation order to allow two juniors to peruse such material: *R. v. Dhaliwal* [2004] Costs L.R. 689. Such work is not remunerated under the graduated fee scheme or indeed at all: *ibid.* Nor does the mere failure of the scheme to accommodate unused material amount to a breach of the principle of equality of arms: *R. v. Marandola, ante.*

An advocate can also claim a special preparation fee where the prosecution evidence exceeds 10,000 pages and the appropriate officer considers that it is reasonable to make a payment in excess of the graduated fee which would otherwise be payable; the fee is calculated by reference to the number of hours which the appropriate officer considers reasonable to read the excess pages, using the current hourly fee rate: S.I. 2013 No. 435, Sched. 1, para. 17(1)(b), (2) and (3)(b); and Sched. 2, para. 20(1)(b). As to this particular provision, see *R. v. Furniss* and *R. v. Jagelo, ante,* G-137.

An advocate making a claim for special preparation should provide the Legal Aid Agency with dates, times and descriptions of the work completed, and the page count of any material considered, and any documents produced as a result of the special preparation should be annexed to the claim form, and the claim should relate each item of special preparation to the very unusual or novel point of law or fact that gave rise to the need for special preparation in the first place: *R. v. French* [2014] Costs L.R. 786.

An advocate's failure to keep a contemporaneous work log may result in rejection of a claim for a special preparation fee: *R. v. Dunne* [2013] Costs L.R. 1031 (considering the corresponding provision in the Criminal Defence Service (Funding) Order 2007 (S.I. 2007 No. 1174).

Evidence served electronically

A special preparation fee may also be claimed where a documentary or pictorial exhibit, which **G-157** has never existed in paper form, is served by the prosecution in electronic form, and the appropriate officer does not consider it appropriate to include it in the pages of prosecution evidence; and such fee may be paid if the appropriate officer considers it reasonable to make a payment in excess of the fee otherwise payable under the graduated fee scheme, with the amount of the payment depending on the number of hours which the appropriate officer considers reasonable to view the exhibit: see Sched. 1, para. 17(1)(c) and (2), and Sched. 2, para. 20(1)(a) and (2). The drafting of these provisions in the two schedules is slightly different, but it is submitted that the intent is the same. As to the drafting, this – taken at face value – gives the appropriate officer a discretion whether to make a payment even where he considers it reasonable to do so. It is submitted, however, that the legislation is unlikely to be so construed: if the appropriate officer considers it reasonable to make a payment, then it is likely to be held that he should do so. The revised wording of these provisions (introduced by the Criminal Defence Service (Funding) (Amendment) Order 2001 (S.I. 2012 No. 750)) was doubtless intended to avoid the difficulties caused by the former wording and which gave rise to a series of decisions, such as *R. v. Rigelsford* [2006] Costs L.R. 518, *R. v. Austin* [2006] Costs L.R. 857, *Lord Chancellor v. Michael J. Reed Ltd* [2010] Costs L.R. 72, QBD (Penry-Davey J.), *Lord Chancellor v. McLarty & Co. Solicitors* [2012] Costs L.R. 190, QBD (Burnett J.), and *R. v. Jones* [2010] Costs L.R. 469. For details of these authorities, which will still have application to cases in which a representation order was granted before April 1, 2012, see previous supplements.

Lord Chancellor v. Michael J. Reed Ltd (ante) was followed in *R. v. Osoteko* [2014] Costs L.R. 190, but the costs judge certified a point of principle of general importance, *viz.* whether that case had created too narrow a definition of pages of prosecution evidence. The appeal to the High Court (see *Maclaverty Cooper Atkins v. Lord Chancellor* [2014] Costs L.R. 629, QBD (Akenhead J.)) was dismissed, the court approving and following *Lord Chancellor v. Michael J. Reed Ltd.*

[The next paragraph is G-159.]

Listening to or viewing tapes

There is now no provision for any separate payment for listening to or viewing tapes. These **G-159** are now treated as being rolled up within the whole of the graduated fee.

Provision of written or oral advice

Any advocate instructed solely to provide written or oral advice shall be paid a fee calculated **G-160** from the reasonable number of hours of preparation for that advice using the appropriate hourly rate in the table following paragraph 24 of Schedule 1 to S.I. 2013 No. 435: see Sched. 1, para. 33(1). The advocate may apply for re-determination of such fee under regulation 28, and he shall supply such information and documents as may be required by the appropriate officer as proof of the number of hours of preparation: *ibid.*, para. 33(2).

As to whether a solicitor may properly instruct counsel other than counsel who appeared at trial to advise on the question of appeal where trial counsel has advised in the negative, see *R. v. Umezie*, § 7-165 in the main work.

R. v. Umezie was considered in *R. v. Bromige* [2011] Costs L.R. 145, in which it was held that where solicitors, on receipt of trial counsel's negative advice as to the prospects of a successful appeal against sentence, instructed fresh counsel to advise on the question, trial counsel's negative advice (whether written or oral) did not terminate the representation order; paragraph A1–2 of the Guide to Commencing Proceedings in the Court of Appeal (Criminal Division) (*post*, Appendix J-4) did not preclude payment of a fee for subsequent advice given by fresh counsel in relation to the appeal, because that paragraph was only concerned with the amendment of representation orders, and no amendment to the representation order granted by the magistrates' court was necessary to instruct fresh counsel to advise; however, fresh counsel's claim for a fee for his advice could only fall within paragraph 6 of Schedule 3 to S.I. 2013 No. 435 (*ante*, G-85), which provides, that upon the determination of an advocate's fees in proceedings in the Court of Appeal, "the appropriate officer must consider the claim ... and must allow such work as appears to him to have been reasonably done"; as a general principle it will not be reasonable to obtain advice on a point that has already been the subject of advice, with the obvious exceptions to this principle being if the initial advice is incompetent or ambiguous, or if there is a change in circumstances or if new evidence has come to light; the reason given in this case for seeking further advice, *viz.* that the solicitors were not convinced as to the correctness of the negative oral advice from trial counsel, was not sufficient; therefore the work done by fresh counsel was not reasonably done for the purposes of paragraph 6 because no good reason had been shown for instructing him to give advice on a point that had already been the subject of advice. For the submission that the costs judge's reliance on paragraph 6 of Schedule 3 is unsustainable, see CLW/11/08/45.

(4) Acting for more than one defendant, or in more than one "case"

G-161   The definition of "case" in paragraph 1(1) of Schedule 2 (*ante*, G-69) could not possibly lead to the conclusion that if a litigator represents more than one defendant charged and tried on the same indictment that litigator is then entitled to be paid on the basis that there are as many cases as there are defendants: *Lord Chancellor v. Eddowes Perry and Osbourne Ltd* [2011] Costs L.R. 498, QBD (Spencer J.). As to this case, see also *post*, G-273.

An uplift of one-fifth for each additional defendant represented may only be claimed where the regulations so provide: S.I. 2013 No. 435, Sched. 1, para. 27(2). Where an advocate acts for more than one defendant, the advocate must select the case on which remuneration is to be based (the principal case). Claims for such uplifts may be made for pleas and directions hearings, some aborted hearings, main hearings, appeals against conviction, committals for sentence, proceedings for a breach of a Crown Court order, disclosure, abuse and witness summons hearings, and confiscation proceedings: S.I. 2013 No. 435, Sched. 1, para. 27(4). But no uplifts for these hearings, with the exception of confiscation proceedings, are payable in cases that were committed to the Crown Court on the election of the defendant, where the magistrates' court had determined that the case was suitable for summary trial: *ibid.*, para. 27(3). In respect of a trial, the uplift is limited to one-fifth of the basic fee and not the basic fee enhanced by reference to the prosecution evidence, witnesses and length of trial uplift: *ibid.*, para. 27(2)(b), *i.e.* where the main hearing in each case was heard concurrently: *R. v. Fletcher*, X6, SCTO 815/97.

The above provisions also apply where the advocate conducts two or more cases concurrently: S.I. 2013 No. 435, Sched. 1, para. 27(2). Proceedings arising out of a single notice of appeal against conviction or sentence, or single committal for sentence, constitute a separate "case": para. 1(1) of Schedule 1 to S.I. 2013 No. 435. However, a committal for sentence together with a committal for breach of a community service order constituted two separate "cases" as the latter was a committal for breach of an earlier order: *R. v. Hines*, X24, SCCO 337/2000. As a case means proceedings on one or more counts of a single indictment, it is submitted that two trials arising from a severed indictment give rise to two separate graduated fees, as the trials are not heard concurrently.

In *R. v. Fury* [2011] Costs L.R. 919, it was said that if a hearing deals with one case then another, independently of each other, it will be hearing them consecutively; hearings will be concurrent only if they are combined or conjoined or somehow interlinked; this will be so where the main hearings of a number of cases against the same defendant are listed together and the defendant either pleads guilty or is to be sentenced in all of the cases; the cases will impact on each other either as to the directions that are given for sentencing or as to the sentences that are imposed; they will not be considered independently of each other. For criticism of the actual decision in this case (cases were not heard concurrently where, as part of an agreed package, defendant pleaded guilty to one indictment and prosecution offered no evidence on the other, all counts having originally been in the same indictment), see CLW/11/40/3.

In *R. v. Sturmer and Lewis* [2009] Costs L.R. 364, it was said that the combined effect of paragraph 15 and the table in paragraph 19 of Schedule 2 to S.I. 2013 No. 435 (*ante*, G-74a, G-75a) is that where a litigator is "instructed in ... a sentencing hearing following a committal for sentence to the Crown Court", the "fee payable ... is that set out in the table" (para. 15), *i.e.* "£210.64" per proceedings (the table). "Proceedings" can involve more than one defendant and, if there is only one "proceedings", only one fee will be payable, however many defendants are represented by the litigator.

[The next paragraph is G-163.]

(5) Abortive hearings

The payment of fixed fees for abortive hearings is limited to ineffective trials: see Sched. 1, para. 16. As to this, see *R. v. Budai, ante*, G-124.   **G-163**

(6) Wasted preparation

Wasted preparation occurs where an advocate does not represent his client because of (a) a clash of listings and the advocate has been unable to secure a change of date for either hearing; or (b) a fixture for a main hearing is altered by the court despite the advocate's objection; or (c) the advocate withdraws with leave of the court because of professional embarrassment; or (d) the advocate is dismissed by the client; or (e) the advocate is obliged to undertake judicial or other public duties: S.I. 2013 No. 435, Sched. 1, para. 18(1). A representation order replacing a single junior with Queen's Counsel acting alone does not entitle junior counsel to claim a wasted preparation fee in respect of the preparation reasonably and properly undertaken; counsel has no redress under the scheme: *R. v. Schultz*, X10, SCTO 552/98. The hourly fee may be claimed only where eight or more hours of preparation have been undertaken, and (a) the trial lasted for five days or more, or (b) in the case of a cracked trial, there are more than 150 pages of prosecution evidence: S.I. 2013 No. 435, Sched. 1, para. 18(2). The wasted preparation fee is calculated by reference to the number of hours of preparation reasonably carried out by the advocate, who must supply such information and documents in support of the claim as may be required: S.I. 2013 No. 435, Sched. 1, para. 18(3) and (5).   **G-164**

The requirements of paragraph 18(1) were satisfied where, following the vacation of the trial date by the trial judge and his proposal of a new date, counsel had written objecting to the new date (on the grounds that he had booked and paid for a holiday abroad that started within 10 days of the new date), but where, despite that objection, the trial had gone ahead on the proposed date, with the result that counsel had had to return the brief: *R. v. Ghaffar* [2009] Costs L.R. 980. The fact that counsel's objection was to the new date, and not to the vacation of the original fixture, was not a valid ground for refusing a wasted preparation fee in respect of the substantial preparation done by counsel prior to the vacation of the original fixture. Changing a fixture is a process and an objection to part of that process is therefore an objection to the change. There was nothing in paragraph 18(1)(b) that restricted it to counsel's professional commitments.

(7) Appeals, pleas before venue, committals and other fees

Graduated fixed fees are also payable in respect of committals for sentence (which include plea   **G-165** before venue cases), appeals from magistrates' courts and breach of Crown Court orders: S.I. 2013 No. 435, Sched. 1, para. 20; noting briefs: *ibid.*, para. 23; bail and other applications, and mentions when not forming part of a main hearing or other hearing for which a fixed fee is provided: *ibid.*, para. 20(3). The appropriate rate is that listed in the table following paragraph 24. After the Crown Court is seized of a case, any bail applications, or executions of bench warrants made in a magistrates' court are remunerated as if made in the Crown Court: *R. v. Bailey*, X16, 378/99. As to trials of Bail Act 1976 offences, see *ante*, G-130.

(8) Contempt proceedings

G-166   Remuneration for proceedings for contempt in the face of the court is fixed at discrete daily rates: S.I. 2013 No. 435, reg. 11, and Sched. 1, para. 21. The fees are fixed and there is no discretion to allow *ex post facto* payment, however regrettable and unfair the result may be: *R. v. Russell* [2006] Costs L.R. 841. Such payments do not fall within the graduated fee scheme and, therefore, such hearings do not form part of the main hearing or the sentencing hearing.

(9) Travel expenses

G-167   Travel and hotel expenses may be claimed subject to the usual 40 kilometre local bar rule: S.I. 2013 No. 435, Sched. 1, para. 29 (see generally *post*, G-253). Expenses should not be paid in respect of conferences for which advocates are not entitled to be remunerated, unless the conference was abortive due to circumstances beyond the advocate's control: *R. v. Pickett*, X39.

(10) Table of offences

G-168   The effect of the table of offences at the end of Schedule 1 to S.I. 2013 No. 435 (as amended by the Protection of Freedoms Act 2012 (Consequential Amendments) Order 2013 (S.I. 2013 No. 862)) is set out in the following paragraphs. Offences are divided into those below £30,000, those where the value is £30,000 or more, but less than £100,000, and those where the value involved is £100,000 or more. As to the method of calculation for the purposes of determining value, see *ante*, G-121. As to conspiracy, incitement and attempt, see *ante*, G-120. It should be noted that there are various errors in the table: for example, it refers to section 39 (rather than section 139) of the CJA 1988 (this has been corrected below) and it refers to various measures that have been repealed and replaced, including the Post Office Act 1953, the Merchant Shipping Act 1970 and the Air Navigation Order 2005 (S.I. 2005 No. 1970)).

An "armed robbery" (see the Theft Act 1968 entries) arises where the offender was armed with a firearm or imitation firearm, or was thought by the victim to have been so armed, or was armed with an offensive weapon: *R. v. Stables*, X12, SCTO 102/99.

Where a judge proposes to try an offence under the Bail Act 1976, s.6, in respect of a defendant who is first brought up before him for non-attendance, then there is a trial or guilty plea under the graduated fee scheme: *R. v. Shaw* [2005] Costs L.R. 326.

G-169   As several statutes are listed under more than one class, the following is a list of the statutes and orders featured in the table, with the classes in which they appear—

Air Navigation Order 2005 (S.I. 2005 No. 1970)	H
Aviation Security Act 1982	B
Bail Act 1976	H
Bribery Act 2010	I
Child Abduction Act 1984	C
Children and Young Persons Act 1933	B, J
Cremation Act 1902	I
Crime and Disorder Act 1998	B, C, H
Criminal Damage Act 1971	B, C
Criminal Justice Act 1961	C
Criminal Justice Act 1967	I
Criminal Justice Act 1988	H

Protection from Eviction Act 1977	H
Protection from Harassment Act 1997	H
Protection of Children Act 1978	J
Public Bodies Corrupt Practices Act 1889	I
Public Order Act 1986	B, C, H
Public Passenger Vehicles Act 1981	H
Road Traffic Act 1960	H
Road Traffic Act 1988	B, H
Road Traffic Regulation Act 1984	H
Sexual Offences Act 1956	D, H, J
Sexual Offences Act 1967	D, H
Sexual Offences Act 2003	D, J
Sexual Offences (Amendment) Act 2000	D
Stamp Duties Management Act 1891	F, G, K
Submarine Telegraph Act 1885	C
Suicide Act 1961	B
Taking of Hostages Act 1982	B
Terrorism Act 2000	B, C
Theatres Act 1968	H
Theft Act 1968	B, C, E, F, G, H, K
Theft Act 1978	F, G, H, K
Trade Descriptions Act 1968	H, I
Treason Act 1842	C
Value Added Tax Act 1994	F, G, K
Vehicle Excise and Registration Act 1994	H

Class A: homicide and related grave offences

(i) *Common law offences*

G-170   Murder and manslaughter

(ii) *Offences created by primary or secondary legislation*
    Those contrary to the following provisions:
        Explosive Substances Act 1883, ss.2 and 3;
        Infant Life (Preservation) Act 1929, s.1(1);
        Infanticide Act 1938, s.1(1);
        Offences against the Person Act 1861, s.4.

Class B: offences involving serious violence or damage, and serious drugs offences

(i) *Common law offences*

G-171   Kidnapping and false imprisonment

(ii) *Offences created by primary or secondary legislation*
    Those contrary to the following provisions:
        Aviation Security Act 1982, s.2(1)(b);
        Crime and Disorder Act 1998, s.30(1);
        Children and Young Persons Act 1933, s.1;
        Criminal Damage Act 1971, s.1(2) and (where the value cxceeds £30,000) s.1(3);

Criminal Justice Act 1991, s.90;

Criminal Justice (International Co-operation) Act 1990, ss.12 and 18;

Customs and Excise Management Act 1979, s.50 (Class A or B drugs), s.85, s.170(2)(b) or
(c) (in relation to Class A or B drugs);

Domestic Violence, Crime and Victims Act 2004, s.5;

Drug Trafficking Act 1994, ss.49, 50, 51, 52 and 53;

Explosive Substances Act 1883, s.4(1);

Firearms Act 1968, ss.5, 16, 17 and 18;

Misuse of Drugs Act 1971, s.4 (Class A or B drug), s.5(3) (Class A or B drug), ss.6, 8, 9, 12
and 13;

Nuclear Material (Offences) Act 1983, s.2;

Offences against the Person Act 1861, ss.16, 17, 18, 21, 22, 23, 28, 29, 30, 32, 33, 34 and
58;

Prison Security Act 1992, s.1;

Proceeds of Crime Act 2002, ss.327, 328, 329, 330, 331, 332, 333, 339(1A);

Public Order Act 1986, ss.1, 2 and 38;

Road Traffic Act 1988, ss.1, 3A and 22A;

Suicide Act 1961, s.2;

Taking of Hostages Act 1982, s.1;

Terrorism Act 2000, ss.11, 12, 13, 15, 16, 17, 18, 39, 54, 56, 57, 58 and 59;

Theft Act 1968, s.8(1) (if "armed"), s.8(2) (if "with weapon"), s.10, s.12A (if resulting in
death) and 21.

Class C: lesser offences involving violence or damage, and less serious drugs offences

(i) *Common law offences*

Permitting an escape, rescue, breach of prison and escaping from lawful custody without **G-172**
force

(ii) *Offences created by primary or secondary legislation*

Those contrary to the following provisions:

Child Abduction Act 1984, ss.1 and 2;

Crime and Disorder Act 1998, ss.29(1) and 30(1);

Criminal Damage Act 1971, s.1(1) and, where the offence does not also fall within section
1(2) and where the value of the damage is less than £30,000, s.1(3), s.2 and s.3;

Criminal Justice Act 1961, s.22;

Criminal Law Act 1977, s.51;

Customs and Excise Management Act 1979, s.50 (in relation to Class C drugs), s.68A(1)
and (2), s.86, s.170(2)(b), (c) (in relation to Class C drugs);

Dangerous Dogs Act 1991, s.3;

Drug Trafficking Offences Act 1986, ss.26B and 26C;

Firearms Act 1968, ss.1, 2, 3, 4, 19, 20, 21(4), 21(5) and 42;

Firearms (Amendment) Act 1988, s.6(1);

Immigration Act 1971, s.25;

Misuse of Drugs Act 1971, s.4 (Class C drug), s.5(2) (Class A drug), s.5(3) (Class C drug);

Offences against the Person Act 1861, ss.20, 24, 26, 27, 31, 37, 47, 59, 60 and 64;

Prison Act 1952, s.39;

Prohibition of Female Circumcision Act 1985, s.1;

Public Order Act 1986, ss.18 to 23;

Submarine Telegraph Act 1885, s.3;

Terrorism Act 2000, s.19;

Theft Act 1968, s.8(1) (other than when "armed");

Treason Act 1842, s.2.

Class D: sexual offences and offences against children

Offences created by primary or secondary legislation

G-173   Those contrary to the following provisions:

Criminal Law Act 1977, s.54;

Mental Health Act 1983, s.127;

Sexual Offences Act 1956, s.4, s.9, s.10 (other than by man with girl under 13), s.11, s.13 (between male aged 21 or over and male under 16), ss.14, 15, 19, 21, 23, 27, 29, 30 and 31;

Sexual Offences Act 1967, s.5;

Sexual Offences Act 2003, s.3, s.4 (without penetration), ss.11 to 13, 15 to 19, 32, 33, 36, 37, 40, 41, 52, 53, 61 to 67, 69 and 70;

Sexual Offences (Amendment) Act 2000, s.3.

Class E: burglary, etc.

Offences created by primary or secondary legislation

G-174   Those contrary to the following provisions:

Theft Act 1968, ss.9 and 25

Classes F, G and K: other offences of dishonesty (offences always in Class F)

Offences created by primary or secondary legislation

G-175   Those contrary to the following provisions:

Forgery Act 1861, ss.36, 37;

Identity Cards Act 2006, s.25(1), (3) and (5).

Classes F, G and K: other offences of dishonesty (offences always in Class G)

Offences created by primary or secondary legislation

G-176   Those contrary to the following provisions:

Customs and Excise Management Act 1979, s.50 (counterfeit notes or coins), s.170(2)(b) or (c) (counterfeit notes or coins);

Forgery and Counterfeiting Act 1981, ss.14 to 17;

Insolvency Act 1986, s.360.

Classes F, G and K: other offences of dishonesty (offences in Class G if value exceeds £30,000, in Class K if value exceeds £100,000 and otherwise in Class F)

Offences created by primary or secondary legislation

G-177   Those contrary to the following provisions:

Customs and Excise Management Act 1979, s.50 (to the extent not specified elsewhere), s.168, s.170(1)(b), s.170(2)(b), (c) (to the extent not specified elsewhere);

Forgery and Counterfeiting Act 1981, ss.1 to 5;

Fraud Act 2006, ss.2, 3, 4, 6, 7, 9 and 11;

Hallmarking Act 1973, s.6;

Stamp Duties Management Act 1891, s.13;

Theft Act 1968, ss.1, 11, 13, 15, 16, 17 and 22;

Theft Act 1978, ss.1 and 2;

Value Added Tax Act 1994, s.72(1)–(8).

Class H: miscellaneous other offences

(i) *Common law offences*

G-178   Keeping a disorderly house, outraging public decency

(ii) *Offences created by primary or secondary legislation*
 Those contrary to the following provisions:
  Air Navigation Order 2005 (S.I. 2005 No. 1970), art. 75;
  Bail Act 1976, s.9(1);
  Crime and Disorder Act 1998, ss.1(10), 2(8), 31(1) and 32(1);
  Criminal Justice Act 1988, s.139;
  Customs and Excise Management Act 1979, ss.13 and 16;
  Disorderly Houses Act 1751, s.8;
  Indecent Displays (Control) Act 1981, s.1;
  Malicious Damage Act 1861, s.36;
  Merchant Shipping Act 1970, s.27;
  Misuse of Drugs Act 1971, s.5(2) (Class B or C drug); s.11;
  Obscene Publications Act 1959, ss.1 and 2;
  Offences against the Person Act 1861, ss.35 and 38;
  Post Office Act 1953, s.11;
  Prevention of Crime Act 1953, s.1;
  Protection from Eviction Act 1977, s.1;
  Protection from Harassment Act 1997, ss.3(6), 4(1) and 5(5);
  Public Order Act 1986, s.3;
  Public Passenger Vehicles Act 1981, s.65;
  Road Traffic Act 1960, s.233;
  Road Traffic Act 1988, ss.2 and 173;
  Road Traffic Regulation Act 1984, s.115;
  Sexual Offences Act 1956, ss.2, 3, 12, 13 (other than where one participant over 21 and the other under 16), 22, 24 and 32;
  Sexual Offences Act 1967, s.4;
  Theatres Act 1968, s.2;
  Theft Act 1968, s.12A (but not where death results);
  Theft Act 1978, s.3;
  Trade Descriptions Act 1968, ss.1, 8, 9, 12, 13 and 14;
  Vehicle Excise and Registration Act 1994, s.44.

Class I: offences against public justice and similar offences

(i) *Common law offences*
  Embracery, fabrication of evidence with intent to mislead tribunal, perverting the course **G-179**
  of justice and personation of jurors

(ii) *Offences created by primary or secondary legislation*
 Those contrary to the following provisions:
  Bribery Act 2010, ss.1, 2 and 6;
  Cremation Act 1902, s.8(2);
  Criminal Justice Act 1967, s.89;
  Criminal Justice (Terrorism and Conspiracy) Act 1998, s.5;
  Criminal Justice and Public Order Act 1994, ss.51(1) and (2), 75(1) and (2);
  Criminal Law Act 1967, ss.4(1) and 5;
  Drug Trafficking Act 1994, s.58(1);
  European Communities Act 1972, s.11;
  Forgery Act 1861, s.34;
  Magistrates' Courts Act 1980, s.106;
  Perjury Act 1911, ss.1 to 7(2);
  Prevention of Corruption Act 1906, s.1;
  Public Bodies Corrupt Practices Act 1889, s.1;

Trade Descriptions Act 1968, s.29(2).

Class J: serious sexual offences

Offences created by primary or secondary legislation

G-180   Those contrary to the following provisions:

> Children and Young Persons Act 1933, ss.25, 26;
> Indecency with Children Act 1960, s.1(1);
> Protection of Children Act 1978, s.1;
> Sexual Offences Act 1956, ss.1(1), 5, 6, 7, 10, 12 (of person under 16), 16, 17, 20, 25, 26 and 28;
> Sexual Offences Act 2003, ss.1, 2, 4 (activity involving penetration), 5 to 10, 14, 25, 26, 30, 31, 34, 35, 38, 39, 47 to 50 and 57 to 59A.

G. Very High Cost Cases

Definition

G-181   For the definition of a "Very High Cost Case", see regulation 2 of S.I. 2013 No. 435 (*ante*, G-7). Regulation 3(8) (*ante*, G-8) provides that the regulations (with the exception of reg. 12 and para. 13(8) and (9) of Schedule 2) do not apply to Very High Costs Cases.

Background

G-182   Unlike the former scheme for the *ex post facto* taxation of fees (as to which, see Appendix G in the supplements to the 2010 edition of this work) and the graduated fee scheme, the Very High Cost Case ("VHCC") regime is not concerned with fee assessment after the completion of a case. VHCCs operate under a contract-based system where litigators' and advocates' tasks and the time allotted for each task are agreed or determined before the work is undertaken. They are managed by the Complex Crime Unit of the Legal Aid Agency (an executive agency of the Ministry of Justice).

Notification and classification

G-183   Litigators (referred to by the Legal Aid Agency as "organisations") are required to notify the Legal Aid Agency of any case which is, or is likely to be, a VHCC: S.I. 2013 No. 435, reg. 12. Notification is effected by submitting a VHCC Notification Request Form 2013, which is available on the agency's website. If a case qualifies, or if an organisation is in any doubt about this, the organisation should make the notification within five business days of the earliest hearing at which the court sets a trial estimate, or the organisation identifying that the case will be or is likely to be a VHCC, or the organisation receiving a VHCC notification request form 2013 from the agency. If the notification requirements are not met, and the agency is likely to or will suffer financial loss as a result, it may, in discharging its functions under the LASPOA 2012: (a) impose any sanction on the organisation in accordance with any other legal aid agreement or contract; (b) exclude the organisation from undertaking VHCC work or Individual Case Contract work on the case that it failed to notify; (c) where it persistently breaches this duty, exclude the organisation from undertaking future VHCC work or Individual Case Contract Work or reduce or refuse any payment to the organisation in relation to the case.

Part A of the current (2013) arrangements sets out the obligations and processes for notification and classification for all cases which may be classified as VHCCs on or after April 1, 2013. Part B applies to cases which fall to be classified on or after that date and where the trial would in the opinion of the Director of Legal Aid Casework be likely to last for more than 60 days (para. 1.4). Part C applies to cases which fall to be classified on or after that date where the case satisfies the definition of a Very High Cost Case (in reg. 2(1) of S.I. 2013 No. 435 (*ante*, G-7)) and the trial would in the opinion of the agency be likely to last for less than 61 days. Paragraph 5.4 of the arrangements states that where it is the opinion of the agency that a case will last no fewer than 25 days and no more than 40 days, it will only be classified as a Very High Cost Case if it is prosecuted by the Serious Fraud Office or it is a terrorism case.

Where a case satisfies the definition of a VHCC for organisations, the agency will issue a VHCC decision letter. If the case is one which in the director's opinion will last more than 60 days, the agency will issue a 2013 VHCC Contract (for organisations). In other cases, the agency will issue a 2013 Individual Case Contract (for organisations).

Where the case satisfies the definition of a VHCC for advocates, and a self-employed advocate has been instructed, the agency will issue a VHCC decision letter and a 2013 VHCC contract (for self-employed advocates) to the self-employed advocate. Exceptional circumstances apart, organisations and advocates must meet the eligibility criteria set out in the arrangements before they can undertake work on a Very High Cost Case.

For information as to the working of earlier arrangements, see the second supplement to the 2013 edition of this work.

Paragraph 13(9) of Schedule 2 is not to be construed literally; where, therefore, a very high cost case panel firm was instructed under the representation order prior to the case being classified as a very high cost case, where it continued to act after such classification and where, after the defendant had pleaded guilty and been put back for sentence, the representation order was withdrawn (apparently on the application of the solicitors) by order of the court, solicitors and counsel fell to be remunerated under the very high cost cases regime, not the graduated fee regime; paragraph 13(9) had no application to this situation; rather, it was intended to deal with the remuneration of a non-panel firm where a case is reclassified as a very high cost case whereupon the representation order is withdrawn (rather than being transferred to another litigator, in which case para. 13(8) is engaged): *Lord Chancellor v. Alexander Johnson & Co. Solicitors and McCarthy* [2011] Costs L.R. 987, QBD (Davis J.).

[The next paragraph is G-187.]

Remuneration

Once a case is classified as a VHCC, the Legal Aid Agency will assign it to one of four categories against the criteria contained in clause 4.21 of the VHCC Specification (see also §§ 4.12 *et seq.* in the VHCC Guidance). For this purpose, the contracted organisation is required to submit a completed VHCC category assessment sheet within 15 business days of the decision letter: Arrangements, para. 8.2(c). The category to which the case is assigned determines the hourly rate payable for preparatory work undertaken by litigators. Advocacy rates are non-category specific. **G-187**

Self-employed advocates are remunerated directly by the Legal Aid Agency: clause 5.21 of the VHCC Specification (for organisations). Where the VHCC has been classified both as a VHCC for organisations and for advocates, self-employed advocates must claim under their VHCC contract. Where the case is a VHCC for organisations but has not been classified as a VHCC for advocates, any self-employed advocate must claim under the advocates' graduated fee scheme. Employed advocates must claim payment through their organisation, whether under the graduated fee scheme (where the VHCC has not been classified as a VHCC for advocates) or under the VHCC scheme (where the VHCC is a VHCC in relation to both organisations and advocates).

As to rates of payments, these are now determined by regulation 12A of, and Schedule 6 (*ante*, G-18a, G-92c, *et seq.*) to the Criminal Legal Aid (Remuneration) Regulations 2013 (S.I. 2013 No. 435) for cases subject to the 2013 VHCC contract, and by the provisions of the Criminal Defence Service (Very High Cost Cases) (Funding) Order 2013 (S.I. 2013 No. 2804) for work undertaken on or after December 2, 2013 (unless the trial date was set before that date and is before April, 2014), in a "pre-commencement case" (as to which, see the Legal Aid, Sentencing and Punishment of Offenders Act 2012 (Consequential, Transitional and Saving Provisions) Regulations 2013 (S.I. 2013 No. 534), reg. 2) that was the subject of a contract made between the Legal Services Commission and members of the (now abolished) Very High Cost Case (Crime) Panel (art. 3 and Sched. 1) or was the subject of a 2010 VHCC contract (art. 4 and Sched. 2). S.I. 2013 No. 2804 also amended paragraph 25 (Very High Cost Cases) of Schedule 2 (litigators' graduated fee scheme) to the Criminal Defence Service (Funding) Order 2007 (S.I. 2007 No. 1174) (which was revoked by the Criminal Defence Service (Funding) (Amendment) Order 2011 (S.I. 2011 No. 2065) in relation to proceedings in which a representation order was granted on or after October 3, 2011) to provide for reduced fees for work done on or after December 2, 2013 (unless the trial date was set before that date and is before April, 2014), in a Very High Costs Case where a litigator instructed an advocate who was not a member of the Very High Cost Case (Crime) Panel.

[The next paragraph is G-195.]

H. Preparation and Submission of Claims

(1) The preparation of claims

G-195   There is no mandatory graduated fee form. The use of computer-generated forms is permitted and this allows only the relevant data to be submitted. As to graduated fees generally, see *ante*, G-115 *et seq.*

(2) Time limits for the submission of claims

G-196   No claim by an advocate for fees for work done shall be entertained unless submitted within three months of the conclusion of the proceedings to which it relates: S.I. 2013 No. 435, reg. 4(3). However, where a confiscation hearing under section 2 of the DTA 1994, section 71 of the CJA 1988 or Part 2 of the PCA 2002 is held more than 28 days after a person has been found or pleaded guilty, a graduated fee claim can be submitted despite the fact that the proceedings have not yet been completed: *ibid.*, reg. 4(6). The time limit may be extended for "good reason": *ibid.*, reg. 31(1); for example, where the claim is particularly complicated and difficult to prepare, where a co-defendant's case is awaiting disposal, or because there is a genuine misunderstanding about the submission of a claim. Extensions should be sought before the time limit expires.

G-197   Where there are no good reasons, the time may be extended in "exceptional circumstances", in which case the appropriate authority shall consider whether it is reasonable to reduce the fee: S.I. 2013 No. 435, reg. 31(2). An advocate should be given a reasonable opportunity to show cause why his costs should not be reduced (*ibid.*). Any reduction may be challenged by appeal to the taxing master: *post*, G-269. As to what may constitute "good reason" or "exceptional circumstances", see *post*, G-269.

    Notwithstanding that a representation order may be expressed to cover proceedings in the Crown Court "and in the event of [the defendant] being convicted or sentenced ..., advice and assistance in regard to the making of an appeal", the legislation is clear as to the need for a claim in relation to work done in the Crown Court to be submitted within three months of the conclusion of the proceedings in that court, rather than within three months of the date on which an application for leave to appeal to the Court of Appeal was refused: *R. v. White* [2008] Costs L.R. 479.

    In *R. v. Dumbaya* [2012] Costs L.R. 976, the costs judge took a different view and held that since "representation" for the purposes of Part I of the Access to Justice Act 1999, "includes ... subject to any time limits which may be prescribed, advice and assistance as to any appeal" (the 1999 Act, s.26), proceedings should not be regarded as "concluded" until any such advice or assistance has been given. For corresponding provision in the LASPOA 2012, see section 42(1).

    The Legal Services Commission disagreed with the judge in *Dumbaya*. Its November, 2012, guidance provides that (i) the "conclusion of the proceedings" for litigators is the date on which the defendant was acquitted or sentenced; where confiscation proceedings follow sentence, these will be treated as separate proceedings; (ii) the "conclusion of the proceedings" for advocates is the date on which the defendant was acquitted or sentenced or on which confiscation proceedings are concluded; (iii) the commission is currently seeking clarification (in light of conflicting authorities) on whether the time taken, following conviction, to obtain and provide advice on appeal can be taken into account when determining when proceedings conclude, but, pending clarification, proposes to use the date of sentence or acquittal as the conclusion of proceedings; advocates or litigators who risk not meeting the three-month time limit as a result of obtaining or providing advice on appeal should contact the commission for an extension; (iv) bereavement, serious illness, burglary, and flooding in an office, are examples of what are likely to constitute "good reason", but delay in obtaining evidence (including prosecution page counts) and administrative errors will not; (v) those who believe that they are unlikely to meet the time limit should email requesting an extension as soon as possible with grounds; advocates, if appropriate, should provide the name of any firm that is refusing to provide relevant documents; (vi) while the disallowance of the entirety of a claim might constitute a disproportionate sanction and, accordingly, an "exceptional" circumstance, as might the length of the delay and the amount of money involved, a rigid framework for imposing financial penalties is not suitable, and claims must instead be assessed on a case-by-case basis; (vii) accordingly, litigators and advocates who submit claims out of time without "good reason" should provide an explanation as to the impact on them of a total disallowance or reduction of fees for the specific case; although the amount of detail need not be equivalent to that provided when asking for payments to be expedited on hardship grounds, it must be sufficient to enable the determining officer to understand the impact of any decision to disallow or reduce fees.

It is submitted that the commission's stance that proceedings conclude upon acquittal or sentence is to be preferred to the approach of the costs judge in *Dumbaya, ante*. As there is no provision under the 2007 order for payment for advice or assistance on appeal, there seems little point in delaying the date on which the proceedings may be said to have concluded. Any other view also introduces uncertainty.

(3) Submitting an amended claim

Where a genuine error is made in submitting a graduated fee claim, counsel should not be **G-198** precluded for all time from submitting an amended claim where the refusal to permit him to do so could result in his being deprived of fees to which he would have been entitled had the claim been advanced correctly in the first place: *R. v. Hann* [2009] Costs L.R. 833. Where, therefore, counsel, as a result of a genuine error, had submitted a claim for a cracked trial where the case was disposed of as a guilty plea (albeit there had been a long delay between plea and sentence, throughout which it had been on the cards that a *Newton* hearing (*R. v. Newton*, 77 Cr.App.R. 13, CA) would eventually be required), it was held that counsel (who had been paid the appropriate graduated fee for a guilty plea) should be granted an extension of time in which to submit an amended claim for a guilty plea plus a special preparation fee (under what is now S.I. 2013 No. 435, Sched. 1 para. 17). See also *R. v. Lafayette* [2010] 4 Costs L.R. 650 (there is no good reason why a lawyer who has submitted a claim should not be permitted to amend it before it has been determined).

[The next paragraph is G-251.]

I. Disbursements and Expenses

(1) Disbursements

A barrister is not entitled to claim for disbursements or expenses other than those permitted **G-251** under S.I. 2013 No. 435.

For an example of the Legal Services Commission successfully questioning, pursuant to regulation 17 of S.I. 2013 No. 435 (*ante*, G-21), the propriety of incurring costs where the defence had sought, and obtained, prior authority to incur those costs, see *R. v. Ward* [2012] Costs L.R. 605. The costs related to the printing of a large quantity of documentation that had been contained on two computer discs and a memory stick. The solicitors had obtained authority on the ground that the files were inaccessible electronically, or that the software would corrupt their own network or that specialist software was needed to download and read the material. However, this only applied to the documents on the memory stick, and when the decision was taken not to print off the material on the memory stick, the solicitors "knew or ought reasonably to have known that the purpose for which authority had been given had failed or had become irrelevant or unnecessary before the disbursements were incurred." It had not been reasonable to incur the considerable costs when the prosecution did not intend to print the material off, and when there was no real difficulty in accessing it electronically. However, it was held that the purchase of a hard drive used by a computer expert instructed to analyse computers that had been seized was reasonable; it was inevitable that the contents would have to be copied on to a new drive, rather than a previously used drive, to avoid contamination, and such a purchase would not be part of the expert's overheads because once the drive was used, it could not be re-used for the same purpose.

(2) Travelling and accommodation expenses

Entitlement under the regulations

G-252   Travel and other expenses incidental to appearance at court may be claimed provided the court is not within 40 kilometres of the advocate's office or chambers. Unless prior approval for the expenditure has been obtained under the regulations, or unless the advocate can justify his attendance having regard to all the relevant circumstances of the case, the amount payable shall not be greater than that, if any, payable to a trial advocate from the nearest local Bar or the nearest advocate's office (whichever is the nearer): S.I. 2013 No. 435, Sched. 1, para. 29. As to interim payment of travel and accommodation expenses, see *ante*, G-110.

Local bars

G-253   In *R. v. Comer* [2009] Costs L.R. 972, it was said that in paragraph 29 of Schedule 1 to S.I. 2013 No. 435 (*ante*, G-62), the juxtaposition of the phrase "local Bar" with the phrase "advocate's office" suggests that a fairly modest number of practitioners can constitute a local bar. The existence of a bar mess is not a prerequisite, and whether the barristers based in an area constitute a local bar will be a question of feel. In this case, the view of the resident judge that "there is a healthy local bar" was considered to be the best evidence of such a bar. As to this case, see also *post*, G-258.

An advocate may be able to justify his attendance in a distant court which is usually serviced by a local bar where:

   (a) the instruction of local counsel might lead to suspicion of prejudice, lack of independence or lack of objectivity (*e.g.* cases of local notoriety involving public figures or officials);

   (b) there are insufficient local counsel whom instructing solicitors consider are sufficiently experienced to undertake the case in question so as to give the client a reasonable choice;

   (c) the services of an advocate who has specialised experience and knowledge of the type of case of an unusual or technical nature are required;

   (d) the advocate has previously been instructed in related matters which would assist him in the presentation or preparation of the case in question: *R. v. Conboy* (1990) Costs L.R. 493; and see *R. v. Gussman*, X14, SCTO 40/99 (counsel had represented his client seven years earlier on a charge of murder; his knowledge of his client's earlier medical condition was relevant to the current charges of rape, and this amounted to special circumstances justifying his attendance).

It is submitted that a further justification arises where an advocate is forced to follow a particular judge on circuit who is seized of his case and it was not reasonable to instruct another local advocate for that particular hearing. Where an advocate is instructed from outside a local bar for any of the above reasons it is advisable that he obtains a letter from his instructing solicitor explaining why he was instructed, and for his clerk to obtain prior approval for incurring such expenses from the court. This applies also to Queen's Counsel practising off-circuit: *post*, G-256.

[The next paragraph is G-256.]

Queen's Counsel and local bars

G-256   Queen's Counsel should not be regarded as being "local" to any particular bar, even though his chambers are in one particular place. Where Queen's Counsel practises on circuit, he should as a general rule receive an amount in respect of travelling and hotel expenses actually and reasonably incurred and necessarily and exclusively attributable to his attendance at a court on the circuit on which he practises: *R. v. Thomas*; *R. v. Davidson*; *R. v. Hutton* (1985) Costs L.R. 469. Where Queen's Counsel practises outside his circuit, the "local bar" rules apply: *ante*, G-253.

Expenses reasonably incurred

G-257   The reasonableness of an advocate's claim for travel and hotel expenses should be judged not by reference to the expenses incurred by other advocates in the same case, but in relation to the demands upon the advocate in putting forward his lay client's case and his own particular circumstances in relation to the conduct of the trial: *R. v. Plews* (1984) Costs L.R. 466; *post*, G-260.

The regulations refer to expenditure "reasonably incurred", whereas earlier regulations referred to expenses "actually and reasonably incurred". In *R. v. Conboy* (1990) Costs L.R. 493, the taxing master observed that the current wording is wider. It is submitted that the alteration acknowledges an advocate's entitlement to recover a reasonable amount in respect of expenses necessarily and exclusively attributable to attendance at court. Thus, where the expense incurred was reasonable, an advocate should recover in full. Where the travel undertaken or accommodation used was reasonable but the cost incurred was excessive, an advocate may only claim for and recover a reasonable amount being a sum no greater than that which he would have incurred had his expenses been reasonable.

Travel to court

In determining what is actually and reasonably incurred the relevant travel is that between **G-258** court and an advocate's chambers: *R. v. Khan*, January 1989, TC C/13. Actual expenses incurred in travelling from an advocate's home to court will only be allowed if his home is nearer to court than his chambers, otherwise his journey is deemed to start from chambers: *R. v. Slessor* (1984) Costs L.R. 438. And, in such a case, he will only be entitled to travelling expenses actually incurred, *i.e.* from home to court: *R. v. Comer* [2009] Costs L.R. 972 (as to which, see also *ante*, G-253).

(i) *Public transport expenses*

Where expenses are recoverable, travel costs are generally limited to the cost of public transport **G-259** actually incurred, together with the expense incurred in getting from the starting point to the railhead or coach station and the expense incurred from getting from the terminal to the court: *Slessor, ante.*

(ii) *Car expenses*

Where an advocate chooses to journey by car, the expenses allowed will not exceed the **G-260** equivalent cost of public transport: *Slessor, ante*; *Conboy, ante*. The expenses of travel by car will be allowed where public transport is not available or is not reasonably convenient. What is "not reasonably convenient" is a matter for the discretion of the taxing officer. What may be convenient in one case may not be convenient in another. The time spent in getting from the starting point to the railhead, and from the terminus to court is always relevant: if it is considerable, the use of a car may be justified. Taxing officers have been urged to adopt a flexible and broad approach to the problem: *Slessor, ante*. Where the case papers are heavy and bulky, an advocate may be justified in using a car (an example given by the taxing officer in argument in *Conboy, ante*). In *R. v. Plews* (1984) Costs L.R. 466, counsel would have had to catch a 7.15 a.m. train from London to allow him to arrive at court in sufficient time to robe, see his client and solicitor, and to hold any pre-hearing discussions. It was therefore reasonable for counsel, bearing in mind that he had to travel from his home to the station and was faced with a full day in court, to travel by car.

(iii) *Expenses for reasonable travel by car*

In *Plews, ante*, counsel's claim, based on a mileage rate less than that prescribed for medical **G-261** practitioners in regulations then current, was considered reasonable, the taxing master observing that a claim based upon the equivalent rate would have been allowed. The usual means of estimating the expenses of travel by car is the standard mileage rate which is calculated by reference to the average cost of running a motor car, including such matters as depreciation, insurance, maintenance, *etc.*, which are referable to the running of a car of the relevant engine capacity. Although the rate is not a precise measure of the actual cost of a particular form of transport, it is intended to provide a mechanism for reimbursing expenses incurred when travelling by car: *Conboy, ante*. Where it is reasonable to incur the expense of travelling by car it must also be reasonable to incur necessary and consequential costs of car parking (if any).

The Legal Services Commission announced an increase in its rates for civil solicitors from 36p per mile to 45p per mile as from April 2, 2001. It is submitted that it is reasonable that similar rates should apply to criminal advocates.

Accommodation expenses

Hotel or accommodation expenses cannot be divorced from travelling expenses. They should **G-262** be paid instead of travelling expenses where an advocate reasonably chooses, or by reason of distance is obliged, to stay near a court distant from his chambers rather than travel daily. If travelling expenses are not payable then neither are hotel or accommodation expenses: *R. v. Khan*, January 1989, TC C/13. Where an advocate claims expenses for overnight accommodation and the cost equals or is less than that of the daily travel for which he would be entitled to be reimbursed, such expenses should be allowed. Where the hotel expenses are more than the cost of daily travel, they should be allowed if, having regard to the demands of the case on an advocate, including the need for conferences after court and overnight preparation, the advocate could not have returned home at a reasonable hour: *Plews, ante.*

Conference travel expenses and travel time

G-263   Travel expenses reasonably incurred and necessarily and exclusively attributable to attending a conference should be reimbursed where an advocate attends a conference in prison where the authorities will only produce the client at the place of detention; the same principle applies when the client is a patient in a psychiatric hospital: *R. v. Hindle* (1987) Costs L.R. 486.

J. Proceedings in the Court of Appeal

General principles

G-264   Payment for proceedings in the Court of Appeal is governed by Schedule 3 to S.I. 2013 No. 435 (*ante*, G-82 *et seq.*), which provides for *ex post facto* taxation, the overriding principles being that the appropriate officer should, in determining fees, allow a "reasonable amount" in respect of all work "actually and reasonably done".

Advice on appeal

G-265   As to this, see, in particular, *R. v. Umezie*, § 7-165 in the main work, and *R. v. Bromige, ante*, G-160.

Solicitor advocates

G-266   In *R. v. Mansell* [2011] Costs L.R. 531, it was held that: (i) under S.I. 2013 No. 435, the fees of a solicitor advocate in the Court of Appeal fall to be determined under Schedule 3 as if he were an advocate, and not a litigator; (ii) a solicitor advocate is an "advocate" for all proceedings covered by S.I. 2013 No. 435, including in the Court of Appeal (see the definition of "advocate" in reg. 2, *ante*, G-7); and (iii) that paragraph 3 of Schedule 3 (determination of litigators' fees (*ante*, G-83)), which permits payment of advocacy by litigators, does not mean that all advocacy by solicitors is payable under that paragraph.

K. Determinations and Appeals

(1) The taxing authorities

G-267   Graduated fee claims are determined by Crown Court taxing officers and should usually be paid within 10 working days of receipt of the claim.

Applications for re-determination are addressed to the chief clerk of the Crown Court or the regional taxation director as appropriate. The re-determination does not have to be carried out by the original officer, although this is usually the case. Where difficult points of principle arise or large sums are in dispute the matter is referred to the regional taxing director or his assistant. Appeals from re-determinations are heard by costs judges appointed by the Lord Chancellor.

(2) Guide to the process of determination and appeal

G-268   A brief outline of the various stages of the determination of an advocate's fees is set out below. The regulations referred to are those of S.I. 2013 No. 435 (*ante*, §§ G-6 *et seq.*). The table below is merely intended as a guide to the relevant procedures.

As to the circumstances in which an advocate or a litigator may apply to the appropriate officer for a redetermination of his fees, for a review of specified decisions or for an offence to be reclassified, see regulation 28 of S.I. 2013 No. 435 (*ante*, G-34).

The references in the last column in the tables below are references to regulations of S.I. 2013 No. 435.

Stage	Description	reg.
Submission of Claim		4
Time limit	Within 3 months of conclusion of proceedings (see *ante*, G-196)	4(3)
Particulars submitted in all cases	In the form and manner directed by the appropriate officer	4(3)
Interim payments (40% of total claim less any sum paid)		19
Definition	Payable where:	18
	(a) the basic fee claimed by any counsel in any related proceedings exceeds £4,000, and	18(2)
	(b) 3 months have elapsed from the date of the conclusion of related proceedings or the date on which the bill is ready to tax, whichever is earlier.	18(4)
Related proceedings	Proceedings involving the same defendant heard or dealt with together or proceedings involving more than one defendant arising out of the same incident so that defendants are charged, tried or disposed of together.	18(3)
When the bill is ready to tax	Date of receipt of last bill in related proceedings.	18(4)
Entitlement	Where counsel is entitled to an interim payment but no interim payment has been made and counsel has submitted his claim.	18(4), (5)
Time limit	6 months after the conclusion of proceedings against the defendant represented.	18(5)
Determination and notification of costs; authorisation of payment		
	Costs determined in accordance with Schedule 1.	23(1)
	Counsel notified of costs payable and payment authorised.	23(1)
Re-calculation of graduated fee or re-determination of decision to allow special or wasted preparation fee, or classification of offence		
Time limit	Within 21 days of receipt or notification of costs payable.	28(3)
Particulars to be submitted	(a) Written notice specifying matters in respect of which application is made, grounds of objection and whether counsel wishes to appear or to be represented.	28(3), (5)
	(b) Documents and information supplied with submission of claim.	28(4)
	(c) Further information, particulars and documents as required by the appropriate officer.	28(6)
Re-determination of decision not to allow conference fee (time limit and particulars as above)		28(1)(b)
Re-determination by the appropriate officer		28(7)
Application for written reasons		28(8)

Stage	Description	reg.
Time limit	21 days of notification of the decision	28(8), (9)
Appeal to costs judge		29(1)
Time limit	21 days of receipt of written reasons.	29(2)
Particulars to be submitted to costs judge and appropriate officer	(a) Copy of written representations on application for re-determination. (b) Appropriate officer's written reasons. (c) All documents supplied hereto.	29(4)
Form of notice of appeal	(a) As directed by the costs judge. (b) Specifying separately each item appealed against, showing amount claimed and determined for each item and the ground of objection. (c) Stating whether appellant wishes to appear or to be represented.	29(5)
Lord Chancellor's written representations	Where the Lord Chancellor makes written representations, counsel shall have a reasonable opportunity to make representations in reply.	29(9)
Notification of hearing	The costs judge shall inform counsel of hearing date and give directions as to conduct of appeal.	29(10)
No further evidence	Unless costs judge otherwise directs no other evidence shall be raised at the hearing nor objection taken which was not raised at redetermination.	29(11)
Notification of costs judge's decision		29(13)
Costs	Costs may be awarded where the appeal is allowed.	29(14)
Appeals to the High Court		30
Right of appeal	Right of appeal to single QBD judge from costs judge's decision on a point of principle of public importance.	30(7)
Application for costs judge's certificate	Counsel may apply to the costs judge to certify a point of principle of general importance.	30(1)
Time limit for application	Within 21 days of notification of costs judge's decision.	30(2)
Time limit for appeal	Within 21 days from receipt of costs judge's certificate.	
Appeal by Lord Chancellor	Within 21 days of notification of costs judge's decision, the Lord Chancellor may appeal the decision if counsel does not do so.	30(5)

(3) The enforcement and extension of time limits

G-269   Time limits may be extended for good reason by the appropriate authority, *i.e.* the appropriate officer, costs judge, or the High Court: S.I. 2013 No. 435, reg. 31(1). Where for no good reason the time limit is not adhered to, the appropriate authority may in exceptional circumstances extend the time limit and shall consider whether it is reasonable in the circumstances to reduce the costs, subject to granting the advocate a reasonable opportunity to state either orally or in writing why the costs should not be reduced: *ibid.*, reg. 31(2). A decision not to extend time, or to reduce costs for claims out of time may be appealed by notice in writing to the senior costs judge specifying the grounds of appeal. The appeal must be instituted within 21 days of the decision being given: *ibid.*, reg. 31(3); and see *ante*, G-198. For the latest guidance from the Legal Services

Commission on the submission of late claims and what may or may not be treated as "good reason" or "exceptional circumstances", see *ante*, G-197.

It was held in *R. v. Mahmood* [2008] Costs L.R. 326, that where a 10 per cent penalty was imposed following a delay of over two months in submitting a claim for costs, but where the representative had only received a notice, prior to the case being tried, stating that all late claims would be the subject of a penalty unless there was a good reason, this did not constitute notice to show cause why the claim should not be reduced. The determining officer had clearly not considered the circumstances of the particular case on its own merits.

In *R. v. Roberts* [2008] Costs L.R. 323, the oversight of two fee earners, the holiday of one of those fee-earners (even if well-deserved), and a subsequent systematic firm-wide failure did not constitute "good reason" or "exceptional circumstances" so as to justify an extension of time, following a delay of 17 months in submitting a claim for costs. Nor did previous good character constitute "exceptional circumstances", although it was said that it might amount to mitigating circumstances when considering the extent of any reduction in costs (were an extension to be granted). This was the case despite a general softening in the attitude to the delay.

A misunderstanding of the legislation cannot amount to "good reason", but could amount to "exceptional circumstances" where the evidence was that other bills that had been submitted late for like reason in the past had been accepted: *R. v. White* [2008] Costs L.R. 479. But a simple failure to follow up a case could rarely constitute "good reason" or "exceptional circumstances", and it made no difference that the firm in question had generally had a good record for submitting claims in time: *R. v. Johnson* [2008] Costs L.R. 983.

Neither "mere oversight" on the part of leading counsel nor a mistaken belief on the part of junior counsel that leading counsel's clerk was dealing with their fees could amount to "good reason" for not submitting their claims on time; but disallowance of fees *in toto* may be so disproportionate as to amount to "exceptional circumstances": see *R. v. Lafayette* [2010] 4 Costs L.R. 650.

In *R. v. Griffin* [2008] Costs L.R. 483, leading counsel had been under the mistaken impression that his junior was going to prepare a taxation note to be agreed between them before submission. However, in the event, his junior submitted his own claim independently and sent a copy of his taxation note to his leader, such note making it plain that he had submitted a claim and asserting, mistakenly, that leading counsel had already submitted his own claim. It was held that as this was already seven months out of time, and leading counsel only submitted his own claim after a further two years, neither the misunderstanding as between leader and junior, nor extreme pressure of work plus some personal pressure over the two years that followed discovery of the fact that his junior had submitted his own claim, could amount to "good reason" for the failure to submit the claim within the three-month time limit; nor could they amount to "exceptional circumstances" so as to justify an extension of time despite the absence of good reason. There had been no obligation on the determining officer to remind counsel that his claim was late and the absence, at the time, of published criteria to be applied to the submission of late claims, did not avail counsel. What was critical to the outcome was the fact that two years before his eventual submission of his claim, he had been alerted by his junior's note to the fact that he would need to submit his own claim and he had failed then to take any steps to address the situation.

In *R. v. Islami* [2009] Costs L.R. 988, following a ruling that total disallowance of a claim by **G-270** solicitors for £58,060.13 (including disbursements and travelling expenses) due to delay (of three years and nine months) would be so disproportionate (because of the substantial effect that this would have on the firm's profits) as to amount to "exceptional circumstances" and that the claim should be re-submitted, albeit that a five per cent penalty should be applied to the sum ultimately allowed, it was held that the fact that an administrative officer at the firm had then not complied with her instructions to submit the relevant documents for taxation, and the fact that this was only discovered during her ensuing extensive sick leave, did not amount to a "good reason" for a further delay of nine months in re-submitting the claim. In these circumstances, total disallowance of the claim, and the ensuing effect on the firm's profits, was no longer a disproportionate penalty sufficient to constitute "exceptional circumstances". Had the sum been needed with the urgency suggested at the original hearing, the firm would have ensured that the claim was re-submitted immediately and carefully tracked. Instead, the administrative problems identified at the original hearing had clearly not been resolved. However, it was said that this conclusion should be applied only to the profit costs and that the claim, so far as it related to disbursements (which had long since been paid out by the firm), should still be determined (without penalty), provided that the necessary papers were lodged within 14 days.

A reduction of an out-of-time claim to zero is not automatically to be regarded as so disproportionate as to give rise to "exceptional circumstances", but the shortness of the delay, the amount of money involved and the impact on the advocate or litigator involved are capable of constituting exceptional circumstances; each case must, however, turn on its own facts; there can be no hard and fast rules or pre-set scales: *R. v. Grigoropolou* [2012] Costs L.R. 982.

G-271   In *R. v. Newport* [2009] Costs L.R. 983, it was said that, although it has often been stated that barristers must have suitable systems in place to ensure that claims for fees and requests for redeterminations are made within the relevant time limits, and although the delay in this particular case was significant (over three years after the determining officer had refused payment), "exceptional circumstances" for extending the time to apply for a redetermination had been made out where counsel had trusted his senior clerk to ensure that the claim and any appeal procedure was appropriately and punctually concluded, but where he had been deliberately misled by the clerk, who failed, despite counsel's regular enquiries, to inform counsel that his claim had been refused *in toto*. This was found to be a rare and regrettable situation and not akin to an argument that "pressures of work" constituted exceptional circumstances (which would not be successful).

(4) Re-determinations and appeals

Graduated fees

G-272   An advocate may only seek re-determination or appeal in respect of graduated fees where, (a) the issue is either whether the graduated fee scheme applied to the relevant proceedings, or (b) complaint is made as to the calculation of the remuneration payable, or (c) where the advocate is dissatisfied with a refusal to allow a special preparation fee or the number of hours allowed in the calculation of such fee; or (d) where the advocate is dissatisfied with the classification of an offence which does not appear in the Table of offences: S.I. 2013 No. 435, reg. 28(3). Under S.I. 2013 No. 435 a re-determination may also be sought in respect of a decision not to allow an hourly fee in respect of attendance at conferences or views at the scene of the alleged offence, or of the number of hours allowed in the calculation of such a fee: see reg. 28(1)(b)(i).

Re-determination

G-273   On an application for re-determination an advocate shall specify the grounds of his objection to all or any part of the determination (S.I. 2013 No. 435, reg. 28(3)(b)) and may appear in person or through another to make representations: S.I. 2013 No. 435, reg. 28(5). An advocate is not obliged to provide fresh information or material to assist the determining officer in the redetermination. If no additional information is provided, the determining officer has a duty to redetermine on the basis of the information already supplied: *R. v. O'Brien* [2003] Costs L.R. 625. Many appeals which might otherwise have succeeded have failed because the representations made to the appropriate officer have been perfunctory and inexplicit: *R. v. Davies* (1985) Costs L.R. 472.

As from January 1, 1994, the General Council of the Bar has agreed that all requests for fees to be re-determined or for written reasons to be provided should be signed by counsel personally.

Re-determination should, where possible, be carried out by the officer who determined costs. Where cases are cited in support of the re-determination, sufficient references must be given to allow an advocate to identify and look them up: *R. v. Pelepenko*, X27A, SCCO 186/2001.

Where the Legal Aid Agency makes a decision to recover an overpayment of fees pursuant to regulation 25 of S.I. 2013 No. 435 (*ante*, G-31) and the litigator requests a review, a subsequent confirmation by the commission of its decision to recoup constitutes a redetermination within the meaning of regulation 28 (*ante*, G-34), so as to allow the litigator to appeal to a costs judge pursuant to regulation 29(1) (*ante*, G-35): *Lord Chancellor v. Eddowes Perry and Osbourne Ltd* [2011] Costs L.R. 498, QBD (Spencer J.) (disapproving *R. v. Charlery*; *R. v. Small* [2011] Costs L.R. 331). As to this case, see also *ante*, G-161.

Further evidence on appeal and supplemental written reasons

G-274   On appeal before a costs judge no further evidence shall be received and no ground of objection shall be valid which was not raised on the application for re-determination unless the costs judge otherwise directs: S.I. 2013 No. 435, reg. 29(11). These provisions are strictly applied. A costs judge will rarely accede to a request to adduce further evidence or allow a fresh objection to be raised. Where written reasons do not address a point raised in the claim, counsel cannot pursue the matter in the appeal. The proper method of dealing with such an omission is to seek supplemental written reasons from the appropriate officer.

Appeals

The right of appeal to a costs judge is effectively limited in that no appeal lies against a **G-275** determination unless the advocate has applied for a re-determination and, thereafter, for written reasons under S.I. 2013 No. 435, reg. 29(1).

An advocate wishing to appeal must have regard to, and be familiar with, the provisions of Part 5 of the *Criminal Costs Practice Directions* (2015) (*ante*, Appendix B-270 *et seq.*) (§§ 6-146 *et seq.*

Representation, costs and expenses of appeal

For the purposes of an appeal to a costs judge, an advocate is treated as the appellant and can **G-276** elect to be represented at the hearing. A successful appellant may be awarded a sum in respect of part or all of any reasonable costs incurred in connection with the appeal: S.I. 2013 No. 435, reg. 29(14); and see *R. v. Boswell*; *R. v. Halliwell* [1987] 1 W.L.R. 705 (Leggatt J.).

A barrister without the intervention of a solicitor may accept a brief or instructions, with or without fee, directly from, and represent, another barrister on that other barrister's appeal as to his fees before a costs judge: see *Code of Conduct*, 8th ed., para. 401 (Appendix C-7, *ante*). A professional fee payable by one barrister to another for conducting the former's appeal is capable of constituting part of the costs incurred by the appellant counsel: *R. v. Boswell*; *R. v. Halliwell*, *ante*. In assessing such costs the costs judge is entitled to take account of time and skill expended by the appellant or his counsel in the drawing of grounds and preparation of the appeal, and the conduct of the hearing, and travel and subsidence costs: *ibid*. Costs incurred in instructing other counsel are clearly reasonable where there is some technical question on the applicability of some part of the regulations or other issue which legitimately deserves the attention of specialist costs counsel. Costs are not reasonably incurred if trial counsel is available, could easily have represented himself and the only real issue is the weight of the case or the value of a particular item of work undertaken: *Jackson v. Lord Chancellor* [2003] Costs L.R. 395; and *R. v. Martin* [2007] Costs L.R. 128. A successful appellant will ordinarily be entitled to the return of the fee payable in respect of the appeal.

Appeals to the single judge

As to appeals from a costs judge to the High Court, see S.I. 2013 No. 435, reg. 30. The ambit **G-277** of an appeal is strictly limited to the point of principle certified by the costs judge as being of general importance (such certificate being a pre-condition to an appeal): *Patten v. Lord Chancellor*, 151 N.L.J. 851, QBD (Leveson J.), not following *Harold v. Lord Chancellor* [1999] Costs L.R. 14. Although *Patten* was concerned with the interpretation of regulation 16 of the Legal Aid in Criminal and Care Proceedings (Costs) Regulations 1989 (S.I. 1989 No. 343), regulation 29 of S.I. 2013 No. 435 is worded in almost identical terms. A refusal of a costs judge to certify that the matter raises a point of principle of general importance is not susceptible to judicial review: *R. v. Supreme Court Taxing Office, exp. John Singh & Co* [1997] 1 Costs L.R. 49, CA (Civ. Div). As to the limited scope for a challenge, by way of judicial review, to the substantive decision of a costs judge where a certificate has been refused, see § 6-75 in the main work.

(5) Recovery of overpayment

Where an advocate receives a sum in excess of his entitlement, the taxing authority may either **G-278** require immediate repayment of that excess, or deduct the excess from any other sum payable to the advocate under the regulations: S.I. 2013 No. 435, reg. 25. These provisions apply notwithstanding the fact that a re-determination or appeal has been or may be requested: S.I. 2013 No. 435, reg. 25(4).

(6) Appeals under VHCCs

Under the arrangements that came into force on April 1, 2013 (*ante*, G-181 *et seq.*), both the **G-279**

VHCC Specification for organisations and that for advocates provide for a right of appeal to the VHCC Appeals Panel. The details are set out in paragraph 6 of the specifications, with paragraph 6.4 listing the issues in relation to which there is a right of appeal (*e.g.* the category to which a case has been assigned) and paragraph 6.5 listing those issues in relation to which there is no right of appeal. The appeal process, including time limits, is provided for by paragraphs 6.6 to 6.30. The appeal will normally be determined by a single adjudicator but may be referred to an appeals committee. The decision of the adjudicator or committee is final (para. 6.28), but is binding only in relation to the particular appeal (para. 6.29). Anonymised versions of decisions will be published on the Legal Aid Agency's website (para. 6.30).

APPENDIX H
Sexual Offences (The Law as at April 30, 2004)

A. Introduction

The history of the sexual offences legislation since 1956 is set out in detail at §§ 20-1 *et seq.* in the main work. All the statutory provisions contained in this appendix were repealed with effect from May 1, 2004, by the SOA 2003, but, as stated in the main work, they have continuing effect in relation to conduct occurring prior to that date. It should be borne in mind that this appendix states the law as at April 30, 2004, and that, therefore, there may yet be prosecutions for offences committed prior to even earlier material changes in the law: see, in particular, the amendments effected by the SOA 1985 and the CJPOA 1994 (summarised at §§ 20-2, 20-3 in the main work). **H-1**

B. Sexual Offences Act 1956

(1) Rape

(a) *Introduction*

Section 1 of the 1956 Act made rape an offence. Section 1(1) of the Sexual Offences (Amendment) Act 1976 provided a statutory definition of rape in terms designed to give effect to the Report of the Advisory Group on the Law of Rape (Cmnd. 6352) and the views expressed by the House of Lords in *DPP v. Morgan* [1976] A.C. 182. Section 1(1) was repealed by the CJPOA 1994, which also substituted a new section 1 in the 1956 Act. The effect of this was to adopt the 1976 definition, but to extend it so as to cover anal intercourse with a woman or a man. In addition, the new provision referred simply to "sexual intercourse" whereas the 1976 Act referred to "unlawful sexual intercourse". The omission of the word "unlawful" made clear Parliament's adoption of the decision of the House of Lords in *R. v. R.* [1992] A.C. 599, that a man may rape his wife. **H-2**

Section 7(2) of the 1976 Act (as amended by the CJA 1988, s.158(1) and (6)) provided that in that Act "a rape offence":

> "means any of the following, namely rape, attempted rape, aiding, abetting, counselling and procuring rape or attempted rape, incitement to commit rape, conspiracy to rape and burglary with intent to rape."

(b) *Statute*

Sexual Offences Act 1956, s.1

Rape of woman or man

    1.—(1) It is an offence for a man to rape a woman or another man. **H-3**

    (2) A man commits rape if—

      (a)   he has sexual intercourse with a person (whether vaginal or anal) who at the time of the intercourse does not consent to it; and

      (b)   at the time he knows that the person does not consent to the intercourse or is reckless as to whether that person consents to it.

    (3) A man also commits rape if he induces a married woman to have sexual intercourse with him by impersonating her husband.

    (4) Subsection (2) applies for the purposes of any enactment.

[This section is printed as substituted (from November 3, 1994) by the CJPOA 1994, s.142.]

Sexual Offences (Amendment) Act 1976, s.1

    1.—(1) [*Repealed by Criminal Justice and Public Order Act 1994, s.168(3) and Sched. 11.*] **H-4**

(2) It is hereby declared that if at a trial for a rape offence the jury has to consider whether a man believed that a woman or man was consenting to sexual intercourse, the presence or absence of reasonable grounds for such a belief is a matter to which the jury is to have regard, in conjunction with any other relevant matters, in considering whether he so believed.

[Subs. (2) is printed as amended by the CJPOA 1994, s.168(2), and Sched. 10, para. 35(1), (2).]

As to the use of the words "man" and "woman", see *post*, H-222. As to the meaning of "a rape offence", see *ante*, H-2.

In the case of a summary trial or a trial by court-martial, the references to the jury in section 1(2) of the 1976 Act are to be construed as references to the court: *ibid.*, s.7(3).

(c) *Anonymity*

H-5   See §§ 20-257 *et seq.* in the main work.

(d) *Indictment*

Statement of Offence

H-6   *Rape, contrary to section 1(1) of the Sexual Offences Act 1956.*

Particulars of Offence

A B on the ____ day of ____, 20__, had sexual intercourse with C D who at the time of the said intercourse did not consent to it, the said A B either knowing that the said C D did not so consent or being reckless as to whether she [or he] so consented.

Where the victim is a woman, the intercourse may be vaginal or anal: s.1(1) of the 1956 Act, *ante*, H-3. It is unnecessary to specify in the indictment whether the allegation is of vaginal or anal intercourse, but there will be cases where it is of assistance to do so. This can be done by adding the words *"per vaginam"* or *"per anum"* after the words "sexual intercourse". The addition of these words will be particularly useful where it is alleged that a woman was raped both vaginally and anally; the counts will reflect this and will ensure, in the event of a conviction on one count only, that the court is aware of the basis of the jury's verdict. As to where it is unclear on the evidence whether penetration was of the vagina or the anus, see *R. v. K. (Robert)* [2009] 1 Cr.App.R. 24, CA (§ 20-20 in the main work).

Good practice does not require that, where the prosecution rely on recklessness as an alternative to knowledge, there should be separate counts (alleging respectively knowledge and recklessness): *R. v. Flitter* [2001] Crim.L.R. 328, CA.

Allegation of joint offence

H-7   Where a person has been raped by more than one man on the same occasion, all the accused should be charged in one count of rape, with no mention of aiders and abettors: see the direction of the House of Lords in *DPP v. Merriman* [1973] A.C. 584. This enables the jury to be told that it matters not whether an individual accused physically committed the act of rape, or assisted or encouraged someone else to; thus, several accused may be convicted where the jury is satisfied only that each played a guilty part, but not as to who committed the physical act.

(e) *Mode of trial and class of offence*

H-8   This offence and an attempt to commit it are triable on indictment only: SOA 1956, s.37(2), and Sched. 2, para. 1. As to the classification of offences, see *ante*, Appendix B-209.

(f) *Alternative verdicts*

H-9   On a count of rape, the accused may be convicted of procurement of a woman by threats (s.2) or false pretences (s.3) or of administering drugs to obtain or facilitate intercourse (s.4): SOA 1956, s.37(4), and Sched. 2, para. 1.

As to alternative verdicts generally, see §§ 4-524 *et seq.* in the main work. Where the alleged victim was a girl under 16 years of age, then whether or not her age is averred in the indictment, a jury may not convict the accused under section 6(3) of the CLA 1967 (§ 4-525 in the main work) of an offence contrary to section 6 of the SOA 1956 (unlawful intercourse with a girl under 16): *R.*

v. Fisher [1969] 2 Q.B. 114, Assizes (Cusack J.); *R. v. Mochan*, 54 Cr.App.R. 5, Assizes (Cusack J.), approved in *R. v. Hodgson* [1973] Q.B. 565, 57 Cr.App.R. 502, CA.

As every charge of rape contains the essential ingredients of indecent assault (*viz.* an assault and indecency), it follows that where a man is acquitted of rape on the ground of the victim's consent, it is open to the jury to convict him where the victim is under 16, of indecent assault, because the consent which provided a defence to a charge of rape cannot, by virtue of the SOA 1956, ss.14(2) and 15(2), provide a defence to a charge of indecent assault. Age is not an ingredient of, nor an essential averment in the framing of a count of indecent assault: *R. v. Hodgson, ante.*

In *R. v. Timmins* [2006] 1 Cr.App.R. 18, CA, it was held that the effect of the decision in *R. v. J.* [2005] 1 A.C. 562, HL (on a true construction of the 1956 Act, it was impermissible to prosecute a charge of indecent assault under section 14(1) (*post*, H-117) in circumstances where the only conduct upon which the charge was based was an act of unlawful sexual intercourse with a girl under the age of 16 in respect of which no prosecution could be commenced under section 6(1) (*post*, H-50) by virtue of the time bar contained in section 37(2) of, and Schedule 2 to, the Act) was not such as to preclude a judge from leaving it to a jury to convict of indecent assault as an alternative to a charge of rape, under section 6(3) of the CLA 1967 (*ante*), where they were satisfied as to the act of sexual intercourse and as to the fact that the girl was under 16 at the time, and where they acquitted of rape on the ground that they were not satisfied as to lack of consent, and this was so notwithstanding that the proceedings for rape had been begun over 12 months after the alleged offence; the decision in *J.* had turned on the words of Schedule 2 to the 1956 Act, which provided that "A prosecution may not be commenced more than 12 months after the offence charged."; leaving a possible alternative verdict to a jury could not be described as a "commencement" of proceedings for the offence; but it would be an abuse of process to bring a charge of rape against a person against whom there was no evidence whatever of rape (in particular lack of consent) in order to circumvent a time limit.

In the earlier case of *R. v. Rabbitts* (2005) 149 S.J. 890, CA, it was held that, *R. v. J.* having decided that, as a matter of statutory construction, it was not open to the prosecution to bring a charge of indecent assault where the conduct on which the prosecution was based was an act of consensual sexual intercourse with a girl under 16, and where the purpose was to circumvent the statutory time limit of 12 months on prosecutions for unlawful sexual intercourse with a girl of that age, it made no difference that the count of indecent assault was included in the indictment as an alternative to a charge of rape to cater for the possibility that the jury would not be satisfied as to lack of consent.

In *R. v. Cottrell; R. v. Fletcher* [2008] 1 Cr.App.R. 7, CA, it was said that to the extent that *Timmins* and *Rabbitts* were inconsistent, they should be followed as they apply to the facts of the individual case. As to the flawed nature of the decision in *Timmins*, see CLW/05/43/4.

(g) *Autrefois acquit and convict*

For the general principles, see §§ 4-183 *et seq.* in the main work. **H-10**

An acquittal upon an indictment for rape was held to be no bar to a subsequent indictment on the same facts for a common assault: *R. v. Dungey* (1864) 4 F. & F. 99 (and see now s.6(3A) of the CLA 1967 (§ 4-525 in the main work), reversing the effect of *R. v. Mearns* [1991] 1 Q.B. 82, 91 Cr.App.R. 312, CA).

An acquittal on an indictment for rape cannot be successfully pleaded as a bar to a subsequent indictment for assault with intent to commit rape: *R. v. Gisson* (1847) 2 C. & K. 781, or, in certain circumstances, to a subsequent indictment for attempted rape, see *R. v. Hearn* [1970] Crim.L.R. 175, CA (§ 4-203 in the main work).

However, it should be noted that there was (as at April 30, 2004), in all probability, no longer an offence of assault with intent to rape, contrary to common law. It did not survive the creation of an identical statutory offence in the Offences against the Person Act 1861, s.38, which was in turn abolished by virtue of section 10 of, and Schedule 3 to, the Criminal Law Act 1967: *R. v. P.* [1990] Crim.L.R. 323, Crown Court (Pill J.) (but note the commentary and reference, by Professor J. C. Smith, to the opposite view expressed by Turner J. in *R. v. J.*, unreported, June 9, 1986). *Cf.* section 16 of the 1956 Act (assault with intent to commit buggery), *post*, H-138.

(h) *Sentence*

Maximum

H-11   Rape: life imprisonment—SOA 1956, s.37(3), and Sched. 2, para. 1(a).

Attempted rape: life imprisonment—SOA 1956, s.37(3), and Sched. 2, para. 1(a) (as amended by the SOA 1985, s.3).

Guidelines

H-12   See *post*, Appendix K-83 *et seq.*

In *R. v. H.* [2012] 2 Cr.App.R.(S.) 21, CA, it was said that in the search for principle, it is impossible to reconcile all the authorities that purport to provide guidance on sentencing for historic sexual offending; that the following considerations, derived from statute (general provisions about sentencing in the CJA 2003, Pt 12, Chap. 1 (ss.142–176), and the Coroners and Justice Act 2009, s.125 (sentencing guidelines: duty of court (§ 5-149 in the main work))) and case law, should be treated as guidance; and that reference to earlier decisions (with the exception of *R. v. Millberry; R. v. Morgan; R. v. Lackenby, post*, Appendix K-83) is unlikely to be helpful and is to be discouraged. First, sentence will be imposed on the basis of the legislative provisions current at the time of sentence, and by measured reference to any definitive sentencing guidelines relevant to the situation revealed by the established facts. Secondly, although sentence must be limited to the maximum permissible at the date when the offence was committed, it is wholly unrealistic to attempt an assessment of sentence by seeking to identify today what the sentence was likely to have been if the offence had come to light at or shortly after its commission. Thirdly, the particular circumstances in which the offence was committed and its seriousness must be the main focus; due allowance for the passage of time may be appropriate; the date may have a considerable bearing on the offender's culpability; for example, if he was young and immature at the time, that remains a continuing feature of the sentencing decision; similarly, if the allegations had come to light many years earlier, and the offender admitted them, but, for whatever reason, the complaint had not been drawn to the attention of, or investigated by, the police, or had been investigated but had not then been pursued to trial, these too would be relevant matters. Fourthly, careful judgment of the harm done to the victim is always a critical feature of the sentencing decision; simultaneously, equal care needs to be taken to assess the true extent of the offender's criminality by reference to what he actually did and the circumstances in which he did it. Fifthly, the passing of the years may demonstrate aggravating features if, for example, the offender has continued to commit sexual crime or he represents a continuing risk to the public; on the other hand, mitigation may be found in an unblemished life over the intervening years, particularly if accompanied by evidence of positive good character. Sixthly, early admissions and a guilty plea are of particular importance in historic cases; given that it is tempting to lie about events long ago, it is greatly to the offender's credit if he makes early admissions; even more powerful mitigation is available to the offender who, out of a sense of guilt and remorse, reports himself to the authorities. The court considered, *inter alia, R. v. Bowers* [1999] 2 Cr.App.R.(S.) 97, CA, *R. v. Fowler* [2002] 2 Cr.App.R.(S.) 99, CA, *Att.-Gen.'s References (Nos 37, 38, 44, 54, 51, 53, 35, 40, 43, 45, 41 and 42 of 2003)* [2004] 1 Cr.App.R.(S.) 84, CA, *R. v. McKendrick* [2005] 2 Cr.App.R.(S.) 68, CA, *R. v. Patterson* [2006] 2 Cr.App.R.(S.) 48, CA, *Att.-Gen.'s Reference (No. 39 of 2006) (R. v. J. (Rodney Clive))* [2007] 1 Cr.App.R.(S.) 34, CA, *R. v. Moon* [2011] 1 Cr.App.R.(S.) 34, CA, *R. v. Hartley (Practice Note)* [2012] 1 Cr.App.R. 7, CA, and *Att.-Gen.'s Reference (No. 78 of 2010)* [2011] 2 Cr.App.R.(S.) 109, CA.

This approach to sentencing historic sexual offences has been specifically endorsed by the Sentencing Council for England and Wales: see Annex B to its definitive guideline on sexual offences (*post*, Appendix K-84).

For a case considering *R. v. H.* (*ante*) see *R. v. Clifford, post*, H-120.

(i) *Ingredients of the offence*

A "man"

H-13   The common law presumption that a boy under the age of 14 was incapable of sexual intercourse was abolished (for both natural and unnatural intercourse) by the SOA 1993, ss.1, 2(2), (3).

A woman may be convicted as an aider and abettor: *R. v. Ram* (1893) 17 Cox 609 at 610n.

A man may be convicted of raping his wife: *R. v. R.* [1992] 1 A.C. 599, HL (confirmed by the revised definition of "rape" introduced by the CJPOA 1994, *ante*, § H-3).

Sexual intercourse

Where it is necessary to prove sexual intercourse (whether natural or unnatural), it shall not be **H-14** necessary to prove the completion of the intercourse by the emission of seed, but it shall be deemed complete upon proof of penetration only: SOA 1956, s.44 (*post*, § H-219). "Unnatural" intercourse in section 44 means buggery (including bestiality): *R. v. Gaston*, 73 Cr.App.R. 164, CA.

The amendment of section 1 of the 1956 Act by the 1994 Act (§ 20-3 in the main work, and *ante*, H-3) did not alter the law (whereunder even the slightest penetration would be sufficient: see *R. v. R'Rue* (1838) 8 C. & P. 641; *R. v. Allen* (1839) 9 C. & P. 31) so as to make penetration of the vagina, properly so-called, an essential ingredient of "vaginal" rape; it is sufficient that there was any degree of penetration by the penis within the labia of the pudendum of the complainant; the word "vaginal" in section 1 is used in comparison with, or in addition to, "anal", and not so as to indicate that the word is being used in the medical sense, rather than the general sense of the female genitalia: *R. v. J.F.*, unreported, December 16, 2002, CA ([2002] EWCA Crim. 2936).

Sexual intercourse is a continuing act; it follows that consensual intercourse will become rape if the woman (or man) ceases to consent during the intercourse, and the man (other man), with the necessary *mens rea*, continues the act: *Kaitamaki v. R.* [1985] A.C. 147, PC (decided on the corresponding New Zealand legislation). It should be noted that these were not the facts in *Kaitamaki*; the facts were that the defendant claimed he only realised the woman was not consenting after intercourse had begun. As to this aspect of the decision, see *post*, H-20. However, the foregoing proposition appears to follow as a matter of logic from the Board's decision on the narrower point.

Absence of consent

General

It must be proved that the accused had sexual intercourse with the complainant without her or **H-15** his consent: s.1(2)(a) of the 1956 Act, *ante*, H-3. This applies even where the offence is alleged to have been committed on a person under the age of 16, though sometimes in such a case the prosecution will not need to prove much more than the age of the victim: *R. v. Harling*, 26 Cr.App.R. 127, CCA. It is not, however, necessary to support a charge of rape that there is evidence that the complainant demonstrated her lack of consent or communicated it to the accused; the minimum requirement is evidence of lack of consent in fact, which might take many forms; the most obvious is the complainant's simple assertion, which may or may not be backed up by evidence of force or threats; alternatively, it may consist of evidence that by reason of drink, drugs, sleep, age or mental handicap the complainant was unaware of what was occurring and/or incapable of giving consent; or it may consist of evidence that the complainant was deceived as to the identity of the man with whom she had intercourse: *R. v. Malone* [1998] 2 Cr.App.R. 447, CA. As to intercourse with a woman known to be asleep, see *R. v. Mayers* (1872) 12 Cox 311; *R. v. Young* (1878) 14 Cox 114.

Lack of consent will have been established if the jury are satisfied that although the complainant did not dissent, her understanding and lack of knowledge were such, whether on account of age, the consumption of drink or drugs or mental handicap, that she was incapable of giving consent or of exercising any judgment on the matter: see *R. v. Howard*, 50 Cr.App.R. 56, CCA (age); *R. v. Lang*, 62 Cr.App.R. 50, CA (drink); *R. v. Fletcher* (1859) Bell 63; *R. v. Ryan* (1846) 2 Cox 115; *R. v. Fletcher* (1866) L.R. 1 C.C.R. 39; *R. v. Barratt* (1873) L.R. 2 C.C.R. 81; *R. v. Pressy* (1867) 10 Cox 635, CCR (mental handicap). To the extent that they suggest that where no force, threat or deceit was used, there must be evidence of some resistance on the part of the complainant, *Howard* and *Lang* should no longer be taken to represent the law: *Malone*, *ante*.

Evidence of resistance may, of course, be highly relevant to the separate issue of the defendant's knowledge or recklessness in relation to the lack of consent.

H-16   Although juries should be told that "consent" in the context of the offence of rape is a word which must be given its ordinary meaning, it is sometimes necessary for the judge to go further. For example, he should point out, if necessary, that there is a difference between consent and submission (as to which, see also § 20-10 in the main work). In cases where intercourse took place after threats not involving violence, or the fear of it, a jury should be directed to concentrate on the state of mind of the victim immediately before the act of intercourse. The jury should be reminded too of the wide spectrum of states of mind which consent could comprehend and that where a dividing line had to be drawn between real consent and mere submission they should apply their combined good sense, experience and knowledge of human nature and modern behaviour to all the relevant facts of the case: *R. v. Olugboja*, 73 Cr.App.R. 344, CA (*cf. R. v. McAllister* [1997] Crim.L.R. 233, CA, *post*, H-124). The word "want" should not be used in directing a jury on the issue of consent, there being a clear difference between "wanting" to have intercourse and "consenting" to it: *R. v. T. (D.)* [2000] 7 *Archbold News* 3, CA.

As to evidence about the lack of sexual experience of a complainant, see § 20-11 in the main work.

As to intercourse with a defective, see also the SOA 1956, ss.7 and 45 (*post*, H-64, H-68).

Intercourse by false pretences

H-17   The only types of fraud which vitiate consent for the purposes of the law of rape are frauds as to the nature of the act or as to the identity of the person doing the act: *R. v. Linekar* [1995] 2 Cr.App.R. 49, CA. As to frauds as to the nature of the act, see *R. v. Case* (1850) 1 Den. 580, and *R. v. Flattery* (1877) 2 Q.B.D. 410, where the consent was induced by the pretence that the act of intercourse was a form of medical treatment, and *R. v. Williams* [1923] 1 K.B. 340, 17 Cr.App.R. 56, CCA, where a choirmaster pretended to be testing a girl's breathing powers with an instrument. As to fraud as to the identity of the perpetrator of the Act, section 1(3) of the SOA 1956 (*ante*, H-3) makes express provision for the case of a man inducing a married woman to have sexual intercourse with him by impersonating her husband. This provision was first introduced by the Criminal Law Amendment Act 1885 for the purpose of reversing the decision in *R. v. Barrow* (1868) L.R. 1 C.C.R. 156. As to other instances of impersonation, it is possible that the principle in *Barrow* will still prevail; but it was dissented from in *R. v. Dee* (1884) 15 Cox C.C. 57, and doubt about the correctness of the decision was expressed in *Flattery*. What was said in *Linekar* as to fraud as to identity vitiating consent was *obiter*, the case not concerning mistake as to identity at all, but it is submitted that the view of the Court of Appeal represents the modern and better view.

See also section 3 of the SOA 1956 (*post*, H-27) in relation to false pretences of a less fundamental character; and *R. v. Tabassum* [2000] 2 Cr.App.R. 328, CA (*post*, H-124) in which it was held that a deception as to the quality of the act vitiated consent in a case of indecent assault.

Recent complaint

H-18   See § 20-12 in the main work.

Distress of victim

H-19   See § 20-13 in the main work.

Mens rea

General

H-20   It must be proved that at the time of the non-consensual intercourse, the defendant either knew that the victim was not consenting or that he was reckless as to whether she or he was consenting: see s.1(2)(b) of the SOA 1956, *ante*, H-3. If the tribunal of fact has to consider whether the defendant believed that a person was consenting to intercourse, the presence or absence of reasonable grounds for such a belief is a matter to which the tribunal is to have regard, in conjunction with any other relevant matters, in considering whether he so believed: Sexual Offences (Amendment) Act 1976, s.1(2), *ante*, H-4.

Sexual intercourse is a continuing act, which ends upon withdrawal. If, therefore, a man becomes aware that the other person is not consenting after intercourse has commenced and he does not desist, he will be guilty of rape from the moment that he realises that she or he is not consenting: *Kaitamaki v. R.* [1985] A.C. 147, PC. This case was decided on sections 127 and 128 of the New Zealand Crimes Act 1961, which are to the same effect as section 44 of the 1956 Act (*post*, H-219) and section 1 of the 1956 Act (*ante*, H-3). As to the situation where the victim was in fact consenting at the outset, but ceases to consent, see *ante*, H-14. This will also be rape provided that the man was aware of the change or was reckless in respect thereof.

Recklessness

Substantive offences. In *R. v. Satnam and Kewal*, 78 Cr.App.R. 149, CA, earlier confusion was **H-21** resolved. The authorities having been reviewed, it was held that any direction as to the definition of rape should be based upon section 1 of the Sexual Offences (Amendment) Act 1976 (see now s.1(2) of the SOA 1956, *ante*, H-3) and upon *DPP v. Morgan* [1976] A.C. 182, HL (§ 17-10 in the main work). The court suggested that a practical definition of recklessness in sexual cases had been given in *R. v. Kimber*, 77 Cr.App.R. 225, CA (a case of indecent assault), namely if the jury were sure that the defendant had been indifferent to the feelings and wishes of the victim, aptly described colloquially as "couldn't care less" then that in law was "reckless". Thus (see pp. 154-155), in summing up a case of rape which involves the issue of consent, the judge should, in dealing with the state of mind of the defendant, direct the jury that before they can convict, the Crown must have proved either that he knew the woman did not consent to sexual intercourse, or that he was reckless as to whether she consented. If the jury are sure he knew she did not consent, they will find him guilty of rape knowing there to be no consent. If they are not sure about that, they will go on to consider reckless rape. If he may genuinely have believed that she did consent, even though he was mistaken in that belief he must be acquitted: see s.1(2) of the 1976 Act, *ante*, H-4. In considering whether his belief may have been genuine, the jury should take into account all the relevant circumstances (including presence or absence of reasonable grounds: see s.1(2)). If, after considering them, the jury are sure that the defendant had no genuine belief that the woman consented to have intercourse, then they will convict. He will be guilty because that finding of fact would mean that his mental state was such that either he knew she was not consenting or he was reckless as to whether she was consenting. If the jury are sure that he could not have cared less whether she wanted to have sexual intercourse or not, but pressed on regardless, then he would have been reckless and could not have believed that she wanted to.

In *R. v. Taylor (Robert)*, 80 Cr.App.R. 327, CA, Lord Lane C.J. said (at p. 332) that in rape, the defendant is reckless if he does not believe the woman is consenting and could not care less whether she is consenting or not but presses on regardless. *Taylor* was followed and applied in *R. v. Adkins* [2000] 2 All E.R. 185, CA, where it was held to be unnecessary to give a direction as to honest belief in every case where consent is in issue; such a direction is only required when, on the evidence in the case, there is room for the possibility of a genuine mistaken belief that the victim had consented; equally, the question of honest belief does not necessarily arise where reckless rape is in issue, for the defendant might have failed to address his mind to the question whether or not there was consent, or have been indifferent as to whether or not there was consent, in circumstances where, if he had addressed his mind to the question, he could not genuinely have believed that there was consent; where, therefore, the defence case was not merely that the complainant consented but that she actively facilitated intercourse, there was no scope for a genuine, but mistaken, belief as to consent.

Attempts. In *R. v. Khan*, 91 Cr.App.R. 29, the Court of Appeal held that precisely the same **H-22** analysis can be made of the offence of attempted rape as that of the full offence, namely: (a) the intention of the offender is to have sexual intercourse with another person; (b) the offence is committed if, but only if, the circumstances are that: (i) the other person does not consent; *and* (ii) the defendant knows that he or she is not consenting or is reckless as to that fact.

Drunkenness and mistake of fact

It is clear from both *DPP v. Majewski* [1977] A.C. 443, HL (§ 17-107 in the main work) and *R.* **H-23** *v. Caldwell* [1982] A.C. 341, HL (§ 17-112 in the main work) that "recklessness" as a consequence of voluntarily induced intoxication cannot amount to a defence.

If the accused was, or may have been, genuinely mistaken as to fact (see generally, §§ 17-10 *et seq.* in the main work, and H-21, *ante*), for example, if he thought or may have thought that the complainant was consenting to sexual intercourse, and the jury are sure that that mistake was a consequence of intoxication, what then is the position? It appears to be this: implicit in such a finding is the finding that but for the voluntary consumption of drink the jury are sure that the accused would have known either that the complainant was not consenting or, at the very least, that there was a risk that she was not consenting. Whatever the true scope of the meaning of "reckless" in the context of sexual offences, it is plain (see *ante*, H-21) that to proceed knowing that there was a risk that the complainant was not consenting and not caring whether she consented or not is to act recklessly. It therefore follows that if the jury are sure that by virtue of drink (or drugs) the accused was not alerted, at the very least to the existence of that risk, that in itself constitutes the necessary recklessness for the purposes of the offence, see *Majewski* (§ 17-109 in the main work); and a genuine mistake as to fact in such circumstances constitutes no defence. This approach is borne out by the decision of the Court of Appeal in *R. v. Woods (W.)*, 74 Cr.App.R. 312. It was conceded on behalf of W that, but for section 1(2) of the Sexual Offences (Amendment) Act 1976 (*ante*, H-4), the principles in *Majewski* and *Caldwell* (as to the relevance of drink to recklessness) would apply and that accordingly a genuine mistake as to fact as a consequence of drink could found no defence. However, it was argued that section 1(2) of the 1976 Act permitted the jury to take into account a defendant's drunken state as a possible reasonable ground for his belief that a woman was consenting to intercourse. The submission was roundly rejected. "Relevant" in that subsection means "*legally* relevant". W's drunkenness was not a matter that the jury were entitled to take into consideration in deciding whether or not reasonable grounds existed for W's belief that the woman consented to intercourse.

The question was considered again in *R. v. Fotheringham*, 88 Cr.App.R. 206, CA, in which the defendant was charged with rape. His defence was that he was so drunk at the time that he believed he was having intercourse with his wife. Applying *Majewski, Caldwell, Woods, ante*, and *R. v. O'Grady* [1987] Q.B. 995, 85 Cr.App.R. 315, CA (§ 17-16 in the main work), the court held that "in rape, self-induced intoxication is no defence, whether the issue be intention, consent or, as here, mistake as to the identity of the victim" (at p. 212).

(j) *Liability of accessories*

H-24   As to indicting accessories to rape, see *ante*, H-7; and as to their liability to conviction, notwithstanding the acquittal of the alleged principal, see *R. v. Cogan and Leak* [1976] Q.B. 217, 61 Cr.App.R. 217, CA (§ 20-26 in the main work).

(k) *Attempts*

H-25   See § 20-27 in the main work, and, in relation to the *mens rea* of an attempt, see *ante*, H-22.

(2) Procurement of intercourse by threats or false pretences

(a) *Statute*

Sexual Offences Act 1956, ss.2, 3

H-26   **2.**—(1) It is an offence for a person to procure a woman, by threats or intimidation, to have ... sexual intercourse in any part of the world.
(2) [*Repealed by CJPOA 1994, s.33(1).*]

[Subs. (1) is printed as repealed in part by the CJPOA 1994, s.168(1) and (3), and Scheds 9, para. 2, and 11.]

H-27   **3.**—(1) It is an offence for a person to procure a woman, by false pretences or false representations, to have ... sexual intercourse in any part of the world.
(2) [*Repealed by Criminal Justice and Public Order Act 1994, s.33(1).*]

[Subs. (1) is printed as repealed in part by the CJPOA 1994, s.168(1) and (3), and Scheds 9, para. 2, and 11.]

As to the meaning of "sexual intercourse", see *post*, H-219; as to the use of the word "woman", see *post*, H-222.

For anonymity provisions, see §§ 20-257 *et seq.* in the main work.

(b) *Indictment*

Statement of Offence

Procuration, contrary to section 3(1) of the Sexual Offences Act 1956.

Particulars of Offence

A B, on the _____ *day of* _____, *20__, procured J N, a woman, to have sexual intercourse with himself* [or *with E F, as the case may be*] *by falsely pretending or representing to her that* [state in ordinary language the false pretence or representation].

The false pretences must be set out: *R. v. Field* (1892) 116 CCC Sess.Pap. 1891–1892, 757; but they need not be expressly negatived: *R. v. Clarke*, 59 J.P. 248.

An indictment for an offence contrary to section 2 may easily be framed from the above specimen.

(c) *Mode of trial and classification of offences*

The offence contrary to section 2 and an attempt to commit it are triable on indictment only: SOA 1956, s.37(2), and Sched. 2, para. 7(a), (b).

The offence contrary to section 3 is triable on indictment only: SOA 1956, s.37(2), and Sched. 2, para. 8.

As to the classification of offences, see *ante*, Appendix B-209.

(d) *Alternative verdicts*

As to the possibility of a conviction of either of these offences on a charge of rape, see *ante*, H-9.

(e) *Sentence*

Either offence, or an attempt to commit the offence contrary to section 2: imprisonment not exceeding two years—SOA 1956, s.37(3), and Sched. 2, paras 7(a), (b), and 8.

(f) *Ingredients of the offences*

"Procure"

See *post*, H-171.

False pretences

Seduction by a married man of a woman under promise of marriage by false representation was held to be within section 3(2) of the Criminal Law Amendment Act 1885 (*rep.*), of which section 3(1) of the Act of 1956 was a replacement: *R. v. Williams*, 62 J.P. 310. It is immaterial whether the intercourse was procured with the defendant or with another: *ibid.*, and see *R. v. Jones* [1896] 1 Q.B. 4.

(3) Administering drugs to obtain or facilitate intercourse

(a) *Statute*

Sexual Offences Act 1956, s.4

4.—(1) It is an offence for a person to apply or administer to, or cause to be taken by, a woman any drug, matter or thing with intent to stupefy or overpower her so as thereby to enable any man to have unlawful sexual intercourse with her.

(2) [*Repealed by Criminal Justice and Public Order Act 1994, s.33(1).*]

As to the meaning of "sexual intercourse", see *post*, H-219; as to the use of the words "man" and "woman", see *post*, H-222.

For anonymity provisions, see *post*, §§ 20-257 *et seq.* in the main work.

(b) *Mode of trial and class of offence*

This offence is triable only on indictment: SOA 1956, s.37(2), and Sched. 2, para. 9. As to the classification of offences, see *ante*, Appendix B-209.

(c) Alternative verdicts

H-36   As to the possibility of a conviction of this offence on a charge of rape, see *ante*, H-9.

(d) Sentence

H-37   Imprisonment not exceeding two years: SOA 1956, s.37(3), and Sched. 2, para. 9.

(e) Ingredients of the offence

H-38   "Unlawful" sexual intercourse means illicit sexual intercourse, *i.e.* outside the bond of marriage: *R. v. Chapman* [1959] 1 Q.B. 100, 42 Cr.App.R. 257, CCA (considering s.19 of the 1956 Act, *post*, H-148).

The essence of the offence is the administering of the drug. If there has been only one administration, there can be only one offence, even though the intention of the administration was to enable more than one man to have intercourse with the woman: *R. v. Shillingford and Vanderwall*, 52 Cr.App.R. 188, CA.

(4) Sexual intercourse with girl under 13

(a) Statute

Sexual Offences Act 1956, s.5

H-39   5. It is an offence for a man to have unlawful sexual intercourse with a girl under the age of thirteen.

[This section is printed as effectively amended by the CLA 1967, s.12(5)(a).]

As to the meaning of "sexual intercourse", see *post*, H-219; as to the use of the words "man" and "girl", see *post*, H-222.

For anonymity provisions, see §§ 20-257 *et seq.* in the main work.

(b) Indictment

Statement of Offence

H-40   *Sexual intercourse with a girl under 13, contrary to section 5 of the Sexual Offences Act 1956.*

Particulars of Offence

A B, on the _____ day of _____, 20__, had sexual intercourse with J N, a girl under the age of 13 years.

(c) Mode of trial and classification of offences

H-41   This offence and an attempt to commit it are triable only on indictment: SOA 1956, s.37(2), and Sched. 2, para. 2(a), (b). As to the classification of offences, see *ante*, Appendix B-209.

(d) Alternative verdicts

H-42   Indecent assault, contrary to section 14(1) of the 1956 Act (*post*, H-117): *R. v. McCormack* [1969] 2 Q.B. 442, 53 Cr.App.R. 514, CA. As to alternative verdicts generally, see §§ 4-524 *et seq.* in the main work.

(e) Sentence

H-43   The full offence: life imprisonment—SOA 1956, s.37(2), and Sched. 2, para. 2(a).

Attempt: imprisonment not exceeding seven years—*ibid.*, para. 2(b).

Custodial sentences are normally imposed, unless the offender is psychologically abnormal or of limited intelligence (see in particular *Att.-Gen.'s Reference (No. 20 of 1994)*, 16 Cr.App.R.(S.) 578, CA.). Some guidance may be obtained from the guideline of the Sentencing Council in relation to offences under the SOA 2003 (*post*, Appendix K-84 *et seq.*); and for guidance as to how to sentence historic offences, see *R. v. H.*, *ante*, H-12.

(f) Ingredients of the offence

Man

H-44   As to the abolition of the presumption that a boy under 14 is incapable of sexual intercourse, see *ante*, H-13.

Consent immaterial

The evidence is the same as in rape, with the exception that it is immaterial whether the act **H-45** was done with or without the consent of the girl. If it was in fact without her consent, an indictment for rape will lie, notwithstanding the age of the child: *R. v. Dicken* (1877) 14 Cox 8; *R. v. Harling*, 26 Cr.App.R. 127, CCA; *R. v. Howard*, 50 Cr.App.R. 56, CCA, *ante*, H-15. So, where the defendant was indicted for an attempt to commit the offence, and the evidence was that he had attempted to have sexual intercourse with the girl, but that she had consented to the attempt, it was held that the fact of her consent was immaterial, and that the defendant was properly convicted: *R. v. Beale* (1865) L.R. 1 C.C.R. 10.

Knowledge of age immaterial

A mistake as to the age of the girl, even if based on reasonable grounds, will not avail a **H-46** defendant: *R. v. Prince* (1875) L.R. 2 C.C.R. 154 (*post*, H-161); *R. v. K.* [2002] 1 A.C. 462, HL; and see the specific defence provided by section 6(3) in relation to the less serious offence of intercourse with a girl under 16 (*post*, H-50).

(g) *Evidence*

Recent complaint

See § 20-12 in the main work.   **H-47**

Distress of victim

See § 20-13 in the main work.   **H-48**

Age

The provisions of section 99(2) of the CYPA 1933 (§ 19-412 in the main work), as to presump- **H-49** tion and determination of age do not apply: see the proviso to Schedule 1 to the 1933 Act (whilst the proviso was repealed by the SOA 2003 (see § 19-412 in the main work), its effect in relation to any prosecution for an offence under the 1956 Act will be saved by virtue of the Interpretation Act 1978, s.16 (*ante*, Appendix F-16)). The girl must be proved to have been under 13 years of age when the offence was committed. The best way of doing this is to produce a duly certified copy of the certificate of birth, coupled with evidence of identity; but the age may be proved by any other legal means: *R. v. Cox* [1898] 1 Q.B. 179 (age could be proved by persons who had seen the child and by a teacher at an elementary school which the child attended). Where a certificate of birth is put in, there must be evidence of identity as well: see *R. v. Nicholls* (1867) 10 Cox 476; *R. v. Bellis*, 6 Cr.App.R. 283, CCA; *R. v. Rogers*, 10 Cr.App.R. 276, CCA.

In the case of an adopted child, the date of birth may be proved by a certified copy of an entry in the Adopted Children Register: Adoption and Children Act 2002, s.77(5).

(5) Sexual intercourse with a girl under 16

(a) *Statute*

Sexual Offences Act 1956, s.6

6.—(1) It is an offence, subject to the exceptions mentioned in this section, for a man to have **H-50** unlawful sexual intercourse with a girl ... under the age of sixteen.

(2) Where a marriage is invalid under section two of the Marriage Act 1949, or section one of the Age of Marriage Act 1929 (the wife being a girl under the age of sixteen), the invalidity does not make the husband guilty of an offence under this section because he has sexual intercourse with her, if he believes her to be his wife, and has reasonable cause for the belief.

(3) A man is not guilty of an offence under this section because he has unlawful sexual intercourse with a girl under the age of sixteen, if he is under the age of twenty-four and has not previously been charged with a like offence, and he believes her to be of the age of sixteen or over and has reasonable cause for the belief.

In this subsection "a like offence" means an offence under this section or an attempt to commit one, or an offence under paragraph (1) of section five of the Criminal Law Amendment Act 1885 (the provision replaced for England and Wales by this section).

[This section is printed as repealed in part by the CLA 1967, s.10(1), and Sched. 2, para. 14.]

As to the meaning of "sexual intercourse", see *post*, H-219; as to the use of the words "man" and "girl", see *post*, H-222.

As to the proof of exceptions, see the SOA 1956, s.47, *post*, H-225.

For anonymity provisions, see §§ 20-257 *et seq.* in the main work.

Marriage Act 1949, s.2

Marriages of persons under sixteen

H-51   2. A marriage solemnized between persons either of whom is under the age of sixteen shall be void.

(b) *Indictment*

Statement of Offence

H-52   *Sexual intercourse with a girl under 16, contrary to section 6(1) of the Sexual Offences Act 1956.*

Particulars of Offence

A B, on the _____ day of _____, 20__, had sexual intercourse with J N, a girl under the age of 16 years.

(c) *Mode of trial and classification of offences*

H-53   This offence and an attempt to commit it are triable either way: MCA 1980, s.17(1), and Sched. 1 (§ 1-130 in the main work). As to the classification of offences, see *ante*, Appendix B-209.

(d) *Alternative verdicts*

H-54   Indecent assault, contrary to section 14(1) of the 1956 Act (*post*, H-117): *R. v. McCormack* [1969] 2 Q.B. 442, 53 Cr.App.R. 514, CA. As to alternative verdicts generally, see §§ 4-524 *et seq.* in the main work.

(e) *Time limit on prosecutions*

H-55   Prosecutions for an offence under section 6 or an attempt to commit such offence may not be commenced more than 12 months after the offence charged: SOA 1956, s.37(2), and Sched. 2, para. 10(a), (b).

As to what is a commencement of the prosecution, see *R. v. West* [1898] 1 Q.B. 174; *R. v. Wakely* [1920] 1 K.B. 688, 14 Cr.App.R. 121, CCA.

In appropriate circumstances, evidence of prior offences by the defendant against the same girl committed outside the 12 months' time limit will be admissible: *R. v. Shellaker* [1914] 1 K.B. 414, 9 Cr.App.R. 240, CCA; *cf. R. v. Hewitt*, 19 Cr.App.R. 64, CCA; *R. v. Adams, The Times*, April 8, 1993, CA.

As to the impropriety of bringing a prosecution for indecent assault, based on an act of consensual sexual intercourse, where a prosecution under section 6 is time barred, see *R. v. J.*, *post*, H-118.

(f) *Sentence*

H-56   The full offence, or an attempt to commit it: imprisonment not exceeding two years' SOA 1956, s.37(3), and Sched. 2, para. 10(a), (b). The penalty on summary conviction is governed by section 32 of the MCA 1980 (§ 1-125 in the main work).

In *R. v. Taylor*, 64 Cr.App.R. 182, CA, the court laid down guidelines for the sentencing of persons convicted of having unlawful sexual intercourse with a girl under the age of 16. Lawton L.J. distinguished between cases where "virtuous friendship" between young people of about the same age ended in sexual intercourse, and cases where a man in a supervisory capacity set out to seduce a girl under 16 who was in his charge. In the first type of case, sentences of a punitive nature were not required; in the second, sentences near the maximum of two years should be passed.

In *R. v. Bayliss* [2000] 1 Cr.App.R.(S.) 412, CA, it was said that attitudes to teenage prostitution had changed since *Taylor*, and that there was a greater appreciation that this offence and that of taking indecent photographs of children, contrary to the Protection of Children Act 1978 (§§ 31-107 *et seq.* in the main work), had been put on the statute book for the protection of children, including against themselves.

(g) *Ingredients of the offence*

Man

As to the abolition of the presumption that a boy under 14 is incapable of sexual intercourse, see *ante*, H-13. **H-57**

A girl under 16 cannot be indicted for "abetting" or "inciting" a man to have unlawful sexual intercourse with herself: *R. v. Tyrrell* [1894] 1 Q.B. 710.

As to doctors who prescribe contraceptive pills to girls under 16, see *Gillick v. West Norfolk and Wisbech Area Health Authority* [1986] A.C. 112, HL, *post*, H-196.

Consent immaterial

See *ante*, H-45, and *R. v. Ratcliffe* (1882) 10 Q.B.D. 74. **H-58**

"Unlawful" sexual intercourse

See *R. v. Chapman, ante,* H-38. **H-59**

(h) *Evidence*

Recent complaint

See § 20-12 in the main work. **H-60**

Distress of victim

See § 20-13 in the main work. **H-61**

Age

See *ante*, H-49, the contents of which apply, *mutatis mutandis*, to the offence under section 6. **H-62**

(i) *Defences*

In the case of a man under the age of 24, the presence of reasonable cause to believe that the **H-63** girl was over the age of 16 years is a valid defence provided that the defendant has not previously been charged with a like offence: SOA 1956, s.6(3) (*ante*, H-50). As to the meaning of the expression "a like offence", see *ibid.* The defence is not incompatible with Article 6 (right to fair trial (§ 16-72 in the main work)) or 14 (prohibition on discrimination (§ 16-177 in the main work)) of the ECHR as being discriminatory on the grounds that, (a) a woman who had sexual intercourse with a boy under 16 would, if prosecuted, be charged with indecent assault, in relation to which she would have a defence, whatever her age, of genuine belief that the boy was 16 or more, and (b) it was restricted to men under the age of 24; as to (b), even though the choice of age was arbitrary, it did not introduce an element of disproportionality into the offence: *R. v. Kirk and Russell* [2002] Crim.L.R. 756, CA.

In *R. v. Rider*, 37 Cr.App.R. 209, Assizes, Streatfeild J. had to construe the wording of the Criminal Law Amendment Act 1922. The proviso to section 2 of that Act gave a man under 24 years of age a defence to a charge of unlawful sexual intercourse with a girl under 16 years of age if at the time of the intercourse he had reasonable cause to believe that the girl was over the age of 16; but the defence was only available "on the first occasion on which he is charged with" such an offence. It was held that "charged" in this context meant "appeared before a court with jurisdiction to deal with the matter". The defendant had been committed for trial on two separate occasions in respect of like allegations relating to different girls. Both allegations were joined in the same indictment and it was held that appearance before the assize was the first occasion on which he appeared before a court with jurisdiction to deal with the matter and, therefore, the defence was available in respect of both counts. Streatfeild J. said, however, that had the magistrates refused to commit for trial in respect of the first matter, the appearance at the assize on the second matter would have been the second occasion. This result seems illogical. It should be borne in mind that at the time of *Rider*, the offence in question could be tried only on indictment. It is now triable either way and it is respectfully submitted that the defence should only be available to a person who at the time of the alleged offence has not been before a court (magistrates' court, whether or not the matter is to be tried summarily, Crown Court or service court) on a charge of such an offence. This gives due effect to the actual decision in *Rider* to the revised formulation of the defence in the 1956 Act and to the changes in the legislation relating to mode of trial. It is also consistent with the rationale underlying the restriction on the defence, *viz.* that once the serious nature of such conduct has been brought to the attention of a man, he can legitimately be expected to be more careful about a girl's age.

To constitute a defence under this proviso, where it applies, the defendant must have reasonable cause to believe, and, in fact, must have believed that the girl was over the age of 16 years: *R. v. Banks* [1916] 2 K.B. 621, 12 Cr.App.R. 74, CCA; *R. v. Harrison*, 26 Cr.App.R. 166, CCA. The question of the existence of reasonable cause to believe is one for the jury: *R. v. Forde* [1923] 2 K.B. 400, 17 Cr.App.R. 99, CCA.

The defence is available not only where intercourse has taken place, but also where it has been merely attempted: *R. v. Collier* [1960] Crim.L.R. 204, Assizes (Streatfeild J.).

As to the burden of proof of the "exceptions" (defences) in subsections (2) and (3) of section 6, see section 47 of the 1956 Act, *post*, H-225.

(6) Intercourse with defectives

(a) *Statute*

Sexual Offences Act 1956, ss.7, 9

Intercourse with defective

H-64   **7.**—(1) It is an offence, subject to the exception mentioned in this section, for a man to have unlawful sexual intercourse with a woman who is a defective.

(2) A man is not guilty of an offence under this section because he has unlawful sexual intercourse with a woman if he does not know and has no reason to suspect her to be a defective.

[This section is printed as substituted by the MHA 1959, s.127(1)(a).]

Procurement of defective

H-65   **9.**—(1) It is an offence, subject to the exception mentioned in this section, for a person to procure a woman who is a defective to have unlawful sexual intercourse in any part of the world.

(2) A person is not guilty of an offence under this section because he procures a defective to have unlawful sexual intercourse, if he does not know and has no reason to suspect her to be a defective.

As to the meaning of "sexual intercourse", see *post*, H-219 as to the use of the words "man" and "woman", see *post*, H-222; as to the meaning of "defective", see *post*, H-68.

For anonymity provisions, see §§ 20-257 *et seq.* in the main work.

As to the burden of proof in relation to the exception in subsection (2) of both sections, see section 47 of the Act, *post*, H-225.

(b) *Mode of trial and classification of offences*

H-66   Offences against sections 7 and 9, and attempts to commit them, are triable only on indictment: SOA 1956, s.37(2), and Sched. 2, paras 11(a), (b), and 13(a), (b). As to the classification of offences, see *ante*, Appendix B-209.

(c) *Sentence*

H-67   Offences against sections 7 and 9, and attempts to commit them: imprisonment not exceeding two years—SOA 1956, s.37(3), and Sched. 2, paras 11(a), (b), and 13(a), (b). For an illustrative example, see *R. v. Adcock* [2000] 1 Cr.App.R.(S.) 563, CA.

(d) *Ingredients of the offences*

"Defective"

Sexual Offences Act 1956, s.45

Meaning of defective

45. In this Act "defective" means a person suffering from a state of arrested or incomplete develop-   **H-68**
ment of mind which includes severe impairment of intelligence and social functioning.

[This section is printed as substituted by the MHA 1959, s.127(1); and as amended by the
Mental Health (Amendment) Act 1982, Sched. 3.]

The words "severe impairment of intelligence and social functioning" are ordinary English
words and not words of art; they were inserted in the definition to protect women, if defectives,
from exploitation. Severe impairment is to be measured against the standards of normal persons:
R. v. Hall (J.H.), 86 Cr.App.R. 159, CA. The trial judge's direction that it was for them to decide
on all the evidence whether the victim was severely impaired within the ordinary meaning of
those words was correct.

"Unlawful" sexual intercourse

See *R. v. Chapman, ante*, H-38.   **H-69**

"Procure"

See *post*, H-171.   **H-70**

(7) Incest by a man

(a) *Statute*

Sexual Offences Act 1956, s.10

10.—(1) It is an offence for a man to have sexual intercourse with a woman whom he knows to be   **H-71**
his grand-daughter, daughter, sister or mother.

(2) In the foregoing subsection "sister" includes half-sister and for the purposes of that subsection
any expression importing a relationship between two people shall be taken to apply notwithstanding
that the relationship is not traced through lawful wedlock.

As to the meaning of "sexual intercourse", see *post*, H-219; as to the use of the words "man"
and "woman", see *post*, § H-222.

For anonymity provisions, see §§ 20-257 *et seq.* in the main work.

(b) *Indictment*

Statement of Offence

Incest, contrary to section 10(1) of the Sexual Offences Act 1956.   **H-72**

Particulars of Offence

A B, being a male person, on the _____ *day of* _____, *20__, had sexual intercourse with J N, whom he knew
to be his daughter* [if under the age of 13, add her age].

An indictment which charged the offence as having been committed "on divers days" between
two specified dates was held to be bad for duplicity: *R. v. Thompson* [1914] 2 K.B. 99, 9 Cr.App.R.
252, CCA.

Where a brother and sister were charged in separate counts of the same indictment with committing incest and were tried separately, with the result that the brother was convicted and the
sister acquitted, it was held that the acquittal of the sister did not make the conviction of the
brother bad: *R. v. Gordon*, 19 Cr.App.R. 20, CCA. As to inconsistent verdicts generally, see §§ 7-70
et seq. in the main work.

(c) *Mode of trial and classification of offences*

This offence, and an attempt to commit it, are triable only on indictment: SOA 1956, s.37(2),   **H-73**
and Sched. 2, para. 14(a), (b). As to the classification of offences, see *ante*, Appendix B-209.

(d) *Alternative verdicts*

H-74   On a charge of the full offence, unlawful sexual intercourse with a girl under 13 (s.5) or with a
girl under 16 (s.6): SOA 1956, s.37(4), and Sched. 2, para. 14(a). Where the girl is under 16,
indecent assault (whether or not the indictment avers her age): *R. v. Rogina*, 64 Cr.App.R. 79, CA.
This possibility arises by virtue of the combination of section 37(5) (*post*, H-226) and the specific
provision in Schedule 2 for a conviction of an offence under either section 5 or 6 (indecent assault
being an alternative on an indictment charging either of those offences, *ante*, H-42, H-54).

(e) *Restriction on prosecution*

H-75   A prosecution for this offence, or an attempt to commit it, may not be commenced except by or
with the consent of the DPP: SOA 1956, s.37(2), and Sched. 2, para. 14(a), (b).

(f) *Sentence*

Maximum

H-76   The full offence and an attempt to commit it: if with a girl under 13, and so charged in the
indictment, life imprisonment, otherwise imprisonment not exceeding seven years— SOA 1956,
s.37(3), and Sched. 2, para. 14(a), (b).

Basis of sentence

H-77   See *R. v. Huchison*, 56 Cr.App.R. 307, CA.

Guidelines

H-78   In *Att.-Gen.'s Reference (No. 1 of 1989)*, 90 Cr.App.R. 141, the Court of Appeal laid down
guidelines for sentencing in cases of incest by a father against a daughter. The court made the following suggestions "as a broad guide" to the level of sentence for various categories of the crime
of incest. All were on the assumption that there had been no plea of guilty. They should be read
subject to *Practice Statement (Crime: Sentencing)* [1992] 1 W.L.R. 948. See, in particular, paragraph
10 thereof.

(i) *Girl aged over 16 years*

H-79   A range from three years' imprisonment down to a nominal penalty would be appropriate
depending in particular on the one hand whether force was used and the degree of harm if any,
to the girl, and, on the other, the desirability where it existed of keeping family disruption to a
minimum. The older the girl the greater the possibility that she might have been willing or even
the instigating party, a factor which would be reflected in the sentence.

(ii) *Girl aged from 13 to 16 years*

H-80   A sentence between about five years' and three years' imprisonment would be appropriate.
Much the same principles would apply as in the case of the girl over 16 years, though the likelihood of corruption increased in inverse proportion to the age of the girl.

(iii) *Girl aged under 13 years*

H-81   It was here that the widest range of sentences was likely to be found. If any case of incest could
properly be described as the "ordinary" type of case, it would be one where the sexual relationship between husband and wife had broken down; the father had probably resorted to excessive
drinking and the eldest daughter was gradually, by way of familiarities, indecent acts and suggestions made the object of the father's frustrated inclinations. If the girl was not far short of her
thirteenth birthday and there were no particularly adverse or favourable features, a term of about
six years' imprisonment would seem to be appropriate. The younger the girl when the sexual approach was started, the more likely it would be that the girl's will was overborne and, accordingly,
the more serious would be the crime.

(iv) *Aggravating factors*

H-82   Whatever the age of the girl, the following, *inter alia*, would aggravate the offence:

(a) physical or psychological suffering from the offence;

(b) the incest taking place at frequent intervals or over a long period;

(c) the use of threats or violence, or the girl being otherwise terrified of her father;

(d) the incest being accompanied by perversions abhorrent to the girl, such as buggery or *fellatio*;

(e) the girl becoming pregnant; and

(f) the commission of similar offences against more than one girl.

(v) *Mitigating features*

Possible mitigating features were, *inter alia*: **H-83**

(a) a plea of guilty;

(b) genuine affection on the defendant's part rather than the intention to use the girl simply as an outlet for his sexual inclinations;

(c) previous sexual experience by the girl; and

(d) deliberate attempts at seduction by the girl.

In relation to a plea of guilty, the court said that such a plea was seldom not entered and it should be met by an appropriate discount, depending on the usual considerations, that is, how promptly the defendant confessed, the degree of contrition and so on. The court also said that occasionally a shorter term of imprisonment than would otherwise be imposed might be justified as being of benefit to the victim and the family.

For cases illustrating the application of these guidelines, see CSP B4–2. For cases of incest by a brother with a sister, see *ibid.*, B4–2.3D; for a case of incest by a mother with her young son, see *ibid.*, B4–2.3E.

(g) *Effect of adoption*

The prohibition contained in section 10(1) applies notwithstanding the adoption of one of the **H-84** parties: Adoption and Children Act 2002, s.74(1)(b) (whilst this provision was amended to substitute a reference to sections 64 and 65 of the SOA 2003 for the references to sections 10 and 11 of the 1956 Act, its previous operation will be saved by virtue of section 16 of the Interpretation Act 1978 (*ante*, Appendix F-16)).

(h) *Ingredients of the offence*

If a man makes a genuine mistake as to the identity of the person with whom he has intercourse, **H-85** he will not commit the offence: *R. v. Baillie-Smith*, 64 Cr.App.R. 76, CA (intercourse with daughter, thinking her to be his wife).

As to the abolition of the common law presumption that a boy under 14 is incapable of sexual intercourse, see *ante*, H-13.

(i) *Evidence*

The relationship between the parties may be proved by oral evidence or by certificates of mar- **H-86** riage and birth, coupled with identification. An admission by the defendant that the person with whom the offence had been committed was his daughter may be sufficient evidence of the relationship: *R. v. Jones (Evan)*, 24 Cr.App.R. 55, CCA.

Evidence tending to show pre-existent sexual passion between the parties is admissible: *R. v. Ball* [1911] A.C. 47, HL.

The defendant was charged with incest with S, who was alleged to be his daughter. His defence was that he had no knowledge that S *was* his daughter. He desired to give evidence:

(a) that he had been told by his first wife (the mother of S) that S had been begotten by another man and that he believed that statement to be true;

(b) that he had told his second wife that he was not the father of S;

(c) explaining statements which he had made on certain occasions acknowledging S to be his daughter.

It was held (on appeal) that this evidence was relevant to the issue whether the defendant *knew* that S was his daughter and that he was entitled to give any evidence relevant to that issue, including evidence of an admission by his first wife: *R. v. Carmichael* [1940] 1 K.B. 630, 27 Cr.App.R. 183, CCA.

(8) Incitement to incest of girls under 16

H-87   See the CLA 1977, s.54, *post*, H-239.

(9) Incest by a woman

(a) *Statute*

Sexual Offences Act 1956, s.11

H-88   **11.**—(1) It is an offence for a woman of the age of sixteen or over to permit a man whom she knows to be her grandfather, father, brother or son to have sexual intercourse with her by her consent.

(2) In the foregoing subsection "brother" includes half-brother, and for the purposes of that subsection any expression importing a relationship between two people shall be taken to apply notwithstanding that the relationship is not traced through lawful wedlock.

As to the meaning of "sexual intercourse", see *post*, H-219; as to the use of the words "woman" and "man", see *post*, H-222.

For anonymity provisions, see §§ 20-257 *et seq.* in the main work.

(b) *Indictment*

Statement of Offence

H-89   *Incest, contrary to section 11(1) of the Sexual Offences Act 1956.*

Particulars of Offence

A B, being a female person of the age of 18, on the _____ day of _____, 20__, with her consent permitted J N, whom she knew to be her father, to have sexual intercourse with her.

As to the form of the indictment, see also *R. v. Thompson, ante,* H-72.

(c) *Mode of trial and classification of offences*

H-90   This offence, and an attempt to commit it, are triable only on indictment: SOA 1956, s.37(2), and Sched. 2, para. 15(a), (b). As to the classification of offences, see *ante*, Appendix B-209.

(d) *Restriction on prosecution*

H-91   A prosecution for this offence or an attempt to commit it may not be commenced except by or with the consent of the DPP: SOA 1956, s.37(2), and Sched. 2, para. 15(a), (b).

(e) *Sentence*

H-92   The full offence: imprisonment not exceeding seven years—SOA 1956, s.37(3), and Sched. 2, para. 15(a).

Attempt: imprisonment not exceeding two years—*ibid.*, para. 15(b).

(f) *Effect of adoption*

H-93   The prohibition contained in section 11(1) applies notwithstanding the adoption of one of the parties: Adoption and Children Act 2002, s.74(1)(b) (as to which, see *ante*, H-84).

(g) *Ingredients of offence*

H-94   The common law presumption as to incapacity in relation to boys under 14 years of age (*ante*, H-13) had no application where a woman was charged with committing incest with such a boy: *R. v. Pickford* [1995] 1 Cr.App.R. 420, CA.

(10) Buggery

(a) *Introduction*

H-95   The SOA 1956 contains two "unnatural offences", namely buggery (with a person or with an animal) and gross indecency between men. There are time limits and requirements as to the consent of the DPP in respect of both offences in certain circumstances.

The SOA 1967 amended the law by providing, in particular, that consenting men over the age of 21 (reduced to 18 by the CJPOA 1994, and to 16 by the Sexual Offences (Amendment) Act 2000) who commit buggery or gross indecency in private, do not commit an offence (s.1, *post*, H-97). There are different rules regarding the lawfulness of procuration of buggery and gross indecency (s.4, *post*, H-236). Section 11(3) provides that section 46 of the 1956 Act (use of words "man", "boy" and other expressions) shall apply for the purposes of the provisions of the 1967 Act as it applies for the purposes of the provisions of that Act. For section 46, see *post*, H-222.

The CJPOA 1994 effected further changes in the law. Apart from reducing the age of consent for homosexual acts to 18 (*ante*), it redefined the offence of rape to include non-consensual anal intercourse with a man or a woman (*ante*, H-3). Non-consensual buggery should, therefore, be charged as rape. Consensual buggery between two people will not be an offence if the act takes place in private and both parties have achieved the age of 16.

As to the offences of indecent assault on a man and assault with intent to commit buggery, which may be on a man or a woman (categorised in the 1956 Act as "assault" offences rather than as "unnatural offences"), see sections 15, *post*, H-127, and 16, *post*, H-138.

(b) *Statute*

Sexual Offences Act 1956, s.12

12.—(1) It is an offence for a person to commit buggery with another person otherwise than in the **H-96** circumstances first described in subsection (1A) or (1AA) below or with an animal.

(1A) The circumstances referred to in subsection (1) are that the act of buggery takes place in private and both parties have attained the age of sixteen.

(1AA) The other circumstances so referred to are that the person is under the age of sixteen and the other person has attained that age.

(1B) An act of buggery by one man with another shall not be treated as taking place in private if it takes place—

(a) when more than two persons take part or are present; or

(b) in a lavatory to which the public have or are permitted to have access, whether on payment or otherwise.

(1C) In any proceedings against a person for buggery with another person it shall be for the prosecutor to prove that the act of buggery took place otherwise than in private or that one of the parties to it had not attained the age of sixteen.

(2), (3) [*Repealed by Police and Criminal Evidence Act 1984, Sched. 7.*]

[Subs. (1) is printed as amended by the CLA 1967, s.12(5)(a); the CJPOA 1994, s.143(1), (2); and the Sexual Offences (Amendment) Act 2000, s.2(1)(a) and (b); subss. (1A), (1B) and (1C) were inserted by the 1994 Act, s.143(1), (3); and are printed as amended by the 2000 Act, s.1(1); subs. (1AA) was inserted by the 2000 Act, s.2(1)(c).]

For anonymity provisions, see §§ 20-257 *et seq.* in the main work.

As to conspiracy or incitement to commit this offence, see *R. v. Boulton* (1871) 12 Cox 87.

Sexual Offences Act 1967, s.1

Amendment of law relating to homosexual acts in private

1.—(1) Notwithstanding any statutory or common law provision, ... **H-97**

(a) a homosexual act in private shall not be an offence provided that the parties consent thereto and have attained the age of sixteen years; and

(b) a homosexual act by any person shall not be an offence if he is under the age of sixteen and the other party has attained that age.

(2) An act which would otherwise be treated for the purposes of this Act as being done in private shall not be so treated if done—

(a) when more than two persons take part or are present; or

(b) in a lavatory to which the public have or are permitted to have access, whether on payment or otherwise.

(3) A man who is suffering from severe mental handicap cannot in law give any consent which, by virtue of subsection (1) of this section, would prevent a homosexual act from being an offence, but a

person shall not be convicted, on account of the incapacity of such a man to consent, of an offence consisting of such an act if he proves that he did not know and had no reason to suspect that man to be suffering from severe mental handicap.

(3A) In subsection (3) of this section "severe mental handicap" means a state of arrested or incomplete development of mind which includes severe impairment of intelligence and social functioning.

(4) Section 128 of the Mental Health Act 1959 (prohibition on men on the staff of a hospital, or otherwise having responsibility for mental patients, having sexual intercourse with women patients) shall have effect as if any reference therein to having unlawful sexual intercourse with a woman included a reference to committing buggery or an act of gross indecency with another man.

(5) [*Repealed by CJPOA 1994, s.168(3) and Sched. 11.*]

(6) It is hereby declared that where in any proceedings it is charged that a homosexual act is an offence the prosecutor shall have the burden of proving that the act was done otherwise than in private or otherwise than with the consent of the parties or that any of the parties had not attained the age of sixteen years.

(7) For the purposes of this section a man shall be treated as doing a homosexual act if, and only if, he commits buggery with another man or commits an act of gross indecency with another man or is a party to the commission by a man of such an act.

[This section is printed as amended and repealed in part by the Mental Health (Amendment) Act 1982, s.65(1), (2), and Scheds 3, para. 34, and 4; the CJPOA 1994, ss.146(1) and 168(3), and Sched. 11; and the Sexual Offences (Amendment) Act 2000, ss.1(2)(a) and 2(3)(a) and (b).]

As to the use of the word "man", see *post*, H-222.

For section 128 of the MHA 1959, see *post*, H-228.

(c) *Indictment for buggery with a person*

Statement of Offence

H-98 *Buggery, contrary to section 12(1) of the Sexual Offences Act 1956.*

Particulars of Offence

A B, a person of [or over] the age of 21 years, on the _____ day of _____, 20__, committed buggery with J N, a person under the age of 18 years.

Because the penalty provisions have the effect of creating a number of separate offences (see *post*, H-103), the particulars should be clear as to which offence is alleged; in the specimen set out above, it is a five year offence that is alleged. Alternative counts may be laid, where appropriate: see *R. v. Reakes* [1974] Crim.L.R. 615, CA.

As to the correct practice where old offences are charged, see *R. v. R.* [1993] Crim.L.R. 541, CA; *R. v. B., ibid.* As to the need for special caution where extremely old offences are alleged, *i.e.* dating back to the period prior to the passing of the SOA 1967 (July 27, 1967), see *R. v. D.* [1993] Crim.L.R. 542, CA.

As to the particulars which need to be averred on a charge of attempted buggery, see *R. v. D., ante.* The principles are the same as for the full offence.

(d) *Indictment for buggery with an animal (bestiality)*

Statement of Offence

H-99 *Buggery, contrary to section 12(1) of the Sexual Offences Act 1956.*

Particulars of Offence

A B, a person of [or over] the age of 21 years, on the _____ day of _____, 20__, committed buggery with a cow [or as the case may be].

(e) *Mode of trial and classification of offences*

H-100   This offence, and an attempt to commit it, are triable only on indictment: SOA 1956, s.37(2), and Sched. 2, para. 3(a), (b). As to the classification of offences, see *ante*, Appendix B-209.

(f) *Time limits*

Sexual Offences Act 1967, s.7

H-101   7.—(1) No proceedings for an offence to which this section applies shall be commenced after the expiration of twelve months from the date on which that offence was committed.

(2) This section applies to—

    (a) any offence under section 13 of the Act of 1956 (gross indecency between men);

    (b) [*repealed by Criminal Law Act 1977, Sched. 13*];

    (c) any offence of buggery by a man with another man not amounting to an assault on that other man and not being an offence by a man with a boy under the age of 16.

For section 13 of the 1956 Act, see *post*, H-107.

Where it was unclear upon the evidence given at the trial whether the offence charged had been committed within the 12 month period prior to the commencement of proceedings for the offence, the court quashed the conviction: *R. v. Lewis*, 68 Cr.App.R. 310, CA. A judge need not in every case to which section 7(1) applies direct the jury that they must be sure the offence was committed within the prescribed period. However, he must do so where an issue under the subsection is raised by the defence, or where it clearly arises on the evidence given at the trial: *ibid.*

(g) *Restriction on prosecutions*

Sexual Offences Act 1967, s.8

8. No proceedings shall be instituted except by or with the consent of the Director of Public **H-102** Prosecutions against any man for the offence of buggery with, or gross indecency with, another man … or for aiding, abetting, counselling, procuring or commanding its commission where either of those men was at the time of its commission under the age of sixteen.

[This section is printed as amended by the Sexual Offences (Amendment) Act 2000, s.1(2)(b); and as repealed in part by the Criminal Jurisdiction Act 1975, s.14(5), and Sched. 6, Pt I; and the Criminal Attempts Act 1981, s.10, and Sched., Pt I.]

Failure to obtain the consent of the DPP will lead to the quashing of the conviction: *R. v. Angel*, 52 Cr.App.R. 280, CA; *Secretary of State for Defence v. Warn* [1970] A.C. 394, HL (proceedings before court-martial).

Section 8 does not apply to proceedings under the Indecency with Children Act 1960 (*post*, H-230): CJA 1972, s.48.

(h) *Sentence*

Maximum

The full offence, or an attempt to commit it: if with a person under the age of 16 or with an **H-103** animal, life imprisonment; if the accused is of or over the age of 21 and the other person is under the age of 18, imprisonment not exceeding five years; otherwise, imprisonment not exceeding two years—SOA 1956, s.37(3), and Sched. 2, para. 3(a), (b) (as substituted by the CJPOA 1994, s.144(1), (2)). (For an offence of non-consensual buggery with a male over 15 committed before the commencement of the amendments effected by the 1994 Act (November 3, 1994), the maximum remains at 10 years: *Att.-Gen.'s Reference (No. 48 of 1994) (R. v. Jeffrey)*, 16 Cr.App.R.(S.) 980, CA.)

The effect of the different penalty provisions is to create distinct offences: see *R. v. Courtie* [1984] A.C. 463, HL.

Absence of consent not being an ingredient of the offence, it is not open to a judge to sentence on the basis that there was lack of consent; if lack of consent is alleged, there should be a charge of rape: *R. v. Davies* [1998] 1 Cr.App.R.(S.) 380, CA; *R. v. D. (Anthony)* [2000] 1 Cr.App.R.(S.) 120, CA.

Guidelines

The bracket of sentencing in cases of homosexual offences against boys with neither aggravat- **H-104** ing nor mitigating factors was set out in *R. v. Willis*, 60 Cr.App.R. 146, CA, as being from three to five years. The court in that case also identified the principal aggravating and mitigating features. In *R. v. A. and W.* [2001] 2 Cr.App.R. 18, CA, the court specifically said that the guidelines in *Willis* remained the starting point. In *R. v. Patterson* [2006] 2 Cr.App.R.(S.) 48, however, the Court of

Appeal said that sentences in historic cases of buggery should now be determined as if the offence were one of rape in accordance with the guidelines in *R. v. Millberry*; *R. v. Morgan*; *R. v. Lackenby* [2003] 1 Cr.App.R. 25, CA, instead of by reference to the *Willis* guidelines. The court said that it is important that the sentence should reflect the gravity of the offence rather than the particular label attached to it, and since there is no distinction in principle or in essential gravity made in the *Millberry* guidelines between rape of a male and rape of a female, it would be wrong for a sentence of buggery to be imposed on any other basis. This approach was taken further in *R. v. Kearns* [2009] 1 Cr.App.R.(S.) 107, CA, where it was applied to what was apparently a case of consensual buggery of a 15-year-old boy. For criticism of the *Patterson/Kearns* approach, see the commentaries at CLW/06/34/24 and CLW/09/16/8. Whilst this criticism remains valid, sentencers dealing with historic offending should now be guided, as to general principles, by the judgment of the Court of Appeal in *R. v. H.*, *ante*, H-12.

(i) *Ingredients of the offence*

H-105   The definition of the offence derives from the common law. It consists of sexual intercourse (*per anum—R. v. Jacobs* (1817) R. & R. 331) by man with man or, in the same manner, by man with woman (*R. v. Wiseman* (1718) Fortescue K.B. 91; Fost. 91), or by man or woman in any manner (*R. v. Bourne*, 36 Cr.App.R. 125, CCA) with beast (also referred to as bestiality): see 1 Hale 669; 1 Hawk. c. 4; 1 East P.C. 480; 1 Russ. Cr., 12th ed., 735. Once penetration is proved, both parties (if consenting) are equally guilty.

Penetration, without emission, is sufficient: *R. v. Reekspear* (1832) 1 Mood. 342.

As to the abolition of the common law presumption that a boy under 14 is incapable of sexual intercourse, see *ante*, H-13.

The offence of bestiality does not depend on consent but on the commission of a particular act: *R. v. Bourne*, *ante* (defendant convicted of aiding and abetting his wife to commit buggery with a dog, it being assumed that she would have been entitled to an acquittal on the ground of duress).

The following direction on the question of privacy (1967 Act, s.1, *ante*) has been approved by the Court of Appeal: "you look at all the circumstances, the time of night, the nature of the place including such matters as lighting and you consider further the likelihood of a third person coming upon the scene": *R. v. Reakes* [1974] Crim.L.R. 615.

In relation to subsection (3A) of section 1 of the 1967 Act, it is open to the prosecution to prove severe mental handicap without calling medical evidence but by inviting the jury to observe the behaviour and reactions of the complainant and to draw what they consider to be an appropriate inference: *R. v. Robbins* [1988] Crim.L.R. 744, CA.

(j) *Evidence*

H-106   The rule as to the admissibility of recent complaints was held to apply in the case of buggery with a youth of 19: *R. v. Wannell*, 17 Cr.App.R. 53, CCA.

(11) Gross indecency

(a) *Statute*

Sexual Offences Act 1956, s.13

H-107   **13.** It is an offence for a man to commit an act of gross indecency with another man otherwise than in the circumstances described below, whether in public or private, or to be a party to the commission by a man of an act of gross indecency with another man, or to procure the commission by a man of an act of gross indecency with another man.

The circumstances referred to above are that the man is under the age of sixteen and the other man has attained that age.

[This section is printed as amended by the Sexual Offences (Amendment) Act 2000, s.2(2)(a) and (b).]

Gross indecency is no longer an offence where the act takes place in private and both parties consent thereto and both have attained the age of 16: see SOA 1967, s.1 (as amended by the Sexual Offences (Amendment) Act 2000, s.1(2)(a)), *ante*, H-97.

Furthermore, it is not an offence under this section for a man to procure the commission by another man of an act of gross indecency with himself which by reason of section 1 of the 1967 Act is not an offence under this section: see section 4(3) of the 1967 Act, *post*, H-236. As to procuration of gross indecency, see further H-113, *post*.

As to the use of the word "man", see *post*, H-222.

(b) *Indictment*

Statement of Offence

Gross indecency, contrary to section 13 of the Sexual Offences Act 1956.   **H-108**

Particulars of Offence

A B, on the _____ day of _____, 20__, being a male person, committed an act of gross indecency with J N, a male person otherwise than in private [or with J N, a male person under the age of 18 years, namely, of the age of _____ years].

(c) *Mode of trial and classification of offences*

Offences contrary to section 13, and an attempt to procure the commission by a man of an act **H-109** of gross indecency with another man, are triable either way: MCA 1980, s.17(1), and Sched. 1 (§ 1-130 in the main work). As to the classification of offences, see *ante*, Appendix B-209.

(d) *Time limits and restrictions on prosecutions*

See *ante*, H-101, H-102.   **H-110**

(e) *Sentence*

Offences contrary to section 13: if by a man of or over the age of 21 with a man under the age **H-111** of 16, imprisonment not exceeding five years, otherwise two years—SOA 1956, s.37(3), and Sched. 2, para. 16(a) (as amended by the CJPOA 1994, s.144(1), (3), and the Sexual Offences (Amendment) Act 2000, s.1(1)).

An attempt to procure the commission by a man of an act of gross indecency with another man: as for the full offences—SOA 1956, s.37(3), and Sched. 2, para. 16(b) (as amended by the CJPOA 1994, s.144(1), (3), and the Sexual Offences (Amendment) Act 2000, s.1(1)).

Penalties on summary conviction are provided for by the MCA 1980, s.32 (§ 1-125 in the main work).

An attempt to commit any other offence than the one specifically provided for by the 1956 Act will be punishable in accordance with the Criminal Attempts Act 1981, ss.1 and 4 (§§ 33-128 *et seq.* in the main work).

(f) *Ingredients of the offences*

Gross indecency

If there is an agreement whereby two male persons act in concert to behave in a grossly **H-112** indecent manner, as, for example, to make a grossly indecent exhibition, the offence is committed even though there has been no actual physical contact: *R. v. Hunt*, 34 Cr.App.R. 135, CCA.

An offence of indecency between men is not committed unless both men participate in the indecency. "With another man" in section 13 cannot be construed as meaning "against" or "directed towards" a person who did not consent: *R. v. Preece and Howells* [1977] Q.B. 370, 63 Cr.App.R. 28, CA, and see *R. v. Hornby and Peaple*, 32 Cr.App.R. 1, CCA, and *R. v. Hunt, ante.*

Where two persons are jointly indicted for an offence under the section, one may be convicted and the other acquitted: *R. v. Jones* [1896] 1 Q.B. 4; *R. v. Pearce*, 35 Cr.App.R. 17, CCA; but see *R. v. Batten, The Times*, March 16, 1990, CA, where two men were charged with committing an act of gross indecency with each other. The jury convicted one defendant, but failed to agree in respect of the other and were discharged. The Court of Appeal quashed the conviction: the issue was the same in the case of both men and it was not a case where there was some evidence such as a confession, implicating one man but not the other. If both are to be convicted, it is important that the jury should be directed that, to establish the offence, it must be proved that there was an act of gross indecency by the one defendant with the other and that the two defendants were acting in concert: *R. v. Hornby and Peaple, ante.*

A conviction for attempting to commit an act of gross indecency may be maintained where one of the persons implicated alone has been charged and the other has not been charged but has been called as a witness for the prosecution and swears that he did not consent to any act of indecency: *R. v. Pearce, ante.*

Procuring gross indecency

H-113   It is an offence within section 13 for a male person to procure the commission with himself of an act of gross indecency by another male person: *R. v. Jones, ante*; *R. v. Cope*, 16 Cr.App.R. 77, CCA. But, if the act itself is not an offence by virtue of section 1 of the SOA 1967, the procuration thereof will not be an offence either: *ibid.*, s.4(3). See *ante*, H-97, and *post*, H-236.

If a male person persuades, or attempts to persuade, a boy to handle him indecently, such person alone may be charged and convicted under this section. In a case where indecent assault may be difficult or impossible to prove, because no threat or hostile act by the defendant towards the boy can easily be established, the proper charge is that of procuring or attempting to procure (as the case may be) an act of gross indecency with the defendant himself: *R. v. Burrows*, 35 Cr.App.R. 180, CCA.

On a charge of incitement to procure an act of gross indecency, it is not necessary that there should be, at the time of the incitement, an ascertained person with whom the act was to be committed: *R. v. Bentley* [1923] 1 K.B. 403, CCA.

As to the meaning of "procure", see also *post*, H-171.

Attempting to procure an act of gross indecency

H-114   Procuring the commission of an act of gross indecency under section 13 of the 1956 Act is itself a substantive offence. Section 1(4)(b) of the Criminal Attempts Act 1981 (§ 33-128 in the main work) does not preclude the charging of an attempt to procure an act of gross indecency under section 1(1) of the 1981 Act because section 1(4)(b) applies in circumstances when the alleged procurement is additional to and not part of the substantive offence: *Chief Constable of Hampshire v. Mace*, 84 Cr.App.R. 40, DC. (The penalty for such attempt is specifically provided for by the 1956 Act: see *ante*, H-111.)

What conduct will be sufficient to constitute an attempt will depend on the application of the formula in section 1(1) of the 1981 Act: was what was done "more than merely preparatory to the commission of the offence"?

Authorities decided prior to the 1981 Act can be no more than illustrative: see *R. v. Cope, ante*; *R. v. Woods*, 22 Cr.App.R. 41, CCA; *R. v. Miskell*, 37 Cr.App.R. 214, Ct-MAC.

(g) *Evidence*

Guilty plea by one defendant

H-115   See *R. v. Mattison* [1990] Crim.L.R. 117, CA (§ 9-90 in the main work).

Recent complaint

H-116   The rule as to admissibility of recent complaints was held not to apply to this offence on the ground that consent of the other male person is immaterial: *R. v. Hoodless*, 64 J.P. 282.

(12) Indecent assault on a woman

(a) *Statute*

Sexual Offences Act 1956, s.14

Indecent assault on a woman
H-117   **14.**—(1) It is an offence, subject to the exception mentioned in subsection (3) of this section, for a person to make an indecent assault on a woman.

(2) A girl under the age of sixteen cannot in law give any consent which would prevent an act being an assault for the purposes of this section.

(3) Where a marriage is invalid under section two of the Marriage Act 1949, or section one of the Age of Marriage Act 1929 (the wife being a girl under the age of sixteen), the invalidity does not make the husband guilty of any offence under this section by reason of her incapacity to consent while under that age, if he believes her to be his wife and has reasonable cause for the belief.

(4) A woman who is a defective cannot in law give any consent which would prevent an act being an assault for the purposes of this section, but a person is only to be treated as guilty of an indecent assault on a defective by reason of that incapacity to consent, if that person knew or had reason to suspect her to be a defective.

As to the use of the words "woman" and "girl", see *post*, H-222.

As to the meaning of "defective", see *ante*, H-68.

For the Marriage Act 1949, s.2, see *ante*, H-51.

For the burden of proof of exceptions, see section 47 of the 1956 Act, *post*, H-225.

For anonymity provisions, see *post*, §§ 20-257 *et seq.* in the main work.

(b) *Indictment*

Statement of Offence

Indecent assault, contrary to section 14(1) of the Sexual Offences Act 1956. **H-118**

Particulars of Offence

A B, on the _____ day of _____, 20__, indecently assaulted J N, a woman.

Age is not an essential ingredient of, nor an essential averment in, the framing of a count under section 14(1): *R. v. Hodgson* [1973] Q.B. 565, 57 Cr.App.R. 502, CA. As to the need, however, to specify the age of the girl in certain old cases, see *post*, H-120.

Where the prosecution case leaves it open to the jury to convict on either of two distinct factual bases, it will be necessary for the judge to direct them as to the need for unanimity as to the basis of any verdict of guilty: see *R. v. Turner* [2000] Crim.L.R. 325, CA, and *R. v. D.* [2001] 1 Cr.App.R. 13, CA.

In *R. v. J.* [2005] 1 A.C. 562, HL, it was held that, on a true construction of the SOA 1956, it is impermissible to prosecute a charge of indecent assault under section 14(1) in circumstances where the only conduct upon which that charge was based was an act of unlawful sexual intercourse with a girl under the age of 16 in respect of which no prosecution might be commenced under section 6(1) (*ante*, H-50) by virtue of the time bar of 12 months contained in section 37(2) of, and Schedule 2, para. 10, to, the Act (as to which, see *ante*, H-55). Their Lordships held that the court was under a duty to give effect to a statute which was plain and unambiguous; it must have been intended that the prohibition in paragraph 10 would have some meaningful effect, otherwise there would have been no possible purpose in prohibiting prosecution under section 6 after a lapse of 12 months if exactly the same conduct could thereafter be prosecuted, with exposure to the same penalty (at the time of enactment), under section 14; but this did not prevent a prosecution being properly founded on independent acts other than sexual intercourse itself or conduct inherent in or forming part of it. As to the effect of this decision in relation to indecent assault as a possible alternative verdict on a charge of rape, see the cases cited at H-9, *ante*.

(c) *Mode of trial and class of offence*

This offence is triable either way: MCA 1980, s.17(1), and Sched. 1 (§ 1-130 in the main work). **H-119** As to the classification of offences, see *ante*, Appendix B-209.

(d) *Sentence*

Imprisonment, not exceeding 10 years: SOA 1956, s.37, and Sched. 2, para. 17 (as amended by **H-120** the SOA 1985, s.3(3)). The 1985 amendment took effect on September 16, 1985: prior to that, the maximum penalty was two years' imprisonment, save where the girl was under 13 and was so stated in the indictment, in which case the maximum was five years' imprisonment. In relation to cases where the facts date back beyond September 16, 1985, see *R. v. R.* [1993] Crim.L.R. 541, CA; *R. v. B.*, *ibid.*

Where a defendant charged with rape of a girl under 16 is acquitted of rape, but convicted of indecent assault on the basis that consent is no defence, the sentence should not exceed the maximum for an offence of unlawful sexual intercourse with a girl under 16 (as to which, see *ante*, H-56): *R. v. Iles* [1998] 2 Cr.App.R.(S.) 63, CA.

The fact that the victim had been abused on a previous occasion does not reduce, but might increase, the gravity of further offending by an adult thereafter. If, however, by reason of being corrupted or precocious, or both, the victim instigated offences against herself, that was an aspect which the judge was entitled to take into account. But it was mitigation only in a negative sense, namely that the child was not being treated in a way which she was personally resisting or found repugnant: *Att.-Gen.'s Reference (No. 36 of 1995) (R. v. Dawson)* [1996] 2 Cr.App.R.(S.) 50, CA.

There is no sentencing principle which precludes the imposition of a custodial sentence on a first conviction of a persistent indecent assault (on a female on an underground train): *R. v. Townsend*, 16 Cr.App.R.(S.) 553, CA, *R. v. Tanyildiz* [1998] 1 Cr.App.R.(S.) 362, CA, and *R. v. Diallo* [2000] 1 Cr.App.R.(S.) 426, CA (not following *R. v. Neem*, 14 Cr.App.R.(S.) 18, CA).

Cases decided prior to the increase in the statutory maximum effected by the SOA 1985 could not be regarded as authoritative in relation to the tariff after the increase; the conclusion in *R. v. Demel* [1997] 2 Cr.App.R.(S.) 5, CA, that the upper end of the tariff for a single incident involving a breach of trust following a trial was in the range of 13 to 18 months' imprisonment should not be followed as the authorities relied on were decided in relation to a different statutory framework or had been decided without apparent appreciation of the effect of the 1985 Act: *R. v. L.* [1999] 1 Cr.App.R. 117, CA (two years' imprisonment following trial for "grave" breach of trust by 52-year-old man on nine-year-old girl upheld; declining to issue guidelines, but observing that in most cases the personal circumstances of the offender would have to take second place to the duty of the court to protect victims). See also *R. v. Wellman* [1999] 2 Cr.App.R.(S.) 162, CA.

For cases of indecent assault, see CSP B4–6.

As to the non-applicability of the Sentencing Guidelines Council's guideline on sexual offences to offences under the 1956 Act, see *Att.-Gen.'s Reference (No. 78 of 2010)* [2011] 2 Cr.App.R.(S.) 109, CA (pointing out that offences under the SOA 2003 are differently defined and have different (more severe) maximum penalties); but see *R. v. H.*, *ante*, H-12, as to the approach to sentencing for historic offences generally.

In *R. v. Clifford* [2015] 1 Cr.App.R.(S.) 32, CA, the appellant (71/ no convictions) was convicted on eight counts of indecent assault, contrary to section 14(1) of the 1956 Act, in respect of four victims, in relation to offences committed between 1977 and 1984 when the statutory maximum was two years' imprisonment. It was held (considering *R. v. H.*, *ante*) that the judge had been entitled in the course of his sentencing remarks to observe that some of the offending would now be charged as rape or assault by penetration, and had been entitled to impose consecutive sentences to reflect the overall criminality involved according to modern standards and attitudes (as reflected in the Sentencing Council for England and Wales's guideline on sexual offences (*post*, Appendix K-84 *et seq.*)). However, the judge had been wrong to take into account when passing sentence the appellant's assertions of innocence (which did not directly impugn the victims (by way of distinction from *Att.-Gen.'s Reference (No. 38 of 2013) (R. v. Hall)* [2014] 1 Cr.App.R.(S.) 61, CA)), his vehement complaints about the fact that the victims were entitled to anonymity, and the fact that he had stood behind a television reporter on camera outside the court, mimicking the reporter's actions (where there was no evidence that the victims were aware of this conduct and the matter had not been dealt with as a contempt of court).

(e) *Ingredients of the offence*

General

H-121   For a full exposition of the elements of the offence, see *R. v. Court* [1989] A.C. 28, HL.

    (a) Most indecent assaults will be clearly of a sexual nature. Some may have only sexual undertones. The jury must decide whether "right-minded persons would consider the conduct indecent or not". The test is whether what occurred was so offensive to contemporary standards of modesty and privacy as to be indecent.

    (b) If the circumstances of the assault are *incapable* of being regarded as indecent, then the undisclosed intention of the accused could not make the assault an indecent one: see *R. v. George* [1956] Crim.L.R. 52, Assizes (Streatfeild J.).

(c) The victim need not be aware of the circumstances of indecency or apprehended indecency.

(d) Cases which ordinarily present no problem are those in which the facts, *devoid of explanation*, will give rise to the irresistible inference that the defendant intended to assault his victim in a manner which right-minded persons would clearly think was indecent. Where the circumstances are such as only to be *capable* of constituting an indecent assault, in order to determine whether or not right-minded persons might think that the assault was indecent the following factors are relevant:

  (i) the relationship of the defendant to the victim (relative, friend, stranger);

  (ii) how the defendant had come to embark on this conduct and why he was so behaving. Such information helps a jury to answer the vital question: are we sure that the defendant not only intended to commit an assault but an assault which was indecent? Any evidence which tends to explain the reason for the defendant's conduct is relevant to establish whether or not he intended to commit not only an assault but an indecent one.

(e) The prosecution must prove: (i) that the accused intentionally assaulted the victim; (ii) that the assault, or the assault and the circumstances accompanying it, are capable of being considered by right-minded persons as indecent; and (iii) that the accused intended to commit such an assault as is referred to in (ii) above.

The above propositions are founded upon Lord Ackner's speech (at p.36), with which the other members of the House concurred, except Lord Goff, who dissented from the decision. It follows that no offence will be committed where the man believes that the woman is consenting to his conduct, whether his belief is based on reasonable grounds or not: this was the effect of the earlier Court of Appeal decision in *R. v. Kimber*, 77 Cr.App.R. 225.

R. v. Court was considered in *R. v. C.* [1992] Crim.L.R. 642, CA, in which it was held that where an assault was indecent in itself, it was unnecessary to establish a specific indecent intent. In *Court*, the issue of whether or not what had occurred amounted to an indecent assault turned on motive and, therefore, specific intent had been necessary to the verdict. Where there was no question whether what had occurred was indecent or not, the basic intent of assault was sufficient. The law before *Court* remained the law and indecent assault remained an offence of basic intent; self-induced voluntary intoxication is not a defence. See also *DPP v. H.* [1992] C.O.D. 266, an earlier decision of the Divisional Court to the same effect.

Court and *George, ante*, were referred to in *R. v. Price* [2004] 1 Cr.App.R. 12, CA, in which it was held that stroking a woman's legs over trousers and below the knee was capable of amounting to an indecent assault.

In *R. v. Kumar* (2006) 150 S.J. 1053, CA, it was said that whilst *Court* was authority for the proposition that a doctor who obtained sexual satisfaction from a necessary medical examination properly conducted was not guilty of indecent assault where the prosecution case was limited to an allegation that he had carried out a medical examination in appropriate circumstances but in an inappropriate way and as a cloak for his own sexual gratification, where the issue had been as to the manner in which the defendant had carried out the examination (*i.e.* in an appropriate way in the presence of a chaperon or in an inappropriate way in the absence of a chaperon), there had been no need to direct the jury as to the remote theoretical possibility suggested in *Court*.

Person

A woman may be guilty of an offence under this section: *R. v. Hare* [1934] 1 K.B. 354, 24   **H-122** Cr.App.R. 108, CCA.

Assault

As to this, see generally, §§ 19-221 *et seq.* in the main work.   **H-123**

In *Fairclough v. Whipp*, 35 Cr.App.R. 138, DC, the respondent exposed himself in the presence of a girl aged nine and invited her to touch his exposed person, which she did. *Held*, an invitation to another person to touch the invitor could not amount to an assault on the invitee, and that therefore there had been no assault and consequently no indecent assault by the respondent: applied in *DPP v. Rogers*, 37 Cr.App.R. 137, DC; and *R. v. Dunn* [2015] 2 Cr.App.R 13, CA; but *cf. Beal v. Kelley*, 35 Cr.App.R. 128, DC, and *R. v. Sargeant*, 161 J.P. 127, CA, *post*, H-133. See also *R.*

v. Sutton, 66 Cr.App.R. 21, CA, *post*, H-134, and the Indecency with Children Act 1960, *post*, H-230 *et seq.*

If a man inserts his finger into the vagina of a girl under 16, this is an indecent assault, however willing or co-operative the girl may be: *R. v. McCormack* [1969] 2 Q.B. 442, 53 Cr.App.R. 514, CA.

Consent

H-124   If the person assaulted is under 16, her consent is no defence: SOA 1956, s.14(2) (*ante*, H-117).

Where the woman's consent was procured by fraud as to the nature (*R. v. Case* (1850) 4 Cox 220) or quality (*R. v. Tabassum* [2000] 2 Cr.App.R. 328, CA) of the act, such consent constitutes no defence. See also § 19-233 in the main work, and *ante*, H-17.

Where a jury asked for the difference between consent and submission to be defined, it was not incumbent on the judge to direct the jury that reluctant acquiescence amounted to consent; it was for the jury to decide whether there was consent and their good sense and experience should lead them to the right conclusion: *R. v. McAllister* [1997] Crim.L.R. 233, CA (*cf. R. v. Olugboja*, 73 Cr.App.R. 344, CA, *ante*, H-16).

Consent cannot be a defence where the indecent assault consists in the infliction of blows intended or likely to cause bodily harm: *R. v. Donovan* [1934] 2 K.B. 498, 25 Cr.App.R. 1, CCA; approved and applied by the House of Lords in *R. v. Brown (Anthony)* [1994] 1 A.C. 212. (As to *Brown*, see also § 19-233 in the main work.) *Donovan* was also referred to in *R. v. Boyea* [1992] Crim.L.R. 574, CA, in which it was held that an assault which was intended or likely to cause bodily harm, and which was accompanied by indecency, constituted the offence of indecent assault regardless of consent, provided that the injury was not "transient or trifling". However, the tribunal of fact must take account of changing social attitudes, particularly in the field of sexual relations between adults. As a generality, the level of vigour in sexual congress which was generally acceptable, and therefore the voluntarily accepted risk of incurring some injury was probably higher now than in 1934, when *Donovan* was decided. It followed that the phrase "transient or trifling" must be understood in the light of current conditions. *Boyea* was approved in *Brown (Anthony)*, *ante*. (See also *R. v. Wilson (A.)* [1996] 2 Cr.App.R. 241, CA (§ 19-235 in the main work).)

Bona fide belief as to age of girl

H-125   Where the complainant was under the age of 16 at the time of the alleged offence, the defendant's genuine belief that she was in fact 16 or over at the time will negative criminal liability if the complainant in fact consented or the defendant genuinely believed that she was consenting: *R. v. K.* [2002] 1 A.C. 462, HL.

Indecent assault within marriage

H-126   A man may be guilty of indecent assault upon his wife: *R. v. Kowalski*, 86 Cr.App.R. 339, CA.

(13) Indecent assault on a man

(a) *Statute*

Sexual Offences Act 1956, s.15

H-127   **15.**—(1) It is an offence for a person to make an indecent assault on a man.

(2) A boy under the age of sixteen cannot in law give any consent which would prevent an act being an assault for the purposes of this section.

(3) A man who is a defective cannot in law give any consent which would prevent an act being an assault for the purposes of this section, but a person is only to be treated as guilty of an indecent assault on a defective by reason of that incapacity to consent, if that person knew or had reason to suspect him to be a defective.

(4), (5) [*Repealed by Police and Criminal Evidence Act 1984, Sched. 7.*]

As to the use of the words "man" and "boy", see *post*, H-222.

As to the meaning of "defective", see *ante*, H-68.

For anonymity provisions, see §§ 20-257 *et seq.* in the main work.

(b) *Indictment*

Statement of Offence

Indecent assault on male person, contrary to section 15(1) of the Sexual Offences Act 1956.

Particulars of Offence

A B, on the _____ day of _____, 20__, indecently assaulted J N, a male person.

In practice, the age of the alleged victim, if he was under the age of 16, was usually averred.

(c) *Mode of trial and class of offence*

This offence is triable either way: MCA 1980, s.17(1), and Sched. 1 (§ 1-130 in the main work). **H-129**
As to the classification of offences, see *ante*, Appendix B-209.

(d) *Sentence*

Imprisonment not exceeding 10 years: SOA 1956, s.37(3), and Sched. 2, para. 18. **H-130**
As to the approach to sentencing for historic offences, see *R. v. H., ante*, H-12.

(e) *Ingredients of the offence*

General

See *R. v. Court* and *R. v. C., ante*, H-121, which, it is submitted, apply equally to this offence. **H-131**

Person

A woman may be guilty of this offence: *R. v. Hare, ante*, H-122. **H-132**

Assault

As to assaults generally, see §§ 19-221 *et seq.* in the main work. **H-133**

An offence under section 15 is committed when a woman immediately prior to having sexual intercourse with a 14-year-old boy holds his penis. The act alleged to constitute the assault is an indecent act, consent is therefore no defence (s.15(2)—see *R. v. Sutton*, 66 Cr.App.R. 21, CA): *Faulkner v. Talbot*, 74 Cr.App.R. 1, DC.

Semble, an allegation of sexual intercourse by a woman with a boy under 16, *per se* connotes an allegation of indecent assault: see *R. v. McCormack* [1969] 2 Q.B. 442, 53 Cr.App.R. 514, CA; *Faulkner v. Talbot, ante.*

If there is an assault committed in circumstances of indecency, then there need not be an indecent touching: see *Beal v. Kelly*, 35 Cr.App.R. 128, DC (when boy refused to touch defendant's penis when asked to do so, defendant pulled boy towards him, but let him go); and *R. v. Sargeant*, 161 J.P. 127, CA (grabbed boy, then used threat of further force to compel boy to masturbate himself). *Cf. Fairclough v. Whipp, ante*, H-123.

In order to constitute an assault against a child under 16, the act complained of either must **H-134** itself be inherently indecent or it must be one that is hostile or threatening or an act which the child is demonstrably reluctant to accept (see *DPP v. Rogers*, 37 Cr.App.R. 137, DC, and *Williams v. Gibbs* [1958] Crim.L.R. 127, DC). Although sections 14(2) and 15(2) of the 1956 Act bar the child's consent from preventing an act being an indecent assault, consent does avail to prevent the act being an assault if the act is not inherently indecent. The proper course where there is an act which could not conceivably be called an assault but which takes place in an indecent situation, is to prosecute under the Indecency with Children Act 1960 (*post*, H-230 *et seq.*): *R. v. Sutton*, 66 Cr.App.R. 21, CA. The defendant photographed partially clothed and unclothed boys, intending to sell the photographs to magazines. In order to arrange poses, he touched the boys on the hands, legs and torso; the actions were not threatening or hostile and the boys consented to them. His convictions under section 15(1) were quashed: touching merely to indicate a pose was not of itself indecent and was consented to. Consent did therefore avail to prevent the acts having been assaults and the question of indecency did not arise.

Consent

H-135   Consent is a defence as it negatives the assault: see *R. v. Wollaston* (1872) 12 Cox 180, CCR. See also *ante*, H-124.

A boy under the age of 16 cannot in law give any consent which would prevent an act being an assault for the purposes of the section: s.15(2), *ante*, H-127; but see the cases cited in the previous paragraph.

Bona fide belief as to age of boy

H-136   See *R. v. K.* [2002] 1 A.C. 462, HL, *ante*, H-125; and *R. v. Fernandez, The Times,* June 26, 2002, CA (confirming that the decision of the House of Lords applies equally to this offence).

(f) Evidence

H-137   The rule as to the admissibility of recent complaints (§§ 8-207 *et seq.* in the main work) was held to apply in the case of an indecent assault upon a boy of 15: *R. v. Camelleri* [1922] 2 K.B. 122, 16 Cr.App.R. 162, CCA.

(14) Assault with intent to commit buggery

(a) Statute

Sexual Offences Act 1956, s.16

H-138   **16.**—(1) It is an offence for a person to assault another person with intent to commit buggery.
(2)–(3) *[Repealed by Police and Criminal Evidence Act 1984, Sched. 7.]*

As to the offence of buggery, see *ante*, H-96 *et seq.*
As to assault, see generally, §§ 19-221 *et seq.* in the main work.
For anonymity provisions, see §§ 20-257 *et seq.* in the main work.

(b) Indictment

Statement of Offence

H-139   *Assault with intent to commit buggery, contrary to section 16(1) of the Sexual Offences Act 1956.*

Particulars of Offence

A B, on the _____ day of _____, 20__, assaulted J N with intent to commit buggery with the said J N.

(c) Mode of trial and class of offence

H-140   This offence is triable only on indictment: SOA 1956, s.37(2), and Sched. 2, para. 19. As to the classification of offences, see *ante*, Appendix B-209.

(d) Sentence

H-141   Imprisonment not exceeding 10 years: SOA 1956, s.37(3), and Sched. 2, para. 19.

(e) Effect of Criminal Justice and Public Order Act 1994

H-142   It seems that no thought could have been given to the effect on this offence of the redefinition of rape to include non-consensual anal intercourse. The logical solution would have been to substitute "rape" for "buggery" at the end of subsection (1). The offence consisting of an assault allied to a specific intent suggests non-consensual buggery, but because of the bizarre nature of the amendments to section 12, not all nonconsensual buggery (*e.g.* both parties over 18 and the act takes place in private) constitutes the *offence* of buggery, although it will always be rape. It is submitted that the proper interpretation is that an offence under section 16 is committed where there is an assault accompanied by the requisite intent regardless of whether or not the act itself, if completed, would constitute the offence of buggery. This does, of course, lead to anomalous results; it would be an offence contrary to this provision to assault a woman intending to have anal intercourse with her but it would not be an offence to do so intending to have vaginal intercourse, although both acts, if completed, would constitute rape. The alternative interpretation would be to confine the offence to the commission of an assault with intent to commit buggery in circumstances which would make the act, if completed, an offence contrary to section 12. Because of the assault ingredient, this would effectively confine the offence to assaults on persons under 18. This seems to be an unwarranted restriction of the scope of the offence; Parliament having, if anything, deemed non-consensual buggery to be a more serious offence than it was previously, it would be an extremely curious result of the legislation if someone who committed an assault with the intention of committing that more serious offence should no longer be guilty of an offence under section 16.

As to whether there was a common law offence of assault with intent to rape, see *ante*, H-10.

(15) Abduction of woman by force or for the sake of her property

(a) *Statute*

Sexual Offences Act 1956, s.17

17.—(1) It is an offence for a person to take away or detain a woman against her will with the   **H-143**
intention that she shall marry or have unlawful sexual intercourse with that or any other person, if she is so taken away or detained either by force or for the sake of her property or expectations of property.

(2) In the foregoing subsection, the reference to a woman's expectations of property relates only to property of a person to whom she is next of kin or one of the next of kin, and "property" includes any interest in property.

[This section is printed as effectively amended by the CLA 1967, s.12(5)(a).]

As to the meaning of "sexual intercourse", see *post*, H-219; as to the use of the word "woman", see *post*, H-222.

(b) *Indictment*

Statement of Offence

Abduction, contrary to section 17(1) of the Sexual Offences Act 1956.   **H-144**

Particulars of Offence

A B, on the _____ day of _____, 20__, took away [or *detained*] *J N against her will and by force* [or *for the sake of her property or expectations of property*] *with the intention that she should have unlawful sexual intercourse with him the said A B or with another* [or *with the intention that she should marry him the said A B or another*].

(c) *Mode of trial and class of offence*

This offence is triable on indictment only: SOA 1956, s.37(2), and Sched. 2, para. 4. As to the   **H-145**
classification of offences, see *ante*, Appendix B-209.

(d) *Sentence*

Imprisonment not exceeding 14 years: SOA 1956, s.37(3), and Sched. 2, para. 4.   **H-146**

(e) *Ingredients of the offence*

As to the meaning of "unlawful" sexual intercourse, see *ante*, H-38.   **H-147**

If the woman is taken away with her own consent, but afterwards refuses to continue further with the offender, and is forcibly detained by him, this is within the statute: see 1 Hawk. c.41 (*Forcible Marriage*), s.7.

(16) Abduction of unmarried girl under 18 from parent or guardian

(a) *Statute*

Sexual Offences Act 1956, s.19

19.—(1) It is an offence, subject to the exception mentioned in this section, for a person to take an   **H-148**

unmarried girl under the age of eighteen out of the possession of her parent or guardian against his will, if she is taken with the intention that she shall have unlawful sexual intercourse with men or with a particular man.

(2) A person is not guilty of an offence under this section because he takes such a girl out of the possession of her parent or guardian as mentioned above, if he believes her to be of the age of eighteen or over and has reasonable cause for the belief.

(3) In this section "guardian" means any person having the parental responsibility for or care of the girl.

[This section is printed as amended by the Children Act 1989, s.108(4), and Sched. 12, para. 11.]

As to the meaning of "sexual intercourse", see *post*, H-219; as to the use of the words "girl" and "man", see *post*, H-222; as to the meaning of "parental responsibility", see *post*, H-224.

For the burden of proof of exceptions, see section 47 of the 1956 Act, *post*, H-225.

(b) *Indictment*

Statement of Offence

H-149   *Abduction of girl, contrary to section 19(1) of the Sexual Offences Act 1956.*

Particulars of Offence

A B, on the _____ day of _____, 20__, unlawfully took or caused to be taken J N, an unmarried girl under the age of 18, out of the possession and against the will of her father [or mother or of C D then having parental responsibility for or care of her] with an intent unlawfully to have sexual intercourse with her [or that she should have unlawful sexual intercourse with E F or generally].

(c) *Mode of trial and class of offence*

H-150   This offence is triable on indictment only: SOA 1956, s.37(2), and Sched. 2, para. 20. As to the classification of offences, see *ante*, Appendix B-209.

(d) *Sentence*

H-151   Imprisonment not exceeding two years: SOA 1956, s.37(3), and Sched. 2, para. 20.

(e) *Ingredients of the offence*

H-152   For the evidence necessary to support this indictment, see *post*, H-157 *et seq.*, *mutatis mutandis*.

As to the meaning of "unlawful" sexual intercourse, see *ante*, H-38.

Upon an indictment under this section for taking a girl out of the possession of her father, it was proved that at the time of the commission of the alleged offence she was employed by another person as barmaid at a distance from her father's home. It was held that she was under the lawful charge of her employer and not in the possession of her father, and that therefore the defendant could not be convicted of the offence with which he was charged: *R. v. Henkers* (1886) 16 Cox 257. The age of the girl must be proved by the prosecution, as *ante*, H-49. The presumption of the CYPA 1933, s.99, does not apply to this offence: see the proviso to Schedule 1 to the 1933 Act (as to which see *ante*, H-49).

(17) Abduction of unmarried girl under 16 from parent or guardian

(a) *Statute*

Sexual Offences Act 1956, s.20

H-153   **20.**—(1) It is an offence for a person acting without lawful authority or excuse to take an unmarried girl under the age of sixteen out of the possession of her parent or guardian against his will.

(2) In the foregoing subsection "guardian" means any person having parental responsibility for or care of the girl.

[This section is printed as amended by the Children Act 1989, s.108(4), and Sched. 12, para. 12.]

As to the use of the word "girl", see *post*, H-222; as to the meaning of "parental responsibility", see *post*, H-224.

See now section 2 of the Child Abduction Act 1984 (§ 19-397 in the main work) which covers much the same ground and is not limited to the abduction of girls.

(b) *Indictment*

Statement of Offence

Abduction of a girl, contrary to section 20(1) of the Sexual Offences Act 1956. **H-154**

Particulars of Offence

A B, on the _____ day of _____, 20__, unlawfully took or caused to be taken J N, an unmarried girl aged 14, out of the possession and against the will of her father [or mother or of E F then having parental responsibility for or care of her].

(c) *Mode of trial and class of offence*

This offence is triable on indictment only: SOA 1956, s.37(2), and Sched. 2, para. 21. As to the **H-155** classification of offences, see *ante*, Appendix B-209.

(d) *Sentence*

Imprisonment not exceeding two years: SOA 1956, s.37(3), and Sched. 2, para. 21. **H-156**

(e) *Ingredients of the offence*

That the girl was in the possession of her father, etc.

This is a question for the jury: *R. v. Mace*, 50 J.P. 776. A girl will still be in the possession of her **H-157** parent/guardian even while she is away from home if she intends to return; and if, when so out of the house, the defendant induces her to run away with him, he is guilty: *R. v. Mycock* (1871) 12 Cox 28. See also *R. v. Baillie* (1859) 8 Cox 238; *R. v. Green* (1862) 3 F. & F. 274; and *R. v. Miller* (1876) 13 Cox 179.

The taking

The taking need not be by force, either actual or constructive, and it is immaterial whether the **H-158** girl consents or not: *R. v. Manktelow* (1853) 6 Cox 143, and see *R. v. Kipps* (1850) 4 Cox 167; *R. v. Booth* (1872) 12 Cox 231; and *R. v. Robins* (1844) 1 C. & K. 456 (where the girl positively encouraged the defendant).

The words "taking out of the possession and against the will" of the parent mean some conduct amounting to a substantial interference with the possessory relationship of parent and child: *R. v. Jones (J.W.)* [1973] Crim.L.R. 621 (Swanwick J.)—attempt to take girls (aged 10) for a walk with a view to indecently assaulting them held not to constitute an attempt to commit the offence. (*Cf. R. v. Leather*, 98 Cr.App.R. 179, CA, decided on the Child Abduction Act 1984 (§ 19-398 in the main work).)

It is no defence that the defendant acted in concert with the girl and had no intention of keeping her away from her home permanently: *R. v. Timmins* (1860) 8 Cox 401; *R. v. Frazer and Norman, ibid.* at 446. See also *R. v. Baillie, ibid.* at 238.

Instead of a taking, it can be shown that a girl left her parent or guardian, in consequence of some persuasion, inducement or blandishment held out to her by the defendant: *R. v. Henkers* (1886) 16 Cox 257, following *R. v. Olifier* (1866) 10 Cox 402.

Where a man induces a girl, by promise of what he will do for her, to leave her father's house **H-159** and live with him, he may be convicted, although he is not actually present or assisting her at the time when she leaves her father's roof: *R. v. Robb* (1864) 4 F. & F. 59. If the girl leaves her father, without any persuasion, inducement or blandishment held out to her by the defendant, so that she has got fairly away from home, and then goes to him, although it may be his moral duty to return her to her father's custody, yet his not doing so is no infringement of this statute, for the statute does not say he shall restore, but only that he shall not take her away: *R. v. Olifier, ante,* and this is so even though it be proved that before she so left he had taken her about to places of amusement and had intercourse with her: *R. v. Kauffman*, 68 J.P. 189. If the suggestion to go away with the defendant comes from the girl only, and he takes merely the passive part of yielding to her suggestion, he is entitled to an acquittal: *R. v. Jarvis* (1903) 20 Cox 249. It is submitted that the ruling to the contrary in *R. v. Biswell* (1847) 2 Cox 279 is not law. For a discussion of the authorities, see *R. v. Mackney* (1903) 29 Vict.L.R. 22, where the English cases are considered.

Against the will, etc.

H-160   If the defendant induced the parents, by false and fraudulent representations, to allow him to take the child away, this is an abduction: *R. v. Hopkins* (1842) C. & Mar. 254.

Where the girl's mother had encouraged her in a lax course of life, by permitting her to go out alone at night and dance at public-houses, from one of which she went away with the defendant, Cockburn C.J. ruled that she could not be said to be taken away against her mother's will: *R. v. Primelt* (1858) 1 F. & F. 50.

To prove this element of the offence, it has been said that the parent or guardian must be called: *R. v. Nash, The Times,* July 2, 1903. *Sed quaere.*

Under 16, etc.

H-161   Prove that she was under the age of 16 years and unmarried. As to the power of a court to presume her age from her appearance, see the CYPA 1933, s.99(2) (§ 19-412 in the main work) and Sched. 1 (§ 19-408 in the main work (prior to its repeal by the SOA 2003, the proviso to Sched. 1 stipulated that s.99(2) did apply to offences under s.20)). It is no defence that the defendant did not know her to be under 16, or might suppose from her appearance that she was older: *R. v. Olifier, ante*; *R. v. Mycock, ante*; *R. v. Booth, ante*; or even that the defendant bona fide believed and had reasonable grounds for believing that she was over 16: *R. v. Prince* (1875) L.R. 2 C.C.R. 154. Doubts about *Prince* were expressed by the House of Lords in *B. (a Minor) v. DPP* [2000] 2 A.C. 428 (*post*, H-235) and *R. v. K.* [2002] 1 A.C. 462 (*ante*, H-125), but its correctness did not fall to be decided upon. Those expressions of doubt are likely to found a challenge to *Prince*, but it is submitted that the express provision of a defence based on mistake as to age in relation to the offence contrary to section 19 (*ante*, H-148) makes it abundantly clear that Parliament intended that there should be no corresponding defence in relation to the abduction of a girl under 16.

Mens rea

H-162   The act of abduction is positively prohibited, and therefore the absence of a corrupt motive is no answer to the charge: see *R. v. Booth, ante.*

If the defendant, at the time he took the girl away, did not know, and had no reason to know, that she was subject to the parental responsibility and care of her father, mother or some other person, he is not guilty of this offence: *R. v. Hibbert* (1869) L.R. 1 C.C.R. 184.

Without lawful authority or excuse

H-163   The defendant must show that he had either lawful authority or a lawful excuse; motive is irrelevant: *R. v. Tegerdine*, 75 Cr.App.R. 298, CA (statutory history reviewed). It is submitted that the burden on the defendant is merely an evidential one, which is discharged if there is sufficient evidence to raise an issue on the matter: *cf.* the specific provision in section 47 (*post*, H-225) in relation to "exceptions" under the Act. And see generally, §§ 4-444 *et seq.* in the main work.

(18) Abduction of defective from parent or guardian

(a) *Statute*

Sexual Offences Act 1956, s.21

H-164   **21.**—(1) It is an offence, subject to the exception mentioned in this section, for a person to take a woman who is a defective out of the possession of her parent or guardian against his will, if she is so taken with the intention that she shall have unlawful sexual intercourse with men or with a particular man.

(2) A person is not guilty of an offence under this section because he takes such a woman out of the possession of her parent or guardian as mentioned above, if he does not know and has no reason to suspect her to be a defective.

(3) In this section "guardian" means any person having parental responsibility for or care of the woman.

[This section is printed as amended by the Children Act 1989, s.108(4), and Sched. 12, para. 13.]

As to the meaning of "sexual intercourse", see *post*, H-219; as to the meaning of "unlawful" sexual intercourse, see *ante*, H-38; as to the use of the words "man" and "woman", see *post*, H-222; as to the meaning of "defective", see *ante*, H-68; as to the meaning of "parental responsibility", see *post*, H-224.

For the burden of proof of exceptions, see section 47 of the 1956 Act, *post*, H-225.

(b) *Mode of trial and class of offence*

This offence is triable on indictment only: SOA 1956, s.37(2), and Sched. 2, para. 22. As to the   **H-165**
classification of offences, see *ante*, Appendix B-209.

(c) *Sentence*

Imprisonment not exceeding two years: SOA 1956, s.37(3), and Sched. 2, para. 22.   **H-166**

(19) Causing prostitution of women

(a) *Statute*

Sexual Offences Act 1956, s.22

22.—(1) It is an offence for a person—   **H-167**
    (a)   to procure a woman to become, in any part of the world, a common prostitute; or
    (b)   to procure a woman to leave the United Kingdom, intending her to become an inmate of or frequent a brothel elsewhere; or
    (c)   to procure a woman to leave her usual place of abode in the United Kingdom, intending her to become an inmate of or frequent a brothel in any part of the world for the purposes of prostitution.

(2) [*Repealed by Criminal Justice and Public Order Act 1994, s.33(1).*]

As to the use of the word "woman", see *post*, H-222.

(b) *Indictment*

Statement of Offence

Procuring a woman to become a common prostitute, contrary to section 22(1)(a) of the Sexual Offences Act 1956.   **H-168**

Particulars of Offence

A B, on or about the _____ day of _____, 20_, at _____ procured C D, a woman, to become a common prostitute.

(c) *Mode of trial and classification of offences*

This offence, and an attempt to commit it, are triable on indictment only: SOA 1956, s.37(2),   **H-169**
and Sched. 2, para. 23(a), (b). As to the classification of offences, see *ante*, Appendix B-209.

(d) *Sentence*

The full offence, and an attempt to commit it: imprisonment not exceeding two years: SOA   **H-170**
1956, s.37(3), and Sched. 2, para. 23(a), (b).

(e) *Ingredients of the offence*

"Procure"

As to the meaning of the word "procure" in general, see §§ 18-22, 18-23 in the main work, and   **H-171**
see *Att.-Gen.'s Reference (No. 1 of 1975)* [1975] Q.B. 773, 61 Cr.App.R. 118, CA; *Re Royal Victoria*

Pavilion, Ramsgate [1961] Ch. 581, Ch D, and *Blakely v. DPP* [1991] R.T.R. 405, DC. In the first of these authorities, Lord Widgery C.J. said that to procure, "means to produce by endeavour. You procure a thing by setting out to see that it happens and taking the appropriate steps to produce that happening" (at pp.779, 121). In *Re Royal Victoria Pavilion, Ramsgate*, Pennycuick J. (at p.587) defined "to procure" as "to obtain by care and effort" or "to see to it".

In *R. v. Broadfoot*, 64 Cr.App.R. 71, CA, the court described *Att.-Gen's Reference (No. 1 of 1975)*, *ante*, as a useful guide. Whilst saying that the interpretation of the word was a matter of common sense for the jury to determine in the light of the particular facts, the court appears to have approved (see p.74) the suggestion of Shaw L.J., during argument, that it could be regarded as bringing about a course of conduct which the woman in question would not have embarked upon of her own volition. *R. v. Christian* (1913) 23 Cox 541, was distinguished. It was there held that procuration could be negatived by evidence showing the girl was not really procured, because she needed no procuring, and acted of her own free will.

If a woman is already a common prostitute she cannot become one and accordingly cannot be procured to become one. It follows that if there is evidence of procuration but "the woman" is a police officer it is a good defence to a charge of attempting to procure a woman to become a prostitute contrary to section 1(1) of the Criminal Attempts Act 1981, that the defendant thought that "the woman" he was attempting to procure was already a prostitute. If he believed (or might have believed) that, it could not be said that he was trying to procure her to become that which he believed she already was. Section 1(3) of the 1981 Act (§ 33-128 in the main work) is concerned with the converse case where the woman is a common prostitute but the defendant believes she is not. In such circumstances, he may be convicted of an attempt even though the commission of the offence is impossible: *R. v. Brown (R.A.)*, 80 Cr.App.R. 36, CA.

As to "attempting to do the impossible", see also § 33-137 in the main work.

"Common prostitute"

H-172   This includes a woman who offiers her body commonly for acts of lewdness for payment although there is no act or offer of an act of ordinary sexual intercourse: *R. v. De Munck* [1918] 1 K.B. 635, 13 Cr.App.R. 113, CCA. The word "common" in the term "common prostitute" is not mere surplusage—a common prostitute is any woman who offers herself commonly for lewdness for reward. Whether or not the performance by a woman of a single act of lewdness with a man on one occasion for reward constitutes the woman a prostitute, it plainly does not make her a woman who offers herself commonly for lewdness. That must be someone who is prepared for reward to engage in acts of lewdness with all and sundry or with anyone who may hire her for that purpose: *R. v. Morris-Lowe*, 80 Cr.App.R. 114, CA, applying *R. v. De Munck, ante*.

It is not necessary that she should have submitted to acts of lewdness in a passive way. Active acts of indecency by the woman herself, *e.g.* masturbation by her of clients when acting as a masseuse will fall within the section: *R. v. Webb* [1964] 1 Q.B. 357, 47 Cr.App.R. 265, CCA.

In *R. v. McFarlane* [1994] Q.B. 419, 99 Cr.App.R. 8, CA, it was held in relation to a prosecution under section 30 of the 1956 Act (*post*, H-197) that the essence of prostitution is the making of an offer of sexual services for reward, and that it is immaterial that the person making the offer does not intend to perform them and does not do so. It is obviously desirable that "prostitution" is given the same meaning wherever it appears in a statute; accordingly, this decision is likely to be applied to section 22. For a criticism of this decision, see the 1996 edition of this work.

(20) Procuration of girl under 21

(a) *Statute*

Sexual Offences Act 1956, s.23

H-173   23.—(1) It is an offence for a person to procure a girl under the age of twenty-one to have unlawful sexual intercourse in any part of the world with a third person.

(2) [*Repealed by Criminal Justice and Public Order Act 1994, s.33(1).*]

As to the meaning of "sexual intercourse", see *post*, H-219; as to the use of the word "girl", see *post*, H-222.

(b) *Mode of trial and classification of offences*

This offence, and an attempt to commit it, are triable on indictment only: SOA 1956, s.37(2), **H-174** and Sched. 2, para. 24(a), (b). As to the classification of offences, see *ante*, Appendix B-209.

(c) *Sentence*

The full offence, and an attempt to commit it: imprisonment not exceeding two years; SOA **H-175** 1956, s.37(3), and Sched. 2, para. 24(a), (b).

(d) *Ingredients of the offence*

As to the meaning of "procure", see *ante*, H-171. As to the meaning of "unlawful" sexual **H-176** intercourse, see *ante*, H-38.

Before the defendant can be found guilty of an offence contrary to this section, it is necessary to prove that unlawful sexual intercourse did take place; if intercourse is not proved to have taken place but procurement with the intention that it should take place is proved, there may be a conviction of an attempt to commit the full offence: *R. v. Johnson* [1964] 2 Q.B. 404, 48 Cr.App.R. 25, CCA. As to the difference between an attempt and an intention, see *R. v. Landow*, 8 Cr.App.R. 218, CCA. As to conspiracy with the procurer, see *R. v. Mackenzie and Higginson*, 6 Cr.App.R. 64, CCA.

(21) Detention of a woman in brothel or other premises

(a) *Statute*

Sexual Offences Act 1956, s.24

24.—(1) It is an offence for a person to detain a woman against her will on any premises with the **H-177** intention that she shall have unlawful sexual intercourse with men or with a particular man, or to detain a woman against her will in a brothel.

(2) Where a woman is on any premises for the purpose of having unlawful sexual intercourse or is in a brothel, a person shall be deemed for the purpose of the foregoing subsection to detain her there if, with the intention of compelling or inducing her to remain there, he either withholds from her her clothes or any other property belonging to her or threatens her with legal proceedings in the event of her taking away clothes provided for her by him or on his directions.

(3) A woman shall not be liable to any legal proceedings, whether civil or criminal, for taking away or being found in possession of any clothes she needed to enable her to leave premises on which she was for the purpose of having unlawful sexual intercourse or to leave a brothel.

As to the meaning of "sexual intercourse", see *post*, H-219; as to the use of the words "man" and "woman", see *post*, H-222.

(b) *Indictment*

Statement of Offence

Detaining a woman against her will for unlawful sexual intercourse [or *in a brothel*], *contrary to section 24(1) of* **H-178** *the Sexual Offences Act 1956.*

Particulars of Offence

A B, on or about the _____ *day of* _____, *20___, detained C D, a woman, against her will at* _____ *intending her to have unlawful sexual intercourse with men* [or *with E F, a man*] [or *detained C D, a woman, against her will at* _____, *a brothel*].

(c) *Mode of trial and class of offence*

This offence is triable on indictment only: SOA 1956, s.37(2), and Sched. 2, para. 25. As to the **H-179** classification of offences, see *ante*, Appendix B-209.

(d) *Sentence*

Imprisonment not exceeding two years: SOA 1956, s.37(3), and Sched. 2, para. 25. **H-180**

(e) *Ingredients of offence*

Unlawful sexual intercourse

See *ante*, H-38. **H-181**

"Brothel"

H-182 See §§ 20-233 *et seq.* in the main work.

(f) *Evidence*

H-183 See § 20-235 in the main work.

(22) Allowing premises to be used for intercourse

(a) *Statute*

Sexual Offences Act 1956, ss.25, 26, 27

Permitting girl under thirteen to use premises for intercourse
H-184   **25.** It is an offence for a person who is the owner or occupier of any premises, or who has, or acts or assists in, the management or control of any premises, to induce or knowingly suffer a girl under the age of thirteen to resort to or be on those premises for the purpose of having unlawful sexual intercourse with men or with a particular man.

[This section is printed as effectively amended by the CLA 1967, s.12(5)(a).]

Permitting girl between thirteen and sixteen to use premises for intercourse
H-185   **26.** It is an offence for a person who is the owner or occupier of any premises, or who has, or acts or assists in, the management or control of any premises, to induce or knowingly suffer a girl ... under the age of sixteen, to resort to or be on those premises for the purpose of having unlawful sexual intercourse with men or with a particular man.

[The words omitted were repealed by the CLA 1967, s.10(1), and Sched. 2, para. 14. This repeal renders the marginal note misleading.]

Permitting defective to use premises for intercourse
H-186   **27.**—(1) It is an offence, subject to the exception mentioned in this section, for a person who is the owner or occupier of any premises, or who has, or acts or assists in, the management or control of any premises, to induce or knowingly suffer a woman who is a defective to resort to or be on those premises for the purpose of having unlawful sexual intercourse with men or with a particular man.

(2) A person is not guilty of an offence under this section because he induces or knowingly suffers a defective to resort to or be on any premises for the purpose mentioned, if he does not know and has no reason to suspect her to be a defective.

As to the meaning of "sexual intercourse", see *post*, H-219; as to the use of the words "man", "woman" and "girl", see *post*, H-222; as to the meaning of "defective", see *ante*, H-68.

For the burden of proof of exceptions, see section 47 of the 1956 Act, *post*, H-225.

(b) *Mode of trial and classification of offences*

H-187   Section 25— this offence is triable only on indictment: SOA 1956, s.37(2), and Sched. 2, para. 6.

Section 26—this offence is triable either way: MCA 1980, s.17(1), and Sched. 1 (§ 1-130 in the main work).

Section 27—this offence is triable only on indictment: SOA 1956, s.37(2), and Sched. 2, para. 27.

As to the classification of offences, see *ante*, Appendix B-209.

(c) *Sentence*

H-188   Section 25—life imprisonment: SOA 1956, s.37(3), and Sched. 2, para. 6.

Section 26—imprisonment not exceeding two years: SOA 1956, s.37(3), and Sched. 2, para. 26. The penalty on summary conviction is provided for by the MCA 1980, s.32 (§ 1-125 in the main work).

Section 27—imprisonment not exceeding two years: SOA 1956, s.37(3), and Sched. 2, para. 27.

(d) *Ingredients of the offences*

"Management", "assists in the management"

H-189   See the following cases, decided in relation to section 33 of the 1956 Act ("assisting in the management of a brothel"): *Abbott v. Smith* [1965] 2 Q.B. 662, DC (meaning of "management"); *Gorman v. Standen*; *Palace-Clark v. Standen* [1964] 1 Q.B. 294, 48 Cr.App.R. 30, DC; *Jones and Wood v. DPP*, 96 Cr.App.R. 130, DC; and *Elliott v. DPP*; *Dublides v. DPP*, *The Times*, January 19, 1989, DC ("assisting in the management"). In the last of these cases, the court appears to have accepted a distinction between assisting in the management of premises and assisting the management of premises.

"Unlawful" sexual intercourse

See *ante*, H-38.   **H-190**

"Knowingly suffer"

In *R. v. Webster* (1885) 16 Q.B.D. 134, it was held that the words "knowingly suffer" mean that   **H-191**
the defendant knew of the girl's purpose in being on the premises and did not prevent the unlawful sexual intercourse from occurring when it was in his power to do so. The girl was the defendant's daughter, and the premises were her home, where she resided with the defendant. But see *R. v. Merthyr Tydfil JJ.* (1894) 10 T.L.R. 375, where a mother was held not within the section, who for the purposes of obtaining conclusive evidence against a man who had seduced her daughter, permitted him to come to her house to repeat his unlawful intercourse.

(23) Causing or encouraging prostitution, etc.

(a) *Statute*

Sexual Offences Act 1956, ss.28, 29

Causing or encouraging prostitution of, intercourse with, or indecent assault on, girl under sixteen
28.—(1) It is an offence for a person to cause or encourage the prostitution of, or the commission   **H-192**
of unlawful sexual intercourse with, or of an indecent assault on, a girl under the age of sixteen for whom he is responsible.

(2) Where a girl has become a prostitute, or has had unlawful sexual intercourse, or has been indecently assaulted, a person shall be deemed for the purposes of this section to have caused or encouraged it, if he knowingly allowed her to consort with, or to enter or continue in the employment of, any prostitute or person of known immoral character.

(3) The persons who are to be treated for the purposes of this section as responsible for a girl are (subject to subsection (4) of this section)—

    (a) her parents;

    (b) any person who is not a parent of hers but who has parental responsibility for her; and

    (c) any person who has care of her.

(4) An individual falling within subsection (3)(a) or (b) of this section is not to be treated as responsible for a girl if—

    (a) a residence order under the Children Act 1989 is in force with respect to her and he is not named in the order as the person with whom she is to live; *or*

    (aa) a special guardianship order under that Act is in force with respect to her and he is not her special guardian; or

    (b) a care order under that Act is in force with respect to her.

(5) If, on a charge of an offence against a girl under this section, the girl appears to the court to have been under the age of sixteen at the time of the offence charged, she shall be presumed for the purposes of this section to have been so, unless the contrary is proved.

[This section is printed as amended by the Children Act 1989, s.108(4), and Sched. 12, para. 14; and the Adoption and Children Act 2002, s.139(1), and Sched. 3, para. 8.]

Causing or encouraging prostitution of defective
29.—(1) It is an offence, subject to the exception mentioned in this section, for a person to cause   **H-193**
or encourage the prostitution in any part of the world of a woman who is a defective.

(2) A person is not guilty of an offence under this section because he causes or encourages the prostitution of such a woman, if he does not know and has no reason to suspect her to be a defective.

As to the meaning of "sexual intercourse", see *post*, H-219; as to the use of the words "woman" and "girl", see *post*, H-222; as to the meaning of "parental responsibility", see *post*, H-224; as to the meaning of "defective", see *ante*, H-68.

For the burden of proof of exceptions, see section 47 of the 1956 Act, *post*, § H-225.

(b) *Mode of trial and classification of offences*

H-194   These offences are triable only on indictment: SOA 1956, s.37(2), and Sched. 2, paras 28 and 29. As to the classification of offences, see *ante*, Appendix B-209.

(c) *Sentence*

H-195   Sections 28 and 29—imprisonment not exceeding two years: SOA 1956, s.37(3), and Sched. 2, paras 28 and 29.

(d) *Ingredients of the offences*

H-196   As to what constitutes "causing" or "encouraging", see *R. v. Ralphs*, 9 Cr.App.R. 86, CCA; *R. v. Chainey* [1914] 1 K.B. 137, 9 Cr.App.R. 175, CCA.

In *R. v. Drury*, 60 Cr.App.R. 195, CA, it was held that there was evidence on which it could be held that a girl (aged 14) was in the care of the defendant where, at the time of the assault by a friend of the defendant, she was babysitting for him. The case was decided on the original wording of section 28(3)(c), *viz.* "any other person who has the custody, charge or care of her". The 1989 amendment (*ante*) would not appear to affect this point. As to encouragement, the court said that there must be encouragement in fact and an intention to encourage.

A doctor who in the exercise of his clinical judgment gives contraceptive advice and treatment to a girl under 16 without her parents' consent does not commit an offence under section 6 or 28 of the 1956 Act, because the bona fide exercise by the doctor of his clinical judgment negates the *mens rea* which is an essential ingredient of those offences: *Gillick v. West Norfolk and Wisbech Area Health Authority* [1986] A.C. 112, HL.

As to the meaning of "unlawful" sexual intercourse, see *ante*, H-38.

(24) Man living on earnings of prostitution

(a) *Statute*

Sexual Offences Act 1956, s.30

H-197   **30.**—(1) It is an offence for a man knowingly to live wholly or in part on the earnings of prostitution.

(2) For the purposes of this section a man who lives with or is habitually in the company of a prostitute, or who exercises control, direction or influence over a prostitute's movements in a way which shows he is aiding, abetting or compelling her prostitution with others, shall be presumed to be knowingly living on the earnings of prostitution, unless he proves the contrary.

As to the use of the word "man", see *post*, H-222.

(b) *Indictment*

Statement of Offence

H-198   *Living on prostitution, contrary to section 30(1) of the Sexual Offences Act 1956.*

Particulars of Offence

A B, being a man, on the _____ day of _____, 20__, and on other days between that date and the _____ day of _____, 20__, knowingly lived wholly or in part on the earnings of the prostitution of J N.

In an indictment for this offence a person may be charged with having committed the offence on one specified day only: *R. v. Hill*, 10 Cr.App.R. 56, CCA. Evidence is admissible to show what the defendant's relations with the woman in question had been either before or after the day specified in the indictment: *ibid.*

As to the application of the alibi notice provisions to this offence, see *R. v. Hassan*, 54 Cr.App.R. 56, CA (§ 12-66 in the main work).

(c) *Mode of trial and class of offence*

H-199   This offence is triable either way: SOA 1956, s.37(2), and Sched. 2, para. 30. As to the classification of offences, see *ante*, Appendix B-209.

(d) Sentence

Maximum

On conviction on indictment, imprisonment not exceeding seven years; on summary convic-   **H-200**
tion, six months, or a fine not exceeding £5,000: SOA 1956, s.37(3), and Sched. 2, para. 30 (as
amended by the Street Offences Act 1959, s.4), and the MCA 1980, ss.32, 34(3)(a).

Guidelines

A sentence exceeding two years should be reserved for cases where there is some evidence of   **H-201**
physical or mental coercion of the prostitutes involved, or of corruption. The existence of such
coercion or corruption is the crucial sentencing factor: *R. v. Farrugia*, 69 Cr.App.R. 108, CA. See
also *R. v. Thomas*, 5 Cr.App.R.(S.) 138, CA; *R. v. El-Gazzar*, 8 Cr.App.R.(S.) 182, CA; *R. v. Malik*
[1998] 1 Cr.App.R.(S.) 115, CA; and CSP B5–1.

(e) Ingredients of the offence

"Man"

In *R. v. Tan* [1983] Q.B. 1053, 76 Cr.App.R. 300, CA, it was held that a person who was born a   **H-202**
man and who remained biologically a man was a man for all purposes although he had undergone
hormone treatment and surgical treatment consisting of sex-change operations and had become
philosophically or psychologically female (applying *Corbett v. Corbett* [1971] P. 83).

Prostitution

As to what constitutes "prostitution", see *ante*, H-172. As to proving that at the material time   **H-203**
the woman was a prostitute, see § 20-235 in the main work, and *R. v. Wilson (D.T.)*, 78 Cr.App.R.
247, CA, in which *Woodhouse v. Hall*, 72 Cr.App.R. 39, DC, was applied in the context of a
prosecution under section 30.

Knowingly living on earnings of prostitution

There are three distinct foundations upon which the prosecution can rely in order to raise a   **H-204**
presumption that an offence has been committed under section 30(2) (*ante*, H-197):
   (a) proof that the accused was at the material time living with the prostitute;
   (b) proof that he was habitually at the material time in her company;
   (c) proof that he exercised control, direction or influence over her movements in a way which
       showed him to be aiding or abetting her prostitution.
Once evidence giving rise to the presumption has been led, it then has two facets: (a) it is
presumed that he is living on immoral earnings; and (b) it is presumed that he is doing so
knowingly: *R. v. Clarke*, 63 Cr.App.R. 16, CA. It is not necessary to prove that he was living with
or habitually in the company of such a prostitute in a way which showed that he was aiding, abetting or compelling her prostitution with others: *ibid*. See also *R. v. Lawrence, post*, H-206.

In *R. v. Stewart*, 83 Cr.App.R. 327, CA, the court was referred to *R. v. Silver*, 40 Cr.App.R. 32,   **H-205**
CCC (Judge Maude); *R. v. Thomas*, 41 Cr.App.R. 121, CCA; *Shaw v. DPP* [1962] A.C. 220, HL; *R.
v. Calderhead and Bidney*, 68 Cr.App.R. 37, CA; and *R. v. Wilson (D.T.)*, *ante*. Mustill L.J. said, in
giving the court's judgment:

> "What we collect from them is as follows: according to the literal meaning of the section any
> person who supplies goods or services to a prostitute is in one sense living off the earnings of
> prostitution: for in part he earns his livelihood from payments which the woman would not be
> able to make but for her trade. This cannot be the right view. There has to be a closer connection
> between the receipt of money and the trade before the recipient commits an offence. We doubt
> whether it is possible to devise a definition of the type and closeness of the necessary connection
> which will deal with all the circumstances which may arise; and, indeed, it is dangerous to treat
> words or phrases from judgments delivered in relation to one set of facts, as if they provided a
> statutory gloss which can be reliably applied to facts of a quite different nature ... .
>   Subject to this reservation, we believe that an approach which will often be useful is to identify
> for the jury the flavour of the words 'living off', and then to express this general concept in the

shape of guidance more directly referable to the case in hand. In our judgment, the word 'parasite' (to be found in the speech of Lord Reid in *Shaw v. DPP* ...), or some expanded equivalent, provides a useful starting point for this exercise, and does express a concept which accounts for all the reported cases except for *Silver*.

Adopting this general approach, and dealing specifically with a defendant who supplies goods or services to a prostitute, a good working test, sufficient to deal with many cases, is whether the fact of supply means that the supplier and the prostitute were engaged in the business of prostitution together: and 'the fact of supply' will include the scale of supply, the price charged and the nature of the goods or services. It will be impossible to say in advance that certain categories of supplies must necessarily fall outside the section, any more than that other categories must be within it, but the idea of participation in the prostitute's business will enable the jury to distinguish readily between (say) the supplier of groceries on the one hand and the publisher of prostitutes' advertisements on the other. There will remain a residue of more difficult cases, and these include the situation where premises are let at a market rent with knowledge of the purpose to which they are to be put. We see no room here for any rule of thumb distinction between premises which are or are not let at abnormally high rates. Certainly, the jury will find it easier to infer in the former case that the lessor participates in the woman's earnings. ... We can, however, see no logic in the suggestion that the lessor cannot be convicted unless the rent is exorbitant and indeed the judgment of Ashworth J. in *Shaw v. DPP* (at p.230) and the speech of Lord Simonds in the same case (at p.265 ... see the words 'whatever the rent') are authority for the view that the presence or absence of this factor is not conclusive. Nor in our opinion is the question whether the premises are occupied or capable of occupation as residential premises to be taken as the touchstone.

Instead, the judge must bear in mind when framing his direction the distinction between the offence under section 30(1), and the offences under sections 34, 35 and 36, and must not allow the jury to believe that knowledge of use to which the premises are put will be sufficient in itself to found a conviction. He must draw the attention of the jury to whatever factors are material to the individual case. These will often include, but not be limited to, the nature and location of the premises, the involvement of the lessor in adapting, furnishing or outfitting the premises for prostitution, the duration of the letting, the hours during which the premises are occupied, the rent at which they are let, the method of payment of rent, the fact that the prostitute does or does not live as well as work at the premises, the presence or absence of a personal relationship between the lessor and the lessee, the steps taken by the lessor to remove the prostitutes from his premises, and the steps taken by the lessor to disguise his relationship with the premises and the persons working there. Having presented the facts to the jury, the judge will invite them to consider whether they are sure that the lessor was involved together with the prostitute in the business of prostitution" (at pp.332–333).

H-206 Mustill L.J. then said that in the opinion of the court, the judge's direction, that where a letting was referable to prostitution and nothing else it was immaterial whether the letting was at a higher than normal rent, was correct, and to the extent that *Silver, ante,* is a decision to the contrary, it should not be followed.

It is essential that a jury should receive a clear and careful direction with regard to this offence and the burden of proof in relation to it. In particular, where the prosecution rely on subsection (2) *(ante,* H-197), the jury's attention should be directed to the various alternatives contained in the subsection, and to any evidence relating to any of those alternatives: *R. v. Lawrence,* 47 Cr.App.R. 72, CCA.

In *R. v. Howard,* 94 Cr.App.R. 89, CA, Lord Lane C.J. said that what is required is a simple direction based primarily on what was said in *Shaw v. DPP, ante,* and *Stewart, ante,* adjusted to the facts of the particular case.

(f) *Evidence*

H-207 That the defendant knowingly lived wholly or in part on the earnings of prostitution is usually proved by evidence that the prostitute paid the rent of rooms where both were living together, or paid for his food, or supplied him with money, or paid for drink consumed by him in public-houses, or the like. Whether conversation and association with a prostitute amounts to proof that the defendant was habitually in her company is a question of fact for the jury: *R. v. Ptohopoulos,* 52 Cr.App.R. 47, CA.

There need not be proof that the prostitute handed money to the defendant if the evidence establishes that what the defendant received was earned by the prostitute (see *Calvert v. Mayes* [1954] 1 Q.B. 242, approved in *Shaw*). Nor, as was held in *R. v. Ansell* [1975] Q.B. 215, 60

Cr.App.R. 45, CA, if the money comes from the men with whom the prostitutes are dealing and not from the prostitutes themselves, does that fact in law prevent the money being the earnings of prostitution: see, for example, *R. v. Farrugia*, 69 Cr.App.R. 108, CA.

(25) Woman exercising control over prostitute

(a) *Statute*

Sexual Offences Act 1956, s.31

31. It is an offence for a woman for purposes of gain to exercise control, direction or influence **H-208** over a prostitute's movements in a way which shows she is aiding, abetting or compelling her prostitution.

As to the use of the word "woman", see *post*, H-222. As to the meaning of "prostitution", see *ante*, H-172.

(b) *Mode of trial and class of offence*

This offence is triable either way: SOA 1956, s.37(2), and Sched. 2, para. 31. As to the classifica- **H-209** tion of offences, see *ante*, Appendix B-209.

(c) *Sentence*

On conviction on indictment, imprisonment not exceeding seven years; on summary convic- **H-210** tion, six months, or a fine not exceeding £5,000: SOA 1956, s.37(3), and Sched. 2, para. 31 (as amended by the Street Offences Act 1959, s.4), and the MCA 1980, ss.32, 34(3)(a).

(26) Solicitation for immoral purposes

(a) *Statute*

Sexual Offences Act 1956, s.32

32. It is an offence for a man persistently to solicit or importune in a public place for immoral **H-211** purposes.

As to the use of the word "man", see *post*, H-222.

(b) *Mode of trial and class of offence*

This offence is triable either way: SOA 1956, s.37(2), and Sched. 2, para. 32. As to the classifica- **H-212** tion of offences, see *ante*, Appendix B-209.

(c) *Sentence*

On conviction on indictment, imprisonment not exceeding two years; on summary conviction, **H-213** six months, or a fine not exceeding £5,000: SOA 1956, s.37(3), and Sched. 2, para. 32, and the MCA 1980, ss.32, 34(3)(a).

(d) *Ingredients of the offence*

"persistently"

Two separate acts of importuning within the period named in the information or indictment **H-214** are sufficient to render the importuning persistent: *Dale v. Smith* [1967] 1 W.L.R. 700, DC (justices entitled to treat the use of the word "Hello" by the defendant to a youth in a public lavatory as an act of importuning, in view of the fact that the same word had been used by the defendant to another youth on the previous evening and had been followed by an undoubted act of importuning, *viz.* an invitation to look at indecent photographs).

"solicit"

In *Behrendt v. Burridge*, 63 Cr.App.R. 202, DC, the defendant was observed for about 50 **H-215** minutes sitting on a high stool in the bay window of a house. She sat silent and motionless, dressed in a low cut top and mini-skirt. The bay window was illuminated by a red light. She was charged with soliciting for the purpose of prostitution, contrary to section 1 of the Street Offences Act 1959. The Divisional Court said that the fact that her behaviour could be described as an explicit form of advertising was not decisive in her favour: advertising and soliciting are not mutually exclusive. It was clear that she was soliciting in the sense of tempting or allowing prospective customers to come in for the purposes of prostitution.

See also *Horton v. Mead* [1913] 1 K.B. 154, DC, and *Burge v. DPP* [1962] 1 W.L.R. 265, DC.

"importune"

H-216   See *Dale v. Smith, ante*, H-214.

"public place"

H-217   No definition appears in the 1956 Act, but it is a frequently used expression in legislation: see, for example, the Public Order Act 1936, s.9 (§ 25-329 in the main work), the Prevention of Crime Act 1953, s.1(4) (§ 24-165 in the main work) and the Firearms Act 1968, s.57(4) (§ 24-120 in the main work).

"for immoral purposes"

H-218   An immoral purpose within section 32 has to be some kind of sexual activity: *Crook v. Edmondson* [1966] 2 Q.B. 81, DC; *R. v. Kirkup*, 96 Cr.App.R. 352, CA.

Section 32 applies both to heterosexual and homosexual behaviour: *R. v. Goddard*, 92 Cr.App.R. 185, CA.

Although section 1 of the SOA 1967 (*ante*, H-97) prevents homosexual practices in private between consenting parties who have attained the age of 16 from being a criminal offence, the 1967 Act did not change the law to the extent of preventing approaches for such purposes from being the offence of persistently importuning for "immoral purposes": *R. v. Ford*, 66 Cr.App.R. 46, CA. The judge correctly ruled that the conduct complained of could amount to an offence and correctly left the jury to decide whether the conduct was or was not immoral.

Similarly, in *R. v. Goddard, ante*, the unchallenged evidence of two young women was that they had had explicit sexual invitations made to them by G. It was held: (a) that it did not matter that the proposed sexual activity may be within the law; and (b) that it was a matter for the jury to decide, whether the invitations were for sexually immoral purposes, considering the circumstances in which the overtures were made and the nature of the overtures. This decision effectively overruled that part of the majority decision in *Crook v. Edmondson, ante*, which had held that "immoral purposes" was to be confined to purposes declared to be offences under other provisions of the 1956 Act.

The correct procedure is for the trial judge to rule whether the acts complained of could amount to an offence and, provided they are so capable, to leave it to the jury to decide whether the conduct, in fact, involved an immoral purpose, applying contemporary standards of morality: *R. v. Goddard, ante*.

(27) Interpretation

(a) Meaning of "sexual intercourse"

Sexual Offences Act 1956, s.44

H-219   **44.** Where, on the trial of any offence under this Act, it is necessary to prove sexual intercourse (whether natural or unnatural), it shall not be necessary to prove the completion of the intercourse by the emission of seed, but the intercourse shall be deemed complete upon proof of penetration only.

See further, *ante*, H-14.

Boys under the age of 14

H-220   As to the abolition of the common law presumption that a boy under the age of 14 is incapable of sexual intercourse, see *ante*, H-13. The presumption did not apply to a charge of aiding and abetting the commission of an offence: 1 Hale 630; *R. v. Williams* [1893] 1 Q.B. 320. Nor would it apply where the boy was not the defendant: see *R. v. Pickford* [1995] 1 Cr.App.R. 420, CA (*ante*, H-94).

(b) *Meaning of "defective"*

See section 45 of the SOA 1956, *ante*, H-68.   **H-221**

(c) *Use of words "man", "boy", "woman" and "girl"*

Sexual Offences Act 1956, s.46

46. The use in any provision of this Act of the word "man" without the addition of the word "boy",   **H-222** or *vice versa*, shall not prevent the provision applying to any person to whom it would have applied if both words had been used, and similarly with the words "woman" and "girl".

As to the use of the word "man", see *R. v. Tan* [1983] Q.B. 1053, 76 Cr.App.R. 300, CA, *ante*, H-202.

Section 46 applies for the purposes of the provisions of the SOA 1967 as it applies for the purposes of the provisions of the 1956 Act: SOA 1967, s.11(3). It also has effect as if the reference to the 1956 Act included a reference to the Sexual Offences (Amendment) Act 1976: Sexual Offences (Amendment) Act 1976, s.7(2).

(d) *Meaning of "parental responsibility"*

Sexual Offences Act 1956, s.46A

46A. In this Act "parental responsibility" has the same meaning as in the Children Act 1989.   **H-223**

[This section was inserted by the Children Act 1989, s.108(4), and Sched. 12, para. 17.]

Section 105(1) of the Act of 1989 provides that in that Act "parental responsibility" has the meaning given by section 3.

Children Act 1989, s.3

3.—(1) In this Act "parental responsibility" means all the rights, duties, powers, responsibilities   **H-224** and authority which by law a parent of a child has in relation to the child and his property.

(2) It also includes the rights, powers and duties which a guardian of the child's estate (appointed, before the commencement of section 5, to act generally) would have had in relation to the child and his property.

(3) The rights referred to in subsection (2) include, in particular, the right of the guardian to receive or recover in his own name, for the benefit of the child, property of whatever description and wherever situated which the child is entitled to receive or recover.

(4) The fact that a person has, or does not have, parental responsibility for a child shall not affect—

(a)   any obligation which he may have in relation to the child (such as a statutory duty to maintain the child); or

(b)   any rights which, in the event of the child's death, he (or any other person) may have in relation to the child's property.

(5) A person who—

(a)   does not have parental responsibility for a particular child; but

(b)   has care of the child,

may (subject to the provisions of this Act) do what is reasonable in all the circumstances of the case for the purpose of safeguarding or promoting the child's welfare.

Further reference may need to be made to sections 2 (parental responsibility for children) and 12 (residence orders and parental responsibility) of the 1989 Act.

(28) Proof of exceptions

Sexual Offences Act 1956, s.47

H-225   **47.** Where in any of the foregoing sections the description of an offence is expressed to be subject to exceptions mentioned in the section, proof of the exception is to lie on the person relying on it.

(29) Powers and procedure for dealing with offenders

Sexual Offences Act 1956, s.37

Prosecution and punishment of offences

H-226   **37.**—(1) The Second Schedule to this Act shall have effect, subject to and in accordance with the following provisions of this section, with respect to the prosecution and punishment of the offences listed in the first column of the Schedule, being the offences under this Act and attempts to commit certain of those offences.

(2) The second column in the Schedule shows, for any offence, if it may be prosecuted on indictment or summarily, or either ... and what special restrictions (if any) there are on the commencement of a prosecution.

(3) The third column in the Schedule shows, for any offence, the punishments which may be imposed on conviction on indictment or on summary conviction, a reference to a period giving the maximum term of imprisonment and a reference to a sum of money the maximum fine.

(4) The fourth column in the Schedule contains provisions which are either supplementary to those in the second or third column or enable a person charged on indictment with the offence specified in the first column to be found guilty of another offence if the jury are not satisfied that he is guilty of the offence charged or of an attempt to commit it, but are satisfied that he is guilty of the other offence.

(5) A provision in the fourth column of the Schedule enabling the jury to find the accused guilty of an offence specified in that provision authorises them, if not satisfied that he is guilty of the offence so specified, to find him guilty of any other offence of which they could find him guilty if he had been indicted for the offence so specified.

(6) Where in the Schedule there is used a phrase descriptive of an offence or group of offences followed by a reference to a section by its number only, the reference is to a section of this Act, and the phrase shall be taken as referring to any offence under the section mentioned.

(7) Nothing in this section or in the Second Schedule to this Act shall exclude the application to any of the offences referred to in the first column of the Schedule—

    (a) of section 24 of the Magistrates' Courts Act 1980 (which relates to the summary trial of young offenders for indictable offences); or

    (b) of subsection (5) of section 121 of the Magistrates' Courts Act 1980 (which limits the punishment which may be imposed by a magistrates' court sitting in an occasional courthouse); or

    (c) of any enactment or rule of law restricting a court's power to imprison; or

    (d) of any enactment or rule of law authorising an offender to be dealt with in a way not authorised by the enactments specially relating to his offence; or

    (e) of any enactment or rule of law authorising a jury to find a person guilty of an offence other than that with which he is charged.

[This section is printed as amended by the MCA 1980, Sched. 7, para. 17; and as repealed in part by the Courts Act 1971, s.56(4), and Sched. 11, Pt IV.]

Subsection (5) was considered in *R. v. Rogina*, 64 Cr.App.R. 79, CA, *ante*, H-74.

Attempts

H-227   Schedule 2 to the 1956 Act is not set out in this appendix. All relevant provisions thereof are referred to in the context of the individual offences, *ante*. Some of the paragraphs in the Schedule specifically refer to an attempt to commit a particular offence (sometimes with a different penalty to the full offence, sometimes with the same penalty). Wherever there is specific reference to an attempt in the schedule, this is referred to in the text in relation to the offence in question; where there is no such reference in the text, this is because there is no separate reference to an attempt in the schedule. In such cases, the Criminal Attempts Act 1981 will exclusively determine liability to prosecution and punishment for an attempt: for the 1981 Act, see §§ 33-128 *et seq.* in the main work.

C. Mental Health Act 1959

Mental Health Act 1959, s.128

Sexual intercourse with patients

128.—(1) Without prejudice to section seven of the Sexual Offences Act 1956, it shall be an of- **H-228**
fence, subject to the exception mentioned in this section,—

    (a) for a man who is an officer on the staff of or is otherwise employed in, or is one of the
managers of, a hospital independent hospital or care home to have unlawful sexual
intercourse with a woman who is for the time being receiving treatment for mental disorder
in that hospital or home, or to have such intercourse on the premises of which the hospital
or home forms part with a woman who is for the time being receiving such treatment there
as an outpatient;

    (b) for a man to have unlawful sexual intercourse with a woman who is a mentally disordered
patient and who is subject to his guardianship under the Mental Health Act 1983 or is
otherwise in his custody or care under the Mental Health Act 1983 or in pursuance of arrangements under ... Part III of the National Assistance Act 1948 ... or the National
Health Service Act 1977, or as a resident in a care home.

(2) It shall not be an offence under this section for a man to have sexual intercourse with a woman
if he does not know and has no reason to suspect her to be a mentally disordered patient.

(3) Any person guilty of an offence under this section shall be liable on conviction on indictment to
imprisonment for a term not exceeding two years.

(4) No proceedings shall be instituted for an offence under this section except by or with the
consent of the Director of Public Prosecutions.

(5) This section shall be construed as one with the Sexual Offences Act 1956; and section 47 of that
Act (which relates to the proof of exceptions) shall apply to the exception mentioned in this section.

(6) In this section "independent hospital" and "care home" have the same meaning as in the Care
Standards Act 2000.

[This section is printed as amended by the National Health Service Act 1977, s.129, Sched. 15,
para. 29, and Sched. 16; the MHA 1983, s.148, and Sched. 3, para. 15; the Registered Homes Act
1984, s.57, and Sched. 1, para. 2; and the Care Standards Act 2000, s.116, and Sched. 4, para. 2.]

As to the meaning of "sexual intercourse", see *ante*, H-219; as to the meaning of "unlawful" **H-229**
sexual intercourse, see *R. v. Chapman*, *ante*, H-38; as to the use of the words "man" and "woman",
see *ante*, H-222.

For anonymity provisions, see §§ 20-257 *et seq.* in the main work.

For section 47 of the 1956 Act (burden of proof of exceptions), see *ante*, H-225.

By section 1(4) of the Sexual Offences Act 1967, section 128 is to have effect as if any reference
therein to having unlawful sexual intercourse with a woman included a reference to committing
buggery or an act of gross indecency with another man.

In connection with the offences created by this section, see *R. v. Davies and Poolton* [2000]
Crim.L.R. 297, CA (§ 19-363 in the main work), decided in relation to the similarly worded section 127 of the 1959 Act.

D. Indecency with Children Act 1960

(1) Statute

Indecency with Children Act 1960, s.1(1)

1.—(1) Any person who commits an act of gross indecency with or towards a child under the age **H-230**
of sixteen, or who incites a child under that age to such an act with him or another, shall be liable on
conviction on indictment to imprisonment for a term not exceeding ten years, or on summary
conviction to imprisonment for a term not exceeding six months, to a fine not exceeding the
prescribed sum, or to both.

(2) [*Repealed by Police and Criminal Evidence Act 1984, Sched. 7.*]

(3) References in the Children and Young Persons Act 1933 ... to the offences mentioned in the
First Schedule to that Act shall include offences under this section.

(4) offences under this section shall be deemed to be offences against the person for the purpose of
section three of the Visiting Forces Act 1952 (which restricts the trial by United Kingdom courts of
offenders connected with visiting forces).

[Subs. (1) is printed as amended by the C(S)A 1997, s.52 (substitution of "ten" for "two"); and the CJCSA 2000, s.39 (substitution of "sixteen" for "fourteen"). The first of these amendments took effect on October 1, 1997, but does not apply to offences committed before that date: Crime (Sentences) Act (Commencement No. 2 and Transitional Provisions) Order 1997 (S.I. 1997 No. 2200). The second amendment took effect on January 11, 2001: Criminal Justice and Court Services Act 2000 (Commencement No. 1) Order 2000 (S.I. 2000 No. 3302).]

As to Schedule 1 to the CYPA 1933, see § 19-408 in the main work.

For anonymity provisions, see §§ 20-257 *et seq.* in the main work.

(2) Indictment

Statement of Offence

H-231   *Indecency with a child, contrary to section 1(1) of the Indecency with Children Act 1960.*

Particulars of offence

A B, on the _____ day of _____, 20__, committed an act of gross indecency with [or towards] J N, a child of the age of 10 years [or incited J N, a child of the age of 10 years to commit an act of gross indecency with him the said A B (or with Y Z)].

It is a prerequisite of a conviction contrary to section 1 that the child was under the age of 16 at the time of the act or incitement: the child's age is an ingredient of the offence about which the jury must be satisfied and, unless age is admitted, calls for an appropriate direction from the judge: see *R. v. Goss and Goss*, 90 Cr.App.R. 400, CA, and *R. v. Radcliffe* [1990] Crim.L.R. 524, CA.

As to the propriety of preferring a charge of outraging public decency although the facts are covered by section 1(1), see *R. v. May (J.)*, 91 Cr.App.R. 157, CA (§ 20-238 in the main work).

(3) Mode of trial and class of offence

H-232   This offence is triable either way: s.1(1), *ante*. As to the classification of offences, see *ante*, Appendix B-209.

(4) Sentence

H-233   See section 1(1), *ante*. As to "the prescribed sum", see section 32 of the MCA 1980 (§ 1-125 in the main work).

(5) Consent of Director of Public Prosecutions

H-234   Section 8 of the SOA 1967 (no proceedings shall be instituted except by or with the consent of the Director against any man for gross indecency or certain other offences where any person involved is under 21) shall not apply to proceedings under the Indecency with Children Act 1960: CJA 1972, s.48.

(6) Ingredients of the offence

H-235   In *R. v. Speck*, 65 Cr.App.R. 161, CA, it was held that section 1 was contravened where S passively permitted a child to keep her hand on his penis for so long (in this case about five minutes) that his inactivity amounted to an invitation to her to continue the activity. If such an invitation could properly be inferred, it would constitute an "act" within section 1(1). Apart from allowing the child's hand to remain where she had placed it, S did nothing to encourage the child. A proper direction to the jury in such circumstances would be that the defendant's conduct might constitute an offence under section 1(1) if it amounted to an invitation from the defendant to the child to continue the activity in question. If they took that view (*i.e.* that there had been an "act") then they should go on to determine whether the act was an act of gross indecency. See also *R. v. B.* [1999] Crim.L.R. 594, CA.

Section 1(1) creates one offence of gross indecency, namely, the committing of an act of gross indecency involving a child; that is, "with or towards a child" is to be read as a phrase: *DPP v. Burgess* [1971] Q.B. 432, DC; *R. v. Francis*, 88 Cr.App.R. 127, CA. In *Francis*, the court considered the circumstances in which a man contravened section 1(1) if he masturbated in the presence of a child: the act had to be directed towards the child, the offender at the very least deriving satisfaction from the knowledge that the child was watching what he was doing.

As to the age of the victim being an essential ingredient of the offence, see *ante*, H-220; and it is necessary for the prosecution to prove the absence of a genuine belief on the part of the defendant that the victim was 16 years or above: *B. (a Minor) v. DPP* [2000] 2 A.C. 428, HL. The presence or absence of reasonable grounds for such belief goes only to whether such belief was genuinely held: *ibid*.

E. Sexual Offences Act 1967

(1) Procuring others to commit homosexual acts

Sexual Offences Act 1967, s.4

4.—(1) A man who procures another man to commit with a third man an act of buggery which by **H-236** reason of section 1 of this Act is not an offence shall be liable on conviction on indictment to imprisonment for a term not exceeding two years.

(2) [*Repealed by Criminal Law Act 1977, Sched. 13.*]

(3) It shall not be an offence under section 13 of the Act of 1956 for a man to procure the commission by another man of an act of gross indecency with the first-mentioned man which by reason of section 1 of this Act is not an offence under the said section 13.

The offence under subsection (1) is triable either way: MCA 1980, s.17(1), and Sched. 1 (§ 1-125 in the main work).

As to the use of the word "man", see *ante*, H-222.

As to the offence of buggery, see *ante*, H-95 *et seq*.

For section 13 of the 1956 Act, see *ante*, H-107.

As to "procures", see *ante*, H-171.

(2) Living on earnings of male prostitution

Sexual Offences Act 1967, s.5

5.—(1) A man or woman who knowingly lives wholly or in part on the earnings of prostitution of **H-237** another man shall be liable—

    (a) on summary conviction to imprisonment for a term not exceeding six months, or

    (b) on conviction on indictment to imprisonment for a term not exceeding seven years.

(2) [*Repealed by Criminal Law Act 1977, Sched. 13.*]

(3) Anyone may arrest without a warrant a person found committing an offence under this section.

As to the use of the words "man" and "woman", see *ante*, H-222 and—in relation to "man"— **H-238** see *R. v. Tan* [1983] Q.B. 1053, 76 Cr.App.R. 300, CA, *ante*, H-202.

As to the classification of offences, see *ante*, Appendix B-209.

Subsection (3) has ceased to have effect by virtue of the PACE Act 1984, s.26(1) (§ 15-133 in the main work).

F. Criminal Law Act 1977

Criminal Law Act 1977, s.54

Incitement of girls under 16

54.—(1) It is an offence for a man to incite to have sexual intercourse with him a girl under the **H-239** age of sixteen whom he knows to be his grand-daughter, daughter or sister.

(2) In the preceding subsection "man" includes boy, "sister" includes half-sister, and for the purposes of that subsection any expression importing a relationship between two people shall be taken to apply notwithstanding that the relationship is not traced through lawful wedlock.

(3) The following provisions of section 1 of the Indecency with Children Act 1960, namely—

    ...

    subsection (3) (references in Children and Young Persons Act 1933 to the offences mentioned in Schedule 1 to that Act to include offences under that section);

    subsection (4) (offences under that section to be deemed offences against the person for the purpose of section 3 of the Visiting Forces Act 1952),

shall apply in relation to offences under this section.

(4) A person guilty of an offence under this section shall be liable—

    (a) on summary conviction, to imprisonment for a term not exceeding six months or to a fine not exceeding the prescribed sum or both;

    (b) on conviction on indictment to imprisonment for a term not exceeding two years.

[This section is printed as effectively amended by the MCA 1980, s.32(2) (substitution of reference to "the prescribed sum"); and as repealed in part by the PACE Act 1984, Sched. 7.]

H-240   As to Schedule 1 to the CYPA 1933, see § 19-408 in the main work.

As to "the prescribed sum", see the MCA 1980, s.32(2) and (9) (§ 1-125 in the main work).

For anonymity provisions, see §§ 20-257 *et seq.* in the main work.

Section 54 filled a *lacuna* in the law, identified in *R. v. Whitehouse* [1977] Q.B. 868, 65 Cr.App.R. 33, CA.

As to incitement at common law, see *ante*, §§ 33-74 *et seq.*

G. Sexual Offences (Amendment) Act 2000

(1) Statute

Sexual Offences (Amendment) Act 2000, ss.3, 4

Abuse of position of trust

H-241   **3.**—(1) Subject to subsections (2) and (3) below, it shall be an offence for a person aged 18 or over—

    (a) to have sexual intercourse (whether vaginal or anal) with a person under that age; or

    (b) to engage in any other sexual activity with or directed towards such a person,

if (in either case) he is in a position of trust in relation to that person.

(2) Where a person ("A") is charged with an offence under this section of having sexual intercourse with, or engaging in any other sexual activity with or directed towards, another person ("B"), it shall be a defence for A to prove that, at the time of the intercourse or activity—

    (a) he did not know, and could not reasonably have been expected to know, that B was under 18;

    (b) he did not know, and could not reasonably have been expected to know, that B was a person in relation to whom he was in a position of trust; or

    (c) he was lawfully married to B.

(3) It shall not be an offence under this section for a person ("A") to have sexual intercourse with, or engage in any other sexual activity with or directed towards, another person ("B") if immediately before the commencement of this Act—

    (a) A was in a position of trust in relation to B; and

    (b) a sexual relationship existed between them.

(4) A person guilty of an offence under this section shall be liable—

    (a) on summary conviction, to imprisonment for a term not exceeding six months, or to a fine not exceeding the statutory maximum, or to both;

    (b) on conviction on indictment, to imprisonment for a term not exceeding five years, or to a fine, or to both.

(5) In this section, "sexual activity"—

    (a) does not include any activity which a reasonable person would regard as sexual only with knowledge of the intentions, motives or feelings of the parties; but

    (b) subject to that, means any activity which such a person would regard as sexual in all the circumstances.

As to "the commencement of this Act", see the Sexual Offences (Amendment) Act 2000 (Commencement No. 1) Order 2000 (S.I. 2000 No. 3303), which brought the Act into force on January 8, 2001.

Meaning of "position of trust"

H-242   **4.**—(1) For the purposes of section 3 above, a person aged 18 or over ("A") is in a position of trust in relation to a person under that age ("B") if any of the four conditions set out below, or any condition specified in an order made by the Secretary of State by statutory instrument, is fulfilled.

(2) The first condition is that A looks after persons under 18 who are detained in an institution by virtue of an order of a court or under an enactment, and B is so detained in that institution.

(3) The second condition is that A looks after persons under 18 who are resident in a home or other place in which—

(a) accommodation and maintenance are provided by an authority under section 23(2) of the Children Act 1989 or Article 27(2) of the Children (Northern Ireland) Order 1995;

(b) accommodation is provided by a voluntary organisation under section 59(1) of that Act or Article 75(1) of that Order; or

(c) accommodation is provided by an authority under section 26(1) of the Children (Scotland) Act 1995,

and B is resident, and is so provided with accommodation and maintenance or accommodation, in that place.

(4) The third condition is that A looks after persons under 18 who are accommodated and cared for in an institution which is—

(a) a hospital;

(b) a residential care home, nursing home, mental nursing home or private hospital;

(c) a community home, voluntary home, children's home or residential establishment; or

(d) a home provided under section 82(5) of the Children Act 1989,

and B is accommodated and cared for in that institution.

(5) The fourth condition is that A looks after persons under 18 who are receiving full-time education at an educational institution, and B is receiving such education at that institution.

(6) No order shall be made under subsection (1) above unless a draft of the order has been laid before and approved by a resolution of each House of Parliament.

(7) A person looks after persons under 18 for the purposes of this section if he is regularly involved in caring for, training, supervising or being in sole charge of such persons.

(8) For the purposes of this section a person receives full-time education at an educational institution if—

(a) he is registered or otherwise enrolled as a full-time pupil or student at the institution; or

(b) he receives education at the institution under arrangements with another educational institution at which he is so registered or otherwise enrolled.

(9) In this section, except where the context otherwise requires—

"authority" means—

(a) in relation to Great Britain, a local authority; and

(b) [*Northern Ireland*];

"children's home" has—

(a) in relation to England and Wales, the meaning which would be given by subsection (3) of section 63 of the Children Act 1989 if the reference in paragraph (a) of that subsection to more than three children were a reference to one or more children; and

(b) [*Northern Ireland*];

"community home" has the meaning given by section 53(1) of the Children Act 1989;

"hospital" has—

(a) in relation to England and Wales, the meaning given by section 128(1) of the National Health Service Act 1977;

(b) [*Scotland*]; and

(c) [*Northern Ireland*];

"mental nursing home" has, in relation to England and Wales, the meaning given by section 22(1) of the Registered Homes Act 1984

"nursing home"—

(a) in relation to England and Wales, has the meaning given by section 21(1) of the Registered Homes Act 1984;

(b) [*Scotland*];

(c) [*Northern Ireland*];

"private hospital" has—

(a) [*Scotland*]; and

(b) [*Northern Ireland*];

"residential care home"—

(a) in relation to England and Wales, has the meaning given by section 1(2) of the Registered Homes Act 1984;

(b) [*Scotland*]; and

(c) [*Northern Ireland*];

"residential establishment" has the meaning given by section 93(1) of the Children (Scotland) Act 1995 as the meaning of that expression in Scotland;

"voluntary home" has—
>   (a) in relation to England and Wales, the meaning given by section 60(3) of the Children
>   Act 1989; and
>   (b) [*Northern Ireland*].

(2) Indictment

Statement of Offence

H-243   *Abuse of a position of trust, contrary to section 3(1)(a) of the Sexual Offences (Amendment) Act 2000.*

Particulars of Offence

A B, on the _____ day of _____, 20__, being a person of the age of at least 18 years, had sexual intercourse with J N, being a person under the age of 18 years, and being at the time in a position of trust in relation to J N, in that at the time he looked after persons under the age of 18 years who were receiving full-time education at _____ school, and J N was at the time in receipt of such education at the aforesaid school.

(3) Mode of trial and class of offence

H-244   This offence is triable either way: s.3(4), *ante*. As to the classification of offences, see *ante*, Appendix B-209.

(4) Sentence

H-245   See s.3(4), *ante*.

The setting out of the various positions of trust in section 4(2) to (5) is not to be taken as indicative of descending seriousness: *R. v. Hubbard* [2002] 2 Cr.App.R.(S.) 101, CA.

APPENDIX J
A Guide to Commencing Proceedings in the Court of Appeal (Criminal Division)

NOTE: the text of the guide that follows has been subjected to some editorial revision (in relation to such matters as punctuation, use of upper and lower case, abbreviations, manner of citation of legislative references and authorities, and in order to correct a small number of obvious, minor errors). None of these revisions has any effect on the sense of the guide.

A GUIDE TO COMMENCING PROCEEDINGS IN THE COURT OF APPEAL (CRIMINAL DIVISION)

Foreword by the Lord Chief Justice of England and Wales

In recent years the Court of Appeal Criminal Division has faced increased complexity in appeals, not only against conviction but also against sentence, particularly in the light of the plethora of recent sentencing legislation. Additionally, the jurisdiction of the court has expanded to encompass a variety of diverse applications and appeals by the defence, the Crown and other interested parties. **J-1**

This guide provides invaluable advice as to the initial steps for commencing proceedings in the Court of Appeal Criminal Division generally and in relation to perhaps unfamiliar provisions.

The first and most important step is, of course, the preparation of the grounds of appeal. The rules prescribe the form and content of the Notice and Grounds of Appeal. Practitioners are also required to summarise the facts and outline their arguments concisely. Well drafted grounds of appeal assist the single judge when considering leave and serve to shorten any hearing before the full court. Ill-prepared and prolix documents necessarily lead to wasted time spent on preparation and unnecessarily protracted hearings.

It is important that we all take seriously our responsibility to ensure the effective progression of cases and keep delay to a minimum. Once an application or appeal is commenced, the responsible officer at the Criminal Appeal Office will be available to assist with any queries on practice or procedure.

The court could not deal with this volume of work efficiently without the support of the Registrar and his staff in the Criminal Appeal Office. Their experience and expertise is invaluable and can always be relied on by those who use the court, not least those who are unfamiliar with its practice and procedures.

Judge C.J.
October 2008

Introduction

Since the publication of the last Guide to Proceedings in the Court of Appeal (Criminal Division), the court's jurisdiction has increased. It hears appeals not only against conviction and sentence, but also against various interlocutory rulings, as well as other appeals and applications. **J-2**

This guide provides practical information about how to commence and conduct proceedings before the court. Once proceedings are commenced, an application will have its own unique reference number and a case progression officer who can help with any difficulties or queries about procedure.

The guide is set out as follows:

    A. General principles of practice and procedure when applying for leave to appeal conviction and sentence.

    B. Guidance on appeals against rulings made in preparatory hearings.

    C. Guidance on prosecution appeals against 'terminating' rulings.

    D. Brief guidance on other appeals in bullet point form showing:
- the type of appeal,
- the relevant section of the statute
- the relevant Criminal Procedure Rules
- who can apply
- the forms to be used and time limits
- respondents' notices,
- whether representation orders are available
- whether leave to appeal is required

E. Guidance on applications for a retrial for a serious offence.

A list of all up to date forms referred to in this guide may be accessed from the HMCS website at www.hmcourts-service.gov.uk or the Criminal Procedure Rules Committee website at www.justice.gov.uk/criminal/procrules. Where the Criminal Procedure Rules do not provide for a specific form, this guide indicates the appropriate form to be used.

This guide was prepared under my direction by the staff of the Criminal Appeal Office, but principally by Ms Alix Beldam and Ms Susan Holdham. It describes the law and practice of the Court as at 1st October 2008.

Master Venne

Registrar of Criminal Appeals

Terminology

J-3   The Criminal Appeal Act 1968 refers to "leave to appeal". This is now referred to as "permission to appeal" in the Criminal Procedure Rules 2007. This guide keeps to the terminology used by the Act.

Also consistently with the Act, an "appellant" is referred to without distinction, but it should be borne in mind that it is the accepted practice of the Criminal Appeal Office (CAO) to refer to a person who has served notice of appeal but not been granted leave to appeal as an "applicant" and use the term "appellant" to refer to a person who has been granted leave to appeal.

Any reference to counsel should be read as including a solicitor advocate as appropriate.

A. General Principles of Practice and Procedure when Applying for Leave to Appeal Conviction and

Sentence

A1 Advice and assistance

J-4   A1-1 Provision for advice or assistance on appeal is included in the trial representation order issued by the Crown Court. Solicitors should not wait to be asked for advice by the defendant. Immediately following the conclusion of the case, the legal representatives should see the defendant and counsel should express orally his final view as to the prospects of a successful appeal (whether against conviction or sentence or both). If there are no reasonable grounds of appeal, that should be confirmed in writing and a copy provided then, or as soon as practicable thereafter, to the defendant by the solicitor. If there are reasonable grounds, grounds of appeal should be drafted, signed and sent to instructing solicitors as soon as possible. Solicitors should immediately send a copy of the documents received from counsel to the defendant.

A1-2 Prior to the lodging of the notice and grounds of appeal by service of Form NG, the Registrar has no power to grant a representation order. Also, the Crown Court can only amend a representation order in favour of fresh legal representatives if advice on appeal has not been given by trial legal representatives and it is necessary and reasonable for another legal representative to be instructed. Where advice on appeal has been given by trial legal representatives, application for funding may only be made to the Legal Services Commission (LSC).

A1-3 Once the Form NG has been lodged, the Registrar is the authority for decisions about representation orders, in accordance with the principle that the court before which there are proceedings is the court with power to grant a right to representation (Access to Justice Act 1999, Sched. 3, affirmed by regulation 10 of the Criminal Defence Service (General) (No. 2) Regulations 2001 (S.I. 2001 No. 1437)).

A1-4 Where, in order to settle grounds of appeal, work of an exceptional nature is contemplated or where the expense will be great, legal representatives should submit a Form NG with provisional grounds of appeal and with a note to the Registrar requesting a representation order to cover the specific work considered necessary to enable proper grounds of appeal to be settled.

A2 Form NG and grounds of appeal

J-5   A2-1 Where counsel has advised an appeal, solicitors should forward the signed grounds of appeal to the Crown Court accompanied by Form NG and such other forms as may be appropriate. It should be noted that Form NG and grounds of appeal are required to be served within the relevant time limit in all cases, whether or not leave to appeal is required (*e.g.* where a trial judge's certificate has been granted). However, on a reference by the Criminal Cases Review Commission (CCRC), if no Form NG and grounds are served within the required period, then the reference shall be treated as the appeal notice: rule 68.5(2).

A2-2 Grounds must be settled with sufficient particularity to enable the Registrar, and subsequently the court, to identify clearly the matters relied upon. A mere formula such as "the conviction is unsafe" or "the sentence is in all the circumstances too severe" will be ineffective as grounds and time will continue to run against the defendant.

A2-3 Rule 68.3(1) sets out the information that must be contained in the appeal notice. The notice must … [*see § 7-382 in the main work*].

A2-4 There is now a requirement for the grounds of appeal to set out the relevant facts and nature of the proceedings concisely in one all encompassing document, not separate grounds and advice. The intended readership of this document is the court and not the lay or professional client. Its purpose is to enable the single judge to grasp quickly the facts and issues in the case. In appropriate cases, draft grounds of appeal may be perfected before submission to the single judge (*see further below para. A5*).

A2-5 Any document mentioned in the grounds should be identified clearly, by exhibit number or otherwise. Similarly, if counsel requires an original exhibit or shorthand writer's tape recording, he should say so well in advance of any determination or hearing.

A2-6 Counsel should not settle or sign grounds unless they are reasonable, have some real prospect of success and are such that he is prepared to argue them before the court. Counsel should not settle grounds he cannot support because he is "instructed" to do so by a defendant.

A2-7 Procedure in relation to particular grounds of appeal

A2-7.1 *Applications to call fresh evidence*

A Form W and a statement from the witness in the form prescribed by section 9 of the CJA 1967 should be lodged in respect of each witness it is proposed to call. The Form W should indicate whether there is an application for a witness order. The Registrar or the single judge may direct the issue of a witness order, but only the court hearing the appeal may give leave for a witness to be called.

The court will require a cogent explanation for the failure to adduce the evidence at trial. A supporting witness statement or affidavit from the appellant's solicitor should be lodged in this regard (*R. v. Gogana, The Times,* July 12, 1999).

If there is to be an application to adduce hearsay and/or evidence of bad character or for special measures, then the appropriate forms should be lodged: rule 68.7(1).

A2-7.2 *Complaints against trial counsel as a ground of appeal*

Where a ground of appeal explicitly criticises trial counsel and/or trial solicitors, the Registrar will institute the "waiver of privilege" procedure. The appellant will be asked to "waive privilege" in respect of instructions to and advice at trial from legal representatives. If he does waive privilege, the grounds of appeal are sent to the appropriate trial representative(s) and they are invited to respond. Any response will be sent to the appellant or his fresh legal representatives for comment. All these documents will be sent to the single judge when considering the application for leave. The single judge may draw inferences from any failure to participate in the process. "Waiver of privilege" is a procedure that should be instigated by the Registrar and not by fresh legal representatives, who should go no further than obtaining a waiver of privilege from the appellant: *R. v. Doherty and McGregor* [1997] 2 Cr.App.R. 218.

A2-7.3 *Insufficient weight given to assistance to prosecution authorities*

Where a ground of appeal against sentence is that the judge has given insufficient weight to the assistance given to the prosecution authorities, the "text" which had been prepared for the sentencing judge is obtained by the Registrar. Grounds of appeal should be drafted in an anodyne form with a note to the Registrar alerting him to the existence of a "text". The single judge will have seen the "text" when considering leave as will the full court before the appeal hearing and it need not be alluded to in open court.

A3 Time limits

A3-1 Notice and grounds should reach the Crown Court within 28 days <u>from the date of the</u> **J-6** <u>conviction</u> in the case of an application for leave to appeal against conviction and within 28 days <u>from the date of sentence</u> in the case of an application for leave to appeal against sentence [CAA 1968, s.18 and rule 68.2(1)]. On a reference by the CCRC, Form NG and grounds should be served on the Registrar not more than 56 days after the Registrar has served notice that the CCRC has referred a conviction and not more than 28 days in the case of a sentence referral: rule 68.2(2).

A3-2 A confiscation order (whether made under the CJA 1988, the DTA 1994 or the PCA 2002) is a sentence [CAA 1968, s.50]. Where sentences are passed in separate proceedings on different dates there may be two appeals against sentence. Thus, there may be an appeal against the custodial part of a sentence and an appeal against a confiscation order (*R. v. Neal* [1999] 2 Cr.App.R.(S.) 352).

A3-3 An application for extension of the 28 day period in which to give notice of application for leave to appeal or notice of appeal must always be supported by reasons why the application for leave was not submitted in time. It is not enough merely to tick the relevant box on Form NG.

A3-4 Such an application should be submitted when the application for leave to appeal against either conviction or sentence is made and not in advance. Notwithstanding the terms of section 18(3) of the CAA 1968, it has long been the practice of the Registrar to require the extension of time application to be made at the time of service of the notice and grounds of appeal. This practice is now reflected by Criminal Procedure Rule 65.4.

A4 Transcript and notes of evidence

J-7

A4-1 In conviction cases, transcripts of the summing up and proceedings up to and including verdict are obtained as a matter of course. Similarly, the transcript of the prosecution opening of facts on a guilty plea and the judge's observations on passing sentence are usually obtained in sentence cases. There is now an obligation under rule 68.3(2) for counsel to identify any further transcript which counsel considers the court will need and to provide a note of names, dates and times to enable an order to be placed with the shorthand writers. Whether or not any further transcript is required is a matter for the judgment of the Registrar or his staff.

A4-2 Transcript should only be requested if it is essential for the proper conduct of the appeal in the light of the grounds. If the Registrar and counsel are unable to agree the extent of the transcript to be obtained, the Registrar may refer that matter to a judge. In some cases the Registrar may propose that counsel agree a note in place of transcript.

A4-3 In certain circumstances the costs of unnecessary transcript could be ordered to be paid by the appellant. Where transcript is obtained otherwise than through the Registrar, he may disallow the cost on taxation of public funding.

A5 Perfection of grounds of appeal

J-8

A5-1 The purpose of perfection is (a) to save valuable judicial time by enabling the court to identify at once the relevant parts of the transcript and (b) to give counsel the opportunity to reconsider his original grounds in the light of the transcript. Perfected grounds should consist of a fresh document which supersedes the original grounds of appeal and contains *inter alia* references by page number and letter (or paragraph number) to all relevant passages in the transcript.

A5-2 In conviction or confiscation cases, the Registrar will almost certainly invite counsel to perfect grounds in the light of the transcript obtained, to assist the single judge or full court. Where counsel indicates a wish to perfect grounds of appeal against sentence, the Registrar will consider the request and will only invite perfection where he considers it necessary for the assistance of the single judge or full court.

A5-3 If perfection is appropriate, counsel will be sent a copy of the transcript and asked to perfect his grounds within 14 days. In the absence of any response from counsel, the existing notice and grounds of appeal will be placed before the single judge or the court without further notice. If counsel does not wish to perfect his grounds, the transcript should be returned with a note to that effect.

A5-4 If, having considered the transcript, counsel is of opinion that there are no valid grounds, he should set out his reasons in a further advice and send it to his instructing solicitors. He should inform the Registrar that he has done so, but should not send him a copy of that advice. Solicitors should send a copy to the appellant and obtain instructions, at the same time explaining that if the appellant persists with his application the court may consider whether to make a loss of time order (*see further below A-13*).

A6 Respondent's notice

J-9

A6-1 The Criminal Procedure Rules 2005 provide for the service of a respondent's notice. Under rule 68.6(1) the Registrar may serve the appeal notice on any party directly affected by the appeal (usually the prosecution) and must do so in a CCRC case. That party may then serve a respondent's notice if it wishes to make representations and must do so if the Registrar so directs: rule 68.6(2). The respondent's notice should be served within 14 days (rule 68.6(4)) on the appellant, the Registrar and any other party on whom the Registrar served the appeal notice (rule 68.6(3)). The respondent's notice must be in the specified form [Form RN], in which a respondent should set out the grounds of opposition (rule 68.6(5)) and which must include the information set out in rule 68.6(6).

A6-2 In practice, this procedure primarily applies prior to consideration of leave by the single judge in both conviction and sentence cases. The Attorney General and the Registrar, following consultation with representatives from the Crown Prosecution Service (CPS) and the Revenue and Customs Prosecution Office (RCPO), have agreed guidance on types of cases and/or issues where the Registrar should consider whether to serve an appeal notice and direct or invite a party to serve a respondent's notice before the consideration of leave by the single judge. Examples of when the Registrar might **direct** a respondent's notice include where the grounds concern matters which were the subject of public interest immunity (PII), allegations of jury irregularity, criticism of the conduct of the judge and complex frauds. Cases where it might be appropriate for the Registrar to **invite** a respondent's notice include, for example, homicide offences, serious sexual offences, cases with national profile or high media interest, cases of violence or domestic violence.

A6-3 In conviction cases where leave has been granted or where the application for leave has been referred to the full court, the Crown is briefed to attend the hearing and required to submit a respondent's notice/skeleton argument. In relation to sentence cases where leave has been granted, referred or an appellant is represented on a renewed application, the sentence protocol set out in paragraph II.1 of the consolidated criminal practice direction [see now *Criminal Practice Direction (Appeal) 68A* [2013] 1 W.L.R. 3164 (§ 7-203 in the main work)] will apply. In those cases, a respondent's notice/skeleton argument will have to be served when the Crown indicates a wish to attend or when the Registrar invites or directs the Crown to attend.

A7 Referral by the Registrar

A7-1 Leave to appeal is required in all cases except where the trial judge or sentencing judge has **J-10** certified that the case is fit for appeal (CAA 1968, ss.1(2) and 11(1A)) or where the case has been referred by the CCRC. The appellant must obtain leave to pursue grounds not related to the Commission's reasons for referral: CAA 1995, s.14(4B).

A7-2 Where leave to appeal is required and the Registrar has obtained the necessary documents, he will refer the application(s) either (a) to a single judge for decision under section 31 of the CAA 1968 or (b) directly to the full court, in which case a representation order is usually granted for the hearing. However, the Registrar will not grant a representation order when the presence of counsel is not required, *e.g.* where the application refers solely to an amendment of the number of days to be credited as "remand time" and the figure is agreed by the parties. Where an application is referred to the full court by the Registrar because an unlawful sentence has been passed or other procedural error identified, a representation order will ordinarily be granted, but counsel should be aware that the court may make observations for the attention of the determining officer that a full fee should not be allowed on taxation.

A7-3 Where leave to appeal is not required, *e.g.* on appeal by certificate of the trial judge, the Registrar will usually grant a representation order for the hearing. On a reference from the CCRC, it is the Registrar's usual practice to grant a representation order in the first instance, to solicitors for them to nominate and instruct counsel to settle grounds of appeal. Once counsel's details are known, a further representation order will be granted to cover the preparation (including settling grounds) and presentation of the appeal by counsel and further work by solicitors, as necessary in light of the grounds.

A8 Bail pending appeal

A8-1 Bail may be granted (a) by a single judge or the full court or (b) by a trial or sentencing **J-11** judge who has certified the case fit for appeal. In the latter case, bail can only be granted within 28 days of the conviction or sentence which is the subject of the appeal and may not be granted if an application for bail has already been made to the Court of Appeal.

A8-2 An application to the Court of Appeal for bail must be supported by a completed Form B, whether or not the application is made at the same time as the notice and grounds are served. The completed Form B must be served on the Registrar <u>and the prosecution</u> at least 24 hours before any application is made to enable the Crown to make representations (either written or oral) about the application and any conditions.

A8-3 An application for bail will not be considered by a single judge or the court until notice of application for leave to appeal or notice of appeal has first been given. In practice, judges will also require the relevant transcripts to be available so they may take a view as to the merits of the substantive application.

A8-4 It is the practice of the court, if bail is granted, to require a condition of residence. An application for variation of conditions of bail may be determined by the Registrar (if unopposed) or a single judge.

A9 Consideration of the applications by single judge

A9-1 Normally a single judge will consider the application for leave to appeal together with any **J-12** ancillary applications, *e.g.* for bail or representation order, without hearing oral argument. Counsel may request an oral hearing, but it is only in very rare circumstances that the Registrar would consider it appropriate to grant a representation order for the proceedings before a single judge at an oral hearing, but counsel may appear to argue the applications before the single judge where instructed to do so, usually appearing either *pro bono* or privately funded. Oral applications for leave and bail are usually heard at 9.30 a.m. before the normal court sittings. Counsel appears unrobed. If counsel considers that an application may take longer than 20 minutes, the Registrar must be informed.

A10 Powers of the single judge

J-13
A10-1 The single judge may grant the application for leave, refuse it or refer it to the full court. In conviction cases and in sentence cases where appropriate, the single judge may grant limited leave, *i.e.* leave to argue some grounds but not others. If the grounds upon which leave has been refused are to be renewed before the full court, counsel must notify the Registrar within 14 days. In the absence of any notification of renewal, it will be assumed that the grounds upon which leave was refused will not be pursued.

The single judge may also grant, refuse or refer any ancillary application.

A11 Grant of leave or reference to full court

J-14
A11-1 Where the single judge grants leave or refers an application to the court, it is usual to grant a representation order for the preparation and presentation of the appeal. This is usually limited to the services of counsel only, in which event counsel will be assigned by the Registrar. In such a case the Registrar will provide a brief but does not act as an appellant's solicitor. Counsel who settled grounds of appeal will usually be assigned. However, the Registrar may assign one counsel to represent more than one appellant if appropriate. If it is considered that a representation order for two counsel and/or solicitors is required, counsel should notify the Registrar and provide written justification in accordance with the Criminal Defence Service (General) (No. 2) Regulations 2001.

A11-2 If solicitors are assigned, it should be noted that by virtue of regulation 13 of the Criminal Defence Service (General) (No. 2) Regulations 2001, a representation order can only be issued to a solicitor if he holds a General Criminal Contract (Crime Franchise) with the LSC. A solicitor not holding such a franchise may apply to the LSC for an individual case contract (by virtue of which the solicitor is employed on behalf of the LSC to represent an appellant in a given case). Such a contract is sufficient for the purposes of regulation 13.

A11-3 In some circumstances, the Registrar may refer an application to the full court. This may be because there is a novel point of law or because in a sentence case, the sentence passed is unlawful and regardless of the merits, the sentence should be amended. A representation order for counsel is usually granted. Counsel for the prosecution usually attends a Registrar's referral.

A12 Refusal by the single judge

J-15
A12-1 Where the single judge refuses leave to appeal, the Registrar sends a notification of the refusal, including any observations which the judge may have made, to the appellant, who is informed that he may require the application to be considered by the court by serving a renewal notice [Form SJ-Renewal] upon the Registrar within 14 days from the date on which the notice of refusal was served on him.

A12-2 A refused application which is not renewed within 14 days lapses. An appellant may apply for an extension of time in which to renew his application for leave: CAA 1968, s.31, and rule 65.5(2). The Registrar will normally refer such an application to the court to be considered at the same time as the renewed application for leave to appeal. An application for extension for time in which to renew must be supported by cogent reasons.

A12-3 If it is intended that counsel should represent the appellant at the hearing of the renewed application for leave to appeal, whether privately instructed or on a *pro bono* basis, such intention must be communicated to the CAO in writing as soon as that decision has been made. Whilst a representation order is not granted by the Registrar in respect of a renewed application for leave, counsel may apply at the hearing to the court for a representation order to cover that appearance. In practice, this is only granted where the application for leave is successful.

A13 Directions for loss of time

J-16
A13-1 The CAA 1968, s. 29, empowers the court to direct that time spent in custody as an appellant shall not count as part of the term of any sentence to which the appellant is for the time being subject. The court will do so where it considers that an application is wholly without merit. Such an order may not be made where leave to appeal or a trial judge's certificate has been granted, on a reference by the CCRC or where an appeal has been abandoned.

A13-2 The mere fact that counsel has advised that there are grounds of appeal will not be a sufficient answer to the question as to whether or not an application has indeed been brought which was wholly without merit: *R. v. Hart; R. v. George; R. v. Clarke; R. v. Brown* [2007] 1 Cr.App.R. 31.

A13-3 The Form SJ, on which the single judge records his decisions, and the reverse of which is used by appellants to indicate their wish to renew, includes:

- a box for the single judge to initial to indicate that that the full court should consider loss of time if the application is renewed and
- a box for the applicant to give reasons why such an order should not be made, whether or not an indication has been given by a single judge.

A14 Abandonment

A14-1 An appeal or application may be abandoned at any time before the hearing without leave by **J-17** completing and lodging Form A. An oral instruction or letter indicating a wish to abandon is insufficient.

A14-2 At the hearing, an application or appeal can only be abandoned with the permission of the court: rule 65.13(2). An appeal or application which is abandoned is treated as having been dismissed or refused by the full court, as the case may be: rule 65.13(4)(c).

A14-3 A notice of abandonment cannot be withdrawn nor can it be conditional. A person who wants to reinstate an application or appeal after abandonment must apply in writing with reasons: rule 65.13(5). The court has power to allow reinstatement only where the purported abandonment can be treated as a nullity (see *R. v. Medway*, 62 Cr.App.R. 85; *R. v. Burt, The Independent,* December 3, 2004; *R. v. Grant* (2005) 149 S.J. 1186).

A15 Case management duties

A15-1 Rule 65.2 gives the court and parties the same powers and duties of case management as in **J-18** Part 3 of the rules. In accordance with those duties, for each application received, the Registrar nominates a case progression officer (the "responsible officer"). There is also a duty on the parties actively to assist the court to progress cases. Close contact between counsel and solicitors and the responsible officer is encouraged in order to facilitate the efficient preparation and listing of appeals, especially in complex cases and those involving witnesses.

A15-2 Powers exercisable by the single judge and the Registrar are contained in the CAA 1968, s.31. These powers include the power to make procedural directions for the efficient and effective preparation of an application or appeal and the power to make an order under section 23(1)(a) of the 1968 Act for the production of evidence etc. necessary for the determination of the case.

A15-3 Procedural directions given by the Registrar may be appealed to a single judge. Those given by a single judge, including a single Lord Justice, are final.

B. INTERLOCUTORY APPEALS AGAINST RULINGS IN PREPARATORY HEARINGS

Appeal against a ruling under section 9 of the Criminal Justice Act 1987 or a decision under section 35 of the Criminal Procedure and Investigations Act 1996 [Part 66 Criminal Procedure Rules 2007]

B1 Where a judge has ordered a preparatory hearing, he may make a ruling as to the admissibil- **J-19** ity of evidence; any other question of law relating to the case or any question as to the severance or joinder of charges. (s.9(3)(b), (c) and (d) of the 1987 Act/s.31(3)(a), (b) and (c) of the 1996 Act)

B2 Under section 9(11) of the 1987 Act/section 35(1) of the 1996 Act the defence or the prosecution may appeal to the CACD (and ultimately to the House of Lords) against such a ruling, but only with the leave of the trial judge, single judge or the full court. As to the scope of a judge's powers in relation to a preparatory hearing and thus the extent of appeal rights, see *R. v. H* (§ 7-310 in the main work).

B3 If the trial date is imminent and the application is urgent, the Registrar should be notified so that he may consider referring the application directly to the full court and make arrangements for listing.

B4 If an application for leave to appeal is made to the trial judge, it should be made orally immediately after the ruling, or within two business days by serving a notice of an application on the appropriate officer of the Crown Court and all parties directly affected: rule 66.4. Notice of appeal or application for leave to appeal [Form NG (Prep)] is to be served on the Registrar, the Crown Court and the parties within five business days of the ruling or the trial judge's decision whether to grant leave: rule 66.2.

B5 The notice and grounds of appeal having been served on the other parties, grounds of opposition should be served in a respondent's notice [Form RN (Prep)] within five business days of service of the appeal notice: rule 66.5.

B6 Defence representatives are usually covered by the Crown Court representation order if one is in force (Access to Justice Act 1999, Sched. 3, para. 2(2)).

B7 If the relevant time limits are not complied with, the court has power to grant an extension of time, but cogent grounds in support of the application will be required. Where a single judge refuses leave to appeal or an extension of time within which to serve a notice, the application may be renewed for determination by the full court by serving the notice of refusal, appropriately completed, upon the Registrar within five business days of the refusal being served (rule 66.7).

C. Appeals by a Prosecutor Against a "Terminating" Ruling

Criminal Justice Act 2003, s.58 [Part 67 Criminal Procedure Rules 2007]

J-20

C1 Section 58 of the 2003 Act gives the prosecution a right of appeal in relation to a "terminating" ruling: in effect where the prosecution agrees to the defendant's acquittal if the appeal against the ruling is not successful (*R. v. Y.* [2008] 1 Cr.App.R. 34). This is wide enough to encompass a case management decision (*R. v. Clarke* [2008] 1 Cr.App.R. 33).

C2 There is no right of appeal in respect of a ruling that the jury be discharged or a ruling in respect of which there is a right of appeal to the Court of Appeal by virtue of another enactment (s.57(2)). The prosecution should therefore consider whether there is a right of appeal under section 9 of the CJA 1987 or section 35 of the CPIA 1996.

C3 The prosecution must inform the court that it intends to appeal or request an adjournment to consider whether to appeal (s.58(4)), which will be until the next business day (rule 67.2(2)). The judge has a discretion to adjourn for longer if there is a real reason for doing so (*R. v. H.* [2008] EWCA Crim. 483). The prosecution can then ask the trial judge to grant leave to appeal (rule 67.5), although leave to appeal can be granted by the trial judge, the single judge or the full court. The Crown must give the undertaking (as to the defendant's acquittal if the appeal is abandoned or leave to appeal is not obtained) at the time when it informs the court of its intention to appeal. The failure to give it then is fatal to an application to the Court of Appeal for leave: s.58(8); *R. v. Arnold* [2008] R.T.R. 25.

C4 Whether or not leave is granted, the trial judge must then decide if the appeal is to be expedited and if so, adjourn the case. If he decides that the appeal should not be expedited, then he can adjourn the case or discharge the jury (s.59). Leave should be granted only where the trial judge considers there is a real prospect of success and not in an attempt to speed up the hearing of the appeal (*R. v. J.G.* [2006] EWCA Crim. 3276).

C5 Whether the appeal is expedited or not affects the time limits for service of the notice of appeal [Form NG (Pros)] and respondent's notice [Form RN (Pros)]. If expedited, the appeal notice must be served the next business day after the decision, if not expedited, it must be served within five business days. Similar time limits apply to the service of the respondent's notice. Defence representatives are usually covered by the Crown Court representation order if one is in force (such proceedings being considered incidental within the Access to Justice Act 1999, Sched. 3, para. 2(2)). If the relevant time limits are not complied with, the court has power to grant an extension of time.

C6 Expedition does not impose time limits on the Registrar or Court of Appeal. However, if leave has not been granted by the trial judge, the application may be referred to the full court by the Registrar to enable the application and appeal to be heard together to ensure that the matter is dealt with quickly.

C7 The Registrar endeavours to list prosecution appeals where a jury has not been discharged as quickly as possible. He is unlikely to be able to list an appeal in less than a week from the ruling because it is necessary for the prosecution to obtain transcripts, papers to be copied and the judges to read their papers. It is of great assistance if it is anticipated that there is to be an appeal against a ruling where the jury has not been discharged, that a telephone call is made to the Registrar or CAO general office (020 7947 6011) notifying the office even before the appeal notice is sent, so that the list office may be put on notice. The listing of an urgent appeal invariably means that other cases have to be removed from the list.

D. Other Appeals

D1 Prosecution appeal against the making of a confiscation order or where the court declines to make one (save on reconsideration of benefit)

J-21

- S.31 of the PCA 2002.
- Parts 71 and 72 of the Criminal Procedure Rules.
- From April 1, 2008 only the prosecution can appeal
- Proceedings are commenced by serving a Form PoCA 1 on the defendant and the Crown Court within 28 days of the decision appealed against. [Proceeds of Crime Act (Appeals under Part 2) Order 2003, art. 3(2)(a).]

- A respondent's notice PoCA 2 is to be served on the Registrar of Criminal Appeals and the appellant not later than 14 days after receiving PoCA 1.
- An undischarged Crown Court representation order will cover advice and assistance on the merits of opposing the appeal and drafting the respondent's notice, otherwise an application for a representation order can be made to the Registrar [Access to Justice Act 1999, ss.12(2)(b), 26]. In any event, where an application for a representation order is made on PoCA 2, the Registrar will consider a representation order for the hearing.
- Leave to appeal can be granted by a single judge or the full court.

D2 Appeal in relation to a restraint order

- S.43 of the PCA 2002.   **J-22**
- Parts 71 and 73 of the Criminal Procedure Rules.
- The prosecution or an accredited financial investigator can appeal a refusal to make a restraint order. A person who applied for an order or who is affected by the order can apply to the Crown Court to vary or discharge the order and then appeal that decision to the Court of Appeal.
- Proceedings are commenced by serving a form PoCA 3 on the Crown Court within 14 days of the decision being appealed. PoCA 3 must then be served on any respondent, and on any person who holds realisable property to which the appeal relates, or is affected by the appeal, not later than seven days after the form is lodged at the Crown Court. The documents which are to be served with PoCA 3 are set out in rule 73.2(3).
- A respondent's notice PoCA 4 is to be served on the Registrar not later than 14 days after the respondent is notified that the appellant has leave to appeal or notified that the application for leave and any appeal are to be heard together. PoCA 4 is then to be served on the appellant and any other respondent as soon as is practicable and not later than seven days after it was served on the Registrar.
- An application for a restraint order can be made as soon as a criminal investigation has begun. The proposed defendant may not have been charged: PCA 2002, s.40. This affects the type of public funding.
- If a defendant has been charged with a criminal offence connected to the restraint order then the restraint proceedings are regarded as incidental to the criminal proceedings and are treated as criminal proceedings for funding purposes [Criminal Defence Service (General) (No. 2) Regulations 2001, reg.3(3)(c)] and the Registrar can grant a representation order if a defendant appeals a decision on an application to vary or discharge the restraint order.
- If the prosecution apply for a restraint order in the Crown Court before the subject of the restraint order has been charged with a criminal offence and the subject of that order wishes to appeal a decision on an application to vary or discharge the restraint order then civil legal aid may be available as these proceedings fall within the Access to Justice Act 1999, Sched. 2, para. 3. The Legal Services Commission should be contacted for funding within the Community Legal Service scheme.
- Similarly, a person affected by the order who wishes to appeal a decision on an application to vary or discharge the restraint order should apply to the Legal Services Commission for funding within the Community Legal Service scheme.
- Leave to appeal can be granted by a single judge or full court.

D3 Appeal in relation to a receivership order

- S.65 of the PCA 2002.   **J-23**
- Parts 71 and 73 of the Criminal Procedure Rules.
- An appeal can be brought by:
  (a) the person who applied for the order,
  (b) a person who is affected by the order or,
  (c) the receiver.
  The orders against which an appeal will lie are:
  (1) the appointment or non-appointment of a receiver,
  (2) the powers of a receiver,
  (3) an order giving a direction to a receiver, and
  (4) the variation or discharge of a receivership order.
- Proceedings are commenced by serving a Form PoCA 3 on the Crown Court within 14 days of the decision being appealed. PoCA 3 must then be served on any respondent and

on any person who holds realisable property to which the appeal relates, or is affected by the appeal, not later than seven days after the form is lodged at the Crown Court. The documents which are to be served with PoCA 3 are set out in rule 73.2(3).

- A respondent's notice PoCA 4 is to be served on the Registrar not later than 14 days after the respondent is notified that the appellant has leave to appeal or is notified that the application for leave and any appeal are to be heard together. PoCA 4 is then to be served on the appellant and any other respondent as soon as is practicable and not later than seven days after it was served on the Registrar.
- If a defendant has been charged with a criminal offence connected to a receivership order then the receivership proceedings are regarded as incidental to the criminal proceedings and are treated as criminal proceedings for funding purposes [Criminal Defence Service (General) (No. 2) Regulations 2001, reg.3(3)(c)] and the Registrar can grant a representation order if a defendant appeals a decision relating to a receivership order.
- If a management receivership order or an application for such an order is made in the Crown Court before a criminal offence has been charged and a person affected by the order (including the proposed defendant) wishes to appeal a decision then civil legal aid may be available as these proceedings fall within Access to Justice Act 1999, Sched. 2, para. 3. The Legal Services Commission should be contacted for funding within the Community Legal Service scheme.
- Leave to appeal can be granted by a single judge or the full court.

D4 Appeal against an order of the Crown Court in the exercise of its jurisdiction to punish for contempt – usually a finding of contempt or sentence for contempt

J-24
- S.13 of the Administration of Justice Act 1960.
- Part 68 of the Criminal Procedure Rules.
- Anyone dealt with by the Crown Court for contempt may appeal.
- Proceedings are commenced by lodging a Form NG at the Crown Court not more than 28 days after the order to be appealed.
- The Registrar may direct a respondent's notice Form RN or the Crown may serve one if they wish to make representations to the court.
- An undischarged Crown Court representation order will cover advice and assistance on appeal. The Registrar will usually grant a representation order for the hearing: Access to Justice Act 1999, s.12(2)(b).
- No leave to appeal is required. The appeal is as of right.
- Appeals occur most frequently when an appellant wishes to appeal a sentence for failing to appear at the Crown Court as the failing to appear is dealt with as if it were contempt.

D5 Appeal against a minimum term set or reviewed by a High Court judge

J-25
- Para. 14 of Schedule 22 to the CJA 2003
- Part 68 of the Criminal Procedure Rules
- A defendant with a mandatory life sentence imposed before December 18, 2003 who has had his minimum term set or reviewed by a High Court judge can appeal.
- Proceedings are commenced by service of Form NG (MT) on the Registrar not more than 28 days after the decision.
- The Registrar may direct a respondent's notice Form RN or the Crown may serve one if they wish to make representations to the court.
- An application for a representation order can be made to the Registrar [Access to Justice Act 1999, s.12(2)(b)].
- Leave to appeal is required and can be granted by the full court or a single judge: Criminal Justice Act 2003 (Mandatory Life Sentences: Appeals in Transitional Cases) Order 2005 (S.I. 2005 No. 2798), art. 8.

D6 Attorney General's reference of an unduly lenient sentence

J-26
- S.36 of the CJA 1988.
- Part 70 of the Criminal Procedure Rules.
- The Attorney General can refer sentences only in relation to specific offences or sentences [CJA 1988, ss.35, 36, and Criminal Justice Act 1988 (Reviews of Sentencing) Order 2006] including a minimum term, set or reviewed by a High Court judge [CJA 2003, Sched. 22, para. 15].

- Although rule 70.3(1) implies there is a specific form to commence proceedings, in practice a standard letter with supporting documents is sent by the Attorney General's office no more than 28 days after sentence.
- If the defendant wishes to make representations to the court he must serve a respondent's notice within 14 days of the Registrar serving the application upon him. Again, there is no specific form designated.
- Representation orders are not issued to respond to an Attorney General's reference but a defendant who appears by counsel is entitled to his reasonable costs from central funds. The cost of instructing leading counsel in addition to or instead of junior counsel is generally not considered reasonable unless there is a compelling reason. It is advisable to consult with the Registrar before leading counsel is instructed.
- The leave of the Court of Appeal is required.

D7 Attorney General's reference of a point of law on an acquittal
J-27
- S.36 of the CJA 1972.
- Part 70 of the Criminal Procedure Rules.
- The Attorney General can refer a point of law to the Court of Appeal for an opinion on the acquittal on indictment of the defendant.
- Although rule 70.3(1) implies there is a specific form to commence proceedings, there is no such form and rule 70.3 sets out what should be included in the reference. The defendant should not be identified.
- There is no time limit.
- If the defendant wishes to make representations to the court he must serve a respondent's notice within 28 days of the Registrar serving the application upon him. Again there is no specific form.
- Representation orders are not issued to respond to an Attorney General's reference but a defendant who appears by counsel is entitled to his reasonable costs from central funds.
- Leave is not required.

D8 Appeal against a finding of unfitness to plead or a finding that the accused did the act or made the omission charged
J-28
- S.15 of the CAA 1968.
- Part 68 of the Criminal Procedure Rules.
- The accused can appeal (by the person appointed to represent the accused) against
  — a finding of unfitness to plead (but not fitness to plead as the defendant can appeal any subsequent conviction in the usual way on the basis he was not fit to plead) or
  — that he did the act or made the omission charged or
  — both findings.
  The appeal does not lie until both findings have been made.
- Proceedings are commenced by the service of Form NG on the Crown Court not more than 28 days after the finding made which the accused wishes to appeal.
- The Crown should serve a respondent's notice Form RN if directed by the Registrar or if they wish to make representations to the court.
- There does not appear to be any statutory provision empowering the grant of a representation order. The Prosecution of Offences Act 1985, s.19, refers to costs from central funds being available to cover the fees of a person appointed by the Crown Court under section 4A of the Criminal Procedure (Insanity) Act 1964. In *R. v. Antoine* ([1999] 2 Cr.App.R 225, CA) this was interpreted to include the costs of an appeal. The Prosecution of Offences Act 1985, s.16(4) provides that where the Court of Appeal allows an appeal under Part 1 of the CAA 1968 against a finding under the Criminal Procedure (Insanity) Act 1964 that the appellant is under a disability, or that he did the act or made the omission charged against him the court may make a defendant's costs order in favour of the accused.
- Leave to appeal may be granted by the Crown Court judge, a single judge or the full court.

D9 Appeal against a verdict of not guilty by reason of insanity
J-29
- S.12 of the CAA 1968.
- Part 68 of the Criminal Procedure Rules.
- The defendant can appeal a verdict of not guilty by reason of insanity.

- Proceedings are commenced by the service of Form NG on the Crown Court not more than 28 days after the verdict.
- The Crown should serve a respondent's notice Form RN if directed by the Registrar or if they wish to make representations to the court.
- There does not appear to be any statutory provision empowering the grant of a representation order. The Prosecution of Offences Act 1985, s.16(4), provides that where the Court of Appeal <u>allows an appeal</u> then the court may make a defendant's costs order. If the appeal is not allowed costs from central funds should be available on the same basis as was allowed in *Antoine* (*ante*) in the absence of any statutory provision.
- Leave to appeal may be granted by the Crown Court judge, a single judge or the full court.

D10 Appeal against the order following a verdict of not guilty by reason of insanity or a finding of unfitness to plead

J-30

- S.16A of the CAA 1968.
- Part 68 of the Criminal Procedure Rules.
- An accused who, as a result of a verdict of not guilty by reason of insanity or a finding of fitness to plead has a hospital order, interim hospital order or supervision order made against him may appeal against the order.
- Proceedings are commenced by the service of Form NG on the Crown Court not more than 28 days after the order.
- [As D9, *ante*.]
- [As D9, *ante*.]
- [As D9, *ante*.]

D11 Appeal against review of sentence

J-31

- S.74(8) of the SOCPA 2005.
- Part 68 of the Criminal Procedure Rules.
- A defendant or specified prosecutor may appeal.
- Proceedings are commenced by serving a Form NG (RD) on the Crown Court not more than 28 days after the review.
- A respondent's notice Form RN should be served if directed by the Registrar or if the respondent wishes to make representations to the Court.
- An application for a representation order can be made to the Registrar: Access to Justice Act 1999, s.12(2)(b).
- Leave to appeal can be granted by the single judge or full court [Serious Organised Crime and Police Act 2005 (Appeals under section 74) Order 2006 (S.I. 2006 No. 2135)].

D12 Appeal against an order for trial by jury of sample counts

J-32

- S.18 of the Domestic Violence, Crime and Victims Act 2004.
- Part 66 of the Criminal Procedure Rules.
- The defendant can appeal.
- An application for the jury to try some counts as sample counts and the judge to try the remainder if the jury convict, must be determined at a preparatory hearing and section 18 confers rights of interlocutory appeal. A Form NG (Prep) must be served on the Crown Court, the Registrar and any party directly affected not more than five business days after the order or the Crown Court judge granting or refusing leave. (*For applications to the Crown Court judge, see Part B above.*)
- A respondent's notice Form RN (Prep) should be served if the court directs or the Crown (or any party affected) wants to make representations to the court.
- Defence representatives are usually covered by the Crown Court representation order if one is in force [Access to Justice Act 1999, Sched. 3, para. 2(2)].
- The Crown Court Judge, single judge or full court can grant leave to appeal.

D13 Appeal against an order relating to a trial to be conducted without a jury where there is a danger of jury tampering

J-33

- S.9(11) of the CJA 1987 and s.35(1) of the CPIA 1996.
- Part 66 of the Criminal Procedure Rules.
- The prosecution can appeal the refusal to make an order; the defence can appeal the making of an order.

- A Form NG (Prep) must be served on the Crown Court, the Registrar and any party directly affected not more than five business days after the order or the Crown Court judge grants or refuses leave. (*For applications to the Crown Court judge, see Part B above.*)
- A respondent's notice Form RN (Prep) should be served if the court directs or the Crown (or any party affected) wants to make representations to the court.
- Defence representatives are usually covered by the Crown Court representation order if one is in force [Access to Justice Act 1999, Sched. 3, para.2 (2)].
- Leave is required. The Crown Court judge, single judge or full court can grant leave to appeal.

D14 Appeal against an order that a trial should continue without a jury or a new trial take place without a jury after jury tampering

- S.47 of the CJA 2003.   **J-34**
- Part 66 of the Criminal Procedure Rules (relating to appeals against an order made in a preparatory hearing notwithstanding the ruling will not have been in the context of a preparatory hearing).
- The defendant can appeal.
- As D13, *ante*
- As D13, *ante*
- As D13, *ante*
- As D13, *ante*

D15 Appeal against orders restricting or preventing reports or restricting public access

- S.159 of the CJA 1988   **J-35**
- Part 69 of the Criminal Procedure Rules
- A person aggrieved may appeal.
- Applications against orders restricting reporting shall be made within 10 business days after the date on which the order was made by serving Form NG (159) on the Registrar, the Crown Court, the prosecutor and defendant and any other affected person. Applications against orders to restrict public access must be made the next business day after the order was made. If advance notice of an order restricting public access is given, then advance notice of an intention to appeal may be made not more than five business days after the advance notice is displayed.
- A person on whom an appeal notice is served should serve a respondent's notice Form RN (159) within three business days if he wishes to make representations to the court or the court so directs.
- The court may make such order as to costs as it thinks fit (CJA 1988, s.159(5)(c)), but not out of central funds - *Holden v. CPS (No. 2)* [1994] 1 A.C. 22, HL.
- A single judge or the full court can grant leave to appeal: CAA 1968, s.31(2B).
- Applications for leave to appeal and appeals in relation to reporting restrictions may be heard in private (rule 65.6 (1)). Applications for leave to appeal and appeals relating to restricting public access must be determined without a hearing (rule 65.6(3)).

D16 Appeal against a wasted costs order and appeal against a third party costs order

- Regulation 3C (costs wasted) and 3E (third party costs) of the Costs in Criminal Cases   **J-36** (General) Regulations 1986.
- A legal or other representative against whom a wasted costs order has been made in the Crown Court or a third party against whom a third party costs order has been made may appeal.
- Notice of appeal should be served on the Crown Court within 21 days of the order being made. There is no specific form. The notice should be served on any interested party (including, if appropriate, the Ministry of Justice).
- Any interested party can make representations orally or in writing.
- There is no power to grant a representation order or to order costs out of central funds as these proceedings are civil in nature.
- Leave to appeal is not required.

D17 Appeal relating to serious crime prevention orders

- S.24 of the SCA 2007.   **J-37**

- Part 68 of the Criminal Procedure Rules.
- A person subject to the order, an applicant authority or anyone given the opportunity to make representations at the Crown Court about the making, refusal to make, variation or non-variation of an order may appeal.
- Proceedings are commenced by the service of Form NG (SCPO) on the Crown Court not more than 28 days after the order.
- A respondent's notice Form RN (SCPO) should be served if directed by the Registrar or if the respondent wishes to make representations to the court.
- Proceedings before the Crown Court or the Court of Appeal relating to serious crime prevention orders and arising by virtue of section 19, 20, 21 or 24 of the SCA 2007 are criminal proceedings for the purposes of section 12(2)(g) of the Access to Justice Act 1999 [see the Criminal Defence Service (General) (No. 2) (Amendment) Regulations (S.I. 2008 No. 725)]. Accordingly, the Registrar may grant a representation order to a person subject to the order. A person who made representations at the Crown Court can apply to the LSC for funding. The court has discretion to order costs as it thinks fit [Serious Crime Act 2007 (Appeals under section 24) Order 2008 (S.I. 2008 No. 1863), Pt 3].
- Leave to appeal can be granted by the Crown Court judge, full court or single judge [S.I. 2008 No. 1863, art. 9].

D18 Appeal against the non-making of a football banning order

J-38
- S.14A(5A) of the Football Spectators Act 1989.
- Part 68 of the Criminal Procedure Rules.
- The prosecution can appeal.
- The appeal notice should be served on the Crown Court within 28 days of the decision not to make an order. However, there is no designated form.
- A respondent's notice should be served if directed by the Registrar or if the respondent wishes to make representations to the court. However, again there is no designated form.
- An application for a representation order may be made to the Registrar - Access to Justice Act 1999, s.12(2)(b).
- Currently, the Court of Appeal has been given no powers to deal with these appeals.

E. Application for a Retrial for a Serious Offence

E1 Application by a prosecutor to quash an acquittal and seek a retrial for a qualifying offence

S.76(1) of the Criminal Justice Act 2003 [Part 41 of the Criminal Procedure Rules]

J-39   E1-1 There must be new and compelling evidence and it must be in the interests of justice for the acquitted person to be retried for a qualifying offence as listed in the CJA 2003, Sched. 5, Pt 1 (CJA 2003, ss.78, 79: see *R. v. Dunlop* [2007] 1 Cr.App.R. 8, and *R. v. Miell* [2008] 1 Cr.App.R. 23).

E1-2 Proceedings can begin in one of two ways.

(1) By serving notice of the application under section 76 on the Court of Appeal and within two days serving the notice on the acquitted person (s.80). This notice charges him with the offence. It requires the personal written consent of the Director of Public Prosecutions (DPP) (s.76(3)). If the acquitted person is not in custody the prosecution can ask the Crown Court to issue:

    (i) a summons for the acquitted person to appear before the Court of Appeal for the hearing of the application or

    (ii) a warrant for his arrest (s.89(3)).

    Once arrested on the warrant the acquitted person must be brought before the Crown Court within 48 hours (s.89(6)).

(2) An acquitted person may be charged with the offence before an application under section 76 has been made. This may be after an arrest in an investigation authorised by the DPP (s.85(2)) or where no authorisation has been given, after arrest under a warrant issued by a justice of the peace (s.87(1)). Having been charged, the acquitted person must be brought before the Crown Court to consider bail within 24 hours (s.88(2)). He can then be remanded in custody or on bail for 42 days whilst an application under s.76 is prepared: s.88(6) unless an extension is granted under subsection (8). Once a notice of application under section 76 has been served, stating that the acquitted person has previously been charged with the offence, the acquitted person must be brought before the Crown Court to consider bail within 48 hours of the notice being given to the Registrar, if the acquitted person is already in custody under secton 88 (*ante*) (s.89(2)).

E1-3 Thus in either case, bail is dealt with largely by the Crown Court. The Court of Appeal only considers bail on the adjournment of the hearing of the application under section 76 (s.90(1)).

E1-4 The notice ["Notice of a s.76 application required by s.80(1) Criminal Justice Act 2003"] should where practicable be accompanied by the witness statements which are relied on as the new and compelling evidence, the original witness statements, unused statements, indictment, paper exhibits from the original trial, any relevant transcripts from the original trial and any other documents relied on: rule 41.2(2).

E1-5 An acquitted person who wants to oppose a section 76 application must serve a response ["Response of the acquitted person under s.80 Criminal Justice Act 2003"] not more than 28 days after receiving the notice: rule 41.3(2).

E2 Application by a prosecutor for a determination whether a foreign acquittal is a bar to a trial and if so, an order that it not be a bar

S.76(2) of the Criminal Justice Act 2003 [Part 41 of the Criminal Procedure Rules]

E2-1 The prosecution can apply, with the personal written consent of the DPP (s.76(3)) for a **J-40** determination whether an acquittal outside the UK is a bar to the acquitted person being tried in England and Wales and if it is found to be so, an order that the acquittal not be a bar. Proceedings can begin in the same way as for an application under section 76(1).

E3 Application for restrictions on publication relating to an application under section 76

S.82 of the Criminal Justice Act 2003 [Part 41 of the Criminal Procedure Rules]

E3-1 An application can be made by the DPP for reporting restrictions. This can be made after a **J-41** notice of an application for a retrial has been made and may also be made by the court of its own motion (s.82(5)). An application can also be made by the DPP for reporting restrictions *before* a notice of an application for a retrial if an investigation has been commenced: s.82(6). The application for reporting restrictions must be served on the Registrar ["Application for restrictions on publication under s.82 Criminal Justice Act 2003"] and (usually) the acquitted person (rule 41.8(1)).

E3-2 A party who wants to vary or revoke an order for restrictions on publication under section 82(7) may apply to the Court of Appeal in writing at any time after the order was made (rule 41.9(1)).

E4 Representation orders

E4-1 The Registrar will usually grant a representation order to the acquitted person for solicitors **J-42** and counsel to respond to any of the above applications.

APPENDIX K
Guidelines issued by the Sentencing Guidelines Council and by the Sentencing Council for England and Wales

I. GUIDELINES

A. REDUCTION IN SENTENCE FOR A GUILTY PLEA

GUIDELINE

CONTENTS

FOREWORD

K-2   One of the first guidelines to be issued by the Sentencing Guidelines Council related to the statutory obligation to take account of any guilty plea when determining sentence. As set out in the foreword to that guideline,[1] the intention was "to promote consistency in sentencing by providing clarity for courts, court users and victims so that everyone knows exactly what to expect". Prior to that guideline there had been different understandings of the purpose of the reduction and the extent of any reduction given.

Since the guideline was issued, there has been much greater clarity but there still remain concerns about some of the content of the guideline and about the extent to which the guideline has been consistently applied. Accordingly the council has undertaken a review of the guideline (in accordance with the statutory obligation placed upon it to do so from time to time[2]); it has also requested that the Judicial Studies Board consider further ways in which judicial training can incorporate the guideline.

The council is extremely grateful to the Sentencing Advisory Panel for the speed and thoroughness with which it has prepared its advice following extensive consultation. The council has accepted almost all the recommendations of the panel; the issues and arguments are set out fully in the panel's advice (see www.sentencing-guidelines.gov.uk). This revised guideline applies to all cases sentenced on or after 23 July 2007.

The council has agreed with the panel that the general approach of the guideline is correct in setting out clearly the purpose of the reduction for a guilty plea, in settling for a reduction no greater than one third (with lower levels of reduction where a plea is entered other than at the first reasonable opportunity) and in continuing to provide for a special approach when fixing the minimum term for a life sentence imposed following conviction for murder.

The council has agreed with the panel that some discretion should be introduced to the approach where the prosecution case is "overwhelming".

The council has not accepted the panel's recommendation in relation to circumstances where a magistrates' court is sentencing an offender for a number of offences where the overall maximum imprisonment is six months. The council continues to consider that there must be some incentive to plead guilty in such circumstances; this is consistent with other aspects of the guideline.

The council has not accepted the panel's recommendation in relation to the "capping" of the effect of reduction on very large fines. The number of such fines is very low and the council was not convinced that the arguments were strong enough to justify a departure from the general approach in the guideline not to "cap" the effect of the reduction. In addition, the revised guideline provides guidance as to when the "first reasonable opportunity" is likely to occur in relation to indictable only offences; emphasises that remorse and material assistance provided to prosecuting authorities are separate issues from those to which the guideline applies and makes clear that the approach to calculation of the reduction where an indeterminate sentence is imposed (other than that following conviction for murder) should be the same as that for determinate sentences.

---

[1] Published December 2004.
[2] Criminal Justice Act 2003, s.170(4).

Since the guideline was issued in 2004, there have been changes in the statutory provisions governing the reduction for guilty plea and in those relating to sentences for public protection. The review has provided an opportunity to bring the guideline up to date and those changes have been incorporated.

The council published a draft guideline in accordance with section 170(8) of the Criminal Justice Act 2003 inviting responses by 14 March 2007. A response has been received from the Home Affairs Committee, a response has been received from the Attorney General and seven other responses have been received. A summary of the responses and the decisions of the council has been published separately.

Chairman of the Council
July 2007

A. STATUTORY PROVISIONS

Section 144 Criminal Justice Act 2003 provides [the guideline here sets out the text of section 144 **K-3** of the 2003 Act, set out in the main work at § 5-107].

Section 174(2) Criminal Justice Act 2003 provides [the guideline here sets out the text of section 174(2)(d) of the 2003 Act, set out in the main work at § 5-165].

1.1 This guideline applies whether a case is dealt with in a magistrates' court or in the Crown Court and whenever practicable in the youth court (taking into account legislative restrictions such as those relevant to the length of detention and training orders).

1.2 The application of this guideline to sentencers when arriving at the appropriate minimum term for the offence of murder is set out in Section F.

1.3 This guideline can also be found at www.sentencing-guidelines.gov.uk or can be obtained from the Council's Secretariat at 4th Floor, 8–10 Great George Street, London SW1P 3AE.

B. STATEMENT OF PURPOSE

2.1 When imposing a custodial sentence, statute requires that a court must impose the shortest **K-4** term that is commensurate with the seriousness of the offence(s)[3]. Similarly, when imposing a community order, the restrictions on liberty must be commensurate with the seriousness of the offence(s)[4]. Once that decision is made, a court is required to give consideration to the reduction for any guilty plea. As a result, the final sentence after the reduction for a guilty plea will be less than the seriousness of the offence requires.

2.2 A reduction in sentence is appropriate because a guilty plea avoids the need for a trial (thus enabling other cases to be disposed of more expeditiously), shortens the gap between charge and sentence, saves considerable cost, and, in the case of an early plea, saves victims and witnesses from the concern about having to give evidence. The reduction principle derives from the need for the effective administration of justice and not as an aspect of mitigation.

2.3 Where a sentencer is in doubt as to whether a custodial sentence is appropriate, the reduction attributable to a guilty plea will be a relevant consideration. Where this is amongst the factors leading to the imposition of a non-custodial sentence, there will be no need to apply a further reduction on account of the guilty plea. A similar approach is appropriate where the reduction for a guilty plea is amongst the factors leading to the imposition of a financial penalty or discharge instead of a community order.

2.4 When deciding the most appropriate length of sentence, the sentencer should address separately the issue of remorse, together with any other mitigating features, before calculating the reduction for the guilty plea. Similarly, assistance to the prosecuting or enforcement authorities is a separate issue which may attract a reduction in sentence under other procedures; care will need to be taken to ensure that there is no "double counting".

2.5 The implications of other offences that an offender has asked to be taken into consideration should be reflected in the sentence before the reduction for guilty plea has been applied.

2.6 A reduction in sentence should only be applied to the punitive elements of a penalty[5]. The guilty plea reduction has no impact on sentencing decisions in relation to ancillary orders, including orders of disqualification from driving.

C. APPLICATION OF THE REDUCTION PRINCIPLE

3.1 Recommended approach **K-5**

---

[3] Criminal Justice Act 2003, s.153(2).
[4] Criminal Justice Act 2003, s.148(2).
[5] Where a court imposes an indeterminate sentence for public protection, the reduction principle applies in the normal way to the determination of the minimum term (see para. 5.1, footnote and para. 7 below) but release from custody requires the authorisation of the Parole Board once that minimum term has been served.

The court decides sentence for the offence(s) taking into account aggravating and mitigating factors and any other offences that have been formally admitted (TICs)

⇩

The court selects the amount of the reduction by reference to the sliding scale

⇩

The court applies the reduction

⇩

When pronouncing sentence the court should usually state what the sentence would have been if there had been no reduction as a result of the guilty plea.

D. Determining the Level of Reduction

K-6
4.1 The level of reduction should be *a proportion of the total sentence* imposed, with the proportion calculated by reference to the circumstances in which the guilty plea was indicated, in particular the stage in the proceedings. The greatest reduction will be given where the plea was indicated at the "first reasonable opportunity".

4.2 Save where section 144(2) of the 2003 Act applies[6], the level of the reduction will be gauged on a *sliding scale* ranging from a recommended *one third* (where the guilty plea was entered at the first reasonable opportunity in relation to the offence for which sentence is being imposed), reducing to a recommended *one quarter* (where a trial date has been set) and to a recommended *one tenth* (for a guilty plea entered at the 'door of the court' or after the trial has begun). *See diagram below.*

4.3 The level of reduction should reflect the stage at which the offender indicated a *willingness to admit guilt* to the offence for which he is eventually sentenced:

(i) the largest recommended reduction will not normally be given unless the offender indicated willingness to admit guilt at the first reasonable opportunity; when this occurs will vary from case to case (see *Annex 1 for illustrative examples*);

(ii) where the admission of guilt comes later than the first reasonable opportunity, the reduction for guilty plea will normally be less than one third;

(iii) where the plea of guilty comes very late, it is still appropriate to give some reduction;

(iv) if after pleading guilty there is a *Newton* hearing and the offender's version of the circumstances of the offence is rejected, this should be taken into account in determining the level of reduction;

(v) if the not guilty plea was entered and maintained for tactical reasons (such as to retain privileges whilst on remand), a late guilty plea should attract very little, if any, discount.

[6] See section A above.

In each category, there is a presumption that the recommended reduction
will be given unless there are good reasons for a lower amount.

First reasonable opportunity	After a trial date is set	Door of the court/ after trial has begun

======= | ============ | =========== |

recommended 1/3   recommended 1/4   recommended 1/10

E. Witholding a Reduction

On the basis of dangerousness

5.1   Where a sentence for a "dangerous offender" is imposed under the provisions in the Criminal **K-7**
Justice Act 2003, whether the sentence requires the calculation of a minimum term or is an extended
sentence, the approach will be the same as for any other determinate sentence (see also section G
below)[7].

Where the prosecution case is overwhelming

5.2   The purpose of giving credit is to encourage those who are guilty to plead at the earliest
opportunity. Any defendant is entitled to put the prosecution to proof and so every defendant who is
guilty should be encouraged to indicate that guilt at the first reasonable opportunity.

5.3   Where the prosecution case is overwhelming, it may not be appropriate to give the full
reduction that would otherwise be given. Whilst there is a presumption in favour of the full reduction being given where a plea has been indicated at the first reasonable opportunity, the fact that the
prosecution case is overwhelming without relying on admissions from the defendant may be a reason
justifying departure from the guideline.

5.4   Where a court is satisfied that a lower reduction should be given for this reason, a recommended reduction of 20% is likely to be appropriate where the guilty plea was indicated at the first
reasonable opportunity.

5.5   A court departing from a guideline must state the reasons for doing so[8].

Where the maximum penalty for the offence is thought to be too low

5.6   The sentencer is bound to sentence for the offence with which the offender has been charged,
and to which he has pleaded guilty. The sentencer cannot remedy perceived defects (for example an
inadequate charge or maximum penalty) by refusal of the appropriate discount.

Where jurisdictional issues arise

(i) Where sentencing powers are limited to six months' imprisonment despite multiple offences

5.7 When the total sentence for both or all of the offences is six months' imprisonment, a court
may determine to impose consecutive sentences which, even allowing for a reduction for a guilty plea
where appropriate on each offence, would still result in the imposition of the maximum sentence
available. In such circumstances, in order to achieve the purpose for which the reduction principle
has been established[9], some modest allowance should normally be given against the total sentence for
the entry of a guilty plea.

(ii) Where a maximum sentence might still be imposed

5.8 Despite a guilty plea being entered which would normally attract a reduction in sentence, a
magistrates' court may impose a sentence of imprisonment of 6 months for a single either-way offence where, but for the plea, that offence would have been committed to the Crown Court for
sentence.

---

[7] There will be some cases arising from offences committed before the commencement of the relevant provisions of the
Criminal Justice Act 2003 in which a court will determine that a longer than commensurate, extended, or
indeterminate sentence is required for the protection of the public. In such a case, the minimum custodial term (but
not the protection of public element of the sentence) should be reduced to reflect the plea.
[8] Criminal Justice Act 2003, s.174(2)(a).
[9] See section B above.

5.9 Similarly, a detention and training order of 24 months may be imposed on an offender aged under 18 if the offence is one which would but for the plea have attracted a sentence of long-term detention in excess of 24 months under the Powers of Criminal Courts (Sentencing) Act 2000, s.91.

F. Application to Sentencing for Murder

K-8

6.1 Murder has always been regarded as the most serious criminal offence and the sentence prescribed is different from other sentences. By law, the sentence for murder is imprisonment (detention) for life and an offender will remain subject to the sentence for the rest of his/her life.

6.2 The decision whether to release the offender from custody during this sentence will be taken by the Parole Board which will consider whether it is safe to release the offender on licence. The court that imposes the sentence is required by law to set a minimum term that has to be served before the Parole Board may start to consider whether to authorise release on licence. If an offender is released, the licence continues for the rest of the offender's life and recall to prison is possible at any time.

6.3 Uniquely, Parliament has set starting points[10] (based on the circumstances of the killing) which a court will apply when it fixes the minimum term. Parliament has further prescribed that, having identified the appropriate starting point, the court must then consider whether to increase or reduce it in the light of aggravating or mitigating factors, some of which are listed in statute. Finally, Parliament specifically provides[11] that the obligation to have regard to any guilty plea applies to the fixing of the minimum term, by making the same statutory provisions that apply to other offences apply to murder without limiting the court's discretion (as it did with other sentences under the Powers of Criminal Courts (Sentencing) Act 2000).

6.4 There are important differences between the usual fixed term sentence and the minimum term set following the imposition of the mandatory life sentence for murder. The most significant of these, from the sentencer's point of view, is that a reduction for a plea of guilty in the case of murder will have double the effect on time served in custody when compared with a determinate sentence. This is because a determinate sentence will provide (in most circumstances) for the release of the offender[12] on licence half way through the total sentence whereas in the case of murder a minimum term is the period in custody before consideration is given by the Parole Board to whether release is appropriate.

6.5 Given this difference, the special characteristic of the offence of murder and the unique statutory provision of starting points, careful consideration will need to be given to the extent of any reduction and to the need to ensure that the minimum term properly reflects the seriousness of the offence. Whilst the general principles continue to apply (both that a guilty plea should be encouraged and that the extent of any reduction should reduce if the indication of plea is later than the first reasonable opportunity), the process of determining the level of reduction will be different.

6.6 Approach

K-9

6.6 1. Where a court determines that there should be a whole life minimum term, there will be no reduction for a guilty plea.

2. In other circumstances,

   (a) the court will weigh carefully the overall length of the minimum term taking into account other reductions for which the offender may be eligible so as to avoid a combination leading to an inappropriately short sentence;

   (b) where it is appropriate to reduce the minimum term having regard to a plea of guilty, the reduction will not exceed one sixth and will never exceed five years;

   (c) the sliding scale will apply so that, where it is appropriate to reduce the minimum term on account of a guilty plea, the maximum reduction (one sixth or five years whichever is the less) is only available where there has been an indication of willingness to plead guilty at the first reasonable opportunity, with a recommended 5% for a late guilty plea;

   (d) the court should then review the sentence to ensure that the minimum term accurately reflects the seriousness of the offence taking account of the statutory starting point, all aggravating and mitigating factors and any guilty plea entered.

[10] Criminal Justice Act 2003, Schedule 21.
[11] Criminal Justice Act 2003, Schedule 1, para 12(c).
[12] In accordance with the provisions of the Criminal Justice Act 2003.

G. Application to other Indeterminate Sentences

7.1 There are other circumstances in which an indeterminate sentence will be imposed. This may **K-10** be a discretionary life sentence or imprisonment for public protection.

7.2 As with the mandatory life sentence imposed following conviction for murder, the court will be obliged to fix a minimum term to be served before the Parole Board is able to consider whether the offender can be safely released.

7.3 However, the process by which that minimum term is fixed is different from that followed in relation to the mandatory life sentence and requires the court first to determine what the equivalent determinate sentence would have been. Accordingly, the approach to the calculation of the reduction for any guilty plea should follow the process and scale adopted in relation to determinate sentences, as set out in section D above.

ANNEX 1

First reasonable opportunity

1. The critical time for determining the maximum reduction for a guilty plea is the first reason- **K-11** able opportunity for the defendant to have indicated a willingness to plead guilty. This opportunity will vary with a wide range of factors and the court will need to make a judgement on the particular facts of the case before it.

2. The key principle is that the purpose of giving a reduction is to recognise the benefits that come from a guilty plea not only for those directly involved in the case in question but also in enabling courts more quickly to deal with other outstanding cases.

3. This Annex seeks to help courts to adopt a consistent approach by giving examples of circumstances where a determination will have to be made:

   (a) the first reasonable opportunity may be the first time that a defendant appears before the court and has the opportunity to plead guilty;

   (b) but the court may consider that it would be reasonable to have expected an indication of willingness even earlier, perhaps whilst under interview;

   Note: For (a) and (b) to apply, the court will need to be satisfied that the defendant (and any legal adviser) would have had sufficient information about the allegations

   (c) where an offence triable either way is committed to the Crown Court for trial and the defendant pleads guilty at the first hearing in that court, the reduction will be less than if there had been an indication of a guilty plea given to the magistrates' court (recommended reduction of one third) but more than if the plea had been entered after a trial date had been set (recommended reduction of one quarter), and is likely to be in the region of 30%;

   (d) where an offence is triable only on indictment, it may well be that the first reasonable opportunity would have been during the police station stage; where that is not the case, the first reasonable opportunity is likely to be at the first hearing in the Crown Court;

   (e) where a defendant is convicted after pleading guilty to an alternative (lesser) charge to that to which he/she had originally pleaded not guilty, the extent of any reduction will be determined by the stage at which the defendant first formally indicated to the court willingness to plead guilty to the lesser charge and the reason why that lesser charge was proceeded with in preference to the original charge.

[The next paragraph is K-13.]

B. Overarching Principles: Seriousness

GUIDELINE

Contents

FOREWORD

K-14   In accordance with the provisions of section 170(9) Criminal Justice Act 2003, the Sentencing Guidelines Council issues this guideline as a definitive guideline. By virtue of section 172 of the Act, every court must have regard to a relevant guideline.

The Council was created in 2004 in order to frame Guidelines to assist Courts as they deal with criminal cases across the whole of England and Wales.

The Council has stated that it intends to follow a principled approach to the formulation of guidelines to assist sentencers which will include consideration of overarching and general principles relating to the sentencing of offenders. Following the planned implementation of many of the sentencing provisions in the 2003 Act in April 2005, this guideline deals with the general concept of seriousness in the light of those provisions and considers how sentencers should determine when the respective sentencing thresholds have been crossed when applying the provisions of the Act.

This guideline applies only to sentences passed under the sentencing framework applicable to those aged 18 or over although there are some aspects that will assist courts assessing the seriousness of offences committed by those under 18. The Council has commissioned separate advice from the Sentencing Advisory Panel on the sentencing of young offenders.

This is the first time that it has been possible to produce definitive guidelines not only before new provisions come into force but also before much of the training of judiciary and practitioners.

The Council has appreciated greatly the work of the Sentencing Advisory Panel in preparing the advice on which this guideline has been based and for the many organisations and individuals who have responded so thoughtfully to the consultation of both the Panel and the Council. The advice and this guideline are available on www.sentencing-guidelines.gov.uk or from the Sentencing Guidelines Secretariat. A summary of the responses to the Council's consultation also appears on the website.

Chairman of the Council

December 2004

SERIOUSNESS

A. STATUTORY PROVISION

K-15   1.1 In every case where the offender is aged 18 or over at the time of conviction, the court must have regard to the five purposes of sentencing contained in section 142(1) Criminal Justice Act 2003:

(a) the punishment of offenders

(b) the reduction of crime (including its reduction by deterrence)

(c) the reform and rehabilitation of offenders

(d) the protection of the public

(e) the making of reparation by offenders to persons affected by their offence

1.2 The Act does not indicate that any one purpose should be more important than any other and in practice they may all be relevant to a greater or lesser degree in any individual case—the sentencer has the task of determining the manner in which they apply.

1.3 The sentencer must start by considering the seriousness of the offence, the assessment of which will:

- determine which of the sentencing thresholds has been crossed;
- indicate whether a custodial, community or other sentence is the most appropriate;
- be the key factor in deciding the length of a custodial sentence, the onerousness of requirements to be incorporated in a community sentence and the amount of any fine imposed.

1.4 A court is required to pass a sentence that is commensurate with the seriousness of the offence. The seriousness of an offence is determined by two main parameters; the **culpability** of the offender and the **harm** caused or risked being caused by the offence

1.5 Section 143(1) Criminal Justice Act 2003 provides [see § 5-67 in the main work].

B. Culpability

1.6 Four levels of criminal culpability can be identified for sentencing purposes: **K-16**

1.7 Where the offender;

> (i) has the **intention** to cause harm, with the highest culpability when an offence is planned. The worse the harm intended, the greater the seriousness.
>
> (ii) is **reckless** as to whether harm is caused, that is, where the offender appreciates at least some harm would be caused but proceeds giving no thought to the consequences even though the extent of the risk would be obvious to most people.
>
> (iii) has **knowledge** of the specific risks entailed by his actions even though he does not intend to cause the harm that results.
>
> (iv) is guilty of **negligence**.

Note: *There are offences where liability is strict and no culpability need be proved for the purposes of obtaining a conviction, but the degree of culpability is still important when deciding sentence. The extent to which reckless-ness, knowledge or negligence are involved in a particular offence will vary.*

C. Harm

1.8 The relevant provision is widely drafted so that it encompasses those offences where harm is   **K-17** caused but also those where neither individuals nor the community suffer harm but a risk of harm is present.

To individual victims

1.9 The types of harm caused or risked by different types of criminal activity are diverse and victims may suffer physical injury, sexual violation, financial loss, damage to health or psychological distress. There are gradations of harm within all of these categories.

1.10 The nature of harm will depend on personal characteristics and circumstances of the victim and the court's assessment of harm will be an effective and important way of taking into considera-tion the impact of a particular crime on the victim.

1.11 In some cases no actual harm may have resulted and the court will be concerned with as-sessing the relative dangerousness of the offender's conduct; it will consider the likelihood of harm occurring and the gravity of the harm that could have resulted.

To the community

1.12 Some offences cause harm to the community at large (instead of or as well as to an individual victim) and may include economic loss, harm to public health, or interference with the administra-tion of justice.

Other types of harm

1.13 There are other types of harm that are more difficult to define or categorise. For example, cruelty to animals certainly causes significant harm to the animal but there may also be a human victim who also suffers psychological distress and/or financial loss.

1.14 Some conduct is criminalised purely by reference to public feeling or social mores. In addi-tion, public concern about the damage caused by some behaviour, both to individuals and to society as a whole, can influence public perception of the harm caused, for example, by the supply of prohibited drugs.

D. The Assessment of Culpability and Harm

1.15 Section 143(1) makes clear that the assessment of the seriousness of any individual offence   **K-18** must take account not only of any harm actually caused by the offence, but also of any harm that was intended to be caused or might foreseeably be caused by the offence.

1.16 Assessing seriousness is a difficult task, particularly where there is an imbalance between culpability and harm:

> • sometimes the harm that actually results is greater than the harm intended by the of-fender;

- in other circumstances, the offender's culpability may be at a higher level than the harm resulting from the offence

1.17 Harm must always be judged in the light of culpability. The precise level of culpability will be determined by such factors as motivation, whether the offence was planned or spontaneous or whether the offender was in a position of trust.

Culpability will be greater if:

- an offender deliberately causes more harm than is necessary for the commission of the offence, or
- where an offender targets a vulnerable victim (because of their old age or youth, disability or by virtue of the job they do).

1.18 Where unusually serious harm results and was unintended and beyond the control of the offender, culpability will be significantly influenced by the extent to which the harm could have been foreseen.

1.19 If much **more** harm, or much **less** harm has been caused by the offence than the offender intended or foresaw, the culpability of the offender, depending on the circumstances, may be regarded as carrying greater or lesser weight as appropriate.

The culpability of the offender in the particular circumstances of an individual case should be the initial factor in determining the seriousness of an offence.

(i) Aggravating factors

K-19

1.20 Sentencing guidelines for a particular offence will normally include a list of aggravating features which, if present in an individual instance of the offence, would indicate *either* a higher than usual level of culpability on the part of the offender, *or* a greater than usual degree of harm caused by the offence (or sometimes both).

1.21 The lists below bring together the most important aggravating features with potential application to more than one offence or class of offences. They include some factors (such as the vulnerability of victims or abuse of trust) which are integral features of certain offences; in such cases, the presence of the aggravating factor is already reflected in the penalty for the offence and **cannot be used as justification for increasing the sentence further**. The lists are not intended to be comprehensive and the aggravating factors are not listed in any particular order of priority. On occasions, two or more of the factors listed will describe the same feature of the offence and care needs to be taken to avoid "double counting". Those factors starred with an asterisk are statutory aggravating factors where the statutory provisions are in force. Those marked with a hash are yet to be brought into force but as factors in an individual case are still relevant and should be taken into account.

1.22 **Factors indicating higher culpability:**

- Offence committed whilst on bail for other offences
- Failure to respond to previous sentences
- Offence was racially or religiously aggravated
- Offence motivated by, or demonstrating, hostility to the victim based on his or her sexual orientation (or presumed sexual orientation)
- Offence motivated by, or demonstrating, hostility based on the victim's disability (or presumed disability)
- Previous conviction(s), particularly where a pattern of repeat offending is disclosed
- Planning of an offence
- An intention to commit more serious harm than actually resulted from the offence
- Offenders operating in groups or gangs
- "Professional" offending
- Commission of the offence for financial gain (where this is not inherent in the offence itself)
- High level of profit from the offence
- An attempt to conceal or dispose of evidence
- Failure to respond to warnings or concerns expressed by others about the offender's behaviour
- Offence committed whilst on licence
- Offence motivated by hostility towards a minority group, or a member or members of it
- Deliberate targeting of vulnerable victim(s)
- Commission of an offence while under the influence of alcohol or drugs
- Use of a weapon to frighten or injure victim

- Deliberate and gratuitous violence or damage to property, over and above what is needed to carry out the offence
- Abuse of power
- Abuse of a position of trust

1.23 **Factors indicating a more than usually serious degree of harm:**
- Multiple victims
- An especially serious physical or psychological effect on the victim, even if unintended
- A sustained assault or repeated assaults on the same victim
- Victim is particularly vulnerable
- Location of the offence (for example, in an isolated place)
- Offence is committed against those working in the public sector or providing a service to the public
- Presence of others *e.g.* relatives, especially children or partner of the victim
- Additional degradation of the victim (*e.g.* taking photographs of a victim as part of a sexual offence)
- In property offences, high value (including sentimental value) of property to the victim, or substantial consequential loss (*e.g.* where the theft of equipment causes serious disruption to a victim's life or business)

(ii) Mitigating factors

1.24 Some factors may indicate that an offender's culpability is **unusually** low, or that the harm **K-20**
caused by an offence is less than usually serious.

1.25 **Factors indicating significantly lower culpability:**
- A greater degree of provocation than normally expected
- Mental illness or disability
- Youth or age, where it affects the responsibility of the individual defendant
- The fact that the offender played only a minor role in the offence

(iii) Personal mitigation

1.26 Section 166(1) Criminal Justice Act 2003 makes provision for a sentencer to take account of **K-21**
any matters that "in the opinion of the court, are relevant in mitigation of sentence".

1.27 When the court has formed an initial assessment of the seriousness of the offence, then it should consider any offender mitigation. The issue of remorse should be taken into account at this point along with other mitigating features such as admissions to the police in interview.

(iv) Reduction for a guilty plea

1.28 Sentencers will normally reduce the severity of a sentence to reflect an early guilty plea. **K-22**
This subject is covered by a separate guideline and provides a sliding scale reduction with a normal maximum one-third reduction being given to offenders who enter a guilty plea at the first reasonable opportunity.

1.29 Credit may also be given for ready co-operation with the authorities. This will depend on the particular circumstances of the individual case.

E. THE SENTENCING THRESHOLDS

1.30 Assessing the seriousness of an offence is only the first step in the process of determining the **K-23**
appropriate sentence in an individual case. Matching the offence to a type and level of sentence is a separate and complex exercise assisted by the application of the respective threshold tests for custodial and community sentences.

The custody threshold

1.31 Section 152(2) Criminal Justice Act 2003 provides [see § 5-458 in the main work]. **K-24**

1.32 In applying the threshold test, sentencers should note: the clear intention of the threshold test is to reserve prison as a punishment for the most serious offences;
- it is impossible to determine definitively which features of a particular offence make it serious enough to merit a custodial sentence;
- passing the custody threshold does not mean that a custodial sentence should be deemed inevitable, and custody can still be avoided in the light of personal mitigation or where there is a suitable intervention in the community which provides sufficient restriction (by

way of punishment) while addressing the rehabilitation of the offender to prevent future crime. For example, a prolific offender who currently could expect a short custodial sentence (which, in advance of custody plus, would have no provision for supervision on release) might more appropriately receive a suitable community sentence.

1.33 The approach to the imposition of a custodial sentence under the new framework should be as follows:

> (a) has the custody threshold been passed?
>
> (b) if so, is it unavoidable that a custodial sentence be imposed?
>
> (c) if so, can that sentence be suspended? (sentencers should be clear that they would have imposed a custodial sentence if the power to suspend had not been available)
>
> (d) if not, can the sentence be served intermittently?
>
> (e) if not, impose a sentence which takes immediate effect for the term commensurate with the seriousness of the offence.

The threshold for community sentences

K-25
1.34 Section 148(1) Criminal Justice Act 2003 provides [see § 5-248 in the main work].

1.35 In addition, the threshold for a community sentence can be crossed even though the seriousness criterion is not met. Section 151 Criminal Justice Act 2003 provides that, in relation to an offender aged 16 or over on whom, on three or more previous occasions, sentences had been passed consisting only of a fine, a community sentence may be imposed (if it is in the interests of justice) despite the fact that the seriousness of the current offence (and others associated with it) might not warrant such a sentence.

1.36 Sentencers should consider all of the disposals available (within or below the threshold passed) at the time of sentence before reaching the provisional decision to make a community sentence, so that, even where the threshold for a community sentence has been passed, a financial penalty or discharge may still be an appropriate penalty.

Summary

K-26
1.37 It would not be feasible to provide a form of words or to devise any formula that would provide a general solution to the problem of where the custody threshold lies. Factors vary too widely between offences for this to be done. It is the task of guidelines for individual offences to provide more detailed guidance on what features within that offence point to a custodial sentence, and also to deal with issues such as sentence length, the appropriate requirements for a community sentence or the use of appropriate ancillary orders.

> **Having assessed the seriousness of an individual offence, sentencers must consult the sentencing guidelines for an offence of that type for guidance on the factors that are likely to indicate whether a custodial sentence or other disposal is most likely to be appropriate.**

F. Prevalence

K-27
1.38 The seriousness of an individual case should be judged on its own dimensions of harm and culpability rather than as part of a collective social harm. It is legitimate for the overall approach to sentencing levels for particular offences to be guided by their cumulative effect. However, it would be wrong to further penalise individual offenders by increasing sentence length for committing an individual offence of that type.

1.39 There may be exceptional local circumstances that arise which may lead a court to decide that prevalence should influence sentencing levels. The pivotal issue in such cases will be the harm being caused to the community. It is essential that sentencers both have supporting evidence from an external source (for example the local Criminal Justice Board) to justify claims that a particular crime is prevalent in their area and are satisfied that there is a compelling need to treat the offence more seriously than elsewhere.

> **The key factor in determining whether sentencing levels should be enhanced in response to prevalence will be the level of harm being caused in the locality. Enhanced sentences should be exceptional and in response to exceptional circumstances. Sentencers must sentence within the sentencing guidelines once the prevalence has been addressed. Having assessed the seriousness of an individual offence, sentencers must consult the sentencing guidelines for an offence of that type for guidance on the factors that are likely to indicate whether a custodial sentence or other disposal is most likely to be appropriate.**

C. New Sentences: Criminal Justice Act 2003

GUIDELINE

Foreword

In accordance with the provisions of section 170(9) Criminal Justice Act 2003, the Sentencing Guidelines Council issues this guideline as a definitive guideline. By virtue of section 172 of the Act, every court must have regard to a relevant guideline.

The Council was created in 2004 in order to frame Guidelines to assist Courts as they deal with criminal cases across the whole of England and Wales.

This guideline relates to the new sentencing framework introduced by the Criminal Justice Act 2003, which affects the nature of community and custodial sentences. Only those sentences and related provisions which are expected to come into force by April 2005 are dealt with in this guideline. It will be followed by further guidelines in due course. This is an unusual guideline since it covers a range of sentences outside the context of individual offences and does so in readiness for the coming into force of the statutory provisions creating the sentences. It is designed with the object of ensuring a consistent approach when the sentences become available.

This guideline applies only to sentences passed under the sentencing framework applicable to those aged 18 or over.

The guideline is divided into two sections:

- Sections 1 covers the practical aspects of implementing the non-custodial powers namely the new community sentence and the new form of deferred sentence;
- Section 2 deals with the new custodial sentence provisions relating to suspended sentences, prison sentences of 12 months or more, and intermittent custody.[13]

The Act also contains an extensive range of provisions to protect the public from dangerous offenders. These will be dealt with separately.

The Advice of the Sentencing Advisory Panel to the Council (published on 20th September 2004) has been broadly accepted by the Council and forms the basis of this guideline. Further information on the issues covered in this guideline can be found in that Advice or in the discussion document that preceded it. All these documents are available on www.sentencing-guidelines.gov.uk or from the Sentencing Guidelines Secretariat.

Chairman of the Council
December 2004

Contents

---

[13] References to the Probation Service reflect current roles and responsibilities. By the time these provisions come into force, some or all of those roles and responsibilities may be those of the National Offender Management Service (NOMS).

SECTION 1 PART 1—COMMUNITY SENTENCES

A. Statutory Provisions

(i) The thresholds for community sentence

K-30   1.1.1   Seriousness—Section 148 Criminal Justice Act 2003 [sets out subsection (1), as to which, see § 5-248 in the main work].

1.1.2   Persistent offenders—Section 151 Criminal Justice Act 2003 [sets out subsections (1) and (2), as to which, see § 5-252 in the main work].

(ii) The sentences available

K-31   1.1.3   Meaning of community sentence—Section 147 Criminal Justice Act 2003 [sets out subsection (1), as to which, see § 5-247 in the main work].

1.1.4   Offenders aged 16 or over—Section 177 Criminal Justice Act 2003 [sets out subsections (1) to (4), as to which, see § 5-253 in the main work].

(iii) Determining which orders to make & requirements to include

K-32   1.1.5   Suitability—Section 148 Criminal Justice Act 2003 [sets out subsection (2), as to which see § 5-248 in the main work].

1.1.6   Restrictions on liberty—Section 148 Criminal Justice Act 2003 [sets out subsection (1), as to which see § 5-248 in the main work].

1.1.7   Compatibility—Section 177 Criminal Justice Act 2003 [sets out subsection (6), as to which see § 5-253 in the main work].

(iv) Electronic monitoring

K-33   1.1.8   Section 177 Criminal Justice Act 2003 [sets out subsections (3) and (4), as to which see § 5-253 in the main work].

B. Imposing a Community Sentence—The Approach

K-34   1.1.9 On pages 8 and 9 of the seriousness guideline the two thresholds for the imposition of a community sentence are considered. Sentencers must consider all of the disposals available (within or below the threshold passed) at the time of sentence, and reject them before reaching the provisional decision to make a community sentence, so that even where the threshold for a community sentence has been passed a financial penalty or discharge may still be an appropriate penalty. Where an offender has a low risk of reoffending, particular care needs to be taken in the light of evidence that indicates that there are circumstances where inappropriate intervention can increase the risk of re-offending rather than decrease it. In addition, recent improvements in enforcement of financial penalties make them a more viable sentence in a wider range of cases.

1.1.10 Where an offender is being sentenced for a non-imprisonable offence or offences, great care will be needed in assessing whether a community sentence is appropriate since failure to comply could result in a custodial sentence.

1.1.11 Having decided (in consultation with the Probation Service where appropriate) that a community sentence is justified, the court must decide which requirements should be included in the community order. The requirements or orders imposed will have the effect of restricting the offender's liberty, whilst providing punishment in the community, rehabilitation for the offender, and/or ensuring that the offender engages in reparative activities.

The key issues arising are:
  (i) which requirements to impose;
  (ii) how to make allowance for time spent on remand; and
  (iii) how to deal with breaches.

(i) Requirements

1.1.12 When deciding which requirements to include, the court must be satisfied on three matters— **K-35**
  (i) that the **restriction on liberty is commensurate with the seriousness** of the offence(s);[14]
  (ii) that the **requirements are the most suitable** for the offender;[15] and
  (iii) that, where there are two or more requirements included, they are **compatible with each other**.[16]

1.1.13 Sentencers should have the possibility of breach firmly in mind when passing sentence for the original offence. If a court is to reflect the seriousness of an offence, there is little value in setting requirements as part of a community sentence that are not demanding enough for an offender. on the other hand, there is equally little value in imposing requirements that would "set an offender up to fail" and almost inevitably lead to sanctions for a breach.

In community sentences, the guiding principles are proportionality and suitability. Once a court has decided that the offence has crossed the community sentence threshold and that a community sentence is justified, the initial factor in defining which requirements to include in a community sentence should be the seriousness of the offence committed.

1.1.14 This means that "seriousness" is an important factor in deciding whether the court chooses the low, medium or high range (see below) but, having taken that decision, selection of the content of the order within the range will be determined by a much wider range of factors.
  • **Sentencing ranges must remain flexible enough to take account of the suitability of the offender, his or her ability to comply with particular requirements and their availability in the local area.**
  • **The justification for imposing a community sentence in response to persistent petty offending is the persistence of the offending behaviour rather than the seriousness of the offences being committed. The requirements imposed should ensure that the restriction on liberty is proportionate to the seriousness of the offending, to reflect the fact that the offences, of themselves, are not sufficiently serious to merit a community sentence.**

(a) Information for sentencers

1.1.15 In many cases, a pre-sentence report[17] will be pivotal in helping a sentencer decide **K-36** whether to impose a custodial sentence or whether to impose a community sentence and, if so, whether particular requirements, or combinations of requirements, are suitable for an individual offender. The court must always ensure (especially where there are multiple requirements) that the restriction on liberty placed on the offender is proportionate to the seriousness of the offence committed.[18] The court must also consider the likely effect of one requirement on another, and that they do not place conflicting demands upon the offender.[19]

1.1.16 The council supports the approach proposed by the panel at paragraph 78 of its advice that, having reached the provisional view that a community sentence is the most appropriate disposal, the sentencer should request a pre-sentence report, indicating which of the three sentencing ranges is relevant and the purpose(s) of sentencing that the package of requirements is required to fulfil. Usually the most helpful way for the court to do this would be to produce a written note for the report writer, copied on the court file. If it is known that the same tribunal and defence advocate will

---

[14] Criminal Justice Act 2003 section 148(2)(b).
[15] *ibid.*, section 148(2)(a).
[16] *ibid.*, section 177(6).
[17] Under the Act, a pre-sentence report includes a full report following adjournment, a specific sentence report, a short format report or an oral report. The type of report supplied will depend on the level of information requested. Wherever it appears, the term "pre-sentence report" includes all these types of report.
[18] Criminal Justice Act 2003 section 148(2).
[19] *ibid.*, section 177(6).

be present at the sentencing hearing and a probation officer is present in court when the request for a report is made, it may not be necessary to commit details of the request to writing. However, events may change during the period of an adjournment and it is good practice to ensure that there is a clear record of the request for the court. These two factors will guide the Probation Service in determining the nature and combination of requirements that may be appropriate and the onerousness and intensity of those requirements. A similar procedure should apply when ordering a pre-sentence report when a custodial sentence is being considered.

1.1.17   There will be occasions when any type of report may be unnecessary despite the intention to pass a community sentence though this is likely to be infrequent. A court could consider dispensing with the need to obtain a pre-sentence report for adult offenders—

- where the offence falls within the LOW range of seriousness (see pp.9-10); and
- where the sentencer was minded to impose a single requirement, such as an exclusion requirement (where the circumstances of the case mean that this would be an appropriate disposal without electronic monitoring); and
- where the sentence will not require the involvement of the Probation Service, for example an electronically monitored curfew (subject to the court being satisfied that there is an appropriate address at which the curfew can operate).

(b) Ranges of sentence within the community sentence band

K-37   1.1.18   To enable the court to benefit from the flexibility that community sentences provide and also to meet its statutory obligations, any structure governing the use of community requirements must allow the courts to choose the most appropriate sentence for each individual offender.

1.1.19   Sentencers have a statutory obligation to pass sentences that are commensurate with the seriousness of an offence. However, within the range of sentence justified by the seriousness of the offence(s), courts will quite properly consider those factors that heighten the risk of the offender committing further offences or causing further harm with a view to lessening that risk. The extent to which requirements are imposed must be capable of being varied to ensure that the restriction on liberty is commensurate with the seriousness of the offence.

1.1.20   The council recognises that it would be helpful for sentencers to have a framework to help them decide on the most appropriate use of the new community sentence. While there is no single guiding principle, the seriousness of the offence that has been committed is an important factor. Three sentencing ranges (low, medium and high) within the community sentence band can be identified. It is not possible to position particular types of offence at firm points within the three ranges because the seriousness level of an offence is largely dependent upon the culpability of the offender and this is uniquely variable. The difficulty is particularly acute in relation to the medium range where it is clear that requirements will need to be tailored across a relatively wide range of offending behaviour.

1.1.21   In general terms, the lowest range of community sentence would be for those offenders whose offence was relatively minor within the community sentence band and would include persistent petty offenders whose offences only merit a community sentence by virtue of failing to respond to the previous imposition of fines. Such offenders would merit a 'light touch' approach, for example, normally a single requirement such as a short period of unpaid work, or a curfew, or a prohibited activity requirement or an exclusion requirement (where the circumstances of the case mean that this would be an appropriate disposal without electronic monitoring).

1.1.22   The top range would be for those offenders who have only just fallen short of a custodial sentence and for those who have passed the threshold but for whom a community sentence is deemed appropriate.

1.1.23   In all three ranges there must be sufficient flexibility to allow the sentence to be varied to take account of the suitability of particular requirements for the individual offender and whether a particular requirement or package of requirements might be more effective at reducing any identified risk of re-offending. It will fall to the sentencer to ensure that the sentence strikes the right balance between proportionality and suitability.

There should be three sentencing ranges (low, medium and high) within the community sentence band based upon seriousness.

It is not intended that an offender necessarily progress from one range to the next on each sentencing occasion. The decision as to the appropriate range each time is based upon the seriousness of the new offence(s).

The decision on the nature and severity of the requirements to be included in a community sentence should be guided by:

(i) the assessment of offence seriousness (low, medium or high);

(ii) the purpose(s) of sentencing the court wishes to achieve;

    (iii) **the risk of re-offending;**

    (iv) **the ability of the offender to comply, and**

    (v) **the availability of requirements in the local area.**

The resulting restriction on liberty must be a proportionate response to the offence that was committed.

1.1.24 Below we set out a non-exhaustive description of examples of requirements that might be appropriate in the three sentencing ranges. These examples focus on punishment in the community, although it is recognised that not all packages will necessarily need to include a punitive requirement. There will clearly be other requirements of a rehabilitative nature, such as a treatment requirement or an accredited programme, which may be appropriate depending on the specific needs of the offender and assessment of suitability. Given the intensity of such interventions, it is expected that these would normally only be appropriate at medium and high levels of seriousness, and where assessed as having a medium or high risk of re-offending. In addition, when passing sentence in any one of the three ranges, the court should consider whether a rehabilitative intervention such as a programme requirement, or a restorative justice intervention might be suitable as an additional or alternative part of the sentence.

Low

1.1.25 For offences only just crossing the community sentence threshold (such as persistent petty offending, some public order offences, some thefts from shops, or interference with a motor vehicle, where the seriousness of the offence or the nature of the offender's record means that a discharge or fine is inappropriate).   **K-38**

1.1.26 Suitable requirements might include:

- 40 to 80 hours of unpaid work; or
- a curfew requirement within the lowest range (*e.g.* up to 12 hours per day for a few weeks); or
- an exclusion requirement (where the circumstances of the case mean that this would be an appropriate disposal without electronic monitoring) lasting a few months; or
- a prohibited activity requirement; or
- an attendance centre requirement (where available).

1.1.27 Since the restriction on liberty must be commensurate with the seriousness of the offence, particular care needs to be taken with this band to ensure that this obligation is complied with. In most cases, only one requirement will be appropriate and the length may be curtailed if additional requirements are necessary.

Medium

1.1.28 For offences that obviously fall within the community sentence band such as handling stolen goods worth less than £1000 acquired for resale or somewhat more valuable goods acquired for the handler's own use, some cases of burglary in commercial premises, some cases of taking a motor vehicle without consent, or some cases of obtaining property by deception.   **K-39**

1.1.29 Suitable requirements might include:

- a greater number (*e.g.* 80 to 150) of hours of unpaid work; or
- an activity requirement in the middle range (20 to 30 days); or
- a curfew requirement within the middle range (*e.g.* up to 12 hours for 2–3 months); or
- an exclusion requirement lasting in the region of six months or
- a prohibited activity requirement.

1.1.30 Since the restriction on liberty must be commensurate with the seriousness of the offence, particular care needs to be taken with this band to ensure that this obligation is complied with.

High

1.1.31 For offences that only just fall below the custody threshold or where the custody threshold is crossed but a community sentence is more appropriate in all the circumstances, for example some cases displaying the features of a standard domestic burglary committed by a first-time offender.   **K-40**

1.1.32 More intensive sentences which combine two or more requirements may be appropriate at this level. Suitable requirements might include an unpaid work order of between 150 and 300 hours; an activity requirement up to the maximum 60 days; an exclusion order lasting in the region of 12 months; a curfew requirement of up to 12 hours a day for 4–6 months.

(c) Electronic monitoring

K-41   1.1.33   The court must also consider whether an electronic monitoring requirement[20] should be imposed which is mandatory[21] in some circumstances.

Electronic monitoring should be used with the primary purpose of promoting and monitoring compliance with other requirements, in circumstances where the punishment of the offender and/or the need to safeguard the public and prevent re-offending are the most important concerns.

(d) Recording the sentence imposed

K-42   1.1.34   Under the new framework there is only one (generic) community sentence provided by statute. This does not mean that offenders who have completed a community sentence and have then re-offended should be regarded as ineligible for a second community sentence on the basis that this has been tried and failed. Further community sentences, perhaps with different requirements, may well be justified.

1.1.35   Those imposing sentence will wish to be clear about the 'purposes' that the community sentence is designed to achieve when setting the requirements. Sharing those purposes with the offender and Probation Service will enable them to be clear about the goals that are to be achieved.

1.1.36   Any future sentencer must have full information about the requirements that were inserted by the court into the previous community sentence imposed on the offender (including whether it was a low/medium/high level order) and also about the offender's response. This will enable the court to consider the merits of imposing the same or different requirements as part of another community sentence. The requirements should be recorded in such a way as to ensure that they can be made available to another court if another offence is committed.

When an offender is required to serve a community sentence, the court records should be clearly annotated to show which particular requirements have been imposed.

(ii)   Time spent on remand

K-43   1.1.37   The court will need to consider whether to give any credit for time spent in custody on remand.[22] (For further detail from the Panel's Advice, see Annex A.)

The court should seek to give credit for time spent on remand (in custody or equivalent status) in all cases. It should make clear, when announcing sentence, whether or not credit for time on remand has been given (bearing in mind that there will be no automatic reduction in sentence once section 67 of the Criminal Justice Act 1967 is repealed) and should explain its reasons for not giving credit when it considers either that this is not justified, would not be practical, or would not be in the best interests of the offender.

1.1.38   Where an offender has spent a period of time in custody on remand, there will be occasions where a custodial sentence is warranted but the length of the sentence justified by the seriousness of the offence would mean that the offender would be released immediately. Under the present framework, it may be more appropriate to pass a community sentence since that will ensure supervision on release.

1.1.39   However, given the changes in the content of the second part of a custodial sentence of 12 months or longer, a court in this situation where the custodial sentence would be 12 months or more should, under the new framework, pass a custodial sentence in the knowledge that licence requirements will be imposed on release from custody. This will ensure that the sentence imposed properly reflects the seriousness of the offence.

1.1.40   Recommendations made by the court at the point of sentence will be of particular importance in influencing the content of the licence. This will properly reflect the gravity of the offence(s) committed.

(iii)   Breaches

K-44   1.1.41   Where an offender fails, without reasonable excuse, to comply with one or more requirements, the 'responsible officer'[23] can either give a warning or initiate breach proceedings. Where the offender fails to comply without reasonable excuse for the second time within a 12-month period, the 'responsible officer' must initiate proceedings.

---

[20] *ibid.*, section 177(3) and (4).
[21] Unless the necessary facilities are not available or, in the particular circumstances of the case, the court considers it inappropriate.
[22] Criminal Justice Act 2003 section 149.
[23] Criminal Justice Act 2003 Schedule 8, paragraphs 5–6.

1.1.42 In such proceedings the court must[24] either **increase the severity of the existing sentence** (*i.e.* impose more onerous conditions including requirements aimed at enforcement, such as a curfew or supervision requirement) or **revoke the existing sentence and proceed as though sentencing for the original offence**. The court is required to take account of the circumstances of the breach,[25] which will inevitably have an impact on its response.

1.1.43 In certain circumstances (where an offender has wilfully and persistently failed to comply with an order made in respect of an offence that is not itself punishable by imprisonment), the court can **impose a maximum of 51 weeks custody**.[26]

1.1.44 When increasing the onerousness of requirements, the court must consider the impact on the offender's ability to comply and the possibility of precipitating a custodial sentence for further breach. For that reason, and particularly where the breach occurs towards the end of the sentence, the court should take account of compliance to date and may consider that extending the supervision or operational periods will be more sensible; in other cases it might choose to add punitive or rehabilitative requirements instead. In making these changes the court must be mindful of the legislative restrictions on the overall length of community sentences and on the supervision and operational periods allowed for each type of requirement.

1.1.45 The court dealing with breach of a community sentence should have as its primary objective ensuring that the requirements of the sentence are finished, and this is important if the court is to have regard to the statutory purposes of sentencing. A court that imposes a custodial sentence for breach without giving adequate consideration to alternatives is in danger of imposing a sentence that is not commensurate with the seriousness of the original offence and is solely a punishment for breach. This risks undermining the purposes it has identified as being important. Nonetheless, courts will need to be vigilant to ensure that there is a realistic prospect of the purposes of the order being achieved.

> **Having decided that a community sentence is commensurate with the seriousness of the offence, the primary objective when sentencing for breach of requirements is to ensure that those requirements are completed.**

1.1.46 A court sentencing for breach must take account of the extent to which the offender has complied with the requirements of the community order, the reasons for breach and the point at which the breach has occurred. Where a breach takes place towards the end of the operational period and the court is satisfied that the offender's appearance before the court is likely to be sufficient in itself to ensure future compliance, then given that it is not open to the court to make no order, an approach that the court might wish to adopt could be to re-sentence in a way that enables the original order to be completed properly—for example, a differently constructed community sentence that aims to secure compliance with the purposes of the original sentence.

1.1.47 If the court decides to increase the onerousness of an order, it must give careful consideration, with advice from the Probation Service, to the offender's ability to comply. A custodial sentence should be the last resort, where all reasonable efforts to ensure that an offender completes a community sentence have failed.

- **The Act allows for a custodial sentence to be imposed in response to breach of a community sentence. Custody should be the last resort, reserved for those cases of deliberate and repeated breach where all reasonable efforts to ensure that the offender complies have failed.**

- **Before increasing the onerousness of requirements, sentencers should take account of the offender's ability to comply and should avoid precipitating further breach by overloading the offender with too many or conflicting requirements.**

- **There may be cases where the court will need to consider re-sentencing to a differently constructed community sentence in order to secure compliance with the purposes of the original sentence, perhaps where there has already been partial compliance or where events since the sentence was imposed have shown that a different course of action is likely to be effective.**

---

[24] *ibid.*, paragraphs 9-10.
[25] *ibid.*, paragraph 9(2).
[26] *ibid.*, paragraph 9(1)(c).

SECTION 1 PART 2—DEFERRED SENTENCES

A. Statutory Provisions

K-45
1.2.1 Under the existing legislation,[27] a court can defer a sentence for up to six months, provided the offender consents and the court considers that deferring the sentence is in the interests of justice.

1.2.2 The new provisions[28] continue to require the consent of the offender and that the court be satisfied that the making of such a decision is in the interests of justice. However, it is also stated that the power to defer sentence can only be exercised where:

> "the offender undertakes to comply with any requirements as to his conduct during the period of the deferment that the court considers it appropriate to impose;".[29]

1.2.3 This enables the court to impose a wide variety of conditions (including a residence requirement).[30] The Act allows the court to appoint the probation service or other responsible person to oversee the offender's conduct during this period and prepare a report for the court at the point of sentence *i.e.* the end of the deferment period.

1.2.4 As under the existing legislation, if the offender commits another offence during the deferment period the court may have the power to sentence for both the original and the new offence at once. Sentence cannot be deferred for more than six months and, in most circumstances, no more than one period of deferment can be granted.[31]

1.2.5 A significant change is the provision enabling a court to deal with an offender before the end of the period of deferment.[32] For example if the court is satisfied that the offender has failed to comply with one or more requirements imposed in connection with the deferment, the offender can be brought back before the court and the court can proceed to sentence.

B. Use of Deferred Sentences

K-46
1.2.6 Under the new framework, there is a wider range of sentencing options open to the courts, including the increased availability of suspended sentences, and deferred sentences are likely to be used in very limited circumstances. A deferred sentence enables the court to review the conduct of the defendant before passing sentence, having first prescribed certain requirements. It also provides several opportunities for an offender to have some influence as to the sentence passed—
> (a) it tests the commitment of the offender not to re-offend;
> (b) it gives the offender an opportunity to do something where progress can be shown within a short period;
> (c) it provides the offender with an opportunity to behave or refrain from behaving in a particular way that will be relevant to sentence.

1.2.7 Given the new power to require undertakings and the ability to enforce those undertakings before the end of the period of deferral, the decision to defer sentence should be predominantly for a small group of cases at either the custody threshold or the community sentence threshold where the sentencer feels that there would be particular value in giving the offender the opportunities listed because, if the offender complies with the requirements, a different sentence will be justified at the end of the deferment period. This could be a community sentence instead of a custodial sentence or a fine or discharge instead of a community sentence. It may, rarely, enable a custodial sentence to be suspended rather than imposed immediately.

> **The use of deferred sentences should be predominantly for a small group of cases close to a significant threshold where, should the defendant be prepared to adapt his behaviour in a way clearly specified by the sentencer, the court may be prepared to impose a lesser sentence.**

1.2.8 A court may impose any conditions during the period of deferment that it considers appropriate.[33] These could be specific requirements as set out in the provisions for community sentences,[34] or requirements that are drawn more widely. These should be specific, measurable conditions so that the offender knows exactly what is required and the court can assess compliance; the restriction on liberty should be limited to ensure that the offender has a reasonable expectation of being able to comply whilst maintaining his or her social responsibilities.

---

[27] Powers of Criminal Courts (Sentencing) Act 2000 sections 1 and 2.
[28] Criminal Justice Act 2003 schedule 23 repealing and replacing sections 1 and 2 of the 2000 Act.
[29] *ibid.*, new section 1(3)(b) as inserted by Schedule 23 to the Criminal Justice Act 2003.
[30] *ibid.*, new section 1A(1).
[31] *ibid.*, new section 1(4).
[32] *ibid.*, new section 1B.
[33] *ibid.*, new section 1 (3)(b) as inserted by Schedule 23 to the Criminal Justice Act 2003.
[34] Criminal Justice Act 2003 section 177.

1.2.9 Given the need for clarity in the mind of the offender and the possibility of sentence by another court, the court should give a clear indication (and make a written record) of the type of sentence it would be minded to impose if it had not decided to defer and ensure that the offender understands the consequences of failure to comply with the court's wishes during the deferral period.

When deferring sentence, the sentencer must make clear the consequence of not complying with any requirements and should indicate the type of sentence it would be minded to impose. Sentencers should impose specific, measurable conditions that do not involve a serious restriction on liberty.

SECTION 2—CUSTODIAL SENTENCES PART 1—CUSTODIAL SENTENCES OF 12 MONTHS OR MORE

A. Statutory Provisions

2.1.1 Under existing legislation: **K-47**
- an adult offender receiving a custodial sentence of at least 12 months and below 4 years will automatically be released at the halfway point and will then be supervised under licence until the three-quarter point of the sentence. [For some, the actual release date may be earlier as a result of release on home detention curfew (HDC).]
- an adult offender receiving a determinate sentence of 4 years or above will be eligible for release from the halfway point and, if not released before, will automatically be released at the two-thirds point. After release, the offender will be supervised under licence until the three-quarter point of the sentence.

2.1.2 Under the new framework, the impact of a custodial sentence will be more severe since the period in custody and under supervision will be for the whole of the sentence term set by the court. Additionally, separate provisions for the protection of the public will be introduced for those offenders designated as "dangerous" under the Act which are designed to ensure that release only occurs when it is considered safe to do so.

2.1.3 Where a prison sentence of 12 months or more is imposed on an offender who is not classified as "dangerous", that offender will be entitled to be released from custody after completing half of the sentence. The whole of the second half of the sentence will be subject to licence requirements. These requirements will be set shortly before release by the Secretary of State (with advice from the Governor responsible for authorising the prisoner's release in consultation with the Probation Service) but a court will be able to make recommendations at the sentencing stage on the content of those requirements.[35] The conditions that the Secretary of State may attach to a licence are to be prescribed by order.[36]

2.1.4 The Act requires that a custodial sentence for a fixed term should be for the shortest term that is commensurate with the seriousness of the offence.[37]

B. Imposition of Custodial Sentences of 12 Months or More

(i) Length of sentence

2.1.5 The requirement that the second half of a prison sentence will be served in the community **K-48** subject to conditions imposed prior to release is a major new development and will require offenders to be under supervision for the full duration of the sentence prescribed by the court. The Probation Service will be able to impose a number of complementary requirements on the offender during the second half of a custodial sentence and these are expected to be more demanding and involve a greater restriction on liberty than current licence conditions.

2.1.6 As well as restricting liberty to a greater extent, the new requirements will last until the very end of the sentence, rather than to the three-quarter point as at present, potentially making a custodial sentence significantly more demanding than under existing legislation. Breach of these requirements at any stage is likely to result in the offender being returned to custody and this risk continues, therefore, for longer under the new framework than under the existing legislation.

Transitional arrangements

2.1.7 In general, a fixed term custodial sentence of 12 months or more under the new framework **K-49** will increase the sentence actually served (whether in custody or in the community) since it continues to the end of the term imposed. Existing guidelines issued since 1991 have been based on a different

[35] Criminal Justice Act 2003 section 238(1).
[36] *ibid.*, section 250.
[37] *ibid.*, section 153(2).

framework and so, in order to maintain consistency between the lengths of sentence under the current and the new framework, there will need to be some adjustment to the starting points for custodial sentences contained in those guidelines (subject to the special sentences under the 2003 Act where the offender is a "dangerous" offender).

2.1.8   This aspect of the guideline will be temporary to overcome the short-term situation where sentencing guidelines (issued since implementation of the reforms to custodial sentences introduced by the Criminal Justice Act 1991) are based on a different framework and the new framework has made those sentences more demanding. As new guidelines are issued they will take into account the new framework in providing starting points and ranges of appropriate sentence lengths for offences and an adjustment will not be necessary.

2.1.9   Since there are so many factors that will vary, it is difficult to calculate precisely how much more demanding a sentence under the new framework will be. The council's conclusion is that the sentencer should seek to achieve the best match between a sentence under the new framework and its equivalent under the old framework so as to maintain the same level of punishment. As a guide, the Council suggests the sentence length should be reduced by in the region of 15%.

2.1.10   The changes in the nature of a custodial sentence will require changes in the way the sentence is announced. Sentencers will need to continue[38] to spell out the practical implications of the sentence being imposed so that offenders, victims and the public alike all understand that the sentence does not end when the offender is released from custody. The fact that a breach of the requirements imposed in the second half of the sentence is likely to result in a return to custody should also be made very clear at the point of sentence.

- **When imposing a fixed term custodial sentence of 12 months or more under the new provisions, courts should consider reducing the overall length of the sentence that would have been imposed under the current provisions by in the region of 15%.**
- **When announcing sentence, sentencers should explain the way in which the sentence has been calculated, how it will be served and the implications of non-compliance with licence requirements. In particular, it needs to be stated clearly that the sentence is in two parts, one in custody and one under supervision in the community.**
- **This proposal does not apply to sentences for dangerous offenders, for which separate provision has been made in the Act.**

(ii) Licence conditions

K-50   2.1.11   Under the Act, a court imposing a prison sentence of 12 months or more may recommend conditions that should be imposed by the Secretary of State (with advice from the governor responsible for authorising the prisoner's release in consultation with the Probation Service) on release from custody.[39] Recommendations do not form part of the sentence and they are not binding on the Secretary of State.[40]

2.1.12   When passing such a sentence, the court will not know with any certainty to what extent the offender's behaviour may have been addressed in custody or what the offender's health and other personal circumstances might be on release and so it will be extremely difficult, especially in the case of longer custodial sentences, for sentencers to make an informed judgement about the most appropriate licence conditions to be imposed on release. However, in most cases, it would be extremely helpful for sentencers to indicate areas of an offender's behaviour about which they have the most concern and to make suggestions about the types of intervention whether this, in practice, takes place in prison or in the community.

2.1.13   The involvement of the Probation Service at the pre-sentence stage will clearly be pivotal. A recommendation on the likely post-release requirements included in a presentence report will assist the court with the decision on overall sentence length, although any recommendation would still have to be open to review when release is being considered. A curfew, exclusion requirement or prohibited activity requirement might be suitable conditions to recommend for the licence period. A court might also wish to suggest that the offender should complete a rehabilitation programme, for example for drug abuse, anger management, or improving skills such as literacy and could recommend that this should be considered as a licence requirement if the programme has not been undertaken or completed in custody.

2.1.14   The governor responsible for authorising the prisoner's release, in consultation with the Probation Service, is best placed to make recommendations at the point of release; this is the case at present and continues to be provided for in the Act. Specific court recommendations will only generally be appropriate in the context of relatively short sentences, where it would not be unreasonable

---

[38] Having reference to the *Consolidated Criminal Practice Direction* [2002] 2 Cr App R 533, Annex C, as suitably amended.
[39] Criminal Justice Act 2003 section 238(1).
[40] *ibid.*, section 250.

for the sentencer to anticipate the relevance of particular requirements at the point of release. Making recommendations in relation to longer sentences (other than suggestions about the types of intervention that might be appropriate at some point during the sentence) would be unrealistic. The governor and Probation Service should have due regard to any recommendations made by the sentencing court and the final recommendation to the Secretary of State on licence conditions will need to build upon any interventions during the custodial period and any other changes in the offender's circumstances.

- **A court may sensibly suggest interventions that could be useful when passing sentence, but should only make specific recommendations about the requirements to be imposed on licence when announcing short sentences and where it is reasonable to anticipate their relevance at the point of release. The governor and Probation Service should have due regard to any recommendations made by the sentencing court but its decision should be contingent upon any changed circumstances during the custodial period.**
- **The court should make it clear, at the point of sentence, that the requirements to be imposed on licence will ultimately be the responsibility of the Governor and Probation Service and that they are entitled to review any recommendations made by the court in the light of any changed circumstances.**

SECTION 2 PART 2—SUSPENDED SENTENCES OF IMPRISONMENT

A. Statutory Provisions

2.2.1 Section 189 Criminal Justice Act 2003 [sets out full text of section 189, as to which, see § 5-547 in the main work]. **K-51**

2.2.2 Imposition of requirements—Section 190 Criminal Justice Act 2003 [sets out full text of section 190, as to which, see § 5-550 in the main work]. **K-52**

2.2.3 Power to provide for review—Section 191 Criminal Justice Act 2003 [sets out full text of section 191, as to which, see § 5-551 in the main work]. **K-53**

2.2.4 Periodic reviews—Section 192 Criminal Justice Act 2003 [sets out full text of section 192, as to which, see § 5-552 in the main work]. **K-54**

2.2.5 Breach, revocation or amendment of orders, and effect of further conviction—Section 193 Criminal Justice Act 2003 [sets out full text of section 193, as to which, see § 5-554 in the main work]. **K-55**

B. Imposing A Suspended Sentence

2.2.6 A suspended sentence is a sentence of imprisonment. it is subject to the same criteria as a sentence of imprisonment which is to commence immediately. in particular, this requires a court to be satisfied that the custody threshold has been passed and that the length of the term is the shortest term commensurate with the seriousness of the offence. **K-56**

2.2.7 A court which passes a prison sentence of less than 12 months may suspend it for between six months and two years (the operational period).[41] During that period, the court can impose one or more requirements for the offender to undertake in the community. The requirements are identical to those available for the new community sentence.

2.2.8 The period during which the offender undertakes community requirements is "the supervision period" when the offender will be under the supervision of a "responsible officer"; this period may be shorter than the operational period. The court may periodically review the progress of the offender in complying with the requirements and the reviews will be informed by a report from the responsible officer.

2.2.9 If the offender fails to comply with a requirement during the supervision period, or commits a further offence during the operational period, the suspended sentence can be activated in full or in part or the terms of the supervision made more onerous. There is a presumption that the suspended sentence will be activated either in full or in part.

(i) The decision to suspend

2.2.10   There are many similarities between the suspended sentence and the community sentence. in both cases, requirements can be imposed during the supervision period and the court can respond to breach by sending the offender to custody. The crucial difference is that the suspended sentence is a prison sentence and is appropriate only for an offence that passes the custody threshold and for which imprisonment is the only option. A community sentence may also be imposed for an offence that passes the custody threshold where the court considers that to be appropriate. **K-57**

---

[41] The power to suspend a sentence is expected to come into force earlier than the provisions implementing "custody plus" and transitional provisions are expected to enable any sentence of imprisonment of under 12 months to be suspended. This guideline therefore is written in the language of the expected transitional provisions.

2.2.11 The full decision making process for imposition of custodial sentences under the new framework (including the custody threshold test) is set out in paragraphs 1.31-1.33 of the seriousness guideline. For the purposes of suspended sentences the relevant steps are:

(a) has the custody threshold been passed?

(b) if so, is it unavoidable that a custodial sentence be imposed?

(c) if so, can that sentence be suspended? (sentencers should be clear that they would have imposed a custodial sentence if the power to suspend had not been available)

(d) if not, can the sentence be served intermittently?

(e) if not, impose a sentence which takes immediate effect for the term commensurate with the seriousness of the offence.

(ii) Length of sentence

K-58

2.2.12 Before making the decision to suspend sentence, the court must already have decided that a prison sentence is justified and should also have decided the length of sentence that would be the shortest term commensurate with the seriousness of the offence if it were to be imposed immediately. The decision to suspend the sentence should not lead to a longer term being imposed than if the sentence were to take effect immediately.

A prison sentence that is suspended should be for the same term that would have applied if the offender were being sentenced to immediate custody.

2.2.13 When assessing the length of the operational period of a suspended sentence, the court should have in mind the relatively short length of the sentence being suspended and the advantages to be gained by retaining the opportunity to extend the operational period at a later stage (see below).

The operational period of a suspended sentence should reflect the length of the sentence being suspended. As an approximate guide, an operational period of up to 12 months might normally be appropriate for a suspended sentence of up to 6 months and an operational period of up to 18 months might normally be appropriate for a suspended sentence of up to 12 months.

(iii) Requirements

K-59

2.2.14 The court will set the requirements to be complied with during the supervision period. Whilst the offence for which a suspended sentence is imposed is generally likely to be more serious than one for which a community sentence is imposed, the imposition of the custodial sentence is a clear punishment and deterrent. In order to ensure that the overall terms of the sentence are commensurate with the seriousness of the offence, it is likely that the requirements to be undertaken during the supervision period would be less onerous than if a community sentence had been imposed. These requirements will need to ensure that they properly address those factors that are most likely to reduce the risk of re-offending.

Because of the very clear deterrent threat involved in a suspended sentence, requirements imposed as part of that sentence should generally be less onerous than those imposed as part of a community sentence. A court wishing to impose onerous or intensive requirements on an offender should reconsider its decision to suspend sentence and consider whether a community sentence might be more appropriate.

C. Breaches

K-60

2.2.15 The essence of a suspended sentence is to make it abundantly clear to an offender that failure to comply with the requirements of the order or commission of another offence will almost certainly result in a custodial sentence. Where an offender has breached any of the requirements without reasonable excuse for the first time, the responsible officer must either give a warning or initiate breach proceedings.[42] Where there is a further breach within a twelve-month period, breach proceedings must be initiated.[43]

2.2.16 Where proceedings are brought the court has several options, including extending the operational period. However, the presumption (which also applies where breach is by virtue of the commission of a further offence) is that the suspended prison sentence will be activated (either with its original custodial term or a lesser term) unless the court takes the view that this would, in all the

---

[42] Criminal Justice Act 2003 schedule 12, para. 4.
[43] *ibid.*, para. 5.

circumstances, be unjust. In reaching that decision, the court may take into account both the extent to which the offender has complied with the requirements and the facts of the new offence.[44]

2.2.17 Where a court considers that the sentence needs to be activated, it may activate it in full or with a reduced term. Again, the extent to which the requirements have been complied with will be very relevant to this decision.

2.2.18 If a court amends the order rather than activating the suspended prison sentence, it must either make the requirements more onerous, or extend the supervision or operational periods (provided that these remain within the limits defined by the Act).[45] In such cases, the court must state its reasons for not activating the prison sentence,[46] which could include the extent to which the offender has complied with requirements or the facts of the subsequent offence.

2.2.19 If an offender near the end of an operational period (having complied with the requirements imposed) commits another offence, it may be more appropriate to amend the order rather than activate it.

2.2.20 If a new offence committed is of a less serious nature than the offence for which the suspended sentence was passed, it may justify activating the sentence with a reduced term or amending the terms of the order.

2.2.21 It is expected that any activated suspended sentence will be consecutive to the sentence imposed for the new offence.

2.2.22 If the new offence is non-imprisonable, the sentencer should consider whether it is appropriate to activate the suspended sentence at all.

Where the court decides to amend a suspended sentence order rather than activate the custodial sentence, it should give serious consideration to extending the supervision or operational periods (within statutory limits) rather than making the requirements more onerous.

ANNEX A

Time spent on remand—Sentencing Advisory Panel's advice

The Act makes provision for a sentencer to give credit for time spent on remand in custody where **K-70** a custodial sentence is passed.[47] It also empowers the court to have regard to time spent on remand in custody when determining the restrictions on liberty to be imposed by a community order or youth community order.[48] Where an offender has spent several weeks in custody, this may affect the nature of the offence that is passed. For example, where the court decides that a custodial sentence is justified some sentencers may decide to pass a community sentence instead, on the basis that the offender has already completed the equivalent of a punitive element in a sentence. The Panel takes the view that, given the changes in the content of the second part of a custodial sentence, in such cases it will be more appropriate to pass a custodial sentence knowing that licence requirements will be imposed on release from custody (which may be immediate). Recommendations made by the court at the point of sentence will then be of particular importance in influencing the content of the licence. This will help to ensure that the record clearly shows the assessment of seriousness of the offending behaviour.

Whereas the Act clearly states that time spent on remand is to be regarded as part of a custodial sentence unless the Court considers it unjust,[49] it states that sentencers passing a community sentence may have regard to time spent on remand, but no further information is given on how this discretion should be exercised. The Panel recognises that giving credit for time spent on remand is likely to be easier to apply in relation to punitive requirements rather than the rehabilitative elements of a community sentence. For example, reducing the number of unpaid work hours could be fairly easy, whereas reducing the length of a rehabilitation programme might not be appropriate as it could undermine its effectiveness. Where an offender has been kept on remand, one could take the view that this action was justified by the bail provisions and that the sentencer should not, therefore, feel obliged to adjust the terms of the community sentence. However, in principle, the Panel recommends that the court should seek to give credit for time spent on remand in all cases and should explain its reasons for not doing so when it considers either that this is not justified, would not be practical, or would not be in the best interests of the offender.

The court should seek to give credit for time spent on remand in all cases. It should make clear, when announc-

---

[44] *ibid.*, para. 8(4).
[45] *ibid.*, section 189(3) and (4).
[46] *ibid.*, schedule 12, para. 8(3).
[47] Criminal Justice Act 2003 section 240.
[48] *ibid.*, section 149.
[49] *ibid.*, section 240 (which will, at a future date, replace Criminal Justice Act 1967, section 67, by which such period is now deducted automatically).

ing sentence, whether or not credit for time on remand has been given and should explain its reasons for not giving credit when it considers either that this is not justified, would not be practical, or would not be in the best interests of the offender.

Where, following a period of time spent in custody on remand, the court decides that a custodial sentence is justified then, given the changes in the content of the second part of a custodial sentence, the court should pass a custodial sentence in the knowledge that licence requirements will be imposed on release from custody. Recommendations made by the court at the point of sentence will be of particular importance in influencing the content of the licence.[50]

D. MANSLAUGHTER BY REASON OF PROVOCATION

GUIDELINE

FOREWORD

K-71   In accordance with section 170(9) of the Criminal Justice Act 2003, the Sentencing Guidelines Council issues this guideline as a definitive guideline. By virtue of section 172 of the Act, every court must have regard to a relevant guideline. This guideline applies to offenders convicted of manslaughter by reason of provocation who are sentenced after 28 November 2005.

This guideline stems from a reference from the Home Secretary for consideration of the issue of sentencing where provocation is argued in cases of homicide, and, in particular, domestic violence homicides. For the purpose of describing "domestic violence", the Home Secretary adopted the Crown Prosecution Service definition.[51] The guideline applies to sentencing of an adult offender for this offence in whatever circumstances it occurs. it identifies the widely varying features of both the provocation and the act of retaliation and sets out the approach to be adopted in deciding both the sentencing range and the starting point within that range.

This guideline is for use where the conviction for manslaughter is clearly founded on provocation alone. There will be additional, different and more complicated matters to be taken into account where the other main partial defence, diminished responsibility, is a factor.

The Council's Guideline *New Sentences: Criminal Justice Act 2003* recognised the potentially more demanding nature of custodial sentences of 12 months or longer imposed under the new framework introduced by the Criminal Justice Act 2003. Consequently the sentencing ranges and starting points in this guideline take that principle into account.

Guidelines are created following extensive consultation. The Sentencing Advisory Panel first consults widely on the basis of a thoroughly researched consultation paper, then provides the Council with advice. Having considered the advice, the Council prepares a draft guideline on which there is further consultation with Parliament, with the Home Secretary and with Ministers of other relevant Government Departments. This guideline is the culmination of that process.

The Council has appreciated greatly the work of the Sentencing Advisory Panel in preparing the advice on which this guideline has been based and for those who have responded so thoughtfully to the consultation of both the Panel and the Council.

The advice and this guideline are available on www.sentencing-guidelines.gov.uk or from the Sentencing Guidelines Secretariat at 85 Buckingham Gate, London SW1E 6PD. A summary of the responses to the Council's consultation also appears on the website.

Chairman of the Council

November 2005

CONTENTS

---

[50] This recommendation only applies to sentences of 12 months and above pending the implementation of 'custody plus'.

[51] "Any criminal offence arising out of physical, sexual, psychological, emotional or financial abuse by one person against a current or former partner in a close relationship, or against a current or former family member." A new definition of domestic violence was agreed in 2004 (and appears in the CPS Policy on Prosecuting cases of Domestic Violence, 2005) "any incident of threatening behaviour, violence or abuse [psychological, physical, sexual, financial or emotional] between adults who are or have been intimate partners or family members, regardless of gender or sexuality".

The extent and timing of the retaliation

Post-offence behaviour

Use of a weapon

D   Sentence Ranges and Starting Points

Identifying sentence ranges

Factors to take into consideration

Guideline

Manslaughter by Reason of Provocation

A. Statutory Provision

1.1 Murder and manslaughter are common law offences and there is no complete statutory defini- **K-73**
tion of either. 'Provocation' is one of the partial defences by which an offence that would otherwise
be murder may be reduced to manslaughter.

1.2 Before the issue of provocation can be considered, the Crown must have proved beyond
reasonable doubt that all the elements of murder were present, including the necessary intent (*i.e.*
the offender must have intended either to kill the victim or to cause grievous bodily harm). The
court must then consider section 3 of the Homicide Act 1957, which provides:

> *Where on a charge of murder there is evidence on which the jury can find that the person charged was
> provoked (whether by things done or by things said or by both together) to lose his self-control, the question
> whether the provocation was enough to make a reasonable man do as he did shall be left to be determined by the
> jury; and in determining that question the jury shall take into account everything both done and said according
> to the effect which, in their opinion, it would have on a reasonable man.*

Although both murder and manslaughter result in death, the difference in the
level of culpability creates offences of a distinctively different character.
Therefore the approach to sentencing in each should start from a different
basis.

B. Establishing the Basis for Sentencing

2.1 The Court of Appeal in *Attorney General's References (Nos. 74, 95 and 118 of 2002) (Suratan and* **K-74**
others),[52] set out a number of assumptions that a judge must make in favour of an offender found not
guilty of murder but guilty of manslaughter by reason of provocation. The assumptions are required
in order to be faithful to the verdict and should be applied equally in all cases whether conviction follows a trial or whether the Crown has accepted a plea of guilty to manslaughter by reason of
provocation:

- first, that the offender had, at the time of the killing, lost self-control; mere loss of temper
  or jealous rage is not sufficient
- second, that the offender was caused to lose self-control by things said or done, normally
  by the person killed
- third, that the offender's loss of control was reasonable in all the circumstances, even
  bearing in mind that people are expected to exercise reasonable control over their emotions and that, as society advances, it ought to call for a higher measure of self-control
- fourth, that the circumstances were such as to make the loss of self-control sufficiently
  excusable to reduce the gravity of the offence from murder to manslaughter.

---

[52] [2003] 2 Cr.App.R.(S.) 42.

Bearing in mind the loss of life caused by manslaughter by reason of provocation, the starting point for sentencing should be a custodial sentence. Only in a very small number of cases involving very exceptional mitigating factors should a judge consider that a non-custodial sentence is justified.

The same general sentencing principles should apply in all cases of manslaughter by reason of provocation irrespective of whether or not the killing takes place in a domestic context.

C. Factors Influencing Sentence

K-75
3.1 A number of elements must be considered and balanced by the sentencer. Some of these are common to all types of manslaughter by reason of provocation; others have a particular relevance in cases of manslaughter in a domestic context.

3.2 **The degree of provocation as shown by its nature and duration**—An assessment of the *degree* of the provocation as shown by its nature and duration is the critical factor in the sentencing decision.

(a) In assessing the *degree* of provocation, account should be taken of the following factors:
- if the provocation (which does not have to be a wrongful act) involves gross and extreme conduct on the part of the victim, it is a more significant mitigating factor than conduct which, although significant, is not as extreme
- the fact that the victim presented a threat not only to the offender, but also to children in his or her care
- the offender's previous experiences of abuse and/or domestic violence either by the victim or by other people
- any mental condition which may affect the offender's perception of what amounts to provocation
- the nature of the conduct, the period of time over which it took place and its cumulative effect
- discovery or knowledge of the fact of infidelity on the part of a partner does not necessarily amount to *high* provocation. The gravity of such provocation depends entirely on all attendant circumstances.

(b) Whether the provocation was suffered over a *long or short* period is important to the assessment of gravity. The following factors should be considered:
- the impact of provocative behaviour on an offender can build up over a period of time
- consideration should not be limited to acts of provocation that occurred immediately before the victim was killed. For example, in domestic violence cases, cumulative provocation may eventually become intolerable, the latest incident seeming all the worse because of what went before.

(c) When looking at the *nature* of the provocation the court should consider both the type of provocation and whether, in the particular case, the actions of the victim would have had a particularly marked effect on the offender:
- actual (or anticipated) violence from the victim will generally be regarded as involving a higher degree of provocation than provocation arising from abuse, infidelity or offensive words unless that amounts to psychological bullying
- in cases involving actual or anticipated violence, the culpability of the offender will therefore generally be less than in cases involving verbal provocation
- where the offender's actions were motivated by fear or desperation, rather than by anger, frustration, resentment or a desire for revenge, the offender's culpability will generally be lower.

3.3 **The extent and timing of the retaliation**—It is implicit in the verdict of manslaughter by reason of provocation that the killing was the result of a loss of self-control because of things said and/or done. The intensity, extent and nature of that loss of control must be assessed in the context of the provocation that preceded it.

3.4 The *circumstances of the killing* itself will be relevant to the offender's culpability, and hence to the appropriate sentence:

- in general, the offender's violent response to provocation is likely to be less culpable the shorter the time gap between the provocation (or the last provocation) and the killing—as evidenced, for example, by the use of a weapon that happened to be available rather than by one that was carried for that purpose or prepared for use in advance
- conversely, it is not necessarily the case that greater culpability will be found where there has been a significant lapse of time between the provocation (or the last provocation) and the killing. Where the provocation is cumulative, and particularly in those circumstances where the offender is found to have suffered domestic violence from the victim over a significant period of time, the required loss of self-control may not be sudden as some experience a "slow-burn" reaction and appear calm
- choosing or taking advantage of favourable circumstances for carrying out the killing (so that the victim was unable to resist, such as where the victim was not on guard, or was asleep) may well be an aggravating factor—unless this is mitigated by the circumstances of the offender, resulting in the offender being the weaker or vulnerable party.

3.5 The *context of the relationship* between the offender and the victim must be borne in mind when **K-76** assessing the nature and degree of the provocation offered by the victim before the crime and the length of time over which the provocation existed. In cases where the parties were still in a relationship at the time of the killing, it will be necessary to examine the balance of power between one party and the other and to consider other family members who may have been drawn into, or been victims of, the provocative behaviour.

> Although there will usually be less culpability when the retaliation to provocation is sudden, it is not always the case that greater culpability will be found where there has been a significant lapse of time between the provocation and the killing.
>
> It is for the sentencer to consider the impact on an offender of provocative behaviour that has built up over a period of time.
>
> An offence should be regarded as aggravated where it is committed in the presence of a child or children or other vulnerable family member, whether or not the offence takes place in a domestic setting.

3.6 **Post-offence behaviour**—The behaviour of the offender after the killing can be relevant to sentence:

- immediate and genuine remorse may be demonstrated by the summoning of medical assistance, remaining at the scene, and co-operation with the authorities
- concealment or attempts to dispose of evidence or dismemberment of the body may aggravate the offence.

> Post-offence behaviour is relevant to the sentence. It may be an aggravating or mitigating factor. When sentencing, the judge should consider the motivation behind the offender's actions.

3.7 **Use of a weapon**

(a) In relation to this offence, as in relation to many different types of offence, the carrying and use of a weapon is an aggravating factor. Courts must consider the type of weapon used and, importantly, whether it was to hand or carried to the scene and who introduced it to the incident.

(b) The use or not of a weapon is a factor heavily influenced by the gender of the offender. Whereas men can and do kill using physical strength alone, women often cannot and thus resort to using a weapon. The issue of key importance is whether the weapon was to hand or carried deliberately to the scene, although the circumstances in which the weapon was brought to the scene will need to be considered carefully.

Archbold
paragraph
numbers

K-76

Archbold's Criminal Pleading—2016 ed.

The use of a weapon should not necessarily move a case into another sentencing bracket.

In cases of manslaughter by reason of provocation, use of a weapon may reflect the imbalance in strength between the offender and the victim and how that weapon came to hand is likely to be far more important than the use of the weapon itself.

It will be an aggravating factor where the weapon is brought to the scene in contemplation of use *before* the loss of self-control (which may occur some time before the fatal incident).

D. Sentence Ranges and Starting Points

K-77 **4.1 Manslaughter is a "serious offence"** for the purposes of the provisions in the Criminal Justice Act 2003[53] for dealing with dangerous offenders. It is possible that a court will be required to use the sentences for public protection prescribed in the Act when sentencing an offender convicted of the offence of manslaughter by reason of provocation. An alternative is a discretionary life sentence. In accordance with normal practice, when setting the minimum term to be served within an indeterminate sentence under these provisions, that term will usually be half the equivalent determinate sentence.

4.1 **Identifying sentence ranges**—The key factor that will be relevant in every case is the nature and the duration of the provocation.

(a) The process to be followed by the court will be:

identify the sentence range by reference to the degree of provocation

adjust the starting point within the range by reference to the length of time over which the provocation took place

take into consideration the circumstances of the killing (e.g. the length of time that had elapsed between the provocation and the retaliation and the circumstances in which any weapon was used)

(b) This guideline establishes that:
  • there are three sentencing ranges defined by the **degree of provocation**—low, substantial and high
  • within the three ranges, the starting point is based on provocation taking place over **a short period of time**.
  • the court will move from the starting point (based upon the degree of provocation) by considering the length of time over which the provocation has taken place, and by reference to any **aggravating and mitigating factors**

MANSLAUGHTER BY REASON OF PROVOCATION

Factors to take into consideration

K-78 1. The sentences for public protection <u>must</u> be considered in all cases of manslaughter.

2. The presence of any of the general aggravating factors identified in the Council's Guideline *Overarching Principles: Seriousness* or any of the additional factors identified in this Guideline will indicate a sentence above the normal starting point.

3. This offence will not be an initial charge but will arise following a charge of murder. The

[53] Sections 224–230.

Council Guideline *Reduction in Sentence for a Guilty Plea* will need to be applied with this in mind. In particular, consideration will need to be given to the time at which it was indicated that the defendant would plead guilty to manslaughter by reason of provocation.

4. An assessment of the *degree* of the provocation as shown by its nature and duration is the critical factor in the sentencing decision.

5. The intensity, extent and nature of the loss of control must be assessed in the context of the provocation that preceded it.

6. Although there will usually be less culpability when the retaliation to provocation is sudden, it is not always the case that greater culpability will be found where there has been a significant lapse of time between the provocation and the killing.

7. It is for the sentencer to consider the impact on an offender of provocative behaviour that has built up over a period of time.

8. The use of a weapon should not necessarily move a case into another sentencing bracket.

9. Use of a weapon may reflect the imbalance in strength between the offender and the victim and how that weapon came to hand is likely to be far more important than the use of the weapon itself.

10. It will be an aggravating factor where the weapon is brought to the scene in contemplation of use *before* the loss of self-control (which may occur some time before the fatal incident).

11. Post-offence behaviour is relevant to the sentence. It may be an aggravating or mitigating factor. When sentencing, the judge should consider the motivation behind the offender's actions.

MANSLAUGHTER BY REASON OF PROVOCATION

This is a serious offence for the purposes of section 224 of the Criminal Justice Act 2003
Maximum penalty: **Life imprisonment**   **K-79**

Type/Nature of Activity	Sentence Ranges & Starting Points
Low degree of provocation: A low degree of provocation occurring over a short period	Sentence Range: 10 years – life Starting Point – 12 years custody
Substantial degree of provocation: A substantial degree of provocation occurring over a short period	Sentence Range: 4 – 9 years Starting Point – 8 years custody
High degree of provocation: A high degree of provocation occurring over a short period	Sentence Range: if custody is necessary, up to 4 years Starting Point – 3 years custody

Additional aggravating factors	Additional mitigating factors
1. Concealment or attempts to dispose of evidence* 2. Dismemberment or mutilation of the body* 3. Offence committed in the presence of a child/ children or other vulnerable family member *subject to para 3.6 above.	1. The offender was acting to protect another 2. Spontaneity and lack of premeditation 3. Previous experiences of abuse and/or domestic violence 4. Evidence that the victim presented an ongoing danger to the offender or another 5. Actual (or reasonably anticipated) violence from the victim

The Council Guideline New Sentences: Criminal Justice Act 2003 recognised the potentially more demanding nature of custodial sentences of 12 months or longer imposed under the new framework introduced by the Criminal Justice Act 2003. The sentencing ranges and starting points in the above guideline take account of this.

E. ROBBERY

(1) Sentencing Guidelines Council

The Sentencing Guidelines Council issued a definitive guideline on robbery (Theft Act 1968,   **★K-80**
s.8(1) (§§ 21-84 in the main work)) in 2006. It dealt with offenders sentenced on or after August 1, 2006. For offenders aged 18 and over who are sentenced on or after April 1, 2016, it will be superseded by a guideline issued by the Sentencing Council of England and Wales (*post*, K-80a *et seq.*). In respect of the limited classes of robberies covered by the 2006 guideline, it will continue to have effect on and after April 1, 2016, therefore, in relation only to the sentencing of youths.

As the drafting of the 2006 guideline was inconsistent and repetitious, and as it lacked a coherent structure and consisted, in large part, of a series of lists and bullet points, its essential contents are summarised here.

The foreword stated that robbery will usually merit a custodial sentence, but that exceptional circumstances may justify a non-custodial penalty for an adult and, more frequently, for a young offender; that the guideline was not, therefore, intended to mark a significant shift in sentencing practice; and that the sentencing ranges and starting points in the guideline take into account the more demanding nature of custodial sentences of 12 months or more under the CJA 2003. The guideline only provides guidance in relation to street robberies, robberies of small businesses, and less sophisticated commercial robberies. No guidance is provided in relation to violent personal robberies in the home and professionally planned commercial robberies.

The sentences suggested by the guideline are determined by the identification of one of three levels of seriousness. These are themselves determined by reference to the type of activity which characterises the offence, and the degree of force or threat present. Level 1 involves a threat and/or minimal use of force. Level 2 involves use of a weapon to threaten and/or use of significant force. Level 3 involves use of a weapon and/or significant force, and the causing of serious injury. Where the offence will fall within a particular level is determined by the presence of one or more aggravating features. However, exceptionally serious aggravating features may have the effect of moving the case to the next level. Aggravating factors which are particularly relevant to the assessment of seriousness are:

(a) the nature and degree of any force or violence used or threatened;

(b) the nature of any weapon carried or used, or the use of which is threatened;

(c) the vulnerability of the victim;

(d) the number of offenders involved and their roles;

(e) the value of the property taken;

(f) the fact that the offence was committed at night or in the hours of darkness; and

(g) the wearing of a disguise.

Mitigating factors which are particularly relevant are:

(a) an unplanned or opportunistic offence;

(b) a peripheral involvement in the offence; and

(c) the voluntary return of the property taken.

Where an offence is committed by a young offender, sentencers should additionally take into account age and immaturity and any group pressure under which the offender may have been acting. Further, in relation to such an offender, the guideline requires that where there is evidence that the offence was committed to fund a drug habit and that treatment might help tackle offending behaviour, the court should consider a drug treatment requirement as part of a supervision order or action plan. In all cases, the court should consider making a restitution or compensation order; in cases where a non-custodial order is made, the court may consider making an anti-social behaviour order.

Starting points and sentencing ranges are prescribed depending on whether the offender is an adult or a young offender. In each case, the starting point is based upon a first time offender who has pleaded not guilty, and who has not been assessed as being dangerous for the purposes of the dangerous offender provisions under the CJA 2003, Pt 12, Chap. 5 (ss.224 *et seq.*) (§§ 5-495 *et seq.* in the main work). In the case of young offenders, the starting points are based on a 17-year-old. Sentencers are required to consider whether a lower starting point is justified on account of the offender's age or immaturity. In the case of an adult offender, the starting point for a level 1 offence is 12 months' custody and the sentence range is from a community order (in exceptional circumstances, as stated in the foreword) to three years' custody. The starting point for a level 2 offence is four years' custody and the sentence range is two to seven years. The starting point for a level 3 offence is eight years' custody and the sentence range is seven to 12 years. In the case of the notional young offender, the starting point for a level 1 offence is a community order and the sentence range is from a community order to a 12-month detention and training order. The starting point for a level 2 offence is three years' detention and the sentence range is one to six years' detention. The starting point for a level 3 offence is seven years' detention and the sentence range is six to 10 years' detention.

(2) Sentencing Council for England and Wales

The Sentencing Council for England and Wales has issued a definitive guideline on robbery offences (Theft Act 1968, s.8(1) (§ 21-84 in the main work)), which comprise "street and less sophisticated commercial" robbery, "professionally planned commercial" robbery, and robbery in a dwelling. It applies to all offenders aged 18 and over who are sentenced on or after April 1, 2016, regardless of the date of the offence. The guideline specifies that, in relation to street and less sophisticated commercial robbery, there is relevant guidance for sentencing young offenders within both the Sentencing Guidelines Council's definitive guidelines on robbery (*ante*, Appendix K-80), and on the overarching principles applicable to the sentencing of youths (*post*, Appendix K-240 *et seq.*). These will continue to apply pending their replacement. **★K-80a**

Step 1 (determining the offence category)

This involves determination of the offence category by reference only to factors listed in each section. In order to do this, the court should make an assessment of culpability and harm. **★K-80b**

Culpability

The level of culpability is determined by weighing up all factors that are relevant to the determination of the offender's culpability. The following indicators of culpability are used throughout the guideline. **★K-80c**

High culpability

HC1:   Use of a weapon to inflict violence

HC2:   Production of a bladed article, firearm or imitation firearm to threaten violence

HC3:   Use of very significant force in the commission of the offence

HC4:   Sophisticated organised nature of offence

HC5:   A leading role where offending is part of a group activity

HC6:   Offence motivated by, or demonstrating hostility based on, any of the following characteristics or presumed characteristics of the victim: religion, race, disability, sexual orientation or trans-gender identity

HC7:   Abuse of position

Medium culpability

MC1:   Production of any other weapon to threaten violence

MC2:   Threat of violence by any weapon (but which is not produced)

MC3:   A significant role where offending is part of a group activity

MC4:   Cases where no indicators of "higher" or "lesser" culpability

Lesser culpability

LC1:   Performed limited function under direction

LC2:   Involved through coercion, intimidation or exploitation

LC3:   Threat or use of minimal force

LC4:   Very little or no planning

LC5:   Mental or learning disability where linked to the commission of the offence

Where there are characteristics present that fall under different levels of culpability, the court should balance them to reach a fair assessment of the offender's culpability.

Harm

The level of harm is determined by considering the factors that are relevant to the harm that has been caused, or was intended to be caused, to the victim (who, in the case of a professionally planned commercial robbery, is specified as including both the commercial organisation that is the victim of the theft and any individual against whom force has been used or threatened). The following indicators of harm are used throughout the guideline: **★K-80d**

729

Category 1
   (a) Serious physical and/ or psychological harm caused to the victim
   (b) Serious detrimental effect on the business
   (c) Very high value goods or sums targeted or obtained (economic, personal or sentimental)
   (d) Soiling, ransacking or vandalism of property
Category 2
   (e) Other cases where characteristics for categories 1 or 3 are not present
Category 3
   (f) No/ minimal physical or psychological harm caused to the victim
   (g) No/ minimal detrimental effect on the business
   (h) Low value goods or sums targeted or obtained (economic, personal or sentimental)
   (i) Limited damage or disturbance to property

Step 2 (starting point and category range)

★**K-80e**   Having determined the category, the court should use the corresponding starting point to reach a sentence within the category range in the tables. The starting points apply to all offenders irrespective of plea and previous convictions. A case of particular gravity, reflected by multiple features of culpability or harm, could merit upward adjustment from the starting point, before further adjustment for aggravating or mitigating features.

Consecutive sentences for multiple offences may be appropriate "particularly where exceptionally high levels of harm have been caused" (the words in quotes appear only in the "professionally planned" and "in a dwelling" guidelines) and reference should be made to the guideline on offences taken into consideration and totality (*post*, Appendix K-280 *et seq.*).

The tables of starting points and category ranges in each section are followed by a "non-exhaustive list of additional factual elements providing the context of the offence and factors relating to the offender." The court should then identify whether any combination of these or other relevant factors should result in an upward or downward adjustment from the sentence arrived at, based on culpability and harm alone. In particular, relevant recent convictions are likely to result in an upward adjustment. In some cases, having considered these factors, it may be appropriate to move outside the identified category range.

The following aggravating and mitigating factors are used throughout the guideline:

Statutory aggravating factors

A1:   Previous convictions, having regard to (a) the nature of the offence to which the conviction relates and its relevance to the current offence; and (b) the time that has elapsed since the conviction
A2:   Offence committed whilst on bail

Other aggravating factors

A3:   High value goods or sums targeted or obtained (economic, personal or sentimental)
A4:   Victim is targeted due to a vulnerability (or a perceived vulnerability)
A5:   Significant planning
A6:   Steps taken to prevent the victim reporting or obtaining assistance and/ or from assisting or supporting the prosecution
A7:   Prolonged nature of event
A8:   Prolonged nature of attack
A9:   Restraint, detention or additional degradation of the victim
A10:   A leading role where offending is part of a group activity
A11:   Involvement of others through coercion, intimidation or exploitation
A12:   Location of the offence (including cases where the location is the victim's residence)

A13:   Timing of the offence

A14:   Attempt to conceal identity (for example, wearing a balaclava or hood)

A15:   Commission of offence whilst under the influence of alcohol or drugs

A16:   Attempts to conceal/ dispose of evidence

A17:   Child or vulnerable person at home (or returns home) when offence committed

A18:   Victim(s) compelled to leave his/ her/ their home

A19:   Established evidence of community/ wider impact

A20:   Failure to comply with current court orders

A21:   Offence committed on licence

A22:   Offences taken into consideration

A23:   Failure to respond to warnings about behaviour

Factors reducing seriousness or reflecting personal mitigation

M1:   No previous convictions or no relevant/ recent convictions

M2:   Remorse, particularly where evidenced by voluntary reparation to the victim

M3:   Good character and/ or exemplary conduct

M4:   Serious medical condition requiring urgent, intensive or long-term treatment

M5:   Age and/ or lack of maturity where it affects the responsibility of the offender

M6:   Mental disorder or learning disability (where not linked to the commission of the offence)

M7:   Little or no planning

M8:   Sole or primary carer for dependent relatives

M9:   Determination, and/ or demonstration of steps having been taken, to address addiction or offending behaviour

Steps 3 to 9

These are standard steps in guidelines issued by the Sentencing Council. They require the ★**K-80f** court to consider the SOCPA 2005, ss.73 and 74 (assistance by defendants: reduction or review of sentence (§§ 5-132, 5-133 in the main work)), and any other rule of law by virtue of which an offender may receive a discounted sentence in consequence of assistance given or offered to the prosecutor or investigator, credit for a guilty plea, whether the offender meets the dangerousness criteria in Chapter 5 of Part 12 of the CJA 2003 (*ibid.*, §§ 5-495 *et seq.*) for a life sentence or an extended sentence, the totality principle, the question of compensation and any appropriate ancillary orders (which may include, where the offence involves a firearm, imitation firearm or offensive weapon, a serious crime prevention order under the SCA 2007, s.19 (*ibid.*, § 5-1168)), and the need to give reasons and to make any appropriate allowance for time spent on bail (2003 Act, s.240A (*ibid.*, § 5-645)).

I. Street and less sophisticated commercial robbery

This refers to robberies committed in public places, including in taxis or on public transport. It ★**K-80g** also refers to "unsophisticated robberies within commercial premises or targeting commercial goods or money."

Step 1: determine the offence category (see generally, ante)
  Culpability

High culpability	Medium culpability	Lesser culpability
HC1-HC3, HC6	MC1, MC2, MC4	LC2, LC3, LC5

Harm

Category 1	Category 2	Category 3
(a), (b)	(e)	(f), (g)

Step 2: identify the starting point and then adjust it for aggravating and mitigating factors (see generally, ante)

	High culpability	Medium culpability	Lesser culpability
	Starting point and ranges	Starting point and ranges	Starting point and ranges
Harm category 1	8 years' custody 7 - 12 years' custody	5 years' custody 4 - 8 years' custody	4 years' custody 3 - 6 years' custody
Harm category 2	5 years' custody 4 - 8 years' custody	4 years' custody 3 - 6 years' custody	2 years' custody 1 - 4 years' custody
Harm category 3	4 years' custody 3 - 6 years' custody	2 years' custody 1 - 4 years' custody	1 year's custody High level community order - 3 years' custody

Adjust the provisional sentence according to the presence of the following factors:

Factors increasing seriousness	Factors reducing seriousness or reflecting personal mitigation
A1-A7, A9-A16, A19-A23	M1-M9

Steps 3 to 9 (see ante)

II. Professionally planned commercial robbery

★**K-80h**   This refers to robberies involving a significant degree of planning, sophistication or organisation.

Step 1: determine the offence category (see generally, ante)
   Culpability

High culpability	Medium culpability	Lesser culpability
HC1-HC3, HC5-HC7	MC1-MC4	LC1-LC3, LC5

Harm

Category 1	Category 2	Category 3
(a), (b), (c)	(e)	(f), (g), (h)

Step 2: identify the starting point and then adjust it for aggravating and mitigating factors (see generally, ante)

	High culpability	Medium culpability	Lesser culpability
	Starting point and ranges	Starting point and ranges	Starting point and ranges
Harm category 1	16 years' custody 12 - 20 years' custody	9 years' custody 7 - 14 years' custody	5 years' custody 4 - 8 years' custody
Harm category 2	9 years' custody 7 - 14 years' custody	5 years' custody 4 - 8 years' custody	3 years' custody 2 - 5 years' custody

	High culpability	Medium culpability	Lesser culpability
	Starting point and ranges	Starting point and ranges	Starting point and ranges
Harm category 3	5 years' custody 4 - 8 years' custody	3 years' custody 2 - 5 years' custody	2 years' custody 18 months' - 4 years' custody

The table refers to single offences. Where multiple offences or a single conspiracy to commit multiple offences of particular severity have taken place, sentences in excess of 20 years may be appropriate.

Adjust the provisional sentence according to the presence of the following factors:

Factors increasing seriousness	Factors reducing seriousness or reflecting personal mitigation
A1, A2, A4, A6, A8, A9, A11-A16, A19-A23	M1-M6, M8, M9

Steps 3 to 9 (see ante)

III. Robbery in a dwelling

Step 1: determine the offence category (see generally, ante)
   Culpability

★**K-80i**

High culpability	Medium culpability	Lesser culpability
HC1-HC7	MC1-MC4	LC1-LC5

Harm

Category 1	Category 2	Category 3
(a), (c), (d)	(e)	(f), (h), (i)

Step 2: identify the starting point and then adjust it for aggravating and mitigating factors (see generally, ante)

	High culpability	Medium culpability	Lesser culpability
	Starting point and ranges	Starting point and ranges	Starting point and ranges
Harm category 1	13 years' custody 10 - 16 years' custody	8 years' custody 6 - 10 years' custody	5 years' custody 4 - 8 years' custody
Harm category 2	8 years' custody 6 - 10 years' custody	5 years' custody 4 - 8 years' custody	3 years' custody 2 - 5 years' custody
Harm category 3	5 years' custody 4 - 8 years' custody	3 years' custody 2 - 5 years' custody	18 months' custody 1 - 3 years' custody

In a case of particular gravity, reflected by extremely serious violence, a sentence in excess of 13 years may be appropriate. The reference to "13 years" here is almost certainly a mistake - it should presumably be a reference to "16 years".

Adjust the provisional sentence according to the presence of the following factors:

Factors increasing seriousness	Factors reducing seriousness or reflecting personal mitigation
A1, A2, A4, A6, A7, A9, A11, A13-A23	M1-M6, M8, M9

Steps 3 to 9 (see ante)

F. BREACH OF A PROTECTIVE ORDER

K-81   The Sentencing Guidelines Council has issued a definitive guideline relating to the sentencing of offenders who have breached either a restraining order under the Protection from Harassment Act 1997, s.5 (§ 19-358a in the main work), or a non-molestation order imposed under section 42 of the Family Law Act 1996 (breach being made an offence by section 42A, which is inserted, as from a day to be appointed, by the Domestic Violence, Crime and Victims Act 2004, s.1). It deals with offenders sentenced on or after December 18, 2006.

Paragraph 2 points out that the facts constituting the breach may amount to a substantive offence in their own right. It advises that in such cases it is desirable that there should be separate counts, and, where necessary, there should be consecutive sentences to reflect the seriousness of the counts and to achieve the appropriate totality. It continues, however, by saying that where there is only the one count, the overall sentence should not generally be affected. If the sole count is the breach, the sentence should reflect the nature of the breach; and if the substantive offence alone has been charged, the fact that it constituted a breach of a court order should be regarded as a matter of aggravation. Where no substantive offence was involved, the sentence should reflect the circumstances of the breach, including whether it was an isolated breach, or part of a course of conduct in breach of the order; whether it was planned or spontaneous; and any consequences of the breach, including psychiatric injury or distress to the person protected by the order.

Paragraph 3 is headed "Factors influencing sentencing". It says that since the order will have been made for the purpose of protecting an individual from harm, the main aim of the sentencer should be to achieve future compliance with the order where that is realistic. The nature of the original conduct or offence is relevant in so far as it allows a judgment to be made on the level of harm caused to the victim by the breach and the extent to which that harm was intended by the offender (para. 3.5). However, sentence following a breach is for the breach alone and must avoid punishing the offender again for the offence or conduct as a result of which the order was made (para. 3.7).

When dealing with a breach, a court will need to consider the extent to which the conduct amounting to the breach put the victim at risk of harm (para. 3.8). Where the order is breached by the use of physical violence, the starting point should normally be a custodial sentence (para. 3.9). Non-violent behaviour and/or indirect contact can also cause (or be intended to cause) a high degree of harm and anxiety. In such circumstances, it is likely that the custody threshold will have been crossed (para. 3.10). Where an order was made in civil proceedings, its purpose may have been to cause the subject of the order to modify behaviour rather than to imply that the conduct was especially serious. If so, it is likely to be disproportionate to impose a custodial sentence for a breach of the order if the breach did not involve threats or violence (para. 3.11). In some cases where a breach might result in a short custodial sentence but the court is satisfied that the offender genuinely intends to reform his behaviour and there is a real prospect of rehabilitation, the court may consider it appropriate to impose a sentence that will allow this. This may mean imposing a suspended sentence order or a community order (where appropriate with a requirement to attend an accredited domestic violence programme) (para. 3.12).

Paragraph 4 deals with matters of aggravation and mitigation. The matters of aggravation mirror those in the guideline on domestic violence (*post*, Appendix K-82), but there is added the fact that the breach was a further breach following previous breach proceedings or that it was committed shortly after the order was made. The matters of mitigation that are listed are that the breach followed a long period of compliance, or that the victim initiated contact.

At the end of the guideline there is a table with suggested starting points. The premise is that the "activity has either been prosecuted separately as an offence or is not of a character sufficient to justify prosecution of it as an offence in its own right". The first column is headed "Nature of activity" and the second column is headed "Starting points". There are five entries in the first column, "Breach (whether one or more) involving significant physical violence and significant physical or psychological harm to the victim", "More than one breach involving some violence and/or significant physical or psychological harm to the victim", "Single breach involving some violence and/or significant physical or psychological harm to the victim", "More than one breach involving no/ minimal contact or some direct contact" and "Single breach involving no/ minimal direct contact". The corresponding entries in the second column are, "More than 12 months. The length of the ... sentence will depend on the nature and seriousness of the breaches.", "26–39 weeks' custody [Medium/High Custody Plus order] (when the relevant provisions of the CJA 2003 are in force)", "13-26 weeks' custody [Low/Medium Custody Plus order] (when the relevant provisions of the CJA 2003 are in force)", "Medium range community order" and "Low range community order".

G. DOMESTIC VIOLENCE

The Sentencing Guidelines Council has issued a definitive guideline for use in all cases that fall **K-82** within the Crown Prosecution Service definition of "domestic violence", *viz.* "Any incident of threatening behaviour, violence or abuse [psychological, physical, sexual, financial or emotional] between adults who are or have been intimate partners or family members, regardless of gender or sexuality." It deals with offenders sentenced on or after December 18, 2006. The guideline makes clear that offences committed in a domestic context should be regarded as being no less serious than offences committed in a non-domestic context. Indeed, because an offence has been committed in a domestic context, there are likely to be aggravating factors present that make it more serious. The foreword, signed by Lord Phillips C.J., as chairman of the council, states that in many situations of domestic violence, the circumstances require the sentence to demonstrate clearly that the conduct is unacceptable, but that there will be cases where all parties genuinely and realistically wish the relationship to continue as long as the violence stops. In such cases, and where the violence is towards the lower end of the scale of seriousness, it is likely to be appropriate for the court to impose a sentence that provides the necessary support.

Paragraph 1 defines "domestic violence" for the purposes of the guideline (*ante*). Paragraph 2 relates to the assessment of seriousness and says nothing new. Paragraph 3 is concerned with matters of aggravation and mitigation. By way of preamble it is stated that the history of the relationship will be relevant to the assessment of seriousness. There follows a non-exhaustive list of aggravating matters, *viz.* abuse of trust or power, that the victim is particularly vulnerable, the exposure of children to an offence (directly or indirectly), using contact arrangements with a child to instigate an offence, a proven history of violence or threats by the offender in a domestic setting, a history of disobedience to court orders and conduct which has forced the victim to leave home. The two matters of mitigation that are listed are positive good character and provocation, but, as to the former, the point is made that the perpetrator of domestic violence may have two personae, and that good character in relation to conduct outside the home should generally be of no relevance where there is a proven pattern of behaviour.

Paragraph 4 deals with the relevance of the wishes of the victim to the sentence. As a matter of general principle, the sentence should be determined by the seriousness of the offence, not by the expressed wishes of the victim. The guideline states that it is particularly important that this principle should be observed in this context, as (a) it is undesirable that a victim should feel a responsibility for the sentence imposed; (b) there is a risk that a plea for mercy made by a victim will be induced by threats made by, or by a fear of, the offender; and (c) the risk of such threats will be increased if it is generally believed that the severity of the sentence may be affected by the wishes of the victim. However, there may be cases in which the court can properly mitigate a sentence to give effect to the expressed wish of the victim that the relationship should be permitted to continue. The court must, however, be confident that such a wish is genuine, and that giving effect to it will not expose the victim to a real risk of further violence. Up-to-date information in a pre-sentence report and victim personal statement will be of vital importance. Either the offender or the victim (or both) may ask the court to take into consideration the interests of any children and to impose a less severe sentence. The court will wish to have regard not only to the effect on the children if the relationship is disrupted but also to the likely effect on the children of any further incidents of domestic violence.

The final section of the guideline is headed "Factors to Take into Consideration". It contains nothing new, save that it advises that where "the custody threshold is only just crossed, so that if a custodial sentence is imposed it will be a short sentence, the court will wish to consider whether the better option is a suspended sentence order or a community order, including in either case a requirement to attend an accredited domestic violence programme. Such an option will only be appropriate where the court is satisfied that the offender genuinely intends to reform his ... behaviour and that there is a real prospect of rehabilitation being successful. Such a situation is unlikely to arise where there has been a pattern of abuse."

H. Sexual Offences

(1) Sentencing Guidelines Council

K-83   The Sentencing Guidelines Council issued a definitive guideline on sexual offences, which applied to offenders sentenced on or after May 14, 2007. For the great majority of sexual offences, this will be overtaken, in relation to offenders sentenced on or after April 1, 2014, by the definitive guideline issued by the Sentencing Council for England and Wales (*post*, K-84 *et seq.*). Those wishing to consult the full detail of the former guideline should refer to the first supplement to this edition.

The new guideline does not cover three offences that were covered by the former guideline, and, since the new guideline does not purport to "revoke" its predecessor, it would appear that the former guideline will still hold sway in relation to those three offences.

At §§ K-83d, K-83e, *post*, Section 7 (sentencing young offenders - offences with a lower statutory maximum) of the Sentencing Guidelines Council's sexual offences guideline is set out. As to the reason for this, see § 20-9c in the main work.

Intercourse with an animal (s.69 of the SOA 2003)

K-83a   For a basic offence assuming no aggravating or mitigating factors, the recommended starting point was a community order and the range was an "appropriate non-custodial sentence". The one specified aggravating feature was "recording activity and circulating pictures/video", and the one specified mitigating factor was "symptom of isolation rather than depravity".

Sexual penetration of a corpse (s.70 of the SOA 2003)

K-83b   For a basic offence assuming no aggravating or mitigating factors, the recommended starting point was a community order and the range was an "appropriate non-custodial sentence". For a case of repeat offending or one accompanied by aggravating factors, the range was four weeks' to 18 months' custody, with a starting point of 26 weeks' custody. There were four aggravating factors that were specifically identified, *viz.* distress caused to relatives or friends of the deceased, physical damage caused to the body of the deceased, corpse was that of a child, and offence was committed in a funeral home or a mortuary.

Sexual activity in a public lavatory (s.71 of the SOA 2003)

K-83c   For a basic offence assuming no aggravating or mitigaging factors, the recommended starting point was a fine, and the range was an "appropriate non-custodial sentence". For a case of repeat offending or one accompanied by aggravating factors, the range was the same but the starting point was a community order. The one aggravating factor specifically identified was "intimidating behaviour/threats of violence to member(s) of the public".

Part 7: Sentencing young offenders—offences with a lower statutory maximum

K-83d   The guidelines in this part are intended for cases where the court considers that the facts found by the court justify the involvement of the criminal law, which findings may be different from those on which a decision to prosecute was made. The guidelines relate to sentencing on conviction of a first time offender. Where a young offender pleads guilty to one of the offences dealt with in this part, a youth court may impose an absolute discharge, a mental health disposal, a custodial sentence, or make a referral order. Where a custodial sentence is imposed in the Crown Court, it may be a detention and training order, or detention under section 91 of the PC-C(S)A 2000 for a period up to the maximum for the offence.

The guideline (as originally drafted) referred to the offences in this part as being contrary to sections 9, 10, 11, 12, 25 and 26 of the 2003 Act. These can be split into two, as slightly different considerations apply to sections 9 to 12 as compared with sections 25 and 26.

As to sections 9 to 12, the guideline was in error in its premise that a person under 18 can commit one of these offences. Each of those offences is defined in such a way that it can only be committed by a person aged 18 or over. If a person under that age does an act proscribed by any of those sections, he does not offend against them. Section 13(1) (not mentioned in the guideline as originally drafted), however, provides that "(1) A person under 18 commits an offence if he does anything which would be an offence under any of sections 9 to 12 if he were aged 18.", and subsection (2) provides for a lesser maximum penalty. A person under 18 who does that which is prohibited by any of those sections would commit an offence under section 13, and should be charged as having committed an offence "contrary to section 13". The guideline has now been corrected in this respect. An offence contrary to section 13 is a specified offence, but not a serious offence for the purposes of Chapter 5 of Part 12 of the CJA 2003.

With sections 25 and 26, the position is less clear-cut. It is subsection (1) in each case that creates the offence and age is not an ingredient of the offence; but subsections (4) and (5) contain different penalty provisions according to whether the offender is aged 18 or over or under 18. Where the offender is under 18, the maximum is five years' custody. Taking the section as a whole, it is submitted, on the basis of *R. v. Courtie* [1984] A.C. 463, HL (the effect of the varying penalty provisions in the SOA 1956, according to the circumstances of an act of buggery, was to create separate offences), that sections 25 and 26 create distinct offences for those under 18. If this is correct, then these offences are specified offences, but not serious offences, because they carry a maximum of five years' custody and they cannot—by definition—be committed by an 18-year-old. The separate listing of these offences in section 91 of the PCC(S)A 2000 (§ 5-610 in the main work) supports this view: an offence under section 25 or 26 committed by an adult carries 14 years' imprisonment and there would have been no need to make special mention of it if there were only one offence.

This view was not accepted by the Sentencing Guidelines Council as the guideline still shows (as it appears on the website of the Sentencing Council (as to which, see § 20-9c in the main work)) the offences contrary to sections 25 and 26, when committed by an under 18-year-old, as "serious offences". It is submitted that the better view is that they are "specified", but not "serious" offences.

Key to table of starting points, etc., for parts 6B to 6D

| † | Denotes that an offence is a "specified offence" for the purposes of section 224 of the Criminal Justice Act 2003 |
| ‡ | Denotes that an offence is a "serious offence" for the purposes of section 224 of the Criminal Justice Act 2003 |

Aggravating factors.

A2:	Background of intimidation or coercion
A3:	Use of drugs, alcohol or other substance to facilitate the offence
A4:	Threats to prevent victim reporting the incident
A5:	Abduction or detention
A6:	Offender aware that he or she is suffering from a sexually transmitted infection
A10:	Images of violent activity

Mitigating factors

M5:	Youth and immaturity of offender
M7:	Offender intervenes to prevent incited offence from taking place
M8:	Small disparity in age between victim and offender
M9:	Relationship of genuine affection

OFFENCE	TYPE/ NATURE OF ACTIVITY	STARTING POINTS (AND SENTENCING RANGES)	AGG. & MIT. FACTORS
Sexual activity with a child 13(9) (intentional sexual touching of a person under 16) (offender under 18) †	Offence involving penetration where one or more aggravating factors exist or where there is a substantial age gap between the parties	12-month detention and training order (6- to 24-month detention and training order)	A2, A3, A4, A5, A6 / M9, M5
	Any form of sexual activity (non–penetrative or penetrative) not involving any aggravating factors	Community order (appropriate non–custodial sentence)	
Causing or inciting a child to engage in sexual activity 13(10) (causing or inciting a child to engage in sexual activity) (offender under 18) †	Offence involving penetration where one or more aggravating factors exist or where there is a substantial age gap between the parties	12-month detention and training order (6- to 24-month detention and training order)	A2, A3, A4, A5, A6 / M9, M7, M5
	Any form of sexual activity (non–penetrative or penetrative) not involving any aggravating factors	Community order (appropriate non-custodial sentence)	
Engaging in sexual activity in the presence of a child 13(11) (engaging in sexual activity in the presence of a child) (offender under 18) †	Sexual activity involving penetration where one or more aggravating factors exist	12-month detention and training order (6- to 24-month detention and training order)	A2, A3, A4, A5 / M5
	Any form of sexual activity (non–penetrative or penetrative) not involving any aggravating factors	Community order (appropriate non-custodial sentence)	
Causing a child to watch a sexual act 13(12) (causing a child to watch a sexual act) (offender under 18) †	Live sexual activity	8-month detention and training order (6- to 12-month detention and training order)	A2, A3, A4, A5, A10
	Moving or still images of people engaged in sexual acts involving penetration	Community order (appropriate non-custodial sentence)	M5
	Moving or still images of people engaged in sexual acts other than penetration	Community order (appropriate non-custodial sentence)	

OFFENCE	TYPE/ NATURE OF ACTIVITY	STARTING POINTS (AND SENTENCING RANGES)	AGG. & MIT. FACTORS
Sexual activity with a child family member and inciting a child family member to engage in sexual activity 25 (sexual activity with a child family member) (offender under 18) ‡ 26 (inciting a child family member to engage in sexual activity) (offender under 18) ‡	Offence involving penetration where one or more aggravating factors exist or where there is a substantial age gap between the parties	18-month detention and training order (6- to 24-month detention and training order)	A2, A3, A4, A6 M8, M9, M5
	Any form of sexual activity that does not involve any aggravating factors	Community order (appropriate non-custodial sentence)	
N.B.: As to whether these offences are "serious offences", see ante.			

(2) Sentencing Council for England and Wales

K-84   The Sentencing Council for England and Wales has issued a definitive guideline covering the sexual offences set out at I to XXXIII, *post*, applying to all offenders aged 18 or over who are sentenced on or after April 1, 2014.

The guideline sets out nine steps to be followed (in order) when sentencing for these offences, which correspond broadly to the steps set out in the guideline on offences against the person (*post*, K-113 *et seq.*). The offence in XVIII, *post*, only has eight steps (missing out the step requiring the court to consider whether an offender meets the dangerousness criteria).

In particular, step one requires the court to determine the offence category, based on harm and culpability. In determining the harm and culpability, the court should refer only to the indicators set out for each offence (*post*) (although this is not specified for XVI, *post*). Step two requires the court to use the starting point identified for the relevant category to reach a sentence within the category range (*post*). The starting point applies to all offenders irrespective of plea or previous convictions. The court should then consider adjustment within the category range for aggravating or mitigating features set out for each offence, *post*, which contain a non-exhaustive list of additional factual elements providing the context of the offence and factors relating to the offender. A case of particular gravity, reflected by multiple features of culpability or harm in step one, could merit upward adjustment of the starting point before further adjustment for aggravating or mitigating features. Having considered all factors, it might be appropriate to move outside the identified category range.

Annex A contains further information about ancillary orders and provisions that apply automatically by operation of law, Annex B describes the approach to sentencing for historic sexual offences (see *R. v. H.*, *ante*, Appendix H-12), Annex C lists the various historic offences and Annex D sets out fine bands, and a non-exhaustive description of examples of requirements that might be appropriate for low, medium and high level community orders, corresponding to those in the guideline on offences against the person (*ante*).

Key to factors indicating varying levels of harm and culpability (step one)

Harm factors

K-84a
1. Severe psychological or physical harm
2. Pregnancy or STI as a consequence of offence
3. Additional degradation/humiliation
4. Abduction
5. Prolonged detention/sustained incident
6. Violence or threats of violence (beyond what is inherent in the offence, where relevant)
7. Forced/uninvited entry into victim's home or residence
8. Victim is particularly vulnerable due to personal circumstances and/or (offences against victims under 13) extreme youth
9. Penetration using large or dangerous object(s)
10. Touching of naked genitalia or naked breasts
11. Penetration of vagina or anus (using body or object) by, or of, the victim
12. Penile penetration of mouth by, or of, the victim
13. Touching, or exposure, of naked genitalia or naked breasts by, or of, the victim
14. Other sexual activity
15. Touching of naked genitalia or naked breasts by, or of, the victim
16. Causing victim to view extreme pornography
17. Causing victim to view indecent/prohibited images of children
18. Engaging in, or causing a victim to view live, sexual activity involving sadism/violence/sexual activity with an animal/child

19. Engaging in, or causing a victim to view images of or view live, sexual activity involving penetration of vagina or anus (using body or object) or penile penetration of the mouth or masturbation

20. Continued contact despite victim's attempts to terminate contact

21. Sexual images exchanged

22. Victim exposed to extreme sexual content (*e.g.* extreme pornography)

23. Abduction/detention

24. Sustained and systematic psychological abuse

25. Individual(s)/those working in brothel forced or coerced to participate in unsafe/degrading sexual activity

26. Individual(s)/those working in brothel forced or coerced into seeing many "customers"

27. Individual(s)/ those working in brothel forced/coerced/deceived into prostitution

28. Under 18-year-olds working in brothel

29. Established evidence of community impact

30. Victims involved in penetrative activity

31. Victim(s) participated in unsafe/ degrading sexual activity beyond that which is inherent in the offence

32. Victim(s) passed around by the offender to other "customers" and/or moved to other brothels

33. Victim subjected to unsafe/degrading sexual activity (beyond that which is inherent in the offence)

34. Victim(s) under 18

35. Victim(s) forced/coerced into prostitution

36. Victim(s) tricked/deceived as to purpose of visit

37. Victim followed/pursued

38. Offender masturbated

39. Image(s) available to be viewed by others

40. Victim observed or recorded in their own home or residence

41. Child conceived

42. Offence committed in victim's home

Culpability factors

K-84b

43. Significant degree of planning

44. Acting with others to commit offence

45. Use of alcohol/drugs on victim to facilitate the offence

46. Abuse of trust

47. Previous violence against victim

48. Offence committed in course of burglary

49. Recording of the offence

50. Commercial exploitation and/or motivation

51. Offence racially or religiously aggravated

52. Offence motivated by, or demonstrating, hostility to the victim based on his sexual orientation (or presumed sexual orientation) or transgender identity (or presumed transgender identity)

53. Offence motivated by, or demonstrating, hostility to the victim based on his disability (or presumed disability)

54. Grooming behaviour used against victim

55. Sexual images of victim recorded, retained, solicited or shared

56. Deliberate isolation of victim

57. Use of threats (including blackmail)

58. Specific targeting of a particularly vulnerable child/victim

59. Offender lied about age

60. Significant disparity in age

61. Communication indicates penetrative sexual activity is intended

62. Offender lied about persona

63. Use of gifts, bribes

64. Abduction/detention

65. Causing, inciting or controlling prostitution/ keeping brothel/ directing or organising child prostitution or pornography/ directing or organising trafficking on significant commercial basis

66. Expectation of significant financial or other gain

67. Exploitation of those known to be trafficked

68. Significant involvement in limiting the freedom of prostitute(s)/ those working in brothel/ victims of child prostitution or pornography/ significant influence over others in trafficking organisation/ hierarchy

69. Grooming of individual(s) to enter prostitution/ child pornography/ work in brothel, including through cultivation of a dependency on drugs or alcohol

70. Close involvement with prostitute(s)/ those working in brothel, *e.g.* control of finances, choice of clients, working conditions, etc., or with inciting, controlling, arranging or facilitating child prostitution or pornography (where offender's involvement is not as a result of coercion)

71. Performs limited function under direction

72. Close involvement but engaged by coercion/intimidation/ exploitation

73. Involvement in keeping a number of brothels

74. Keeping/ managing premises

75. Use of alcohol/ drugs on victim

76. Blackmail or other threats made

77. Offender aware that he has a sexually transmitted disease

78. Offender aware victim has been trafficked

79. Significant influence over others in trafficking organisation/ hierarchy

80. Operational or management function within hierarchy

81. Involves others in operation whether by coercion/ intimidation/ exploitation or reward (and offender's involvement is not as a result of coercion)

82. Specific or previous targeting of a particularly vulnerable victim

83. Image(s) recorded

84. Intended sexual offence carries a statutory maximum of life imprisonment

85. Possession of weapon or other item to frighten or injure

Key to aggravating and mitigating factors (step two)

Statutory aggravating factors

86. Previous convictions (CJA 2003, s.143(2) (§ 5-67 in the main work))
87. Offence committed whilst on bail (*ibid.*, s.143(3))

Other aggravating factors

88. Specific targeting of a particularly vulnerable victim
89. Ejaculation (where not taken into account at step one)
90. Blackmail or other threats made (where not taken into account at step one)
91. Location of offence
92. Timing of offence
93. Use of weapon or other item to frighten or injure
94. Victim compelled to leave their home, institution, school, etc.
95. Failure to comply with current court orders
96. Offence committed whilst on licence
97. Exploiting contact arrangements with a child to commit an offence
98. Presence of others, especially children
99. Any steps taken to prevent the reporting of an incident, obtaining assistance and/ or from assisting or supporting the prosecution
100. Attempts to dispose of or conceal evidence
101. Commission of offence whilst under the influence of alcohol or drugs
102. Victim encouraged to recruit others
103. Pregnancy or STI as a consequence of offence
104. Failure of offender to respond to previous warnings
105. Period over which offence committed/ operation has been run
106. Severe psychological or physical harm
107. Age and/ or vulnerability of the child depicted (this should be given significant weight; in cases where the actual age is difficult to determine, sentencers should consider the development of the child – infant, pre-pubescent, post-pubescent)
108. Discernible pain or distress suffered by child depicted
109. High volume of images possessed, distributed or produced
110. Placing images where there is the potential for a high volume of viewers
111. Collection includes moving images
112. Abuse of trust
113. Child depicted known to offender
114. Active involvement in a network or process that facilitates or commissions the creation or sharing of indecent images of children
115. Commercial exploitation and/ or motivation
116. Deliberate or systematic searching for images portraying young children, category A images or the portrayal of familial sexual abuse
117. Large number of different victims
118. Child depicted intoxicated or drugged
119. Deliberate isolation of victim(s)/ prostitute(s)/ those working in brothel

120. Threats made to expose victim(s)/ prostitute(s)/ those working in brothel to the authorities (*e.g.* immigration or police), family/ friends or others

121. Harm threatened against the family/ friends of victim(s)/ prostitute(s)/ those working in brothel

122. Passport/ identity documents removed

123. Victim(s)/ prostitute(s)/ those working in brothel prevented from seeking medical treatment

124. Food withheld

125. Earnings withheld/ kept by offender or evidence of excessive wage reduction or debt bondage, inflated travel or living expenses or unreasonable interest rates

126. Prostitute/ those working in brothel forced or coerced into pornography

127. Those working in brothel passed around by offender and moved to other brothels

128. Vulnerability of victim(s)

129. Victim prevented from attending school

130. Children of victim(s) left in home country due to trafficking

131. Exploitation of victim(s) from particularly vulnerable backgrounds

132. Victim(s) previously trafficked/ sold/ passed around

133. Use of drugs/ alcohol or other substance to secure victim's compliance

134. Distribution of images, whether or not for gain

135. Placing images where there is the potential for a high volume of viewers

136. Period over which victim observed

137. Period over which images were made or distributed

Mitigating factors

K-84e

138. No previous convictions or no relevant/recent convictions

139. Remorse

140. Previous good character and/ or exemplary conduct (but the more serious the offence the less weight should be attributed to this factor, particularly where it has been used to facilitate the offence, when it may well be an aggravating factor; where this number is followed by a *, the factor should not normally be given any significant weight or justify a reduction in what would otherwise be the appropriate sentence)

141. Age and/ or lack of maturity where it affects the responsibility of the offender

142. Mental disorder or learning disability, particularly where linked to the commission of the offence

143. Demonstration of steps taken to address offending behaviour

144. Sexual activity was incited but no activity took place because the offender voluntarily desisted or intervened to prevent it

Consideration of custody threshold

K-84f   In the following sections, where there is a sufficient prospect of rehabilitation, a community order with a sex offender treatment programme requirement can be a proper alternative to a short or moderate custodial sentence: II to IV, VII, IX to XI, XIV, and XV to XXX.

When sentencing for some or all of the categories within the various offences, it is sometimes indicated that the court should consider whether the custody threshold has been passed, if so, whether it is unavoidable that a custodial sentence be imposed, and, if so, whether that sentence can be suspended, or whether the community order threshold has been passed. The categories for which these should be considered, if at all, are indicated at the end of step two for each section, *e.g.*, as follows:

Consideration of custody threshold: category 2 or 3

Consideration of community order threshold: category 3

I. Rape (SOA 2003, s.1 (§ 20-19 in the main work))

Offences here may be of such severity, for example including a campaign of rape, that sentences **K-85**
of 20 years and above may be appropriate.

Factors indicating harm and culpability (step one)

Harm

Category 1:	The extreme nature of one or more category 2 factors or the extreme impact caused by a combination of category 2 factors **may** elevate to category 1
Category 2:	Factors 1–8
Category 3:	Factor(s) in categories 1 and 2 not present

Culpability

Category A:	Factors 43–53
Category B:	Factor(s) in category A not present

Starting point and category range (step two)

	A	B
Category 1	**Starting point** 15 years **Range** 13 – 19 years	**Starting point** 12 years **Range** 10 – 15 years
Category 2	**Starting point** 10 years **Range** 9 – 13 years	**Starting point** 8 years **Range** 7 – 9 years
Category 3	**Starting point** 7 years **Range** 6 – 9 years	**Starting point** 5 years **Range** 4 – 7 years

Aggravating and mitigating factors

Aggravating factors:	Factors 86-101
Mitigating factors:	Factors 138, 139, 140*, 141, 142

II. Assault by penetration (2003 Act, s.2 (ibid., § 20-28))

Factors indicating harm and culpability (step one)

Harm **K-85b**

Category 1:	The extreme nature of one or more category 2 factors or the extreme impact caused by a combination of category 2 factors **may** elevate to category 1
Category 2:	Factors 1, 3–9
Category 3:	Factor(s) in categories 1 and 2 not present

Culpability

Same as I *(ante)*

Starting point and category range (step two)

	A	B

Category 1	**Starting point** 15 years **Range** 13 – 19 years	**Starting point** 12 years **Range** 10 – 15 years
Category 2	**Starting point** 8 years **Range** 5 – 13 years	**Starting point** 6 years **Range** 4 – 9 years
Category 3	**Starting point** 4 years **Range** 2 – 6 years	**Starting point** 2 years **Range** high level community order – 4 years

Consideration of custody threshold: category 3

Aggravating and mitigating factors

Aggravating factors: Factors 86–88, 90–101

Mitigating factors: Factors 138, 139, 140*, 141, 142

III. Sexual assault (2003 Act, s.3 (ibid., § 20-29))

Factors indicating harm and culpability (step one)

K-85c   *Harm*

         Category 1:   Factors 1, 4, 6, 7

         Category 2:   Factors 3, 5, 8, 10

         Category 3:   Factor(s) in categories 1 and 2 not present

Culpability

         Same as I (*ante*)

Starting point and category range (step two)

	A	B
Category 1	**Starting point** 4 years **Range** 3 – 7 years	**Starting point** 2.5 years **Range** 2 – 4 years
Category 2	**Starting point** 2 years **Range** 1 – 4 years	**Starting point** 1 year **Range** high level community order – 2 years
Category 3	**Starting point** 26 weeks **Range** high level community order – 1 year	**Starting point** high level community order **Range** medium level community order – 26 weeks

Consideration of custody threshold: category 2 or 3

Aggravating and mitigating factors

Aggravating factors: Factors 86–88, 90–101

Mitigating factors: Factors 138-143

IV. Causing a person to engage in sexual activity without consent (2003 Act, s.4 (ibid., § 20-40))

Factors indicating harm and culpability (step one)

K-86   *Harm*

Category 1:	The extreme nature of one or more category 2 factors or the extreme impact caused by a combination of category 2 factors **may** elevate to category 1
Category 2:	Factors 1–9
Category 3:	Factor(s) in categories 1 and 2 not present

Culpability

Same as I (*ante*)

Starting point and category range (step two)

Where offence involved penetration: same as II (*ante*)

Where offence did not involve penetration: same as III (*ante*)

Consideration of custody threshold: category 2 or 3

Aggravating and mitigating factors

Same as I (*ante*)

V. Rape of a child under 13 (2003 Act, s.5 (ibid., § 20-49))

Offences here may be of such severity, for example including a campaign of rape, that sentences **K-87** of 20 years and above may be appropriate. Sentencers should have particular regard to the fact that these offences are not only committed through force or fear of force but may include exploitative behaviour towards a child, that should be considered to indicate high culpability. This guideline is designed to deal with the majority of offending behaviour but there may be exceptional cases where a lengthy community order with a requirement to participate in a sex of- fender treatment programme may be the best way of changing the offender's behaviour and of protecting the public by preventing any repetition of the offence.

This guideline may not be appropriate where the sentencer is satisfied that on the available evidence, and in the absence of exploitation, a young or particularly immature defendant genuinely believed, on reasonable grounds, that the victim was aged 16 or over and that they were engaging in lawful sexual activity.

Factors indicating harm and culpability (step one)

Harm

Same as I (*ante*)

Culpability

Category A:	Factors 43–48, 50–56
Category B:	Factor(s) in category A not present

Starting point and category range (step two)

	A	B
Category 1	**Starting point** 16 years **Range** 13 – 19 years	**Starting point** 13 years **Range** 11 – 17 years
Category 2	**Starting point** 13 years **Range** 11 – 17 years	**Starting point** 10 years **Range** 8 – 13 years
Category 3	**Starting point** 10 years	**Starting point** 8 years

	Range 8 – 13 years	**Range** 6 – 11 years

Aggravating and mitigating factors

Aggravating factors:	Factors 86–102
Mitigating factors:	Factors 138, 139, 140*, 141, 142

VI. Assault of a child under 13 by penetration (2003 Act, s.6 (ibid., § 20-50))

Factors indicating harm and culpability (step one)

K-87a *Harm*

  Same as II (*ante*)

Culpability

  Same as V (*ante*)

Starting point and category range (step two)

	A	**B**
Category 1	**Starting point** 16 years **Range** 13 – 19 years	**Starting point** 13 years **Range** 11 – 17 years
Category 2	**Starting point** 11 years **Range** 7 – 15 years	**Starting point** 8 years **Range** 5 – 13 years
Category 3	**Starting point** 6 years **Range** 4 – 9 years	**Starting point** 4 years **Range** 2 – 6 years

Aggravating and mitigating factors

Aggravating factors:	Factors 86–88, 90–102
Mitigating factors:	Factors 138, 139, 140*, 141, 142

VII. Sexual assault of a child under 13 (2003 Act, s.7 (ibid., § 20-51))

Factors indicating harm and culpability (step one)

K-87b *Harm*

  Same as III (*ante*)

Culpability

  Same as V (*ante*)

Starting point and category range (step two)

	A	**B**
Category 1	**Starting point** 6 years **Range** 4 – 9 years	**Starting point** 4 years **Range** 3 – 7 years
Category 2	**Starting point** 4 years **Range** 3 – 7 years	**Starting point** 2 years **Range** 1 – 4 years
Category 3	**Starting point** 1 year	**Starting point** 26 weeks

	Range 26 weeks – 2 years	**Range** high level community order – 1 year

Aggravating and mitigating factors

Same as VI (*ante*)

VIII. Causing or inciting a child under 13 to engage in sexual activity (2003 Act, s.8 (ibid., § 20-52))

Factors indicating harm and culpability (step one)

Harm   **K-87c**

    Category 1:   The extreme nature of one or more category 2 factors or the extreme impact caused by a combination of category 2 factors **may** elevate to category 1

    Category 2:   Factors 1, 3–8, 11, 12

    Category 3:   Factor(s) in categories 1 and 2 not present

Culpability

    Same as V (*ante*)

Starting point and category range (step two)

	A	**B**
Category 1	**Starting point** 13 years **Range** 11 – 17 years	**Starting point** 11 years **Range** 10 – 15 years
Category 2	**Starting point** 8 years **Range** 5 – 10 years	**Starting point** 6 years **Range** 3 – 9 years
Category 3	**Starting point** 5 years **Range** 3 – 8 years	**Starting point** 2 years **Range** 1 – 4 years

Aggravating and mitigating factors

    Aggravating factors: Factors 86–103

    Mitigating factors: Factors 138, 139, 140*, 141, 142, 144

IX. Sexual activity with a child (2003 Act, s.9 (ibid., § 20-58)); causing or inciting a child to engage in sexual activity (2003 Act, s.10 (ibid., § 20-64))

Factors indicating harm and culpability (step one)

Harm   **K-88**

      Category 1:   Factors 11, 12

      Category 2:   Factor 13

      Category 3:   Factor 14

Culpability

      Category A: Factors 43–46, 50–55, 57–60

      Category B: Factor(s) in category A not present

Starting point and category range (step two)

	A	B
Category 1	**Starting point** 5 years **Range** 4 – 10 years	**Starting point** 1 year **Range** high level community order – 2 years
Category 2	**Starting point** 3 years **Range** 2 – 6 years	**Starting point** 26 weeks **Range** high level community order – 1 year
Category 3	**Starting point** 26 weeks **Range** high level community order – 3 years	**Starting point** medium level community order **Range** low level – high level community order

Consideration of custody threshold: category 2 or 3

Aggravating and mitigating factors

Aggravating factors: Factors 86, 87, 89, 91, 92, 94–106
Mitigating factors: Factors 138, 139, 140*, 141, 142, 144

X. Sexual activity with a child family member (2003 Act, s.25 (ibid., § 20-110)); inciting a child family member to engage in sexual activity (2003 Act, s.26 (ibid., § 20-111))

K-89 It should be assumed that the greater the trust, the more serious the offence.

Factors indicating harm and culpability (step one)

Harm
    Category 1:   Factors 11, 12
    Category 2:   Factor 15
    Category 3:   Factor 14

Culpability
    Category A: Factors 43–45, 50–55, 57, 58, 60
    Category B: Factor(s) in category A not present

Starting point and category range (step two)

	A	B
Category 1	**Starting point** 6 years **Range** 4 – 10 years	**Starting point** 3.5 years **Range** 2.5 – 5 years
Category 2	**Starting point** 4 years **Range** 2 – 6 years	**Starting point** 18 months **Range** 26 weeks – 2.5 years
Category 3	**Starting point** 1 year **Range** high level community order – 3 years	**Starting point** medium level community order **Range** low level – high level community order

Consideration of custody threshold: category 3

Aggravating and mitigating factors

Same as IX (*ante*)

XI. Engaging in sexual activity in the presence of a child (2003 Act, s.11 (ibid., § 20-69)); causing a child to watch a sexual act (2003 Act, s.12 (ibid., § 20-74))

Factors indicating harm and culpability (step one)

Harm   **K-90**

Category 1:	Factors 16–18
Category 2:	Factor 19
Category 3:	Factor(s) in categories 1 and 2 not present

Culpability

Category A:	Factors 43–46, 50–54, 57, 58, 60
Category B:	Factor(s) in category A not present

Starting point and category range (step two)

	A	B
Category 1	**Starting point** 4 years **Range** 3 – 6 years	**Starting point** 2 years **Range** 1 – 3 years
Category 2	**Starting point** 2 years **Range** 1 – 3 years	**Starting point** 1 year **Range** high level community order – 18 months
Category 3	**Starting point** 26 weeks **Range** high level community order – 1 year	**Starting point** medium level community order **Range** low level – high level community order

Consideration of custody threshold: category 2 or 3

Aggravating and mitigating factors

| Aggravating factors: | Factors 86, 87, 91, 92, 94–102, 104 |
| Mitigating factors: | Factors 138–143 |

XII. Arranging or facilitating the commission of a child sex offence (2003 Act, s.14 (ibid., § 20-85))

Sentencers should refer to the guideline for the applicable, substantive offences under sections **K-90a** IX and XI. The level of harm should be determined by reference to the type of activity arranged or facilitated. For offences involving significant commercial exploitation and/ or an international element, it may, in the interests of justice, be appropriate to increase a sentence to a point above the category range. In exceptional cases, such as where a vulnerable offender performed a limited role, having been coerced or exploited by others, sentences below the starting point and range may be appropriate.

XIII. Meeting a child following sexual grooming (2003 Act, s.15 (ibid., § 20-91))

Factors indicating harm and culpability (step one)

K-90b
     Category 1:   Raised harm **and** raised culpability
     Category 2:   Raised harm **or** raised culpability
     Category 3:   Grooming **without** raised harm or culpability factors present

    Where an offence does not fall squarely into a category, individual factors may require a degree of weighting before making an overall assessment and determining the appropriate offence category.

Indicators of raised harm
     Factors 8, 20–22

Indicators of raised culpability
     Factors 44, 46, 50–53, 57–59, 61–64

Starting point and category range (step two)

Category 1	**Starting point** 4 years **Range** 3 – 7 years
Category 2	**Starting point** 2 years **Range** 1 – 4 years
Category 3	**Starting point** 18 months **Range** 1 – 2.5 years

Aggravating and mitigating factors

    Aggravating factors: Factors 86, 87, 95, 96, 99, 100, 102
    Mitigating factors: Factors 138–143

XIV. Abuse of position of trust: sexual activity with a child (2003 Act, s.16 (ibid., § 20-96)); abuse of position of trust: causing a child to engage in sexual activity (2003 Act, s.17 (ibid., § 20-97))

Factors indicating harm and culpability (step one)

K-90c *Harm*
     Category 1:   Factors 11, 12
     Category 2:   Factor 13
     Category 3:   Factor(s) in categories 1 and 2 not present

Culpability
     Category A: Factors 43–45, 50–55, 57, 58
     Category B: Factor(s) in category A not present

Starting point and category range (step two)

	A	B
Category 1	**Starting point** 18 months	**Starting point** 1 year

	Range 1 – 2 years	**Range** 26 weeks – 18 months
Category 2	**Starting point** 1 year **Range** 26 weeks – 18 months	**Starting point** 26 weeks **Range** high level community order – 1 year
Category 3	**Starting point** 26 weeks **Range** high level community order – 1 year	**Starting point** medium level community order **Range** low level – high level community order

Consideration of custody threshold: category 2 or 3

Aggravating and mitigating factors

Aggravating factors: Factors 86, 87, 89, 91, 92, 94–96, 98–104

Mitigating factors: Factors 138–144

XV. Abuse of position of trust: sexual activity in the presence of a child (2003 Act, s.18 (ibid., § 20-98)); abuse of position of trust: causing a child to watch a sexual act (2003 Act, s.19 (ibid., § 20-99))

Factors indicating harm and culpability (step one)

Harm   **K-90d**

     Same as XI (*ante*)

Culpability

     Category A: Factors 43–45, 50–54, 57, 58

     Category B: Factor(s) in category A not present

Starting point and category range (step two)

     Same as XIV (*ante*)

Consideration of custody threshold: category 2 or 3

Aggravating and mitigating factors

Aggravating factors: Factors 86, 87, 91, 92, 94–96, 98–102, 104

Mitigating factors: Factors 138–143

XVI. Possession of indecent photograph of child (CJA 1988, s.160 (ibid., § 31-115)); indecent photographs of children (Protection of Children Act 1978, s.1 (ibid., § 31-107))

Factors indicating harm and culpability (step one)

	Possession	**Distribution**	**Production**	**K-91**
Category A	Of images involving penetrative sexual activity	Sharing such images	Creating such images	
	Of images involving sexual activity with an animal or sadism	Sharing such images	Creating such images	

Category B	Of images involving non-penetrative sexual activity	Sharing such images	Creating such images
Category C	Of other indecent images not falling within categories A or B	Sharing such images	Creating such images

Distribution includes possession with a view to distributing or sharing images. Production includes the taking or making of any image at source, for instance the original image. Making an image by simple downloading should be treated as possession for the purposes of sentencing.

In most cases the intrinsic character of the most serious of the offending images will initially determine the appropriate category. If, however, the most serious images are unrepresentative of the offender's conduct, a lower category may be appropriate. A lower category will not, however, be appropriate if the offender has produced or taken (*e.g.* photographed) images of a higher category.

Starting point and category range (step two)

	Possession	Distribution	Production
Category A	**Starting point** 1 year **Range** 26 weeks – 3 years	**Starting point** 3 years **Range** 2 – 5 years	**Starting point** 6 years **Range** 4 – 9 years
Category B	**Starting point** 26 weeks **Range** high level community order – 18 months	**Starting point** 1 year **Range** 26 weeks – 2 years	**Starting point** 2 years **Range** 1 – 4 years
Category C	**Starting point** high level community order **Range** medium level community order – 26 weeks	**Starting point** 13 weeks **Range** high level community order – 26 weeks	**Starting point** 18 months **Range** 1 – 3 years

Consideration of custody threshold: category 2 or 3

Aggravating and mitigating factors

Aggravating factors: Factors 86, 87, 95, 96, 100, 105, 107–118
Mitigating factors: Factors 138–143

XVII. Causing or inciting prostitution for gain (2003 Act, s.52 (ibid., § 20–172)); controlling prostitution for gain (2003 Act, s.53 (ibid., § 20–173))

Factors indicating harm and culpability (step one)

K-92 *Harm*

        Category 1:   Factors 6, 23–27
        Category 2:   Factor(s) in category 1 not present

Culpability

        Category A: Factors 46, 65–69
        Category B: Factor 70
        Category C: Factors 71, 72

Starting point and category range (step two)

	A	B	C
Category 1	**Starting point** 4 years **Range** 3 – 6 years	**Starting point** 2.5 years **Range** 2 – 4 years	**Starting point** 1 year **Range** 26 weeks – 2 years
Category 2	**Starting point** 2.5 years **Range** 2 – 5 years	**Starting point** 1 year **Range** high level community order – 2 years	**Starting point** medium level community order **Range** low level – high level community order

Consideration of custody threshold: category 2 or 3

Aggravating and mitigating factors

Aggravating factors: Factors 86, 87, 95, 96, 99, 100, 105, 119–126

Mitigating factors: Factors 138–143

XVIII. Keeping a brothel used for prostitution (SOA 1956, s.33A (ibid., § 20-229))

Factors indicating harm and culpability (step one)

Harm   **K-92a**

       Category 1:   Factors 6, 23–29

       Category 2:   Factor(s) in category 1 not present

Culpability

       Category A: Factors 46, 65–69, 73

       Category B: Factors 70, 74

       Category C: Factors 71, 72

Starting point and category range (step two)

	A	B	C
Category 1	**Starting point** 5 years **Range** 3 – 6 years	**Starting point** 3.5 years **Range** 2 – 5 years	**Starting point** 1 year **Range** high level community order – 18 months
Category 2	**Starting point** 3 years **Range** 2 – 5 years	**Starting point** 1 year **Range** 26 weeks – 2 years	**Starting point** medium level community order **Range** low level – high level community order

Consideration of custody threshold: category 1

Aggravating and mitigating factors

Aggravating factors: Factors 86, 87, 95, 96, 99, 100, 105, 119–127

Mitigating factors: Factors 138–143

XIX. Causing or inciting child prostitution or pornography (2003 Act, s.48 (ibid., § 20-160)); controlling a child prostitute or child involved in pornography (2003 Act, s.49 (ibid., § 20-167)); arranging or facilitating child prostitution or pornography (2003 Act, s.50 (ibid., § 20-161))

Factors indicating harm and culpability (step one)

K-92b *Harm*

Category 1:   Factors 6, 23, 24, 30–32

Category 2:   Factor(s) in category 1 not present

Culpability

Same as XVII (*ante*)

Starting point and category range (step two)

	Age of victim	A	B	C
Category 1	U13	**Starting point** 10 years **Range** 8 – 13 years	**Starting point** 8 years **Range** 6 – 11 years	**Starting point** 5 years **Range** 2 – 6 years
	13–15	**Starting point** 8 years **Range** 6 – 11 years	**Starting point** 5 years **Range** 4 – 8 years	**Starting point** 2.5 years **Range** 1 – 4 years
	16–17	**Starting point** 4 years **Range** 3 – 7 years	**Starting point** 2 years **Range** 1 – 4 years	**Starting point** 1 year **Range** 26 weeks – 2 years
Category 2	U13	**Starting point** 8 years **Range** 6 – 11 years	**Starting point** 6 years **Range** 4 – 9 years	**Starting point** 2 years **Range** 1 – 4 years
	13–15	**Starting point** 6 years **Range** 4 – 9 years	**Starting point** 3 years **Range** 2 – 5 years	**Starting point** 1 year **Range** 26 weeks – 2 years
	16–17	**Starting point** 3 years **Range** 2 – 5 years	**Starting point** 1 year **Range** 26 weeks – 2 years	**Starting point** 26 weeks **Range** high level community order – 1 year

Consideration of custody threshold: category 2

Aggravating and mitigating factors

Aggravating factors: Factors 86, 87, 95, 96, 99, 100, 105, 119-125, 128, 129

Mitigating factors: Factors 138, 139, 140*, 141, 142

XX. Paying for the sexual services of a child (2003 Act, s.47 (ibid., § 20-155))

K-92c   This guideline should only be used where the victim was aged 16 or 17.

Factors indicating harm and culpability (step one)

Harm

Category 1:	Factors 6, 11, 12, 33
Category 2:	Factor 15
Category 3:	Factor 14

Culpability

Category A:	Factors 44, 46, 47, 55, 64, 75–78
Category B:	Factor(s) in category A not present

Starting point and category range (step two)

	A	B
Category 1	**Starting point** 4 years **Range** 2 – 5 years	**Starting point** 2 years **Range** 1 – 4 years
Category 2	**Starting point** 3 years **Range** 1 – 4 years	**Starting point** 1 year **Range** 26 weeks – 2 years
Category 3	**Starting point** 1 year **Range** 26 weeks – 2 years	**Starting point** 26 weeks **Range** high level community order – 1 year

Consideration of custody threshold: category 3

Aggravating and mitigating factors

Aggravating factors:	Factors 86, 87, 89, 95, 96, 99, 100
Mitigating factors:	Factors 138–143

XXI. Trafficking people for sexual exploitation (2003 Act, s.59A (ibid., § 20-179)) (and also ss.57–59 before their replacement by s.59A)

Factors indicating harm and culpability (step one)

Harm **K-93**

Category 1:	Factors 6, 23–25, 34–36
Category 2:	Factor(s) in category 1 not present

Culpability

Category A:	Factors 46, 65, 66, 68
Category B:	Factors 80, 81
Category C:	Factors 71, 72

Starting point and category range (step two)

	A	B	C
Category 1	**Starting point** 8 years **Range** 6 – 12 years	**Starting point** 6 years **Range** 4 – 8 years	**Starting point** 18 months

			Range 26 weeks – 2 years
Category 2	**Starting point** 6 years **Range** 4 – 8 years	**Starting point** 4 years **Range** 2 – 6 years	**Starting point** 26 weeks **Range** high level community order – 18 months

Consideration of custody threshold: category 2

Aggravating and mitigating factors

Aggravating factors: Factors 86, 87, 95, 96, 99, 100, 105, 119–125, 131–133

Mitigating factors: Factors 138, 139, 140*, 141, 142

XXII. Sexual activity with a person with a mental disorder impeding choice (2003 Act, s.30 (ibid., § 20-125)); causing or inciting such a person to engage in a sexual activity (2003 Act, s.31 (ibid., § 20-126))

Factors indicating harm and culpability (step one)

K-94   *Harm*

Category 1:   The extreme nature of one or more category 2 factors or the extreme impact caused by a combination of category 2 factors **may** elevate to category 1

Category 2:   Factors 1–7

Category 3:   Factor(s) in categories 1 and 2 not present

Culpability

Category A: Factors 43–48, 50–56

Category B: Factor(s) in category A not present

Starting point and category range (step two)

Where offence involved penetration: same as V (*ante*)

Where offence did not involve penetration: same as VII (*ante*)

Consideration of custody threshold: when appropriate

Aggravating and mitigating factors

Aggravating factors: Factors 86, 87, 89, 90–96, 98–101

Mitigating factors: Factors 138, 139, 140*, 141, 142, 144

XXIII. Engaging in sexual activity in the presence of a person with a mental disorder impeding choice (2003 Act, s.32 (ibid., § 20-127)); causing such a person to watch a sexual act (2003 Act, s.33 (ibid., § 20-128))

Factors indicating harm and culpability (step one)

K-95   *Harm*

Same as XI (*ante*)

Culpability

    Category A: Factors 43–46, 50–54, 57

    Category B: Factor(s) in category A not present

Starting point and category range (step two)

    Same as XI (*ante*)

  Consideration of custody threshold: category 2 or 3

Aggravating and mitigating factors

Aggravating factors: Factors 86, 87, 91, 92, 95, 96, 99–101

Mitigating factors: Factors 138–143

XXIV. Inducement, threat or deception to procure sexual activity with a person with a mental disorder (2003 Act, s.34 (ibid., § 20-134)); causing such a person to engage in or agree to engage in sexual activity by inducement, threat or deception (2003 Act, s.35 (ibid., § 20-135))

Factors indicating harm and culpability (step one)

Harm   **K-96**

    Same as IX (*ante*)

Culpability

    Category A: Factors 43–46, 50–53, 55

    Category B: Factor(s) in category A not present

Starting point and category range (step two)

    Same as IX (*ante*)

  Consideration of custody threshold: category 2 or 3

Aggravating and mitigating factors

Aggravating factors: Factors 86, 87, 89, 91, 92, 94–96, 99–101, 103, 106

Mitigating factors: Factors 138, 139, 140*, 141, 142

XXV. Engaging in sexual activity in the presence, procured by inducement, threat or deception, of a person with a mental disorder (2003 Act, s.36 (ibid., § 20-136)); causing such a person to watch a sexual act by inducement, threat or deception (2003 Act, s.37 (ibid., § 20-137))

Factors indicating harm and culpability (step one)

Harm   **K-97**

    Same as XI (*ante*)

Culpability

    Category A: Factors 43–46, 50–53

    Category B: Factor(s) in category A not present

Starting point and category range (step two)

> Same as XI (*ante*)

> Consideration of custody threshold: category 2 or 3

Aggravating and mitigating factors

> Aggravating factors: Factors 86, 87, 91, 92, 95, 96, 99–101
> Mitigating factors: Factors 138–143

XXVI. Care workers: sexual activity with a person with a mental disorder (2003 Act, s.38 (ibid., § 20-143)); care workers: causing or inciting sexual activity (2003 Act, s.39 (ibid., § 20-144))

Factors indicating harm and culpability (step one)

K-98   *Harm*

> Same as XIV (*ante*)

Culpability

> Category A: Factors 43–45, 50–55, 57
> Category B: Factor(s) in category A not present

Starting point and category range (step two)

	A	B
Category 1	**Starting point** 5 years **Range** 4 – 10 years	**Starting point** 18 months **Range** 1 – 2 years
Category 2	**Starting point** 3 years **Range** 2 – 6 years	**Starting point** 26 weeks **Range** medium level community order – 1 year
Category 3	**Starting point** 26 weeks **Range** high level community order – 3 years	**Starting point** medium level community order **Range** low level – high level community order

> Consideration of custody threshold: category 2 or 3

Aggravating and mitigating factors

> Aggravating factors: Factors 86, 87, 89, 91, 92, 94–96, 99–101, 103, 104
> Mitigating factors: Factors 138, 139, 140*, 141, 142, 144

XXVII. Care workers: sexual activity in the presence of a person with a mental disorder (2003 Act, s.40 (ibid., § 20-145)); care workers: causing such a person to watch a sexual act (2003 Act, s.41 (ibid., § 20-146))

Factors indicating harm and culpability (step one)

K-99   *Harm*

> Same as XI (*ante*)

Culpability

Category A: Factors 43–45, 50–54, 57

Category B: Factor(s) in category A not present

Starting point and category range (step two)

Same as XIV (*ante*)

Consideration of custody threshold: category 2 or 3

Aggravating and mitigating factors

Aggravating factors: Factors 86, 87, 91, 92, 95, 96, 99–101, 104

Mitigating factors: Factors 138–143

XXVIII. Exposure (2003 Act, s.66 (ibid., § 20-208))

Factors indicating harm and culpability (step one)

Category 1:   Raised harm **and** raised culpability   **K-100**

Category 2:   Raised harm **or** raised culpability

Category 3:   Exposure **without** raised harm or culpability factors present

Where an offence does not fall squarely into a category, individual factors may require a degree of weighting before making an overall assessment and determining the appropriate offence category.

Indicators of raised harm

Factors 37, 38

Indicators of raised culpability

Factors 46, 51–53, 57, 82

Starting point and category range (step two)

Category 1	**Starting point** 26 weeks **Range** 12 weeks – 1 year
Category 2	**Starting point** high level community order **Range** medium level community order – 26 weeks
Category 3	**Starting point** medium level community order **Range** band A fine – high level community order

Consideration of custody threshold: category 2
Consideration of community order threshold: category 3

Aggravating and mitigating factors

Aggravating factors: Factors 86, 87, 91, 92, 95, 96, 98, 99, 101

Mitigating factors: Factors 138–143

XXIX. Voyeurism (2003 Act, s.67 (ibid., § 20-212))

Factors indicating harm and culpability (step one)

K-101   Category 1:   Raised harm **and** raised culpability

Category 2:   Raised harm **or** raised culpability

Category 3:   Voyeurism **without** raised harm or culpability factors present

Where an offence does not fall squarely into a category, individual factors may require a degree of weighting before making an overall assessment and determining the appropriate offence category.

Indicators of raised harm

Factors 39, 40

Indicators of raised culpability

Factors 43, 46, 50–53, 82, 83

Starting point and category range (step two)

Category 1	**Starting point** 26 weeks **Range** 12 weeks – 18 months
Category 2	**Starting point** high level community order **Range** medium level community order – 26 weeks
Category 3	**Starting point** medium level community order **Range** band A fine – high level community order

Consideration of custody threshold: category 2
Consideration of community order threshold: category 3

Aggravating and mitigating factors

Aggravating factors: Factors 86, 87, 91, 92, 95, 96, 99, 100, 134–137

Mitigating factors: Factors 138–143

XXX. Sex with an adult relative: penetration (2003 Act, s.64 (ibid., § 20-202)); sex with an adult relative: consenting to penetration (2003 Act, s.65 (ibid., § 20-203))

Factors indicating harm and culpability (step one)

K-102   Category 1:   Raised harm **and** raised culpability

Category 2:   Raised harm **or** raised culpability

Category 3:   Sex with an adult relative **without** raised harm or culpability factors present

Where an offence does not fall squarely into a category, individual factors may require a degree of weighting before making an overall assessment and determining the appropriate offence category.

Indicators of raised harm

Factors 8, 41

Indicators of raised culpability

Factors 54, 57

Starting point and category range (step two)

Category 1	**Starting point** 1 year **Range** 26 weeks – 2 years
Category 2	**Starting point** high level community order **Range** medium level community order – 1 year
Category 3	**Starting point** medium level community order **Range** band A fine – high level community order

Consideration of custody threshold: category 2
Consideration of community order threshold: category 3

Aggravating and mitigating factors

Aggravating factors: Factors 86, 87, 95, 96, 99, 100, 104
Mitigating factors: Factors 138–143

XXXI. Administering a substance with intent (2003 Act, s.61 (ibid., § 20-187))

Factors indicating harm and culpability (step one)

Category 1: Raised harm **and** raised culpability **K-103**

Category 2: Raised harm **or** raised culpability

Category 3: Administering a substance with intent **without** raised harm or culpability
factors present

Where an offence does not fall squarely into a category, individual factors may require a degree of weighting before making an overall assessment and determining the appropriate offence category. Where no substantive sexual offence has been committed the main consideration for the court will be the offender's conduct as a whole including, but not exclusively, the offender's intention.

Indicators of raised harm
Factors 1, 3, 5

Indicators of raised culpability
Factors 43, 44, 46, 49–53, 58, 84

Starting point and category range (step two)

Category 1	**Starting point** 6 years **Range** 4 – 9 years
Category 2	**Starting point** 4 years **Range** 3 – 7 years
Category 3	**Starting point** 2 years **Range** 1 – 5 years

Aggravating and mitigating factors

Aggravating factors: Factors 86, 87, 91, 92, 95, 96, 99, 100
Mitigating factors: Factors 138–143

763

XXXII. Committing an offence with intent to commit a sexual offence (2003 Act, s.62 (ibid., § 20-192))

K-104   The starting point and range should be commensurate with that for the preliminary offence actually committed, but with an enhancement to reflect the intention to commit a sexual offence. This will vary depending on the nature and seriousness of the intended sexual offence, but two years is suggested as a suitable enhancement where the intent was to commit rape or assault by penetration.

XXXIII. Trespass with intent to commit a sexual offence (2003 Act, s.63 (ibid., § 20-197))

Factors indicating harm and culpability (step one)

K-105   Category 1:   Raised harm **and** raised culpability

Category 2:   Raised harm **or** raised culpability

Category 3:   Trespass with intent to commit a sexual offence **without** raised harm or culpability factors present

Where an offence does not fall squarely into a category, individual factors may require a degree of weighting before making an overall assessment and determining the appropriate offence category. Where no substantive sexual offence has been committed the main consideration for the court will be the offender's conduct as a whole including, but not exclusively, the offender's intention.

Indicators of raised harm

Factors 3, 5, 42

Indicators of raised culpability

Factors 43, 44, 46, 50–53, 58, 84, 85

Starting point and category range (step two)

Same as XXXI (*ante*)

Aggravating and mitigating factors

Same as XXXI (*ante*)

Errors

K-106   In XXVII, the starting point for a category 1A offence is given as 18 years' custody. It has been assumed that this should be 18 months. In XI, XXIII and XXV, the top of the range for a category 3B offence is given as a medium level community order (the same as the starting point), and thus it has been assumed that the top of the range should be a high level community order.

I. FAILING TO SURRENDER TO BAIL

K-107   The Sentencing Guidelines Council has issued a definitive guideline on failing to surrender to bail (Bail Act 1976, s.6(1) and (2) (§ 3-31 in the main work)). It deals with offenders sentenced on or after December 10, 2007, and only relates to the sentencing of those aged 18 or over.

Assessment of seriousness

K-108   The seriousness of an offence is to be determined by: (a) the offender's culpability (in particular, whether the failure to surrender was intended to cause harm and, if so, what level of harm), and (b) any harm which the offence caused, was intended to cause or might foreseeably have caused (in particular, to what extent the failure to surrender impeded the course of justice), and "harm" includes not only harm caused to victims and witnesses but also the consequential drain on the police and the courts and the wider negative impact on public confidence in the criminal justice system. The same approach to sentencing should be adopted for offences under both section 6(1) and (2), though the seriousness is likely to be less for an offence under subsection (2). The assessment of culpability requires consideration of the immediate reason why the defendant failed to appear, which can range from forgetfulness or fear of the outcome of the hearing to a deliberate act, and where the failure to surrender was deliberate, it will be relevant whether it was designed to disrupt the system to the defendant's advantage or whether the defendant simply gave no thought at all to the consequences. Failure to surrender will always cause some degree of harm, will inevitably delay justice, and will almost always waste public money. The circumstances of an offence, and the harm likely to be caused, will range from failure to appear for a first hearing but attending shortly afterwards (where the only harm caused is likely to be financial and procedural), to failure to appear for trial or sentence, especially where the trial does not proceed in the defendant's absence (where the harm caused may extend to the prevention of justice). Generally, the same approach should be taken whether the failure to surrender is to a court or to a police station, but the harm caused is likely to be less in the case of a police station, and there are also circumstances where the culpability may be less. Where sentence is passed in advance of the offence in respect of which bail was granted, the seriousness of that offence should not affect the assessment of seriousness, but the nature of that offence may affect the degree or likelihood of harm caused, such as where it is a violent or sexual offence, and an acquittal for that offence will not affect the seriousness of the failure to surrender.

Aggravating factors that are particularly relevant to the assessment of seriousness are: (a) repeated offences under section 6; (b) the absence of the offender causing a lengthy delay to the administration of justice; and (c) a determined effort to avoid the jurisdiction of the court or to undermine the course of justice. Mitigating factors that are particularly relevant are: (a) prompt voluntary surrender (if initiated by the offender); (b) misunderstanding (which must be differentiated from a mistake on the part of the offender); (c) a failure to comprehend the requirements or significance of bail; and (d) caring responsibilities (where these are the cause of the failure to surrender). The fact that the offender has a disorganised or chaotic lifestyle (which may be due to dependence on drugs or alcohol) does not mitigate the seriousness of the offence (though it may amount to personal mitigation).

Procedural issues

As to when to sentence, the key principle is stated to be that a court should deal with a defendant **K-109** who fails to surrender as soon as it is practicable, even if the trial or other hearing for the offence in respect of which bail was granted is adjourned. Relevant factors when deciding what is practicable include: (a) when the proceedings in respect of which bail was granted are expected to conclude; (b) the seriousness of that offence; and (c) the type of penalty that might be imposed for that offence and for the failure to surrender. Liability for the section 6 offence should be determined as soon as possible, since it will be central to the issue of whether bail should be renewed; accordingly, a trial should be held on the first appearance after arrest or surrender, unless an adjournment is necessary. Occasions on which it may be more appropriate to sentence both offences together include circumstances where the totality of sentence may affect sentence type and where the harm caused cannot be assessed at an earlier stage.

As to sentencing, the alternatives to immediate custody are a community order, including an **K-110** electronically monitored curfew requirement and, perhaps, a supervision or activity requirement, and, in more serious cases, a suspended sentence. Where custodial sentences are imposed both for the section 6 offence and for the substantive offence, they should normally be consecutive, but should be concurrent where otherwise the overall sentence would be disproportionate to the combined seriousness of the offences.

As to trial in the defendant's absence, where it has proved possible to proceed to trial or conclude **K-111** proceedings in the absence of the defendant, this should have no bearing on culpability, but may be relevant to the assessment of harm, if the harm caused by the failure to attend has been reduced or avoided by such a course.

Sentencing ranges and starting points

The sentencing ranges and starting points relate to persons convicted following a plea of not **K-112** guilty, and who do not have a conviction which, by virtue of the CJA 2003, s.143(2) (§ 5-67 in the main work), must be treated as an aggravating factor. A court should identify the description that most nearly matches the facts of the offence and this will identify a starting point, from which a provisional sentence can be reached. The sentencing range is the bracket into which the provisional sentence will fall after consideration of aggravating or mitigating factors (although particular circumstances, particular matters of aggravation or mitigation or the reduction for a guilty plea may require a sentence outside of that range). A court should give reasons for imposing a sentence of a different kind or outside the range provided in the guideline.

For a deliberate failure to attend causing delay and/or interference with the administration of justice, the starting point is 14 days' custody, and the range, in a magistrates' court, should be from a community order (low) to 10 weeks' custody, and in the Crown Court, should be from a community order (medium) to 40 weeks' custody, with the type and degree of harm actually caused affecting where in the range the case falls. For a negligent or non-deliberate failure to attend causing delay and/or interference with the administration of justice, the starting point should be a fine, and the range (regardless of court) should be from a fine to a community order (medium). Where the defendant surrenders late, but the case proceeds as planned, the starting point and the range should be a fine.

J. Assault and Other Offences Against the Person

K-113   The Sentencing Council for England and Wales has issued a definitive guideline on non-fatal offences against the person, applying to all offenders aged 18 or over who are sentenced on or after June 13, 2011, regardless of the date of their offence. The offences covered are: (A) causing grievous bodily harm, or wounding, with intent to do grievous bodily harm (Offences against the Person Act 1861, s.18 (§ 19-251 in the main work)), (B) inflicting grievous bodily harm or unlawful wounding (1861 Act, s.20 (*ibid.*, § 19-252)) and racially or religiously aggravated grievous bodily harm or unlawful wounding (CDA 1998, s.29 (*ibid.*, § 19-266)), (C) assault occasioning actual bodily harm (1861 Act, s.47 (*ibid.*, § 19-242)) and racially or religiously aggravated actual bodily harm (1998 Act, s.29), (D) assault with intent to resist arrest (1861 Act, s.38 (*ibid.*, § 19-316)), (E) assault on a police constable in execution of his duty (Police Act 1996, s.89), and (F) common assault (CJA 1988, s.39) and racially or religiously aggravated common assault (1998 Act, s.29).

K-114   The guideline sets out eight to nine steps to be followed (in order) when sentencing for these offences, which are as follows, subject to any modifications set out in the specific sections relating to each group (*post*).

Step one requires the court to determine within which of three categories reflecting various degrees of seriousness the offence falls. Category 1 requires greater harm and higher culpability, category 2 requires either greater harm and lower culpability or lesser harm and higher culpability, and category 3 requires lesser harm and lower culpability. In determining the offender's culpability and the harm caused (or intended), the court should refer only to the factors indicating harm and culpability set out in the specific sections relating to A to F, *post*, which comprise the principal factual elements of the offence.

Step two requires the court to use the starting point identified for the relevant category (as to which, see also the specific sections relating to A-F, *post*) to reach a sentence within the category range (*post*). The starting point applies to all offenders irrespective of plea or previous convictions. A case of particular gravity, reflected by multiple features of culpability in step one, could merit upward adjustment from the starting point before further adjustment is made for the aggravating or mitigating factors increasing or reducing seriousness or reflecting personal mitigation set out in the specific sections relating to A to F, post, which contain a non-exhaustive list of additional factual elements providing the context of the offence and factors relating to the offender. Having considered all these, and other relevant factors, it might be appropriate to move outside the identified category range.

At step three, the court should take into account sections 73 and 74 of the SOCPA 2005 (assistance by defendants: reduction or review of sentence (*ibid.*, §§ 5-132, 5-133)), and any other rule of law by virtue of which an offender may receive a discounted sentence in consequence of assistance given (or offered) to the prosecutor or investigator.

At step four, the court should take account of any potential reduction for a guilty plea in accordance with section 144 of the CJA 2003 (*ibid.*, § 5-107) and the revised guideline on reductions in sentence for guilty pleas (*ante*, Appendix K-1 *et seq.*).

At step five, which does not apply to the offence in E (assault on a police constable in execution of his duty), the court will consider whether the offender meets the dangerousness criteria for a life sentence or imprisonment for public protection (in respect of those offences which are serious offences within the meaning of the 2003 Act, Ch. 5 (*ibid.*, §§ 5-495 *et seq.*), in which case the notional determinate sentence should be used as the basis for setting the minimum term) or an extended sentence (in respect of those offences which are specified offences within the meaning of the 2003 Act, Ch. 5).

At step six (or five), the court should apply the totality principle, step seven (or six), consider whether to make compensation or other ancillary orders or both, step eight (or seven), give its reasons for, and explain the effect of, the sentence (2003 Act, s.174 (*ibid.*, § 5-165)), and step nine (or eight) take into account any time spent on remand in custody or on bail (2003 Act, ss.240 and 240A (*ibid.*, §§ 5-640, 5-645)).

For offences under the 1998 Act, s.29, only, the court should determine the appropriate sentence for the offence without taking account of the element of aggravation, and then make an addition to the sentence, considering the level of aggravation involved. It may be appropriate to move outside the identified category range, taking into account the increased statutory maximum.

Key to factors indicating greater harm and higher or lower culpability (step one)

Factors indicating greater harm

- a. Injury (which includes disease transmission and/ or psychological harm) which is serious in the context of the offence (must normally be present). **K-115**
- b. Victim is particularly vulnerable because of personal circumstances.
- c. Sustained or repeated assault on the same victim.
- d. Injury or fear of injury which is serious in the context of the offence (must normally be present).

Factors indicating higher culpability

Statutory aggravating factors: **K-116**
- e. offence racially or religiously aggravated.
- f. offence motivated by, or demonstrating, hostility to the victim based on his or her sexual orientation (or presumed sexual orientation).
- g. offence motivated by, or demonstrating, hostility to the victim based on the victim's disability (or presumed disability).

Other aggravating factors:
- h. A significant degree of premeditation.
- i. Use of weapon or weapon equivalent (*e.g.* shod foot, headbutting, use of acid, use of animal).
- j. Threatened use of weapon or weapon equivalent.
- k. Intention to commit more serious harm than actually resulted from the offence.
- l. Deliberately causes more harm than is necessary for commission of offence.
- m. Deliberate targeting of vulnerable victim.
- n. Leading role in group or gang.
- o. Offence motivated by, or demonstrating, hostility based on the victim's age, sex, gender identity (or presumed gender identity).

Factors indicating lower culpability

- p. Subordinate role in group or gang. **K-117**
- q. A greater degree of provocation than normally expected.
- r. Lack of premeditation.
- s. Mental disorder or learning disability, where linked to commission of the offence.
- t. Excessive self defence.

Key to factors increasing or reducing seriousness or reflecting personal mitigation (step 2)

Factors increasing seriousness

Statutory aggravating factors: **K-118**

u. Previous convictions (in accordance with the 2003 Act, s.143(2) (§ 5-67 in the main work)).

v. Offence committed whilst on bail (2003 Act, s.143(3)).

Other aggravating factors include:

w. Location of the offence.

x. Timing of the offence.

y. Continuing effect upon the victim.

z. Offence committed against those working in the public sector or providing a service to the public.

aa. Presence of others including relatives, especially children or partner of the victim.

bb. Gratuitous degradation of victim.

cc. In domestic violence cases, victim forced to leave home.

dd. Failure to comply with current court orders.

ee. Offence committed whilst on licence.

ff. An attempt to conceal or dispose of evidence.

gg. Failure to respond to warnings or concerns expressed by others about the offender's behaviour.

hh. Commission of offence whilst under the influence of alcohol or drugs.

ii. Abuse of power and/ or position of trust.

jj. Exploiting contact arrangements with a child to commit an offence.

kk. Any steps taken to prevent the victim reporting an incident, obtaining assistance and/ or from assisting or supporting the prosecution.

ll. Offences taken into consideration.

Factors reducing seriousness or reflecting personal mitigation

K-119

mm. No previous convictions or no relevant/ recent convictions.

nn. Single blow.

oo. Remorse.

pp. Good character and/ or exemplary conduct.

qq. Determination and/ or demonstration of steps taken to address addiction or offending behaviour.

rr. serious medical conditions requiring urgent, intensive or long-term treatment.

ss. isolated incident.

tt. Age and/ or lack of maturity where it affects the responsibility of the offender.

uu. Lapse of time since the offence where this is not the fault of the offender.

vv. Mental disorder or learning disability, where not linked to the commission of the offence.

ww. Sole or primary carer for dependent relatives.

Fine bands

K-120

Fine band	Starting point (applicable to all offenders)	Category range (applicable to all offenders)
band A	50% of relevant weekly income	25 – 75% of relevant weekly income
band B	100% of relevant weekly income	75 – 125% of relevant weekly income
band C	150% of relevant weekly income	125 – 175% of relevant weekly income

Community orders

K-121   The following table sets out a non-exhaustive description of examples of requirements that might be appropriate for low, medium and high level community orders (respectively). Where two or more requirements are ordered, they must be compatible with each other.

Low	Medium	High
In general, only one requirement will be appropriate and the length may be curtailed if additional requirements are necessary		More intensive sentences which combine two or more requirements may be appropriate
Suitable requirements might include: • 40 – 80 hours unpaid work • curfew requirement within the lowest range (*e.g.* up to 12 hours per day for a few weeks) • exclusion requirement, without electronic monitoring, for a few months • prohibited activity requirement • attendance centre requirement (where available)	Suitable requirements might include: • greater number of hours of unpaid work (*e.g.* 80 – 150 hours) • an activity requirement in the middle range (20 – 30 days) • curfew requirement within the middle range (*e.g.* up to 12 hours for two – three months) • exclusion requirement, lasting in the region of six months • prohibited activity requirement	Suitable requirements might include: • 150 – 300 hours unpaid work • activity requirement up to the maximum of 60 days • curfew requirement up to 12 hours per day for four – six months • exclusion order lasting in the region of 12 months

A. Causing grievous bodily harm, or wounding, with intent to do grievous bodily harm

In assessing whether there has been greater harm for the purposes of determining the offence **K-122** category in respect of these offences, serious injury must normally be present.

Factors indicating harm and culpability (step one)
> Greater harm: a–c
> Lesser harm: injury which is less serious in the context of the offence
> Higher culpability: e–i, k–o
> Lower culpability: p–t

Starting point and category range (step two)

Offence category		Starting point (applicable to all offenders)	Category range (applicable to all offenders)
category 1		12 years' custody	nine – 16 years' custody
category 2		six years' custody	five – nine years' custody
category 3		four years' custody	three – five years' custody

Factors increasing or reducing seriousness or reflecting personal mitigation
> Factors increasing seriousness: u–z, aa–ll
> Factors reducing seriousness or reflecting personal mitigation: mm–ww

B. Inflicting grievous bodily harm or unlawful wounding and racially or religiously aggravated grievous bodily harm or unlawful wounding

K-123   In assessing whether there has been greater harm for the purposes of determining the offence category in respect of these offences, serious injury must normally be present.

Factors indicating harm and culpability (step one)

Greater harm: a–c
Lesser harm: injury which is less serious in the context of the offence
Higher culpability: f–i, k–o
Lower culpability: p–t

Starting point and category range (step two)

Offence category	Starting point (applicable to all offenders)	Category range (applicable to all offenders)
category 1	three years' custody	30 months' – four years' custody
category 2	18 months' custody	one – three years' custody
category 3	high level community order	low level community order – 51 weeks' custody

When sentencing for category three offences, the court should consider whether the custody threshold has been passed, if so, whether it is unavoidable that a custodial sentence be imposed and, if so, whether that sentence can be suspended.

Factors increasing or reducing seriousness or reflecting personal mitigation

Same as for A, *ante*.

C. Assault occasioning actual bodily harm and racially or religiously aggravated actual bodily harm

K-124   In assessing whether there has been "greater harm" for the purposes of determining the offence category in respect of these offences, serious injury must normally be present.

Factors indicating harm and culpability (step one)

Same as for B, *ante*.

Starting point and category range (step two)

Offence category	Starting point (applicable to all offenders)	Category range (applicable to all offenders)
category 1	18 months' custody	one – three years' custody
category 2	26 weeks' custody	low level community order – 51 weeks' custody
category 3	medium level community order	band A fine – high level community order

When sentencing for category two offences, the court should consider whether the custody threshold has been passed, if so, whether it is unavoidable that a custodial sentence be imposed and, if so, whether that sentence can be suspended; and in sentencing for category three offences, the court should also consider whether the community order threshold has been passed.

Factors increasing or reducing seriousness or reflecting personal mitigation

Same as for A and B, *ante*.

D. Assault with intent to resist arrest

Factors indicating harm and culpability (step one)

K-125   Greater harm: c

Lesser harm: injury which is less serious in the context of the offence
Higher culpability: e–i, k–l, n, o
Lower culpability: p, r, s

Starting point and category range (step two)

Offence category	Starting point (applicable to all offenders)	Category range (applicable to all offenders)
category 1	26 weeks' custody	12 – 51 weeks' custody
category 2	medium level community order	low level community order – high level community order
category 3	band B fine	band A fine – band C fine

When sentencing for category one offences, the court should consider whether the sentence can be suspended.

Factors increasing or reducing seriousness or reflecting personal mitigation
Factors increasing seriousness: u–y, bb, dd–hh, kk, ll
Factors reducing seriousness or reflecting personal mitigation: mm–tt, vv, ww

E. Assault on a police constable in execution of his duty

Factors indicating harm and culpability (step one)
Same as for D, *ante*.

K-126

Starting point and category range (step two)

Offence category	Starting point (applicable to all offenders)	Category range (applicable to all offenders)
category 1	12 weeks' custody	low level community order – 26 weeks' custody
category 2	medium level community order	low level community order – high level community order
category 3	band B fine	band A fine – band C fine

When sentencing for category one offences, the court should consider whether the custody threshold has been passed, if so, whether it is unavoidable that a custodial sentence be imposed and, if so, whether that sentence can be suspended.

Factors increasing or reducing seriousness or reflecting personal mitigation
Factors increasing seriousness: u–y, bb, dd–hh, kk, ll
Factors reducing seriousness or reflecting personal mitigation: mm–ww

F. Common assault and racially or religiously aggravated common assault

In assessing whether there has been "greater harm" for the purposes of determining the of- **K-127** fence category in respect of these offences, injury or fear of injury must normally be present.

Factors indicating harm and culpability (step one)
Greater harm: b–d
Lesser harm: injury which is less serious in the context of the offence
Higher culpability: f–o
Lower culpability: p–t

Starting point and category range (step two)

Offence category	Starting point (applicable to all offenders)	Category range (applicable to all offenders)
category 1	high level community order	low level community order – 26 weeks' custody
category 2	medium level community order	band A fine – high level community order
category 3	band A fine	discharge – band C fine

When sentencing for category one offences, the court should consider whether the custody threshold has been passed, if so, whether it is unavoidable that a custodial sentence be imposed and, if so, whether that sentence can be suspended. When sentencing for category two offences, the court should consider whether the community order threshold has been crossed.

Factors increasing or reducing seriousness or reflecting personal mitigation
    Same as for A, B and C, *ante.*

[The next paragraph is K-131.]

K. Assaults on Children and Cruelty to a Child

K-131   The Sentencing Guidelines Council has issued a definitive guideline (i) supplementing the guideline on assaults and other offences against the person (*ante*, K-113 *et seq.*) by detailing additional principles which apply where the victim of the offence was aged 15 or under and (ii) on the offence of cruelty to a child (CYPA 1933, s.1(1)). It deals with offenders sentenced on or after March 3, 2008, and only relates to the sentencing of those aged 18 or over.

Part 1: Assaults on children: general principles

Assessing seriousness

K-132   The seriousness of an offence is to be determined by (a) the culpability of the offender and (b) the harm caused, intended or reasonably foreseeable, and guidance on whether sentencing thresholds have been reached is provided by the guideline on seriousness. Where an offender has previous convictions, the court must consider whether it should treat any of them as an aggravating factor, having regard to the nature and relevance of each offence and the time that has elapsed since the conviction. The fact that the victim is a child is likely to aggravate the seriousness of the offence where the offender is an adult.

Aggravation

K-133   The fact that the victim of an assault is a child will often mean that the offence involves a particularly vulnerable victim. The most relevant aggravating factors are: (i) the victim is particularly vulnerable; (ii) an abuse of power; (iii) an abuse of a position of trust; (iv) an especially serious physical or psychological effect on the victim, even if unintended; (v) the presence of others, *e.g.* relatives, especially other children; and (vi) additional degradation of the victim. Additional aggravating factors are: (i) sadistic behaviour; (ii) the making of threats to prevent the victim reporting the offence; (iii) the deliberate concealment of the victim from the authorities; and (iv) a failure to seek medical help. The location and particular circumstances of the offence may also be relevant aggravating factors.

Mitigation

K-134   The defence of lawful chastisement is only available on a charge of common assault, and where that defence is not available or is not made out, sentencing for the offence should normally be approached in the same way as for any other assault, even where an offender held a genuine belief that his actions amounted to no more than a legitimate form of physical punishment. However, if an offender has been charged with assault occasioning actual bodily harm and the court has found that he only intended to administer lawful chastisement to the child, and that the injury that was inflicted was neither intended nor foreseen by him, there should be a substantial reduction in sentence and a custodial sentence should not normally be imposed. Where the injury was neither intended nor foreseen, and was not even reasonably foreseeable, then a discharge might be appropriate.

Other factors relevant to sentencing

Adverse effect of the sentence on the victim

Imposition of a custodial sentence will often protect a victim from further harm and anguish, **K-135** and some children will be less traumatised once they are no longer living with an abusive carer, but where imprisonment of the offender deprives a child victim of his sole or main carer (and may result in the child being taken into care), it may punish and re-victimise the child. Imposing a custodial sentence on the offender may be the only option, but where other sentencing options remain open, the court should take into account the impact that a custodial sentence for the offender might have on the victim. The court also needs to be aware of the progress of any concurrent family proceedings.

Offenders who have primary care responsibilities

Where the offender is the sole or primary carer of the victim or other dependants, this should **K-136** potentially be taken into account for sentencing purposes, regardless of whether the offender is male or female. In such cases, an immediate custodial sentence may not be appropriate and, subject to a risk assessment, the offender may be able to resume care of or have contact with the victim.

Part 2:　Cruelty to a child

Assessing seriousness

One category of child cruelty is not automatically more serious than another and, in order **K-137** properly to assess the seriousness of an offence, its precise nature must be established before consideration is given to a range of contingent factors, including the defendant's intent, the length of time over which the cruelty took place, and the degree of physical and psychological harm suffered by the victim.

Culpability

Culpability should be the initial factor in determining the seriousness of an offence. An offence **K-138** may be the consequence of a wide range of factors including: (i) sadism; (ii) violence resulting from any number of causes; (iii) a reduced ability to protect a child in the face of aggression from an overbearing partner; (iv) indifference or apathy resulting from low intelligence or induced by alcohol or drug dependence; (v) immaturity or social deprivation resulting in an inability to cope with the pressures of caring for children; and (vi) psychiatric illness. It might also arise as the result of a momentary lack of control by an otherwise responsible and loving carer. The extent to which any of these factors might have contributed to the commission of an offence will be important in determining the culpability of the offender. A court must strike a balance between the need to reflect the serious view which society takes of the ill-treatment of young children and the need to protect those children, and also the pressures upon immature and inadequate parents attempting to cope with the problems of infancy, and the extent to which remorse should influence sentence will always have to be judged in the light of all the circumstances. The normal starting point should be a custodial sentence, the length of which should be influenced by the circumstances surrounding the offence.

Harm

It is helpful if the indictment clearly states the nature of the offender's conduct, but even where **K-139** this is clear, difficulties arise in determining the relative seriousness of the different forms of child cruelty. There is, however, a significant distinction between cases of wilful ill-treatment which usually involve positive acts of abuse and physical violence, and cases of neglect which are typified by the absence of actions. There is also a distinction between cases involving physical injury, whether resulting directly from an assault or ill-treatment or resulting from a period of abandonment or neglect, and cases where the harm occasioned is exposure to the risk of harm or lack of proper care, attention or supervision. In addition, whether one form of cruelty is worse than another will depend not only on the degree to which the victim suffers as a result but also on the motivation and culpability of the offender.

Aggravating and mitigating factors

K-140   The guideline refers to the guideline on seriousness for general aggravating and mitigating factors. In particular, care should be taken to avoid "double-counting" when an essential element of an offence might, in other circumstances, be an aggravating factor, and the abuse of trust or abuse of power inherent in the offence have been built into the guideline and should not be treated as aggravating factors. Relevant aggravating factors are targeting one particular child from the family and the four additional aggravating factors listed under "Assaults on children: general principles" (*ante*). The sole relevant mitigating factor is seeking medical help or bringing the situation to the notice of the authorities.

Other factors relevant to sentencing

Long-term psychological harm

K-141   The starting points have been calculated to reflect the likelihood of psychological harm and this cannot be treated as an aggravating factor. Where there is an especially serious physical or psychological effect on the victim, even if unintended, this should result in an increased sentence.

Adverse effect of the sentence on the victim

K-142   As in Part 1, *ante*.

Offenders who have primary care responsibilities

K-143   As in Part 1, *ante*.

Personal mitigation

K-144   The most relevant areas of personal mitigation are likely to be: (i) mental illness/ depression; (ii) inability to cope with the pressures of parenthood; (iii) lack of support; (iv) sleep deprivation; (v) domination of the offender by an abusive or stronger partner; (vi) extreme behavioural difficulties in the child, often coupled with a lack of support; and (vii) inability to secure assistance or support services in spite of every effort having been made by the offender. However, some of these factors could be regarded as an inherent part of caring for children, especially with young children, and so before they are accepted in mitigation, there must be evidence that these factors were present to a high degree and had an identifiable and significant impact on the offender's behaviour.

Factors to take into consideration

K-145   *Dangerous offenders*: the offence is a "specified offence" within the CJA 2003, s.224, and so a court must consider the imposition of a sentence for public protection. The guideline only applies to offenders who have not been classed as dangerous.

Categories of offence: the same starting point applies regardless of which of the various ways in which the offence can be committed is in point, and it already assumes an abuse of trust or power and the likelihood of psychological harm, and is designed to reflect the seriousness with which society as a whole regards these offences.

Additional factors: only additional aggravating and mitigating factors specifically relevant to this offence are included in the guideline, and a court must always take into account the full list of factors in the guideline on seriousness.

Sentencing ranges and starting points

K-146   The sentencing ranges and starting points relate to persons convicted following a plea of not guilty, and who do not have a conviction which, by virtue of the 2003 Act, s.143(2) (§ 5-67 in the main work), must be treated as an aggravating factor. A court should identify the description that most nearly matches the facts of the offence and this will identify a starting point, from which a provisional sentence can be reached. The sentencing range is the bracket into which the provisional sentence will fall after consideration of aggravating or mitigating factors (although particular circumstances, particular matters of aggravation or mitigation, or the reduction for a guilty plea may require a sentence outside of that range). The provisional sentence may then be reduced by matters of personal mitigation, which may also take it outside the appropriate sentencing range. A court should give reasons for imposing a sentence of a different kind or outside the range provided in the guideline.

Where there has been (i) serious cruelty over a period of time, (ii) serious long-term neglect, or (iii) a failure to protect a child from either of these, the starting point is six years' custody and the sentencing range is five to nine years' custody.

Where there has been (i) a series of assaults (the more serious the individual assaults and the longer the period over which they are perpetrated, the more serious the offence), (ii) protracted neglect or ill-treatment (the longer the period of ill-treatment or neglect and the longer the period over which it takes place, the more serious the offence), or (iii) a failure to protect a child from either of these, the starting point is three years' custody and the sentencing range is two to five years' custody.

Where there has been (i) an assault resulting in injuries consistent with assault occasioning actual bodily harm, (ii) more than one incident of neglect or ill-treatment (but not amounting to long-term behaviour), (iii) a single incident of long-term abandonment or regular incidents of short-term abandonment (the longer the period of long-term abandonment or the greater the number of incidents of short-term abandonment, the more serious the offence), or (iv) a failure to protect a child from any of these, the starting point is 36 weeks' custody and the sentencing range is 26 weeks' to two years' custody.

Where there has been (i) short-term neglect or ill-treatment, (ii) a single incident of shortterm abandonment, or (iii) a failure to protect a child from any of these, the starting point is 12 weeks' custody and the sentencing range is a community order (low) to 26 weeks' custody.

L. SENTENCING IN MAGISTRATES' COURTS

Introduction

The Sentencing Guidelines Council has issued a guideline on offences for which sentence is **K-147** frequently imposed in magistrates' courts when dealing with adult offenders, which replaces the guidelines which were effective from January 1, 2004. The foreword and introduction state that they are to apply to all relevant cases appearing for allocation (mode of trial) or for sentence on or after August 4, 2008, not only in magistrates' courts, but also in the Crown Court when dealing with appeals against sentence and when sentencing for summary only offences. The guideline should be consulted when dealing with an either-way offence for which there is no plea or an indication of a not guilty plea, since it will be relevant to the mode of trial decision. The guideline will also be relevant to decisions as to committal for sentence.

There have been 13 updates to these guidelines. An update that took effect on January 5, 2009, made changes to Parts 1 (indices), 3 (offence guidelines) and 5 (explanatory material). The effect of the changes to Part 3 was (i) to include extracts from the guideline on breach of an anti-social behaviour order (*post*, K-196 *et seq.*) and the guideline on theft and burglary in a building other than a dwelling (*post*, K-209 *et seq.*) in these guidelines in the appropriate places, and (ii) to make a clarificatory amendment to the existing guideline for burglary in a dwelling. Consequential amendments were made to the section in Part 5 that relates to ancillary orders, in respect of anti-social behaviour orders, and an amendment was also made to that section in respect of orders disqualifying an offender from driving, to reflect recent case law.

An update implemented on August 4, 2008, made equivalent changes to Part 3 in relation to the guideline on causing death by driving (*post*, K-185 *et seq.*) and modified Part 5 in respect of explanatory material relating to dangerous offenders (to take account of changes made by the CJIA 2008).

The third update was published on October 13, 2009. This included new guidelines for statutory offences of fraud (reflective of the guideline for such offences (*post*, K-228 *et seq.*). In addition, supplementary guidance was provided in relation to sentencing for health and safety offences following changes to the maximum penalty for certain offences effected by the Health and Safety (Offences) Act 2008 and which came into effect on January 16, 2009.

As from June 13, 2011, a fourth update will apply to all offenders aged 18 or over who are sentenced on or after that date, regardless of the date of their offence, with the effect that the new guideline on offences against the person (as to which, see *ante*, K-113 *et seq.*) is imported, except for those parts dealing with indictable-only offences, with the imposition of sentences which magistrates are not entitled to impose, and with sections 73 and 74 of the SOCPA 2005 (§§ 5-132, 5-133 in the main work), since they apply only in the Crown Court.

A fifth update was issued on October 13, 2011, and applies to all offenders aged 18 or over who are sentenced on or after January 16, 2012, regardless of the date of their offence. The effect is to import the guidelines on domestic and non-domestic burglary (but not aggravated burglary, which is an indictable-only offence) (as to which, see *post*, K-259 *et seq.*), except that, at step three, there is no mention of sections 73 and 74 of the SOCPA 2005 (§§ 5-132, 5-133 in the main work), since they apply only in the Crown Court. The starting points and category ranges apply to all offenders in all cases, irrespective of plea or previous convictions.

A sixth update was issued on January 24, 2012. This applies to all offenders aged 18 or over who are sentenced on or after February 27, 2012, regardless of the date of their offence. The effect is to import the guidelines on drug offences (*post*, K-271 *et seq.*).

As from June 11, 2012, a seventh update applies to all offenders aged 18 or over who are sentenced on or after that date, regardless of the date of their offence, with the effect that a new definitive guideline on the allocation of offences (see *ante*, § 1-97) and a guideline on offences taken into consideration (*ante*, §§ 5-160 *et seq.*) and totality (*post*, K-280 *et seq.*) are imported. It also corrects an error in one of the drug offence guidelines (importation) issued in the sixth update (this correction has been incorporated into the supplement at K-275, *post*).

As from August 20, 2012, an eighth update applies to all offenders aged 18 or over who are sentenced on or after that date, regardless of the date of their offence, with the effect that a new definitive guideline on dangerous dog offences (*post*, K-291 *et seq.*) is imported into the guideline.

A ninth update makes alterations to Part 5 (explanatory material) to reflect changes made to the victim surcharge by the Criminal Justice Act 2003 (Surcharge) Order 2012 (S.I. 2012 No. 1696) (see §§ 5-1300 *et seq.* in the main work) and amendments (not yet in force) to sentencing legislation effected by the LASPOA 2012. As to the latter, the new material deals, in particular, with the new requirements (foreign travel prohibition and alcohol abstinence and monitoring) that may be attached to a community sentence or a suspended sentence, the new law relating to suspended sentences (their length and the necessity or otherwise to attach community requirements) and the making of hostility based on transgender identity a statutory aggravating factor.

The Sentencing Council issued a tenth update, applying to all offenders aged 18 or over who are sentenced on or after April 1, 2014. The principal effect was to replace the incorporation of the previous Sentencing Guideline's Council guideline on sexual offences with the new Sentencing Council's guideline on sexual offences (*ante*, K-84 *et seq.*), save for such parts thereof as can only have any application in the Crown Court. The starting points apply in all cases, irrespective of previous convictions or plea.

The update also revised the explanatory material in Part 5 relating to road traffic offences. The starting point when considering disqualification from driving in a defendant's absence is now that disqualification should be imposed in an offender's absence if there is no reason to believe that the defendant is unaware of the proceedings and where the statutory notice has been served pursuant to the MCA 1980, s.11(4). It should not be imposed in the absence of the offender where there is evidence that there is an acceptable reason for the defendant's absence or where there are reasons to believe it would be contrary to the interests of justice.

As from July 1, 2014, an eleventh update to the sentencing guidelines for magistrates' courts applies to all offenders aged 18 or over who are sentenced on or after that date, the principal effect of which was to incorporate the Sentencing Council's guideline on environmental offences (as to which, see § 5-147 in the main work), and to expand the explanatory material relating to health and safety offences to include environmental offences. The update also corrects an error in the section of the tenth update (*ante*) relating to indecent photographs of children.

As from October 1, 2014, a twelfth update to the sentencing guidelines for magistrates' courts applies to all offenders aged 18 or over who are sentenced on or after that date. The principal effect is to incorporate the Sentencing Council's guideline on fraud, money laundering and bribery offences (*post*, Appendix K-297 *et seq.*), but the opportunity has also been taken to bring up to date the table of offences for which fixed penalty notices are available and the amount of such penalties in Annex B to the explanatory material.

A thirteenth update to the sentencing guidelines for magistrates' courts applies to all offenders aged 18 or over who are sentenced on or after February 1, 2016. Its effect is to incorporate the Sentencing Council's guideline on "theft offences" (*post*, K-315 *et seq.*).

A fourteenth update to the sentencing guidelines for magistrates' courts applies to all organisa- ★ tions and offenders aged 18 or over who are sentenced on or after February 1, 2016. The effect is to incorporate the council's guideline on offences under legislation relating to health and safety and food safety and hygiene (as to which, see *ante*, § 5-147, and *post*, Appendix K-252).

Recommendations

The following recommendations are sentence recommendations where the starting points are **K-148** based on a first time offender who has pleaded not guilty. However, the guideline makes plain that they are to be used by magistrates in making decisions as to whether or not an offender should be tried or sentenced in the magistrates' court or the Crown Court. What is set out below is confined to that which is material to the latter decision. It follows, therefore, that the full range of recommendations is not necessarily set out. For example, in the case of burglary of a dwelling, for a case involving an unforced entry with property of low value being stolen and no aggravating features, the top end of the recommended range is 12 weeks' custody, which is well within the maximum available to a magistrates' court. Any description of offence which is of a less serious nature than the descriptions set out below may, therefore, be taken to be suitable for summary trial.

Whilst the guideline itself lists aggravating and mitigating features for all the offences, these are only set out below where the presence or absence of such features is relevant to the decision as to the appropriate court for trial or sentence.

Burglary in a dwelling

Reference should now be made to the guideline issued by the Sentencing Council of England **K-149** and Wales: see *post*, K-259 *et seq.*

Handling stolen goods

Reference should now be made to the guideline issued by the Sentencing Council of England **K-150** and Wales: see *post*, K-323.

Going equipped for theft

Reference should now be made to the guideline issued by the Sentencing Council of England **K-151** and Wales: see *post*, K-324.

[The next paragraph is K-154.]

False statements/representations to obtain social security benefits

For offences under the Social Security Administration Act 1992, s.111A, see the fraud guideline, **K-154** *post*, K-297 *et seq.*

Vehicle licence/registration fraud (Vehicle Excise and Registration Act 1994, s.44)

The guideline recommends sentence in the Crown Court in the case of (a) use of number **K-155** plates from another vehicle, or (b) the forging or altering of licence/ number plates for sale to another.

Assault occasioning actual bodily harm and racially/religiously aggravated versions

Reference should now be made to the relevant section in the Sentencing Council's guideline on **K-156** assault and other non-fatal offences against the person: see *ante*, K-124.

Inflicting grievous bodily harm/wounding and racially/religiously aggravated versions

K-157   Reference should now be made to the relevant section in the Sentencing Council's guideline on assault and other non-fatal offences against the person: see *ante*, Appendix K-123.

Assault with intent to resist arrest

K-158   Reference should now be made to the relevant section in the Sentencing Council's guideline on assault and other non-fatal offences against the person: see *ante*, Appendix K-125.

Threats to kill

K-159   The guideline recommends sentence in the Crown Court for repeated threats or a threat accompanied by a visible weapon.

Firearm, carrying in public place (Firearms Act 1968, s.19)

K-160   The guideline recommends (but note that certain offences under this section are triable only on indictment (not mentioned in the guideline) and certain offences are triable only summarily, as to which, see § 24-72 in the main work)—

   (i) a starting point of a high level community order and a range of a medium level community order to sentence in the Crown Court for the carrying of an imitation firearm or an unloaded shot gun without ammunition;

   (ii) sentence in the Crown Court for the carrying of a loaded shot gun or for the carrying of a shot gun or any other firearm together with ammunition for it.

Bladed article/offensive weapon (possession of)

K-161   The guideline recommends—

   (i) a starting point of six weeks' custody and a range of a high level community order to sentence in the Crown Court where the weapon was not used to threaten or cause fear but the offence was committed in dangerous circumstances;

   (ii) sentence in the Crown Court where the weapon was used to threaten or cause fear and the offence was committed in dangerous circumstances.

Cruelty to a child

K-162   The guideline recommends—

   (i) a starting point of sentence in the Crown Court and a range of 26 weeks' custody to sentence in the Crown Court for an assault (assaults) resulting in injuries consistent with actual bodily harm, more than one incident of neglect or ill-treatment (but not amounting to long-term behaviour), a single incident of long-term abandonment or regular incidents of short-term abandonment (the longer the period of abandonment or the greater the number of incidents of short-term abandonment, the more serious the offence) or failure to protect a child from any of the foregoing;

   (ii) sentence in the Crown Court for a series of assaults, protracted neglect or ill- treatment, serious cruelty over a period of time or failure to protect a child from any of the foregoing.

Affray

K-163   The guideline recommends 18 weeks' custody as a starting point and a range of 12 weeks' custody to sentence in the Crown Court in the case of a fight involving a weapon or the throwing of objects or conduct causing risk of serious injury.

Harassment (putting people in fear of violence) (Protection from Harassment Act 1997, s.4), and the racially/religiously aggravated version

K-164   The guideline recommends—

   (i) a starting point of 18 weeks' custody and a range of 12 weeks' custody to sentence in the Crown Court for a case involving deliberate threats or persistent action over a longer period or an intention to cause a fear of violence;

(ii) sentence in the Crown Court for "sexual threats, vulnerable person targeted".

Breach of a protective order (other than in a domestic context)

The guideline recommends— **K-165**
   (i) a starting point of sentence in the Crown Court and a range of 26 weeks' custody to sentence in the Crown Court for more than one breach involving some violence and/or significant physical or psychological harm to the victim;
  (ii) sentence in the Crown Court for a breach (one or more) involving significant physical violence and significant physical or psychological harm to the victim.

Witness intimidation

The guideline recommends— **K-166**
   (i) a starting point of 18 weeks' custody and a range of 12 weeks' custody to sentence in the Crown Court for conduct amounting to a threat, staring at, approaching or following witnesses, talking about the case, trying to alter or stop evidence;
  (ii) sentence in the Crown Court for threats of violence to witnesses and/or their families or for deliberately seeking out witnesses.

Sexual assault (SOA 2003, ss.3, 7)

See Sections III and VII of the sexual offences guideline, *ante*, K-85c, K-87b. **K-167**

Child prostitution and pornography

Reference should now be made to the relevant section in the Sentencing Council's guideline on **K-168** sexual offences: see *ante*, Appendix K-92b.

Exploitation of prostitution (SOA 2003, ss.52, 53)

See Section XVII of the sexual offences guideline, *ante*, K-92. **K-169**

Exposure (SOA 2003, s.66)

See Section XXVIII of the sexual offences guideline, *ante*, K-100. **K-170**

Voyeurism (SOA 2003, s.67)

See Section XXIX of the sexual offences guideline, *ante*, K-101. **K-171**

Keeping a brothel used for prostitution (SOA 1956, s.33A)

See Section XVIII of the sexual offences guideline, *ante*, K-92a. **K-172**

Indecent photographs of children

See Section XVI of the sexual offences guideline, *ante*, K-91. **K-173**

Failure to comply with the notification requirements applicable to sex offenders

The guideline recommends a starting point of 18 weeks' custody and a range of six weeks' **K-174** custody to sentence in the Crown Court for a deliberate failure to comply or the supply of information known to be false accompanied by long-period of non-compliance or attempts to avoid detection.

Drugs

See *ante*, K-147; and *post*, K-271 *et seq.* **K-175**

[The next paragraph is K-179.]

Dangerous driving

The guideline recommends sentence in the Crown Court for (a) prolonged bad driving involv- **K-179** ing deliberate disregard for the safety of others, (b) incidents involving excessive speed or showing off, especially on busy roads or in a built up area, by a disqualified driver, or while driver was being pursued by the police.

Aggravated vehicle-taking (damage to property other than the vehicle taken in accident or to the vehicle)

K-180   The guideline recommends sentence in the Crown Court if the vehicle was taken as part of a burglary or from private premises and the damage caused was valued at in excess of £5,000.

Aggravated vehicle-taking (dangerous driving or accident causing injury)

K-181   The guideline recommends sentence in the Crown Court if there was a course of prolonged bad driving involving deliberate disregard for the safety of others.

Arson

K-182   The guideline recommends sentence in the Crown Court in the case of "significant" damage.

Criminal damage (not arson) and racially/religiously aggravated version of offence

K-183   The guideline recommends sentence in the Crown Court if the value of the damage done was in excess of £10,000.

Identity documents (possession of false or of another's improperly obtained) (Identity Cards Act 2006, s.25(5))

K-184   The guideline recommends—
   (i) a starting point of 12 weeks' custody and a range of a six weeks' custody to sentence in the Crown Court for a small number of documents where there is no evidence of dealing;
   (ii) sentence in the Crown Court for "considerable number of documents possessed, evidence of involvement in larger operation".

M. Causing Death by Driving

K-185   The Sentencing Guidelines Council has issued a guideline on the offences of causing death by dangerous driving (RTA 1988, s.1), causing death by careless driving when under the influence of drink or drugs or having failed without reasonable excuse either to provide a specimen for analysis or to permit the analysis of a blood sample (*ibid.*, s.3A), causing death by careless or inconsiderate driving (*ibid.*, s.2B) and causing death by driving while unlicensed, disqualified or uninsured (*ibid.*, s.3ZB). The guideline applies to offenders aged 18 or over who are sentenced on or after August 4, 2008, and is based on first-time offenders convicted after trial.

The guideline has an introduction and four parts. Part A sets out factors relating to the assessment of seriousness, Part B relates to ancillary orders, Part C contains explanatory material relating to sentencing ranges and starting points, and a description of the decision making process, and Part D contains the offence guidelines. The introduction also refers to Annex A which sets out the statutory definitions of dangerous driving, careless driving and inconsiderate driving, and gives examples.

The introduction makes plain that since the causing of death is common to all offences covered by the guideline, the factor that is going to have the greatest weight in determining a starting point for any particular offence will be the culpability of the offender and, accordingly, the primary task for the court (apart from s.3ZB cases) will be an evaluation of the quality of the driving involved and the degree of danger that it foreseeably created. The degree of intoxication must also be considered where this is an element of the offence. The introduction further points out that the guideline draws a distinction between those factors of an offence that are intrinsic to the quality of the driving ("determinants of seriousness") and those which, while they aggravate the offence (*e.g.* more than one death), are not.

Part A: Assessing seriousness

Determinants of seriousness

K-186   There are five determinants of seriousness, for each of which the guideline sets out examples:

(i) the offender's awareness of risk (*e.g.* typified by a prolonged, persistent and deliberate course of bad driving), (ii) where the presence of alcohol or drugs is not an element of the offence, the effect of consumption of any alcohol or drugs (which includes a failure to supply a specimen for analysis (unless inherent in the offence or charged separately) and the consumption of legal drugs where this impaired the offender's ability to drive and the offender knew or should have known about the likelihood of impairment), (iii) whether the offender was driving at an inappropriate speed, (iv) whether the offender behaved in a seriously culpable manner, and (v) the identity of the victim (*e.g.* failing to have regard to, and to take extra care when driving near, vulnerable road users such as cyclists, motorcyclists, horse riders, pedestrians and those working in the road).

Examples of (iv), *ante*, are aggressive driving, driving whilst using a hand-held mobile telephone, driving whilst the driver's attention is avoidably distracted (*e.g.* reading or adjusting the controls of electronic equipment), driving when knowingly suffering from a medical or physical condition that significantly impairs the offender's driving skills (including failure to take prescribed medication), driving when knowingly deprived of adequate sleep or rest, particularly where this is caused by commercial concerns, and driving a poorly maintained or dangerously loaded vehicle, again, particularly where this is caused by commercial concerns. A distinction is drawn between ordinary avoidable distractions and gross avoidable distractions (*e.g.* reading or composing a text message over a period of time), but where the degree of impairment is so serious that it is used to determine whether the offence is based on dangerous or careless driving, care must be taken to avoid double counting.

Aggravating and mitigating factors

Once the court has considered the determinants of seriousness, it must then consider whether **K-187** any aggravating or mitigating factors affect culpability so as to increase or decrease the starting point, or move the offence into a different sentencing range. When assessing seriousness, the court should have regard to the full list of aggravating and mitigating factors set out in the guideline on seriousness (*ante*, § K-13) and the particular aggravating and mitigating factors applicable to each offence, a key to which is set out, *post*:

Key to aggravating factors:

		K-188
1	Previous convictions for motoring offences, particularly offences that involve bad driving or the consumption of excessive alcohol or drugs before driving.	
2	Previous convictions for motoring offences, particularly offences that involve bad driving.	
3	Previous convictions for motoring offences, whether involving bad driving or an offence of the same kind that forms part of the present conviction.	
4	More than one person killed as a result of the offence. Where the number of deaths is high and that was reasonably foreseeable, this is likely to provide sufficient justification for moving an offence into the next highest sentencing range.	
5	Serious injury to one or more victims, in addition to the death(s).	
6	Disregard of warnings.	
7	Other offences committed at the same time, such as driving other than in accordance with the terms of a valid licence, driving while disqualified, etc.	
8	Irresponsible behaviour such as failing to stop, falsely claiming that one of the victims was responsible, or trying to throw the victim off the car by swerving in order to escape.	
9	Irresponsible behaviour such as failing to stop or falsely claiming that one of the victims was responsible for the collision.	
10	Driving off in an attempt to avoid detection or apprehension.	

Key to mitigating factors:

		K-189
11	Alcohol or drugs consumed unwittingly.	
12	Offender was seriously injured in the collision, but the greater the driver's fault, the less effect this factor should have on mitigation.	

13   The victim was a close friend or relative, but the greater the driver's fault, the less effect
this factor should have on mitigation.

14   Actions of the victim or a third party contributed significantly to the likelihood of a
collision occurring and/ or death resulting.

15   Actions of the victim or a third party contributed to the commission of the offence.

16   The offender's lack of driving experience contributed significantly to the likelihood of a
collision occurring and/ or death resulting.

17   The offender's lack of driving experience contributed to the commission of the offence.

18   The driving was in response to a proven and genuine emergency falling short of a
defence.

19   The offender genuinely believed that he or she was insured or licensed to drive.

Personal mitigation

K-190   If the offender can show that he previously had a good driving record, or can demonstrate
remorse or that he provided direct and positive assistance to a victim at the scene of the accident,
this may justify a reduction in sentence.

Part B: Ancillary orders

K-191   An order disqualifying an offender from driving is usually a mandatory requirement when
sentencing for these offences. In principle, the minimum period of disqualification should either
equate to the length of the custodial sentence imposed or the relevant statutory minimum
disqualification period, whichever results in the longer period of disqualification.

The court may also consider whether to impose an order depriving the offender of property,
e.g., a vehicle.

Part D: Offence guidelines

Causing death by dangerous driving

K-192   There are three levels of seriousness which relate predominantly to the standard of driving.

Level 1 (starting point 8 years, sentencing range of 7–14 years): driving that involved a deliberate decision to ignore (or a flagrant disregard for) the rules of the road and an apparent disregard
for the great danger being caused to others. Determinants of seriousness (as identified *ante*) that
will fix a case at this level include (a) a prolonged, persistent and deliberate course of bad driving,
(b) consumption of substantial amounts of alcohol or drugs leading to gross impairment, and/or
(c) a group of determinants of seriousness which in isolation or smaller number would place the
offence in level 2. The presence of both (a) and (b), particularly if accompanied by aggravating
factors will move the offence towards the top of the sentencing range.

Level 2 (starting point 5 years, sentencing range of 4–7 years): driving that created a *substantial*
risk of danger. Determinants of seriousness that will fix a case at this level include greatly excessive speed, racing or competitive driving, gross avoidable distraction, driving whilst ability to
drive is impaired as a result of consumption of alcohol or drugs, failing to take prescribed
medication or a known medical condition, or a group of determinants of seriousness which in
isolation or smaller number would place the offence in level 3.

Level 3 (starting point 3 years, sentencing range of 2–5 years): driving that created a *significant*
risk of danger. Relevant determinants of seriousness include driving above the speed limit or at a
speed that is inappropriate for the prevailing conditions, driving when knowingly deprived of
adequate sleep or rest or knowing that the vehicle has a dangerous defect or is poorly maintained
or is dangerously loaded, a brief but obvious danger arising from a seriously dangerous
manoeuvre, driving whilst avoidably distracted, or failing to have proper regard to vulnerable
road users. Where the driving is markedly less serious than this level, reference should be made
to the starting point for the most serious level of causing death by careless driving.

Additional aggravating and mitigating factors applicable to sentencing for this offence: 1, 4–8,
10-13, 16, 17 (as to which, see the key, *ante*).

Causing death by careless driving when under the influuence of drink or drugs etc.

The legal limit of alcohol is 35µg breath (80mg in blood and 107mg in urine)	Careless/inconsiderate driving arising from momentary inattention with no aggravating factors	Other cases of careless/inconsiderate driving	Careless/inconsiderate driving falling not far short of dangerousness
Level 1 71µg or above of alcohol/ high quantity of drugs OR deliberate non-provision of specimen where evidence of serious impairment	Starting point 6 years Sentencing range 5–10 years	Starting point 7 years Sentencing range 6–12 years	Starting point 8 years Sentencing range 7–14 years
Level 2 51–70µg of alcohol/ moderate quantity of drugs OR deliberate non-provision of specimen	Starting point 4 years Sentencing range 3–7 years	Starting point 5 years Sentencing range 4–8 years	Starting point 6 years Sentencing range 5–9 years
Level 3 35–50µg of alcohol/ minimum quantity of drugs OR test refused because of honestly held but unreasonable belief	Starting point 18 months Sentencing range 26 weeks–4 years	Starting point 3 years Sentencing range 2–5 years	Starting point 4 years Sentencing range 3–6 years

Additional aggravating and mitigating factors applicable to sentencing for this offence: 1, 4, 5, 7, 9, 11–14, 18 (as to which, see the key, *ante*).

Causing death by careless or inconsiderate driving

There are three levels of seriousness defined by the degree of carelessness involved in the **K-194** standard of driving. A fine is unlikely to be an appropriate sentence for this offence. The most likely requirements to be included in a community order are unpaid work requirements, activity requirements, programme requirements and curfew requirements.

Level 1 (starting point 15 months, sentencing range of 36 weeks–3 years): careless or inconsiderate driving falling not far short of dangerous driving.

Level 2 (starting point 36 weeks, sentencing range of community order (high)–2 years): other cases of careless or inconsiderate driving.

Level 3 (starting point community order (medium), sentencing range of community order (low)-community order (high)): careless or inconsiderate driving arising from momentary inattention with no aggravating features. Examples include misjudging the speed of a vehicle or turning without seeing an oncoming vehicle because of restricted visibility.

Additional aggravating and mitigating factors applicable to sentencing for this offence: 2, 4, 5, 7, 9, 11, 12, 14, 15, 17 (as to which, see the key, *ante*).

Causing death by driving while unlicensed, disqualified or uninsured

A fine is unlikely to be an appropriate sentence for this offence. **K-195**

Level 1 (starting point 12 months, sentencing range 36 weeks–2 years): (i) the offender was disqualified from driving or (ii) the offender was unlicensed or uninsured and there are two or more aggravating features from the list, *post*.

Level 2 (starting point 26 weeks, sentencing range of community order (high)–36 weeks): the offender was unlicensed or uninsured and there was at least one aggravating factor from the list, *post*.

Level 3 (starting point community order (medium), sentencing range of community order (low)-community order (high)): the offender was unlicensed or uninsured, with no aggravating factors.

Additional aggravating and mitigating factors applicable to sentencing for this offence: 3, 4, 5, 9, 11, 12, 17, 19 (as to which, see the key, *ante*).

N. Breach of an Anti-Social Behaviour Order

Summary

K-196   The Sentencing Guidelines Council issued a guideline on the sentencing of offenders convicted of breaching an anti-social behaviour order. It applies to the sentencing of adult and young offenders, who are sentenced on or after January 5, 2009, and is based on first-time offenders (*i.e.* in respect of adult offenders, those who do not have a previous conviction for breach of an anti-social behaviour order and, in respect of young offenders, to have its usual meaning) convicted after trial. Since the sentencing framework for offenders under 18 is significantly different from that for older offenders, the guidance for young offenders is in the form of principles (see Part E, *post*). It is noted that regard should also be had to the approach to sentencing for breaches of orders set out in the guideline on new sentences (*ante*, K-28 *et seq.*) and the guideline on breach of a protective order (*ante*, K-81).

The guideline is in five parts. Part A sets out section 1(10), and summarises the effect of section 1(11), of the CDA 1998, Part B is an introduction, Part C sets out factors relating to the assessment of seriousness, Part D contains explanatory material relating to sentencing ranges and starting points, a description of the decision making process, and the sentencing guideline for adult offenders, and Part E sets out sentencing principles in relation to young offenders.

Anti-social behaviour orders in criminal proceedings have now been replaced by criminal behaviour orders: see §§ 5-1198 *et seq.* in the main work. As there are few significant differences between the old and the new orders, there seems to be no reason why this guideline should not be applied to breaches of criminal behaviour orders.

Part B: introduction

K-197   The main aim of sentencing for breach of an order is to achieve the purpose of the order. When sentencing, the primary consideration should therefore be to reflect the harassment, alarm or distress involved, with the fact that it constituted a breach of a court order (and the consequent harm caused by the undermining of public confidence in the effective administration of justice) being a secondary consideration.

Part C: assessing seriousness

K-198   This must be assessed by considering the offender's culpability in committing the offence and the harm which the offence caused, was intended to cause, or might foreseeably have caused. In order properly to assess the seriousness of a breach, a court needs to be aware of the purpose of the order and the context in which it was made. To this end, Annex A summarises the key principles and considerations applicable when making an order. Whereas a breach may be of one or more prohibitions in an order, the approach to sentencing should be based on an assessment of the seriousness of the harm arising from the breach (or intended by the offender) rather than the number of prohibitions not complied with.

Culpability and harm

K-199   When determining the seriousness of a breach, the court will need to consider (a) the degree to which the offender intended to breach the order, and (b) the degree to which the offender intended to cause the harm that resulted (or could have resulted).

Relevance of the originating conduct

K-200   As stated in previous guidelines, the original conduct that led to the making of an order is relevant in so far as it indicates the level of harm caused and whether this was intended. High culpability and/ or harm may be indicated if the breach continues a pattern of behaviour against an identifiable victim, but the offence may be less serious if there is little connection between the breach and the behaviour that the order was aimed at. The court should examine the prohibitions of the order itself (particularly those in older orders made without the benefit of the guidance set out in Annex A), and their necessity and reasonableness in the circumstances.

Breach of an interim order

Breach of such an order is as serious as breach of a final order, and the same approach to **K-201** sentencing should be taken. If the hearing regarding the final order can be brought forward, this should be done so that the two issues can be considered together, but sentencing for the interim breach should not be delayed for this purpose and should take place as soon as possible. The court should also consider the extent to which an urgent need for specific interim prohibitions was originally demonstrated, or if the interim order was sought principally in order to obtain additional time to prepare a case for the full hearing.

Breach that also constitutes another criminal offence

If the substantive offence only has been charged, the fact that it also constitutes breach of an **K-202** anti-social behaviour order should be treated as an aggravating factor.

If breach of the order only has been charged, the sentence should reflect the full circumstances of the breach, which will include the conduct that could have been charged as a substantive offence.

Where breach of the order also constitutes another offence with a lower maximum penalty, that penalty is an element to be considered in the interests of proportionality, although the court will not be limited by it.

Aggravating and mitigating factors

For ease of reference, Annex B sets out the aggravating and mitigating factors in the guideline **K-203** on seriousness (*ante*, K-13 *et seq.*) that might increase or mitigate the seriousness of an offence. Additional aggravating and mitigating factors are identified in the guideline (*post*).

Personal mitigation

This is particularly relevant to breach of an anti-social behaviour order, since compliance **K-204** depends on an ability to understand its terms and make rational decisions. Sentence may be mitigated where the offender has a lower level of understanding due to mental health issues or learning difficulties, was acting under the influence of an older or more experienced offender or has complied with an individual support order or intervention order imposed at the same time as the anti-social behaviour order.

Part D: sentencing guideline—adult offenders

There are three levels of seriousness: **K-205**

    (i) *serious harm caused or intended*: examples may involve the use of violence, significant threats or intimidation, or the targeting of individuals or groups of people in a manner that leads to a fear of violence;

    (ii) *lesser degree of harm intended or likely*: examples may include lesser degrees of threats or intimidation, the use of seriously abusive language or causing more than minor damage to property;

    (iii) *no harm caused or intended*: examples may involve being drunk or begging, the prohibited use of public transport, or entry into a prohibited area, provided there is no evidence that harassment, alarm or distress was caused or intended.

The suggested starting points, *post*, are based on the assumption that the offender had the **K-206** highest level of culpability (*i.e.* he intended the breach). Care needs to be taken to ensure that there is no double counting when an element of the breach determines the level of seriousness where it might in other circumstances be an aggravating factor. In the most serious cases involving repeat offending and a breach causing serious harassment, together with the presence of several aggravating factors such as the use of violence, a sentence beyond the highest range will be justified.

A conditional discharge is not available as a sentence for this offence.

Nature of failure and harm	Starting point	Sentencing range
Serious harassment, alarm or distress has been caused or where such harm was intended	26 weeks' custody	Custody threshold–2 years' custody
Lesser degree of harassment, alarm or distress, where such harm was intended, or where it would have been likely if the offender had not been apprehended	6 weeks' custody	Community order (medium)–26 weeks' custody
No harassment, alarm or distress was actually caused by the breach and none was intended by the offender	Community order (low)	Fine (Band B)–community order (medium)

K-207   Additional aggravating factors:
  (i) offender has a history of disobedience to court orders;
  (ii) breach was committed immediately or shortly after the order was made;
  (iii) breach was committed subsequent to earlier breach proceedings arising from the same order;
  (iv) targeting of a person the order was made to protect or a witness in the original proceedings.

Additional mitigating factors:
  (i) breach occurred after a long period of compliance;
  (ii) the prohibition(s) breached was/were not fully understood, especially where an interim order was made without notice.

Part E: sentencing guideline—young offenders

K-208   It is noted that the principles covered in Part C apply equally to young offenders.

Apart from those cases where the court is bound to make a referral order, in less serious cases, such as where the breach has not involved any harassment, alarm or distress, a fine may be appropriate if it will be paid by the offender; otherwise a reparation order. In most cases, however, the appropriate sentence will be a community sentence. The custody threshold should be set at a significantly higher level than for adults, and will usually not be crossed unless the breach involves serious harassment alarm or distress (as to which, see the levels of seriousness, *ante*). Exceptionally, the custody threshold may also be crossed where a youth is being sentenced for more than one offence of breach (committed on separate occasions within a short period) involving a lesser but substantial degree of harassment, alarm or distress. Even where the custody threshold is crossed, the court should normally impose a community sentence in preference to a detention and training order and custody should be used only as a last resort. Where custody is unavoidable, the starting point for sentencing should be four months' detention, with a range of up to 12 months. Where the youth is being sentenced for more than one breach involving serious harassment, alarm or distress, however, the sentence may go beyond that range.

Factors likely to aggravate or mitigate a breach are the same as the additional factors listed in the guideline for adult offenders (*ante*) and the principles relating to personal mitigation (*ante*) also apply. In addition, peer pressure and lack of parental support may justify mitigation of sentence.

When imposing a community sentence, a court must consider what requirements will best prevent further offending and the individual circumstances of the offender, including his particular stage of intellectual or emotional maturity. Any requirements imposed must be compatible both with each other and with the prohibitions of the anti-social behaviour order, if it remains in force, and the combination of both must not be so onerous as to make further breaches likely.

O. Theft and Burglary in a Building Other Than a Dwelling

Summary

The Sentencing Guidelines Council issued a guideline on these offences. It applies only to of- **K-209**
fenders aged 18 and over, who fell to be sentenced on or after January 5, 2009, and is based on
first-time offenders convicted after trial.

As to burglary, it has been overtaken by a guideline issued by the Sentencing Council of
England and Wales: see K-259 *et seq., post.*

With effect from February 1, 2016, this guideline will also be superseded, in relation to theft,
by the Sentencing Council's guideline on "theft offences" (*post,* K-315 *et seq.*).

The guideline is in five parts. Part A sets out the statutory provisions relating to the offences,
Part B sets out factors relating to the assessment of seriousness, Part C relates to ancillary orders,
Part D contains explanatory material relating to sentencing ranges and starting points, and a
description of the decision making process, and Part E contains the offence guidelines.

Part A: statutory provisions

In addition to setting out the relevant statutory provisions, the mode of trial and the maximum **K-210**
penalties, Part A states that (i) in relation to burglary, the guideline relates solely to cases in which
an offender enters a building other than a dwelling as a trespasser with intent to steal or, having
entered a building as a trespasser, actually goes on to steal, and (ii) the forms of theft covered by
the guideline are theft in breach of trust, theft in a dwelling, theft from persons, and theft from
shops; but that (iii) the principles in Parts B and C are of general application and likely to be of
assistance where a court is sentencing for any other form of theft.

Part B: assessing seriousness

This must be assessed by considering the offender's culpability in committing the offence and **K-211**
the harm which the offence caused, was intended to cause, or might foreseeably have caused.
When assessing the harm caused, the starting point should be the loss suffered by the victim.
However, the monetary value might not reflect the full extent of the harm and the court should
take into account the impact of the offence on the particular victim (*e.g.* where the value of the
loss is high in proportion to the victim's financial circumstances), any harm to a person other than
the immediate victim, and any harm in the form of public concern or erosion of public confidence.

Aggravating and mitigating factors which may affect the seriousness of the offence must be
considered, including those identified in the guideline on seriousness (*ante,* K-13 *et seq.*) (and set
out in Annex A) and the additional factors identified in each offence guideline. Since the suggested starting points and sentencing ranges are based on the assumption that the offender was
motivated by greed or a desire to live beyond his means, in order to avoid double counting, such
a motivation should not be treated as a factor that increases culpability. The aggravating factors
from the seriousness guideline most relevant to these offences are planning, offenders operating
in groups or gangs and deliberate targeting of vulnerable victims, and the most relevant aggravating factors indicating a more than usually serious degree of harm are particularly vulnerable
victims, high levels of gain and the high value (including sentimental value) of property to the
victim or substantial consequential loss.

The court must also consider the following matters of personal mitigation: return of stolen
property (depending on voluntariness and timeliness of return), whether the offender has been
motivated by addiction (in which case, while seriousness will not be mitigated, it may be appropriate to impose a drug rehabilitation requirement, alcohol treatment requirement or activity or
supervision requirement, as part of a community or suspended sentence order), and whether the
offender has been motivated by desperation or need (which may count as personal mitigation in
exceptional circumstances).

Part C: ancillary orders

The ancillary orders which a court must consider are restitution (PCC(S)A 2000, s.148 (§ 5-711 **K-212**
in the main work)), compensation (*ibid.,* s.130 (§ 5-691 in the main work)), deprivation (*ibid.,* s.143
(§ 5-726 in the main work)) and confiscation (PCA 2002, s.6 (§ 5-805 in the main work)). Neither

restitution nor compensation orders should normally impact or influence the choice of sentence. However, where an offender has acted (as opposed to offered) to free assets in order to pay compensation, this is akin to making voluntary restitution and may be regarded as personal mitigation. In making compensation orders, consideration should be given to the wishes of the victim and, where it is difficult to ascertain the full amount of the loss suffered, the making of an order for an amount representing the agreed or likely loss.

Part D: offence guidelines

Theft in breach of trust

K-213   While the seriousness of the offence will generally increase in line with the level of trust breached, the extent to which the nature and degree of trust placed in an offender should be regarded as increasing seriousness will depend on a careful assessment of the circumstances of each individual case, including the type and terms of the relationship between the offender and victim. A court should also consider whether a suspended sentence would be appropriate, particularly where this may allow reparation to be made either to the victim or to the community at large.

Type/ nature of activity	Starting point	Sentencing range
Theft of £125,000 or more **or** theft of £20,000 or more in breach of a high degree of trust	3 years' custody	2–6 years' custody
Theft of £20,000 or more but less than £125,000 **or** theft of £2,000 or more but less than £20,000 in breach of a high degree of trust	2 years' custody	12 months–3 years' custody
Theft of £2,000 or more but less than £20,000 **or** theft of less than £2,000 in breach of a high degree of trust	18 weeks' custody	Community order (high)–12 months' custody
Theft of less than £2,000	Community order (medium)	Fine–26 weeks' custody

K-214   Additional aggravating factors:
  (i) long course of offending;
  (ii) suspicion deliberately thrown on others;
  (iii) offender motivated by intention to cause harm or out of revenge.
    Additional mitigating factors:
  (i) offender has been given inappropriate degree of trust or responsibility;
  (ii) genuine cessation of offending before discovery (particularly where evidence of remorse);
  (iii) offender reports undiscovered offending;
  (iv) other than in the most exceptional of circumstances, loss of employment and any consequential hardship should *not* constitute personal mitigation.

Theft in a dwelling

K-215   It is noted that the guideline does not apply where the offender has been convicted of a burglary.
    For the purposes of the table, post, property should generally be regarded as having a high monetary value if it is worth more than £2,000 and a victim is vulnerable if he is targeted by the offender because it is anticipated that he will be unlikely or unable to resist the theft.

Type/ nature of activity	Starting point	Sentencing range
Where the effect on the victim is particularly severe, the stolen property is of high value (see ante), or substantial consequential loss (e.g. serious disruption to victim's life or business)		

Type/ nature of activity	Starting point	Sentencing range
results, a sentence higher than the range into which the offence otherwise would fall may be appropriate		
Theft from a vulnerable victim (see *ante*) involving intimidation or the use or threat of force (falling short of robbery) or the use of deception	18 months' custody	12 months–3 years' custody
Theft from a vulnerable victim	18 weeks' custody	Community order (high)–12 months' custody
Theft not involving vulnerable victim	Community order (medium)	Fine–18 weeks' custody

Additional aggravating factors: **K-216**
  (i) offender motivated by intention to cause harm or out of revenge;
  (ii) intimidation or face-to-face confrontation with victim (except where this takes the offence into a higher sentencing range);
  (iii) use of force, or threat of force, against victim (not amounting to robbery) (except where this takes the offence into a higher sentencing range);
  (iv) use of deception (except where this takes the offence into a higher sentencing range);
  (v) offender takes steps to prevent the victim from reporting the crime or seeking help.

Theft from the person
  It is noted that the guideline does not apply where the offender has been convicted of robbery **K-216a**
(the guideline for which is set out *ante*, K-80 *et seq.*). As to the approach, to issues of local prevalence, see the seriousness guideline (*ante*, K-27). Issues of national prevalence should *not* be used by sentencers to justify including a deterrent element as this is already taken into account in these and other guidelines.
  For the purposes of the table, post, property should generally be regarded as having a high monetary value if it is worth more than £2,000 and a victim is vulnerable if he is targeted by the offender because it is anticipated that he will be unlikely or unable to resist the theft (*e.g.* because of youth or age or disability).

Type/ nature of activity	Starting point	Sentencing range
Where the effect on the victim is particularly severe, the stolen property is of high value (see ante), or substantial consequential loss (e.g. serious disruption to victim's life or business) results, a sentence higher than the range into which the offence otherwise would fall may be appropriate		
Theft from a vulnerable victim (see *ante*) involving intimidation or the use or threat of force (falling short of robbery)	18 months' custody	12 months–3 years' custody
Theft from a vulnerable victim	18 weeks' custody	Community order (high)–12 months' custody
Theft not involving vulnerable victim	Community order (medium)	Fine–18 weeks' custody

Additional aggravating factors: **K-216b**
  (i) offender motivated by intention to cause harm or out of revenge;
  (ii) intimidation or face-to-face confrontation with victim (except where this takes the offence into a higher sentencing range);
  (iii) use of force, or threat of force, against victim (not amounting to robbery) (except where this takes the offence into a higher sentencing range);

(iv) high level of inconvenience caused to victim, *e.g.* replacing house keys, credit cards, etc., or where the victim is a tourist.

Theft from a shop

K-217   When assessing the level of harm, the circumstances of the retailer (*e.g.* size) are a proper consideration. However, the seriousness of an individual case must be judged on its own dimension of harm and culpability and the sentence on an individual offender should not be increased to reflect the harm caused to retailers in general by the totality of this type of offending (*e.g.* higher insurance premiums, cost of preventative security measures). Whereas the seriousness guideline requires the value of goods to be taken into account in property offences, where this is associated with other aggravating factors such as the degree of planning and/or operating in a group, care will need to be taken to avoid double counting.

When taking previous convictions into account, if the offender demonstrates a level of persistent or seriously persistent offending, the community and custody thresholds may be crossed even though the other characteristics of the offence would otherwise warrant a lesser sentence.

Type/ nature of activity	Starting point	Sentencing range
Organised gang/ group **and** intimidation or the use or threat of force (short of robbery)	12 months' custody	36 weeks–4 years' custody
Significant intimidation or threats **or** use of force resulting in slight injury **or** very high level of planning **or** significant related damage	6 weeks' custody	Community order (high)–36 weeks' custody
Low level intimidation or threats **or** some planning, *e.g.* a session of stealing on the same day or going equipped **or** some related damage	Community order (low)	Fine–community order (medium)
Little or no planning or sophistication **and** goods stolen of low value	Fine	Conditional discharge–community order (low)

K-218   Additional aggravating factors:
  (i) child accompanying offender where child is involved or aware of theft;
  (ii) offender is subject to a banning order that includes the store targeted (care to be taken to avoid double counting where offender also being sentenced for breach of order);
  (iii) offender motivated by intention to cause harm or out of revenge;
  (iv) professional offending;
  (v) victim particularly vulnerable (*e.g.* small, independent shop);
  (vi) offender targeted high value goods;
  (vii) intimidation, threat or use of force (falling short of robbery) and additional damage to property.

[The next paragraph is K-221.]

P. ATTEMPTED MURDER

K-221   The Sentencing Guidelines Council has issued a guideline which applies only to the sentencing of offenders aged 18 and over, who are sentenced on or after July 27, 2009, and is based on first-time offenders convicted after trial. The guideline is not intended to provide for an offence found to be based on a genuine belief that murder would be an act of mercy, although the approach to assessing the seriousness in such cases might be similar.

Part A: Assessing seriousness

This must be assessed, first, by considering the offender's culpability in committing the offence. **K-222**
While an offender convicted of an offence of attempted murder will have already demonstrated a
high level of culpability (intention to kill), the precise level of culpability will vary in line with the
circumstances of the offence (*e.g.* whether a weapon was used) and whether it was planned or
spontaneous.

Next, the court must consider the harm caused. Since there is a potential imbalance between
culpability and harm, the degree of (or lack of) physical or psychological harm suffered by a
victim may generally influence sentence, in particular where the degree of harm actually caused
to the victim is negligible.

Aggravating and mitigating factors will also affect the seriousness of the offence. The court
should consider (i) the specific factors identified in Part D (*post*), which follow those set out in the
CJA 2003, Sched. 21 (§ 5-425 in the main work), (ii) the factors identified in the guideline on
seriousness (*ante*, K-13 *et seq.*), although, here, care needs to be taken to ensure that there is no
double counting where an essential element of the offence charged might, in other circumstances,
be an aggravating factor, and (iii) the additional statutory aggravating factor introduced by the
Counter-Terrorism Act 2008, s.30 (§ 25-213 in the main work) and Sched. 2 (offence having a terrorist connection).

Part B: ancillary orders

A court must consider making a compensation order.   **K-223**

Part C: sentencing ranges and starting points

Part C contains explanatory material relating to sentencing ranges and starting points, and a   **K-224**
description of the decision making process. This is largely repetitious of material that appears in
previous guidelines (see, in particular, the guideline on the assessment of seriousness, *ante*, K-13
et seq., and, in relation to sexual offences, *ante*, K-85).

Part D: offence guidelines

K-225

Nature of offence	Starting point	Sentencing range
Level 1		
The most serious offences including those which (if the charge had been murder) would come within the 2003 Act, Sched. 21, paras 4 and 5		
Serious and long term physical or psychological harm	30 years' custody	27–35 years' custody
Some physical or psychological harm	20 years" custody	17–25 years' custody
Little or no physical or psychological harm	15 years' custody	12–20 years' custody
Level 2		
Other planned attempt to kill		
Serious and long term physical or psychological harm	20 years' custody	17–25 years' custody
Some physical or psychological harm	15 years' custody	12–20 years' custody
Little or no physical or psychological harm	10 years' custody	7–15 years' custody
Level 3		
Other spontaneous attempt to kill		
Serious and long term physical or psychological harm	15 years' custody	12–20 years' custody
Some physical or psychological harm	12 years' custody	9–17 years' custody
Little or no physical or psychological harm	9 years' custody	6–14 years' custody

K-226   Specific aggravating factors:
   (i) the fact that the victim was particularly vulnerable, *e.g.*, because of age or disability;
   (ii) mental or physical suffering inflicted on the victim;
   (iii) the abuse of a position of trust;
   (iv) the use of duress or threats against another person to facilitate the commission of the offence;
   (v) the fact that the victim was providing a public service or performing a public duty.

K-227   Specific mitigating factors:
   (i) the fact that the offender suffered from any mental disorder or mental disability which lowered his degree of culpability;
   (ii) the fact that the offender was provoked (for example, by prolonged stress);
   (iii) the fact that the offender acted to any extent in self-defence;
   (iv) the age of the offender.

[The next paragraph is K-240.]

Q. Sentencing Youths

K-240   The Sentencing Guidelines Council issued a definitive guideline in relation to the sentencing of offenders who are under 18 years of age. It applies to any sentence imposed on or after November 30, 2009. The foreword states that the offence-specific guidelines for youths convicted of offences under the SOA 2003 which have a lower maximum penalty when committed by a person under the age of 18 (*ante*, K-83 *et seq.*), and of robbery (*ante*, K-80), continue to apply and are not superseded by these guidelines. As with other guidelines issued by the council, there is a great deal of repetition both within the guideline itself and of material from other guidelines.

General approach

Statutory provisions

K-241   As well as summarising key statutory provisions, this section reminds sentencers that they must be aware of a range of international conventions which emphasise the importance of avoiding "criminalisation" of young people while ensuring that they are held responsible for their actions and, where possible, take part in repairing the damage that they have caused, the intention being to establish responsibility and to promote re-integration rather than to impose retribution.

Sentencing principles

K-242   The approach will be individualistic, with the response varying significantly according to the actual age and maturity of the offender. Sentences must remain proportionate (except in the case of dangerous offenders), with particular care needing to be taken where a young person has committed a relatively less serious offence but there is a high risk of re-offending. Whilst a court is sometimes required to treat the seriousness of an offence as aggravated where there are previous convictions (CJA 2003, s.143(2) (§ 5-67 in the main work)), a sentence that follows re-offending does not need to be more severe than a previous sentence solely because of the previous conviction.

   As to the CDA 1998, s.37 (principal aim of the youth justice system is to prevent offending by children and young people (§ 5-63 in the main work)), the guideline points out that, in relation to the offender, this incorporates the need to demonstrate that his conduct is not acceptable in a way that makes an impact on him whilst also identifying and seeking to address any other factors that make offending more likely; and that, for any victim and society as a whole, it incorporates the need to demonstrate that the law is being effectively enforced and to sustain confidence in the rule of law. Overall, the emphasis should be on approaches that seem most likely to be effective in realising the aim set out in section 37.

   As to the duty to have regard to the welfare of the offender (CYPA 1933, s.44 (§ 5-64 in the main work)), a court should ensure that it is alert to—
   (i) the high incidence of mental health problems and learning difficulties or disabilities amongst young people in the criminal justice system;

(ii) the effect that speech and language difficulties might have on the ability of the young person (or any adult with them) to communicate with the court, to understand the sanction imposed or to fulfil the obligations resulting from that sanction;

(iii) the extent to which young people anticipate that they will be discriminated against by those in authority and the effect that it has on the way that they conduct themselves during court proceedings;

(iv) the vulnerability of young people to self harm, particularly within a custodial environment;

(v) the extent to which the changes which take place during adolescence can lead to experimentation; and

(vi) the effect on young people of experiences of loss or abuse.

Effect on sentence of the offender being a young person

There is an expectation that, generally, a youth will be dealt with less severely than an adult, **K-243** although the distinction diminishes as the offender approaches the age of 18. Factors which govern the approach to the sentencing of young people who offend (compared with the approach for adult offenders), and which will affect the sentence imposed in individual cases, include:

(i) offending by a young person is frequently a phase which passes fairly rapidly and therefore the reaction to it needs to be kept well balanced in order to avoid alienating the young person from society;

(ii) a criminal conviction at this stage of a person's life may have a disproportionate impact on the ability of the offender to gain meaningful employment and play a worthwhile role in society;

(iii) the impact of punishment is felt more heavily by young people in the sense that any sentence will seem far longer in comparison with their relative age than a like sentence imposed on an adult;

(iv) young people may be receptive to changing the way they conduct themselves and should be able to respond more quickly to interventions;

(v) young people should be given greater opportunity to learn from their mistakes; and

(vi) young people will be no less vulnerable than adults to the contaminating influences that can be expected within a custodial context and probably more so.

Having taken account of all relevant considerations, the court should, within a disposal that is no more restrictive of liberty than is proportionate to the seriousness of the offence(s), impose a sentence which:

(i) confronts the young offender with the consequences of the offending (either for the offender himself, his family, the victim(s) or the community), and helps him to develop a sense of personal responsibility;

(ii) tackles the particular factors (personal, family, social, educational or health) that put the young person at risk of offending;

(iii) strengthens those factors that reduce the risk that the young person will continue to offend;

(iv) encourages reparation; and

(v) defines, agrees and reinforces the responsibilities of the parents.

Crossing a significant age threshold between commission of an offence and sentence

Where an increase in the age of an offender results in the maximum sentence on the date of **K-244** conviction being greater than that available on the date on which the offence was committed, a court should take as its starting point the sentence likely to have been imposed on the date on which the offence was committed. It would be rare for a court to have to consider passing a sentence more severe than the maximum it would have had jurisdiction to pass at the time the offence was committed even where the offender has subsequently attained the age of 18. However, a sentence at or close to the maximum may be appropriate, especially where a serious offence was committed by an offender close to the age threshold.

Persistent offenders

Whereas certain sentences are available only where the offender is a "persistent offender", in **K-245** determining whether a young person is a persistent offender for these purposes a court should consider simply whether he is someone who persists in offending. A finding of persistence may be derived from previous convictions but may also arise from other orders or disposals which require an admission or finding of guilt. A finding of persistence is likely where an offender has been convicted of, or made subject of a pre-court disposal that involved an admission or finding of guilt in relation to, imprisonable offences on at least three occasions in a 12-month period.

Enforcing the responsibilities of parents and guardians

K-246   In considering whether to make a parenting order under the CDA 1998, s.8(6) (§ 5-1282 in the main work), a court must consider the strength of familial relationships and any diversity issues, in particular relating to sexual orientation or race, which might impact on the achievement of the purpose of the order.

Particular sentences and orders

Referral orders

K-247   A court should be prepared to use the full range of periods allowed; in general, orders of 10 to 12 months should be made only for more serious offences. Typically, the length of an order should be three to five months, five to seven months or seven to nine months according to whether the court assesses the seriousness of the offending to be relatively low, of medium seriousness or relatively high.

Financial orders

K-248   It will rarely be appropriate to take an education maintenance allowance or a similar means-related provision into account as a resource from which a young person may pay a financial penalty, especially where the recipient is a young person who is living independently or as part of a household primarily dependent on state benefit.

Youth rehabilitation orders

K-249   From the commencement (on November 30, 2009) of section 1 of the CJIA 2008 (§ 5-314 in the main work), youth rehabilitation orders have been the sole available community sentence for young offenders. Where a court is considering sentence for an offence for which a custodial sentence is justified, a guilty plea may be one of the factors that persuades a court that it can properly impose a youth rehabilitation order instead, and in those circumstances no further adjustment to that sentence would need to be made in order to fulfil the obligation to give credit for the plea. Where, however, the provisional sentence is already a youth rehabilitation order, the necessary reduction for a guilty plea should apply to those requirements within the order that are primarily punitive rather than those which are primarily rehabilitative.

K-249a   **Determining the requirements and the length of an order:** where a court concludes that a youth rehabilitation order is appropriate, taking account of the assessment in the presentence report, the court should consider (i) the requirements that are most suitable for the offender, (ii) what period is necessary to ensure that all requirements may be satisfactorily completed, and (iii) whether the restrictions on liberty that result from those requirements are commensurate with the seriousness of the offence.

K-249b   **Orders with intensive supervision and surveillance:** when imposing a youth rehabilitation order with intensive supervision and surveillance a court must ensure that the requirements are not so onerous as to make the likelihood of a breach almost inevitable.

K-249c   **Orders with a fostering requirement:** it is unlikely that the statutory criteria, contained in Schedule 1, para. 4, to the 2008 Act (§ 5-315 in the main work), will be met in many cases; where they are met and the court is considering making an order, care should be taken to ensure that there is a well developed plan for the care and support of the young person throughout the period of the order and following conclusion of the order.

K-249d   **Breaches:** the primary objective when dealing with a breach of an order is to ensure that the young person completes the requirements imposed by the court. Where the failure arises primarily from non-compliance with reporting or other similar obligations, if a sanction is necessary, the most appropriate one is likely to be the inclusion of, or increase in, a primarily punitive requirement. A court must ensure that it has sufficient information to enable it to understand why the order has been breached and that all steps have been taken by relevant authorities to give the young person appropriate opportunity and support. This will be particularly important if the court is considering imposing a custodial sentence as a result of the breach. Where a court is considering whether a young person has "wilfully and persistently" breached an order, it should apply the same approach as when determining whether an offender is a "persistent offender" (as to which, see *ante*). In particular, a young person almost certainly will have "persistently" breached an order where there have been three breaches (each resulting in an appearance before the court) demonstrating a lack of willingness to comply with the order.

Custodial sentences

Threshold and approach: a pre-sentence report must be considered in all cases before a   **K-250** custodial sentence is imposed. Even where the custody threshold (*viz.* that the youth cannot properly be dealt with by a fine alone or by a youth rehabilitation order) has been crossed, a court is not required to impose a custodial sentence. This is likely only to be the case where a custodial sentence will be more effective in preventing offending by children and young persons. The obligation to have regard to the welfare of the offender will require the court to take account of a wide range of issues including those relating to mental health, capability and maturity.

Length of sentence (offenders aged 15, 16 or 17): where the offender is aged 15, 16 or 17, the   **K-250a** court will need to consider the maturity of the offender as well as age. Where there is no offence-specific guideline it may be appropriate, depending on maturity, to consider a starting point from half to three-quarters of that which would have been identified for an adult offender. The closer the offender was to being 18 when the offence was committed, and the greater the maturity of the offender, or the sophistication of the offence, the closer the starting point is likely to be to that appropriate for an adult. For younger offenders, greater flexibility is required to reflect the potentially wider range of culpability. Where an offence shows considerable planning or sophistication, a court may need to adjust this approach upwards; conversely, where an offender is particularly immature, the approach may need to be adjusted downwards. It will be particularly important to consider maturity when the court has to sentence multiple offenders. When the offenders are of different ages, including when one or more is over 18, the court will also need to have proper regard to parity between their sentences.

Length of sentence (offenders aged under 15): where the offender is under 15, sentence   **K-250b** should normally be imposed in a youth court, and the length of sentence will normally be shorter than for an older offender convicted of the same offence. An offender should be sentenced to detention under the PCC(S)A 2000, s.91 (§ 5-610 in the main work), only where necessary for the protection of the public, either because of the risk of harm from future offending or the persistence of the offending behaviour, or, exceptionally, because the seriousness of the offence alone warrants such a disposal.

Length of sentence (detention and training orders): in determining the term of a detention   **K-250c** and training order the proper approach to taking account of any period for which the offender has been remanded in custody or on bail subject to a qualifying curfew condition and electronic monitoring (see s.101(8) of the Act of 2000 (*ibid.*, § 5-598)) is to reduce, if possible, the length of the part of the sentence that is to be served in custody from what would otherwise have been appropriate, in order to reflect that period.

Trial and sentencing of cases in the Crown Court

A youth will appear for trial and sentence in the Crown Court only when charged with   **K-251** homicide, when subject to a statutory minimum sentence, when charged with a "grave crime" and a youth court has determined that, if convicted, its powers of sentence would be insufficient, or when charged together with an adult offender who has been sent to the Crown Court and it has been determined that the cases should be kept together. Where a sentence under the "dangerous offender" provisions is likely to be needed the youth may be committed for trial or for sentence.

"Grave crimes"

The power of a youth court to commit a young person charged with a "grave crime" for trial   **K-251a** (MCA 1980, s.24 (§ 1-110 in the main work)) should be exercised sparingly, since (i) it is the general policy of Parliament that those under 18 should be tried in a youth court wherever possible, (ii) trial in the Crown Court should be reserved for the most serious cases, recognising the greater formality of the proceedings and the greatly increased number of people involved, and (iii) offenders aged under 15 will rarely attract a period of detention under the "grave crimes" provision, and those under 12 even more rarely. A child aged 10 or 11 (or aged 12 to 14 but not a persistent offender) should be committed to the Crown Court only when charged with an offence of such gravity that, despite the normal prohibition on a custodial sentence for a person of that age, a sentence exceeding two years is a realistic possibility. A young person aged 12 to 17 (for whom a detention and training order could have been imposed) should be committed to the Crown Court only when charged with an offence of such gravity that a sentence substantially beyond the two year maximum for a detention and training order is a realistic possibility.

Dangerous offenders

K-251b   A sentence under the dangerous offender provisions of the CJA 2003 (§§ 5-497, 5-499 in the main work) may be imposed only where an equivalent determinate sentence of at least four years would have been imposed. Criteria relating to future offending and the risk of serious harm must be assessed in light of the maturity of the offender, the possibility of change in a much shorter time than would apply for an adult, and the wider circumstances of a young person. Where a young person charged with a specified offence would not otherwise be committed or sent to the Crown Court for trial, it is generally preferable for the decision whether to commit under these provisions to be taken after conviction.

Remittal from the Crown Court

K-251c   Where a child or young person is convicted before the Crown Court of an offence other than homicide there is an obligation to remit to a youth court for sentence unless it would be undesirable to do so. In considering whether remittal is undesirable, a court should balance the need for expertise in the sentencing of young offenders with the benefits of sentence being imposed by the court which has determined guilt. Particular attention should be given to the obligation to remit where a young person appears before the Crown Court only because he was jointly charged with an adult.

For the full text of the guidelines, see www.sentencing-guidelines.gov.uk/guidelines/council/final.html.

R. Corporate Manslaughter

★K-252   The Sentencing Council for England and Wales has issued a definitive guideline on health and safety offences, corporate manslaughter, and food safety and hygiene offences, applying to all organisations and individuals aged 18 or over, sentenced on or after February 1, 2016, regardless of the date of the offence.

The offences are split into five sections: (i) (applying only to organisations) breach of an employer's duty to employees and non-employees, and breach of health and safety regulations (Health and Safety at Work etc. Act 1974, ss.2, 3 and 33(1)(a) and (c)); (ii) (applying only to individuals) breach of an employer's duty to employees and non-employees, breach of a self-employed person's duty to others, breach of health and safety regulations, and secondary liability (1974 Act, ss.2, 3, 7, 33(1)(a) and (c), 36 and 37); (iii) corporate manslaughter (Corporate Manslaughter and Corporate Homicide Act 2007, s.1 (§ 19-138 in the main work)); (iv) (applying to organisations only) and (v) (applying to individuals only) breach of food safety and hygiene regulations (Food Safety and Hygiene (England) Regulations 2013 (S.I. 2013 No. 2996), reg. 19(1), Food Hygiene (Wales) Regulations 2006 (S.I. 2006 No. 31), reg. 17(1), and the General Food Regulations 2004 (S.I. 2004 No. 3279), reg. 4).

Each of the five sections sets out the steps to be followed to determine the appropriate sentence. In particular, in all cases step two requires the court to use the starting point identified for the relevant category to reach a sentence within the category range. The starting point applies to all offenders irrespective of plea or previous convictions. The court will also need to consider adjustment within the category range for the aggravating or mitigating features set out for each section (based on the key, *post*). These constitute a non-exhaustive list of additional factual elements providing the context of the offence and factors relating to the offender.

As health and safety offences and food safety and food hygiene offences fall outside the scope of this work, only the detail in relation to the offence of corporate manslaughter is included here.

Corporate manslaughter

Key to aggravating and mitigating factors (step two (factors irrelevant to corporate manslaughter have been omitted))

Statutory aggravating factors

A1: Previous convictions, having regard to (a) the nature of the offence to which the conviction relates and its relevance to the current offence; and (b) the time that has elapsed since the conviction. ★K-253

Other aggravating factors

A3: Cost-cutting at the expense of safety

A4: Deliberate concealment of illegal nature of activity

A5: Breach of any court order

A6: Obstruction of justice

A7: Poor health and safety record

A8: Falsification of documentation or licences

A9: Deliberate failure to obtain or comply with relevant licences in order to avoid scrutiny by authorities

A11: Exploiting vulnerable victims

Factors reducing seriousness or reflecting mitigation

M1: No previous convictions or no relevant/ recent convictions

M2: Evidence of steps taken voluntarily to remedy problem

M3: High level of co-operation with the investigation, beyond that which will always be expected

M4: Good health and safety record

M5: Effective health and safety procedures in place

M6: Self-reporting, co-operation and acceptance of responsibility

M14: Other events beyond offender's responsibility contributed to death (likely to exclude actions of victims)

Step one (determining seriousness of offence)

The court should assess factors affecting the seriousness of the offence (where harm and ★K-254 culpability are by definition high) by asking four questions.

(a) How foreseeable was serious injury? Failure to heed warnings or advice from the authorities, employees or others or to respond appropriately to "near misses" in like circumstances may be relevant.

(b) How far short of the appropriate standard did the offender fall? Failure to abide by recognised standards or to provide adequate training or supervision or to have suitable reporting arrangements in place may be relevant.

(c) How common is this kind of breach in this organisation? Was it an isolated incident or representative of systemic failings?

(d) Was there more than one death, or a high risk of further deaths, or serious personal injury in addition to death?

Offence category A: where answers to questions (a) to (d) indicate a high level of harm or culpability.

Offence category B: where answers to questions (a) to (d) indicate a lower level of culpability.

Step two (starting point and category range)

Having determined the category, the court should use the table (*post*) to identify the relevant ★K-255 starting point and range. It should focus on the organisation's annual turnover or equivalent to reach a starting point and then consider further adjustment within the category range for aggravating and mitigating features (*post*).

Obtaining financial information

★K-256   The offender is expected to provide comprehensive accounts for the last three years and the guideline sets out which documents a court would require for companies, partnerships, local authorities, fire authorities and similar bodies, health trusts and charities. For companies, partnerships and charities, accounts should be produced; in the case of companies, limited partnerships and charities, these should be audited accounts. In the case of companies and partnerships, particular attention should be paid to turnover, profit before tax, directors' remuneration (partners' drawings), loan accounts and pension provision, and assets, as disclosed by the balance sheet. For local authorities, police and fire authorities and similar public bodies, it is said that reference should be made to their annual revenue budget. For health trusts, reference should be made to the quarterly reports and annual figures as to their financial strength and stability published by Monitor, their regulator. Without this information, or where the court is not satisfied that it has been given sufficient reliable information, it is entitled to draw reasonable inferences as to the offender's means, which may include the inference that the offender can pay any fine. Normally, only information relating to the organisation before the court will be relevant, unless exceptionally it is demonstrated that resources of a linked organisation are available and can properly be taken into account.

★K-257   The table sets out the starting point and ranges of fines in pounds sterling for large ("LO") (turnover or equivalent of more than £50 million), medium ("MO") (turnover or equivalent of between £10 million and £50 million), small ("SO") (turnover or equivalent of between £2 million and £10 million) and micro ("MIO") (turnover or equivalent of not more than £2 million) organisations. For very large organisations (*viz.* turnover or equivalent that greatly exceeds the threshold for large organisations), it may be necessary to move outside the suggested range to achieve a proportionate sentence.

	Starting point				**Category range**			
	LO	**MO**	**SO**	**MIO**	**LO**	**MO**	**SO**	**MIO**
Offence category								
A	7.5m	3m	800k	450k	4.8 - 20m	1.8 - 7.5m	540k - 2.8m	270 - 800k
B	5m	2m	540k	300k	3 - 12.5m	1.2 - 5m	350k - 2m	180 - 540k

Aggravating and mitigating factors

Factors increasing seriousness	**Factors reducing seriousness or reflecting mitigation**
A1, A3-A9, A11	M1-M6, M14

Step three (checking whether proposed fine based on turnover is proportionate to offender's means)

General principles to follow in setting a fine

★K-258   The court should finalise the level of fine in accordance with the CJA 2003, s.164 (fixing of fines (§ 5-674 in the main work)). Fines cannot and do not attempt to value a human life in money. They should meet the objectives of punishment, the reduction of offending through deterrence and the removal of any gain through the commission of the offence. They must be sufficiently substantial to have a real economic impact that will bring home to the management and shareholders the need to achieve a safe environment for workers and members of the public affected by their activities.

Review of fine based on turnover

★K-258a   The court should "step back", review and, if necessary, adjust the initial fine upwards or downwards to ensure that it meets the general principles, including outside the range. The court should examine the financial circumstances of the organisation in the round to assess the economic realities of the organisation and the most efficacious way of giving effect to the purposes of sentencing. In finalising sentence, the court should have regard to (a) the profitability of an organisation, (b) any quantifiable economic benefit derived from the offence, and (c) whether the fine will put the offender out of business. As to (b), this should normally be added to the fine arrived at in step two. Where information as to this is not readily available, the court may draw on information from enforcement authorities about the costs of operating within the law. The court can also take into account the power to allow time for payment in instalments, if necessary over a number of years.

Step four (consider other factors that may warrant adjustment of proposed fine)

The court should consider any wider impact of the fine within the organisation or on innocent ★**K-258b** third parties, such as (but not limited to): its impact on the offender's ability to improve conditions to comply with the law; and its impact on staff, customers, service users and the local economy (but not on shareholders or directors). Where the fine will fall on public or charitable bodies, it should normally be substantially reduced if the organisation can demonstrate that it would have a significant impact on service provision.

Steps five to nine

These are standard steps in guidelines issued by the Sentencing Council. They require the ★**K-258c** court to consider the SOCPA 2005, ss.73 and 74 (assistance by defendants: reduction or review of sentence (§§ 5-132, 5-133 in the main work)), credit for a guilty plea, the totality principle, the question of confiscation, compensation and any appropriate ancillary orders, and the need to give reasons. As to ancillary orders, particular attention is drawn to remediation and publicity orders under sections 9 and 10 of the 2007 Act (§§ 19-148, 19-149 in the main work). The cost of compliance with a remediation order should not normally be taken into account in fixing the fine, but any exceptional cost of compliance with a publicity order should be considered in fixing the fine, but it is not necessary to fix the fine and then deduct the cost of compliance.

S. Aggravated Burglary and Burglary

On October 13, 2011, the Sentencing Council for England and Wales issued a definitive **K-259** guideline on burglary, applying to all offenders aged 18 or over who are sentenced on or after January 16, 2012, regardless of the date of their offence. The offences covered are: (A) aggravated burglary (Theft Act 1968, s.10 (§ 21-129 in the main work)), (B) domestic burglary (1968 Act, s.9 (*ibid.*, § 21-108)) and (C) non-domestic burglary (1968 Act, s.9).

The guideline sets out nine steps to be followed (in order) when sentencing for these offences, which correspond to the steps set out in the guideline on assault and other offences against the person (*ante*, K-114), subject to the modifications set out in the specific sections A to C relating to each offence (*post*).

In particular, step one requires the court to determine within which of three categories reflecting various degrees of seriousness the offence falls. Category 1 requires greater harm and higher culpability, category 2 requires either greater harm and lower culpability or lesser harm and higher culpability, and category 3 requires lesser harm and lower culpability. In determining the offender's culpability and the harm caused or intended, the court should refer only to the factors indicating harm and culpability set out in the specific sections relating to A to C, *post*, which comprise the principal factual elements of the offence. Where an offence does not fall squarely into a category, individual factors may require a degree of weighting before making an overall assessment and determining the appropriate offence category.

Step two requires the court to use the starting point identified for the relevant category (as to which, see also the specific sections relating to A-C, *post*) to reach a sentence within the category range (*post*). The starting point applies to all offenders irrespective of plea or previous convictions. A case of particular gravity, reflected by multiple features of culpability in step one, could merit upward adjustment from the starting point before further adjustment is made for the aggravating or mitigating factors increasing or reducing seriousness or reflecting personal mitigation set out in the specific sections A to C, *post*, which contain a non-exhaustive list of additional factual elements providing the context of the offence and factors relating to the offender. In particular, relevant recent convictions are likely to result in an upward adjustment. Having considered all these, and other relevant factors, it might be appropriate to move outside the identified category range.

Fine bands, and a non-exhaustive description of examples of requirements that might be appropriate for low, medium and high level community orders, correspond to those set out in the guideline on assaults and other offences against the person (*ante*), and are set out in the annex to the guideline.

Key to factors indicating greater or lesser harm and higher or lower culpability (step one)

K-260   A number of the following factors may apply when determining the offence category for aggravated burglary, and domestic and non-domestic burglary. As to which factors may apply to each type of offence, see the specific sections A–C, *post*.

(a) *Factors indicating greater harm*

K-261   i. Theft of/damage to property causing a significant degree of loss to the victim (whether economic, sentimental or personal).

ii. Soiling, ransacking or vandalism of property.

iii. Occupier and/or victim at home or on the premises (or returns) while offender present.

iv. Significant physical or psychological injury or other significant trauma to the victim.

v. Violence used or threatened against victim (particularly, in relation to offences of aggravated burglary, involving a weapon).

vi. Context of general public disorder.

vii. Trauma to the victim, beyond the normal inevitable consequence of intrusion and theft.

(b) *Factors indicating lesser harm*

K-262   i. No physical or psychological injury or other significant trauma to the victim.

ii. No violence used or threatened and a weapon is not produced.

iii. Nothing stolen or only property of very low value to the victim (whether economic, sentimental or personal).

iv. Limited damage or disturbance to property.

(c) *Factors indicating higher culpability*

K-263   i. Victim or premises deliberately targeted (for example, due to vulnerability or hostility based on disability, race, sexual orientation, and, in relation to offences of non-domestic burglary, to include a pharmacy or doctor's surgery).

ii. A significant degree of planning or organisation.

iii. Equipped for burglary (for example, implements carried and/or use of vehicle).

iv. Weapon present on entry.

v. Member of a group or gang.

vi. Knife or other weapon carried (where not charged separately).

(d) *Factors indicating lower culpability*

K-264   i. Offender exploited by others.

ii. Mental disorder or learning disability, where linked to the commission of the offence.

iii. Offence committed on impulse, with limited intrusion into property.

Key to factors increasing or reducing seriousness or reflecting personal mitigation (step 2)

K-265   A number of the following factors may apply when determining the sentence within the category range for offences of aggravated burglary, and domestic and non-domestic burglary. As to which factors may apply to each type of offence, see the specific sections A-C, *post*.

(e) *Factors increasing seriousness*

Statutory aggravating factors:

K-266   i. Previous convictions (in accordance with the Criminal Justice Act 2003, s.143(2) (*ibid.*, § 5-67)).

ii. Offence committed whilst on bail (2003 Act, s.143(3)).

Other aggravating factors include:

iii. Child at home (or returns home) when offence committed.

iv. Offence committed at night (particularly, in relation to offences of non-domestic burglary, where staff are, or are likely to be, present).

v. Abuse of power and/or position of trust.

vi. Gratuitous degradation of victim.

vii. Any steps taken to prevent the victim reporting the incident or obtaining assistance and/or from assisting or supporting the prosecution.

viii. Victim compelled to leave home (in particular victims of domestic violence).

ix. Established evidence of community impact.

x. Commission of offence whilst under the influence of alcohol or drugs.

xi. Failure to comply with current court orders.

xii. Offence committed whilst on licence.

viii. Offences taken into consideration.

(f) *Factors reducing seriousness or reflecting personal mitigation*

i. Subordinate role in a group or gang.   **K-267**

ii. Injuries caused recklessly.

iii. Nothing stolen or only property of low value to the victim (whether economic, commercial, sentimental or personal).

iv. Offender has made voluntary reparation to the victim.

v. No previous convictions or no relevant/recent convictions.

vi. Remorse.

vii. Good character and/or exemplary conduct.

viii. Determination, and/or demonstration of steps taken to address addiction or offending behaviour.

ix. Serious medical condition requiring urgent, intensive or long-term treatment.

x. Age and/or lack of maturity where it affects the responsibility of the offender.

xi. Lapse of time since the offence where this is not the fault of the offender.

xii. Mental disorder or learning disability, where not linked to the commission of the offence.

xiii Sole or primary carer for dependent relatives.

A. Aggravated burglary

Factors indicating harm and culpability (step one)

		K-268
Greater harm *list (a)*	i–vi	
Lesser harm *list (b)*	i, ii	
Higher culpability *list (c)*	i–iii, v, vi	
Lower culpability *list (d)*	i–iii	

Starting point and category range (step two)

Offence category	*Starting point (applicable to all offenders)*	*Category range (applicable to all offenders)*
category 1	10 years' custody	nine –13 years' custody
category 2	six years' custody	four –nine years' custody

Offence category	Starting point (applicable to all offenders)	Category range (applicable to all offenders)
category 3	two years' custody	one –four years' custody

Factors increasing or reducing seriousness or reflecting personal mitigation

Factors increasing seriousness *list (e)*	i–xiii
Factors reducing seriousness or reflecting personal mitigation *list (f)*	i–xiii

B. Domestic burglary

Factors indicating harm and culpability (step one)

Greater harm *list (a)*	i–iii, v–vii
Lesser harm *list (b)*	iii, iv
Higher culpability *list (c)*	i–iii, v, vi
Lower culpability *list (d)*	i–iii

Starting point and category range (step two)

Offence category	Starting point (applicable to all offenders)	Category range (applicable to all offenders)
category 1	three years' custody	two –six years' custody
category 2	one year's custody	high level community order –two years' custody
category 3	high level community order	low level community order –26 weeks' custody

Where the defendant is dependent on, or has a propensity to misuse, drugs and there is sufficient prospect of success, a community order with a drug rehabilitation requirement under section 209 of the 2003 Act (*ibid.*, § 5-275) may be a proper alternative to a short or moderate custodial sentence.

When sentencing for category 2 or 3 offences, the court should consider whether the custody threshold has been passed, if so, whether it is unavoidable that a custodial sentence be imposed and, if so, whether that sentence can be suspended.

Factors increasing or reducing seriousness or reflecting personal mitigation

Factors increasing seriousness *list (e)*	i–iv, vi–xiii
Factors reducing seriousness or reflecting personal mitigation *list (f)*	i, iv–xiii

C. Non-domestic burglary

Factors indicating harm and culpability (step one)
   As for B, *ante*.   **K-270**

Starting point and category range (step two)

Offence category	Starting point (applicable to all offenders)	Category range (applicable to all offenders)
category 1	two years' custody	one –five years' custody
category 2	18 weeks' custody	low level community order –51 weeks' custody
category 3	medium level community order	band B fine –18 weeks' custody

Where the defendant is dependent on, or has a propensity to misuse, drugs and there is sufficient prospect of success, a community order with a drug rehabilitation requirement under section 209 of the 2003 Act may be a proper alternative to a short or moderate custodial sentence.

When sentencing for category 2 or 3 offences, the court should consider whether the custody threshold has been passed, if so, whether it is unavoidable that a custodial sentence be imposed and, if so, whether that sentence can be suspended; and in sentencing for category three offences, the court should also consider whether the community order threshold has been passed.

Factors increasing or reducing seriousness or reflecting personal mitigation

Factors increasing seriousness *list (e)*	i, ii, iv–vii, ix–xiii
Factors reducing seriousness or reflecting personal mitigation *list (f)*	i, iv–xiii

T. Drug Offences

On January 24, 2012, the Sentencing Council for England and Wales issued a definitive **K-271** guideline, applying to all offenders aged 18 or over who are sentenced on or after February 27, 2012, regardless of the date of their offence. The offences covered are:

   I. fraudulent evasion of a prohibition on the importation or exportation of a controlled drug (CEMA 1979, s.170(2) (§ 25-474 in the main work));

   II. supplying or offering to supply such a drug (Misuse of Drugs Act 1971, s.4(3) (*ibid.*, § 27-28)) and possession of such a drug with intent to supply it to another (1971 Act, s.5(3) (*ibid.*, § 27-50));

   III. production of such a drug (1971 Act, s.4(2)(a) or (b)) and cultivation of a cannabis plant (1971 Act, s.6(2) (*ibid.*, § 27-79)));

   IV. permitting premises to be used (1971 Act, s.8 (*ibid.*, § 27-84)); and

   V. possession of a controlled drug (1971 Act, s.5(2)).

The guideline sets out eight steps to be followed (in order), which broadly correspond to the steps set out in the guideline on offences against the person (*ante*, Appendix K-113 *et seq.*), except that there is no step requiring the court to consider whether an offender meets the dangerousness criteria.

Step one requires the court to determine the offence category based on varying factors set out in the specific sections I to V (*post*).

Step two requires the court to use the starting point identified for the relevant category (as to which, see also the specific sections relating to I-V, *post*) to reach a sentence within the category range (*post*) dependent on whether the offence in question relates to a Class A, B or C drug. The starting point applies to all offenders. The court should then consider adjustment within the category range for aggravating or mitigating features set out in the specific sections I to V, *post*, which contain a non-exhaustive list of additional factual elements providing the context of the offence and factors relating to the offender. Having considered all these, and other relevant factors, it might be appropriate to move outside the identified category range. In cases where the offender is regarded as being at the very top of a "leading role" (which does not apply to section IV and V offences), it may be justifiable for the court to depart from the guideline. Where the defendant is dependent on, or has a propensity to misuse, drugs and there is a sufficient prospect of success, a community order with a drug rehabilitation requirement under the CJA 2003, s.209 (§ 5-275 in the main work), can be a proper alternative to a short or moderate length custodial sentence. As with previous guidelines, the council emphasises that, where appropriate, courts should consider whether community or custodial thresholds have been passed and, if the latter threshold has been passed, whether it is unavoidable that a custodial sentence be imposed and, if so, whether that sentence can be suspended. The guidelines are subject to section 110 of the PC-C(S)A 2000 (minimum sentences for third drug trafficking offence (*ibid.*, § 5-443)).

In addition to considering whether to make ancillary orders, step six also requires the court, except for section V offences, to consider confiscation where the Crown invokes the process or where it considers it appropriate.

Fine bands, and a non-exhaustive description of examples of requirements that might be appropriate for low, medium and high level community orders, correspond to those in the guideline on offences against the person (*ante*), and are set out in the annex to the guideline.

Key to factors increasing or reducing seriousness or reflecting personal mitigation (step two)

K-272 A number of the following factors may apply when determining the sentence within the category range. As to which factors may apply to each type of offence, see the specific sections I to V, *post*.

(a) *Factors increasing seriousness*

Statutory aggravating factors:

K-273 (i) Previous convictions (CJA 2003, s.143(2) (§ 5-67 in the main work)).

(ii) using or permitting a person under 18 to deliver a controlled drug to a third person (1971 Act, s.4A (*ibid.*, § 27-28a)).

(iii) Supplying or offering to supply a drug on, or in the vicinity of, school premises (1971 Act, s.4A).

(iv) Offence committed on bail (2003 Act, s.143(3)).

Other aggravating factors include:

(v) Targeting of any premises to locate vulnerable individuals or supply to such individuals and/ or supply to those under 18.

(vi) Nature of any likely supply.

(vii) Level of any profit element.

(viii) Use of premises accompanied by unlawful access to electricity/ other utility supply.

(ix) Continuing/ large scale operation as evidenced by presence and nature of specialist equipment.

(x) Exposure of others to more than usual danger, *e.g.* drugs cut with harmful substances.

(xi) Length of time over which premises used for drug activity.

(xii) Volume of drug activity permitted.

(xiii) Premises adapted to facilitate drug activity.

(xiv) Location of premises, *e.g.* proximity to school.

(xv) Attempts to conceal or dispose of evidence, where not charged separately.

(xvi) Possession of drug in prison or in a school or licensed premises.

(xvii) Presence of others, especially children and/ or non-users.

(xviii) Presence of weapon(s), where not charged separately.

(xix) Charged as importation of a very small amount.

(xx) High purity or high potential yield.

(xxi) Failure to comply with current court orders or offence committed on licence.

(xxii) Established evidence of community impact.

(b) *Factors reducing seriousness or reflecting personal mitigation*
  (i) Involvement due to pressure, intimidation or coercion, except where already taken into **K-274**
      account at step one.
 (ii) Supply only of drug to which offender addicted.
(iii) Mistaken belief as to type of drug, taking into account the reasonableness of such belief.
 (iv) Isolated incident.
  (v) Low purity.
 (vi) No previous convictions or no relevant or recent convictions.
(vii) Offender's vulnerability was exploited.
(viii) Remorse.
 (ix) Good character and/ or exemplary conduct.
  (x) Offender is using cannabis to help with a diagnosed medical condition.
 (xi) Determination and/ or demonstration of steps having been taken to address addiction or
      offending behaviour.
(xii) Serious medical conditions requiring urgent, intensive or long-term treatment.
(xiii) Age and/ or lack of maturity where it affects the responsibility of the offender.
(xiv) Mental disorder or learning disability.
 (xv) Sole or primary carer for dependent relatives.

I. Fraudulent evasion of a prohibition on importation or exportation

Determining the offence category (step one)
    The court should determine the weight of the drugs involved and the offender's culpability **K-275**
demonstrated by his role, by reference to the tables below. Where there are characteristics
present that fall under different role categories, the court should balance them to reach a fair assessment of the offender's culpability.

Culpability demonstrated by offender's role
One or more of these characteristics may demonstrate the offender's role. These lists are not exhaustive.
LEADING role: • directing or organising buying and selling on a commercial scale; • substantial links to, and influence on, others in a chain; • close links to original source; • expectation of substantial financial gain; • use of business as cover; • abuse of a position of trust or responsibility.
SIGNIFICANT role: • operational or management function within a chain; • involvement of others whether by pressure, influence, intimidation or reward; • motivated by financial or other advantage, whether or not operating alone; • some awareness and understanding of scale of operation.
LESSER role: • performance of limited function under direction; • engaged by pressure, coercion, intimidation; • involvement through naïvety/ exploitation; • no influence on those above in a chain; • little, if any, awareness or understanding of the scale of operation; • if own operation, solely for own use (considering reasonableness of account).

Category of harm
Indicative quantity of drug concerned (upon which the starting point is based):
Category 1 - heroin, cocaine - 5 kg; Ecstasy - 10,000 tablets; LSD - 250,000 squares; amphetamine - 20 kg; cannabis - 200 kg; ketamine - 5 kg.
Category 2 - heroin, cocaine - 1 kg; Ecstasy - 2,000 tablets; LSD - 25,000 squares; amphetamine - 4 kg; cannabis - 40 kg; ketamine - 1 kg.
Category 3 - heroin, cocaine - 150g; Ecstasy - 300 tablets; LSD - 2,500 squares; amphetamine - 750g; cannabis - 6 kg; ketamine - 150g.
Category 4 - heroin, cocaine - 5g; Ecstasy - 20 tablets; LSD - 170 squares; amphetamine - 20g; cannabis - 100g; ketamine - 5g.

Where the operation is on the most serious and commercial scale, involving a quantity of drugs significantly higher than category 1, sentences of 20 years and above may be appropriate, depending on the role of the offender.

Starting point and category range (step two)

Class A	**Leading role**	**Significant role**	**Lesser role**
Category 1	*Starting point*	*Starting point*	*Starting point*
	14 years	10 years	8 years
	Category range	*Category range*	*Category range*
	12 –16 years	9 –12 years	6 –9 years
Category 2	*Starting point*	*Starting point*	*Starting point*
	11 years	8 years	6 years
	Category range	*Category range*	*Category range*
	9 –13 years	6.5 –10 years	5 –7 years
Category 3	*Starting point*	*Starting point*	*Starting point*
	8.5 years	6 years	4.5 years
	Category range	*Category range*	*Category range*
	6.5 –10 years	5 –7 years	3.5 –5 years
Category 4	Where the quantity falls below the indicative amount set out for category 4 in the "category of harm" table (*ante*), first identify the role for the importation offence, then refer to the starting point and ranges for possession or supply offences, depending on intent.		
	Where the quantity is significantly larger than the indicative amounts for category 4 but below category 3 amounts, refer to the category 3 ranges above.		

Class B	**Leading role**	**Significant role**	**Lesser role**
Category 1	*Starting point*	*Starting point*	*Starting point*
	8 years	5.5 years	4 years
	Category range	*Category range*	*Category range*
	7 –10 years	5 –7 years	2.5 –5 years
Category 2	*Starting point*	*Starting point*	*Starting point*
	6 years	4 years	2 years
	Category range	*Category range*	*Category range*
	4.5 –8 years	2.5 –5 years	1.5 –3 years
Category 3	*Starting point*	*Starting point*	*Starting point*

	4 years	2 years	1 year
	Category range	*Category range*	*Category range*
	2.5 –5 years	1.5 –3 years	12 weeks –18 months
Category 4	As for "Category 4" Class A offences, *ante*.		

Class C	Leading role	Significant role	Lesser role
Category 1	*Starting point*	*Starting point*	*Starting point*
	5 years	3 years	1.5 years
	Category range	*Category range*	*Category range*
	4 –8 years	2 –5 years	1 –3 years
Category 2	*Starting point*	*Starting point*	*Starting point*
	3.5 years	1.5 years	26 weeks
	Category range	*Category range*	*Category range*
	2 –5 years	1 –3 years	12 weeks –18 months
Category 3	*Starting point*	*Starting point*	*Starting point*
	1.5 years	26 weeks	high level community order
	Category range	*Category range*	*Category range*
	1 –3 years	12 weeks – 18 months	medium level community order – 12 weeks
Category 4	As for "Category 4" class A offences, *ante*.		

Factors increasing or reducing seriousness or reflecting personal mitigation

Factors increasing seriousness	i, iv, xi–xv, xvii, xviii, xx–xxii
Factors reducing seriousness or reflecting personal mitigation	i, iv–ix, xi–xv

II. Supplying, offering to supply, possession with intent to supply

Determining the offence category (step one)

The court should determine the weight of the drugs and the offender's culpability demonstrated **K-276** by his role, by reference to the tables below. Where there are characteristics present that fall under different role categories, the court should balance them to reach a fair assessment of the offender's culpability.

Culpability demonstrated by offender's role
One or more of these characteristics may demonstrate the offender's role. These lists are not exhaustive.
LEADING role:
As for "Leading role" in section I, *ante*.
SIGNIFICANT role:
As for "Significant role" in section I, *ante*, but also:
supply, other than by a person in a position of responsibility, to a prisoner for gain without coercion.
LESSER role:
As for "Lesser role" in section I, *ante*, save that:

if own operation, absence of any financial gain, *e.g.* joint purchase for no profit, or sharing minimal quantity between peers on non-commercial basis.

Category of harm
Indicative quantity of drug concerned (upon which the starting point is based):
Category 1
As for "Category 1" in section I, *ante.*
Category 2
As for "Category 2" in section I, *ante.*
Category 3
As for "Category 3" in section I, *ante.*   OR   supplying drugs in prison by a prison employee or "street dealing", *i.e.* selling directly to users (including test purchase officers).
Category 4
As for "Category 4" in section I, *ante,*

Where the operation is on the most serious and commercial scale, involving a quantity of drugs significantly higher than category 1, sentences of 20 years and above may be appropriate, depending on the role of the offender.

Starting point and category range (step two)

Class A	**Leading role**	**Significant role**	**Lesser role**
Category 1	*Starting point* 14 years *Category range* 12 – 16 years	*Starting point* 10 years *Category range* 9 – 12 years	*Starting point* 7 years Category range 6 – 9 years
Category 2	*Starting point* 11 years *Category range* 9 – 13 years	*Starting point* 8 years *Category range* 6.5 – 10 years	*Starting point* 5 years *Category range* 3.5 – 7 years
Category 3	*Starting point* 8.5 years *Category range* 6.5 – 10 years	*Starting point* 4.5 years *Category range* 3.5 – 7 years	*Starting point* 3 years *Category range* 2 – 4.5 years
Category 4	*Starting point* 5.5 years *Category range* 4.5 – 7.5 years	*Starting point* 3.5 years *Category range* 2 – 5 years	*Starting point* 1.5 years *Category range* high level community order – 3 years

Class B	**Leading role**	**Significant role**	**Lesser role**
Category 1	*Starting point* 8 years *Category range* 7 – 10 years	*Starting point* 5.5 years *Category range* 5 – 7 years	*Starting point* 3 years Category range 2.5 – 5 years
Category 2	*Starting point* 6 years *Category range*	*Starting point* 4 years *Category range*	*Starting point* 1 year *Category range*

	4.5 – 8 years	2.5 – 5 years	26 weeks – 3 years
Category 3	*Starting point* 4 years *Category range* 2.5 – 5 years	*Starting point* 1 year *Category range* 26 weeks – 3 years	*Starting point* high level community order *Category range* low level community order – 26 weeks
Category 4	*Starting point* 1.5 years *Category range* 26 weeks – 3 years	*Starting point* high level community order *Category range* medium level community order – 26 weeks	*Starting point* low level community order *Category range* band B fine – medium level community order

Class C	Leading role	Significant role	Lesser role
Category 1	*Starting point* 5 years *Category range* 4 – 8 years	*Starting point* 3 years *Category range* 2 – 5 years	*Starting point* 1.5 years Category range 1 – 3 years
Category 2	*Starting point* 3.5 years *Category range* 2 – 5 years	*Starting point* 1.5 years *Category range* 1 – 3 years	*Starting point* 26 years *Category range* 12 weeks – 1.5 years
Category 3	*Starting point* 1.5 years *Category range* 1 – 3 years	*Starting point* 26 years *Category range* 12 weeks – 1.5 years	*Starting point* high level community order *Category range* low level community order – 12 weeks
Category 4	*Starting point* 26 years *Category range* high level community order – 1.5 years	*Starting point* high level community order *Category range* low level community order – 12 weeks	*Starting point* low level community order *Category range* band A fine – medium level community order

Factors increasing or reducing seriousness or reflecting personal mitigation

Factors increasing seriousness	i–v, x, xv, xvii–xxii
Factors reducing seriousness or reflecting personal mitigation	i–ix, xi–xv

III. Production of a controlled drug OR cultivation of a cannabis plant

Determining the offence category (step one)

The court should determine the offender's culpability demonstrated by his role and the output **K-277** or potential output based on the weight of the product or number of plants/ scale of operation, by reference to the tables below. Where there are characteristics present that fall under different role categories, the court should balance them to reach a fair assessment of the offender's culpability.

Culpability demonstrated by offender's role
One or more of these characteristics may demonstrate the offender's role. These lists are not exhaustive.
LEADING role:
As for "Leading role" in section I, *ante*, save that there is no reference here to closeness to the original source.
SIGNIFICANT role:
As for "Significant role" in section I, *ante*.
LESSER role:
As for "Lesser role" in section I, *ante*.
Category of harm Indicative quantity of drug concerned (upon which the starting point is based):
Category 1 As for "Category 1" in section I, *ante*, except that the quantity specified for cannabis is an operation capable of producing industrial quantities for commercial use.
Category 2 As for "Category 2" in section I, *ante*, except that the quantity specified for cannabis is an operation capable of producing significant quantities for commercial use.
Category 3 As for "Category 3" in section I, *ante*, except that the quantity specified for cannabis is 28 plants (with an assumed yield of 40g per plant).
Category 4 As for "Category 4" in section I, *ante*, except that the quantity specified for cannabis is nine plants (with an assumed yield of 40g per plant) (domestic operation).

Where the operation is on the most serious and commercial scale, involving a quantity of drugs significantly higher than category 1, sentences of 20 years and above may be appropriate, depending on the role of the offender.

Starting point and category range (step two)

For Class A offences, as for "Class A" in section II, *ante*, except for category 3:

Class A	Leading role	Significant role	Lesser role
Category 3	*Starting point* 8.5 years *Category range* 6.5 – 10 years	*Starting point* 5 years *Category range* 3.5 – 7 years	*Starting point* 3.5 years *Category range* 2 – 5 years

For Class B offences, as for "Class B" in section II, *ante*, except for category 4:

Class B	Leading role	Significant role	Lesser role
Category 4	*Starting point* 1 year *Category range* high level community order – 3 years	*Starting point* high level community order *Category range* medium level community order – 26 weeks	*Starting point* band C fine *Category range* discharge – medium level community order

Class C	Leading role	Significant role	Lesser role
Category 1	*Starting point*	*Starting point*	*Starting point*

	5 years *Category range* 4 – 8 years	3 years *Category range* 2 – 5 years	1.5 years *Category range* 1 – 3 years
Category 2	*Starting point* 3.5 years *Category range* 2 – 5 years	*Starting point* 1.5 years *Category range* 1 – 3 years	*Starting point* 26 weeks *Category range* high level community order – 1.5 years
Category 3	*Starting point* 1.5 years *Category range* 1 – 3 years	*Starting point* 26 weeks *Category range* high level community order – 1.5 years	*Starting point* high level community order *Category range* low level community order – 12 weeks
Category 4	*Starting point* 26 weeks *Category range* high level community order – 1.5 years	*Starting point* high level community order *Category range* low level community order – 12 weeks	*Starting point* band C fine *Category range* discharge – medium level community order

Factors increasing or reducing seriousness or reflecting personal mitigation

Factors increasing seriousness	i, iv, vi–x, xv, xvii, xviii, xx–xxii
Factors reducing seriousness or reflecting personal mitigation	i, iv–ix, xi–xv

IV. Permitting premises to be used

Determining the offence category (step one)

The court should determine into which of three categories the offence falls by reference to the **K-278** offender's culpability and the harm caused (which will be based on the extent of the activity and/ or the quantity of drugs). Category 1 requires greater harm and higher culpability, category 2 requires either greater harm and lower culpability or lesser harm and higher culpability, and category 3 requires lesser harm and lower culpability.

Factors indicating higher culpability (non-exhaustive):
- Premises used primarily for drug activity, *e.g.* crack house.
- Expectation of substantial financial gain.
- Use of legitimate business premises to aid and/ or conceal illegal activity, *e.g.* public house or club.

Factors indicating lower culpability (non-exhaustive):
- Limited or no financial gain.
- No active role in any supply taking place.
- Involvement through naivety.

Factors indicating greater harm (non-exhaustive):
- Regular drug-related activity.
- Higher quantity of drugs, *e.g.* more than 5g of heroin or cocaine or more than 50g of cannabis.

Factors indicating lesser harm (non-exhaustive):
- Infrequent drug-related activity.
- Lower quantity of drugs.

Starting point and category range (step two)

Class A	Starting point	Category range
Category 1	2.5 years	1.5 – 4 year
Category 2	36 weeks	high level community order – 1.5 years
Category 3	medium level community order	low level community order – high level community order

Class B	Starting point	Category range
Category 1	1 year	26 weeks – 1.5 years
Category 2	high level community order	low level community order – 26 weeks
Category 3	band C fine	band A fine – low level community order

Class C	Starting point	Category range
Category 1	12 weeks	high level community order – 26 weeks (3 months if tried summarily)
Category 2	low level community order	band C fine – high level community order
Category 3	band A fine	discharge – band C fine

Factors increasing or reducing seriousness or reflecting personal mitigation

Factors increasing seriousness	i, iv, xi–xv, xvii, xviii, xx–xxii
Factors reducing seriousness or reflecting personal mitigation	i, iv–ix, xi–xv

V. Possession of a controlled drug

Determining the offence category (step one)

K-279   The court should determine the offence category based on the class of drug involved.

Starting point and category range (step two)

Offence category	Starting point	Category range
Category 1 (Class A)	band C fine	band A fine – 51 weeks
Category 2 (Class B)	band B fine	discharge – 26 weeks
Category 3 (Class C)	band A fine	discharge – medium level community order

Factors increasing or reducing seriousness or reflecting personal mitigation

Factors increasing seriousness	i, iv, xv–xvii, xix, xxi, xxii
Factors reducing seriousness or reflecting personal mitigation	iv, vi, viii–xv

U. Offences Taken into Consideration and Totality

K-280   The Sentencing Council issued a guideline on the related topics of taking offences into consideration (TICs) and totality, applying to all offenders whose cases are dealt with on or after

June 11, 2012. In addition to setting out the applicable principles to be gleaned from legislation and case-law, the guideline covers the following.

A. Offences taken into consideration

See §§ 5-160 *et seq.* in the main work.   **K-281**

B. Totality

This part of the guideline applies to the sentencing of an offender for multiple offences or   **K-282**
when he is serving an existing sentence. The principle of totality comprises two elements: (i) all courts when sentencing for more than a single offence should pass a just and proportionate total sentence that reflects all the offending behaviour, whether the sentences are structured as concurrent or consecutive (in respect of which there is no inflexible rule); (ii) it is usually impossible to arrive at a just and proportionate total sentence simply by adding together notional single sentences - it is necessary to address the offending behaviour, together with the factors personal to the offender, as a whole.

The general approach (as applied to determinate custodial sentences) consists of four steps:
  (i) consider the sentence for each individual offence;
  (ii) determine whether the case calls for concurrent or consecutive sentences;
  (iii) test the overall sentence against the requirement that it should be just and proportionate; and
  (iv) consider whether the sentence is structured in a way that will be best understood by all concerned with it.

As to (ii), concurrent sentences will ordinarily be appropriate where the offences arise out of the same incident or facts or where there is a series of offences of the same or similar kind, especially when committed against the same person, with examples of both being set out in the guideline. Consecutive offences will be appropriate where the offences arise out of unrelated facts or incidents, where the offences are of the same or similar kind, but where the overall criminality will not sufficiently be reflected by concurrent sentences, or where one or more offence qualifies for a statutory minimum sentence and concurrent sentences would improperly undermine that minimum. Examples are again set out, including ways in which the court can reach a just and proportionate sentence where this is not achieved by simply aggregating the consecutive sentences (*e.g.* with offences of a similar level of severity, by reducing all of the sentences proportionately or by identifying the most serious principal offence and reducing the remainder proportionately; with offences of differing levels of seriousness, by recording lesser offences as "no separate penalty" or by ordering the lesser sentences to run concurrently).

Tables follow the guideline, setting out the approach to be taken when applying the totality principle in specified circumstances (this is in large part based on existing legislation and case-law).

Determinate custodial sentence to be passed
  a. where the offender is serving an existing custodial determinate sentence: if the new of-   **K-283**
     fence was committed before the imposition of that sentence, the court should consider what sentence would have been imposed if the court had dealt with the offences at the same time; if it was committed after that sentence, then generally the sentence will be consecutive;
  b. where the offender is serving a custodial determinate sentence, but had been released from custody prior to being recalled, the court should follow *R. v. Costello* [2010] 2 Cr.App.R.(S.) 94, CA (§ 5-669 in the main work);
  c. where the offender is liable to be returned to custody under the PCC(S)A 2000, s.116, see subsection (6)(c);
  d. where the offender is in breach of a suspended sentence, the additional sentence will generally be consecutive to the activated suspended sentence;

Extended sentences
  e. when using multiple offences to calculate the requisite determinate term (in accordance   **K-284**

with *R. v. Joyce*; *R. v. Pinnell* [2011] 2 Cr.App.R.(S.) 30, CA (§ 5-523 in the main work)), the custodial period must be adjusted for totality in the same way as determinate sentences would be;

Indeterminate sentences

K-285 f. when imposing multiple indeterminate sentences and using multiple offences to calculate the minimum term for an indeterminate sentence, assess the notional determinate term for all offences (serious, specified or otherwise) in the usual way, adjusting for totality, and then, normally, impose the indeterminate sentence on all serious specified offences concurrently;

g. where the offender is already serving an existing determinate sentence, the court should order the sentence to run concurrently but adjust the minimum term to reflect half of any period still remaining to be served under the existing sentence; where the offender is already serving an existing indeterminate sentence, the court may order the sentence to run consecutively to the existing sentence (*R. v. Hills* [2009] 1 Cr.App.R.(S.) 75, CA (§ 5-523 in the main work)), but the aggregate minimum terms should be adjusted if this is not just and proportionate;

h. when ordering a determinate sentence to run consecutively to an indeterminate sentence, the court should consider the total sentence that the offender will serve before becoming eligible for consideration for release, achieving justice and proportionality, if necessary, by reducing the length of the determinate sentence or, alternatively, ordering the second sentence to be served concurrently;

Multiple fines for non-imprisonable offences

K-286 i. where the offender has been convicted of more than one offence where a fine is appropriate, there are various ways in which the court can achieve a just and proportionate fine if this is not achieved by simply totting up the fines; the court should also consider *R. v. John Pointon & Sons Ltd* [2008] 2 Cr.App.R.(S.) 82, CA (as to the need to avoid double counting);

Fines in combination with other sentences

K-287 j. a fine may be imposed in addition to any other sentence (subject to statutory exceptions), but combining a fine with an immediate custodial sentence is only likely to be justifiable if a confiscation order is not contemplated, there is no obvious victim to receive compensation and the offender has the means to pay;

Community orders

K-288 k. multiple offences that do not individually cross the custody threshold may do so when taken in combination;

l. where there is more than one offence, with one meriting immediate custody and one meriting a community order, the custodial sentence should be enhanced by virtue of the associated offence or no separate penalty should be imposed for the lesser offence;

m. where the offender has been convicted of more than one offence where a community order is appropriate, the court should generally impose a single community order that reflects the overall criminality of the offending behaviour; where it is necessary to impose more than one community order, these should be ordered to run concurrently and, for ease of administration, each of the orders should be identical;

n. where the offender is convicted of an offence while serving a community order, the court should consider if the overall seriousness of the offending behaviour justifies a custodial sentence; if not, it should impose a single community order reflecting the overall totality of criminality; and it should take into account the extent to which the offender complied with the requirements of the previous order;

Disqualifications from driving

K-289 o. where the offender has been convicted of two or more obligatory disqualification offences, the court should take into account all offences when determining the disqualification periods and should generally impose like periods for each offence (which have to be concurrent);

p. where the offender has been convicted of two or more offences and is liable to disqualification under the "totting up" provisions of the RTOA 1988, s.35 (§ 32-264 in the main work), the guideline simply sets out the effect of subsection (3);

q. where the offender has otherwise been convicted of two or more offences involving discretionary disqualification, it is generally desirable for the court to impose a single disqualification order that reflects the overall criminality of the offending behaviour;

Compensation orders

r. a global compensation order should not be made unless the offences were committed　**K-290** against the same victim; where there are competing claims for limited funds, the amount available should normally be apportioned on a *pro rata* basis;

s. compensation may be combined with a fine (with priority to compensation), a confiscation order, a community order, a suspended sentence or an immediate custodial sentence (where the offender is clearly able to pay or has good prospects of employment on release).

V. Dangerous Dog Offences

The Sentencing Council for England and Wales issued a definitive guideline, applying to all of-　**K-291** fenders aged 18 or over who were sentenced on or after August 20, 2012, regardless of the date of the offence. The offences covered are: (A) owning or being in charge of a dog that injures a person whilst dangerously out of control in a public place (Dangerous Dogs Act 1991, s.3(1) (§ 31-35 in the main work)), and allowing a dog to enter a private place where the dog is not permitted to be, where it then injures any person (1991 Act, s.3(3)(a)), (B) owning or being in charge of a dog dangerously out of control in a public place (1991 Act, s.3(1)), and allowing a dog to enter a private place where the dog is not permitted to be, and, while it is there, there are grounds for reasonable apprehension that it will injure any person (1991 Act, s.3(3)(b)), and (C) possession of a prohibited dog (1991 Act, s.1(3)), and breeding, selling, exchanging or advertising a prohibited dog (1991 Act, s.1(2)).

In view of the legislative changes made to the 1991 Act by the Anti-social Behaviour, Crime and Policing Act 2014, including by way of abolishing the offences under section 3(3), extending the offence under section 3(1) to private places as well as public places, and increasing the penalties for aggravated offences under section 3(1), the guideline now needs to be approached with considerable caution.

The guideline sets out eight steps to be followed (in order), which broadly correspond to the steps set out in the guideline on offences against the person (*ante*, K-113 *et seq.*), except that there is no step requiring the court to consider whether an offender meets the dangerousness criteria, and consideration of compensation and/ or ancillary orders is step five (as to which, see the specific sections relating to A to C, *post*), preceding consideration of the totality principle (now step six).

Step one requires the court to determine within which of three categories reflecting various degrees of seriousness the offence falls. In determining the offender's culpability and the harm caused (or intended), the court should refer only to the factors indicating harm and culpability set out in the specific sections relating to A to C, *post*, which comprise the principal factual elements of the offence.

Step two requires the court to use the starting point identified for the relevant category (as to which, see also the specific sections relating to A to C, *post*) to reach a sentence within the category range. The starting point applies to all offenders irrespective of plea or previous convictions. The court should then consider adjustment within the category range for aggravating or mitigating features set out in the specific sections A to C, *post*, which contain a non-exhaustive list of additional factual elements providing the context of the offence and factors relating to the offender. Having considered all these, and other relevant factors, it might be appropriate to move outside the identified category range. As with previous guidelines, the council emphasises that, where appropriate, courts should consider whether community or custodial thresholds have been passed and, if the latter threshold has been passed, whether it is unavoidable that a custodial sentence be imposed and, if so, whether that sentence can be suspended.

Fine bands, and a non-exhaustive description of examples of requirements that might be appropriate for low, medium and high level community orders, correspond to those in the guideline on offences against the person (*ante*), and are set out in the annex to the guideline.

Consultation on a new guideline on dangerous dog offences closed on June 9, 2015.

Key to factors increasing or reducing seriousness or reflecting personal mitigation (step two)

K-292   A number of the following factors may apply when determining the sentence within the category range. As to which factors may apply to each type of offence, see the specific sections A to C, *post.*

(a) *Factors increasing seriousness*
    Statutory aggravating factors:
      i. Previous convictions.
      ii. Offence committed on bail.
    Other aggravating factors include:
      iii. Injury to other animal(s).
      iv. Location of offence.
      v. Continuing effect upon victim and/ or others.
      vi. Failure to take adequate precautions to prevent dog escaping.
      vii. Allowing insufficiently experienced or trained person to be in charge of dog.
      viii. Presence of children or others who are vulnerable because of personal circumstances.
      ix. Ill-treatment or failure to ensure welfare needs of dog, where not charged separately.
      x. Dog known to be prohibited.
      xi. Lack or loss of control of dog due to influence of alcohol or drugs.
      xii. Offence committed against those working in the public sector or providing a service to the public.
      xiii. Established evidence of community impact.
      xiv. Failure to comply with current court orders or offence committed on licence.

(b) *Factors reducing seriousness or reflecting personal mitigation*
      i. No previous convictions or no relevant/ recent convictions.
      ii. Isolated incident.
      iii. No previous complaints against, or incidents involving, the dog.
      iv. Unaware that dog was prohibited type despite reasonable efforts to identify type.
      v. Evidence of safety or control measures having been taken by owner.
      vi. Prosecution results from owner notification.
      vii. Remorse.
      viii. Good character and/ or exemplary conduct.
      ix. Evidence of responsible ownership.
      x. Determination, and/ or demonstration of steps taken, to address addiction or offending behaviour.
      xi. Serious medical condition requiring urgent, intensive or long-term treatment.
      xii. Age and/ or lack of maturity where it affects the responsibility of the offender.
      xiii. Lapse of time since the offence where this was not the fault of the offender.
      xiv. Mental disorder or learning disability (for offences in sections A and B only, where not linked to commission of the offence).
      xv. Sole or primary carer for dependent relatives.

A. Dog dangerously out of control in a public place, injuring any person, or allowing a dog to enter a private place where the dog is not permitted to be, where it then injures any person

Determining the offence category (step one)

K-293   Category 1 requires greater harm and higher culpability, category 2 requires either greater harm and lower culpability or lesser harm and higher culpability, and category 3 requires lesser harm and lower culpability.

Factors indicating greater harm
- Serious injury (including disease transmission and/ or psychological harm)
- Sustained or repeated attack
- Victim is a child or otherwise vulnerable because of personal circumstances

Factors indicating lesser harm
- Minor injury

Factors indicating higher culpability

Statutory aggravating factors:
- Offence racially or religiously aggravated
- Offence motivated by, or demonstrating, hostility to the victim based on sexual orientation or disability (or presumed sexual orientation or disability)

Other aggravating factors:
- Failure to respond to others' warnings or concerns about dog's behaviour
- Goading, or allowing goading, of dog
- Dog used as weapon to intimidate victim
- Offence motivated by, or demonstrating, hostility to the victim based on age, sex, or (presumed) gender identity

Factors indicating lower culpability
- Attempts made to regain control of dog and/ or intervene
- Provocation of dog without fault of offender
- Evidence of safety or control measures taken
- Mental disorder or disability, where linked to the commission of the offence

Starting point and category range (step two)

Offence category	Starting point (applicable to all offenders)	Category range (applicable to all offenders)
category 1	six months' custody	medium level community order - 18 months' custody
category 2	medium level community order	band B fine - six months' custody
category 3	band B fine	discharge - band C fine

Factors increasing or reducing seriousness or reflecting personal mitigation

Factors increasing seriousness: i-vii, ix-xiv

Factors reducing seriousness or reflecting personal mitigation: i-iii, vii-xii, xiv, xv

Compensation and ancillary orders (step five)

The court should consider whether to make a compensation order and/ or other ancillary orders. The court may disqualify the offender from having custody of a dog, the test being whether the offender is a fit and proper person to have custody of a dog. The court shall make a destruction order (after giving the owner, where not the offender, an opportunity to be present and make representations) unless satisfied that the dog would not constitute a danger to public safety. In reaching a decision, the court should consider the relevant circumstances, which include (i) the incident — what degree of harm was caused by the dog's behaviour, (ii) past behaviour of the dog — whether this was an isolated incident or whether there have been previous warnings or incidents, and (iii) the owner's character — whether the owner is a fit and proper person to own the particular dog. If satisfied that the dog would not constitute a danger to public safety, the court shall make a contingent destruction order imposing certain conditions. Where the court makes a destruction order, it may order the offender to pay reasonable expenses.

B. Dog dangerously out of control in a public place, or allowing a dog to enter a private place where the dog is not permitted to be, where there are grounds for reasonable apprehension that it will injure any person

Determining the offence category (step one)

K-294   Same categories as for A, *ante.*

Factors indicating greater harm
- Presence of children or others who are vulnerable because of personal circumstances
- Injury to another animal(s)

Factors indicating lesser harm
- Low risk to the public

Factors indicating higher culpability
- Same as for A, *ante*

Factors indicating lower culpability
- Same as for A, *ante*

Starting point and category range (step two)

Offence category	Starting point (applicable to all offenders)	Category range (applicable to all offenders)
category 1	medium level community order	band C fine - six months' custody
category 2	band B fine	band A fine - low level community order
category 3	band A fine	discharge - band B fine

Factors increasing or reducing seriousness or reflecting personal mitigation
    Factors increasing seriousness: i, ii, iv-vii, ix-xiv
    Factors reducing seriousness or reflecting personal mitigation: i-iii, vii-xii, xiv, xv

Compensation and ancillary orders (step five)
    Same as for A, *ante*, except the court is permitted (rather than required) to make a destruction order or contingent destruction order. In reaching a decision, the court should consider the relevant circumstances, which include those set out in section A, *ante*.

C. Possession of a prohibited dog, or breeding, selling, exchanging or advertising a prohibited dog

Determining the offence category (step one)

K-295   Category 1 requires greater harm and higher culpability, category 2 requires either greater harm or higher culpability, and category 3 requires that there be neither greater harm nor higher culpability.

Factors indicating greater harm
- Injury to person
- Injury to another animal(s)

Factors indicating higher culpability
- Dog known to be prohibited
- Offence committed for gain
- Dog used to threaten or intimidate

- Permitting fighting
- Training and/ or possession of paraphernalia for dog fighting

Starting point and category range (step two)

Offence category	Starting point (applicable to all offenders)	Category range (applicable to all offenders)
category 1	medium level community order	band C fine - six months' custody
category 2	band C fine	band A fine - medium level community order
category 3	band A fine	discharge - band B fine

Factors increasing or reducing seriousness or reflecting personal mitigation

Factors increasing seriousness: i, ii, viii, ix, xiii, xiv

Factors reducing seriousness or reflecting personal mitigation: i, iv-xv.

Ancillary orders (step five)

The court may disqualify the offender from having custody of a dog, the test being whether the **K-296**
offender is a fit and proper person to have custody of a dog. The court shall make a destruction
order unless satisfied that the dog would not constitute a danger to public safety. In reaching a
decision, the court should consider the relevant circumstances, which include those set out in section A, *ante.* If the court does not make a destruction order, the court shall make a contingent
destruction order providing that unless the dog is exempted from the prohibition within two
months it shall be destroyed. Where the offender is the owner of the dog, it would not normally
be appropriate to make a contingent destruction order in conjunction with a disqualification
order. Further, the court must not transfer ownership of the dog to another. Where the court
makes a destruction order, it may order the offender to pay reasonable expenses.

W. Fraud, Bribery and Money Laundering

The Sentencing Council for England and Wales has issued a definitive guideline for offences of **K-297**
fraud, money laundering and bribery falling to be sentenced on or after October 1, 2014. The
guideline is in seven sections, the seventh of which relates to corporate offenders and incorporates
an earlier guideline issued by the Sentencing Council.

Each section (apart from Section VII, which is dealt with separately, *post*) describes eight steps
to be gone through.

Step 1 (determining the offence category)

This involves determination of the offence category by reference to the tables in each section. **K-298**
In order to do this, the court should make an assessment of culpability and harm. The level of
culpability is determined by weighing up all the factors of the case to determine the offender's
role and the extent to which the offending was planned and the sophistication with which it was
carried out.

The following indicators of culpability are used throughout the guideline (apart from Section
VII, which is dealt with separately (*post*)).

Higher culpability (A)

HC1:   A leading role where offending is part of a group activity

HC2:   Involvement of others through pressure, influence

HC3:   Abuse of position of power, trust or responsibility

HC4:   Sophisticated nature of offence/ significant planning

HC5:   Fraudulent activity conducted over sustained period of time

HC6: Large number of victims

HC7: Deliberate targeting of victim on basis of vulnerability

HC8: Articles deliberately designed to target victims on basis of vulnerability

HC9: Criminal activity/ offending conducted over sustained period of time

HC10: Intended corruption (directly or indirectly) of a senior official performing a public function or of a law enforcement officer

HC11: Motivated by expectation of substantial financial, commercial or political gain

Medium culpability (B)

MC1: Other cases where characteristics for categories A or C are not present

MC2: A significant role where offending is part of a group activity

MC3: Claim not fraudulent from outset

Lesser culpability (C)

LC1: Involved through coercion, intimidation or exploitation

LC2: Not motivated by personal gain

LC3: Peripheral role in organised fraud

LC4: Opportunistic "one-off" offence

LC5: Limited awareness or understanding of the extent of the fraudulent activity

LC6: Performed limited function under direction

Where there are characteristics present that fall under different levels of culpability, the court should balance them to reach a fair assessment of the offender's culpability.

As to the assessment of harm, see the individual sections.

Step 2 (starting point and category range)

K-299   Having determined the category, the court should use the appropriate starting point to reach a sentence within the category range in the tables. The starting points apply to all offenders irrespective of plea and previous convictions. Where the starting point is based on a particular value (as in Sections I, III, IV and V), this should be adjusted upwards or downwards according to the actual value involved. Where the value greatly exceeds the amount of the starting point for a category 1 case, it may be appropriate to move outside the identified range.

The tables of starting points and category ranges in each section are followed by a "non-exhaustive list of additional factual elements providing the context of the offence and factors relating to the offender." The court is then to identify whether any combination of these or other relevant factors should result in an upward or downward adjustment from the sentence arrived at based on culpability and harm alone. In each section, it is also stated that consecutive sentences for multiple offences may be appropriate where large sums are involved.

The following aggravating and mitigating factors are used throughout the guideline (apart from Section VII, which is dealt with separately (*post*)).

Aggravating factors

A1: Previous convictions, having regard to (a) the nature of the offence to which the conviction relates and its relevance to the current offence; and (b) the time that has elapsed since the conviction

A2: Offence committed whilst on bail

A3: Steps taken to prevent the victim reporting or obtaining assistance and/ or from assisting or supporting the prosecution

A4: Attempts to conceal/ dispose of evidence

A5:   Established evidence of community/ wider impact

A6:   Failure to comply with current court orders

A7:   Offence committed on licence

A8:   Offences taken into consideration

A9:   Failure to respond to warnings about behaviour

A10:   Offences committed across borders

A11:   Blame wrongly placed on others

A12:   Involves multiple frauds

A13:   Number of false declarations

A14:   Damage to third party (*e.g.* as a result of identity theft, or loss of employment to legitimate employees)

A15:   Dealing with goods with an additional health risk

A16:   Disposing of goods to under age purchasers

A17:   Claim fraudulent from outset

A18:   Proceeds of fraud funded lavish lifestyle

A19:   Length of time over which offending was committed

A20:   Pressure exerted on another party

A21:   Offence committed to facilitate other criminal activity

Mitigating factors

M1:   No previous convictions or no relevant/ recent convictions

M2:   Remorse

M3:   Good character and/ or exemplary conduct

M4:   Little or no prospect of success

M5:   Serious medical conditions requiring urgent, intensive or long-term treatment

M6:   Age and/ or lack of maturity where it affects the responsibility of the offender

M7:   Lapse of time since apprehension where this does not arise from the conduct of the offender

M8:   Mental disorder or learning disability

M9:   Sole or primary carer for dependent relatives

M10:   Offender co-operated with investigation, made early admissions and/ or voluntarily reported offending

M11:   Determination and/ or demonstration of steps having been taken to address addiction or offending behaviour

M12:   Activity originally legitimate

M13:   Legitimate entitlement to benefits not claimed

M14:   Offender experiencing significant financial hardship or pressure at time fraud was committed due to exceptional circumstances

Steps 3–8

These are standard steps in guidelines issued by the Sentencing Council. They require the **K-300** court to consider the SOCPA 2005, ss.73 and 74 (assistance by defendants; reduction or review of sentence (§§ 5-132, 5-133 in the main work)), credit for a guilty plea, the totality principle, the question of confiscation, compensation and any appropriate ancillary orders, the need to give reasons and to make any appropriate allowance for time spent on bail (CJA 2003, s.240A (§ 5-645 in the main work)).

I. Fraud

K-301   This section covers fraud (Fraud Act 2006, s.1, (§ 21-310 in the main work)), conspiracy to defraud (§§ 33-37 *et seq.* in the main work) and false accounting (Theft Act 1968, s.17 (§ 21-177 in the main work)), but none of these if the fraud is a revenue or benefit fraud (as to which, see Sections III and IV, *post*).

Step 1: determine the level of culpability and the harm category (and see generally, ante)
     Culpability

High culpability (HC)	Medium culpability (MC)	Lesser culpability (LC)
HC1–HC7	MC1, MC2	LC1–LC5

     Harm
     This is initially assessed by the actual, intended or risked loss that may arise from the offence. The values in the table below are to be used for actual or intended loss only. Intended loss relates to offences where circumstances prevent the actual loss that is intended to be caused by the fraudulent activity. Risk of loss (*e.g.* in mortgage frauds) involves consideration of the likelihood of harm occurring and its extent if it does, and is less serious than actual or intended loss. Where the offence has caused risk of loss but no (or much less) actual loss, the normal approach is to move down to the corresponding point in the next category. This may be inappropriate if the likelihood or extent of risked loss is particularly high.

Category 1	£500k or more	Starting point based on £1m
Category 2	£100k–£500k or risk of category 1 harm	Starting point based on £300k
Category 3	£20k–£100k or risk of category 2 harm	Starting point based on £50k
Category 4	£5k–20k or risk of category 3 harm	Starting point based on £12.5k
Category 5	Less than £5k or risk of category 4 harm	Starting point based on £2.5k

     If there is risk of category 5 harm, the court should move further down the range within the category.
     Harm B — Victim impact
     The court should then take into account the level of harm caused to the victim or others to determine whether it warrants the sentence being moved up to the corresponding point in the next category or further up the range of the initial category.

> **High impact** — move up a category; if in category 1 move up the range
> - Serious detrimental effect on the victim whether financial or otherwise, *e.g.* substantial damage to credit rating.
> - Victim particularly vulnerable (due to factors including, but not limited to, age, financial circumstances and mental capacity).

> **Medium impact** — move upwards within the category range
> - Considerable detrimental effect on the victim, financial or otherwise.

> **Lesser impact** — no adjustment
> - Some detrimental impact on victim, financial or otherwise.

Step 2: use the following tables to reach a provisional sentence (and see generally, ante)
     Table 1 (fraud and conspiracy to defraud)

Harm	Culpability (A)	Culpability (B)	Culpability (C)
	Starting points and ranges	*Starting points and ranges*	*Starting points and ranges*
Category 1	7 years 5–8 years	5 years 3–6 years	3 years 1.5–4 years
Category 2	5 years 3–6 years	3 years 1.5–4 years	1.5 years 26 weeks–3 years
Category 3	3 years 1.5–4 years	1.5 years 26 weeks–3 years	26 weeks Medium level community order–12 months
Category 4	1.5 years 26 weeks–3 years	26 weeks Medium level community order–12 months	Medium level community order Band B fine–high level community order
Category 5	36 weeks' custody High level community order–12 months	Medium level community order Band B fine–26 weeks	Band B fine Discharge–medium level community order

Table 2 (false accounting)

Harm	Culpability (A)	Culpability (B)	Culpability (C)
	Starting points and ranges	*Starting points and ranges*	*Starting points and ranges*
Category 1	5.5 years 4–6.5 years	4 years 2.5–5 years	2.5 years 15 months–3.5 years
Category 2	4 years 2.5–5 years	2.5 years 15 months–3.5 years	15 months 26 weeks–2.5 years
Category 3	2.5 years 15 months–3.5 years	15 months High level community order–2.5 years	High level community order Low level community order–36 weeks
Category 4	15 months High level community order–2.5 years	High level community order Low level community order–36 weeks	Low level community order Band B fine–medium level community order
Category 5	26 weeks Medium level community order–36 weeks	Low level community order Band B fine–medium level community order	Band B fine Discharge–low level community order

Adjust the provisional sentence according to the presence of the following factors:

Factors increasing seriousness	Factors reducing seriousness or reflecting personal mitigation
A1–A11	M1–M12

Steps 3–8: see *ante*

II. Possessing, making or supplying articles for use in fraud

This section covers the offences contrary to sections 6 and 7 of the Fraud Act 2006 (§§ 21-345, **K-302**
21-346 in the main work)).

Step 1: determine the level of culpability and the harm category (and see generally, ante).
  Culpability

High culpability (A)	Medium culpability (B)	Lesser culpability (C)
HC1–HC5, HC8	MC1, MC2	LC1, LC2, LC4–LC6

Harm

The level of harm is determined by weighing up all the factors to determine the harm that would be caused if the article(s) was (were) used to commit a substantive offence.

Greater harm
- Large number of articles created/ supplied/ in possession.
- Article has potential to facilitate fraudulent acts affecting large number of victims.
- Article has potential to facilitate fraudulent acts involving significant sums.
- Use of third party identities.
- Offender making considerable gain as result of the offence.

Lesser harm
- All other offences.

Step 2: use the following tables to reach a provisional sentence (and see generally, ante).
Table 1 (possessing articles for use in fraud (2006 Act, s.6))

Harm	Culpability (A)	Culpability (B)	Culpability (C)
	Starting points and ranges	*Starting points and ranges*	*Starting points and ranges*
Greater	1.5 years 36 weeks–3 years	36 weeks High level community order–2 years	High level community order Medium level community order–26 weeks
Lesser	26 weeks High level community order–1.5 years	Medium level community order Low level community order–26 weeks	Band B fine Band A fine–medium level community order

Table 2 (making, adapting or supplying articles for use in fraud (2006 Act, s.7))

Harm	Culpability (A)	Culpability (B)	Culpability (C)
	Starting points and ranges	*Starting points and ranges*	*Starting points and ranges*
Greater	4.5 years 3–7 years	2.5 years 1.5–5 years	12 months High level community order–3 years
Lesser	2 years 26 weeks–4 years	36 weeks Low level community order–2 years	Medium level community order Band C fine–26 weeks

The table of additional factual elements providing the context of the offence and factors relating to the offender is the same as in Section I (*ante*).

Steps 3–8: see *ante*.

III. Revenue fraud

K-303   This section covers the same offences as in Section I, plus cheating the public revenue and offences under the Taxes Management Act 1970, s.106A (fraudulent evasion of income tax), the CEMA 1979, ss.50, 170 and 170B (fraudulent evasion of duty; improper importation of goods (§§ 25-430, 25-474, 25-505 in the main work)), and the Value Added Tax Act 1994, s.72 (§ 25-532 in the main work).

Step 1: determine the level of culpability and the harm category (and see generally, ante).
  Culpability

High culpability (A)	Medium culpability (B)	Lesser culpability (C)
HC1–HC5	MC1, MC2	LC1, LC2, LC4–LC6

  Harm
  Gain or intended gain, or loss or intended loss.

Category 1	£50m or more	Starting point based on £80m
Category 2	£10m–£50m	Starting point based on £30m
Category 3	£2m–£10m	Starting point based on £5m
Category 4	£500k–£2m	Starting point based on £1m
Category 5	£100k–£500k	Starting point based on £300k
Category 6	£20k–100k	Starting point based on £50k
Category 7	Less than £20k	Starting point based on £12.5k

Step 2: use the following tables to reach a provisional sentence (and see generally, ante).
  Table 1 (2006 Act, s.1, conspiracy to defraud)
  Where the value of the fraud is over £2 million, the court should refer to the corresponding
category in Table 3, subject to the maximum sentence of 10 years for these offences.

Harm	Culpability (A)	Culpability (B)	Culpability (C)
	Starting points and ranges	*Starting points and ranges*	*Starting points and ranges*
Category 4	7 years 5–8 years	5 years 3–6 years	3 years 1.5–4 years
Category 5	5 years 3–6 years	3 years 1.5–4 years	1.5 years 26 weeks–3 years
Category 6	3 years 1.5–4 years	1.5 years 26 weeks–3 years	26 weeks Medium level community order–12 months
Category 7	1.5 years 36 weeks–3 years	36 weeks Medium level community order–18 months	Medium level community order Low–high level community order

  Table 2 (1968 Act, s.17, 1970 Act, s.106(a), 1979 Act, ss.50(1)(a) and (2), 170(1)(a)(i) and (ii), (1)(b),
and (2)(a), and 170B, and 1994 Act, s.72(1), (3) and (8))

Harm	Culpability (A)	Culpability (B)	Culpability (C)
	Starting points and ranges	*Starting points and ranges*	*Starting points and ranges*
Category 4	5.5 years 4–6.5 years	4 years 2.5–5 years	2.5 years 15 months–3.5 years
Category 5	4 years 2.5–5 years	2.5 years 15 months–3.5 years	15 months 26 weeks–2.5 years
Category 6	2.5 years 15 months–3.5 years	15 months High level community order–2.5 years	High level community order Low level community order–36 weeks

Harm	Culpability (A)	Culpability (B)	Culpability (C)
	Starting points and ranges	*Starting points and ranges*	*Starting points and ranges*
Category 7	15 months 26 weeks–2.5 years	26 weeks Medium level community order–15 months	Medium level community order Band C fine–high level community order

Table 3 (cheating the revenue)

Where the offending is on the most serious scale, involving sums significantly higher than the starting point in category 1, sentences of 15 years and above may be appropriate. In cases involving sums below £2 million, the court should refer to Table 1.

Harm	Culpability (A)	Culpability (B)	Culpability (C)
	Starting points and ranges	*Starting points and ranges*	*Starting points and ranges*
Category 1	12 years 10–17 years	8 years 7–12 years	6 years 4–8 years
Category 2	10 years 8–13 years	7 years 5–9 years	5 years 3–6 years
Category 3	8 years 6–10 years	6 years 4–7 years	4 years 3–5 years

Adjust the provisional sentence according to the presence of the following factors:

Factors increasing seriousness	Factors reducing seriousness or reflecting personal mitigation
A1, A2, A4, A6–A9, A11–A16	M1–M12

Steps 3–8: see *ante.*

IV. Benefit fraud

K-304   This section covers the offences in Section I, plus offences under the Social Security Administration Act 1992, ss.111A (dishonest representations for obtaining benefit, *etc.*) and 112 (false representations for obtaining benefit, *etc.*), and the Tax Credits Act 2002, s.35 (tax credit fraud).

Step 1: determine the level of culpability and the harm category (and see generally, ante).
   Culpability

High culpability (A)	Medium culpability (B)	Lesser culpability (C)
HC1-HC4	MC1-MC3	LC1, LC6

Harm
Amount obtained or intended to be obtained:

Category 1	£500k–£2m [sic]	Starting point based on £1m
Category 2	£100k–£500k	Starting point based on £300k
Category 3	£50k–£100k	Starting point based on £75k
Category 4	£10k–£50k	Starting point based on £30k
Category 5	£2.5k–£10k	Starting point based on £5k
Category 6	Less than £2.5k	Starting point based on £1k

Step 2: use the following tables to reach a provisional sentence (and see generally, ante).
  Table 1 (1968 Act, s.17, 1992 Act, s.111A, 2002 Act, s.35)

Harm	Culpability (A)	Culpability (B)	Culpability (C)
	Starting points and ranges	*Starting points and ranges*	*Starting points and ranges*
Category 1 £500k or more [*sic*]	5.5 years 4–6.5 years	4 years 2.5–5 years	2.5 years 15 months–3.5 years
Category 2	4 years 2.5–5 years	2.5 years 15 months–3.5 years	12 months 26 weeks–2.5 years
Category 3	2.5 years 2–3.5 years	12 months 26 weeks–2.5 years	26 weeks High level community order–36 weeks
Category 4	1.5 years 36 weeks–2.5 years	36 weeks Medium level community order–21 months	Medium level community order Low level community order–26 weeks
Category 5	36 weeks Medium level community order–1.5 years	Medium level community order Low level community order–26 weeks	Low level community order Band B fine–medium level community order
Category 6	Medium level community order Low level community order–26 weeks	Low level community order Band A fine–medium level community order	Band A fine Discharge–band B fine

Table 2 (1992 Act, s.112)

Harm	Culpability (A)	Culpability (B)	Culpability (C)
	Starting points and ranges	*Starting points and ranges*	*Starting points and ranges*
Category 5 Above £2.5k	High level community order	Medium level community order	Low level community order
Starting point based on £5k	Medium level community order–12 weeks	Band B fine–high level community order	Band A fine–medium level community order
Category 6 Less than £2.5k	Medium level community order	Band B fine	Band A fine
Starting point based on £1k	Low–high level community order	Band A–band C fine	Discharge–band B fine

Table 3 (2006 Act, s.1, conspiracy to defraud)

Harm	Culpability (A)	Culpability (B)	Culpability (C)
	Starting points and ranges	*Starting points and ranges*	*Starting points and ranges*
Category 1 £500k or more [*sic*]	7 years	5 years	3 years
Starting point based on £1m	5–8 years	3–6 years	1.5–4 years

Harm	Culpability (A)	Culpability (B)	Culpability (C)
	Starting points and ranges	*Starting points and ranges*	*Starting points and ranges*
Category 2	5 years 3–6 years	3 years 1.5–4 years	15 months 26 weeks–3 years
Category 3	3 years 2.5–4 years	15 months 36 weeks–3 years	36 weeks 26 weeks–12 months
Category 4	21 months 12 months–3 years	12 months High level community order–2 years	High level community order Low level community order–26 weeks
Category 5	12 months High level community order–2 years	High level community order Low level community order–26 weeks	Medium level community order Band C fine–high level community order
Category 6	High level community order Low level community order–26 weeks	Low level community order Band B fine–medium level community order	Band B fine Discharge–band C fine

Adjust the provisional sentence according to the presence of the following factors:

Factors increasing seriousness	Factors reducing seriousness or reflecting personal mitigation
A1, A2, A4, A6–A9, A11, A13, A14, A17–A19	M1–M11, M13, M14

Steps 3–8: see *ante*.

V. Money laundering

K-305   This section covers offences contrary to the PCA 2002, ss.327–329 (§§ 26-11 *et seq.* in the main work).

Step 1: determine the level of culpability and the harm category (and see generally, ante).
Culpability

High culpability (A)	Medium culpability (B)	Lesser culpability (C)
HC1–HC4, HC9	MC1, MC2	LC1, LC2, LC4–LC6

Harm A
Harm is initially assessed by the value of the money laundered.

Category 1	£10m or more	Starting point based on £30m
Category 2	£2m–£10m	Starting point based on £5m
Category 3	£500k–£2m	Starting point based on £1m
Category 4	£100k–£500k	Starting point based on £300k
Category 5	£10k–£100k	Starting point based on £50k
Category 6	Less than £10k	Starting point based on £5k

Harm B
   To complete the assessment of harm, the court should take into account the level of harm associated with the underlying offence to determine whether it warrants upward adjustment of the starting point within the range, or in appropriate cases, outside the range. Where it is possible to identify the underlying offence, the court should have regard to the relevant sentencing levels for that offence.

Step 2: use the following table to reach a provisional sentence (and see generally, ante).

Harm	Culpability (A)	Culpability (B)	Culpability (C)
Category 1	*Starting points and ranges* 10 years 8–13 years	*Starting points and ranges* 7 years 5–10 years	*Starting points and ranges* 4 years 3–6 years
Category 2	8 years 6–9 years	5 years 3.5–7 years	3.5 years 2–5 years
Category 3	7 years 5–8 years	5 years 3–6 years	3 years 1.5–4 years
Category 4	5 years 3–6 years	3 years 1.5–4 years	1.5 years 26 weeks–3 years
Category 5	3 years 1.5–4 years	1.5 years 26 weeks–3 years	26 weeks Medium level community order–12 months
Category 6	12 months 26 weeks–2 years	High level community order Low level community order–12 months	Low level community order Band B fine–medium level community order

Adjust the provisional sentence according to the presence of the following factors:

Factors increasing seriousness	Factors reducing seriousness or reflecting personal mitigation
A1, A2, A4–A11, A14.	M1–M12

Steps 3–8: see *ante*.

VI. Bribery

This section covers offences under sections 1, 2 and 6 of the Bribery Act 2010 (§§ 31-171, 31- **K-306** 172, 31-176 in the main work).

Step 1: determine the level of culpability and the harm category (and see generally, ante).
Culpability

High culpability (A)	Medium culpability (B)	Lesser culpability (C)
HC1–HC4, HC9–HC11	MC1, MC2	LC1–LC5

Harm is to be assessed in relation to any impact caused by the offending (whether to identifiable victims or in a wider context) and the actual or intended gain to the offender, and it is demonstrated by one or more of the following factors:

Category 1	• Serious detrimental effect on individuals (*e.g.* by provision of sub-standard goods or services resulting from the corrupt behaviour). • Serious environmental impact. • Serious undermining of the proper function of local or national government, business or public services. • Substantial actual or intended financial gain to offender or another or loss caused to others.
Category 2	• Significant detrimental effect on individuals.

	• As 2–4 in Category 1, but with substitution of "Significant" for "Serious" (2 & 3) and "Substantial" (4) • Risk of category 1 harm.
Category 3	• Limited detrimental impact on individuals, the environment, government, business or public services. • Risk of category 2 harm.
Category 4	• Risk of category 3 harm.

Step 2: use the following table to reach a provisional sentence (and see generally, ante).

Harm	Culpability (A)	Culpability (B)	Culpability (C)
	Starting points and ranges	*Starting points and ranges*	*Starting points and ranges*
Category 1	7 years 5–8 years	5 years 3–6 years	3 years 1.5–4 years
Category 2	5 years 3–6 years	3 years 1.5–4 years	1.5 years 26 weeks–3 years
Category 3	3 years 1.5–4 years	1.5 years 26 weeks–3 years	26 weeks Medium level community order–12 months
Category 4	1.5 years 26 weeks–3 years	26 weeks Medium level community order–12 months	Medium level community order Band B fine–high level community order

Adjust the provisional sentence according to the presence of the following factors:

Factors increasing seriousness	*Factors reducing seriousness or reflecting personal mitigation*
A1, A2, A3–A11, A20, A21	M1–M10

Steps 3–8: see *ante*.

VII. Corporate offenders

K-307   This section applies to corporate offenders and covers the offences in Sections I, II, V and VI plus cheating the public revenue, fraudulent evasion of value added tax (Value Added Tax Act 1994, s.72 (§ 25-532 in the main work)), fraudulent evasion of duty (CEMA 1979, s.170 (§ 25-474 in the main work)), and failure of commercial organisations to prevent bribery (Bribery Act 2010, s.7 (§ 31-177 in the main work)).

K-308   The guideline sets out 10 steps to be followed when sentencing for these offences. Step one requires the court to consider making a compensation order. Step two requires the court to consider confiscation. Step three requires the court to determine the level of culpability and the harm caused or intended. Where there are characteristics present that fall under different categories, the court should balance them to reach a fair assessment of the offender's culpability. The culpability attaching to the offender's role and motivation may be demonstrated by one or more of the following non-exhaustive characteristics:

High culpability (A)	Medium culpability (B)	Lesser culpability (C)
Plays a leading role in organised, planned activity (whether acting alone or with others). Wilful obstruction of detection (*e.g.* destruction of evidence, misleading investigators, suborning employees).	Plays a significant role in activity organised by others. Activity not unlawful from the outset. Recklessness in making false statement (1994 Act, s.72).	Plays a minor, peripheral role in activity organised by others. Some effort made to put bribery prevention measures in place but insufficient to amount to a defence (2010 Act, s.7).
Involving others through pressure or coercion (*e.g.* employees or suppliers). Targeting of vulnerable victims or large number of victims. Corruption of local or national government officials or ministers, or of law enforcement officials. Abuse of dominant market position or position of trust or responsibility. Offending committed over a sustained period of time. Culture of wilful disregard of offences by employees or agents with no effort to put effective systems in place (2010 Act, s.7, only).	All other cases where characteristics for categories A or C are not present.	Involvement through coercion, intimidation or exploitation.

Harm is represented by a financial sum calculated by reference to the table below: **K-309**

Fraud	For fraud, conspiracy to defraud, cheating the Revenue and fraudulent evasion of duty or value added tax, harm will normally be the actual or intended gross gain to the offender.
Bribery	The appropriate figure will normally be the gross profit from the contract obtained, retained or sought as a result of the offending. An alternative measure for offences under s.7 may be the likely cost avoided by failing to put in place appropriate measures to prevent bribery.
Money laundering	The appropriate figure will normally be the amount laundered or, alternatively, the likely cost avoided by failing to put in place an effective anti-money laundering programme if this is higher.
General	Where the actual or intended gain cannot be established, the appropriate measure will be the amount that the court considers was likely to be achieved in all the circumstances. In the absence of sufficient evidence of the amount that was likely to be obtained, 10–20 per cent of the relevant revenue (*e.g.* 10–20 per cent of the worldwide revenue derived from the product or business area to which the offence relates for the period of the offending) may be an appropriate measure. There may be large cases in which the true harm is to commerce or markets generally. That may justify adopting a harm figure beyond the normal measures here set out.

K-310   Having determined the culpability level, step four requires the court to determine the starting point within the category range using the table below. The harm figure from step three is multiplied by the relevant percentage figure representing culpability.

	A (high)	*B (medium)*	*C (low)*
Harm figure multiplier	*Starting point 300%* *Category range 250% to 400%*	*Starting point 200%* *Category range 100% to 300%*	*Starting point 100%* *Category range 20% to 150%*

K-311   After determining the appropriate starting point, the court should then consider adjustment within the category range for aggravating or mitigating features. In some cases it may be appropriate to move outside the identified category range. The following is a non-exhaustive list of aggravating and mitigating factors:

Increasing seriousness	*Reducing seriousness or reflecting mitigation*
Previous relevant convictions or subject to previous relevant civil or regulatory enforcement action.	No previous relevant convictions or previous relevant civil or regulatory enforcement action.
Corporation or subsidiary set up to commit fraudulent activity.	Victims voluntarily reimbursed/compensated.
Fraudulent activity endemic within corporation.	No actual loss to victims.
Attempts made to conceal misconduct.	Corporation co-operated with investigation, made early admissions and/or voluntarily reported offending.
Substantial harm (whether financial or otherwise) suffered by victims of offending or by third parties affected by offending.	Offending committed under previous director(s)/manager(s).
Risk of harm greater than actual or intended harm (*e.g.* in banking/credit fraud).	Little or no actual gain to corporation from offending.
Substantial harm to integrity or confidence of markets.	
Substantial harm to integrity of local or national governments.	
Serious nature of underlying criminal activity (money laundering offences).	
Offence committed across borders or jurisdictions.	

K-312   The court should determine the appropriate level of fine in accordance with the CJA 2003, s.164 (§ 5-674 in the main work). Where the offender fails to provide comprehensive accounts for the last three years, or where the court is not satisfied that it has been given sufficiently reliable information, the court will be entitled to draw reasonable inferences as to the offender's means from evidence it has heard and from all the circumstances of the case. The information that should be examined in relation to different companies and bodies is then set out (this coincides with the guidance in the Sentencing Guidelines Council's guideline on corporate manslaughter and health and safety offences causing death (*ante*, K-258)).

K-313   Under step five, the court should consider the overall effect of its orders and whether there are any further factors that require an adjustment in the level of the fine. The combination of orders ought to achieve the removal of all gain, appropriate additional punishment and deterrence. The court may adjust the fine to ensure that these objectives are met in a fair way, and should consider any further factors relevant to the setting of the fine to ensure that it is proportionate, with regard to the seriousness of the offence and the size and financial position of the organisation. The fine must be substantial enough to have a real economic impact. Whether the fine will put the offender out of business will be relevant, and in some bad cases this may be an acceptable consequence. The court should consider whether the level of fine would cause unacceptable harm to third parties (bearing in mind that the payment of any compensation should take priority over any fine). Below is a non-exhaustive list of additional factual elements to consider in adjusting the level of fine:

- whether it fulfils the objectives of punishment, deterrence and removal of gain;
- the offender's value, worth or available means;
- whether the fine impairs the offender's ability to make restitution to the victims;
- the fine's impact on the offender's ability to implement effective compliance programmes;
- the fine's impact on the employment of staff, service users, customers and the local economy (but not shareholders);
- the fine's impact on the performance of public or charitable functions.

At step six, the court should take into account the SOCPA 2005, ss.73 (assistance by defendant: **K-314** reduction of sentence (§ 5-132 in the main work)) and 74 (assistance by defendant: review of sentence (*ibid.*, § 5-133)), and any other rule of law by virtue of which an offender may receive a discounted sentence in consequence of assistance given (or offered) to the prosecutor or investigator. At step seven, the court should take into account any potential reduction for a guilty plea. At step eight, the court must consider whether to make any ancillary orders, and at step nine, if sentencing the offender for more than one offence, it must consider the totality principle. At step 10, the court must give reasons for and explain the effect of the sentence.

X. "Theft Offences"

The Sentencing Council for England and Wales has issued a definitive guideline covering the **★K-315** offences set out at I to VI, *post*, applying to all offenders aged 18 or over who are sentenced on or after February 1, 2016. Each section describes a process of eight steps. The annex sets out fine bands, and a non-exhaustive list of examples of requirements that might be appropriate for low, medium and high level community orders.

Step 1 (determining the offence category)

This involves determination of the offence category by reference **only** to the tables in each **K-316** section. In order to do this, the court should make an assessment of culpability and harm.

Culpability

The level of culpability is determined by weighing up all factors that are relevant to the **K-317** determination of the offender's role and the extent to which the offending was planned and the sophistication with which it was carried out. The following indicators of culpability are used throughout the guideline.

High culpability

HC1:	A leading role where offending is part of a group activity
HC2:	Involvement of others through coercion, intimidation or exploitation
HC3:	Breach of a high degree of trust or responsibility
HC4:	Sophisticated nature of offence/ significant planning
HC5:	Offence involving intimidation or the use or threat of force
HC6:	Deliberately targeting victim on basis of vulnerability
HC7:	Significant use or threat of force
HC8:	Offender subject to a banning order from the relevant store
HC9:	Child accompanying offender is actively used to facilitate offence (not merely present when offence committed)
HC10:	Abuse of position of power, trust or responsibility
HC11:	Professional and sophisticated offence
HC12:	Advance knowledge of primary offence
HC13:	Possession of very recently stolen goods from a domestic burglary or robbery
HC14:	Significant steps taken to conceal identity and/ or avoid detection
HC15:	Offender equipped for robbery or domestic burglary

HC16:   Commission of offence in association with, or to further, other criminal activity

Medium culpability

MC1:   A significant role where offending is part of a group activity

MC2:   Some degree of planning involved

MC3:   Breach of some degree of trust or responsibility

MC4:   Limited use or threat of force

MC5:   Offender acquires goods for resale

MC6:   All other cases where indicators of high or lesser culpability are not present

Lesser culpability

LC1:   Performed limited function under direction

LC2:   Involved through coercion, intimidation or exploitation

LC3:   Little or no planning

LC4:   Limited awareness or understanding of offence

LC5:   Mental disorder/ learning disability where linked to the commission of offence

LC6:   Goods acquired for offender's personal use

Where there are characteristics present that fall under different levels of culpability, the court should balance them to reach a fair assessment of the offender's culpability.

Harm

K-318   As to the assessment of harm, see the individual sections.

Step 2 (starting point and category range)

K-319   Having determined the category, the court should use the appropriate starting point to reach a sentence within the category range in the tables. The starting points apply to all offenders irrespective of plea and previous convictions.

The tables of starting points and category ranges in each section are followed by a "non-exhaustive list of additional factual elements providing the context of the offence and factors relating to the offender." The court is then to identify whether any combination of these or other relevant factors should result in an upward or downward adjustment from the sentence arrived at based on culpability and harm alone.

The following aggravating and mitigating factors are used throughout the guideline.

Aggravating factors

A1:   Previous convictions, having regard to (a) the nature of the offence to which the conviction relates and its relevance to the current offence, and (b) the time that has elapsed since any previous conviction

A2:   Offence committed whilst on bail

A3:   Offence motivated by, or demonstrating hostility based on, any of the following characteristics or presumed characteristics of the victim: religion, race, disability, sexual orientation or transgender identity

A4:   Stealing goods to order

A5:   Steps taken to prevent the victim reporting offence or obtaining assistance and/ or from assisting or supporting the prosecution

A6:   Offender motivated by intention to cause harm or take revenge

A7:   Offence committed over sustained period of time

A8:   Attempts to conceal/ dispose of evidence

A9:   Failure to comply with current court orders

A10: Offence committed on licence

A11: Offences taken into consideration

A12: Blame wrongly placed on others

A13: Established evidence of community/ wider impact (in relation to I and II, *post*, for issues other than prevalence)

A14: Prevalence. There may be exceptional local circumstances that may lead a court to decide that prevalence should influence sentencing levels. The pivotal issue in such cases will be the harm caused to the community. It is essential that the court before taking account of prevalence (a) has supporting evidence from an external source, *e.g.*, community impact statements, to justify claims that a particular crime is prevalent in the area, and is causing particular harm in that community, and (b) is satisfied that there is a compelling need to treat the offence more seriously than elsewhere.

A15: Seriousness of the underlying offence, *e.g.*, armed robbery

A16: Deliberate destruction, disposal or defacing of stolen property

A17: Damage to a third party

A18: Electricity abstracted from another person's property

Mitigating factors

M1: No previous convictions **or** no relevant/ recent convictions

M2: Remorse, particularly where evidenced by voluntary reparation to the victim

M3: Good character and/ or exemplary conduct

M4: Serious medical conditions requiring urgent, intensive or long-term treatment

M5: Age and/ or lack of maturity where it affects the responsibility of the offender

M6: Mental disorder or learning disability

M7: Sole or primary carer for dependent relatives

M8: Determination and/ or demonstration of steps having been taken to address addiction or offending behaviour

M9: Inappropriate degree of trust or responsibility

M10: Offender experiencing exceptional financial hardship

Steps 3-8

These are standard steps in guidelines issued by the Sentencing Council. They require the **K-320** court to consider the SOCPA 2005, ss.73 and 74 (assistance by defendants: reduction or review of sentence (§§ 5-132, 5-133 in the main work)), credit for a guilty plea, the totality principle, the question of confiscation, compensation and any appropriate ancillary orders, and the need to give reasons and to make any appropriate allowance for time spent on bail (CJA 2003, s.240A (*ibid.*, 5-645)).

I. General theft (Theft Act 1968, s.1 (§ 21-15 in the main work))

This covers all offences of theft other than from a shop or stall (as to which, see II, *post*). **K-321**

Step 1: determine the level of culpability and the harm category (and see generally, ante)
Culpability

High culpability	Medium culpability	Lesser culpability
HC1-HC6	MC1-MC3, MC6	LC1-LC4

Harm

Harm is assessed by reference to the financial loss that results from the theft and any significant additional harm suffered by the victim or others. Intended loss should be used where actual loss has been prevented. Examples of significant additional harm may include, but are not limited to:

    (i) items stolen were of substantial value to the loser, regardless of monetary worth,

    (ii) high level of inconvenience caused to the victim or others,

    (iii) consequential financial harm to victim or others,

    (iv) emotional distress,

    (v) fear/ loss of confidence caused by the crime,

    (vi) risk of or actual injury to persons or damage to property,

    (vii) impact of theft on a business,

    (viii) damage to heritage assets,

    (ix) disruption caused to infrastructure.

Category 1	Very high value goods stolen (above £100,000) **or** High value with significant additional harm to the victim or others
Category 2	High value goods stolen (£10,000 to £100,000) **and** no significant additional harm **or** Medium value with significant additional harm to the victim or others
Category 3	Medium value goods stolen (£500 to £10,000) **and** no significant additional harm **or** Low value with significant additional harm to the victim or others
Category 4	Low value goods stolen (up to £500) **and** Little or no significant additional harm to the victim or others

Step 2: use the following tables to reach a provisional sentence (and see generally, ante)

Harm	High culpability	Medium culpability	Lesser culpability
	Starting point and ranges	*Starting point and ranges*	*Starting point and ranges*
Category 1 Adjustment should be made for any significant additional harm factors where very high value goods are stolen.	3.5 years' custody 2.5 - 6 years' custody	2 years' custody 1 - 3.5 years' custody	12 months' custody 26 weeks' - 2 years' custody
Category 2	2 years' custody 12 months' - 3.5 years' custody	12 months' custody 26 weeks' - 2 years' custody	High level community order Low-level community order - 36 weeks' custody
Category 3	12 months' custody 26 weeks' - 2 years' custody	High level community order Low-level community order - 36 weeks' custody	Band C fine Band B fine - Low level community order
Category 4	High level community order Medium-level community order - 36 weeks' custody	Low level community order Band C fine - Medium level community order	Band B fine Discharge - Band C fine

    This table refers to single offences. Where there are multiple offences, consecutive sentences may be appropriate. Where multiple offences are committed in circumstances that justify consecutive sentences, and the total amount stolen is in excess of £1 million, then an aggregate sentence in excess of seven years' custody may be appropriate.

Where the offender is dependent on or has a propensity to misuse drugs or alcohol and there is sufficient prospect of success, a community order with a drug rehabilitation requirement under section 209 (§ 5-275 in the main work), or an alcohol treatment requirement under section 212 (*ibid.*, § 5-278), of the CJA 2003 may be a proper alternative to a short or moderate custodial sentence.

Where the offender suffers from a medical condition that is susceptible to treatment but does not warrant detention under a hospital order, a community order with a mental health treatment requirement under section 207 (*ibid.*, § 5-273) of the 2003 Act may be a proper alternative to a short or moderate custodial sentence.

Adjust the provisional sentence according to the presence of the following factors:

Factors increasing seriousness	*Factors reducing seriousness or reflecting personal mitigation*
A1-A14	M1-M9

II. Theft from a shop or stall (Theft Act 1968, s.1 (§ 21-15 in the main work))

Step 1: determine the level of culpability and the harm category (and see generally, ante)
Culpability

High culpability	*Medium culpability*	*Lesser culpability*
HC1, HC2, HC4, HC7-HC9	MC1, MC2, MC4, MC6	LC1-LC3, LC5

Harm

Harm is assessed by reference to the financial loss that results from the theft and any significant additional harm suffered by the victim. Intended loss should be used where actual loss has been prevented. Examples of significant additional harm may include, but are not limited to:
   (i) emotional distress,
   (ii) damage to property,
   (iii) effect on business,
   (iv) a greater impact on the victim due to the size or type of the business,
   (v) a particularly vulnerable victim.

Category 1	High value goods stolen (above £1,000) **or** Medium value with significant additional harm to the victim
Category 2	Medium value goods stolen (£200 to £1,000) **and** no significant additional harm **or** Low value with significant additional harm to the victim
Category 3	Low value goods stolen (up to £200) **and** Little or no significant additional harm to the victim

Step 2: use the following tables to reach a provisional sentence (and see generally, ante)

Harm	*High culpability*	*Medium culpability*	*Lesser culpability*
	Starting point and ranges	*Starting point and ranges*	*Starting point and ranges*
Category 1 Where the value greatly exceeds £1,000 it may be appropriate to move outside the	26 weeks' custody 12 weeks - 3 years' custody	Medium level community order Low level community order - 26 weeks' custody	Band C fine Band B fine - Low level community order

Harm	High culpability	Medium culpability	Lesser culpability
	Starting point and ranges	*Starting point and ranges*	*Starting point and ranges*
identified range. Adjustment should be made for any significant additional harm where high value goods are stolen.			
Category 2	12 weeks' custody High level community order - 26 weeks' custody	Low level community order Band C fine - Medium level community order	Band B fine Band A fine - Band C fine
Category 3	High level community order Low level community order - 12 weeks' custody	Band C fine Band B fine - Low level community order	Band A fine Discharge - Band B fine

Where there are multiple offences, consecutive sentences may be appropriate.

Previous diversionary work with an offender does not preclude the court from considering this type of sentencing option again if appropriate.

The same guidance applies as that under section I (*ante*) in relation to offenders who misuse drugs or alcohol, and those who suffer from a medical condition.

Adjust the provisional sentence according to the presence of the following factors:

Factors increasing seriousness	*Factors reducing seriousness or reflecting personal mitigation*
A1-A6, A8-A11, A13, A14	M1-M8, M10

As to A1 "previous convictions", relevant recent convictions may justify an upward adjustment, including outside the category range. In cases involving significant persistent offending, the community and custody thresholds may be crossed even though the offence otherwise warrants a lesser sentence. Any custodial sentence must be kept to the necessary minimum.

III. Handling stolen goods (Theft Act 1968, s.22 (§ 21-221 in the main work))

Step 1: determine the level of culpability and the harm category (and see generally, ante)

K-323 *Culpability*

High culpability	*Medium culpability*	*Lesser culpability*
HC1, HC2, HC10-HC13	MC1, MC5, MC6	LC1-LC4, LC6

Harm

Harm is assessed by reference to the financial value (to the loser) of the handled goods and any significant additional harm associated with the underlying offence on the victim or others. Examples of additional harm may include, but are not limited to:

(i) property stolen from a domestic burglary or a robbery (unless this has already been taken into account in assessing culpability),

(ii) items stolen were of substantial value to the loser, regardless of monetary worth,

(iii) metal theft causing disruption to infrastructure,

(iv) damage to heritage assets.

Category 1	Very high value goods stolen (above £100,000) **or** High value with significant additional harm to the victim or others
Category 2	High value goods stolen (£10,000 to £100,000) **and** no significant additional harm **or** Medium value with significant additional harm to the victim or others
Category 3	Medium value goods stolen (£1,000 to £10,000) **and** no significant additional harm **or** Low value with significant additional harm to the victim or others
Category 4	Low value goods stolen (up to £1,000) **and** Little or no significant additional harm to the victim or others

Step 2: use the following tables to reach a provisional sentence (and see generally, ante)

Harm	High culpability	Medium culpability	Lesser culpability
	Starting point and ranges	*Starting point and ranges*	*Starting point and ranges*
Category 1 Where the value greatly exceeds £100,000, it may be appropriate to move outside the identified range. Adjustment should be made for any significant additional harm where very high value stolen goods are handled.	5 years' custody 3 - 8 years' custody	3 years' custody 1.5 - 4 years' custody	12 months' custody 26 weeks - 1.5 years' custody
Category 2	3 years' custody 1.5 - 4 years' custody	12 months' custody 26 weeks' - 1.5 years' custody	High level community order Low level community order - 26 weeks' custody
Category 3	12 months' custody 26 weeks' - 2 years' custody	High level community order Low level community order - 26 weeks' custody	Band C fine Band B fine - Low level community order
Category 4	High level community order Medium level community order - 26 weeks	Low level community order Band C fine - High level community order	Band B fine Discharge - Band C fine

Where there are multiple offences, consecutive sentences may be appropriate.
Adjust the provisional sentence according to the presence of the following factors:

Factors increasing seriousness	Factors reducing seriousness or reflecting personal mitigation
A1, A2, A9-A11, A13, A15-A17	M1, M3-M8

IV. Going equipped for theft or burglary (Theft Act 1968, s.25 (§ 21-288 in the main work))

Step 1: determine the level of culpability and the harm category (and see generally, ante)

K-324   *Culpability*

High culpability	Medium culpability	Lesser culpability
HC1, HC2, HC4, HC14, HC15	MC1, MC6	LC2-LC4

Harm

The level of harm is determined by weighing up all the factors of the case to determine the harm that would be caused if the item or items were used to commit a substantive offence.

Greater harm	Possession of item or items that have the potential to facilitate an offence affecting a large number of victims
	Possession of item or items that have the potential to facilitate an offence involving high value items
Lesser harm	All other cases

Step 2: use the following tables to reach a provisional sentence (and see generally, ante)

Harm	High culpability	Medium culpability	Lesser culpability
	Starting point and ranges	*Starting point and ranges*	*Starting point and ranges*
Greater	12 months' custody 26 weeks'- 1.5 years' custody	18 weeks' custody High level community order - 36 weeks' custody	Medium level community order Low level community order - High level community order
Lesser	26 weeks' custody 12 - 36 weeks' custody	High level community order Medium level community order - 12 weeks' custody	Band C fine Discharge - Medium level community order

Where there are multiple offences, consecutive sentences may be appropriate.

Adjust the provisional sentence according to the presence of the following factors:

Factors increasing seriousness	Factors reducing seriousness or reflecting personal mitigation
A1, A2, A8-A11, A13	M1, M3-M8

V. Abstracting electricity (Theft Act 1968, s.13 (§ 21-169 in the main work))

Step 1: determine the level of culpability and the harm category (and see generally, ante)

K-325   *Culpability*

High culpability	Medium culpability	Lesser culpability
HC1, HC2, HC4, HC10, HC16	MC1, MC6	LC1, LC2, LC4

Harm

The level of harm is determined by weighing up all the factors of the case to determine the harm caused.

Greater harm	A significant risk of, or actual, injury to persons or damage to property Significant volume of electricity extracted [*sic*] as evidenced by length of time of offending and/ or advanced type of illegal process used
Lesser harm	All other cases

Step 2: use the following tables to reach a provisional sentence (and see generally, ante)

Harm	High culpability	Medium culpability	Lesser culpability
	Starting point and ranges	*Starting point and ranges*	*Starting point and ranges*
Greater	12 weeks' custody High level community order - 12 months' custody	Medium level community order Low level community order - 12 weeks' custody	Band C fine Band B fine - Low level community order
Lesser	High level community order Medium level community order - 12 weeks' custody	Low level community order Band C fine - Medium level community order	Band A fine Discharge - Band C fine

Adjust the provisional sentence according to the presence of the following factors:

Factors increasing seriousness	*Factors reducing seriousness or reflecting personal mitigation*
A1, A2, A8-A13, A18	M1, M3-M8

VI. Making off without payment (Theft Act 1978, s.3 (§ 21-303 in the main work))

Step 1: determine the level of culpability and the harm category (and see generally, ante)
Culpability

High culpability	Medium culpability	Lesser culpability
HC1, HC2, HC4-HC6	MC1, MC2, MC6	LC1-LC4

Harm

Harm is assessed by reference to the actual loss that results from the offence and any significant additional harm suffered by the victim. Examples of additional harm may include, but are not limited to:

   (i) a high level of inconvenience caused to the victim,
  (ii) emotional distress,
 (iii) fear/ loss of confidence caused by the crime,
 (iv) a greater impact on the victim due to the size or type of the business.

Category 1	Goods or services obtained above £200 **or** Goods/ services up to £200 with significant additional harm to the victim
Category 2	Goods or services obtained up to £200 **and** Little or no significant additional harm to the victim

Step 2: use the following tables to reach a provisional sentence (and see generally, ante)

Harm	High culpability	Medium culpability	Lesser culpability
	Starting point and ranges	*Starting point and ranges*	*Starting point and ranges*
Category 1 Where the value greatly exceeds £200, it may be appropriate to move outside the identified range. Adjustment should be made for any significant additional harm for offences above £200.	12 weeks' custody High level community order - 36 weeks' custody	Low level community order Band C fine - High level community order	Band B fine Band A fine - Low level community order
Category 2	Medium level community order Low level community order - 12 weeks' custody	Band C fine Band B fine - Low level community order	Band A fine Discharge - Band B fine

Where there are multiple offences, consecutive sentences may be appropriate.
Adjust the provisional sentence according to the presence of the following factors:

Factors increasing seriousness	Factors reducing seriousness or reflecting personal mitigation
A1-A3, A5, A8-A11, A13	M1-M8

II. AUTHORITIES ON OFFICIAL GUIDELINES

A. Reduction in Sentence for Guilty Plea

Introduction

K-350   The purpose of this section of this appendix is to give details of authorities considering particular aspects of final guidelines issued by the Sentencing Guidelines Council and which are set out in full or summarised in the previous section of this appendix. There is, however, a fine line that divides cases specifically on some aspect of a guideline from those considering a statutory provision or some more general aspect of sentencing. Accordingly, practitioners looking for authorities on sentencing in relation to one of the guideline subjects should also make reference to the relevant paragraphs of the main work.

Relevant main work references

K-351   For sentencing guidelines generally, see section 125 of the Coroners and Justice Act 2009 (§ 5-149 in the main work); and for the reduction in sentence for a guilty plea, see section 144 of that Act (*ibid.*, § 5-107), and the authorities set out at §§ 5-109 *et seq.*, and, in particular, §§ 5-115, 5-118.

First reasonable opportunity

K-351a   See *R. v. Caley*, § 5-114 in the main work.

Credit in overwhelming cases

K-352   Even in overwhelming cases, a plea of guilty was a distinct public benefit and the earlier it was put forward the better it was for everyone; where, therefore, the judge had given no credit for a plea of guilty on the basis that the evidence was such that the offender had had no option but to plead guilty, and where no specific feature of the case required the Sentencing Guidelines Council's guidance on credit for pleas of guilty (*ante*, K-7) to be disapplied, it was appropriate to vary the sentence to allow limited credit; it would be productive ultimately of chaos, and would undermine consistency in sentencing and the value of a guilty plea to the criminal justice system, if an existing guideline could be disregarded, unless it was possible to find that the interests of justice required its disapplication; it was important to underline that part of the advice that would be given to a defendant was that a guilty plea, even in an extreme case, would attract some discount: *R. v. Wilson* [2012] 2 Cr.App.R.(S.) 77, CA.

Wilson, ante, was considered in *R. v. Caley*, § 5-115 in the main work.

In *R. v. Walter* [2015] 1 Cr.App.R.(S.) 22, CA, it was held that a judge had been entitled to take the view that the evidence was overwhelming and, in consequence, to reduce the standard discount for a plea of guilty to one of 20 per cent in accordance with the Sentencing Guidelines Council's guideline, notwithstanding that, at the preliminary hearing at which the defendant had indicated a wish to plead guilty, there had been no indictment, the prosecution indicating that they were awaiting an expert report before finalising the indictment (which was not the principal evidence).

Walter, ante, was a case of causing death by dangerous driving (RTA 1988, s.1 (§ 32-2 in the main work)). For two cases of causing serious injury by dangerous driving (RTA 1988, s.1A (§ 32-25 in the main work)), where the evidence was said to have been overwhelming, see *R. v. Jenkins* [2015] 1 Cr.App.R.(S.) 70, CA (discount should have been limited to 20 per cent), and *R. v. Buckle* [2015] 1 Cr.App.R.(S.) 68, CA (discount of 30 per cent was "generous").

[The next paragraph is K-360.]

B. Overarching Principles: Seriousness

Introduction

As to the purpose of this section of this appendix, see *ante*, K-350. **K-360**

Relevant main work references

For sentencing guidelines generally, see section 125 of the Coroners and Justice Act 2009 (§ **K-361** 5-149 in the main work); and for the determination of the seriousness of an offence, see section 143 of that Act (*ibid.*, § 5-67).

Vulnerability of victim

It had not been open to the Crown Court to sentence on the basis that the victim of a domestic **K-362** assault was particularly vulnerable where none of the features of vulnerability mentioned in paragraph 1.17 of the guideline on overarching principles (*ante*, K-18) or in paragraph 3 of the domestic violence guideline (*ante*, K-82 *et seq.*) were present, with the finding instead being based on the complainant's timid demeanour when giving evidence: *Barnard v. DPP* [2011] A.C.D. 108, DC.

[The next paragraph is K-370.]

C. New Sentences: Criminal Justice Act 2003

Introduction

As to the purpose of this section of this appendix, see *ante*, K-350. **K-370**

Relevant main work references

For sentencing guidelines generally, see section 125 of the Coroners and Justice Act 2009 (§ **K-371** 5-149 in the main work). As to community sentences generally, see § 5-185 *et seq.* in the main work; as to the restrictions on the imposition of such sentences, see *ibid.*, § 5-248; as to community orders generally, see *ibid.*, §§ 5-253 *et seq.*; as to the requirements that may be included in a community order, see *ibid.*, §§ 5-265 *et seq.*; as to the misleading terminology adopted in this guideline, see *ibid.*, § 5-288.

Transitional arrangements

K-372   In *R. v. Whittle* (2007) 151 S.J. 398, CA, it was said that whereas paragraph 2.1.9 suggests that any sentence of 12 months or more should be reduced by in the region of 15 per cent to reflect the more onerous nature of the release on licence regime under the CJA 2003, where an offender is sentenced to a term of four years or more, the sentencer may be entitled not to reduce the sentence to the full extent or at all; in relation to such sentences, the increased onerousness of the licence conditions would be more or less in balance with the fact that the offender would be entitled to release at the half way point under the new regime instead of at the two-thirds point under the pre-existing regime.

[The next paragraph is K-380.]

D. Manslaughter by Reason of Provocation

Introduction

K-380   As to the purpose of this section of this appendix, see *ante*, K-350.

Relevant main work references

K-381   For sentencing guidelines generally, see section 125 of the Coroners and Justice Act 2009 (§ 5-149 in the main work); and for provocation as a defence to a charge of murder generally, see *ante*, §§ 19-65 *et seq.* For "loss of control" as a defence to murder, see §§ 19-54 *et seq.* in the main work. It is submitted that pending the issuing of any new guideline, the existing guideline may be applied to the new defence, with appropriate caution to take account of the differing ingredients of the two defences.

Approach to guideline

K-382   Referring to heightened and justifiable public concern about cases involving the stabbing of one teenager by another, the court in *R. v. Daley* [2008] 2 Cr.App.R.(S.) 95, CA, said that the guideline had not been intended to lay down fixed or rigid boundaries.

In *Att.-Gen.'s Reference (No. 8 of 2011) (R. v. Edwards)* [2012] 1 Cr.App.R.(S.) 53, CA, the court emphasised that the guideline on manslaughter by reason of provocation should be approached with caution. It did not reflect the impact on sentencing for murder of Schedule 21 to the CJA 2003 (§§ 5-425 *et seq.* in the main work); and, in a series of cases, it had now been recognised that the upward shift in sentencing for murder required a corresponding upward shift in sentencing for manslaughter (see, in particular, *R. v. Thornley*, *post*, K-383). The court commented that the apparently higher threshold for the loss of control defence under the Coroners and Justice Act 2009 (§§ 19-55, 19-56 in the main work), as compared with the common law defence of provocation, may impact on sentencing both for murder and for manslaughter.

For a case considering *Att.-Gen.'s Reference (No. 8 of 2011) (R. v. Edwards)*, and its significance for manslaughter by reason of loss of control, see *R. v. Ward* (§ 19-64 in the main work).

Use of a knife

K-383   Just as sentencing guidelines are not tramlines, nor are they ring-fenced; the interests of justice require that consideration be given to any subsequent thinking of the Court of Appeal and the legislature on sentencing issues which may impact on any definitive guideline; since the guideline on manslaughter by reason of provocation was issued, there had been at least four developments relevant to the sentencing of manslaughter by provocation using a knife (*viz.* (a) the Court of Appeal had, in *R. v. Povey* (§ 24-168 in the main work), addressed the issue of knife crime generally, and the need for the courts to be alert on appropriate occasions to impose deterrent sentences on those who carry knives, (b) the court had come to appreciate the impact of Schedule 21 to the CJA 2003 (*ibid.*, §§ 5-425 *et seq.*) on cases of manslaughter because of the need for there to be a proportionate relationship with sentences for murder, (c) a specific provision relating to the use of a knife as a murder weapon had been introduced into Schedule 21, and (d) the entire law on provocation had been changed by legislation); as to (a) and (b), the weight to be attached to decisions of the Court of Appeal on sentencing issues or policy was undiminished by the issue of guidelines; as to (c) and (d), these changes could not be ignored on the basis of a guideline issued in 2005; accordingly, the use of a knife should now be regarded as a more significant feature of aggravation than it was when the guideline was published: *R. v. Thornley* [2011] 2 Cr.App.R.(S.) 62, CA.

[The next paragraph is K-390.]

E. ROBBERY

Introduction

As to the purpose of this section of this appendix, see *ante*, K-350.　　　　　**K-390**

Relevant main work references

For sentencing guidelines generally, see section 125 of the Coroners and Justice Act 2009 (§ **K-391** 5-149 in the main work)). As to this guideline, see, in particular, § 21-93 in the main work; as to sentencing for armed robbery, for robbery in the course of burglary and for the hijacking of cars, see *ibid.*, §§ 21-91, 21-92 and 21-95 respectively. For examples of the application of the dangerous offender provisions of the 2003 Act to cases of robbery, see *ibid.*, § 5-520.

"less sophisticated commercial robbery"

In *Att.-Gen.'s References (Nos 32, 33 and 34 of 2007) (R. v. Bate)* [2008] 1 Cr.App.R.(S.) 35, CA, it **K-392** was held that for the purposes of the guideline on robbery, (i) the boundary between a "less sophisticated commercial robbery" falling within the guideline and a "professionally planned commercial robbery" falling without the guideline is not a hard and fast one (to like effect, see *R. v. Lafferty* [2012] 2 Cr.App.R.(S.) 93, CA, and *R. v. O'Bryan* [2013] 2 Cr.App.R.(S.) 16, CA (a case which fell on or just over the borderline)) and many cases would properly be regarded as falling on either side of the line; and a judge had been entitled to regard as falling within the guideline (and to regard the case as a level 1 case) two robberies during normal working hours (involving prior reconnaissance or information and the use of a stolen car) in which the three unarmed defendants, wearing masks and using a stolen car, had intercepted unaccompanied lorry drivers making deliveries of cigarettes to shops; and (ii) whereas "vulnerability of the victim" as an aggravating factor is expressly stated to be "targeting the elderly, the young, those with disabilities and persons performing a service to the public, especially outside normal working hours", there was nonetheless a low level of vulnerability (and hence aggravation) where the targets of the robberies were delivery drivers working alone, albeit delivering to shops where there were people to receive them.

Whilst the CJA 2003, s.172, required a court to have regard to a relevant sentencing guideline (see now the Coroners and Justice Act 2009, s.125 (§ 5-149 in the main work)), a guideline is only a guideline and the guideline on robbery cannot cover each and every category because of the immense variety of circumstances in which offences of robbery are committed, and as such there is a wide spectrum of offences that fall between "less sophisticated commercial robberies" and "professionally-planned commercial robberies", as described in the guideline; where, therefore, four men had "swiftly" robbed the driver of a delivery van in a robbery that was "cynically and callously planned" with one of the men persuading him to drive with them to a secluded place whilst wearing a mask and rubber gloves and being armed with a knife, the case did not fall neatly and cleanly within the category of the "less sophisticated commercial robbery" (which has an indicated starting point of four years' custody) and instead fell within a range of six to 10 years (possibly more for a ring leader); and, in the case of the respondent (40), who acted as the driver of the robbers' vehicle, three years' imprisonment on conviction was unduly lenient given that, although he was not a prime mover and did not wield the knife, it must have been within his contemplation that some degree of threat or force would be used on the victim; taking account, however, of the fact that he suffered from Asperger's syndrome, which made him vulnerable to being manipulated by more sophisticated offenders, the appropriate bracket was six to eight years' imprisonment: *Att.-Gen.'s Reference (No. 147 of 2006) (R. v. Gunner)* [2008] 1 Cr.App.R.(S.) 9(2), CA (substituting six years).

As to there being a category of case that falls between the "less sophisticated commercial robbery" and the "professionally planned commercial robbery", see also *R. v. Eccleston* [2008] 2 Cr.App.R.(S.) 56, CA.

In *R. v. Yarboi* [2010] 2 Cr.App.R.(S.) 40, CA, one of the defendants snatched a cash box containing £11,530 from a security guard who was attempting to deliver it to a cash machine. He ran to a car (the number plates of which had been removed) being driven by another of the defendants and, after half a mile, they abandoned the car and got into a third vehicle driven by a further defendant. The Court of Appeal found that the case did not fit easily within any of the categories within the Sentencing Guidelines Council's guideline (see *ante*, K-80), being close to the border between "less sophisticated commercial robberies" and "professionally planned robberies". The most aggravating feature was that the robbery had been pre-planned, although cases could come within the least serious category even where there had been some pre-planning. The removal of the first car's number plates, and the use of a second "clean" getaway car, however, made the case rather more unusual, and showed a significant degree of planning. On the other hand, the force used was minimal, being only that which was necessary in order to snatch the container from the security guard, there was only a single robber involved at that stage, and there was no intimidation from a group, no weapon, no threat of force, and no disguises were used. The court said that whilst the planning, therefore, might have taken the case out of the least serious category, it was difficult to conclude that it was of such sophistication as to justify a starting point of double the maximum for that category. In all the circumstances, it was decided that the proper starting point was four-and-a-half years.

"vulnerability of the victim"

K-393   See *Att.-Gen.'s References (Nos 32, 33 and 34 of 2007) (R. v. Bate)*, *ante*, § K-392.

Ranges

K-394   For an example of a sentence that was significantly above the recommended range being upheld on account of "additional aggravating features", albeit that most of them are foreshadowed in the guideline, see *R. v. Sheller* [2010] 1 Cr.App.R.(S.) 107, CA.

In *R. v. Taylor (Shaun)* [2012] 2 Cr.App.R.(S.) 98, CA, it was held that the judge had been wrong to sentence on the basis that the guideline sentences were out of date and that it had been "almost a different world when they came into force"; when appropriate, the court added, it is of course open to a judge to sentence outside guidelines and to support such a course by giving reasons for doing so; but personal disagreement with a guideline will not furnish a good reason for departing from them; and the guideline was not out of date.

Violent robbery in the home

K-395   It was said in *R. v. Smith (Claire Louise)* [2015] 2 Cr.App.R.(S.) 35, CA, that whilst the guideline expressly states that it does not provide guidance for violent robberies in the home, but then indicates a sentencing range of 13 to 16 years' imprisonment for such offences where a high level of violence is involved, where an offence could be seen as a violent personal robbery in the home or an aggravated burglary, reference to the Sentencing Council's guideline on aggravated burglary (*ante*, K-259 *et seq.*) was likely to be more helpful than that one brief observation in the robbery guideline.

[The next paragraph is K-400.]

F. Breach of a Protective Order

Introduction

K-400   As to the purpose of this section of this appendix, see *ante*, K-350.

Relevant main work references

For sentencing guidelines generally, see section 125 of the Coroners and Justice Act 2009 (§ 5-149 in the main work); for restraining orders under the Protection from Harassment Act 1997, see *ibid.*, §§ 19-358a *et seq.*; and for sexual harm prevention orders, see *ibid.*, §§ 20-323 *et seq.* As to breach of an anti-social [criminal] behaviour order, see *ante*, K-196 *et seq.* **K-401**

Taking the original offence into account

As to the importance of avoiding sentencing again for the original offence when sentencing for a breach, and as to the need to reserve the maximum sentence for the most serious of breaches, see *R. v. McDonald* [2013] 1 Cr.App.R.(S.) 3, CA. **K-401a**

Repeated breaches

For a case in which a sentence substantially outside the guidelines was upheld where there had been repeated (low-level) breaches of a restraining order over a long period, see *R. v. Todd* [2013] 1 Cr.App.R.(S.) 89, CA. **K-402**

[The next paragraph is K-410.]

G. DOMESTIC VIOLENCE

Introduction

As to the purpose of this section of this appendix, see *ante*, K-350. **K-410**

Relevant main work references

For sentencing guidelines generally, see section 125 of the Coroners and Justice Act 2009 (§ 5-149 in the main work); and for restraining orders under the Protection from Harassment Act 1997, see §§ 19-358a *et seq.* in the main work. **K-411**

Attitude of victim

In *R. v. Fazli*, unreported, April 24, 2009, CA ([2009] EWCA Crim. 939), the court emphasised that the principle (see para. 4 of the guideline) that a sentence should not be determined by the expressed wishes of the victim, was of particular importance in cases of domestic violence. The court said that, in the case with which it was concerned, the victim (the defendant's wife) had been made to feel responsible for his incarceration, and that such feelings on the part of the victim were a familiar consequence of controlling and intimidating behaviour such as that of the offender. The responsibility for what had happened to him lay entirely with him. **K-412**

To similar effect, see *R. v. Moore* [2016] Crim.L.R. 133, CA (the guideline emphasises the necessity to exercise real care before imposing a more lenient sentence because of representations on the victim's behalf - a course that should not be taken lightly). ★

Vulnerability of victim

See *Barnard v. DPP*, *ante*, K-362. **K-413**

Aggravating factors

In *R. v. Caceres* [2014] 1 Cr.App.R.(S.) 23, CA, it was said that whilst the guideline stressed that violence in the home was no less serious than violence elsewhere simply because it was committed in the home, and whilst this was correct in so far as it went, where someone is put in constant peril and fear in their own home as a result of repetitive domestic abuse, that was potentially a substantial aggravating factor. The court said that the aggravation is compounded where the perpetrator is in reality controlling the victim and abusing his position in the home, and the victim is, in the domestic context, vulnerable; and a further aggravating feature is where the **K-414** victim is effectively forced to leave home as a consequence of the abuse.

[The next paragraph is K-420.]

H. Sexual Offences

Introduction

K-420   As to the purpose of this section of this appendix, see *ante*, K-350.

Relevant main work references

K-421   For sentencing guidelines generally, see section 125 of the Coroners and Justice Act 2009 (§ 5-149 in the main work).

Gender

K-421a   Sentencing guidelines for sexual offences are gender-neutral: *Att.-Gen.'s Reference (No. 85 of 2014) (R. v. A.)* [2015] 1 Cr.App.R.(S.) 14, CA. As to this case, see also *ante*, § 5-110.

Historic offences

K-422   See *R. v. H.*, *ante*, H-12 *et seq.*

For a case considering the application of the Sentencing Council's guideline on sexual offences to historic offences, see *R. v. Clifford*, *ante*, Appendix H-120.

Rehabilitation

K-423   In *R. v. Jones (David William)* [2015] 1 Cr.App.R.(S.) 9, CA, a community order with a sex offender treatment programme requirement was considered a proper alternative to a moderate custodial sentence in accordance with the guideline of the Sentencing Council (see Appendix K-84f). The 64-year-old offender (who had previously served a short prison sentence for similar offences but had received no treatment) had pleaded guilty to making (Protection of Children Act 1978, s.1(1)(a) (§ 31-107 in the main work)) and possessing (CJA 1988, s.160(1) (*ibid.*, § 31-115)) indecent photographs of a child. Reports before the judge suggested that there was little likelihood of the offender moving on to contact offences, and that he would be likely to benefit from a sex offender treatment programme. It was held that the public would be better protected by a disposal that might prevent further offending than by a short sentence that was unlikely to have that result.

Rape

K-423a   It was held in *R. v. O. (D.)* [2015] 1 Cr.App.R.(S.) 41, CA, that not every case of rape within an established relationship should be treated as an "abuse of trust" for the purposes of the guideline (*ante*, K-84).

For an example of a case falling within the rubric in the guideline (*ante*, K-85), *viz.* that "Offences may be of such severity, for example involving a campaign of rape, that sentences of 20 years and above may be appropriate.", see *R. v. J.H.* [2015] 1 Cr.App.R.(S.) 59, CA (appellant convicted of a number of sexual offences, including rape, against his daughter, aged 11 to 15 at the time, committed over a prolonged period, "in gross breach of trust", involving planning, emotional and sometimes physical pressure, plus an element of degradation and humiliation).

Rape of a child under 13

★K-424   In *R. v. Watkins* [2015] 1 Cr.App.R.(S.) 6, CA, total sentences of 29 years' imprisonment (15 years for two attempted rapes, plus an extended sentence of 20 years (14 + 6) for sexual assault and conspiracy to rape a child under 13 (including concurrent lesser sentences on other related counts)) for the first defendant (lead singer of a rock band), and 17 years' imprisonment (14 years and four months for assault by penetration and conspiracy to rape, plus two years and eight

months for sexual assault) for the second defendant, were upheld where the second defendant
and another woman (who did not appeal her sentence), acting independently of one another, allowed the first defendant to abuse their own infant children (including the almost completed oral
and anal rape of one child) and to abuse them themselves with his encouragement and also to
participate in his filming of these activities and the planning of further such activities.

Sexual activity with a child

In *Att.-Gen.'s Reference (No. 53 of 2013) (R. v. Wilson)* [2014] 2 Cr.App.R.(S.) 1, CA, it was said **K-425**
that the fact that the complainant had initiated the activity was an aggravating rather than
mitigating factor; it has long been clear that Parliament's purpose in passing legislation making it
a crime to have sexual relations with those under 16 was to protect those under 16; to reduce the
punishment on the basis that the person needing protection encouraged the offence is simply
wrong; an under-age person who encourages sexual relations with herself needs more not less
protection.

Causing or inciting a child to engage in sexual activity

In *R. v. Buchanan* [2015] 2 Cr.App.R.(S.) 13, CA, it was said that the absence of any physical **K-426**
contact between victim and offender is highly material to sentence. The appellant's sentence was
reduced from 12 to eight months' imprisonment where he had made online contact with a 14-
year-old girl and the messages had become sexually explicit to the point where he indicated a
wish to have sex with her and solicited her to send him photographs of herself naked, but where
the prosecution accepted that he had no intention of engaging in sexual activity. The court said
that there was considerable doubt about whether the guideline (*ante*, K-88) addressed this type of
offending, but that the most appropriate category was 3A (starting point of 26 weeks, range of
high-level community order to three years).

[The next paragraph is K-430.]

I. FAILING TO SURRENDER TO BAIL

Introduction

As to the purpose of this section of this appendix, see *ante*, K-350. **K-430**

Relevant main work references

For sentencing guidelines generally, see section 125 of the Coroners and Justice Act 2009 (§ **K-431**
5-149 in the main work); for *Criminal Practice Direction III (Custody and bail) 14C* (which covers the
same ground), see *ante*, Appendix B-70 *et seq.*

Sentencing outside recommended range

For a case where the imposition of the maximum sentence, outside the recommended range in **K-432**
the guideline, was upheld on appeal, see *R. v. Chowdhury* [2014] 1 Cr.App.R.(S.) 27, CA (defendant had been at large for 13 years; trial of the substantive offence had become impossible as a
result of the delay).

In *R. v. Armaselu* [2014] 2 Cr.App.R.(S.) 65, CA, six months' imprisonment for failing to surrender after the offender had been at large for 15 months was upheld. The court said that whilst
it was aware of the Sentencing Guidelines Council's guideline (*ante*, K-107 *et seq.*), the Court of
Appeal had on a number of occasions since then upheld sentences in the range of six months'
custody for absences of 18 months to two years.

J. ASSAULT AND OTHER OFFENCES AGAINST THE PERSON

Introduction

As to the purpose of this section of this appendix, see *ante*, K-350. **K-433**

Relevant main work references

For sentencing guidelines generally, see section 125 of the Coroners and Justice Act 2009 (§ **K-434**
5-149 in the main work).

Use in case of young offenders

K-434a   In *R. v. Bowley* [2009] 1 Cr.App.R.(S.) 79, CA, where a 17-year-old pleaded guilty to causing grievous bodily harm with intent after stabbing a rival gang member, the court said (i) that the judge had been entitled to look to the guideline of the Sentencing Guidelines Council for assistance, even though it did not apply to offenders under 18 and (ii) in making use of it, the judge need not have been unduly constrained by the particular sentencing brackets set out therein, because the case was one where an element of deterrence was an essential ingredient of the sentencing decision.

Ranges

K-434b   Where an offence of assault occasioning actual bodily harm fell within category 2 as being one of lesser harm and greater culpability, the judge had been entitled to go outside the category range where there were present six factors from the non-exhaustive list of 18 factors that are capable of increasing the seriousness of the offence and there was just one factor reducing its seriousness: *R. v. Nelson, The Times,* October 27, 2011, CA.

As to departure from the guidelines when sentencing those convicted of an offence committed during the widespread public disorder of the kind seen in the riots that occurred around the country in August, 2011, and as to the appropriateness of sentences beyond the range set out in those guidelines, see *R. v. Blackshaw,* § 29-8 in the main work.

"particularly vulnerable"

K-434c   It was held in *R. v. Halane* [2014] 2 Cr.App.R.(S.) 46, CA that, in a case of assault, a victim's state of intoxication may be such that he may properly be regarded as being "particularly vulnerable" for the purposes of the Sentencing Council's guideline (Appendix K-113 *et seq.*), and where such a person struck the first blow, that did not necessarily mean that he could no longer be treated as having been particularly vulnerable.

It was held in *R. v. Maloney* [2015] 2 Cr.App.R.(S.) 32, CA, that the deliberate targeting of a vulnerable victim as an indicator of higher culpability is not engaged where the victim is particularly vulnerable, but is not targeted because of that vulnerability.

★   In *R. v. Smith (Grant Christopher)* [2016] 1 Cr.App.R.(S.) 8, CA, it was said that a person may be vulnerable for reasons that are not extraneous to the offence itself (such as age, medical condition or infirmity); thus an attack on a person already dazed, prone and unable to defend himself due to events directly connected to the offence, might be an attack on a "vulnerable" person for this purpose; the victim's circumstances include the condition he has been placed in by what has gone before (including any preliminary assault by the offender).

Section 18

Use of a knife

K-434d   In *R. v. Fadairo* [2013] 1 Cr.App.R.(S.) 66, CA, a case of "wounding" (not "causing grievous bodily harm") in which "lesser harm" was caused but with higher culpability, the court said that a starting point above the category two range was justified because of the use of a knife. Parliament had dictated, the court said, in enacting section 18 of the 1861 Act, that assaults with a knife or other bladed weapon should be regarded and punished more seriously than assaults without a weapon or with another kind of weapon; and there was a need for deterrence. For critical consideration of this approach to the guideline, see CLW/12/27/3.

Sections 18 and 20 ("particularly grave injury")

★**K-434e**   A fractured ankle and torn knee ligaments were not injuries constituting "greater harm" within the Sentencing Council's guideline (*ante*, K-113 *et seq.*), but were to be classified as being injuries of the normal level that constituted grievous bodily harm: *R. v. McIntosh* [2014] 2 Cr.App.R.(S.) 64, CA.

★   In *R. v. Smith (Grant Christopher), ante*, K-434c, it was said, in relation to an offence under section 18, that the purpose of the reference to "serious in the context of the offence" is to distinguish between the level of violence inherent in the offence, and that which will by definition go beyond what is par for the course; and that, as there is such a disparity in starting points between the categories, the harm and violence for a category 1 offence must be significantly above the serious level of harm that is normal for the purpose of the offence.

"sustained or repeated assault on the same victim"

In *R. v. Smith (Grant Christopher)*, *ante*, K-434c, it was said that "sustained" and "repeated" may ★K-435 imply different things; an assault may be "sustained" because it continued over significant time, even though it may not have involved a substantial number of blows; or it may be "repeated" because it involves multiple blows over a short time; they both import some degree of persistent repetition; and they must be read in the light of the major difference in starting point between the categories, such that it must be doubtful whether the difference between one and two blows could move a case from category 2 to category 1 (otherwise there would be few cases that were not category 1).

K. Assaults on Children and Cruelty to a Child

Introduction

As to the purpose of this section of this appendix, see *ante*, K-350. K-436

Relevant main work references

For sentencing guidelines generally, see section 125 of the Coroners and Justice Act 2009 (§ K-437 5-149 in the main work).

The four categories of seriousness

In *R. v. S. (Will)* [2009] 1 Cr.App.R.(S.) 40, CA, the offender (30/good character/no previous K-438 parenting experience) subjected a "challenging" five-year-old, one of the four children of his (now ex-)partner, to a particularly harsh regime of discipline. She was shouted at, made to feel unwanted, and sent to her room for long periods (sometimes day after day). No violence was used except on one occasion, when the offender put masking tape over her mouth (for which he later expressed regret). At school, it was noticed that the child, from being a relatively happy child, became tearful and unsettled. On pleas of guilty to two counts of "causing cruelty to a child", 30 months' imprisonment was held to be manifestly and grossly excessive. The court found that it was clear that the offender's actions were not those of a gratuitous bully, but of an inexperienced parent, at the end of his tether, who, together with the mother, was doing what he mistakenly believed to be the right thing in respect of what he saw as an ill-behaved child. In particular, it was said that the judge had wrongly identified the case as falling within the second of the four categories of seriousness in the guideline, which, the court noted, should more properly be reserved for cases of actual abuse, either through physical violence or deprivation of food, clothing, shelter or attendance. A community order with a supervision requirement (to include a parenting course) was substituted.

It had been open to a judge to place the offender's intense neglect of her child into the category of "protracted" neglect (*ante*, Appendix K-146), where it took place over a period that adults might regard as a relatively short period (a few days): *R. v. Sutherland* [2011] 1 Cr.App.R.(S.) 90, CA.

L. Sentencing in Magistrates' Courts

Introduction

As to the purpose of this section of this appendix, see *ante*, K-350. K-439

Relevant main work references

For sentencing guidelines generally, see section 125 of the Coroners and Justice Act 2009 (§ K-440 5-149 in the main work); for general mode of trial considerations, see *Criminal Practice Direction II (Preliminary proceedings) 9A*, *ante*, Appendix B-62.

[The next paragraph is K-442.]

M. Causing Death by Driving

Introduction

K-442   As to the purpose of this section of this appendix, see *ante*, K-350.

Relevant main work references

K-443   For sentencing guidelines generally, see section 125 of the Coroners and Justice Act 2009 (§ 5-149 in the main work). For the penalty provisions relating to the offences covered by this guideline, see § 32-6 (causing death by dangerous driving); § 32-50 (causing death by careless or inconsiderate driving); § 32-66 (causing death by careless driving when under the influence of drink or drugs or having failed without reasonable excuse either to provide a specimen for analysis or to permit the analysis of a blood sample) and § 32-75 (causing death by driving while unlicensed, disqualified or uninsured). As to disqualification and endorsement, see §§ 32-227 *et seq.*

Aggravating and mitigating factors

K-444   As to the importance of taking care to ensure that factors which put an offence into a particular category are not then double-counted as matters of aggravation, see *R. v. Watson* [2010] 1 Cr.App.R.(S.) 29, CA.

In *R. v. Lawes* [2010] 2 Cr.App.R.(S.) 43, CA, it was held that the potentially aggravating feature, identified in the guideline, of more than one death was not intended to apply to the case of a pregnant mother and her unborn child.

Borderline between careless and dangerous driving

K-445   For a case of dangerous driving that was close to the borderline with careless driving, see *R. v. Foster* [2010] 1 Cr.App.R.(S.) 36, CA. A 64-year-old man had been driving his wife, who suffered from motor neurone disease, home from the hospital, where she had been told that her condition had deteriorated to the point that her treatment should no longer be continued, when he crossed onto the wrong side of the road and collided with a motorcyclist. The central issue at trial had been whether the defendant had crossed onto the wrong side of the road because he had "blacked out"; in passing sentence, the judge proceeded on the basis that the defendant had convinced himself that that was what had happened. On appeal, the court reduced a sentence of 18 months' imprisonment to 12 months' imprisonment suspended for two years, on the basis that the appellant was distracted for a "matter of seconds at most" and, importantly, when his emotions as a result of the hospital visit must have made him susceptible to distraction. The court pointed out that the guideline on causing death by driving states (see *ante*, K-192) that where the driving is markedly less culpable than for the lowest of the three categories for the offence of causing death by dangerous driving, reference should be made to the starting point for the most serious level of causing death by careless driving (starting point 15 months' imprisonment, range of 36 weeks to three years) and that, having regard to this, and to the other mitigation, in particular the appellant's character and his deep and genuine remorse, that starting point could be reduced. The court concluded that if it be a merciful sentence to suspend the term of imprisonment, this was a proper case for mercy.

In *R. v. Crew* [2010] 2 Cr.App.R.(S.) 23, CA, a 52-year-old, the day after an overnight flight from the United States (where he lived), fell asleep momentarily at the wheel of his car while travelling along a long straight road in daylight hours. It was likely that, on waking, he instinctively over-corrected the car's direction of travel as he was used to driving on the opposite side of the road, and in so doing he collided with an oncoming car. A sentence of 14 months' imprisonment on a plea of guilty, entered at the earliest opportunity, was upheld by the Court of Appeal. It was said that the case fell into the most serious category identified in the Sentencing Guidelines Council's guideline (*ante*, Appendix K-194), and that the carelessness had bordered on dangerous driving. The offender had had no more than five hours' sleep in the previous 24 hours, during which he had twice been disturbed to take his young son to the lavatory, and, as an experienced traveller, he must have known the risk he was taking, so his culpability was accordingly high.

Causing death by careless or inconsiderate driving

In *R. v. Campbell (Karl)* [2010] 2 Cr.App.R.(S.) 28, CA, the court said that whereas the guideline **K-446** (*ante*, K-194) identified three categories of case, the most serious being cases where the driving was not far short of dangerous driving and the least serious comprising cases of momentary inattention with no aggravating features, the guideline provided no assistance as to the intermediate category of "other cases", but this could include cases of single misjudgments, such as a failure to see a vehicle approaching from the right when emerging from a minor road and when the visibility permitted the vehicle to have been seen in good time.

Campbell (Karl) was considered in *R. v. Odedara* [2010] 2 Cr.App.R.(S.) 51, CA, in which the court said of a case of momentary inattention with no aggravating features and some mitigating features, that it did not pass the custody threshold on a plea of guilty and probably would not have done so on conviction.

Ranges

In *R. v. Shepherd* [2010] 2 Cr.App.R.(S.) 54, CA, it was pointed out that since the recommended **K-447** range for the most serious of the three categories of cases of causing death by careless driving stops short (at four years' custody) of the statutory maximum (five years), there must be cases in which a judge will be entitled to go above the recommended range.

Where the offender, despite being aware that the braking system of the coach he was driving was not operating satisfactorily, drove the coach in terrain where there were regular hills, the driving created a "substantial risk of danger" such that the case fell within level 2, rather than a "significant risk of danger" such that the case would fall within level 3, of the guideline relating to causing death by dangerous driving (*ante*, K-192): *R. v. Oughton* [2011] 1 Cr.App.R.(S.) 62, CA.

Foreign drivers

Where a fatal accident is caused by a person driving on the wrong side of the road at night, the **K-448** culpability involved will be a good deal lower for a person who is used to driving on the right-hand side of the road, and who has only just arrived in this country: *R. v. Fleury* [2014] 2 Cr.App.R.(S.) 14, CA.

[The next paragraph is K-450.]

N. Breach of an Anti-Social Behaviour Order

Introduction

As to the purpose of this section of this appendix, see *ante*, K-350. **K-450**

Relevant main work references

For sentencing guidelines generally, see section 125 of the Coroners and Justice Act 2009 (§ **K-451** 5-149 in the main work). For the power to make an anti-social behaviour order on conviction, see section 1C of the CDA 1998 (§ 5-1198 in the main work). For authorities considering the imposition of an anti-social behaviour order, see § 5-1202 in the main work.

As to the replacement of anti-social behaviour orders by criminal behaviour orders, see *ante*, K-196.

Ranges

In *R. v. Fagan* [2011] 1 Cr.App.R.(S.) 105, CA, the court upheld a sentence that was above the **K-452** upper bracket for the most serious category in the guideline (*ante*, K-206), even though it was accepted that the case fell within the intermediate category. Referring to the maximum permissible sentence of five years' imprisonment, the court said that it followed that the guideline (which recommended a maximum of two years for a single offence) was not appropriate in the case of a persistent offender such as the appellant.

[The next paragraph is K-475.]

O. Theft and Burglary in a Building Other Than a Dwelling

Introduction

K-475   As to the purpose of this section of this appendix, see *ante*, K-350.

Relevant main work references

K-476   For sentencing guidelines generally, see section 125 of the Coroners and Justice Act 2009 (§ 5-149 in the main work). For previous guidelines in relation to various types of theft, see §§ 21-11 *et seq.* in the main work.

Theft in breach of trust

K-477   In *R. v. Hakimzadeh* [2010] 1 Cr.App.R.(S.) 8, CA, the appellant was a 61-year-old American of Iranian origin, who was an expert on cultural relations between Iran and the western world. He owned an extensive collection of materials relating to that topic and considered his library to be the fourth most significant in the world. Over a substantial period, in order to improve his personal library, he stole maps and illustrations from books and some books themselves from the British and Bodleian libraries. The court said that whilst the guideline did not specifically address such cases, the section on theft in breach of trust provided some relevant basis of comparison; the offender was able to access the books in the manner that he did partly because of his reputation and partly because he was trusted to treat them in the way that scholars should treat such important resources. See also § 5-1267 in the main work.

R. v. Hakimzadeh, ante, was considered in *R. v. Jacques* [2011] 2 Cr.App.R.(S.) 39, CA, a case that involved the theft of a set of 13 rare books from The Linley, the public library of the Royal Horticultural Society, which were valued at £40,000 for insurance purposes (but could have been sold for £27,000). The offender had gained access using a reader's card under an assumed name and was found to be in possession of a list of 70 other books and their valuations. The court held that the case was wholly different to *R. v. Hakimzadeh, ante,* because none of what was regarded as exceptional mitigation in that case applied here. As to the guideline, it was said that this provided an inadequate foundation for identifying the appropriate level of sentence in a case such as this; to categorise this case as a breach of trust was a poor guide to the gravity of this type of offending, which constituted a deliberate attack undermining the importance of libraries.

Theft from the person

K-478   In *R. v. De Weever* [2010] 1 Cr.App.R.(S.) 3, CA, the appellant had pushed a woman as she boarded a tube train and stolen a purse from her shoulder bag. The Court of Appeal found that the offence fell into the bottom level of seriousness identified in the Sentencing Guidelines Council's guidelines on theft from the person (see *ante*, K-215). However, they considered that there were a number of grave aggravating factors (*viz.* the offence was clearly planned and was carried out in a highly professional manner, it involved the use of force (a push) short of robbery and resulted in a high level of inconvenience to the victim, the offender had a number of like convictions, albeit from many years ago, and he had failed to respond to his most recent sentences) which took the offence out of the lowest level in the guideline, and to the top of the level above it, where the starting point would be 12 months' imprisonment.

De Weever (ante) was considered in *R. v. Sayed* [2014] 2 Cr.App.R.(S.) 39, CA, where it was held that the reference to a victim being "vulnerable" in the guideline on theft from the person referred to the personal characteristics of the victim, rather than circumstances in which a victim was vulnerable to theft.

In *R. v. Bond* [2014] 2 Cr.App.R.(S) 3, CA, the court upheld a sentence of four years' imprisonment for a professional thief with an "appalling criminal record" who had stolen luggage, while operating with accomplices, from victims at Heathrow Airport on two occasions. The court said that it was clear from the narrative accompanying the guideline on "theft from the person" (*ante*, K-216a) that it did not provide for circumstances such as those in the present case where the court was sentencing a defendant for crimes involving a high degree of planning and sophistication, where the victims were targeted because they were likely to be travelling with considerable amounts of money or highly valuable property, and where the defendant had a criminal background of persistent and grave offending, frequently carried out in circumstances identical to the offences before the court.

Offences occurring in the context of widespread public disorder

As to departure from the guidelines when sentencing those convicted of theft and burglary in the context of widespread public disorder of the kind seen in the riots that occurred around the country in August, 2011, and as to the appropriateness of sentences beyond the range set out in those guidelines, see *R. v. Blackshaw*, § 29-8 in the main work. **K-479**

[The next paragraph is K-500.]

P. Attempted Murder

Introduction

As to the purpose of this section of this appendix, see *ante*, § K-350. **K-500**

Relevant main work references

For sentencing guidelines generally, see section 125 of the Coroners and Justice Act 2009 (§ 5-149 in the main work). For the statutory guidelines on fixing the minimum term in a case of murder, see Schedule 21 to the CJA 2003 (§§ 5-425 *et seq.* in the main work). **K-501**

Conspiracy to murder

It was correct for the judge to have considered the Sentencing Guidelines Council's guideline on attempted murder in a case charged as a conspiracy to murder but in which the facts would have supported a charge of attempted murder: *R. v. Jolie* [2011] 1 Cr.App.R.(S.) 87, CA. **K-502**

Ranges

The Sentencing Guidelines Council's guideline had no application to the scale of criminality involved in a "hideous" case where the offender woke the lone female victim at night, stole from her and subjected her to rape, beatings, stabbings and set fire to her clothes and her home after tying her up, see *Att.-Gen.'s Reference (No. 37 of 2011) (R. v. Parsons)* [2012] 1 Cr.App.R.(S.) 84, CA. **K-503**

An indeterminate sentence with a minimum term which reflected a notional determinate term that was way above the top of the recommended range for a determinate sentence was justified where the term was intended to reflect a course of violent offending (including a second attempted murder and two offences of wounding with intent to cause grievous bodily harm): *R. v. Onyenaychi* [2013] 1 Cr.App.R.(S.) 59, CA.

Use of a knife or other weapon

Although the guideline was published prior to the insertion of paragraph 5A (taking a knife or other weapon to the scene/25-year starting point) in Schedule 21 to the 2003 Act (*ante*), given the way the guideline was constructed with direct reference to Schedule 21, it was incumbent on a judge to take account of the amendment of the law in relation to knives in a case involving the use of a knife: *R. v. Barnaby* [2013] 1 Cr.App.R.(S.) 53, CA; and, to similar effect, see *R. v. Gayzer-Tomlinson* [2013] 1 Cr.App.R.(S.) 98, CA. **K-504**

[The next paragraph is K-550.]

Q. Sentencing Youths

Introduction

As to the purpose of this section of this appendix, see *ante*, K-350. **K-550**

Relevant main work references

K-551   As to the aim of the youth justice system, see section 37 of the CDA 1998 (§ 5-63 in the main work); as to the requirement for a court to have regard to the welfare of a child or young person, see section 44 of the CYPA 1933 (*ibid.*, § 5-64); as to the purposes of sentencing when dealing with young offenders, see section 142A of the CJA 2003 (*ibid.*, § 5-66) (not in force as at October 17, 2014); as to youth rehabilitation orders, see §§ 5-314 *et seq.* in the main work; as to the enforcement of such orders, see §§ 5-380 *et seq.* in the main work; as to detention and training orders, see sections 100 to 107 of the PCC(S)A 2000 (§§ 5-597 *et seq.* in the main work); and as to the detention of young offenders convicted of certain grave crimes, see section 91 of the 2000 Act (*ibid.*, § 5-610).

For sentencing guidelines generally, see section 125 of the Coroners and Justice Act 2009 (§ 5-149 in the main work).

[The next paragraph is K-575.]

R. Corporate Manslaughter

Introduction

K-575   As to the purpose of this section of this appendix, see *ante*, K-350.

Relevant main work references

K-576   For sentencing guidelines generally, see section 125 of the Coroners and Justice Act 2009 (§ 5-149 in the main work). As to the offence of corporate manslaughter, see §§ 19-138 *et seq.* in the main work. For the maximum sentence, for the power to order the taking of remedial action and for the power to order a conviction to be publicised, see sections 1(2), 9 and 10 of the Corporate Manslaughter and Corporate Homicide Act 2007 respectively (§§ 19-138, 19-148, 19-149 in the main work). For decisions of the Court of Appeal considering the proper approach to determining the amount of a fine, see § 5-685 in the main work.

[The next paragraph is K-600.]

S. Aggravated Burglary and Burglary

Introduction

K-600   As to the purpose of this section of this appendix, see *ante*, K-350.

Relevant main work references

K-601   For sentencing guidelines generally, see section 125 of the Coroners and Justice Act 2009 (§ 5-149 in the main work). For section 9 of the Theft Act 1968 (burglary), see § 21-108 in the main work; and for section 10 of the 1968 Act (aggravated burglary, see § 21-129 in the main work).

Harm

K-602   Whereas one of the factors indicative of greater harm is "theft of/damage to property causing a significant degree of loss to the victim (whether economic, sentimental or personal value)", this is primarily addressing the position at the time of the theft or damage; subsequent recovery of the property, particularly if it is through voluntary reparation, may be a mitigating factor, but it does not change the character of the offence: *R. v. Franks* [2013] 1 Cr.App.R.(S.) 65, CA.

Distraction burglaries

K-603   In *R. v. Dance* [2014] 1 Cr.App.R.(S.) 51, CA, the court held that while courts must apply the guideline when passing sentence for distraction burglaries, judges are entitled to have regard to previous decisions of the Court of Appeal, provided that they bear in mind that those cases were decided before the guideline came into force. The earlier authorities provided a useful reminder that distraction burglaries targeted at vulnerable victims are a very serious crime, despite the fact that they may involve no violence to person or property. Such offences may well merit a sentence higher than the top of the range in the guidelines, particularly if there is a pattern of repeat offending of this kind.

"group" or "gang"

It was held in *R. v. Blaydes* [2014] 2 Cr.App.R.(S.) 55, CA, that where two people take part in a dwelling-house burglary, that is a clear and substantial aggravating feature for the purposes of the guideline, and it was not necessary to go into the semantics of whether two people amount to a "group" or "gang" (a factor indicating higher culpability in the guideline (see *ante*, K-263)). See also *R. v. Taylor* [2014] 2 Cr.App.R.(S.) 85, CA, where it was held that two persons acting together in committing a burglary do constitute a "group" for the purposes of the guideline. ★K-604

[The next paragraph is K-625.]

T. Drug Offences

Introduction

As to the purpose of this section of this appendix, see *ante*, K-350. **K-625**

Relevant main work references

For sentencing guidelines generally, see section 125 of the Coroners and Justice Act 2009 (§ 5-149). For section 170 of the CEMA 1979, see § 25-474; and for the penalty provisions in Schedule 1 to that Act, see § 25-508; for section 4 of the Misuse of Drugs Act 1971 (restriction of production and supply of controlled drugs), see § 27-28; for section 4A of the 1971 Act (aggravation of offence of supply of controlled drug), see § 27-28a; for section 5 of the 1971 Act (restriction of possession of controlled drug), see § 27-50; for section 6 of the 1971 Act (restriction of cultivation of cannabis plant), see § 27-79; for section 8 of the 1971 Act (occupiers of premises), see § 27-84; for section 25 of the 1971 Act (prosecution and punishment of offences), see § 27-105; for the sentencing guidelines of the Court of Appeal, see §§ 27-107 *et seq.*; and for the table of maximum penalties under the 1971 Act (and mode of trial provisions), see § 27-130. **K-626**

Scope of the guideline

The Sentencing Council's guideline on drug offences does not cover the offence of taking a prohibited article into prison, contrary to the Prison Act 1952, s.40B (§ 28-194 in the main work), where the article in question is a controlled drug and it is supplied to, or intended for supply to, a prisoner: *R. v. Simmons* [2013] 1 Cr.App.R.(S.) 109, CA. For critical consideration of this approach, see CLW/13/20/4. **K-626a**

The guideline should be applied to an offence of conspiracy to supply a controlled drug, but it should be approached with a degree of common sense and flexibility; whilst a judge should reflect the individual's culpability in the sentence passed, perhaps by adjusting the category to one better reflecting the reality, the fact of involvement in a conspiracy is an aggravating feature, since each conspirator playing his part gives comfort and assistance to others knowing that he is doing so, and the greater his awareness of the scale of the enterprise in which he is assisting, the greater his culpability: *R. v. Khan (Kazim Ali), Khan (Umar), Khan (Mohammed Arfan) and Khan (Mohammed Ahsan)* [2014] 1 Cr.App.R.(S.) 10, CA. The court also held that a judge was not confined to category 3 of the guideline because the end point activity of a conspiracy was street dealing; the words in the guideline "Where the offence is street dealing ... the quantity of the product is less indicative of the harm caused and therefore the starting point is not based on quantity." were plainly intended to move what would otherwise be category 4 offending into category 3; and it did not follow that those involved in street dealing of quantities which in aggregate went far beyond the amounts shown in category 4 can limit themselves to category 3 no matter what the scale of their dealing. As to street dealing, see also *R. v. Dyer, post,* § K-629.

R. v. Khan, ante, was referred to in *R. v. Pitts* [2014] Crim.L.R. 834, CA, where it was said that while the parameters of the guideline do not explicitly encompass the offences of conspiracy to import, supply or produce drugs, there was no error in the judge seeking to derive some assistance as to starting points by reference to the weights of drugs recovered, but this was subject to recognition that the criminality of a conspiracy is not necessarily thereby confined. The court emphasised that the degree of participation in the illegal agreement and its scope must also be considered. It added that the broad brush of defining leading, significant and lesser roles may be a helpful indicator as to participation, but these categories would be likely to be subject to further refinement on the facts. The court also warned against a slavish following of the guidelines on the basis of weights of drugs discovered at the conclusion of a surveillance operation when sentencing for drugs conspiracies. As to *Pitts,* see also *post,* K-632.

★   Where the appellants were convicted of conspiracy to convert criminal property, contrary to section 1 of the CLA 1977 (§ 33-2 in the main work), and section 327(1)(c) of the PCA 2002 (*ibid.,* § 26-11), but where the prosecution argued, and the judge accepted, that it was essentially a case about the supply of controlled drugs and that the only reason why charges were preferred by reference to the money laundering legislation was because of evidential difficulties in identifying, with sufficient clarity, which type of drugs were involved in individual cases and that, accordingly, the drug sentencing guideline, rather than the money laundering guideline (*ante,* K-297 *et seq.*), was to be applied, the solution was to take a figure between the figures indicated by the two guidelines: *R. v. Ogden,* unreported, January 26, 2016, CA ([2016] EWCA Crim. 6) (adjusting downwards sentences that were too heavily weighted towards the sentences indicated by the (heavier) drugs guideline). As to this case, see also *ante,* § 26-12.

Prospective or retrospective

K-627   The guideline is not retrospective: *R. v. Boakye and other cases* [2013] 1 Cr.App.R.(S.) 2, CA.

Categorisation of role

K-628   In *Att.-Gen.'s References (Nos 15, 16 and 17 of 2012) (R. v. Lewis)* [2013] 1 Cr.App.R.(S.) 52, CA, it was said that there may be a misunderstanding as to how to categorise the role of an offender; the essential nature of a drugs hierarchy remains the same even if the terminology in the guideline ("leading", "significant" and "lesser" roles) has changed; the guideline provides a list of characteristics to guide the judge in his task, but the list is not exhaustive, and it is not necessary for an offender to possess every characteristic before he can be described as fulfilling any particular role; there may be a tendency to focus on the "non-exhaustive" list of characteristics provided and to give them far too strict a meaning; the words chosen have a broad meaning and judges should be astute not to place offenders in a lower category than is appropriate; the judge should declare his conclusions on step one in his sentencing remarks, for the benefit of the offender, those advising the offender, and the Court of Appeal; at step two, having determined the offender's role and the category of harm, the judge should "use the corresponding starting point to reach a sentence within the category ranges" which follow, and then factor in any aggravating or mitigating features.

It is not the case that a "leading role" should be reserved for cases where there is an operational hierarchy and a chain of employees, and that a "significant role" should apply to an organiser where there is no such chain: *R. v. Descombre and Thomas* [2013] 2 Cr.App.R.(S.) 51, CA (considering *R. v. Healey, post,* K-630).

Categorisation of harm

K-628a   For a case applying the principle that the quantities of drug listed in the categories of harm in the drugs guideline are not thresholds but indicative quantities, see *R. v. Henry* [2014] 1 Cr.App.R.(S.) 55, CA.

★   Whereas the guideline specifies 20 kilogrammes of amphetamine as an indicative weight for a case falling into category 1, and four kilogrammes for a category 2 case, where the appellants were found with five vacuum packs of wet amphetamine with a total weight of 9,950 grammes, but which weighed 5,421 grammes when dried, the judge had been entitled to place the case at the lower end of category 1 or the extreme end of category 2; there is an expectation that drug dealers will be dealt with according to the weight of the drugs they have in their possession when they are caught; if the use of water was simply for the purposes of transport or to maintain the condition of the drugs, then evidence of that would need to have been adduced: *R. v. Kerley* [2015] 2 Cr.App.R.(S.) 69, CA.

Community impact

Where the offender, having installed a sophisticated cannabis cultivation set-up at his home, fell **K-628b** to be sentenced for an offence of production of a controlled drug, the judge had been entitled to take the case to the top of the relevant bracket having regard to the evidence provided by a community impact statement of a detective inspector, which dealt with the effect of drugs in the South Yorkshire area, and which noted that there was a significant risk of harm to communities from associated crime, namely, violence directed at cannabis producers in order to "tax" them ("taxing" being the street term used to describe the taking of drugs and other assets from those engaged in crime), and that innocent victims were also sometimes the target of "taxing" due to mistaken identity: *R. v. Wicks* [2014] 1 Cr.App.R.(S.) 57, CA.

Supply

In *R. v. Dyer* [2014] 2 Cr.App.R.(S.) 11, CA, it was held: (i) against the background of the **K-629** Sentencing Council's definitive guideline, earlier authorities have limited, if any, relevance, and further reliance on *R. v. Afonso; R. v. Sajid; R. v. Andrews* [2005] 1 Cr.App.R.(S.) 99, CA (sentencing of unemployed drug addicts), is inappropriate; (ii) in relation to selling directly to users ("street dealing"), harm is not categorised by quantity in the guideline; the fact of street dealing is sufficient to put the offending into Category 3 irrespective of the quantity involved; street dealing will inevitably be in quantities far smaller than those listed in the guideline (but see *R. v. Khan (Kazim Ali), Khan (Umar), Khan (Mohammed Arfan) and Khan (Mohammed Ahsan), ante,* K-626a); (iii) the fact that drugs have been supplied to a test purchase or undercover officer is not a reason to reduce the category; (iv) whereas "lesser role" in the guideline includes "if own operation, absence of any financial gain, for example joint purchase for no profit, or sharing minimal quantity between peers on non-commercial basis", street dealers funding their own habit, or perhaps an extremely meagre living, are motivated by financial and other advantage and are not the same as those who, for example, are funded by friends to buy drugs for the group without any question of financial or other reward; and (v) as street dealing is always likely to be at a low level and the category is fixed, the descriptors "some awareness and understanding of the scale of the operation" in relation to "significant role", and "very little, if any, awareness or understanding of the scale of the operation" in relation to "lesser role", are of far greater relevance to those being sentenced on the basis of the quantity of the drug concerned (*e.g.* a courier or low-level participant in a substantial drug dealing operation). As to this case, see also *ante*, §§ 5-141, 5-159.

Att.-Gen.'s References (Nos 82–96 and 104–109 of 2011) (R. v. Page) [2012] 2 Cr.App.R.(S.) 56, CA, was a pre-guideline case. However, the court's general observations as to the assessment of roles would seem to carry over to sentencing under the guideline (*Dyer, ante,* notwithstanding). The court said that all dealers are not the same; on the whole, the greater the quantity, the longer the period over which supplies were made, and the greater the profit, the more serious the offence is likely to be, with wholesale supply likely to be more serious than retail supply because of the quantity involved; and just as dealers vary, so do transporters or "couriers"; some people fulfilling the role of transporting drugs may in fact be very close to the central organisers of the trade, the "entrepreneurs"; other couriers, however, are little more than hired hands, operating under the direction of the entrepreneurs, and are likely to be paid per task; when sentencing, therefore, it is necessary to ensure that couriers or other handlers of drugs are placed in the right relationship with the entrepreneurs, especially the principals (those responsible for large scale purchase and sale), but also the entrepreneurs who are dealers, wholesale or retail.

In *R. v. Leigh* [2015] 2 Cr.App.R.(S.) 42, CA, the court considered the different roles that can be categorised as "street dealing" for the purposes of deciding whether a person falls into category 3 for harm. It was said that a number of people can play different roles in street dealing, including the organiser, someone running a phone line, runners who deliver the drugs to the point of supply, others who supply deals one at a time from a central store, and persons who courier drugs. It was, therefore, nonsense to argue that the secretion of drugs in the anus of an offender acting as a courier meant his case could not be treated as street dealing as there was no possibility of a street deal taking place during his particular journey.

R. v. Kelly [2014] 2 Cr.App.R.(S.) 70, CA, was a conspiracy to supply case to which the guidelines had no direct application. However, it was held that the judge had been entitled to take account of the purity of the drugs found, first, in assigning roles to the defendants and, secondly, in deciding into which harm category to place the case, despite the guideline stating (see Appendix K-276) that quantity alone is to be assessed at step 1 (when the decision as to category of harm should be taken) and purity should be taken into account only as a potentially aggravating feature at step 2.

In *R. v. Nnamani* [2015] 2 Cr.App.R.(S.) 23, CA, the appellant was found with a quantity of cocaine (695.65 grammes) and a cutting agent (595.48 grammes) that together added up to more than one kilogramme. It was held that the judge had been correct to regard it as a category 2 case (for which the specified indicative weight is one kilogramme of heroin or cocaine) within the guideline. The guideline had to be applied with "a due sense of realism". The quantity of cocaine could not be viewed in isolation and, had the drugs been cut, there would have been a considerably larger amount available for distribution.

In *R. v. Williams* [2014] 2 Cr.App.R.(S.) 58, CA, it was held that a judge had been entitled to place an offence of possession of a Class A drug (heroin) with intent to supply into category 3 of the guideline (*ante*, K-275) where the offender was found in possession of 54 grammes of powder containing diamorphine mixed with caffeine and paracetamol, being enough to be divided into 288 separate deals, and where he entered his plea on the basis that he was storing the goods for his supplier to whom he was in debt. The court said that whilst the indicative quantity for category 3 was 150 grammes, category 3 also embraced "street dealing", in which case the starting point was not based on a quantity of drugs. Whilst the appellant was not street dealing himself, the court found that his involvement was, if anything, higher up the chain, given that he was fully aware that he was holding a stock of heroin which would be used to supply street dealers.

In *R. v. Sanchez-Canadas* [2013] 1 Cr.App.R.(S.) 114, CA, it was said that the judge had been wrong to elevate a case from category 4 to category 3 on the ground that the supply was to a prisoner; as to culpability, however, the court said that the supply of drugs into a prison ought normally to be regarded as best fitting the description of "significant role"; and it will ordinarily demand a prison sentence, even when there is no commercial motive, and even where the supplier has come under some moral pressure.

Where the person supplied dies as a result of taking the drug supplied, this had to be treated as a substantial aggravating feature notwithstanding that it was not intended, it was not anticipated, it was greatly regretted, and there was no reason for the offender to consider that it would result, except for the fact that any supply of Class A drugs carries risks: *R. v. Harrod* [2014] 1 Cr.App.R.(S.) 76, CA.

In *R. v. Bush* [2014] 1 Cr.App.R.(S.) 40, CA, the court held that anyone involved in selling drugs at summer music festivals, even on a relatively low level basis, must expect an immediate custodial sentence; such festivals are an increasingly important part of the popular culture and teenagers, who are often away from direct parental control for the first time, attend them in groups and are thus particularly vulnerable to those trying to sell them drugs.

Where the drug being sold turns out to be Class A, not Class B, as the seller believed, this should not lead to the seller being sentenced as if he were selling a Class B drug; however, a genuine misunderstanding as to the nature of a drug was relevant, because it is more culpable to sell a Class A drug, knowing it to be Class A, than to sell a Class A drug, reasonably believing it to be Class B: *R. v. Bird* [2014] 1 Cr.App.R.(S.) 77, CA.

In *R. v. Tumara and Wheaton* [2014] 8 Archbold Review 3, CA, it was held that where offences of supply and importation of cannabis were committed at a time when cannabis had been re-classified as a Class C drug from a Class B drug (between 2004 and 2009), a judge was not required to impose sentences in accordance with the guideline for a Class C offence. When cannabis was first classified as a Class C drug in 2004 the maximum sentences for the supply and importation of Class C drugs were increased to 14 years' imprisonment (CJA 2003, s.284, and Sched. 28) which brought them into line with the maximum for Class B drugs. Parliament had thus intended the penalty to be the same for both classes of drugs.

Cultivation and production

K-630   In *R. v. Healey* [2013] 1 Cr.App.R.(S.) 33, CA, it was said that whereas the guideline uses pictorial boxes to describe the broad categories of offence, adjacent boxes are not mutually exclusive; there is an inevitable overlap between the scenarios described; the guideline sets out to describe such sliding scales and graduations as occur in real-life offending; the quantities which appear in the boxes as broad indicators of harm are neither fixed points nor thresholds; they are "indicative" quantities designed to enable the experienced judge to put the case into the right context on the sliding scale. In production cases, the court continued, it is the output or the potential output that counts, and the number of plants is to be considered only as a route to the more fundamental question of output or potential output; there may be evidence that the yield per plant is higher than the assumption used in the guideline, in which case the application of the guideline must be adjusted accordingly. It was held that those who create a purpose-built room in their loft, cellar or garage, or who dedicate a bedroom to cultivating cannabis, having invested substantially in professional equipment for watering, for lighting and/or for electronically controlled timing, can perfectly properly be described as being at the next level up (*viz.* having a "significant role") from those who are at the lowest level; and where there is a real likelihood of additional wider circulation, in other words supply, whether for money or not, they are to be positioned higher up in the "significant role" category; as the quantity of cannabis increases, the likelihood of it being intended for the sole consumption of the defendant reduces; and a judge faced with a defendant who asserts that an improbably large quantity of cannabis is entirely for his own use should indicate that he is not presently inclined to accept that assertion, and give the defendant and his counsel the opportunity to give evidence about it if he wishes; what a judge is not entitled to do is to say that he accepts the assertion that the drug cultivation was all for the defendant's own use and yet sentence on the basis that there is likely to be a supply to somebody else. As to this case, and what was said about guidelines generally, see also §§ 5-152, 5-153 in the main work. *Healey* (which was considered in *R. v. Descombre and Thomas, ante,* K-628) may be contrasted with *R. v. Bamford* [2013] 1 Cr.App.R.(S.) 4, CA, which was decided a month earlier, where the defendant had converted a bedroom into a professionally-equipped small cannabis farm. The court said that, as it was accepted that it was all for his own use, he was properly to be described as having a "lesser role".

In *R. v. Wiseman* [2014] 2 Cr.App.R.(S.) 23, CA, it was held that whilst the Sentencing Council's definitive guideline in relation to the production of a controlled drug or cultivation of cannabis (*ante,* K-277 *et seq.*), did not provide any indicative weight or quantity of plants to assist the sentencer in the descriptions of cases that may fall into category 1 ("operation capable of producing industrial quantities for commercial use") or category 2 ("operation capable of producing significant quantities for commercial use"), a comparison with the guidelines for the importation (*ante,* K-275) and supply (*ante,* K-276) of drugs, where indicative weight was listed, was not appropriate. There was a crucial distinction between the offences of importation and supply on the one hand, and production of drugs on the other. When a controlled drug was imported or supplied, the charge in most cases related to an identified quantity of that drug where a particular seizure has been made or a particular sale and purchase has been intercepted. In contrast, many offences involving the production of a controlled drug did not involve a specific quantity that was never going to be exceeded.

It was held in *R. v. Dang* [2014] 2 Cr.App.R.(S.) 49, CA, (i) that a judge was not permitted to sentence according to his personal opinion that the starting points and ranges for cannabis offences in the guideline on drugs offences (*ante,* K-271 *et seq.*) were in general too low for "skunk" offences, and that "the distinction to be drawn between cultivated skunk and Class A drugs is not a large one", and (ii) that the above average potency of the particular drugs seized was properly to be regarded as an aggravating factor.

The guideline does not require "slide-rule sentencing": *R. v. Soloman* [2015] 1 Cr.App.R.(S.) 57, CA (judge had been entitled to sentence on the basis that the case was more akin to category 3 than category 4 where the evidence suggested that the anticipated yield from the cannabis operation that the appellant was involved in setting up was closer to category 3 than category 4, and where it was more akin to a commercial, than to a domestic operation).

Importation

In *R. v. Jaramillo* [2013] 1 Cr.App.R.(S.) 110, CA, the court considered what is said in the **K-631** guideline about a starting point of 20 years (*ante,* K-275), but said that such a starting point is likely to be reserved for cases of commercial importation where the amount of drugs involved is enormous, the offender is an organiser, he has taken part in more than one importation, or he has a record of serious drug dealing.

In *Att.-Gen.'s References (Nos 82 and 90 of 2014) (R. v. Ebanks)* [2015] 2 Cr.App.R.(S.) 1, CA, it was held that *Jaramillo* had not imposed an artificial or inflexible limitation on the circumstances in which a sentence exceeding 20 years would be appropriate. It was said that the correct sentence for importations in the most serious commercial cases depended on a variety of factors, of which the precise amount of drugs was clearly important, but the court had to stand back and look at the operation as a whole.

It was held in *R. v. Sidlauskas* [2015] Crim.L.R. 297, CA, that importing 14.5 kilogrammes of khat (Class C) (representing a potential 140 deals) was enough to put the offence into category 3 of the guideline (despite it containing no indicative weights for khat).

Cannabis

K-631a   As the sentencing of cannabis offences committed at a time when cannabis had been re-classified as a Class C drug, see *R. v. Tumara and Wheaton, ante,* K-629; and as to whether it was legitimate to align "skunk cannabis" with Class A drugs, see *R. v. Dang, ante,* § K-630.

MDPV and M-Kat

K-632   In determining the category of harm into which an offence falls, the harm associated with the synthetic Class B drug methylenedioxypyrovalerone (or "MDPV"), a derivative of cathinone, is to be treated as commensurate to the harm associated with amphetamine, and the potential of a particular quantity of MDPV for causing harm is to be taken to be the same as the potential for the same quantity of amphetamine; the purity of any given quantity was to be taken into account at step 2, that is when determining where in the range the sentence should be positioned: *R. v. Brown* [2014] 1 Cr.App.R.(S.) 84, CA.

R. v. Brown, ante, was considered in *R. v. Pitts* [2014] Crim.L.R. 834, CA (as to which, see also *ante,* K-626a), where it was similarly held that, in the case of mephedrone (or M-Kat), a Class B drug that, along with its associated cathinone derivatives, is not explicitly covered by the guideline, the correct weight comparator for deciding the entry point into the guideline is amphetamine and not cannabis.

[The next paragraph is K-650.]

U. Offences Taken into Consideration and Totality

Introduction

K-650   As to the purpose of this section of this appendix, see *ante,* K-350.

Relevant main work references

K-651   For sentencing guidelines generally, see section 125 of the Coroners and Justice Act 2009 (§ 5-149).

As to offences taken into consideration, see §§ 5-160 *et seq.*

As to "totality" and consecutive or concurrent sentences, see the CJA 2003, ss.166(3)(b) (§ 5-126) and 265 (§ 5-668); and for the existing case law, see §§ 5-585 *et seq.*

[The next paragraph is K-675.]

V. Dangerous Dog Offences

Introduction

K-675   As to the purpose of this section of this appendix, see *ante,* K-350.

Relevant main work references

K-676   For sentencing guidelines generally, see section 125 of the Coroners and Justice Act 2009 (§

5-149). For sections 3, 4 and 4A of the Dangerous Dogs Act 1991, see §§ 31-35, 31-38 and 31-38a respectively (and *ante*).

[The next paragraph is K-700.]

W. Fraud, Bribery and Money Laundering

Introduction

As to the purpose of this section of this appendix, see *ante*, K-350.　　**K-700**

Relevant main work references

For sentencing guidelines generally, see section 125 of the Coroners and Justice Act 2009 (§　**K-701** 5-149). For conspiracy to defraud, see §§ 33-37 *et seq*.; for false accounting (Theft Act 1968, s.17), see § 21-177; for possession, etc., of articles for use in fraud (2006 Act, s.6), see § 21-345; for making or supplying articles for use in fraud (2006 Act, s.7), see § 21-346; for fraudulent evasion of value added tax (Value Added Tax Act 1994, s.72), see § 25-532, for improper importation of goods (CEMA 1979, s.50), see § 25-430; for fraudulent evasion of duty (CEMA 1979, s.170), see § 25-474; for taking steps to evade duty (CEMA 1979, s.170B), see § 25-505; for cheating the public revenue, see §§ 25-409 *et seq*.; for money laundering (PCA 2002, ss.327 to 329), see §§ 26-11 *et seq*; for bribery (Bribery Act 2010, ss.1, 2 and 6), see §§ 31-171, 31-172, 31-176; and for failure of commercial organisations to prevent bribery (2010 Act, s.7), see § 31-177.

Money laundering

As to whether, where the appellants were convicted of conspiracy to convert criminal property,　**★K-702** contrary to section 1 of the CLA 1977 (§ 33-2 in the main work), and section 327 of the PCA 2002 (*ibid*., § 26-11), but where the prosecution argued that it was essentially a case about the supply of controlled drugs and that the only reason why charges were preferred by reference to the money laundering legislation was because of evidential difficulties in identifying which type of drugs were involved, the drug sentencing guideline (*ante*, K-271 *et seq*.) or the money laundering guideline should be applied, see *R. v. Ogden, ante*, K-626a.

X. "Theft Offences"

Introduction

As to the purpose of this section of the appendix, see *ante*, K-350.　　**K-725**

Relevant main work references

For sentencing guidelines generally, see section 125 of the Coroners and Justice Act 2009 (§　**K-726** 5-149). For theft (Theft Act 1968, s.1), see §§ 21-15 *et seq*; for abstracting electricity (1968 Act, s.13), see §§ 21-159 et seq.; for handling stolen goods (1968 Act, s.22), see §§ 21-221 *et seq*; for going equipped (1968 Act, s.25), see §§ 21-288 *et seq*.; and for making off without payment (Theft Act 1978, s.3), see §§ 21-303 *et seq*.

[The next paragraph is K-1000.]

III. COMPENDIUM OF GUIDELINE CASES

The Sentencing Guidelines Council has published a compendium of those cases that it regards　**K-1000** as constituting considered guidance and issued over the past 30 years. The list is in two parts, "Generic sentencing principles" and "Offences". It has been updated five times, with some cases having been removed from the original list.

As at October, 8, 2014, there was a note on the website of the Sentencing Council stating that the case compendium is no longer being updated and should be referred to for reference only.

In the first list are: *R. v. Martin (Selina)* [2007] 1 Cr.App.R.(S.) 3 (**approach to sentencing**); *Att.-Gen.'s Reference (No. 4 of 1989) (R. v. Brunt)*, 11 Cr.App.R.(S.) 517 (**Attorney-General's references**); *R. v. Montgomery*, 16 Cr.App.R.(S.) 274 (**contempt**); *R. v. Bernard* [1997] 1 Cr.App.R.(S.) 135 (**health of the offender**); *R. v. Goodyear* [2005] 3 All E.R. 117; *R. v. Kulah* [2008] 1 Cr.App.R.(S.) 85 (**indication of sentence**); *R. v. Buckland* [2000] 1 W.L.R. 1262 (**automatic life sentences**); *R. v. Hodgson*, 52 Cr.App.R. 113; *R. v. Chapman* [2000] 1 Cr.App.R. 77; *R. v. McNee, Gunn and Russell* [2008] 1 Cr.App.R.(S.) 24; *R. v. Kehoe* [2009] 1 Cr.App.R.(S.) 9; *R. v. Davies* [2009] 1 Cr.App.R.(S.) 15 (**discretionary life sentences**); *R. v. M. (Discretionary Life Sentence)*; *R. v. L.* [1999] 1 W.L.R. 485; *R. v. Szczerba* [2002] 2 Cr.App.R.(S.) 86 (**life sentence—specified period**); *R. v. McLean*, 6 Cr.App.R. 26; *R. v. Simons*, 37 Cr.App.R. 120; *R. v. Walsh*, unreported, March 8, 1973 (**taking offences into consideration**); *Att.-Gen.'s Reference (No. 52 of 2003) (R. v. Webb)* [2004] Crim.L.R. 306 (**prosecution duty**); *R. v. Kelly and Donnelly* [2001] 2 Cr.App.R.(S.) 73; *R. v. McGillivray* [2005] 2 Cr.App.R.(S.) 60; *R. v. O'Callaghan* [2005] 2 Cr.App.R.(S.) 83 (**racially aggravated offences**); *R. v. A. and B.* [1999] 1 Cr.App.R.(S.) 52; *R. v. Guy* [1999] 2 Cr.App.R.(S.) 24; *R. v. X. (No. 2)* [1999] 2 Cr.App.R.(S.) 294; *R. v. R. (Informer: Reduction in sentence)*, *The Times*, February 18, 2002; *R. v. P.*; *R. v. Blackburn* [2008] 2 Cr.App.R.(S.) 5 (**discount on account of assistance given to the police**); *R. v. Bird*, 9 Cr.App.R.(S.) 77; *R. v. Tiso*, 12 Cr.App.R.(S.) 122 (**discount on account of lapse of time since offence**); *R. v. Bibi* [1980] 1 W.L.R. 1193; *R. v. Ollerenshaw* [1999] 1 Cr.App.R.(S.) 65; *R. v. Kefford* [2002] 2 Cr.App.R.(S.) 106 (**length of custodial sentences**); *R. v. Nelson* [2002] 1 Cr.App.R.(S.) 134; *R. v. Cornelius* [2002] 2 Cr.App.R.(S.) 69; *R. v. Pepper* [2006] 1 Cr.App.R.(S.) 20 (**length of extended sentences**); *R. v. Lang* [2006] 2 Cr.App.R.(S.) 3; *R. v. S.*; *R. v. Burt* [2006] 2 Cr.App.R.(S.) 35; *CPS v. South East Surrey Youth Court* [2006] 2 Cr.App.R.(S.) 26 (**dangerousness**); *R. v. Reynolds* [2007] 2 Cr.App.R.(S.) 87; *R. v. Johnson* [2007] 1 Cr.App.R.(S.) 112; *R. v. O'Brien* [2007] 1 Cr.App.R.(S.) 75; *R. v. O'Halloran*, unreported, November 14, 2006 ([2006] EWCA Crim. 3148) (**dangerousness: imprisonment for public protection**); *R. v. Brown and Butterworth* [2007] 1 Cr.App.R.(S.) 77; *R. v. Lay* [2007] 2 Cr.App.R.(S.) 4; *R. v. C.*; *R. v. Bartley* [2007] 2 Cr.App.R.(S.) 98 (**dangerousness: extended sentences**); *Att.-Gen.'s Reference (No. 101 of 2006) (R. v. P.)*, unreported, December 8, 2006 ([2006] EWCA Crim. 3335) (**deferment of sentence**); *R. v. Cain* [2007] 2 Cr.App.R.(S.) 25 (**prosecution and defence duty to assist at sentencing**); *R. v. Seed; R. v. Stark* [2007] 2 Cr.App.R.(S.) 69 (**sentence length: custodial sentences**); *R. (Stellato) v. Secretary of State for the Home Department* [2007] 2 A.C. 70 (**sentence length: licence period**); *Att.-Gen.'s Reference (No. 6 of 2006) (R. v. Farish)* [2007] 1 Cr.App.R.(S.) 12 (**sentence length: minimum sentences**); *R. v. Gordon* [2007] 2 All E.R. 768 (**sentence length: time spent in custody on remand**); *R. v. Tyre*, 6 Cr.App.R.(S.) 247 (**sentence length: joint conviction with a juvenile offender**); *R. v. Davies* [2009] 1 Cr.App.R.(S.) 15 (**sentence length: standard of proof**); *R. v. Raza* [2010] 1 Cr.App.R.(S.) 56, CA (**sentence length: discounts; totality and mandatory minimum sentences**); *R. v. Round; R. v. Dunn* [2010] 2 Cr.App.R.(S.) 45, CA (**sentence length: early release provisions**); *Att.-Gen.'s Reference (No. 55 of 2008) (R. v. C.)* [2009] 2 Cr.App.R.(S.) 22, CA (**sentence length: imprisonment for public protection**); *R. v. Costello* [2010] 2 Cr.App.R.(S.) 94, CA (**sentence length: offence committed whilst on licence**); *R. v. McGrath* [2005] 2 Cr.App.R.(S.). 85; *R. v. Morrison* [2006] 1 Cr.App.R.(S.) 85; *R. v. Lamb* [2006] 2 Cr.App.R.(S.) 11 (**anti-social behaviour orders**); *R. v. P. (Shane Tony)* [2004] 2 Cr.App.R.(S.) 63 (**anti-social behaviour order imposed with custody**); *R. v. Sullivan* [2003] EWCA Crim. 1736 (**compensation with custody**); *R. v. Robinson* [2002] 2 Cr.App.R.(S.) 95; *Att.-Gen.'s Reference (No. 64 of 2003)* [2004] 2 Cr.App.R.(S.) 22; *R. v. Woods and Collins* [2006] 1 Cr.App.R.(S.) 83 (**drug treatment and testing orders**); *R. v. Richards* [2007] 1 Cr.App.R.(S.) 120 (**sexual offences prevention orders**); *R. v. Kidd; R. v. Canavan; R. v. Shaw (Dennis)* [1998] 1 W.L.R. 604; *R. v. Tovey; R. v. Smith* [2005] 2 Cr.App.R.(S.) 100 (**specimen offences**); *R. v. Perks* [2001] 1 Cr.App.R.(S.) 66; *R. v. Ismail* [2005] 2 Cr.App.R.(S.) 88 (**victim's wishes**); *R. v. Danga*, 13 Cr.App.R.(S.) 408 (**age for purpose of sentencing**); *R. (W.) v. Southampton Youth Court*; *R. (K.) v. Wirral Borough Magistrates' Court* [2003] 1 Cr.App.R.(S.) 87 (**venue for trial**); *R. v. Sharma* [2006] 2 Cr.App.R.(S.) 63 (**confiscation orders**); *R. v. Oshungbure and Odewale* [2005] 2 Cr.App.R.(S.) 102 (**confiscation proceedings following sentence**); *R. v. Richards (Michael)* [2005] 2 Cr.App.R.(S.) 97 (**confiscation order: obtaining social security benefits by false representations**); *R. v. Debnath* [2006] 2 Cr.App.R.(S.) 25 (**restraining orders**); *R. v. Lees-Wolfenden* [2007] 1 Cr.App.R.(S.) 119 (**suspended sentence orders**); *R. v. Sheppard* [2008] 2 Cr.App.R.(S.) 93, CA; *R. v. Chalmers*, unreported, August 7, 2009, CA ([2009] EWCA Crim. 1814) (**activation of suspended sentences**).

In the second list are:—

affray—*R. v. Fox and Hicks* [2006] 1 Cr.App.R.(S.) 17;

breach of licence—*R. v. Pick and Dillon* [2006] 1 Cr.App.R.(S.) 61;

burglary (domestic)—*R. v. McInerney; R. v. Keating* [2003] 1 All E.R. 1089; *R. v. Saw* [2009] 2 Cr.App.R.(S.) 54, CA [but see now *R. v. Dance, ante,* K-603];

counterfeiting and forgery—*R. v. Howard,* 7 Cr.App.R.(S.) 320 (dealing in counterfeit currency); *R. v. Crick,* 3 Cr.App.R.(S.) 275 (counterfeiting coins); *R. v. Kolawole* [2005] 2 Cr.App.R.(S.) 14; *R. v. Mutede* [2006] 2 Cr.App.R.(S.) 22; *Att.-Gen.'s Reference (Nos 1 and 6 of 2008) (R. v. Dziruni and Laby)* [2008] 2 Cr.App.R.(S.) 99; *R. v. Mabengo, Lomoka, Salang and Birindwa, The Times,* July 17, 2008, CA; and *R. v. Ovieriakhi* [2009] 2 Cr.App.R.(S.) 91, CA (false passports);

drugs—[for a listing of the cases included in the compendium, see the first supplement to this edition; they have not been included here in light of the observations of the Court of Appeal in *R. v. Dyer, ante,* K-629 about the citation of pre-guideline authorities];

explosive offences—*R. v. Martin* [1999] 1 Cr.App.R.(S.) 477;

firearms offences—*R. v. Avis; R. v. Barton; R. v. Thomas; R. v. Torrington; R. v. Marquez; R. v. Goldsmith* [1998] 1 Cr.App.R. 420; *Att.-Gen.'s Reference (No. 43 of 2009) (R. v. Bennett); R. v. Wilkinson* [2010] 1 Cr.App.R.(S.) 100; *R. v. Rehman; R. v. Wood* [2006] 1 Cr.App.R.(S.) 77 (exceptional circumstances);

fraud—*R. v. Feld* [1999] 1 Cr.App.R.(S.) 1 (company management); *R. v. Palk and Smith* [1997] 2 Cr.App.R.(S.) 167 (fraudulent trading); *R. v. Roach* [2002] 1 Cr.App.R.(S.) 12 (obtaining money transfer by deception);

handling stolen goods—*R. v. Webbe* [2002] 1 Cr.App.R.(S.) 22;

health and safety offences—*R. v. F. Howe and Son (Engineers) Ltd* [1999] 2 All E.R. 249; *R. v. Rollco Screw and Rivet Co Ltd* [1999] 2 Cr.App.R.(S.) 436; *R. v. Balfour Beatty Infrastructure Ltd* [2007] 1 Cr.App.R.(S.) 65;

immigration—*R. v. Le and Stark* [1999] 1 Cr.App.R.(S.) 422; *R. v. Ai (Lu Zhu)* [2006] 1 Cr.App.R.(S.) 5 (failing to produce an immigration document);

incest—*Att.-Gen.'s Reference (No. 1 of 1989),* 11 Cr.App.R.(S.) 409;

indecent assault—*Att.-Gen.'s References (Nos 120, 91 and 119 of 2002)* [2003] 2 All E.R. 955 (general); *R. v. Lennon* [1999] 1 Cr.App.R. 117 (on male);

insider dealing—*R. v. McQuoid* [2010] 1 Cr.App.R.(S.) 43, CA;

intimidation of witness—*R. v. Williams* [1997] 2 Cr.App.R.(S.) 221; *R. v. Chinery* [2002] 2 Cr.App.R.(S.) 244(55);

kidnapping—*R. v. Spence and Thomas,* 5 Cr.App.R.(S.) 413;

manslaughter—*R. v. Chambers,* 5 Cr.App.R.(S.) 190 (diminished responsibility); *R. v. Furby* [2006] 2 Cr.App.R.(S.) 8; *Att.-Gen.'s Reference (No. 60 of 2009) (R. v. Appleby)* [2010] 2 Cr.App.R.(S.) 46, CA ("single punch"); *Att.-Gen.'s Reference (No. 111 of 2006) (R. v. Hussain)* [2007] 2 Cr.App.R.(S.) 26 ("motor"); *R. v. Wood* [2010] 1 Cr.App.R.(S.) 2, CA (diminished responsibility);

money laundering—*R. v. Basra* [2002] 2 Cr.App.R.(S.) 100; *R. v. Gonzalez and Sarmineto* [2003] 2 Cr.App.R.(S.) 9 (general); *R. v. El-Delbi* [2003] 7 Archbold News 1 (proceeds of drug trafficking);

murder—*R. v. Jones* [2006] 2 Cr.App.R.(S.) 19; *R. v. Barot* [2008] 1 Cr.App.R.(S.) 31; *R. v. McNee, Gunn and Russell* [2008] 1 Cr.App.R.(S.) 24 (conspiracy); *R. v. Davies* [2009] 1 Cr.App.R.(S.) 15 (minimum term); *R. v. Javed* [2008] 2 Cr.App.R.(S.) 12 (soliciting); *R. v. M.; R. v. A.M.; R. v. Kika* [2010] 2 Cr.App.R.(S.) 19, CA (with a knife);

offensive weapons—*R. v. Poulton; R. v. Celaire* [2003] 4 All E.R. 869; *R. v. Povey* [2009] 1 Cr.App.R.(S.) 42;

perjury—*R. v. Archer* [2003] 1 Cr.App.R.(S.) 86;

perverting the course of justice—*R. v. Walsh and Nightingale,* 14 Cr.App.R.(S.) 671; *R. v. Tunney* [2007] 1 Cr.App.R.(S.) 91, CA;

pornography—*R. v. Holloway,* 4 Cr.App.R.(S.) 128 (having obscene articles for publication for gain); *R. v. Nooy and Schyff,* 4 Cr.App.R.(S.) 308 (importation of indecent or obscene publications);

prison breaking (escape)—*R. v. Coughtrey* [1997] 2 Cr.App.R.(S.) 269;

public nuisance—*R. v. Kavanagh* [2008] 2 Cr.App.R.(S.) 86;

riot—*R. v. Najeeb* [2003] 2 Cr.App.R.(S.) 69;

robbery—*R. v. Snowden, The Times,* November 11, 2002 (hijacking of cars);

sex offenders' register—*Att.-Gen.'s Reference (No. 50 of 1997) (R. v. V.)* [1998] 2 Cr.App.R.(S.) 155;

theft—*R. v. Evans* [1996] 1 Cr.App.R.(S.) 105 ("ringing" stolen cars);

trafficking women for prostitution—*Att.-Gen.'s Reference (No. 6 of 2004) (R. v. Plakici)* [2005] 1 Cr.App.R.(S.) 19;

violent disorder—*R. v. Chapman* (2002) 146 S.J. (LB 242);

APPENDIX N
Protocols

A. Cᴏɴᴛʀᴏʟ ᴀɴᴅ Mᴀɴᴀɢᴇᴍᴇɴᴛ ᴏғ Hᴇᴀᴠʏ Fʀᴀᴜᴅ ᴀɴᴅ ᴏᴛʜᴇʀ Cᴏᴍᴘʟᴇx Cʀɪᴍɪɴᴀʟ Cᴀsᴇs

A protocol issued by the Lord Chief Justice of England and Wales **N-1**

22 March 2005

Introduction

The investigation

> The role of the prosecuting authority and the judge
>
> Interviews
>
> The prosecution and defence teams
>
> Initial consideration of the length of a case
>
> Notification of cases likely to last more than 8 weeks
>
> Notification of cases likely to last more than 8 weeks
>
> Venue

Designation of the trial judge

> The assignment of a judge

Case management

> Objectives
>
> The assignment of a judge

Case management

> Objectives
>
> Fixing the trial date
>
> The first hearing for the giving of initial directions
>
> The first Case Management Hearing
>
> Further Case Management Hearings
>
> Consideration of the length of the trial
>
> The exercise of the powers
>
> Fixing the trial date
>
> The first hearing for the giving of initial directions
>
> The first Case Management Hearing
>
> Further Case Management Hearings
>
> Consideration of the length of the trial
>
> The exercise of the powers
>
> Expert Evidence
>
> Surveillance Evidence

Disclosure

Abuse of process

The trial

> The particular hazard of heavy fraud trials
>
> Judicial mastery of the case
>
> The order of the evidence
>
> Case management sessions

Controlling prolix cross-examination
Electronic presentation of evidence
Use of interviews
Jury Management
Maxwell hours
Livenote

Other issues

Defence representation and defence costs
Assistance to the Judge
Jury Management
Maxwell hours
Livenote

Other issues

Defence representation and defence costs
Assistance to the Judge

Introduction

N-2   There is a broad consensus that the length of fraud and trials of other complex crimes must be controlled within proper bounds in order:

(i) To enable the jury to retain and assess the evidence which they have heard. If the trial is so long that the jury cannot do this, then the trial is not fair either to the prosecution or the defence.

(ii) To make proper use of limited public resources: see *Jisl* [2004] EWCA Crim. 696 at [113]-[121].

There is also a consensus that no trial should be permitted to exceed a given period, save in exceptional circumstances; some favour 3 months, others an outer limit of 6 months. Whatever view is taken, it is essential that the current length of trials is brought back to an acceptable and proper duration.

This Protocol supplements the Criminal Procedure Rules and summarises good practice which experience has shown may assist in bringing about some reduction in the length of trials of fraud and other crimes that result in complex trials. Flexibility of application of this Protocol according to the needs of each case is essential; it is designed to inform but not to proscribe.

This Protocol is primarily directed towards cases which are likely to last eight weeks or longer. It should also be followed, however, in all cases estimated to last more than four weeks. This Protocol applies to trials by jury, but many of the principles will be applicable if trials without a jury are permitted under s.43 of the Criminal Justice Act 2003.

The best handling technique for a long case is continuous management by an experienced Judge nominated for the purpose.

It is intended that this Protocol be kept up to date; any further practices or techniques found to be successful in the management of complex cases should be notified to the office of the Lord Chief Justice.

1. The investigation

(i) The role of the prosecuting authority and the judge

N-3   (a) Unlike other European countries, a judge in England and Wales does not directly control the investigation process; that is the responsibility of the Investigating Authority, and in turn the Prosecuting Authority and the prosecution advocate. Experience has shown that a prosecution lawyer (who must be of sufficient experience and who will be a member of the team at trial) and the prosecution advocate, if different, should be involved in the investigation as soon as it appears that a heavy fraud trial or other complex criminal trial is likely to ensue. The costs that this early preparation will incur will be saved many times over in the long run.

(b) The judge can and should exert a substantial and beneficial influence by making it clear that, generally speaking, trials should be kept within manageable limits. In most cases 3 months should be the target outer limit, but there will be cases where a duration of 6 months, or in exceptional circumstances, even longer may be inevitable.

(ii) Interviews

(a) At present many interviews are too long and too unstructured. This has a knock-on effect **N-4** on the length of trials. Interviews should provide an opportunity for suspects to respond to the allegations against them. They should not be an occasion to discuss every document in the case. It should become clear from judicial rulings that interviews of this kind are a waste of resources.

(b) The suspect must be given sufficient information before or at the interview to enable them to meet the questions fairly and answer them honestly; the information is not provided to give him the opportunity to manufacture a false story which fits undisputable facts.

(c) It is often helpful if the principal documents are provided either in advance of the interview or shown as the interview progresses; asking detailed questions about events a considerable period in the past without reference to the documents is often not very helpful.

(iii) The prosecution and defence teams

(a) **The Prosecution Team**

While instructed it is for the lead advocate for the prosecution to take all necessary deci- **N-5** sions in the presentation and general conduct of the prosecution case. The prosecution lead advocate will be treated by the court as having that responsibility.

However, in relation to policy decisions the lead advocate for the prosecution must not give an indication or undertaking which binds the prosecution without first discussing the issue with Director of the Prosecuting authority or other senior officer.

"Policy" decisions should be understood as referring to non-evidential decisions on: the acceptance of pleas of guilty to lesser counts or groups of counts or available alternatives: offering no evidence on particular counts; consideration of a re-trial; whether to lodge an appeal; certification of a point of law; and the withdrawal of the prosecution as a whole (for further information see the "Farquharson Guidelines" on the role and responsibilities of the prosecution advocate).

(b) **The Defence Team**

In each case, the lead advocate for the defence will be treated by the court as having responsibility to the court for the presentation and general conduct of the defence case.

(c) In each case, a case progression officer must be assigned by the court, prosecution and defence from the time of the first hearing when directions are given (as referred to in paragraph 3(iii)) until the conclusion of the trial.

(d) In each case where there are multiple defendants, the LSC will need to consider carefully the extent and level of representation necessary.

(iv) Initial consideration of the length of a case

If the prosecutor in charge of the case from the Prosecuting Authority or the lead advocate for the **N-6** prosecution consider that the case as formulated is likely to last more than 8 weeks, the case should be referred in accordance with arrangements made by the Prosecuting Authority to a more senior prosecutor. The senior prosecutor will consider whether it is desirable for the case to be prosecuted in that way or whether some steps might be taken to reduce its likely length, whilst at the same time ensuring that the public interest is served.

Any case likely to last 6 months or more must be referred to the Director of the Prosecuting Authority so that similar considerations can take place.

(v) Notification of cases likely to last more than 8 weeks

Special arrangements will be put in place for the early notification by the CPS and other Prosecut- **N-7** ing Authorities, to the LSC and to a single designated officer of the Court in each Region (Circuit) of any case which the CPS or other Prosecuting Authority consider likely to last over 8 weeks.

(vi) Venue

The court will allocate such cases and other complex cases likely to last 4 weeks or more to a **N-8** specific venue suitable for the trial in question, taking into account the convenience to witnesses, the parties, the availability of time at that location, and all other relevant considerations.

2. Designation of the trial judge

The assignment of a judge

N-9
   (a) In any complex case which is expected to last more than four weeks, the trial judge will be assigned under the direction of the Presiding Judges at the earliest possible moment.

   (b) Thereafter the assigned judge should manage that case "from cradle to grave"; it is essential that the same judge manages the case from the time of his assignment and that arrangements are made for him to be able to do so. It is recognised that in certain court centres with a large turnover of heavy cases (*e.g.* Southwark) this objective is more difficult to achieve. But in those court centres there are teams of specialist judges, who are more readily able to handle cases which the assigned judge cannot continue with because of unexpected events; even at such courts, there must be no exception to the principle that one judge must handle all the pre-trial hearings until the case is assigned to another judge.

3. Case management

(i) Objectives

N-10
   (a) The number, length and organisation of case management hearings will, of course, depend critically on the circumstances and complexity of the individual case. However, thorough, well-prepared and extended case management hearings will save court time and costs overall.

   (b) Effective case management of heavy fraud and other complex criminal cases requires the judge to have a much more detailed grasp of the case than may be necessary for many other Plea and Case Management Hearings (PCMHs). Though it is for the judge in each case to decide how much pre-reading time he needs so that the judge is on top of the case, it is not always a sensible use of judicial time to allocate a series of reading days, during which the judge sits alone in his room, working through numerous boxes of ring binders.

See paragraph 3(iv)(e) below

(ii) Fixing the trial date

N-11
   Although it is important that the trial date should be fixed as early as possible, this may not always be the right course. There are two principal alternatives:

   (a) The trial date should be fixed at the first opportunity—*i.e.* at the first (and usually short) directions hearing referred to in The first hearing for the giving of initial directions. From then on everyone must work to that date. All orders and pre-trial steps should be timetabled to fit in with that date. All advocates and the judge should take note of this date, in the expectation that the trial will proceed on the date determined.

   (b) The trial date should not be fixed until the issues have been explored at a full case management hearing (referred to in The first Case Management Hearing), after the advocates on both sides have done some serious work on the case. Only then can the length of the trial be estimated.

Which is apposite must depend on the circumstances of each case, but the earlier it is possible to fix a trial date, by reference to a proper estimate and a timetable set by reference to the trial date, the better.

   It is generally to be expected that once a trial is fixed on the basis of the estimate provided, that it will not be **increased** if, and only if, the party seeking to extend the time justifies why the original estimate is no longer appropriate.

(iii) The first hearing for the giving of initial directions

N-12
   At the first opportunity the assigned judge should hold a short hearing to give initial directions. The directions on this occasion might well include:

   (a) That there should be a full case management hearing on, or commencing on, a specified future date by which time the parties will be properly prepared for a meaningful hearing and the defence will have full instructions.

   (b) That the prosecution should provide an outline written statement of the prosecution case at least one week in advance of that case management hearing, outlining in simple terms:

   (i) the key facts on which it relies;

   (ii) the key evidence by which the prosecution seeks to prove the facts.

The statement must be sufficient to permit the judge to understand the case and for the defence to appreciate the basic elements of its case against each defendant. The prosecution may be invited to highlight the key points of the case orally at the case management hearing by way of a short mini-opening. The outline statement should not be considered binding, but it will serve the essential purpose in telling the judge, and everyone else, what the case is really about and identifying the key issues.

(c) That a core reading list and core bundle for the case management hearing should be delivered at least one week in advance.

(d) Preliminary directions about disclosure: see paragraph 4.

(iv) *The first case management hearing*

(a) At the first case management hearing: **N-13**

(1) the prosecution advocate should be given the opportunity to highlight any points from the prosecution outline statement of case (which will have been delivered at least a week in advance;

(2) each defence advocate should be asked to outline the defence.

If the defence advocate is not in a position to say what is in issue and what is not in issue, then the case management hearing can be adjourned for a short and limited time and to a fixed date to enable the advocate to take instructions; such an adjournment should only be necessary in exceptional circumstances, as the defence advocate should be properly instructed by the time of the first case management hearing and in any event is under an obligation to take sufficient instructions to fulfil the obligations contained in sections 33–39 of Criminal Justice Act 2003.

(b) There should then be a real dialogue between the judge and all advocates for the purpose of identifying:

(i) the focus of the prosecution case;

(ii) the common ground;

(iii) the real issues in the case. (Rule 3.2 of the Criminal Procedure Rules.)

(c) The judge will try to generate a spirit of co-operation between the court and the advocates on all sides. The expeditious conduct of the trial and a focussing on the real issues must be in the interests of **all** parties. It cannot be in the interests of any defendant for his good points to become lost in a welter of uncontroversial or irrelevant evidence.

(d) In many fraud cases the primary facts are not seriously disputed. The real issue is what each defendant knew and whether that defendant was dishonest. Once the judge has identified what is in dispute and what is not in dispute, the judge can then discuss with the advocate how the trial should be structured, what can be dealt with by admissions or agreed facts, what uncontroversial matters should be proved by concise oral evidence, what timetabling can be required under Rule 3.10 Criminal Procedure Rules, and other directions.

(e) In particularly heavy fraud or complex cases the judge may possibly consider it necessary to allocate a whole week for a case management hearing. If that week is used wisely, many further weeks of trial time can be saved. In the gaps which will inevitably arise during that week (for example while the advocates are exploring matters raised by the judge) the judge can do a substantial amount of informed reading. The case has come "alive" at this stage. Indeed, in a really heavy fraud case, if the judge fixes one or more case management hearings on this scale, there will be need for fewer formal reading days. Moreover a huge amount can be achieved in the pre-trial stage, if all trial advocates are gathered in the same place, focussing on the case **at the same time**, for several days consecutively.

(f) Requiring the defence to serve proper case statements may enable the court to identify

(i) what is common ground and

(ii) the real issues.

It is therefore important that proper defence case statements be provided as required by the Criminal Procedure Rules; judges will use the powers contained in ss.28–34 of the Criminal Proceedings and Evidence Act 1996 [*sic*] (and the corresponding provisions of the CJA 1987, ss.33 and following of the Criminal Justice Act 2003) and the Criminal Procedure Rules to ensure that realistic defence case statements are provided.

(g) Likewise this objective may be achieved by requiring the prosecution to serve draft admissions by a specified date and by requiring the defence to respond within a specified number of weeks.

(v) *Further case management hearings*

(a) The date of the next case management hearing should be fixed at the conclusion of the **N-14** hearing so that there is no delay in having to fix the date through listing offices, clerks and others.

(b) If one is looking at a trial which threatens to run for months, pre-trial case management on an intensive scale is essential.

(vi) Consideration of the length of the trial

N-15

(a) Case management on the above lines, the procedure set out in paragraph 1(iv), may still be insufficient to reduce the trial to a manageable length; generally a trial of 3 months should be the target, but there will be cases where a duration of 6 months or, in exceptional circumstances, even longer may be inevitable.

(b) If the trial is not estimated to be within a manageable length, it will be necessary for the judge to consider what steps should be taken to reduce the length of the trial, whilst still ensuring that the prosecution has the opportunity of placing the full criminality before the court.

(c) To assist the judge in this task,

(i) the lead advocate for the prosecution should be asked to explain why the prosecution have rejected a shorter way of proceeding; they may also be asked to divide the case into sections of evidence and explain the scope of each section and the need for each section;

(ii) the lead advocates for the prosecution and for the defence should be prepared to put forward in writing, if requested, ways in which a case estimated to last more than three months can be shortened, including possible severance of counts or defendants, exclusions of sections of the case or of evidence or areas of the case where admissions can be made.

(d) One course the judge may consider is pruning the indictment by omitting certain charges and/or by omitting certain defendants. The judge must not usurp the function of the prosecution in this regard, and he must bear in mind that he will, at the outset, know less about the case than the advocates. The aim is achieve [*sic*] fairness to all parties

(e) Nevertheless, the judge does have two methods of pruning available for use in appropriate circumstances:

(i) persuading the prosecution that it is not worthwhile pursuing certain charges and/or certain defendants;

(ii) severing the indictment. Severance for reasons of case management alone is perfectly proper, although judges should have regard to any representations made by the prosecution that severance would weaken their case. Indeed the judge's hand will be strengthened in this regard by rule 1.1(2)(g) of the Criminal Procedure Rules. However, before using what may be seen as a blunt instrument, the judge should insist on seeing full defence statements of all affected defendants. Severance may be unfair to the prosecution if, for example, there is a cut-throat defence in prospect. For example, the defence of the principal defendant may be that the defendant relied on the advice of his accountant or solicitor that what was happening was acceptable. The defence of the professional may be that he gave no such advice. Against that background, it might be unfair to the prosecution to order separate trials of the two defendants.

(vii) The exercise of the powers

N-16

(a) The Criminal Procedure Rules require the court to take a more active part in case management. These are salutary provisions which should bring to an end interminable criminal trials of the kind which the Court of Appeal criticised in *Jisl* [2004] EWCA 696 at [113]-[121].

(b) Nevertheless these salutary provisions do not have to be used on every occasion. Where the advocates have done their job properly, by narrowing the issues, pruning the evidence and so forth, it may be quite inappropriate for the judge to "weigh in" and start cutting out more evidence or more charges of his own volition. It behoves the judge to make a careful assessment of the degree of judicial intervention which is warranted in each case.

(c) The note of caution in the previous paragraph is supported by certain experience which has been gained of the Civil Procedure Rules (on which the Criminal Procedure Rules are based). The CPR contain valuable and efficacious provisions for case management by the judge on his own initiative which have led to huge savings of court time and costs. Surveys by the Law Society have shown that the CPR have been generally welcomed by court users and the profession, but there have been reported to have been isolated instances in which the parties to civil litigation have faithfully complied with both the letter and the spirit of the CPR, and have then been aggrieved by what was perceived to be unnecessary intermeddling by the court.

(viii) Expert evidence

(a) Early identification of the subject matter of expert evidence to be adduced by the prosecution and the defence should be made as early as possible, preferably at the directions hearing. **N-17**

(b) Following the exchange of expert evidence, any areas of disagreement should be identified and a direction should generally be made requiring the experts to meet and prepare, after discussion, a joint statement identifying points of agreement and contention and areas where the prosecution is put to proof on matters of which a positive case to the contrary is not advanced by the defence. After the statement has been prepared it should be served on the court, the prosecution and the defence. In some cases, it might be appropriate to provide that to the jury.

(ix) Surveillance evidence

(a) Where a prosecution is based upon many months' observation or surveillance evidence and it appears that it is capable of effective presentation based on a shorter period, the advocate should be required to justify the evidence of such observations before it is permitted to be adduced, either substantially or in its entirety. **N-18**

(b) Schedules should be provided to cover as much of the evidence as possible and admissions sought.

4. Disclosure

[*Replaced by the 2013 judicial protocol on disclosure: see* post, N-52 *et seq.*] **N-19**

5. Abuse of process

(i) Applications to stay or dismiss for abuse of process have become a normal feature of heavy and complex cases. Such applications may be based upon delay and the health of defendants. **N-20**

(ii) Applications in relation to absent special circumstances [*sic*] tend to be unsuccessful and not to be pursued on appeal. For this reason there is comparatively little Court of Appeal guidance: but see: *Harris and Howells* [2003] EWCA Crim. 486. It should be noted that abuse of process is not there to discipline the prosecution or the police.

(iii) The arguments on both sides must be reduced to writing. Oral evidence is seldom relevant.

(iv) The judge should direct full written submissions (rather than "skeleton arguments") on any abuse application in accordance with a timetable set by him; these should identify any element of prejudice the defendant is alleged to have suffered.

(v) The judge should normally aim to conclude the hearing within an absolute maximum limit of one day, if necessary in accordance with a timetable. The parties should therefore prepare their papers on this basis and not expect the judge to allow the oral hearing to be anything more than an occasion to highlight concisely their arguments and answer any questions the court may have of them; applications will not be allowed drag on.

6. The trial

(i) The particular hazard of heavy fraud trials

A heavy fraud or other complex trial has the potential to lose direction and focus. This is a disaster for three reasons: **N-21**

(a) the jury will lose track of the evidence, thereby prejudicing both prosecution and defence;

(b) the burden on the defendants, the judge and indeed all involved will become intolerable;

(c) scarce public resources are wasted. Other prosecutions are delayed or—worse—may never happen. Fraud which is detected but not prosecuted (for resource reasons) undermines confidence.

(ii) Judicial mastery of the case

(a) It is necessary for the judge to exercise firm control over the conduct of the trial at all stages. **N-22**

(b) In order to do this the judge must read the witness statements and the documents, so that the judge can discuss case management issues with the advocates on—almost—an equal footing.

(c) To this end, the judge should not set aside weeks or even days for pre-reading (see paragraph 3(i)(b)). Hopefully the judge will have gained a good grasp of the evidence during the case management hearings. Nevertheless, realistic reading time must be provided for the judge in advance of trial.

(d) The role of the judge in a heavy fraud or other complex criminal trial is different from his/ her role in a "conventional" criminal trial. So far as possible, the judge should be freed from other duties and burdens, so that he/she can give the high degree of commitment which a heavy fraud trial requires. This will pay dividends in terms of saving weeks or months of court time.

(iii) The order of the evidence

N-23

(a) By the outset of the trial at the latest (and in most cases very much earlier) the judge must be provided with a schedule, showing the sequence of prosecution (and in an appropriate case defence) witnesses and the dates upon which they are expected to be called. This can only be prepared by discussion between prosecution and defence which the judge should expect, and say he/she expects, to take place: See: Criminal Procedure Rule 3.10. The schedule should, in so far as it relates to prosecution witnesses, be developed in consultation with the witnesses, via the witness care units, and with consideration given to their personal needs. Copies of the schedule should be provided for the Witness Service.

(b) The schedule should be kept under review by the trial judge and by the parties. If a case is running behind or ahead of schedule, each witness affected must be advised by the party who is calling that witness at the earliest opportunity.

(c) If an excessive amount of time is allowed for any witness, the judge can ask why. The judge may probe with the advocates whether the time envisaged for the evidence-in-chief or cross-examination (as the case may be) of a particular witness is really necessary.

(iv) Case management sessions

N-24

(a) The order of the evidence may have legitimately to be departed from. It will, however, be a useful for tool for monitoring the progress of the case. There should be periodic case management sessions, during which the judge engages the advocates upon a stock-taking exercise: asking, amongst other questions, "where are we going?" and "what is the relevance of the next three witnesses?". This will be a valuable means of keeping the case on track. Rule 3.10 of the Criminal Procedure Rules will again assist the judge.

(b) The judge may wish to consider issuing the occasional use of "case management notes" to the advocates, in order to set out the judge's tentative views on where the trial may be going off track, which areas of future evidence are relevant and which may have become irrelevant (*e.g.* because of concessions, admissions in cross-examination and so forth). Such notes from the judge plus written responses from the advocates can, cautiously used, provide a valuable focus for debate during the periodic case management reviews held during the course of the trial.

(v) Controlling prolix cross-examination

N-25

(a) Setting **rigid** time limits in advance for cross-examination is rarely appropriate—as experience has shown in civil cases; but a timetable is essential so that the judge can exercise control and so that there is a clear target to aim at for the completion of the evidence of each witness. Moreover the judge can and should indicate when cross-examination is irrelevant, unnecessary or time wasting. The judge may limit the time for further cross-examination of a particular witness.

(vi) Electronic presentation of evidence

N-26

(a) Electronic presentation of evidence (EPE) has the potential to save huge amounts of time in fraud and other complex criminal trials and should be used more widely.

(b) HMCS is providing facilities for the easier use of EPE with a standard audio visual facility. Effectively managed, the savings in court time achieved by EPE more than justify the cost.

(c) There should still be a core bundle of those documents to which frequent reference will be made during the trial. The jury may wish to mark that bundle or to refer back to particular pages as the evidence progresses. EPE can be used for presenting all documents not contained in the core bundle.

(d) Greater use of other modern forms of graphical presentations should be made wherever possible.

(vii) Use of interviews

The judge should consider extensive editing of self serving interviews, even when the defence **N-27** want the jury to hear them in their entirety; such interviews are not evidence of the truth of their contents but merely of the defendant's reaction to the allegation.

(viii) Jury management

(a) The jury should be informed as early as possible in the case as to what the issues are in a **N-28** manner directed by the Judge.

(b) The jury must be regularly updated as to the trial timetable and the progress of the trial, subject to warnings as to the predictability of the trial process.

(c) Legal argument should be heard at times that causes the least inconvenience to jurors.

(d) It is useful to consider with the advocates whether written directions should be given to the jury and, if so, in what form.

(ix) Maxwell hours

(a) Maxwell hours should only be permitted after careful consideration and consultation with **N-29** the Presiding Judge.

(b) Considerations in favour include:
   (i) legal argument can be accommodated without disturbing the jury;
   (ii) there is a better chance of a representative jury;
   (iii) time is made available to the judge, advocates and experts to do useful work in the afternoons

(c) Considerations against include:
   (i) the lengthening of trials and the consequent waste of court time;
   (ii) the desirability of making full use of the jury once they have arrived at court;
   (iii) shorter trials tend to diminish the need for special provisions *e.g.* there are fewer difficulties in empanelling more representative juries;
   (iv) they are unavailable if any defendant is in custody.

(d) It may often be the case that a maximum of one day of Maxwell hours a week is sufficient; if so, it should be timetabled in advance to enable all submissions by advocates, supported by skeleton arguments served in advance, to be dealt with in the period after 1:30 pm on that day.

(x) Livenote

If Livenote is used, it is important that all users continue to take a note of the evidence, otherwise **N-30** considerable time is wasted in detailed reading of the entire daily transcript.

7. Other issues

(i) Defence representation and defence costs

(a) Applications for change in representation in complex trials need special consideration; **N-31** the ruling of HH Judge Wakerley QC (as he then was) in *Asghar Ali* has been circulated by the JSB.

(b) Problems have arisen when the Legal Services Commission have declined to allow advocates or solicitors to do certain work; on occasions the matter has been raised with the judge managing or trying the case.

(c) The Legal Services Commission has provided guidance to judges on how they can obtain information from the LSC as to the reasons for their decisions; further information in relation to this can be obtained from *Nigel Field, Head of the Complex Crime Unit, Legal Services Commission, 29–37 Red Lion Street, London, WC1R 4PP.*

(ii) Assistance to the judge

Experience has shown that in some very heavy cases, the judge's burden can be substantially offset **N-32** with the provision of a judicial assistant or other support and assistance.

[The next paragraph is N-52.]

B. Disclosure of Unused Material in Criminal Cases

Foreword

N-52   [*Identical to the foreword to the Attorney-General's guidelines*: ante, § A-242a.]

Introduction

N-53   This protocol is prescribed for use by CPD IV Disclosure 22A: Disclosure of Unused Material. It is applicable in all the criminal courts of England and Wales, including the Crown Court, the Court Martial[1] and the magistrates' courts. It replaces the previous judicial document 'Disclosure: a Protocol for the Control and Management of Unused Material in the Crown Court'[2] and it also replaces section 4 'Disclosure' of the Lord Chief Justice's Protocol on the Control and Management of Heavy Fraud and Other Complex Criminal Cases, dated 22 March 2005.[3]

This protocol is intended to provide a central source of guidance for the judiciary, although that produced by the Attorney General also requires attention.

In summary, this judicial protocol sets out the principles to be applied to, and the importance of, disclosure; the expectations of the court and its role in disclosure, in particular in relation to case management; and the consequences if there is a failure by the prosecution or defence to comply with their obligations.

Readers should note that a review of disclosure in the magistrates' courts is currently being undertaken by H.H.J. Kinch Q.C. and the Chief Magistrate, on behalf of Lord Justice Gross, the Senior Presiding Judge. Amendments may therefore be made following the recommendations of that review, and in accordance with other forthcoming changes to the criminal justice system.

The importance of disclosure for fair trials

N-54   1. Disclosure remains one of the most important – as well as one of the most misunderstood and abused – of the procedures relating to criminal trials. Lord Justice Gross' review has reemphasised the need for all those involved to understand the statutory requirements and to undertake their roles with rigour, in a timely manner.

2. The House of Lords stated in *R. v. H.* [2004] UKHL 3; [2004] 2 A.C. 134; [2004] 2 Cr.App.R. 10:

> "Fairness ordinarily requires that any material held by the prosecution which weakens its case or strengthens that of the defendant, if not relied on as part of its formal case against the defendant, should be disclosed to the defence. Bitter experience has shown that miscarriages of justice may occur where such material is withheld from disclosure. The golden rule is that full disclosure of such material should be made" ([2004] 2 A.C. 134, at 147).

The Criminal Cases Review Commission has recently noted that failure to disclose material to the defence to which they were entitled remains the biggest single cause of miscarriages of justice.

3. However, it is also essential that the trial process is not overburdened or diverted by erroneous and inappropriate disclosure of unused prosecution material or by misconceived applications. Although the drafters of the Criminal Procedure and Investigations Act 1996 ('CPIA 1996') cannot have anticipated the vast increase in the amount of electronic material that has been generated in recent years, nevertheless the principles of that Act still hold true. Applications by the parties or decisions by judges based on misconceptions of the law or a general laxity of approach (however well-intentioned) which result in an improper application of the disclosure regime have, time and again, proved unnecessarily costly and have obstructed justice. As Lord Justice Gross noted, the burden of disclosure must not be allowed to render the prosecution of cases impracticable.

4. The overarching principle is that unused prosecution material will fall to be disclosed if, and only if, it satisfies the test for disclosure applicable to the proceedings in question, subject to any over-

---

[1] The timetables given here may vary in the Court Martial and reference should be made to the Criminal Procedure and Investigations Act 1996 (Application to the Armed Forces) Order 2009 and to any practice note issued by the Judge Advocate General.
[2] The previous judicial protocol was endorsed by the Court of Appeal in *R. v. K.* [2006] EWCA Crim. 724; [2006] 2 All ER 552 (Note).
[3] This protocol also replaces the Protocol for the Provision of Advance Information, Prosecution Evidence and Disclosure of Unused Material in the Magistrates' Courts, dated 12 May 2006, which was adopted as part of the Stop Delaying Justice initiative.

riding public interest considerations. The test for disclosure will depend on the date the criminal investigation in question commenced, as this will determine whether the common law disclosure regime applies, or either of the two disclosure regimes under the CPIA 1996.

5. The test for disclosure under section 3 of the CPIA 1996 as amended will be applicable in nearly every case and all those involved in the process will need to be familiar with it. Material fulfils the test if – but only if – it "might reasonably be considered capable of undermining the case for the prosecution ... or of assisting the case for the accused."

6. The disclosure process must be led by the prosecution so as to trigger comprehensive defence engagement, supported by robust judicial case management. Active participation by the court in the disclosure process is a critical means of ensuring that delays and adjournments are avoided, given failures by the parties to comply with their obligations may disrupt and (in some cases) frustrate the course of justice.

Disclosure of unused material in criminal cases

7. The court should keep the timetable for prosecution and defence disclosure under review from **N-55** the first hearing. Judges should as a matter of course ask the parties to identify the issues in the case, and invite the parties to indicate whether further disclosure is sought, and on what topics. For example, it is not enough for the judge to rely on the content of the PCMH form. Proper completion of the disclosure process is a vital part of case preparation, and it may well affect the progress of the case. The court will expect disclosure to have been considered from the outset; the prosecution and defence advocates need to be aware of any potential problems and substantive difficulties should be explained to the judge; and the parties should propose a sensible timetable. Realism is preferable to optimistic but unachievable deadlines which may dislocate the court schedule and imperil the date of trial. It follows that judges should not impose deadlines for service of the case papers or disclosure until they are confident that the prosecution advocate has taken instructions from the individuals who are best placed to evaluate the work to be undertaken.

8. The advocates – both prosecution and defence – must be kept fully informed throughout the course of the proceedings as to any difficulties which may prevent them from complying with their disclosure obligations. When problems arise or come to light after directions have been given, the advocates should notify the court and the other party (or parties) immediately rather than waiting until the date set by the court for the service of the material is imminent or has passed, and they must provide the court with a suggested timetable in order to resolve the problem. The progress of the disclosure process should be reviewed at every hearing. There remains no basis in practice or law for counsel to counsel disclosure.

9. If there is a preliminary hearing the judge should seize the opportunity to impose an early timetable for disclosure and to identify any likely problems including as regards third party material and material that will require an application to the Family Court. In an appropriate case the court should consider holding a joint criminal/care directions hearing. See "Material held by Third Parties", from paragraph 44 below.

10. For the PCMH to be effective, the defence must have a proper opportunity to review the case papers and consider initial disclosure, with a view to preparing a properly completed defence statement which will inform the judge's conduct of the PCMH, and inform the prosecution of the matters required by sections 5, 6A and 6C of the CPIA. As the Court of Appeal noted in *R. v. Newell* [2012] EWCA Crim. 650; [2012] 2 Cr.App.R. 10, "a typed defence statement must be provided before the PCMH. If there is no defence statement by the time of the PCMH, then a judge will usually require the trial advocate to see that such a statement is provided and not proceed with the PCMH until that is done. In the ordinary case the trial advocate will be required to do that at the court and the PCMH resumed later in the day to avoid delay". There may be some instances when there will be a well-founded defence application to extend the 28-day time limit for serving a proper defence statement. In a proper case (but never routinely), it may be appropriate to put the PCMH back by a week or more, to enable an appropriate defence statement to be filed.

11. The defence statement can be admitted into evidence under section 6E(4) of the CPIA 1996. However, information included on the PCMH form (which is primarily an administrative form) will not usually be admitted in evidence when the defence advocate has complied with the letter and the spirit of the Criminal Procedure Rules.[4] Introducing the PCMH form (or part of it) during the trial is likely to be an exceptional event. The status of the trial preparation form in the magistrates' court is somewhat different, as discussed below.

12. The court should not extend time lightly or as a matter of course. If an extension is sought, it ought to be accompanied by an appropriate explanation. For instance, it is not sufficient for the prosecutor merely to say that the investigator has delivered the papers late: the underlying reasons

---

[4] *R. v. Newell* [2012] EWCA Crim. 650; [2012] 2 Cr.App.R. 10.

are to be provided to the court. The same applies if the defence statement is delayed. Whichever party is at fault, realistic proposals for service are to be set out.

13. Judges should not allow the prosecution to avoid their statutory responsibility for reviewing the unused material by the expedient of permitting the defence to have access to (or providing the defence with copies of) the material listed in the schedules of non-sensitive unused prosecution material irrespective of whether it satisfies, wholly or in part, the relevant test for disclosure. Additionally, it is for the prosecutor to decide on the manner of disclosure, and it does not have to mirror the form in which the information was originally recorded. Rose L.J. gave guidance on case management issues in this context in *R. v. CPS (Interlocutory Application under sections 35/36 CPIA)* [2005] EWCA Crim. 2342. Allowing the defence to inspect items that fulfil the disclosure test is also a valid means of providing disclosure.

14. The larger and more complex the case, the more important it is for the prosecution to adhere to the overarching principle and ensure that sufficient prosecution attention and resources are allocated to the task. Handing the defendant the "keys to the warehouse" has been the cause of many gross abuses in the past, resulting in considerable expenditure by the defence without any material benefit to the course of justice. The circumstances relating to large and complex cases are outlined below.

15. The court will require the defence to engage and assist in the early identification of the real issues in the case and, particularly in the larger and more complex cases, to contribute to the search terms to be used for, and the parameters of, the review of any electronically held material (which can be very considerable). Any defence criticisms of the prosecution approach to disclosure should be timely and reasoned; there is no place for disclosure "ambushes" or for late or uninformative defence statements. Admissions should be used so far as possible to narrow the real issues in dispute.

16. A constructive approach to disclosure is a necessary part of professional best practice, for the defence and prosecution. This does not undermine the defendant's legitimate interests, it accords with his or her obligations under the rules and it ensures that all the relevant material is provided. Delays and failures by the prosecution and the defence are equally damaging to a timely, fair and efficient trial, and judges should be vigilant in preventing and addressing abuses. Accordingly, whenever there are potential failings by either the defence or the prosecution, judges, in exercising appropriate oversight of disclosure, should carefully investigate the suggested default and give timely directions.

17. In the Crown Court, the defence statement is to be served within 28 days of the date when the prosecution complies with its duty of initial disclosure (or purports to do so) and whenever section 5(5) of the CPIA applies to the proceedings, and the defence statement must comply with section 6A of the CPIA. Service of the defence statement is a most important stage in the disclosure process, and timely service is necessary to facilitate proper consideration of the disclosure issues well in advance of the trial date. Judges expect a defence statement to contain a clear and detailed exposition of the issues of fact and law. Defence statements that merely rehearse the suggestion that the defendant is innocent do not comply with the requirements of the CPIA.

18. The prosecutor should consider the defence statement carefully and promptly provide a copy to the disclosure officer, to assist the prosecution in its continuing disclosure obligations. The court expects the Crown to identify any suggested deficiencies in the defence statement, and to draw these to the attention of the defence and the court; in particular in large and complex cases, it will assist the court if this is in writing. Although the prosecution's ability to request, and the court's jurisdiction to give, an adverse inference direction under section 11 of CPIA is not contingent on the prosecution having earlier identified any suggested deficiencies, nevertheless the prosecutor must provide a timely written explanation of its position.

19. Judges should examine the defence statement with care to ensure that it complies with the formalities required by the CPIA. As stated in *R. v. H.* (*supra*) (para. 35):

> "If material does not weaken the prosecution case or strengthen that of the defendant, there is no requirement to disclose it. For this purpose the parties' respective cases should not be restrictively analysed. But they must be carefully analysed, to ascertain the specific facts the prosecution seek to establish and the specific grounds on which the charges are resisted. The trial process is not well served if the defence are permitted to make general and unspecified allegations and then seek far-reaching disclosure in the hope that material may turn up to make them good. Neutral material or material damaging to the defendant need not be disclosed and should not be brought to the attention of the court."

20. If no defence statement – or an inadequate defence statement – is served within the relevant time limits, the judge should investigate the position. At every PCMH where there is no defence statement, including those where an extension has been given, or the time for filing has not yet expired, the defence should be warned in appropriate terms that pursuant to section 6E(2) of the

CPIA an adverse inference may be drawn during the trial, and this result is likely if there is no justification for the deficiency. The fact that a warning has been given should be noted.

21. An adverse inference may be drawn under section 11 of the CPIA if the accused fails to discharge his or her disclosure obligations. Whenever the amended CPIA regime applies, the prosecution may comment on any failure in defence disclosure (except where the failure relates to a point of law) without leave of the court, but counsel should use a measure of judgment as to whether it is wise to embark on cross-examination about such a failure.[5] If the accused is cross-examined about discrepancies between his evidence and his defence statement, or if adverse comment is made, the judge must give appropriate guidance to the jury.[6]

22. In order to secure a fair trial, it is vital that the prosecution is mindful of its continuing duty of disclosure. Once the defence statement has been received, the Crown must review disclosure in the light of the issues identified in the defence statement. In cases of complexity, the following steps are then likely to be necessary:

    i. service by the prosecution of any further material due to the defence following receipt of the defence statement;

    ii. any defence request to the prosecution for service of additional specific items; as discussed below, these requests must be justified by reference to the defence statement and they should be submitted on the section 8 form;

    iii. prosecution response to the defence request;

    iv. if the defence considers that disclosable items are still outstanding, a section 8 application should be made using the appropriate form.

23. It follows that all requests by the defence to the prosecution for disclosure should be made on the section 8 application form, even if no hearing is sought in the first instance. Discussion and co-operation between the parties outside of court is encouraged in order to ensure that the court is only asked to issue a ruling when strictly necessary. However, use of the section 8 form will ensure that focussed requests are clearly set out in one place.

24. The judge should set a date as part of the timetabling exercise by which any application under section 8 is to be made, if this appears to be a likely eventuality.

25. The court will require the section 8 application to be served on the prosecution well in advance of the hearing – indeed, prior to requesting the hearing – to enable the Crown to identify and serve any items that meet the test for disclosure.

26. Service of a defence statement is an essential precondition for an application under section 8, and applications should not be heard or directions for disclosure issued in the absence of a properly completed statement (see Part 22 of the Criminal Procedure Rules). In particular, blanket orders in this context are inconsistent with the statutory framework for disclosure laid down by the CPIA and the decision of the House of Lords in *R. v. H.* (*supra*). It follows that defence requests for disclosure of particular pieces of unused prosecution material which are not referable to any issue in the case identified in the defence statement should be rejected.

27. Judges must ensure that defendants are not prejudiced on account of the failures of their lawyers, and, when necessary, the professions should be reminded that if justice is to be done, and if disclosure is to be dealt with fairly in accordance with the law, a full and careful defence statement and a reasoned approach to section 8 applications are essential. In exploring the adequacy of the defence statement, a judge should always ask what the issues are and upon what matters of fact the defendant intends to rely[7] and on what matters of fact the defendant takes issue.

Listing

28. Sufficient time is necessary for the judge properly to undertake the PCMH, and this is a **N-56** paramount consideration when listing cases. Unless the court is able to sit early, judges who are part heard on trials are probably not best placed to conduct PCMHs.

29. Cases that raise particularly difficult issues of disclosure should be referred to the resident judge for directions (unless a trial judge has been allocated) and, for trials of real complexity, the trial judge should be identified at an early stage, prior to the PCMH if possible. Listing officers, work-ing in consultation with the resident judge and, if allocated, the trial judge, should ensure that sufficient time is allowed for judges to prepare and deal with prosecution and defence applications relat-ing to disclosure, particularly in the more complex cases.

Magistrates' courts (including the youth court)

30. The principles relating to disclosure apply equally in the magistrates' courts. It follows that **N-57**

---

[5] *R. v. Essa* [2009] EWCA Crim. 43, para. 22.
[6] *R. v. Hanyes* [2011] EWCA Crim. 3281.
[7] *R. v. Rochford* [2010] EWCA Crim. 1928; [2011] 1 Cr.App.R. 11.

whilst disclosure of unused material in compliance with the statutory test is undoubtedly essential in order to achieve justice, it is critical that summary trials are not delayed or made over-complicated by misconceived applications for, or inappropriate disclosure of, prosecution material.

31. Magistrates will rely on their legal advisers for guidance, and the latter should draw the attention of the parties and the court to the statutory provisions and the applicable case law. Cases raising disclosure issues of particular complexity should be referred to a District Judge (Magistrates' Courts), if available.

32. Although service of a defence statement is voluntary for summary trials (s.6 CPIA), the defendant cannot make an application for specific disclosure under section 8 CPIA, and the court cannot make any orders in this regard, unless a proper defence statement has been provided. It follows that although providing a defence statement is not mandatory, it remains a critical stage in the disclosure process. If disclosure issues are to be raised by the defence, a defence statement must be served well in advance of the trial date. Any section 8 application must be made in strict compliance with the rules.

33. The case-management forms used in the magistrates' courts fulfil some of the functions of a defence statement, and the prosecution must take into account the information provided as to the defence case when conducting its on-going review of unused material. As the Court of Appeal noted in *R. v. Newell* (*supra*), admissions can be made in the trial preparation form and the defence is able to identify the matters that are not in issue. Admissions made in these circumstances may be admissible during the trial. However, other information on the form that does not come within the section relating to admissions should be treated in the same way as the contents of a PCMH form in the Crown Court and it should not generally be introduced as part of the evidence at trial. However, the contents of the trial preparation form do not replace the need to serve a defence statement if the defendant seeks to apply for disclosure under section 8 CPIA.

34. The standard directions require that any defence statement is to be served within 14 days of the date upon which the prosecution has complied with, or purported to comply with, the duty to provide initial disclosure. There may be some instances when there will be a wellfounded defence application to extend the 14-day time limit for serving the defence statement. These applications must be made in accordance with the Criminal Procedure Rules, in writing and before the time limit expires.

35. Although CCTV footage frequently causes difficulties, it is to be treated as any other category of unused material and it should only be disclosed if the material meets the appropriate test for disclosure under the CPIA. The defence should either be provided with copies of the sections of the CCTV or afforded an opportunity to view them. If the prosecution refuses to disclose CCTV material that the defence considers to be discloseable, the courts should not make standard or general directions requiring the prosecutor to disclose material of this kind in the absence of an application under section 8. When potentially relevant CCTV footage is not in the possession of the police, the guidance in relation to third party material will apply, although the police remain under a duty to pursue all reasonable lines of inquiry, including those leading away from a suspect, whether or not defence requests are made.

36. The previous convictions of witnesses and any disciplinary findings against officers in the case are frequently discloseable and care should be taken to disclose them as appropriate. Documents such as crime reports or records of emergency calls should not be provided on a routine basis, for instance as part of a bundle of disclosed documents, irrespective of whether the material satisfies the appropriate test for disclosure. Defence advocates should not request this material in standard or routine correspondence, and instead focussed consideration should be given to the circumstances of the particular case. Unjustified requests for disclosure of material of this kind are routinely made, frequently leading to unnecessary delays and adjournments. The prosecution should always consider whether the request is properly made out.

37. The supervisory role of the courts is critical in this context, and magistrates must guard against granting unnecessary adjournments and issuing unjustified directions.

Large and complex cases in the Crown Court

N-58

38. Disclosure is a particular problem with the larger and more complex cases, which require a scrupulous approach by the parties and robust case management by the judiciary. If possible, the trial judge should be identified at the outset.

39. The legal representatives need to fulfil their duties in this context with care and efficiency; they should co-operate with the other party (or parties) and the court; and the judge and the other party (or parties) are to be informed of any difficulties, as soon as they arise. The court should be provided with an up-to-date timetable for disclosure whenever there are material changes in this regard. A disclosure-management document, or similar, prepared by the prosecution will be of particular assistance to the court in large and complex cases.

40. Judges should be prepared to give early guidance as to the prosecution's approach to disclosure, thereby ensuring early engagement by the defence.

41. Cases of this nature frequently include large volumes of digitally stored material. The Attorney General's 2011 guidance (now included as an annex to the Attorney General's Guidelines on Disclosure 2013) is of particular relevance and assistance in this context.

42. Applications for witness anonymity orders require particular attention; as the Court of Appeal noted in *R. v. Mayers* [2008] EWCA Crim. 2989; [2009] 1 Cr.App.R. 30, in making such an application, the prosecution's obligations of disclosure "go much further than the ordinary duties of disclosure".

43. If the judge considers that there are reasonable grounds to doubt the good faith of the investigation, he or she will be concerned to see that there has been independent and effective appraisal of the documents contained in the disclosure schedule and that its contents are adequate. In appropriate cases where this issue has arisen and there are grounds which show there is a real issue, consideration should be given to receiving evidence on oath from the senior investigating officer at an early case management hearing.

Material held by third parties

44. Where material is held by a third party such as a local authority, a social services department, **N-59** hospital or business, the investigators and the prosecution may need to make enquiries of the third party, with a view to inspecting the material and assessing whether the relevant test for disclosure is met and determining whether any or all of the material should be retained, recorded and, in due course, disclosed to the accused. If access by the prosecution is granted, the investigators and the prosecution will need to establish whether the custodian of the material intends to raise PII issues, as a result of which the material may have to be placed before the court for a decision. This does not obviate the need for the defence to conduct its own enquiries as appropriate. Speculative enquiries without any proper basis in relation to third party material – whether by the prosecution or the defence – are to be discouraged, and, in appropriate cases, the court will consider making an order for costs where an application is clearly unmeritorious and misconceived.

45. The 2013 Protocol and Good Practice Model on Disclosure of Information in Cases of Alleged Child Abuse and Linked Criminal and Care Directions Hearings has recently been published. It provides a framework and timetable for the police and CPS to obtain discloseable material from local authorities, and for applications to be made to the Family Court. It is applicable to all cases of alleged child abuse where the child is aged 17 years or under. It is not binding on local authorities, but it does represent best practice and therefore should be consulted in all such cases. Delays in obtaining this type of material have led to unacceptable delays to trials involving particularly vulnerable witnesses and every effort must be made to ensure that all discloseable material is identified at an early stage so that any necessary applications can be made and the defence receive material to which they are entitled in good time.

46. There is no specific procedure for disclosure of material held by third parties in criminal proceedings, although the procedure established under section 2 of the Criminal Procedure (Attendance of Witnesses) Act 1965 or section 97 of the Magistrates' Courts Act 1980 is often used for this purpose. Where the third party in question declines to allow inspection of the material, or requires the prosecution to obtain an order before providing copies, the prosecutor will need to consider whether it is appropriate to obtain a witness summons under either section 2 of the Criminal Procedure (Attendance of Witnesses) Act 1965 or section 97 of the Magistrates' Courts Act 1980. Part 28 of the Criminal Procedure Rules and paragraphs 3.5 and 3.6 of the Code of Practice under the CPIA 1996 should be followed.

47. Applications for third party disclosure must identify the documents that are sought and provide full details of why they are discloseable. This is particularly relevant when access is sought to the medical records of those who allege they are victims of crime. It should be appreciated that a duty to assert confidentiality may arise when a third party receives a request for disclosure, or the right to privacy may be claimed under Article 8 of the ECHR (see in particular Crim. P.R., Pt 28.6). Victims do not waive the confidentiality of their medical records, or their right to privacy under Article 8 of the ECHR, by making a complaint against the accused. The court, as a public authority, must ensure that any interference with the right to privacy under Article 8 is in accordance with the law, and is necessary in pursuit of a legitimate public interest. General and unspecified requests to trawl through such records should be refused. Confidentiality rests with the subject of the material, not with the authority holding it. The subject is entitled to service of the application and has the right to make representations: Criminal Procedure Rule 22.3 and *R. (B.) v. Stafford Combined Court* [2006] EWHC 1645 (Admin.); [2006] 2 Cr.App.R. 34. The 2013 Protocol and Good Practice Model at paragraph 13 should be followed. It is likely that the judge will need to issue directions when issues of this kind are raised (*e.g.* whether enquiries with the third party are likely to be appropriate; who is to make the request; what material is to be sought, and from whom; and a timetable should be set).

48. The judge should consider whether to take any steps if a third party fails, or refuses, to comply with a request for disclosure, including suggesting that either of the parties pursue the request and, if necessary, make an application for a witness summons. In these circumstances, the court will need to set an appropriate timetable for compliance with Part 28 of the rules. Any failure to comply with the timetable must immediately be referred back to the court for further directions, although a hearing will not always be necessary. Generally, it may be appropriate for the defence to pursue requests of this kind when the prosecution, for good reason, decline to do so and the court will need to ensure that this procedure does not delay the trial.

49. There are very limited circumstances in which information relating to Family Court proceedings (*e.g.* where there have been care proceedings in relation to a child who has complained to the police of mistreatment) may be communicated without a court order: see the Family Procedure Rules 12.73. Reference should be made to the 2013 Protocol and Good Practice Model. In most circumstances, a court order will be required and paragraph 11 of the Protocol which sets out how an application should be made should be followed.

Other government departments

N-60
50. Material held by other government departments or other Crown agencies will not be prosecution material for the purposes of section 3(2) or section 8(4) of the CPIA if it has not been inspected, recorded and retained during the course of the relevant criminal investigation. The *CPIA Code of Practice and the Attorney General's Guidelines on Disclosure*, however, impose a duty upon the investigators and the prosecution to pursue all reasonable lines of inquiry and that may involve seeking disclosure from the relevant body.

International matters

N-61
51. The obligations of the Crown in relation to relevant third-party material held overseas are as set out in *R. v. Flook* [2009] EWCA Crim. 682; [2010] 1 Cr.App.R. 30: the Crown must pursue reasonable lines of enquiry and if it appears there is relevant material, all reasonable steps must be taken to obtain it, whether formally or otherwise. To a great extent, the success of these enquiries will depend on the laws of the country where the material is held and the facts of the individual case. It needs to be recognised that when the material is held in a country outside of the European Union, the power of the Crown and the courts of England and Wales to obtain third-party material may well be limited. If informal requests are unsuccessful, the avenues are limited to the Crime (International Co-operation) Act 2003 and any applicable international conventions. It cannot, in any sense, be guaranteed that a request to a foreign government, court or body will produce the material sought. Additionally, some foreign authorities may be prepared to show the material in question to the investigating officers, whilst refusing to allow the material to be copied or otherwise made available.

52. As the Court of Appeal observed in *R. v. Khyam* [2008] EWCA Crim. 1612; [2009] 1 Cr.App.R.(S.) 77:

"The prosecuting authorities in this jurisdiction simply cannot compel authorities in a foreign country to acknowledge, let alone comply with, our disclosure principles" (at [37]).

The obligation is therefore to take reasonable steps. Whether the Crown has complied with that obligation is for the courts to judge in each case.

53. It is, therefore, important that the prosecution sets out the position clearly in writing, including any inability to inspect or retrieve any material that potentially ought to be disclosed, along with the steps that have been taken.

Applications for non-disclosure in the public interest

N-62
54. Applications in this context, whenever possible, should be considered by the trial judge. The House of Lords in *R. v. H.* (*supra*) has provided useful guidance as to the proper approach to be applied (para. [36]):

"When any issue of derogation from the golden rule of full disclosure comes before it, the court must address a series of questions:
    (1) What is the material which the prosecution seek to withhold? This must be considered by the court in detail.
    (2) Is the material such as may weaken the prosecution case or strengthen that of the defence? If No, disclosure should not be ordered. If Yes, full disclosure should (subject to (3), (4) and (5) below) be ordered.
    (3) Is there a real risk of serious prejudice to an important public interest (and, if so, what) if full disclosure of the material is ordered? If No, full disclosure should be ordered.

(4) If the answer to (2) and (3) is Yes, can the defendant's interest be protected without disclosure or disclosure be ordered to an extent or in a way which will give adequate protection to the public interest in question and also afford adequate protection to the interests of the defence?

> This question requires the court to consider, with specific reference to the material which the prosecution seek to withhold and the facts of the case and the defence as disclosed, whether the prosecution should formally admit what the defence seek to establish or whether disclosure short of full disclosure may be ordered. This may be done in appropriate cases by the preparation of summaries or extracts of evidence, or the provision of documents in an edited or anonymised form, provided the documents supplied are in each instance approved by the judge. In appropriate cases the appointment of special counsel may be a necessary step to ensure that the contentions of the prosecution are tested and the interests of the defendant protected (see para. [22] above). In cases of exceptional difficulty the court may require the appointment of special counsel to ensure a correct answer to questions (2) and (3) as well as (4).

(5) Do the measures proposed in answer to (4) represent the minimum derogation necessary to protect the public interest in question? If No, the court should order such greater disclosure as will represent the minimum derogation from the golden rule of full disclosure.

(6) If limited disclosure is ordered pursuant to (4) or (5), may the effect be to render the trial process, viewed as a whole, unfair to the defendant? If Yes, then fuller disclosure should be ordered even if this leads or may lead the prosecution to discontinue the proceedings so as to avoid having to make disclosure.

(7) If the answer to (6) when first given is No, does that remain the correct answer as the trial unfolds, evidence is adduced and the defence advanced?

It is important that the answer to (6) should not be treated as a final, once-and-for-all, answer but as a provisional answer which the court must keep under review."

55. In this context, the following matters are to be emphasised:

a. the procedure for making applications to the court is set out in the Criminal Procedure Rules, Pt 22;

b. when the PII application is a Type 1 or Type 2 application, proper notice to the defence is necessary to enable the accused to make focused submissions to the court and the notice should be as specific as the nature of the material allows; it is appreciated that in some cases only the generic nature of the material can be identified; in some wholly exceptional cases (Type 3 cases) it may be justified to give no notice at all; the judge should always ask the prosecution to justify the form of notice (or the decision to give no notice at all);

c. the prosecution should be alert to the possibility of disclosing a statement in a redacted form by, for example, simply removing personal details; this may obviate the need for a PII application, unless the redacted material satisfies the test for disclosure;

d. except when the material is very short (for instance only a few sheets), or for reasons of sensitivity, the prosecution should supply securely sealed copies to the judge in advance, together with a short statement explaining the relevance of each document, how it satisfies the disclosure test and why it is suggested that disclosure would result in a real risk of serious prejudice to an important public interest; in undertaking this task, the use of merely formulaic expressions is to be discouraged; in any case of complexity a schedule of the material should be provided, identifying the particular objection to disclosure in relation to each item, and leaving a space for the judge's decision;

e. the application, even if held in private or in secret, should be recorded; the judge should give some short statement of reasons; this is often best done document by document as the hearing proceeds;

f. the recording, copies of the judge's orders (and any copies of the material retained by the court) should be clearly identified, securely sealed and kept in the court building in a safe or locked cabinet consistent with its security classification, and there should be a proper register of the contents; arrangements should be made for the return of the material to the prosecution once the case is concluded and the time for an appeal has elapsed.

Conclusion

56. Historically, disclosure was viewed essentially as being a matter to be resolved between the par- **N-63**

ties, and the court only became engaged if a particular issue or complaint was raised. That perception is now wholly out of date. The regime established under the Criminal Justice Act 2003 and the Criminal Procedure Rules gives judges the power – indeed, it imposes a duty on the judiciary – actively to manage disclosure in every case. The efficient, effective and timely resolution of these issues is a critical element in meeting the overriding objective of the Criminal Procedure Rules of dealing with cases justly.

ALMANAC

TABLE OF CONTENTS

2012

JANUARY
M	T	W	Th	F	Sa	Su
2	3	4	5	6	7	1
9	10	11	12	13	14	8
16	17	18	19	20	21	15
23	24	25	26	27	28	22
30	31					29

FEBRUARY
M	T	W	Th	F	Sa	Su
6	7	1	2	3	4	5
13	14	8	9	10	11	12
20	21	15	16	17	18	19
27	28	22	23	24	25	26
		29				

MARCH
M	T	W	Th	F	Sa	Su
5	6	7	1	2	3	4
12	13	14	8	9	10	11
19	20	21	15	16	17	18
26	27	28	22	23	24	25
			29	30	31	

APRIL
M	T	W	Th	F	Sa	Su
2	3	4	5	6	7	1
9	10	11	12	13	14	8
16	17	18	19	20	21	15
23	24	25	26	27	28	22
30						29

MAY
M	T	W	Th	F	Sa	Su
7	1	2	3	4	5	6
14	8	9	10	11	12	13
21	15	16	17	18	19	20
28	22	23	24	25	26	27
	29	30	31			

JUNE
M	T	W	Th	F	Sa	Su
4	5	6	7	1	2	3
11	12	13	14	8	9	10
18	19	20	21	15	16	17
25	26	27	28	22	23	24
				29	30	

JULY
M	T	W	Th	F	Sa	Su
2	3	4	5	6	7	1
9	10	11	12	13	14	8
16	17	18	19	20	21	15
23	24	25	26	27	28	22
30	31					29

AUGUST
M	T	W	Th	F	Sa	Su
6	7	1	2	3	4	5
13	14	8	9	10	11	12
20	21	15	16	17	18	19
27	28	22	23	24	25	26
		29	30	31		

SEPTEMBER
M	T	W	Th	F	Sa	Su
3	4	5	6	7	1	2
10	11	12	13	14	8	9
17	18	19	20	21	15	16
24	25	26	27	28	22	23
					29	30

OCTOBER
M	T	W	Th	F	Sa	Su
1	2	3	4	5	6	7
8	9	10	11	12	13	14
15	16	17	18	19	20	21
22	23	24	25	26	27	28
29	30	31				

NOVEMBER
M	T	W	Th	F	Sa	Su
5	6	7	1	2	3	4
12	13	14	8	9	10	11
19	20	21	15	16	17	18
26	27	28	22	23	24	25
			29	30		

DECEMBER
M	T	W	Th	F	Sa	Su
3	4	5	6	7	1	2
10	11	12	13	14	8	9
17	18	19	20	21	15	16
24	25	26	27	28	22	23
31					29	30

2013

JANUARY

M	T	W	Th	F	Sa	Su
	1	2	3	4	5	6
7	8	9	10	11	12	13
14	15	16	17	18	19	20
21	22	23	24	25	26	27
28	29	30	31			

FEBRUARY

M	T	W	Th	F	Sa	Su
			1	1	2	3
4	5	6	7	8	9	10
11	12	13	14	15	16	17
18	19	20	21	22	23	24
25	26	27	28			

MARCH

M	T	W	Th	F	Sa	Su
				1	2	3
4	5	6	7	8	9	10
11	12	13	14	15	16	17
18	19	20	21	22	23	24
25	26	27	28	29	30	31

APRIL

M	T	W	Th	F	Sa	Su
1	2	3	4	5	6	7
8	9	10	11	12	13	14
15	16	17	18	19	20	21
22	23	24	25	26	27	28
29	30					

MAY

M	T	W	Th	F	Sa	Su
	1	1	2	3	4	5
6	7	8	9	10	11	12
13	14	15	16	17	18	19
20	21	22	23	24	25	26
27	28	29	30	31		

JUNE

M	T	W	Th	F	Sa	Su
					1	2
3	4	5	6	7	8	9
10	11	12	13	14	15	16
17	18	19	20	21	22	23
24	25	26	27	28	29	30

JULY

M	T	W	Th	F	Sa	Su
1	2	3	4	5	6	7
8	9	10	11	12	13	14
15	16	17	18	19	20	21
22	23	24	25	26	27	28
29	30	31				

AUGUST

M	T	W	Th	F	Sa	Su
			1	2	3	4
5	6	7	8	9	10	11
12	13	14	15	16	17	18
19	20	21	22	23	24	25
26	27	28	29	30	31	

SEPTEMBER

M	T	W	Th	F	Sa	Su
						1
2	3	4	5	6	7	8
9	10	11	12	13	14	15
16	17	18	19	20	21	22
23	24	25	26	27	28	29
30						

OCTOBER

M	T	W	Th	F	Sa	Su
	1	2	3	4	5	6
7	8	9	10	11	12	13
14	15	16	17	18	19	20
21	22	23	24	25	26	27
28	29	30	31			

NOVEMBER

M	T	W	Th	F	Sa	Su
				1	2	3
4	5	6	7	8	9	10
11	12	13	14	15	16	17
18	19	20	21	22	23	24
25	26	27	28	29	30	

DECEMBER

M	T	W	Th	F	Sa	Su
						1
2	3	4	5	6	7	8
9	10	11	12	13	14	15
16	17	18	19	20	21	22
23	24	25	26	27	28	29
30	31					

2014

JANUARY

M	T	W	Th	F	Sa	Su
6	7	1	2	3	4	5
13	14	8	9	10	11	12
20	21	15	16	17	18	19
27	28	22	23	24	25	26
		29	30	31		

FEBRUARY

M	T	W	Th	F	Sa	Su
3	4	5	6	7	1	2
10	11	12	13	14	8	9
17	18	19	20	21	15	16
24	25	26	27	28	22	23

MARCH

M	T	W	Th	F	Sa	Su
3	4	5	6	7	1	2
10	11	12	13	14	8	9
17	18	19	20	21	15	16
24	25	26	27	28	22	23
31					29	30

APRIL

M	T	W	Th	F	Sa	Su
	1	2	3	4	5	6
7	8	9	10	11	12	13
14	15	16	17	18	19	20
21	22	23	24	25	26	27
28	29	30				

MAY

M	T	W	Th	F	Sa	Su
5	6	7	1	2	3	4
12	13	14	8	9	10	11
19	20	21	15	16	17	18
26	27	28	22	23	24	25
			29	30	31	

JUNE

M	T	W	Th	F	Sa	Su
2	3	4	5	6	7	1
9	10	11	12	13	14	8
16	17	18	19	20	21	15
23	24	25	26	27	28	22
30						29

JULY

M	T	W	Th	F	Sa	Su
	1	2	3	4	5	6
7	8	9	10	11	12	13
14	15	16	17	18	19	20
21	22	23	24	25	26	27
28	29	30	31			

AUGUST

M	T	W	Th	F	Sa	Su
4	5	6	7	1	2	3
11	12	13	14	8	9	10
18	19	20	21	15	16	17
25	26	27	28	22	23	24
				29	30	31

SEPTEMBER

M	T	W	Th	F	Sa	Su
1	2	3	4	5	6	7
8	9	10	11	12	13	14
15	16	17	18	19	20	21
22	23	24	25	26	27	28
29	30					

OCTOBER

M	T	W	Th	F	Sa	Su
6	7	1	2	3	4	5
13	14	8	9	10	11	12
20	21	15	16	17	18	19
27	28	22	23	24	25	26
		29	30	31		

NOVEMBER

M	T	W	Th	F	Sa	Su
3	4	5	6	7	1	2
10	11	12	13	14	8	9
17	18	19	20	21	15	16
24	25	26	27	28	22	23
					29	30

DECEMBER

M	T	W	Th	F	Sa	Su
1	2	3	4	5	6	7
8	9	10	11	12	13	14
15	16	17	18	19	20	21
22	23	24	25	26	27	28
29	30	31				

2015

JANUARY

M	T	W	Th	F	Sa	Su
			1	2	3	4
5	6	7	8	9	10	11
12	13	14	15	16	17	18
19	20	21	22	23	24	25
26	27	28	29	30	31	

FEBRUARY

M	T	W	Th	F	Sa	Su
						1
2	3	4	5	6	7	8
9	10	11	12	13	14	15
16	17	18	19	20	21	22
23	24	25	26	27	28	

MARCH

M	T	W	Th	F	Sa	Su
						1
2	3	4	5	6	7	8
9	10	11	12	13	14	15
16	17	18	19	20	21	22
23	24	25	26	27	28	29
30	31					

APRIL

M	T	W	Th	F	Sa	Su
		1	2	3	4	5
6	7	8	9	10	11	12
13	14	15	16	17	18	19
20	21	22	23	24	25	26
27	28	29	30			

MAY

M	T	W	Th	F	Sa	Su
				1	2	3
4	5	6	7	8	9	10
11	12	13	14	15	16	17
18	19	20	21	22	23	24
25	26	27	28	29	30	31

JUNE

M	T	W	Th	F	Sa	Su
1	2	3	4	5	6	7
8	9	10	11	12	13	14
15	16	17	18	19	20	21
22	23	24	25	26	27	28
29	30					

JULY

M	T	W	Th	F	Sa	Su
		1	2	3	4	5
6	7	8	9	10	11	12
13	14	15	16	17	18	19
20	21	22	23	24	25	26
27	28	29	30	31		

AUGUST

M	T	W	Th	F	Sa	Su
					1	2
3	4	5	6	7	8	9
10	11	12	13	14	15	16
17	18	19	20	21	22	23
24	25	26	27	28	29	30
31						

SEPTEMBER

M	T	W	Th	F	Sa	Su
	1	2	3	4	5	6
7	8	9	10	11	12	13
14	15	16	17	18	19	20
21	22	23	24	25	26	27
28	29	30				

OCTOBER

M	T	W	Th	F	Sa	Su
			1	2	3	4
5	6	7	8	9	10	11
12	13	14	15	16	17	18
19	20	21	22	23	24	25
26	27	28	29	30	31	

NOVEMBER

M	T	W	Th	F	Sa	Su
						1
2	3	4	5	6	7	8
9	10	11	12	13	14	15
16	17	18	19	20	21	22
23	24	25	26	27	28	29
30						

DECEMBER

M	T	W	Th	F	Sa	Su
	1	2	3	4	5	6
7	8	9	10	11	12	13
14	15	16	17	18	19	20
21	22	23	24	25	26	27
28	29	30	31			

2016

JANUARY

M	T	W	Th	F	Sa	Su
				1	2	3
4	5	6	7	8	9	10
11	12	13	14	15	16	17
18	19	20	21	22	23	24
25	26	27	28	29	30	31

FEBRUARY

M	T	W	Th	F	Sa	Su
1	2	3	4	5	6	7
8	9	10	11	12	13	14
15	16	17	18	19	20	21
22	23	24	25	26	27	28
29						

MARCH

M	T	W	Th	F	Sa	Su
	1	2	3	4	5	6
7	8	9	10	11	12	13
14	15	16	17	18	19	20
21	22	23	24	25	26	27
28	29	30	31			

APRIL

M	T	W	Th	F	Sa	Su
				1	2	3
4	5	6	7	8	9	10
11	12	13	14	15	16	17
18	19	20	21	22	23	24
25	26	27	28	29	30	

MAY

M	T	W	Th	F	Sa	Su
						1
2	3	4	5	6	7	8
9	10	11	12	13	14	15
16	17	18	19	20	21	22
23	24	25	26	27	28	29
30	31					

JUNE

M	T	W	Th	F	Sa	Su
		1	2	3	4	5
6	7	8	9	10	11	12
13	14	15	16	17	18	19
20	21	22	23	24	25	26
27	28	29	30			

JULY

M	T	W	Th	F	Sa	Su
				1	2	3
4	5	6	7	8	9	10
11	12	13	14	15	16	17
18	19	20	21	22	23	24
25	26	27	28	29	30	31

AUGUST

M	T	W	Th	F	Sa	Su
1	2	3	4	5	6	7
8	9	10	11	12	13	14
15	16	17	18	19	20	21
22	23	24	25	26	27	28
29	30	31				

SEPTEMBER

M	T	W	Th	F	Sa	Su
			1	2	3	4
5	6	7	8	9	10	11
12	13	14	15	16	17	18
19	20	21	22	23	24	25
26	27	28	29	30		

OCTOBER

M	T	W	Th	F	Sa	Su
					1	2
3	4	5	6	7	8	9
10	11	12	13	14	15	16
17	18	19	20	21	22	23
24	25	26	27	28	29	30
31						

NOVEMBER

M	T	W	Th	F	Sa	Su
	1	2	3	4	5	6
7	8	9	10	11	12	13
14	15	16	17	18	19	20
21	22	23	24	25	26	27
28	29	30				

DECEMBER

M	T	W	Th	F	Sa	Su
			1	2	3	4
5	6	7	8	9	10	11
12	13	14	15	16	17	18
19	20	21	22	23	24	25
26	27	28	29	30	31	

2017

JANUARY

M	T	W	Th	F	Sa	Su
2	3	4	5	6	7	1
9	10	11	12	13	14	8
16	17	18	19	20	21	15
23	24	25	26	27	28	22
30	31					29

FEBRUARY

M	T	W	Th	F	Sa	Su
6	7	1	2	3	4	5
13	14	8	9	10	11	12
20	21	15	16	17	18	19
27	28	22	23	24	25	26

MARCH

M	T	W	Th	F	Sa	Su
6	7	1	2	3	4	5
13	14	8	9	10	11	12
20	21	15	16	17	18	19
27	28	22	23	24	25	26
		29	30	31		

APRIL

M	T	W	Th	F	Sa	Su
3	4	5	6	7	1	2
10	11	12	13	14	8	9
17	18	19	20	21	15	16
24	25	26	27	28	22	23
					29	30

MAY

M	T	W	Th	F	Sa	Su
1	2	3	4	5	6	7
8	9	10	11	12	13	14
15	16	17	18	19	20	21
22	23	24	25	26	27	28
29	30	31				

JUNE

M	T	W	Th	F	Sa	Su
5	6	7	8	9	3	4
12	13	14	15	16	10	11
19	20	21	22	23	17	18
26	27	28	29	30	24	25

JULY

M	T	W	Th	F	Sa	Su
3	4	5	6	7	1	2
10	11	12	13	14	8	9
17	18	19	20	21	15	16
24	25	26	27	28	22	23
31					29	30

AUGUST

M	T	W	Th	F	Sa	Su
7	1	2	3	4	5	6
14	8	9	10	11	12	13
21	15	16	17	18	19	20
28	22	23	24	25	26	27
	29	30	31			

SEPTEMBER

M	T	W	Th	F	Sa	Su
4	5	6	7	1	2	3
11	12	13	14	8	9	10
18	19	20	21	15	16	17
25	26	27	28	22	23	24
				29	30	

OCTOBER

M	T	W	Th	F	Sa	Su
2	3	4	5	6	7	1
9	10	11	12	13	14	8
16	17	18	19	20	21	15
23	24	25	26	27	28	22
30	31					29

NOVEMBER

M	T	W	Th	F	Sa	Su
6	7	1	2	3	4	5
13	14	8	9	10	11	12
20	21	15	16	17	18	19
27	28	22	23	24	25	26
		29	30			

DECEMBER

M	T	W	Th	F	Sa	Su
4	5	6	7	1	2	3
11	12	13	14	8	9	10
18	19	20	21	15	16	17
25	26	27	28	22	23	24
				29	30	31

2018

JANUARY

M	T	W	Th	F	Sa	Su
1	2	3	4	5	6	7
8	9	10	11	12	13	14
15	16	17	18	19	20	21
22	23	24	25	26	27	28
29	30	31				

FEBRUARY

M	T	W	Th	F	Sa	Su
			1	2	3	4
5	6	7	8	9	10	11
12	13	14	15	16	17	18
19	20	21	22	23	24	25
26	27	28				

MARCH

M	T	W	Th	F	Sa	Su
			1	2	3	4
5	6	7	8	9	10	11
12	13	14	15	16	17	18
19	20	21	22	23	24	25
26	27	28	29	30	31	

APRIL

M	T	W	Th	F	Sa	Su
						1
2	3	4	5	6	7	8
9	10	11	12	13	14	15
16	17	18	19	20	21	22
23	24	25	26	27	28	29
30						

MAY

M	T	W	Th	F	Sa	Su
	1	2	3	4	5	6
7	8	9	10	11	12	13
14	15	16	17	18	19	20
21	22	23	24	25	26	27
28	29	30	31			

JUNE

M	T	W	Th	F	Sa	Su
				1	2	3
4	5	6	7	8	9	10
11	12	13	14	15	16	17
18	19	20	21	22	23	24
25	26	27	28	29	30	

JULY

M	T	W	Th	F	Sa	Su
						1
2	3	4	5	6	7	8
9	10	11	12	13	14	15
16	17	18	19	20	21	22
23	24	25	26	27	28	29
30	31					

AUGUST

M	T	W	Th	F	Sa	Su
		1	2	3	4	5
6	7	8	9	10	11	12
13	14	15	16	17	18	19
20	21	22	23	24	25	26
27	28	29	30	31		

SEPTEMBER

M	T	W	Th	F	Sa	Su
					1	2
3	4	5	6	7	8	9
10	11	12	13	14	15	16
17	18	19	20	21	22	23
24	25	26	27	28	29	30

OCTOBER

M	T	W	Th	F	Sa	Su
1	2	3	4	5	6	7
8	9	10	11	12	13	14
15	16	17	18	19	20	21
22	23	24	25	26	27	28
29	30	31				

NOVEMBER

M	T	W	Th	F	Sa	Su
			1	2	3	4
5	6	7	8	9	10	11
12	13	14	15	16	17	18
19	20	21	22	23	24	25
26	27	28	29	30		

DECEMBER

M	T	W	Th	F	Sa	Su
					1	2
3	4	5	6	7	8	9
10	11	12	13	14	15	16
17	18	19	20	21	22	23
24	25	26	27	28	29	30
31						

2019

JANUARY

M	T	W	Th	F	Sa	Su
7	1	2	3	4	5	6
14	8	9	10	11	12	13
21	15	16	17	18	19	20
28	22	23	24	25	26	27
	29	30	31			

FEBRUARY

M	T	W	Th	F	Sa	Su
4	5	6	7	1	2	3
11	12	13	14	8	9	10
18	19	20	21	15	16	17
25	26	27	28	22	23	24

MARCH

M	T	W	Th	F	Sa	Su
4	5	6	7	1	2	3
11	12	13	14	8	9	10
18	19	20	21	15	16	17
25	26	27	28	22	23	24
				29	30	31

APRIL

M	T	W	Th	F	Sa	Su
1	2	3	4	5	6	7
8	9	10	11	12	13	14
15	16	17	18	19	20	21
22	23	24	25	26	27	28
29	30					

MAY

M	T	W	Th	F	Sa	Su
6	7	1	2	3	4	5
13	14	8	9	10	11	12
20	21	15	16	17	18	19
27	28	22	23	24	25	26
		29	30	31		

JUNE

M	T	W	Th	F	Sa	Su
3	4	5	6	7	1	2
10	11	12	13	14	8	9
17	18	19	20	21	15	16
24	25	26	27	28	22	23
					29	30

JULY

M	T	W	Th	F	Sa	Su
1	2	3	4	5	6	7
8	9	10	11	12	13	14
15	16	17	18	19	20	21
22	23	24	25	26	27	28
29	30	31				

AUGUST

M	T	W	Th	F	Sa	Su
5	6	7	1	2	3	4
12	13	14	8	9	10	11
19	20	21	15	16	17	18
26	27	28	22	23	24	25
			29	30	31	

SEPTEMBER

M	T	W	Th	F	Sa	Su
2	3	4	5	6	7	1
9	10	11	12	13	14	8
16	17	18	19	20	21	15
23	24	25	26	27	28	22
30						29

OCTOBER

M	T	W	Th	F	Sa	Su
7	1	2	3	4	5	6
14	8	9	10	11	12	13
21	15	16	17	18	19	20
28	22	23	24	25	26	27
	29	30	31			

NOVEMBER

M	T	W	Th	F	Sa	Su
4	5	6	7	1	2	3
11	12	13	14	8	9	10
18	19	20	21	15	16	17
25	26	27	28	22	23	24
				29	30	

DECEMBER

M	T	W	Th	F	Sa	Su
2	3	4	5	6	7	1
9	10	11	12	13	14	8
16	17	18	19	20	21	15
23	24	25	26	27	28	22
30	31					29

Holidays and Notable Dates

Holiday, etc.	2012	2013	2014	2015	2016	2017	2018	2019
New Year's Day	Jan. 1	Jan. 1	Jan. 1	Jan. 1	Jan. 1	Jan. 1	Jan. 1	Jan. 1
New Year Holiday (England)	Jan. 2	—	—	—	—	—	—	—
New Year Holiday (Scotland)	Jan. 3	Jan. 2	Jan. 2	Jan. 2	Jan. 2	Jan. 2	Jan. 2	Jan. 2
St David's Day (Wales)	Mar. 1	Mar. 1	Mar. 1	Mar. 1	Mar. 1	Mar. 1	Mar. 1	Mar. 1
St Patrick's Day (Ireland)	Mar. 17	Mar. 17	Mar. 17	Mar. 17	Mar. 17	Mar. 17	Mar. 17	Mar. 18
Good Friday	Apr. 6	Mar. 29	Apr.18	Apr. 3	Mar. 25	Apr. 14	Mar. 30	Apr. 19
Easter Monday	Apr. 9	Apr. 1	Apr.21	Apr. 6	Apr. 28	Apr. 17	Apr. 2	Apr. 22
St George's Day (England)	Apr. 23	Apr. 23	Apr. 23	Apr. 23	Apr. 23	Apr. 23	Apr. 23	Apr. 23
May Day Holiday	May 7	May 2	May 5	May 4	May 2	May 1	May 7	May 6
Queen's Diamond Jubilee	Jun. 4	—	—	—	—	—	—	—
Spring Bank Holiday	Jun. 5	May 27	May 26	May 25	May 30	May 29	May 28	May 27
August Bank Holiday	Aug. 27	Aug. 26	Aug. 25	Aug. 24	Aug. 29	Aug. 28	Aug. 27	Aug. 26
St Andrew's Day (Scotland)	Nov. 30	Nov. 30	Nov. 30	Nov. 30	Nov. 30	Nov. 30	Nov. 30	Nov. 30
Christmas Day	Dec. 25	Dec. 25	Dec. 25	Dec. 25	Dec. 25	Dec. 25	Dec. 25	Dec. 25
Boxing Day	Dec. 26	Dec. 26	Dec. 26	Dec. 26	Dec. 26	Dec. 26	Dec. 26	Dec. 26
Christmas Holiday(s)	—	—	—	—	Dec. 27	—	—	—

Measurement Conversion Tables

The measurements set out below are based upon the following standards set by the Weights **AL-10** and Measures Act 1985, Sched. 1, Pts I to V:

YARD = 0.9144 metre; GALLON = 4.546 09 cubic decimetres or litres; POUND = 0.453 592 37 kilograms

Archbold
paragraph
numbers

AL-10

Archbold's Criminal Pleading—2016 ed.

AL-11

Measurements of Length

Imperial Units of Length		Metric Equivalents
Mil	1/1000 inch	0.0254 millimetres
Inch	1000 mils	2.54 centimetres
Link	7.92 inches	20.1168 centimetres
Foot	12 inches	0.3048 metres
Yard	3 feet	0.9144 metres
Fathom	6 feet	1.8288 metres
Cable	60 feet or 10 fathoms	18.288 metres
Chain	22 yards (100 links)	20.1168 metres
Furlong	220 yards	201.168 metres
Mile	1,760 yards (8 furlongs)	1.609344 kilometres
Nautical mile	6080 feet	1.853184 kilometres

Metric Units of Length		Imperial Equivalents
Micron	1/1000 millimetre	0.03937007 mils
Millimetre	1/1000 metre	0.03937007 inches
Centimetre	1/100 metre	0.3937 inches
Decimetre	1/10 metre	3.937 inches
Metre	Metre	1.09361329 yards
Kilometre	1000 metres	0.62137712 miles or 0.53961 nautical miles

Measurements of Area

Imperial Units of Area		Metric Equivailents
Square inch	1/144 square feet	6,4516 square centimetres
Square foot	1/9 square yard	929.0304 square centimetres
Square yard	Square yard	0.83613 square metres

Imperial Units of Area		*Metric Equivalents*
Square chain	484 square yards	404.685642 square metres
Rood	1,210 square yards	1011.714 square metres
Acre	4 roods or 4840 square yards	4046.85642 sq. ms or 40.4685642 acres
Square mile	640 acres	258.998811 hectares

Metric Units of Area		*Imperial Equivalents*
Square millimetre	1/100 square centimetre	0.00155 square inches
Square centimetre	1/100 square decimetre	0.155 square inches
Square decimetre	1/100 metre	15.5 square inches
Square metre	Square metre	1.1959 sq. yards or 10.7639 sq. ft
Are	100 square metres	119.599 sq. yds or 0.09884 roods
Dekare	10 ares	0.2471 acres
Hectare	100 ares (1,000 square metres)	2.47105 acres
Square kilometre	100 hectares	247.105 acres or 0.3861 square miles

Measurements of Volume

Imperial Units of Volume		*Metric Equivalents*
Cubic inch	Cubic inch	16.387064 cubic centimetres
Cubic foot	1,728 cubic inches	28.3168465 decimetres
Cubic yard	27 cubic feet	0.76455485 cubic metres

Metric Units of Volume		*Imperial Equivalents*
Cubic centimetre	1,000 cubic millimetres	0.06102374 cubic inches
Cubic decimetre	1,000 cubic centimetres	0.0353466 cubic feet
Cubic metre	1,000 cubic decimetres	1.30795061 cubic yards or 35.3147 cu. ft

899

Archbold
paragraph
numbers

AL-13

Archbold's Criminal Pleading—2016 ed.

AL-13

Measurements of Capacity

Imperial, Apothecaries and US Units of Capacity		*Metric Equivalents*
Minim	Minim	0.0591938 millilitres
Fluid Drachm	60 minims	0.35516328 centilitres
Fluid ounce	8 fluid drachms	2.84130625 centilitres
US fluid ounce	1.0408 UK fluid ounces	29.573522656 millilitres
Gill	5 fluid ounces	1.42065312 decilitres
Pint	4 gills or 20 fluid ounces	0.56826125 litres
US pint	0.8327 UK pints or 16 US fluid ounces	0.47317636 litres
Quart	2 pints or 8 gills	1.1365225 litres
Gallon	4 quarts or 1.20095 US gallons	4.54609 litres
US gallon	0.08327 UK gallons	3.7854109 litres
Peck	2 gallons or 16 pints	9.09218 litres
Bushel	4 pecks or 8 gallons	36.36872 litres
Quarter	8 bushels or 36 pecks	2.9094976 hectolitres
Chaldron	36 bushels or 4 ½ quarters	13.0927392 hectolitres

Metric Units of Capacity		*Imperial Equivalents*
Millilitre	Millilitre	0.28156064 fluid drachms
Centilitre	10 millilitres	0.35195080 fluid ounces
Decilitre	10 centilitres	0.70390160 gills
Litre	10 decilitres	1.75975398 pints or 0.21996924 UK gallons
Dekalitre	10 litres	2.1996924 UK gallons
Hectolitre	10 dekalitres or 100 litres	21.996824 UK gallons

Measurements of Weight

Imperial and Apothecaries Units of Weight		*Metric Equivalents*
Grain	Grain	64.79891 milligrams

Imperial and Apothecaries Units of Weight		Metric Equivalents
Scruple	20 grains	1.2959782 grams
Pennyweight	24 grains	1.55517384 grams
Drachm	3 scruples or 60 grains	3.8879346 grams
Troy ounce	8 drachms or 480 grains	31.1034768 grams
Dram	1/16 ounce	1.77184519 grams
Ounce	16 drams or 437.5 grains	28.3495231 grams
Troy pound (US)	12 troy ounces or 5,760 grains	373.241721 grams
Pound	16 ounces or 7,000 grains	453.59237 grams or 0.45359237 kilograms
Stone	14 pounds	6.3502318 kilograms
Quarter	28 pounds or 2 stone	12.7005863 kilograms
Cental	100 pounds	45.359237 kilograms
Hundredweight	4 quarters or 112 pounds	50.8023454 kilograms
Short hundredweight (US)	100 pounds	45.359237 kilograms
Ton (UK or long ton)	20 cwt or 2,240 pounds	1.0160469 metric tonnes (tonne)
Ton (US or short ton)	2,000 pounds	0.90718474 metric tonnes

Metric Units of Weight		Imperial Equivalents
Milligram	.001 grams	0.012432 grains
Centigram	.01 grams	0.15432 grains
Decigram	.1 grams	1.5432 grains
Gram	1 gram	0.03527396 ounces or 0.03215 troy ounces
Dekagram	10 grams	0.35273961 ounces
Hectogram	100 grams	3.52739619 ounces
Kilogram	1,000 grams	2.20462262 pounds
Myriagram	10 kilograms	22.0462 pounds
Quintal	100 kilograms	1.9684 hundredweight
Tonne	1,000 kilograms	0.984207 UK tons or 1.10231 US tons

Measurements of Velocity

Per Hour	Per Minute	Per Second
Mile	88 feet	17.6 inches per second
1.609344 kph	26.8224 metres	44.704 centimetres per second
Kilometres	16.6667 metres	27.7778 centimetres
0.62137 mph	54.6806 feet	10.9361 inches

Système Internationale D'unites or SI Units

1. SI units are increasingly being used to report laboratory results. They have largely replaced **AL-16**
earlier systems such as c.g.s. units (centimetre, gram, second), m.k.s. or Giorgi units
(metre, kilogram, second), and Imperial units (yard, pound, second).
2. S.I. Units comprise 7 base units and 2 supplementary units. Other units are derived from
these. 18 derived units are currently widely accepted.

Base SI Units

Physical Quantity	Unit	Symbol	
Length	metre	m	**AL-17**
Mass	kilogram	kg	
Time	second	s	
Electric current	ampere	A	
Temperature	kelvin	K	
Luminosity	candela	cd	
Amount of substance	mole	mol	
Plane angle*	radian*	rad	
Solid angle*	steradian*	sr	

*Supplementary Units

Derived SI Units

Physical Quantity	Unit	Symbol	
Frequency	hertz	Hz	**AL-18**
Energy	joule	J	
Force	newton	N	
Power	watt	W	
Pressure	pascal	Pa	
Electric charge	coulomb	C	
Electric potential difference	volt	V	
Electrical resistance	ohm	Ω	
Electric conductance	siemens	S	
Electric capacitance	farad	F	
Magnetic flux	weber	Wb	
Inductance	henry	H	
Magnetic flux density	tesla	T	
Luminous flux	lumen	lm	
Illuminance	lux	lx	
Absorbed dose	gray	Gy	
Activity	becquerel	Bq	
Dose Equivalence	sievert	Sv	

Multiples and Subdivisions of SI Units

Prefix	Symbol	Power	Value	
exa	E	10^{18}	1,000,000,000,000,000,000	**AL-19**
peta	P	10^{15}	1,000,000,000,000,000	

Prefix	Symbol	Power	Value
tera	T	10^{12}	1,000,000,000,000
giga	G	10^{9}	1,000,000,000
mega	M	10^{6}	1,000,000
kilo	k	10^{3}	1,000
hecto	h	10^{2}	100
deca	da	10	10
-			1
deci	d	10^{-1}	1/10
centi	c	10^{-2}	1/100
milli	m	10^{-3}	1/1,000
micro	μ	10^{-6}	1/1,000,000
nano	n	10^{-9}	1/1,000,000,000
pico	p	10^{-12}	1/1,000,000,000,000
femto	f	10^{-15}	1/1,000,000,000,000,000
atto	a	10^{-18}	1/1,000,000,000,000,000,000

International Time Differences

AL-20   The following time differences are based upon Greenwich Mean Time (GMT).
British Summer Time (BST) is one hour in advance of GMT.

Country		Hours +/-
Algeria		+1 hour
Argentina		-3 hours
Australia	South Australia	+9½ hours
	New South Wales	+10 hours
	Tasmania	+10 hours
	Victoria	+10 hours
Austria		+1 hour
Belgium		+1 hour
Bolivia		-4 hours
Brazil		-3 hours
Bulgaria		+2 hours
Canada	Newfoundland	-3½ hours
	Atlantic	-4 hours
	Eastern	-5 hours
	Central	-6 hours
	Mountain	-7 hours
	Pacific	-8 hours
	Yukon	-9 hours
Chile		-4 hours
China		+8 hours
Columbia		-5 hours
Czech Lands		+1 hour
Denmark		+1 hour
Egypt		+2 hours
Finland		+2 hours

AL-21

Country	Hours +/-
France	+1 hour
Germany	+1 hour
Ghana	
Greece	+2 hours
Holland	+1 hour
Hong Kong	+8 hours
Hungary	+1 hour
India	+5½ hours
Iraq	+3 hours
Ireland	
Israel	+2 hours
Italy	+1 hour
Jamaica	-5 hours
Japan	+9 hours
Kenya	+3 hours

Country	Hours +/-
Luxembourg	+1 hour
Malaysia	+8 hours
Malta	+1 hour
Morocco	
New Zealand	+12 hours
Nigeria	+1 hour
Norway	+1 hour
Peru	-5 hours
Philippines	+8 hours
Poland	+1 hour

Country		Hours +/-
Portugal		
Romania		+2 hours
Russia	Moscow	+3 hours
	Vladivostock	+10 hours
Saudi Arabia		+3 hours
Serbia		+1 hours
Singapore		+8 hours
South Africa		+2 hours
Spain		+1 hour
Sri Lanka		+5½ hours
Sweden		+1 hour
Switzerland		+1 hour
Taiwan		+8 hours
Thailand		+7 hours
Tunisia		+1 hour
Turkey		+2 hours
Ukraine		+3 hours
United Arab Emirates		+4 hours
United States	Eastern	-5 hours
	Central	-6 hours
	Mountain	-7 hours
	Pacific	-8 hours
Zambia		+2 hours
Zimbabwe		+2 hours

Stopping Distances

AL-22

Speed (m.p.h.)	Stopping distance (feet)
20	40
30	75
40	120
50	175
60	240
70	315

Useful Contact Details

	Telephone	Email
Courts, etc.		
House of Lords, Judicial Office	(020) 7219 3111	
Royal Courts of Justice	(020) 7947 6000	
Registrar, Criminal Appeals	(020) 7947 6103	
Criminal Appeal Office	(020) 7947 6011	Criminalappealoffice.generaloffice@hmcourts-service.x.gsi.gov.uk
Administrative Court Office	(020) 7947 6205	
Official Bodies		
Home Office	(020) 7035 4848	public.enquiries@homeoffice.gsi.gov.uk
Serious Fraud Office	(020) 7239 7272	public.enquiries@sfo.gsi.gov.uk
H.M. Revenue and Customs	0845 010 9000	Enquiries.estn@hmrc.gsi.gov.uk This address handles all enquiries related to VAT, Excise and other duties formerly administered by HM Customs and Excise (with the exception of International Trade)
New Scotland Yard	(020) 7230 1212	new.scotland.yard@met.police.uk
City of London Police	(020) 7601 2222	postmaster@cityoflondon.police.uk
British Transport Police	0800 40 50 40	
Others		
Justice	(020) 7329 5100	admin@justice.org.uk
Liberty	(020) 7403 3888	
Bar Council	(020) 7242 0082	
Bar Council Ethical Enquiries Line	(020) 7611 1307	
Bar Standards Board	(020) 7611 1444	

	Telephone	*Email*
Law Society — Lawyerline	0870 606 2588	
Law Society — Practice Advice Service	0870 606 2522	

INDEX

LEGAL TAXONOMY
FROM SWEET & MAXWELL

This index has been prepared using Sweet and Maxwell's Legal Taxonomy. Main index entries conform to keywords provided by the Legal Taxonomy except where references to specific documents or non-standard terms (denoted by quotation marks) have been included. These keywords provide a means of identifying similar concepts in other Sweet & Maxwell publications and online services to which keywords from the Legal Taxonomy have been applied. Readers may find some minor differences between terms used in the text and those which appear in the index. **Suggestions to** *sweetandmaxwell.taxonomy@thomson.com.*

All references are to paragraph numbers.

6